A History of the United States

Our Land, Our Time

Annotated Teacher's Edition

Joseph R. Conlin

 CORONADO PUBLISHERS

San Diego   Chicago   Orlando   Dallas

Editorial Development: Kirchoff/Wohlberg, Inc.
Design, Production: Kirchoff/Wohlberg, Inc.

Printed in the United States of America   ISBN 0–15–772001–2

CONTENTS

TO THE TEACHER

STUDENT TEXT ORGANIZATION

Convenient Design

The student edition of *A History of the United States: Our Land, Our Time* is organized to present American history and related skills strategies clearly and logically in order to convey to students the excitement and importance of America's story. Content is presented in lesson-sized chunks. Each lesson to be studied is easily perceived by students because study objectives begin—and checkpoints punctuate—each chapter. A glossary of terms; an atlas and reference section containing maps, tables, charts, and graphs; and an index appear at the end of the book for convenient reference. Special features that support the running text add punch to each unit of study.

The organization of the text is compatible with the school year and with weekly lesson plans. There are 10 units and 34 chapters. Each chapter has three or four sections; in general, the chapters are a week's work with the sections representing a day's lesson. Section Reviews and Chapter Reviews provide regular surveys. Chapter Reviews also provide skills instruction and open-book testing, and a Unit Test is included to wrap up each of the ten major study sections. In-text maps, charts, graphs, tables, and special features are listed separately, and their pages given, in the table of contents.

The pedagogical design of the book is predictable in order to make study easy. To encourage student awareness of how to use the book for study, metacognition strategies are built into the book's organization.

Predictable Format

Each unit and chapter is titled succinctly, and dates covered in each are always given. Units are signaled by the title and by two-page paintings that capture the era and show how America changed during its development. Each chapter is signaled by a two-page opener that has several design features: the title, a set-off quotation, a gray-screened introduction, the start of the first section of the chapter, and a full-page picture.

After every Chapter Title and time span, there is a quotation from an American essayist, novelist, playwright, or poet. These quotations were chosen because they characterize some aspect of the period to be studied. They represent an artistic expression of some of the events and times covered in the chapter. Annotations give the teacher the source from which the quotation was taken, the years of the author's life, and other published works of the author.

The introduction to each chapter is titled Making Connections. It is always in a three-part, gray-screened initial column. (Throughout the book, a gray screen is used to signal material that is not part of the running text. It is either study-aid information or material that requires student response.) This metacognition feature appears in the book to help students set realistic goals for studying and to serve as a model for good self-study methods.

The first part of the introduction is a lead-in statement about the time period. Next is a study-aid preview in which students are told specifically what to look for as they read. In a highlighted list of who, what, were, when, how, and why topic statements, students are presented with a survey of major ideas and concepts that will be discussed in the chapter. In this way, students are told what to expect and what ideas to focus on as they read the chapter. The last part of this introductory column is a statement that makes pertinent connections between what students have learned in previous chapters and what they will learn in the current chapter. They are instructed to note these connections as they read.

Section Reviews

Each chapter has numbered sections and each section is divided into subsections set off by run-in boldface subheadings. The sections were planned to represent one day's lesson, although a few may take longer. Section Reviews follow each section and signal the section's end. They may be used as independent, written follow-up work; as a quick, oral wrap-up at the end of a lesson; or as a review/survey before beginning a new section. These Section Reviews, like the Making Connections feature, always appear in a gray box, signaling that they are study material.

Chapter Reviews

At the end of each chapter is a Chapter Review. It also appears on a gray screen to signal student response. This feature has four parts, time lines and related questions, skills strategy lessons, test and, for all except the last chapter in a unit, a writing assignment.

Time Line Questions

The first part of each Chapter Review is a vertical Time Line, followed by questions pertaining to it. Answering these questions requires that students examine the Time Line in detail to note relationships, draw conclusions, or infer cause and effect, as well as to see a sequence of events. The Time Line also serves as a quick synthesis of the events just studied—the chapter at a glance.

Skills Strategy

The Skills Strategy presents a skill important to the study of history, as well as strategies for acquiring, improving, and applying that skill. Skills taught in the book range from notetaking and outlining to skills involving reading charts, graphs, captions, and pictures. Primary sources, such as editorials, news stories, speeches, and documents, are included and discussed.

Skills are always introduced in the following way: Students first are told why having the skill is beneficial, and how the skill can be used. Then the skill is explained in detail in order to teach the skill—it is not merely mentioned or assigned. An example is given above the text to illustrate the skill. This example also extends the content of the chapter. The third step directs students to apply the skill in written form. Again the task uses facts and concepts from the chapter and serves as a part of the review. The skills application work is often used as a tool or a base to help students write the paragraph that is assigned at the end of every Chapter Test.

Chapter Tests

The Chapter Test is an open-book, learning-oriented test. It is presented in two parts: Text Review and Critical Thinking. The first part asks students questions that can be answered by recalling or rereading the text. The second part requires students to integrate information, understand causes and effects, be able to summarize, and, in general, to demonstrate in-depth knowledge of material covered in the chapter. The last chapter of each unit is tested in the Unit Test. (Additional Chapter Tests are also provided in Test Books.)

Writing a Paragraph

This task usually relates directly to the Skills Strategy lesson and always extends the chapter content; therefore, it too is part of the history skills scope and sequence plan. It may be used as an extension of the Chapter Test. Its primary purpose, however, is to help students to synthesize their ideas in a basic unit of written expression, the paragraph. Students are given specific instructions for constructing a good paragraph. Topic sentences are supplied in the early chapters. Later, supporting-detail sentences, sequencing sentences, and concluding sentences are discussed. If students can master paragraph organization, and, implicitly, sentences as well, they will not be hampered or discouraged by an inability to organize their thoughts and express what they have learned. When the skill of writing one good paragraph is mastered, putting paragraphs together becomes easier. In short, the objective of this part of the Chapter Review is to help students become more literate, more at home with written language, and more able to use writing as a tool. (When a Chapter Review coincides with a Unit Test, students are not asked to write a paragraph.)

Unit Tests

The Unit Tests present assessment strategies that survey the unit. Each Unit Test has four sections, titled Chapter Survey, Text Review, Critical Thinking, and Skills Review.

In the first portion of the test, titled Chapter Survey, students are directed to write a brief summary of each chapter in the unit. They are presented with important terms from each chapter to help them set chapter parameters. They are also asked to select one of the terms from each chapter to identify.

In the Text Review section, students are asked questions involving text recall. The questions are arranged in chapter order and are titled by chapter number.

The Critical Thinking section presents questions that require students to integrate information and note relationships. A variety of critical thinking skills involving high-level thought makes this section a challenging one.

Answering the questions in the Skills Review part of the test involves the use of skills that were taught in the Skills Strategy sections of the Chapter Reviews in the unit. Students are asked to demonstrate a working knowledge of these skills.

The predictable format of test content, initiated by a study plan, punctuated by section checkpoints, and culminating with chapter or unit reviews provides a built-in lesson plan for the teacher. More importantly, it leads students through the history of the United States in a manner geared to optimum comprehension.

Special Features

The special features in *A History of the United States: Our Land, Our Time* add to the book's lively style and sense of immediacy. They give spark to the running text and stress the importance of individual contributions to the growth of the United States and the American character. The features help students understand that history is the record of what *people* did, and not just a compressed account of important events such as wars, economic cycles, elections, and life-style trends. Each of these textbook features is also represented in the Workbook.

The Movers and Shapers feature—short biographies of interesting people who lived during the time covered in a unit—appears throughout the book. The "Movers and Shapers" made a difference to American history by their unique contributions, problem-solving abilities, and often by the force of their will to make life better for themselves and their country.

This text feature is supported by similar biographical sketches in the Workbook. The sketches are used for study-skills development and reading comprehension. In the Workbook, these features are titled both by the skills emphasized and by the subject of the biography.

Primary-source materials are featured in Going to the Source, which appears in each unit. This feature presents original writings from the period covered in the chapters where they appear, including personal letters, diary entries, speeches, and other documents. These primary sources are offered as examples of then-current thoughts about an historical subject, and add the flavor of the period to the secondary-source text account. Skills Strategy pages in the textbook present detailed lessons about primary and secondary sources and provide skills applications.

This feature is extended by the inclusion of additional source material in the Workbook. These activity pages provide opportunities for student analysis of original sources.

Another feature, Profiles of the Presidency, gives special attention to a quotation from each president. These quotes are from speeches, diaries, letters, and documents. They are presented in the text as primary sources, at the point of a president's incumbency, to give students insight into the person in the presidential office.

In the Workbook, a feature about presidential crises extends this textbook feature. It deals with the "buck stops here" aspect of the presidency—how each president dealt with one particular crisis.

In each unit, there is a colorful two-page spread titled American Ingenuity. Ten of these poster-like spreads highlight technological expertise, which has long been an American hallmark. Paintings of five to seven inventions that changed American life are shown, accompanied by brief descriptions. Under this display is a Changing Technology time line listing other inventions that were widely used. These range from small items, such as the zipper, to big ones, such as open hearth steel mills.

The maps in the textbook are outstanding in several ways. The maps are easy to read because of their size and use of color. Map labels bear a direct relation to the text, making them immediately useful. All of the maps support the text, and some maps support each other. They may illustrate the same historical subject, for example, but over a period of time, so that students can make visual comparisons of information. Charts, graphs, and tables are equally clear and easy to interpret. In fact, a unique feature of the book is the use of visuals in the Skills Strategies—the interpretation of visuals is taught, enabling students to grasp the complexity and make better use of maps, charts, and graphs as they read the text.

There are four assessment features in this American History program. The first three features are informally introduced into the pedagogical design of the student book: the in-book Section Reviews, which wrap up each day's work; Chapter Tests, which consist of ten questions involving text recall and critical thinking; and Unit Tests, which are composed of 20 items. These features are designed mainly to be open-book learning or self-assessment tools, although they certainly may be used in a variety of ways, such as oral discussions, group reports, or graded tests.

The fourth formal assessment tool is the Test Book. The Test Book provides a test for every chapter. These tests differ from the in-book tests, which reinforce learning and allow students to review because they are intended mainly for teacher-evaluated testing and use a standardized-test format. A more complete description of the Test Book follows.

Additional Tools

In the Test Book, a test is provided for every chapter. These tests differ from the in-book tests in five ways: They are intended mainly for testing, although they can also be used for teaching and learning. These tests use a standardized test format. The answers are shorter, are written on test sheets, and can be graded readily by using the answer key provided. The questioning format includes paragraph comprehension, controlled completion, and matching.

The questions themselves involve text recall and critical thinking. Skills taught in the Skills Strategy sections of the book as well as paragraph writing are also offered for optional testing.

Philosophies about testing are legion, and may vary from teacher to teacher according to the needs of each class. For this reason, testing materials and accompanying procedures are offered as optional tools with optional application. However, research shows that the most benefit is derived from a testing program that involves each student in evaluating his or her own test. So, whatever testing options are chosen, it is time well spent to have students involved in checking their own tests to reinforce correct responses and to explore and correct wrong answers.

Each page in the Workbook is designed to extend the content of a chapter section. In addition, the activity pages extend skills taught in the Skills Strategy sections of the student book and include map-reading skills, chart-analysis techniques and applications, outlining, comprehension, critical-thinking skills and applications, visual-analysis techniques and applications, and analyses of primary and secondary sources.

The Workbook is planned to be used as an American history hands-on, learning-resource tool, supplementary to the student text. The pages may be used for independent work or for class activity.

The title of each Workbook page includes an objective so that both students and teachers are aware of the major goal of each activity. Secondary goals are always present and, of course, the content material used as a skills vehicle is always relevant to the chapter as it presents new information.

There are various kinds of pages, such as biographies, charts, presidential crises, crossword puzzles, maps, newspaper editorials, and graphs. Each page integrates skills with content to help keep student interest high and to offer opportunities for learning. Emphasis is on instruction; there are no true-false or matching-activity pages with limited learning value. With the exception of a few crossword puzzles, vocabulary work is done incidentally in context, not as a separate exercise.

USING THE TEACHER'S EDITION

Answers For Written Activities

Answers for questions, model answers for answers that vary, and answers for Writing a Paragraph assignments occurring in Section Reviews, Chapter Reviews, and Unit Reviews, are provided in the front matter of the teacher's edition. For every question or direction that appears in a student textbook gray-screened portion, there is an answer or suggested model in the answer key of the teacher's edition.

Unit Overview Pages

The teacher's edition has a unique feature to make lesson-planning for each unit and chapter convenient. In the student book, each Unit Opener is a two-page spread that displays a painting of an area of the United States. These paintings show the changing contour of the United States from a pastoral landscape to an urban and industrial image. These Unit Opener pages help track the book and signal the beginning of a new unit. In the teacher's edition, the paintings have been reduced; they appear in the upper left corner of the spread to facilitate tracking and identification. This allows space for pedagogical material in the teacher's edition where it is most useful—at the beginning of each unit.

These unit-opener pages contain the following helpful features:
    a survey of the unit's content
    a list of basic unit concepts
    titles of each unit chapter
    a synopsis of each chapter's content
    a list of each chapter's special features
    a list of historical generalizations as chapter objectives
    skills covered in each chapter
This brief overview of each unit is organized in chapter form close to the point of teaching, instead of being removed to a separate section, in order to make planning convenient for the teacher.

Annotations

Annotations appear in blue at the bottom of the student pages and give additional material relevant to the content of the student pages. This includes information about tests, illustrations, captions, or special features. The teacher can use this material to add pertinent and interesting details to a lesson without doing exhaustive research to find those "extras" that can lend a spark to a discussion or to quickly answer student questions. Annotations may also be teaching strategies or suggestions in the form of questions to ask or topics to discuss. Annotations were written by teachers for teachers, to help make a lesson go smoothly and to add interest to class discussions.

The nature of the textbook page dictates the kind of annotation that appears on it. Chapter Review and Section Review pages tend to have additional questions; pages with maps and charts may have questions, but more likely will have teaching strategies. Special feature pages may have background information relevant to the featured subject.

Bibliography

The bibliography is arranged by unit to make it as accessible and useful as possible.

The books in the bibliography have been selected for both teachers and students to use in carrying out further research on the topics covered. References are discussed and suggestions are given for their use.

**Scope and Sequence
Skills Chart
for
A History of the United States
Our Land, Our Time**

SCOPE AND SEQUENCE CHART

READING SKILLS

COMPREHENSION		UNIT 1	2	3	4	
READ TO GET LITERAL MEANING	●	12, 16, 25, 33, 37, 44, 49, 59, 66, 69, 73, 77, 83, 87, 91, 92	103, 107, 111, 115, 117, 127, 128, 133, 138, 145, 147, 151, 158, 162, 167, 189, 194, 198, 200, 207, 211	220, 225, 232, 235, 237, 245, 248, 252, 257, 261, 266, 271, 276, 281, 283, 289, 291, 294, 305, 307	316, 322, 329, 333, 342, 346, 353, 357, 359, 368, 373, 382, 387, 389, 395, 400, 405, 407, 409	
	▲	19	122, 126, 130, 131, 164, 166, 171, 201	229	382, 399, 400	
USE CHAPTER & SECTION HEADINGS, TOPIC SENTENCES, AND SUMMARY SENTENCES TO SELECT MAIN IDEAS	●	26, 27, 49, 73	211			
	▲	29, 51, 75		215		
	■			11.3		
DIFFERENTIATE BETWEEN MAIN AND SUBORDINATE IDEAS	●	49, 73	189, 211			
	▲	29, 75		215		
	■	3.1, 4.2				
SELECT PASSAGES THAT ARE PERTINENT TO THE TOPIC BEING STUDIED	●	12, 16, 25, 27, 33, 37, 44, 49, 59, 66, 69, 73, 77, 83, 87, 91, 92	103, 107, 111, 115, 117, 127, 128, 133, 138, 145, 147, 151, 158, 162, 167, 189, 194, 198, 200, 207, 211	220, 225, 232, 235, 237, 245, 248, 252, 257, 261, 266, 271, 276, 281, 283, 289, 291, 294, 305, 307	316, 322, 329, 333, 342, 346, 353, 357, 359, 368, 373, 382, 387, 389, 395, 400, 405, 407, 409	
	▲	8, 9, 46, 55, 61, 69, 76, 83, 84, 90	106, 109, 114, 115, 126, 133, 150, 151, 160, 163, 198, 204–206	215, 222, 223, 240, 266, 304	352, 401	
	■	2.1				
INTERPRET WHAT IS READ BY DRAWING INFERENCES	●	37, 49, 69, 73, 77, 83, 87, 92	103, 107, 111, 115, 117, 128, 138, 147, 151, 158, 167, 189, 198, 200, 207, 211	237, 257, 271, 283	316, 322, 329, 333, 353, 357, 359, 382, 389, 409	
	▲	47, 53, 61, 76, 77, 90	106, 114, 115, 122, 151	266, 286, 291	321, 352, 381	
	■	2.3				
DETECT CAUSE AND EFFECT RELATIONSHIPS	●	12, 37, 49, 66, 73, 83, 87, 92	115, 158, 189, 207	232, 235, 237, 248, 252, 261, 276, 283, 289, 305, 307	316, 353, 357, 359, 368, 389, 400, 407, 409	
	▲	8, 15, 26, 27, 37, 44, 45, 47, 61	106, 109, 151			
	■	4.4	8.3	12.2, 12.3	16.2	
DISTINGUISH BETWEEN FACT AND OPINION; RECOGNIZE PROPAGANDA	●	49	117, 147	261, 283, 307	359, 389, 409	
	▲	38, 39, 41	126, 130, 131, 164		324, 325, 327, 361, 370	
	■		6.1, 6.2	12.4	13.1, 13.2	

● = book (pages)   ▲ = annotations (pages)   ■ = workbook (chapter section)

5	6	7	8	9	10
420, 423, 427, 430, 431, 435, 441, 453, 455, 457, 463, 467, 474, 477, 481–483	492, 496, 501, 502, 505, 507, 512, 515, 520, 521, 525, 530, 533, 538, 545, 547	556, 561, 563, 565, 567, 572, 576, 580, 583, 587, 592, 596, 603, 607, 609, 611	618, 623, 627, 629, 635, 643, 647, 651, 657, 661, 667, 671, 673	679, 688, 691, 701, 705, 712, 721, 725, 727, 735, 738, 741, 745	759, 764, 769, 771, 779, 783, 786, 789, 791, 799, 805, 807, 811
		598, 608			
482					
457, 467, 482					
17.4					
420, 423, 427, 430, 431, 435, 441, 453, 455, 457, 463, 467, 474, 477, 481–483	492, 496, 501, 502, 505, 507, 512, 515, 520, 521, 525, 530, 533, 538, 545, 547	556, 561, 563, 565, 567, 572, 576, 580, 583, 587, 592, 596, 603, 607, 609, 611	618, 623, 627, 629, 635, 643, 647, 651, 657, 661, 667, 671, 673	668, 679, 691, 701, 705, 712, 721, 725, 727, 735, 738, 741, 745	759, 764, 769, 771, 779, 783, 786, 789, 791, 799, 805, 807, 811
461, 468	533, 542		624, 635		
19.2	20.3, 21.2		27.1	31.6	32.3
420, 435, 474		587, 603, 611	629, 651, 661, 673		811
416, 417, 442, 461, 483	528	556, 577, 578, 593, 594	623, 624, 635, 642		
19.5b					
420, 430, 435, 455	492, 502, 507, 512, 515, 521, 525, 533, 538, 547	580, 587, 596, 603, 607, 611	627, 629, 647, 651, 661, 667, 671, 673	679, 688, 712, 721, 725, 727, 741, 745	759, 771, 783, 791, 811
414		556, 592, 593, 594, 599	623, 643, 648		764
17.5					33.2
435, 457	501, 505, 525, 547	611		705, 745	
	503, 527, 534	601, 606	642	689, 692, 707	
19.3	20.2, 21.4	23.2, 25.4	26.1	30.2	

Skills Designations reprinted and adapted with the permission of The National Council for the Social Studies.

		UNIT 1	2	3	4	
RECOGNIZE AUTHOR BIAS	●	49	117, 147	261, 283, 307	359, 389, 409	
	▲	9, 77	98, 99, 126, 130, 131, 201		324, 325, 327, 361	
	■			12.1, 12.3, 12.4	13.1, 13.2, 16.1	
USE PICTURE CLUES AND PICTURE CAPTIONS TO AID COMPREHENSION	●			306		
	▲			296	311, 405	
	■					
USE LITERATURE TO ENRICH MEANING	▲	14	98, 99	293	318	
	■		6.1	10.1, 12.3	13.2	
READ FOR A VARIETY OF PURPOSES: CRITICALLY, ANALYTICALLY, TO PREDICT OUTCOMES, TO ANSWER A QUESTION, TO FORM AN OPINION, TO SKIM FOR FACTS	●				359	
	▲	14	122, 130, 131, 158, 162, 166	263, 293	318, 346, 361, 396, 403	
	■		6.1	12.2	16.1	
READ VARIOUS FORMS OF PRINTED MATERIAL: BOOKS, NEWSPAPERS, JOURNALS	●				359	
	▲	14	99, 162, 169, 170	293, 298, 305	312, 313, 318, 324, 325, 342, 361, 403	
	■			12.4	13.2, 15.2	

READING SKILLS

VOCABULARY

		UNIT 1	2	3	4	
USE USUAL WORD ATTACK SKILLS: SIGHT RECOGNITION, PHONETIC ANALYSIS, STRUCTURAL ANALYSIS	●				333	
	▲	66		300	404	
USE CONTEXT CLUES TO GAIN MEANING	●				333	
	▲	3, 11, 16, 18, 30, 66		229, 242, 300, 301	384, 393, 404	
USE APPROPRIATE SOURCES TO GAIN MEANING OF ESSENTIAL TERMS AND VOCABULARY	●			291	333	
	▲			229	335, 378	
	■	1.4, 2.2	5.2, 7.1		14.1	
RECOGNIZE AND UNDERSTAND AN INCREASING NUMBER OF SOCIAL STUDIES TERMS	●				333	
	▲	3		242, 271, 301	384, 393	

● = book (pages)   ▲ = annotations (pages)   ■ = workbook (chapter section)

5	6	7	8	9	10
435	547	611	629, 672, 673		771
			642		
19.1, 19.3	20.2, 21.4	23.2	26.1	30.2	
461, 470	488	558, 603		667	786, 799
19.4	20.4				
	540	561			
19.1	20.2	23.2	26.2		
453		561	642	685, 701	
18.2	20.2, 21.4	23.2	26.1, 26.2, 28.3	30.2	
	525				
453, 459	509, 516, 527, 534	561, 603	642		799
18.3, 19.1, 19.3	20.2, 21.4	23.2	26.1, 26.2, 28.3	30.2	

5	6	7	8	9	10
	497		616	739	757
				745	811
470	497, 498, 505, 513, 519		616, 621	723, 735, 739	757
					811
	497				
18.1		23.4		31.2	33.1
					811
	516			667, 735	

Skills Designations reprinted and adapted with the permission of
The National Council for the Social Studies.

STUDY SKILLS

FIND INFORMATION

	UNIT 1	2	3	4	
METACOGNITION PLAN IN ANTICIPATION OF STUDY (EACH CHAPTER AND END OF CHAPTER ANNOTATION) ●	2, 28, 50, 74	96, 118, 148, 190	214, 238, 262, 284	310, 334, 360, 390	
▲	26, 27, 48, 49, 72, 73, 92, 93	116, 117, 146, 147, 188, 189, 210, 211	236, 237, 260, 261, 282, 283, 306, 307	332, 333, 358, 359, 388, 389, 410, 411	
EVALUATE SOURCES OF INFORMATION ●					
▲		98, 99, 100, 125, 126, 127, 130, 131, 162, 194, 201		346, 403	
USE APPROPRIATE SOURCE OF INFORMATION ●					
▲				403	
USE THE COMMUNITY AS A RESOURCE ▲	4–7, 30	172	250	355	

STUDY SKILLS

ARRANGE INFORMATION

	UNIT 1	2	3	4	
MAKE OUTLINE OF TOPIC ●	26, 27, 49	189, 211			
▲	29, 51, 75		215		
■	2.1, 3.1, 4.2	8.2			
PREPARE SUMMARIES ●		138	261, 307	389, 409	
▲	10, 11, 37, 55, 58	114, 115, 203	216, 274, 285, 290	366, 392	
■		7.4, 8.2, 8.3		15.1	
MAKE TIMELINES ●		211			
▲		199	251		
■	3.3b	8.1	10.2, 10.4	13.3b, 15.2	
TAKE NOTES ●	26, 27				
▲	29, 51, 75				
■	1.3, 2.1				
LISTEN FOR INFORMATION ▲	15, 22, 23, 34, 35, 81, 87	107, 159, 161, 172, 206, 207	217, 244	316, 317, 353, 356, 357, 372–374	
FOLLOW DIRECTIONS ●	26, 27, 48, 49, 72, 73, 92, 93	116, 117, 146, 147, 188, 189	236, 237, 260, 261, 282, 283, 306	332, 333, 358, 359, 388, 389, 408	

● = book (pages)　　▲ = annotations (pages)　　■ = workbook (chapter section)

5	6	7	8	9	10
412, 436, 458	486, 508, 526	550, 568, 588	614, 630, 652	676, 706, 728	748, 772, 792
434, 435, 456, 457, 482, 483	506, 507, 524, 525, 546, 547	566, 567, 586, 587, 610, 611	628, 629, 650, 651, 672, 673	704, 705, 726, 727, 744, 745	770, 771, 790, 791, 810, 811
					810
	509		631	689, 741	
					810, 811
	509				749
421, 438, 467, 471, 481			659, 665, 666	741	786

5	6	7	8	9	10
17.3			28.4	30.1	
457, 482	507, 547		627, 635, 651, 673	705, 727	791
420, 424, 477	487	561, 564	619, 653, 662, 663, 670	681, 729, 731	764, 777, 779, 793, 805
17.4, 19.2, 19.5	20.1, 20.3, 21.3	24.3	27.2, 28.2		34.1
		611			
		584, 597			
	22.4				32.2
	546				
429, 471	495, 532, 540	555, 562, 563, 565, 575, 581, 590, 602	622, 638, 671	684, 694, 700, 702	756, 766, 781
431, 432, 456, 457, 482	506, 507, 524, 525, 546	566, 567, 610	628, 629, 650, 651, 672	704, 705, 726, 727, 744	770, 771, 790, 791, 810

Skills Designations reprinted and adapted with the permission of
The National Council for the Social Studies.

T21

	UNIT 1	2	3	4	
WRITE REPORTS AND RESEARCH PAPERS ●			237		
▲	4–7, 14, 24, 30, 31, 40, 58, 62, 64, 68, 69, 78, 89	99, 100, 101, 136, 143, 152, 158, 162, 194	220, 222, 223, 226–229, 231–233, 240, 250, 252, 288, 289, 293, 296–298, 302	312, 315, 318, 320, 323, 329, 340, 346, 355, 368, 371, 380, 387, 395, 397, 403, 404	
■				16.1	

REFERENCE AND INFORMATION SEARCH SKILLS

THE LIBRARY

	UNIT 1	2	3	4	
USE CARD CATALOG TO LOCATE BOOKS ●					
▲					
USE *READERS' GUIDE TO PERIODICAL LITERATURE* AND OTHER INDEXES ●					
▲					

SPECIAL REFERENCES

	UNIT 1	2	3	4	
ALMANACS ●					
▲				350	
ENCYCLOPEDIAS ●			237, 283	408	
▲			239	336	
DICTIONARIES ●				333	
▲			229		
GOVERNMENT PUBLICATIONS ●		189			
▲		164, 166, 168, 171, 197, 201, 205–207	222, 223, 232–234, 276, 277	312, 313, 342, 378, 382, 393, 397, 399, 400	
■	3.2, 4.3				
NEWS SOURCES: NEWSPAPERS, MAGAZINES ●				359	
▲	84	125, 169, 170	298, 305	320, 324, 325, 342, 354, 361, 403	
■			12.4	15.2	

● = book (pages)　　▲ = annotations (pages)　　■ = workbook (chapter section)

5	6	7	8	9	10	
420, 424, 432, 433, 438, 454, 455, 467, 469, 480	488, 491, 492, 499, 501, 515, 527, 536, 538, 539	554, 560, 561, 572, 573, 594, 596, 600, 604, 605	618, 637, 639, 640, 649, 655, 659, 664–666, 669	680, 685, 689, 698, 715, 734, 737, 743	755, 759, 760, 779, 782, 804, 806	● ▲ ■

5	6	7	8	9	10	
		567, 587, 611				
		589				
			629, 673			
			631			

5	6	7	8	9	10	
				744		
					749	
					807	
	542, 544	596, 598, 608	667	690, 719		
	525		629			
453, 459	490, 503, 516, 521, 527, 534	569, 601, 603, 606	637, 642, 645, 656, 658, 665, 666	667, 685, 692, 701, 741	759, 768, 769, 799	
18.3, 19.3	21.4		26.1, 28.3	30.2		

Skills Designations reprinted and adapted with the permission of The National Council for the Social Studies.

REFERENCE AND INFORMATION SEARCH SKILLS

MAPS, GLOBES, GRAPHS

		UNIT 1	2	3	4	
MAP AND GLOBE ORIENT A MAP AND NOTE DIRECTIONS	●		147			
	▲	13	149	249, 254		
	■	1.1	7.2	10.3		
LOCATE PLACES ON A MAP	●		147		408	
	▲	13	149	249, 254	336	
	■	1.1	5.1	9.2, 10.3	14.1	
USE SCALE AND COMPUTE DISTANCES	●		117, 147			
	■				14.1	
INTERPRET MAP SYMBOLS AND VISUALIZE WHAT THEY MEAN	●		117		408	
	▲		119			
	■	2.4		10.3	15.1	
COMPARE MAPS AND MAKE INFERENCES	●		117, 211			
	▲	13		254		
	■	2.4, 4.1				
EXPRESS RELATIVE LOCATION	●		147			
	▲	13	149	249, 254		
	■	2.4	5.1, 7.2		14.1	
INTERPRET GRAPHS	●	26, 48, 72, 92	116, 146, 188, 210	236, 260, 282, 283, 306	332, 358, 388, 408	
	▲	44, 45, 58	160, 199, 203		362, 363	
	■	2.4	5.3, 5.4, 6.3, 8.3	9.3, 11.1	14.3	
DETECT BIAS IN VISUAL MATERIALS	●					
	▲					
	■					
INTERPRET SOCIAL AND POLITICAL MESSAGES OF CARTOONS	▲		110		405	
	■			11.4	16.4	
INTERPRET HISTORY THROUGH ARTIFACTS	●			306		
	▲	6, 7		246, 302	320, 324, 325, 369–371	
	■				13.2, 16.1	

● = book (pages)   ▲ = annotations (pages)   ■ = workbook (chapter section)

5	6	7	8	9	10
435					
465					
17.2					
413, 465		574	665, 666		
17.2				30.3	
435					
		610			
437, 465					
17.1	22.2			30.3	
435					
437, 465		574	615		
17.1	22.2			29.2, 30.3	
435					791
			615, 665, 666		
17.2					
434, 456, 482	506, 546	566, 586, 610	628, 650, 651, 672, 673	704, 726, 727, 744, 745	790, 791, 810
444, 477			663, 670	681, 729	
17.2, 19.5	20.1, 20.3, 21.1, 21.3	24.3	27.2, 27.3	29.3, 31.3	32.1, 33.2, 34.3
457				705	
		606			
	22.3				
439, 455, 459		606			
18.2		24.1, 25.4		29.1	
457	507, 525		672, 673	705	
432, 433, 472, 473	503, 521, 534	606	642, 658, 665, 666	677, 685, 692, 701	768, 769, 786, 799
19.4					

Skills Designations reprinted and adapted with the permission of
The National Council for the Social Studies.

T25

REFERENCE AND INFORMATION SEARCH SKILLS

COMMUNITY RESOURCE		UNIT 1	2	3	4	
USE SOURCES OF INFORMATION IN THE COMMUNITY	▲	4–7, 30	172	250	355	
CONDUCT INTERVIEWS OF INDIVIDUALS IN THE COMMUNITY	▲					

ELECTRONIC SKILLS

COMPUTER		UNIT 1	2	3	4	
OPERATE A COMPUTER USING PREPARED INSTRUCTIONAL OR REFERENCE PROGRAMS	▲		97			
OPERATE A COMPUTER TO ENTER AND RETRIEVE INFO.	▲					

INTELLECTUAL SKILLS

CLASSIFY INFORMATION		UNIT 1	2	3	4	
IDENTIFY RELEVANT FACTUAL MATERIAL	●	12, 16, 25–27, 33, 37, 44, 49, 77, 83, 87, 91, 92	103, 107, 111, 115, 117, 127, 128, 133, 138, 145, 147, 151, 158, 162, 167, 189, 194, 200, 207, 211	220, 225, 232, 235, 237, 245, 248, 252, 257, 261, 266, 271, 276, 281, 283, 289, 291, 294, 305, 307	316, 322, 329, 333, 342, 346, 353, 357, 359, 368, 373, 382, 387, 389, 395, 400, 405, 407, 409	
	▲	9–11, 14, 22, 23, 29–33, 37, 44–47, 51, 53, 56, 57, 58, 61, 68–69, 75–79, 89, 90	97, 100–102, 106, 108, 114, 115, 119, 125, 126, 130, 131, 133, 136, 143, 144, 149–152, 156, 158, 162–164, 168–170, 194, 195, 197–199, 203–207	215, 216, 218–220, 222–224, 226, 227, 229, 231–232, 240–243, 250–253, 265, 268, 269, 274, 276–279, 288–291, 295–298, 302, 304	312–315, 324, 325, 330, 331, 340, 350, 355, 366, 368, 387, 392, 395, 398, 400, 401, 404	
	□	3.1, 4.2	8.2			
SENSE RELATIONSHIP BETWEEN ITEMS OF FACTUAL INFORMATION	●	12, 16, 25–27, 33, 49, 77, 83, 87, 92	103, 107, 111, 117, 127, 133, 145, 147, 151, 158, 167, 189, 198, 200, 207, 211	232, 235, 237, 248, 252, 261, 271, 276, 283, 289, 291, 294, 305, 307	316, 322, 329, 333, 346, 357, 359, 368, 373, 382, 387, 389, 395, 400, 405, 407, 409	
	▲	8–11, 13, 15, 22, 23, 26, 27, 30, 32, 33, 36, 37, 44–47, 51, 55–57, 61, 68, 69, 72, 73, 75, 76, 78, 79, 90, 92, 93	97, 100–102, 106, 114, 115, 126, 130, 131, 136, 146, 150, 151, 158, 160–163, 168–170, 195, 197–199, 205	215, 218, 219, 221–227, 229, 231, 240–243, 248, 250–252, 269, 270, 276–279, 288–291, 296, 297, 302, 304	312–315, 321, 324, 325, 330, 331, 352, 362, 363, 395, 399, 401	
	□	3.1, 4.2			13.3	

● = book (pages)   ▲ = annotations (pages)   □ = workbook (chapter section)

5	6	7	8	9	10	
421, 467, 471, 481			659, 665, 666	741	786	▲
467			659, 665, 666, 669	689	751, 760, 776, 789	▲

5	6	7	8	9	10	
			653, 663		755, 779	▲
			653, 663		755, 779	▲

5	6	7	8	9	10	
420, 423, 427, 430, 431, 435, 441, 453, 455, 457, 463, 467, 477, 481–483	492, 496, 501, 502, 505, 507, 512, 515, 520, 521, 525, 530, 533, 538, 545, 547	556, 561, 563, 565, 567, 572, 576, 583, 587, 592, 596, 603, 607, 609, 611	618, 623, 627, 629, 635, 643, 647, 651, 657, 661, 667, 671, 673	679, 688, 691, 701, 705, 712, 721, 725, 727, 735, 738, 741, 745	759, 764, 769, 771, 779, 783, 786, 789, 791, 799, 805, 807, 811	●
414, 416, 417, 440, 451, 453, 454, 461, 463, 467–469, 472, 473, 481	489, 491, 499, 501, 503, 515, 521, 529, 538, 539	554, 559, 573, 577, 578, 592, 596	618, 624, 635, 645, 663, 670	681, 724		▲
17.3			28.4	30.1		■
420, 427, 430, 431, 435, 455, 457, 467, 474, 482, 483	501, 502, 505, 512, 515, 521, 530, 533, 547	547, 563, 567, 572, 583, 587, 596, 609, 611	618, 623, 629, 635, 651, 657, 661, 667, 671, 673	679, 688, 691, 701, 712, 721, 725, 727, 735, 738, 741, 745	559, 771, 779, 783, 789, 791, 799, 811	●
416, 417, 424, 463, 465, 477	492, 515, 521, 529, 533, 534, 538, 544	560, 561, 579, 583, 593, 594, 606	623, 639, 642, 643	681, 701, 710, 717, 724, 733, 737	755, 766, 777, 783, 793, 797, 805, 807	▲
			28.4			■

Skills Designations reprinted and adapted with the permission of The National Council for the Social Studies.

		UNIT 1	2	3	4	
GROUP DATA IN CATEGORIES ACCORDING TO APPROPRIATE CRITERIA	●	27, 49	138, 189, 211		359, 373, 409	
	▲	10, 11, 32, 33, 37, 55, 58, 68–69, 76, 78, 79, 89, 90	97, 100, 101, 109, 114, 115, 135, 151, 152, 156, 163, 166, 168, 203	215, 216, 225, 240, 248, 250, 265, 268, 276, 277, 290, 295	366, 392	
	■	3.1, 4.2	7.5, 8.3		13.3	
PLACE IN PROPER SEQUENCE: 1) ORDER OF OCCURRENCE 2) ORDER OF IMPORTANCE	●	26	211	307		
	▲	15, 26, 27, 37, 51, 75	199	217, 251, 296, 297	362, 363	
	■	4.4				
PLACE IN TABULAR FORM: CHARTS, GRAPHS, ILLUSTRATIONS	●		138		409	
	▲	10, 11, 55, 58	97, 119, 144, 166, 199, 203	216, 274, 285, 290	366, 392	
	■		8.3		13.3b, 15.1	

INTERPRET INFORMATION		UNIT 1	2	3	4	
STATE RELATIONSHIPS BETWEEN CATEGORIES OF INFORMATION	●	12, 27, 33, 49, 77, 83, 87	103, 107, 111, 117, 147, 198, 200, 207, 211	232, 237, 248, 252, 261, 271, 276, 283, 289, 291, 294, 305, 307	316, 329, 333, 346, 353, 357, 359, 368, 373, 382, 387, 389, 395, 400, 405, 407, 409	
	▲	8, 10, 11, 13, 24, 26–27, 32, 33, 36, 44–47, 55–58, 72, 73, 76, 78, 79, 89, 92, 93	97, 100, 101, 106, 109, 114, 115, 119, 136, 151, 152, 156, 158, 162, 164, 166, 168, 171, 195, 197–199, 203, 205–207	215, 216, 218, 219, 221–227, 229, 231, 240–243, 248, 250, 252, 253, 265, 268, 276–279, 285, 288–290, 298, 301, 304	312, 313, 318, 320, 322, 324, 338, 342, 343, 362, 363, 379, 381, 384, 394, 396–398, 400, 401	
	■	3.1, 4.2	7.3, 8.3		13.3	
NOTE CAUSE AND EFFECT RELATIONSHIPS	●	12, 27, 37, 49, 77, 83, 87, 92	115, 158, 189, 207	232, 235, 237, 248, 252, 261, 276, 283, 289, 305, 307	316, 353, 357, 359, 368, 389, 400, 407, 409	
	▲	8, 13, 15, 22–24, 26–27, 37, 44–47, 58, 92, 93	100–102, 106, 109, 144, 151, 199, 204	225, 227, 231, 251–253, 265, 266, 270, 276–279, 288, 289	312–317, 321, 322, 330, 331, 338, 352, 362, 363	
	■	4.4	8.3	12.2	16.2	
DRAW INFERENCES FROM FACTUAL MATERIAL	●	12, 27, 37, 49	103, 107, 111, 115, 117, 128, 147, 151, 158, 167, 189, 194, 200, 207, 211	237, 257, 271, 283	316, 322, 329, 333, 353, 357, 359, 382, 409	
	▲	8, 9, 19, 26, 27, 32, 33, 36, 37, 41, 47, 53, 58, 72, 73, 76, 77, 83, 84, 90	100–102, 106, 108, 114, 115, 133, 150, 151, 152, 156, 160, 162, 164, 171, 195, 199, 204–207	218, 219, 221, 224, 225, 231, 241–243, 248, 250, 286, 291, 293, 298, 304	312–315, 321, 324, 325, 338, 343, 362, 363, 379, 381, 384, 392, 395, 396, 398	
	■	2.3				

 = book (pages)   = annotations (pages)   ■ = workbook (chapter section)

5	6	7	8	9	10
	525, 545			727	791
468, 477	515	564, 579, 583, 597		681, 731	764, 777, 805
17.3				30.1	
				727	559, 771, 783, 791, 807
		584, 592		729	793, 805
17.4					
457			651	727	791
420, 424, 432, 433, 477		564, 584, 597	615, 619, 653, 662, 665, 666, 690	681, 729, 731	
19.2	21.3	24.3	27.2, 27.3, 28.2		

5	6	7	8	9	10
430, 435, 453, 455, 457, 467, 477, 483	496, 501, 507, 512, 520, 521, 525, 530, 533, 547	563, 565, 567, 576, 587, 596, 607, 611	623, 629, 643, 647, 651, 657, 673	679, 688, 691, 705, 721, 727, 738, 745	759, 764, 769, 771, 786, 789, 791, 811
414, 432, 433, 444, 453, 463, 468, 469, 477, 481	489, 492, 514, 515, 522, 528, 533, 544	559–561, 577, 579, 583, 592, 597, 601, 606	619, 620, 623, 637, 642, 643, 648, 649, 658	681, 689, 699, 710, 714, 718, 719, 731	762, 773, 777, 783, 797, 800, 805, 808
17.3, 19.5	21.1	23.3	26.1		
423, 430, 435, 455	492, 502, 507, 512, 515, 521, 525, 533, 538, 547	580, 587, 596, 603, 607, 611	623, 629, 647, 651, 661, 667, 671, 673	679, 688, 712, 721, 725, 727, 741, 745	759, 771, 783, 791, 811
414, 467	489	556, 592, 593, 594, 599	623, 624, 643, 648		764
17.5, 19.5b					
420, 435, 474	547	587, 603, 611	629, 651		811
414, 416, 417, 440, 442, 444, 455, 463, 465, 472, 473, 481	487, 492, 521, 522, 528, 533, 544	556, 560, 577, 578, 593, 594, 596	623, 624, 635, 639, 642, 643, 658, 667	681	

Skills Designations reprinted and adapted with the permission of
The National Council for the Social Studies.

T29

	UNIT 1	2	3	4	
PREDICT LIKELY OUTCOMES BASED ON FACTUAL MATERIAL ▲	37, 46	102	225	312–315, 324, 325	
RECOGNIZE THE VALUE DIMENSION OF INTERPRETING FACTUAL MATERIAL ●	49	117	261, 283	359	
▲	9, 10, 22–24, 26–27, 41, 77	98, 99, 110, 114, 115, 126, 129–131, 156, 162, 164, 194, 195, 205	218, 219, 221–224, 248, 296	346, 403	
■		6.1, 6.2	12.2, 12.4	13.1, 13.4	
RECOGNIZE INSTANCES WHERE MORE THAN ONE INTERPRETATION OF FACTUAL MATERIAL IS VALID ●				359	
▲		98, 99, 114, 115, 195	221–224, 241	403	
■		6.2		13.2	

INTELLECTUAL SKILLS

ANALYZE INFORMATION

	UNIT 1	2	3	4	
FORM A SIMPLE ORGANIZATION OF KEY IDEAS RELATED TO A TOPIC ●	26, 27, 49, 73	138, 189, 211		409	
▲	10, 11, 37, 51, 55, 75, 78, 79	97, 100, 101, 114, 115, 119, 130, 131, 133, 151, 166, 199, 203	215, 216, 274, 290	366, 392	
■	3.1, 4.2	7.5			
SEPARATE A TOPIC INTO MAJOR COMPONENTS ACCORDING TO APPROPRIATE CRITERIA ●	26, 27, 49, 73	138, 189, 211	291, 294, 307	342, 346, 409	
▲	9–11, 32, 33, 47, 51, 55, 78, 79	97, 100, 101, 106, 109, 114, 115, 130, 131, 133, 136, 150–152, 156, 158, 162–164, 171, 197–199, 203	215, 216, 224, 225, 250, 276, 277, 290, 295, 298–302	366, 392, 400	
■	3.1, 4.2	7.5			
EXAMINE CRITICALLY THE RELATIONSHIPS BETWEEN AND AMONG ELEMENTS OF A TOPIC ●	16, 27, 33, 37, 49, 59, 66, 69, 73, 77, 83, 87, 92	107, 111, 115, 117, 147, 158, 189, 200, 207, 211	232, 237, 248, 261, 276, 283	316, 322, 329, 333, 346, 357, 359, 382, 389, 395, 400, 407, 409	
▲	8, 13, 14, 19, 24, 26–27, 32, 33, 36, 37, 44–47, 53, 58, 72, 73, 76	100, 101, 106, 109, 114, 115, 130, 131, 136, 150, 151, 156, 158, 160, 162–164, 166, 171, 195, 197–199, 203–207	221–224, 227, 229, 231, 240–243, 248, 252, 253, 265, 268, 276–279, 291, 293, 295, 298–302, 304	312–315, 318, 321, 322, 330, 331, 338, 340, 342, 343, 362, 363, 379, 384, 394–396, 398, 400, 401	
■					

 = book (pages)   = annotations (pages)   = workbook (chapter section)

5	6	7	8	9	10	
	489	594	648	689, 692	783, 807, 809	
	507, 525, 547	611	629			
418, 419, 440, 455, 472, 473, 483	501, 503, 527	606	636, 642	689, 707		
17.6, 19.3	20.2, 21.4	23.2	26.1, 26.2, 28.3	30.2		
			629			
472, 473					776	
19.3	22.3		26.1			

5	6	7	8	9	10	
457				727	791	
420, 424, 477		564, 584, 597	619, 662	681, 729, 731	764, 777, 779	
17.3, 19.2			28.4	30.1		
457, 482					791	
463, 468, 477		579, 583, 597	619, 623, 635, 658, 667	714, 731	777	
17.3			28.4	30.1		
420, 431, 435, 477	533	611	629, 651	725, 727	759, 771, 791	
416, 417, 431–433, 437, 440, 447–454, 455, 459, 463, 467, 469, 472, 473, 477, 481, 483	489, 492, 514, 515, 521, 522, 527, 528, 533, 538, 542, 544	559, 560, 577, 579, 583, 591–594, 599, 605	618, 620, 623, 624, 635–637, 643, 648, 649	681, 689, 699, 701, 710, 714, 717, 731	755, 762, 773, 777, 784	
			27.3			

Skills Designations reprinted and adapted with the permission of The National Council for the Social Studies.

	UNIT 1	2	3	4	
DETECT BIAS IN DATA IN VARIOUS FORMS: PRINT, TABLE, GRAPH, VISUAL ●	49	117	261, 283, 307	359, 389, 409	
▲	9, 19, 26, 27, 77	97, 98, 110, 114, 115, 125, 126, 129–131, 162, 194, 201, 204, 205	249, 269, 278, 279, 296	324–327, 346, 361, 370, 403, 405	
■			12.1, 12.2, 12.3, 12.4	13.1, 13.2	
COMPARE AND CONTRAST CREDIBILITY OF DIFFERING ACCOUNTS OF THE SAME EVENT ●	49	117	220, 261, 307	359, 405	
▲	24, 36, 41	98, 99, 110, 114, 115, 125, 126, 129–131, 163, 194, 195	221, 224, 276, 277	324–327, 346, 403	
■				13.1, 13.2	

SUMMARIZE INFORMATION

	UNIT 1	2	3	4	
EXTRACT SIGNIFICANT IDEAS FROM SUPPORTING ILLUSTRATIVE DETAILS ●	26, 27, 33, 37, 49, 69, 73, 77, 87, 91, 92	103, 107, 115, 133, 147, 167, 189, 198, 200, 211	237, 248, 261, 283, 294, 307	316, 322, 329, 333, 357, 382, 389, 407, 409	
▲	9, 32, 33, 37, 44–47, 51, 53, 55, 58, 75–79, 90	97, 100, 101, 102, 106, 107, 110, 114, 115, 119, 130, 131, 133, 136, 150–152, 156, 160, 162–164, 169, 170, 195, 199–203, 205–207	215, 216, 218, 219, 221–225, 229, 231–233, 240–243, 265, 268, 270, 286, 290, 291, 293, 301, 304	312–317, 321, 322, 330, 331, 338, 379, 381, 382, 384, 394–396, 398, 399, 401	
■	3.1, 4.2	8.2		13.3b, 16.1	
COMBINE CRITICAL CONCEPTS INTO A STATEMENT OF CONCLUSIONS BASED ON INFORMATION ●	73, 77, 83, 87, 92	115, 117, 128, 145, 147, 211	237, 283, 307	316, 322, 329, 333, 357, 359, 400, 409	
▲	9, 36, 44–47, 53, 58, 76, 77, 83, 84	100–102, 109, 114, 115, 150, 151, 156, 162–164, 195, 197–205	218, 219, 221–225, 242, 243, 248, 269, 276, 277, 291, 293, 295, 298, 304	314, 315, 321, 322, 338, 362, 363, 379, 394, 395, 398, 400	
■			12.2	14.3, 16.1	
RESTATE MAJOR IDEAS OF A COMPLEX TOPIC IN CONCISE FORM ●	12, 26, 27, 49, 73	138, 189, 211		409	
▲	8–11, 32, 33, 37, 51, 55, 75, 78, 79	97, 114, 115, 130, 131, 150, 156, 166, 203	215, 216, 274, 290	366, 392	
■	3.1, 4.2	7.5, 8.2			

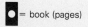

● = book (pages)   ▲ = annotations (pages)   ■ = workbook (chapter section)

5	6	7	8	9	10
435, 457	505, 507, 525, 547	611	629	705	
439, 455, 459, 461	488, 501, 503, 514, 515, 521, 522, 527, 534	601, 606	636, 642	689, 692, 707	
19.3	20.2, 21.4	23.2, 25.4	26.1	30.2	
	501, 505, 507, 525, 547				
418, 419, 440, 472, 473, 483	503, 527	596	642, 669	689	776, 784
18.3, 19.3	20.2, 22.3		26.1	30.2	

5	6	7	8	9	10
420, 435, 457	507, 530, 547	580, 587, 611	629, 651	691, 727	771, 791, 811
414, 418, 419, 431, 440, 442, 444, 454, 455, 461, 463, 465, 468, 474	489, 492, 499, 515, 516, 521, 522, 529, 533, 542	559, 560, 564, 577–579, 583, 591–594, 596, 601	623, 635–637, 643, 648, 658	681, 689, 699, 701, 731	773
17.3, 17.4, 19.2, 19.5	20.1, 20.3, 20.4, 21.1, 21.3		28.4	29.3, 30.1, 31.3	33.2, 34.1
435	507	580, 587, 611	629, 651	727	771, 791
414, 416, 417, 463, 472–474	487, 489, 492, 514, 515, 521, 522, 527, 529, 533, 534, 542, 544	556, 559, 560, 577–579, 583	618, 620, 623, 624, 658	681, 689, 699, 701, 709, 717, 729	756, 773, 784
17.4, 19.5	20.3, 20.4, 21.1, 21.3				33.2, 34.3
457, 482				727	791
420, 424, 468, 477		564, 584, 597	619, 662	681, 729, 731	764, 777
17.3, 17.4, 19.2			28.4	30.1	

Skills Designations reprinted and adapted with the permission of The National Council for the Social Studies.

	UNIT	1	2	3	4	
FORM OPINION BASED ON CRITICAL EXAMINATION OF RELEVANT INFORMATION	●				409	
	▲	9, 19, 36, 53, 76, 83, 84	102, 108, 156, 197, 203	218, 219, 221, 225, 241, 265, 268, 278, 279, 296	312, 313, 384, 395–397	

INTELLECTUAL SKILLS
SYNTHESIZE INFORMATION

	UNIT	1	2	3	4	
REINTERPRET EVENTS IN TERMS OF WHAT MIGHT HAVE HAPPENED, AND SHOW THE LIKELY EFFECTS ON SUBSEQUENT EVENTS	●	27				
	▲		114, 115	225		
PRESENT VISUALLY (CHART, GRAPH, DIAGRAM, MODEL, ETC.) INFORMATION EXTRACTED FROM PRINT	●		138		409	
	▲	10, 11, 55	97, 119, 113, 144, 149, 199, 203	216, 220, 274, 285, 290, 305	329, 336, 366, 369, 370, 371, 392	
	■				13.3b, 15.1	
PREPARE A RESEARCH PAPER THAT REQUIRES A CREATIVE SOLUTION TO A PROBLEM	▲		114, 115			
COMMUNICATE ORALLY AND IN WRITING	●	12, 16, 25–27, 33, 37, 44, 49, 59, 66, 69, 73, 77, 83, 87, 91, 92	103, 107, 111, 115, 117, 127, 128, 133, 145, 147, 151, 158, 167, 188, 189, 194, 200, 207, 211	220, 225, 232, 235, 236, 237, 245, 248, 252, 257, 261, 266, 271, 276, 281–283, 289, 291, 294, 305–307	316, 322, 329, 332, 333, 342, 346, 353, 357–359, 368, 373, 382, 387–389, 395, 400, 405, 407–409	
	▲	4–7, 14, 17, 19, 24, 30–33, 36, 37, 40, 41, 44–47, 51, 53, 58, 62, 64, 68–69, 75–79, 83–84, 89, 90	97, 99, 100, 102, 106, 109, 110, 114, 115, 119, 122, 125, 126, 129–131, 133, 136, 143, 150–152, 156, 158, 160, 162–164, 168, 171, 172, 194, 195, 197–207	215, 216, 218–227, 229, 231–233, 240–243, 248, 250, 252, 253, 265, 266, 268–270, 274, 276–279, 286, 288, 289, 291, 293, 295–298, 301, 302, 304	312–318, 320–327, 329–331, 338, 340, 342, 343, 346, 352, 354, 355, 361–363, 368–370, 379–382, 384, 387, 394–397, 399–401, 403, 404	
	■	2.1, 2.4, 3.3, 4.1, 4.4	6.1, 6.2, 6.4, 8.2	9.1, 11.3, 12.1, 12.3	14.1, 16.1, 16.4	

● = book (pages)   ▲ = annotations (pages)   ■ = workbook (chapter section)

5	6	7	8	9	10	
		611		727	771, 811	●
418, 419, 431–433, 474, 481	496	599	618, 620, 639, 649	699, 701, 710, 729	752, 778–780, 783, 798, 807	▲

5	6	7	8	9	10	
457			651			●
		599		719	783	▲
457			651	727	791	●
420, 424, 432, 433, 453, 455, 477, 480	488, 521, 531	564, 584, 597, 606	615, 619, 637, 653, 662, 665, 666, 670	681, 729, 731	759, 764, 777	▲
19.2		24.3	27.2, 28.2		34.1	■
						▲
420, 423, 427, 430, 431, 434, 435, 441, 453, 455–457, 463, 467, 477, 481–483	492, 496, 501, 502, 505–507, 512, 515, 520, 521, 524, 525, 530, 533, 538, 545–547	556, 561, 563, 565–567, 572, 576, 583, 586, 587, 592, 596, 603, 607, 609–611	618, 623, 627–629, 635, 643, 647, 650, 651, 657, 661, 667, 671–673	679, 688, 691, 701, 704, 705, 712, 721, 725–727, 735, 738, 741, 744, 745	759, 764, 769, 770, 771, 779, 783, 786, 789–791, 799, 805, 807, 810, 811	●
414, 416–421, 424, 431, 433, 438, 440, 442, 451, 453, 454, 455, 461, 463, 465, 467–469, 472–474, 477, 480	488–492, 496, 499, 501, 503, 509, 514–516, 522, 527–529, 533, 534, 536, 538, 539, 542, 544	554, 556, 559–561, 572, 573, 577, 579, 583, 592–594, 596, 599–601, 604–606, 608	618, 620, 623, 624, 631, 635–637, 639, 640, 642, 643, 648, 649, 655, 658, 659, 663–667, 669, 670	680, 681, 685, 689, 690, 692, 698, 699, 701, 708, 710, 715, 724, 730, 733, 734, 737, 742, 743	752, 755, 756, 759, 760, 762, 778–780, 782–784, 797, 800, 803–809	▲
17.1, 17.6, 19.3, 19.5	20.3, 20.4, 21.1, 21.2, 22.2, 22.3	24.3, 25.3	27.1, 27.2, 28.4	29.1–29.3, 30.3, 31.3	32.3, 33.2, 33.3, 34.3	■

Skills Designations reprinted and adapted with the permission of The National Council for the Social Studies.

EVALUATE INFORMATION

	UNIT	1	2	3	4	
DETERMINE WHETHER OR NOT THE INFORMATION IS PERTINENT TO THE TOPIC	●	26, 27				
	▲	9–11, 29, 36, 37, 44, 45, 51, 55, 58, 75, 90	97, 100–102, 106, 109, 114, 115, 119, 133, 136, 143, 150–152, 158, 169, 170, 195, 199, 204–207	215, 216, 222, 223, 240, 250, 293, 295, 298	329, 346, 361, 370	
	■	3.1, 4.2				
ESTIMATE THE ADEQUACY OF THE INFORMATION	●	37, 41	114, 115, 125	266	396, 398, 403	
	■					
TEST THE VALIDITY OF INFORMATION IN TERMS OF SOURCE, CREDIBILITY, AND TECHNICAL CORRECTNESS	●	49	117, 147	261, 283, 307	359, 409	
	▲	24	98, 99, 110, 126, 130, 131, 194	218, 219, 221, 224, 278, 279	327, 398, 403	
	■			12.4	13.1, 13.2	

DECISION-MAKING SKILLS

	UNIT	1	2	3	4	
IDENTIFY SITUATION WHERE A DECISION IS REQUIRED	▲	56, 57	114, 115			
SECURE THE NEEDED FACTUAL INFORMATION RELEVANT TO THE DECISION	▲	36, 56, 57	102, 114, 115, 150			
RECOGNIZE VALUES IMPLICIT IN THE SITUATION & ISSUES THAT FLOW FROM THEM	▲					
		36, 56, 57	102, 114, 115			
IDENTIFY ALTERNATIVE COURSES OF ACTION AND PREDICT LIKELY CONSEQUENCE OF EACH	▲		102, 114, 115, 150			
MAKE DECISION BASED ON THE DATA OBTAINED	▲	56, 57	114, 115, 150			
TAKE ACTION TO IMPLEMENT THE DECISION	▲		114, 115			

 = book (pages)　　 = annotations (pages)　　 = workbook (chapter section)

5	6	7	8	9	10	
						●
453				773		▲
						■
				689		●
	22.3					■
	501, 505, 507, 525, 547		629	705, 745		●
418, 419	503, 527	601, 606	642	689, 707		▲
19.3	20.2, 21.4, 22.3	23.2	26.1, 26.2, 28.3	30.2		■

5	6	7	8	9	10	
						▲
						▲
						▲
						▲
						▲
						▲

Skills Designations reprinted and adapted with the permission of
The National Council for the Social Studies.

PERSONAL SKILLS

	UNIT 1	2	3	4	
COMMUNICATE OWN BELIEFS, FEELINGS, AND CONVICTIONS ▲	36, 53, 56, 57, 83, 84	102, 150		395	
ADJUST OWN BEHAVIOR TO FIT THE DYNAMICS OF VARIOUS GROUP SITUATIONS ▲	56, 57	114, 115			
RECOGNIZE THE MUTUAL RELATIONSHIP BETWEEN HUMAN BEINGS IN SATISFYING EACH OTHER'S NEEDS ▲	56, 57	114, 115, 150			

GROUP INTERACTION SKILLS

	UNIT 1	2	3	4	
CONTRIBUTE TO DEVELOPMENT OF SUPPORTIVE GROUP CLIMATES ▲	56, 57	150			
PARTICIPATE IN MAKING RULES AND GUIDELINES FOR GROUP LIFE ▲	56, 57	114, 115, 150			
ASSIST IN SETTING GROUP GOALS ▲	56, 57	150			
PARTICIPATE IN DELEGATING DUTIES, ORGANIZING, PLANNING, MAKING DECISIONS AND TAKING ACTION IN A GROUP SETTING ● ▲		114, 115	261		
PARTICIPATE IN PERSUADING, COMPROMISING, DEBATING, AND NEGOTIATING RESOLUTION OF CONFLICTS AND DIFFERENCES ▲ ■	56, 57	150, 163 6.2	276, 277		

SOCIAL AND POLITICAL PARTICIPATION SKILLS

	UNIT 1	2	3	4	
KEEP INFORMED ON ISSUES THAT AFFECT SOCIETY ▲ ■	36, 53, 68, 69, 72, 73, 76, 83, 84	169, 170, 172	218, 219, 241, 248, 265, 268, 278, 279, 288, 289, 295, 298 12.4		

 = book (pages)   = annotations (pages)   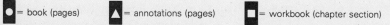 = workbook (chapter section)

5	6	7	8	9	10	
418, 419, 474, 481	496		618, 620	699, 701	752, 778, 780, 798	▲
						▲
						▲

5	6	7	8	9	10	
						▲
						▲
						▲
						●
						▲
418, 419		605				▲
						■

5	6	7	8	9	10	
451, 453, 459, 469, 471, 481	491, 496, 514, 515, 516, 521, 538	560, 598	618, 620, 623, 635, 639, 642, 663	708	755, 778, 788, 789	▲
					33.3, 34.2	■

Skills Designations reprinted and adapted with the permission of
The National Council for the Social Studies.

ANSWERS TO STUDENT EDITION QUESTIONS

CHAPTER 1

Section Review (text page 12)

1. Students' sentences will vary. Information about the names and terms can be found on the pages given in parentheses: Machu Picchu (6), the Inca (6–7), ideographs (7), counting coup (11), League of the Iroquois (12).
2. (a) over 25,000 years ago, (b) Asia
3. Students' responses should indicate that the Native Americans developed many different ways of life, or cultures, because of the need to adapt to the very great variety of physical environments in the Americas.
4. (a) Mayas, (b) Toltecs, (c) Eastern Woodlands Indians, (d) Plains Indians
5. The Hopi and Zuñi farmers used irrigation to bring water from springs and mountains to their farm fields.

Section Review (text page 16)

1. Students' sentences will vary. Information about the names can be found on the pages given in parentheses: the Indies (12–13), Prince Henry (14–15), Vasco da Gama (16).
2. (a) Crusaders who returned to Europe told of rich goods they had known in the East, such as food (sugar, oranges), cloth (cotton, silks), spices, drugs for pain and disease, and jewels that were rare in Europe, (b) The Renaissance opened the European mind to new ideas in writing, science, and philosophy, and it spurred explorers to reach beyond the boundaries of Europe to a ''New World'' far across the ocean, (c) Merchants of Italian city-states monopolized trade in Eastern luxuries, and their powerful navies controlled trade routes that excluded other Europeans, (d) Polo's book described a great ocean to the east of China, and Northern Europeans came to believe that a trade route could be found that would bypass the routes of the Italian merchants.
3. Possible answers include the following: Portugal led the way because of a strong seafaring tradition, because it was unified under a powerful ruling family, because of a strong national identity, because of the work of Prince Henry the Navigator.
4. Columbus suggested that Portugese ships catch westerly winds and sail directly to the Indies. He

believed that the ships would cross the Atlantic Ocean.

Section Review (text page 25)

1. Students' sentences will vary. Information about the names and terms can be found on the pages given in parentheses: Martin Waldesmuller (18), privateer (20), The *Victoria* (20), scurvy (20), conquistador (21, 24–25).
2. Columbus believed he had reached the Indies, so he called the Arawaks ''Indians.''
3. Ponce de Leon found Florida, a part of the ''unknown continent,'' instead of Asia, and Balboa crossed the Isthmus of Panama and found the Pacific Ocean, which meant that another sea voyage lay between Spain's Caribbean colonies and East Asia. Both explorations proved Vespucci correct in saying that Columbus discovered an unknown continent.
4. (a) Cortez—Mexico, (b) Pizarro—empire of Incas in western South America, (c) Esteban and de Niza—present-day New Mexico, (d) de Soto—southeastern part of what is now the U.S., as far north as Tennessee and Arkansas, and the Mississippi River, (e) Coronado—southwestern U.S., as far north as Kansas, the Grand Canyon, and lands of the Pueblo Indians.

Time Line Questions (text page 26)

1. 26, 542 years.
2. 1492 and 1542
3. 25,000 BC and 8,000 BC

Skills Strategy: Note–Taking (text pages 26–27)

The person formed the question from the text heading that best reflects the content of the remaining parts of Section 1 of the chapter.

1. What parts of the United States were settled by the first Americans?
   Southwestern Indians—Hopis, Zuñis, Navajos, Apache
2. Remaining notes should contain the subheadings on pages 10–11, each followed by the name(s) of Indians or some information about them.
3. Check to see that students have done necessary editing of their notes. (Note: Students will use their outlines for ''Writing a Paragraph.'')

Chapter Test (text page 27)

Text Review

1. Possible answers are that they may have been following migrating animals, or fleeing advancing glaciers, or trying to escape enemies.

2. The number of people in these Indian groups was small relative to the vast areas they settled. These first Americans had to spread out to grow or to hunt for food. Such a small population could not support centralized empires with advanced cultures like those found in Central and South America.

3. Possible answers are Prince Henry's establishment of a center for the advancement of the maritime arts at Sagres, the exploratory voyages along the Cape of Good Hope at Africa's tip, da Gama's voyage around the Cape of Good Hope and then on to India, and the founding of trading posts in East Africa, India, Indonesia, and Macao.

4. Possible answers are Columbus—Bahamas and parts of the American mainland, Ponce de Leon—Florida, Balboa—Isthmus of Panama, Cortez—Mexico, Pizarro—west coast of South America, Esteban and de Niza—New Mexico, de Soto—southeastern United States, Coronado—southwestern United States.

5. England—Cabot gave claim to what is now Newfoundland; France—Verrazano claimed lands of present-day North Carolina northward to Newfoundland, and Cartier claimed lands along the St. Lawrence River, sites of modern Quebec and Montreal.

6. The Aztecs—looking for gold, conquistadors under Cortez, through battle, treachery, and disease, conquered the Aztecs, destroyed their culture, and made Aztec people and lands part of the Spanish American empire. The Incas—led by Pizarro, other conquistadors cruelly overcame Incans' resistance to their advances and brought their empire under the control of Spain.

Critical Thinking

7. The Aztec emperor was thought to be a descendant of the chief Aztec god, but he was elected by the Aztec nobles and was not all-powerful like the Inca. The Incan emperor, called the Inca, was considered a god and had absolute power. All property was owned by the Inca and all his subjects paid him the *mita* (a labor tax), which represented the earnings of a specified number of days of labor done for the emperor.

8. Students' conclusions will vary. However, they should take into account the contrasting manifestations of Cortez's character—his bravery in overcoming hardship, suffering, and the larger Aztec forces, as well as his apparent greed for gold, his treachery in dealing with the Aztec emperor, and his bloody suppression of the Aztecs.

9. Students' hypotheses will vary. If left undisturbed for another hundred years, the Mayas might have developed their system of writing, as well as the sciences of astronomy, mathematics, and medicine, to a very advanced degree. Responses might take into account the Mayan practice of human sacrifice.

10. Students may choose from the Southwestern Indians, the people of the Great Basin, Indians of California, Pacific Northwest Indians, Eastern Woodlands Indians. Some students may choose to name specific tribes within these larger groups. (Note: Descriptions of these groups are given on pages 8–12.)

Writing a Paragraph
Sample paragraph:

The first Americans settled in different parts of what is now the United States. People known as Hopis, Zuñis, Navajos, and Apache farmed in the harsh environment of the Southwest. The Utes, Paiutes, and Shoshones managed to find food in the forbidding area of the Great Basin, between the Rockies and the Sierra Nevada. The Modoc, Mojave, and numerous other tribes lived in what is now California. Early people such as the Chinook and Nootka settled in the Pacific Northwest coastal areas. Eastward were the hunters and trappers of the plateau region, including the Nez Perce and Yakima. The Plains Indians lived between the Rockies and the Mississippi River. The tribes of the Southeast included the Creeks, Choctaws, and Cherokees. Indians who settled in the Northeast included the Algonkian-speaking Lenni Lenape and Narragansett. The Great Lakes region was inhabited by the Iroquois, Mohawk, Oneida, Seneca, Cayuga, and Onondaga.

CHAPTER 2

Section Review (text page 33)

1. Students' sentences will vary. Information about the names and terms can be found on the pages given in parentheses: encomienda system (30–31), presidio (32), Bartolomé de Las Casas (31), Junipero Serra (32), viceroy (33).

2. Establishment of a Spanish Empire had begun by 1550 because no more Indian kingdoms rich in gold

and silver were left to conquer, and more than five million Spanish settlers found new wealth in mining, farming, ranching, and trading rather than in conquests.

3. The economic philosophy was mercantilism. By exporting more than it imported, Spain could make money to build new businesses that would make more money. In this way, Spain would be less dependent on foreign goods. Under mercantilism, the Spanish colonies were expected to send natural resources to Spain, where they would be turned into finished goods to be sold back to the colonies. The Spanish colonists were only allowed to trade with merchants from Spain, and foreign ships were forbidden to enter Spanish ports in America.

4. In theory, the Spanish monarch had complete control over his American empire through four appointed viceroys. Actually, the Spanish monarch left control of the empire to six nobles in Spain who made up the Council of the Indies.

Section Review (text page 37)

1. Students' sentences will vary. Information about the names and terms can be found on the pages given in parentheses: Spanish Main (34), sea dog (34), galleon (35), *Golden Hind* (35–36), Sir Humphrey Gilbert (36).

2. England, France, and the Netherlands did not challenge Spain's monopoly because they did not have the wealth to build powerful armies and navies that could confront Spanish military power and because each country had problems at home: The Netherlands were in rebellion against Spain; France was divided by a civil war; England was torn by religious strife.

3. In England's name, Drake defied Spanish power. He smuggled slaves into the Caribbean, raided Spanish ports in the Caribbean and along the Pacific coast of Spanish America, brought thousands of pounds of Spanish silver and gold back to England, and destroyed 33 Spanish ships.

4. King Philip ordered the construction of a huge fleet, the Armada, to be used for an invasion of England. In 1588, he prepared 130 ships and 30,000 soldiers for battle.

Section Review (text page 44)

1. Students' sentences will vary. Information about the names and terms can be found on the pages given in parentheses: corporate charter (38), Powhatan (39), John Smith (39), headright system (40), indentured servant (40).

2. The London Company and the Plymouth Company founded colonies. They hoped to make money by

finding gold, by finding a route to Asia, or by buying animal hides and furs from Native Americans.

3. Rolfe raised tobacco and sold it to the English, who sold it throughout Europe for less money than the Spanish charged for their tobacco, thus creating a profitable tobacco trade which saved Jamestown from failure.

4. The Plymouth Company shareholders never made a profit from the colony. They wanted to salvage their investment and may have feared that the king would make Plymouth a royal colony, so they sold their charter to the colonists.

Section Review (text page 47)

1. Students' sentences will vary. Information about the names and terms can be found on the pages given in parentheses: Champlain (46, 47), Peter Minuit (47), patroon, (47), log cabin (47).

2. The Netherlands; Sweden; France.

3. Deer were rare in Europe and fur-bearing animals were nearly extinct. The Hurons and Algonkians traded with the French, but the Indians of the Iroquois Confederacy were hostile because Champlain had fired upon members of the Five Nations. Indians were not hostile to the Dutch, because the Dutch purchased land from them rather than simply taking it as the English sometimes did.

4. Peter Minuit and two dozen settlers build a fort in present-day Delaware and call it Christina; Johann Printz becomes governor and lures more settlers; new governor Johann Rising attacks Dutch fort; Dutch retaliate by taking control of New Sweden.

Time Line Questions (text page 48)

1. 61 years
2. Sir Francis Drake circumnavigated the globe
3. Virginia House of Burgesses established
4. 1607

Skills Strategy: Two-Level Outline (text pages 48–49)

1. Base the title on the heading or headings of the part of a chapter on which the outline is based.
2. The main topics are indicated by Roman numerals followed by periods.
3. The subtopics are indicated by capital letters followed by periods.
4. The word that begins each main topic and subtopic is capitalized. The first word of a main topic begins at the left margin. The first word of a subtopic is indented.
5. II. The Netherlands' Colonies
    A. New Amsterdam in New York

B. Fort Orange in New York

C. Newcastle in Delaware

(Note: Students will use their outlines for "Writing a Paragragh.")

Chapter Test (text page 49)

Text Review

1. The Spanish colonies were expected to send natural resources to Spain and then buy the finished goods Spanish workers made from them. In addition, colonists had to use only Spanish merchant vessels for the shipment of resources and finished goods that went to and from Spain. The colonists could buy only articles made in Spain and had to do without articles that were not made in Spain. In short, under mercantilism, the chief purpose of the Spanish colonies was the enrichment of their parent country.

2. Spanish colonial society was a hierarchy made up of people of many races. At the highest level were the white Spaniards from Spain. Then came criollos (Spaniards born in America), mestizos (of mixed Spanish and Indian blood) blacks, Indians, and zamboes (of mixed Indian and black blood). All of these groups were represented in all social classes and economic levels.

3. Viceroy of New Spain: Mexico to Costa Rica; Viceroy of New Granada: Panama, Colombia, Venezuela, Ecuador; Viceroyalty of La Plata: most of southern South America, including Uruguay, Argentina, Paraguay, Bolivia, and Chile.

4. Sir Francis Drake smuggled slaves into Spanish Caribbean colonies, attacked coastal cities on the Spanish Main and in California, stole Spanish gold and silver and sent it to England, destroyed 33 ships of the Spanish Armada in the harbor of Cadiz, Spain. Other sea dogs were Humphrey Gilbert, who challenged Spain by attempting to found an English settlement in Newfoundland; Walter Raleigh, who established the first English settlement at Roanoke, Virginia (the colonists disappeared mysteriously). Drake and other sea dogs helped to defeat the Spanish Armada.

5. The Spanish king, Philip II, recognized that the sea dogs represented an English threat to Spanish power in the Americas, so he decided to send the Armada to try to invade and conquer England before the threat became more serious.

6. Students' responses should refer to the strong leadership of John Smith in dealing with both the reluctance of the settlers to work and the enmity of the Powhatan Indians. Reference to John Rolfe's success in growing tobacco should also be included.

7. The second permanent English colony was in Plymouth, Massachusetts. It was settled by an English religious group known as Separatists (later, Pilgrims) who had sought refuge from persecution.

8. France—New France (St. Croix, Maine; Port Royal, Nova Scotia; Quebec); The Netherlands—New Amsterdam (Manhattan), Fort Orange (Albany, New York), Newcastle (Delaware); Sweden—Christina (Wilmington, Delaware).

Critical Thinking

9. Most students will agree that the de Las Casas book would be a more accurate source because of this priest's protests over Spanish treatment of the Indians. A Spanish encomendero's letter to the king of Spain would probably distort accounts or avoid mention of the harsh treatment of the Indians.

10. Virginia had a House of Burgesses elected (by wealthy landowner voters only), establishing the principle of representative government. Massachusetts had the Mayflower Compact, which laid the basis for participatory government.

Writing a Paragraph

Sample Paragraph:

Four European countries decided to challenge Spain's power in the New World by building colonies in North America. In what is now Virginia, English settlers founded Jamestown, England's first permanent North American colony. Plymouth, England's second colony, was settled in present-day Massachusetts. France built a trading post at Quebec and a number of forts in today's Canada. In present-day New York, the Netherlands built New Amsterdam and Fort Orange, and they settled Newcastle in what is now Delaware. Delaware was also the site of the Swedish colony of Wilmington (which was later taken over by the Netherlands.)

CHAPTER 3

Section Review (text page 59)

1. Students' sentences will vary. Information about the names and terms can be found on the pages given in parentheses: John Winthrop (52), Great Migration (52–53), General Court (53), Fundamental Orders of Government (56).

2. The Puritans worried about their future under James I because they knew he hated them. When Charles I introduced Catholic-like rituals into English worship services, the Puritans thought that God

would punish them as well as England for embracing a false religion. Under the leadership of John Winthrop, they came to the conclusion that they should set up a new England in America to save themselves from God's anger by practicing the true religion.

3. In American, the Puritans gave the right to vote to settlers instead of those who had invested money. Freemen—people who owned land and were members of the official church—made up the representative assembly, or General Court. Non-Puritans could not participate in government.

4. They disagreed with Puritan leaders over their religious intolerance, their refusal to let women speak out on religious practices, and their practice of allowing only church members to vote.

Section Review (text page 66)

1. Students' sentences will vary. Information about the names and terms can be found on the pages given in parentheses: Cecilius Calvert (60–61), Anthony Ashley Cooper (63), Act of Toleration (61), Fundamental Constitutions of Carolina (63).

2. Maryland was founded as a refuge for Catholics who were persecuted in England. Carolina was founded on land given to eight supporters of Charles II as repayment of debts. Georgia was founded as a buffer between South Carolina and Spanish Florida and as a social experiment to give impoverished English people a chance for a better life.

3. Maryland was taken over by the Puritans, who repealed the Act of Toleration. Slavery was introduced by tobacco plantation owners who needed farm laborers. Carolina split into North Carolina and South Carolina. South Carolina had many rice and indigo plantations, worked by slaves. North Carolina was settled by poor farmers who raised tobacco, usually without slaves. Georgia failed as an experiment in social reform but succeeded as a buffer between South Carolina and Spanish Florida. Despite laws against slavery, slaveowners moved in and established a rice and indigo plantation economy.

4. The southern farmers favored quit-rents because the rents were small, in some places only two pennies an acre. The southern proprietors favored quit-rents because, even though the rents were small, the proprietors collected them from thousands of farmers and made large sums of money.

5. Profitable plantation farming required huge tracts of land and great numbers of laborers. Planters at first used indentured servants, but for various reasons found them unsatisfactory and unprofitable. To solve their labor problems, the planters turned to enslavement of Africans. The first American blacks had the same status as white indentured servants. However, by the 1660s, laws were passed stating that black servants and their descendants must serve a plantation owner *durante vita,* or "during life," leading to widespread slavery.

Section Review (text page 69)

1. Students' sentences will vary. Information about the names and terms can be found on the pages given in parentheses: Duke of York (67), Peter Stuyvesant (67), Society of Friends (67–68), Holy Experiment (69), Philadelphia (69).

2. Possible answers are that the lands between Maryland and Connecticut were not allotted to the English colonies in their original charters. The civil war between Charles I and Parliament barred English activities in the Dutch and Swedish colonies. Cromwell had no interest in colonization, and the English colonies had more than enough land for expansion within their own borders.

3. The Dutch welcomed the English takeover. They showed their feelings by refusing to fight the English and, later, by exhibiting their displeasure when the Dutch briefly recaptured the colony.

4. These beliefs caused the Quakers to adopt practices that went against all of British society. If every human had an "inner light," the ability to communicate directly with God, then no priests or ministers were needed for worship. Because Quakers believed that all men and women were equal before God, they refused to take off their hats in the presence of nobles. If women were equal to men, they had the right to preach. If all people had a spark of divinity, it was wrong to fight wars or support armies by paying taxes. Ministers and preachers, the wealthy and powerful, and government leaders in Britain saw the Quaker beliefs as threats to the foundation of their society.

Time Line Questions (text page 72)

1. Massachusetts, Maryland, Rhode Island, Connecticut, Carolina
2. Plymouth, Massachusetts, Rhode Island, Connecticut, Maryland, Pennsylvania
3. 1679—New Hampshire, 1685—New York, 1702—New Jersey, 1729—North and South Carolina
4. Pennsylvania (1681)

Skills Strategy: Three-Level Outline (text pages 72–73)

1. The outline on page 72 is a topic outline; main topics, subtopics, and numbered details are phras-

es. In the outline on page 73, the main topics, subtopics, and numbered details are sentences.

2. Skim the chapter main sections using the names of cities in the southern colonies as key words.

3. These are possible cities for subtopics A. and B. under main topic II.: New York, Philadelphia. These are possible subtopics for main topic III.: Charleston, Savannah. Details for these subtopics can be found under these main section headings of the chapter: ''2. Southern Colonies'' and ''3. Middle Colonies.'' All main topics, subtopics, and details should be written as sentences. (Note: Students will use their outlines for ''Writing a Paragraph.'')

Chapter Test (text page 73)

Text Review

1. Puritans: King James tried to cut Puritan influence in both the Church of England and the English government. King Charles I introduced to English church services Catholic rituals that the Puritans considered wrong and deserving of God's punishment of England and of them. They went to North America to found a colony that would be such an outstanding example to England of how God wanted people to live that England would invite the Puritans back to reform the country. Catholics sought refuge in Maryland from religious persecution at home in England. Quakers were persecuted in England because their religious beliefs caused them to adopt practices that seemed threatening to those in power.

2. Blue laws required that on Sundays no whistling, game-playing, sports, singing of nonreligious songs, running, or walking in a garden would be allowed. Penalties included fines, sitting in town stocks, standing in the pillory, jailing at the lawbreaker's expense, banishment, public whipping for less serious offenses, and death for serious lawbreaking.

3. Roger Williams attacked Puritan government for taking Indian lands rather than buying them, he disagreed that government had the right to make everyone observe Puritan religious practices, and he argued that government had no right to say that only church members could vote. Anne Hutchinson held meetings in her home after church services to discuss sermons of the leading ministers of the Massachusetts colony, a practice considered irreverent by the Puritans.

4. Religious provisions were to guarantee religious freedom for all; governmental provisions stated that a colony made up of huge estates owned by nobles be worked willingly by serfs and slaves and that a legislature of two houses—nobles and commoners—be set up, with only nobles proposing legislation.

5. Planters in Virginia and Maryland lived on isolated plantations; planters in South Carolina lived in Charleston most of the year to enjoy the social activities, leaving their plantations in the care of overseers.

6. Oglethorpe and his associates intended Georgia to be a place where the poor of England could settle and lead better lives; slavery was outlawed; and alcoholic beverages were prohibited.

7. The English colony founded by Dutch settlers was New York. Its original name was New Netherland.

Critical Thinking

8. Pennsylvania was the ''Holy Experiment.'' Students who think it was a successful experiment can support their opinion by pointing to the Quakers' attitude toward Indians that led to peace, the orderly design of the city, and the rapid growth of Philadelphia to become the second-largest city in the English-speaking world. Students who think Pennsylvania was unsuccessful should back up their opinion with facts, reasons, and examples.

9. The Dutch developed New Netherland along the Hudson River. Just before war broke out between the Dutch and the English, the Duke of York sent four warships to New Amsterdam at the foot of Manhattan Island. Because of local opposition to the Dutch governor, Peter Stuyvesant, the English were able to take the colony of New Netherland without firing a shot. The Dutch briefly recaptured New Netherland several years later, but they were not welcomed by the colonists, including the Dutch majority.

10. Institutions developed as part of democratic government were the General Court in Massachusetts Bay colony; the Fundamental Orders of Government of Connecticut, allowing settlers to vote and share political power; the right of most farmers to vote in North Carolina; and self-government of people in Delaware and parts of New Jersey under William Penn. Public education institutions included Harvard College (funded by the Massachusetts General Court), and the New England public school system (supported by taxes).

Writing a Paragraph
Sample Paragraph:

Providence, an important city in the United States today, had its origins in the English colony of Rhode Island. Roger Williams, the city's founder, disagreed with Puritan leaders. He left Massachusetts in 1636 and founded a settlement that later became the city of Providence.

CHAPTER 4

Section Review (text page 77)

1. Students' sentences will vary. Information about the terms can be found on the pages given in parentheses: economic self-sufficiency (76), entrepot (76–77), enumerated article (77).
2. Colonies were a source of prestige, they provided land for England's population to expand, and this larger population would provide soldiers and sailors in time of crisis. Also, they were expected to enrich England even at their own expense.
3. Parliament passed the Navigation Acts to ensure that profits from the colonies would return to England and not go to other countries. All colonial trade had to be carried on ships built and owned by English or colonial merchants. Three-quarters of each crew had to be English subjects. English colonies were required to purchase all of their imports from England. Goods that England did not produce and that the colonists purchased elsewhere had to be brought to English ports and recorded and taxed before the ships could proceed to the colonies. Colonial crops and goods that were to be exported to places other than England had to be taken to England, where they were recorded and taxed before the ships carrying them could proceed to their destinations.
4. New Englanders did not object to the first Navigation Act, because it put their ships on equal footing with those of England. But almost all other Americans opposed the law because it caused delays in shipment and added to the cost of products.

Section Review (text page 83)

1. Students' answers will vary. Information about the terms can be found on the pages given in parentheses: Tidewater (78), slave code (80), Yankee (80), Middle Passage (81).
2. Colonies like these were almost entirely agricultural; they produced a cash crop and manufactured nothing. Therefore, English merchants profited by shipping the crops of these colonies, and English manufacturers profited by selling manufactured goods to them.
3. Slaves were less expensive to maintain and more easily identified than other workers; British slave traders encouraged colonists to purchase slaves by selling them at increasingly cheaper prices.
4. In the Southern colonies colonists felt restricted: tobacco prices fell; colonists had to mortgage future crops to pay for luxuries and necessities and were in chronic debt. In the New England colonies

colonists benefited: they had no cash crop and traded for the cash or goods they needed to purchase manufactured items from England. As a result, the New Englanders competed with the British in practically everything they did for a living. The middle colonies were the least affected by mercantilism: They produced more food than their population consumed, and the Navigation Acts placed few restrictions on the sale of their surplus foodstuffs to the West Indies.
5. See the text and map on pages 80–81 of the student edition. Students will describe one of the trade routes pictured there.

Section Review (text page 87)

1. Students' sentences will vary. Information about the terms can be found on the pages given in parentheses: Pine Tree Shillings (83), power of the purse (83), salutary neglect (84), Dominion of New England (85), Glorious Revolution (85), limited suffrage (87).
2. Possible answers, first part: the minting of coins by Massachusetts, failure to obey such British laws as the Iron Act, the colonial assemblies' use of the "power of the purse" to lessen the power of royal governors, rebellions of individuals and whole colonies against the authority of royal governors. Possible answers, second part: the similar situation in England, where there was popular demand for "the rights of the English" and for the increase of power for the Parliament; the colonies' habit of self-government from the start, further developed during the time Cromwell left them on their own; Walpole's policy of salutory neglect.
3. Maryland: John Coode imprisoned the Catholic governor and escaped punishment because he proclaimed his loyalty to William and Mary; New York: Jacob Leisler led a rebellion against the government of New York; New England: Connecticut, Rhode Island, and Massachusetts rebelled. In Maryland, the Crown's authority won out; Maryland was taken away from its Catholic proprietors and made a royal colony; in New York, the dispute concluded in a draw between the colonists and the Crown; Connecticut and Rhode Island regained their charters and restored their assemblies, and Massachusetts had its assembly, but not its charter, restored and became a royal colony.
4. No people in the world enjoyed the rights of British subjects. For example, under English law Parliament or elected colonial assemblies had to consent to all laws. There was free debate in Parliament and colonial assemblies. Everyone had the right to trial by jury. Bail could not be used as a punishment for a

person accused of crime. The right to keep arms was guaranteed to all Protestant British subjects. The government could not maintain an army during peace time without Parliament's consent. Many of these rights were incorporated into the United States Constitution and its Bill of Rights.

Section Review (text page 91)

1. Students' sentences will vary. Information about the names and terms can be found on the pages given in parentheses: Marquette and Joliet (89), La Salle (89), *petit guerre,* (90), Port Royal (90), Louisbourg (91).
2. New France was not able to support itself or make a profit for France as an agricultural colony because of its poor soil and short growing season. French kings would not allow religious dissenters (Huguenots) to emigrate. The peasants in France did not show any inclination to become settlers in New France.
3. War of the League of Augsburg—King William's War; War of the Spanish Succession—Queen Anne's War; War of the Austrian Succession—King George's War.

Time Line Questions (text page 92)

1. 1745—surrender of Louisbourg
2. 1689-1697—King William's War, 1702-1713—Queen Anne's War, 1740-1748—King George's War
3. 1660—First Navigation Act

Skills Strategy: Line Graphs (text page 92)

1. North—about 30,000; South—about 205,000
2. 1700 and 1750

UNIT 1 TEST (text page 93)

Chapter Survey

1. Sample summary sentence(s): Chapter 1 describes how the ancestors of present-day Indians came from Asia to become the original settlers of North and South America. The chapter also tells of the Europeans' discovery of the Americas as they searched for a route to Asia and of the founding of Spanish colonies in the New World. Pages containing information about names and terms: the Inca (6–7), League of the Iroquois (12), the Indies (12–13), Prince Henry (14–15), conquistador (21, 24–25).
2. Sample summary sentence(s): Chapter 2 describes Spain's mighty American empire, recounts the development of the first two English settlements, and traces the growth of colonies begun by France, the Netherlands, and Sweden. Pages containing information about terms: Junipero Serra (32), viceroy (33), *Golden Hind* (35–36), Roanoke (36), John Smith (39).
3. Sample summary sentence(s): Chapter 3 tells the story of how and why each of the thirteen English colonies got its start and what life was like in each. Pages containing information about terms: Great Migration (52–53), blue law (53–54), Fundamental Constitutions of Carolina (63), Society of Friends (67–68), the Holy Experiment (69).
4. Sample summary sentence(s): Chapter 4 discusses the effects of British mercantilism on the American colonies, the reactions of the different colonies to this policy, and the growing rivalry of the French and British over North America. Pages containing information about terms: enumerated article (77), Middle Passage (81), Dominion of New England (85), Marquette and Joliet (89), Louisbourg (91).

Text Review

5. The first settlers of North and South America were Asian people. One theory of how they got from Asia to the Americas says that thousands of years ago, an ice age caused the level of the oceans to drop. The waters of the Bering Strait dropped so low that a land bridge connecting Asia and North America appeared. The Asian people crossed this "bridge" to what is now Alaska and from there, over thousands of years, they went to different parts of North and South America.
6. Students should describe one of the following cultures, including details given on the text pages shown in parentheses: the Incas (6–7, 24), the Mayas (7), the Toltecs (8–11), the Aztecs (8, 21, 24).
7. Portugal took the lead in exploring the world. After Vasco da Gama became the first European to round the southern tip of Africa and go on to India, the Portuguese decided that their future lay on da Gama's route and not in the Americas.
8. On his first trip, Columbus thought he was heading for the Indies. When he reached San Salvador, off the coast of North America, he assumed that it was one of the islands of the Indies, so he called the inhabitants of San Salvador "Indians."
9. Verrazano: France; Columbus: Spain; Cabot: England; Ponce de Leon: Spain; Cartier: France; Cortez, Pizarro, Coronado: Spain.
10. Spain's King Philip II was outraged by the plunder-

ing of Spanish ships and American colonies by Francis Drake and other English sea dogs. England represented a growing threat to Spanish control of America, so Philip ordered the construction of a fleet of 130 warships—the Armada—with which he intended to invade and defeat England. On the way to England, the Armada was confronted in the English Channel by ships under the command of Drake and other sea dogs. In hit and run battles, the English destroyed or badly damaged many Spanish ships. To escape attack, the Armada headed north around Scotland and Ireland, where it was further damaged by a series of violent storms. Together, Drake and the forces of nature destroyed about half of the Armada. Instead of going through with the invasion of England, the Armada sailed back to Spain. The defeat of the Armada made Europeans think that if Spain could be defeated in Europe, it could be defeated in America, too, and they decided to challenge Spain by building colonies in the Americas.

11. Possible answers: England—Roanoke, Jamestown, Plymouth; France—New France (Ile de Saint Croix, Port Royal, Quebec); the Netherlands—New Amsterdam, Fort Orange Newcastle; Sweden—New Sweden (Christina).

12. New Hampshire, Massachusetts, Rhode Island, Connecticut, New York, New Jersey, Pennsylvania, Delaware, Maryland, Virginia, North Carolina, South Carolina, and Georgia were English colonies that became the first states.

13. Before the American Revolution, most slaves were kept by southern planters (about 206,000 slaves in 1750), although there were slaves in the northern colonies too (about 30,000 in 1750). In 1750, slaves made up about two thirds of South Carolina's population. Slaves were regarded as chattel and were controlled by harsh slave codes. Planters in the South needed many laborers to operate their huge tobacco and rice plantations. They chose slaves to work for them because slaves were less expensive than indentured servants and could be easily identified. In addition, the British encouraged colonists to buy slaves by offering them at low prices.

14. According to the economic philosophy of mercantalism, colonies existed to enrich the parent country. Colonial raw materials were sent only to the parent country. There, they were used to manufacture goods that the colonists had to buy from the parent country. The colonists could neither sell raw materials to, nor buy manfuactured goods from, any country but the parent country. Among the colonies in America, the New England colonies and the southern colonies opposed English mercantilists policies. New Englanders depended on trade, and because of mercantilist policies, found themselves in competition with British traders. Southern planters had no cash with which to buy manfuactured luxuries and necessities from England. As a result, they had to mortgage future crops to pay for these goods. Often this practice led them into debt, which they blamed on mercantilism.

Critical Thinking

15. The English: thirteen colonies along the Atlantic seaboard; The French: eastern parts of present-day Canada; The Spanish: Florida, parts of Central America, and South Florida.

16. Students' responses may include references to Europeans who simply took the Indians' land as well as those, like the Dutch and Quakers, who compensated the Indians for their land.

17. Among the principles and practices students may include in their answers are the following: Roger Williams' view on religious tolerance, Connecticut's Fundamental Orders of Government, Maryland's Act of Toleration, the Fundamental Constitutions of Carolina, the tolerance of all religions in New York after the English took it from the Dutch.

Skills Review

18. Tenochtitlán; Columbus; Jamestown; Massachusetts Bay Colony; Manhattan; Georgia; King William's, Queen Anne's, and King George's wars.

19. Sample completed outline:
    Colonial Origins of American Cities
    I. Some Cities began in New England.
    A. Providence was founded in the Rhode Island Colony.
    1. The city was founded in 1636.
    2. Roger Williams was its founder.
    3. He founded it after disagreeing with Massachusetts Puritan leaders.
    Additions to the outline may include the following: B. Hartford (or New Haven) and appropriate details numbers 1, 2, 3; II. Some cities began in the Middle Colonies; A. New York was once the Dutch New Netherland (and a listing of appropriate details); B. Philadelphia was founded in Pennsylvania (plus appropriate details). A similar major section on cities in the southern colonies (for example, Charleston and Savannah) may be added. Topics, subtopics, and details should be sentences.

20. Students' graphs should follow the form of the similar graph on page 92 of the student edition. Each graph should have an appropriate title (Popu-

lation of the English Colonies, 1660–1750), labels, number values or years on the vertical and horizontal axes, and a legend.

CHAPTER 5

Section Review (text page 103)

1. Students' sentences will vary. Information about the names can be found on the pages given in parentheses: William Pitt (96, 100), Fort Duquesne (98), General Braddock (100).
2. Franklin proposed the Albany Plan of Union. It was meant to eliminate the threat of French expansion into the Ohio Valley and the threat that the Indians would present once the French were defeated in the war that everyone knew was coming.
3. Whoever controlled the junction of the three rivers controlled the entire Ohio River Valley.
4. Quebec was the root of the tree and the source of French power in America. Wolfe reasoned he could fell the tree (New France) by striking at its root in Quebec.
5. In the terms of the treaty, England acquired Spanish Florida and all of French Canada; Spain received Louisiana; France retained two small islands off the coast of Nova Scotia and the islands of Martinique and Guadeloupe in the Caribbean. In effect, England had the whole eastern seaboard of North America under its flag.

Section Review (text page 107)

1. Students' sentences will vary. Information about the names and terms can be found on the pages given in parentheses: General Amherst (105, 106), Bushy Run (105), King George III (106), Proclamation of 1763 (106).
2. Religion—Canadians were Catholic, but most English colonists were Protestants; language—Canadians spoke French, but most English colonists spoke English; culture—Unlike the English colonists, French Canadians had no experience with political institutions such as representative government. The French were used to a king who ruled with absolute authority.
3. Pontiac led several Indian tribes in a revolt, attacking forts and raiding farms because General Amherst would not continue the French practice of giving the Ottawas and other tribes regular gifts. The tribes regarded these gifts as compensation for land the Europeans had taken away from them.
4. Although the cost was high, few colonists at first

protested the Quartering Act. They recognized the need for British soldiers to provide them with protection against the powerful Indian tribes.

Section Review (text page 111)

1. Students' sentences will vary. Information about the terms can be found on the pages given in parentheses: Sugar Act (107–108), Sons of Liberty (109), Stamp Act Congress (109–110).
2. Although he neither knew nor cared to learn much about the colonists, Grenville reasoned that the colonists came from England, were governed by England, were treated as English subjects, and so should be taxed like English subjects.
3. No one paid attention to Otis's plan. Americans did not want to be represented in Parliament because their delegation would be small and weak. Americans wanted Parliament's recognition that they could be taxed only by colonial assemblies.
4. Reactions to the Stamp Act ranged from John Dickinson's stinging attack on its illegality to violence. The Sons of Liberty burned the special stamped paper in warehouses in some colonies, and in Boston they looted the homes of several British officials in protest. Peaceful boycott of taxed English goods rather than riots was the strategy of the colonists in their protest against the Townshend Acts. As a result of the boycott, trade between the colonies and Britain was cut in half. British merchants demanded the repeal of the Townshend Acts and got it.

Section Review (text page 115)

1. Students' sentences will vary. Information about the names and terms can be found on the pages given in parentheses: Crispus Attucks (111), Lord North (113–115), Quebec Act (115).
2. Some British soldiers had been quartered in Boston since 1765. However, even more troops had come to the city to enforce the hated Stamp Act and Townshend Acts.
3. No. The presence of Redcoats in colonial cities increased American resentment of them, but even the attempt by Samuel Adams to spark the revolution by using the Redcoats' part in the "Boston Massacre" as propaganda failed to arouse massive protest in the colonies.
4. The Tea Act led to the Tea Parties because of the opposition to the tax on tea. As a result of the Tea Parties, Lord North tried to punish Boston and all of Massachusetts through the Coercive Acts. When the Quebec Act passed, the colonists saw it as another step toward tyranny, since it did not allow for an elected assembly, and as an attempt to deny

them the right to westward expansion. After a request by Massachusetts for a continental congress, every colony except Georgia sent delegates to Philadélphia to discuss united action. This was the turning point in the relations between Great Britain and the colonies.

Time Line Questions (text page 116)

1. 20 years
2. 1763
3. 1763, 1764, 1765, 1766, 1767, 1770, 1772, 1773, 1774
4. 11 years

Skills Strategy: Physical and Political Maps (text pages 116–117)

1. The Colony of Massachusetts, 1774
2. Connecticut and New Hampshire
3. All the major cities grew along the rivers. The flat land and the rivers made travel easier.
4. 110 miles or 175 km

Chapter Test (text page 117)

Text Review

1. The junction of the Allegheny, Monongahela, and Ohio rivers was a strategic location, because whoever controlled it controlled the whole of the Ohio River Valley and could use the rivers as avenues of trade and travel to the interior of America. The river junction belonged to Virginia according to its 1609 charter. However, the French moved into the area and started building forts there. British leaders decided to go to war to break the French influence not only in the Ohio Territory, but also in the whole of North America.
2. Wolfe saw New France as a tree with its roots and source of power in the city of Quebec. He reasoned that by striking at the city, the roots of French power would be destroyed and New France would fall.
3. In the treaty, France agreed to surrender Canada to Great Britain and retained only a few islands in the Caribbean and off the coast of Nova Scotia. France was no longer a power in North America.
4. The French-speaking, Roman Catholic Canadians and the Indian allies of the French who lived in the Great Lakes area (who had not surrendered to the English nor signed the Treaty of Paris) fell under British rule.
5. They argued that Canada was worthless, that the Indians who lived there had been traditional enemies of the British, and that with the French threat gone, the American colonists might not remain loyal to Great Britain.
6. The Proclamation of 1763 forbade colonists to purchase or settle on lands west of the crest of the Appalachian Mountains. Although some colonists had settled in the area, most Americans did not protest the proclamation at the time. Later, however, they remembered it as the first attempt of King George III to control their lives. In the Quartering Act of 1765, Parliament gave the commander of the British forces in America 10,000 men to defend the colonies against Indian attack. However, the colonial governments were expected to foot the bills for housing, feeding, and paying the British soldiers. The colonists did not immediately object to the act because they realized they needed portection against the powerful Indian tribes. Nevertheless, the Quartering Act raised a question about a principle that led the colonists to fight the War for Independence: Did Parliament have the authority to pass laws that applied to the colonies?
7. First, Parliament needed money because the French and Indian War had nearly bankrupted Great Britain, and the British people were already so heavily taxed that they could be taxed no further. Second, Parliament saw a need to set up a rational, uniform government for all the colonies that made up the worldwide British Empire.
8. In convening the continental congress, the colonists were in effect saying that since all other efforts toward resolving their disputes with Britain had failed, they were contemplating a serious break with the parent country.

Critical Thinking

9. Possible answers: Samuel Adams termed the regrettable incident a *massacre*. In an inflammatory pamphlet, he described the incident as a brutal military action against innocent civilians. Some colonial newspapers printed their reports of the incident surrounded by a black border.
10. Lord North's biased purpose in having the Tea Act of 1773 passed was to save the East India Company from bankruptcy. The British government depended on this company to help with the governing of British colonies in India. North insisted on keeping a small duty on tea (although this was unnecessary) because he wanted the colonists to show their loyalty to the king by obeying Parliament's tax law.

Writing a Paragraph

Sample Paragraph:

Both Samuel and John Adams deplored the Boston Massacre, but each viewed the incident in a different way. Samuel Adams, an agitator for American independence, viewed the incident as an opportunity to spread propaganda to gain support for the cause of independence. It was he who described the incident as a massacre in an inflammatory pamphlet. On the other hand, John Adams took a less biased view. In the court trial following the incident, he was the lawyer for the British soldiers who were accused of killing the five Boston civilians. Although he felt that the redcoats did not belong in Boston, he apparently was determined to see that they got a fair trial.

CHAPTER 6

Section Review (text page 127)

1. Students' sentences will vary. Information about the terms can be found on the pages given in parentheses; Benedict Arnold (124–125), Green Mountain Boys (124), *Common Sense* (125–126), ''the Royal Brute'' (126).
2. The Intolerable Acts should be repealed because they violated the rights of British subjects. Massachusetts should form its own government and until the Intolerable Acts were repealed, keep the taxes that usually went to the royal governor. All colonies should form and train armed militias. Trade with Great Britain should be boycotted.
3. Possible answers: Lexington-Concord—Americans; Bunker Hill—British; Ticonderoga—Americans; Crown Point—Americans; Quebec—British; Lake Champlain—British.
4. The delgates sent King George III a letter entitled ''A Declaration of the Cause and Necessity of Taking Up Arms,'' an appeal for the king's support. King George was infuriated. He refused to read the letter and told Lord North that ''blows must decide whether they are to be subject to the country or independent.''

Section Review (text page 128)

1. Patriots were American colonists who supported independence. Southern patriots favored independence because they believed that British mercantilism drained their wealth. Loyalists were American colonists who remained loyal to Great Britain; most were in the middle colonies but there were some Loyalists in every colony; they did not believe that Americans had the right or any good reason to rebel.
2. The five delegates the Continental Congress chose to write a draft of the Declaration of Independence were John Adams—Massachusetts, Roger Sherman—Connecticut, Robert Livingston—New York, Benjamin Franklin—Pennsylvania, Thomas Jefferson—Virginia.
3. Delegates to the Continental Congress formally accepted the Declaration of Independence on July 4, 1776.

Section Review (text page 133)

1. Students' sentences will vary. Information about the names and terms can be found on the pages given in parentheses: Enlightenment (129), John Locke (129), propaganda (129, 132), natural rights (129).
2. The Declaration is addressed to the whole world; Jefferson and most of the delegates believed that what they did in Philadelphia in July 1776 had meaning for all people everywhere.
3. Three natural rights were said to be self-evident: life, liberty, and property; property was changed to the pursuit of happiness in the final version.
4. Jefferson never mentioned Parliament in the Declaration because Americans denied that Parliament had ever had any authority to make laws for them; according to Americans, the colonial assemblies were equal to and independent of Parliament. Loyalty to George III tied Americans to Great Britain, not loyalty to Parliament.

Section Review (text page 138)

1. Students' sentences will vary. Information about the names and terms can be found on the pages given in parentheses: General William Howe (133, 135–136, 137), Continental Army (133), mercenary (133), Count Vergennes (135).
2. British: b, d, f; American: a, c, e.
3. The American victory at Saratoga ruined the British plan to isolate New England and thereby force the southern colonies to surrender.

Section Review (text page 145)

1. Students' sentences will vary. Information about the names and terms can be found on the pages given in parentheses: John Paul Jones (139), ''America's Oldest Friend'' (139–140), ''Swamp Fox'' (141), ''The World Turned Upside Down'' (144–145).

2. Lord North was willing to end the war by meeting all the demands the Americans had made up until July 2, 1776 (repeal of Intolerable Acts; colonists could control own internal affairs; no punishment if loyalty to the Crown was sworn).
3. Possible answers: Lafayette—field commander; Pulaski—cavalry commander; Johann Kalb—cavalry officer; Kosciusko—military engineer; Von Steuben—trainer of troops.
4. If Arnold's betrayal had not been discovered, the British could have controlled the Hudson River and been in a position to retake New England.

Time Line Questions (text page 146)

1. The first battles of the American Revolution occurred first.
2. 6 years (8 years to Treaty of Paris in 1783)
3. 1778
4. British evacuated Boston

Skills Strategy: Map Grids (text pages 146–147)

1. 15°, 30°, 45°, 60°
2. Newark—about 41°N; Maryland capital (Annapolis) —about 39°N; Syracuse—about 43°N
3. Between Delaware capital (Dover) and Connecticut capital (Hartford)—about 240 miles or 384 kilometers; between Harrisburg and Richmond—about 200 miles or 320 kilometers
4. Parallels and meridians form a grid, and any place on the earth's surface can be pinpointed on the grid if the parallel and meridian on which it is located is known.

Chapter Test (text page 147)

Text Review

1. Although the delegates to the First Continental Congress were angry about the Intolerable Acts and had no intention of submitting to Lord North and Parliament, they considered themselves British subjects and were more interested in reaching a compromise with Parliament than in declaring independence from Great Britain. To show their intentions, the delegates at the Congress addressed the Suffolk Resolves to King George III, thinking that, as their friend, he would convince Parliament to back down and compromise. It was only a year and a half later, after compromise was proven a useless hope and fighting with the British had already begun, that Americans went the route of revolution and independence.

2. Concord and Lexington; Bunker Hill; Fort Ticonderoga and Crown Point; Quebec.
3. Benedict Arnold delayed Carleton's progress down the Hudson River to New York City, which, if it had been accomplished, would have cut off New England from the rest of the colonies.
4. While colonists battled British forces, the Second Continental Congress, which would eventually declare America's independence, met in Philadelphia starting in May of 1775. The delegates initially hoped to find a way to restore peace, but as events progressed they sent George Washington to lead the Minutemen, making the fight an American rather than a Massachusetts one.
5. First, Thomas Paine's *Common Sense* pictured King George III as a tyrant, a "Royal Brute," and changed Americans' attitudes towards him. Second, Paine's pamphlet extended the importance of the revolt in Massachusetts from a defense of the rights of British subjects to a revolution on behalf of the liberty of peoples the world over.
6. New Englanders and southerners generally supported the ideas in the Declaration of Independence because they had felt the effects of the disputes with Parliament most. People in the middle colonies, having felt less of these effects, were divided about the Declaration of Independence. Some people in every colony, the Tories, remained loyal to Great Britain and disagreed with the Declaration's ideas. Still other colonists felt that change should be effected by political process and not by rebellion, which they considered wrong.
7. Locke had stated that the natural rights of all human beings include life, liberty, and property, and Jefferson borrowed ideas from his philosophy when writing the Declaration. However, after some discussion, the delegates enumerated these rights as life, liberty, and the pursuit of happiness.
8. The Americans' defeat of the British at Yorktown was extraordinary, as Cornwallis acknowledged, perhaps ironically, when he had the British band play "The World Turned Upside Down." With some help from their French allies, the relatively inexperienced, ill-equipped, and poorly trained Americans had defeated what was recognized as the best fighting force on earth.

Critical Thinking

9. Students' hypotheses may differ. However, they should recognize that, today, they might be British "overseas" subjects rather than citizens of an

independent country. Accept all reasonable answers.

10. Possible answers are that Jefferson appealed to the belief that God had created all men equal and given them certain "natural" rights that were "self-evident" and that no government could take away; that he depicted King George III as a tyrant; that he presented the idea that Americans were acting on behalf of all people in their struggle against tyranny and for human freedom.

Writing a Paragraph

Sample Paragraph:

The general American attitude toward King George III gradually changed for the worse as difficulties with Great Britain developed. At the time of the First Continental Congress in 1774, Americans generally liked the king and thought of him as their friend. Feelings toward King George were similar in the following year, at the beginning of the Second Continental Congress, which sent a letter to him appealing for his help in the American cause. The king, however, refused to read the Congress's letter. Then, in January 1776, Thomas Paine attacked King George as a "Royal Brute" in the pamphlet *Common Sense*, helping to shatter the loyalty and affection many Americans had for the monarch. By July of the same year, Thomas Jefferson, in writing the Declaration of Independence, appealed to the king's general lack of popularity among Americans in an attempt to win them over to the cause of the Patriots.

Chapter 7

Section Review (text page 151)

1. Students' sentences will vary. Information about the terms can be found on the pages given in parentheses: Magna Carta (148), separation of church and state (150), enfranchise (150).

2. England has no one document on which its government is founded. With the exception of the Magna Carta and the English Bill of Rights, most of the duties and powers of the Crown, Parliament, and the judiciary system are not written down. They developed over time as customs and became accepted as law.

3. Americans wanted their system of government, and particularly the powers of their leaders and their rights as citizens, written out for all to see in case of disputes and abuses.

4. Possible answers are that the right to vote was limited to males who paid taxes in Pennsylvania and Vermont and to men who owned property in most other states. New Jersey, at first the only state that allowed women to vote, disenfranchised them in 1807. Catholics were not allowed to hold office in North Carolina until 1835. In most states, many men who could vote could not hold office because of property qualifications. Only in Massachusetts were black people covered by a bill of rights, and some southern states explicitly stated that their bill of rights did not apply to slaves or free blacks.

Section Review (text page 158)

1. Students' sentences will vary. Information about the names and terms can be found on the pages given in parentheses: Confederation (151), national domain (153), continentals (154), Sandy Hook lighthouse (157).

2. The need for a national government to keep the states united was recognized by American leaders. A committee was formed by the Second Continental Congress to write a constitution (the Articles) and create a national government.

3. The Northwest Territory was the area bounded by the Great Lakes, the Ohio River, and the Mississippi River.

4. Gold and silver coins were scarce during the colonial period. British trade laws required colonists to exchange their products for English manufactured goods rather than money. During the Revolution, states were slow to vote money for the Continental Congress, so the Congress issued paper money (continentals) which it promised to redeem for silver and gold. The value of the continentals dropped. Congress had very restrictive taxing powers, so it could not raise much money. Rhode Island caused the defeat of an amendment that would have given Congress the power to tax imports, thereby frustrating the attempts of Congress to stabilize the paper currency.

5. Great Britain refused to honor the Treaty of Paris by withdrawing its troops from U.S. territory. It schemed to detach Vermont from the U.S. and did not send an ambassador to the U. S. as agreed in the Treaty of Paris. In London, the U. S. ambassador was ridiculed.

France refused to lend money to the Confederation Congress during peacetime because Congress could not tax the states and would be unable to repay the loan.

Spain attempted to split the northern and southern states by offering to open Spanish ports to American ships (which were mostly owned by the North) in exchange for Congress giving up its claims to free navigation of the Mississippi for 25 years.

Section Review (text page 162)

1. Students' sentences will vary. Information about the names and terms can be found on the pages given in parentheses: Edmund Randolph (158), the Founding Fathers (158–159, nationalist (159), conservative (159–160).
2. To amend the Articles of Confederation in order to provide a government that really could govern.
3. The Connecticut Compromise was designed to resolve a problem of representation where the small states were pitted against the large states. The small states feared they would constantly be outvoted by the large states. According to the Connecticut Compromise, each state legislature would elect two senators to the upper house (Senate), thus protecting the smaller states by giving them equal representation. The people of the country as a whole would be represented in the lower house (House of Representatives). Each state's delegation in the House was to be determined by the state's population.
4. Small states feared they would have too little influence in a direct national election of the president. They were joined by conservatives who did not want common people to have a direct say in choosing the president. George Mason proposed a compromise. All voters would participate in the election, thus making the president a representative of the people and not the states. The people would not vote directly for the president. They would choose electors who would convene as an electoral college after the election. The president would be elected by a majority vote of the electoral college. If the electoral college could not agree, the house of Representatives (each state having one vote) would make the decision.

Section Review (text page 164)

1. Students' sentences will vary. Information about the names and terms can be found on the pages given in parentheses: the *Federalist Papers* (162–163), quorum (164), Samuel Adams (164).
2. The Federalists were for the Constitution and against the Articles of Confederation. They believed that clinging to the Articles would guarantee a weak and divided United States that would invite European meddling in American affairs. The Federalists wanted a strong central government. The Anti-Federalists were against the Constitution because they believed the Articles should be improved and

not abandoned. They argued that, under Confederation, independence of the states was guaranteed and that freedoms would be protected when smaller state governments were more powerful than the federal government. The Anti-Federalists urged voters to reject the Constitution.
3. On December 7, Delaware became the first state to ratify the Constitution. New Hampshire was the ninth state to ratify the Constitution, thus putting the document into effect. No, Rhode Islanders had been dragging their feet since the end of the Revolution. They thought they would not be protected by the Constitution. They knew, however, that the new central government would not tolerate an independent country of Rhode Island, so they joined the Union reluctantly.

Section Review (text page 167)

1. Student sentences will vary. Information about the terms can be found on the pages given in parentheses: federalism (165), mixed government (165), separation of powers (165), Bill of Rights (167).
2. James Madison wanted to replace the weak Confederation with strong central government. He did not get as strong a central government as he wanted, because power was divided between the federal government and the states. Alexander Hamilton distrusted democracy, but many of his wishes were satisfied. The people would be allowed to vote directly only for members of the House of Representatives. The president and senators would be elected indirectly (with senators chosen by state legislatures and the president by electoral college). Federal justices would be appointed by the president and not elected. John Adams got his mixed government. A single, strong president embodied his monarchic principle, the Senate and Supreme Court his aristocratic principle, and the House of Representatives his democratic principle.
3. The executive branch includes the president, the president's advisors, and the vice president. The legislative branch is Congress, comprised of the Senate, and the House of Representatives. The judicial branch includes the Supreme Court and other federal courts.
4. Possible answers: The president can veto an act passed by Congress. Congress can override the president's veto and enact the law. The Supreme Court can declare federal laws unconstitutional, but the president (because he appoints Supreme Court justices) has some control over the Supreme Court. The Senate has to approve the president's appointees to the Supreme Court. The House of Representatives has power to impeach Supreme Court jus-

tices and other federal officials, including the president.

Time Line Questions (text page 188)

1. 1781; Land Ordinance of 1785; Northwest Ordinance of 1787
2. 7 years

Skills Strategy: Primary Sources (text pages 168–169)

1. Fourth Amendment
2. Fifth Amendment
3. First Amendment
4. First Amendment
5. No; First Amendment; No national religion will be established.
6. None of the first five amendments guarantee this right; it is guaranteed by the Eighth Amendment.
7. Military personnel on active duty during a war or time of public danger do not have this right.
8. Third Amendment

Chapter Test (text page 189)

Text Review

1. After independence, Americans insisted on written constitutions rather than on an unwritten constitution such as that of Great Britain. Differences in interpreting England's unwritten constitution had been the cause of many abuses of Americans' rights by Parliament that had led to the Revolution. To avoid repeating such circumstances, Americans wanted to have a tangible document to turn to if their rights were violated. In their written state constitutions, they insisted on listing their rights and defining in detail the powers they were willing to let their executives and legislators exercise over them.
2. In dealing with both domestic and foreign issues, the central government under the Articles was largely ineffective because American citizens had created a weak central government so that their rights could not be taken away from them. The experiences with Great Britain were still fresh in Americans' minds.
3. Because the states agreed to cede their western lands to the confederation government after some discussion and compromise, a national domain, which included the Northwest Territory, was formed. Through the Land Ordinance of 1785 and the Northwest Ordinance of 1787, the Confederation provided for the sale of land and the procedure by which the lands could become territories and then states. Eventually, the states of Ohio, Indiana, Illinois, Wisconsin, and Michigan were formed from the Northwest Territory.
4. The attempt by the Confederation Congress to gain power to raise taxes in 1781 was in the form of an amendment to the Articles. Such an amendment had to be approved by all 13 states. Twelve states had approved the tax amendment, but since Rhode Island refused to approve it, the state prevented the amendment from going into effect.
5. Student responses should indicate their understanding that the Founding Fathers did indeed accomplish a second, peaceful revolution. Through the Constitution, they set up a completely different national government, one with powers that far exceeded the powers of the Confederation government.
6. Among the facts students may use are the following: the Connecticut Compromise, which gave all states equal representation in the Senate, calmed the fears of smaller states. The Three-Fifths Compromise, which allowed the counting of slaves to determine the size of a state's delegation in the House of Representatives, was agreed to in order to mollify the southern states. The electoral college was established as a means of satisfying both the strong nationalists who wanted all people to participate in presidential elections and the strong conservatives who did not want common people to directly elect the president. The Bill of Rights was included to induce Massachusetts to ratify the Constitution.
7. The president had the power to veto acts passed by Congress. He could appoint justices to the Supreme Court. Congress could override the president's veto of an act. The Senate had the power to approve certain presidential appointments. The House of Representatives had the power to impeach federal officials, including the president and Supreme Court justices. One House of Congress could reject a law proposed by the other. The Supreme Court could declare a federal law unconstitutional. The division of powers between state governments and the federal government is another way the Constitution provided for checks and balances in government.
8. From the outset, Rhode Island had opposed amending the Articles because it did not want a central government to have more power than the Confederation government. After the Constitution was written, Rhode Island was opposed to ratifying it, but decided to join the union because state leaders knew that the new central government would not tolerate an independent country of Rhode Island. Delaware thought the Constitution protected small states.

9. Steps to statehood: When the population of any region within the Northwest Territory reached 60,000, it could (1) write a constitution, (2) apply to Congress for statehood, (3) become a state on equal footing with the other states when its constitution was approved.

10. Sample two-level outline:

    The Separation of Powers
    I. The Legislative Branch
        A. Congress—Senate and House of Representatives
        B. Power to make laws for the nation
    II. The Executive Branch
        A. The president and advisors
        B. Power to enforce the laws
    III. The Judicial Branch
        A. The Supreme Court
        B. Other federal courts
        C. Power to make judgments according to the law
        D. Ensures that executive branch does not act unjustly

Writing a Paragraph

Sample Paragraph:

The government of the United States under the Articles of Confederation was largely ineffective. Most important as a reason was the determination of the states to maintain their individual rights by keeping the central government weak. Of almost equal importance was the inability of the central government to solve the country's money problems because of the states' refusal to give Congress the power to tax them adequately. Another important reason for the new government's ineffectiveness was its powerlessness to inspire the confidence and respect of other countries. Of less importance was the disloyalty of some citizens, such as the New England merchants and the Allen brothers of Vermont.

CHAPTER 8

Section Review (text page 194)

1. Students' sentences will vary. Information about the names can be found in the pages given in parentheses: John Adams (190), John Jay (192), Henry Knox (194), Alexander Hamilton (194).
2. Possible answers are that Washington was the unanimous choice of the electoral college. He knew how to lead and inspired people to respect the presidency; Washington knew he was setting standards for future presidents. He remained above squabbling, knew his limitations, and listened to the advice of others. He approved policies that set the republic on a solid foundation.
3. State legislatures chose senators. Voters chose representatives. Members of the electoral college unanimously chose George Washington as president.
4. The Judiciary Act of 1789 provided for thirteen federal district courts with powers over state governments and three federal circuit courts to hear appeals from district court decisions. The Judiciary Act of 1789 also set up the Supreme Court. The act was of great importance because it created the third branch of federal government—the judicial—and completed the system of checks and balances. Disputes over the meaning of federal law and treaties would be settled by the Supreme Court as would disputes over state and federal laws.

    The Tariff of 1789 placed a tax of five to fifteen percent on some imported goods. The tariff was important as a symbol of the new government's strength. It also opened the doors of Congress to a financial policy that went beyond a simple tax.

Section Review (text page 198)

1. Students' sentences will vary. Information about the terms can be found on the pages given in parentheses: government bond (194–195), national debt (195), protective tariff (194,197), excise tax (194, 197).
2. Hamilton wanted to put the new government on a firm financial footing and to encourage American economic development.
3. The southern states opposed this proposal because, for the most part, they had been repaying their war debts while the northern states had practically ignored their debts, and interest was piling up on them. The southerners, led by Madison, did not feel that southern taxpayers should help pick up the debts of the northern states.
4. Loose construction means the government has the right to exercise any power the Constitution does not explicitly deny to it or reserve for the states. This construction, or interpretation, is based on the elastic clause in the Constitution, which allows Congress to make any laws that are ''necessary and proper'' to execute the government's powers. Hamilton's national bank, or Bank of the United States, was created as a result of loose construction.

Section Review (text page 200)

1. Students' sentences will vary. Information about the names and terms can be found on the pages

given in parentheses: impressment (200), Treaty of San Lorenzo (200), Louisiana (200), right of deposit (200).

2. At first, almost all Americans favored the French Revolution, but as the excesses of the revolution increased, Americans became divided in their feelings. For example, Hamilton and Washington changed their minds, while Jefferson, with some reservations, continued to back the revolution in France.

3. French ambassador Genêt acted as if he had official power in the United States. He empowered adventurers to invade Spanish Louisiana, and privateers he commissioned captured and brought more than 80 British ships into American ports. Washington was furious. He had declared the United States neutral in the British-French War. He ordered Genêt to stop his political activities and to bring no British ships into United States waters.

4. When the terms of the Jay Treaty were finally revealed, there were riots. John Jay was burned in effigy. Washington was the subject of personal abusive attacks, and he and his administration were called toadies of the British. The Jay Treaty provided nothing for the United States but a promise of peace. It mentioned nothing about the impressment of American sailors.

Section Review (text page 207)

1. Students' sentences will vary. Information about the names and terms can be found on the pages given in parentheses: Farewell Address (203), High Federalist (204), Aaron Burr (206), midnight judge (206).

2. Hamilton spawned the Federalist party; Jefferson's ideas led to the Democratic Republican, or Republican party.

3. The Kentucky Resolutions by Jefferson and the Virginia Resolutions by Madison argued that the union of states was a compact, in which individual states agree to give up their independence but still remain sovereign. Because each state was sovereign, the state legislature had the right to decide if a federal action was constitutional. If the federal action was not, the legislature had the right to nullify it within the state. This compact theory meant that the Constitutional government was not much different from the old Confederation government.

4. By complimenting Jefferson and saying Burr was dangerous because he had no principles, Hamilton helped bring about, in the House of Representatives, the election of Jefferson as president.

5. The principle of judicial review was established in *Marbury* v. *Madison*. Marshall's purpose was to avoid a direct conflict with the executive branch, which he might have lost. Instead, Marshall claimed the authority of the Supreme Court to declare unconstitutional a law passed by Congress and signed by the president, and extended the power of the federal judiciary.

Time Line Questions (text page 210)

1. 8 years
2. Jefferson (*Marbury* v. *Madison*); Washington (establishment of first national bank); John Adams (XYZ Affair, Sedition Act)
3. Kentucky (1792), Tennessee (1796), Ohio (1803)

Skills Strategy: Summarizing (text page 210)

1. The first main section (''The Course Is Set'')
2. The main headings and subheadings of the first section
3. The New Government Takes Shape

- Washington sworn in at New York, temporary capital
- April 10, 1789

The Importance of George Washington

- natural leadership ability and almost royal dignity
- awareness of role in setting precedents

An Active Congress

- Judiciary Act, 1789: circuit courts and Supreme Court
- Passed Bill of Rights, reenacted Northwest Ordinance
- Tariff of 1789—tax on imports as symbol of new government's strength

The Cabinet

- committee of advisors created by Congress to assist president
- made up of executive offices and departments, each headed by secretary

UNIT 2 TEST (text page 211)

Chapter Survey

1. Sample summary sentence(s): Chapter 5 begins with an account of the French and Indian War, which expelled France from America, and continues with a discussion of the growing quarrel between the colonists and the British Parliament

over the right to levy taxes. The chapter traces the action of Parliament and the reaction of the colonists that finally led to the convening of the first Continental Congress, a turning point in relations between the colonies and Britain. Pages containing information about names and terms: Proclamation of 1763 (106), Sons of Liberty (109), Stamp Act Congress (109–110), Crispus Attucks (111), Boston Tea Party (113–114).

2. Sample summary sentence(s): Chapter 6 describes the failure of the first Continental Congress to persuade King George III to intervene with Parliament on behalf of the colonists, the first battles of the Revolution, and the declaration of the American colonies' independence at the Second Continental Congress. The chapter also presents a detailed analysis of the Declaration of Independence. Pages containing information about terms: Minutemen (121), Breed's Hill (123), Continental Army (133), Valley Forge (140), ''The World Turned Upside Down'' (144–145).

3. Sample summary sentence(s): Chapter 7 explains that the weaknesses of the postwar national government under the Articles of Confederation were due to the unwillingness of the states to give the national government the powers it needed. The chapter goes on to discuss the writing and ratification of the Constitution and, finally, investigates the ideas it contains. Pages containing information about terms: separation of church and state (150), Confederation (151), the Founding Fathers (158–159), Samuel Adams (164), Bill of Rights (167).

4. Sample summary sentence(s): Chapter 8 gives an account of the domestic and foreign activities of the new Constitutional government of the United States under the Congress and such Federalist and Democratic Republican leaders as George Washington, John Adams, Thomas Jefferson, Alexander Hamilton, and John Marshall. Pages containing information about names and terms: President John Adams (190), Alexander Hamilton (194), impressment (200), Farewell Address (203), midnight judges (206).

Text Review

5. The French and Indian War was fought between the English colonists and the settlers of New France, both with the help of Indian allies. Even before the war, the British government had decided to break French influence in North America. Both France and England wanted to control the valuable Ohio River Valley. England believed it had a right to the region because it had been given to Virginia in its colonial charter of 1609. However, the French had begun to build forts in the valley, making their intentions obvious.

6. Under the terms of the treaty, France surrendered all its territory in mainland North America to England, retaining only a few islands off Nova Scotia and in the Caribbean. England also received Florida, formerly owned by Spain, which was given control of French Louisiana. In short, the French flag flew over no lands in North America, and the English flag flew over the lands along the entire Atlantic seaboard. Some English wanted to return Canada to France because Canada was mostly wilderness populated by Indians hostile to Great Britain.

7. Among the events students may list are the following: the Sugar Act of 1764, and the colonial protests of it; the Stamp Act, the riots it evoked, and the calling of the Stamp Act Congress by the colonists; the Declaratory Act, the Townshend Acts and the colonists' boycott; the Boston Massacre and Samuel Adams's manipulation of it; the Tea Act of 1773 and the resulting ''tea parties''; the Intolerable Acts imposed on the colony of Massachusetts; in general, the inability of Parliament and the colonists to compromise over the question of who had the right to make tax laws for the colonies. The calling of the First Continental Congress could be considered a turning point in British-American relations because, in taking this action, the colonists were in effect saying that they were willing to consider breaking away from England if some compromise with Britian's leaders could not be reached.

8. The delegates to the First Continental Congress considered themselves loyal British subjects. They even addressed their grievances to King George III, hoping that he could persuade Parliament to compromise on its stand. The delegates to the Second Continental Congress were generally more belligerent and less willing to compromise than the delegates to the First Continental Congress. However, they were not united in the intention of declaring independence from Great Britain. Delegates from New England and the southern colonies were, for the most part, in favor of a break with England. Those from the middle colonies were divided about the possibility of a break.

9. Lexington and Concord were the first battles of the Revolution. The Minutemen showed that they could hold their own in fighting the Redcoats. These two battles convinced the delegates to the Second Continental Congress that they should make the battles an American fight rather than a

Massachusetts fight. General George Washington took command of the Continental Army and state militias, a ragged and inexperienced fighting force, and by exercise of exceptional leadership, led this force through discouragements and defeats to final victory over the British army, reputedly the best in the world. Benjamin Franklin, as ambassador to France, kept French aid coming to the Americas as the war went on. After the American victory at Saratoga, he was able to convince the French government to bring their forces into the war on the American side. French, Prussian, and Polish friends: Professional soldiers from other countries contributed their expertise to American fighting forces and helped them win the Revolution. Among these foreign professionals were the Frenchman Lafayette, the Poles Pulaski and Kosciusko, and the Prussian von Steuben. Saratoga was the most important American victory of the Revolution up to 1777. The victory saved New England from the British forces and brought France into the war as an American ally. Yorktown was the battle in which the Continental Army finally defeated the British forces and confirmed the independence of the United States.

10. The weakness of the national government under the Articles of Confederation was due to the refusal of the states to give it the money and power it needed to run the nation and deal with other nations. The effectiveness of the national government under the Constitution was made possible because, through the Constitution, the states empowered the government to carry out its necessary functions.

11. The Connecticut Compromise resolved the issue of the number of representatives each state would have in the national legislature. Edmund Randolph's Virginia Plan proposed that the number of a state's representatives in both houses of the legislature would be determined by the size of the state's population. The small states objected to this plan because they felt that they would be constantly outvoted by the large states. Some small states wanted to follow the New Jersey Plan, according to which there would be only one house in the legislature and every state would have the same number of representatives. The Connecticut Compromise broke the stalemate that developed over the Virginia and New Jersey plans. According to the Connecticut Compromise, each state would have two representatives in the Senate, the upper house of the national legislature. The number of each state's representatives in the lower house would be decided by the size of the state's population. The Three-Fifths Compro-

mise resolved the issue summed up in this question: Should slaves be counted in determining the number of representatives a state would have in the House, the lower house in the national legislature? Northerners answered no, but demanded that slaves be counted when taxes were levied on a state. Southerners answered yes because the slave population was large in the southern states, and not counting the slaves would have meant that the South's representation in the House would have been reduced drastically. The Three-Fifths Compromise proposed that, in determining representation and taxation, five slaves be counted as three people. In accepting the compromise, the delegates at the Constitutional Convention were in effect saying that a slave was only three-fifths of a person, something less than a human being.

12. Among the leaders of the first administration were George Washington, Alexander Hamilton, Thomas Jefferson, and James Madison. Students will evaluate the importance of one of these leaders. Points that may be included in the evaluation follow. Washington was a good leader; he commanded respect for the presidency; he recognized that he was setting precedents for subsequent presidents; he left the running of the government to the more able men in his cabinet; he placed the nation on a solid foundation. Hamilton put the government on a firm financial footing and encouraged American economic development; he was personally involved in the suppression of the Whiskey Rebellion, thus establishing the authority of the national government; he was instrumental in founding the Federalist party. Jefferson acted as "the loyal opposition" during Washington's administrations; he was instrumental in forming the (Democratic) Republican party; he advocated a strict construction of the Constitution. Madison generally sided with Jefferson in opposing Hamilton's policies.

13. Foreign problems: (1) the Citizen Genêt incident (Washington ordered Genêt to stop his political activities, to refrain from bringing captured British ships into American waters, and, finally, to return to France); (2) the impressment of American sailors by British ship captains (Washington saved the peace by agreeing to the terms of Jay's Treaty, which did nothing to resolve the impressment problem, and he received severe criticism for his actions); (3) disputes with Spain (In Pinckney's Treaty, Spain recognized American claims to lands bordering Louisiana, allowed American farmers to use the Mississippi River, and granted Americans the right of deposit at New Orleans). Domestic

problems: (1) Madison's opposition to Hamilton's plan to redeem the Confederation's bonds, which originally had been purchased by private citizens and then bought by unscrupulous, wealthy speculators (Hamilton's arguments for the rich as the nation's most important class won Congress funding of a bill to redeem the bonds); (2) the opposition of Madison and other southerners to payment of the debts of the northern states (a funding of the debts was defeated in the House; however, Hamilton made a deal to support a southern site for the national capital in return for a favorable vote on another funding bill); (3) the opposition of Madison and Jefferson to Hamilton's national bank (Hamilton persuaded Washington to sign a bill establishing the bank); (4) southern opposition to Hamilton's high protective tariff (the tariff bill was defeated in the House of Representatives); (5) the Whiskey Rebellion (Washington and Hamilton led troups to western Pennsylvania, where the rebellion was put down and the authority of the national government was affirmed).

Critical Thinking

14. Cartographers draw parallels and meridians to form a grid on maps and globes. Any place on the earth's surface can be pinpointed on the grid if the parallel and meridian at which the place is located is known.

15. Thomas Paine: In his pamphlet *Common Sense*, he attacked the idea of monarchy, particularly as it was represented in King George III, whom Paine referred to as "the Royal Brute." The Declaration of Independence alluded to the "tyranny" of King George and listed more than two dozen of the King's violations of the natural rights of Americans. Enlightenment philosophers taught that the Creator bestowed certain natural rights on all human beings, rights that could not be taken away by government. The second paragraph of the Declaration enumerates some of these rights (life, liberty, the pursuit of happiness), and justifies the colonies' break with Great Britain by stating that it had violated these natural rights.

16. The Federalists argued that the new national government outlined in the Constitution was badly needed. They said that a government as weak as the Confederation would invite powerful European countries to meddle in American affairs. The Federalists' arguments found support because of the Confederation's ineffective response to such foreign actions as the following: Great Britain's refusal to send an ambassador to the United States and to withdraw its troops from American territory; France's refusal to lend money to the weak Confederation government; the harassment of American ships by the Barbary Pirates. The Anti-Federalists argued that the Articles of Confederation could be improved and did not have to be replaced. The Anti-Federalist argument also contended that the Confederation government was beginning to work well and that it did not take away the independence of the states. The Confederation's success in acquiring the western lands from the various states and the passage of the Land Ordinance of 1785 and the Northwest Ordinance of 1787 seemed to bear out one part of the Anti-Federalist argument. The other part was supported by the extreme reluctance of many of the states to give to the Confederation government any more power than they thought was necessary.

Skills Review

17. Surrender of Canada (1760); Boston Tea Party (1773); Declaration of Independence (1776); Battle of Yorktown (1781); Constitutional Convention (1787); John Adams inaugurated (1793).

18. A physical (topographic) map shows natural features such as mountains, valleys, and bodies of water. A political map shows manmade features such as boundaries, cities, and railroads. Both show some of the same features. Four elements that appear on every good map are a title, a scale, a legend, and a compass rose.

19. A primary source is an account of an event or events of a particular period of history given by a person or persons who lived through the event or events. It is an "eye-witness" account. Some examples of primary sources are newspapers, books, letters, diaries, and official documents. A secondary source is an interpretation of historical events produced by someone who neither participated in the events nor was closely involved with them. One example of a secondary source is a history textbook.

20. Sample scratch outline:

The Cabinet
- committee of advisors created by Congress to assist president
- made up of secretaries, or heads, of executives offices and departments
- Secretary of War—Henry Knox
- Secretary of State—Thomas Jefferson
- Secretary of the Treasury—Alexander Hamilton
- Attorney General and Postmaster General met with Cabinet, but did not have full cabinet rank

Students' paragraphs should open or close with an appropriate topic sentence. Supporting sentences should include details noted in the scratch outline.

CHAPTER 9

Section Review

1. Students' sentences will vary. Information about the names can be found on the pages given in parentheses: Justice Samuel Chase (216–217), James Monroe (218), Robert Livingston (218), Sacajawea (219).
2. France no longer had to feed the slaves of Santo Domingo, and so the need for grain and livestock from Louisiana lessened. Great Britain, with whom Napolean was planning a war, could easily conquer the thinly populated territory.
3. Lewis and Clark were the first people to cross the North American continent. They started in St. Louis and traveled up the Missouri River to what is now Great Falls, Montana. With the help of Sacajawea and several different Indian tribes, they discovered and followed a river flowing west, which took them to the Pacific. Indian tribes they met were curious, friendly, and helpful. Zebulon Pike traveled up the Missouri River deep into Minnesota and then down the Mississippi. In 1806 and 1807, Pike led an expedition up the Arkansas River into territory claimed by Spain, discovering the mountain in Colorado that bears his name (Pikes Peak). He returned along the Rio Grande. In his travels, Pike was treated well by the Indians.
4. One theory was that Burr was plotting a revolution that would detach Louisiana from the United States. The second theory was that Burr was planning to conquer Mexico and make himself emperor. Burr was tried for treason and acquitted.

Section Review (text page 225)

1. Students' sentences will vary. Information about the names and terms can be found on the pages given in parentheses: Tripoli (221–222), Stephen Decatur (222), *Leopard* and *Chesapeake* (223), War Hawks (224).
2. England had devastated the French fleet and dominated the seas. France had defeated the armies of Austria, Prussia, and Russia; and its army became supreme in Europe. This created a military standoff between England and France; they could wage only an economic war. Great Britain issued the Orders in Council, which fobade neutral nations to trade in European ports unless their ships stopped first in England for inspection and licensing. France countered with the Milan Decree, stating that neutral ships that observed the Orders in Council would be seized. The ships of American merchants were seized by both countries.
3. Because of Jefferson's Embargo Act, American trade came to a standstill, ships rotted at anchor in New England ports, and some capsized from neglect.
4. Madison's Nonintercourse Act (1809) allowed Americans to trade with all nations except England and France but provided that the United States would resume trade with whichever of the two warring countries stopped seizing American ships. The Act seemed to work; the British ambassador signed a treaty, and Madison reopened trade. But the British foreign minister in London rejected the treaty. Under the provisions of *Macon's Bill No. 2* (1810), Americans were permitted to trade with both France and England. As soon as one of the two powers stopped seizing American ships, the United States would cease trading with the other. Thus, when France lifted the Milan Decree, America cut off trade with Great Britain, whereupon the British prime minister repealed the Orders in Council on June 16, 1812.

Section Review (text page 232)

1. Students' sentences will vary. Information about the names and terms can be found on the pages given in parentheses: General Harrison (225, 227), Put-in-Bay (228), Treaty of Ghent (229), General Andrew Jackson (229).
2. American advantages were that Congress voted money for an army of more than 100,000 soldiers; their land neighbors to the north, the Canadians, expected to welcome the Americans as liberators. British advantages were that their navy had hundreds of ships, and they were used to "ruling the seas."
3. Monroe's achievements included the Rush-Bagot Agreement, which limited the number of U.S. and British warships on Great Lakes, setting the pattern for a later U.S.-Canadian boundary agreement; the establishment of the present U.S.-Canada boundary from the Great Lakes to the Rockies at 49° north latitude; the Oregon country—U.S. and Great Britain agreed to share sovereignty, and this land later peacefully became the states of Oregon and Washington and the province of British Columbia; Florida—Spain was persuaded to sell Florida; the Monroe Doctrine—the United States pledged not to interfere in European affairs, and Europe was not to interfere in the Western Hemisphere, Americans would respect existing colonies but would not tolerate attempts to gain new colonies (the doctrine set the course for United States-Latin American policy for many years).
4. John Marshall established the authority of the federal government and the Supreme Court over state legislatures; he committed the Supreme

Court to the Hamiltonian principle of loose construction of the Constitution.

Section Review (text page 235)

1. Students' sentences will vary. Information about the names and terms can be found on the pages given in parentheses: Tallmadge amendment (233), Henry Clay (233, 234–235), Virginia Dynasty (234), Twelfth Amendment (234).

2. To preserve the balance of free and slave states, Missouri was admitted as a slave state and Maine was admitted as a free state. Only free states could be created out of land north of the line at 36° 30' north latitude extending from the southern boundary of Missouri to the Rockies; states created from lands south of this line could be either slave states or free states.

3. None of the four candidates received an absolute majority of the electoral vote. Jackson won more votes (popular and electoral) than any other candidate. Adams was second. Therefore, the choice of the sixth president went to the House of Representatives. The House chose John Quincy Adams.

4. Jackson angrily resigned from the Senate. He probably thought he had won the election because of the popular and electoral vote; he was the only candidate to win states in all three sections of the country, and he and his followers claimed that Adams and Clay had made a "corrupt bargain" to make Adams president.

Time Line Questions (text page 236)

1. James Madison's
2. Louisiana Purchase, start of Lewis and Clark expedition, Treaty of Ghent, battle of New Orleans, Adams-Oñis Treaty, Monroe Doctrine
3. Orders in Council, Milan Decree, Embargo Act, Nonintercourse Act, Macon's Bill No. 2

Skills Strategy: Encyclopedia Indexes (text pages 236–237)

1. D: 68a
2. The section entitled "Boyhood" in the article, "Jefferson, Thomas" (J:58)
3. Marshall, John
4. *Information*—the section of the article, "Marine Corps, United States," with the heading "The War of 1812" on page 168 of volume M; *picture*—page 165 of volume M
5. In the "Related Articles" list in the article, "War of 1812

Chapter Test (text page 237)

Text Review

1. Chase was impeached under President Jefferson. The members of the Senate recognized that Chase was not guilty of the "high crimes and misdemeanors" that are the Constitutional grounds for impeachment. The senators also realized that Jefferson was striking back at Chief Justice Marshall and the independence of the federal judicial branch. Therefore, the Senate refused to find Chase guilty.

2. Nothing in the Constitution gave President Jefferson the right to buy Louisiana. Because the Constitution did not specifically forbid his action, Jefferson assumed he had the right to buy the area from the French.

3. Possible answers: by buying the Louisiana Territory, Jefferson would be able to assure the right of western farmers not only to use the port of New Orleans but also the entire Mississippi River, eliminating any French threat to the United States; the purchase of Louisiana would double the size of the United States (at 3 cents an acre, it was the greatest real estate bargain in history).

4. Students' answers may refer to the British seizure of many American ships, the impressment of thousands of American sailors by British captains, the *Leopard* and *Chesapeake* incident, pressure from the War Hawks in Congress, and the failure of the British government to notify the United States that the Orders in Council had been repealed.

5. During the "Era of Good Feelings," American nationalism exploded: the Fourth of July became an important celebration, patriotic books were published and patriotic songs were written, orators boasted of the superiority of the United States, Noah Webster differentiated between American English and British English in his dictionary, the United States and Great Britain peacefully established the western part of the boundary between Canada and the United States, Florida was purchased from Spain, the boundary between the United States and Spanish lands was peacefully set, the Monroe Doctrine was promulgated, and John Marshall's decisions established the authority of the federal government over the states.

6. When the Missouri territory applied for admission as a state, the number of free and slave states was equal with 11 states north of the Mason-Dixon line and 11 south of it. The admission of Missouri would undo the balance; emotions in both North and South ran high. For the first time, the North denounced slavery, and the South, on the defensive, demanded that its people be allowed to settle their own problems. The Missouri Compromise was intended to settle the dispute.

7. Jefferson found the strife between northerners and southerners "terrifying." John Quincy Adams saw the issue as "a title-page to a great tragic

volume." Neither of these former presidents believed that the compromise settled the dispute over slavery. Their negative reactions were prophetic of the continuation of the dispute and, eventually, of the Civil War.

8. The candidates in the 1824 presidential election were John Quincy Adams of Massachusetts, William Crawford of Georgia, Henry Clay of Kentucky, and Andrew Jackson of Tennessee. Only Jackson had nationwide support, carrying states in the West, the South, and the Northeast, and winning more popular and electoral votes than any other candidate. However, Jackson did not receive an absolute majority of either popular or electoral votes, so the election went to the House of Representatives, which chose John Quincy Adams as president.

Critical Thinking

9. Students' responses should indicate that the information regarding the Indians, geography, and the animal and plant life of Louisiana brought back by Lewis and Clark reflected some of Jefferson's universal interests.

10. Student conclusions may differ, but possible responses are that Jackson's furious resignation from the Senate, his supporters' cry of "Corrupt Bargain" and work to organize for a Jackson victory in 1828, and the harassment of President Adams all indicated that Jackson very much wanted to be president.

Writing a Paragraph

Sample Paragraph:

Andrew Jackson was a no-nonsense man of action. Jackson sometimes went outside the law to get things done. For example, he illegally battled and defeated powerful southeastern Indian tribes and executed two British subjects for treason against the United States. In the election of 1824, the House of Representatives made John Quincy Adams President, although Jackson had won a plurality of both the popular and electoral votes. When Adams named Clay his Secretary of State, Jackson took action. Furious, he resigned from the Senate, raised the cry "Corrupt Bargain!," and saw to it that Adams did not have an easy time as President.

If time permits, encourage students to read their sketches to the class.

CHAPTER 10

Section Review (text page 245)

1. Students' sentences will vary. Information about the names and terms can be found on the pages given in parentheses: Moses Brown (241), Yankee ingenuity (241), Oliver Evans (241), Lowell girls (243–244).

2. They got nails and flour from specialists like blacksmiths and millers. The wealthy bought clothes, shoes, and other goods from artisans who made them by hand. People in the middle (not rich or poor) made most of the goods they used, and treasured the things they had to buy. Those who lived far from towns (farmers and westerners) had to be "handy" at a large number of crafts.

3. With such cloth-making machines, other countries could set up textile mills to compete with the British, and the British would lose their profitable monopoly. Samuel Slater, a British machinist, heard that American state legislatures offered large amounts of money to machinery experts who would defy British law and come to the United States. Slater managed to slip out of England and get to New York with the plans for an entire spinning factory in his head. The Scholfield brothers and the American Francis Lowell also brought English industrial secrets to the United States.

4. Items are made by machine—parts are interchangeable—rather than made by hand by skilled craft workers. Different machines make hundreds of precise copies of each part of an item at a much lower cost than a handmade item. When a machine-made item breaks down, repair is easier, faster, and cheaper. The owner simply replaces the worn-out part with a machine-made copy of the part, rather than having skilled craft workers make the part by hand.

5. Possible answers: New England had many fast-flowing rivers and streams to supply power for the factories, and plenty of wood from forests for fuel; the War of 1812 convinced merchants to get out of maritime trade and put their money into manufacturing; American banks helped to finance industrialization; loans from state banks made it possible for investors to build the mills they could not otherwise afford; farm families provided a ready-made labor force for the new industry (farms were too small to support large families).

Section Review (text page 248)

1. Students' sentences will vary. Information about the names and terms can be found on the pages given in parentheses: American Colonization Society (245–246), Eli Whitney (246), short-staple cotton (246).

2. *Webster* spoke for the industrial Northeast and came to favor a high protective tariff. He advocated a strong sovereign national government. *Calhoun* at first was a strong nationalist and advocated a high protective tariff. Later, he opposed the protective tariff and became a spokesman for the agricultural

South. Believing that the states should have more authority than the central government, he supported his state's attempt to nullify a tariff law.

3. Practical reasons: plantation system was dying; there was no market for tobacco, indigo, and rice, which were the major slave crops; slavery seemed to be losing its reason for existing. Moral reasons: Some plantation owners, troubled by the statement in the Declaration of Independence that "all men are created equal" freed their slaves; others freed slaves in their wills; Madison, Monroe, Marshall supported the American Colonization Society, which encouraged slave owners to free their slaves and pay their passage to Africa. Reason for slavery's revival: The invention of the cotton gin made cotton a cash crop that could be grown efficiently and profitably on a large plantation with large numbers of slaves.

4. The South lacked the fast rivers necessary to power mills; Southern planters with rich land and a long agricultural tradition were less inclined than New Englanders to turn to manufacture as a way of making a living; growing cotton was so profitable that it seemed a waste of energy and money to manufacture cloth.

Section Review (text page 252)

1. Students' sentences will vary. Information about the names and terms can be found on the pages given in parentheses: Conestoga Wagon (249), Alexis de Tocqueville (249), squatter's rights (252), Thomas Hart Benton (252).

2. "The West" of the early nineteenth century was forested country beginning at the Appalachian Ridge and running 100 miles or so west of the Mississippi River. "The West" was an idea as well as a region.

3. Detroit, Michigan; Cincinnati, Ohio; Louisville and Lexington, Kentucky; Nashville, Tennessee.

4. Land speculators borrowed money to buy land and sell it at a profit; prices became too high, and people refused to buy. Prices started to drop and finally crashed as more and more speculators threw their land on the market. Wildcat banks loaned money to any speculator or planter willing to pay the inflated prices for land. Such banks gambled that the price of land would keep rising. When the price of land crashed, and banks could not get their money back from the speculators and planters who had borrowed it, many banks closed, and their depositors lost all their money. The Bank of the United States loaned money to wildcat banks, but panicked when land prices crashed; the Bank then demanded the money that the wildcat banks owed; the wildcat banks in turn ordered speculators and planters to pay off their loans so the wildcat banks could pay the Bank of the United

States. Unable to do so, the speculators and planters were ruined.

Sen. Thos. Benton pressed for *pre-emption* (squatter's rights) and *graduation* (lowering the cost of unsold lands).

Section Review (text page 257)

1. Students' sentences will vary. Information about the names and terms can be found on the pages given in parentheses: turnpikes (253), National Road (253), DeWitt Clinton (255), Mainline Canal (256).

2. Possible answers: Much of the land beyond the Appalachian was settled by southerners, especially Virginians. Like people of the South, most westerners were farmers. Slavery was a common bond in southwestern states where cotton was the cash crop (in Louisiana, sugar cane competed with cotton). States of the Old Northwest (Ohio, Indiana, Illinois) were isolated from the Northeast by the Appalachians and closely tied to the South by the Mississippi, which was used to get products to southern markets.

3. Clay's American System did not offer southerners anything they did not already have and would create higher prices for manufactured goods, and higher taxes to pay for the internal improvements to Northeastern mills. Because England bought all the cotton the South produced, Southerners saw no reason to subsidize New England mills through a protective tariff. Farmers from the Old Northwest supplied southern plantations with food via the Mississippi River, so benefit could come to the South by connecting the West to the Northeast.

4. The Erie Canal connected the Hudson River at Albany with the Great Lakes at Buffalo. The canal opened up the whole Northwest to merchants from New York; New York City became the nation's leading commercial center.

5. Fulton's steamboat was flat-bottomed and could travel in the very shallow water of the Mississippi and Missouri rivers, where shifting sandbars could change a clear channel into an obstacle course overnight. Conclusions: Steamboats became increasingly popular because they provided dependable, fast, and cheap transportation for people and goods. The steamboats made the Mississippi and Missouri commercially important waterways.

Time Line Questions (text page 260)

1. Fitch builds steamboat, invention of cotton gin, interchangeable parts demonstration, voyage of *Clermont*

2. 8 years (1817–1825)

3. 32 years

Skills Strategy: Opinions and Fact
(text pages 260–261)

1. The first paragraph; it contains strong opinions supported by examples of past experiences and historical facts.
2. The second paragraph; the initial opinion is supported by other opinions that are weak because they are based on feelings rather than facts, reasons, and examples.
3. Factual information can be found under the chapter subheadings indicated: *first opinion*—"Steamboats" and "Old Man River"; *second opinion*—"Cities on the Frontier"; *third opinion*—"People on the Move".

Chapter Test (text page 261)

Text Review

1. Alexander Hamilton viewed the Industrial Revolution as the path to prosperity in the United States. He believed that if the United States could manufacture what is needed rather than buying from abroad, it would become wealthier and more powerful than if it remained an agricultural nation. In contrast, Thomas Jefferson saw the benefits of industrialization, but preferred to keep the United States a farming country. He objected to the shift of the British population from farm to city and did not want the same thing to happen in the United States. Furthermore, he believed that for democracy to work in a country, landowners had to make up the core of the country.

2. Students will identify three of the following: Samuel Slater memorized plans for a complete spinning factory and brought them from England to the United States. He worked with Moses Brown, a wealthy merchant, to build a cotton-manufacturing factory in Rhode Island. Eli Whitney's principle of interchangeable parts opened the door to the application of mass production to the production of iron and steel goods and, therefore, to the manufacture of industrial machines. State banks in New England loaned money to investors which made it possible for them to build mills and factories which they could not have financed on their own. Francis Lowell smuggled plans for a power loom out of England and set up a weaving mill in Waltham, Massachusetts. He used local farm girls—the "Lowell girls"—to run the mill. His Lowell system was meant to be a way to manufacture cloth without disturbing traditional New England ways. Daniel Webster represented New Hampshire farmers when he was elected to Congress the first time. After he moved to Massachusetts, he became the attorney for the Second Bank of the United States and began to sympathize with the industrialists. By the time he was elected to Congress from Massachusetts, he had become a strong defender of the high tariffs that helped American industry develop.

3. A factor that contributed to the decline of slavery was that the American Colonization Society urged slaveowners to free their slaves and pay the slaves' passage to Africa if they wished it. The free blacks who chose to go to Africa founded the African republic of Liberia. Another factor was the belief of many planters in the natural rights of all people, which led them to free their slaves.

4. After the invention of the cotton gin, cotton became a crop that could make a planter with slaves and many acres very wealthy. Growing cotton was potentially so profitable that planters chose to invest their money on slaves rather than in cloth maufacturing and other southern industries.

5. Possible answers: New England couples in large numbers uprooted themselves and headed west as soon as they married. So many Virginians went west, that people in towns along their route could make a living by supplying the needs of the emigrants. Alexis de Toqueville wrote that "in the United States a man builds a house in which to spend his old age, and he sells it before the roof is on." Pioneers like Abraham Lincoln's father moved several times during their lives.

6. All western lands were owned by the government. They were for sale to anyone. However, purchasers had to buy at least 640 acres (259 hectares) at $1 an acre. To the average settler, 640 acres was more land than they needed, and $640 was more money than they could afford. Speculators, on the other hand, came with the purpose of buying large amounts of land at $1 an acre and making their profit by dividing large holdings into smaller plots and selling these at $2 or $3 an acre. Government policy favored this kind of land speculation until the Panic of 1819 brought in its wake reforms in land-sale policy.

7. Henry Clay persuaded Congress to pay for building the National Road from Cumberland, Maryland, to Vandalia, Illinois. He also proposed unsuccessfully the American System, which was to be a federally financed network of roads that would link the Northeast, South, and West. DeWitt Clinton, the governor of New York, was the chief mover in the building of the Erie Canal, which opened up the entire Northwest to New York City merchants and quickly made New York the nation's leading commercial center. Robert Fulton improved on the design of John Fitch's steamboat. Fulton's steamboat could float in a mere seven feet of

water, making it ideal for navigating the shallow parts of the Mississippi, and for reaching inland river ports. In this way steamboats like Fulton's quickly connected many river ports to other parts of the United States.

Critical Thinking

8. Industry failed to develop in the South for several reasons. Chief among these was the revival of the plantation system and slavery after the invention of the cotton gin, although southerners like John Calhoun wanted to build cotton mills near the southern cotton fields and thus create a cloth manufacturing industry. However, with cotton gins and slaves, owners of large plantations could make such enormous profits from raising cotton that they saw little point to investing money in a cloth manufacturing industry. Another factor that thwarted the growth of southern industry was the lack of fast rivers to provide power for running industrial machinery.

9. A high tariff was most favorable to the Northeast where most of the nation's manufacturing was done. A high tariff would add to the price of imported manufactured goods and promote the sale of the cheaper goods manufactured in the factories of the Northeast.

10. Whitney's cotton gin revived slavery, which, as time went on, became an issue over which North and South disagreed and eventually fought a civil war.

Writing a Paragraph

Sample Paragraph:

The people of the Northeast would benefit in three ways from the internal improvements proposed in my American System. The roads would cost the taxpayers of the Northeast huge sums of money, but roads connecting the Northeast to the West could be used to transport manufactured goods to a constantly growing market. The same roads could be used to bring back large amounts of cheap food from western farms. Thus, the prices of food in the Northeast would drop, and manufacturing workers would not need such high wages. In addition, my proposal for the American System includes a recommendation for a high tariff designed to protect northeastern industries from overseas competition.

CHAPTER 11

Section Review (text page 266)

1. Students' sentences will vary. Information about the names and terms can be found on the pages

given in parentheses: mechanics (265), Fanny Wright (265), debtors prisons (265), Masonic Order (265).

2. Adams was a private man, aloof from the crowd in an age of magnetic "charismatic" politicians. He openly took pride in his distinguished ancestry, superior intelligence, and education, as well as his record of accomplishment when Americans liked their leaders to claim that they were ordinary citizens. During his presidency, Adams was haunted by charges that he had made a "corrupt bargain" with Henry Clay. Jackson, meanwhile, worked behind the scenes to get support of powerful politicians for the next presidential election.

3. One reason for the upsurge of democracy was that people demanded that Jeffersonian principles be put into practice (e.g., common people should vote in elections). Also, the West was settled mostly by people who were not of privileged classes, so western states generally opened polls to all white adult males. Eastern states, fearing a loss of population, reformed their election laws. *Possible examples:* Property requirements were gradually eliminated, and by 1830, only three states required voters to own property. By 1832, voters, rather than legislatures, chose presidential electors in all states except South Carolina. By the end of the 1820s, nearly every white male could participate in government. By 1840, three-quarters of the eligible voters cast ballots in contrast to 1828 when only half voted.

4. the "Workies" were new voters who organized Workingpeople's parties among the mechanics, or skilled craftspeople in New York and other eastern cities. Reforms suggested by the Workies included abolition of debtors prisons, a mechanic's lien law, and free public education for all children.

5. The Anti-Masonic Party was formed because of Morgan's disappearance. Members of this party believed that Morgan was murdered by the Masons because he was writing a book revealing their secrets.

Section Review (text page 271)

1. Students' sentences will vary. Information about the terms can be found on the pages given in parentheses: "Old Hickory" (267), Whigs (269), "Trail of Tears" (269–270), Force Bill (270).

2. The campaign of 1828 was a mudslinging campaign with personal attacks on Adams and Jackson by their followers. *Adams* was depicted as an elitist snob who preferred fancy British manners to forthright American ways. He was said to be given to gambling and personally immoral. *Jackson* was labeled a murderer, and posters were published

listing the names of his supposed victims. Opponents also claimed that he had married his wife before her divorce from a previous husband was final.

3. Women, blacks, and Indians did not benefit from Jacksonian democracy. Equal opportunity, during that era, was reserved for free and white adult males. Women, blacks, and Indians did not have the right to participate in either business or politics. The attitude toward women was that their place was in the home, and that by preserving the home as a place of culture and a refuge of morality, women kept men from lapsing into savagery. Blacks were considered inferior to white people, and therefore, slavery was justified. Indians were considered culturally different, incompatible with whites but not inferior. They were seen as competitors with Jacksonians for land ownership. Jacksonians argued that white settlers developed land more intensively, and therefore had more right to the land than Indians.

4. The Supreme Court ruled that Georgia had no authority over the Cherokees. The court also ruled that Samuel A. Worcester, a white minister living in Cherokee land who had been arrested for refusing to take an oath of allegiance to Georgia, should be released from prison. When Georgia ignored the Supreme Court ruling, Jackson refused to enforce the decision. In 1838 the Cherokees and other southeastern tribes were forced to move to Oklahoma, and thousands of them died on the "Trail of Tears."

Section Review (text page 276)

1. Students' sentences will vary. Information about the terms can be found on the pages given in parentheses: Nicholas Biddle (273–275), hard money (274), "The Monster" (274), pet banks (275).

2. Jackson began to distance himself from Calhoun because of the Peggy Eaton affair. Jackson ordered his cabinet members to socialize. And Jackson discovered that Calhoun, as Secretary of War, had wanted him punished when he was fighting the Indians and hanging British subjects in Florida. Calhoun supported nullification; Jackson believed in a strong central government. Calhoun took a personal slap at Jackson by casting the deciding vote in the Senate against confirmation of Martin Van Buren, Jackson's choice for ambassador to England. Jackson named Van Buren to succeed Calhoun as his new running mate for Vice President.

3. In general, Jackson, by taking the actions he did, hurt the people he most wanted to help. His actions also led to boom, bust, and depression, and resulted in a wave of bank failures, wiping out the savings of thousands of people.

4. The Specie Circular required payment of debts to the government in gold or silver, so people lost faith in paper money. Banks failed because they did not have gold and silver to back paper money. People who believed their paper money was redeemable in gold found that it was worthless. Farmers lost their land, businesses went bankrupt because of bank failures, and people were thrown out of work.

Section Review (text page 281)

1. Students' sentences will vary. Information about the terms can be found on the pages given in parentheses: "King Andrew I" (276), subtreasuries (277), "Tippecanoe and Tyler, Too" (278–279), Lord Ashburton (280–281).

2. The candidates and their party were Van Buren— Democratic; Daniel Webster, Hugh L. White, and General William Henry Harrison—Whig. The Whig strategy was to run three candidates, so the election would be thrown into the House of Representatives where Whigs could out-vote Democrats. The strategy failed because Whig candidates did not carry enough states. Van Buren won with 170 electoral votes.

3. Weed pointed out that Jackson won the election of 1828 because he was a military hero and no one knew where he stood on any issues. Weed wanted to nominate William Henry Harrison because, like Jackson, he was a military hero, and no one knew where he stood on the issues. The Whigs would emphasize his career as an Indian fighter.

4. Harrison died one month after he was sworn into office. Vice President Tyler succeeded him. Tyler vetoed Clay's attempts to design a new Bank of the United States. The Clay Whigs expelled Tyler and all of his cabinet except Daniel Webster from the Whig party.

Time Line Questions (text page 282)

1. 1828, Tariff of Abominations; 1828, South Carolina Exposition and Protest; 1832, Tariff, South Carolina nullification convention; 1833, Force Bill

2. Depression of 1837, "Trail of Tears" in 1838

3. Anti-Masonic party–1826, Whig party–1834

Skills Strategy: Pie Graphs (text pages 282–283)

1. Election of 1828

2. Divide the electoral votes of each candidate by the total electoral votes (261)

3. 261 electoral votes

4. 1,155,370 popular votes

5. Andrew Jackson won the election of 1828 with 178 electoral votes to John Quincy Adams's 83, and he received almost 150,000 more popular votes than Adams.

Chapter Test (text page 283)

Text Review

1. The Workingpeople's parties were composed of "Workies," skilled craftspeople who had received the vote in the upsurge of democracy that swept the nation in the early nineteenth century. They pressed for democratic reforms such as the abolition of debtors' prisons and the increase of free public education for all children. That a woman, Frances Wright, should be their most effective leader is indicative of the democratic spirit of the Workies.

2. The two principles that constitute the key to Jacksonian Democracy are, *first,* Jackson's belief that every American should have the opportunity to succeed in life as he had done and, *second,* his belief that government should ensure that everyone had an equal opportunity to succeed.

3. Upon taking office, President Jackson openly used political patronage to reward his Democratic supporters, following a practice that became known as the spoils system. Jackson did not abuse this practice. Of the 20,000 federal jobs available when he began his presidency, he gave only about 4,000 to fellow Democrats. His opponents and critics, the National Republicans (later called Whigs), used the spoils system much more than Jackson did.

4. Students will probably cite Calhoun's toast at a dinner in April of 1830 as his most disloyal action. Jackson had looked directly at Calhoun and offered the toast, "Our Union, it must be preserved." Calhoun, in front of all those present at the dinner, countered with another toast, "The Union, next to our liberty, the most dear." Accept other appropriate answers that students reasonably support.

5. Jackson believed in hard money, gold and silver coin. He felt that it was wrong for banks to loan money in the form of bank notes if they did not have enough gold and silver to redeem them on demand. Such a practice could result in bank failures and the financial ruin of a bank's depositors. Jackson believed that the Bank of the United States (which he called "The Monster") was unconstitutional. He especially resented the fact that a few wealthy people owned 80 percent of the Bank's stock and therefore controlled the Bank and, in Jackson's opinion, the lives of the common people.

6. Jackson ordered the Secretary of the Treasury to stop depositing government money in the Bank of the United States and instead to deposit the money in state banks, the so-called "pet banks." The need to continue paying the government's bills caused the Bank to call in loans it had made to the state banks. This resulted in the failure of many of the banks that wiped out the savings of many common people, the opposite of what Jackson wanted. Jackson's issuance of the Specie Circular, which required payment for government land in hard money resulted eventually in the depression of 1837 in which common people suffered—farmers lost their land, bank depositors lost their savings, and workers lost their jobs because of business failures.

7. The Whigs (formerly the National Republicans) became important in the election of 1836. Because the Whigs were unable to unite on anything except their dislike of Andrew Jackson, they did not get behind a single presidential candidate in 1836, and they lost the election that year. In 1840, the Whigs won the presidency because of several factors. The voters blamed the 1837 depression on Democratic President Van Buren. Following the successful strategy of the Democrats in the 1828 election, the Whigs nominated William Henry Harrison who, like Jackson in 1828, was a military hero who made no public statement about his stand on the issues. A Democratic politician blundered by making a sneering and snobbish comparison between Van Buren and Harrison which backfired. John Tyler, the Whig vice-presidential nominee, attracted southern votes.

8. John Tyler became president when William Harrison died. When he vetoed a proposal to establish a new national bank, the furious Whigs expelled him and his whole cabinet (except for Daniel Webster) from the party. The Webster-Ashburton Treaty was President Tyler's major accomplishment. Negotiated by Secretary of State Daniel Webster, the treaty peacefully resolved several potentially dangerous British-American disputes, most of them over the boundary between Canada and the United States.

Critical Thinking

9. Students should support their opinions with details from the text.

10. The campaign of 1828 could be called a propagandist's dream. The Adams and Jackson supporters used highly emotional techniques to win voters for their candidates. Jacksonians depicted Adams as an elitist and snob who preferred fancy British manners to honest and straightforward American

ways. Adams was also said to be a gambler and an immoral person. Adams's people labeled Jackson a murderer and published a poster with the names of those he was supposed to have killed. They also claimed that Jackson had married his wife before her divorce from her previous husband was final.

Writing a Paragraph

Among the "history makers" students may choose are the following: John Quincy Adams, Frances Wright, John C. Calhoun, Martin Van Buren, Sequoyah, Peggy Eaton, Nicholas Biddle, Thomas Hart Benton, Henry Clay, Daniel Webster, William Henry Harrison, John Tyler. Students' paragraphs should begin or end with a topic sentence. The supporting sentences should contain at least three details that have not been included in the text thus far about the person.

CHAPTER 12

Section Review (text page 289)

1. Students' sentences will vary. Information about the names and terms can be found on the pages given in parentheses: deists (284), William Ellery Channing (286), Seventh-Day Adventists (288), Joseph Smith (288–289).
2. The Anglicans lost influence because many Anglican priests had been Loyalists during the Revolution. Congregationalists also suffered losses because people now felt that their economic and political lives were in their own hands and found it difficult to continue belief in the Puritan doctrine of predestination. They also opposed the Jeffersonian Republicans.
3. The revivalists preached a democratic version of Puritanism. Camp meetings were run by the revivalists. The meetings were announced months in advance and took place on the frontier. They lasted a week or more, featured outdoor sermons and hymn singing, and were deeply emotional. Baptists and Methodists were the most popular denominations in the trans-Appalachian West because they were most active in organizing these frontier revivals. Circuit riders were commissioned by Methodist ministers because some people went to camp meetings for entertainment rather than religion. Each of these traveling ministers visited a dozen or more western settlements too poor to support a permanent minister. The circuit riders preached, performed marriages and baptisms, and gave counsel. The riders were housed and fed by the people of one settlement before riding off with gun and bible to the next stop on the circuit.

4. Because of ridicule by neighbors, Joseph Smith eventually led the Latter-Day Saints from New York to Missouri, and then to Nauvoo, Illinois, in 1840. The Mormons were hated there for their polygamy, for their prosperity during the 1837 depression, and for shutting themselves off from neighbors. In 1844, Smith announced his candidacy for the United States presidency, was arrested, taken from jail, and murdered. Brigham Young emerged as the strong new leader of the Mormons. He decided the Mormons would never flourish in the United States, so in 1847, he led the Mormons west.

Section Review (text page 291)

1. Students' sentences will vary. Information about the terms can be found on the pages given in parentheses: Sir Thomas More (290), George Rapp (290), Mother Ann Lee (290).
2. A utopia is a perfect society where there is no evil. The Rappites and Shakers were two religious utopian groups. Shakers survived longer because even though they forbade marriage, practiced celibacy, and held property in common like the Rappites, they welcomed any true believer into their communities and adopted children to carry on their faith.
3. Followers of Etienne Cabet, the Icarians, established settlements in Texas and Nauvoo, Illinois. New England writers and philosophers founded Brook Farm, near Concord, Massachusetts. Robert Owen founded New Harmony in Indiana.
4. Other utopias were based on the belief that private property and competition for money were the causes of unhappiness in society, so each utopia held property in common. John Humphrey Noyes added marriage as a source of evil. He believed marriage was a form of property. So Noyes devised the idea of complex marriages for his Oneida community. Each man was married to all the women there, each woman to all the men.

Section Review (text page 294)

1. Students' sentences will vary. Information about the names and terms can be found on the pages given in parentheses: Transcendentalism (291-293), Nathaniel Hawthorne (293), *Moby Dick* (293), Natty Bumppo (294).
2. Many of the men and women, who in the 1830s and earlier, created an impressive body of American literature, were New England Transcendentalists. This emergence of American writing and culture is often called "The Flowering of New England." James Fenimore Cooper, as well as Edgar Allan Poe and Henry Wadsworth Longellow.

3. Emerson looked to find God in nature. He felt that personal morality was superior to laws.

4. Thoreau tried to break away from society. He built a cabin on Walden Pond and wrote a book called *Walden* which is a transcendental masterpiece and a beautifully written celebration of nature. Both Emerson and Thoreau claimed to be above and to reject American materialism, but both enjoyed its benefits. Margaret Fuller sensed the problems of Transcendentalism. She, like Emerson, was a romantic. She grew restless with her conventional life as editor and essayist for the Transcendentalist magazine, *The Dial.* Lashing out, she wrote a criticism of the role Americans allowed women. Fuller went to Italy and participated in the 1848 revolution.

5. Possible answers: Nathaniel Hawthorne explored evil. Herman Melville explored evil in the world. James Fenimore Cooper wrote about life on the American frontier. Washington Irving wrote humorous sketches and folk tales. Edgar Allan Poe invented the modern ghost story and modern detective story. Henry Wadsworth Longfellow wrote on American themes in long epics such as *The Song of Hiawatha.* John Greenleaf Whittier wrote poems with American themes, such as ''Barefoot Boy with Cheek of Tan.''

Section Review (text page 305)

1. Students' sentences will vary. Information about the names and terms can be found on the pages given in parentheses: *laissez faire* (295), Fifteen Gallon Law (300), Samuel F. B. Morse (302), Seneca Falls Convention (305).

2. Deaf people: Thomas Gallaudet; blind people: Samuel Gridley Howe, the mentally ill: Dorothea Dix; prisoners: Prison Discipline Society; alcoholics: Sylvester Graham, Washington Temperance Society, Dr. Benjamin Rush, Sons of Temperance, John B. Gough, NEal Dow, Father Theobald Mathew

3. Know-Nothings began as the secret anti-Catholic Order of the Star-Spangled Banner. Members were instructed to answer all questions about their organization with ''I know nothing.'' Then, at the urging of prominent American anti-Catholics, Know-Nothings became the Native American party and entered politics. The new party capitalized on the decline of the Whigs and became a major force in American elections. It swept to power in several states and controlled Massachusetts. At its peak, the party had 75 members in Congress. Millard Fillmore ran as the party's presidential nominee in 1856. The American Bible Society was made up of missionaries who distributed Protestant pamphlets and Bibles to Catholics and in other ways attempted to convert them.

4. Elizabeth Cady Stanton was one of founders and the guiding spirit of the women's movement. She wrote the *Declaration of Sentiments and Resolutions.* Lucretia Coffin Mott was an important leader in the women's movement. Amelia Bloomer was the editor of the temperance newspaper *The Lily* and a crusader for women's right to vote. Susan B. Anthony also played a major role in the women's suffrage movement.

Time Line Questions (text page 306)

1. Universalism,1779; American Unitarianism,1785; American Bible Society,1816; American Tract Society,1825; Millerites,1831; Mormons move to Nauvoo,1839; Mormons move to Utah, 1847

2. 6 years

3. 26 years

Skills Strategy: Text, Pictures, and Captions (text page 306)

1. The information given in the sentence beginning ''One of the spectators. . . .'' (under the heading ''The Seneca Falls Convention'')

2. Because of the pantaloons under her dress; from the name of Amelia Bloomer who recommended wearing them as a symbol of feminist ideas.

3. The pleasant appearance of the woman indicates an approving attitude. However, the picture was meant to be appealing to sell sheet music and may not reveal a widespread attitude. In fact, the text reveals that attitudes of the times towards feminists were at least not totally sympathetic.

4. Where the picture appeared, a possible motive for using the picture, and the origin of the clothing worn by the woman.

UNIT 3 TEST (text page 307)

Chapter Survey

1. Sample summary sentence(s): Chapter 9 treats the presidencies of Thomas Jefferson, James Madison, and James Monroe, and the disputed election of John Quincy Adams. The chapter presents such important events as the Louisiana Purchase, the War of 1812, the Era of Good Feelings under President Monroe, and the Missouri Compromise, among the first steps on the tragic path to the Civil War. Pages containing information about names and terms: Robert Livingston (218), Sacajawea (219–220), General Andrew Jackson (229), Twelfth Amendment (234).

2. Sample summary sentence(s): Chapter 10 traces the origins of the industrialization of the United

States, explains the near demise and sudden revival of slavery, follows pioneers who settled "the West," and describes the developments in transportation that helped to unite the regions of the expanding United States. Pages containing information about terms: Lowell girls (243–244), Eli Whitney (242, 246), Conestoga wagon (249), National Road (253), Mainline Canal (256).

3. Sample summary sentence(s): Chapter 11 analyzes the growth of democracy under President Andrew Jackson and reveals its exclusion of women, Indians, and blacks. The chapter also discusses the brief rise of the nullification issue; the actions of President Jackson that led to a boom, a bust, and a depression; and the administrations of Van Buren, Harrison, and Tyler, who became a president without a party. Pages containing information about terms: "Trail of Tears" (269–270), Sequoyah (269), Nicholas Biddle (273, 274, 275), "Tippecanoe and Tyler, Too" (278, 279).

4. Sample summary sentence(s): Chapter 12 begins with a discussion of the rise of various new religions and utopian groups in the United States in the nineteenth century. The chapter also examines the flowering of American literature, the many reform movements of the period, the origins of the women's rights struggle, and the growth of strong feelings against immigrants. Pages containing information about names and terms: Joseph Smith (288–289), Mother Ann Lee (290), Utopia (290–291), Transcendentalism (291, 293), Know-Nothings (302).

Text Review

5. Student answers will vary. Among the achievements of Jefferson's presidency they may choose are the purchase and exploration of Louisiana, the end of the Alien and Sedition Acts and Jefferson's pardon of people jailed under them, the repeal of the law that required a foreigner to wait 14 years to become a citizen, or Jefferson's introduction of informality to the new capital in Washington. Student choices should be backed up by appropriate reasons.

6. The impressment of American sailors was only one of the reasons for the War of 1812. Pressure from a patriotic group of congressmen had a great deal of influence on President Madison's decision to ask for a declaration of war. These congressmen, known as the War Hawks, had several motives: they wanted to avenge the "injuries and indignities" the British had heaped on the United States; they wanted to prevent the British from capturing New Orleans and closing the Mississippi River to western exports; and they wanted to annex Canada to the United States.

7. "Era of Good Feelings" as a description of the Monroe presidency is not completely accurate. At the end of Monroe's term, Missouri's application for statehood began a dispute between slave states and free states in which the immorality of slavery was discussed for the first time. The dispute was ended temporarily by the Missouri Compromise. However, John Quincy Adams and Thomas Jefferson looked on the compromise with foreboding, as a grim harbinger of further problems over slavery and, eventually, civil war.

8. Three types of machines that made the English Industrial Revolution possible were James Hargreaves's spinning jenny, Sir Richard Arkwright's machine for changing wool or cotton into yarn or thread and Edmund Cartwright's rope-making machine, and the steam engine. Machines like these were kept secret by law in England. However, state legislatures in the United States offered money rewards to English machine experts who would defy British law and bring their knowledge to the United States. In response, machines were smuggled into the United States by English machinists Samuel Slater, Paul and Arthur Schofield, and the American entrepreneur Francis Cabot Lowell.

9. With Eli Whitney's invention of the cotton gin and the use of steam engines to run it, cotton became a valuable crop in the South, a crop that could be easily sold in great quantity to the cloth-weaving mills that had developed in England and the Northeast as a result of the Industrial Revolution. Southern planters had to grow enough cotton to keep these mills supplied, and to do so economically, the planters chose to use slave labor on their plantations.

10. Land speculation in the West was based on credit. Speculators made down payments on land and agreed to pay the balance over four years, gambling that buyers would come along before payment of the balance was due. Wildcat banks, western banks with irresponsible lending policies, fueled the land speculation by advancing money somewhat indiscriminately to speculators. The Bank of the United States, which had loaned money to the wildcat banks, demanded repayment of loans from these banks when land prices crashed. This caused the failure of many wildcat banks which had insufficient money to repay the loans. People who had savings in the wildcat banks lost all their money when the banks closed.

11. The West: The western states, settled by people who were not of the privileged class, gave the vote to all white adult males in order to attract

more settlers. Because the eastern states did not want to lose their population to the West, they also reformed their election laws. Thomas Jefferson believed that "common" people should take part in elections. Andrew Jackson believed that government should protect the opportunity of every American to succeed. He claimed to favor the "common person" over the "rich and powerful" and a strong, democratic central government over state governments controlled by small groups of aristocrats. In defending his practice of awarding government jobs to "common" people, he said that the "common person" was quite able to perform any government job in a democracy.

12. Calhoun's compact theory of government held that the federal government was an agreement, or "compact," among the states. According to this theory, the Union was formed by people acting through their state governments, not by the people themselves, and that the states were sovereign, not the federal government. The theory also stated that when the compact of states passed a law, each and every state had the right to nullify the law within its own boundaries. In 1832, when Congress passed a tariff bill that South Carolinians did not want, they met in convention and nullified the law. In response, Jackson asked for, and Congress passed, the Force Bill which gave him power to use force to ensure that the tariff law was obeyed. South Carolina nullified the Force Bill, too, and announced its intentions to fight any federal troops that crossed its borders. However, a compromise was reached before the situation went any further.

13. Students will list five of the following and give essential facts about one: revivalists (286–288), Millerites (288), Latter-Day Saints (288–289), Rappites (290), Shakers (290), Robert Owen's New Harmony group (290), Icarians (290), Phalanxes (290), Brook Farm (290), Oneida (290–291). Facts about each religious or utopian group can be found on the pages given in parentheses.

14. Students may include reforms of the following in their answers: treatment and education of deaf and blind people (295–96), treatment of the insane (296), the prison system (298–299), excessive drinking and alcoholism (299–300), the treatment of women (297, 303–305). Information about individual reformers can be found on the pages given in parentheses.

Critical Thinking

15. Student responses should suggest that, if Marshall had not ruled as he did, the relationship between states and the federal government might

have followed the lines described by Calhoun's compact theory of government; that is, the federal government would not have real authority over the states.

16. Student answers should reflect the understanding that the West in the early 1800s was made up of lands between the Appalachian ridge and a line about 100 miles west of the Mississippi River. It included none of the areas the students may think of as the West today.

17. Agreed with Transcendentalism: Henry David Thoreau, Margaret Fuller; disagreed with Transcendentalism: Nathaniel Hawthorne, Herman Melville.

Skills Review

18. Louisiana Purchase (1803), British burn Washington, D.C. (1814), Erie Canal built (1817–1825), Andrew Jackson first inaugurated (1829), South Carolina nullification convention (1832), Mormons move to Nauvoo, Illinois (1839), Seneca Falls convention on women's rights (1848).

19. The second statement is a fact. The first statement is an opinion. The opinion can be validated by reference to the unfortunate aspects of slavery —the poor treatment of the slaves—and the slave rebellions that occurred in slave states.

20. Sentences will vary. Examples might be: The War of 1812 brought about a sharp delineation of U.S. boundaries and territorial rights. The development of strong national spirit provided a basis for America to grow into a powerful, proud nation. Industrialization changed the world's way of life from agrarian to technology-based. Heightened protest against slavery led to a belief in equality for all. Social reform movements brought about humane treatment for handicapped and mentally ill people, and for prisoners.

CHAPTER 13

Section Review (text page 316)

1. Students' sentences will vary. Information about the names and terms can be found on the pages given in parentheses: Thomas Roderick Dew (313), *The Impending Crisis* (313), George Fitzhugh (314).

2. Four slave rebellions that took place in the South were Cato's revolt, 1739; Gabriel Prosser's rebellion, 1801; Denmark Vesey's revolt, 1822; Nat Turner's rebellion, 1831. Turner and his followers killed more than 60 whites in Southampton County, Virginia. A band of 60 followers was rounded up, and Turner gave himself up. Turner and 16 others were hanged. The other slaves were sold out of

state, and new restrictions were placed on all slaves.

3. The major points of the Floyd plan included a gradual abolition of slavery where slaveowners would free slaves and be compensated for their loss of property out of Virginia's state treasury. If the plan had passed, the northernmost southern states—Delaware, Maryland, Kentucky, and possibly North Carolina—might have abolished slavery. Also, slavery might have been restricted to the cotton states which, by themselves, might not have considered seceding from the Union.

4. Religious: Because some Biblical figures favored by God owned slaves, God must have approved of slavery. Jesus Christ had told a runaway slave to return to his master. Historical: Greece and Rome were slave-holding societies. Artistic and philosophical accomplishments of the upper classes of these countries were made possible because slaves did labor for them. Cultural: The South had three times as many people attending colleges as New England, even though populations were about the same. Racial: According to George Fitzhugh, owning blacks was justified because they were racially inferior to whites. They were incapable of competing with whites, so slaveowners did blacks a favor by protecting them from freedom. Sociological: Fitzhugh also argued that slaves lived a better life than most northern industrial workers. In return for their labor, they were cared for by their masters from cradle to grave. Slaves were happy to be slaves, and children, the elderly, and handicapped and injured blacks who could not work at all were provided with the necessities of life. Refutations: Students should realize that the refutation to all arguments is that none of them did, or could, justify the basic essence of slavery—the denial of the freedom and other natural rights of human beings.

Section Review (text page 322)

1. Students' sentences will vary. Information about the terms can be found on the pages given in parentheses: Mary Boykin Chesnut (317), task system (318), Simon Gray (320), Fugitive Slave Act (321).

2. Slavery was a "peculiar institution" in that it was unique as practiced in the American South. Every Western nation had abolished slavery except Brazil. However, the slaves in Brazil had legal rights that American slaves did not have.

3. Members of the planter elite led elegant, aristocratic lives and lived in big houses. Thanks to slavery, they could devote themselves to cultural pursuits and to governing the South. In their view, they lived

this way not for selfish reasons, but for the good of all. Their society was patriarchal, not democratic. Planters were a small minority in the South. Three-quarters of those who lived in the South were not slaveowners. Most of those who were, besides the big planters, had at most two or three slaves. The majority of white southerners worked hard for a living. Unlike the planters, they did not have the leisure or the wealth for a life of culture and genteel pursuits. Yet, most of these other white southerners defended slavery. Many of the white farmers hoped to prosper in the future and become planters themselves. The poorest whites supported slavery because, with the existence of slaves, the poor whites were not at the bottom of the social ladder.

4. Wise slaveowners did not mistreat their slaves. Slaves were expensive. A master who beat a slave to death destroyed a valuable piece of property. A master who fed, housed, and clothed slaves so badly that they could not work was a poor business person. Out of self-interest, some masters encouraged their slaves to own small things, to sell things, and to marry. The reasoning was that a slave who had a husband, wife, or property would be unlikely to run away.

Section Review (text page 329)

1. Students' sentences will vary. Information about the names and terms can be found on the pages given in parentheses: manumit (322), Benjamin Banneker (322–323), Angelina and Sarah Grimké (326), Underground Railway (329).

2. Lundy's approach was in the tradition of the early Quaker protests and far more moderate than that of Walker or Garrison. Lundy called on the southern states to abolish slavery and on the entire nation to raise money to help freed blacks move to Haiti, Canada, or Texas, then a part of Mexico. Lundy tried to communicate reasonably with slaveowners rather than attack them. Walker believed that, if slavery was not abolished, blacks had the right to rise up in violent revolution. In *The Liberator*, Garrison took such a fierce anti-slavery stance that he seemed to be calling for war. Garrison attacked not only the evils of slavery but also the evil of slaveowners. Garrison was not interested in discussing the practical problems involved in any plan to end slavery.

3. *American Slavery As It Is* was a collection of newspaper articles that detailed the mistreatment and outright cruelty that slaves had to endure. The articles were collected and published by Theodore Dwight Weld. Weld deliberately included newspaper accounts of whippings and brandings and of slaves starving or freezing to death. He did this to

counteract claims by some southerners that north-erners only imagined such things.

4. Frederick Douglass, who escaped from slavery, was an author and orator who gave a first-hand account of what it meant to be human property. Sojourner Truth was a former slave and an inspired speaker who combined antislavery feelings with support for women's rights in her speeches. Harriet Tubman was a conductor on the Underground Railway. Tubman risked her freedom and possibly her life by returning 19 times to slave states in order to lead other blacks to freedom.

Time Line Questions (text page 332)

1. 1801, 1822, 1831, 1849, 1850
2. 1808
3. *The Appeal, The Liberator, American Slavery As It Is,* Douglass's *Autobiography, The Impending Crisis*

Skills Strategy: Dictionaries (text pages 332–333)

1. (1) main entry word; (2) phonetic respelling; (3) numbered definition; (4) lettered definition; (5) sample phrase; (6) part of speech; (7) usage label; (8) word history, or origin; (9) another form of the word
2. (a) verb—I;a; (b) adjective—2; (c) noun—2

Chapter Test (text page 333)

Text Review

1. The last debate on slavery in the Virginia legislature was brought about by a slave rebellion led by Nat Turner in Virginia's Southampton County in 1831. The subject of the debate was Governor John Floyd's proposal for the gradual abolition of slavery in Virginia—slaveowners would be paid cash by the state to free their slaves. After three weeks of discussion, the state representatives—believing that blacks and whites could not live together as equals—rejected Governor Floyd's plan by a vote of 94 to 40. After the debate, slavery was no longer considered a debatable issue in the South.

2. Southern representatives blocked debate on slavery in Congress by instituting the "gag rule" in 1836. This rule called on the House to table, or set aside, any proposal for Congress to discuss the question of slavery, insisting that the decision to abolish or retain slavery was up to each state and was not a part of the Congress's business.

3. Possible answers: Every southern state had laws that forced blacks to remain in bondage. Other laws made it impossible for slaveowners to free

even one of their slaves. Some states required free blacks to leave or to live in cities where they could not influence slaves. In most states of the South, teaching a slave to read was a crime. Southern county governments were required to finance slave patrols to keep track of the comings and goings of slaves. Slaves who had permission to be away from their master's property had to carry passes. Slave codes in the southern states denied civil and human rights to the slaves. Slaves could not own property, buy or sell things, make contracts, enter into legal marriage, testify against whites in court, or have even their right to life protected legally.

4. Some slaveowners ignored the slave codes out of self-interest. A slave who was allowed to own property had something to lose and would be less likely to run away. Slaves who were allowed to marry would be unwilling to escape and leave a husband or wife behind. For other reasons, some slaveowners allowed slaves to hunt with guns and to learn to read and write.

5. Possible answers: A minority of slaves rebelled against their enslavement. Many others chose to run away. Almost all expressed thinly veiled protests in spirituals they sang or in folk tales they told.

6. Slaves created their own culture and social life. They found ways to keep up their spirits, preserve their will to live, and teach their children to have courage. Many slaves found strength in the practice of religion and hope in Biblical stories.

7. The American Colonization Society urged slaveowners to free their slaves and raised money to pay for the passage of free blacks to West Africa. Neither of these programs offered any real solution to the slavery question. The blacks who chose to return to Africa were already free. Since cotton continued to boom in the South, slaveowning planters were not willing to free the slaves whose labor on the cotton plantations was making them rich.

8. Conventional Americans were distracted from the ideas the two sisters spoke of because they were shocked to see women speaking in public against slavery.

Critical Thinking

9. Sample sentences are given. Black woman: How can slavery be good when it takes a man away from his wife and children? Extreme abolitionist: Slavery has to be ended at any cost because it's wrong. Member of the planter class: I need my slaves to run this plantation, and on this plantation

they're treated better than most of the poor white workers in the factories up north.

10. Accept opinions that are supported by appropriate facts. Most students will disagree with the statement, and should note that unlike industrial workers, slaves were methodically and rigorously denied their civil and human rights, including their right to freedom.

Writing a Paragraph

The topic sentence of the paragraph on the problem of slavery should state the problem and the fact that various attempts at solving the problem were offered by the different groups specified. Among the details that could be included in the supporting sentences are the following: the Constitutional Convention of 1787; Congressional outlawing of the slave trade in 1807; William B. Preston's plan; the rebellions and other actions of the slaves themselves; the abolitionists; the Tallmadge Amendment; the Colonization Movement; the extremist abolitionists; the moderate abolitionists, northern and southern, black and white.

CHAPTER 14

Section Review (text page 342)

1. Students' sentences will vary. Information about the names and terms can be found on the pages given in parentheses: Camino Real (336), Santa Fe Trail (336–337), Stephen Austin (337), Sam Houston (338–339).

2. Except for Missouri, Arkansas, and Louisiana, the United States lay east of Lake Superior and the Mississippi River in 1840. The Mexican territory and the Oregon Country interested Americans of the times. Although American farmers were not interested in the prairies and plains west of the Mississippi because they believed the land would not support crops, mountain men—explorers and trappers—were interested in the fur-bearing animals and the rugged adventure of exploring the Rockies. The mountain men awakened the interest of eastern missionaries and midwesterners with their descriptions of the Oregon Country. Missouri merchants saw opportunity for enrichment and began to trade with Santa Fe, New Mexico. Other Americans poured into Texas looking for land to grow cotton and graze cattle.

3. The present-day American Southwest and California were owned by Spain in the 1840s. Russia had vague claims to the Oregon Country. Britain also had a vague claim to the Oregon Country based on the presence of the Hudson Bay Company in the territory.

4. Student histories should include the following points: the American Fur Company was established. American missionaries made their appearance in the 1830s. Beginning in 1840, thousands of Americans followed the Oregon Trail to settle in the Oregon Country. In 1842, the Webster-Ashburton Treaty provided that Oregon Country be jointly governed by the British and Americans. Most Americans settled south of the Columbia River. In July 1843, a group of Americans proclaimed Oregon a territory of the United States and informed President Tyler of their action.

Section Review (text page 346)

1. Students' sentences will vary. Information about the names and terms can be found on the pages given in parentheses: manifest destiny (342), "Fifty-four Forty or Fight" (342), Zachary Taylor (345), Bear Flag Republic (345).

2. Both Tyler and Calhoun were expansionists. Because slavery was legal in Texas, both men were interested in the annexation of Texas. Calhoun, in particular, feared for the future of the southern way of life because the Missouri Compromise effectively shut slavery out of the remaining territories. Expansionists of the North were not concerned with slavery. They mainly wanted the United States to grow.

3. In 1844, Henry Clay was the Whig candidate, and James K. Polk was the Democratic candidate. Because Clay needed the votes of both the North's Conscience Whigs (anti-slavery and anti-annexation) and the South's Cotton Whigs (pro-slavery and pro-annexation), he never took a firm stand on either side of the annexation issue. Polk was for the annexation of Texas.

4. In the treaty of Guadalupe Hidalgo which ended the war between Mexico and the United States, Mexico agreed to recognize the Rio Grande as the boundary of Texas, and ceded California and New Mexico to the United States for $15 million.

Section Review (text page 353)

1. Students' sentences will vary. Information about the terms can be found on the pages given in parentheses: Wilmot Proviso (346), Forty-niners (346), Doughfaces (349), "Bleeding Kansas" (352).

2. The Free Soil party was the third party in 1848. With Martin Van Buren as their candidate, the Free Soilers made the Wilmot Proviso their guiding principle. They did not want to abolish slavery where it already existed. They insisted that the western lands be reserved for small family farms. Where there was slavery, they argued, wealthy planters dominated politics.

3. The Omnibus Bill was a compromise plan. The northerners would get California admitted to the Union as a free state, and the slave trade would be abolished in the District of Columbia. For the southerners, Clay proposed that slavery be kept legal in the District of Columbia. His plan organized two federal territories, one to include present-day Utah and Nevada, the other present-day New Mexico and Arizona. Clay left open the possibility that one or both of these might become slave states. To further satisfy southerners, the bill also included a new Fugitive Slave Act in which federal marshals in northern states would receive broader powers to arrest and return runaway slaves.
4. According to the Kansas-Nebraska Act, slavery would no longer be forbidden north of 36° 30'. The new territories of Kansas and Nebraska could be either slave states or free according to *popular sovereignty*. That is, the voters living in the territories would choose whether or not to legalize slavery.
5. Many northerners were stunned by the passage of the Kansas-Nebraska Act. For 34 years slavery had been illegal in the northern Louisiana area. Now voters in the Nebraska or Kansas territories that had been the northern part of the Louisiana territory could legalize slavery if they chose to. In reaction, anti-slavery northerners formed the new Republican party in 1854. The Republicans were committed to keep slavery out of all territories.

Section Review (text page 357)

1. Students' sentences will vary. Information about the terms can be found on the pages given in parentheses: slavocrats (354), Harpers Ferry (354), Robert E. Lee (354), James Buchanan (357).
2. Dred Scott was a slave of a Missouri army officer who sued his master for his freedom because he had lived for a time in territories where slavery was illegal. Scott won his suit. However, the decision was appealed and reached the Supreme Court. Chief Justice Taney and the Court ruled that Scott was a slave in Missouri and had no legal right to sue because he was not a citizen of Missouri. Scott remained a slave. Taney, in writing the majority opinion, said the Constitution provided that citizens could not be deprived of their property in federal territories without due process. Because slaves were considered property, Congress could not forbid slave ownership in the lands of the Northwest Ordinance and the Missouri Compromise. The Missouri Compromise, under which slavery had been illegal in all territories north of 36° 30', was thus invalid. Then Taney went even further. Under the Kansas-Nebraska Act, slavery could be legalized in those territories only if the settlers chose to do so.

Taney, however, ruled that territories did not have the same sovereignty as states and therefore could not outlaw slavery, even if the majority of settlers did not want slavery. The Kansas-Nebraska Act was therefore rendered invalid also. Slavery could not be kept out of federal territories.
3. Lincoln pointed out that, after the Dred Scott decision, northerners could do nothing to prevent the expansion of slavery except to pass a Constitutional amendment. Douglas replied that, in practice, territorial legislatures could keep slavery out simply by failing to pass laws protecting the rights of slaveowners.
4. In 1860 the presidential candidates and their parties were Abraham Lincoln (Republican party), John Bell (Constitutional Union party), John Breckinridge (Southern Democrats), and Stephen Douglas (Northern Democrats). After Lincoln was elected, South Carolina seceded from the Union in December of 1860, and six other southern states seceded in January of 1861. The slave states of Virginia, Kentucky, and North Carolina voted against secession. However, they warned Lincoln not to use force against the states that had seceded. The country was no longer united.

Time Line Questions (text page 358)

1. 9 years
2. 4 years; party founded in 1854, first election after party was founded was 1856, Lincoln elected in 1860.

Skills Strategy: News Stories and Editorials (text pages 358–359)

1. ''The massacre of almost 200 Texans . . .''
2. All but *Why*?
3. *Feelings*: indignation, restrained outrage, sympathy for the dead and their survivors; *attitudes*: American Texan cause is just, U.S. government is too slow in acting; *opinions*: All Americans want government to take action, government should give Texas territorial status
4. To get an idea of the feelings, attitudes, and opinions of people at the time of the Alamo massacre
5. To get the basic facts about the Alamo (Who? What? Where?, etc.)
6. The first sentence of each

Chapter Test (text page 359)

Text Review

1. They protected their settlements by founding presidios, or forts. They needed protection from nearby Indians.
2. In addition to the present state of Oregon, the

Oregon Country also included the present-day Washington, part of Idaho, and the Canadian province of British Columbia.

3. To many Americans, *manifest destiny* meant that the United States was ordained in some way to rule North American lands from the Atlantic to the Pacific. President Polk's dream of a United States that stretched from coast to coast was in accord with the American belief in manifest destiny. As president, Polk wanted to annex Texas, as much as possible of Oregon, and he wanted to buy New Mexico and California from Mexico.

4. Polk, in a speech to Congress, declared that a state of war already existed between Mexico and the United States. According to the Constitution, only Congress, not the president, has the power to declare war.

5. The South wanted the western territories admitted as slave states that would support the institution of slavery. Many people in the North did not want to abolish slavery, but they wanted the western territories admitted as free states because they thought these lands should be reserved for small farmers and not taken over by wealthy slaveowning planters. Other northerners wanted the territories admitted as free states because they opposed slavery on moral grounds.

6. The Compromise of 1850 (Omnibus Bill) gave northerners California as a free state and the abolition of the slave trade in the District of Columbia. To compensate proslavery southerners, it provided that slavery would remain legal in the District of Columbia; organized two federal territories, one or both of which might become slave states; and proposed a new and stronger Fugitive Slave Act. Senator Stephen A. Douglas reworked the Omnibus Bill into five different bills known as the Compromise of 1850, which Congress passed. The Kansas-Nebrasks Act was meant to mollify both northerners and southerners by eliminating the Missouri Compromise line. The choice of whether to legalize slavery was left to the voters of the Kansas and Nebraska territories.

7. The Wilmot Proviso stated that slavery would be illegal in any territory taken from Mexico after the war. It was meant as a challenge to the South and was the first in a series of events that led the South toward secession and civil war. California's admission to the Union as a free state destroyed the balance of 15 free states and 15 slave states and lessened the southerners' voting power in the Senate. Extremist southern Fire-eaters spoke of seceding from the Union until the Compromise of 1850 temporarily mollified them. John Brown's attack at Harpers Ferry awakened the South's fear of slave rebellion when they heard that slaves in the area were about to rebel and join Brown. When some prominent northerners spoke of Brown as a saint, southerners began to lose hope that their states had any future within the Union.

Critical Thinking

8. Henry Clay and John C. Calhoun, though strong proponents of their viewpoints, were usually able to compromise their differences with their opponents. The Fire-eaters, however, had few able or willing compromisers within their ranks.

9. *Proslavery*: Doughfaces, southern Democrats; *antislavery*: Free Soilers, Charles Sumner, Republican party.

10. Douglas had devised a plan that would bring the transcontinental railroad to his own state of Illinois. In order to realize his plan, he had to organize territories in the prairies of the Midwest. He knew southerners would not support the organization of territories in an area where, under the Missouri Compromise, slavery would be illegal. So, in order to bring his railroad plan to reality, he repealed the Missouri Compromise line in the Kansas-Nebraska Act and left the choice of legalizing slavery to popular sovereignty.

Writing a Paragraph

Sample Editorial:

Accept western territories as states? Never! Making these lands states would add nothing to the United States but useless desert and wilderness. Do we Americans forget ourselves? Other people—the Indians and Spanish settlers—have prior claims to these lands. Shall we now disregard these claims and be seen before the world as unjust aggressors? Will the Spanish and Indians stand by passively as we snatch their lands away from them? And on what basis would these territories be admitted—as free states or slave states? The bitter struggle over this question between proslavery and antislavery proponents would surely increase the already divisive bitterness between North and South, and in all probability would divide the nation.

Sample Letter:

To the Editor:

Your editorial writer has ignored one important consideration: It is the duty, even the destiny, of Americans to bring the blessings of civilization to all parts of this vast continent. I say that the American people would benefit from the further expansion of territories into statehood because of our ability to transform the lands using our expertise.

Sincerely,
Caleb Witherspoon

Some students may wish to write letters to the

editor of the local newspaper, responding to a recent news story or editorial.

CHAPTER 15

Section Review (text page 368)

1. Students' sentences will vary. Information about the names and terms can be found on the pages given in parentheses: Jefferson Davis (360), April 12, 1861 (363), Robert E. Lee (367).
2. The slave states that joined the Confederacy were South Carolina, Texas, Georgia, Florida, Alabama, Mississippi, Louisiana, Virginia, North Carolina, Arkansas, and Tennessee. The slave states that remained in the Union were Delaware, Maryland, and Missouri. West Virginia was the new state admitted to the Union in 1863.
3. Supplies were running low at Fort Sumter. Lincoln wrote South Carolina Governor Picket that he was sending food but no troops to the fort on a supply ship. Jefferson Davis ordered Pickett to turn back any attempt to supply the fort. When the supply ship tried to enter Charleston's harbor on April 12, 1861, Sumter was fired upon. The bombardment lasted for 40 hours. With no ammunition left and the fort nearly demolished, the Union commander surrendered. Consequently, Lincoln asked for 75,000 troops to combat the Confederates. The Civil War had begun.
4. The Union's advantages over the South could be seen in its great population, better transportation system, overwhelming industrial capacity, and its 40-ship navy. The South thought they could win for a number of reasons. First, the southern defensive position gave them several advantages; for example, the rebels knew their terrain better than invading northerners would. Second, the South expected British aid. Third, in the early part of the war, Confederate military commanders were superior to those of the North.

Section Review (text page 373)

1. Students' sentences will vary. Information about the terms can be found on the pages given in parentheses: draft laws (369–370), Anaconda Plan (370), Army of the Potomac (373), Army of Northern Virginia (373).
2. The Civil War armies were divided into calvalry, artillery, and infantry fighting groups. These basic groups were supported by the Corps of Engineers and the Quartermaster Corps. *Sample answer to second part*: Artillery was critical to both attack and defense. A bombardment by the big guns could "soften up" enemy fortifications before an infantry attack. On the other hand, the defenders' big guns could repulse an enemy attack before it got within shooting range.
3. In July of 1861, the first battle of the Civil War was fought in Virginia. Southerners called it the Battle of Manassas Junction, and northerners called it the first Battle of Bull Run. The battle ended in a rout of Union forces. The Union soldiers threw down their weapons and ran in panic. The battle taught both sides that the war would not end quickly and that the key to victory was to train their troops thoroughly.
4. *Union*: The war would be fought on three fronts. (1) The Army of the Potomac would keep constant pressure on Richmond. (2) Union forces were to push down the Mississippi River in order to open the river to trade by states of the Old Northwest and to split the Confederacy in half. (3) A naval blockade would prevent the Confederacy from selling cotton abroad and also choke off the imports of manufactured goods, including arms, that the Confederates needed to continue the war. *Confederacy*: Aid from Britain or France was central to southern strategy. Jefferson Davis and his advisors hoped to win a major battle and form an alliance with one or the other of these great powers.

Section Review (text page 382)

1. Students' sentences will vary. Information about the terms can be found on the pages given in parentheses: Stonewall Jackson (373, 376–377), *Merrimack* and *Monitor* (375–376), Admiral Farragut (379), Pickett's Charge (381–382).
2. Union victories were: Fort Donelson and Fort Henry, Shiloh, Antietam, Vicksburg, Gettysburg, Chattanooga; Confederate victories were: Seven Days Battle, Second Battle of Bull Run, Fredericksburg, Chancellorsville, Chickamauga Creek.
3. Sample answer: Lee was a great strategist and field commander. For example, the Confederates were greatly outnumbered during the Peninsular Campaign. However, because of Lee's leadership and ability to maneuver his troops, McClellan's offensive turned into a desperate defensive struggle to keep the Union forces from being destroyed. McClellan was a superb trainer and organizer of the Union Army. However, he was too cautious as a field commander. His caution during the Peninsular Campaign allowed the Confederates under Lee to get the upper hand and push the Union forces back to the James River where the Peninsular campaign had started.

4. By making public the Emancipation Proclamation in September of 1862, Lincoln was telling the Confederates that if they laid down their arms by January 1, 1863, they could keep their slaves. The Emancipation Proclamation helped the Union war effort in these ways: First, Union morale was improved by giving the troops a positive goal—they were fighting ''to make men free.'' Second, blacks now had reason to join the army and they rushed to join up. Slaves near the northern lines deserted their plantations by the thousands. Third, it prepared the way for the abolition of slavery. As a military policy, northerners would accept the destruction of slavery.

Section Review (text page 387)

1. Students' sentences will vary. Information about the terms can be found on the pages given in parentheses: attrition (384), ''March to the Sea'' (385), Hampton Roads (385), John Wilkes Booth (386).
2. President Lincoln appointed General Grant as commander of all the Union forces because he was convinced that Grant was the only Union military leader who could destroy Lee's army. Grant's success in the West, especially his rescue of Chattanooga from the Confederates, led Lincoln to that conviction. William Tecumseh Sherman was nominated by Grant as commander of Union forces in the West.
3. General Sheridan laid waste the fertile Shenandoah Valley, thus depriving Lee's army of future food supplies. The capture and burning of Atlanta by General Sherman in the heart of the previously untouched South was a devastating psychological blow to the Confederacy. Both events painfully taught southerners how destructive war could be.
4. George McClellan was the Democratic nominee in 1864. Lincoln knew he was unpopular with some groups. The northern Democrats increasingly criticized him as the war dragged on. Radicals among the Republicans thought he was too generous to the South. Black leaders knew that he did not believe in racial equality. People of all points of view poked fun at his awkward appearance.
5. The words of Lincoln's Second Inaugural Address suggest that he hoped for true reconciliation of the North with the South. He called for northerners to move toward the postwar period ''with firmness in the right, as God gives us to see the right.''

Time Line Questions (test page 388)

1. 4 years (1861–1865)
2. Confederacy formed, fall of Fort Sumter, *Merrimack* versus *Monitor*, Emancipation Proclamation, Battle of Gettysburg, Gettysburg Address, Sherman's March to the Sea, Lincoln assassinated
3. approximately 10 months later

Skills Strategy: Quotations and Footnotes (text pages 338–389)

1. Two quotations; the first is longer
2. It is broken out of the paragraph and indented.
3. Below the sentence ending with the words ''historian pointed out,'' break it out and indent the entire quotation.
4. Two sets of ellipsis points
5. Two footnote reference numbers and two footnotes
6. Women played active roles in the Civil War, as one historian pointed out.

> '' . . .Northern and Southern women may have considered themselves 'ladies,' but they were not content to sit demurely and hopefully waiting for their men to come home . . . Scornful of social censure, women in both the South and the North worked as nurses tending the wounded of the many bloody battles. Others willingly, and successfully, took over for their soldier spouses on farms and plantations.''[1]

Civil War women made clothes and collected supplies for the armies, worked as government clerks, and even spied. Their work was valuable. Indeed, ''neither the Union nor the Confederacy could long have prosecuted the war without the help of its women.''[2]

1. Nancy Jane Weiss, *The Not So Weaker Sex,* p. 93.
2. Edgar Morris, *Civil War Asides,* p. 713.

Chapter Test (text page 389)

Text Review

1. The four border states that joined the Confederacy were Arkansas, Tennessee, Virginia, and North Carolina. Many western North Carolinians did not want to go to war to protect slavery.
2. Delaware's culture and location made its people's sympathies more northern than southern. Because Maryland surrounded Washington, D.C., Lincoln stationed troops there to keep it in the Union. Missouri was kept in the Union by the swift action of Union troops. Lincoln assured leaders in Kentucky that he would declare war only on disunion, not on slavery.

teeing slavery in territories south of it. As a politician, if Lincoln accepted Crittenden's plan, he would have been rejected by his Republican party which was held together by the principle that slavery could not be allowed in the territories.

4. Student responses should include references to some of the following: the many battles between large armies and the resulting huge numbers of casualties; General Winfield Scott's Anaconda Plan; the Union's use of a naval blockade to destroy the economy of the Confederacy; the Confederacy's use of commerce raiders to sink or capture northern merchant vessels; the use of ironclad gunboats by both North and South; the psychological warfare and propaganda aspects of the Emancipation Proclamation; Grant's belief in and practice of a war of attrition; Sheridan's destruction of the Shenandoah Valley that was the chief supplier of food for the Confederate army; Sherman's burning of Atlanta and his devastating March to the Sea.

5. Americans in both the North and the South expected the war would last only for the summer of 1861. They looked forward to the first battle of the war as they would to a sporting event. Congressmen, their wives, and journalists in a holiday mood and carrying picnic lunches accompanied Union troops as they marched toward the Confederate capital of Richmond. After the first Battle of Bull Run, people on both sides had a very different attitude toward the war.

6. Grant and Sherman used battle tactics designed to grind down the enemy in a war of attrition. Lee was a master of hit-and-run tactics and extremely skilled in out-maneuvering the enemy and neutralizing their superior forces. Recognizing Lee's superiority, Grant refused to be drawn into battles of maneuver with Lee. Instead, he took advantage of his larger army, pressed the enemy, and eventually wore them down.

7. Political abilities: Lincoln was a shrewd politician who knew how to use patronage to gain support, and he chose his Cabinet members with an eye to satisfying the greatest number of voters.
Personal qualities: To the hostility and ridicule of his critics, Lincoln showed his determination to end the war victoriously. Also, his sense of human decency, his personal humility, and his great eloquence was known to the voters. Events on the battlefield: After Grant's takeover, Union forces had some significant successes: Grant's continuing advance toward Richmond and his siege of that city and Petersburg; Sheridan's destruction of the Shenandoah Valley; and Sherman's occupation and burning of Atlanta and his March to the Sea are a few examples.

8. Sherman occupied Atlanta, evacuated its citizens, and burned the city to the ground. He moved his troops from Atlanta to Savannah, stripping the land along the way of almost all buildings, crops, and livestock in a path 60 miles wide. Sherman had two reasons for causing this devastation. First, he wanted to make it difficult for Confederate forces to pursue him. Second, he wanted to punish the South for rebelling.

Critical Thinking

9. On April 2, Lee tried to draw Grant away from his siege of Richmond before the stronger Union forces trapped him. Grant and Sheridan cut him off as he tried to link up with Johnston's army to make a last stand for the Confederacy. Lee asked for terms of surrender, and he and Grant met at Appomattox Courthouse, where Lee agreed to Grant's simple and generous terms and surrendered his forces to the Union commander. On April 18, Joseph Johnston also surrendered to Sherman at Durham, North Carolina.

10. To show that the sentence is an opinion, the author uses the words *might* and *if*. To lend weight to his opinion, the author quotes from Lincoln's Second Inaugural Address, in which the president seems to indicate that he was intending to be generous in his postwar dealings with the South.

Writing a Paragraph

Students' paragraphs should adhere to basic structural principles: a beginning or concluding topic sentence stating the main idea, and supporting sentences with details that support the main idea. The use of quotations and footnotes should follow the methods taught in the chapter's Skills Strategy section.

CHAPTER 16

Section Review (text page 395)

1. Students' sentences will vary. Information about the terms can be found on the pages given in parentheses: Pacific Railways Act (392), Morrill Land Grant Act (393), Copperheads (393–394), Radical Republicans (394).

2. (1) Nine out of fifteen presidents before Lincoln were southerners. (2) Two of the six northern presidents were strongly pro-southern (Pierce and Buchanan). (3) In the House, southerners and their northern allies were able to restrain, if not prevent, Whig and Republican economic policies. (4) In the Senate, the slave states had equal representation until 1850, and after California's admission to the Union had nearly a working majority because of the

Doughface senators. (5) Even the Supreme Court, as the Dred Scott decision shows, was friendly to southern interests.

3. Railroads: Both the North and the South wanted a transcontinental railroad. However, they had never been able to agree on a route. Both wanted the railroad to benefit their section of the country. So southern legislators would have blocked passage of the Pacific Railway Act of 1862 and the act of 1864 which authorized the building of a transcontinental railroad through northern states and territories. Neither would the southern Congressmen have allowed the lavish giveaway of land to build the railroads. Tariff: The southern Congressmen would have blocked passage of the Morrill Tariff Act because the south had an agricultural economy, and the tariff raised the prices of the manufactured goods southerners needed. Southern Democrats had consistently pushed the tariff rate downward from 1832 to 1860. National Bank: Southern Democrats had successfully opposed the old Whig plan for a central banking system. Opposition to a national bank was one of the foundation stones of the Democratic Party. The idea of a national bank regulating the flow of paper money would have been intolerable to southerners. Paper money: The Southern Democrats would have blocked the federal government from issuing paper money—greenbacks. Opposition to the printing of paper money was also one of the foundation stones of the Democratic Party.

4. Lincoln proposed that at the end of hostilities, and as soon as ten percent of the voters in each rebellious state took an oath of allegiance to the Union, the people could organize a government and elect senators and representatives to Congress. Three occupied southern states quickly met these "easy" terms. Radical Republicans in Congress felt that if southern states were reconstructed so easily, they would act in the same way as they did before the war, and the fighting and sacrifice would have been for nothing. Moderate Republicans did not want to see former Confederates coming to Washington, especially with the war still going on. Congress, as a result of a coalition of Radical and Moderate Republicans, refused to recognize the governments of the three southern states that met Lincoln's terms.

5. According to the Wade-Davis Bill, over 50 percent of registered southern voters must take the oath of loyalty before any reconstruction could take place. The bill also stated that Congress, not the president, would determine when a state had met the requirements for readmission to the Union. Lincoln killed the Wade-Davis Bill with a pocket veto, so it never became law.

Section Review (text page 400)

1. Students' sentences will vary. Information about the terms can be found on the pages given in parentheses: black codes (397), Freedmen's Bureau (398), *Ex parte Milligan* (399), Fourteenth Amendment (399-400).

2. None of the black codes that were adopted by southern state governments gave blacks the rights of full citizenship. Instead, the codes created second-class citizens with few civil rights. For example, some codes permitted blacks to work only as domestic servants or in agriculture. In other codes, blacks were not permitted to live in towns and cities. No southern state allowed blacks the right to vote or bear arms.

3. The Constitution: Johnson maintained that it was constitutionally impossible for states to secede from the Union. In his view, the people, not the states, formed the nation. Therefore, the Confederate states were still part of the Union. Johnson believed that individual rebels should be punished, not the states. The Thirteenth Amendment: In President Johnson's plan, each new state government must ratify the Thirteenth Amendment which ended slavery. The Wade-Davis Bill: President Johnson's plan for reconstruction was similar to the Wade-Davis Bill, in that his plan called for 50 percent of the voters to take the loyalty oath. However, in Johnson's plan, the president, not Congress, would decide when the states could take full part in political life. The administrative duties of the president: According to Johnson, reconstructing the Confederate states was not a Congressional matter but merely an administrative matter, and administration was the president's job.

4. Johnson thought that, by appealing to midwestern voters' strong racial prejudice, he could induce them to vote against Radical Republican candidates in the Congressional elections of 1866. However, he miscalculated. The Radicals won an overwhelming victory because midwestern voters feared that Johnson's Reconstruction plan would put the Confederate elite back into power. The victory of the Radicals meant that they controlled the two-thirds majority needed to override any presidential veto and could put their own Reconstruction plan into effect.

Section Review (text page 405)

1. Students' sentences will vary. Information about the names and terms can be found on the pages given in parentheses: impeachment (401), carpetbaggers (402), Redeemers (405), Nathan Bedford Forrest (405).

2. Some of the charges were true but silly. For

example, Johnson was charged with (1) undignified behavior and (2) disrespect for Congress. Neither is one of the "high crimes and misdemeanors" that the Constitution says are the grounds for impeachment. Johnson was also charged with (3) violating the Tenure of Office Act. According to this act, no presidential appointee confirmed by the Senate could be dismissed by the president without the Senate's approval. Johnson had dismissed Edwin M. Stanton, Lincoln's Senate-confirmed Secretary of War. The constitutionality of the Tenure of Office Act was debatable. (It was later repealed.) Even if it was constitutional, the act might not even apply to the case. Stanton had been appointed by Lincoln and approved by the Senate before the law was passed in 1867. The real reason for the impeachment was that the Radicals wanted to humiliate Johnson and complete their control of the federal government.

3. The Fifteenth Amendment forbade the states to deny the vote to any person on the basis of "race, color or previous condition of servitude."

4. Southern whites thought of Reconstruction as a time when they were bullied by Union soldiers, exploited by carpetbaggers and scalawags, and lorded over by ignorant former slaves. Southern blacks remembered Reconstruction as a short period of political freedom between the miseries of slavery and the ruthless repression of their rights after Reconstruction ended. Northern whites thought of Reconstruction as a tragic mistake. In their view, vindictive Radicals forced on the South unworkable policies, including racial equality.

Section Review (text page 407)

1. Students' sentences will vary. Information about the terms can be found on the pages given in parentheses: Liberal Republicans (405), "Lily-Whites" (407), Civil Rights Act of 1875 (407), South Carolina, Florida, and Louisiana in 1876 (407).

2. A group calling themselves the Liberal Republicans broke away from their party and formed a brief alliance with the Democrats in an attempt to deny reelection to President Grant. They were disillusioned with the widespread corruption in Grant's government. They believed that the only way to preserve the rights of southern blacks was to keep large units of the army stationed in the south. Also, they came to the conclusion that only the white Redeemers could bring social stability to the South and end terrorism there.

3. Grant became increasingly reluctant to send federal troops to the South to maintain order and to help keep Republicans in power. As a result, by 1876, only three southern states were controlled by the

Radical Republicans. These states were South Carolina, Florida, and Louisiana. As the white Redeemers took over the other southern state governments, the black southerners lost the right to vote and other civil liberties. The Republicans abandoned the freed people, for the new western states were predominately Republican, and southern votes were no longer needed to maintain a Republican majority. The final blow to Reconstruction came when Hayes was elected president. Hayes withdrew federal troops from the remaining three states controlled by Radical Republicans. The Compromise of 1877 was an informal agreement by a group of northern and southern politicians and businessmen in order to settle the election dispute over Hayes and Tilden. The South agreed to go along with the electoral results of the election, which made Hayes president, and some conservative southerners agreed to build a "lily-white" Republican party, based on views they shared with northern conservatives. In return, Hayes removed troops from the South.

Time Line Questions (text page 408)

1. 1862
2. Between Wade-Davis Bill and Reconstruction Proclamation
3. *Ex parte Milligan*

Skills Strategy: Atlas References (text page 408)

Atlanta	E–3	Montgomery	E–4
Austin	A–5	Nashville	D–2
Baton Rouge	C–5	Raleigh	G–2
Columbia	F–3	Richmond	G–1
Jackson	C–4	Tallahassee	E/F–5
Little Rock	C–3		

UNIT 4 TEST (text page 409)

Chapter Survey

1. Sample summary sentence(s): Chapter 13 explains the South's decision to continue the practice of slavery and discusses the difficulties most slaves faced. The chapter also presents the views of a variety of people and groups who worked for the abolition of slavery. Pages containing information about terms: The Impending Crisis (313), the

peculiar institution (316), chattel property (318), *The Liberator* (324–325), Angelina Grimké (326).

2. Sample summary sentence(s): Chapter 14 reveals where a belief in manifest destiny led Americans: to the establishment of new territories in Oregon Country and in Mexican lands after a war with Mexico. The chapter then traces the bitter dispute over the status of slavery in the new territories and tells how the dispute concluded with the secession of several Southern states. Pages containing information about terms: Wilmot Proviso (346), Alamo (337–338, 340), "Oregon or Bust" (341), Bear Flag Republic (345), Harpers Ferry (354).

3. Sample summary sentence(s): Chapter 15 deals with the tragic Civil War, from the first shot at Fort Sumter, through the many destructive battles, to the dignified surrender of General Lee at Appomattox. The chapter concludes with an account of the assassination of President Lincoln. Pages containing information on names and terms: Jefferson Davis (360), Johnny Reb (369–370), Billy Yank (369–370), the *Monitor* (375–376), "the butcher" (384), John Wilkes Booth (386).

4. Sample summary sentence(s): Chapter 16 opens with a discussion of the domestic changes Congress made during the Civil War in the absence of southern legislators. The chapter goes on to explain how the Radical Republican Reconstruction plan was implemented in the South, and why the fate of southern blacks was finally left in the hands of white supremacist southern leaders. Pages containing information about terms: Radical Republicans (394), black codes (397), Fourteenth Amendment (399–400), carpetbaggers (402), "Lily-Whites" (407).

Text Review

5. Among the facts students may use to verify the statement are the following: the slave revolts that brought in their train the harsh black codes; the great numbers of runaway slaves; the thinly veiled protests that slaves expressed in their spirituals and folk songs; the lively social, religious, and cultural life the slaves developed to help them cope with their enslavement; the slaves' practice of working only as hard as was necessary to escape punishment; the work of Harriet Tubman in helping slaves to escape; the writings and speeches of the escaped slave Frederick Douglass urging the abolition of slavery.

6. Student's answers will include a brief explanation and evaluation of three of the following. Religious: God must approve of slavery because some Biblical figures favored by God had owned slaves.

Jesus had told a runaway slave to return to his master. Historical and cultural: The great accomplishments of Greece and Rome were made possible because slaves freed the upper classes from labor and gave them time to create. Educational: In response to New Englanders' arguments that their primary and secondary school systems were superior to those of the South, southerners said that they were interested in providing high culture for the few and not in teaching everyone just to read and write. The South had three times as many college graduates as New England, even though the two regions had about the same number of people. Racial: Owning blacks was justified because blacks were racially inferior to whites; they were incapable of competing with whites, and slaveowners did blacks a favor by protecting them from freedom. Sociological: Slaves had better lives than most northern white industrial workers. Slaves—even the injured, handicapped, and elderly—were cared for by their masters from cradle to grave. Because of the northern workers' poor living conditions, disruptive reformers and revolutionaries were able to lead riots and strikes in the North. These social problems were not present in the South. Evaluation: Accept reasonable evaluations of the arguments if they bring out that none of the arguments did, or could, justify the central injustice of slavery—the denial of freedom and other natural rights of human beings.

7. Theodore Dwight Weld published a collection of newspaper articles (*American Slavery As It Is*) which gave details of the mistreatment and cruelty slaves had to endure—whippings, brandings, starvation, freezing to death. Dwight published the collection to refute southern claims that northerners only imagined such things. James G. Birney, a southern planter, freed his slaves after considering Weld's ideas. Birney thought that slavery should be fought in political debate rather than by attacks and denunciations. William Lloyd Garrison published an inflammatory anti-slavery newspaper called *The Liberator*. Garrison took an extreme position, arguing the evil of both slavery and slaveowners. His position admitted no possibility of reasonable discussion with slaveowners and saw no point in talking about practical problems involved in freeing slaves. To Garrison, slavery was wrong and must be abolished, period. Sojourner Truth, a former slave, traveled to various parts of the country giving inspired speeches and singing songs against slavery. She also worked on behalf of women's rights.

8. Four western areas that became states before 1860 were Missouri, Texas, Calfiornia, and Ore-

gon. The South wanted the western territories admitted as slave states that would support the institution of slavery and the southern way of life. Some northerners wanted the territories admitted as free states, not because they wanted to abolish slavery, but because they thought these new lands should be reserved for small farmers and not taken over by wealthy, slave owning planters.

9. Like Polk, many Americans believed that it was the *manifest destiny* of the United States to rule the lands of North America from the Atlantic Ocean to the Pacific Ocean. Polk and such Americans saw the war with Mexico as a way of fulfiling this destiny by acquiring some of Mexico's lands in North America. In the Treaty of Guadalupe Hidalgo which ended the war with Mexico, the Rio Grande was recognized as the boundary of Texas, and Mexico ceded California and New Mexico to the United States in exchange for $15 million.

10. In the years before the election, relations between North and South were steadily moving toward a crisis. Not long before the election, southern Fire-eaters warned northern voters that if they elected Lincoln to the presidency the southern states would leave the Union. About a month after Lincoln won the election, the South Carolina legislature voted to secede. The next month, six more southern states seceded, and southerners began taking over military installations and federal offices and agencies. The scene was set for the Civil War, a tragic turning point in American history.

11. The eleven Confederate states were South Carolina, Texas, Georgia, Florida, Alabama, Mississippi, Louisiana, Virginia, North Carolina, Arkansas, and Tennessee. Jefferson Davis was the president of the Confederacy, and the Confederate capital city was Richmond, Virginia. Confederate gun batteries opened fire on Fort Sumter in the Charleston, South Carolina, harbor when a ship tried to bring supplies to the Union forces manning the fort. This action began the Civil War.

12. April 9, 1865, at Appomattox, Virginia: General Lee surrendered the Confederate armies under his command to Union General Grant; April 18, 1865, at Durham, North Carolina: General Joseph Johnson surrendered the remaining Confederate forces to Union General Sherman; April 15, 1865, in Washington, D.C.: President Lincoln was assassinated at a theater by a pro-Confederate actor, John Wilkes Booth.

13. Students' answers should refer to three of the following: authorizations for the Union Pacific, Central Pacific, and Northern Pacific railways to build transcontinental lines; passage of the Morrill Tariff; printing of paper money—greenbacks—not redeemable in gold; establishment of Jay Cooke's bank to act as the financial agent for the federal government; passage of the Homestead Act and the Morrill Land Grant Act in 1862. The reason why southern legislators would have opposed each of the preceding is given in parentheses: railroads (southerners would have fought for southern routes to benefit the South); tariff (southerners consistently opposed high tariffs and had referred to a similar tariff of 1828 as the Tariff of Abominations); paper money and a central bank (opposition to paper money and a national bank were foundation stones of southerners in the Democratic party); Homestead and Morrill Acts (the giveaway of land to small farmers in the Homestead Act and the free spending of money for agricultural colleges in the Morrill Act would have been strongly opposed by Southerners.)

14. President Lincoln: After the fighting ended, and as soon as ten percent of the voters in each Confederate state had taken an oath of allegiance to the Union, the people could organize a government and elect senators and representatives to Congress. The Wade-Davis Bill: More than 50 percent of registered southern voters had to take an oath of loyalty before any reconstruction could take place, and Congress rather than the president would determine when a state had met the requirements for readmission to the Union. Radical Republicans: The Confederacy would be divided into five military districts governed by martial law. The army would enforce order and supervise voter registration. (Adult black males could register, but not Confederate officals, who were disenfranchised by the Fourteenth Amendment.) Voters would elect a state convention to ratify the Thirteenth, Fourteenth (and, for the last four states, the Fifteenth) Amendment and to draw up a state constitution. Once Congress approved the Constitution, the reconstructed state could elect a state legislature, a governor, two senators, and members of the House of Representatives.

15. The Radical Reconstruction program was put into effect. Short-term effects for blacks were positive. They were free; their right to vote was recognized; they could, and did, participate in government as elected officials; the law protected them from discrimination. Long-term effects for blacks were negative. After Reconstruction ended, southern state governments were taken over by white supremacists who systematically denied the human and civil rights of black citizens.

16. Widespread corruption in Grant's first administration caused the Liberal Republicans to become disillusioned. They abandoned their commitment to the ideal of black civil equality, coming to the

conclusion that the only way to assure social stability in the South, other than by stationing army units there indefinitely, was to let the Redeemers—white supremacists—take over the state governments. Presidents Grant and Hayes eventually managed, between them, to withdraw all federal troops from the South.

Critical Thinking

17. Students' summaries may refer to the following: the hard labor most slaves did "from first light to last light"; the frequent whippings and other mistreatment; the indignities of being bought and sold; the pain caused by the separation of husbands and wives and parents and children; denial of civil rights under the slave codes. Students' views of the greatest deprivation slaves suffered may differ. However, they should recognize that the deprivation of their freedom as human beings was at the root of all their other miseries.

18. Thirteenth Amendement: ended slavery; Fourteenth Amendment: Confederate leaders must be pardoned by Congress before holding any federal office, equal citizenship guaranteed to all persons born or naturalized in the United States; Fifteenth Amendment: voting rights guaranteed to all citizens. (Note: Alabama, Arkansas, Florida, Louisiana, North Carolina, and South Carolina had to ratify the Thirteenth Amendment and the Fourteenth Amendment; Georgia, Mississippi, Texas, and Virginia had to ratify the Fifteenth Amendment as well as the other two.)

Skills Review

19. The excerpt is from an editorial. Students should recognize this from the emotional tone of the language and the use of the word *should* in the first sentence. They should also recognize the absence of the straightforward presentation of essential facts that the first paragraph, or lead, of a new story always contains.

20. Symbols like D7, 13, and B10 would appear in the gazatteer at the back of an atlas. The symbols refer to the locations of places on the grid of one of the atlas maps. By following along to where the letter and number lines intersect on a map grid, the places can be found.

CHAPTER 17

Section Review (text page 420)

1. Students' sentences will vary. Information about the terms can be found on the pages given in

parentheses: agrarian (412), robber barons (416), Promontory Point (417), "money power" (420).

2. Before 1860, the United States had been, for the most part, an agrarian society. More than 70 percent of the people lived on farms or in small farm towns. Scarcely more than 1.5 million people worked in industrial jobs, even though the United States was the fifth largest industrial power in the world. Because many of the industrial workers were women and children who could not vote, they were an insignificant political force. By 1900, the United States was the most productive industrial nation in the world. Investment in American factories totaled $8 billion, and more than 5.5 million people worked in industrial jobs. For good or for ill, Americans lived in an industrial, capitalist society and no longer in an agrarian republic.

3. Sample answer: Steam-powered locomotives made it possible for steelmakers in Pittsburgh, Pennsylvania, to bring together coal from Scranton in Pennsylvania and iron ore from the Mesabi Range in Minnesota as though mines of both regions were just a few miles away. Because most western railroads found their way into Chicago, the city became the meat packing center of America. Livestock fattened in a distant place rolled into Chicago alive on railway cars. There, the animals would be butchered and processed. Then the meat would be shipped by rail to the East Coast and from there around the world.

4. Among railroad entrepreneurs students may name are the following: J. Edgar Thompson, Cornelius Vanderbilt, Daniel Drew, James Fisk, Jay Gould, and the Big Four of California—Collis P. Huntington, Leland Stanford, Mark Hopkins, and Charles Crocker. The goals of these railroaders were similar: to bring economic and technological order to American transportation and to become personally very rich in the process.

5. Because of abuses of power and general corruption among many railroad officials, the Interstate Commerce Act was passed by Congress. The act outlawed the excessive rates charged by the national railroads and created an independent commission, the ICC, to keep an eye on railroad rates and practices. The ICC was given little power of enforcement and, moreover, had to take its decisions to courts that favored the railroads. Furthermore, the Interstate Commerce Act itself did not forbid interlocking directorates or mergers which were very effective ways for the railroads to avoid competition.

Section Review (text page 423)

1. Students' sentences will vary. Information about the terms can be found on the pages given in

parentheses: condensed milk (420), refined flour (421), "disassembly line" (421–422), *Boston Cooking School Cookbook* (423).

2. Students should name and discuss two of the following: Gail Borden (420–421), H.J. Heinz (421), Philip D. Armour (421–422), Gustavus Swift (422), Fannie Farmer (423). Details concerning each "food revolutionary" are given on the text pages shown.

3. The railroads were a key in bringing about the food processing revolution which changed American eating habits. Because the railroads had access to the West, where wheat and livestock could be grown on a large scale and therefore more cheaply than in the East, they funneled grain and cattle into cities such as Minneapolis—St. Paul, Chicago, and St. Louis, which had rail connections with the East Coast. In these transfer cities, gigantic processing companies such as General Mills, Swift, Ralston, Purina, and Armour turned the wheat and meat into consumer goods such as refined flour and packaged meats.

4. Fannie Merritt Farmer started the practice of advising beginning cooks to use standardized measurements—level teaspoon, one-half cup, etc.—in the preparation of food. In Boston, she started Miss Farmer's School of Cookery. Her cookbook, first published in 1896, is still in print today.

Section Review (text page 427)

1. Students' sentences will vary. Information about the names and terms can be found on the pages given in parentheses: William "Pig Iron" Kelly (423), Henry Bessemer (423), vertical integration (425), Standard Oil Company (426).

2. Cutting costs was at the heart of Carnegie's business method. His fundamental way of reducing costs was vertical integration of his steel business. Carnegie did not buy iron and coal from independent mining companies who had to make their own profit. He purchased his own iron and coal mines, often taking advantage of bankruptcies. Carnegie was never totally independent of trunkline railways but assumed as much control of shipping as he could. By eliminating the middlemen—independent suppliers, distributors, and carriers—Carnegie was able to undersell his competitors who had to include the profits of the middlemen in their prices.

3. Benjamin Silliman was a chemist who isolated kerosene from crude oil while looking for a replacement for whale oil as an illuminant. Thereafter, kerosene became a major lighting and heating source. Edwin Drake developed a drill and pump system to extract crude oil from deep within the earth. His successful breakthrough in Titusville in 1859 caused a rush to Titusville much like the earlier California gold rush. Oil soon became an essential energy source for the machines of American industry.

4. John D. Rockefeller's horizontal integration (the control of an industry by dominating the "strategic stage") was his most distinctive innovation in the movement to consolidate American industry. The refining process was the strategic stage in the oil industry. Few people could afford to compete with Rockefeller by going into refining because of the huge investment required.

Section Review (text page 430)

1. Students' sentences will vary. Information about the names and terms can be found on the pages given in parentheses: American Telephone and Telegraph Company (428), Harvey Firestone (428), Menlo Park (428), reaper (428).

2. Thomas Alva Edison invented the incandescent light bulb. Elisha Otis was responsible for the elevator. Cyrus Hall McCormick invented the reaper for harvesting grain. Christopher Latham Sholes perfected the typewriter. George Westinghouse created the air brake and a method for transmitting alternating current.

3. Elevators made possible the construction of tall office buildings. These skyscrapers encouraged the centralization of business administration. Telephones became the nervous system of American business. "Writing machines"—typewriters—eliminated illegible handwriting that was potentially costly to business and brought more women into the business sector. Air brakes for trains increased safety and led to bigger profits for railroads because the brakes made longer trains possible.

4. The purpose of Bell's original device was to allow some people with hearing impairments to hear. Then Bell recognized other possibilities for the device. If two of the hearing aids were connected by wire, voices could be transmitted over long distances. Thus, the telephone came into existence. Bell tested his device and exhibited it at the 1876 Centennial Exposition in Philadelphia. The telephone was the hit of the show. But he could not sell it. Western Union showed no interest whatsoever. Bell had to set up his own pilot company in New York. The invention quickly caught on.

Section Review (text page 431)

1. Students' sentences will vary. Information about the names and terms can be found on the pages

given in parentheses: corporation (430), shareholders (430), trust (431), James Buchanan Duke (431).

2. Before limited liability, owners of a bankrupt business could have everything they owned, even their homes and personal possessions, seized and sold by creditors to satisfy their debts. After limited liability, only the corporation's assets were subject to seizure by creditors. Creditors could not touch the personal property of shareholders or their shares in other businesses. This privilege made it easier for entrepreneurs to raise high-risk venture capital.

3. Under the Fourteenth Amendment, a corporation came to be viewed as a person with legal rights. States were forbidden to pass laws that applied specifically to corporations, because the laws would deny the corporate person the civil rights that were granted to other persons. Because of the Fourteenth Amendment, the corporation had all the legal civil rights of a human being but none of the responsibilities. Nineteenth century entrepreneurs found corporations greatly to their liking.

4. Public pressure caused Congress to pass the Sherman Antitrust Act. The public was convinced that, when a few men could control a whole industry, the principle of economic opportunity was a mockery and the foundations of American democracy were jeopardized. The Act declared business could not legally form any kind of trust or combination that restrained trade or commerce among the states or foreign nations. The Attorney General was authorized to move against such combinations or trusts and force them to disolve into smaller businesses.

Time Line Questions (text page 434)

1. 1869
2. 1876
3. Sherman Antitrust Act, 1890
4. 1859, Pennsylvania

Skills Strategy: Thematic Maps (text page 435)

1. None in 1870; 240 miles in 1900.
2. Yes
3. New Mexico, Arizona, Texas, Oklahoma, Oregon, Washington, Idaho, Montana, North Dakota, South Dakota, and Colorado did not have railroads in 1870, but did by 1900.
4. The eastern half. The eastern half of the country was more developed, and had a much larger population, making it more profitable for the railroad companies.

Chapter Test (text page 435)

Text Review

1. Answers will vary, but may include that the United States during this period had a peaceful and stable political environment. Large amounts of foreign and domestic capital were available for investment, and vast stretches of usable land and large deposits of natural resources could be found in the United States.

2. Population more than doubled. The number of states increased from 36 to 45. Wealth, as measured by the annual production of goods, jumped from $2 billion to $13 billion between 1865 and 1900.

3. Since women, children, Indians, and blacks did not vote, politicians of this period did not consider them important.

4. Most of the regional railroads in 1865 did not link up with one another which caused great inefficiency and inconvenience in transporting people and goods over long distances. Adding to the inefficiency were the different gauge tracks used by the various regional railroads. The inefficiency tended to isolate and slow the growth of the areas served by these independent systems. The Northeast and South, though already crowded, continued to grow.

5. Sample answer: J. Edgar Thompson secretly bought stock in small lines in Pennsylvania and Ohio and gradually put the Pennsylvania Railroad together. Once in control, Thompson waged fierce rate wars with companies that had resisted his attempts to acquire control of them.

6. With the aid of new technology, several inventors and entrepreneurs developed new ways to process food, revolutionizing the way Americans ate. Gail Borden worked out a process for evaporating milk and canning it. H. J. Heinz applied industrial methods to canning pickles, fruits, vegetables, and ketchup. Companies such as General Mills, Ralston, Purina, Swift, Armour, Wilson, and Cudahy found new ways to process America's staples —wheat and meat. Fanny Farmer was the first to recommend the use of standardized measures in cooking. She included these measurements in recipes in her *Boston Cooking School Cookbook*. The revolution in the oil industry was also brought about by new technology and entrepreneurs who recognized the monetary potential. John D. Rockefeller, for example, saw the business possibilities of oil, and built the Standard Oil Company, the first billion-dollar industry. Rockefeller controlled his oil business through both vertical and horizontal integration.

7. The Pacific Railway Act of 1862 granted the Union Pacific and Central Pacific a right of way 200 feet (60 meters) wide from Omaha, Nebraska, to Sacramento, California. The two companies were given ten alternate sections (square miles) on both sides of each mile of tracks they laid. This created a belt of land in a checkerboard pattern on each side of a rail line. The belts were 40 miles (64 kilometers) wide. Half of this land became the property of the Union Pacific and the Central Pacific. The other half was kept for the government to distribute under the Homestead Act or to sell directly. The Fourteenth Amendment allowed business corporations to be viewed as legal persons. Thus, states were unable to pass laws that applied specifically to corporations since those laws would deny the "corporate persons" the civil rights granted to flesh-and-blood persons. The Sherman Antitrust Act stated that "every contract, combination, in the form of trust or otherwise, or conspiracy, in restraint of trade or commerce among the several states, or with foreign nations, is hereby declared to be illegal." The act authorized the Attorney General to force such combinations to break up into smaller businesses.

8. In most parts of the West, only one rail line handled all the traffic, so the railroad could charge farmers whatever it wished to ship their crops and livestock. This practice often ate up all the profits of farmers. The railroad also controlled storage facilities near its depots and charged farmers fees to store their products while awaiting a train to take the products away. Frequently, the railroad delayed sending trains to collect higher storage fees.

Critical Thinking

9. Students should support their opinions with specific facts, reasons, and/or examples from the text. Although responses will most likely describe the entrepreneurs in a negative light, students should also indicate the contributions made by them.

10. Sample statements are given. *Favoring*: Through the financial wizardry of talented, aggressive business leaders and the hard labor of workers from all regions of the country and many parts of the world, the railroads have given a new meaning to the name of this great nation. Thanks to the railroads that crisscross the land, the states are now truly united. *Opposing*: The building of the transcontinental railroads is a marvelous accomplishment, but the price is too high. American traditions and principles have been sullied by the greedy, corrupt robber barons who financed railroad construction, not to make the United States a better place, but to increase their personal wealth and power.

Writing a Paragraph

A sample paragraph is given. Additional details may be added by students.

If not for the inventive genius of Americans, farmers and industrial leaders could not have made the progress they did. McCormick's mechanical reaper made it possible for grain farmers to increase their profits by planting more acres. In industry, leaders of steel and oil companies owed thanks to Kelley's cheaper method for making steel and Drake's drill and pump system for tapping crude oil deposits. Once installed in offices throughout the country, Bell's telephones became the nervous system of American business. Sholes's typewriter eliminated illegible, potentially costly, handwritten business reports, bills, and correspondence. Bigger profits for the railroads and increased safety were among the results of Westinghouse's airbrake, which also made longer trains possible.

Students may wish to consider submitting their paragraphs for publication in the school magazine or newspaper.

CHAPTER 18

Section Review (text page 441)

1. Students' sentences will vary. Information about the names and terms can be found on the pages given in parentheses: Boss William Tweed (438), Cornelius Corson (439), Dick Connolly (440), "Gray Wolves" (440).

2. These powerful organizations that took over the politics of big cities were called political machines.

3. A political machine made money in a number of ways. Bribery: In return for cash, law enforcement officials would ignore the operations of illegal business. Influence peddling: Boss Tweed, although not a lawyer, was on the Vanderbilt payroll as a "legal adviser." What Vanderbilt was paying for were favorable rulings by judges controlled by Tweed. Kickbacks: Companies that wished to do business with a city government were told to submit inflated bids and then give back part of the money to the political machine. Sandbagging: In return for a bribe, the political machine granted a company permission to partially complete something. Thus, the

owners of the company had to pay time and time again until the entire project is completed. Working at nonexistent or meaningless city jobs: Members of political machines would be on a city's payroll for jobs that did not really exist. Despite the machine candidates' obvious profiteering, poor and immigrant voters elected them time after time. These voters often had difficult lives, and they were grateful to the machines for the needed political favors and informal social services the machines provided.

4. The Goo-Goos were the tax paying, middle-class property owners who periodically conducted campaigns for good government. They believed that good government was the same as inexpensive government. The Goo-Goos did not offer alternatives to the informal social services that the machines provided to the poor. Often, they combined attacks on political corruption with attacks on new ethnic groups. As a consequence, their candidates' terms in office were short; that is, if they were elected at all.

Section Review (text page 453)

1. Students' sentences will vary. Information about the terms can be found on the pages given in parentheses: "waving the bloody shirt" (442), Black Friday (444–445), Mugwumps (446), "rum, Romanism, and rebellion" (452).

2. Corrupt practices were common. Neither of the national parties was organized around an ideology by which members believed the nation could be governed. The national parties were loose coalitions of regional, state, and city political organizations. Politicians on the national level thought of their calling as a business, or at best a profession, that involved organizing majorities, winning public office, and using governmental power to bestow benefits on party members.

3. Sample answer: The original pension law covered Union veterans who were disabled by wartime wounds and diseases. The law was so strictly worded that some legitimately handicapped veterans did not qualify for benefits. Republicans, instead of changing the law, introduced special pension bills for individuals from their districts. In 1888, a new pension law was passed that granted an income to every veteran who served at least 90 days in wartime and who was disabled for any reason whatsoever. This bill was vetoed by President Cleveland. Republicans ran against Cleveland in 1888 with the slogan "Vote Yourself a Pension" and won the election. The Dependent Pensions Act was passed the next year. It was even more

generous than the previous bill. James Tanner, appointed by President Harrison to distribute the money, increased the total annual payment of pensions to $135 million by the end of Harrison's term.

4. Greeley, the candidate of the Liberal Republicans, was a lifelong eccentric who had advocated every reform, from abolition to phrenology. Because Greeley needed the support of the Democrats to win against Grant, he proposed to "clasp hands across the bloody chasm." The Democrats did give him their nomination. However, Republican party regulars who disapproved of Grant disapproved of southern Democrats more. In seven southern states, white voters who found it difficult to support Greeley voted for Grant. Blacks, too, gave their vote to Grant. Grant was comfortably reelected.

5. After 1872, The Republican Party was divided into the Half-Breeds, headed by James G. Blaine, and the Stalwarts, headed by Roscoe Conkling.

Section Review (text page 455)

1. Students' sentences will vary. Information about the terms can be found on the pages given in parentheses: Pan-American Union (454), Wilson-Gorman Act (454), deflation (455), Greenback Labor party (455).

2. Relations with Great Britain generally improved. For example, the Treaty of Washington was signed. Under the treaty, American shipowners were compensated for damage done to their ships during the Civil War by the British-built Confederate raider, the Alabama. Squabbles between New Englanders and Canada over fishing rights were smoothed. A minor boundary dispute between the territory of Washington and the province of British Columbia was ironed out. Closer relations with Latin America had been a longtime goal of the United States. In 1889, Secretary of State Blaine hosted the Pan-American Congress in Washington. The delegates agreed to the establishment of a Pan-American Union in Washington as a clearinghouse for diplomatic dealings within the Americas. However, delegates would not agree to a customs union that would encourage free trade within the Americas with tariff protection against the rest of the world. Hispaniola (today, the Dominican Republic) was almost annexed by the United States under President Grant. However, Liberal Republicans prevented the annexation.

3. Low tariffs were favored by most southern and western Democrats from agricultural areas as well as by some Republicans from rural areas. Most American farmers had no fear of foreign competi-

tion because of the abundance of farm products. They also felt that low duties on manufactured goods meant lower prices for the imported items they had to buy. Railroaders and bankers often supported low tariffs because more goods being transported meant more profits for them. Protective tariffs were favored by American manufacturers and industrial workers because they believed the size of their profits and wages depended on keeping out foreign competition.

4. What should be the basis of the nation's medium of exchange? Should gold in a vault back every piece of paper money? Or, should the money supply be increased by the government to benefit workers and, especially, farmers?

5. After the war, secretaries of the Treasury retired greenbacks. When the paper money flowed into the Treasury, it was destroyed and not replaced by new bills. This resulted in deflation, or a reduction in the amount of money in circulation, and an increase in the value of gold and paper money redeemable in gold. Prices and wages fell. Western farmers suffered most from deflation. When greenbacks were plentiful and prices high, farmers had borrowed money to increase their acreage and to buy machinery. When money became scarce and more valuable, they had difficulty repaying their loans because they were receiving less for their efforts.

Time Line Questions (text page 456)

1. Pendleton—Arthur; Pan-American Congress—Harrison; Greenback Labor party—Grant; McKinley Tariff—Harrison
2. Grover Cleveland
3. Garfield; assassinated

Skills Strategy: Political Cartoons (text pages 456–457)

1. The group that favors public financing of political campaigns.
2. The size of the figure, the greedy look on the figure's face, the dollar sign on his hat
3. He appears to feel somewhat overwhelmed and helpless, and perhaps a little frightened.
4. Students' responses to the cartoon will vary, but should indicate that the cartoon arouses negative feelings toward public financing.
5. Political cartoons always appeal to emotion and present information in a one-sided, biased way in order to win others to the viewpoint the cartoonist espouses.

Chapter Test (text page 457)

Text Review

1. Students' answers should include reference to some or all of the following: political machines (Tammany Hall in New York); bosses (William Tweed); bribes, kickbacks, sandbagging, payment for nonexistent city jobs, illegal voting practices; attempts at reform (the "Goo-Goos"); ethnic aspects of city politics.

2. Students' answers should compare city and national politics and should include references to the following: widespread existence of corruption at both levels of government; similar lack of political ideology, or principles of government; similar consolidation of groups who would keep politicians in power for their own advantage; similar attitudes toward government as a business; similar methods for winning elections and for distributing government jobs and other benefits; similar attitudes of voters toward corruption. (See text pages 441–442).

3. Grant accepted cash and other gifts from groups and individuals without completely understanding that the gifts were meant as payment for his future favors. He apparently saw no great wrong in repaying these gifts with the resources he had at his disposal as president. When he realized how he was being used in the gold futures manipulations of Jay Gould, Jim Fisk, and his brother-in-law, Grant took immediate, but unsuccessful, action to frustrate their plans.

4. Voters consistently voted for corrupt rather than reform politicians for several reasons. In the cities, ward bosses gave out jobs, fixed up minor and major scrapes with the law, and brightened up the lives of the poor with parties. In addition, many of the city politicians were immigrants, and they helped new immigrants assimilate. They also served as role models for the new immigrants. Nationally, voters kept corrupt politicians in office for many of the same reasons. Reform groups did not offer voters an alternative to the informal social services the corrupt politicians provided, and reformers often attacked ethnic groups who constituted an influential part of the electorate.

5. Among examples students may include in their answers are the following: the awarding of well-paying but nonexistent jobs to faithful machine workers; the unwritten rule that party members who got political jobs would kick back a percentage of their salaries to finance political campaigns; the granting of government contracts to party supporters through pork barrel bills; the practice

of senatorial courtesy, by which senators and representatives submitted lists of party supporters and the jobs they wanted for automatic presidential approval.

6. The chart should contain the following headings and information: Republican—New Englanders, northern and midwestern upper- and middle-class people, blacks; Democratic—city residents, ethnic groups, southerners.

7. James G. Blaine of Maine led a faction of the Republican party known as Half-Breeds. Blaine skillfully distributed patronage through the spoils system. He came into conflict with Grant when he somewhat hypocritically depicted the president as the man who silently allowed corruption. Blaine tried unsuccessfully for the Republican presidential nomination in 1880. President Garfield appointed Blaine Secretary of State, but he resigned under President Arthur, Garfield's successor. In 1884, Blaine easily won the Republican nomination for president, but lost the election to Grover Cleveland. Throughout his career, Blaine was a strong, formative force in national politics. Roscoe Conkling started off as a Republican party boss in New York and rose through party ranks to become President Grant's chief aide. Conkling headed the Stalwart faction of the Republican party, the opponents of Blaine's Half-Breeds. He originated the senatorial courtesy system of distributing patronage. Conkling exerted great influence on President Grant and remained a power to be dealt with in the Republican party even after Grant left office.

8. Students should list the following big political issues and give essential details about one of them: relations with Canada, Great Britain, and Latin America; the tariff; the dispute over whether paper money should or should not be backed by gold (which led to a deflation and the rise of the Greenback Labor Party). Details about each of these issues can be found on text pages 453–455.

Critical Thinking

9. Students' responses should indicate that both poor working-class voters and recent immigrant voters generally favored political machines because the machines provided them with jobs, informal social services, and other kinds of help that both groups needed. Responses should also point out that the property-owning middle class opposed the machines because they had to pay the bills for the machines' corruption with their taxes.

10. Accept hypotheses that are based upon the text

depiction of Arthur's character as an uncorrupt, competent, and dignified president.

Writing a Paragraph
Sample Paragraph:

The political machines that controlled the governments of some American cities had both good and bad points. Ward bosses helped fill the material needs of poor people, gave them jobs, and added some joy to their dismal lives by providing entertainment. And since many of the bosses were immigrants themselves, they became role models for other immigrants and helped these people assimilate into a new and different way of life. On the other hand, the political machines were corrupt. Members of these machines made money in a number of illegal ways. For example, ward bosses placed themselves on city payrolls and were paid for jobs that did not exist. In addition, some city "machine" officials accepted bribes in return for ignoring criminal actions, or demanded kickbacks from companies to whom they awarded city contracts.

CHAPTER 19

Section Review (text page 463)

1. Students' sentences will vary. Information about the names and terms can be found on the pages given in parentheses: Newport, Rhode Island (461), *Progress and Poverty* (461), Horatio Alger (462–463), philanthropy (463).

2. Most Americans believed that in the United States there were opportunities for success, so they did not have to remain at the economic level at which they had been born. Americans felt that, to improve their economic situations, they had to work hard and practice thrift.

3. Spencer argued that the "fittest" people rise to the top in the social competition for riches, while weaker people who are not fit fall behind. He took his argument from a biological theory about survival in nature.

4. Sample answer: Nowhere was conspicuous consumption more evident than in Newport, Rhode Island, where a 30-room summer "cottage" used for only 3 months cost $1 million. William K. Vanderbilt outdid everyone at Newport with a cottage that cost $2 million to build and $9 million to furnish. Conspicuous waste was evidenced by the summer people at Newport. They hosted lavish parties for one another, purchased large yachts that were good for little more than show, and used their "cottages" for only the three months of the summer social season.

Section Review (text page 467)

1. Students' sentences will vary. Information about the terms can be found on the pages given in parentheses: cash wages versus real wages (465), "black lung" (466), scrip (466–467), Lowell System (467).

2. In 1860, most Americans were working on farms or working alone in small family businesses. Only 1.5 million worked in workshops, and 700,000 worked in mining and construction. In 1870, the average workshop employed eight people. By 1900, factories that employed 1,000 were common, and a few listed 10,000 people on the payroll. Between the 1860s and 1900, annual production of goods in the United States increased from $2 billion to $13 billion.

3. The work force in factories became predominantly male. However, because one salary often was not enough to support a family, working-class women continued to work for wages even after they were married. In 1900, 20 percent of the total work force were women. Women made up 50 percent of the textile workers. Generally, women were paid much less than men for doing the same work for the same number of hours. About 1,750,000 children under 16 were employed full time in 1900. They did all but the heaviest kinds of work. They worked in factories, mines, and city sweatshops. Because children had no nonworking dependents, they were paid less than adults. However, because children could be hired for less, they replaced adults in the work force. For example, "mill daddies" were commonplace in southern textile towns. Unable to work because his children could be hired for less, the mill daddy was reduced to carrying his children's lunches to the factory at noon.

4. During the late nineteenth century, the use of steam power and constantly improving machinery increased tremendously. As a result, the use of highly skilled craftspeople (who trained for years in the use of hand tools) was no longer the most important factor in manufacturing. Their places were taken by unskilled or semiskilled machine tenders who guided the machines. These workers required little training and were poorly paid.

5. Wages: Wages were low for manufacturing workers. Women and children received the lowest wages. Workers skilled in certain areas, such as engineers and machinists, improved their earnings much more than unskilled workers. Cash wages of working people remained about the same or declined. Real wages increased. As a whole, industrial workers enjoyed about 50 percent more purchasing power in 1900 than in 1860. Hours: The number of hours on the job varied widely. Government employees worked eight hours a day. Skilled craftspeople worked 10 hours a day. Factory workers were lucky if they worked as little as 12 hours a day. Working conditions: A safe work place was not the general rule. Textile workers with missing fingers and ex-textile workers without hands were common sights in mill towns. Victims of work-related accidents might or might not receive compensation. Work-related diseases such as "black lung" among coalminers were not considered "occupational," and workers received no compensation. Company towns: Companies used the company towns as a way of controlling their employees. Some built their towns in isolated places so workers could not organize and push up wages. If workers went on strike, they risked not only losing their jobs but being evicted from their company-owned homes. Also, the company-owned stores in the company towns gave the company owners additional control over their employees.

Section Review (text page 474)

1. Students' sentences will vary. Information about the terms can be found on the pages given in parentheses: Molly Maguires (468–469), William Sylvis (469), Haymarket Square incident (470–471), American Federation of Labor (471–472).

2. The National Labor Union and the Knights of Labor were both founded before the AFL. The NLU broke up after the poor showing of the candidates put up by their National Labor party in the presidential election of 1872. NLU members were demoralized and the union quickly dissolved. The Knights of Labor fell to pieces after the 1886 Haymarket Square incident to which they were unfairly linked. Membership dropped from 700,000 to 100,000. However, the union dragged on until almost the turn of the century.

3. First, Gompers held that only skilled craftspeople could effectively force employers to bargain with them. Second, the goal of the AFL was higher wages, shorter hours, and better working conditions. Third, the strike as peaceful coercion was the union's best weapon.

4. With words like these, Jay Gould vowed to destroy the Knights of Labor. The Knights of Labor had gone on strike successfully against Gould's Missouri Pacific Railroad.

5. Unskilled workers, women, and blacks were not unionized in 1900.

Section Review (text page 477)

1. Students' sentences will vary. Information about the names and terms can be found on the pages given in parentheses: New Immigration (474), Foran Act (474), Carl Schurz (476), ghettos (477).

2. Before1880, only about 200,000 people of southern and eastern European origin had immigrated to the United States. Between 1880 and 1896, about 8.4 million of these people arrived. In 1896, the flow of people from southern and eastern Europe exceeded the flow from northern and western Europe. By 1907, southern and eastern Europeans were almost the whole of the influx. Industrialists generally liked European immigrant labor because it invariably was cheaper than American labor, and because immigrants were less inclined to join unions.

3. Ireland: potato crop failure and famine; China: overpopulation, flood, famine, epidemic disease, civil warfare; Philippines: becoming an American colony in 1898, Filipinos had free access to the U.S.; Germany: Failure of liberal revolutions and exile of revolutionaries; Russia and Italy: persecution of Jews and desire for prosperity and freedom of opportunity.

4. Not all Americans welcomed the New Immigrants. Many people whose families had been in America for generations looked on the different ethnic communities that formed as detrimental to the American culture they loved. Unlike the older immigrants, the New Immigrants seemed determined not to become Americans. Pressure groups such as the Immigration Restriction League began to call for immigration laws that would keep southern and eastern Europeans from entering the United States in any significant numbers.

Section Review (text page 481)

1. Students' sentences will vary. Information about the names and terms can be found on the pages given in parentheses: metropolis (478), John A. Roebling (479), tenements (479), Jane Addams (480–481).

2. Immigrants and people from American farms and rural towns added to their growth.

3. Innovations in mass trnasportation could be seen in the cities' horse-drawn public carriages, on rails, electric trolley cars, and subways. Innovations in architecture included multistoried skyscrapers and suspension bridges.

4. Among the challenges that city governments faced were overcrowding in tenements, health problems such as outbreaks of epidemics, and sanitation problems such as keeping up with waste disposal. City governments had to provide running water to tenements. Crimes such as homicide and theft, which saw dramatic increases, were also major challenges. City governments passed ordinances to regulate housing conditions, license saloons, regulate water supplies, increase the size of sanitation departments, appoint fire inspectors to inspect buildings for safety hazards, and establish police detective departments to fight organized crime. Private groups also tried to solve city problems. The YMCA provided sanitary and moral housing and recreational facilities in city centers. The Salvation Army distributed hot meals and clothing and started a work program for hungry and seemingly hopeless men. The Hebrew Immigrant Aid Society ministered to the needs of penniless Eastern European Jews who flocked to the cities. Individuals, too, offered help. Frederick Law Olmstead designed and lobbied for city parks so that poor people could get away from city bustle and noise for a few hours. Jane Addams, Robert A. Woods, and Lillian Wald founded settlement houses which not only provided food and drink, but also established places where the young, elderly, and those in between could go for a wide range of services and programs such as child care, recreation, counsel, and study.

Time Line Questions (text page 482)

1. 1886, Haymarket Square incident
2. 1866, 1869, 1886
3. New York elevated line, Brooklyn Bridge, Boston subway.
4. 1889

Skills Strategy: Summarizing and Drawing Conclusions (text page 482)

Information for the scratch outlines may be found on pages 463–467 and on pages 474 and 476–478. The sample paragraph below summarizes information in an imaginative way and is written in the first person. Students may choose to write more conventional summaries.

It's 6 A.M., time for me to leave for the factory where I work six days a week. I am only twelve, so I was lucky to get a job there. I tend a machine that spins thread from cotton. The machine is big and noisy, and I'm afraid of it, but it pays $2 a week unless I'm fined for being late or absent. The best time of the day is noon, when Daddy brings my lunch and throws it over the fence around the factory. The afternoons are long and boring, and I have to keep from falling asleep so I don't catch my fingers in the machine. At 6 P.M., I leave my job to go home. After eating supper, I'm too tired to do much of anything.

UNIT 5 TEST (text page 483)

Chapter Survey

1. Sample summary sentence(s): Chapter 17 examines the people, the technological developments, and the inventions that transformed the United States from a nation of farmers to the greatest industrial power on earth. The chapter also discusses the attempts of government to deal with a phenomenon that accompanied industrial growth —the greed and increasing power of some big business leaders. Pages containing information about terms: Big Four (416), robber barons (416), Promontory Point (417), condensed milk (420–421), *Boston Cooking School Cookbook* (423), William ''Pig Iron'' Kelly (423), Titusville (425), Harvey Firestone (428), James Buchanan Duke (431).

2. Sample summary sentence(s): Chapter 18 takes an objective look at corruption in American governments at the city and national level—the big city political machines, the businessman-politician on the national level, dishonesty in the Grant administration, the uses and abuses of political patronage, and the voters' acquiescence in all of this. Pages containing information about names and terms: Boss William Tweed (438), Goo-goos (440–441), Mugwumps (446), ''waving the bloody shirt'' (442, 443), patronage (443), Charles Guiteau (450–451), Pan-American Union (454), Wilson-Gorman Act (454), Greenback Labor party (455).

3. Sample summary sentence(s): Chapter 19 opens with an examination of the very rich and the reactions of ordinary Americans to them and their ostentatious lifestyle. The chapter continues with discussions of working conditions in the new factories, the early growth of labor unions, the role of immigrants, and the phenomenal growth of American cities. Pages containing information about terms: Newport, Rhode Island (461), Horatio Alger (462–463), scrip (466–467), Lowell system (467), Molly Maguires (468–469), New Immigration (474), tenements (479), Robert A. Wood (481).

Text Review

4. Between 1865 and 1900, the United States changed from a basically agrarian nation to a modern capitalistic industrial power. Among the factors that help account for this change are the following: a stable political environment conducive to industrial growth; the investment of domestic and foreign capital; a large laboring population; the growth of railroads; vast stretches of usable land; apparently endless resources; the genius of American inventors and entrepreneurs; government's favorable policies toward business.

5. Jay Gould: railroads; Gustavus Swift: meatpacking; Gail Borden: condensed milk; John D. Rockefeller: oil; Andrew Carnegie: steel

6. Cyrus McCormick: The reaper and other farm machinery produced at McCormick's International Harvester Company greatly increased the yield of American farms. Christopher Sholes: His invention, the typewriter, increased the efficiency of American business and attracted more women to the labor force. Elisha Otis: His invention and manufacture of safe elevators made possible deeper mines and taller office buildings, the latter encouraging the centralization of American business administration in the cities. Alexander Graham Bell: His telephones became the nervous system of American business and an important means of communication among American homes. George Westinghouse: The air brake he invented for trains increased their safety and added to their length. His method of transmitting alternating current made possible the transmission of electricity over long distances. Thomas Edison: His incandescent light bulb lighted the homes, offices, schools, and streets of America. Edison's storage battery, movie projector, and phonograph gave rise to new American industries.

7. The Fourteenth Amendment served the interests of big business corporate managers and stockholders. Because the amendment defined a business corporation as a person, with the same civil rights as a human person, states could not pass laws directed at a corporation, because such laws would deny the corporate person the civil rights guaranteed to human persons. However, while a corporation had all the rights of a person, it had none of the responsibilities. Thus, a corporation could not be sent to jail for violating the law. The Interstate Commerce Act and the Interstate Commerce Commission (ICC) set up to enforce it were meant to control the railroads by prohibiting excessive rates. However, the act did not forbid mergers or interlocking directorates, both of which were effective means of eliminating competition. In addition, the ICC was given little real power and, within a few years of its passage, was composed mostly of railroaders and the lawyers friendly to them. The Pacific Railway Act of 1862 in effect subsidized railroad construction by giving the Union Pacific and Central Pacific railway companies large sections of the public domain for every mile of track they built. The Sherman Anti-

trust Act, passed in response to public pressure, declared trusts unlawful and gave the Attorney General the power to move against such business combinations and force them to break up into smaller, separate companies.

8. Students' summaries should indicate that dishonesty and corruption in city and national politics led to cynical attitudes toward government and politics among most voters, who were often interested chiefly in what they could get in return for their votes. Widespread abuses of patronage were common. Although some groups of Americans called for reforms, many Americans voted to keep corrupt and dishonest politicians in office.

9. Students' responses will differ. However, their assessments of Grant's personal responsibility should be supported by facts given on text pages 444–449.

10. Students' answers should reflect their understanding that voters of the time were acting out of motives of self-interest. Corrupt politicians were willing to fulfill what the voters saw as their needs; reform candidates were not. Student reactions to this behavior of the voters will vary.

11. Students' answers should include two of the following: Foreign affairs: The Treaty of Washington settled British-American disputes over damages done by the British-built raider, the *Alabama*, used by the Confederacy during the Civil War; smoothed squabbles between New Englanders and Canadians over North Atlantic fishing rights; and ironed out problems about the boundary between the state of Washington and the province of British Columbia. President Grant, motivated by American investors and a pro-American faction, tried unsuccessfully to annex Santo Domingo (present-day Dominican Republic) to the United States. The tariff: High tariff interests (manufacturers and most industrial workers) generally had their way in the late nineteenth century. The McKinley Tariff raised rates to 50 percent. A subsequent depression led to the election of President Cleveland, who had campaigned against the high tariff rates. A proposal for a new tariff—The Wilson-Gorman Act—lowered rates only slightly, so Cleveland vetoed it. The money question: The government brought on a deflation when they took greenbacks out of circulation, thus increasing the value of gold and paper money redeemable in gold, and reducing wages and prices. Farmers, who were hardest hit by the deflation, formed the Greenback Labor Party. It had little success in bringing about the farmers' goal: to increase the money supply by printing of paper money not backed by gold.

12. Henry George advocated a 100 percent tax on the "unearned increment" of the wealthy, that is, on the income derived from wealthy people's mere ownership of property—income for which they had to do no work, expend no effort, and apply no ingenuity. George called his tax the "single tax," saying that it would eliminate the need for all other taxes and destroy the idle rich as a social class. George did not blame industrialization or capitalism as a system for the inequalities in American life. In fact, he believed that his single tax would allow everyone to compete for comfort and security on an equal basis. Herbert Spencer and his American disciple William Graham Summer attempted to explain and justify great success and wealth by applying a biological theory to human society. As animals and plants freely compete for life, Spencer argued, so do people. Those who are "fittest" survive, whereas the weak die out. In the United States, business leaders and pro-business politicians used Spencer's ideas as a basis for their opposition to giving aid to the poor and to regulating business, maintaining that such policies would interfere with the "natural" processes Spencer described.

13. Students' descriptions should include references to the following. Wages: Cash wages remained constant or declined, but real wages, or purchasing power, rose. As a whole, workingpeople had 50 percent more buying power in 1900 than they had forty years earlier. Hours: Time on the job varied widely. Government employees had an eight-hour day. Skilled workers generally worked about ten hours daily. Unskilled workers and factory workers averaged 12 hours on the job each day, with mills in some parts of the country running as long as 16 hours a day in summer. Working conditions: In most industries, a safe workplace was not the rule. Furthermore, employers offered little compensation for job-related deaths, injuries, and illness. Company towns made workers almost completely dependent on their employers and lessened their freedom to protest injustice. The higher prices charged in company stores often put workers into debt and increased their dependence on employers. Women: Plans like the Lowell system encouraged unmarried women to work at factory jobs until they were ready to marry. Although the increasing demands of industry for workers and the heavy nature of much factory work resulted in a predominantly male work force, many women continued to work in order to help their families make ends meet. About 20 percent of the total work force in 1900 was composed of women, who were usually paid

as much as one-half less for doing the same jobs as men. Child laborers: About 1,750,000 children under 16 worked full time in 1900, doing all but the heaviest labor, often working in dangerous conditions. Because their children could be hired for less, some men were unable to find work.

14. Students should list items in this order and give details about one item from pages shown in parentheses: National Labor Union (469), Knights of Labor (469–470, 471), Haymarket Square incident (470–471), American Federation of Labor (471–473), National Civic Federation (472).

15. Before 1880, most immigrants came from northern and western Europe; only about 200,000 southern and eastern Europeans came to the United States at this time. After 1880, about 8.4 million people emigrated from southern and eastern Europe, far exceeding the number of immigrants from northern and western Europe. Unlike those who had preceded them, most of those who came to the United States after 1880 had little money, were illiterate, had little experience which could prepare them for life in a great industrial nation, and often chose to maintain their original national identities. American industrialists generally welcomed immigrants, because they could be paid less and were less likely to join unions. However, not all Americans welcomed the newcomers. Older Americans saw the new people as detrimental to American life, and formed pressure groups such as the Immigration Restriction League to keep immigration from southern and eastern Europe to a minimum.

16. Students' descriptions of an immigrant's impressions of a large American city will vary. Information given on text pages 478–481 may suggest ideas.

Critical Thinking

17. A business manager benefits from a corporation's broad financial base, influence, and limited liability protection, but some of the individual's decision-making authority may be limited by or relinquished to the corporate directorship. A working person may benefit from the potential high productivity, stability, and possible profits of a corporation, yet is also subject to its decisions. A shareholder assumes financial risk—with potential for loss or gain.

18. The growth of industry: Many immigrants took jobs in factories and mines. Others, such as steel entrepreneur Andrew Carnegie, promoted the growth and efficiency of the major industries of the nation. Advances in the labor movement: Immigrants played a significant role in the emergence of American labor unions. Among the immigrants were the Irish Molly Maguires and Samuel Gompers of the AFL. Improvement of transportation: Chinese and Irish laborers played a large part in the construction of the Union Pacific and Central Pacific railways that joined at Promontory Point, Utah, to become the nation's first transcontinental railroad. A German immigrant, Henry Villard, was a key figure in the building of the Northern Pacific Railroad.

Skills Review (text page 483)

19. Thematic maps present specific information in a concise, pictorial form. They are often used for comparing changes in geographic features over a specified period of time. Political maps are one type of thematic map which show political boundaries. They are most often used to show changes in international borders and political alignments.

20. Political cartoons are a form of propaganda aimed at influencing the reader toward a particular point of view. They are a biased, not an objective, presentation of information.

CHAPTER 20

Section Review (text page 492)

1. Students' sentences will vary. Information about the names and terms can be found on the pages given in parentheses: the frontier (486), Indian Territory (488), "Buffalo Bill" Cody (491), buffalo robes (491).

2. The frontier was where the nation's settled lands ended and its undeveloped region began. After the Civil War, the frontier was about 150 to 200 miles beyond the Mississippi and just beyond the western boundaries of Minnesota, Iowa, Missouri, Arkansas, and the eastern half of Texas.

3. Possible answers: The Ute, Paiute, and Shoshone lived in the Great Basin area. The Pima, Zuñi and Hopi lived in pueblos in a region that is now Arizona and New Mexico.

4. The near extinction of the Plains Indians was a result of the destruction of the buffalo herds by hunters like "Buffalo Bill" Cody. These hunters were hired to provide meat for railroad workers. Later, when buffalo robes were in fashion, teams of sharpshooters and skinners slaughtered countless bison. Railroad companies encouraged the slaughter because their iron train tracks were being destroyed by buffalo herds that crossed over them.

Wealthy eastern and British hunters chartered special trains to take them to the plains so they could shoot trophies for their mansions and clubs. The economy, social structure, religion, diet, and dress of the Plains Indians revolved around the bison and the horse. The Plains Indians grew no crops. To get their food, they trailed after the herds of bison on their horses—to southern grazing grounds in the winter and then back to northern grazing grounds in the summer. The bison provided food, and its hide was made into clothing, footwear, blankets, portable shelters, bowstrings, and canvasses. The bison's manure was used as fuel for cooking and warmth.

Section Review (text page 496)

1. Students' sentences will vary. Information about the names and terms can be found on the pages given in parentheses: General George Crook (492), *A Century of Dishonor* (494), Wovoka (494), Pine Ridge Reservation (494).
2. The Indian Wars began with an uprising of the Sioux in Minnesota in 1862 and ended with the defeat of the Dakotas at Wounded Knee in South Dakota in 1890. The peak years of the fighting were between 1869 and 1876.
3. In June 1876, General Custer led 265 men of the Seventh Cavalry into a battle with the Sioux at the Little Big Horn River in Montana. The battle was a total victory for the Indians. Custer and all his men were killed.
4. The Dawes Act (1887) was an attempt to Americanize the Indians by making them self-sufficient farmers and citizens. The Indian tribes were dissolved, and their lands were divided into homesteads. A totally alien way of life was forced on the Indians. Furthermore, the defeated and demoralized Indians were now susceptible to being defrauded of their lands. Wovoka, a Paiute, spread a religion that appealed to thousands of defeated and demoralized Indians in the West. He taught that, by performing a Ghost Dance, the Indians—who were God's chosen people—could prevail upon the Great Spirit to bring back the old way of life. The Dakota Sioux was one tribe that became avid believers in the Ghost Dance Religion. The soldiers guarding them were uneasy about this, and they grew even more nervous when they heard the Sioux had guns in their camp at Wounded Knee Creek on the reservation. A shoving incident caused the soldiers to open fire on the Indians there with rifles and artillery. About 200 Sioux men, women, and children were killed on that December day in 1890.
5. The final decades of the nineteenth century stand

as the era of the greatest economic expansion in American history. The output of lumber more than tripled from 1870 to 1900. The number of cattle raised nearly tripled from 1870 to 1900. Annual gold production by the end of the century nearly doubled the total produced in 1850. The annual production of silver in 1870 was 2.4 million troy ounces and in 1900 reached 57.7 million troy ounces.

Section Review (text page 501)

1. Students' sentences will vary. Information about the names and terms can be found on the pages given in parentheses: *vaquero* (497), Chisholm Trail (498), Abilene (498), Sitting Bull (500–501).
2. McCoy promoted the first successful long-distance commerce in beef. In 1866, when the Kansas Pacific Railroad reached Abilene, Kansas, McCoy saw the possibilities of underselling Eastern steers by selling half-wild Texas longhorns. He sent agents to southern Texas to convince Texans to round up longhorns from the open range, where they were nearly worthless, and drive them to Abilene on the Chisholm Trail. He built holding pens on the outskirts of Abilene and arranged with the Kansas Pacific to ship the longhorns to Chicago butchers and meatpackers. In 1867, McCoy shipped 35,000 longhorns and made enormous profits. Chicago meatpackers wanted more of the cheap longhorns, so the next year, McCoy shipped 75,000 longhorns. In 1871, 600,000 longhorns left Abilene on the Kansas Pacific for the meatpacking plants in Chicago.
3. Between 1867 and 1886, the West's cattle industry became enormously profitable. Investors (speculators) from as far away as England came to the West to establish cattle businesses. Cattle owners ignored the natural limits of the range and by the mid-1880s had overstocked the ranges with huge herds. Clear-running springs were trampled into mud holes with undrinkable water. Weeds replaced the overgrazed grasses. In 1886, a series of natural disasters devastated the cattle industry. After 1886, the cattle industry was reorganized. Methodical ranchers replaced speculators. Clever manipulators of the federal law, like cattle baron Richard King, built huge ranches. They were not willing to risk their all on the open range ever again. When new east-west railroads snaked into Texas and the states along the Canadian border, and the Union Pacific and Kansas Pacific extended feeder lines north and south into cow country, the days of the long cattle drive and the legendary cowboy were over.
4. Sample answers: Jesse James was really a bank

and train robber, but after Jesse's death, his mother made a tourist attraction of his grave, charged admission, and explained that her son was a Bible-reading Christian. Jesse James was romanticized into a modern-day Robin Hood who gave the money he robbed to the poor. Billy the Kid, or William Bonney, a Brooklyn-born criminal, was romanticized as a tragic hero who had been forced into a life of crime. Among other legendary western characters students may choose to discuss are Belle Starr, ''Wild Bill'' Hickok, and Calamity Jane. Student opinions of why such legends began and spread should contain references to the influence of Wild West shows and other commercial merchandising of popular entertainment.

Section Review (text page 502)

1. Students' sentences will vary. Information about the names and terms can be found on the pages given in parentheses: Great American Desert (501), Indian Territory (501), Joseph Glidden (501), President Benjamin Harrison (502).

2. Pioneers had to endure plagues of grasshoppers and violent winter and summer storms. Because the plains had almost no trees, instead of building log cabins, the pioneers built one-room houses from grass sod. Also, because there were so few trees, farmers could not build fences to protect their crops from cattle. They experimented with hedges of various kinds and wire strung between posts. However, nothing was really effective until Joseph Glidden invented barbed wire in 1874. The shortage of water prevented farmers from growing corn. They could not get to the water deep in the earth with simple tools. In the 1860s, petroleum companies developed machinery which could drill far down beneath the earth's surface. Farmers adapted these drilling machines to tap underground water. Then, the farmers used windmills to bring the water up to ground level. They used the pumped water to irrigate the soil and made prairie farming feasible.

3. The Homestead Act granted 160 acres of free land to anyone who could live on the land for five years. Civil War veterans, farm families from New England, and immigrants from Scandinavia, Germany, and Russia took advantage of the opportunities the law offered.

4. About 100,000 eager pioneers responded to President Harrison's proclamation opening up the territory of Oklahoma for settlement on April 22, 1889. They hovered along the Oklahoma border waiting for the signal gun to fire. Then they darted across the line to stake out homestead claims. Within a few hours, the territory was completely overrun with homesteaders. This event was a disadvantage for the Indian tribes because it took land that was formerly reserved for them—the so-called Indian Territory.

Section Review (text page 505)

1. Students' sentences will vary. Information about the terms can be found on the pages given in parentheses: Virginia City (503, 504), Jim Butler (504), Demonetization Act of 1873 (504).

2. Among western mining towns were Deadwood Gulch, Leadville, Virginia City, Tombstone, and Goldfield. Fictional pictures of these towns as boisterous and colorful were not altogether imaginary. However, these mining areas were also an integral and important part of the country's economy.

3. The value of paper money in the United States had value according to the amount of gold and silver the issuing banks kept in their vaults to back it. In 1873, Congress passed the Demonetization Act which demonetized silver, taking the silver dollar off the coinage list. With greenbacks being retired, gold became the only basis of American money. Silver was demonetized because the American gold supply increased while the supply of silver decreased. The value of silver on the open market rose above the officially pegged value of 16 ounces of silver to one ounce of gold. Silver dollars ceased to circulate because they brought more than 100 cents when they were melted down and sold for the metal they contained.

4. Silver had been demonetized. New discoveries in Nevada caused the market to be flooded with silver. Since the government was buying none of this silver, the price plunged. Supply had exceeded demand.

5. Western farmers attributed their problems to bankers' manipulation of the currency. Mine owners agreed with the farmers. They wanted the Treasury to buy more silver because production of silver was steadily increasing and its price was falling. Both would have been happy to see the Treasury buy more silver and mint more silver coins.

Time Line Questions (text page 506)

1. 5 years
2. massacre at Wounded Knee
3. 6 years

Skills Strategy: Primary Sources (text pages 506–507)

1. The conflict between Indians and white settlers of the West is the subject.

2. Although Flint lived on the frontier, he was probably not as involved as Black Hawk, who actually took part in the battles.

3. Black Hawk's statements contain some fact (Whites did take Indian lands and drive them from their homes, he did fight them, and things did get worse for the Indians) and many emotional opinions (White men despised the Indians and looked at them spitefully). Except for the fact of Indian-White conflict, Flint's article is made up of opinions and assumptions.

4. Black Hawk had just been defeated and taken prisoner. As a leader, his concern for his people may have aroused deep feelings.

5. He seems to assume that the white takeover of the continent was the "order of Providence," growing out of "the laws of nature and the universal march of human events."

6. Flint's article portrays Indians as bloodthirsty, warlike savages, a stereotype prevalent at the time and one that was reinforced later in popular literature, movies, and television.

7. Ellipsis points are used to show that some original text has been left out; they can be used to save space.

8. Both sources chiefly convey attitudes and feelings, although both articles do contain some facts. However, neither source is suitable as an accurate, factual account.

Chapter Test (text page 507)

Text Review

1. The frontier was where the nation's settled lands ended and its undeveloped region began, a place —so people thought—with no history and no law. The frontier usually took the form of a north-south line moving constantly westward. Between 1865 and 1900, the frontier was about 150 to 200 miles beyond the Mississippi, just beyond the western boundaries of Minnesota, Iowa, Missouri, Arkansas, and almost all of the western part of Texas. The West at this time was made up of all the undeveloped lands on the other side of the frontier, comprising nearly half of the total area of the United States. Farther west, in what are now California, Oregon, Washington, and New Mexico, there were relatively large pockets of settlement.

2. The slaughter began when the Union Pacific Railroad Company hired hunters such as "Buffalo Bill" Cody to kill buffalo so that crews constructing a rail line to the Pacific could be fed. Hunting teams continued the slaughter of the bison to meet the demand for "buffalo robes," which had become very popular back east. When the railroads learned that bison herds were destroying their tracks, they encouraged even more slaughter. Finally, wealthy hunters from Great Britain and the East chartered special buffalo-hunting trains and killed the bison so they could display their heads as trophies in their homes and clubs. By the end of the century, only a few hundred bison were alive.

3. Students answer only one part of the following items: The resistance of Plains Indians to white settlement—The construction of the railroads and white settlement in their hunting lands threatened the bison herds upon which the Plains people's way of life was totally dependent. They had no choice but to resist such a destructive threat. The massacre at Wounded Knee—After the Dakota Sioux had been defeated in the wars with the whites, they were herded onto the Pine Ridge Reservation in South Dakota, where they were guarded by American soldiers. The soldiers became nervous when they heard that some of the Dakotas had guns in their camp at Wounded Knee Creek. One day a shoving incident led the soldiers to open fire on the Indians. After the smoke cleared, about 200 Dakotas lay dead.

4. General George Crook respected the Indian tribes and their rights and tried to deal fairly with them. However, he was an exception among the cavalry men and officers in the West. Their sympathies were with the white railroaders, miners, cattle owners, and farmers. Many of these whites and their cavalry supporters felt that, because the Indians used land so inefficiently, their claim to it was not equal to the claim of the more efficient newcomers.

5. Students' answers should include references to the following: tthe roundup of half-wild longhorn cattle by enterprising Texans in the late 1850s and their shipping of cattle to Chicago; the long cattle drive to Sedalia, Missouri, a rail town with connections to Chicago; Missouri law against importing Texas cattle caused the failure of the Texans' enterprise; the extension of the transcontinental railroad to Abilene, Kansas, and Joseph McCoy's successful idea for selling the Texas longhorns to cities in the East; the profitable cattle drives from Texas to the cattle pens in railheads like Abilene; the destruction of the thriving cattle industry by the great winter blizzard and summer drought of 1886 and the second blizzard of 1887; the reorganization of the cattle industry by cattle barons like Richard King of Texas, who raised cattle on mammoth ranches rather than rounding them up from the open range; the effect of the expansion of the railroads on the decline of the long cattle drives and the cowboys.

6. Students should name and give important details

about the following: the Homestead Act of 1862 (page 501), the Oklahoma Land Rush of April 22, 1889 (page 502). Details about each can be found on the pages given in parentheses.

7. Students should list these steps that led to the demonetization of silver: before 1849, one ounce of gold was worth 16 ounces of silver because more silver was being mined; after 1849, silver mines began to run out and the metal became more valuable; people began to sell 16 ounces of silver for more than one ounce of gold and melted silver dollars to sell at more than 100 cents to jewelers, speculators, and foreign buyers; silver dollars ceased to circulate; Congress demonetized silver in 1873, making silver dollars valueless as U.S. currency and establishing gold as the sole basis of American paper money. Demonetization brought about passage of the Bland-Allison Act. At about the same time that the Demonetization Act was passed, rich new veins of silver were discovered, and silver flooded the market at increasingly lower prices. Greenbackers and inflation-minded representatives began to refer to demonetization as the "Crime of '73" as though it had been deliberately designed by bankers and financial conservatives to keep money scarce. The public outcry led to the passage of the Bland-Allison Act of 1878 which, as it was originally introduced, was meant to remonetize silver, but in its final version did not. The silver dollars minted after passage had value only because they were backed by gold deposits.

Critical Thinking

8. Students' summaries should stress that white westward expansion deprived the original Indian inhabitants of the West not only of their lands but of their very way of life, relegating a once-proud people to useless lives on government reservations.

9. Students' responses should indicate their understanding that, for the most part, the West as most Americans thought of it was the creation of highly commercial merchandisers of books and popular entertainment. Examples should be included in the responses.

10. Students' contrasts should bring out the conflicting needs of both farmers and Indians for land to support their differing ways of daily living. For example, the Plains Indians needed untouched land that would provide forage for the bison herds that supplied their daily needs. The pioneer farmers, by cultivating the land to feed themselves, were destroying the bison grazing lands.

Writing a Paragraph

Students' paragraphs should describe one or more aspects of a cowboy's work on the trail, with appropriate details. Ideas for the paragraph and words and terms used by cowboys can be found under these chapter headings: "The Cowboy," "The Cowboy's Life," "Getting Meat to Market" (pages 497–498), "The Cattle Drive," and "The Cowboy's Job" (page 499).

CHAPTER 21

Section Review (text page 512)

1. Students' sentences will vary. Information about the terms can be found on the pages given in parentheses: "bone and sinew" (508), Johnson County (510), staples (510–511), harrows and threshers (511–512).

2. Thomas Jefferson and four generations of politicians had told American farmers that those who toiled the earth were the "bone and sinew" of the republic. In the final decades of the nineteenth century, farmers began to suspect that they were no longer "society's most valuable citizens" but just another interest group among many. And in an urban and industrialized America, they were not a very important interest group at that. Farmers were apt to be viewed humorously and disparagingly by the general public.

3. Farmers fenced their holdings with barbed wire, which prevented some cattle from reaching streams and water holes. The cattle owners fought back by damming up streams and cutting barbed wire fences. However, most of the disputes between the two were settled on the local level by legislation and through the courts.

4. The expansion of agriculture in the last three decades of the nineteenth century has never been rivaled. For example, a single generation of farmers put 431 million acres of virgin soil into cultivation, averaging 14.4 million acres each year. In 1900, farmers were producing 150 percent more staples than they had in 1870. Hogs numbered 25 million in 1870 and 63 million in 1900. Improvements in farming equipment furthered the agricultural expansion. New plows, harrows, reapers, and threshers did things like slice through sod, plant seeds, shuck corn, thresh wheat, bind shocks, and shred fodder for livestock. These machines also allowed farmers to reduce waste, raise more livestock, and care for more acreage than was thought possible by earlier generations. The new machinery greatly reduced the number of hours a farmer spent working.

Section Review (text page 515)

1. Students' sentences will vary. Information about the names and terms can be found on the pages given in parentheses: real income (512), sharecropper system (513), Mary Elizabeth Lease (514), Hamlin Garland (515).

2. The price of staples such as wheat, corn, and livestock fell so low that the real income of western farmers in 1896 was half that of 1872. In other words, western farmers had to produce twice as much to make the same money they did in 1872. One reason for the drop in prices was that there were too many farmers producing too much grain and livestock. The supply became greater than the demand, forcing prices down. For the most part, farmers in the Northeast and those in the Ohio and upper Mississippi watershed prospered. They had stopped growing staples, instead producing dairy goods, poultry, eggs, and garden vegetables to supply nearby urban markets.

3. Manufacturers who depended on Cooke & Company for credit had to close down. The tens of thousands of workers who worked for them lost their jobs. These unemployed workers cut down on the money they spent on food, thus reducing demand and forcing down the price of agricultural products.

4. Tens of thousands of the sons and daughters of farmers fled to the cities because they saw how difficult it was to earn a living from the soil and because they were lured by the social and cultural attractions of city life. They wanted no more of the dreary routine of farm life.

Section Review (text page 520)

1. Students' sentences will vary. Information about the names and terms can be found on the pages given in parentheses: cooperative (515), Agricultural Wheel (515–516), Eugene V. Debs (518), Sherman Silver Purchase Act (519).

2. Possible answers: (1) The Populist Party wanted election of United States Senators by popular vote rather than by state legislatures; (2) The party endorsed the adoption of a secret ballot to prevent intimidation of voters; (3) They encouraged the use of the initiative, which would allow voters through petition to put measures on the ballot independent of action by legislatures and thus avert possible manipulation by lobbies; (4) The party sought the use of the recall, which would allow voters through petition to force a public official to stand for election before his or her term expired; (5) They called for the use of the referendum, which would allow voters to vote directly on laws rather than indirectly through their representatives (referendum was the means by which initiative measures and recall petitions could be decided.); (6) The Populist party demanded public ownership of natural monopolies such as the railroads and telegraph, which could be run efficiently under a single management; (7) The Populists called for adoption of a postal savings system to allow ordinary people to avoid depositing their money in the hated banks; (8) It advocated an adoption of a graduated income tax, which would make the wealthy pay a higher percentage of their income than the modest farmer or the wage worker; (9) The Populist Party wanted national banks to be abolished; (10) They wanted an increase in the amount of money in circulation through the free and unlimited coinage of silver at the old ratio of 16 ounces of silver to one ounce of gold.

3. Watson was a leading advocate of the principle that social class was more important than race. Watson's reasoning was that whites and blacks were made to hate each other so that each could be "separately fleeced" of their earnings. Democratic politicians such as Benjamin Tillman appealed to poor white farmers on the same class issues as Watson. However, these politicians did not call for an alliance of blacks and whites. Rather, they attacked the blacks more viciously than during the Reconstruction. They promised to preserve white domination of the South by completely excluding blacks from political life. Tillman and others wanted blacks to observe a strict and humiliating color line in every aspect of daily life. Embittered by his failure to bring about racial cooperation, Watson did an about-face and became one of Georgia's fiercest race baiters.

4. The Populists felt that the free coinage of silver was the key to prosperity. The Populist stand on free silver captured the voters' attention after 1893 and destroyed voters' interest in the rest of the Populists' program in the election of 1896.

5. The point of view on free silver of the silver mine operators and the pro-silver Democrats was essentially the same as the Populists' point of view. However, neither group had any interest in other reforms proposed by the Populists. As wealthy capitalists, mine operators were hostile to most Populist demands. Although pro-silver Democrats had a slight interest in some of the other Populist reforms, they strongly opposed such other reforms as the nationalization of the railroads and the telegraph.

Section Review (text page 521)

1. Students' sentences will vary. Information about the terms can be found on the pages given in

parentheses: ''Pittsburgh of the South'' (520), ''pigs'' (520); Spindletop (520), tobacco trust (521).

2. Grady's reason for giving the speech was to make the point that the South must abandon its total reliance on agriculture and promote industrialization. The North's industry explained why the Confederacy had been defeated. Only by accepting the realities of the modern world would the South prosper.

3. Beginning with the federal donation of almost six million acres of forest land, southern syndicates laid the basis for the lumber and turpentine industry in the vast pine forests of the South. The discovery of coal and iron in northern Alabama led to Birmingham's becoming the ''Pittsburgh of the South'' and the center of a booming steel industry. The oil industry was a twentieth-century development in the South that began with the oil gusher Spindletop in Texas in 1901. Most of New England's textile industry moved south after 1900.

4. Cigarettes were a minor tobacco product, so Duke had to change the image of cigarette smokers. Soldiers had smoked cigarettes during the Civil War because they could easily carry the papers and pouches of tobacco. After the war, cigarettes were considered unmanly, and only boys smoked them behind the barn. After Duke bought the patent rights to a cigarette-rolling machine, he set about pulling together a long-term market for his products. He encouraged adolescents to smoke by selling a pack of cigarettes for only a nickel. Inside each pack was a trading card that featured a picture and a brief biography of a military hero or a popular athlete. At the same time that Duke created a consumer market, he improved machinery and bought out competitors. In 1890, Duke set up a trust similar to John D. Rockefeller's. Through the trust, he gained control of his major competitors (R. J. Reynolds, P. H. J. Lorillard) and built an almost perfect monopoly. Through loose arrangements with British cigarette manufacturers, Duke had a major say in the tobacco industry on two continents. In 1911, he was forced to disband his gigantic corporation which, by then, controlled 150 factories.

Time Line Questions (text page 524)

1. 1894, Wilson-Gorman Tariff
2. 1913, Sixteenth Amendment
3. 1891, 1894
4. 1901, Spindletop gusher in Texas

Skills Strategy: News Stories As Primary Sources (text pages 524–525)

1. The second story contains a nonfactual headline.

2. The first story; Who? What? Where? When? How? Why?

3. Emotional nouns such as *rebel* and *revolutionaries*, and modifiers such as *wild-eyed*, and *disloyal*, show the writer's bias.

4. The writer of the second news story appeals to feelings of loyalty and patriotism (loyal observers, American way of life, Founding Fathers) and fear (wild-eyed spokesperson, fiery rebels, revolutionary plans, utter ruin).

5. Facts such as names of people who headed the meeting, examples of bold new proposals, and reasons why ordinary Americans felt they needed a greater say in government could have been included.

6. The first story; the second story could be used for insight into attitudes and feelings of people of the time.

7. The first story presents facts in an unbiased, unemotional manner.

Chapter Test (text page 525)

Text Review

1. The expansion of the railroads and the development of new farming machinery and techniques were two chief reasons for the phenomenal expansion of American agriculture during the last three decades of the nineteenth century. Large-scale commercial agriculture was not feasible until the railroad arrived to transport farm products to other parts of the country and to seaports from which they could be exported to other countries. Steel plows, harrows, threshers, reapers, and other agricultural machinery made farmers' work easier and faster. Potentially, a farmer with such machinery could cultivate six times more land in 1890 than was possible without machinery before the Civil War.

2. Agriculture made a remarkable recovery in the South after the Civil War. Cotton production soared above prewar levels. This was possible because the war had done nothing to harm the fertile soil of the region, and most of all because the black farm laborers remained and were exploited by cotton growers.

3. Instead of dividing the old plantations into homesteads for freed blacks after the war, the Radical Republicans left the land in the hands of its prewar owners. The landowners had no cash to pay gangs of farm laborers; even if they had had the cash, freed blacks probably would not have worked within a gang-labor system because it resembled slavery. To get their lands producing again, the owners divided plantations into family-size farm plots, and a cabin was built on each. Landowners

gave the houses, plots of land, mules, plows, and seed in exchange for up to half of each year's crop. In practice, the landlord or a merchant took the other half as well, causing sharecropper families to buy what they needed and live on credit, using the next season's harvest as collateral. When the harvest failed or crop prices declined, the black tenant families had no crop to sell to pay their debts. All they had was an open line of credit based on crops not yet planted—a kind of debt bondage or economic slavery.

4. After the failure of Jay Cooke & Company in 1873, businesses failed; workers lost their jobs and cut their spending for food, forcing down prices; wholesale agricultural prices dropped almost 30 percent; and many farmers were ruined. Economists explained that the agricultural depression was brought on by the working of the law of supply and demand. Farmers were producing much more than society could consume. In other words, supply was greater than demand and prices dropped.

5. Both money pools and farmers' alliances were among the organizations farmers formed in response to the many problems they faced in the late 1800s. Money pools were nonprofit organizations capitalized by farmer members, making loans to members at low interest rates. Money pools were started to eliminate farmers' dependence on the banks they distrusted so greatly. They were opposed by banks and were often mismanaged. Regional and state farmers' alliances were political action organizations formed in the late 1880s. By 1889, the various alliances had merged into three major groups: one representing western farmers, one representing white southern farmers, and one representing black southern farmers. At first, the alliances endorsed politicians of any party who supported their points of view. However, many of the politicians they backed let themselves be seduced by lobbyists representing opposing points of view. Therefore, the three major alliances began to think seriously of forming a new political party. In December of 1890, representatives of the three groups met in Ocala, Florida, to draw up a list of their grievances.

6. In February 1892, the three major farmers' alliances sent delegates to Omaha, Nebraska, to form a new political party—the People's party, or the Populists, as they were better known. Through this party, the farmers and their allies hoped to overcome what they perceived as the bankers' control of American currency and to take control of American government policy away from bankers, railroaders, and industrialists. They saw themselves as bringing the nation back to the democratic virtue intended by the Founding Fathers.

7. Possible answers are the election of United States senators directly by the people; universal adoption of the secret ballot; introduction of the initiative, recall, and referendum; a graduated income tax.

8. Lloyd said that because the free silver issue was given disproportionate attention in public discussion, it would distract people's attention from other important parts of the Populist program. Since the Democrats also backed free silver and the voters were not kept aware of the other parts of the Populist platform, the Populists' chances for winning the 1896 election would be lessened. The Populist defeat in 1896 proved him correct.

Critical Thinking

9. Students' responses should indicate their understanding that Watson originally advocated that social class was more important than race and urged black and white farmers to work together against the "financial despotism" that hurt both.

10. *Populist*: a, c; *Democrat/Republican*: b, d.

Writing a Paragraph

Sample Paragraph:

LEGISLATURE SETTLES LONG-STANDING DISPUTE

Today, responding to strong pressure from farmers' groups, lawmakers in Sacramento settled an old dispute between farmers and gold miners here in California. According to the new state law passed in this morning's session, miners must follow specified procedures when extracting gold ore. Adherence to the procedures will prevent further pollution of the rivers that farmers depend on to irrigate their crops.

CHAPTER 22

Section Review (text page 530)

1. Students' sentences will vary. Information about the names and terms can be found on the pages given in parentheses: Marcus Hanna (526), "Cross of Gold" speech (528), Canton (530), "the enemy's country" (530).

2. McKinley was nominated by the Republicans because of the efforts of his close friend Marcus Hanna, the master strategist of the Republican party. Bryan was by no means the front-running candidate at the Democratic Convention, but his thrilling words in the "Cross of Gold" speech so aroused the delegates at the convention that they gave him the party's nomination for president. The Populists who were in opposition to the Republicans called for the nomination of Bryan on the

Populist ticket as well as the Democratic. Although Bryan accepted only the free silver coinage plank of their platform, the Populists reasoned he would win if he had their support.

3. Bryan campaigned vigorously. His speaking tour took him more than 13,000 miles by train. He delivered 600 speeches in 29 states in only 14 weeks. On the other hand, knowing that McKinley could not rival Bryan's oratory flamboyance, Hanna kept his candidate at his modest home in Canton, Ohio. Steady streams of Republican delegations marched behind a brass band to McKinley's home. McKinley would make a short speech and answer a few prearranged questions. In addition, Hanna had spent more money on posters, rallies, picnics, advertisements, and speakers for McKinley than had been spent by both parties in all the elections since the Civil War.

4. Farmers of the Midwest did not vote for Bryan because they believed the Republicans when they had labeled him a radical. Industrial and city workers did not vote for Bryan, because his free silver campaign offered them little. They voted Republican because they believed the Republicans' high protective tariff would protect their jobs and because Bryan had called New York City "the enemy's country." The growing middle class, considering themselves the new bone and sinew of the American republic, voted for McKinley because they were frightened by Bryan.

5. The Populist party was doomed by its collaboration with the Democrats. They had sacrificed their reform program for the chance of winning free silver with Bryan. In the South, white Populists turned against the blacks and became the leading exponents of Democratic party rule and white supremacy. In the West, the party simply withered away, in part because the wholesale prices of farm products were rising.

Section Review (text page 533)

1. Students' sentences will vary. Information about the terms can be found on the pages given in parentheses: Alaska and Midway Island (532), jingoism (532), expansionists (532), Pearl Harbor (533).

2. First, the country had been founded in a war against imperial control, and Americans opposed colonialism. Second, the vastness of the American continent provided a more than adequate outlet for American energies.

3. Most Americans felt they were the heirs of the first great anti-colonial rebellion and should not take control over other people.

4. Lodge and Roosevelt openly said that the United States must seize colonies before there were none left to be taken. They worried publicly that, in their prosperity, Americans were becoming soft and flabby. They believed that Anglo-Saxons (English and Americans) were divinely commissioned to spread their institutions to other people. Alfred Thayer Mahan, in his book *The Influence of Sea Power Upon History*, argued that great nations were always seafaring nations that had powerful navies. Scolding the Americans for allowing their fleet to decay, Mahan urged a massive program of fleet construction. Congress agreed and made large appropriations. A modern navy needed fueling stations at scattered points worldwide. This meant taking colonies, even if they were only small islands in the Pacific. It also meant building bases in Hawaii. In 1887, the United States established a naval base in Pearl Harbor.

5. Turner theorized that the frontier had been the key to the vitality of American democracy, social stability, and prosperity. With the frontier gone, Turner asked, was the United States doomed to stagnation and social upheaval? Those who found Turner convincing looked to establishing new frontiers abroad. In the 1890s, American financiers invested millions of dollars in China and Latin America because they felt opportunities for investment within the United States were shrinking.

Section Review (text page 538)

1. Students' sentences will vary. Information about the names and terms can be found on the pages given in parentheses: yellow press (533), U.S.S. *Maine* (534), Commodore George Dewey (535), Rough Riders (536).

2. Cuba was in the midst of a serious uprising that was being fought like a classic guerrilla war. Valeriano Weyler was the Spanish military commander in Cuba. His repressive policies against Cubans earned him the nickname "The Butcher."

3. The *Journal* and *World* were in a circulation war and decided that the Cuban rebellion could be used as ammunition in that war. They used all the tricks of the "yellow press" to luridly publicize atrocities such as those of Valeriano Weyler. In addition, they transformed simple incidents into horror stories and even invented atrocities. The yellow press wanted war with Spain. They worked Americans into a war fever. President McKinley tried to pursue a peaceful policy. He asked Spain to abandon its harsh policies and placate both Cubans and outspoken Americans. In 1898, Madrid withdrew Weyler and proposed autonomy for Cuba. However, Hearst's *Journal* on February 9 published a letter written by the Spanish Ambassador in Washington. The letter was

insulting, describing McKinley as a "weak bidder for public admiration." McKinley was riled and war fever flared higher. On February 15, the battleship *Maine* exploded in the harbor at Havana, causing the loss of 260 lives. No one knows to this day what caused the disaster. However, influenced by the yellow press, the public blamed Spain.

4. McKinley feared that to continue to resist the war fever would cost the Republicans control of Congress in the fall elections. On April 11, practically ignoring the Spanish capitulation to all his demands, McKinley asked Congress for a declaration of war—and got it.

5. Sample answer: The Tenth Negro Cavalry played a crucial part in the taking of San Juan Hill by assisting the Rough Riders. They raked the Spanish with constant rifle fire, saving the Rough Riders from destruction.

6. An American fleet under the command of Admiral William Sampson and Commodore W.S. Schley destroyed or captured every ship in the Spanish fleet trying to leave Cuba on July 3, 1898. This proved to be the last straw for the Spanish in Cuba, and on July 15, the Spanish commander surrendered.

Section Review (text page 545)

1. Students' sentences will vary. Information about the names and terms can be found on the pages given in parentheses: Queen Liliuokalani (540–541), Open Door policy (542–543), Roosevelt Corollary (544), dollar diplomacy (545).

2. Gained in peace treaty with Spain: the Philippines, Guam, Puerto Rico; Gained at another time: Hawaii, Alaska.

3. While Roosevelt was governor of New York, he alienated Thomas C. Platt, the Republican boss of the state, by refusing to take orders and by attacking members of Platt's organization. In retaliation, Platt got Roosevelt the vice-presidential nomination, believing he was ending Roosevelt's political career. The vice presidency was considered a dead-end position in politics, a powerless post that was usually assigned to political hacks who could carry swing states.

4. In Asia, Roosevelt continued John Jay's Open Door policy toward China, thus maintaining the independence of China and keeping it open to the trade of all. In 1905, Roosevelt applied his theory of equilibrium to end the war between Japan and Russia in Manchuria. In Latin America, Roosevelt proclaimed what came to be called the "Roosevelt Corollary to the Monroe Doctrine," when several European nations threatened to invade the Dominican Republic to collect debts owed to their citizens. In order to protect the American states, Roosevelt said that the United States would, if necessary, exercise an "international police power" in the Western Hemisphere. Roosevelt conspired with Philippe Jean Bunau-Varilla to start a revolution in Panama, then a part of Colombia. Riots erupted in Panama and the province declared its independence from Colombia. The United States recognized the new republic of Panama, and the first foreign minister of the new republic, Bunau-Varilla, signed a treaty with the United States. The treaty guaranteed the United States' perpetual use of a ten-mile-wide "canal zone" across the isthmus. In 1904, Roosevelt sent United States Marines to the Dominican Republic to collect customs in order to pay off the country's foreign creditors.

Time Line Questions (text page 546)

1. 1867
2. opening of U.S. naval base at Pearl Harbor
3. 1901

Skills Strategy: Note-Taking (text page 546)

1. There were several reasons for the negative feelings of many Latin American people toward the United States government.
2. The card marked "The Philippines" would have to be eliminated because it does not deal with Latin America.
3. Details for supporting sentences in the paragraph
4. Cards for notes on Colombia and/or the Panama Canal
5. Students' note cards should contain information that can be included in the topic sentence and supporting sentences of a paragraph.

UNIT 6 TEST (text page 547)

Chapter Survey

1. Sample summary sentence(s): Chapter 20 begins with a definition-description of the changing frontier and "the West" that was always just beyond it. The chapter continues with an account of the Indian Wars and a survey of the pioneer farmers, miners, and cattle owners and cowboys who settled and developed the West. Pages containing information about terms: Indian Territory (488), "Buffalo Bill" Cody (491), Little Big Horn (494), General George Crook (492), Chisholm Trail (498), Homestead Act (501), Demonetization Act of 1873 (504–505).

2. Sample summary sentence(s): Chapter 21 discusses the phenomenal growth of American agriculture, the hard times many farmers had in spite of this growth, the formation and proposed reforms of the farmers' Populist party, and the rise of a new industrial South. Pages containing information about terms: bone and sinew of the Republic (508), ''hayseed'' (510), Mary Elizabeth Lease (514), Populist party (516–520), ''Pittsburgh of the South''(520), Spindletop (520), James Buchanan Duke (521).

3. Sample summary sentence(s): Chapter 22 opens with a presentation of the election of 1896 that marked a turning point in United States history. The chapter continues with an examination of the causes and outcome of a war between the United States and Mexico and a discussion of American imperialism. Pages containing information about terms: ''Cross of Gold'' (528), Frederick Jackson Turner (533), Tenth Negro Cavalry (536–537), Queen Liliuokalani (540–541).

Text Review

4. Student answers should reflect the understanding that, between 1865 and 1900, the frontier was the north-south line that divided settled areas from unsettled areas, and that this line of settlement was more or less constantly moving westward.

5. The Plains Indians realized that, if the whites settled on their lands, they would destroy the grazing grounds of the bison herds. Without the bison, the Plains Indians' way of life would be destroyed, too, for everything in their lives—economy, social structure, religion, diet, dress, housing—depended upon the buffalo. Student descriptions of the battle that shattered the last resistance of one group of Plains Indians may include the following facts: After their war with the whites, the Dakota Sioux were sent to the Pine Ridge Reservations in South Dakota. There, on Wounded Knee Creek, the Dakotas took avidly to the Ghost Dance religion. This made the soldiers who were guarding them uneasy. When the soldiers heard the Dakotas had guns in their camp, they became more nervous. In December 1890, a shoving incident erupted into a tragedy. The soldiers fired on the Dakotas with rifles and artillery, killing about 200 of the Indian people, about half of them women and children. Student comments on Wounded Knee will vary.

6. One type of person who invested in the cattle industry in the 1870s was the wheeling and dealing speculator, for example, Joseph G. McCoy. McCoy initiated the drives of longhorn cattle from the ranges in southern Texas, along the Chisholm Trail, to the railroad at Abilene, Kansas. From there, they were shipped to meatpacking plants in Chicago. McCoy made great profits from his wheeling and dealing. Other investors in the cattle industry came from the East and as far away as England. These people, who rarely sat on a horse, established ranches that were as comfortable as big-city private clubs. They, like McCoy, made huge profits on their investments. The people who actually took care of the cattle—trail crews made up of cowboys, trail bosses, segundos, cooks, and wranglers—had very different lives than those like McCoy and the wealthy ranch owners. The trail crew had the difficult and often dangerous task of driving 2,500–3,000 cattle from the ranges to railhead towns. After a long day, the crew could look forward to a dinner from the chuckwagon and a bed on the sod of the Great Plains. In return for their labor, they were paid a wage as low as $1 a day.

7. After 1886, the cattle industry was taken over from the speculators by methodical owners who kept cattle on large ranches rather than letting them roam free on the open range. The reorganization was made necessary by a destructive winter blizzard and summer drought in 1886 which killed many cowboys and decimated a large percentage of the cattle on the eastern and southern plains. The following year, another powerful blizzard destroyed more cattle.

8. American pioneers were encouraged to settle lands in the West by the Homestead Act of 1862 and President Harrison's proclamation of 1889 opening up the Oklahoma Territory (formerly reserved for Indian tribes) to settlement. Hardships faced by settlers of the Great Plains were typical: lack of trees for houses and fences, the scanty rainfall and the consequent water shortage, violent blizzards and tornadoes, and swarms of crop-devouring grasshoppers.

9. By 1873, because American silver mines seemed to be running out, the value of silver rose, and silver dollars ceased to circulate because they brought more than 100 cents if melted down and sold to jewelers, speculators, or foreign buyers. Recognizing this, Congress passed the Demonetization Act of 1873. This meant that the silver dollar was dropped from the coinage list and could no longer be used as money. Prior to the passage of this act, both gold and silver had been the basis for the value of paper currency. After the act was passed, gold became the sole basis of American paper money. No sooner was the Demonetization Act passed than new discoveries by Nevada miners flooded the market with silver. Because the

government was buying none of it, the price of silver plunged. Advocates of paper money, silver mine owners, and miners raised a great hue and cry and referred to the Demonetization Act as the "Crime of '73." A bill to remonetize silver was introduced in the House of Representatives. However, financial conservatives in the House forced the passage of a compromise bill—The Bland-Allison Act. The provisions of this 1878 law follow: The Secretary of the Treasury had to purchase $2-4 million in silver monthly at the market price. The silver purchased by the government would be minted into silver dollars, but this did not mean that silver was remonetized. The silver dollars, like paper dollars, were tokens, valuable only because they were backed up by gold stored in the vaults of banks and the federal treasury.

10. Students should use adjectives like *unrivaled* and *phenomenal* to characterize the advance of agriculture in the last three decades of the 1800s. Among reasons students may cite for this advance are the following: (1) new and improved farm machinery that enabled farmers to reap larger crops in less time than formerly—steel plows; disc harrows; machines that threshed wheat, bound the shocks, and shredded fodder for livestock; (2) the expansion of railroads into farming areas that made large-scale farming feasible because they could carry crops in quantity to eastern cities and to ports where the crops could be exported to foreign cities.

11. Among the effects of the agricultural depression of the 1890s were the following: the drop in prices for cotton, corn, and other crops; the loss of farmland and farm homes because of inability to make mortgage payments; the abandonment of farms and the increase of farm tenant families in western Kansas and Nebraska; the growing debt bondage and the common occurrence of pellagra, a vitamin-deficiency among southern tenant farmers most of whom were blacks. The economic law of supply and demand was the root cause of the agricultural depression. American agricultural production had expanded too quickly. Farmers were supplying more agricultural products than consumers were demanding and, therefore, agricultural prices dropped. However, the failure of the Reading Railroad and the resulting unemployment which caused people to spend less on food also contributed to touching off the depression.

12. American farmers were the founders of the Populist party. They founded the party because they believed that the control of the currency by bankers and control of government policy by bankers, railroaders, and industrialists were the ultimate causes for their problems. They intended to solve their problems by capturing control of the government through the Populist party. Reforms proposed by the party include the following: (1) direct election of United States Senators by the voters; (2) use of the secret ballot; (3) introduction of the initiative, the recall, and the referendum; (4) public ownership of such "natural" monopolies as railroads and the telegraph; (5) abolition of national banks; (6) establishment of a postal savings system; (7) introduction of a graduated income tax.

13. In speech after speech, Grady told his "funeral story" in which he pointed out that the South provided none of the trappings of the funeral except "the corpse and the hole in the ground." He was emphasizing the South's need to turn from its dependence on agriculture to the development of industry if it wanted to prosper and overcome its reputation as the nation's backwater. After Grady's death, his dream was realized by the emergence of thriving lumber, steel, oil, textile, and tobacco industries in the New South.

14. Prior to the latter years of the nineteenth century, American expansion had been for the most part confined to lands within the borders of the United States as they existed at that time. During the final years of the century, however, the United States began to look for new frontiers outside its own borders. The international push for colonies: Many European nations had established colonies in Africa and Asia, profiting economically, in national pride, and in international prestige. By 1897, the United States had become the most important industrial power in the world, and many Americans felt that their country should take their rightful place among the other powerful nations of the world. One way to do this was to establish its own colonies. Theories of racial supremacy: Americans like Henry Cabot Lodge and Theodore Roosevelt believed that Anglo-Saxons (the English and Americans) should take colonies because the Anglo-Saxon race was superior and was divinely commissioned to govern the people of inferior races in other parts of the world. Alfred Thayer Mahan: Mahan wanted the United States, like other great nations of the past and present, to build a powerful navy. Congress agreed and appropriated funds to expand and modernize the American navy. However, a modern navy of steamships needed refueling stations and bases at various places around the world—for example, Midway and Hawaii in the Pacific. Frederick Jackson Turner's frontier theory: In 1893, Turner theorized that the frontier was the basis for American democracy, social stability, and prosperity. However, the frontier had

officially closed in 1890, and many Americans felt the only way for the United States to avoid social upheaval and economic stagnation was to establish American colonies in other parts of the world.

15. The "yellow press" referred to newspapers like Hearst's New York *Journal* and Pulitzer's New York *World*. Instead of reporting news in a straightforward way, the yellow press featured sensational accounts of lurid murder and sex cases. Using the same kind of sensational approach, the Hearst and Pulitzer newspaper chains featured stories on Spanish atrocities against the rebels in Cuba. Sometimes, they reported simple incidents as horror stories, and when no real atrocities occurred, they invented some. Yellow press coverage of the explosion of the American battleship *Maine* in Havana harbor and the printing of a letter written by the Spanish ambassador which was insulting to President McKinley created a war fever which finally influenced McKinley to ask Congress to declare war on Spain.

16. Student answers should give the details about two of the following. The annexation of Hawaii: When Liliuokalani became queen of Hawaii in 1891, she made the theme of her reign "Hawaii for the Hawaiians" and took steps to lessen the political and economic power of white American planters in the island. With the help of the American ambassador, the planters convinced the United States government to send Marines to take control of Hawaii. Newly elected President Cleveland withdrew a Senate proposal to annex Hawaii, but the planters declared Hawaii a republic and waited until Cleveland left office. Then, under President McKinley, the islands were annexed in 1898. The Open Door Policy and the Boxer Rebellion: Acting in the spirit of McKinley's Open Door Policy, Theodore Roosevelt led the imperial powers to pledge that they would seize no more territory in China and leave the door to trade with China open to all of them. To test the international domination of China, the dowager empress encouraged a group known as the Boxers to rebel. The Boxers terrorized the murdered westerners and besieged 900 foreigners in the British legation in Peking. A combined force of American, British, French, German, Austrian, Italian, Japanese, and Russian troops marched on Peking, defeated the Boxers, and ensured the continuation of the Open Door Policy. The death of President McKinley: McKinley was visiting the Pan American Exposition in Buffalo on September 6, 1901. He was greeting a long line of guests when Leon Czolgosz shot him several times. Eight days after he was shot, President McKinley died.

Critical Thinking

17. Students should give the points of view of two of the following: President McKinley had no wish for the United States to acquire colonies; however, public opinion and political pressure overcame his wishes. Senator Henry Cabot Lodge favored imperialistic expansion because of his belief that Americans, as part of the Anglo-Saxon race, had a duty to govern inferior races. Alfred Thayer Mahan favored imperialistic expansion because he wanted fueling stops and bases for the ships of the United States Navy. Queen Liliuokalani opposed American imperial expansion in Hawaii. She wanted to keep Hawaii independent under her rule and believed that Hawaii should be for Hawaiians, not Americans. Emilio Aguinaldo was one of the Filipino guerrilla leaders who fought fiercely to prevent annexation of the Philippines by the United States.

18. Student summaries should include the following: the killing of bison to feed railroad construction workers; the wholesale slaughter of the bison herds to fulfill the demand for "buffalo robes"; the railroads' encouragement of the slaughter to protect its rails from damage and destruction by the herds; the shooting of bison by wealthy eastern and British hunters in order to get trophies for their mansions and clubs.

Skills Review

19. A primary source is an oral or written "eyewitness" account of an event given by a person who was closely involved in it. Speeches, diaries, and contemporary news stories are some primary sources. A secondary source is an interpretation of historical events by a person who did not witness the events and was not closely involved with them. History textbooks and magazine articles about historical events are examples of secondary sources.

20. The following standards can be used to evaluate the factuality of a news story: (1) The headline is factual; (2) the lead, or first paragraph, includes facts that answer *who*, *what*, *where*, *when*, *why*, and *how* questions and excludes any statement of opinion; (3) the body contains paragraphs with less important facts. In short, a news story is a straight report of the facts of a news event and never includes statements of opinion.

CHAPTER 23

Section Review (text page 556)

1. Students' sentences will vary. Information about the terms can be found on the pages given in parentheses: Triangle Shirtwaist factory (552), Gay Nineties (552), lyceum (555), Chautauqua (555).
2. Indians were stripped of tribal power and confined to bleak reservations without the benefits of citizenship. Black office holding in the South was eliminated by the rise of political movements based on white supremacy. The lynching of blacks became commonplace. Workers and bosses clashed in bloody strikes in Homestead, Pennsylvania; Pullman, Illinois; and Coeur d' Alene, Idaho. Unemployment reached such high levels that, in 1894, thousands of workers in Coxey's Army marched to Washington to demand that the government provide jobs for them.
3. Theodore Roosevelt was president from 1901 to 1909. He was so in tune with the forces of his time that he became the symbol of his age. The new middle class thought him a grand fellow, calling him "TR" and "Teddy" and naming the Teddy Bear after him. He was popular with blacks, even though he believed in the superiority of the "Angle-Saxon race," because he ignored segregationists and invited Booker T. Washington to the White House. Women suffragists, campaigning to win votes for women, also approved of him. Most college professors and intellectuals liked the President because he was a scholar and author with more than a dozen books to his credit.
4. Higher education remained largely the privilege of white males during the period. Women who were willing to put up with ridicule and discrimination could attend most of the midwestern and western state universities. In the East, they could study at separate women's colleges such as Barnard, Bryn Mawr, Radcliffe, Vassar, Wellesley, and Smith. These institutions offered courses as challenging as the best men's colleges. Secondary school students could attend the growing number of free junior and senior high schools. There were 6,000 such secondary schools in 1900, and 12,000 by 1915. Blacks could attend segregated institutions like Lincoln University, Fisk University, Howard University, and Tuskegee Institute, and the older colleges and universities, including Harvard and West Point, admitted a few blacks. Blacks who were willing to stand up to prejudice could even complete graduate training, as W. E. B. Du Bois did at Harvard. Graduate students, having completed four years of college, could study for advanced degrees in the professions (law, engineering, etc.) in the new graduate schools. Previously, these professions had been learned by working as an apprentice for a professional such as a lawyer or engineer.

Section Review (text page 561)

1. Students' sentences will vary. Information about the names can be found on the pages given in parentheses: Kitty Hawk (558), Jack Johnson (559), Edith Wharton (559), Cyrus Curtis (560).
2. Before the turn of the century, only the very wealthiest of people could even think of going on a vacation. At the start of the twentieth century, large numbers of less well-to-do Americans had the time and money to travel and live away from home for a few weeks each year. Tens of thousands of ordinary Americans each summer boarded trains to travel to the mountains or seaside where they could participate in the activities of a number of educational, religious, or health resorts.
3. Some praised bicycling as a "health-giving outdoor exercise." Others complained that bicycling created opportunities for young men and women to break away from the watchful eyes of their chaperones. Tennis, croquet, roller-skating, professional baseball, and boxing were other popular participant and spectator sports at the turn of the century.
4. Muckrakers such as Ida M. Tarbell, Lincoln Steffens, and Upton Sinclair wrote books and magazine articles exposing corruption and dishonesty in government and business. Tarbell, Steffens, and Sinclair were idealists who were convinced that, once wrongdoing was made known to middle-class Americans, they would bring about reforms.

Section Review (text page 563)

1. Students' sentences will vary. Information about the names and terms can be found on the pages given in parentheses: Louis Brandeis (561), *The Promise of American Life* (562), Ray Stannard Baker (562), Jane Addams (562).
2. Progressives were middle-class doctors, lawyers, teachers, journalists, social workers, and middle-class business people and their families. They believed themselves to be truer to the American ideals of democracy than either the great capitalists or the very poor working people. Progressives felt themselves—and the best American ideals of democracy and liberty—threatened by big business

from above and by a dangerous mob of poor workers and immigrants from below.

3. Both the Progressives and the Populists wanted social and political reform. However, the Progressives were urban people, while the majority of Populists came from rural areas.

4. Almost all Progressives looked to government to solve the nation's problems. They believed that, once they had captured the powers of the state, they could use those powers to correct what was wrong in America. Progressives disagreed about labor unions, the issue of child labor, and racial equality.

5. Minorities were represented among the leading progressives. For example, Louis Brandeis, a Jew, crusaded against corrupt railroad practices. W. E. B. DuBois and other prominent blacks joined with Jane Addams to organize the National Association for the Advancement of Colored People (NAACP). Catholic political leaders Alfred E. Smith and Robert Wagner were other well-known Progressives.

6. Wilson would not compromise with political opponents, even when his stubbornness meant complete defeat rather than partial victory.

Section Review (text page 565)

1. Students' sentences will vary. Information about the names and terms can be found on the pages given in parentheses: city manager (564), William S. U'ren (564), Robert M. La Follette (564), Wisconsin Idea (564–565).

2. First, the good government reformers were effective administrators who stayed in power and made their reforms permanent. Second, they went beyond mere honesty, making basic and enduring structural changes in the way cities, and eventually the nation, were operated.

3. In Staunton, Virginia, Progressives in the city council abolished the office of mayor. They thought that vesting a mayor with so much power made it easier for special interests to corrupt government. In his place, the city council hired a city manager—a professionally trained expert—who administered the day-to-day workings of the city according to policies adopted by the elected city council. The Oregon System was developed by Governor U'ren of Oregon. The system was designed to prevent special interest groups from pressuring lawmakers to depart from the people's best interest. U'ren persuaded the legislature to adopt the initiative, the recall, and the referendum. The initiative allowed voters to bypass irresponsible elected legislators with their own proposals for laws; when a sufficient number of voters' signatures were collected for

them on petitions, these laws could be put on the ballot for voter approval or disapproval. An election in which such issues were decided was called a referendum. The recall worked in a similar way. Voters displeased by an elected official could collect voters' signatures petitioning for the official's recall from office. The official under recall would have to resign or submit to an election, even if his or her term had not expired.

4. Jones, an honest businessman before he became mayor, rooted graft out of Toledo's government and proved to be a skillful and successful city administrator.

5. Both Socialists and Progressives appealed to voters with essentially the same program of reforms. However, progressives staunchly defended the free enterprise system, whereas the Socialist party worked to overthrow capitalism peacefully by winning the support of the voters.

Time Line Questions (text page 566)

1. Coxey's march on Washington—1894
2. 5 years
3. Jack Johnson wins heavyweight championship, founding of NAACP

Skills Strategy: Library Sources (text pages 566–567)

592.6W—Pure Science
769.35A—Fine Arts
911.3P—Travel
485.16L—Language
172.47T—Philosophy
652.24S—Applied Science
816.7C—Literature
901.38E—History
938.6R—History
386.9D—Social Sciences

Chapter Test (text page 567)

Text Review

1. The years of the Progressive Era were not a good time for Indians, blacks, or most workers. The Indian tribes were broken up after the Wounded Knee Massacre of 1890, and the people were sent to government reservations, often located on the worst lands. They were not given American citizenship, and their own cultures began to decay. In addition, they were faced with increasing poverty. Blacks in the South lost their last political leaders, and their lives were subjected to the whims of white supremacist politicians. Lynchings of blacks

became commonplace. Workers' strikes in various parts of the country resulted in bloody suppressions. Unemployment reached unusually high levels, and workers' protests demanding jobs were ignored or put down violently.

2. To many, Theodore Roosevelt symbolized the Progressive Era. He was in tune with the forces of his times; always moving about the country, mixing with crowds and joyfully posing for photographers. He became the first president to travel outside the country's borders when he visited the site of the Panama Canal. He typified the determination of the rising middle class to enjoy life. Everything he did was done with fanfare. "TR" or "Teddy" seemed to have something for everyone. Blacks liked him because he defied segregationists and invited Booker T. Washington to the White House. Women suffragists approved of him. As a scholar and prolific writer, he appealed to most college professors and intellectuals. He backed many of the reforms that middle-class people of the era were demanding.

3. Among the facts students may include in their responses are the following: the increase in free public secondary schools between 1860 and 1900; the growing number of college graduates during the same period; the founding and endowment of many private universities by millionaires; the growth of educational opportunities for women in midwestern or western state universities, and the founding of separate women's colleges in the East; the institution of the elective system in many colleges and graduate schools, the opening of separate colleges for blacks and Catholics; the founding of women's medical colleges.

4. The lyceum was a lecture program in which distinguished ministers, statesmen, and educators traveled to hundreds of small American cities and towns to give lectures to eager citizens who were otherwise isolated from culture. The Chautauqua was a resort in upstate New York where middle-class people could combine vacationing with varied programs of learning and entertainment—lectures by experts, slide shows on distant lands, and many kinds of popular exhibitions.

5. Among the leisure activities available to Americans of the 1890s and early 1910s were vacations at health resorts' "curative" hot mineral springs and mud baths; weekend and holiday visits to city-built public parks and amusement parks built by trolley companies at the ends of their lines; bicycling, roller-skating, croquet playing, or tennis; watching professional baseball games and boxing matches; reading new books and magazines.

6. Books published around the turn of the century include Mark Twain's *The Adventures of Tom Sawyer* and *The Adventures of Huckleberry Finn;* Edith Wharton's *Ethan Frome* and *The Age of Innocence;* Upton Sinclair's *The Jungle,* Herbert Croly's *The Promise of American Life;* Ray Stannard Baker's *Following the Color Line;* and Lincoln Steffens's *The Shame of the Cities.* Magazines published at the time included *Atlantic Monthly, Harper's, Forum, The Arena, Ladies Home Journal, Saturday Evening Post, McClure's, Munsey's,* and *Cosmopolitan.* Muckracking magazines featured exposés—articles that revealed corruption and dishonesty in business and government.

7. Student profiles of the Progressives should give the following information about the following points: "in-between" status—The Progressives felt threatened by both big business and the poor worker and immigrant groups; relationship to cities—Progressivism was a movement made up of urban residents; self-righteous tendencies—Progressives were not broadminded and tended to evaluate actions as absolute rights or wrongs; role of government in reform—Almost all progressives looked to the government to find solutions to what they found wrong with America; issues on which they differed—Progressives individually had varying views on labor unions, child labor laws, and the status of blacks in American society.

8. City government reforms of the Progressives included Samuel M. Jones's elimination of graft from Toledo; Thomas L. Johnson's cleanup of Cleveland's government, reform of juvenile courts, elimination of bribery by city public utilities companies, Staunton's introduction of the city manager/council form of government; Hiram Johnson's prosecution of corrupt city politicians in San Francisco. State and national government reforms by Progressives included the initiative, the recall, and the referendum of Governor William S. U'ren's Oregon System; primary elections and the popular election of United States senators, also introduced by U'ren; Governor Robert La Follette's Wisconsin Idea, which enlisted state experts to counter experts employed by special interest groups; La Follette's honest use of the methods of political machines; Charles Evans Hughes's investigations of public utilities and insurance companies; Idaho Senator William F. Borah's work with the Progressives in the Senate.

Critical Thinking

9. The Socialists sought the same kinds of reforms as the Progressives; however, they differed from the Progressives in actively seeking to peacefully

overthrow capitalism. Since reforms advocated by the Socialists were almost identical to those advocated by Progressives, and because most voters tended to see Socialists as wild-eyed radicals, the Socialist party made little headway in American national politics.

10. Boss Tweed and others like him used political machines in a corrupt way, usually to enrich themselves and their cronies. La Follette used the same political machinery honestly to elect his party to office and to provide good government to the people.

Writing a Paragraph

Students' paragraphs should begin or end with an appropriate topic sentence. Details in the supporting sentences may be gathered from the chapter, from an encyclopedia, or from another appropriate reference. If you wish, lead a follow-up discussion based on the reforms students refer to in their paragraphs, especially any that have influenced the local or state government.

CHAPTER 24

Section Review (text page 572)

1. Students' sentences will vary. Information about the names and terms can be found on the pages given in parentheses: Northern Securities Company (570), arbiters (571), United Mine Workers (571), John Mitchell (571).

2. It was because the political boss of New York State, Tom Platt, could not control Roosevelt as governor that in 1900, he foisted him off on the Republican party as its vice-presidential nominee. However, McKinley's death brought Roosevelt the presidency. To head off Mark Hanna's plan to deny him the Republican nomination for the presidency in 1908, Roosevelt tried to win the support of the conservative Republicans. He kept most of President McKinley's cabinet, and by allowing them more control over their departments, won them and their followers over to his side.

3. Trust buster: Roosevelt initiated 44 antitrust suits and won 25. However, his successor, William Howard Taft, filed 90 suits in fewer years as president. Once Roosevelt was confident that big business acknowledged the superiority of government, he resumed the quiet ironing out of problems with big business leaders that had characterized McKinley's administration. In fact, in 1907, when J. P. Morgan sent U. S. Steel president Elbert H. Gary to ask

permission to take over a major regional competitor, Roosevelt agreed. The radical's enemy: Roosevelt was hostile toward union leaders who advocated socialism. For example, in 1906, while the president and secretary-treasurer of the radical Western Federation of Miners were on trial for conspiracy to murder the former governor of Idaho, Roosevelt publicly called them "undesirable citizens." Unlike his pro-miner actions in the coal strike of 1902, Roosevelt sent troops into Goldfield, Nevada, when radical unionists nearly took over the town, and, despite the fact that there was little violence, left troops at the disposal of Goldfield mine owners, even after he suspected his action was unneccessary.

4. Roosevelt was the Republican candidate. Alton B. Parker was the candidate of the Democratic party. A quiet and distinguished man, Parker could not compete with the energetic and bombastic president during the campaign. Roosevelt won the Progressive vote as well as the vote of Conservative Republicans, tallying up 57.4 percent of the popular vote and an electoral college victory of 336 to Parker's 140.

Section Review (text page 576)

1. Students' sentences will vary. Information about the names and terms can be found on the pages given in parentheses: adulterants (573), John Muir (575), Gifford Pinchot (575), forest reserves (575).

2. At the beginning of his second term, Roosevelt, along with many Progressives, believed that if he could reform the worst business practices of nineteenth century capitalists, the impact of the Socialist party's call for reforms would be negated. Students' explanations of why Roosevelt's belief was valid or invalid should be based upon information given in the text. For example, students who think the belief valid may follow a line of reasoning such as this: Some capitalists conducted illegal business practices. Americans were dissatisfied with these practices. Socialists were offering solutions. Socialists had made small gains in the previous election, but they had risen to power in Europe from small beginings in a similar situation. Roosevelt knew all of this.

3. Newlands Reclamation Act: unrestricted exploitation of land; Hepburn Act: abuses and illegal practices of railroads; Pure Food and Drug Acts: unsanitary and sometimes dangerous practice of commercial food processors, unregulated use of narcotics, and high percentages of alcohol in patient medicines; Elkins Act: rebates to shippers that railroads used to eliminate their competition.

4. Roosevelt technically could have run again, since he had been elected president only once. However, he agreed with the precedent set by Washington, Jefferson, and Jackson that limited presidents to two terms, and announced during the 1904 campaign that he would not again be a candidate for president or accept the nomination. The candidates were William Howard Taft (Republican), William Jennings Bryan (Democrat), and Eugene V. Debs (Socialist). William Howard Taft, Roosevelt's hand-picked successor, won.

Section Review (text page 580)

1. Students' sentences will vary. Information about the terms can be found on the pages given in parentheses: Mann-Elkins Act (577), Sixteenth Amendment (578), Insurgents (579), New Nationalism (579).
2. Students who choose to prove the statement true will use some or all of the following facts: Taft sponsored twice as many antitrust suits as Roosevelt. Under Taft, the Mann-Elkins Act gave the ICC authority to regulate telephone, telegraph, cable, and radio companies. The Taft administration cut the work day of companies with government contracts to no more than eight hours. Taft did not use fanfare to announce his progressive accomplishments, as Roosevelt had. Taft's nineteenth-century belief was that the president's job was not to seek publicity or take the initiative of government, but to act as chief administrator and let Congress take the initiative. This belief as well as his political blunders caused the Progressives in his own party to unfairly label him reactionary. Students who choose to disprove the statment should cite appropriate information from the text.
3. Payne-Aldrich Tariff: Taft signed and praised the tariff bill instead of vetoing it even though it contained 800 pro-business amendments. "Uncle Joe" Cannon's methods as Speaker of the House: Taft supported Cannon, who often used his powers to support business and to thwart Progressive house members. For example, he appointed Progressives mostly to unimportant committees, and during debate, he often refused to recognize Progressives. Republican Progressives, calling themselves Insurgents, joined with House Democrats to curtail Cannon's power, although Taft supported him. In retaliation, Taft refused to let the Insurgents use funds that the Republicans had raised in the election of 1910. The Democrats then gained control of the House for the first time in 16 years. Interior Secretary Ballinger's decisions on conservation: Ballinger opened several hundred hydroelectric sites to private developers, claiming they had been wrongly reserved. Pinchot of the Forestry Service protested loudly and Taft overruled Ballinger. Then Ballinger opened government forest and coal reserved in Alaska for private exploitation. Pinchot protested again to Taft, but this time Taft sided with Ballinger. Taft fired Pichot when he supported Louis Glavis, who had attacked Ballinger in a magazine article. Pinchot went immediately to Europe to see Theodore Roosevelt.
4. Roosevelt returning to New York from Europe contacted many old supporters who added their criticism to Pinchot's. In September, 1910, at Ossawatomie, Kansas, he proclaimed a progressive program for the nation, called the New Nationalism. Among the things called for in the new progressive program were women's suffrage; restriction of child labor; strict limitations on the courts to issue injunctions against labor unions; a national retirement insurance plan; the establishment of a commission to set tariff rates "scientifically"; support for the initiative, recall, and referendum; and a national primary to replace political conventions in nominating presidental candidates. Roosevelt denied his presidential ambition to La Follette, who planned to challenge Taft. However, while delivering a speech, La Follette collapsed from exhaustion, allowing Roosevelt the opportunity to declare his own candidacy, which caused Progressives to desert La Follette. Roosevelt won primaries in states that held them, but Taft controlled the Republican party machinery. Federal office holders owed their jobs to him, and in nonprimary states they picked convention delegates. When Roosevelt realized he could not win the nomination of the Republican party, he and the Progressive Republicans walked out of the Republican convention and held one of their own. The Progressives nominated Roosevelt as candidate of the Bull Moose Party.

Section Review (text page 583)

1. Students' sentences will vary. Information about the names and terms can be found on the pages given in parentheses: Keating-Owne Act (583), Colonel Edward M. House (581), Underwood Tariff (581), Smith-Lever Act (583).
2. Wilson was able to sweep the electoral college in 1912 because of the split of Republican votes between Roosevelt and Taft and an unusually high vote for Socialist candidate Eugene Debs.
3. Wilson's New Freedom program emphasized (1) states rights, (2) breakup rather than regulation of trusts, and (3) restoration of competition to American economic life, counter to Roosevelt's demand

that the economy be regulated and managed as "a partnership between the government and the trust." Wilson converted to a program like Roosevelt's New Nationalism because (1) The election of 1916 was approaching, and Wilson knew that his only chance for reelection was to convince the Progressive voters that he was more likely to continue reform than anyone the reunited Republicans named to oppose him, and (2) his interest in domestic affairs was declining, and more and more of his attention was drawn to the war in Europe where both sides were trying to get American support.

4. The Sixteenth Amendment made the graduated income tax constitutional. Congress levied taxes that hit the wealthy harder than it hit lower- and middle-income groups. The Federal Reserve System was a compromise between conservatives and progressives. The system established 12 district banks and a semi-public central bank. The system was privately owned; however, the president appointed the highest officials. The Federal Reserve banks dealt only with other banks. By increasing or decreasing the money supply, the Federal Reserve maintained some control over the economy. The Clayton Antitrust Act carefully defined the unfair business practices for which a corporation could be punished: (1) interlocking directorates were illegal, and (2) officers of corporations were personally responsible for violations of the law carried out by their companies. The FTC (Federal Trade Commission) was designed to control corporations rather than break them up. The five members of the commission appointed by the president were empowered to demand annual reports from major corporations, to investigate unfair business practices, and to order corporations to stop unfair business practices.

Time Line Questions (text page 586)

1. two terms
2. 1892, 1902
3. Northern Securities case—1902; Elkins Act—1903; Payne-Aldrich Tariff—1909

Skills Strategy: Card Catalog (text page 586–587)

Students' cards should follow the form of those in the second exhibit and should include the information shown on the book in the first exhibit. Be sure each card gives the location of the publisher, the date of publication, and the number of pages. Students may choose to omit the illustration note.

Chapter Test (text page 587)

Text Review

1. Among the reasons why Theodore Roosevelt allied himself with the Progressives are the following: despite his personal distaste for reformers, he needed the support of the many middle-class voters who were Progressives to remain a viable politician; as a member of the wealthy aristocratic class that felt that industrialists and financiers had rudely pushed them aside, Roosevelt found it easy to oppose the "malefactors" of great wealth; in the early twentieth century, Progressivism was a vital force, and this appealed to Roosevelt.

2. In the election of 1904, in which Roosevelt won the presidency, the Socialists received four times the number of votes they had received in the 1900 election. European Socialists had begun their rise to power with just such small gains. Realizing this soon after he began his second term, Roosevelt introduced several reform bills aimed at cutting the Socialists' appeal by correcting the worst business practices of the time.

3. Harnessing the railroads: The Elkins Act forbade shippers to accept rebates from railroads, adding power to the Interstate Commerce Act, which forbade the railroads to offer rebates to shippers. Thus, the ICC was able to prosecute both shippers and railroads. The Hepburn Act curtailed the railroads' practice of giving free passes to politicians and their families, authorized the ICC to set maximum rates that the railroads could charge, and made it more difficult for railroad bookkeepers to falsify records by requiring all railroads to use the same accounting methods. An additional law held the railroads liable for injuries employees suffered while working.

   Curbing destructive exploitation of natural resources: Roosevelt helped John Muir found the Sierra Club. Congress created forest reserves in 1891. Roosevelt added almost 125 million acres of protected forest land to the 46 million set aside by the two previous presidents; he made Gifford Pinchot Chief Forester; and he transferred authority over the national forests from the Interior Department to the Agriculture Department. He also refused to allow commercial exploitation of large mineral deposits, oil fields, and potential sites for dams that could be used for irrigation and hydroelectricity production. The Newlands Reclamation Act allowed money obtained from public land sales to be used to develop irrigation projects and to restore land damaged by past exploitation.

4. Roosevelt decided not to run for a third term, but

he picked William Howard Taft as his successor, assuming that Taft would carry on Roosevelt's progressive policies. When he entered office, Taft surprised Roosevelt. Because of his style more than his political beliefs, Taft was unfairly condemned as a reactionary and a tool of big business. Not only did he sign the Payne-Aldrich Tariff (which Progressives opposed because of over 800 pro-business amendments attached to it), but he publicly praised it as the best tariff law in the nation's history. In a battle for control of the House of Representatives, Taft gave his support to Speaker Joseph Cannon, a dictatorial, pro-business opponent of House Progressives. Finally, he opened government forest reserves and coal deposits in Alaska to private exploitation over the protests of Gifford Pinchot, whom Taft fired shortly afterwards.

5. Students should list the following causes for the formation of the Bull Moose party: Roosevelt sided with Pinchot and other Progressives against Taft; he proclaimed the New Nationalism, a progressive program for America, at Osawatomie, Kansas; he publicly gave his support to many traditional Progressive reform proposals and added a proposal that would allow a referendum on court decisions; he called for a national primary to replace conventions in nominating presidential candidates; he withheld his support from La Follette, who had decided to run against Taft; he declared his candidacy during a short illness of La Follette; when it became clear that Taft's control of Republican party machinery withheld the nomination from Roosevelt, he and his Progressive supporters walked out of the convention and held one of their own. Roosevelt's comment that he was "as fit as a Bull Moose" gave the Progressive party its nickname.

6. In 1912, Wilson espoused a New Freedom program that differed in many particulars from Roosevelt's progressive ideas. By 1916, Wilson had converted to a program best described as the Republican Progressive program, incorporating most of the 1912 Progressive party platform. Wilson had two important reasons for this change. First, Progressive party members showed signs of returning to the Republican party, which made it necessary to convince Progressive voters that Wilson would continue Progressive reforms. Second, Wilson's attention was being directed away from domestic issues and drawn more and more toward the war in Europe, where the fighting threatened to involve the United States.

7. Debs was a dramatic and electrifying speaker, and he drew large audiences because Americans were fond of him. They also liked the shows he put on, for example, the "Red Special," a train in which Debs campaigned throughout the nation. However, Americans voted for Taft or Bryant in 1908 because Roosevelt had undercut the appeal of the Socialists by reforming the worst practices of big business.

8. The Clayton Act held officers of corporations personally responsible for crimes their organizations committed, in an attempt to curb violations. The FTC (Federal Trade Commission) was meant to control corporations in order to stop unfair business practices. The Adamson Act required railroads involved in interstate commerce to institute the eight-hour day without cutting workers' wages. The Keating-Owens Act was also reformist, strictly regulating most child employment.

Critical Thinking

9. Roosevelt decided not to serve a third term because he did not want to break the tradition set by Washington, Jefferson, and Jackson. Actually, he could have run again, because he had first become president when McKinley was assassinated, which meant that he had been elected only once. Considering his personality, Roosevelt may have made his decision public in the hope that he would be urged to change his mind and run.

10. Roosevelt knew that because of his great popularity with voters, he would be the most likely winner of a national presidential primary.

Writing a Paragraph

Students should choose an appropriate "doing" to write about. Use of the first person, accuracy of detail, and an appropriate tone are criteria for evaluating students' paragraphs.

CHAPTER 25

Section Review (text page 592)

1. Students' sentences will vary. Information about the names and terms can be found on the pages given in parentheses: "cooling off" treaties (590), Henry T. Mayo (590), ABC powers (591), John J. Pershing (591–592).

2. Wilson's moral principles were very strict. He believed it was wrong to bully smaller nations with "gunboat diplomacy." Wilson was also suspicious of big business. He disapproved of "dollar diplomacy" because he did not believe that the blood of the American armed forces should be spilled to protect

the interests of wealthy bankers in foreign countries. However, Wilson himself used both "gunboat diplomacy" and "dollar diplomacy." He used "gunboat diplomacy" when he ordered marines into the Dominican Republic. Wilson used both "dollar diplomacy" and "gunboat diplomacy" when he involved the navy and army in Mexican internal affairs.

3. Porfirio Diaz, the pro-American dictator of Mexico, was overthrown by Francisco Madero in a revolution in 1911. Shortly after winning power, Madero was overthrown, murdered, and replaced by Victoriano Huerta. Wilson was opposed to Huerta because he believed Huerta's regime was undemocratic and immoral. General Venustiano Carranza rebelled against Huerta; Wilson decided to help Carranza overthrow Huerta. Carranza defeated Huerta and assumed power. Pancho Villa rebelled and tried to provoke the United States into intervening in Mexican affairs again, so he could overthrow Carranza.

4. Wilson used the ships of the American fleet to blockade Mexican ports so that Huerta would not receive arms from Europe. Wilson used the Tampico incident as an excuse to use the marines to occupy Vera Cruz, thus preventing the landing of a German ship carrying arms to Huerta. Pancho Villa successfully provoked Wilson by attacking and killing Americans. Wilson ordered General Pershing and 6,000 troops to go into Mexico to capture Villa.

Section Review (text page 596)

1. Students' sentences will vary. Information about the names and terms can be found on the pages given in parentheses: Kaiser Wilhelm II (593), Battle of the Somme (593), *Lusitania* (596), Sussex Pledge (596.)

2. Students' answers should include (1) the Austrian ultimatum to Serbia, which Gemany and Austria knew Serbia would not accept; (2) Serbia's appeal to Russia; (3) Russia's massing troops on the border of Austria—Hungary; (4) Germany's declaration of war on Russia and France; (5) England's involvement in the war as a member of the Triple Entente.

3. According to the Schlieffen Plan, Germany would give up land to Russia in the east in order to first concentrate on achieving victory in the west. German forces would sweep through Belgium in six days, preventing Britain from landing an army by occupying channel ports, knock France out of the war by capturing Paris, and only then deal with Russia in the east. The German armies were slowed down by heroic Belgian resistance. It took 18 days for the Germans to get through Belgium. Thus, Britain had time to land a large army to help France. German commanders lost their nerve, changed tactics, and sent crack troops from the western front to fight Russia in the east. The loss of these troops weakened the Germans' western thrust. The British and French were able to stop the Germans at the outskirts of Paris, and the war bogged down into a deadlock.

4. Among the new weapons of World War I were the following: machine guns, tanks, poison gas, and submarines. The German use of submarine warfare helped to bring the United States into World War I. The Germans had declared the waters surrounding Britain a war zone. All enemy ships within the war zone were subject to submarine attack, and Germany would not guarantee the safety of neutrals. Wilson informed the Germans that he intended to enforce American freedom of the seas and would hold Germany to strict accountability if American lives were lost. In May 1915, a German submarine sank the British liner *Lusitania* without warning. Among the 1,200 passengers that drowned were 128 Americans. The United States was outraged. Wilson sent another note to Germany that seemed like a declaration of war, and Germany stopped sinking passenger vessels. Then the Allies announced they were arming all merchant ships. Germany declared that all Allied ships were subject to submarine attack. In March 1916, a submarine sank the *Sussex*, a British channel steamer. An American was among those drowned. Wilson threatened to break off diplomatic relations if the unrestricted warfare did not immediately stop.

Section Review (text page 603)

1. Students' sentences will vary. Information about the names and terms can be found on the pages given in parentheses: Charles Evans Hughes (598), "bridge of ships" (599–600), Château-Thierry (603), November 11, 1918 (603).

2. Americans were not impartial. Most Americans, whose ancestors were English, sympathized with England. About eight million Americans of German or Austro-Hungarian ancestry sympathized with Germany and Austria-Hungary but did not want the United States to intervene on the side of the Triple Alliance. Many of the 4.5 million Irish-Americans favored Germany because they hated the British. However, as the war dragged on, there was a shift in feeling. More and more Americans came to prefer the British and French. British propagandists were extremely successful in bringing about this shift in feeling.

3. Wilson asked that belligerents on both sides declare an armistice and forge a "peace among equals" in which national self-determination and absolute freedom of the seas would be recognized by all. Wilson also proposed the formation of some kind of international organization to prevent future wars. However, three German actions brought the United States into the war: (1) Germany resumed unrestricted submarine warfare, threatening to sink all ships in the war zone; (2) The German foreign minister promised Mexico its "lost provinces" of Arizona and New Mexico if it would declare war on the United States; (3) Germany sank three American ships.

4. A possible answer is that Germany probably would have conquered Europe. It might have been able to starve England out of the war. A quarter of the British fleet had been sunk by submarines. At one point, Britain had only enough food to feed its population for three weeks. When Russia and Rumania left the war, Germany would no longer have to fight on the eastern front. The entire German army could have been used to fight and win on the western front.

Section Review (text page 607)

1. Students' sentences will vary. Information about the terms can be found on the pages given in parentheses: "victory gardens" (604), Nineteenth Amendment (606), CPI (606), ACLU (607).

2. The Shipping Board, the United States Railway Administration, the War Industries Board, and the Food Administration helped organize the American economy during World War I. Instead of rationing food, Hoover urged Americans to conserve food voluntarily. Americans observed wheatless Mondays, meatless Tuesdays, and porkless Thursdays. By giving up one commodity on different days of the week, Americans felt they were involved with the fighting machine. Hoover also encouraged people to grow "victory gardens" in their backyards so commercially grown foods could be channeled to the army and the European allies.

3. In return for Wilson's concessions to organized labor and the recognition that labor leaders were partners in running the country, most AFL unions pledged not to strike during wartime. The IWW opposed, but did not work actively against, the war. Samuel Gompers, the head of the AFL, was appointed by Wilson to sit on the War Industries Board. William Wilson, an AFL official, became Secretary of Labor. The government moved rigorously against the IWW, which it regarded as radical. Union halls were raided from coast to coast. More

than 100 IWW officials were jailed for espionage and sedition. The IWW was destroyed.

4. Immediate: Women's contributions in the armed services, in industry, and in patriotic organizations helped to bring victory. Eventual: Men's resistance to women's suffrage collapsed because of the part women played in helping to win the war. Less than a year after the war, the Nineteenth Amendment recognized women's right to vote.

Section Review (text page 609)

1. Students' sentences will vary. Information about the terms can be found on the pages given in parentheses: Article 10 (609), irreconcilables (609), reservationists (609), isolationism (609).

2. Clemenceau, Lloyd-George, and other victorious European leaders wanted Germany to pay their nation's huge reparations in money and goods to replace their war losses. They also wanted Germany to acknowledge complete blame for the war. These demands violated Wilson's principle against revenge on the defeated nations. Allied leaders agreed to Wilson's principle of self-determination of nations only when the defeated powers had to give up territory. Thus, for example, Poland was created out of territory formerly possessed by Germany and Russia; Czechoslovakia was created out of Austria; Austrian territory was given to Serbia, which became Yugoslavia. Wilson's ideas were compromised when national self-determination meant taking away territory from the victors.

3. Personal: Henry Cabot Lodge detested President Wilson. Political: As a Republican leader, Lodge wanted to defeat the Democrat Wilson politically. Patriotic: Lodge thought that the covenant of the League of Nations limited American freedom of action. Lodge and other senators most distrusted Section 10 of the covenant, which seemed to say that all members of the League, including the United States, must protect the territory of any League member, even if it meant going to war.

4. Wilson refused to accept Senate changes in the League covenant. As the time grew near for the Senate to vote on the peace treaty and the League, Wilson went on a speaking tour to rally public support of the League. Wilson seemed to be succeeding when he had a stroke or the beginning of a nervous breakdown. If Wilson had agreed to the Republican reservationists' modifications of section 10, the League would have been ratified. In March 1920, half of the Democrats wanted to join with the Republican reservationists in support of a modified covenant. Wilson, however, refused to compromise and the covenant was finally rejected.

Time Line Questions (text page 610)

1. 3 years, 1914–1917
2. 1920 to the present
3. 1917
4. Marines land on Dominican Republic; Pershing pursues Villa.

Skills Strategy: Thematic Maps (text page 610)

1. European military casualties during World War I
2. To represent the approximate number of casualties suffered by various European countries
3. *Pink*, smallest number of casualties; *orange*, greatest number of casualties
4. France, Austria-Hungary, Germany, Russia

UNIT 7 TEST (text page 611)

Chapter Survey

1. Sample summary sentence(s): Chapter 23 discusses various aspects of the United States at the turn of the century: the leadership of Theodore Roosevelt, the growing opportunities for education, the leisure activities of the time, the influence of muckraking writers, the rise of the Progressive reformers, and the lasting changes in government made by the Progressives. Pages containing information about names and terms: Triangle Shirtwaist fire (552), Kitty Hawk (558), Red Stockings (559), Jane Addams (562), Robert M. La Follette (564).

2. Sample summary sentence(s): Chapter 24 opens with a survey of the two terms of popular reformer President Theodore Roosevelt. The chapter continues with an explanation of how President Taft's actions provoked the formation of the Bull Moose party with Roosevelt as its presidential candidate, and concludes by tracing President Wilson's move away from his idealistic New Freedom program to a program more in line with Progressive demands. Pages containing information about names and terms: United Mine Workers (571), "trust buster" (571), John Muir (575), Insurgents (579), "Red Special" (576), New Freedom program (581).

3. Sample summary sentence(s): Chapter 25 examines President Woodrow Wilson's eight years in office: his dealings with Latin American nations, including an undeclared war with Mexico; his unsuccessful attempts to keep the United States out of World War I; his leadership during the war; and his failure to bring the United States into the League of Nations after the war. Pages containing information about terms: Pancho Villa (591–592), Franz Ferdinand (593), Kaiser Wilhelm II (593), Sussex Pledge (596), November 11, 1918 (603), Nineteenth Amendment (606).

Text Review

4. Information given on pages 552–554, 568, and 570–576 will suggest ideas for student sketches. Sketches should include these points: the Progressive Era was a time of enjoyment of life and Roosevelt was a person who enjoyed every aspect of living; Roosevelt's desire to be in the thick of things was suited perfectly to the reforming spirit of the Progressives; Roosevelt's activities as president were, for the most part, completely in line with the general aims of the Progressives.

5. Student answers should include references to the following: the admission of some blacks to older universities and colleges, including West Point and Harvard; the increase in the number of black institutions of higher learning—Lincoln University in Pennsylvania, Fisk University in Nashville, Howard University in Washington, D.C., Tuskegee Institute in Alabama; the founding of universities for Catholics—Notre Dame in Indiana, Boston College and Holy Cross in Massachusetts. Students who choose to include women should mention the following: admission of women to some programs of western and midwestern universities; the founding of women's institutions in the East—Barnard, Bryn Mawr, Radcliffe, Smith, Vassar, Wellesley; the establishment of medical colleges for women in New York City and in Pennsylvania.

6. *Shame of the Cities,* a series of articles, is an example of a kind of writing called muckraking. This kind of writing was found in magazines published in the early twentieth century. The purpose of such writing was twofold: to expose corruption and dishonesty in business and government, and thereby to motivate middle-class Americans to take actions to eliminate the corruption and dishonesty.

7. Four characteristics common to the Progressives were: (1) their middle-class status in between the industrial and financial elite and the laborers and farmers, (2) their urban origins, (3) their self-righteousness, (4) their belief that only government had the power to fight corruption in American institutions. Progressives differed on these issues: labor unions, child labor laws, and black equality.

8. City managers: Progressives in Staunton, Virginia, abolished the office of mayor and replaced the

mayor with a city manager, a professionally trained expert hired by the city council. The city manager would handle the day-to-day administrative tasks of city government, following policies adopted by the council. Progressives believed that giving a mayor great power often resulted in corruption by special interests, and that not having to face election, a city manager would be free of the influence of special interest groups. The initiative allowed voters to bypass elected legislators with their own proposals for laws. A sufficient number of voters' signatures on a petititon could put a law on the ballot for voters' approval or disapproval. The recall was similar. People dissatisfied with an elected official could collect voters' signatures petitioning for that official's recall from office. The official would have to resign or submit to an election, even if his or her term had not expired. The referendum was the special election in which an initiative or recall petition was decided by the voters. Primary elections: The Progressives substituted primary elections, in which voters chose party candidates, for the practice of party bosses choosing candidates. In so doing, Progressives were affirming their belief in the superiority of democratic procedures. The Popular election of United States sentators was a Populist idea taken over by the Progressives that became law in the Seventeenth Amendment, ratified in 1913.

9. "Trust buster": Roosevelt evoked the provisions of the Sherman Antitrust law to break up a trust (the Northern Securities Company) formed by J. P. Morgan, James J. Hill, and Edward H. Harriman, all archvillains to the Progressives. When Morgan approached Roosevelt in an attempt to fix things up as he had been used to doing with McKinley, he was turned down; as a result, newspaper editors and cartoonists began to refer to Roosevelt as the "trust buster." However, this image was not completely valid. Roosevelt filed less than half as many antitrust suits as his more conservative successor, William Howard Taft, and, once he felt that he had established government's proper authority over business, resumed the quiet ironing out of problems that had been characteristic of McKinley. "The worker's friend": This image of Roosevelt resulted from his siding with the United Mine Workers (UMW) in their strike against Pennsylvania mine owners, even though the UMW was opposed to socialism. Toward union leaders and unions who advocated socialism, Roosevelt was hostile and aggressive. For example, while two socialist union leaders were on trial in Idaho, Roosevelt publicly called them "undesirable citizens," possibly prejudicing the jury against them.

Also, he kept troops in Goldfield, Nevada, where radical unionists had seemed about to take over the town, even after it became clear that little violence was involved.

10. Students' answers should include an evaluation and examples of two of the following: Control of the railroads: Students' evaluation of Roosevelt's performance will vary. Among the examples they may offer are the Elkins Act (1903), the Hepburn Act (1906), the 1906 law that made railroads liable for on-the-job injuries suffered by their employees. Making food and drugs safe: Students' evaluations of Roosevelt's performance will vary. The Pure Food and Drug Acts exemplify Roosevelt's performance in this area. Natural resources of the nation: Students' evaluation of Roosevelt's performance will vary. Among the examples they may offer are Roosevelt's support of preservationists like John Muir and conservationists like Gifford Pinchot; his addition of 125 million acres (50 million hectares) to the nation's forest reserves; his appointment of Gifford Pinchot as Chief Forester; his application of conservation measures to grasslands; his refusal to allow private exploitation of mineral deposits, oil fields, and prospective sites for irrigation and hydroelectric projects; his support of the Newlands Reclamation Act of 1902; his reluctant signing of a bill that forbade the government to reserve additional forestland in the states of Washington, Oregon, Idaho, Montana, Wyoming, and Colorado, which he countered by reserving 17 million acres (7 million hectares) of forests in those states before he signed the bill.

11. The focus of students' responses should be that Taft belonged to an earlier generation and that his adherence to the principles of that generation caused him to perform in blundering ways that went counter to progressive thinking of the time (e.g., the Dingley Tariff, the support of House Speaker Joseph G. Cannon, his dispute with Gifford Pinchot). Taft's style differed radically from Theodore Roosevelt's. Whereas Roosevelt surrounded his presidential actions with fanfare and profound pronouncements, Taft acted quietly. He believed that a president should not seek the initiative (or publicity) in matters of government, but should instead act as chief administrator and let Congress take the lead. In addition, Taft, a strict constructionist, was far more cautious than Roosevelt about using presidential powers.

12. The Clayton Act: One of the goals of Wilson's New Freedom program was to break up, rather than regulate, trusts. Under the provisions of the Clayton Act, Wilson had an outstanding opportunity to do this. However, Wilson chose not to use

the trust-busting powers of this act to their fullest. The Federal Trade Commission (FTC) was designed to control trusts instead of breaking them up. Although this was the reverse of Wilson's New Freedom goal, the President gave his approval to the establishment of the commission. The Smith-Lever Act directly provided federal money for rural schools too poor to pay the price of maintaining high educational standards. The act allowed federal intervention in affairs traditionally considered the business of state or local governments. Although Smith-Lever went counter to Wilson's New Freedom guarantee of protecting states rights, Wilson approved it.

13. Roosevelt's "gunboat diplomacy": Roosevelt used navy gunboats and other military forces to protect what he saw as American rights in Latin America. Taft's "dollar diplomacy": Taft assured American investors that, if necessary, American military power would be used to protect their investments in other countries. Wilson's "moral diplomacy": Wilson proclaimed that his administration would deal with the weak Latin American republics "upon terms of equality and honor," thus upholding the highest principles of justice and morality. In dealing with events in Mexico in 1914, Wilson used "gunboat diplomacy." For example, he sent the American navy to blockade Mexican ports so that Mexican leader Huerta, whom he opposed, could not receive weapons from Europe. Also, an incident involving American sailors in Tampico gave Wilson an excuse to send marines to occupy the Mexican port of Vera Cruz and thus prevent the landing of a German arms ship carrying arms to Huerta. Finally, Wilson dispatched General John J. Pershing and 6,000 troops to Mexico to pursue Pancho Villa, a Mexican general who had killed 16 American passengers on a Mexican train and killed 17 more Americans in a raid across the border between Mexico and New Mexico.

14. Student answers should include references to the following: (1) the assassination of Franz Ferdinand, heir to the throne of Austria-Hungary, by a Serbian nationalist; (2) The Austrian ultimatum to Serbia which Germany and Austria knew Serbia could not accept; (3) Serbia's appeal to Russia and the consequent massing of Russian troops on the border of Austria-Hungary, (4) Germany's declaration of war on Russia and France, Russia's Triple Entente ally; (5) England's entrance to the war as the third member of the Triple Entente; (6) the fighting on two fronts in Europe; (7) the sinking of the Lusitania and the Sussex by German U-boats (8) Wilson's threat to break diplomatic relations with Germany if unrestricted U-boat attacks continued; (9) British diplomats' use of anti-German propaganda which caused more and more Americans to sympathize with the British side; (10) German resumption of indiscriminate U-boat warfare; (11) German promise to give Mexico its "lost provinces" of Arizona and New Mexico in exchange for Mexico's declaration of war against the United States; (12) German sinking of three American ships in March of 1917; (13) Wilson's war message to Congress on April 2, 1917.

15. The home front: "Bridges of ships" brought food and other vital supplies from the United States across the Atlantic to its European allies. American farmers grew the food, and other Americans conserved food so that more could be sent overseas. American shipbuilders produced vessels as quickly as German U-boats sank them. Americans factory workers, including women, turned out clothing, vehicles, airplanes, and weapons in quantities the Germans and Austrians could not match. Women became members of the armed forces. Thousands of other women engaged in activities designed to support the "boys in France"— working for the Red Cross, rolling bandages, knitting sweaters and socks, and baking cookies and cakes to be sent overseas. On the battlefield: The American Navy took over defense of the Western Hemisphere. Two million American soldiers were sent to fight in Europe. They participated in battles at Château-Thierry, the Marne River, and the Argonne Forest, helping to defeat the Germans. About 112,000 Americans lost their lives in the fighting.

16. Henry Cabot Lodge and other senators objected to Article 10 in the covenant of the League. This section provided that League members, including the United States, would go to war to protect each other's territory if necessary. However, the League could have been ratified if Wilson had been willing to insert some reservations in Article 10 of the covenant. Wilson would not agree, and the Senate finally voted to reject the League.

Critical Thinking

17. Student sentences should suggest the negative point of view of bosses like Tweed toward such progressive political reforms as the city manager-council form of city government, primary elections, the initiative, the recall, and the referendum. Students should recognize that reforms like these would greatly reduce the power of political bosses.

18. Student summaries should refer to several of the

following actions of the federal government: the Committee on Public Information's censorship of negative reports from the battlefield and exaggeration of positive reports, as well as its propaganda messages implying that any dissent from the government's war policies was disloyal; the refusal of the Post Office to handle Socialist newspapers; the refusal of the New York assembly to let Socialist members take their seats; the refusal of the House of Representatives to seat a Socialist representative; the imprisonment of Socialists Kate Richards O'Hare and Eugene V. Debs for opposing the draft; Supreme Court Justice Holmes's approval of a federal law restricting free speech; the federal government's quiet encouragement of the sometimes violent harassment of people with German last names; the questionably fair trial and imprisonment of 100 leaders of the radical and antiwar International Workers of the World on charges of espionage and sedition. Student comments should show an understanding that many of the government's actions seriously threatened the American tradition of individual liberties guaranteed in the Bill of Rights.

Skills Review

19. The Dewey Decimal System is used by many libraries to organize nonfiction books into ten subject-area categories, each of which is given a different number. For example, history books have any of the Dewey numbers from 900 through 909 and from 930 through 999. One of these Dewey numbers plus additional identifying numbers and letters is placed on the spine of each history book in a library. All the history books are placed on the library shelves in numerical order in one section of the library. Nonfiction books in other subject areas are organized and shelved in a similar way. A growing number of libraries with very large collections use the more specific Library of Congress cataloging system.

20. The drawers in a library card catalog and the cards inside them are arranged alphabetically. Title cards are filed alphabetically by the first word in the title other than A, An, or The. Title cards are helpful in locating books whose titles library users know. Author cards are filed alphabetically by the author's last name and are helpful in locating books if the authors' last names are known. Subject cards are useful in locating books on particular subjects. These cards are also filed alphabetically, and the subjects are printed in capital letters. In the upper left corner of the three catalog cards for each book

is a call number, the Dewey or Library of Congress number on the spine of the book. This call number directs a library user to the shelf on which the book can be found.

CHAPTER 26

Section Review (text page 618)

1. Students' sentences will vary. Information about the names and terms can be found on the pages given in parentheses. xenophobia (616), general strike (616), Calvin Coolidge (617), Attorney General Palmer (618).

2. Three strikes that occurred in 1919 were the general strike in Seattle, Washington, the strike of workers in the steel industry, and the Boston police strike. The strikes were quickly suppressed because of the public's fear of communism, and because bad economic conditions made striking risky.

3. First, the Johnson-Reed Act would cut the yearly quota of immigrants from 354,000 to 164,447. Second, the United States would accept from other countries only a number of immigrants equal to two percent of the number of people of that nationality who had resided in the United States in 1890. This base year was deliberately chosen to discriminate against southern and eastern Europeans, most of whom had come to the United States after 1890, and created a quota system that favored northern and western Europeans.

4. Sacco and Vanzetti were accused of armed robbery and the murder of a paymaster and guard. The ACLU, as well as a number of Italian-American groups, investigated the case and found that the evidence against the two men was weak. Some of the evidence seems to have been invented by the prosecution.

Section Review (text page 623)

1. Student sentences will vary. Information about the names and terms can be found on the pages given in parentheses: NAWSA (618–619), Harlem Renaissance (620), "Wets" and "Drys" (620), Al Capone (622–623).

2. In 1890, several women's suffrage groups had banded together to form the National American Woman's Suffrage Association (NAWSA). By focusing on women's right to vote, the NAWSA soon became a powerful social force. Women gained strength in their pursuit of voting rights through their growing social role during World War I and

their work in state legislatures. Women had gained suffrage in 37 states by 1919. The Nineteenth Amendment, which gave women the vote, was adopted in 1920. In contrast, Alice Paul undertook a more radical approach to women's suffrage. She and her followers drew national attention to the cause by picketing the White House; they were subsequently jailed and went on a hunger strike in protest.

3. Garvey's ideas were pro-black and anti-white. He urged blacks to withdraw from white society and form black nationalist movements based on pride in being black. Garvey formed the Universal Negro Improvement Association which emphasized black culture. With time and work, Garvey believed, American blacks would be able to return to Africa and establish their own nation. Garvey's ideas on black culture had positive effects as blacks in neighborhoods like New York City's Harlem took pride in the black culture that was emerging. The Harlem Renaissance of the 1920's was significant for an outpouring of prose and poetry by black writers such as Countee Cullen, James Weldon Johnson, and Langston Hughes. Urban blacks in the 1920s supported halls and nightclubs where they turned their rich musical heritage into sophisticated blues and jazz.

4. The southern Klan preached black inferiority and the necessity of white supremacy. As warnings, Klan members burned crosses in front of black homes, churches, and businesses, and blacks and whites who criticized the Klan were harassed and beaten. In the Northeast and Midwest, the Klan preached hatred of foreigners and appealed to anti-Catholic and anti-Semitic feelings. The Klan burned crosses in front of synagogues, Catholic churches, and the homes of white Protestants who were friendly to Catholics and Jews.

5. Student answers should indicate their understanding that the prohibition of the manufacture and sale of liquor is the connection among the temperance movement, the Eighteenth Amendment, the Volstead Act, bootleggers, speakeasies, and gangland slayings.

Section Review (text page 627)

1. Students' sentences will vary. Information about the names and terms can be found on the pages given in parentheses: James Cox (623), Franklin D. Roosevelt (623), smoke-filled room (624), Coolidge luck (627).

2. Harding and his supporters sensed that Americans wanted to forget the turmoil associated with progressivism and World War I and that what they most wanted was a return to "normalcy." His assessment of the American people's desire for normalcy was apparently correct, for, after a campaign in which he waffled on the important issues, 61 percent of the voters gave him their votes.

3. Hoover attempted to pursuade farmers and businesspeople that cooperation among themselves and self-regulation was in their own interest. He suggested that each area of the economy set up private associations through which members would determine ways of cooperating voluntarily with the government to eliminate inefficiency. Hoover's role as Secretary of Commerce would be to provide advice and information to these associations. Hughes offered a solution to the problem caused by the Senate's refusal to ratify the Treaty of Versailles by asking that Congress simply resolve that World War I was over and that a state of peace existed between the United States and Germany. Hughes also presented an alternative plan for keeping world peace whereby in the Treaty of Washington of 1921, France, Great Britain, Italy, and Japan all agreed to limit the size of their navies in proportion to their defensive needs.

4. Attorney General Harry Daugherty winked at the corrupt schemes of his friends and did not enforce the nation's laws. Charles Forbes headed the Veteran's Bureau and pocketed tens of thousands of dollars meant to build hospitals for the soldiers of World War I. Secretary of the Interior Albert Fall abused his power in disposing of naval oil reserves at Elk Hills, California, and Teapot Dome, Wyoming. He persuaded Harding to transfer authority over the reserves to his own Department of the Interior, and then leased the two rich oil fields to Harry Sinclair and Edward Doheny, who in turn "loaned" Fall over $400,000.

5. Calvin Coolidge was sworn in as President after Harding, who was returning from a vacation in Alaska, died of either a suspicious ptomaine poisoning, or as later research suggested, a massive heart attack.

Time Line Questions (text page 628)

1. 2 years (1921–1923)
2. Red Scare
3. Eighteenth Amendment and Volstead Act (Prohibition begins)
4. Treaty of Washington

Skills Strategy: The *Readers' Guide* (text pages 628–629)

Students' listings should follow exactly the style of the two sample listings in the Skills Strategy.

Chapter Test (text page 629)

Text Review

1. The postwar depression period was a time of high unemployment. Striking workers were no threat to employers, because employers knew they could replace the strikers with the unemployed. Fear of communists and of anarchists marked the postwar period. Attorney General Palmer believed that these groups were responsible for the many strikes, bombings, and other disturbances and had Justice Department agents raid the headquarters of radical groups all over the United States, arresting hundreds. Some were Communists and anarchists, who were deported to the Soviet Union. Others, however, were American citizens guilty of no crimes. Sacco and Vanzetti, two Italian anarchists, were charged with the murder of a paymaster and a guard in a bank robbery in Massachusetts. They were tried, found guilty, and executed. Many people protested that the two men were victims of anti-foreign prejudice aroused by anarchist activities of the time, executed for their controversial political views, not for the crimes they were charged with.

2. Marcus Garvey led a black nationalist movement that gave black Americans pride in black accomplishments. His ideas had little influence in the South white supremacists dominated. However, in northern urban neighborhoods, black people began to take pride in their heritage and in the emerging American black culture exemplified by the outpouring of literature, music, and other arts, in what has been called the Harlem Renaissance.

3. The Eighteenth Amendment and the Volstead Act, both enacted in 1919, made alcoholic drinks illegal. Americans who wished to continue drinking ignored the law, creating a thriving business for bootleggers and owners of "speakeasies." Even the governor of New York State and the mayor of New York City publicly broke the laws. In addition, the demand for illegal liquor gave rise to criminal organizations that were willing to supply it. Frequently, such organizations also became involved in other crimes, including murder, in their attempts to get a share of the illegal liquor trade.

4. Democrats tried to make a referendum on the League of Nations the major issue of the presidential election of 1920.

5. Students will answer one part of the question. Hoover's private associations promoted self-regulating associations in order to phase out wasteful all-out economic competition. The government would act only as an advisor and informa-tion source. Such organizations provided no way to restrain businesses if they chose to engage in unfair practices. Treasury Secretary Mellon's policies could be seen as favoring business and people with high income.

6. The Treaty of Washington of 1921 limited the size of the navies of France, Great Britain, Italy, Japan, and the United States. Each country would maintain navies only large enough to defend themselves. The United States and Great Britain needed fleets on two oceans, so they were allowed to keep the most ships. Japan was allowed fewer ships because it was a power only in the Pacific. Except for Japan, the treaty countries were happy to be rid of their excess naval vessels because of the costs of maintaining them. Japan saw the cutting of the size of its navy as anti-Asiatic prejudice.

7. President Harding's appointees to his administration—Harry Daugherty as Attorney General, Charles Forbes as head of the Veteran's Bureau, and Albert Fall as Secretary of the Interior—betrayed Harding by becoming involved in scandals. For example, Fall used his friend Harding to have the oil reserves placed under his jurisdiction. Then he leased the oilfields to two oilmen in return for a "loan" of over $400,000. Daugherty and Forbes took advantage of their friendship with Harding in similar ways.

8. After the scandals of the Harding administration, Coolidge's proper personal habits and an untainted political record seemed to assure honesty in his administration.

Critical Thinking

9. Student conclusions will vary but should be supported with appropriate information from the text. Sample conclusions: As a politician, Harding was accommodating but incompetent. As a national leader, he cut a fine figure and gave the American people a sense of security with his presence in the White House. However, he did not really lead the nation. As a person, Harding was likable, humane, and decent. He pardoned Socialist Eugene Debs, persuaded leaders of the steel industry to cut their workers' day to eight hours, and he suffered greatly from the betrayal of his friends.

10. Undoubtedly, some of the facts of the Sacco-Vanzetti trial could be learned from consulting the newspapers and magazines of the time. However, the emotion and controversy surrounding the trial most likely affected the news accounts. For this reason, these sources would best be used to get an impression of the public feeling of the time.

If students do not have access to the *Readers' Guide*, provide copies of recent magazines for their research. You may wish to have students write *Readers' Guide* author listings and/or subject listings for the articles they use. They should provide a quoted passage and use a footnote.

CHAPTER 27

Section Review (text page 635)

1. Students' sentences will vary. Information about the terms can be found on the pages given in parentheses: William G. McAdoo (630, 632), fiscal year (633), trickle-down economics (632), New Era (632).

2. Republican Calvin Coolidge was the winner. John W. Davis (Democrat) and Robert La Follette (Progressive) were Coolidge's opponents.

3. The words are those of Calvin Coolidge. All of Mellon's policies were designed to favor American business. He believed that national prosperity depended on constant economic growth; therefore, the government should make sure that as much money as possible found its way into the hands of wealthy capitalists who would then reinvest it. When the capital investment expanded, jobs and opportunities would be created for the working people, and prosperity would "trickle down" to them. Mellon drastically slashed income taxes for those who made over $60,000 yearly, and made only minor adjustments in the tax rates paid by people with lower incomes. As a consequence, the Treasury was paying refunds to very rich individuals and corporations. To make up part of the government revenues lost by Mellon's income tax policy, he increased many taxes that everyone paid—for example, excise taxes and the price of postage stamps. Mellon also introduced new federal taxes on such items as automobiles. Government revenues were lost when, through high protective tariffs (such as the Fordney-McCumber tariff), Mellon virtually froze foreign manufacturers out of the American market. Americans bought fewer of the high-priced imported products, and as a consequence, the government received no duties on the lost imports. Because he had reduced government revenues, Mellon also had to cut government expenditures. Mellon did this by (1) canceling construction of expensive battleships and cruisers; (2) abolishing many governmental regulatory agencies; (3) cutting the payrolls of other government agencies; (4) sponsoring the creation of the Bureau of the Budget, which was to predict revenues and expenditures for the fiscal year and suggest budgets for that year.

4. The Dawes and Young plans: Britain and France were given more time to repay their war loans. Germany was given more time to pay reparations. Kellogg-Briand Pact: This treaty between the United States and France outlawed war between the two nations. In time, 62 nations signed the pact, promising never to war against one another. However, the pact had no provisions for enforcing peace. New Era Latin-American diplomacy: The United States became the major investor in Latin America, controlling, directly or indirectly, the finances of ten Latin American countries. To protect American business interests, United States marines occupied Nicaragua, Honduras, Cuba, Haiti, and the Dominican Republic at various times.

Section Review (text page 643)

1. Students' sentences will vary. Information about the names and terms can be found on the pages given in parentheses: Boosterism (636), "tin lizzie" (637), *The Jazz Singer* (639), Charles Lindbergh (642, 643).

2. Sample answers: John D. Rockefeller, unpopular with the previous generation of progressives, became an object of respect and affection to most Americans. Bruce Barton was an advertising entrepreneur whose book, *The Man Nobody Knows*, remained a best-seller for two years. John J. Rascob wrote articles for popular magazines that encouraged the admiration of businesspeople.

3. Students will name three of the following: Ty Cobb, the "Georgia Peach," and George Herman "Babe" Ruth (baseball); Jack Dempsey, the "Manassa Mauler" (boxing); Harold "Red" Grange, the "Galloping Ghost" (football).

4. Students should list six of the following industries and explain how each affected the American lifestyle: automobile manufacturing industry; automobile servicing industries—service stations, automobile parts shops; motels; supermarket industry; road construction industry; electric power industry; electrical appliance industry—refrigerators, washing machines, etc.; radio broadcasting and manufacturing industries; phonograph and record industry; movie industry; advertising industry. Students' explanations of the effect of each industry they listed on the American lifestyle should include information discussed on text pages 637–643.

5. To sell newspapers, the tabloids specialized in sensational stories rather than hard news. Murder

trials, which earlier would have gone unnoticed, became the center of national attention when dressed up in colorful language and accompanied by "exclusive photographs." Tabloids even invented sensational stories.

Section Review (text page 647)

1. Students' sentences will vary. Information about the names and terms can be found on the pages given in parentheses: buying on margin (645), Black Thursday (645–646), McNary-Haugen Bills (646), Alfred E. Smith (647).
2. Buying on the installment plan is actually a form of borrowing in which the customer pays back the cost of an item plus interest over a specified period of time. Merchants successfully changed American ideas that people should avoid debt and do without goods until they had saved the money to pay for them. The installment plan made it easy to buy an item with a small down payment and enjoy using the item immediately. Consumers eagerly bought and bought, enjoying the automobiles, radios, refrigerators, and other gadgets until most of them were deeply in debt and living beyond their means.
3. The following are considered causes of the Great Depression: businesses' overreliance on the sale of expensive consumer goods, playing the stock market, and low income of a large portion of the population.

Time Line Questions (text page 650)

1. 1924—Dawes Plan; 1929—Young Plan
2. 5 years
3. KDKA radio broadcasts, Bureau of the Budget established, Babe Ruth hits 60 home runs, Lindbergh's flight, Kellogg-Briand Pact

Skills Strategy: Line Bar, and Pie Graphs (text pages 650–651)

1. 3 percent
2. 1931
3. Between 1929 and 1933
4. 1933 (1934 may also be considered correct.)
5. Students' bar graphs should have the same title, labels, percentages, and years as the line graph. The tops of the bars should align with the percentages indicated by dots on the line graph.

Chapter Test (text page 651)

Text Review

1. Students' answers should include references to the following: Coolidge's strong belief that "the business of America is business" and his willingness to let Mellon handle the government's economic dealings; Mellon's Hamiltonian notion that the wealthy were America's most valuable citizens because they had the money to invest in the country's growth; Mellon's trickle-down economic theory; Mellon's sharp reduction of taxes on the rich and increase of taxes that almost all ordinary and poor citizens had to pay; Mellon's raising of tariff rates, authorized by the Fordney-McCumber Tariff, which kept foreign competitors out of the market and left it open to American industrialists.
2. Secretary Mellon's reduction of taxes and his tariff policies reduced government revenues. Consequently, he had to find a way to reduce government expenses. He created the Bureau of the Budget to predict revenues and expenditures and suggest a budget for each year. Government would be limited to the amounts specified in the budgets.
3. International economy: Student answers should include references to the Fordney-McCumber Tariff; the Coolidge-Mellon policy on repayment of loans made by the United States to its European allies of World War I and the effect this had on the German economy; the Dawes Plan; and the Young Plan. World peace: Students should refer to the Kellogg-Briand Pact, its main provision to eliminate war, and the reason for its ineffectiveness. Latin America: Students should indicate their understanding that protection of Americans' investments in Latin America was part of Coolidge's policies. This protection included military intervention. Students should note that although this American policy aided the interests of United States business, it aroused anger toward the United States on the part of Latin Americans.
4. Among the elements students may suggest are the following: sports; material goods such as cars, electrical appliances, radios, Victrolas and records, movies. Changes in behavior: Students' suggestions should refer to the fact that ideas and attitudes in movies and the freedom from traditional restraints permitted by the automobile contributed to the changing behavior of middle-class youth.
5. Installment-plan buying encouraged American consumers to take on debts by purchasing goods "on time." Traditional American buying habits and ethics stressed avoidance of debt, doing without goods that were not affordable, and spending money only on essentials. Merchants used advertising to overcome these traditional consumer attitudes. Advertisers learned how to create a

demand for goods by developing images of people who used various products as tasteful, sporty, proper, liberated, modern, or popular, among other qualities.

6. Two speculative crazes that swept the nation in the 1920s were investment in land along the southern Florida coast and investment in the stock market.

7. Over-reliance on the sale of consumer goods: For almost all consumers, durable goods such as cars and washing machines lasted a long time and therefore were purchased infrequently. Eventually, demand for these goods leveled off, and this had a negative impact on the economy. Government policy toward depressed sectors of the economy: Government did nothing to help northern blacks and farmers whose incomes were at very low levels during the 1920s. Since these groups had little money to spend on anything but basics, they could not afford the consumer goods on the sale of which the American "boom" prosperity was based.

Critical Thinking

8. Immediate effects: The high rates allowed by the Fordney-McCumber Tariff prevented Germany from selling its manufactured goods in the United States, the world's best market, causing a decrease of cash income. This fact, plus the need to pay war reparation debts, kept money flowing out of the country, so the German government printed increasing amounts of paper money to meet its domestic needs. Inflation rapidly resulted from this government action. Long-range effects: The instability of the German economy brought about by inflation was of deep concern to the German people, and some considered the extremist political philosophy of Hitler as a solution to their national difficulties.

9. The pro-business stance of the Coolidge administration led the American government to protect business investments in Latin America by keeping in power military dictators who were sympathetic to American business interests but exploitative of the people they ruled. These dictators knew they could depend upon American intervention when the hard-pressed common people attempted rebellion. Animosity might not have developed if not for U.S. policy at that time.

10. Students' responses should indicate their understanding that Hoover's ability, which he had demonstrated frequently before the Great Depression, showed that he should have been an outstanding president. However, he came into office at the wrong time. He inherited the Depression, which was the result of economic policies of the Coolidge administration, over which he had little or no control.

Writing a Paragraph
Sample Paragraph:

The Roosevelt administration dealt far more effectively with unemployment during the Great Depression than did the Hoover administration. When President Hoover took office in 1929, only about 3 percent of the total work force was jobless. However, during each of the four years of his presidency, the percentage of jobless workers rose dramatically, peaking at almost 25 percent in 1933, the year FDR took over the reins of government. Apparently, FDR's program to put people back to work was successful, for in the first two years of his presidency, a sharp downward trend in unemployment began—from a high of above 25 percent in 1933 to 20 percent in 1935.

CHAPTER 28

Section Review (text page 657)

1. Students' sentences will vary. Information about the terms can be found on the pages given in parentheses: "Okies" and "Arkies" (655), Will Rogers (656), "Hoovervilles" (656), Norman Thomas (657).

2. Students' answers should include three of the following: employment—1932, 13 million or 25 percent of work force unemployed, 35 percent of blacks unemployed (see also the chart on page 654); earnings—average earnings fell from $25 to less than $17; savings—$3.2 billion lost in one year; hunger—85,000 free meals daily in New York City, 20 percent of poor families received $4.23 a week to buy food in Philadelphia; homelessness—estimated 1.5 million wandered the country looking for work, 25 percent of farmers in South and Midwest could not pay mortgages and were forced off land, people of whole counties in Oklahoma, Arkansas, and surrounding states headed for California to find work; business—32,000 businesses failed in 1932; banking—5,000 bank failures by 1932. (See also the chart on page 655.)

3. Americans distracted themselves by going to the movies, which were cheap. Hollywood featured films about people who "beat the system," as well as films with escapist themes, such as Shirley Temple and Busby Berkeley musicals.

4. Communism and Socialism, which blamed capitalism for the depression, won very few supporters among American voters of the time. For example,

the Communists won only 49,000 votes in 1928 and 103,000 in 1932; Socialists with presidential candidate Norman Thomas won only 882,000 votes in 1932, a small percentage of the 40 million votes cast. Many Americans blamed themselves rather than the capitalist system. However, a large majority of people blamed the Republican party, the businesspeople associated with the party, and, most of all, Republican Herbert Hoover.

Section Review (text page 661)

1. Students' sentences will vary. Information about the terms can be found on the pages given in parentheses: *Kreditanstalt* (659), "rugged individualism" (658), "Brain Trust" (661).

2. Hoover believed that the success of the United States was due to "rugged individualism," or the willingness of an individual to stand alone and struggle on the basis of his or her own resources. To Hoover, government interference in solving the problems of the depression meant that individual initiative—the genius of America—would be sapped and destroyed. So Hoover did not act during the first year of the depression. He waited for the prosperity that he unrealistically believed was "just around the corner."

3. Hoover pumped $500 million into the economy through a public works program and established the Reconstruction Finance Corporation (RFC), which loaned more than $2 billion to major banks, railroad companies, and factories, so they could avoid failure and possibly recover from the shock of the depression.

4. Veterans of World War I had been awarded life insurance policies which could be redeemed in 1943. Unemployed veterans asked that they be given early payment to help them through the hard times. Hoover refused. In the summer of 1932, 20,000 veterans and their families—the Bonus Expeditionary Force—went to Washington to demand payment. They said they would stay until Hoover gave in and took over several federal office buildings, setting up a shantytown at the edge of the city. Despite the fact that the marchers were peaceful, Hoover became nervous because 1932 was an election year. Finally, in July, the police were ordered to clear the veterans out of the federal office buildings. Riots followed. On July 29, Hoover ordered General Douglas MacArthur to clear the veterans out of their shantytown on the outskirts of Washington. MacArthur's soldiers attacked the veterans using tear gas and armored vehicles. Three veterans were killed in the fight.

5. The winner of the 1932 election was Franklin Delano Roosevelt. Roosevelt promised an end to Prohibition and a "New Deal" for the American people. However, it was unclear what specific actions FDR intended to take.

Section Review (text page 667)

1. Students' sentences will vary. Information about the terms can be found on the pages given in parentheses: Hundred Days (661), Twenty-First Amendment (665), Harry Hopkins (665), American Liberty League (667).

2. Banks: The day after he was inaugurated, Roosevelt declared a bank holiday so that bank examiners could determine which banks could be saved with loans from the Federal Reserve System. He also stopped the drain of gold from the Treasury by forbidding the export of gold. In April, he took the United States off the gold standard. At FDR's request, Congress made it illegal for private citizens to hoard gold. People were required to sell their gold to the government at a fixed price. Farms: An emergency measure, the Farm Credit Administration, allowed farmers who had missed mortgage payments and were in danger of losing their land to refinance their mortgages. The Agricultural Adjustment Administration helped farmers restore their purchasing power. Farmers were paid a subsidy to plow under one-quarter to one-half of their 1933 crops. Farmers were also paid a subsidy to slaughter part of their livestock to keep it off the market. The subsidies were not available to tenant farmers, and many of these were thrown off the land.

3. FERA—Federal Emergency Relief Act; CCC—Civilian Conservation Corps; CWA—Civil Works Administration; WPA—Works Progress Administration; TVA—Tennessee Valley Authority; NRA—National Recovery Administration.

4. The Supreme Court had declared the NRA and the AAA unconstitutional. To protect his New Deal programs, FDR proposed packing the Supreme Court with justices who would support New Deal laws. Roosevelt asked Congress to allow him to increase the Court to 15 justices. To pack the Court, he would appoint a new justice each time a sitting justice reaching the age of 70 did not retire. The Congress refused his request. After his court-packing attempt, and perhaps because of it, the Supreme Court upheld the constitutionality of several New Deal laws. Also, Roosevelt was able to appoint a majority of justices that favored the New Deal because of deaths in and resignations from the Court.

Section Review (text page 671)

1. Students' sentences will vary. Information about the names and terms can be found on the pages

given in parentheses: Social Security Act (668–669), John L. Lewis (670), sit-down strike (671), Memorial Day Massacre (671).

2. Father Charles Coughlin, Dr. Francis Townsend, Huey P. Long.

3. Roosevelt's opponents: Al Landon—Republican, William Lemke—Union party; Popular and electoral votes: FDR—27.7 million popular, 472 electoral; Landon—16.6 million popular, 59 electoral; Lemke 900,000 popular, 0 electoral.

4. Three leaders of the AFL—John L. Lewis of the United Mine Workers, David Dubinsky of the garment workers union, and Sidney Hillman of the needle workers union—did not agree with other AFL leaders that only skilled workers should be organized. Lewis formed the committee on Industrial Organization within the AFL, aiming to organize workers by industry rather than skill. The AFL expelled the committee in 1936 because of their ideas and tactics. Instead of disbanding, the committee re-formed as the Congress of Industrial Organizations (CIO).

5. Since the Civil War, almost all blacks had voted Republican, the party of Lincoln. Southern segregationists—enemies of the blacks—were all staunch Democrats. However, in the election of 1936, 75 percent of the blacks voted Democratic, which amounted to a revolution in the black voting pattern and contributed to FDR's landslide victory in that election.

Time Line Questions (text page 672)

1. 4 years (1929–1933)
2. 1937
3. Social Security Act
4. Wall Street crash, TVA established, WPA begun, Roosevelt reelected

Skills Strategy: Pictures and Captions (text page 672)

First paragraph questions: the woman's children; that the children are tired and unhappy.

1. Students may see the photo as a supplement to the descriptions of the plight of the farmers given on page 654 or as a fleshing out of the information following the heading "Saving Farms" (page 663).

2. The caption gives factual information about the photographer and the circumstances under which the photo was taken.

3. The photograph is more important as a suggestion of the feelings of the time, but it also—to some extent—presents facts about the poverty of the woman and children.

UNIT 8 TEST (text page 673)

Chapter Survey

1. Sample summary sentence(s): Chapter 26 opens with a discussion of the changes in America after World War I: a depression, a wave of xenophobia, a series of unsuccessful strikes, restrictions on immigration, a Red Scare, a controversial murder trial, a black nationalist movement, a Ku Klux Klan revival, and Prohibition. The chapter concludes with an account of Warren G. Harding's scandal-tainted administration, Harding's death, and the accession of Calvin Coolidge to the presidency. Pages containing information about terms: xenophobia (616), "Red Scare" (617), Marcus Garvey (619–620), speakeasies (622), smoke-filled room (624).

2. Sample summary sentence(s): Chapter 27 examines the Mellon-inspired pro-business bias of the Coolidge administration that led to a deceptive prosperity at home and economic difficulties abroad, especially in Germany. The chapter continues with a depiction of the excitement as well as the credit-based materialism of the Roaring Twenties that preceded the Stock Market Crash of 1929, the opening act of the Great Depression. Pages containing information about terms: trickle-down economics (632), Andrew Mellon (632), *The Jazz Singer* (639), Black Thursday (645–646), Kellogg-Briand Pact (634–635).

3. Sample summary sentence(s): Chapter 28 portrays the courage, spirit, and humor of the American people that helped them survive the woeful effects of the Great Depression. The chapter also contrasts President Hoover's inability to overcome the Depression with President Roosevelt's bold and pragmatic, if sometimes controversial, programs that started the nation on the road to economic recovery. Pages containing information about terms: "Okies" and "Arkies" (655), "Hoovervilles" (656), "Brain Trust" (661), Hundred Days (661), John L. Lewis (671).

Text Review

4. Strikes of 1919: During the war, most people's wages did not keep up with rising prices. Workers waited until after the war to demand higher pay, and they were willing to go on strike to get it. When the city government refused to recognize the Boston police union, and increase their pay, the entire police force went out on strike. Failure of these strikes: Most of the strikes failed for two main reasons. First, employers were able to re-

fuse the demands of their workers because they knew they could replace striking workers with the many people who were out of work at the time. Employers could also afford to close down for a time or operate with fewer workers. Second, many Americans of the period thought of unions as radical, that unionism was the same as communism, and that unions had links with the Bolsheviks of the Soviet Union. Johnson-Reed Act of 1924: After the war, a great flood of eastern and southern European immigrants came to the United States. Fearing that radicals would be among these immigrants, some Americans clamored for more restrictive immigration laws. The Johnson-Reed Act practically shut out people from eastern and southern Europe while favoring northern and western Europeans. Red Scare of 1919: Deaths caused by terrorist bombings prepared Americans for a Communist and anarchist hunt by Attorney General Palmer in 1919. Palmer, calculating that his actions would make him a national hero and perhaps win him the Democratic presidential nomination, ordered highly publicized raids on dozens of radical organizations throughout the nation. Sacco-Vanzetti trial: The ACLU and Italian-American groups claimed that the two Italian anarchists were tried for their political beliefs, not for the robbery and murders with which they were charged.

5. Students' summaries should include the following points. Positive factors: Marcus Garvey's black nationalist ideas gave rise to black pride in black heritage and culture. The Harlem Renaissance of the 1920s saw an outpouring of black literature and music. Negative factors: Lynching of blacks became a frequent phenomenon. Race riots broke out in 26 cities. The revived Ku Klux Klan preached black inferiority in the South and the need to maintain white supremacists in government. Klan members burned wooden crosses in front of black homes, churches, and businesses. They also harassed and beat blacks and white critics of Klan ideas and actions.

6. The Eighteenth Amendment outlawed the manufacture, sale, and transportation of alcoholic beverages. In effect, the amendment encouraged crime and disrespect for the law. Illegal businesses developed to supply Americans' demand for liquor by bootlegging it from Canada, Mexico, and the West Indies. Rival businesses fought gang wars for the control of the illegal liquor trade. In Chicago alone, over 400 people were murdered in these wars. Ordinary citizens and political leaders showed their contempt for Prohibition. Some city and state leaders allowed illegal "speakeasies" to operate, publicly went to speakeasies themselves, and served liquor at public functions.

7. Americans were saddened by the sacrifices made during the war and were weary over the turmoil caused by the fighting for Progressive idealistic goals. Sensing this, Republicans avoided discussion of the League of Nations, which Democrats wanted to make the major issue in the 1920 campaign. Republican party leaders promoted Harding as the "candidate of normalcy." In many campaign speeches, Harding himself urged Americans to put the war and the League behind them and to forget the turmoil of the Progressive movement. American voters responded by electing Harding as their president. Student evaluations of Harding's success as president will vary. However, evaluations should be backed up by information given on text pages 625–627.

8. Students' answers should include references to the following. Pro-business domestic policies are exemplified in Coolidge's "the business of America is business"; Secretary of the Treasury Mellon's trickle-down economics; Mellon's tax policies; Mellon's endorsement of the high rates of the Fordney-McCumber Tariff; Mellon's businesslike running of the national government, in his creation of the Bureau of the Budget, for example. Pro-business foreign policies are exemplified in Mellon's refusal to reduce tariff rates and Coolidge's refusal to cancel repayment of French and British war debts to the United States, both of which would have helped Germany out of its grave economic difficulties and in the New Era policy toward Latin America which was designed chiefly to protect American investments in the nations of the region.

9. Student discussion of two aspects of the 1920s should include facts given on the pages shown in parentheses: entertainment and sports (636–637, 639–640); technological advances (637–638—automobiles and electricity, 639—the radio, phonographs and records, the movies); advertising, ballyhoo. and hoopla (641–643); the revolution in morals (641).

10. Over-reliance on the sale of consumer goods: This policy was one of the causes of the Great Depression. The prosperity of the 1920s was based on the sale of long-lasting goods such as cars and refrigerators. So, eventually, sales leveled off, and the drop in sales affected the economy negatively. "Playing the stock market": This widespread practice touched off the crash but did not cause it. By playing the market, investors forced up stock prices; in reality, the stocks had no value. Government policy toward the depressed sectors of the

economy was another one of the causes of the Great Depression. The income of groups like the blacks and farmers was hardly large enough to buy the basic necessities of life. People in such groups had no money to spend on the durable goods upon the sale of which continued prosperity depended. However, the government did nothing about their plight. Since these groups made up a significant portion of the population, the prosperity was bound to end without their participation.

11. Negative effects of the Great Depression: Student answers should include references to unemployment, reduction in earnings, loss of savings, hunger, failures of banks and businesses, loss of homes and farms. Evidence of Americans' spirit and courage: Students' responses should mention the fact that Americans were able to make jokes about their plight even in the worst of times (page 656) and showed their faith in the capitalist system by refusing to elect candidates of the Communist and Socialist parties, both of which hoped to gain power by blaming the capitalist system for the Great Depression.

12. Student responses should indicate the understanding that Hoover's philosophy of rugged individualism led him to believe that government intervention to bring about an end to the depression would sap and destroy individual initiative, which he saw as the source of the strength and success of the United States. These ideals and his unfounded belief that prosperity was ''just around the corner'' kept Hoover from acting to lead the nation out of the depression, though in the past he had more than amply demonstrated that he had the talent and skills necessary to do so.

13. To explain the comment, students should cite the ''alphabet soup'' abbreviations of the many agencies FDR set up to deal with the problems of the depression, for example: FERA (Federal Emergency Relief Act), CCC (Civilian Conservation Corps), NRA (National Recovery Administration), and WPA (Works Progress Administration).

14. Student answers will include two of the following. Opposition to Franklin Roosevelt's policies: The American Liberty League charged that programs like the TVA and NRA were a threat to the American tradition of free enterprise. In two separate decisions, the Supreme Court ruled the NRA and the AAA unconstitutional. Father Charles Coughlin, Dr. James Townsend, and Governor Huey Long all proposed plans that opposed Roosevelt's programs. (See page 668). Gains for labor and management's reactions: Within a few years, labor unions went from near powerlessness to becoming a major force in the economic life of the country. The founding and growth in the power of organizations such as the Congress of Industrial Organizations, the United Steel Workers, and the United Auto Workers testify to gains made by labor, as does the use of successful new tactics against employers such as the sit-down strike. Management's reactions include the threat to use force to fight union organizers made by the president of Republic Steel; the Memorial Day Massacre in Chicago, which resulted in the killing of ten union demonstrators and the injury of 100 more by the Chicago police; the hiring of toughs by the Ford Motor Company to attack and beat several union organizers. ''The revolution in the voting patterns of American blacks'': Since the Civil War, blacks had consistently voted for the candidates of the Republican party, the party of Lincoln. In the election of 1936, however, 75 percent of the nation's black electorate voted for Roosevelt, a Democrat. This constituted a revolution in black voting patterns and was one reason for Roosevelt's landslide victory that year. The positive legacy of the New Deal: Its greatest accomplishment was the relief it brought to many needy Americans, starting in 1933, possibly heading off widespread riot and rebellion. The negative legacy of the New Deal: Its most significant negative consequence was the tremendous growth of government bureaucracy. Some students may see the emergence of the Democratic party to political predominance as a positive or negative legacy of the New Deal.

Critical Thinking

15. Student responses should indicate the understanding that Secretary of the Treasury Mellon's pro-business policies during the Coolidge presidency would most likely lead wealthy Americans of the 1920s to the point of view expressed in the quotation.

16. Accept reasonable hypotheses. Some students may hypothesize that, in the circumstances described, eventually Americans may have rebelled against the government. Others may hypothesize that, in those circumstances, Americans may have become a grim and dispirited people.

17. Student conclusions about the leadership abilities of Roosevelt and Hoover should be based upon and supported by facts from the text. Although most students will make positive judgments about Roosevelt and negative judgments about Hoover, all reasonable conclusions that are backed up by references to text information should be accepted.

Skills Review

18. The *Readers' Guide* should be consulted to find a specific magazine article. The *Readers' Guide* contains subject listings and author listings. Both types of listings contain the following information: the title of the article, the author's initials and last name, the abbreviation of the magazine's name, the volume number of the magazine, the numbers of the pages on which the article appears, and the abbreviation of the month and last two numbers of the year the magazine was published.

19. Percentage of electoral and popular votes: pie graph; number (in millions) of homeless people: bar or line graph; government expenditures: line or bar graph

20. Students' answers will vary with the text photograph selected but should include answers to all the questions listed.

CHAPTER 29

Section Review (text page 679)

1. Students' sentences will vary. Information about the names and terms can be found on the pages given in parentheses: Cordell Hull (676), Platt Amendment (678), Manchuria and Shanghai (678), reciprocity (678).

2. Roosevelt and Hull adopted Hoover's term "Good Neighbor Policy" to describe the role the United States meant to play in Central and South America. No longer would the United States interfere in the internal affairs of their neighbors in the south. How Roosevelt applied it: (1) Roosevelt withdrew marines from Nicaragua, the Dominican Republic, and Haiti; (2) He refused to intervene in the Cuban civil war, and when peace was restored in 1934, he repudiated the Platt Amendment, which stated that the United States could interfere in Cuban affairs; (3) In 1938, he resisted the demands for action made by powerful American oil companies when Mexico seized property owned by those companies and paid them very little compensation, remained friendly with the Mexican government, and a few years later, worked out a satisfactory settlement.

3. The Stimson Doctrine was directed toward Japan. Japan had moved into the Chinese province of Manchuria and had set up a puppet government there. Hoover and Stimson wanted to protect American trading rights in China (the Open Door Policy). Roosevelt continued the doctrine because he was preoccupied by the depression and was reluctant to cut off profitable exports to Japan.

4. In his investigations, Senator Nye wanted to show that munitions makers ("merchants of death") and bankers generally favored American participation in World War I. However, Nye went further than the evidence warranted, saying that the arms-makers and bankers were responsible for Wilson's declaration of war. Although Nye's conclusion could not be proved, some Americans believed it. This put them on guard for signs that certain interests were trying to drag the United States into war.

Section Review (text page 688)

1. Students' sentences will vary. Information about the names and terms can be found on the pages given in parentheses: Allied Powers (684), Edward Murrow (684), RAF (684), "Blitz" (684), Tojo (687).

2. (1) Well-armed Italy invaded Ethiopia. Many Ethiopians struggled against Italian tanks and planes with primitive weapons. Despite American sympathy, Ethiopia could not buy American arms because of the Neutrality Act, which forbade the sale of arms to warring nations. Italy had other sources of arms, but Ethiopia had none. (2) Japan invaded China in 1937. However, President Roosevelt did not invoke his power to cut off arms sales to warring nations and announced that China would be allowed to buy arms and munitions for defense. This meant that Japan could buy them also. Because Japan's navy and merchant marine were far superior to China's and because Japan controlled much of China's coast, it could buy tons of scrap iron in the United States to make weapons, while very few American-made arms could make their way to the Chinese. (3) Mussolini and Hitler aided Francisco Franco's fascists in a civil war against Spanish republicans who believed in democracy. Although the western democracies sympathized with the Spanish republicans, they gave the republicans little direct aid because they feared a war with Italy and Germany. President Roosevelt invoked the Neutrality Act, thus denying trade with the Spanish republicans while Italy and Germany kept the Spanish fascists well supplied.

3. (1) Germany, Italy, and Japan denounced democracy and human liberties as symptoms of social decay. (2) The leaders of all three countries preached a creed of racism. For example, in Germany, the belief in a "master race" led to massive persecution and murder of German Jews. During World War II, German Nazis systematically murdered Jews and other groups in other countries. (3) The three countries exalted the totalitarian state as personified by a single leader who was to be worshipped almost as a god.

4. 1936: Hitler marched troops into the German

Rhineland, which had been demilitarized under the Treaty of Versailles. March 1938: Hitler, with the help of Austrian Nazis, joined Austria to Germany in the *Anschluss.* September 1938: Hitler demanded that Czechoslovakia cede the Sudetenland, a section of Czechoslovakia, to Germany. Britain and France appeased Hitler to avoid war and sacrificed the Sudetenland. March 1939: Hitler seized the rest of Czechoslovakia. September 1, 1939: Germany invaded Poland.

5. The direct attack on the United States, causing the loss of battleships, warships, airplanes, and lives of American servicemen, practically forced the United States to declare war on Japan, and, later, Italy and Germany.

Section Review (text page 691)

1. Students' sentences will vary. Information about the terms can be found on the pages given in parentheses: "Rosie the Riveter" (689–690), Lend-Lease Act (689), rationing (690), Nisei (690).

2. The wartime production of large and small American manufacturers was "little short of miraculous." Airplane production increased from 5,865 in 1939 to 96,369 in 1944. Construction of merchant ships went from 1 million tons in 1941 to 19 million tons in 1943. Workers on American assembly lines produced 17 million rifles, 2.7 million machine guns, and 41.4 billion rounds of ammunition.

3. Women went to work in unprecedented numbers doing jobs that had been held previously by men only. Blacks got high-paying jobs in industry that had been previously closed to them. President Roosevelt issued an order forbidding racial discrimination by companies that benefited from government contracts. Not since Reconstruction had such strides been taken toward racial justice. Unions increased in size and power. Membership increased from 10.5 million before the war to 14.7 million. White-collar workers grew at a dizzying rate, increasing from 1 million in 1940 to 2.8 million in 1945. The increase of government white-collar jobs opened opportunities that earlier generations of men and women could not have dreamed possible.

4. Students' answers should include three of the following: (1) consumer goods were hard to find, so civilians saved their money; (2) automobile production was completely cut off in 1942 so that automobile workers could turn out tanks, trucks, jeeps, and airplanes; (3) gasoline was rationed and a presidential proclamation limited speed to 35 miles per hour; (4) tires were hard to get because Japan controlled Malaya, the source of 97 percent of the world's rubber supply; in 1942, the government forbade the sale of new tires; huge scrap drives were held to collect rubber for the government; (5) some foods were rationed, for example, butter, coffee, and meat.

5. Japanese-Americans, especially those on the West Coast, suffered most from wartime discrimination. Early in 1942, more than 100,000 Japanese-Americans (including many native-born citizens) were forced to leave their California homes to be interned in concentration camps. The Japanese-Americans were considered to be security risks merely because of their ancestry. The Supreme Court upheld their internment. Governor Earl Warren of California proposed excluding Japanese-Americans permanently from his state. More than $350 million worth of property had been taken from Japanese-Americans before the end of the war.

Section Review (text page 701)

1. Students' sentences will vary. Information about the terms can be found on the pages given in parentheses: Chiang Kai-shek (699), Mao Tse-tung (699), J. Robert Oppeheimer (699), Hiroshima (700).

2. The battles of Bataan and Corregidor were the worst military defeats in American history. The victorious Japanese forced 75,000 American prisoners of war to march to prison camps in the interior of the Philippines. The men on this "Bataan Death March" were so cruelly treated that only 54,000 survived the war.

3. The Battle of the Coral Sea and the Battle of Midway put Japan on the defensive so early in the war that it was easier for President Roosevelt to pursue his first objective, the defeat of Germany.

4. On June 6, 1944, Americans, British, Free French, and Polish forces hit the beaches of Normandy in northwestern France. After being pinned down on the beaches, the Allied invaders broke through the German defenses. With surprising speed, they rolled back the German forces and entered Paris on August 25. Less than three weeks later (September 12), the Allies were across the border of Germany.

5. First, after the German surrender, Germany would be divided into four occupation zones. Britain, France, the United States, and the Soviet Union each would be responsible for a different zone. Berlin would be governed jointly by all four powers. Second, Roosevelt reluctantly agreed to allow the Soviets to remain in Poland and to annex eastern Poland to the Soviet Union. The Soviets pledged that the new government of Poland would be freely elected. Third, Roosevelt and Churchill persuaded

Stalin to launch a Soviet attack against Japan soon after Germany surrendered. In exchange, they would allow the Soviets to take the Kurile Islands from Japan, and they would recognize Soviet control of Outer Mongolia. Fourth, the three leaders worked out the details of a new international organization to be called the United Nations. To ensure Soviet participation, Roosevelt agreed to an arrangement that in effect gave the Soviet Union power to cast three votes on any issue debated in the UN's General Assembly.

6. American strategists had planned a three-pronged attack on Japan. The Chinese armies of Chiang Kai-shek and Mao Tse-tung were to pin down the 2 million-man Japanese army on the Chinese mainland. Because Chiang hated his communist allies more than he hated the Japanese, he refused to go for an all-out attack. The Japanese army remained in excellent condition. The first prong of the attack was unsuccessful. The two American prongs were very successful. However, the number of American casualties was staggering. General MacArthur and Admiral Nimitz had succeeded in capturing strategic islands from which bombers could strike at Japan. By the summer of 1945, American troops were ready for the invasion of Japan. American planners did not look forward to the invasion. The Japanese army was still 2.5 million strong. Planners believed that the invasion would cost the United States a million casualties, as many as had been suffered in over three years of fighting in both Europe and the Pacific.

Time Line Questions (text page 704)

1. Italy—1922, Germany—1933
2. 6 years (1939–1945)
3. Japan invades China, Pearl Harbor attacked, Battle of Coral Sea and Midway, Allied invasion of Europe, President Roosevelt dies, atomic bomb dropped.

Skills Strategy: Propaganda (text pages 704–705)

1. Nazi—lefthand poster; American—righthand poster
2. The poster shows a young German man, and evokes feelings of security, nationalism, and patriotism.
3. The propagandist is trying to say that the Germans are good people and should be looked up to as shining examples of good citizens.
4. The second poster evokes fear, repugnance, and anger because of the grim and coldly efficient look on the man's face as he observes the hanging (a symbol of Nazi brutality) reflected in his monocle.
5. The second poster uses *name calling*—pictorially,

the poster calls the Nazis heartless brutes, butchers, and automatons. It also uses *glittering generality*—all Nazis are like the man in the poster.

Chapter Test (text page 705)

Text Review

1. President Roosevelt had two reasons for continuing Herbert Hoover's foreign policy. First and most important was the need to give almost all of his attention to the depression at home rather than foreign affairs. Second, Roosevelt's secretary of state, Cordell Hull, was a politician from Tennessee, not an experienced career diplomat, and he adopted Hoover's policies rather than creating his own.

2. Students will answer two items. Good Neighbor Policy in 1938: In that year, the Mexican government seized property belonging to American oil companies and paid little compensation in return. Roosevelt refused to be pressured into action by the oil companies. Keeping cool and remaining friendly with Mexico, he negotiated an acceptable settlement a few years later. Roosevelt's response to the Shanghai air attack: The air attack in 1932 was the worst instance of making war on civilians up to that time. However, Roosevelt did nothing because the United States was in the grips of the depression, and Roosevelt was reluctant to take any action that might result in the loss of profitable exports to Japan. Formal recognition of the Soviet Union: Although Roosevelt was not sympathetic to Soviet Communism or Joseph Stalin's dictatorship, he recognized realistically that the Soviet regime was going to survive. Roosevelt also hoped that the depressed economy of the United States could be helped by developing trade with the Soviet Union. However, due to lack of money in the Soviet Union to pay for American goods, the hoped-for trade never developed.

3. The three main provisions of the Neutrality Acts were (1) a warning to Americans against traveling on the ships of the warring nations; (2) a stipulation that warring nations must pay cash for American products and haul these products in their own ships; (3) a prohibition on the sale of arms to belligerent nations by American manufacturers. American public opinion saw these provisions as means of avoiding entanglement in war.

4. Among the examples students may cite are the following: Roosevelt's sale of 50 American destroyers to the British for their use in anti-submarine warfare; his call for a peacetime draft in 1940; his proposal of the Lend-Lease Bill to

Congress, designed to make America the "arsenal of democracy"; his proclamation of a neutral zone between the United States and Iceland, giving the protection of American destroyers to British trans-Atlantic shipping and freeing the British Navy to guard the waters around their home islands; his order sending American troops to occupy Greenland; his meeting with Churchill to draw up the Atlantic Charter.

5. The words were spoken by Japanese Admiral Isoroku Yamamoto, who was in command of the attack on Pearl Harbor. The admiral spoke the words after canceling one final attack on three American aircraft carriers which were at sea during the attack on the American naval base in Hawaii. Yamamoto perhaps understood the potential of the United States to wage war when "awakened."

6. The Battle of Britain: Under the inspiring and defiant leadership of Winston Churchill, the Royal Air Force and the British people heroically resisted and finally overcame the Nazi "Blitz," the relentless aerial bombardment of England. The Battle of Stalingrad: The Soviet army surrounded and captured 300,000 German soldiers who had been besieging the Russian city of Stalingrad.

7. The Battle of the Coral Sea was fought entirely by planes from Japanese and American aircraft carriers that were never within sight of each other. Although Admiral Yamamoto claimed victory, he was prevented from carrying out the Japanese strategy of pushing as far south in the Pacific as possible before the Americans recovered from Pearl Harbor and went on the offensive. The Battle of Midway was a decisive defeat for Japan. Four Japanese aircraft carriers, which resource-poor Japan could not replace, were sunk. Admiral Yamamoto was forced on the defensive and began to fortify the Pacific islands under Japanese control. The United States retained control of the strategically important island of Midway and was on the verge of taking the offensive.

Critical Thinking

8. The quotation is from President Roosevelt, who was responding to the Japanese bombing of the American naval base at Pearl Harbor on December 7, 1941.

9. The Axis Powers held these three beliefs in common: Democracy and human liberties are symptoms of social decay; the totalitarian state, with a leader regarded almost as a god at the head, is the proper form of government; certain groups of people are racially inferior to the citizens of the Axis Powers.

10. The Atlantic Charter provisions: First, all nations would be free to determine their own destinies. Second, freedom of the seas and free trade would be maintained. Third, the aggressor Axis Powers would be disarmed. Fourth, a world organization would be set up where all nations could meet to resolve their differences peacefully. Provisions of the Yalta agreement: First, after German surrender, Germany would be divided into British, French, Russian, and American occupation zones, and Berlin would be governed by all four powers. Second, the Soviet Union would be allowed to continue its occupation of Poland and annex eastern Poland in exchange for its pledge that the new government would be freely elected. Third, the Soviet Union would be allowed to take Japan's Kurile Islands, and its control of Outer Mongolia would be recognized in exchange for a Soviet attack on Japanese armies after the surrender of Germany. Fourth, the international organization to maintain peace after the war would be called the United Nations, and to insure the participation of the Soviet Union, they would have the power to cast three votes in the General Assembly of the United Nations.

Writing a Paragraph
Sample Paragraph:

Good evening, ladies and gentlemen. This is Lois Kirk asking you to join with me and other patriotic Americans to do your bit in fighting the Axis monsters who want to enslave us. Here in Hollywood, we conserve gasoline and rubber tires by walking, taking public transportation, or sharing rides. At home, I myself save tin cans and cooking fats and turn them over to the collection center here in town. I'm doing all I can to see that our men and women in the armed forces have all the materials they need to win this world struggle for freedom. Won't you do the same?

CHAPTER 30

Section Review (text page 712)

1. Students' sentences will vary. Information about the names and terms can be found on the pages given in parentheses: Trygve Lie (708), "iron curtain" (710), Soviet satellites (711), Berlin airlift (711–712).

2. The three most important bodies of the United Nations are the Secretariat, the General Assembly, and the Security Council. The Secretariat, headed by the Secretary General, administers the day-to-day affairs of the UN. The General Assembly, made

up of ambassadors from every member nation, has very little power because none of the powerful nations want to be bound by decisions of smaller nations. It is a place in which nations can talk out their differences as an alternative to war. The Security Council is composed of five permanent member nations (the United States, the Soviet Union, France, Britain, China) and representatives of ten (originally six) smaller member nations. Each of these ten nations are elected for two years. The Security Council has the authority to enforce UN policy with military action. However, each of the five member nations has the power to veto any Security Council resolution. Therefore, the council has real power only in disputes between smaller nations, and then, only when the "Big Five" agree to use force.

3. The origins of the Cold War go back to the Communist Revolution in Russia in 1917. The United States government did not want the Soviets to spread communism to other countries. In 1918 and 1919, American, British, and French troops landed in Russia to help Russian anti-Communists fight the Communists. Many Russians were convinced that the western powers wanted to destroy their country. After World War II, the feelings of mutual distrust were again aroused by political disagreements about Eastern Europe. In March 1946, Poland was not allowed to hold the free elections that would have resulted in a government favorable to the West, because Soviet troops still occupied it. Winston Churchill called for western democracies to halt the expansion of Communism in his "iron curtain" speech in March 1946. By the end of 1947, Stalin, in violation of previous promises, was interested only in setting up satellites, or pro-Soviet governments, in Eastern Europe. The Cold War had been declared.

4. The Marshall Plan had the broader scope. It was a much more ambitious program than the Truman Doctrine, which offered only military aid to anti-Communist nations. The Marshall Plan, however, offered vast amounts of money to help European countries rebuild their war-devastated economies. Although the Marshall Plan aid was offered to the Soviet Union and Eastern European countries, they rejected it.

Section Review (text page 715)

1. Students' sentences will vary. Information about the names and terms can be found on the pages given in parentheses: elections of 1946 (712), NAACP (713), Hubert Humphrey (713), "do-nothing Congress" (714).

2. Senator Taft proposed the Taft-Hartley Act. Among its provisions were the following: (1) it outlawed the closed shop (which excluded all non-union labor); (2) it permitted employers to sue unions for breach of contract; (3) it permitted the president to declare a "cooling off" period before workers in a vital industry could strike. Republicans in Congress mustered enough support to override President Truman's veto of the act.

3. The Progressives, under the leadership of Henry Wallace, blamed Truman for the Cold War. Wallace insisted that the United States and the Soviet Union should cooperate rather than attack one another. The Dixiecrats bolted from the Democratic party because of their opposition to civil rights. They hoped to help defeat Truman and win Republican support for continued segregation in the South.

4. Adopted: (1) increase of federal minimum wage from 40 to 75 cents an hour; (2) Social Security Act amended to increase benefits for retired workers; (3) authorization of the construction of housing for low-income families; rejected: (1) federally supported health insurance plan; (2) repeal of Taft-Hartley Act; (3) laws protecting civil rights of black citizens.

Section Review (text page 721)

1. Students' sentences will vary. Information about the names and terms can be found on the pages given in parentheses: Red China (715, 717), Third World countries (716), Dean Acheson (717), thirty-eighth parallel (717).

2. The three events were (1) a Soviet nuclear bomb exploded in 1949; (2) Mao Tse-tung and the Communists defeated the pro-American Nationalist government of Chiang Kai-shek, who fled to Taiwan; (3) the Communist government of North Korea, with the apparent approval of Red China and the Soviet Union, invaded pro-American South Korea in 1950.

3. The Twenty-Second Amendment prohibits any person from being elected to the presidency more than twice. Alger Hiss was convicted of perjury when he testified before the House Committee on Un-American Activities. Whittaker Chambers claimed that in the 1930s he had received secret information from Hiss, who was then a high-level government employee. Hiss denied the charge under oath. Richard Nixon, a member of the committee, collected evidence showing that Hiss was lying about some things. The Rosenbergs, a married couple, were implicated in a plot to sell atomic secrets to the Soviets. Both admitted they were Communists but denied any guilt. They claimed they were being tried for their political beliefs rather

than for any crime. The Rosenbergs were found guilty and executed although evidence against them was questionable. McCarthyism meant labeling as a traitor anyone who dissented from approved ideas or who was even thought to have done so. The term comes from the name of Senator Joseph McCarthy, who used Red Scare tactics to win reelection to the United States Senate and become nationally prominent and powerful.

4. General MacArthur assured President Truman and the United Nations that the Chinese would not intervene if he invaded North Korea. The president and UN approved of the invasion. But MacArthur was wrong. Fearing that MacArthur's troops would cross the Yalu River, which separates China from Korea, the Chinese government sent 200,000 "volunteers" across the Yalu to attack MacArthur's weary troops.

Section Review (text page 725)

1. Students' sentences will vary. Information about the names and terms can be found on the pages given in parentheses: John Kenneth Galbraith (722), GI Bill of Rights (723).

2. An affluent society is one in which people have surplus income to buy consumer goods rather than to save the extra money. During World War II, people could not spend all the money they earned because of rationing and because factories were producing armaments. People saved the money because they could not buy such things as better housing, automobiles, or radios. Americans entered the postwar period with money in the bank and the desire to spend it. Also, rising wages throughout the 1940s and 1950s contributed to the trend.

3. The "baby boom" was the upward trend in the number of American babies born, starting in 1946, peaking in 1961, and continuing at a high rate until the 1970s. The tremendous leap in the number of American children caused a great increase in the demand for housing and child-related goods and services.

4. The suburbs where veterans and other Americans bought housing were far from workplaces and shops, so automobiles became a vital means of transportation in American life. More automobiles meant more highway construction firms and automobile-related businesses, motels, drive-in movies, drive-in restaurants, and shopping malls.

5. During the war, women had held men's jobs and attended college in significant numbers. When the men returned from the war, many women assumed their traditional roles. College became a place to find suitable husbands. Women were supposed to take pride in the roles of homemaker,

wife, and mother. However, their wartime experiences gave them a different viewpoint of their place in society. In the 1950s, women became the backbone of social, political, and religious organizations. The social activism of the women's rights movement of the 1960s and 1970s built upon this previous involvement.

Time Line Questions (text page 726)

1. 1954
2. Soviet Union explodes atomic bomb
3. Truman Doctrine; Marshall Plan
4. Eisenhower's administration

Skills Strategy: Flow Charts (text pages 726–727)

"Boom babies" flow charts should show the following information: infants (housing, diaper services, baby food); toddlers (toys); schoolchildren (schools); teenagers (records, clothing). Encourage students to include other goods and services they can think of.

Flow charts depicting the process of mass-production of houses should show the steps given in the second paragraph under the subheading "Growth of Suburbs" in the order given.

Flow charts should have a title and may include appropriate illustrations.

Chapter Test (text page 727)

Text Review

1. The United Nations General Assembly has little real power because none of the powerful nations, including the United States, want to be bound by the policies of smaller nations. The Assembly attempts to keep the peace by serving as a "town meeting of the world" in which nations can talk out their differences rather than going to war.

2. The Cold War was a non-shooting but nevertheless intense and bitter conflict between the United States and the Soviet Union. The United States was determined to put an end to Soviet expansion in Europe by supporting anti-communist regimes with massive military aid. This policy became known as the Truman Doctrine. The Marshall Plan helped to prevent the rise of Communist power in the war-ravaged countries of Western Europe by providing them with vast amounts of money to help these countries reconstruct their economies. In both cases, American financial aid was used as a weapon against communism.

3. George Kennan's policy of containment outlined how the United States should deal with Soviet expansion. Because the Soviets feared an attack

from the West, the United States must draw clear lines beyond which it would not tolerate Russian expansion. When the Soviets cut off all ground access to West Berlin and Stalin stated that all of the city was within the Soviet Union's sphere of influence, the United States applied Kennan's containment policy. By instituting a massive airlift of needed supplies to West Berlin, the United States was telling the Russians it would defend its rights. Convinced that Americans were serious and would continue the airlift indefinitely, the Soviets eventually backed down and lifted the blockade.

4. Truman called his ambitious program of reform legislation the Fair Deal. Only a few parts of it were passed by Congress—the federal minimum wage was raised from 40 to 75 cents an hour; Social Security benefits for retired workers were increased; and the construction of housing for low-income families was authorized. However, conservative Republicans would not accept a federally supported health insurance plan, and southern Democrats rejected laws meant to protect civil rights for blacks.

5. United States membership in NATO was a drastic departure from American isolationist tradition. The United States joined nine Western European nations in NATO as a defense measure in case of attack and as one means of fighting the Cold War with the Soviet Union.

6. While Truman was in office, Republicans began to allege that Democrats were tolerating Communist government workers. As a result, Truman ordered all federal employees and applicants for federal assistance to sign loyalty oaths (which were probably unconstitutional). In signing such oaths, people swore that they were not members of the Communist party or members of any group connected with the Communist party, and that they did not support the overthrow of the United States government by force.

7. Students will respond to one part of the question. The China lobby and the communist takeover of China: This was a group of influential Americans who supported the Nationalist government of China under Generalissimo Chiang Kai-shek. The lobby opposed Chinese Communist leader Mao Tse-tung, whom they said was a Soviet puppet. The members of the Truman administration took the lobby seriously and were stunned when Mao and the Communists drove Chiang out of China and set up a Communist government in China. The UN and the war in Korea: After the withdrawal of American and Soviet troops from Korea in 1949, the country divided into two parts—Communist North Korea and democratic South Korea, both of which claimed the right to rule the entire country. In 1950, North Korea invaded South Korea. In the absence of the Soviet delegate, the United Nations Security Council branded North Korea an aggressor and called upon UN member nations to go to the aid of South Korea. Many responded but only the U.S. provided massive assistance. The U.S. became involved in an unwinnable war that, four years later, ended in a truce that is still in effect. The Rosenbergs and atomic secrets: In 1950, Klaus Fuchs admitted that he and several others had conspired to give American atomic secrets to the Soviet Union. Julius and Ethel Rosenberg, self-admitted Communist party members, were implicated in the plot, although the evidence was questionable. The Rosenbergs were tried for treason, found guilty, and executed. Many liberal Americans agreed with the Rosenbergs when they protested that they had been tried for their political beliefs and not for any crime. McCarthyism and the election of 1952: Senator Joseph McCarthy of Wisconsin feared that he would not be reelected in 1952, so he looked for an issue: He chose Communist infiltration of the federal government. With no facts to back him up, McCarthy alleged that over 200 Communists were working for the State Department and thereby implied that their superiors were actively supporting the subversion of the United States government. (He later admitted these charges were false.) He continued with such actions—and in the process destroyed the reputations of many innocent Americans—until 1954, when his lack of evidence was exposed during nationally televised hearings investigating Communist infiltration of the Army. Soon afterward, the Senate censured him.

8. During World War II, rationing and extreme shortages of consumer goods prevented people from spending money. Consequently, there was a growth in personal savings accounts. Americans began the postwar period with a lot of accumulated money and were eager to spend it, which they did, on consumer goods such as homes (which caused the growth of suburbs), cars (which gave rise to a host of businesses such as service stations, motels, and shopping malls), and television sets. America became an affluent society, one in which income enabled people to buy many goods beyond those which were necessary to maintain life.

Critical Thinking

9. Kennan correctly predicted that the Soviets would back down when the United States let them know that it would not permit them to expand beyond a

specified limit. Kennan's prediction was not merely a guess. Like all serious predictions, it was based upon reliable knowledge—in Kennan's case, his knowledge of the history and behavior of Russia.

10. Students' responses should indicate their understanding that McCarthy's claims were, in large part, made possible because of Americans' ignorance of national issues.

Writing a Paragraph

Sample Paragraph:

After World War II, the passage of the GI Bill of Rights had a number of effects in the United States. Under one provision of the GI Bill, low-interest, government-backed home loans were made available to returning veterans. This led to a move to the suburbs, where contractors were building houses in record numbers to take advantage of the GI home buyers' spending ability. As a result, suburbanites needed more cars, causing a rapid expansion in the automobile and highway construction industries. Consequently, other related businesses grew—service stations; auto parts stores; car washes; drive-in restaurants, theaters, and banks; and shopping malls. The end effect of the home-loan provision of the GI Bill was a dramatic change in how and where Americans lived and worked.

CHAPTER 31

Section Review (text page 735)

1. Students' sentences will vary. Information about the terms can be found on the pages given in parentheses: Adlai E. Stevenson (728, 730), Jonas Salk (731), Justice Earl Warren (732–733), Thurgood Marshall (732).

2. According to the concept of nonviolent civil disobedience, citizens have a moral duty to disobey unjust laws in peaceful ways. Because the disobedience is moral, and enforcement of the law is sometimes brutal, public opinion would support the nonviolent protesters and cause the abandonment of the unjust laws. Rosa Parks, a black woman, refused to give up her seat on a crowded bus to a white person in Montgomery, Alabama, thus disobeying one of Montgomery's civil laws. She was arrested. Under the leadership of Martin Luther King, Jr., blacks boycotted the city-owned busline. Soon it was in economic difficulty. After considerable time, the boycott was successful, and the law was removed.

3. Economic and social politics: Eisenhower wanted to sell the TVA to private industry and did not put pressure on Southern schools to integrate. Ability to compromise: Oveta Culp Hobby warned that if the government funded a massive polio immunization program the United States would drift toward socialism. Eisenhower compromised, and the government paid only for part of that program. Secretary Benson had to swallow his opposition to agricultural subsidies when farmers produced such huge surpluses that they could not get enough money for their grain to pay for the cost of growing it. Again there was compromise, and the Soil Bank Act of 1956 became law. The government paid farmers for every acre they did not cultivate.

4. The White Citizens' Council was organized in the deep South to evade the Supreme Court integration order. Governor Faubus called out the Arkansas National Guard to prevent the enrollment of black students at Central High School in Little Rock. After talking to Faubus, Eisenhower countermanded the governor's order. Then, Faubus used the local police to prevent integration. Eisenhower ordered the Arkansas National Guard to defend the rights of black students to enroll and protect them from the mob. The NAACP led the attack on the 1896 Supreme Court ruling in *Plessy* v. *Ferguson,* which held that "separate but equal" facilities for blacks and whites did not discriminate against the civil rights of black citizens. The NAACP believed that integration was the key to black equality. CORE (Congress for Racial Equality) was an organization that worked for equal rights for blacks in the North.

5. In *Brown* v. *Board of Education of Topeka*, the Supreme Court ruled that racially segregated schools violated the Fourteenth Amendment guarantee of equal treatment for all citizens, thus reversing the Court's ruling in *Plessy* v. *Ferguson.*

Section Review (text page 738)

1. Students' sentences will vary. Information about the names and terms can be found on the pages given in parentheses: emerging nations (735), Nikita Khrushchev (735, 737), Ho Chi Minh (736–737), Ngo Dinh Diem (737).

2. Dulles's personality: Dulles was a very direct, serious, and somber man with a powerful personality. He maintained strong and unswerving convictions about communism. Dulles's political beliefs: Dulles firmly believed that Soviet leaders lacked credibility or honest intentions. The conviction that "good" nations should not cooperate with "bad" nations influenced his approach to Communist bloc countries. Dulles looked upon neutral nations that had good relations with the Soviet Union as suspect. He did not recognize the genuine desire some of them

had to remain neutral. In this way, Dulles put the United States at a disadvantage in trying to win friends among the emerging nations of the Third World. In addition, the policy of brinkmanship affected American prestige abroad. Nations viewed American diplomacy as uncertain.

3. In all four cases, the United States' commitment to protecting Third World nations, as well as allies, was uncertain. Quemoy and Matsu: Chinese Nationalists on the islands of Quemoy and Matsu began shelling mainland China on the order of Chiang Kai-shek. Chiang believed that the Eisenhower administration would "unleash" him to invade the Chinese mainland. The Red Chinese, in return, started bombing Quemoy and Matsu. The United States refused to give Chiang the military support he needed for the invasion. Hungary: Anti-Communists in Hungary rebelled against the puppet government the Soviets had installed there. The anti-Communists captured Budapest, the Hungarian capital. The Soviets hesitated to reassert their control, as if waiting to see what the United States would do. When no support came from the United States, Soviet tanks and infantry easily crushed the rebellion. Egypt: Israel, Great Britain, and France seized the Suez Canal, which had been nationalized by Egyptian leader Gamal Abdel Nasser. The three nations assumed they had the support of the United States because Nasser had established ties with the Soviet Union. A crisis situation developed. Eisenhower was prepared to use American troops if the Soviets sent military aid to Egypt. When the Soviets did not send military support, Eisenhower openly criticized Israel, France, and Great Britain for invading Egypt. The three had to withdraw from the canal because of world censure of their action. Indochina: France was losing its fight against the anti-colonial movement in Indochina. The French believed that the United States would help them in their fight against the Viet Minh guerrilas because in 1953, the United States had given France $60 million to continue its rule of Indochina. The French controlled the major cities of the country. However, much of the countryside was controlled by the Viet Minh guerrillas, especially at night. The French established a powerful fort at Dien Bien Phu to challenge the Viet Minh. The Viet Minh attacked the fort. Within weeks, the French at Dien Bien Phu were surrounded and struggling to survive. They asked the United States to bomb the attackers. Dulles urged Eisenhower to do so. Eisenhower refused because he feared the bombing would lead to the use of United States ground troops. Dien Bien Phu fell. In the Geneva Accords of 1954, Indochina was portioned into two

parts—North Vietnam and South Vietnam. By 1956, the United States was giving South Vietnam substantial military aid because it was anti-Communist.

5. In 1955, President Eisenhower met with Premier Nikolai Bulganin in Geneva, and agreed to a "new spirit of cooperation" between the Soviet Union and the United States. Then, in 1956, Khrushchev condemned Stalin for his bloodthirsty policies and for creating a "cult of personality."

Section Review (text page 741)

1. Students' sentences will vary. Information about the names and terms can be found on the pages given in parentheses: Bernard Goldfine (739), Francis Gary Powers (740), missile gap (740), media election (741).

2. The launching of Sputnik called into question Americans' assumptions about their country's technological superiority and the "drift" that Democrats blamed on Eisenhower. Americans had assumed that the Soviet Union had been able to produce the atomic and hydrogen bombs using vital secrets stolen from the United States. However, Sputnik proved that Soviet space scientists were several years ahead of the United States. Americans responded to the challenge, taking new interest in education. Science and math were emphasized in order to "catch up" with the Russians. Many critics blamed America's failings on the lack of leadership in Washington.

3. The tour of the Soviet Union by Vice President Nixon in July 1959 and the return visit of Soviet Premier Khrushchev in September 1959 are evidence of the improved relations between the United States and the Soviet Union. Khrushchev came to the United States even though Nixon had upstaged him in the so-called "kitchen debate" at a trade show in Moscow. President Eisenhower planned to go to Russia in May 1960.

4. For several years, American U-2 planes had been flying high above the Soviet Union, photographing military installations. On May 1, 1960, one plane piloted by Francis Gary Powers, disappeared. President Eisenhower believed that the plane had been destroyed and the pilot killed. He announced that a plane used in weather forecasting had mistakenly wandered into Soviet territory. However, the pilot had safely parachuted to the ground. Francis Gary Powers confessed the nature of his mission to the Soviets. Khrushchev was delighted at the diplomatic coup—a major victory in the Russian-American competition. Khrushchev hinted he still wanted Eisenhower to visit the Soviet Union, implying that the President may not have known about the U-2

flights. Eisenhower refused to accept Khrushchev's help. To say that he had not known about the U-2 flights would give ammunition to the Democrats, who claimed that subordinates of Eisenhower were making key decisions. Therefore, he acknowledged that he had approved every U-2 flight. Khrushchev cancelled Eisenhower's invitation.

5. In 1960, John F. Kennedy (Democrat) and Richard M. Nixon (Republican) were the presidential candidates. Kennedy won the election.

Time Line Questions (text page 744)

1. 1955
2. Khrushchev's anti-Stalin speech
3. Egypt invaded by England, France, and Israel—1956
4. Soviets launch Sputnik—1957

Skills Strategy: Almanacs (text page 744)

1. Quick Reference Index; pages 148–149
2. Space walks—148; space shuttles—149, 664, 872, 884, 889, 894
3. Any other General Index entries under "Space developments" that have not been used could be consulted.

UNIT 9 TEST (text page 745)

Chapter Survey

1. Sample summary sentence(s): Chapter 29 traces the events that brought the United States out of the depression and into war in Europe and the Pacific under the strong leadership of Franklin Roosevelt. The chapter continues with a survey of the outstanding contributions made by Americans —on the battlefield and at home—that led to the defeat of the totalitarian Axis powers, and concludes with President Truman's momentous decision to drop two atom bombs on Japan. Pages containing information about terms: Manchuria and Shanghai (678), Edward R. Murrow (684), RAF (684), Nisei (690), J. Robert Oppenheimer (699).

2. Sample summary sentence(s): Chapter 30 discusses President Truman's leadership of the American people through the ups and downs of the promising, as well as threatening, years following World War II—the tensions of the Cold War with the Soviet Union; the Berlin blockade and the American airlift; the rise of the communist government in China; NATO and the Marshall Plan; the attempt to contain communism in Asia by

fighting an unwinnable war in Korea; the hysteria of the Red Scare provoked mostly by Senator Joseph McCarthy; and the rise of an affluent society in the United States. Pages containing information about terms: "iron curtain" (710), Third World (716), thirty-eighth parallel (717), GI Bill of Rights (723).

3. Sample summary sentence(s): Chapter 31 opens with the election of President Dwight D. Eisenhower and concludes with the election of President John F. Kennedy. The chapter discusses Ike's ending of the Korean War, the landmark *Brown* v. *Board of Education* Supreme Court decision, the beginnings of the black struggle for civil rights in Little Rock and Montgomery and the rise of Martin Luther King, Jr.'s leadership, the brinksmanship and the foreign policy of Eisenhower and Dulles, the good life for Americans in the 1950s, the warming and then chilling of the Cold War, and the "media election" of 1960. Pages containing information about terms: Thurgood Marshall (732), peaceful coexistence (737), Camelot (741).

Text Review

4. Roosevelt spent a minimum of time on foreign policy during his first years in office. Roosevelt and Secretary of State Cordell Hull, inexperienced as a diplomat, continued the foreign policies of Hoover and his more experienced Secretary of State Henry L. Stimson. They introduced significant changes only where foreign policy would help in the fight against the Great Depression, which was the chief focus of Roosevelt's activities. Pages on which examples of the "Hoover-Roosevelt foreign policy" can be found are given: Latin America (the Good Neighbor policy, pages 676, 678), Asia (the Stimson Doctrine, page 678), the Soviet Union (formal recognition of the Soviet regime, page 678).

5. Fifty old American destroyers: In September 1940, Roosevelt gave the destroyers to the British who needed them to hunt and destroy German submarines. In exchange, Britain gave the United States naval bases in Bermuda and Newfoundland which Roosevelt said were needed for defending the nation. The Burke-Wadsworth Act was the first peacetime draft law in American history and was meant to increase the country's preparedness for war. Congress appropriated $37 billion to build up the navy and the army air corps. The Lend-Lease Bill was a response to Winston Churchill's appeal for more American help. Under the provisions of this bill, American factories pro-

duced arms and other war materials for Britain, making the United States what Roosevelt termed the "arsenal of democracy." These materials were "loaned" rather than sold to Great Britain. Neutral zone from the United States to Greenland: American destroyers patrolled the waters of this zone, warning British ships and protecting them from "wolf packs" of German submarines. This was, in effect, an informal limited war with Germany and freed the British to use their navy to defend the waters around Great Britain. Adding to this informal state of war, Roosevelt also sent American troops to occupy Greenland, a possession of Denmark which was itself occupied by German forces. Atlantic Charter: Roosevelt showed his intentions with regard to going to war against Germany by meeting with Churchill on a ship off the coast of Newfoundland where he and the British leader agreed on the principles of the Atlantic Charter, a statement of their aims for the postwar world.

6. On the morning of December 7, 1941, the Japanese sent waves of Japanese bombers to make a surprise attack on the naval base at Pearl Harbor in Hawaii. The bombers destroyed or badly damaged fifteen American warships and 188 American planes. Close to 3,500 American servicemen were killed or wounded in the Japanese air attack. All but one member of Congress voted to declare war on Japan at Roosevelt's request the day after Pearl Harbor. The single holdout was Montana congresswoman Jeanette Rankin who had also voted against war in 1917, because of her anti-war stance.

7. Battle of Midway: The American fleet, led by Admirals Raymond A. Spruance and Frank J. Fletcher, defeated the Japanese fleet decisively, sinking four Japanese aircraft carriers. As a result of this battle, Americans were able to hold on to strategically important Midway Island and to put the Japanese on the defensive. The United States was almost ready to take the offensive in the Pacific war with Japan. Stalingrad: The Soviet Army destroyed a German force of 300,000 at Stalingrad, halting the eastward advance of Hitler's armies which the Soviets slowly began to push back. D-Day: On June 6, 1944, Allied forces under the command of American General Dwight D. Eisenhower began an amphibious invasion of Hitler's Fortress Europe on the beaches of Normandy, France. In a short time they pushed back the German forces and by August 25, the Allies entered Paris. By September 12, they were across the German border. Battle of the Bulge: In December 1944, the Germans delayed the Allied

advance toward Germany for six weeks by successfully attacking a weak point in the Allied lines. The German attack was overcome, and after the battle, all German resistance collapsed. Yalta, a resort city in the Soviet Union, was the site of a meeting of the "Big Three"—Roosevelt, Churchill, and Stalin. The purpose of the meeting was to decide on postwar plans for Europe. Four points were agreed upon: (1) Germany would be divided into four occupation zones, each occupied by one of the four powers, the United States, Britain, Russia, and France. Berlin would be jointly governed by all four. (2) The Soviets would continue their occupation of Poland, in exchange for a Soviet promise to allow the free election of a postwar Polish government. (3) The Soviets would be given Japan's Kurile Islands and recognition of their control of Outer Mongolia in exchange for entering the war against Japan when fighting with Germany ceased. (4) A new international organization to be called the United Nations would be formed after the war. To ensure the Soviet Union's involvement, Roosevelt agreed to an arrangement whereby the Communist country would have three votes on any issue debated in the UN General Assembly. April 12, 1945, was the day President Roosevelt died of a massive stroke, not long after he had been inaugurated for a fourth term. Hiroshima was one of the two Japanese cities on which atom bombs were dropped. On August 6, 1945, about 100,000 people in Hiroshima died in an instant. A similar number died over the years from the effects of radiation poisoning. A second city, Nagasaki, was destroyed by another atom bomb three days after Hiroshima. Less than a month later, Japan formally surrendered on the deck of the American battleship *Missouri*.

8. The Cold War was an intense and bitter conflict between the United States and the Soviet Union that began a few years after World War II ended. Both sides used money and propaganda rather than guns, tanks, and planes as weapons to wage this war. Among such weapons used by the United States are the following: The Marshall Plan: In 1947, Secretary of State George Marshall pointed out that economic difficulties in some of the war-ravaged countries of Western Europe were helping the Communists gain power. He convinced Congress to appropriate large sums to help these countries reconstruct their economies. Such assistance was offered to the Soviet Union and the countries of Eastern Europe, but they refused the offer. Policy of containment: This policy was proposed by State Department Soviet expert George Kennan as a way of halting Soviet

expansion in Europe. Kennan pointed out the long history of westward expansion by Russia and emphasized the Soviets' fear of attack from the capitalist nations. Kennan argued that Stalin could not be trusted to honor any agreement he made with the United States. What had to be done, Kennan argued, was to make it clear to the Soviets that the United States would tolerate no further expansion in Europe. He warned that the United States must be firm because the Soviets would test American determination but would pull back when they saw that the United States was serious. Kennan's containment policy proved to be a successful American weapon in the Cold War. The Berlin blockade and airlift: In 1948, violating the Yalta agreement, Stalin declared that all of Berlin was within the Soviet sphere of influence, including West Berlin which was occupied by French, British, and American troops. West Berlin was deep within the Soviet zone of Germany and supplies for the city had to be transported over roads and railroads that ran through the Soviet zone. Stalin cut off the supply routes to West Berlin. Instead of going to war or abandoning West Berlin, the United States began to airlift supplies to the city. After a year, the Soviets realized the United States would continue the airlift as long as necessary, and they lifted their blockade of West Berlin. Soviet expansion was contained. NATO (North Atlantic Treaty Organization): The founding of NATO was one of the points in President Truman's four-point program for winning the Cold War with the Soviet Union. NATO was an alliance of the United States, Great Britain, France, West Germany, Canada, Iceland, and other countries of the North Atlantic region. In the NATO treaty, all these nations agreed to go to the aid of any one of the nations that was attacked. General Dwight Eisenhower was made supreme commander of the NATO military forces.

9. Congress passed these parts of Truman's Fair Deal: the increase of the federal minimum wage from 40 to 75 cents an hour, amendment of the Social Security Act to increase benefits for retired workers, and an act authorizing construction of housing for low-income families. Congress rejected these parts of the Fair Deal: a proposal for federally financed health insurance, repeal of the Taft-Hartley Act, laws protecting civil rights. Democratic members of Congress: the Southern Democrats fended off Truman's efforts for laws protecting civil rights.

10. Student answers should include two of the following. Events in China after World War II: The Chinese Communists under Mao Tse-tung defeated Chiang Kai-shek's Nationalist forces and drove them from mainland China to the island of Taiwan. Korean War and American containment policy: The United States applied the policy of containment of communism to Korea in 1950. In that year, North Korean communists crossed the thirty-eighth parallel and invaded South Korea, an anti-communist nation, friendly to the United States. The United Nations called upon all members to go to the aid of South Korea. Many responded but only the U.S. provided massive assistance. After three years, the fighting was ended with a truce in 1953. However, neither side could claim victory. McCarthyism and its ultimate end: In an attempt to be reelected in 1952, Senator Joseph McCarthy of Wisconsin caused great turmoil in the United States with his claim that Communists were infiltrating the federal government. McCarthy had no factual evidence to support his claims, but many people believed he was telling the truth. For two years McCarthy had great power which he used to destroy the reputations of innocent people by merely suggesting that they had Communist sympathies. McCarthyism came to mean accusing as a traitor anyone who dissented from approved ideas, or who was even thought to have done so. During nationally televised hearings into the charge that Communists had infiltrated the Army, McCarthy's power was destroyed and he was completely discredited. In 1954, he was censured by his colleagues in the Senate. GIs, teenagers, and women in the postwar era: Under the Serviceman's Readjustment Act (the GI Bill of Rights), veterans of World War II were given help in buying homes, finding medical care, and getting an education. GI housing loans contributed to the rapid growth of suburbs, the increase in automobile production, and the building of highways. About 8 million veterans took advantage of the education benefits offered in the GI Bill. Teenagers developed their own styles in music and dress. Many emulated movie actors who played young, rebellious people. As in the 1920s, many teenagers clashed with their parents over standards of acceptable conduct. Women who had held jobs during the war were expected to return to the traditional roles of homemakers, wives, and mothers, and most did. However, they also took leadership roles in religious, civic, and political organizations. Experience they gained in these roles prepared them to take part in the social activism that contributed to the women's rights movement of the 1960s and 1970s.

11. The winner of the 1952 election was Republican Dwight D. Eisenhower. Soon after taking office, he went to Korea where he let it be known that, if the North Koreans did not compromise on the truce talks then being carried on, he might use nuclear weapons. Under the moderate Soviet leadership that succeeded Stalin, the Soviet delegate to the UN suggested a settlement, and a truce ending the fighting in Korea was signed on July 27, 1953.

12. Supreme Court: In *Brown* v. *Board of Education*, the Court ruled that racially segregated schools violated the Fourteenth Amendment of the Constitution, and ordered segregated schools in 17 states and the District of Columbia to integrate "with all deliberate speed." This ruling became the legal basis for the black civil rights struggle of the 1950s and the 1960s. Central High School in Little Rock, Arkansas, was the scene of a struggle over the attempt to register black students. Segregationists, backed by the governor of Arkansas, opposed the attempt with violence. However, President Eisenhower used the National Guard, and the black students were able to enroll and attend classes in the school. Rosa Parks of Montgomery, Alabama, refused one day to give up her seat on a city bus to a white person. Her arrest precipitated a protest of Montgomery blacks led by Dr. Martin Luther King, Jr. King urged black citizens to boycott the Montgomery bus company. When the company began to lose money, the boycott achieved success. The event thrust Dr. King into national prominence as leader of the Southern Christian Leadership Conference. Nonviolent civil disobedience was the method Dr. King believed would bring success to black people in their struggle for civil rights. King believed citizens had a moral duty to disobey unjust laws in peaceful ways. He believed that when authorities arrested or even beat protesters, the protesters should submit without resistance. King felt that unjust laws would be abandoned by the use of this method; public opinion would support the protesters when people recognized the justice of their cause and observed the sometimes brutal enforcement actions of authorities. Thoreau's philosophy: Nonviolent civil disobedience had been written about and practiced by Henry David Thoreau.

13. Students' answers should point out that American reactions to incidents in all four places confused the allies of the United States. The reactions seemed to contradict the Eisenhower-Dulles "saber-rattling" stance toward Communism. For example, Chiang Kai-shek began shelling mainland China, believing that the United States would "unleash" him to invade the mainland. The Nationalist leader was surprised when this didn't happen. Likewise, the Hungarian rebels believed the United States would support their actions against the Soviet-backed regime of their country. However, when no such support came, the rebellion was put down by Soviet tanks and troops. American reactions to the Israeli, French, and British takeover of the Suez Canal and to the French plight at Dien Bien Phu in Indochina were similar and caused similar consternation in friendly nations.

14. The U-2 was one of many that had for several years been flying over the Soviet Union photographing defense installations. President Eisenhower at first claimed that the U-2 was a weather plane that had strayed off course, not knowing that the pilot had already admitted the real mission of the plane. Khrushchev scored a diplomatic triumph when he publicly revealed the pilot's admission. However, he implied that Eisenhower might not have known about the U-2 flights and left open his invitation to the president to visit Russia. Eisenhower responded negatively. He knew of the flights and to say otherwise would substantiate Democratic claims that his subordinates, not he, made the key government decisions. He acknowledged that he had ordered the U-2 flights, and Khrushchev had to cancel his invitation. The whole incident resulted in a serious chilling in United States-Soviet relations.

15. In 1960, John F. Kennedy was the Democratic presidential candidate and Richard M. Nixon ran on the Republican ticket. In the sense that the candidates engaged in a highly touted series of four televised debates, the 1960 election was a "media election."

Critical Thinking

16. Students' answers should indicate an understanding that, for example, Americans' fear of Communism and frustration over Communist successes had an indirect effect on the formation of postwar foreign policy toward the Soviet Union and other Communist powers. Students should support their answers with facts.

17. Students should list the following groups, summarizing and evaluating the gains and setbacks of two: women (pages 689–690, 725), blacks (pages 690, 713, 732–735), Japahese-Americans (690). Note that students can find information for summaries on the text pages given in parentheses. Women, in the majority in this country, are some-

times inaccurately thought of as a minority because they have often been victims of the same kinds of injustices as minorities.

18. Students' evaluations of Truman and Eisenhower as presidents will vary. Accept all responses that are supported by text information.

Skills Review

19. Among the communications media in which propaganda may be found are books, magazines, newspapers, songs, and speeches. Students should name and describe four of the following propaganda techniques: name calling, glittering generalities, transfer, "just plain folks," card stacking, and bandwagon. Students' descriptions of techniques should approximate the descriptions given in the Skills Strategy on pages 704–705.

20. A flow chart is a type of diagram that can help to clarify the relationships among ideas and details presented in written materials. Some flow charts show casual relationships among groups of events. Other flow charts clarify the chronological relationships among events.

CHAPTER 32

Section Review (text page 759)

1. Students' sentences will vary. Information about the terms can be found on the pages given in parentheses: New Frontier (748–750), Robert Kennedy (751), Fidel Castro (755–756), Berlin Wall (757).

2. Domestic legislative reforms: Kennedy had little help from Congress. In both the Senate and the House, Southern Democrats joined with the Republican minority to block New Frontier legislation. Bills proposing such things as low-interest federal loans to college students, federal funds to help depressed Appalachia, and aid to redevelop old cities were either defeated or passed in watered-down form. Kennedy's Medicare program to provide medical insurance for the elderly was defeated after lobbying by the American Medical Association. Among the projects the conservatives supported was the infant space technology industry, which was to be centered in the southern states. Civil Rights: At first, Kennedy moved very cautiously on civil rights because he hoped that, with the help of Vice President Johnson, southern Democratic legislators could be persuaded to support his New Frontier. Therefore, he offered no new civil rights legislation, but he had the laws already on the books enforced. Relations with the Third World: Kennedy began to more actively support the civil rights movement because he was determined to win the friendship of Third World nations. He also organized the Peace Corps and founded the Alliance for Progress with this goal in view. The West Berlin Crisis: Khrushchev apparently concluded that Kennedy's inexperience provided an opportunity to strike at West Berlin. Thousands of East Germans were fleeing to West Berlin, among them well-educated professionals and technicians who were looking for greater opportunities in the West. To stop this "brain drain," Khrushchev threatened to seal off West Berlin. The President told Khrushchev that sealing off West Berlin would mean war. Then Kennedy increased American military preparedness. Khrushchev got the message and decided West Berlin was not worth a war. A short time later, however, the East Germans built the "Berlin Wall." The Wall was a defeat for Kennedy, but war had been averted.

3. In October 1962, American reconnaissance planes flying over Cuba returned with photographs showing the construction of several bases for Soviet offensive missiles capable of hitting many large American cities. President Kennedy considered an invasion of Cuba or a pre-emptive air strike to destroy the missile sites. But because the bases were not yet operational, he decided to blockade Cuba to prevent the arming of the missiles. Kennedy announced that Soviet ships bound for Cuba would be stopped. Khrushchev insisted that the missiles were defensive and posed no threat unless Cuba was attacked. President Kennedy repeated his intention to maintain the blockade. The Soviets backed down, and the missile-carrying ships stopped in mid-ocean. On October 26, Khrushchev sent a letter to Kennedy offering to dismantle the bases if Kennedy would promise in writing not to attack Cuba. A second letter from Khrushchev arrived the next day stating that he would withdraw the missiles from Cuba if Kennedy withdrew American missiles from Turkey. Kennedy ignored the second letter. However, he agreed to the terms of the first letter, and Khrushchev accepted his agreement. Both leaders, shaken by their flirtation with nuclear war, agreed to install a "hot line" between the White House and the Kremlin so that in another crisis both leaders would be able to contact one another in an instant.

4. The Warren Commission was set up at the request of President Johnson to investigate the assassination of President Kennedy. After exhaustive research, the commission could find no reason to link Oswald or Ruby to any conspiracy. But many Ameri-

cans were not satisfied with the commission's report.

Section Review (text page 764)

1. Students' sentences will vary. Information about the names and terms can be found on the pages given in parentheses: OEO (761), VISTA (761), James Meredith (762), ''black power'' (762).
2. Johnson vastly expanded Kennedy's New Frontier program into the most significant governmental shaping of American Society since FDR's New Deal, and he pushed it through Congress as the first wave of the Great Society. Johnson idolized Roosevelt and saw his own presidential mission as the completion of Roosevelt's program of social justice for the weak and poor.
3. The Civil Rights Act of 1964 and the Voting Rights Act of 1965 were perhaps Johnson's greatest achievements. The 1964 law forbade segregation and discrimination on the basis of race in all schools and public accommodations and in all private companies or institutions receiving federal funds. The 1965 law put the Fifteenth Amendment (which forbade states to deny voting rights to anyone) into practice. The Attorney General could send officials into any area where a charge of discrimination at the polls had been filed.
4. Senator Goldwater claimed that Johnson's social welfare programs ate at the vitality of America. During the campaign, the Democrats successfully depicted Goldwater as a trigger-happy man who would start World War III.

Section Review (text page 769)

1. Students' sentences will vary. Information about the names and terms can be found on the pages given in parentheses: New Left (767), Sirhan B. Sirhan (768), Yippies (769).
2. The following are among the reasons some South Vietnamese were sympathetic toward the Viet Cong. (1) Diem canceled the election required by the Geneva Accords to determine the permanent government of a united Vietnam so he could stay in power. (2) Diem, a Roman Catholic, was hostile to the Buddhist majority of Vietnam. (3) Diem supported the interests of the large landowners against the peasants. (4) Diem's government was corrupt. (5) The NLF (Viet Cong) murdered many officials of Diem's government, thus weakening Diem's authority.
3. President Kennedy's plan was to use some military personnel (the Green Berets) to train the South Vietnamese army to counter guerrilla rebellion while urging the Vietnamese government to eliminate the social injustice that caused the rebellions. He used other military personnel (marines) to guard American bases in South Vietnam. After the overthrow and murder of Diem in mid-1963, a rapid succession of military dictators ruled South Vietnam. Most had no interest in social reform and wanted more American troops. Kennedy refused, resisting any action that would deepen American involvement in Vietnam. President Johnson did not refuse troops. He did not want Southeast Asia to go Communist. In August of 1964, Johnson found a way to step up the war. He asked Congress for powers to repel any armed attack against the forces of the United States and to prevent further aggression. With the Tonkin Gulf Resolution as his justification, Johnson increased the number of American troops from 28,000 in 1964 to a total of 541,000 in 1969. As the war deepened and dragged on, many Americans became attracted to an antiwar movement. As the American involvement in Vietnam deepened, the ranks of the antiwar protesters grew. Antiwar leaders began to organize nonviolent demonstrations. As a result of the growing opposition to the war, President Johnson announced that he would not run again.
4. Eugene McCarthy, Hubert Humphrey, and Robert Kennedy were contenders for the Democratic party presidential nomination.
5. The candidates of the three parties in the 1968 election were Hubert Humphrey (Democratic party), Richard Nixon (Republican party), and George Wallace (American Independent party). Richard Nixon won the election with 301 electoral votes and a slim margin of 500,000 popular votes.

Time Line Questions (text page 770)

1. about 3 years (1961–1963)
2. Medgar Evers, John Kennedy, Malcolm X, Martin Luther King, Jr., Robert Kennedy
3. 1962, 1963, 1964, 1965
4. Cuban missile crisis, 1962

Skills Strategy: Hypotheses from Photographs (text pages 770–771)

1. The lefthand photo shows an antiwar rally; the righthand photo shows a civil rights demonstration.
2. Students' answers should show their recognition of the determination of the civil rights marchers and the anger of the antiwar rally.
3. Captions should reflect the events shown in the photos.
4. Hypothesis statements should reflect students' answers to the previous question and the details in the photos.

Chapter Test (text page 771)

Text Review

1. Johnson's Great Society domestic legislation program was a greatly expanded version of Kennedy's New Frontier program. The two programs differed because Kennedy moved cautiously in the area of civil rights, whereas Johnson's program brought about the Civil Rights Act of 1964 and the Voting Rights Act of 1965. Kennedy's proposal to provide medical insurance for the elderly was defeated because of heavy lobbying by the American Medical Association, whose physician-members opposed government involvement in health care. Other of Kennedy's New Frontier proposals were defeated or watered down by southern Democrats and Republican conservatives who were opposed to many of the expensive government programs. The first wave of Johnson's Great Society programs was passed by Congress because of a wish to honor the assassinated Kennedy. The second and greater wave of Johnson's legislative programs passed after he was reelected. The ease with which they got through Congress is, in part, a testimony to the influence, knowledge, and skill Johnson had gained as Senate majority leader.

2. Kennedy was planning to introduce a sweeping Civil Rights Act to Congress in 1964 when he was also planning to seek reelection. Although he was sure of support in the northern states, he anticipated opposition to his reelection in the South because of his stance on civil rights. As part of a plan to win at least some support from southerners, Kennedy and Johnson went to Dallas and Houston to win over as many Texans as possible.

3. Students should include the following steps in their answers: in August of 1964, Johnson used the Tonkin Gulf incident as a justification for sending more American troops to Vietnam; in November of 1964, there were 28,000 American troops in Vietnam; by September 1965, Johnson had increased this number to 130,000.

4. Students will answer two items in the question. James Meredith won a court order affirming his right to enroll at the all-white University of Mississippi in 1962. After a rash of riots by segregationists, Meredith was finally admitted. Four years later, Meredith was shot when he started a "Walk Against Fear" across Mississippi. George Wallace, who had been elected governor of Alabama on a "Segregation Forever" platform, personally blocked the door when two black students, accompanied by United States marshalls, attempted to enroll at the University of Alabama. Robert Kennedy was converted to deep sympathy with the plight of American blacks by the University of Mississippi and the University of Alabama incidents, the bombing of black churches, and the killing of black activists, including Medgar Evers. Malcolm X, a Black Muslim, gave radical speeches urging blacks to take pride in their color and to break free of white domination. Before he was assassinated, he was beginning to call for some degree of cooperation between blacks and whites to bring about social change. Martin Luther King, Jr., was a spokesman for nonviolent civil disobedience as a means for achieving black civil rights. He was the founder and president of the Southern Christian Leadership Conference. King rose to national prominence when he organized a boycott of the city of Montgomery's segregated buses. His influence on American blacks grew after that, and his leadership had its greatest effect in his organizing the March on Washington, during which he gave his memorable "I Have a Dream" speech. Dr. King was assassinated in Memphis, Tennessee, in 1968.

5. The Tonkin Gulf Resolution, giving the president power to repel any armed attack against the forces of the United States, and to prevent further aggression, became President Johnson's justification for sending more troops to Vietnam, thus escalating American involvement in the war.

6. Students' answers may include the following: Hans Morgenthau—he believed that the United States, with no vital interest in Vietnam, was exhausting its power while Russia and China were untouched; Senators Fulbright, Nelson, and Morse—they believed that the United States was alienating the Third World by its unwanted presence in Vietnam; pacifists—they opposed this war, as they opposed all wars; moralists such as Dr. Benjamin Spock—they condemned the war as unjust and immoral; students and college professors—they opposed the war on a number of grounds, including the students' fear that they would be drafted and sent to fight in Vietnam; civil rights leaders—they protested the disproportionate number of black soldiers in Vietnam.

7. The Democratic Convention: Inside the convention hall in Chicago, the Democratic party nominated Hubert Humphrey and Edmund Muskie as their presidential and vice-presidential candidates over the opposition of antiwar delegates. Outside the hall, what was later described as a "police riot"

was going on. A group of young members of the Youth International Party (Yippies) had come to Chicago from all over the country to stage nonviolent demonstrations against the war. However, they had not been given an official permit for the demonstration by city officials. Eventually, police and demonstrators met, and before the eyes of millions of television viewers the police beat demonstrators, journalists, and passersby. The 1968 Republican Convention in Miami, in contrast, nominated Richard Nixon and Spiro Agnew in an orderly and peaceful manner. Richard Nixon's nomination was an astonishing comeback, the result of four years of hard work by the presidential candidate. In 1964 he had won the loyalty of the conservative Republicans by supporting their unpopular presidential candidate, Barry Goldwater. In the four years that followed, Nixon made himself available for Republican fund-raising events whenever invited. In such quiet ways, he tirelessly built up a following so strong that he easily got the nomination at the 1968 Republican convention.

Critical Thinking

8. Students' responses should indicate their realization of the feelings of fear, tension, helplessness, and anxiety aroused in the people of the United States and the Soviet Union by the threat of imminent nuclear holocaust.

9. Johnson idolized President Roosevelt. When he himself became president, Johnson saw his mission as the completion of the New Deal, Roosevelt's program aimed at giving social justice to the weak and poor. Much of Johnson's Great Society domestic legislation reflected this influence.

10. Students' reactions to the lifestyle of the "flower children" and evaluations of the flower children's reasons for choosing it will vary. However, all responses should be based on information given in the text.

Writing a Paragraph

Students' paragraphs should be written in the first person, from the point of view of the woman reporter. The topic sentence should make a general statement about her perceptions of the general mood or feelings of the 1960s. The remaining sentences should support these perceptions with the reporter's impressions of particular events and people's reactions to them.

Some students may wish to make recordings of their paragraphs and play them for the class.

CHAPTER 33

Section Review (text page 779)

1. Students' sentences will vary. Information about the names and terms can be found on the pages given in parentheses: Spiro Agnew (774–775), Kent State University (775), SALT (777), Salvador Allende (778–779).

2. In Nixon and Henry Kissinger's plan for Vietnamization of the war, American soldiers were gradually withdrawn from front lines and sent home. Their places were taken by South Vietnamese troops trained by American advisors. The number of American troops was reduced from a high of 541,000 in 1969 to 24,000 by 1972. But the Nixon-Kissinger plan had a flaw. In 1965, the South Vietnamese army had been losing when there were few, if any, North Vietnamese soldiers fighting. In 1969, several hundred thousand North Vietnamese soldiers were fighting, and they proved to be a superior fighting force. As long as they were winning, North Vietnam refused every attempt to negotiate a conclusion to the war. Nixon tried to force North Vietnam to the bargaining table; while he continued to remove ground troops from Vietnam, he was actually expanding the scope of the war through the increased use of air power. In 1972, after the failure of the secret talks between Kissinger and Le Duc Tho, Nixon ordered the bombing of Haiphong and Hanoi in North Vietnam.

3. After the heavy bombing of Hanoi and Haiphong, Le Duc Tho returned to the bargaining table. In January 1973, a ceasefire agreement was signed, enabling Nixon to withdraw the remaining American troops. In 1975, North Vietnam broke the ceasefire and launched a major offensive that concluded with the capture of Saigon. The conflict in Vietnam could be called the most tragic war in United States history. Not one of the goals for which more than 200,000 Americans were killed or wounded and $140 billion spent was achieved. And the war demoralized the American people. It cost Lyndon Johnson and many of his advisors their historical reputations and damaged the prestige of the United States. Vietnam veterans were neglected and shunned as if they had been responsible for the war, instead of its victims. Finally, the huge expenditure of money probably contributed to the nation's economic difficulties in the early 1980s.

4. According to Kissinger's *realpolitik*, ideology should not be the chief force determining how nations act toward one another. To allow such elements as

religious or anti-Communist feelings, for example, to determine national policy would be foolish and self-destructive. Instead, it should be the policy of the United States to seek a balance of power among nations in which it had the edge and the initiative. Realpolitik appealed to Nixon, so he was able to reverse his lifelong condemnation of Red China, and sent Henry Kissinger on a secret mission to that country to arrange for his own far more dramatic visit. In February 1972, Nixon went to China and laid the groundwork for diplomatic recognition of the People's Republic of China and for its admission to the UN, where it would replace the Nationalist government of Taiwan.

Section Review (text page 783)

1. Students' sentences will vary. Information about the terms can be found on the pages given in parentheses: inflationary spiral (779), Environmental Protection Agency (780), Burger Court (780), Twenty-Sixth Amendment (780).
2. Astronaut Neil Armstrong made the statement on July 20, 1969, at the moment when he became the first person to step on the moon.
3. Sample answer: Nixon angered his conservative Republican supporters by (1) instituting wage and price controls, and (2) establishing the Cost of Living Council to monitor inflation and set guidelines for it. To these supporters, Nixon seemed to be acting against the conservative principles for which they had elected him.
4. Among the events students should refer to in their answers are the following: (1) the arrest of five men for burglarizing Democratic party headquarters in the Watergate complex, including the security chief for the Republican Committee to Reelect the President; (2) the Democrats' unsuccessful attempt to exploit the burglary; (3) the news stories of two investigative reporters that seemed to implicate members of the Nixon administration and Nixon's campaign committee in the burglary; (4) Judge Sirica's demand for more information during the trial of the five Watergate burglars; (5) the Senate bipartisan investigation revealing that top Nixon aides, and perhaps the President himself, may have known about the burglary and may have tried to cover it up; (6) the evidence on tape recordings that Nixon was ordered to turn over to Judge Sirica—the President had clearly been involved in the cover-up; (7) the three resolutions by the Judiciary Committee of the House of Representatives calling for Nixon's impeachment; (8) Nixon's resignation from the presidency. Nixon caused his own downfall

because of his practice of taping meetings held in his office.

Section Review (text page 786)

1. Students' sentences will vary. Information about the terms can be found on the pages given in parentheses: fossil fuels (784), OPEC (784–785), stagflation (785), *Mayaguez* (785).
2. By pardoning Richard Nixon for any crimes he might have committed, Gerald Ford seemed to be damaging his popularity with the American people.
3. The oil embargo by the Arab members of OPEC was a blow to the United States because it could no longer count on cheap, abundant energy. Approximately 35 to 40 percent of the oil Americans consumed was imported, much of it from the Middle East. Now, because of the embargo, American motorists had to wait in long lines to fill their gas tanks. Gasoline also became very expensive. Saudi Arabian leaders pointed out that if the industrialized countries went bankrupt, the oil-producing countries would suffer too, because their oil sales and revenues would drop significantly.
4. An annual inflation rate of 11 percent means that prices rise 11 cents on the dollar in a year. Both of President Ford's attempts to reduce inflation failed. Americans thought of themselves as the victims of inflation rather than as the cause of it; consequently, few people paid attention to President Ford's Whip Inflation Now campaign. The reduction of money in circulation and the raising of the prime interest rate as well as the interest rate banks charged their customers, did succeed in discouraging spending. However, this in turn resulted in the most serious recession since the end of World War II. With people spending less, factories had to cut production and lay off workers. Unemployment rose to 8.5 percent. Stagflation—that is, a stagnant economy and inflation at the same time—resulted.

Section Review (text page 789)

1. Students' sentences will vary. Information about the names and terms can be found on the pages given in parentheses: Natchez Trace (786), "Earth Days" (788), Betty Friedan (788), ERA (789).
2. Involvement in political and social issues seemed to characterize the American spirit in the 1960s. However, after the deaths of four students at Kent State in May 1970, the American people seemed to withdraw into their own private, personal concerns. The writer Tom Wolfe called the 1970s "the Me decade." The difference between people's concerns in the 1960s and the 1970s was reflected in a boom in sales of recreational equipment and other

commodities designed for personal enjoyment. Americans spent billions on such items as ski equipment, tennis equipment, hang gliders, and snowmobiles. No activity was exempt from commercial exploitation; even running, which would seem to require no equipment at all, spawned multi-million dollar sales of special shoes and fashionable jogging clothes. Some Americans turned to new religions or cults. Although some of these were relatively harmless, others demanded complete loyalty to their leaders, which worried many Americans.

3. During the 1970s, American society was influenced by the belief that traditional moral codes were out of date. To many, marriage and families seemed less important. The birthrate dropped from 25 per 1,000 people in 1955 to 14.8 in 1975. Among the reasons for the decrease in births were people's concerns about overpopulation and the responsibility of raising children. With the divorce rate hovering near 50 percent, the family seemed threatened. Marriage was often viewed as a means for self-fulfillment rather than as a social or religious contract.

4. The goal of affirmative action was to place women, blacks, Hispanics, and physically handicapped people in jobs traditionally held by white males. Women allied themselves with racial and ethnic minorities to demand affirmative action. As a result, federal and state officials began requiring government agencies, universities, law schools, medical schools, and corporations to hire members of these underemployed groups rather than white males, when they were equally qualified.

5. The bicentennial celebration took many forms. It was celebrated in different ways across the nation. Historic buildings were restored, trees were planted in public parks, parades and picnics were held, and people retraced historic trails like the Natchez Trace or the Oregon Trail. Most seafaring countries sent antique sailing ships to New York to participate in the celebration.

Time Line Questions (text page 790)

1. Yom Kippur War, SALT agreement
2. 1972
3. National Organization for Women founded; Congress approves Equal Rights Amendment
4. Possible answers: Nixon's trip to China; SALT agreement

Skills Strategy: Pie Graphs (text pages 790–791)

Students' graphs should contain a title, the label *1980*, and a key matching colors and energy resources. The wedge representing each resource should be the color shown in the key, and its size should represent the percentage of use. The missing percentage is 45%. The 1980 graph should be completed before students answer questions 1–5.

1. 1925 to 1950
2. Oil
3. Increased by 16 percent
4. Increased by 3.5 percent
5. Increase in use of natural gas, hydroelectric and geothermal power, nuclear power

Chapter Test (text page 791)

Text Review

1. Students' answers should include the following: ending the Vietnam War, laying the groundwork for diplomatic recognition of Communist China and for its admission to the UN, signing the SALT treaty on a 1973 trip to the Soviet Union, achieving détente with the Soviet Union, bringing peace between the Arabs and Israelis by sanctioning the shuttle diplomacy of Secretary of State Henry Kissinger.

2. When Kissinger was Nixon's chief advisor on foreign policy and, even more, when he became Secretary of State, he helped to bring about a revolution in American diplomacy through the application of his *realpolitik*, or "realistic policy." According to this theory of international relations, allowing religious or political ideology to determine foreign policy would be foolish, dangerous, and self-destructive for the United States. Instead, Kissinger insisted, the United States should work for a balance of power among nations, holding the edge and initiative.

3. Students' answers should include the following: the opposition of Republican conservatives who disliked recognition of Communist China and détente with the Soviet Union; the failure of *realpolitik* in Angola, which prolonged an ugly civil war there; Kissinger's approval of the CIA's part in the overthrow of the democratically elected president of Chile.

4. Nixon nominated and the Senate approved Warren Burger as Chief Justice of the Supreme Court and Harry Blackmun as one of the justices. However, because of their questionable records on civil rights, two other Nixon nominees for the Court—Clement Haynesworth and Harold Carswell—were rejected by the Senate.

5. The initials EPA stand for Environmental Protection Agency. This government agency was made responsible for overseeing the conservation of the nation's resources. It was given the power to prosecute companies and individuals who violated

laws designed to eliminate pollution of air and water and other threats to the environment.

6. Students' chronological accounts should refer to the following events: the burglary of the national headquarters of the Democratic party in Washington by the security chief of the Committee to Reelect the President and others; the unsuccessful initial attempts of the Democrats to exploit the burglary; the implication of important members of the Nixon administration and campaign committee brought about by the investigative reporting of journalists Woodward and Bernstein; Judge Sirica's demand for more details about the burglary during the trial of five of the burglars; the Senate investigating committee's findings that Nixon aides had known about the burglary and that the President himself may have attempted a cover-up of the affair; the resignation of Vice President Agnew and Nixon's replacement of him with Gerald Ford; the firing of Special Prosecutor Archibald Cox by Nixon's order; the discovery of tape recordings that clearly showed that Nixon was involved in the cover-up; the House Judiciary Committee's recommendation for impeachment; Nixon's resignation; Gerald Ford's presidency; Ford's pardon of Nixon.

7. The OPEC oil embargo was meant as a protest against United States support of Israel, which had just won the Yom Kippur War against Egypt and Syria. Among the effects the embargo had in the United States were long lines at gas stations, the extreme scarcity of gas in some American cities and throughout the state of Hawaii for weeks; the skyrocketing of gasoline prices to as much as $2 a gallon.

Critical Thinking

8. American prestige among nations of the world sank to a lower point than ever before in history. The morale of the American people also sank to a new low, and they lost confidence in their government. The war haunted people who lived through it, just as the Civil War had haunted Americans of earlier generations. Returning veterans were ostracized and treated as if they were responsible for the war instead of being its victims. The economic difficulties of America in the late 1970s were, in large part, the result of the huge expenditures made to fight the war.

9. Possible response: Ford's words and actions indicate that he apparently felt that the country's morale needed to be boosted after Vietnam and Watergate.

10. Whereas Americans of the 1960s sought involvement in political and social issues, Americans of the 1970s seemed to be asking only what they could do for themselves. One writer labeled the 1970s "the Me decade."

Writing a Paragraph

Students' paragraphs should begin or end with a topic sentence predicting the degree of importance of one of the given alternate energy sources in the future. The other sentences should support the prediction with appropriate facts, reasons, and/or examples. Samples:

Hydroelectric and geothermal power will remain important in areas where water power and underground thermal sources are available, but probably neither will ever have the worldwide importance of oil.

Solar and wind power may develop as important local energy sources if the necessary technology develops beyond present initial phases.

Nuclear power could replace oil because the technology is already in place; however, current serious questions about the dangers of nuclear reactors must be answered satisfactorily.

CHAPTER 34

Section Review (text page 799)

1. Students' sentences will vary. Information about the names and terms can be found on the pages given in parentheses: windfall profits tax (795), Andrew Young (795), PLO (795), Solidarity (797).

2. In 1976, when Jimmy Carter announced that he would run for the presidency, one poll showed that only two percent of Democratic voters knew his name. Yet Carter surprised experts and confounded party professionals by winning most of the state primaries he entered. At the Democratic Convention, he was nominated on the first ballot, and in the election received 50 percent of the popular vote and 297 votes of the electoral college. Gerald Ford was his Republican opponent.

3. Among the examples of President Carter's problems at home are the following. Poor relations with Congress: None of the major bills Carter submitted were passed in the form he wanted in the first year of his presidency. A worsening economy: Inflation ran at more than 10 percent each year during his presidency; Carter's actions in fighting inflation increased an already high rate of unemployment; high interest rates caused by actions of the Federal Reserve System alienated voters who wanted to buy homes, cars, and other goods. The energy crisis: The rise of OPEC oil prices (1980 total, $73

billion) fueled inflation; Carter could not get people to cut down consumption of petroleum products, nor could he get Congress to pass a windfall profits tax on oil companies to finance the search for new sources of energy. Students will cite one of Carter's diplomatic breakthroughs: the appointment of Andrew Young as UN ambassador; the treaty giving Panama control of the Canal Zone; the Camp David Accords between Egypt and Israel.

4. President Carter's popularity in November 1979, before the hostages were taken in Iran, was at a record low. Polls showed that Senator Edward Kennedy could have easily defeated Carter in the Democratic primaries. However, after the hostages were seized, many Americans, standing behind their president in a time of crisis, increased Carter's popularity. After a hard-fought campaign against Kennedy, and because of Carter's power as the incumbent president, as well as voters' anxiety about the hostages, Carter was nominated at the Democratic convention. Ronald Reagan won the presidential election of 1980. He represented the views of the conservative wing of the Republican party.

Section Review (text page 806)

1. Students' sentences will vary. Information about the names and terms can be found on the pages given in parentheses: ''boll weevils'' (800), Beirut (802, 804), Reaganomics (804), Jesse Jackson (804).

2. Cutting $35 billion from the budgets of social programs: Reagan argued that inflation was caused by huge government expenditures and the resulting budget deficits. Cutting taxes: President Reagan's supply-side economic theory held that the way to cure unemployment was to cut taxes and reduce government regulations. In theory, the untaxed money would be invested in industry, thus creating jobs for working people. In the short run, Reagan said, his policies would bring about higher unemployment. If, however, Americans would ''stay the course,'' by 1981 the economy would swing upward. Increasing expenditures for the military: Reagan claimed that increased spending for the military was necessary to restore America's prestige in the world.

3. Reagan used his influence in the Senate to block the SALT II treaty because he believed that America made too many concessions to the Soviets, receiving none in return.

4. The victory of the Sandinistas in Nicaragua alarmed Reagan and his advisors. They feared that other nations in Latin America might also fall prey to rebel forces trained and equipped by Cuba. Despite the cruel tactics of El Salvador's military regime, Reagan won Congressional approval for increasing military aid to El Salvador to stop the Cuban-supported rebels from taking over the government. In 1983, Reagan announced that United States marines and paratroopers had invaded the tiny island-nation of Grenada because a brief civil war had endangered the lives of 700 American students there. The victory of the Cuban-backed rebels was also a primary reason for the Grenada invasion.

Section Review (text page 807)

1. Black Americans: the number of black Americans was 26 million in 1980, an increase of 12.1 percent since 1970. The number of blacks who held positions of prominence rose significantly. Black businesspeople and executives numbered in the thousands. By 1984, there were 20 blacks in the Congress and 19 black mayors governing large cities. Hispanics: The population of the Hispanics increased 61 percent between 1970 and 1980. By 1990, Hispanic-Americans, according to estimates, would outnumber blacks and become the largest ethnic American minority. Asian immigrants: Asian immigrants from Korea, Japan, Vietnam, India, Taiwan, and the Philippines increased by 128 percent between 1970 and 1980. About 3.5 million Asian immigrants lived in the cities of the United States. The Frostbelt and the Sunbelt: Responding to the attraction of lower taxes, major corporations shifted their headquarters from cities in the Frostbelt to cities in the warmer and newer regions of the Sunbelt. Thousands of those who moved to the Sunbelt were immigrants from Asia and Latin America.

2. In the 1950s: The policy set by the Indian Reorganization Act of 1934 was reversed. President Eisenhower encouraged migration of American Indians from reservations into the mainstream of American society. In the late 1960s: The National Congress of American Indians was founded and began to push for legal rights for American Indians. The more militant American Indian Movement was organized at about the same time. This organization sought (sometimes violently) Indian treaty rights. In the 1970s: President Nixon announced a policy of self-determination for American Indians, whereby Indians could establish their own tribal systems and customs on the reservations. The Federal government would help with housing, vocational training, and economic development. President Carter established the post of Assistant Secretary of the Interior for Indian Affairs and named a Blackfoot

Indian to the post. In the 1980s: Indians on reservations developed sophisticated organizations to protect their legal rights and to advance their economic power.

3. Possible answers: Computers, robots, and lasers were growing in importance during the 1980s. Users of home computers could play games, keep records, conserve heating fuel, and defend against burglars. Computers were also used on farms, and in factories, hospitals, stores, airports, and schools, as well as for processing information, delivering services, and distributing goods. Robots were used on assembly lines in the most advanced American factories. Lasers were used by surgeons and by the military to defend against enemy missiles and satellites.

4. President Reagan repeatedly said in his television speeches that the United States had survived past challenges and that America's future growth and security were assured if Americans would only remember their courageous heritage and live up to the pioneering spirit of earlier generations.

Time Line Questions (text page 810)

1. Soviet Union invades Afghanistan
2. 1978
3. Jimmy Carter inaugurated, People's Republic of China recognized, Americans taken hostage in Iran, national debt rises to over one trillion dollars

Skills Strategy: Selecting References (text page 810)

1. The author card for the book in the library card catalog
2. Encyclopedia
3. Atlas
4. A dictionary
5. *Readers' Guide to Periodical Literature*
6. Almanac or magazine found in *Readers' Guide*

UNIT 10 TEST (TEXT PAGE 811)

Chapter Survey

1. Sample summary sentence(s): Chapter 32 opens with a presentation of President Kennedy's Thousand Days—the blacks' continuing quest for their rights, the confrontation of the United States and Russia over missiles in Cuba, and the assassination of President Kennedy. The chapter continues with an account of Lyndon Johnson's success in establishing his monumental Great Society and concludes with analysis of his Vietnam policy that brought turmoil at home, the Johnson decision not to run again, and the defeat of the Democrats by Richard Nixon in 1968. Pages containing information about terms: Peace Corps (753), Warren Commission (759), James Meredith (753, 762), Watts (762), Ho Chi Minh (764).

2. Sample summary sentence(s): Chapter 33 is an account of the negative and positive aspects of the Nixon and Ford years: the growing intensification of the antiwar movement that brought about the withdrawal of United States forces from Vietnam; recognition of Communist China, temporary peace in the Middle East, and the signing of the SALT treaty; the anger of Republican conservatives over Nixon's foreign and economic domestic policies; the resignation of Spiro Agnew and appointment of Gerald Ford as vice president; the first American moon landing; Watergate scandal and Nixon's resignation; President Ford's pardon of Nixon; the OPEC oil embargo; the Bicentennial celebration; the rise of the "Me Generation"; and women's fight to have the Equal Rights Amendment ratified. Pages containing information about terms: Kent State (775), Strategic Arms Limitations Talks (777), Burger Court (780), Organization of Petroleum Exporting Countries (784–785), Betty Friedan (788).

3. Sample summary sentence(s): Chapter 34 begins with President Jimmy Carter's accomplishments and frustrations and continues with Ronald Reagan's presidency. The chapter concludes with a summation on the status of minorities in the 1980s, an examination of three technological marvels, and a look into America's future. Pages containing information about terms: Andrew Young (795), Palestine Liberation Organization (795, 803), Reaganomics (804), Jesse Jackson (804), Sunbelt (805).

Text Review

4. Kennedy moved very cautiously on the issues raised by the growing civil rights movement in the 1960s because he hoped to get support for his New Frontier programs from southern Democrats in Congress.

5. Students' answers should refer to the following domestic legislation: Medicare and Medicaid; laws conserving wilderness areas for recreation; laws providing for aid to education, the building of public transportation systems, and the renewal of blighted neighborhoods; laws establishing the Department of Housing and Urban Development and the Office of Economic Opportunity (which directed VISTA and other aspects of Johnson's War on Poverty), the Civil Rights Act of 1964, the Voting Rights Act of 1965.

6. Students' answers should reflect the following understandings: Kennedy's Vietnam policy was one of limited use of American military personnel to train the South Vietnamese army (Green Berets) and to guard American bases in South Vietnam (marines), supplemented by attempts to persuade the South Vietnamese leaders to eliminate social injustice. Kennedy was opposed to deepening American involvement in Vietnam. Johnson's Vietnam policy was one of escalation of American involvement in Vietnam. Under the provisions of the Tonkin Gulf Resolution, which gave Johnson the power to repel attacks against American forces and to stop further aggression, he increased the number of American troops in Vietnam from 28,000 (1964) to over 500,000 (1969). Johnson's Vietnam policy caused him to lose popularity among Americans. Many joined the antiwar movement. As a result of his unpopularity and the growing opposition to the war, Johnson decided not to run again.

7. The candidates and platforms of the three parties: Democrat Hubert Humphrey campaigned on a platform that was an attempt at balancing loyalty to Johnson with cautious opposition to the war. Republican Richard Nixon campaigned on a platform that promised to end the Vietnam War and the instability of the Johnson years. Nixon's running mate, Spiro Agnew, took a hard line against rioters and antiwar "peaceniks" and said that Nixon would restore "law and order." American Independent party candidate George Wallace's campaign criticized black rioters and professors, whom he said encouraged student disloyalty to the United States, and promised a victorious conclusion of the Vietnam War. The winner of the election was Richard Nixon, the Republican candidate. Students' choices of the main reason for Nixon's victory will differ. Among the possible choices are the promise to end the war in Vietnam, the promise to end the turmoil of the Johnson years and restore "law and order," or the weakness of the Democratic party.

8. Students should list all of the following and describe one in detail: ending the Vietnam War (page 775), recognition of the People's Republic of China and Nixon's visit there (page 776), signing and ratifying the SALT treaty of 1973 (777), Kissinger's shuttle diplomacy, which resulted in a cease-fire between Israel and its Egyptian and Syrian foes, as well as Egyptian leader Sadat's recognition of and exchange of ambassadors with Israel (pages 777–778). In their description of one of these achievements, students should include details given on the page references in parentheses.

9. Henry Kissinger was Secretary of State under both Nixon and Ford. Students' explanations of Kissinger's role in the nation's foreign policy successes should focus on the Secretary of State's application of *realpolitik* to relations between the United States and other countries.

10. Gerald Ford was appointed vice president by President Nixon when Spiro Agnew resigned after being charged with falsifying his tax returns and accepting bribes as governor of Maryland. Ford then became president when Richard Nixon resigned as a result of his involvement in the Watergate scandal.

11. Many Americans in the 1970s seemed to be interested only in what they could do for themselves. Political radicalism, black demands for civil rights, and the peace movement all disappeared. "Me-ism" was reflected in self-centered fads, fashions, and religious cults.

12. Carter's was a moralistic foreign policy aimed at people's moral sensibilities and dedicated to exposing violations of human rights whenever they occurred. Carter cut off foreign aid to countries where leaders denied basic rights to their people. Kissinger's *realpolitik* was based on the idea that ideology should not be the basis for relations with other countries and that to allow ideas about religion or anti-communism to determine United States foreign policy was foolish, dangerous, and self-destructive. By emphasizing morality in foreign policy, Carter hoped to contrast his moral approach to world affairs with Kissinger's *realpolitik*. Camp David was considered a diplomatic triumph for Carter because Israeli leader Begin's reluctance to return the Sinai Peninsula to Egypt and his refusal to agree to establishing a site for the Palestinians almost caused Egyptian leader Sadat to end the meetings and go home. Through his persuasion of both men, Carter was able to lead them to a compromise, which resulted in Egypt's formal recognition of Israel and a chance for peace in the Middle East.

13. After the Shah left Iran, the Ayatollah Khomeini began to villify the United States. When Carter admitted the Shah to the United States for medical treatment in October of 1979, Iranian students stormed the American embassy in Teheran, took 53 Americans hostage, and held them captive for more than a year in spite of Carter's diplomatic and military attempts to free them. The hostage crisis helped Carter win the Democratic nomination for president. Prior to the taking of the hostages, his popularity was at an all-time low. After the hostages were taken, however, Americans united behind him and his popularity increased. This

development, plus his control of the Democratic party machinery, gave him the party's nomination. By election day, Carter's failure to free the hostages convinced many voters that he lacked the leadership qualities needed by a president, and they voted for Republican candidate Ronald Reagan.

14. Students' answers should include three of the following. Social programs: Reagan convinced Congress to cut $35 billion from such social welfare programs as Medicare, food stamps, and free lunches for some school children. Tax cuts: With the stated purpose of curbing unemployment, Reagan cut taxes, particularly for the wealthy. Theoretically, the wealthy would invest the tax money in industry, thus creating jobs. Military expenditures: In accordance with his "get tough" policy toward the Communists and his declared intention of restoring the nation's prestige, Reagan increased military expenditures, which resulted in increases in the ceiling of the national debt. Relations with Latin America: Reagan was alarmed by the victory of the Communists in taking over the government of Nicaragua. Therefore, when it seemed that the same thing might happen in El Salvador, he increased military aid to the country's anti-Communist military leaders. Reagan said that his intention in sending marines to Grenada was to protect the lives of Americans studying at a medical college there. School prayer: Reagan backed a proposed constitutional amendment that would allow voluntary prayer in school activities. However, the proposal failed. The Equal Rights Amendment: both before and after his election, Reagan opposed the amendment. He also approved some policies that seemed to threaten social gains made by women in the 1960s and 1970s.

15. Students will answer one part of the question. Changes for minorities between 1970 and 1980: Discussions will summarize information found under the headings "Rise of Minorities in the Sunbelt" and "American Indians" on pages 805–806. High technology in the 1980s: Discussions will summarize information given under the three headings on pages 806–807.

Critical Thinking

16. Martin Luther King, Jr., advocated nonviolent disobedience of unjust laws with the goal of changing the laws or having them taken off the books and, ultimately, achieving integration of blacks in American society. Advocates of black power such as Stokely Carmichael, Rap Brown, and the Black Panthers called on blacks to cut themselves off from white society instead of seeking integration. Some black power leaders preached active violence, while others said blacks should arm themselves only for self-defense. Malcolm X started off as a member of the Black Muslims, a group that advocated the arming of blacks for self-defense. He urged blacks to take pride in their blackness and to break loose from white domination. However, his speeches urged violence, and the Black Muslims expelled him. Just before Malcolm X was assassinated, he was beginning to call for a degree of cooperation between blacks and whites who were seeking social change.

17. Students should recognize that White's statement contrasts Johnson's phenomenally successful domestic legislation program with his dismal handling of the Vietnam situation. To verify White's opinion, students should refer to examples of Johnson's domestic successes as well as to examples of his mishandling of the war.

18. Students' comments should indicate their awareness of the responsibility they will have for the future growth and security of America as future voters, mature citizens, and leaders of the United States. Their present study of American history will help them "remember their courageous heritage" and "the pioneering spirit of earlier generations" in anticipation of their future roles.

Skills Review

19. A hypothesis, or theory, is a tentative conclusion based upon the study of available evidence. It is not a final conclusion, and its degree of validity rests upon the accuracy with which sources used to form it are interpreted. A hypothesis about a historical era can be formed by carefully examining and thoughtfully interpreting various primary sources of the era: books, magazines, newspapers, songs, laws, photographs, public opinion polls, oral testimony of people living during the era, and so forth. A hypothesis about an historical era can be tested for validity by referring to conclusions about the era reached by a majority of historians. Where possible, further testing can be done by interviewing a sampling of reliable people who lived through the era.

20. Students can name any of the following: encyclopedia (and index), dictionaries of various types, atlases, almanacs, the *Readers' Guide,* and the library catalog. Students' explanations of how to use the *Readers' Guide* should approximate the instruction in the Skills Strategy on pages 628–629. Explanations of how to use a library card catalog should reflect information give in the Skills Strategy on pages 586–587.

BIBLIOGRAPHY

UNIT 1 **One Land, Many Peoples (25,000 BC–1754 AD)**

Chapter 1

For information about the people who were already in the Americas, see A.M. Josephy, Jr., *The Indian Heritage of America* (1968).

J.H. Elliott, *The Old World and the New* (1970), deals with interactions between Europe and America.

Chapter 2

Designed as a textbook, but also an authoritative history, is Curtis PI Nettels, *The Roots of American Civilization* (1938).

The reigning classic about English colonization is still

Charles M. Andrews' *The Colonial Period of American History* (1934–38).

Chapter 3

Wesley, F. Craven, *The Southern Colonies in the Seventeenth Century* (1949), is an excellent brief account of Virginia and Maryland.

For a crystal-clear understanding of Puritanism, see Larzer Ziff, *Puritanism in Old and New England* (1973).

On the Middle Colonies, see T.J. Wertenbaker, *The Founding of American Civilization: The Middle Colonies* (1938).

Chapter 4

See the first volume of G.M. Wrong, *The Rise and Fall of New France* (1928).

For information about slavery in colonial Virginia, see E.S. Morgan, *American Slavery, American Freedom* (1975).

UNIT 2 **The Making of a Nation (1754–1801)**

Chapter 5

See Francis Parkman, *A Half Century of Conflict* (1892), an epic work on the French in North America.

A.M. Schlesinger, *The Colonial Merchants and the American Revolution, 1763–1776* (1951), is a specialized study that has greatly influenced historians of the period.

Chapter 6

See Carl Becker, *The Declaration of Independence* (1922), for an intensive study of the great document that is still revealing.

D. Higginbotham, *The War of American Independence: Military Attitudes, Policies, and Practice* (1971), offers a military history of the Revolutionary War.

Chapter 7

John Fiske, *The Critical Period of American History, 1783–1789* (1883), gives the classic account of the Confederation period as a dismal time for the young country.

A largely discredited work is still the first book to read about the writing of the Constitution. According to Charles A. Beard, *Economic Interpretation of the Constitution of the United States* (1913), the long-lived frame of government was written largely because men who held Confederation notes wanted to profit from their speculations.

Chapter 8	J.T. Flexner focuses on the president himself in *George Washington and the New Nation* (1970). J.C. Miller, *The Federalist Era* (1960), is the standard study of the 1790s.

UNIT 3 The Bold Republic (1801–1850)

Chapter 9	On the War of 1812, see Bradford Perkins, *Prologue to War: England and the United States, 1805–1812* (1961). Dexter Perkins, *The Monroe Doctrine* (1927), deals with the successful foreign policy of the Monroe administration.
Chapter 10	Essential background for understanding the significance of every ''West'' in American history is F.J. Turner, *The Frontier in American History* (1920). L.C. Hunter, *Steamboats on the Western Rivers* (1949), treats in detail two aspects of the revolution in transportation.
Chapter 11	G.G. Van Deusen, *The Jacksonian Era, 1828–1848* (1959), is still the best general history of the Jacksonian period. O.D. Lambert follows the aftermath of the election of 1840 in *Presidential Politics in the United States 1841–1844* (1936).
Chapter 12	On the reform movements of the first half of the nineteenth century, the classic study is A.F. Tyler, *Freedom's Ferment: Phases of American Social History to 1860* (1944). Eleanor Flexner, *Century of Struggle: The Woman's Rights Movement in the United States* (1975), for feminist history.

UNIT 4 Division and Reunion (1820–1877)

Chapter 13	The neglected prominence of blacks in the antislavery movement is remedied in J.H. and W.H. Pease, *They Who Would Be Free: Blacks' Search for Freedom, 1830–1861* (1974). If students are to read only one book on slavery, it ought to be Eugene Genovese, *Roll, Jordan, Roll* (1975).
Chapter 14	The best single book to bring the many aspects of expansion together is Ray A. Billington, *The Far Western Frontier, 1830–1860* (1956). David M. Potter, *The Impending Crisis,* 1848–1861 (1976), is also a useful source.
Chapter 15	The most comprehensive account of the first half of the Civil War is Allan Nevins, *Ordeal of the Union* (1947). A collection of essays edited by David Donald, *Why the North Won the Civil War* (1960), is recommended.
Chapter 16	J.G. Randall and David Donald, *The Civil War and Reconstruction* (1961) is the standard one-volume account. W.A. Dunning, *Reconstruction: Political and Economic* (1907), is the classic depiction of Reconstruction as a time of brutal oppression for the South.

UNIT 5   The Transformation of America (1865–1900)

Chapter 17

For a general discussion of technology and inventors, see Roger Burlingame, *Engines of Democracy: Inventions and Society in Mature America* (1940).

Also see Sigmund Diamond, *The Reputation of the American Businessman* (1955).

Chapter 18

The most comprehensive study of politics during the late nineteenth century is H. Wayne Morgan, *From Hayes to McKinley: National Party Politics, 1877–1896* (1969).

D.J. Rothman, *Politics and Power, The United States Senate, 1869–1901* (1966), focuses on the Senate, where the balance of power rested during this period.

Chapter 19

For a good history of the organized labor movement in the late nineteenth century, see Norman J. Ware, *The Labor Movement in the United States, 1860–1893* (1929).

For an introduction to the immigrant experience, see Maldwyn A. Jones, *American Immigration* (1960).

UNIT 6   The Closing of the Frontier (1865–1903)

Chapter 20

See Ray A. Billington, *Westward Expansion: A History of the American Frontier* (1967).

For a study of the cattleman's frontier, see E.S. Osgood, *The Day of the Cattleman* (1929).

Chapter 21

For the problems that American farmers experienced, see Fred A. Shannon, *The Farmer's Last Frontier: Agriculture, 1860–1897* (1945).

Also see John D. Hicks, *The Populist Revolt* (1931).

Chapter 22

See S.L. Jones, *The Presidential Election of 1896* (1964).

For a great shift in American foreign policy, see Ernest R. May, *Imperial Democracy: The Emergence of America as a Great Power* (1961).

UNIT 7   The Progressive Era (1890–1920)

Chapter 23

Frederick Lewis Allen, *The Big Change* (1952), provides a good brief overview of American society as it evolved around the turn of the century.

Also see Foster Rhea Dulles, *America Learns to Play* (1940).

Chapter 24

George Mowry, *The Era of Theodore Roosevelt* (1958), discusses the early period of reform.

P.E. Coletta focuses on the events of the Taft years in *The Presidency of William Howard Taft* (1973).

Chapter 25	See Arthur S. Link, *Woodrow Wilson and the Progressive Era* (1954).

Also see N.G. Levin, Jr., *Woodrow Wilson and World Politics: America's Response to War and Revolution* (1968).

Ralph Stone, *The Irreconcilables: The Fight Against the League of Nations* (1970), discusses the rejection of the treaty.

UNIT 8   Good Times, Bad Times (1920–1937)

Chapter 26   See Robert K. Murray, *The Harding Era* (1969).

A good general overview is George Soule, *Prosperity Decade: From War to Depression, 1917–1929* (1947).

Chapter 27   See D.R. McCoy, *Calvin Coolidge: The Quiet President* (1967).

J.H. Wilson, *Herbert Hoover: Forgotten Progressive* (1975), presents a somewhat different picture of the president who is best remembered for having presided over the Great Crash and Great Depression.

Chapter 28   A must for the first years of the national trauma is Jordan A. Schwarz, *The Interregnum of Despair: Hoover, Congress, and the Depression* (1970).

On the difference that Franklin D. Roosevelt meant for the United States, see Arthur M. Schlesinger, Jr., *The Coming of the New Deal* (1959).

UNIT 9   America in a Turbulent World (1930–1960)

Chapter 29   The debate between "isolationists" and "interventionists" is dealt with in Robert A. Divine, *The Illusion of Neutrality* (1962).

For the controversies surrounding America's defeat at Pearl Harbor, see Herbert Feis, *The Road to Pearl Harbor* (1950).

The standard military history of the Second World War is A.R. Buchanan, *The United States and World War II* (1962).

Chapter 30   On the Truman administration, see R.F. Haynes, *The Awesome Power: Harry S. Truman as Commander in Chief* (1973).

On Senator Joseph McCarthy, the oldest book remains the most authoritative: Richard H. Rovere, *Senator Joe McCarthy* (1959).

Chapter 31   Eric Goldman, *The Crucial Decade—and After: America, 1945–1960* (1961), is political in focus but helps give a feel for Ike's America.

Also see C.C. Alexander, *Holding the Line: The Eisenhower Era, 1952–1961* (1975).

UNIT 10   New American Frontiers (1960–Present)

Chapter 32   Arthur M. Schlesinger, Jr. *A Thousand Days* (1965), is the memoir of a distinguished historian who served in the Kennedy administration.

Also see Doris Kearns, *Lyndon Johnson and the American Dream* (1976).

On the black movement, see Martin Luther King, Jr., *Where Do We Go From Here: Chaos or Community?* (1967).

Chapter 33

Theodore H. White wrote a study of Nixon's elections in *The Making of the President, 1968, 1972* (1969, 1973).

Also see A.E. Goodman, *The Lost Peace: America's Search for a Negotiated Settlement of the Vietnam War* (1978).

For Watergate, the standard work is by the two *Washington Post* reporters who broke the story, Carl Bernstein and Robert Woodward, *All the President's Men* (1974).

Chapter 34

See Laurence Barrett, *Gambling with History* (1983), on the Reagan Administration.

Also see Lee Edwards, *Ronald Reagan, A Political Biography* (1981).

A History
of the United States

*Our Land,
Our Time*

A History
of the United States

Our Land,
Our Time

Joseph R. Conlin

CORONADO PUBLISHERS

San Diego   Chicago   Orlando   Dallas

Joseph R. Conlin is Professor of History at the California State University
in Chico, California.

REVIEWERS

The publisher wishes to thank the following reviewers of *A History of the United States: Our Land, Our Time* for their comments. They provided specific comments on the content, organization, and difficulty level of the material. Their assistance has been invaluable in creating a textbook that will be usable for the teacher and profitable for the students.

Henry Billings
Social Studies Educator
Hamilton-Wenham Regional High School
South Hamilton, Massachusetts

Gerald Jackson
Social Studies Educator
Caney High School
Caney, Oklahoma

Leone Little
Director of the Social Studies Department
Thomas Carr Howe High School
Indianapolis, Indiana

Suzanne McDaniels
Social Studies Consultant
Spartanburg County School District No. 7
Spartanburg, South Carolina

Clifford O'Harrow
Social Studies Department Coordinator
Sandy Union High School
Sandy, Oregon

John Porterfield
Secondary Curriculum Coordinator
and General Supervisor
Lewis County Schools
Weston, West Virginia

Margaret Ward
Social Studies Curriculum Program Supervisor
Polk County Schools
Bartow, Florida

Karen Wiggins
Consultant for Social Studies and Foreign Languages
Richardson Independent School District
Richardson, Texas

James Wilson
U.S. History and Government Educator
Bonita Vista High School
Chula Vista, California

Acknowledgments for material quoted from other sources will be found on page 870 which is an extension of this page.

A History of the United States: Our Land, Our Time is organized to make your study of American history more valuable. As you thumb through the book, note how the book design signals the beginning of each unit and chapter. Each of the ten units opens with a two-page painting that reflects the changes in America as it grew and developed. These unit pages list the chapters to be found in each unit. Within the units, every chapter begins with a two-page opening spread. There is introductory text on the left page and a full-page picture on the right. Chapters have several opening features. The number, title, and dates covered in each chapter are given. Below the title is a quotation from an American writer. These quotations are 34 writers' responses in prose or poetry to the general time period or to a particular event that is covered in each chapter.

Notice that some parts of the text in each chapter have a gray background. These gray-screened portions signal that there is an extra message, apart from the historical account in the chapter. On the opening page of each chapter, the extra message is called Making Connections. It always has three parts. First, it briefly sets the scene for the chapter. Second, it gives you a list of specific points to look for as you read. And third, it reminds you about something you have already learned that has a bearing on what you are about to learn. In this way, you are provided with a convenient plan for studying a chapter at a time.

The questions that form each Section Review allow you to check your own understanding of the section of the chapter you have just read. The two-page reviews that come at the end of each chapter are also set apart from the text by a gray screen. The first part of each review is the Time Line. Several time line questions allow you to review the sequence of the chapter's events and to jog your memory about causes and effects. The next section of each Chapter Review is called Skills Strategy. It is there to provide review and practice of a skill that is valuable to the study of history. The last part is a Chapter Test. The conclusion of every Chapter Test involves writing a paragraph. The paragraph will always be about the chapter you have just read.

Unit Tests are like the Chapter Tests, except that they are more comprehensive. They assess skills and ask for summaries of each unit's content. They ask questions involving Text Review and Critical Thinking. The last chapter in each unit is tested in the Unit Test.

Following Chapter 34 is an Atlas and Reference Section. It includes additional maps, charts, graphs, and tables that will prove helpful throughout the reading of this book. A list of what is in the Atlas and Reference Section is on page 813. A glossary and index complete the book.

The maps and other displays throughout this book were especially created to complement the text.

Each unit has features that offer interesting sidelights to the period you are studying. Profiles of the Presidency and Going to the Source offer you important primary source readings. Movers and Shapers provides biographies of people who contributed to our nation's greatness. American Ingenuity and its accompanying Changing Technology time line show how life in the United States changed as new machines and techniques were invented.

The paintings and photographs in this book document the people, places, and events discussed in the text and add visual information about American history. The captions next to the pictures identify them and bring together information in the text or add relevant, new information.

MAPS

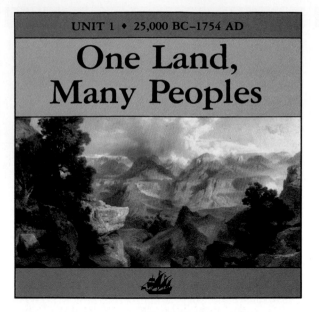

UNIT 1 ♦ 25,000 BC–1754 AD

One Land, Many Peoples

Unit One Overview:

Unit One takes students from a hazy time in the distant past when Asian people came to the vast, empty, and bountiful continents we know as North and South America to a time closer to us, when the English colonies in North America were at the brink of revolt from Great Britain.

Basic Unit Concepts

1. The ancestors of American Indians were the first settlers of the Americas.
2. Thousands of years later, people from several European nations founded American colonies.
3. Native Americans often suffered serious injustices at the hands of European settlers.
4. English colonists built the Thirteen Colonies that later became the first thirteen United States.
5. African people were forced to come to the English colonies as slaves.
6. Governmental institutions of the English colonists sowed the seeds of participatory government in the United States.

Chapter 1: "A Meeting of Two Worlds" (25,000 BC–1550 AD)

In Chapter 1, students survey the remarkable variety of cultures developed by the First Americans; they follow the daring sea voyages that resulted in the European discovery of America; and they witness the often tragic encounters of Native Americans and Europeans.

Features

Movers and Shapers: Henry the Navigator and Queen Isabella (page 15)
Going to the Source: Excerpt from Christopher Columbus's *Letter on His Discoveries* (page 19)

Learning Objectives
History Generalizations

Students will gain knowledge that supports the following generalizations:

1. People from Asia, the ancestors of American Indians, were the first settlers of North and South America.
2. The First Americans developed a great variety of remarkable cultures over thousands of years.
3. The cultures these people developed were, in part, an intelligent response to the environments in the parts of America where they settled.
4. Tens of thousands of years later, Europeans in search of trade routes to the riches of Asia found the Americas.
5. People from several European nations explored North and South America and founded colonies there. The Europeans adapted the cultures of their homelands to their new American environments.

Study Skills

Students will:

1. interpret a time line to answer questions.
2. identify the main ideas and supporting details of the chapter and its sections.
3. use key words and chapter headings in skimming text to find answers to previously formulated questions.
Note: The three study skills mentioned above are used by students as they read each chapter of the text.
4. take notes on specified text information.
5. write a paragraph from the notes taken.
6. relate graphic materials to the text of the chapter.
7. practice these **critical thinking skills:** generating questions about material to be read, summarizing, drawing conclusions, hypothesizing, classifying.

Chapter 2: "European Empires in America" (1525–1625)

Chapter 2 traces the growth of a mighty Spanish Empire in Latin America and follows the first tentative steps of English, French, Dutch and Swedish colonies in North America.

Feature

Going to the Source: Selection from William Bradford's history, *Of Plymouth Plantation* (page 43)

Learning Objectives
History Generalizations

Students will gain knowledge that supports the following generalizations:

1. The relationship between the American colonies and their parent countries was based on the economic philosophy of mercantilism.
2. For a time, Spain monopolized control of the New World because wealth it acquired there enabled Spanish rulers to build a strong army and navy to keep other nations out.
3. Because of the actions of the "sea dogs" and the defeat of the Spanish Armada, the English successfully challenged Spain's monopoly in the New World.
4. English colonists—some seeking religious freedom, others hoping for riches—founded colonies that later were among the thirteen original United States.
5. Except for strong leadership and cultivation of tobacco, Jamestown—the first English colony—would have been abandoned.

6. Following England's lead, France, the Netherlands, and Sweden challenged Spain by founding colonies and settlements in North America.
7. Religion was an important factor in the founding and daily life in the colonies of some European countries, especially England and Spain.
8. Native Americans suffered serious injustices at the hands of some European settlers.

Skills
In addition to the three skills noted for chapter 1 which are standard to every chapter, students will:
1. make a two-level topic outline of information in specified chapter sections.
2. write a paragraph from a two-level outline.
3. relate graphic materials to the text of the chapter.
4. practice these **critical thinking skills:** generating questions about materials to be read, evaluating sources, determining possible causes and effects.

Chapter 3: "The Thirteen Colonies" (1625–1732)
In Chapter 3, students learn of the English colonists' various motives for emigrating to America, the circumstances of the founding of each of the thirteen colonies, and the religious characteristics and political and social developments within the colonies.

Features
Movers and Shapers: Eliza Lucas Pinckney (page 64)
American Ingenuity chart (pages 70–71)

Learning Objectives
History Generalizations
Students will gain knowledge that supports the following generalizations:
1. Some English colonists—the Puritans, Catholics, and the Society of Friends (Quakers)—came to North America seeking religious freedom and settled corporate colonies there.
2. Some proprietary colonies were founded to enrich their proprietors; others were founded as social or religious experiments.
3. Religious and political dissenters were banished from or chose to leave the colonies where they first settled and some founded other colonies.
4. The thirteen colonies built by all these colonists later became the thirteen original states.
5. Although the colonies tried to remain as free as possible of control by the English monarch, several eventually became royal colonies.
6. African people were brought to the thirteen colonies and forced to work as slaves on huge Southern plantations and elsewhere.
7. The settlers in the thirteen colonies developed institutions that sowed the seeds of democratic government, public education, and religious tolerance in the United States.

Study Skills
In addition to the three skills noted in chapter 1 which are standard to every chapter, students will:
1. make a three-level sentence outline of information in specified chapter sections.
2. write a paragraph from a three-level outline.
3. relate graphic materials to the text of the chapter.

4. practice these **critical thinking skills:** generating questions about materials to be read, supporting opinions, summarizing, classifying.

Chapter 4: "Colonial Americans" (1650–1754)
In Chapter 4, students examine the position of the colonies in the British Empire under British mercantilism, the growing rivalry among the European powers, and the eventual predominance of the English in eastern North America. Students will recognize the initial stirrings of ideas that are woven deeply into their lives as Americans today.

Learning Objectives
History Generalizations
Students will gain knowledge that supports the following generalizations:
1. Through various economic and political means, the monarch, Parliament, and others who ruled Great Britain attempted to extend control over the colonies to increase Britain's wealth and power.
2. The American colonists, eager to retain control of their own destinies, resisted Britain's attempts at dominating them, but not always successfully.
3. In the New England and southern colonies, bitter resentment against Britain's mercantilist policies grew. In the Middle Colonies, least affected by these policies, loyalty to Great Britain remained strong.
4. New England competition with Britain for the slave trade and economic difficulties of southern planters contributed to the spread of slavery, especially in the southern colonies.
5. Suffrage was extended to a limited group of colonists, in most colonies to those who had a specified amount of property or money.
6. Along with British colonies, French settlements were developing in North America. However, the French settlements were different from the English colonies in several ways.
7. Because of their fair behavior, the French benefited from peaceful and friendly relations with Indian groups in New France.
8. To protect their American empires, France and Great Britain involved their colonists and settlers in North American extensions of wars the two nations were fighting in Europe.

Study Skills
In addition to the three skills noted in chapter 1 which are standard to every chapter, students will:
1. interpret and compare information presented on a line graph.
2. write a paragraph, arranging detail sentences in logical order.
3. relate graphic materials to the text of the chapter.
4. practice these **critical thinking skills:** generating questions about materials to be read, recognizing reasons for different points of view, classifying information.

Quotation: from the play *The Mound Builders.* Other plays by Lanford Wilson (born 1938) include *Balm in Gilead, The Rimers of Eldritch, The Gingham Dog, Lemon Sky, The Hot L Baltimore, 5th of July, A Tale Told, Angels Fall,* and the 1980 Pulitzer Prize-winning *Talley's Folly.*

CHAPTER 1

A MEETING OF TWO WORLDS

25,000 BC–1754 AD

A great amount of work has been done on the early cultures of North America and we have found only the periphery of the culture. LANFORD WILSON

Making Connections. People sometimes call Europe the "Old World" and America the "New World." In 1492, these two worlds met when Christopher Columbus sailed from Europe to America. The land Columbus found was new to him, but people had been living there for thousands of years. The real history of America began with the arrival of the earliest Americans.

In this chapter, you will learn:
- When the first people came to America and how they populated two continents
- What kind of civilization the first Americans had and how they lived
- Why the peoples of the Americas developed diverse cultures
- What caused Europeans to search for a sea route to the Indies
- Who were the first Europeans to explore the Americas

You know the United States as a powerful country with worldwide influence. But what was it like even before there was a United States? What other cultures existed here? What happened to them?

Sections
1. The First Americans
2. An Old World Awakens
3. Spain Claims America

1. THE FIRST AMERICANS

The first people to populate the Americas arrived from Asia over 25,000 years ago. For them, simple survival was a daily struggle. They spent most of their days searching for food and stalking animals with weapons made of wood, bone, and stone. The animals that these early American inhabitants hunted provided meat for food, skins for clothing, and bone and sinew for utensils and thread.

A Land Crossing to the Americas. Today, 55 miles (90 kilometers) of icy, choppy water called the Bering Strait separate Siberia in Asia from the Seward Peninsula of Alaska. But this was not always so.

Much scientific evidence indicates that the earth's climate zones have changed several times. As recently as 10,000 years ago, the earth was locked in an Ice Age. Temperatures were lower throughout the planet than they are now. During this time at the North Pole and in what is now Canada, snow accumulated much faster than it melted. Layer after layer of snow and ice built up, creating huge glaciers that began to move southward, partially covering North America.

More and more of the earth's water became trapped in the growing glaciers; consequently, the oceans dropped. As this happened, the land under the Bering Strait gradually appeared. For a long

The Great Serpent Mound in Adams County, Ohio was an ancient burial site of the Native Americans known as the Adenans. The various mounds these people built were in the forms of animals.

2

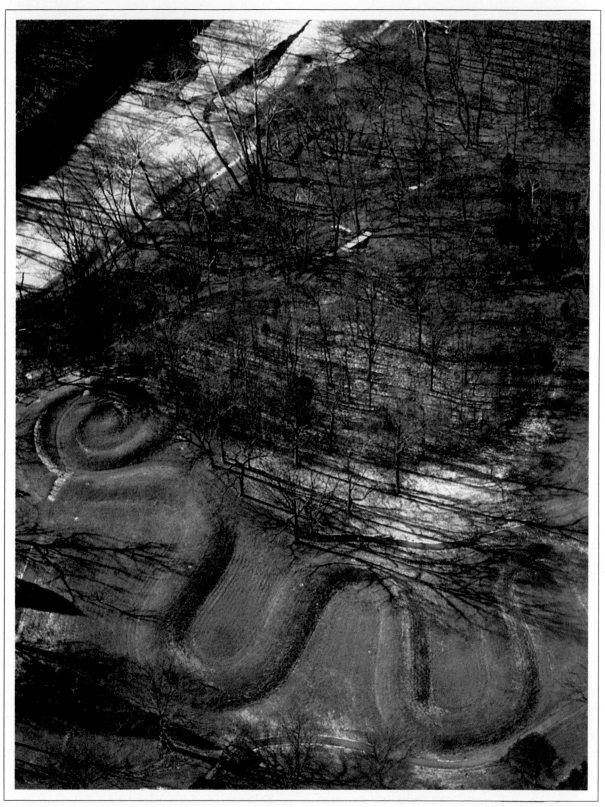

Migration is an especially important concept for understanding American history. Its significance should be stressed in covering the original Asian migrations, the various European migrations, the concept of Manifest Destiny, and migrations of the 1800s by Asian and "Third World" peoples, as well as the present-day migrations by these peoples.

 3

Portage Glacier in Chugach National Forest, Alaska, is one of the many glaciers left over from the Ice Age. It is slowly melting into the lake.

time, until water again covered it, this land connected the continents of Asia and North America. The "bridge" allowed animals and humans to cross between the land masses of Asia and North America.

Settling Two Continents. Between two huge glaciers, an ice-free corridor just east of the Rocky Mountains stretched from Alaska southward. People passed through this corridor, settled for a while and then moved on again. It took thousands of years to populate the Americas.

Some *anthropologists* believe that 16–20 million Indians lived in North and South America, with 7–9 million of them living in what is now the United States. Thus, the population density was much lower than it is today. This spreading out was necessary because the Indians' hunting and farming practices required a great deal of land to feed each group.

With so much land available, most tribes probably found it fairly easy to move from one place to another. Attacks by other tribes, lack of animals to hunt, need for more water or plant food, local overpopulation, or a search for a warmer climate might have caused population shifts. As the tribes

moved, they developed practices to cope with their new homes.

Many Tribes, Many Cultures. People worked out very different ways of life according to how they adapted to the environment in which they settled. The great variety of America's climates, landforms, and forests contributed to the amazing number of distinct prehistoric cultures.

By the time Europeans came to the American continents during the 1500s, there were 500 basic language groups among the Indians! Each language had particular dialects, developed by different subgroups and based on unique experiences or conditions. Oftentimes, neighboring tribes had difficulty understanding each other, even though their language origin was similar. Each different language probably represented a cultural variety —a slightly different way of life.

The variety of Indian cultures was reflected in other ways, too. Some tribes, such as the Shoshones and Paiutes of present-day Nevada and Utah, lived very hard lives, surviving in deserts where food and water were extremely scarce. Other peoples, like the Arawaks of the West Indies or the California Indians, lived where the climate was

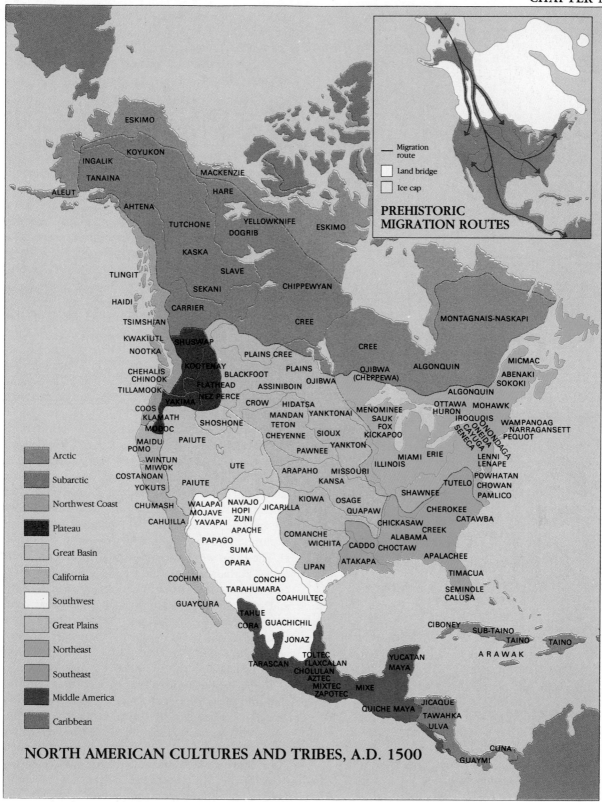

Migration route

Land bridge

Ice cap

PREHISTORIC MIGRATION ROUTES

ESKIMO

KOYUKON

INGALIK

TANAINA

ALEUT

AHTENA

TUTCHONE

YELLOWKNIFE

DOGRIB

KASKA

SLAVE

TLINGIT

SEKANI

HAIDI

CARRIER

TSIMSHIAN

KWAKIUTL

NOOTKA

SHUSWAP

CHEHALIS

CHINOOK

KOOTENAY

TILLAMOOK

FLATHEAD

NEZ PERCE

COOS

YAKIMA

KLAMATH

MODOC

MAIDU

POMO

WINTUN

MIWOK

COSTANOAN

YOKUTS

CHUMASH

CAHUILLA

COCHIMI

GUAYCURA

MACKENZIE

HARE

ESKIMO

CHIPPEWYAN

CREE

MONTAGNAIS-NASKAPI

PLAINS CREE

CREE

PLAINS

BLACKFOOT

OJIBWA

ALGONQUIN

ASSINIBOIN

OJIBWA
(CHIPPEWA)

MICMAC

ABENAKI

SOKOKI

ALGONQUIN

CROW

HIDATSA

MANDAN

TETON

CHEYENNE

SHOSHONE

PAIUTE

SIOUX

YANKTONAI

YANKTON

MENOMINEE

SAUK

FOX

KICKAPOO

OTTAWA

HURON

MOHAWK

IROQUOIS

ONONDAGA

ONEIDA

CAYUGA

SENECA

WAMPANOAG

NARRAGANSETT

PEQUOT

UTE

PAWNEE

ARAPAHO

MISSOURI

KANSA

MIAMI

ILLINOIS

ERIE

LENNI

LENAPE

POWHATAN

PAIUTE

WALAPAI

MOJAVE

YAVAPAI

NAVAJO

HOPI

ZUNI

APACHE

JICARILLA

KIOWA

OSAGE

QUAPAW

SHAWNEE

TUTELO

CHOWAN

PAMLICO

CHEROKEE

CATAWBA

CHICKASAW

CREEK

ALABAMA

CADDO

CHOCTAW

APALACHEE

PAPAGO

SUMA

OPARA

COMANCHE

WICHITA

LIPAN

ATAKAPA

TIMACUA

CONCHO

TARAHUMARA

COAHUILTEC

SEMINOLE

CALUSA

CIBONEY

SUB-TAINO

TAINO

TAINO

ARAWAK

TAHUE

CORA

GUACHICHIL

JONAZ

TARASCAN

TOLTEC

TLAXCALAN

CHOLULAN

AZTEC

MIXTEC

ZAPOTEC

MIXE

YUCATAN

MAYA

JICAQUE

TAWAHKA

ULVA

QUICHE MAYA

CUNA

GUAYMI

Legend

- Arctic
- Subarctic
- Northwest Coast
- Plateau
- Great Basin
- California
- Southwest
- Great Plains
- Northeast
- Southeast
- Middle America
- Caribbean

NORTH AMERICAN CULTURES AND TRIBES, A.D. 1500

Remnants of that epoch are found today in many parts of the country. For example, Long Island, New York, is believed to be a glacial moraine—residue left by glaciers as they moved northward. Have students use local colleges, libraries, or historical societies as sources of information.

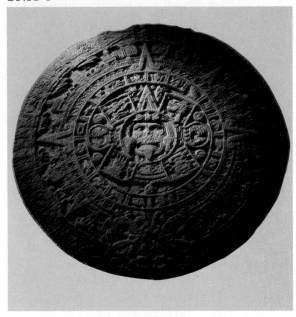

Aztec calendars were used by priests trained in astrology to make predictions on special occasions.

Machu Picchu was a city built by skillful Incan builders on the top of a steep mountain in the Andes Mountain range in Peru. When it was inhabited, food was provided locally by farmers who grew crops in a series of hillside terraces. The city's ruins were discovered by the American explorer Hiram Bingham in 1911.

milder and food was easier to get. Some tribes lived very simple lives. Others, such as the Aztecs and Mayas, developed cultures as advanced as the highest civilizations of Africa, Asia, or Europe of that time.

The Advanced Cultures of the South. The most advanced Indian cultures developed in South America, Central America, and Mexico. In the highlands of Mexico the Aztec civilization was the last and greatest of a line of empires that existed before Europeans arrived. In the Yucatan peninsula of southern Mexico and in Guatemala, a people known as the Mayas erected massive *pyramids* that still exist and may be climbed to this day. And high in the mountains of Ecuador and Peru the Incas created the greatest prehistoric American empire of all.

The Incas. The Incas' homeland lay in the towering Andes Mountains of South America. In valleys between snow-capped peaks the Incas farmed potatoes and corn. They domesticated llamas and alpacas, and raised them as pack animals and for their soft wool. Dogs and guinea pigs were kept for food.

The Incas rank among the greatest builders in the world. One of their greatest cities was Machu Picchu (mä′chōō pēk′chōō) in Peru. It covered 5 square miles (13 square kilometers), and must have been home to thousands of people. The city's location is so remote that the city was unknown to the outside world until 1911 when an American explorer, Hiram Bingham, discovered its ruins.

The Incas were also master road builders. Their paved paths snaked hundreds of miles over difficult terrain—around mountains, through forests, and over cliffs. Like the Romans, the great road builders of ancient Europe, the Incas used their transportation system to unite their vast empire, which stretched 2,500 miles (4,200 kilometers) from Ecuador to the northern part of Chile.

Remarkably, the Inca Empire was ruled without a system of writing. Runners carried news reports into the capital city of Cuzco (kōōs′kō) and the emperor's proclamations out to the borders. Relay teams of runners could cover 150 miles (240 kilometers) of steep mountain roads in a day.

Although the Inca empire was rich in lands, gold, and tribute from conquered peoples, the

Research Assignment: Have students report on some aspect of the life of an Indian culture, perhaps one in your area. Encourage students to use models, photographs, or actual artifacts to illustrate their projects. (Topics to study could include housing, social life, clothing, jewelry, customs, inventions, and language.) Developing a slide presentation could spark interest and provide a useful tool for a class activity.

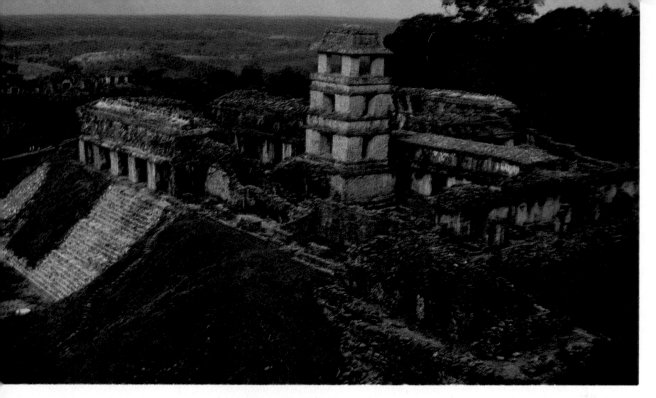

Mayan ruins dating back to far before Columbus's arrival in the New World provide evidence of an advanced culture as early as 300 AD. These ruins are in Palenque, Mexico.

common people had little personal freedom. The emperor, who was called the Inca, was considered a god and had absolute power. Every imperial order had to be obeyed without question. All property, except for houses and goods such as furniture and tools, was owned by the emperor. Every subject was expected to enrich the emperor by paying taxes in the form of crops or gold and by working for the Inca a certain number of days each year. This "labor tax" was called the *mita*, and resembled the medieval obligations of the European common people to their nobles.

Also like the Europeans, the Incas were frequently at war. They conquered other people and beat back invaders tempted by Incan riches. The Incan nobles also fought among themselves to determine who would be emperor.

The Mayas. Guatemala and the Yucatan peninsula were home to the Mayas, whose advanced culture dates back as far as the year 300. But their great civilization did not survive—the religious centers at Chichén Itzá (chē-chĕn' ĕt-sä') and Mayapan were abandoned before the Europeans arrived. We could have learned a great deal about pre-Columbian (before Columbus) America from the Mayas, because they had developed a form of writing using pictographs and ideographs. The *pictographs* were pictures representing objects; for example, two parallel lines symbolized a road. The *ideographs* were pictures representing ideas. The ideograph for "travel," for example, was a drawing of a human foot next to a pictograph for "road." About 850 different Mayan characters have been identified. However no one has translated more than a few of them.

The Mayas also excelled in astronomy, mathematics, and medicine. Their calendar was much like ours, based on the sun and having a 365-day year. They had a sophisticated number system based on 20 that allowed them to make complex calculations. Mayan physicians performed brain operations, and made their own medicines.

Most Mayan individuals probably had more freedom than the Incas. They had no all-powerful emperor; instead, they lived in farming towns and villages that may have been independent of one another. However, there was another side to Mayan culture—as part of their worship of the sun, the Mayas practiced human sacrifice.

Mayan temples are still a source of mystery. Given the tools and technology available, it is unclear how the Mayas carved perfectly square 5- to 10-ton blocks out of granite and built them into perfectly symmetrical temples.

The Toltecs and Aztecs. Farther north, on the central plateau of Mexico where most Mexicans live today, was the Aztec empire. Here is one of only two places in the world where anthropologists are sure that agriculture was invented, the other place being Mesopotamia (in present-day Iraq).

The chief crops of the Toltecs, who ruled central Mexico before the Aztecs, were maize (corn), beans, and squash. They also grew and ate tomatoes and chili peppers. All of these foods were unknown to people in Europe, Africa, and Asia.

Sometime before 1300, the Toltec lands were invaded by a poor, primitive, and warlike people, the Aztecs. The Aztecs quickly learned skills from the Toltecs, becoming excellent farmers. The Aztecs also learned how to mine gold, silver, and copper, and how to turn these metals into magnificent jewelry, art, and sculpture. In about 1325 the Aztecs built their capital Tenochtitlán (tē-nôch'tē-tlän'), which sat on an island in the center of a lake. (This site is now included in Mexico's capital—Mexico City.) The capital city was easily defended because it could be entered only over a few causeways joined to the shore by drawbridges that could be pulled up. In the safety of the large lake,

The Aztec Indians learned from the Toltecs how to mine gold. In time, they also became expert jewelry-makers and artisans. Today their pre-Columbian artifacts can be found in many museum collections.

the Aztecs used large woven reed baskets covered with earth to make artificial islands on which people lived and even farmed.

Like the Incas, the Aztecs had an emperor. However, the emperor was not all-powerful. The nobles elected the emperor, who needed their support in order to rule. Even though he was elected, the emperor was considered to be a descendant of the chief Aztec god, Quetzalcoatl (kĕt-säl'kō-ät'əl).

The Aztecs were wealthy, but they were cruel to the people they conquered. The subject tribes hated the Aztecs for the taxes they had to pay. When the Spaniards arrived, these tribes became willing partners in the Spanish conquest of the Aztecs, and ultimately of all Mexico.

The Indians of the United States. In contrast to the empires of the Incas and the Aztecs, the northern tribes had no great centers such as Cuzco or Tenochtitlán. In so vast an area, the Native American population was too small to support a centralized empire with an advanced culture. In 1492, approximately 1 million people lived in what is now the United States and Canada; about 5 million lived in Mexico. Therefore, the northern Indians, who lived in an area ten times larger than Mexico, had only one-fifth the population.

Although the Indians of the area that is now the United States did not have high cultures, they were ingenious in their ways of adapting to the various environments of the land. From the dry deserts of the Southwest to the dense forests of the Northeast, American Indian cultures were wondrously diverse.

Southwestern Indians. In the southwestern part of the United States, the Hopis and Zuñis adapted to an extremely harsh environment. With few large game animals in this area, they had to grow their food using the little rainfall that fell in this desert land. They used irrigation to solve their problem, digging long ditches to bring water from springs and mountain streams to their fields. They became the best farmers north of Mexico, raising corn, beans, and squash.

These Indians lived in multi-storied houses made of adobe (ə-dō'bē), or sun-dried bricks. The Spanish explorers called these people Pueblos

Discussion Question: How did climate and environment affect the way of life and culture of many Indian tribes? Have students examine factors such as why the desert dwellers used adobe to build pueblos; why the Utes were nomadic; why salmon became an important trade item to Pacific Northwest tribes.

8

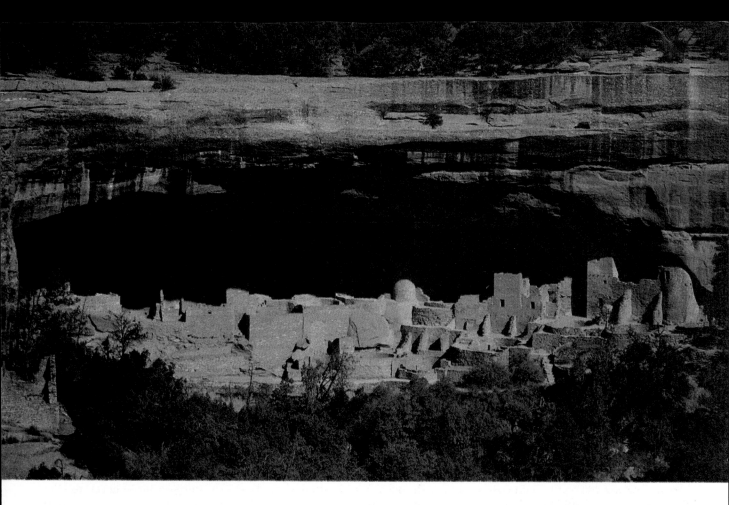

because the villages reminded the Spaniards of their own villages back home. In Spanish, *pueblo* means both "village" and "people." The houses were often built as cliffside "apartment houses" entered via ladders leading to doors in upper floors, or in villages on top of mesas (flat-topped mountains). It seems that the Pueblos chose such remote sites for their homes because they were easy to defend.

Another people of the southwestern desert developed an entirely different way of life. Instead of living in villages and farming large fields, the Navajos split up into family groups and spread out in the desert, living far from one another in round houses called *hogans*. This pattern of small scattered groups enabled the Navajos to survive on the scarce game of the desert without overhunting the wildlife.

The Navajos were fine artists, a talent they still possess. They were the best weavers in the United States, and used cotton and wool for their magnificent fabrics. For the unique Navajo art of sand painting, artists devote hours to creating brilliantly

Cliff Palace (above) is the largest Pueblo in Mesa Verde National Park, located in southwestern Colorado. Built into the side of a cliff, it contains dozens of rooms built centuries before Columbus's voyages to the New World. Petroglyphs (below) are line drawings or carvings on rock. These petroglyphs are typical of the ones created by American Indians centuries ago in what is now Utah.

Discussion Question: What are characteristics of an advanced civilization? Referring to individual tribes, have students use criteria such as governmental organization, technical skill, knowledge and inventions, architecture, and wealth (farming, mining). Discuss the propriety of judging "civilization" by these criteria. Do they bias our view?

 9

executed designs, using different colored sands, that will be destroyed by nightfall. To the Navajo, the brief experience of beauty by a few is enough to justify long, hard labor.

A third tribe of the Southwest was the Apache, who came north out of Mexico. They learned farming and later sheep herding. But as recently as 100 years ago many still preferred the freedom of their traditional wandering life.

People of the Great Basin.

Nevada and Utah form a "basin." Although the land is not low, it is between two lofty mountain ranges—the Sierra Nevada and the Rocky Mountains. Even today, the Great Basin is a forbidding place, and is home to relatively few people. It is a land of spectacular scenery, extreme temperatures, and little rainfall.

The Utes, Paiutes, and Shoshones of the Great Basin did not live in tribes. They lived in small family units and wandered the sagebrush desert and mountains, scraping out a living from pine nuts, berries, small animals, snakes, and lizards.

Today, anthropologists understand that although the Indians of the Great Basin lived in a land where few of what we would call "necessities of life" were available, they were extremely resourceful. Their survival was a result of their will and ingenuity.

Indians of California.

Just across the Sierra Nevada from the Great Basin, in what is now California, lived the largest number of Indians in the United States. Mild weather meant food was more abundant and easier to collect. Some tribes dug for edible roots; others gathered acorns from forests of oak trees; and those others who lived near the sea fished and gathered shellfish from bays and tidepools.

Despite the concentration of people in California, and the relatively easy life there, the culture of the California Indians was not advanced. Not that the California Indians were without skills. In fact, they rivaled the Paiutes and Shoshones as basket makers. They wove their baskets so tightly that the baskets were actually watertight and were used for cooking.

Although the number of people in California would appear to promote a stable and unified nation, there were numerous California tribes. Different villages in an area often spoke the same language, traded with one another, and occasionally formed defense alliances. But they prized their independence and easygoing life above all else. Among the larger tribes were the Wintun, Pomo, Modoc (mō'dŏc), Maidu, and Mojave (mō-hä'vē). Most California Indians were peaceful and tolerant of one another, but a few, like the Modoc and Mojave, were warriors every bit as fearful as the Apache.

Pacific Northwest Indians.

The Indians of coastal Oregon and Washington (and British Columbia in Canada) were the richest in North America. Their staple food was the salmon that teemed in the rivers of the Pacific Northwest. Thus, the Coos, Tillamook, Chehalis, Chinook, Nootka, and other smaller tribes had an excellent, protein-rich diet.

Dried or smoked salmon was also a valuable trade item, so the Indians of the Pacific Northwest had their pick of what other peoples brought to them. As a result, material possessions played an important part in their culture, but in a curious way.

Instead of winning the respect of others by displaying their accumulated baskets, weavings, tools, wood and bone carvings, copper articles, and metal jewelry, the Northwest Indians gave away their wealth, and sometimes destroyed it. For years every member of a family worked hard and saved, making or buying as many goods as possible. Then the family announced a *potlatch*. At these parties, the hosts gave away their wealth to invited guests.

Families who hosted potlatches were generally of high rank, and gifts were distributed to guests according to their rank. These ceremonies served to mark milestones, such as assumption of a title or high position in the tribe. This desire to amass an impressive display of goods to give away made the Northwest Indians hard workers, thus ensuring the prosperity of the tribe.

These Indians generally lived in large log houses. Outside their homes, which usually faced the water, they placed their carved and colorfully painted *totem poles*. The totem poles were really decorations, artwork that identified the people who lived in a particular village or house. They served the same purpose as the coat of arms of a European knight.

Class Activity: Charts can be useful tools in making comparisons. Using either an overhead projector or the chalkboard, develop a chart comparing the various Indian civilizations. Have students list the tribes in one column and follow these with separate columns for area of settlement, environment, government, major accomplishments, family structure, and other cultural aspects such as food, clothing, or art. Discuss how these may be related.

10

People of the Plateau. In the high country to the east of the coastal Indians lived the Klamath, Nez Perce (nĕz′ pûrs′), Kootenay, Yakima (yăk′ə-mə), and Flathead tribes. They all lived by hunting and trapping the abundant game of the mountains. However, their languages differed and their tribal loyalties were very strong.

The people of the *plateau* were almost always at war with one another. When hunting parties from different tribes met, they fought. These battles were not very dangerous, but were a form of ritual or a demonstration of bravery. Most tribes thought it just as brave to simply touch an opponent during battle as to wound or kill. This touch was called *counting coup.* In order to count coup, a warrior had to have witnesses to testify that he had indeed done the act he claimed.

Indians of the Plains. The best known American Indians are the Great Plains Indians, whose home was the rolling grasslands stretching from the Rocky Mountains almost to the Mississippi River. For the Sioux (soo), Blackfoot, Crow, Cheyenne, and Comanche, the horse was the key to their culture. On their unsaddled ponies they followed the herds of bison, or buffalo, that provided them with their food, their clothing, and the coverings of their famous cone-shaped *wicki-ups,* their mobile houses.

However, the Plains Indians became horse-riders late in their history, because there were no horses in America until the Europeans brought them. Before the 1600s, the Plains Indians were farmers and hunters. They traveled on foot. Although having horses made their lives much easier, their way of life did not change that much.

The Plains Indians were also capable warriors. But the object of war was much like the object of the hunt. Plains tribes raided one another to seize food and to win glory for bravery.

Southeastern Indians. It seems that the Indians of the Southeast United States probably had some contact with the Aztecs of Mexico, because they practiced a similar kind of sun worship, though it did not include human sacrifice. The Creeks, Choctaws, Chickasaws, Cherokees, and other tribes of present-day Georgia, South Carolina, Alabama, Tennessee, and Mississippi spoke related languages of the Muskogean group and had similar life styles. They hunted, trapped, fished, and farmed. Their chief crop was maize, and they also grew squash, pumpkins, and beans.

Unlike the Aztec and Pueblo farmers, the Southeastern Indians lived in forestland. They used a type of agriculture called *slash-and-burn.* First fields were cleared from the forest by girdling the trees, or cutting a circle around the bark. This prevented soil nutrients from reaching the leaves, thus killing the trees. After a year, the trees were without leaves and the plants and bushes around the trees were burned, fertilizing the soil. When the sun's rays could reach the ground through the leafless trees, the plot was ready for planting.

These people had a well-structured tribal organization. Their style of farming required them to plan ahead, so they had regular governing councils. Their class system was strict. The people with the highest standing were called Suns, and the lowest were known as Stinkards.

Eastern Woodlands Indians. As did the Southeastern Indians, the Indians of the Eastern Woodlands farmed by the slash-and-burn method; hunted and trapped deer, bear, and smaller animals; gathered wild nuts and berries; and fished the streams and bays. The Northeastern Indians used waterways to move about and invented the birchbark canoe, a light boat made of bent saplings covered with patches of bark. The Northeastern Indians also invented the snowshoe to cope with the often snowy winters of their land.

Mexican Indian influences may have reached tribes living as far north as Illinois. At Cahokia, there is a mysterious group of 85 earthen mounds, some of them small and some huge. Because an astronomical laboratory such as Mexican Indians built stood there, it is possible that Toltecs, fleeing their Aztec conquerors, tried to rebuild their culture far up the Mississippi River.

A majority of Northeastern Indians spoke an Algonkian language. Among the Algonkian tribes were the Lenni Lenape, Wampanoag (wäm′pə-nō′ăg), Pequot (pē′kwät), Narragansett, and Powhatan (pou′hə-tăn′). The Algonkian tribes and towns were usually quite small, and organized action was difficult. As a result, their enemies, the Iroquois, were able to control the lands around the Great Lakes, especially in New York State.

Slash-and-burn agriculture was developed to compensate for poor soil, and was used in the absence of other fertilizer. It is still used in some parts of the world today, such as Africa and Indonesia.

The Iroquois banded together in fewer but larger tribes than the Algonkians. Around 1500, five of these nations—the Mohawk, Oneida, Seneca, Cayuga, and Onondaga—did what few people in history have managed to do. They decided to stop fighting one another and they succeeded.

In their legends, a Mohawk chief named Hiawatha founded the *League of the Iroquois*. Each summer thereafter, the women of each of the five tribes chose 50 men, called *sachems*, to meet with the sachems from the other tribes the following autumn. For 300 years the Iroquois kept the peace among themselves.

SECTION REVIEW

1. Write a sentence to identify: Machu Picchu, the Inca, ideographs, counting coup, League of the Iroquois.

2. (a) When did the ancestors of present day American Indians arrive in the Americas? (b) Where did they come from?

3. Explain how the different ways of life among the Native Americans were determined by the places in which they lived.

4. Which Native Americans (a) developed writing, (b) invented farming, (c) used birch bark canoes, (d) lived in wickiups?

5. How did the Hopi and Zuñi farmers adapt to the harsh conditions of their land?

2. AN OLD WORLD AWAKENS

Unknown to the people of the Americas was the gradual changing of civilization in Europe. Although the Inca and Aztec civilizations were at one point possibly more advanced than the European, a giant leap was occurring in European affairs. During the fourteenth and fifteenth centuries Europeans began to take an intense interest in the learning and art of the golden age of the ancient Greeks and Romans. Because of this, Europeans believed that a golden age was being reborn. The French word for rebirth is *renaissance*; thus, this period in European history is called the Renaissance.

Studying the ideas and ways of thinking of the Greeks and Romans opened European minds to new ideas as well. The Renaissance was an age of great writers, daring philosophers, and inventive scientists. It was also an age of adventurous explorers who reached beyond the boundaries of their world and came upon a "New World" far across the ocean.

The Crusades and the Lure of the East. Events that led to the European discovery of America began as far back as the religious wars known as the Crusades. Beginning in 1095, armies made of thousands of European peasants and nobles traveled to the eastern end of the Mediterranean Sea. Their goal was to capture the holy places of the Christian religion—Bethlehem, Nazareth, and Jerusalem. These cities were held by *Moslems*, Arabs who had been converted to the religion of Islam.

At first the Christians were victorious, and set up Crusader states. However, they were outnumbered and were eventually defeated. Those who returned to Europe brought back memories of a different style of living in the Arab lands. They had learned to like the foods found in warm climates, such as oranges and sugar. They wanted the comfortable clothing made of cotton, and the jewels, such as pearls, that were rare in Europe. Old enemies soon became new trading partners. The people of the Levant (present-day Lebanon, Syria, and Israel) were happy to have European markets for their goods and other products that came from far beyond the Middle East. In great demand were incense and perfumes; silks; drugs for the treatment of pain and disease; and pepper, cloves, cinnamon, and nutmeg. These treasures came from Zanzibar in East Africa; India and Sri Lanka; and Indonesia, China, and Japan. Europeans did not know exactly where these countries were; these mysterious lands were simply called *the Indies*. All most people knew was that they lay far to the East.

The goods from the Indies were extremely expensive. Transportation costs were high, as the 4,000-mile (6,400-kilometer) overland trip from the East, by donkey or camel, took a year or longer. Even ships hauling their cargoes through the Persian Gulf or the Red Sea could take that long. The wages of animal tenders, sailors, and

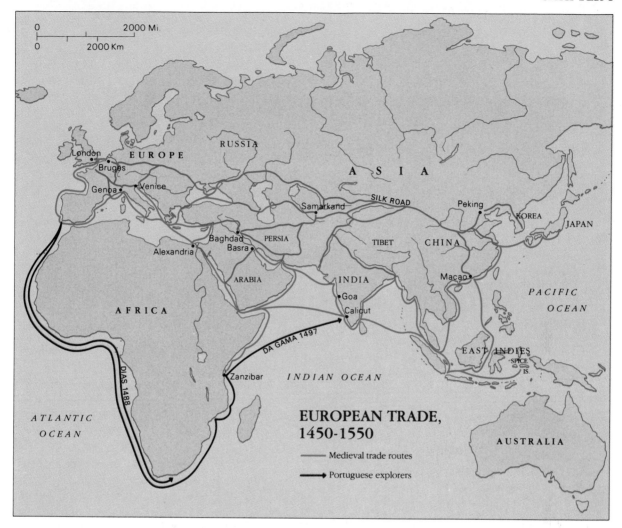

EUROPEAN TRADE, 1450-1550

—— Medieval trade routes

➤ Portuguese explorers

soldiers who guarded such valuable goods were added into the retail price. Dozens of merchants bought and sold the shipments along the way, and each took a profit. At the western end of the route were the powerful Italian city-states, such as Genoa and Venice, which monopolized the sale of Eastern goods to northern Europe. Their merchants charged the highest prices possible.

Northern Europeans resented the high prices they had to pay for the Eastern luxuries. But there seemed little they could do against the powerful Genoan and Venetian navies. If their ships sailed through the Mediterranean Sea to the Levant, their crews risked capture, slavery, and death. And they could do less about the high prices of the products after the long trip from the East.

Then, around 1300, a remarkable book began to turn up in royal courts. It was entitled *Voyages of Sir Marco Polo*, and detailed the 17-year experience of Marco Polo with the emperor of China. It took some time for all of Europe to discover the book, for printing presses were unknown and books were copied by hand. But the stories of the Chinese court traveled rapidly, and convinced the Northern Europeans of the need to find their own way to the Indies.

In his travels around China, Polo had discovered that the country was bounded by a great ocean to the east. If the Northern Europeans could find a sea route to the Indies that bypassed the Italian city-states and the Asian merchants, their treasuries would grow rich from trade.

Class Activity: Using a map to gain important information is an important skill. Using the map on this page, have the class discuss why Genoa and Venice were more involved in earlier trade with Asia, and how this changed with the opening of all-water routes. Reinforce the idea that economic behavior is influenced by location.

Marco Polo's departure from Venice is depicted in this illuminated manuscript.

Portugal Leads the Way. Portugal was the first country to search for a new route to the East. Portugal was a small country, cut off from Spain by mountains. However, it faced the Atlantic Ocean, and the Portuguese built a strong seafaring tradition—both fishing and trading. They also developed a strong national identity from isolation and a long struggle to drive out the *Moors*. (The Moors were Moslems from northwestern Africa who had conquered Portugal and Spain in the 700s.)

Prince Henry the Navigator. The guiding light of Portuguese exploration was a younger brother of the king, Prince Henry the Navigator.

Henry was fascinated by anything having to do with ships and sailing. In 1418, he founded a research center and school for sailors at Sagres, in southern Portugal.

The most important of the innovations that came from Sagres was a new kind of ship—the *caravel*. These ships were smaller than other trading vessels of the fifteenth century. Their three-cornered sails made them much faster and able to sail more easily against the wind. This increased maneuverability was essential to the Portuguese dream of sailing south around the tip of Africa to the Indies.

However, no one knew how large Africa was, and not until 1498 would anyone sail around the

Research Assignment: Have students do a report on Marco Polo's voyages. Have them examine his first contact with new people and find how his prior cultural experiences caused him to react to these new cultures.

14

MOVERS AND SHAPERS

Henry the Navigator

The man known to history as Henry the Navigator, or Don Henrique Navegadore (1394–1460), was a Portuguese prince. He was one of the most important Europeans of his time. The guiding force behind a series of voyages that led to the establishment of the Portuguese *maritime* empire, he made all European overseas empires possible.

Henry's exciting career got under way in 1415 when he and his brothers captured the Moorish city of Ceuta in Africa. As governor of that city he sponsored voyages of exploration along the African coast.

In 1419 he returned to Portugal and became governor of Algarve. At his seaside home in Sagres he studied oceangoing ships and established a center for the advancement of the maritime arts.

Henry's interest in exploration was twofold: he was anxious to explore the unknown, and he wanted to spread Christianity. His sea captains set out on dangerous voyages in ships that bore the red cross of the crusader on their sails.

The caravel, representing a great advance in ship design, was a swift, light, graceful, three-masted vessel that could outperform the *barchas* previously in use. Henry used the newly designed ships to further explore the African coast.

Henry the Navigator never embarked on any of the sea explorations he advanced. In later life he remained at Sagres, surrounded by experts in mapmaking, navigation, and ship design. These nautical scholars, sponsored by Henry, became teachers to the seafaring nations of Europe.

Queen Isabella

Queen Isabella of Spain (1451–1504) was a powerful, successful leader. Unlike many queens, she shared Spain's monarchy equally with the king.

During the monarchy of Isabella and her husband, King Ferdinand, weak laws were strengthened, roads and bridges were built, and people were engaged to find new markets for Spain. Church reforms to end corruption were also instituted. And a holy war against Granada, the last Moslem stronghold in Spain, was begun.

The conquest of Granada became the monarchs' obsession, and to do it they committed all their resources. In 1482 troops attacked the Moors in Granada. Fighting did not cease until 1492, when a victorious Isabella and Ferdinand entered Granada's magnificent palace, the Alhambra. Seven centuries of Moslem reign was ended, and the drain on the treasury was stopped.

It is reported that among the crowd at the conquest of Granada was Christopher Columbus. For six years he had hounded the court with his dream of sailing west to the Indies, but there was no money in Spain's treasury for a high-risk voyage of exploration. However, with Granada overcome, Isabella was ready to talk to Columbus. She agreed to obtain financial support and offered him the command of the three ships which she had received from the city of Palos as payment of a debt. Elated, Columbus prepared for his epic voyage.

Aristotle (350 BC) was the first to conclude the earth was a sphere. Another Greek, Eratosthenes, calculated its circumference to within 4,000 miles. Though these estimations weren't known by common people, scholars were aware of them. The printing press (1450) made these ideas and Marco Polo's travels public knowledge, influencing Prince Henry and others.

continent. Therefore, while pushing farther south with each voyage, the Portuguese developed trade with the Africans.

Frustration and a New Plan. For 60 years the quest for an African route to the East was frustrated. Navigators pushed far beyond the equator, but one after another turned back to Portugal with the same news. Africa seemed never to end.

Even the contact with West Africa was disappointing. The Portuguese, who dreamed of having the silk and spice trade of the Indies, found that West Africa had few of the goods Europeans wanted. Some chieftains did offer slaves for sale. The Portuguese then established forts at the mouths of major rivers and began carrying on that tragic human trade.

Then, in 1484, Christopher Columbus, an Italian navigator living in Portugal, suggested a new plan to King John II. The sea that bordered China and Japan to the east, Columbus claimed, was surely the Atlantic Ocean. By catching westerly winds, ships from Portugal could sail directly to the Indies.

Columbus did not have to persuade the king that the world was round. Although uneducated people thought the earth was flat, and that a ship would sail off the edge into unknown horrors, sailors and educated people knew better. The weakness of Columbus's plan, King John's advisors told him, was that the distance was too great. Japan was thought to be 8,000–9,000 miles (13,000–14,000 kilometers) from Europe. The actual distance is closer to 12,000 miles (19,000 kilometers). Not even a speedy caravel could sail that far without resupplying. Columbus persisted, however, insisting that he would land in Asia after a voyage of 2,000–3,000 miles (3,000–4,800 kilometers). Until 1488 he continued to hope. Then a ship arrived in Lisbon that ended Columbus's hopes for Portuguese support.

Portugal Chooses the African Route. In 1488, Bartholomeu Dias (dē'əs) reached the southern tip of Africa, which he named the Cape of Good Hope. He went no farther, but rushed the news back to Portugal. It was not until 1498 that another Portuguese captain, Vasco da Gama (dă găm'ə), actually rounded the Cape of Good

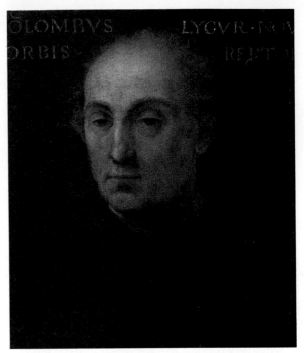

Christopher Columbus believed that he could reach Asia by sailing from Europe across the Atlantic. Although he did not reach Asia, he did find a "New World"—the Americas.

Hope and went on to India. But Dias's voyage convinced the Portuguese that their future lay on the African route. Over the next half-century they established trading posts and forts in East Africa, India, Indonesia, and as far as Macao (mə-kou') in southern China.

SECTION REVIEW

1. Write a sentence to identify: the Indies, Prince Henry, Vasco da Gama.

2. Why did the following cause Europeans to look for a way to the Indies: (a) the Crusades, (b) the Renaissance, (c) merchants of Italian city-states, (d) *Voyages of Sir Marco Polo?*

3. Give two reasons why Portugal led the way in the search for the Indies.

4. What plan for reaching the Indies did Christopher Columbus suggest to King John II of Portugal.

Slavery and the trade in slaves was common among African tribes long before the Europeans arrived. Slavery was common in ancient times among the conquering nations of the present-day Middle East and was also practiced by Europeans during the Middle Ages. It was not an American invention, but its use was greatly expanded here.

3. SPAIN CLAIMS AMERICA

Christopher Columbus traveled to Spain after the Portuguese had rejected his plan. Although the Spanish did not have a strong seafaring tradition and the nation had only recently been united by the marriage of King Ferdinand of Aragon and Queen Isabella of Castile, Columbus hoped to gain Spanish backing for his plan.

Ferdinand never took much of an interest in Columbus. Isabella at first turned Columbus down, but then changed her mind and sent for him. Perhaps it was that his expedition would cost only about $14,000 and the town of Palos owed her a debt that could be paid by providing Columbus with three ships, the *Niña*, the *Pinta*, and the *Santa Maria*. Suddenly, Isabella enthusiastically supported the Italian sailor.

Columbus's Fateful Voyage. Columbus left Spain in August 1492. His ships, which were no more than 75 feet (23 meters) long and 25 feet (8 meters) wide, stopped for supplies at Spain's Canary Islands and began their voyage into the unknown on September 6.

Although the expedition was to have a smooth crossing, Columbus risked his life for his dream. His crews, out of sight of land, were frightened. He deceived them as to how far they had traveled by keeping two *logs*, or records, of the voyage. He hid the log with his true calculations of the distance covered. Whenever the crew grumbled, he showed them false figures that indicated they were not far from home. Even then, a few threatened to throw Columbus overboard. Finally, in early October, he promised that if they did not reach land within a few days, they would return to Spain.

On October 11 leaves were spotted floating in the ocean and there was a smell of soil in the air. The next day the sailors saw a green tropical island. Columbus named it San Salvador.

This print shows Columbus leaving to board the Santa Maria. Queen Isabella and King Ferdinand are on the right. On August 3, 1492, Christopher Columbus, an Italian navigator, took command of three ships—the Santa Maria, *the* Niña, *and the* Pinta, *loaned to him by Queen Isabella of Spain—and set sail from the port city of Palos, Spain.*

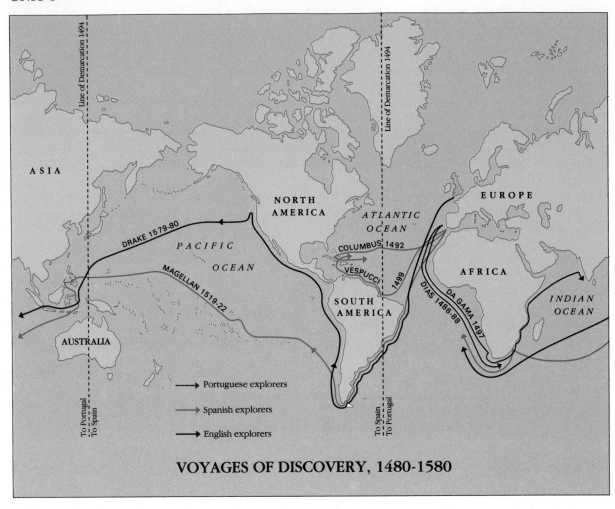

VOYAGES OF DISCOVERY, 1480-1580

Although the friendly people who greeted Columbus knew nothing of the Emperor of Japan, Columbus believed he had reached the Indies and called the people he met "Indians." Today we know that the people who greeted him were Arawaks; and San Salvador is an island of the Bahamas off the coast of Florida.

Columbus made three more voyages across the Atlantic, founded several Spanish colonies, and actually explored part of the American mainland. However, he never admitted that instead of reaching Asia he had actually discovered a new world. In 1504, another Italian explorer named Amerigo Vespucci (věs-po͞ot′chē), wrote a series of letters about his experiences in which he stated that the land formed "a very great continent hitherto unknown." A German mapmaker named Martin Waldesmuller read them, believed Vespucci was the discoverer, and wrote "America" on his charts.

Columbus's discoveries in the western world brought about sharp conflict between Spain and Portugal. Spanish and Portuguese ships now competed fiercely for trade. To lessen the conflict, and to do a favor for the Spanish, Pope Alexander IV "divided" the world in 1493. He decided that everything discovered west of a line running north and south through the Atlantic Ocean would be Spain's; everything to the east of the line would be Portugal's. The *Treaty of Tordesillas* (tôr-dä-sē-yəs) in 1494, between Spain and Portugal, moved the line farther west. Consequently, Spain controlled the Americas and everything westward, and Portugal claimed Brazil (in South America), Africa, and everything eastward.

America was not named after Columbus for yet another reason. Until his dying day, Columbus fervently believed that he had landed in the Far East and would not admit he had found a new world by accident.

GOING TO THE SOURCE

It has often occurred when I have sent two or three of my men to any of the villages to speak with the natives, that they have come out in a disorderly troop and have fled in such haste at the approach of our men that the fathers forsook their children and the children their fathers. This timidity did not arise from any loss or injury that they had received from us; for, on the contrary, I gave to all I approached whatever articles I had about me, such as cloth and many other things, taking nothing of theirs in return; but they are naturally timid and fearful.

> *Although they have been with us now a long time, they continue to entertain the idea that I have descended from heaven; and on our arrival at any new place they published this, crying out immediately with a loud voice to the other Indians, "Come, come and look upon beings of a celestial race. . . ."*
>
> CHRISTOPHER COLUMBUS,
> *LETTER ON HIS DISCOVERIES*

As soon, however, as they see that they are safe and have laid aside all fear, they are very simple and honest and exceedingly liberal with all they have. . . . They exhibit great love toward all others in preference to themselves. They also give objects of great value for trifles and content themselves with very little or nothing in return.

. . . They practice no kind of idolatry, but have a firm belief that all strength and power, and indeed all good things, are in heaven, and that I had descended from thence with these ships and sailors, and under this impression was I received after they had thrown aside their fears. Nor are they slow or stupid, but of very clear understanding; and those men who have crossed to the neighboring islands give an admirable description of everything they observed; but they never saw any people clothed nor any ships like ours.

On my arrival at that sea, I had taken some Indians by force from the first island that I came to, in order that they might learn our language and communicate to us what they knew respecting the country; which plan succeeded excellently and was a great advantage to us, for in a short time, either by gestures and signs or by words, we were enabled to understand each other. These men are still traveling with me, and although they have been with us now a long time, they continue to entertain the idea that I have descended from heaven; and on our arrival at any new place they published this, crying out immediately with a loud voice to the other Indians, "Come, come and look upon beings of a celestial race"; upon which both women and men, children and adults, young men and old, when they got rid of the fear they at first entertained, would come out in throngs, crowding the roads to see us, some bringing food, others drink, with astonishing affection and kindness.

Each of these islands has a great number of canoes, built of solid wood, narrow and not unlike our double-banked boats in length and shape, but swifter in their motion; they steer them only by the oar. These canoes are of various sizes . . . and with these they cross to the other islands. . . . I saw some of these canoes that held as many as seventy-eight rowers. In all these islands there is no difference of physiognomy [physical features], of manners, or of language, but they all clearly understand each other, a circumstance very propitious for the realization of what I conceive to be the principal wish of our most serene King, namely, the conversion of these people to the holy faith of Christ, to which indeed, as far as I can judge, they are very favorable and well-disposed.

Christopher Columbus completed his first voyage of discovery in 1493. From Portugal, he sent a long letter to Spain to report his discoveries. In this excerpt from his Letter on His Discoveries, *he describes the peoples he met.*

Discussion Question: Did Columbus really discover America? Why is it significant that we refer to Columbus as its "discoverer"? Have students realize that America existed and was populated before Columbus found it. Discuss how this perception of the New World may have influenced the European attitude toward the Native Americans and their treatment of them.

England and France Look for the Indies.

Few of the explorers who followed Columbus were interested in a new world. Their goal remained a direct trade route to the Indies. Thus, in 1497, King Henry VII of England sent John Cabot, an Italian, across the Atlantic. Cabot landed at Newfoundland, which is part of present day Canada, and claimed it for England. Like Columbus, he was sure he was on the verge of reaching Asia. A short time after returning to London, he once again set sail, but he never returned, and England's claims were unexploited for another 80 years. The rulers of France took no interest in sending out explorers until 1522 when a French *privateer,* a private ship under contract to the government, captured a Spanish ship loaded with gold. King Francis I quickly fitted out a voyage led by yet another Italian captain, Giovanni da Verrazano (věr'ə-zä'nō), to see if there might be treasure in the New World for France, too.

But Verrazano had less interest in gold than in getting to Asia. From present-day North Carolina he sailed north, always looking for a waterway to the East. He continued as far north as Newfoundland before returning to France.

In 1535, Jacques Cartier (kär-tyä') carried the flag of France up the St. Lawrence River, which he hoped might lead to Asia. Suffering dreadful hardships, the expedition sailed about 1,000 miles (1,600 kilometers) up the St. Lawrence, locating the sites of Montreal and Quebec. The crew spent a terrible winter at Quebec, and were hard hit by scurvy, a vitamin C deficiency. Enough crew members survived for Cartier to return to France. However, like the English, the French did not exploit their American claims for another two generations.

Spanish Explorers Learn the Truth.

In the meantime, Spanish explorers learned just how far they were from the Indies. In 1513, Juan Ponce de León (pōn' seh deh lā-on'), had set out to find the Caribbean island called Bimini (bĭm'ə-nē). There, Indians had told him, drinking from a "Fountain of Youth" made a person forever young and healthy.

Ponce de León may not have been searching for youth as much as he was searching for a route to Asia. What he found instead was Florida. He was the first European to explore land that is now part of the United States.

Another expedition confirmed that the Americas were continents. In 1513, Vasco Nuñez de Balboa (băl-bo'ə) led an expedition across the Isthmus of Panama in search of a country he had been told was "flowing with gold." They found little gold, but Balboa earned immortality by being the first European to see the Pacific Ocean from the Americas. Balboa's discovery meant that another sea voyage lay between the Spanish colonies in the Caribbean and East Asia.

Magellan and Del Cano.

In 1519, Ferdinand Magellan (mə-jěl'ən) sailed south from Spain with five ships and 265 crew members. It took him a year and cost him one of his ships to reach the tip of South America. There he discovered a natural phenomenon that almost ended his trip. Because the level of the Pacific is higher than that of the Atlantic, the currents and winds where the two oceans meet run strongly from west to east. It took five weeks for Magellan to sail 350 miles (560 kilometers) through the icy, treacherous strait (which was named after him) to get to the Pacific.

Crossing the Pacific presented other trials, as there were no places to resupply. Magellan himself was killed in battle when the fleet finally reached the Philippines. Only one of the ships, the *Victoria,* commanded by Juan Sebastian Del Cano and carrying the remaining 18 sailors of the expedition, reached Spain after three years of exploration.

Magellan and Del Cano proved that Asia could be reached by sailing west. However, they also showed that the western route was not practical. Portugal's route around Africa would be used for the East Asian trade.

Gold!

A huge New World was out there, but what was it worth? While the Portuguese grew rich from their African route to Asia, the Spanish men and women who came to the colonies Columbus had founded were often disappointed. A few prospered through trade with the Indians, and gold and silver trickled into the little outposts. Back in Spain, King Charles V took little interest in his subjects overseas. All this changed in 1522 when startling news arrived in Spain. A Spanish soldier in Cuba, Hernando Cortez, had sent King Charles three ships packed with gold!

Sailors bound for Asia by way of Africa were able to find their way by keeping within sight of land. When travel moved to open sea, the compass and the astrolabe told navigators in which direction they were going and where they were in relation to lines of latitude (distance from a position to the equator.)

Balboa, a Spanish explorer, led an expedition across the Isthmus of Panama in September of 1513. What he saw—the Pacific Ocean—confirmed that not one ocean but two oceans and a huge continent lay between Europe and Asia.

The gold never actually reached Charles. Not far from Spain, the ships were captured by a French privateer who turned the treasure over to the French rulers. Nevertheless, tons of gold and silver remained in America for each bar of precious metal that was lost. Spain's *siglo de oro* (sē′glō dä ôr′ō), or "golden century," had begun.

Hernando Cortez, The First Conquistador.
Tales of a rich Indian empire had drifted into Cuba for years. Native American traders and captives claimed that the Aztec nobles of Mexico ate from golden dishes and washed their hands in silver basins. In 1519, Cortez took about 500 soldiers armed with swords, pikes, muskets, cannon, and horses to investigate the rumors.

In one way, Cortez was the best person for the job. He was brave almost beyond belief. Hardship and suffering did not sway him from his purpose, which was to conquer a people who far outnumbered his little army.

In another way, Cortez was not a good leader. Like other *conquistadors* to follow him (*conquistador* means "conqueror" in Spanish), Cortez was ruthless when gold was the prize. He would just as soon destroy the whole Aztec nation for all of their gold, as trade with them for part of their gold.

Cortez Wins an Empire.
Cortez moved slowly toward Tenochtitlán, the Aztec capital, fighting his way through the lands of several tribes. Although always outnumbered, his men had several overwhelming advantages. Their armor protected them from most arrows and spears. They had firearms, including cannon, which terrified their opponents. Because the Indians had never seen horses, many were frightened of a mounted soldier.

Cortez also had two powerful allies. First, because tribes like the Tlaxcalans (tläs-kä′lənz), and Cholulans (chô-loo′lənz) hated the Aztecs,

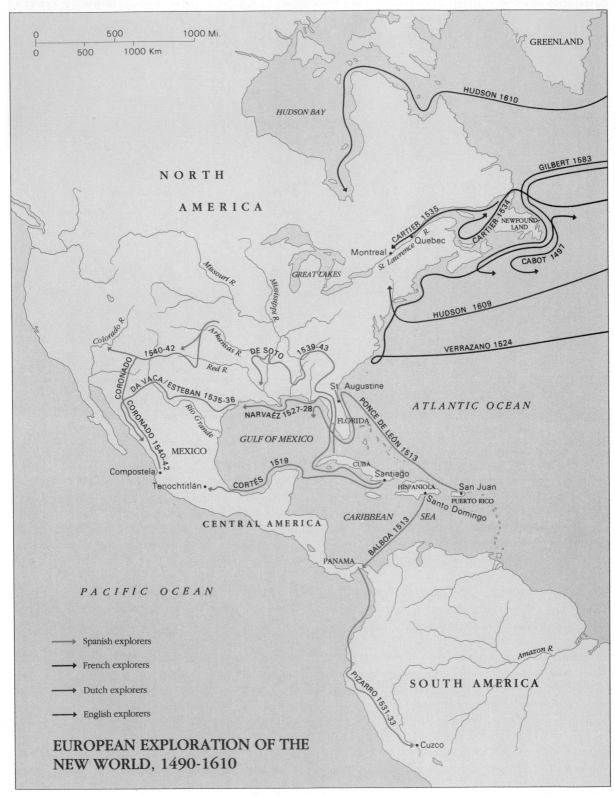

GREENLAND

HUDSON 1610

HUDSON BAY

NORTH

AMERICA

GILBERT 1583

CARTIER 1535

CARTIER 1534

NEWFOUND-LAND

Montreal

St. Lawrence R.

Quebec

CABOT 1497

Missouri R.

GREAT LAKES

Mississippi R.

HUDSON 1609

Colorado R.

1540-42

Arkansas R.

DE SOTO

1539-43

VERRAZANO 1524

CORONADO

Red R.

DA VACA/ESTEBAN 1535-36

St. Augustine

ATLANTIC OCEAN

CORONADO 1540-42

Rio Grande

NARVAÉZ 1527-28

FLORIDA

PONCE DE LEÓN 1513

MEXICO

GULF OF MEXICO

Compostela

1519

CUBA

Tenochtitlán

CORTÉS

Santiago

HISPANIOLA

San Juan

PUERTO RICO

Santo Domingo

CENTRAL AMERICA

CARIBBEAN

SEA

BALBOA 1513

PANAMA

PACIFIC OCEAN

Amazon R.

→ Spanish explorers

→ French explorers

PIZARRO 1531-33

SOUTH AMERICA

→ Dutch explorers

→ English explorers

EUROPEAN EXPLORATION OF THE NEW WORLD, 1490-1610

Cuzco

To stress why it is important for events to fit into a chain of events to affect history, remind students that Leif Ericson was actually the first European to land in America (1000 AD). The Norse already had settlements in Iceland and Greenland before that date. It is believed that Ericson was blown off course while on a trip to Greenland. Although guesses about where he landed have put

EUROPEAN EXPLORERS
1492–1542

	DATE	EXPLORER	MONARCH	OBJECTIVE	ACHIEVEMENT
SPAIN	1492–1504	Christopher Columbus	Ferdinand and Isabella	Find western route to Asia	Discovered West Indies
	1513	Juan Ponce de León	Ferdinand	Search for gold	Explored Florida
	1513	Vasco Nuñez de Balboa	Ferdinand	Search for gold	Crossed Panama and reached Pacific Ocean
	1519–1521	Hernando Cortez	Carlos I	Search for gold	Explored Mexico, conquered Aztecs
	1519–1522	Ferdinand Magellan	Carlos I	Find western route to Asia	Landed in Philippines, survivors circled globe
	1528–1536	Cabeza de Vaca, Esteban	Carlos I	Search for gold	Explored American Southwest and Mexico
	1531–1533	Francisco Pizarro	Carlos I	Search for gold	Explored Peru, conquered Incas
	1539–1542	Hernando de Soto	Carlos I	Search for gold	Explored Florida and Mississippi River Valley
	1540–1542	Francisco Coronado	Carlos I	Search for gold	Explored American Southwest and Mexico
ENGLAND	1497–1498	John Cabot	Henry VII	Find Northwest Passage	Explored North American coast
	1507–1508	Sebastian Cabot	Elizabeth I	Find Northwest Passage	Explored Labrador and Newfoundland
FRANCE	1524	Giovanni da Verrazano	Francis I	Find water route to Asia	Explored North American coastline
	1535	Jacques Cartier	Francis I	Find water route to Asia	Explored St. Lawrence River, founded Montreal and Quebec
PORTUGAL	1488	Bartholomeu Dias	Manuel I	Find southern tip of Africa	Sailed around Cape of Good Hope into Indian Ocean
	1498	Vasco da Gama	Manuel I	Sail around Africa to India	Reached India
	1500	Pedro Cabral	Manuel I	Sail around Africa to India	Landed in Brazil
	1501–1502	Amerigo Vespucci	Manuel I	Explore Americas	Explored South American coastline and discovered that Americas are continents

him anywhere from the Carolinas to Nova Scotia, Maine and Newfoundland are the two most plausible sites. The reason Ericson is not remembered as the discoverer of America is that his discovery did not add to a chain of meaningful events affecting history.

When Cortez conquered Mexico, thousands of Aztecs died and much of their culture was destroyed.

Cortez, and would one day return from the East to rule the Aztecs.

Some Aztec nobles, however, disagreed with Montezuma. They argued that the Spaniards did not act very much like gods. But before the emperor could change his mind, Cortez imprisoned him.

Tenochtitlán was peaceful for several months, but the Aztecs eventually became alarmed at the Spaniards' ungodlike behavior. In June 1520, the Aztecs revolted and forced Cortez out of the city and back to the coast. During the fighting, 2,000 Aztecs and 600 Spaniards were killed. The loss to the Aztecs would not have been so great, except that one of the dead was Montezuma.

The Aztecs were to discover that conquistadors rarely gave up when gold was the prize. New recruits from Cuba increased Cortez's army to 1,000 soldiers, and about 75,000 Indians joined him, too. In the summer of 1521 they attacked Tenochtitlán. Slowly but steadily they pushed the Aztecs back and finally surrounded them. Disease and starvation also took their toll. Then, on August 13, 1521, Cortez launched a massive and bloody assault. Within a few hours over 15,000 Aztecs lay dead. Mexico was Spain's, and the Spaniards changed their minds about the New World.

The Conquistadors. Spanish soldiers continued to sail across the ocean to the New World. But only one conquistador found riches to compare to those of Mexico. In 1532, Francisco Pizarro (pĭ-zär′ō) led a band of 180 soldiers down the western coast of South America, where he captured Atahualpa (ăt′ə-hwäl′pə), the emperor of the Incas. Pizarro told the Incas he would release Atahualpa if they filled a room with gold. The Inca empire was so efficient that within a short time Pizarro was in possession of a fortune worth $10 million. However, instead of freeing Atahualpa, Pizarro murdered him. All Incan resistance collapsed, and the Spanish took control of the empire.

From a conquistador named Esteban, who had been held captive by Indians in what is now Texas, the Spanish heard of a kingdom called Quivira where the people hung bells of gold on trees. Supposedly, even richer were the Seven Cities of Cibola (sĭ-bō′lə). In these places the buildings were said to be made of gold.

Cortez was easily able to persuade them to join him. By the time he arrived at the lake that surrounded Tenochtitlán, his 500 Spanish soldiers were backed by thousands of Indians. Second, the European diseases his men carried with them —smallpox, measles, influenza, and others—were devastating to the Indians, who possessed no natural immunities to them.

At first it seemed he did not need his allies. Cortez was able to march peacefully into the city of 250,000 because Montezuma, the emperor, believed Cortez was divine. Aztec legends told of the god Quetzalcoatl, who had light skin like

Research Assignment: Have students write a paper on misconceptions that have affected history. Examples might include how the fear of falling off the edge of the world inhibited

In 1539, Esteban and a Roman Catholic priest, Marcos de Niza, explored what is now New Mexico. From a distance they saw several Pueblo Indian towns and their reports inspired several other explorers to look farther. Hernando de Soto explored the southeastern part of the United States between 1539 and 1542, pushing as far north as Tennessee and Arkansas, and discovered the Mississippi River. But de Soto never returned. He died of fever and was buried in the Mississippi River.

Another early explorer of the United States, Francisco Coronado (kôr-ō-nä′dō), covered more distance than any other conquistador. From 1540 to 1542, he ranged over much of southwestern United States and pushed north as far as Kansas. An expedition he sent to the west discovered the Grand Canyon. Coronado also made contact with the Pueblo Indians and found them to be farmers and artisans. But no golden cities were discovered. Not until 300 more years had passed would huge gold and silver mines be found there.

The explorers of the southern United States found no rich empires to compare with those of Mexico and South America. However, they claimed much territory for Spain, opening the land for settlement by Europeans.

SECTION REVIEW

1. Write a sentence to identify: Martin Waldesmuller, privateer, the Victoria, scurvy, conquistador.
2. Why did Columbus call the Arawaks of San Salvador "Indians"?
3. How did the explorations of Juan Ponce de León and Vasco Nuñez de Balboa prove Amerigo Vespucci correct?
4. Which places did these explorers claim for Spain: (a) Hernando Cortez, (b) Francisco Pizarro, (c) Esteban and Marcos de Niza, (d) Hernando de Soto, (e) Francisco Coronado?

The Spanish explorer Coronado traveled in search of fabled cities of gold in North America. Though he never found any such cities of legend, he did discover the Grand Canyon and traveled extensively in what is now California, Arizona, and Texas.

exploration; why Columbus thought he would find Asia; how the Aztecs believed Cortez to be a deity; and how the belief that Prester John was a real person influenced the Crusades.

CHAPTER REVIEW

TIME LINE

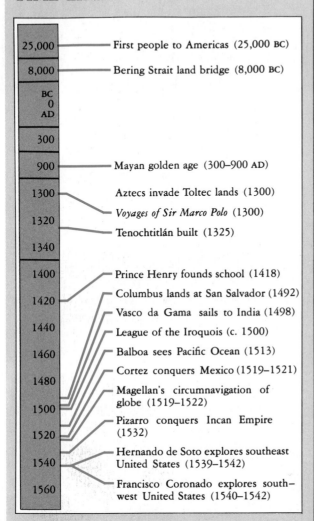

25,000	First people to Americas (25,000 BC)
8,000	Bering Strait land bridge (8,000 BC)
BC 0 AD	
300	
900	Mayan golden age (300–900 AD)
1300	Aztecs invade Toltec lands (1300)
1320	*Voyages of Sir Marco Polo* (1300)
	Tenochtitlán built (1325)
1340	
1400	Prince Henry founds school (1418)
1420	Columbus lands at San Salvador (1492)
	Vasco da Gama sails to India (1498)
1440	League of the Iroquois (c. 1500)
1460	Balboa sees Pacific Ocean (1513)
	Cortez conquers Mexico (1519–1521)
1480	Magellan's circumnavigation of globe (1519–1522)
1500	
1520	Pizarro conquers Incan Empire (1532)
1540	Hernando de Soto explores southeast United States (1539–1542)
1560	Francisco Coronado explores south-west United States (1540–1542)

TIME LINE QUESTIONS

This time line represents a tremendous length of time. In the Christian calendar, which almost all Americans use, dates that occurred *Before Christ's* birth are indicated with the letters BC. Those events that occurred after Christ's birth are indicated by the letters AD (*Anno Domini*, which is Latin for "in the year of our Lord").

1. How many years does this time line span?
2. Between which years are explorations noted on this time line?
3. Between which entries is the greatest amount of time shown?

SKILLS STRATEGY

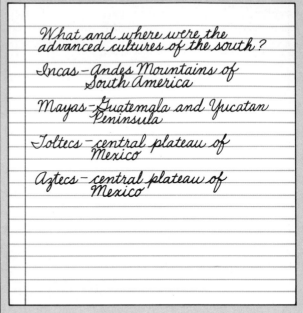

What and where were the advanced cultures of the south?

Incas — Andes Mountains of South America

Mayas — Guatemala and Yucatan Peninsula

Toltecs — central plateau of Mexico

Aztecs — central plateau of Mexico

TAKING NOTES

Taking good notes will help you to remember important information and to understand the relationships of the ideas being presented. The time you spend in note-taking will be worth your while. You can use your notes for class discussion, for quick recall before a test, or to organize a report.

To be most useful, your notes should have headings, be brief, accurate, and easy to read. You can summarize information and jot down phrases or sentences that you consider to be important. If your notes deal with data only, you may want to write them in a list.

One technique for note-taking is to change major text headings into questions and to use minor text headings and text skimming to answer the questions. Text skimming involves looking quickly at a passage without reading every word. When you skim, you pick up important words and phrases to survey the content and get the chief ideas contained within a section of text. This method helps you to think about and concentrate on the most important ideas in the text.

The notes in the exhibit above were taken

Making Connections: Review the questions and topics presented in the Making Connections section opening this chapter. Pay particular attention to making students aware that there were highly civilized cultures among the Indians living here; to make students understand and

---

*What parts of the
United States were settled by
the First Americans?*

CHAPTER 1 TEST

TEXT REVIEW

1. Give two possible reasons for the migration of the first Americans from Asia to the American continents.
2. Why didn't the first Americans who settled what is now the United States develop advanced cultures like Central and South America?
3. Describe two ways in which Portugal led the way in the European exploration of other parts of the world.
4. Name four explorers who gave Spain a claim to lands in the Americas, and name the areas they explored.
5. Which two European countries besides Portugal and Spain established claims to lands in the Americas?
6. Describe the circumstances that led to the drastic changes in the lives of the Aztecs and Incas in the 1500 s.

CRITICAL THINKING

7. Summarize the differences in the roles of the Aztec and Inca emperors.
8. What positive and negative conclusions have you reached about Cortez? Support your conclusions.
9. If the European explorers had reached the Americas 100 years later, what do you think might have happened to the civilization of the Mayas?
10. Compare the life of two early North American Indian tribes.

while reading the subsections on the Incas, Mayas, Toltecs, and Aztecs in Chapter 1 (pages 6–8). The person taking the notes changed the text heading to a question reflecting the content of the section. This question serves as the note heading. The details beneath it answer the question and contain the most important information in the text.

APPLYING SKILLS

Look at the subheading "The Indians of the United States" on page 8 and skim the eight subheadings and text that follow it in the section (pages 8–12). Can you see why the person taking notes on the section formed the question above?

1. Copy the question and write the first item you think belongs under it.
2. Complete your notes on this section.
3. When you have finished, compare your notes with the text. Do they all relate to the note heading? Eliminate any that do not.

Keep these notes. You will be asked to write about the first Americans. Your notes will make the task easier and help you to create a well-organized paragraph.

WRITING A PARAGRAPH

A paragraph should have a topic sentence expressing the main idea and detail sentences supporting the main idea.

Write a paragraph that begins or ends with the topic sentence below. The section notes you took will help you write this paragraph. Notice the relationship of your note heading and the topic sentence.

Topic Sentence: The first Americans settled in different parts of what is now the United States.

appreciate the chain of events that led to the discovery of America by Europeans; and to make certain that students grasp the significance of European attitudes toward the Native Americans and how they would affect future relations.

CHAPTER 2

EUROPEAN EMPIRES IN AMERICA

1525–1625

Marriage, tobacco, and slavery,
initiated liberty
when the Deliverance brought seed
of that new controversial weed—
MARIANNE MOORE

Making Connections. The Europeans first came to the Americas for "God, gold, and glory." However, gold existed in only a few areas, and glory was tempered by the harsh wilderness. Many did find a place where they could worship without persecution. They all came to find a better way of life in the new American colonies.

In this chapter you will learn:
- How American colonies brought wealth to their parent countries
- How Europeans treated Native Americans
- Why Spain gained control over much of the New World
- Who the "sea dogs" were and how they helped England challenge Spain
- What saved the English colony of Jamestown
- Which European countries established colonies

You know that the Europeans explored the New World hoping to find the riches of the Indies to take back to their homelands and that, for the most part, those riches did not exist in the Americas. Consequently, this emphasis had to change if Europe was to benefit from the New World. As you read, note how European activity and interest shifted from conquest to colonization after it became clear that plunder and pillage did not enrich European treasuries.

Sections
1. The Spanish Empire
2. Spain's Challengers
3. English Colonies
4. French, Dutch, and Swedish Colonies

1. THE SPANISH EMPIRE

The conquistadors served Spain well. By 1550, they had explored the Americas as far north as Kansas and as far south as the very tip of South America. They had paved the way for Spanish settlement of all but the most remote jungles and mountains. They assumed the role of the Native American nobility in the Aztec and Inca lands, and simply overwhelmed the smaller tribes. But with the fall of the Incas, the conquistadors' job was finished. There were no more Indian kingdoms that were rich in gold and silver left to be conquered. Spanish America was becoming a more settled and varied land: mines, ranches, farms, and trade were providing the new wealth.

Mercantilism. The economic philosophy behind empire building was called *mercantilism.* According to this doctrine, a country could make itself stronger by exporting more than it imported. By selling more goods to foreign countries than it bought from them, money would flow into the country. That money could then be invested in new business ventures to make more money, and to make the country less dependent on foreign

The 102 English settlers aboard the Mayflower (right)—one third of whom were Separatists—arrived on the coast of what is now Massachusetts in November 1620. While remaining aboard, they drew up a governing agreement called the Mayflower Compact.

Skills Review: Have students reinforce their knowledge of one-level outlines by having them outline this chapter according to the method given in the Skills Strategy in chapter 1.

goods. The money could also be used to finance larger armies and navies, and so increase a country's military power.

Colonies were thought to be part of the parent country for mercantilist purposes. Natural resources were sent to the parent country and turned into finished goods, which were then shipped back to the colonies. In order to enrich the country's merchant fleet, all goods moving between the colonies and the parent country had to be carried on the parent country's ships. Colonists could buy only those articles made in the parent country, whether or not they needed something made in another country.

Spain, Portugal, and the other European powers all followed this policy. This caused friction because each country wanted to sell its products to other countries while keeping its own harbors closed to foreign traders. Eventually, the policy would hamper the growth of colonies, and the colonists would have to turn to other means, including smuggling and building their own trading fleets, to get what they needed. But during the early colonial years, and especially in Spanish America, mercantilism prevailed.

Economic Policy. As in all empires, it was believed that the colonies existed for the good of the parent country. The crown received the "royal fifth" of all precious metals mined in America. Trade with Spanish America was restricted to merchants from Spain. Ships from all other nations were forbidden to enter Spanish American ports.

A major feature of the Spanish-American colonies was the *encomienda* (ĕn-kō′mē-ĕn′də) system. Under this system the Spanish monarch granted tracts of land to Spaniards who settled in America. With the land came the right to the labor of the Indians who lived on it. The encomiendas were self-sufficient units, growing food for local consumption and some export crops. The system was also designed to protect the Indians and convert them to Christianity, but it actually caused their enslavement.

Although the Aztec and Incan empires were already rich in gold and silver, the Spaniards extended and developed the mines. Using forced Indian labor and the additional labor of slaves brought from Africa, the Spanish shipped about

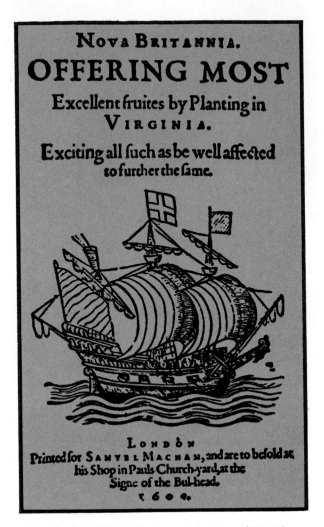

Early "broadside" advertisements encouraged British subjects to emigrate to the English colonies in the New World.

$12 million of the precious metals back to Spain every year.

A People of Many Races. Although they regarded the Indians as their subjects, the Spanish did not think of them as inferior because of their color. In fact, the children of most of the conquistadors had mixed Spanish and Indian blood, and were called *mestizos* (mĕs-tē′zōz). Although the first 30 Spanish women came to America on Columbus's third voyage in 1498, almost all the early settlers were men, most of whom were soldiers. As a result, when the Spanish men married, most of them married Indian women.

Research Assignment: Using local colleges, libraries, or historical societies, have students research the origins of place names in your area. From this starting point, have students further examine the history of the people responsible for the naming of these places and find other contributions these people may have made to the development of the area.

Black people were also present in Spanish America. One of the sailors with Columbus on his first voyage may have been a black man. But most of the blacks in the New World came unwillingly, as slaves from Africa to replace the Indians in the labor force. Blacks were a majority of the population in many islands of the West Indies and on the mainland surrounding the Caribbean Sea. Brazil also had a large black population because the Portuguese dominated the African end of the slave trade.

Within a few generations, a multi-racial society emerged. In addition to the Indians, mestizos, white Spaniards, and *criollos* (krē ō′ yōz) —Spaniards born in America—there were *mulattoes*, people of Spanish and African descent, and *zamboes*, people of Indian and African descent. People from each group were found in all of the social classes, from richest to poorest. In general, though, the white Spaniards had the highest levels of society to themselves. From the moment Spanish natives set foot in America, they enjoyed greater economic and political privileges than every criollo, and thus every other group in Spanish America.

The Tragedy of the Indians.

Although the wealth of Spain was based on the abundance of the Americas, very few Indians shared in the prosperity. The advanced Aztecs and Incas were forced to abandon their religious practices and folkways. They had to work for their new rulers as they did for their old emperors, but the work was much harder. Indians everywhere died under the Spanish conquerors. The Native American population of Mexico, about 5 million when Cortez arrived, declined to 1 million by 1600. It is estimated that the total Indian population of the area the Spanish conquered was 25 million in 1492 and only 4 million two centuries later.

How did so many die? The conquistadors killed tens of thousands in battle. Hundreds of thousands more died when forced to work at a pace to which they were not accustomed. Conditions in the mines and on the encomiendas were poor, and overseers were at times brutal. Although the *encomenderos* (ĕn-kō′mən-dê′rōz), or Spanish-American landowners, were expected to protect the welfare of their workers, enforcement of the law was uneven during the early years of the empire. Rough Spanish soldiers, who had seen much hardship and bloodshed, were rarely gentle.

Most of all, the Indians died from disease. Smallpox, measles, mumps, and influenza were unknown in the Western Hemisphere before Europeans arrived. Therefore, the Indians had no natural immunities to these diseases. Even a comparatively minor European illness like chicken pox could be fatal to Native Americans. The Arawaks of San Salvador, already weakened by forced labor, were completely destroyed by epidemic diseases, and the Indians elsewhere suffered much the same fate.

The Importance of Religion.

The Catholic Church was a powerful force in Spanish America because the Spaniards were an intensely religious people. Even the most hard-bitten and greedy conquistadors were devoted to spreading Christianity, and along with the friars, they were remarkably successful. Today, a large majority of Central and South Americans are Catholic.

There was little religious tolerance in the Spanish Empire. In Europe, the sixteenth century was a time of bitter religious warfare between Catholics and Protestants. In Spanish America, people who did not practice the Roman Catholic faith were persecuted, forced to change their religion or leave the empire, and occasionally put to death. For example, Jewish conquistadors helped win the empire. They fought alongside Cortez and Pizarro, and according to a census of 1545, one-fourth of the Spanish population of Mexico City was Jewish. But by 1600 almost all Spanish Americans were Catholics—the nonbelievers had been expelled or converted.

There was another side of the Catholic religion. A few Roman Catholic priests like Bartolomé de Las Casas tried to protect the Indians from their Spanish overlords. Himself an encomendero as a young man, de Las Casas was shocked by the brutality of his neighbors toward the Native Americans. He became a priest, wrote books condemning Spanish cruelty and exploitation, and continually traveled from his home in Guatemala to Spain, where he implored King Charles to protect the Native Americans.

De Las Casas achieved many victories. The king empowered him and other friars to found *missions*, self-sufficient communities of free Indians where

Research Assignment: Have students read the biography of one of the religious leaders or missionaries who influenced relations with the Indians. Examine both the religious and nonreligious contributions of these people and how they got along with the Indians. Some possible subjects would include: Junípero Serra, de Las Casas, Kino, and Marquette.

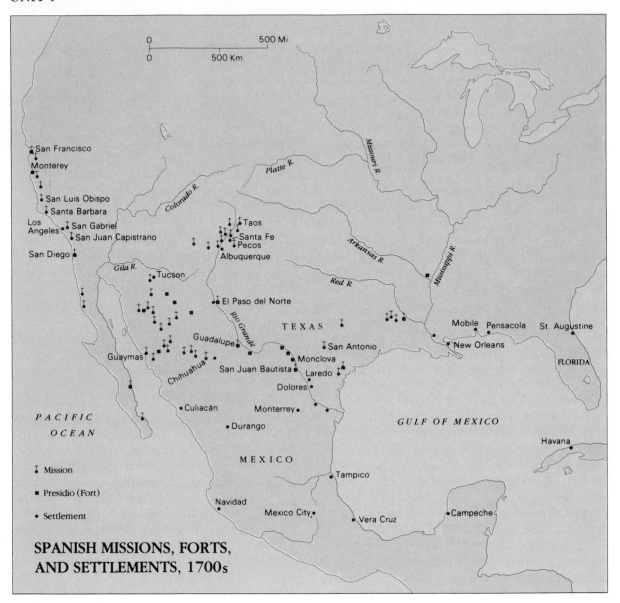

SPANISH MISSIONS, FORTS, AND SETTLEMENTS, 1700s

treatment was much better than it was on the encomiendas. With a missionary desire to convert the Indians to the Roman Catholic faith, Franciscan and Dominican priests ventured far beyond the Spanish cities, pueblos, and *presidios*, or military forts.

Much of northern Mexico was brought under Spanish control by these spiritual conquistadors. Beginning in 1712, they established missions along the Rio Grande and the San Antonio River in Texas. Somewhat later, Father Junipero Serra began a chain of missions in California which was

so complete that a traveler going from San Diego to San Francisco never had to spend a night outside.

Governing an Empire. By 1550, half a century before the first permanent English and French settlements in the New World were founded, more than 5 million Spaniards called America their home. At least 200 cities, towns, missions, and presidios swore loyalty to the Spanish Crown. Lavishly decorated churches overlooked every pueblo. Cathedrals soared over the cities. Priests,

Discussion Question: In what ways were the Indian civilizations similar and dissimilar to European civilizations? Were they more similar than dissimilar? Parallel Inca and Spanish kings and how both derived authority from God. Examine totalitarian and more democratic govern-

32

nuns, ranchers, farmers, laborers, and slaves gathered in the broad plazas located at the center of every Spanish town. The seaports teemed with ships engaged in a busy trade with Spain. There were universities in Mexico City and Lima, Peru.

In theory, this sprawling empire was firmly in the grip of the Spanish monarch. The monarchs of Spain were *absolute rulers*. That is, they claimed to derive their power from God and to be responsible only to God. Their proclamations were law, and their subjects were expected to obey them without question. In order to carry out their will in America, the Spanish rulers appointed four *viceroys*, or deputy rulers. The Viceroy of New Spain governed the area from Mexico to Costa Rica. The Viceroy of New Granada was responsible for modern-day Panama, Colombia, Venezuela, and Ecuador. The Viceroyalty of Peru was the old Inca empire. The Viceroyalty of La Plata included Uruguay, Argentina, Paraguay, Bolivia, and Chile.

In practice, the influence in the Americas of the monarch and the viceroys was limited. The Spanish rulers were more interested in European wars than in their American empire. They left most decisions on colonial policy to the *Council of the Indies*, a group of six nobles. However, it took a long time for a viceroy's report or request for instructions to reach the Council. Indeed, because ships were sometimes lost at sea, some letters never arrived in Spain at all, and a year or more might pass before the viceroy realized what had happened. Even when the Council received a report, the time lost between the sending of the report and the receipt of a reply in America often made the reply outdated.

Communication within the Americas was not much more efficient. As a result, day-to-day decisions rested with the great landowners, the Catholic bishops, and the local military commanders. Although they often disagreed on how to run their sections of the empire, they all had to be careful to obey the laws of the Council.

Some towns elected governing councils called *cabildos* (kə-bīl′dōz), and mayors (who were also judges) called *alcaldes* (äl-käl′däz). But elections were not an important part of Spanish-American tradition. As in Spain, authority was held by a single person or a small group, that directed the lives of the others.

SECTION REVIEW

1. Write a sentence to identify: encomienda system, presidio, Bartolomé de Las Casas, Junipero Serra, viceroy.

2. Explain why Spanish exploration and conquest had stopped and the establishment of the Spanish Empire had begun by 1550 in the Americas.

3. Name and describe the economic philosophy behind the building of the Spanish Empire.

4. How did the theory of the role of the Spanish monarch in the American empire differ from that monarch's actual role?

2. SPAIN'S CHALLENGERS

The strict economic and political restrictions of the Spanish Empire had effects outside the Americas. Seafaring merchants from other countries resented these policies. They wanted to compete for a share of the rich trading opportunities in the New World. There was a great deal of smuggling in the Caribbean Islands as Dutch, French, and English merchants sought to get around Spain's rules. When foreign captains arrived in Jamaica or Puerto Rico with slaves for sale, or to offer good prices for sugar and other tropical products, Spanish plantation owners were usually willing to bargain. They were also able to get products that were not available from Spanish traders.

Spain's Early Dominance. Because they brought great wealth to their countries, merchants had great influence with their rulers. Until the end of the sixteenth century, however, they could not officially break Spain's monopoly. Spain was a formidable enemy. Since wealth from America enabled the Spanish to raise powerful armies and navies, other European countries could not afford confrontations.

Another reason that Spain and Portugal had the New World to themselves for so long was that the other seafaring nations of Europe were troubled by problems at home. Until 1562, the Netherlands were ruled by Spain. After ten years of

ments in Native American and European cultures. Also compare methods of taxation and laws in both cultures and reasons for going to war of countries and groups on both sides of the Atlantic.

rebellion, Holland and several other Dutch provinces drove the Spaniards out. The little country prospered. Trade and industry, especially the manufacture of cloth, enabled the little Netherlands to become a rich naval power. But as long as Spanish armies threatened their country's independence, the Dutch could not devote their energies to overseas colonization.

Until 1589, France was torn by a vicious civil war. Two and sometimes three great nobles battled one another to wear the crown and to determine whether France would be a Roman Catholic or Protestant country. As long as the French people were fighting among themselves, the explorations and claims of Verrazano and Cartier were neglected.

England's wars to decide which family would rule ended a century earlier, in 1485, when the Tudor dynasty was established on the throne. However, Spain's golden century was a time of religious uncertainty for the English. King Henry VIII took England out of the Roman Catholic Church. Under his son, Edward VI, England became more Protestant. But Edward died after only six years on the throne and the new queen, Mary I, married Philip II of Spain and tried to bring the English back to the Catholic religion. Then, in 1558, after only five years, Mary died.

Her successor, Elizabeth I, was a shrewd and cautious woman. Because her strongest supporters belonged to the moderate Church of England, she favored that religion but without persecuting people who practiced other faiths quietly. Elizabeth was also friendly to trade; and England prospered as never before, growing stronger with each year that passed. Ever richer and more confident seafarers urged her to challenge the Spanish monopoly in America. But Elizabeth moved carefully in foreign relations, too. For the first 25 years of her reign, she kept the peace with Spain. In order to avoid a war, Elizabeth even led Philip II to believe she might marry him. But a conflict was inevitable.

The Exploits of Sir Francis Drake.

By the 1570s, England was no longer a minor nation on the northern fringes of Europe, but the home of a restless and ambitious people. One who was more restless than most was Francis Drake. By the age of 27, he had already defied Spanish rule by smuggling slaves to the Caribbean, and had battled Spanish ships. He hated the Spanish and did his best to bring on war with them.

In 1572, with only two ships and 73 men, including blacks who had escaped from slavery in the West Indies, Drake sailed boldly into the *Spanish Main*, the waters off the northern coast of South America. He raided several rich ports and cities, and also captured a mule train carrying 60,000 pounds (27,000 kilograms) of silver. King Philip II of Spain was furious, and complained to Queen Elizabeth that Drake was a common pirate and should be hanged. Legally, Philip was right, but Elizabeth stalled. She was fascinated by the English "*sea dog*," as Drake and other raiders of the Spanish colonies were called, and his raids were very popular in England.

Drake knew how difficult it would be to duplicate his exploits in the Caribbean. Spanish warships gathered there in large numbers, waiting for him or some other adventurer. So he decided to attack the Spanish cities on the west coast of South

Under the firm leadership of Queen Elizabeth I, England prospered financially and proved militarily superior to the Spanish.

Sir Francis Drake hated the Spanish because of events on one of his sea voyages. In 1567, Drake commanded one of several ships under the leadership of John Hawkins, a relative of Drake's. The ships were on a peaceful trading expedition when they were attacked by Spanish warships.

The English "sea dog" Sir Francis Drake (right) raided Spanish colonies in the Americas and returned to England by sailing around the world. The engraving above is of Drake capturing St. Augustine, Florida, on June 7, 1586.

America. These cities were lightly defended because the only vessels in those waters were large Spanish freighters, called *galleons*, sailing from the Philippines.

In 1577, Drake set out on his mission. He began with five ships, but three were wrecked in storms, and one later turned back to England.

Yet Drake continued on in his flagship, the *Golden Hind*. He sailed through the Straits of Magellan and north up the Pacific Coast of Spanish America. He pillaged the Spanish cities, murdering people and burning buildings. Drake's men loaded so much stolen gold on the ship that it was difficult to sail it on an even keel.

Hawkins died in the attack, and most of the unarmed British ships were destroyed. With two ships and 73 men, Drake began his marauding days in 1572.

Drake Circles the Globe.
Drake knew he probably wouldn't escape the Spanish if he returned through the Straits of Magellan. So he continued north, hoping to find a water route through America into the North Atlantic. He established the English claim to California, and may have visited San Francisco Bay. But when he found no passageway he did what Magellan had done—turned westward to cross the Pacific.

Drake finally returned to England in 1580, the captain of only the second voyage around the world. When the profits of the voyage were counted, the investors who had financed the expedition reaped a gain of 4,700 percent! King Philip of Spain again demanded that Drake be punished. But Elizabeth decided England was ready to challenge Spain's power, and she boarded the *Golden Hind* and honored Drake by making him a knight.

Sea Dog Colonies.
Other sea dogs challenged Spain by establishing English settlements in America. In 1583 Sir Humphrey Gilbert tried to prepare a site in Newfoundland for settlement. Gilbert picked this area because it was far north of

Sir Walter Raleigh explored the eastern coast of North America from Florida to North Carolina.

the centers of Spanish power. His goal was to establish a base from which he could pursue the old dream of reaching Asia by sailing west. But the long Canadian winter proved too hard and Gilbert started back to England. On September 9, 1583, his ship sank in a storm and Gilbert was drowned.

Walter Raleigh, Gilbert's half-brother, organized another expedition in 1587 that resulted in the "lost colony" of Roanoke. The settlement was originally intended to be near Chesapeake Bay in what is now Virginia, but the ships were blown southward and landed at Roanoke Island, off the coast of what is now North Carolina. But under Governor John White, the 118 men and women built cabins surrounded by protective log walls. Governor White's daughter gave birth to the first English child born in America, Virginia Dare.

Although the colony's start was good, its end was mystifying. When Raleigh was finally able to send supplies to the colonists on the island in 1590, the little village was found deserted. The only clue to the whereabouts of the missing people was the word CROATOAN carved on a tree. Croatoan was the name of a nearby island and the ships sailed there. The sailors shouted and sang English songs but received no response. No graves or other signs of the colonists' existence were found.

England Defeats Spain.
Raleigh took so long to send Roanoke supplies because England and Spain had gone to war. Philip II had had his fill of the sea dogs and had ordered the construction of a great fleet, called the *Armada*, for the invasion of England. The fact that Drake destroyed 33 of the ships in the habor at Cadiz, Spain, only increased Philip's determination. In 1588 he sent 130 ships carrying 30,000 soldiers to a part of the Netherlands that Spain still controlled, where more soldiers were waiting. Philip intended to use all of Spain's might against England.

The English had other ideas. Drake and other sea dogs knew their fleet could not defeat the Armada in an old-fashioned naval battle, in which enemy ships would pull alongside one another and armored soldiers would fight with swords and pikes on the decks. To avoid such a battle, the English met the Armada with small, quick ships that the lumbering Spanish troop carriers could not catch. The English blasted the Spanish ships

Discussion Questions: Should Great Britain have been held responsible for the actions of the sea dogs? Relate this question not only to the issue at hand, but to more recent situations that may parallel it. Should the Iranian government be held responsible for terrorist attacks by Shiite Moslems? Teach students to present coherent, logical arguments.

36

Pomeiock (above) was a village located in what is now North Carolina. The construction of a pole fence around the village was a typical feature of the Algonquin Indian settlements of the seventeenth century.

with long-range cannon, and then sent burning ships toward the Armada as it retreated toward Calais on the French coast. Fearing that the flaming vessels were loaded with enough gunpowder to destroy them all, the Spaniards headed for open water without proper preparation. Again the English launched hit-and-run attacks.

To escape the attacks in the narrow English Channel, the Armada headed north around Scotland and Ireland. But a series of storms further devastated the once proud fleet. Only about half the ships that had set out to conquer England returned to Spain. English church bells rang victoriously for days. Soon the English people began to think that if Spain could be defeated in Europe, perhaps it could be challenged in the Americas. The victory over the Armada thus emboldened England and other countries to build empires.

SECTION REVIEW

1. Write a sentence to identify: Spanish Main, sea dog, galleon, Golden Hind, Sir Humphrey Gilbert.

2. Explain why the Netherlands, France, and England let Spain's monopoly of the rich trade with the New World go unchallenged until the end of the sixteenth century.

3. How did the actions of Sir Francis Drake bring on the conflict between England and Spain?

4. What was Spain's response to the behavior of the English Queen Elizabeth and her subjects?

Class Activity: Have students use outside research along with information in the textbook to formulate a chronological order of events leading to the war between Spain and Great Britain. List these on the board and present some events that are unrelated. Label the events presented as *direct, indirect,* or *no effect.*

3. ENGLISH COLONIES

Although Elizabeth I defeated Spain, she did not live to see English colonies in America. Only after her cousin, James I, assumed the throne was the Spanish colonial monopoly in America finally broken.

In 1606, James granted charters to the London Company and the Plymouth Company, allowing them to create colonies in America. The most favorable locations were to go to the company that established the first colony. In 1607, the London Company won the race by founding Jamestown, in present-day Virginia. Plymouth, in present-day Massachusetts, was founded by people sailing for the Plymouth Company in 1620. In 1609, another English colony was begun by accident in Bermuda, a group of islands off the coast of present-day North Carolina, when a ship bound for Jamestown was wrecked there.

How Colonies Were Founded. English colonies in North America, as well as Dutch and French colonies, were not founded directly by European governments. Private companies applied for and received royal permission, in the form of corporate charters, to begin colonies in the New World. To raise money for the ventures, shares in the companies were sold to rich nobles and merchants. These combinations of investors were called *joint-stock companies*. Their goal was profit, divided up according to how many shares

English women were present in the New World from the time of the first English colony at Jamestown, Virginia.

Many foods were introduced to the Americas by the Europeans. Some of these were wheat, barley, citrus fruits, and sugar cane. In return, Europeans were introduced to potatoes, corn, beans, peppers, and tomatoes. Some of the latter did not immediately find their way into the European diet. Many Europeans would not eat tomatoes, for example. Some thought they were each member owned. Although the profit would be divided, this form of business organization appealed to merchants and other investors because, if a venture failed, they would lose only the value of their shares.

The shareholders in the London Company and the Plymouth Company hoped to make money by finding American gold, by finding a route to Asia, or by purchasing animal furs and hides from Native Americans.

The First English Colony. The 104 London Company colonists landed on a low-lying spit of land on the James River of Virginia. It was a difficult place to establish a colony, being marshy and plagued by mosquito-borne diseases. The founders, who arrived in May 1607, chose it because their orders told them to locate far up a river. They also chose the site because a peninsula could be more easily defended against the nearby Powhatan Indians, a loose confederation of about 34 Algonkian tribes who were sometimes friendly and sometimes hostile.

Few of the original settlers were farmers. Most were soldiers and adventurers who had no intention of working. There were brickmakers and a few glassmakers from Poland who were willing to labor but knew nothing of surviving in a wilderness. The first Virginians could not hunt as skillfully as the Indians, and were suspicious of wild plants that were unfamiliar to them. Instead of planting crops, they wandered the forests in search of gold, confident that English ships would bring them food.

Had it not been for the presence of a crusty soldier named John Smith, Jamestown would probably have failed. Smith made the settlers work hard. He denied food to men and boys who would not work, and threatened them with execution. Through persuasion and force he got corn from the Powhatan Indians. Still, half the settlers died during Virginia's first year and most of the survivors begged to be taken back to England when a relief ship arrived in January 1608.

The reinforced population was again reduced by half during the second year. After Smith was injured in a gunpowder explosion and had to return to England, matters grew even worse. A population of about 500 in the fall of 1609 was reduced to 60 by May 1610. This starving group

John Smith, an English soldier, maintained discipline among the hard-pressed members of early Jamestown. Without him, more settlers would probably have died during Virginia's first year.

was found several miles from Jamestown. They had been living on little more than oysters scraped from shallow waters in Chesapeake Bay.

The new governor, Sir Thomas Dale, wrote to the London Company that "everie man allmost laments himself of being here." At his suggestion, convicts who had no choice were sent to Jamestown. Orphans, and probably other poor children from the streets of London, were seized and shipped to Virginia. Still the colony had difficulty growing. By 1617, more than 2,000 people had come to Jamestown, yet the population of the colony was only about 400.

The investors of the London Company were discouraged. Little gold had been found. Virginia boasted no water route to Asia. The Company had made some money from furs and hides that the Powhatan Indians had sold to the colonists. They had also made some money from lumber and naval stores, and from pitch and tar extracted from pine trees. But income never managed to cover the expenses of supporting Jamestown. King James

poisonous; others thought them an aphrodisiac and, therefore, immoral. Only in the 1700s did Europeans change their ways. Change in the United States was slower. In the mid-1800s a man in Newport, R.I., caused a sensation by eating a raw tomato in front of a crowd.

might have taken pride in the little American settlement that bore his name, but early Jamestown was a commercial failure.

Tobacco Saves Jamestown.

The business that finally saved Virginia was the tobacco trade. The person who developed it was John Rolfe, an early settler who was married to a Powhatan princess, Pocahontas. The habit of smoking tobacco had been spreading in the Old World for a century after it was introduced from Spanish America. It was the cost of Spanish tobacco that set Rolfe to experimenting in his garden with West Indian seed.

By 1617, he was satisfied with his home-grown crop. He shipped a few barrels to a merchant friend in England, and it caused a sensation. The tobacco was cheaper than Spanish tobacco, and the English could then sell it throughout Europe for less money than the Spanish charged. At last Virginia had an economic reason to exist. Indeed, the colony began to boom immediately.

Growth of Virginia.

Sensing a bright future, the London Company tried to make Virginia more attractive to settlers. In 1619, the Company gave up its tight control over the colonies, allowing the election of a 22-member House of Burgesses, the first elected assembly in North America. The House was not a truly democratic body because not all people could vote, and only wealthy landowners could hold office. Nevertheless, the principle of *representation*—the belief that members of a community have a say in making the laws by which they are governed—was established in America.

The London Company also made it easier to own property in Virginia. The *headright system* was established in 1619 as a means to attract colonists. Instead of working as employees of the Company, each person able to pay passage from England to Jamestown received 50 acres of land. A person who transported a family (including servants) to the colony had a right to 50 acres "per head."

The headright also promoted the growth of the servant population in Virginia. People with enough money to transport several servants to Virginia often hired *indentured servants*, who received their passage to the New World in return for legally contracting their services to their mas-

Étatis suæ 21. Aⁿ 1616.

Matoaks als Rebecka daughter to the mighty Prince Powhatan Emperour of Attanoughkomouck als Virginia converted and baptized in the Christian faith, and wife to the wor.ᵇˡ Mʳ Tho: Rolff.

Pocahontas, a Powhatan Indian princess, extended aid to early Jamestown settlers. She also married one of them—John Rolfe—who developed the tobacco trade in America.

ters for a certain number of years. A common length of time was seven years, but if the demand for servants was high, that number decreased to five and even three years. For more than a century, indentured servants were the backbone of the agricultural workforce in Virginia.

The year 1619 also saw the first unmarried women arrive in Virginia, as the Company began to promote a natural increase in the colony's population. Sixty single women came to Virginia. They married some of the planters and began families. More women arrived in 1620 and 1621.

Finally, 1619 marked the arrival of the first black people in English America. The first group consisted of 20 captives, Africans who had been purchased in their homeland or seized on their way to the Spanish West Indies. These first black Americans were probably not lifetime slaves, but servants who, after seven years, were granted their freedom. While a few English people, like Francis Drake, had been involved in the slave trade, slavery was offensive to others.

Research Assignment: Women did not arrive in the English colonies until settlements were established. Students may wish to write a report describing what life was like for the first women who came to the colony of Virginia.

NEW WORLD LAND GRANTS, 1600

Map legend:
- Settlement rights granted to Virginia Co. of London, 1606
- Settlement rights granted to Virginia Co. Plymouth (Eng.), 1609
- Neutral Zone: Territory open to settlement by both companies

Map labels: 0 150 300 Mi / 0 150 300 Km; St. Lawrence R.; MASSACHUSETTS BAY 1629; Boston 1630; Plymouth; PLYMOUTH 1620; Hudson R.; VIRGINIA COMPANY OF LONDON 1609; Chesapeake Bay; ATLANTIC OCEAN; James R.; Jamestown 1607; ROANOKE I.; 100 Mi.

The Crown Takes Over. In 1621, Virginia was finally becoming prosperous. In that year, however, the Powhatans named a new chief, Opecanough (ō-pĕk′ə-nō). The old chief, the father of Pocahontas, had been friendly to the people at Jamestown. Opecanough recognized that with the success of the tobacco trade, the colonists were pushing rapidly into his tribe's lands and growing more powerful. To him the trade goods the colonists offered were not worth the loss of land.

In March 1622, Opecanough and his warriors entered Jamestown as if to trade or talk. Suddenly, they attacked the Virginians and killed 350 people within a few hours. This attack became known as the *Jamestown Massacre*, and almost destroyed the colony. However, it was the Powhatans' last uprising, as the Virginians regrouped and used their superior firearms to drive the Powhatans deep into the forest, breaking the tribe's power forever.

When King James heard of the Jamestown Massacre, he blamed it on the London Company's poor management. James revoked the London Company's charter in 1624 and took control, turning Virginia into the first *royal colony*, or colony. ruled directly by the Crown. The Crown collected Virginia's revenues and appointed the governor who, like a Spanish viceroy, enforced royal policies. However, the settlers also continued to have a voice in local laws. The House of Burgesses continued to meet informally, and was officially reopened in 1629.

Under royal rule, Virginia continued to develop steadily. Although its growth was not spectacular, there was no more need to force settlers to immigrate there. Those who came to the colony did so of their own free will in search of better economic possibilities. But they were no longer looking for gold or a route to Asia and then a quick return to England. Opportunity to begin a new life was now the magnet that drew people from the Old World to the New.

The Second English Colony. Many of the people who settled the second English colony on the mainland—Plymouth, in what is now Massachusetts—had a reason other than economic opportunity for coming to the New World. They were members of a small group of Protestants— the *Separatists*—which suffered from religious intolerance in England. They called themselves Sep-

In time, this attitude toward slavery was modified. As tobacco plantations grew larger, the landowners found slave labor to be less costly than indentured or free labor. By 1700, the majority of slaves in Virginia were bonded for life.

Discussion Question: Tobacco was thought by the early English to have disease-fighting qualities. Indians, who smoked it often, seldom got sick. Use this point to open a discussion on making inferences. What other things might have been thought to provide the Indians with great health?

 41

aratists because they believed in worshiping separately from the official Church of England, which they thought was too much like the Roman Catholic Church in both beliefs and practices. Although the Separatists who eventually came to America were not given the name Pilgrims until the 1800s, that name is appropriate. For like pilgrims who travel to a holy place, the Separatists journeyed to find a place where they could practice their religion without interference.

The Pilgrims.

In England, the Separatists were ridiculed for their religious practices, fined for refusing to attend services of the Church of England, and even beaten. Under King James I, who strongly disliked their beliefs, the Separatists feared continuing persecution. Thus, in 1608, they began to emigrate. A small band of Separatists from the village of Scrooby in the English Midlands traveled to the city of Leiden (lī'dən) in Holland in search of a haven.

For nearly twelve years they lived in Leiden, but they were not happy. Although all religions were tolerated in the Netherlands, the Separatists did not believe in freedom of religion for all. Rather, they believed that all religions but their own were sinful. The Separatists were also disturbed because their children, like children of most immigrants in another country, were *assimilating*, or becoming as much Dutch as English. For though the Separatists may have disliked the Church of England, they still favored their English language and culture. What they wanted was a new England, a place where all people worshiped as they did, and where they could keep their national traditions.

The Plymouth Company, which had lost the colonization race to the London Company, provided the Separatists their chance. A leading shareholder in the Plymouth Company, Sir Edwin Sandys, persuaded James I to leave the Separatists alone if they returned to England and then went to America.

The *Pilgrims* actually set out for America in two ships—the *Speedwell* and the *Mayflower*. However, the *Speedwell* had to turn back when it began to leak. The *Mayflower* successfully crossed the Atlantic and anchored in present-day Massachusetts Bay in November 1620. There, the group waited on board for a month while an exploration party selected a town site. The chosen site, called Plymouth, had been earlier abandoned by Indians because of a smallpox epidemic. To the deeply pious Pilgrims, who looked for messages from God in natural events, the land seemed to have been "cleared" of other people so that they could live there.

The Mayflower Compact.

The Pilgrims' choice for a home presented them a legal challenge. They had located Plymouth north of the land grant King James had made to the Plymouth Company in 1606. This meant that the Plymouth Company's charter had no legal force until the *Mayflower* could return to England and the Company officials could win the Crown's approval.

Two-thirds of the 102 settlers were not Separatists, and they made it clear that once they were ashore they would take orders from no one. In order to avoid this situation, Pilgrim leaders William Bradford and William Brewster, and the colony's military officer, Captain Miles Standish, drew up a *compact*, or an agreement, known as the *Mayflower Compact*. In the compact, 41 male colonists pledged their loyalty to King James I and stated that for the purposes of preserving order, those who signed the paper promised to meet "from time to time" to make laws and ordinances necessary to have a stable, orderly society. Nothing was said of elections, and as it turned out, the colony was run by only a few people—all Puritans—for its first 40 years. But because the compact bound everyone within the community to obey the colony's laws, the document laid the basis for participatory government.

After a difficult first winter, in which 47 of the original settlers died, the population began to grow. And Plymouth proved to be a far healthier site than Jamestown had been. Local Indians, the Wampanoags, were friendly toward the Pilgrims, and the two groups cooperated in farming and hunting. In fact, some of the Indians spoke English. One of them, named Squanto, had been to Europe and had lived at an English home before returning to America, where he became the English settlers' guide, translator, and teacher.

The Separatists never discovered a valuable cash crop like tobacco. They concentrated instead on farming and fishing so that they were able to survive without outside help. Consequently, like

Plymouth Rock was the place where the Mayflower Pilgrims disembarked. What is not usually known is that the site was chosen only after several others were examined and rejected. The notion that Indians greeted the Pilgrims at Plymouth Rock is untrue.

GOING TO THE SOURCE

But that which was most sad and lamentable was that in two or three months' time half of their company died, especially in January and February, being the depth of winter, and wanting houses and other comforts; being infected with the scurvy and other diseases which this long voyage and their inaccommodate condition had brought upon them. So as there died sometimes two or three of a day in the aforesaid time, that of one hundred and odd persons, scarce fifty remained. . . .

All this while the Indians . . . would sometimes show themselves aloof off, but when any approached near them, they would run away; and once they stole away their tools where they had been at work and were gone to dinner. But about the 16th of March, a certain Indian came boldly among them and spoke to them in broken English, which they could well understand but marveled at. At length they understood by discourse with him that he was not of these parts but belonged to the eastern parts where some English ships came to fish, with whom he was acquainted and could name sundry of them by their names, among whom he had got his language. He become profitable to them in acquainting them with many things concerning the state of the country in the east parts where he lived, which was afterward profitable unto them; as also of the people here, of their names, number and strength, of their situation and distance from this place, and who was chief among them. His name was Samoset. He told them also of another Indian whose name was Squanto, a native of this place, who had been in England and could speak better English than himself.

Being, after some time of entertainment and

> *So as there died sometimes two or three of a day . . . that of one hundred and odd persons, scarce fifty remained. . . . But about the 16th of March, a certain Indian came boldly among them and spoke to them in broken English, which they could well understand. . . .*
>
> WILLIAM BRADFORD, *OF PLYMOUTH PLANTATION*

gifts dismissed, a while after he came again, and five more with him, and they brought again all the tools that were stolen away before, and made way for the coming of their great sachem, called Massasoit, who, about four or five days after, came with the chief of his friends and other attendants, with the aforesaid Squanto; [and] with whom, after friendly entertainment and some gifts given him, they made a peace . . . (which has now continued this twenty-four years) in these terms:

1. That neither he nor any of his should injure or do hurt to any of their people.

2. That if any of his did hurt to any of theirs, he should send the offender that they might punish him.

3. That if anything were taken away from any of theirs, he should cause it to be restored; and they should do the like to his.

4. If any did unjustly war against him, they would aid him; if any did war against them, he should aid them.

After these things, he returned to his place called Sowams, some forty miles from this place, but Squanto continued with them and was their first interpreter and was a special instrument sent by God for their good beyond their expectation. He directed them how to set their corn, where to take fish, and to procure other commodities, and was also their pilot to bring them to unknown places for their profit, and never left them till he died. . . .

William Bradford, elected year after year as governor of Plymouth colony, also wrote a valuable history of the colony, Of Plymouth Plantation, *which includes this account of the Pilgrim's first struggling year, 1620–1621.*

Miles Standish is incorrectly known as the romantic interest of Priscilla Alden. Although she was a real person, the story of the romance, as depicted by Henry Wadsworth Longfellow in "The Courtship of Miles Standish," is purely fictional—another example of fact taking a back seat to popular myth.

The Mayflower Compact was drawn up by William Bradford (seated in the center) while the Plymouth settlers were still aboard the Mayflower. Its purpose was to legally bind the group together so that once ashore, the colony could run smoothly.

their rivals in the London Company, Sir Edwin Sandys and his partners never made a profit from Plymouth. Anxious to salvage their investment, and perhaps fearful that the king would make Plymouth a royal colony, the shareholders in the Plymouth Company sold their charter to the colonists.

The Plymouth colonists used their purchased charter as their constitution. *Freeholders*, or those who owned land, could vote for officials and approve or disapprove all laws. The Pilgrims were careful to recognize the authority of the English Crown and to adopt no laws that might cause their charter to be revoked. Within these limits, however, Plymouth was self-governing. It was the first *corporate colony* in North America; that is, it was a colony in which authority was based on a corporation charter.

SECTION REVIEW

1. Write a sentence to identify: corporate charter, Powhatan, John Smith, headright system, indentured servant.

2. What two English joint-stock companies founded colonies in North America in 1606 and 1620? How did these two companies hope to make money from the colonies?

3. How did John Rolfe turn Jamestown from a commercial failure into a commercial success?

4. Why did the Plymouth Company sell their charter to the people who actually settled Plymouth?

Class Activity: To provide a concept of the order of events in the various European countries' explorations of the Americas, make a time line chronicling the various events presented in the text. By doing this on an overhead projector, a different transparency can be made for each

EUROPEAN COLONIES IN AMERICA · 1638

YEAR FOUNDED	COLONY	COUNTRY	DISCOVERER OR FOUNDER	REASON FOR DEVELOPMENT
1492	Hispaniola	Spain	Christopher Columbus	Lumber, sugar
1492	Bahamas	Spain	Christopher Columbus	Source of slaves for Hispaniola
1492	Cuba	Spain	Christopher Columbus	Trading and exploration base, later sugar plantations
1493	Puerto Rico	Spain	Christopher Columbus	Strategic outpost, gold, sugar
1494	Jamaica	Spain	Christopher Columbus	Cattle ranching, supply base later sugar plantations
1497	Newfoundland	England	John Cabot	Fishing base for Grand Banks
1498	Trinidad and Tobago	Spain	Christopher Columbus	Trade, tobacco
1500	Brazil	Portugal	Pedro Cabral	Brazilwood, sugar, tobacco
1521	Mexico	Spain	Hernando Cortez	Gold, conquest
1533	Peru	Spain	Francisco Pizarro	Gold, silver, conquest
1565	Florida	Spain	Pedro Menéndez de Avilés	Exploration, fur trade, competition with France and England
1604	Acadia	France	Samuel de Champlain	Fur trade, exploration
1605	Bermuda	England	English settlers	Sugar
1607	Virginia	England	English settlers	Tobacco, fur trade
1608	Quebec	France	Samuel de Champlain	Fur trade, exploration, naval stores
1609	Bermuda	England	Sir George Somers	Trading post
1610	Hudson Bay	England	Henry Hudson	Fishing, fur trapping
1620	Plymouth	England	Pilgrims	Freedom of religion
1626	Guadeloupe	France	Pierre Belain	Trade, sugar, competition with Spain
1626	New Netherland	Netherlands	Dutch West India Company	Farming, fur trade
1638	New Sweden	Sweden	Peter Minuit	Farming, fur trade

country and presented in an overlay format. Discuss related events on the time line that may show how the developments in one country affected those in another.

4. FRENCH, DUTCH, AND SWEDISH COLONIES

The first permanent French colony in North America was founded in 1608, a year after Jamestown. The Dutch began their explorations in 1609 and established their first settlement in 1624, four years after Plymouth was settled. Sweden formed a colonization company in 1626, but did not actually send people across the Atlantic until 1638.

New France. In 1608, Samuel de Champlain (shăm-plān') was sent to retrace the North American explorations of Verrazano and Cartier for the French. Champlain's instructions were to establish forts that would be safe from Indian attack, and to open trading posts to purchase deer hides and furs from the Indians. Deer were rare in Europe and fur-bearing animals were nearly extinct, so hides and pelts brought high prices. They could be bought in Russia, but the French preferred to found colonies where furs and hides were plentiful and then to compete with the Russians in selling them to other nations.

Champlain first tried to settle at Ile de Saint Croix in what is now Maine. However, after a harsh winter he abandoned the frigid site. He then built a fort at Port Royal in Nova Scotia to guard the mouth of the St. Lawrence River, and sailed up the river to the site of Quebec, a more easily defended place at the foot of steep cliffs.

New France grew slowly but was extremely profitable. The Hurons, an independent Iroquois tribe, and the Algonquin tribes of the Great Lakes region annually brought tons of hides and furs to Quebec, trading them for iron goods, wool blankets, firearms, and other manufactured goods. Small numbers of French people came to Quebec, but instead of settling down as farmers or town dwellers, they usually adopted the Indian ways. Many French men married Indian women and joined the Indian tribes, becoming fur trappers themselves. Consequently, although French North America covered a huge area, the French never had very strong control over the territory.

In this sixteenth-century engraving, Native American hunters with bows and arrows (on the left) are depicted using disguises in order to approach the deer on the right.

The Dutch tried to promote settlement by promising large land grants along the Hudson River to wealthy Dutch citizens, who were required to settle at least 50 peasants on the land. But only one landowner, or *patroon*, succeeded in doing this. The colony remained a small, prosperous trading center. However, it had an international air to it, as the Dutch permitted anyone to settle there as long as they added to the colony's wealth.

Peter Minuit left the Dutch West India Company in 1637 to become the head of a Swedish colony in America. He and about two dozen settlers built a fort at the present site of Wilmington, Delaware, and named it Christina, after the Swedish queen. Johann Printz, who became governor in 1643, managed to lure more Swedish and Finnish people to the colony. But the next governor of New Sweden, Johan Rising, made the mistake of attacking a Dutch fort at Newcastle, Delaware, and the Dutch responded by attacking and taking over New Sweden.

New Netherland and New Sweden. The Dutch West Indies Company, chartered in 1621, was also interested in the profitable hide and fur trade. Following the French example, a Dutch expedition established a fort at the mouth of the Hudson River on Manhattan Island, which they named New Amsterdam, and a trading post where furs were purchased at Fort Orange (present-day Albany, New York).

The Iroquois Confederacy, which had sworn hostility to the French after Champlain fired on members of the Five Nations in 1609, agreed to supply the Dutch settlers at Fort Orange with furs and hides. In contrast to the French settlers, few Dutch settlers took to the woods.

Most Dutch were careful to maintain friendly relations with the Indians. Unlike the English in Jamestown and Plymouth, who simply took the land on which they settled, the Dutch purchased their townsites. It did not cost them very much. In 1626, for about $24 worth of beads, mirrors, and other trinkets, Governor Peter Minuit purchased the whole of Manhattan Island from the tribe that controlled it.

The most important Swedish legacy for early America was the log cabin. Prior to this innovation, the settlers needed a trained carpenter to put

Algonquin Indians are seen in this sixteenth-century watercolor fishing off the coast of what is now the Carolinas.

up a frame and to cut clapboard siding in order to build a house. In contrast, a log cabin could be constructed with little skill and only one tool—an axe. The Swedish log cabin was perfect for frontier life in forested America.

SECTION REVIEW

1. Write a sentence to identify: Champlain, Peter Minuit, patroon, log cabin.

2. Name the countries that founded settlements in North America at the following times: four years after Plymouth was settled; twelve years after the country formed a colonization company; one year after Jamestown was settled.

3. Why did the French and Dutch want hides and furs from the American Indians? How did the Indians feel about the French and Dutch? Why?

4. Summarize the history of New Sweden.

Discussion Question: How did relations between the Indians and different European groups vary? How do you think this would affect future relations? Include such things as the French trading with Indians, the Dutch being the only ones who made it a practice to buy Indian lands.

 47

CHAPTER REVIEW

TIME LINE

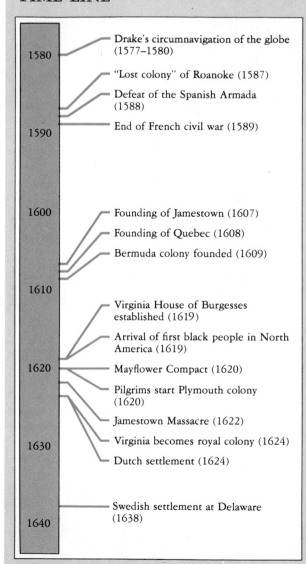

1580	Drake's circumnavigation of the globe (1577–1580)
	"Lost colony" of Roanoke (1587)
	Defeat of the Spanish Armada (1588)
1590	End of French civil war (1589)
1600	Founding of Jamestown (1607)
	Founding of Quebec (1608)
	Bermuda colony founded (1609)
1610	
	Virginia House of Burgesses established (1619)
	Arrival of first black people in North America (1619)
1620	Mayflower Compact (1620)
	Pilgrims start Plymouth colony (1620)
	Jamestown Massacre (1622)
1630	Virginia becomes royal colony (1624)
	Dutch settlement (1624)
1640	Swedish settlement at Delaware (1638)

TIME LINE QUESTIONS

1. How many years of history are covered on this time line?
2. What important event happened between 1577 and 1580?
3. Why is 1619 an important date in the history of democracy?
4. In what year was the first permanent English colony founded?

SKILLS STRATEGY

Notes

What four European countries challenged Spain's power by building colonies in North America?

—England built colonies at Jamestown in Virginia and Plymouth in Massachusetts.

—France built forts and trading posts like Quebec.

—The Netherlands built colonies at New Amsterdam and Fort Orange in New York and at New Castle in Delaware.

—Sweden started a settlement at Wilmington, Delaware, which was later taken over by the Netherlands.

TWO-LEVEL OUTLINES

You will find that making an outline is valuable for the same purpose as taking notes. Both help you think first about the main points of a text passage and then deal with supporting details. As you consider outlining as a study skill, refer to the notes and to the outline in the two exhibits above. Both notes and outlines may be written to answer a question about one or more main sections of a textbook chapter. Notice that the question in the notes above is based on the three main headings on pages 28, 33, and 38 of this chapter. Notice also that the title of the outline reflects these chapter headings. The notes and the outline were written after skimming the text that appears under the chapter headings.

The form of a set of notes is different from the form of an outline. You could say that making an outline is a more formal, more highly organized way of studying than note-taking. An outline form shows the relationships of facts and ideas more specifically than notes do and requires you to use high-level organizational skills. Thinking about

Making Connections: Review the questions and topics presented in the Making Connections section opening this chapter. Pay special attention to making certain students are aware of how the various cultures came to blend and how evidence of this exists today. Also show how, in very

48

```
                    Outline
           European Colonies
             Challenge Spain

    I. England's colonies
       A. Jamestown in Virginia
       B. Plymouth in Massachusetts

   II. France's settlements
       A. Forts for protection
       B. Trading post at Quebec

   _____
   _____
   _____

   IV. Sweden's colony
       A. A fort at Wilmington,
          Delaware
       B. Later taken over by the
          Netherlands
```

the order and relationships of ideas and facts helps you to understand text materials.

The information in *main topic I* of the outline is taken from the first note. The information in *subtopics A and B* is also taken from this note. The title of the outline is centered, and all important words are capitalized. The Roman numeral before each main topic is at the left margin; it is followed by a period; and the first word of the topic is capitalized. The capital letter before each subtopic is followed by a period, and the first word of the subtopic is capitalized. Each subtopic is indented.

APPLYING SKILLS

Refer to the outline above as you do the following.
1. How do you choose the title of an outline?
2. How are the main topics indicated?
3. How are the subtopics indicated?
4. What should you remember about the word that begins a main topic and subtopic?
5. Complete the outline. Save your work. It will be useful when you do the Writing a Paragraph assignment on this page.

CHAPTER 2 TEST

TEXT REVIEW

1. Explain the following statement: "Spanish-American colonies were considered part of Spain for mercantilist purposes."
2. Describe the society that emerged in the Spanish colonies within a few generations of their founding.
3. Give the modern-day names of the areas governed by the Spanish viceroys of New Spain, New Granada, and La Plata.
4. List some exploits of Sir Francis Drake and other English sea dogs.
5. What did the actions of Sir Francis Drake and other English sea dogs have to do with the launching of the Spanish Armada?
6. Explain why England's first permanent colony in North America succeeded.
7. Name the second permanent English colony. Who were its settlers, and what motivated them to come to North America?
8. List three other countries that founded colonies in North America, and name the colonies they founded.

CRITICAL THINKING

9. If you were researching information about the treatment of Native Americans in the Spanish Empire, which source would you consider most accurate—a book by de Las Casas, or letters from Spanish encomenderos to the king of Spain? Why?
10. Which two colonies in the Americas contributed most to the growth of democratic government? Explain your reasons.

WRITING A PARAGRAPH

Use the outline you completed to write a paragraph. The topic sentence below should express the main idea. In your other sentences, use the information from each main topic and subtopic of your outline. Include only details that support your paragraph's main idea.

Topic Sentence: Four European countries decided to challenge Spain's power in the New World by building colonies in North America.

much the same situation, the different European groups that came to America had different relationships with the Native Americans, and governed their colonies differently.

CHAPTER 3

THE THIRTEEN COLONIES

1625–1732

We are the pioneers of the world; the advance guard sent on through the wilderness of untried things to break a new path in the New World that is ours. In our youth is our strength; in our inexperience, our wisdom. HERMAN MELVILLE

Making Connections. One by one, vigorous new colonies were established on the east coast of North America. Although life was difficult America attracted many who were willing to work hard and sacrifice in order to improve their own lives and the lives of their children. Were they successful? Did their dreams come true?

In this chapter, you will learn:
- Which group left Massachusetts and settled in Rhode Island
- How the quit-rent system enabled some people to get their own land
- What southern colony was founded to alleviate poverty
- How the British appropriated a Dutch colony without firing a shot
- Why the English king gave away Pennsylvania

Knowing about the disastrous beginnings of the early colonists, you might wonder that they succeeded at all. The fact that they did learn to adapt to their new environment inspired and enabled others to pursue the same course. The first hard-won communities served as examples and as springboards for subsequent ones. As you read about later English colonies in North America, note customs and attitudes that prevailed and how colonists established a stronghold in three regions of the new land.

Sections
1. New England Colonies
2. Southern Colonies
3. Middle Colonies

1. NEW ENGLAND COLONIES

The promise of freedom of worship brought another Englsih group to North America—the *Puritans*. Like the Pilgrims, they were followers of John Calvin, and wanted to purify the Church of England of all Roman Catholic elements. They believed that man was sinful by nature and could achieve good only by severe and unremitting self-discipline and hard work.

The Puritans differed from the Pilgrims because they wanted to reform the Church of England from within. They did not want to leave the Church. Many English people believed the way they did, and the Puritans were numerous, politically influential, and wealthy. They were favored by Queen Elizabeth for their support against Catholic Spain, and many of their leaders found positions in government. However, their influence declined when James I became king of England in 1603.

Why the Puritans Came to America. The Puritans began to worry about their future when James became king. James detested Puritans and tried to cut their influence in both the Church of England and the government. However, to the Puritans, Charles I, who became king in 1625, was

William Penn, a Quaker, tried to live in peace with the Indians who lived in what is now Pennsylvania. At a meeting in 1682 (right) they signed a treaty confirming their friendship.

Skills Review: Have students reinforce their knowledge of making a two-level outline by having them outline this chapter according to the method presented in the Skills Strategy for Chapter 2.

John Winthrop, an English Puritan lawyer, left England in 1630. He hoped that the new Massachusetts Bay Colony, of which he became the first governor, would be a model society for others.

Cotton Mather was born in Boston; graduated from America's first college, Harvard; and was ordained a clergyman in 1685. Seven years later, he participated in the Salem witchcraft trials.

even more dangerous. Possibly influenced by his wife, who was a French Catholic, Charles ordered Thomas Laud, Archbishop of Canterbury, to introduce numerous Catholic-like rituals to English worship services. To the Puritans, these changes showed that England was embracing what to them was a false religion. They believed that God would punish England for this sin, and by association, they would be punished too.

The leader of this worried group, a wealthy landowner named John Winthrop, came to the conclusion that in order to save themselves from God's anger, the Puritans should found a new England in America. Based on true religious principles, as Winthrop saw them, this colony would be a shining example to old England of how God wanted people to live. Winthrop's supporters expected that in time England would be converted to their way of life, and would then invite the Puritans back to reform the old country.

The Puritans did not come to Massachusetts to create a society based on freedom of worship for everyone. Rather, it is closer to the truth to say that the Puritans came to America to create a society in which everyone worshiped as the Puritans did. With this distinction in mind, we can understand why daily life in Massachusetts was strictly regulated and why other religions were not tolerated. The Puritan's goal was not "freedom of religion," but "true [Puritan] religion."

The Great Migration. The Puritans were cautious and methodical, and had learned from the experiences of those who had come to America before them. While the Pilgrims arrived in one small ship and struggled to survive as employees of the Plymouth Company, the well-financed Puritans planned their journey to America for more than a year. In June 1630, about 40 miles up the coast from Plymouth, four ships arrived to prepare the way for seven more vessels a month behind them. By the fall there were more than 1,000 people in the Massachusetts Bay colony. Supplies were abundant; a first crop had been harvested; and towns had been built at Salem, Boston, and other sites. During the next ten years, 15,000

Because of the infamy attached to the Salem witchcraft trials, the magnitude of the trials has been distorted. Instead of the hundreds of innocent people said to have been burned alive at the stake, 19 were hanged. The one male "witch" was pressed to death under heavy weights for refusing to confess to being a witch.

English men and women, most of them Puritans, arrived in Massachusetts and established dozens of towns in a planned, orderly fashion. This mass movement was called the "Great Migration."

Self-Government. The Puritans also made sure that they would have nearly complete control of their colony. Their company, the Massachusetts Bay Company, had a commercial charter much like the charters of Virginia and Plymouth. However, before they left England, the leaders of the Great Migration met with those shareholders who wished to remain in England and persuaded them to sell all of their shares to those who planned to go to America. Then the new shareholders voted to move the company to Massachusetts. In this way, the Puritans were able to take their charter to America, out of the Crown's immediate reach.

Self-government was important to the Massachusetts Puritans because they were interested in more than just making money in the New World. They believed that they had a higher purpose to serve, one that was intertwined with their religious beliefs and their discontent in England. What they did to create their ideal state may well have been vetoed by the Crown if they had left their charter in England.

Once in America, the Puritans gave the right to vote for company officials, who became colony officials, to actual settlers instead of to those who had merely invested money. Before their first year in Massachusetts was out, the Puritans established a representative assembly called the General Court. It consisted of 130 *freemen*, or people who owned land and were members of the official church. Non-Puritans were excluded from the government, and although this violated the colony's charter, there was no counter-order from England. Distance made it difficult for Charles I to control the Puritans, and the colonists found that as long as they acknowledged the Crown's authority, they were able to do much as they pleased in their new home.

New England Laws. The lawbooks of Massachusetts and most other New England colonies were filled with rules that most twentieth-century Americans, who place heavy emphasis on individual freedom, would not tolerate. Because the Puritans believed that God wanted the sabbath to

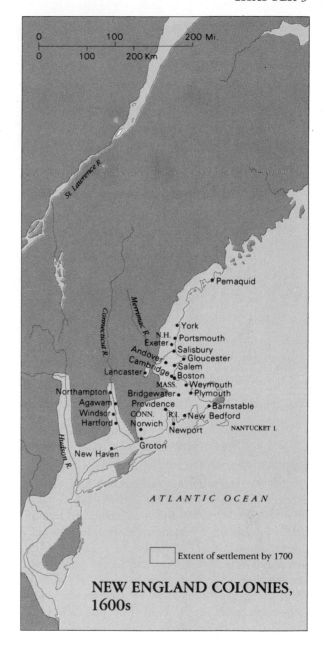

NEW ENGLAND COLONIES, 1600s

☐ Extent of settlement by 1700

be devoted to worship, they forbade nonreligious activities on Sunday. Playing games and sports, which was a popular Sunday activity in England, was forbidden in New England. People could be fined for whistling on Sunday, for singing nonreligious songs, for breaking into a run, or walking in a garden. This strictness was not because the Puritans believed men and women should not enjoy these activities, but because they felt that Sunday was for religion only.

The town pillory or stocks were used by New England Puritans in order to hold those who had committed minor crimes up to public ridicule.

The most common punishment for breaking these *blue laws*, as they came to be called, was a fine. However, the Puritans also believed in holding law-breakers up to ridicule. People who committed minor crimes were often sentenced to sit in the town *stocks* or stand in the *pillory* on a market day. Hopefully, the criminals would be so humiliated they would mend their ways. In fact, the man who built Boston's first stocks was also the first to sit in them. The crime was overcharging the city for the work!

The punishment for more serious crimes was designed to match the crime. A man who beat his wife, for example, was whipped in public. Lawbreakers were not sentenced to long prison terms, and those who were jailed had to pay the expenses of their imprisonment. The most serious crimes were punished by death or by *banishment* —expulsion from the colony so God would not hold the other members responsible for the sinner's actions.

Rhode Island. Because the population of Massachusetts was large, and the rule of Governor Winthrop and his supporters was so strict, Massachusetts became something of a springboard for other New England colonies when it was still a very young settlement itself. Providence, Rhode Island, was founded in 1636 by a Massachusetts minister who protested against several Puritan beliefs. The population of that new colony grew in 1638 after the trial of a Massachusetts woman who challenged church authority.

Roger Williams. Roger Williams came to Plymouth in 1632 and to Massachusetts Bay in 1634. His belief in church reform was as strong as that of any other Puritan, but Williams attacked the Massachusetts Bay government for not buying land from the Indians before settling it. How could a society be righteous, Williams asked, when it was built on stolen land? Williams also disagreed with the Puritan insistence that everyone in the

Some of the blue laws are still on the books in a few New England states. One blue law that forbade the opening of supermarkets and other stores on Sunday was revoked by the Massachusetts General Court only a few years ago.

colony observe Puritan religious practices. He claimed that only God knew for certain who was chosen to reach heaven and who was not. Therefore, since the government did not know God's intentions, it had no right to demand that people attend services in an approved church. Nor did the government have the right to say only church members could vote. Williams did not believe that all religions were equal in God's eyes. However, because he insisted that God alone decided who was saved, he said that human government must tolerate all religions.

The most serious sin a man or woman could commit in Massachusetts was irreverence toward God, as the Puritans defined it. Many colonists believed that Williams' criticisms of the government were words against God. In 1635, the General Court ordered Williams sent back to England. However, because John Winthrop respected the troublesome preacher, Williams was allowed to escape and spend the winter with the Narragansett Indians to the south. He purchased land from them, and early in 1636, founded Providence in Rhode Island. Williams was a realistic man, and feared royal intervention, so in 1644 he traveled to England and received a charter that guaranteed Rhode Island's independence from Massachusetts.

Anne Hutchinson. Anne Hutchinson ran afoul of Governor Winthrop and the Massachusetts General Court because, after church services, she held meetings in her home at which she discussed the sermons of the colony's leading ministers. With a deep intelligence and a sharp, quick tongue, Hutchinson soon made enemies of many preachers, including John Cotton, who was respected in both England and America. Cotton and Winthrop believed that women should be seen at church, but not heard on religious subjects, but Hutchinson debated the issues in public.

Hutchinson was banished for her irreverence, and in 1638 started a settlement in Rhode Island. One of her followers, John Wheelwright, chose to go north to New Hampshire, which had been granted to several wealthy English citizens in the 1620s. Wheelwright founded Exeter, but except for the town and a few rude outposts, New Hampshire remained thinly populated until the last half of the seventeenth century.

After having spent the winter of 1635–1636 with Narragansett Indians from whom he purchased land, Roger Williams, a Puritan preacher, founded Providence, Rhode Island. Williams believed that governments must tolerate all religions.

Connecticut. The colony of Connecticut dates from 1636 when another Massachusetts minister was asked to leave the colony. Thomas Hooker had criticized the Winthrop government for allowing only church members to vote. Hooker was allowed to lead his followers south of the boundaries of Massachusetts to the site of Hartford (then a Dutch trading post) on the Connecticut River. In 1639, Hooker helped write the *Fundamental Orders of Government,* the agreement among the settlers for governing the colony. The Orders allowed those who were not Puritans to vote and share in political power.

In 1638, a Puritan merchant from England, Theophilus Eaton, and a friend, the Reverend John Davenport, established New Haven near the Connecticut colony on Long Island Sound. New Haven's laws were stricter than those in Massachusetts, and Governor Eaton enforced them rigorously. Eaton died in 1658, and New Haven was absorbed into the Connecticut colony in 1665, Although Connecticut was more liberal than Massachusetts in political matters, it retained New Haven's strict standards for behavior.

New Hampshire. One New England colony that was not an offshoot of Massachusetts was New Hampshire. In the 1620s, King James I gave land grants in that area to James Mason, Ferdinando Gorges, and others. These landholders became *proprietors,* for the land became their private property. They could do whatever they wished with the land. Although a fishing and trading settlement was established in 1623, the proprietors were unable to attract many people to their cold, rocky land.

New Hampshire did fall under the domination of Massachusetts from 1641 to 1679, but there was continual religious and territorial feuding between Massachusetts and the heirs of the original proprietors. Finally, in 1679, New Hampshire was separated from Massachusetts and became a royal colony.

The six engravings below and on the next page illustrate a variety of common occupations in colonial America. Most jobs were learned at a young age under an apprentice system. In time, an apprentice would become a master craftsperson, and then would take on one or more apprentices. In this way, the young country replenished and expanded its pool of skilled craftspeople.

Mariner.

A Sawyer.

A Cooper

Class Activity: Divide the class into small groups and have them imagine they are colonists. Have each group decide upon a plan for settlement that would include location of the colony, principles and laws, type of leadership, selection of leadership, and type of economic activity they will pursue. The activity may be done separately by the groups during the course of the chapter and

A Varied Economy. The people who settled New England were an industrious and ambitious people. Puritans believed that a person should "labor diligently at his calling" because work was a religious duty. Extreme poverty was unusual in Plymouth, Massachusetts, Rhode Island, New Hampshire, and Connecticut.

The governments of every New England colony, except Rhode Island, regulated their economies as closely as they watched the morals of their people. People who were convicted of cheating in business or charging what the assemblies regarded as unfair prices were punished, because these practices placed individual riches above the common good.

In the early colonial years, small towns grew up in New England. People opened shops in the towns to provide finished goods to the colonists and carry on some trade with other countries. However, most New Englanders were engaged in two other occupations—farming and fishing.

Farming the Land. Most New Englanders were farmers, raising the corn, squash, beans, and livestock they needed in order to survive. However, New England landowners were not to grow rich from farming, as did landowners in more southerly colonies. Most New England farms were small, as townships (the local government that allotted land) provided just enough acreage for a family to support itself and raise a small surplus for sale to the town dwellers. Another block to large-scale farming was the availability of labor in the early years of the colony. Since people could easily get land, few would work for wages or as servants. Therefore, the farmer who had a large plot had difficulty getting people to work the land, and had to pay premium wages for those people who would work for another person.

Operating a New England farm, large or small, presented more difficult challenges. Winters in New England were long, the growing season short. The country was thickly forested and the soil rocky. To clear land for plowing took years of cutting down and burning trees and decades of removing rocks. Each spring thaw brought new boulders to the surface that had to be blasted into pieces and piled into stone walls. These walls, which can still be seen running along roads and cutting through woods, symbolize the New England farmer's continuing struggle to produce a livelihood. The whole family—wife and husband

Shipwright.

A Wool Comber.

A Basket-maker.

presented at its conclusion. Examine the reasoning behind the choices of each group. See if group ideas are based on a good sense of reality (what life might have been like then) and on logical reasoning in making choices.

and children beyond the toddler stage—helped in the heavy labor. The result was not great riches, but an abundant, self-sufficient life.

Harvest of the Sea.

The New Englanders had some of the best fishing areas in the world. Europeans had been coming to fish the Grand Banks of Newfoundland, a huge ocean area stretching from Cape Cod in Massachusetts to near Newfoundland, long before any North American colonies were established. The colonists were quick to take advantage of the area, netting lobsters, herring, and cod in great numbers.

On the island of Nantucket and in New Bedford, Massachusetts, settlers turned to hunting whales. Whale oil was used for making candles and *ambergris*, an extremely valuable substance used for making perfumes. Although the whaling industry was small during the *colonial* period, New Englanders would virtually monopolize it by the nineteenth century, when the development of other energy sources caused a decline in the demand for whale oil.

New Englanders also developed a shipbuilding industry, without which the fishing and whaling industries could not have been so successful.

An Educated People.

In most respects, the New England colonists were not much different from any other English colonists. However, their

Harvard College, founded in 1636 in Cambridge, Massachusetts, was the first college in colonial America. Its name comes from John Harvard, who donated his personal library to the college. Harvard College's first mission was to train ministers.

Research Assignment: Stress the importance of education to the early New Englanders and the role it plays in present attitudes. Have students do research and write a report on one of the early colleges or make a chart for several colleges showing the dates they were opened, or do research and write a report on elementary education in the colonies.

religious beliefs were unique. The Puritans believed that the Bible was the only place where the
word of God could be found. Their religion, like
the religion of the ancient Hebrews, with whom
the Puritans liked to compare themselves, was
based on the written word. The Puritans also
believed that no one person possessed any spiritual powers that were denied to others.

Consequently, the Puritans believed their ministers should be well-educated so that they could
interpret sacred scriptures in their sermons. The
first college in America was founded in 1636 in
Cambridge, Massachusetts, only six years after the
first house was constructed in the town. The
Massachusetts General Court gave funds so the
school could train ministers. In 1638, John Harvard died and left his library and some money to
the school, which became Harvard College.

The Puritans also believed that people should
read the Bible at home. A law of 1642 fined
families which did not educate their children. In
1647, every township with more than 50 families
was required to appoint a school teacher, and each
township with more than 100 families was required to open a grammar school. Some schools
were free, supported by taxes on the residents.
Others required the pupils' parents to pay a fee.
By the end of the 1600s, all the New England
colonies, except Rhode Island, boasted a comprehensive public school system unlike any other
school system in the world. As a result the New
England population was the most literate in the
world.

2. SOUTHERN COLONIES

The first two English colonies, Virginia and Plymouth, were corporate colonies. Rhode Island and
Connecticut were also corporate colonies. New
Hampshire, however, was a *proprietary colony*.
James I had given the land to Ferdinando Gorges,
James Mason, and others as their private property,
to dispose of as they chose. They could settle
people there, sell the land, or just leave the colony
alone. The proprietary system was also the means
by which England settled the southern colonies
—Maryland, the Carolinas, and Georgia.

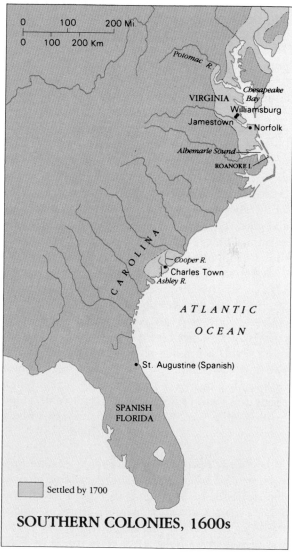

SOUTHERN COLONIES, 1600s

SECTION REVIEW

1. Write a sentence to identify: John Winthrop, Great Migration, General Court,
   Fundamental Orders of Government.

2. Why did the Puritans leave England and
   found the Massachusetts Bay Colony?

3. Who could vote and take part in the
   government of Massachusetts?

4. For what general reason did Roger Williams, Ann Hutchinson, and Thomas
   Hooker leave Massachusetts?

5. Give two reasons why farming was a
   challenge for early New Englanders.

Harvard College was founded in 1636. It was originally surrounded by a stockade fence to keep
out Indians as well as prowling wolves. Until 1769, class standing was not based on grades, but
on social standing and status.

Making Money from America. *Proprietors* were wealthy people, often nobles, who had won the friendship of the Crown. By granting them huge tracts of American land, the monarchs ensured their loyalty and settled America more quickly. While the Crown was too busy with other matters to devote enough attention to encouraging people to go to America, proprietors could concentrate on promoting their colonies. They had good reason to do so. Owning and disposing of land in America could be a very profitable enterprise.

Only a little land was sold or rented out. The people who were willing to risk a life in the American wilderness were rarely rich enough to buy the land. As for those already in the colonies, they did not want to rent from others when there was seemingly limitless land all around them. They wanted to be landowners themselves. The proprietors' solution was the headright system developed in Virginia and the *quit-rent*, an English custom developed at the end of the Middle Ages.

During the Middle Ages, European serfs earned the right to farm the land on which they lived by laboring for the landowners for a certain number of days each year. The system was useful until money began to circulate freely and the landowners discovered they preferred cash to labor. They freed the serfs of their old obligations and gave them their land. In return, the serfs paid an annual quit-rent, so called because by paying it, they were quit of their former duties.

America was also a place in which money was scarce. So, the proprietors gave land to immigrants according to the headright system, and collected quit-rents in return when the settlers could pay. Few settlers protested. Quit-rents were quite small. A tobacco grower in Maryland had to pay only two pennies an acre. A New York farmer owed only a bushel of wheat per 100 acres. When thousands were paying, however, quit-rents added up to a large sum. A noble lucky enough to be a proprietor could get very rich indeed.

Maryland: Haven for Catholics. Some proprietors had more in mind than making money. The founder of Maryland, George Calvert, was such a man. Calvert, a high government official raised to the nobility as the first Lord Baltimore, was a Roman Catholic. As a close friend of King

Charles I, he was not persecuted because of his religion. But many poorer Catholics were and Calvert thought of himself as the protector of these people. He asked the king for a tract of land in America that could serve as a refuge for them.

In 1632, Charles I detached the land north of the Potomac River and east of Chesapeake Bay from Virginia and gave it to Calvert's son, Cecilius. (George Calvert had died that year.) Two years later, 200 colonists, including two Catholic priests, bought a village from the Indians and founded

Charles I of England granted land in North America to the son of George Calvert as a place where English Catholics would immigrate to if they wished. Eventually, however, more English Puritans than Catholics settled in what came to be Maryland.

One of the earliest and longest wars in the colonies was the Oyster War. When King Charles I drew the dividing line between Maryland and Virginia, he drew it at the high-water mark on the Virginia side of Chesapeake Bay rather than at its middle. From 1632 to 1959, this has led to occasional fights among oystermen. At least 50 men have died.

Maryland. There were no "starving times" in Maryland. Tobacco was booming in the 1630s and the Virginians were able to help with food and other assistance. But few English Catholics came to the colony. From the beginning Maryland attracted many Puritans, and the Catholics were a minority.

In 1649, Cecilius Calvert feared that the Puritan majority would persecute members of his faith, so he proclaimed the *Act of Toleration*, which guaranteed freedom of worship in the colony for virtually all Christians. In 1654, Calvert's fears became reality when Puritans seized control of Maryland, repealed the Act of Toleration, and adopted laws discriminating against Catholics and supporters of the Church of England.

The Puritan majority of Maryland was able to defy the power of the Catholic proprietor because King Charles I, who had been so generous to the Calvert family, was dead. Charles I was executed in 1649 after losing a civil war to Puritans under the command of Oliver Cromwell. Cromwell ruled England as a military dictator during the 1650s. While he revolutionized English life, enforcing "blue laws" of his own, he paid little attention to the colonies.

Although Catholics lost control of the government of Maryland, they were able to defend themselves and their faith. In fact, while only a few of the colonies had laws guaranteeing freedom of worship, serious religious persecution was rare outside of Massachusetts.

Slavery. As in Virginia, the economy of Maryland was based on the growth and sale of tobacco. A tobacco planter generally worked a larger acreage than a New England farmer. However, a chronic labor shortage prevented the Virginians and Marylanders from expanding their holdings into the huge plantations that could make them very rich. The planters could hire servants from England, but the passage to the colonies was expensive. The planter who did so had the use of the servant's labor for seven years, and in some cases a shorter period. The servants had written contracts, and they could appeal to the colonial courts to see that the contracts were enforced.

Disease was also a problem, as were runaway servants. In the semitropical summers of Virginia and Maryland, servants often died before they had

Broadsides, like the one above from 1774, were used to announce slave auctions, land sales, or job opportunities. Tobacco labels like the one below—showing slaves working while landowners smoked—were common in the eighteenth century.

Discussion Question: How did the Protestant Reformation help colonize the U.S.? Answers should mention the various religious groups that came to this country, as well as the Reformation's contribution to conflicts in Europe that would pour over into the colonies. Stress the interconnection of events.

 61

Owners of large plantations purchased thousands of African and West Indian slaves and forced them to work in their fields. In colonial America, slavery was legal in every colony.

Phillis Wheatley was an African child who was kidnaped, shipped to Boston, and sold as a slave. However, she taught herself to write in English and eventually became a celebrated poet.

begun to pay their masters' expenses. And it was not difficult for a bold and imaginative servant to run away. Plantations were tiny clearings in· a gigantic wilderness. With luck and proper planning, a white servant could escape to another colony and disappear into the population.

The colonists' solution to the labor problem proved to be the enslavement of Africans and their descendants. Although the first American blacks enjoyed the same status as white servants, they lacked written contracts and an understanding of English traditions of individual freedom. Moreover, because they could be identified by their skin color, black servants could not run away as easily as white servants. Where a strange white person in a town could claim to be a free, recent arrival from Great Britain, a strange black person was arrested immediately on the assumption that he or she had a master somewhere.

By the 1660s, the status of black servants had changed to enslavement. The representative assemblies in Virginia and Maryland, which the tobacco planters controlled, passed laws stating that blacks served *durante vita*, or "during life," and that the children of a slave woman were also slaves, and the property of their mother's master. In this way, as the solution to a labor shortage, blacks were cut off from the mainstream of American development. Whereas white servants could watch out for their own rights and steadily improve their condition, blacks, most of them from Africa during the early years, had no one to protect their rights.

Blacks remained a minority of the field hands of Maryland, Virginia, and the other colonies during the 1600s. After 1700, however, black slaves became the backbone of southern agriculture, and until the American Revolution, slavery was legal in every colony.

The Carolinas. When Oliver Cromwell died in 1658, England was weary of Puritan rule. In 1660, the English Parliament invited Charles II, the son of the beheaded Charles I, to be king on

Research Assignment: An interesting, yet often overlooked factor in colonial history was the nature of the system of indentured white servants in this country. Students may do a report on how these people lived and how they became servants.

the condition he recognize the power of Parliament. Charles II, a personable man who liked to live luxuriously, agreed. When he arrived in London, he brought with him a host of debts to those who had supported him during his exile and helped him regain the throne. Although he had little money with which to pay these people, he did own plenty of American land. He rewarded eight of his supporters by making them proprietors of the territory south of Virginia where, in 1587, Sir Walter Raleigh had founded the doomed Roanoke Colony. The proprietors named the colony Carolina after the king (*Carolus* is Latin for Charles) and hatched a scheme to govern their colony as if they were medieval barons and the settlers were serfs.

The Fundamental Constitutions of Carolina.

One of the proprietors, Anthony Ashley Cooper, directed his secretary to draw up a document called the *Fundamental Constitutions of Carolina.* The document guaranteed religious freedom, but the system of government was otherwise unrealistic. Cooper imagined a colony of serfs and slaves laboring faithfully on huge estates owned by nobles. The legislature would be made up of two houses—the nobles and the commoners, as in England—but only the upper house would be able to propose legislation.

The Fundamental Constitutions never really went into effect. While slavery did develop from the planters' need for labor, the plan for the Carolinas was completely at odds with American and English experience. English men and women, who were not serfs at home, had no intention of becoming serfs in an environment that encouraged owning land and getting ahead. And the lower house of the legislature did not remain powerless for long. In fact, by 1700 the Fundamental Constitutions were largely ignored, and a rebellion in 1719 changed the whole structure of the government.

Two Different Carolinas.

Charles II and the eight proprietors expected Carolina to be one colony. This expectation was unrealized, too, as the geography of the area created two different ways of life. One way of life centered around Charleston in the south. The other developed around Albemarle Sound in the north.

The illustration below shows a colonial settlement in the Carolinas in 1673.

Indians were also treated as slaves in some parts of the country until well into the 1700s. In 1708, North Carolina had 2,000 black slaves and 1,400 Indian.

MOVERS AND SHAPERS

The engraving above shows an eighteenth century indigo plantation.

Elizabeth Lucas Pinckney

As a teenage girl on a colonial plantation, Eliza Lucas (1722?–1793) possessed an astonishing range of talents and interests. Educated in England, she was an accomplished musician, an avid reader of classical literature, and a fluent speaker of both French and English. Her father, an officer in the British army, had so much confidence in her ability that when he was called to military duty in the West Indies, he left 17-year-old Eliza in charge of his three plantations in South Carolina.

It was as a young woman that Eliza Lucas made her most significant contribution to colonial life. South Carolina's economy was then totally dependent on a single cash crop —rice. When Eliza began managing her father's plantations, the price of Carolina rice was badly depressed. The problem was critical and something had to be done about it. What crop besides rice, Eliza wondered, could profitably be grown on her father's Wappoo plantation?

There were several possibilities, but Eliza decided to concentrate on indigo, the plant that produced a beautiful blue dye. Other planters before her had experimented with indigo and failed. Eliza admitted in letters to her father that she knew nothing about the nature of the indigo seed. But she persevered for a number of years with experiments. Finally, in 1744, her determination was rewarded when a good crop of indigo was harvested at Wappoo, processed into blocks of blue dyestuff, and shipped to England for sale. In that same year, she married Charles Pinckney, with whom she had four children.

Neighbors of the Pinckneys soon learned from Eliza how indigo could be successfully planted and harvested. The effect of her experiments on South Carolina's economy was immediate and profound. The indigo dye, widely used for making blue cloth, was in great demand among British merchants. The sale of indigo sustained South Carolina's economy until the American Revolution.

During her later years, Eliza spent most of her time with her family at her daughter's plantation at Hampton, helping to rear her grandchildren. Among the many distinguished guests she entertained at Hampton was President Washington, who paid her a visit while on his southern tour in May 1791. She died in 1793, and was buried in Philadelphia.

Research Assignment: As a follow-up to an earlier Research Assignment, students may do a report on a famous New England woman. Suggestions could include Anne Hutchinson, Anne Bradstreet, and Phillis Wheatley.

Until 1712, the two Carolinas were ruled by one proprietary governor in Charleston, who appointed a deputy governor for the north. In 1712, separate assemblies were approved and equal governors appointed for North Carolina and South Carolina. Both South Carolina and North Carolina became royal colonies in 1729.

South Carolina was settled first by former sugar planters from the English West Indian colony of Barbados. Although sugar cane did not flourish around the mouth of the Ashley and Cooper Rivers, the site of Charleston, rice did.

Like tobacco and sugar, rice was most efficiently grown on large plantations. Therefore, South Carolina's society came to be dominated by a few families that owned huge tracts of land and many slaves. Later, through the efforts of Eliza Pinckney, the South Carolinians began growing a second profitable crop, *indigo*, from which a magnificent blue dye was manufactured. Indigo was a perfect companion for rice because it required attention at seasons when there was little work to be done in rice fields. In fact, the swampy lowlands where rice grew were so unhealthy during the summer that it was necessary to move slaves to higher elevations where the indigo flourished.

Unlike planters in Virginia and Maryland, who lived on their isolated plantations, wealthy South Carolinians liked the social whirl of town life. Leaving their lands under the care of overseers most of the year, they made Charleston a sophisticated city of elegant townhouses and fashionably dressed ladies and gentlemen. The city resembled the rich cities of the sugar islands of Barbados and the West Indies.

Charleston was one of the few true cities in the southern colonies. It was a busy trading center with a cosmopolitan and tolerant upper class. For example, Jews from Spain and Portugal found little prejudice against them in South Carolina. By the American Revolution, more Jews lived in Charleston than in any other American city, and they took full part in South Carolina's social and economic life.

The northern part of Carolina was settled by people from Virginia who were unable to secure farmland in their old colony. Their chief cash crop was tobacco, but because they arrived poor, the North Carolinians owned few slaves. Lacking a first-rate seaport, and isolated from Virginia and South Carolina by huge swamps, North Carolina grew slowly. Its inhabitants were proud of their independence and protective of their comparatively democratic society, in which most small farmers could vote.

Georgia: A Social Experiment. The final southern colony to be founded—and the last English colony founded on the North American mainland—was Georgia. Chartered in 1732, and named after King George II, Georgia was neither a corporate, proprietary, nor royal colony, but an experiment in social reform.

The Crown's motive in colonizing the region was defensive. South Carolina was prospering, and an attack on Charleston by the Spaniards in Florida was feared. Therefore the person who was entrusted to establish this buffer colony was an experienced soldier, General James Oglethorpe. Oglethorpe and his associates would be allowed to govern the colony as trustees for 21 years, after which the colony would be turned over to the Crown as a royal colony.

However, Oglethorpe and his friends wanted to build more than just a fortified outpost of the empire. They saw Georgia as the answer to poverty, a serious social problem in England. Terrible poverty led many individuals to commit crimes, and others were imprisoned simply because they could not pay their debts. The debtors were not criminals, but they were kept in overflowing prisons until they or someone else paid their debts.

The first settlement in the colony, Savannah, was a planned village. Oglethorpe carefully selected the first settlers to ensure there were no hardened criminals among them, and brought them to the colony. He outlawed slavery to avoid domination of the colony by a few wealthy planters, and also tried to prevent the importation of alcoholic beverages. Like many reformers, Oglethorpe believed that drunkenness was a cause of poverty.

As a colony Georgia succeeded. As an experiment in reform, however, it failed. Few debtors actually came to the colony, although some poor merchants and tradespeople did. Even the earliest settlers insisted on drinking. Coastal Georgia was swampy and plagued by mosquito-borne diseases such as malaria. The settlers mistakenly believed that cheap rum, made from West Indian sugar, prevented the disease, or at least made it and hard labor more bearable.

Once Savannah was secure against Spanish attack, slaveowners moved in and defied Oglethorpe's authority. A rice and indigo plantation economy much like South Carolina's developed on the Georgia shore. The well-meaning Oglethorpe returned discouraged to England in 1743, long before his trusteeship was over. Although he lived to be 91, he never returned to the scene of his failed experiment.

SECTION REVIEW

1. Write a sentence to identify: Cecilius Calvert, Anthony Ashley Cooper, Act of Toleration, Fundamental Constitutions of Carolina.

2. Describe the circumstances that led to the founding of Maryland, Carolina, and Georgia.

3. Describe how each of these colonies changed in the years after its founding: Maryland; Carolina; Georgia.

4. Why did southern farmers and proprietors favor quit-rents?

5. What labor problem faced large plantation owners in the southern colonies? What solution did they choose to correct this problem?

---

3. MIDDLE COLONIES

Between Maryland and Connecticut lay some of the best harbors and farmland in North America. The territory had rolling hills, deep forests, several major waterways, and many streams. The Dutch and Swedes had placed small colonies there, but very little of the land was settled.

Still, no English colonies were founded here until after 1660. This neglect arose from a provision in the original charters of the London and Plymouth Companies: the land was simply outside the territory allotted to Virginia to the south and the New England colonies to the north. In this neutral zone, New Sweden had developed at the mouth of the Delaware River, and New Netherland along the Hudson River.

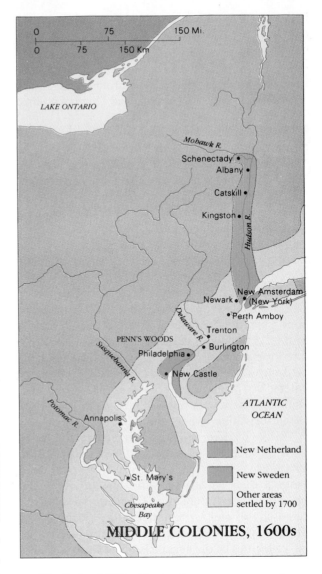

MIDDLE COLONIES, 1600s

Until the 1660s, England was content to leave New Sweden and New Netherland alone, even though after 1655 the Dutch controlled both major waterways of the area and were aggressively expanding their trading operations. The civil war between King Charles I and Parliament, and then Oliver Cromwell's disinterest in colonization barred English activity there. Moreover, Virginia, Maryland, and the New England colonies provided the English people with more than enough opportunity for expansion.

New Netherland Becomes New York. In 1664, however, the Dutch and English trading conflict was about to break out in war. James,

---

Yankee has several believed origins. Most likely it is a Dutch word. *Janke* is the Dutch equivalent of "Johnny," and was pronounced "Yankee." It was commonly applied to New Englanders by the Dutch from New York.

Duke of York and brother of King Charles II, ordered Colonel Richard Nicolls to sail four warships to New Amsterdam at the foot of Manhattan Island and demand the colony's surrender. The governor of New Netherland, Peter Stuyvesant, an ornery old soldier who stormed along the battlements of his fort on a wooden leg, wanted to fight, but no one backed him! Stuyvesant's temper and dictatorial laws had made enemies of practically everyone in the colony. The British were able to take the colony without firing a shot. King Charles gave the colony to James, and it was renamed New York. It remained a proprietary colony until 1685, when it became a royal colony as the Duke became King James II.

James was a popular proprietor. He guaranteed all grants of land made under Dutch rule. Although he became a Catholic, he allowed worship in the Dutch Reformed Church and tolerated the practice of other religions. James also eased the strict laws that had made Stuyvesant so unpopular. When a Dutch squadron briefly recaptured the colony in 1673, the officers discovered that few of the inhabitants, including the Dutch majority, were pleased to see them.

New York developed slowly, even after it was taken over by the British. The land-grant system that existed in the colony did not promote settlement, as most settlers would have to be tenants of large landholders. Settlers could find better opportunities elsewhere. Also, the French influence was strong north of Albany, and Indian tribes that were allied with the French were very active on the frontier. The colony's rise as an agricultural and trading center would occur in the later colonial period, when New Englanders moved across the border looking for more land, and New York City became a leading shipping center for the middle colonies.

Pennsylvania. In 1681, Charles II gave a tract of land between New York and Maryland to William Penn as payment of a debt he owed Penn's father. (His father, Sir William Penn, was an admiral in the Royal Navy, and Charles had been unable to pay his salary.) Although Charles was generally free in giving away his American possessions, the grant of Pennsylvania ("Penn's Woods") was unusual. William Penn was a member of the *Society of Friends (Quakers)*, a religious sect that

Before 1664, New York City was called New Amsterdam. The picture below shows New Amsterdam, located at the southeastern tip of Manhattan Island, around 1650.

was the object of amusement, scorn, and fear to almost every other group in England.

The Society of Friends was founded by a wandering preacher named George Fox. Appealing mostly to the poor of England, Fox taught that all men and women were equal before God. To him, true religion required no priests with spiritual powers such as in the Roman Catholic Church or Church of England, nor learned ministers, such as for the Puritans. According to Fox, every human being was possessed with an "inner light"—the capacity to communicate directly with God.

This doctrine by itself offended powerful priests and preachers. It also caused the Quakers to adopt practices that went against all of British society, and for which they were persecuted.

For example, if all men and women were equal before God, it was wrong for the poor and humble to take off their hats in the presence of nobles. If women were equal to men, they had the right to preach what God had inspired in them, too. If all people had a spark of divinity within them, fighting wars or even paying taxes to support armies was wrong. To the wealthy and powerful, to people who believed women should be subordinate to men, and to governments involved constantly in warfare, such beliefs threatened the very basis of society.

Charles II found Quaker teachings absurd. However, he liked William Penn. It amused him that a wealthy and educated gentleman should speak for a religion that appealed to the poor and

Quakers settled in Pennsylvania. They welcomed anyone who believed in one God, regardless of their individual religious practices. Quakers experienced very few problems with the Indians who lived nearby because the Quakers kept their promises.

Research Assignment: As a long-term research assignment, you may have students study the concept of religious freedom and its development in the course of U.S. history. Starting with the English colonists, discuss the issue of religious freedom in other groups, such as the Mormons, the Jews, and some of the present-day religious groups. Direct students to include the powerless. And giving Pennsylvania to Penn would also have the practical advantage of ridding England of the troublesome Society of Friends.

The Holy Experiment.

Penn was delighted to take American land instead of the money Charles owed him. Not only did he want to protect Quakers from persecution, he wanted to use Pennsylvania as the scene of a "Holy Experiment" in Quaker principles.

Penn's colony was to be substantially different from the other colonies. Penn believed in religious toleration, and all people who believed in one God were welcome in Pennsylvania. (Note that this does not mean that all people were welcome.) Penn also believed in recognizing the rights of the Indians. Instead of simply seizing land, the Quakers explained their principles to the tribes that lived in the Delaware River Valley and purchased the land, usually at a fair price. The Indians, already accustomed to unjust treatment by colonists, were surprised, and respected the Quakers. Only rarely were members of the Society of Friends attacked, even on the edges of the colony.

Penn also experimented with city design. Whereas most cities of the time, like Boston and New York, grew haphazardly, Penn's capital of Philadelphia (which means "City of Brotherly Love") was laid out before any buildings were constructed. Like Charleston, South Carolina, the first planned city in America, Philadelphia was designed on a gridiron pattern that made moving about and finding an address a simple matter. Because Penn envisioned "a greene countrie towne" even when Philadelphia was large, he reserved five squares as public parks.

Under Penn's liberal policies, Pennsylvania grew more quickly than any other colony. Peasants from Switzerland and Germany, who were persecuted at home for beliefs like those of the Quakers, streamed into the fertile, rolling hills of southeastern Pennsylvania. Today, their descendants are known as the "Pennsylvania Dutch" and still practice some seventeenth-century customs. Philadelphia also grew rapidly. Although much younger than Boston or New York, it quickly became the largest English-speaking city in North America. In fact, by the American Revolution, the only city in the British Empire that was larger was London itself.

Delaware and New Jersey.

William Penn's land grant also included the present state of Delaware and parts of New Jersey. Officially, Delaware remained a part of Pennsylvania until the Revolution. However, Penn allowed the people there, including the original Swedish and Dutch settlers, to govern themselves in most matters.

Delaware was never dominated by the Quakers to the degree Pennsylvania was. One consequence of this was that Pennsylvania was an early source of antislavery feeling in America, whereas Delaware borrowed the institution from the nearby tobacco colonies of Maryland and Virginia. Although never critical to its small farm economy, slavery remained legal in Delaware until the American Civil War.

New Jersey was originally two colonies that became one. The land, which had been part of New Netherland, was given to two proprietors, Lord Berkeley and Sir George Carteret, who also held great tracts of land in the Carolinas. The western part, bordering on the Delaware River, was settled largely by Quaker farmers, and developed much like Pennsylvania. Eastern New Jersey, with its capital at Perth Amboy, was settled by people from New York and New England. The original proprietors had to sell off their holdings, as they were able to attract few settlers, and the land changed owners several times. In 1702, New Jersey became a royal colony.

SECTION REVIEW

1. Write a sentence to identify: Duke of York, Peter Stuyvesant, Society of Friends, Holy Experiment, Philadelphia.

2. Give two reasons why the English colonies at first did not interfere with Dutch and Swedish colonies.

3. How did the Dutch of New Amsterdam show how they felt about the English takeover of the colony?

4. Explain how the following beliefs caused Quakers persecution in England: Every human has an "inner light". Men and women are equal before God. All people have a spark of divinity within them.

Constitutional interpretation of religious freedom and the separation of church and state. Include major court cases and present issues about school prayer. This type of on-going research project will provide valuable preparation for the kind of work students may find themselves doing in some college classes.

The quipu (kē'po͞o), a system of knotted strings for counting and recording numbers, was invented by the Incas. From the main pendant hung many smaller strings of different colors, tied at intervals.

The Incas made the first suspension bridges. The rope sides and webbed walkway swayed in the wind.

In the 1500s oceangoing caravels made possible the discovery of new lands by the Portuguese and Spanish. Although most caravels had four masts, three-masted caravels were used by Columbus on his first voyage across the Atlantic.

C H A N G I N G   T E C H N O L O G Y

Pre 1000 AD

Before the year 1,000 A.D. people invented thousands of useful items to make their lives easier. Among them were:

The lever (Paleolithic)
The wedge (Paleolithic)

The inclined plane (Paleolithic)
The plow (5,000-3,000 BC)
The wheel and axle (3,000 BC)
System of writing (3,000 BC)
The sail (3,000 BC)
The pulley (700 BC)

The pump (300 BC)
The lathe (200 BC)
The waterwheel (100 BC)
The screw press (100 BC)

Reseach Assignment: Have students do research to find how long it took for trans-Atlantic crossings in a caravel. Some students might be interested in conducting an on-going research report on how travel time has decreased with technological advances in transportation. Students

Spectacular stained glass windows were found in twelfth century churches, but glass was too expensive for use in private homes until the late 1700s, when the construction of windows with small squares of clear glass became feasible.

Cultivation of the indigo plant, enabled early people to dye fabrics. It was the best source of a dark blue dye. Its pods look like small sausages.

Before the invention of the wheel, loads were dragged on a travois (trä-vwä'), arranged like a platform. The plains Indians used the travois first with dogs and later with horses.

10	00	13	50	16	00
Vertical windmill built	Movable type developed	Air pump produced
Spinning wheel invented	Rifle built	Pendulum clock built
Cannon developed	Knitting machine produced	Steam pump developed
Mechanical clock designed	Adding machine designed	Steam engine introduced
		Flying shuttle constructed
		Lightning rod invented

should note the impact that these advances have had on politics and economics on both sides of the Atlantic.

CHAPTER REVIEW

TIME LINE

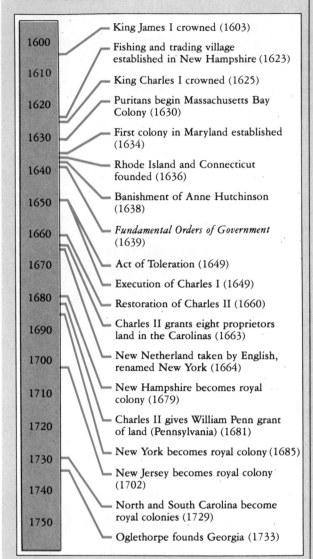

1600	King James I crowned (1603)
	Fishing and trading village established in New Hampshire (1623)
1610	
	King Charles I crowned (1625)
1620	Puritans begin Massachusetts Bay Colony (1630)
1630	First colony in Maryland established (1634)
1640	Rhode Island and Connecticut founded (1636)
1650	Banishment of Anne Hutchinson (1638)
1660	*Fundamental Orders of Government* (1639)
1670	Act of Toleration (1649)
	Execution of Charles I (1649)
1680	Restoration of Charles II (1660)
1690	Charles II grants eight proprietors land in the Carolinas (1663)
1700	New Netherland taken by English, renamed New York (1664)
1710	New Hampshire becomes royal colony (1679)
1720	Charles II gives William Penn grant of land (Pennsylvania) (1681)
1730	New York becomes royal colony (1685)
	New Jersey becomes royal colony (1702)
1740	North and South Carolina become royal colonies (1729)
1750	Oglethorpe founds Georgia (1733)

TIME LINE QUESTIONS

1. Write the names of these colonies in the order in which they were founded: Rhode Island, Connecticut, Massachusetts, Carolina, Maryland.
2. Name four colonies founded by people searching for religious liberty.
3. Which places became royal colonies, and in what years?
4. Which began first, Georgia or Pennsylvania?

SKILLS STRATEGY

> **City Beginnings in the English Colonies**
> I. The New England Colonies
>   A. Boston in Massachusetts Bay Colony
>   1. Founded in 1630
>   2. Puritan founders
>   3. Grew haphazardly
>   B. Providence in Rhode Island Colony
>   1. Founded in 1636
>   2. Roger Williams the founder
>   3. Williams's disagreements with Puritans
> II. The Middle Colonies
>   A. New York City in New York Colony
>   1. Founded by Dutch as New Amsterdam
>   2. Taken over by English in 1664
>   3. Renamed to honor Duke of York
>   4. Became leading shipping center
>   B. Philadelphia in Pennsylvania Colony
>   1. Founded by William Penn and Quakers
>   2. A planned city
>   3. Became largest English-speaking city in North America

THREE-LEVEL OUTLINES

If you compare the outline above with the outline on page 49 you will see that something has been added—*details* numbered with Arabic numerals under each lettered subtopic.

The outline above was written to answer the question, "Which present-day cities in the United States had their origins in the 13 English colonies?" Notice that the title of this outline is not this question, but reflects it. The information given in main topic *I*, subtopics *A* and *B*, and details *1*, *2*, and *3* was found by skimming the text under the three main headings in this chapter. In skimming the chapter, the key words *Boston* and *Providence* became subtopics *A* and *B*. Details about these two New England cities became part of the outline under each of the cities.

Now compare the two outlines above. Notice that, in the first outline above, phrases are used to give information in the main topics, the subtopics, and the details. Sentences give this same information in the second outline. The first outline above is known as a *topic outline*. The second is called a *sentence outline*.

Making Connections: Review the questions and topics presented in the Making Connections section opening this chapter. Make clear to students the variety of motives the colonists had for

72

Cities Begin in the English Colonies

I. Some cities started in New England.
  A. Boston started in the Massachusetts Bay Colony.
    1. The city was founded in 1630.
    2. The Puritans founded it.
    3. Boston grew haphazardly.
  B. Providence began in the Rhode Island Colony.
    1. The city was founded in 1636.
    2. Roger Williams was its founder.
    3. He founded it because he disagreed with the Puritans in Massachusetts.
II. Other cities grew in the Middle Colonies.
  A. _____
    1. _____
    2. _____
    3. _____
  ___ _____
III. Cities were begun in the Southern Colonies, too.

Parts of the second outline are missing. In order to complete this outline, you should skim the three chapter sections. Use the names of cities in the middle and southern colonies as key words and read carefully for detail information to list under them.

APPLYING SKILLS

Refer to the two outlines as you do the following.
1. How do the above outlines differ from one another?
2. Where and how would you find the information for section III?
3. Copy and complete the outline above. As you skim the chapter, look for information about cities in the middle and southern colonies that answers questions like these: When was the city founded? Who founded it? Why? How did the city grow? Notice other important information the chapter gives about a city. Under each main topic, list two or more subtopics and details. Save your completed outline for use in the Writing a Paragraph assignment on this page.

CHAPTER 3 TEST

TEXT REVIEW

1. Explain why each of these religious groups came to North America: Puritans, Catholics, Quakers.
2. Name some Puritan blue laws and their penalties.
3. Give reasons why Roger Williams and Anne Hutchinson were dissenters.
4. Describe the religious and governmental provisions of the Fundamental Constitutions of Carolina.
5. How was the life of the South Carolina planters different from the lives of planters in Virginia and Maryland?
6. Explain how the founders of the last English colony intended it to be an experiment in social reform.
7. Which English colony was founded by Dutch settlers? What was the original name of this colony?

CRITICAL THINKING

8. Which of the thirteen colonies was founded as a "Holy Experiment"? Explain why you think this experiment was successful or unsuccessful.
9. Summarize the Dutch experience in colonial America.
10. List any institutions developed in the colonies that fit under one of these headings: *democratic government, public education*. Include the colonies in which they developed.

WRITING A PARAGRAPH

Use the sentence outline you completed to write a paragraph on the colonial origins of a present-day city. The information under one main topic should be used to write your paragraph. Complete the topic sentence below to express the main idea. Your topic sentence should be based on one of the main topics in your sentence outline. You choose which one.

  Topic Sentence: _____, an important city in the United States today, had its origins in the English colony of _____.

coming here and how these translated into ways of life and principles, many of which are still espoused today.

Quotation: from the essay *Common Sense.* Other works by Thomas Paine (1737–1809) include *The Rights of Man* and *The Age of Reason.*

CHAPTER 4

COLONIAL AMERICANS

1650–1754

Not a place upon the earth might be so happy as America. Her situation is remote from all the wrangling world, and she has nothing to do but to trade with them. THOMAS PAINE

Making Connections. As the American colonies grew in size, their economic importance grew, too. Consequently, the English Parliament passed laws to guarantee that the profitable colonial trade would remain in British hands. Many colonists resented these laws because they felt that what was good for the English was not necessarily good for the Americans.

In this chapter, you will learn:
- How mercantilism affected the development of the English colonies
- Why the British encouraged Americans to use slave labor
- How colonial assemblies used the "power of the purse" to whittle away the power of colonial governors
- Who led the colonial rebellions
- Why French colonies in the New World did not grow rapidly
- How European wars spilled over into the New World

You know that the economic policy of mercantilism required Europeans to establish colonies and to maintain rigid control of their colonies. However, this policy did not always sit well with the colonists. As you read, note how Great Britain enforced its mercantilist policies and how the Americans reacted.

Sections
1. Mercantilism
2. Colonial Economy
3. Colonial Government
4. Contest for Empire

1. MERCANTILISM

The people who governed England—monarchs, powerful nobles and leaders of Parliament, wealthy merchants and great landowners— believed that the colonies existed to serve the interests of the parent country. Colonies were a source of prestige. Royalty and commoners alike were proud of and benefited from their overseas possessions.

Colonies also meant greater military strength in times of crisis. England was crowded, but land was abundant in the colonies. Therefore, a population loyal to the Crown could increase its numbers indefinitely and provide soldiers and sailors in time of war.

Most of all, the colonies were expected to enrich the English people. It was all right for the colonials to prosper, too. But the economic philosophy of mercantilism required that colonial well-being come second to England's prosperity. When the economic interests of colonials conflicted with the interests of England, the colonials' interests were almost always sacrificed.

Mercantilist Principles. Mercantilism was economic nationalism, and was designed to strengthen a nation by economic means. The

Maritime trade made docks like the Old East India Wharf (right) centers of commercial activity. English ships, laden with manufactured goods, sailed to North America and returned with tobacco, furs, and lumber.

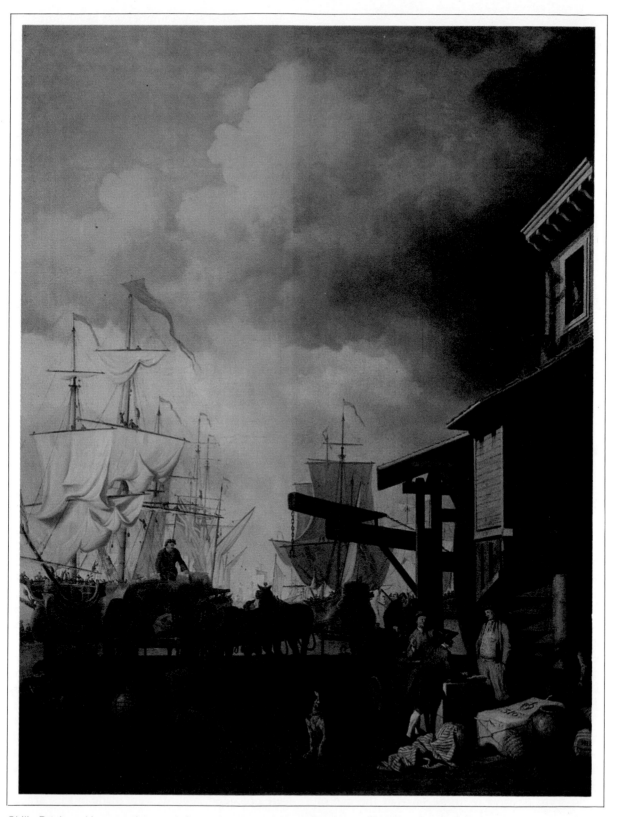

Skills Review: Have students reinforce their knowledge of making a three-level outline by having them outline this chapter according to the method presented in the previous Skills Strategy.

 75

Merchants had to account for the many goods shipped between England and America.

simple central idea of the policy was to build up the national supply of gold and silver, but not just in the government's treasury. Mercantilists thought in terms of a richer nation: richer merchants, richer manufacturers, richer bankers, and richer nobles and landowners.

In order to build up gold and silver reserves, subjects were discouraged from spending money abroad. Foreign cash was attracted by exporting favorably priced goods. Economic self-sufficiency was necessary so that the country would sell more to other countries than it bought from them.

Ideally, English farmers would produce all the food the nation needed and English manufacturers would make every product the nation used. However, a small island nation like England could not produce everything its people consumed. If England were to have a strong navy in the age of fragile wooden ships, lumber and naval stores had to be imported from forested countries like Norway and Sweden. Furs were needed to manufacture felt, a fabric used in making hats and many other products. Only Russia had fur-bearing animals. The Asian spices and perfumes, and exotic products like wine, sugar, citrus fruits, and tobacco, could not be successfully raised in England.

England's colonies filled these needs. From colonies England could purchase lumber, furs, sugar, rice, and tobacco and pay for them not in gold and silver but with *bills of credit* that colonials could redeem only in English manufactured goods. And to ensure that English merchants monopolized the profit from the colonies, the colonials were required to sell valuable products and to buy manufactured goods only in England.

The Navigation Acts. The *Navigation Acts* were enacted under Charles II after 1660. The first law provided that all colonial trade be carried by ships built and owned by English or colonial merchants. Three-quarters of the crew on these ships had to be British subjects. This law ensured that profits from the colonies would return to England, and closed the lucrative business to other countries. The Netherlands, whose merchants had been very active in the tobacco colonies before the Navigation Acts, declared war on England in an effort to force a change.

Great Britain won the trade wars with the Netherlands. This was a loss to colonial tobacco planters because the Dutch often offered higher prices than the English did. And the planters were at the mercy of the English market. In the 1660s and 1670s, the planters produced so much tobacco that England could not buy all of it, and the price of tobacco fell. However, New Englanders did not object to the law. It put their ships on an equal footing with those of Great Britain.

The second important Navigation Act required that colonials purchase all their imports from England. The purpose of this law was to ensure that England profited even on trade goods that originated elsewhere. Goods that England did not produce had to be brought to an English port before going to the colonies. At the docks of these *entrepots* (än'trə-pō')—the word means warehouse or, in this case, a port for clearing goods—ships were unloaded, records were made of the cargo, a

Discussion Questions: What are some of the possible positive and negative effects of mercantilism on a country's economy? Are there possible political ramifications of this?

76

Stamps like the one pictured above were affixed to different products manufactured in England and shipped to America. Colonial merchants were forced to pay the taxes indicated on the stamps. The painting below is of a seventeenth century merchant and his clerk.

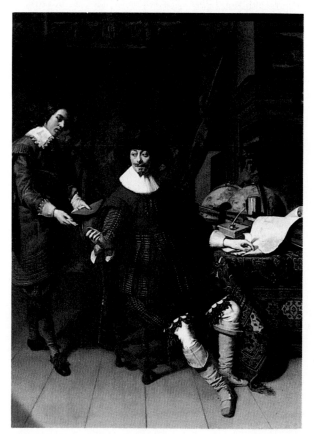

tax was collected on most shipments, and the ships were reloaded for the voyage to the colonies.

Unsurprisingly, almost every American who used imported goods resented this law. A tobacco planter who drank French wines had to pay more because the wines could not be shipped directly from France. Merchants resented the delay and the added costs.

The third basic provision of the Navigation Acts applied the entrepot principle to products the colonies exported. It created a list of certain colonial crops and goods that had to be taken to England, even if they were to be sold in another country. These enumerated articles included almost everything Americans grew or made that had a cash value in world trade. Tobacco was enumerated, as were cotton and indigo. Furs and hides (the only source of income for many frontier settlers), timber, *naval stores* (tar, pitch, and turpentine used to make wooden ships watertight), and molasses and rum were all listed. Two salable products that were not originally enumerated were rice and salted fish, and rice was enumerated in 1705.

SECTION REVIEW

1. Write a sentence to identify: economic self-sufficiency, entrepot, enumerated article.

2. Give three reasons for England's desire to hold on to its American colonies.

3. How did England ensure that its colonies would help it maintain economic self-sufficiency?

4. Which group in the American colonies did not object to the first Navigation Act? Why? Which groups opposed the entrepot principle? Why?

---

2. COLONIAL ECONOMY

No colonial economy better served mercantilist purposes than one that was entirely agricultural, produced a cash crop, and manufactured nothing. The mercantilists' favorite colonies were the sugar islands of the West Indies. On Jamaica and Barbados, a few wealthy planters supervised huge gangs

Discussion Question: Read the first sentence in section 2 on this page aloud. Then ask, "What did the author mean by this statement?" Use this exercise to check that students can read into what an author may be implying.

 77

of slaves to produce sugar, which could be sold anywhere in the world. English merchants made money by handling the sugar, molasses, and rum (which is made from molasses). English manufacturers profited by supplying the planters with luxuries, and cheap clothing and tools for the laborers.

Like the sugar islands, the tobacco colonies of Virginia and Maryland and the rice and indigo colonies of South Carolina and Georgia were almost exclusively agricultural. This was partly because of mercantilist laws, and partly because of geography.

The Rural South.

The Chesapeake Bay region, where most tobacco grew, is a country of low land between broad rivers and creeks that are deep enough for small trading ships to sail on. Because the land was washed by ocean tides, the country is known as the *Tidewater*. No large cities developed here in colonial times because none were necessary. In the Tidewater, English merchants could sail their vessels right up to docks of the larger plantations. There, once a year, the activities associated with cities—buying, selling, banking, social life—held sway for a week or two.

Life was exciting when the ships arrived. Servants and slaves rolled the barrels of tobacco onto the ships. Poorer farmers without wharves of their own gathered to bargain, dance, and race. The sailors enlivened the scene with tales of the strange lands they had visited. The tobacco was sold, and goods the tobacco planters had ordered the previous year were received.

The tobacco planters rarely received gold and silver coin for their crop. Mercantilist policy discouraged cash payment to colonials. And, in practice, it did not matter. Because mercantilism also forbade most forms of manufacture in the colonies and trade with other countries, the planters needed the goods the tobacco ships carried. When planters had tobacco worth more than the goods they ordered, they received bills of credit, which could be redeemed in goods at some future time.

Elegance and Debt.

Although not much cash circulated in the southern colonies, Tidewater planters still lived a comfortable, even elegant life. With close connections to England through the tobacco merchants, the wealthier planters imitated

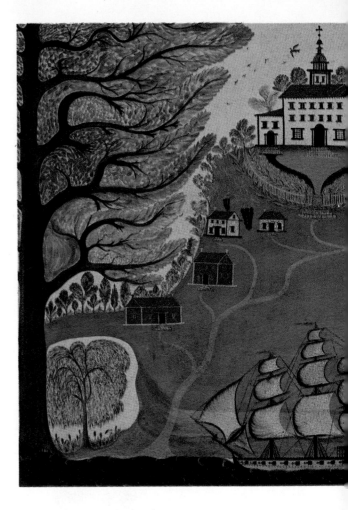

In the Chesapeake Bay region, larger tobacco plantations had their own docks. English ships could pick up the season's crops and deliver any goods ordered the previous season.

the manners and fashions of the English upper class. By the eighteenth century, sizeable homes in the style of English manors dotted the Tidewater and even the foothills of the Appalachians where later settlers had built their plantations.

These mansions were often filled with the finest furniture, china, and decorations. Because there were no large cities to serve as social centers, the homes were always open to neighbors and strangers.

The tradition of southern hospitality, a generous willingness to serve as host and hostess at parties, balls, and dinners, had its origins in the isolation of southern plantation life. Tobacco

Class Activity: This activity will examine the differences in the ways of life in different regions of the colonies and in different social groups. Divide the class into small groups. Assign each group member the task of researching one of the following five aspects in the life of either a colonial slave, an Indian, a plantation owner, a Boston merchant, a small farmer in New England, a ers with the goods they wanted in return for a *lien* (lēn), or claim, on the next year's crop—at a reduced price.

By the end of the colonial period, many planters were at least a year behind in their debts. Tobacco that had not even been planted had already been sold to pay for the year's luxuries and necessities. Their chronic debt helps to explain why, despite their admiration for the English way of life, the Tidewater planters were strong supporters of local government. They bitterly resented the mercantilist policies on which they blamed their high debts.

The Growth of Slavery. The difficulty the tobacco growers had in making ends meet also helped to spread slavery. There were only about 1,600 black slaves in English America in 1650, with more in the northern colonies than in the South. But by 1700 almost 28,000 blacks were slaves for life, most of them in the South. By 1750, about 206,000 slaves toiled in southern tobacco and rice fields; 30,000 were enslaved in the northern colonies.

A work force of slaves was less expensive to maintain than a group of servants who went free after several years. Planters also found black workers preferable because their skin color identified them as slaves unless they could produce a document that said they were free. Thus, it was very difficult for blacks to run away. By the 1700s, moreover, the British were encouraging colonials to purchase slaves. In the Treaty of Utrecht (1713) ending the War of the Spanish Succession, the British were granted the right to import 4,800 African slaves a year to Spanish colonies. Slave trading thus became a major British activity.

As British traders provided slaves at ever cheaper prices, slaves replaced more servants in

planters worked hard to supervise the complex operation of raising crops and running plantations. If anything, the mistress of a plantation worked harder and longer than her husband. She had to run a large household and to care for the family, servants, and slaves. As a result, both wife and husband were starved for company. They were sincerely delighted when a stranger appeared, glad to make a bed and set a table for all visitors, and sorry (most of the time) when their company departed.

Free-spending habits made debtors of many tobacco planters. As the price of tobacco fell and the fertility of the land declined, the planters found it increasingly difficult to pay for the imports on which their elegant life-style depended., They mortgaged future crops to pay for their comforts, and the English tobacco merchants were usually willing to oblige. They provided the plant-

TO BE SOLD,
A likely ſtrong Negro Girl, abc ut 17 Years of Age ; fold by Reaſon that a Boy would fuit the Owner better. Enquire at R. & S. *Draper*'s Printing Office

This was a slave advertisement in the December 9, 1763 edition of the Massachusetts Gazette.

government official in one of the middle colonies, or a Philadelphia shopkeeper: 1) common foods and their preparation, 2) clothing, 3) entertainment, 4) arts and crafts, 5) perceptions of people they might meet in a normal day. Have groups present their findings to the class.

the agricultural work force. Nowhere was the institution more important than in South Carolina. By 1750, about two-thirds of the colony's population was black. This majority was controlled by means of a harsh *slave code,* or collection of laws that defined the blacks as chattels.

The word *chattel* is related to the word *cattle,* which almost sums up the slaves' status. They were legally much like livestock or even a piece of furniture. The master or mistress of a plantation or household had nearly complete control over the slaves, including the right to whip them.

New England.

While a large majority of slaves lived in the southern colonies, New Englanders from coastal cities like Newport, Rhode Island, were active in the slave trade. Lacking a cash crop they could trade for British goods, the New Englanders needed cash or goods from other places to purchase manufactured goods.

In order to get the money and goods, they turned to trade, including the slave trade. This put the New Englanders into direct competition with 'the English slave traders. In fact, the *Yankees,* as New Englanders were called, competed with the British in practically everything they did for a living. This competition helps to explain why New Englanders were the first Americans to rebel violently against British rule.

Earning Cold Cash.

New England did produce some goods that English merchants wanted. The abundant forests provided lumber and naval stores. There was some trade in New England deerhides and beaver furs until the animals were overhunted. New Englanders also found a ready market in southern Europe for salted codfish. (Fish was not an enumerated article.)

But these products were never enough to pay for imports from English manufacturers. New Englanders depended on profits from the exchange of goods produced by others to raise money for their purchases from England. Except that they had to spend their cash in England, the Yankees had their own mercantilist system.

The Triangular Trade.

The *triangular trade* was the way New England merchants earned cash for their colonies. The merchants traveled from the colonies to England or Africa, then back across the Atlantic to the West Indies, and then back north to New England. By making a profit on the transactions after each leg of a journey, ships' captains were able to return home with gold and silver despite the lack of a New England cash crop.

There were several triangular routes. One started in the middle colonies where grain and livestock were purchased. These foodstuffs were sold at a large profit in the Spanish or French West Indies for gold and silver or traded in the English West Indies for sugar and molasses. These items were taken to England. There, the Yankee captains picked up manufactured goods ranging from nails to books for sale in New England.

A second triangle began with tobacco from Maryland and Virginia. It took a ship to England where the tobacco was exchanged for iron goods, textiles, and other commodities desired by West Africans. In Africa, these goods were traded for slaves, who were then taken to the tobacco colonies. Again, on each leg the shrewd trader could pocket a large profit.

The 1775 engraving below shows a Virginia wharf, where barrels of tobacco are being rolled down to the ships. The ships would then go to England, West Africa, and back to America.

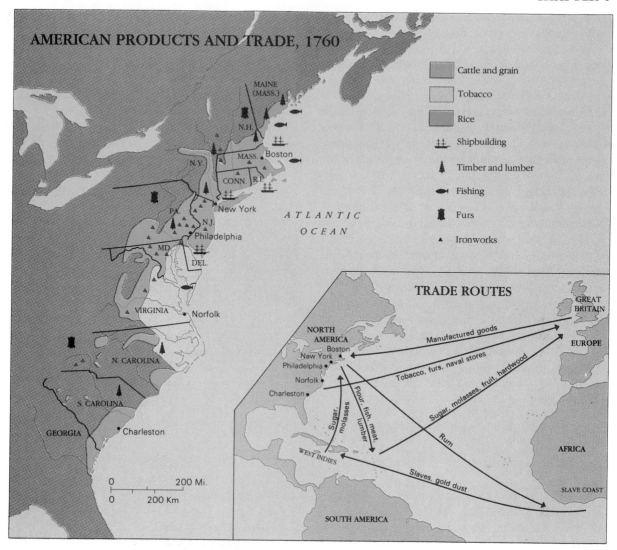

AMERICAN PRODUCTS AND TRADE, 1760

Legend:
- Cattle and grain
- Tobacco
- Rice
- Shipbuilding
- Timber and lumber
- Fishing
- Furs
- Ironworks

ATLANTIC OCEAN

MAINE (MASS.)
N.H.
MASS. • Boston
N.Y.
CONN. R.I.
• New York
PA.
N.J.
• Philadelphia
MD.
DEL.
VIRGINIA • Norfolk
N. CAROLINA
S. CAROLINA
GEORGIA • Charleston

0   200 Mi.
0   200 Km

TRADE ROUTES

NORTH AMERICA
— Boston
New York •
Philadelphia •
Norfolk •
Charleston •

GREAT BRITAIN
EUROPE
AFRICA
SLAVE COAST
WEST INDIES
SOUTH AMERICA

Manufactured goods
Tobacco, furs, naval stores
Sugar, molasses, fruit, hardwood
Sugar, molasses
Flour, fish, meat, lumber
Rum
Slaves, gold dust

A third triangular route also included slave trading. Molasses from the sugar islands was carried to New England, where the molasses was distilled into rum. The rum went to West Africa, where it was exchanged for slaves. This human property was carried back to the West Indies. This trade was very profitable because West Indian planters were always in the market for human chattels. Conditions there were so bad—much worse than in the tobacco colonies—that many slaves died quickly and had to be replaced.

The Middle Passage. While slaves were treated as less than human from the moment they were captured in West Africa, the worst experience for the enslaved Africans was the sea crossing from their homeland to America. The Africans called the crossing the Middle Passage. The First Passage was their journey to the coast as captives. The Third Passage was their final sale to their owners in the Americas.

Because slave traders knew that under the best conditions their captives would die in large numbers, they sought to pack their ships with as many humans as possible. The blacks were crowded into decks that were more like shelves, where they were chained wrist-to-wrist and leg-to-leg. Food was little better than gruel, and sanitation was no more than an occasional hosing down. Disease spread quickly under such conditions. The wretched captives often broke down under the stress and killed themselves or others.

As early as 1700, a Boston judge, Samuel Sewall, was outraged over the miseries his fellow New Englanders caused the blacks. Some Quakers, like John Woolman of New Jersey, traveled from farm to farm urging people to free their slaves. But antislavery feeling among whites was weak. Slavery made the plantations work, and the slave trade brought money into New England.

The Middle Colonies. New York, New Jersey, and Pennsylvania were least affected by mercantilist policies. This is a possible reason for the large number of people in the middle colonies who were loyal to Great Britain. The rich farmlands of New York's Hudson Valley and Pennsylvania's rolling hills provided more food than the population could consume. Because the Navigation Acts placed few restrictions on the sale of foodstuffs, this surplus was shipped to the West Indies to feed the slave population there. The trade made middle colony farmers and merchants wealthy.

A slave trade vessel, the Vigilante, *was captured by an English naval ship near the coast of Africa. On board were 345 slaves held in chains in the cramped conditions shown in the engraving above.*

Wealthier colonial families would sometimes commission painters to paint their portraits. The portrait below is of the Sargent family.

Smuggling and Bribery. Most colonists operated within the limits of the Navigation Acts. However, more than a few managed to thrive only by ignoring mercantilist restrictions. *Smuggling* —illegal trade—was a thriving business in America.

Puritans and Quakers who were strict moralists in all other matters thought they were doing nothing wrong when they sold enumerated tobacco in France or purchased cheap imports from Dutch traders. They regarded the Navigation Acts as unfair restraint of their trade. They sometimes forged documents so that if their ships were inspected by British customs collectors, they would appear to have obeyed the law.

Forgery was rarely necessary because customs officials were paid very poorly and were easily bribed. The Royal Navy did not have enough ships to patrol the 1,100-mile (1,760-kilometer) American coast. It was not difficult to unload an illegal cargo in a hidden cove.

When smugglers were caught, royal governors found it almost impossible to convict them. The juries that heard the cases consisted of the accused smugglers' neighbors, who were often smugglers.

Smuggling was difficult to stamp out because it was profitable. The colonists wanted foreign products. They wanted to be able to sell their goods to other countries besides England, but the mercantilist policies of England did not allow this. Therefore, in order to expand their economy, the colonists found it necessary to break the law.

SECTION REVIEW

1. Write a sentence to identify: Tidewater, slave code, Yankee, Middle Passage.

2. Why did English mercantilists favor colonies such as Virginia, Maryland, and the Carolinas?

3. What helped to spread slavery in English America between 1650 and 1750?

4. In which colonies did the colonists feel restricted by mercantilist policies? In which colonies did colonists benefit from the policies? Give reasons.

5. Describe one of the three triangular trade routes followed by New England merchants to earn cash for their colonies.

---

3. COLONIAL GOVERNMENT

Smugglers were not the only Americans to play loose with British authority. In 1652, the colony of Massachusetts actually minted its own coins, defying the ancient principle that only a *sovereign*, or completely independent, government could coin money. The Pine Tree Shillings circulated for more than 30 years before British officials were able to outlaw them.

In 1750, urged on by British iron manufacturers, Parliament passed the *Iron Act*. It forbade the colonists to make any finished iron products. But sizeable forges that were already open continued to operate; and a new mill was founded in Philadelphia within sight, sound, and smell of the governor's home. Nothing was done about it.

The Colonial Assemblies. Such disobedience of British laws shows that, long before the War for Independence, Americans acted independently in many ways. In the corporate colonies, of course, almost all public officials were elected. Connecticut until 1665, Plymouth and Massachusetts until 1691, and Rhode Island until the Revolution were governed like independent commonwealths under the Crown.

In the royal and proprietary colonies, the governors were appointed by the Crown or by the proprietors. However, the governors had to deal with elected assemblies that watched them closely. The members of these bodies insisted that, like Parliament in England, the assemblies possessed the right to rule on all matters involving money —how it was raised through taxes, and how it was spent.

This "power of the purse" is the most important power in government. By exercising it, the colonial assemblies gradually whittled away at the authority of even royal governors. On more than one occasion, assemblies forced governors to approve of their policies by refusing to vote the governors their salaries and the money to keep their houses. Because most colonial governors had come to the colonies from England to make their fortunes, denying them their pay was an extremely effective tactic.

If the Crown had cracked down consistently on the colonials, the trend toward self-government might have been halted, or at least delayed. How-

In colonial America, town meetings were held to discuss local issues. These meetings set the stage for later participatory democracy.

Bacon's Rebellion. The establishment of self-government was not entirely peaceful. For example, in Virginia in 1676, many of the people who had settled in the backcountry rebelled against the Tidewater elite and forced the governor to flee.

The governor was William Berkeley. Although he owned tobacco lands, Berkeley and other Tidewater planters depended increasingly on trade with the Indians. The price of tobacco was low during the 1660s and 1670s, but furs and hides, which the Indians brought into Jamestown, commanded high prices.

During these same years, other Virginians pushed inland to the foothills of the Appalachians. Most of these people were former servants who hoped to build plantations of their own on lands occupied by Indians. Their most prominent leader was Nathaniel Bacon.

Nathaniel Bacon burned Jamestown, Virginia, threatened to hang Governor Berkeley, and demanded that local residents pledge allegiance to him.

ever, the 1600s and 1700s were a time when "the rights of the English" was a popular cry in Great Britain, too. People fighting to increase the power of Parliament at home were not inclined to criticize colonial assemblies for doing the same thing.

Moreover, during the 1650s, when Oliver Cromwell ruled England, the colonies were left on their own, and developed the habit of self-government. During the first half of the eighteenth century, the colonies were so profitable for British merchants that they urged Prime Minister Robert Walpole to do nothing that would disturb prosperity. Walpole's policy was called *salutary* (or healthful) *neglect*. He left the colonies alone.

Discussion Question: Do you agree that the "power of the purse" is the most important power of the government? Defend your position. Is this still the government's most important power? Relate this question to recent appropriations issues that might be in the news.

When the Indians fought back against the invaders, Bacon and others demanded that Governor Berkeley help them defeat the tribes. Berkeley agreed to build a line of defensive forts to protect the pioneers. But he was unwilling to attack the Indians and ruin relations with his fur and hide suppliers.

The forts were not enough for Bacon and his supporters. When the death toll of frontier settlers topped 100, Bacon attacked one tribe on his own and then marched to Jamestown, where he threatened to hang the governor. Berkeley fled across the Chesapeake.

After October 1676, however, the rebellion quickly quieted. Bacon died of a fever and his followers were lost without him. Returning to the colony, Berkeley captured and hanged 23 rebels. The power of the royal governor was confirmed. However, frontier resentments did not die so easily. In almost every colony throughout the colonial period, poorer backcountry settlers were at odds with the wealthier, better-established people who lived near the coasts.

James II and the Dominion of New England.

Another attempt at controlling the colonies occurred in 1685, when Charles II died and was succeeded by his brother, James II. James was a Roman Catholic, which disturbed many Protestants in England and the colonies. However, because he was more than 50 years old and his daughters, Mary and Anne, were both Protestants, they hoped for a short and uneventful reign. After the experience with Oliver Cromwell, few people in England were interested in overthrowing another king.

James's plan for the colonies included combining all the New England colonies plus New York and New Jersey into a single *Dominion of New England*. The Dominion would be ruled by a royal governor, and there would be no elected assemblies.

The Americans did not want to lose their old colonial governments. The people of Massachusetts were devoted to their colony, the people of New Jersey to New Jersey, and so on. The colonists had also become used to having a say in how they were governed. Therefore, they were very uncomfortable with the rule of the Dominion's governor, Sir Edmund Andros.

Sir Edmund Andros was appointed in 1686 by King James II of England to be the Royal Governor of the newly formed Dominion of New England.

Andros was an effective administrator, but was also a tactless person. Since there were no assemblies to vote for taxes, Andros had to raise money by proclamation. The colonists soon began to resist his rule. Andros still tried to impose his will on the colonists, but with no loyal militia and no representative assemblies to work through, his job was impossible.

The Glorious Revolution.

In 1688, a son was born to James II's queen, and was baptized Catholic. Because the English law of succession to the throne gave the eldest son of a monarch priority over all daughters, powerful nobles rebelled. The *Glorious Revolution*, so-called because not a shot was fired, put James II's daughter Mary and her husband William of Orange, a Dutch Protestant, on the English throne.

News of the Glorious Revolution of 1688 was received with celebrations in the colonies. As soon as they heard that James had been overthrown, people in the colonies rebelled. In Maryland, a Protestant planter named John Coode marched on the capital at St. Mary's and imprisoned the

Roman Catholic governor. Because Coode was careful to proclaim his loyalty to William and Mary, he was not punished. In fact, Maryland was taken away from its Roman Catholic proprietors, the Calvert family, and made a royal colony. Only in 1715, when the Calverts became Protestants, was Maryland restored to them.

A wealthy merchant in New York, Jacob Leisler, led a rebellion against the Dominion of New England in that colony. For two years he governed New York with the help of a small army of supporters. However, when a royal representative arrived in New York in 1691, Leisler refused to give up control. After a short battle in March 1691, Leisler was arrested, convicted of treason, and hanged. New York's assembly was restored, but the colony continued as a royal colony.

New Englanders also rebelled. They imprisoned Andros and restored the assemblies of all the New England colonies. Connecticut and Rhode Island regained their charters and remained corporate colonies until independence. Plymouth, however, was judged too small to continue as a separate colony, and became part of Massachusetts.

Massachusetts did not have its charter restored. In 1691, it became a royal colony with a governor appointed by the new king and queen. William and Mary wisely recognized the importance the colonials placed on their elected assemblies. The Massachusetts voters continued to elect representatives who approved all laws dealing with taxation and government spending.

The Rights of British Subjects.

As British subjects, the colonists possessed certain rights that were enjoyed by no other people in the world. According to the *English Bill of Rights*, accepted by William and Mary in 1689 as the price of taking the throne, Parliament (or the elected assemblies in the colonies) had to consent to all laws. Debate in Parliament (and the assemblies) was to be free. That is, a member could not be punished for expressing an opinion.

Everyone had the right to a trial by jury. Judges could not set the bail of an accused law-breaker so high that it amounted to a punishment in itself. All Protestant British subjects had the right to keep arms. The government could not maintain an army during peacetime unless Parliament agreed.

King William III (left) and Queen Mary II (right) were invited to rule England as joint sovereigns by powerful nobles fearful of a future Catholic monarch.

You will recognize many of these rights as part of the United States *Constitution* and Bill of Rights. Indeed, much of our heritage of rights and liberties originated in England.

Limited Suffrage. The Glorious Revolution confirmed the rights of the colonists to choose representatives, but elections were not democratic by our standards. *Limited suffrage* was practiced in the colonies, meaning that not everyone was entitled to vote. Women did not vote because they were rarely heads of households, a requirement in every colony. Blacks, except perhaps for a very few well-to-do free blacks, did not vote. Nor did the few Indians who lived within colonies rather than with their tribes.

In fact, with the exception of Rhode Island, where the property requirement was low, only a minority of free white male heads of households voted. Every colony had a property requirement. A man had to possess a certain number of acres of land or be worth a certain amount of money to be eligible to vote. In most colonies, a person had to own even more property to be eligible for office. Consequently, government was dominated by a comparatively few wealthy families. Moreover, in every colony the inhabitants of the areas that were settled earliest, the Tidewater in the South and the seaports in the North, dominated the colonial assemblies and discriminated against newer arrivals who moved to the West.

New Ethnic Groups. When Nathaniel Bacon led his rebellion in Virginia, it was English colonist versus English colonist. During the 1700s, however, more and more colonials were not English, but members of other ethnic groups. Germans flocked to Pennsylvania, and some western counties of the colony were more German than English.

An even more numerous ethnic group was the Scotch-Irish. These people were originally Scots whom King James I settled in northern Ireland in the early 1600s after he defeated a Catholic army there. However, after Queen Anne was crowned in 1702, Parliament adopted laws that almost wiped out the weaving trade on which the Scotch-Irish depended. Looking for a livelihood, the Scotch-Irish came to America by the thousands and settled in the western parts of Pennsylvania, Maryland, Virginia, and North Carolina.

The Scotch-Irish were independent people with a Presbyterian religion that was as strict as oldtime Massachusetts Puritanism. They wanted to clear the western lands of Indians. Just like Nathaniel Bacon in 1676, they found themselves at odds with the people of the eastern parts of their colonies.

SECTION REVIEW

1. Write a sentence to identify: power of the purse, salutary neglect, Dominion of New England, limited suffrage.

2. Name two ways that the American colonists "played loose" with British authority in the 1600s and 1700s. Give two reasons explaining the Crown's failure to crack down on the continuing movement toward self-government in the American colonies.

3. List the effects of the Glorious Revolution in Maryland, New York, and New England. After the incidents in these places, did the Crown or the colonists prevail? Explain your answer.

4. Why did the English Bill of Rights make English subjects unique in the world? What would it become a model for?

---

4. CONTEST FOR EMPIRE

A factor that had a great effect on life in the English colonies was the French presence in North America. Quebec was founded in 1608, just a year after Jamestown, Virginia. However, the development of *New France*, which was made up of the provinces of Canada and Louisiana (and the French West Indies), was considerably different from the development of the 13 English colonies. The most important difference was size. While the French claims were much larger than English claims, far fewer people lived in New France. By 1713, when New France was more than a century old, the total French population of the colony was about 25,000. At least that many people lived in Pennsylvania alone, and Pennsylvania was but 30 years old. In 1713, more than 400,000 people lived in the 13 English colonies.

It is correct to refer to the colonies as the English colonies prior to 1707 and as the British colonies after that year. Prior to 1707 and the Act of Union, England and Scotland had the same monarch but different laws and parliaments. They joined in 1707. England financed, founded, and claimed the original colonies. After 1707, all belonged to Britain.

The French explorer La Salle traveled south on the Mississippi River and claimed Louisiana for France. Subsequently, La Salle was appointed Viceroy of North America.

Why New France Was Small.

The first reason New France's population grew so slowly was geography. The St. Lawrence River Valley, which was the center of settlement, had soil no better than rocky New England's, and a growing season that was shorter. New France would not be able to support itself or make profits for France as an agricultural colony.

Second, the French kings would not allow religious dissenters to emigrate. The *Huguenots*, Calvinistic Protestants like the English Puritans, showed some interest in going to America. A numerous and energetic people, they might have established large, prosperous colonies of seafarers and traders like Massachusetts and Pennsylvania. But the French kings Louis XIII and Louis XIV were determined that New France be totally Roman Catholic.

However, the Catholic French peasantry did not have the same impulse to emigrate that the English did. Although France's population was larger than England's, France had more land and was less crowded. Good quality land was more abundant. Peasants had not been pushed off the land into squalid cities as much as in England.

The French Crown had to force people to go to New France. They were arrested in the countryside and on the streets for no crime but poverty, and shipped across the Atlantic. Such unwilling emigrants did not make for a contented population. New France remained largely a colony of soldiers, fur trappers, and missionaries.

French Friendship With the Indians.

One advantage of a small population was better relations with the Indians. Whereas English farmers were constantly pushing into the hunting grounds of the Native Americans, the French settlements remained around small forts. Quebec and Montreal were sizeable villages. Other, smaller strategic points were Detroit on the Great Lakes, Vincennes near the Ohio River, and Cahokia and St. Louis on the Mississippi River.

The Hurons (an Iroquois tribe) and the Algonkian Indians willingly traded furs and skins for French textiles, iron goods, tools, and firearms. French Jesuit priests also encouraged friendship with the Indians by their missionary work. The Jesuits underwent severe hardships to spread their faith, but were remarkably successful. Not every tribe of New France embraced Roman Catholicism, but the religion spread quickly.

French-Indian friendship was also sealed by marriage. As in the Spanish Empire, relatively few French women came to America. The male population—soldiers and *trappeurs* (trä-pōōrz'), men who took to the forests to hunt and trap with the Indians—married Indian women.

The Iroquois: Allies of England.

Not every tribe was friendly to the French. In 1609, Samuel de Champlain (shăm-plān') had pleased his Algonkian companions by shooting at a party of Iroquois, who were the Algonkians' enemies. Therefore, when the Dutch founded Fort Orange (Albany, New York), the five Iroquois nations immediately sought an alliance with them in order to take revenge on the French. When the English replaced the Dutch in New York, the Iroquois allied with them.

Missionaries and Explorers.

A priest, Jacques Marquette (mär-kĕt'), became one of New France's greatest explorers. In 1673, along with Ottawa Indians and Louis Joliet (jō'lē-ĕt'), a *coureur du bois* (kōō-rër' dyü bwä'), or runner-of-the-woods, Marquette paddled through the Mackinac Straits to Lake Michigan, and across the lake to the Fox River. The party followed the Fox River and then discovered a short *portage* (a place where canoes are carried from river to river) through the pine forests to the Wisconsin River, which flowed into the Mississippi River.

Marquette and Joliet followed the Mississippi as far south as the mouth of the Arkansas River. When Indians there told them of whites to the south, the two Frenchmen correctly guessed they were Spaniards, who were enemies. They had traversed almost all of the western land that would become British territory in 1763 at a time when no English colonist had yet seen the crest of the Appalachians. They returned up the Mississippi, but Marquette never saw Quebec again. He died quite near the present site of Chicago.

In 1682, Robert Cavelier, Sieur (syōōr) de La Salle, followed the Mississippi to its mouth. This exploration laid the basis for the founding of the second French province in North America, Louisiana. In 1699, Pierre Le Moyne began the series of settlements that became New Orleans.

This 1738 engraving depicts Canadian Indians hunting beaver with rifles. Traditionally, however, the Indians used traps.

World Wars, Colonial Wars.

There was plenty of room in North America for the English and the French. For the most part, the two colonial powers easily avoided one another during the seventeenth century. When war did break out in 1689, the participation of the English colonials was uneven. Because each colony acted independently of the others, it was not unusual for Massachusetts to be fighting the French while Pennsylvania was carrying on a brisk trade with them.

The causes of the three French-English wars between 1689 and 1748 were unrelated to America. The American part of these conflicts was quite minor. The colonists knew this, as was reflected in the names they gave the wars. What in Europe was called the War of the League of Augsburg, which lasted from 1689 to 1697, was known as King William's War in America. The American name for the War of the Spanish Succession (1702–1713) was Queen Anne's War. The War of the Austrian Succession (1740–1748) was called King George's War in the colonies. It was almost as if the Americans were saying that these wars were none of their business—that they belonged to the Europeans.

Research Assignment: The Iroquois Indians became British allies and would play an important part in upcoming wars in North America. Assign a report on the Iroquois, detailing their way of life, where they lived, and their experiences with Europeans.

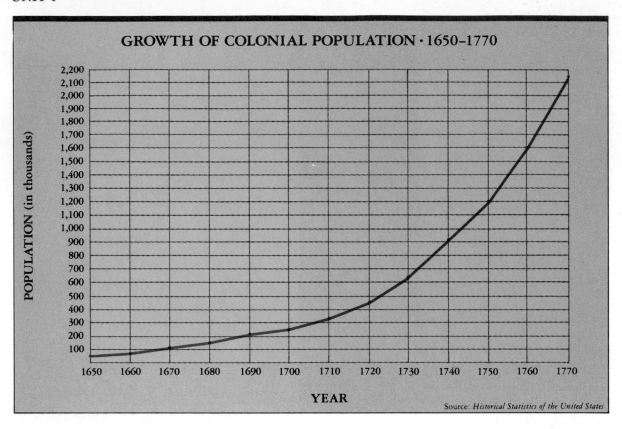

GROWTH OF COLONIAL POPULATION · 1650–1770

POPULATION (in thousands)

YEAR

Source: *Historical Statistics of the United States*

King William's War. The cause of King William's War was a long-standing rivalry between King William, who also ruled the Netherlands, and Louis XIV of France. In America the hostilities began when a few French soldiers and Algonkian and Huron Indians attacked frontier settlements in New York, New Hampshire, and Maine (then part of Massachusetts).

There were no large pitched battles between armies in America. The French called the raid-and-run style of fighting *petit guerre* (pə-tē′ gär), or little war, and had learned it from the Indians.

Massachusetts ships and troops helped a British fleet capture the important French stronghold of Port Royal in Acadia, as the French called Nova Scotia. However, because English armies had been defeated in Europe, Port Royal was returned to France at the peace conference in 1697. The people of Massachusetts were not happy about the return of Port Royal because French privateers constantly harassed their merchant ships and fishing boats. But King William had not fought the war to serve colonial interests.

Queen Anne's War. When the King of Spain died in 1700 without leaving any clear heirs to the throne, Louis XIV tried to get the Spanish throne for his nephew. When Austria, England's ally, tried to stop Louis from uniting Spain and France, England declared war on France again.

This time, southerners who had taken no part in King William's War were in the thick of the fight. Although the South Carolinians had developed a thriving fur and hide trade with southeastern Indians and competed with the French and Spanish on the Gulf of Mexico, the most powerful tribes in the area, the Creeks and Cherokees, sided with the French. The South Carolinians had enraged them by raids against them to recapture runaway slaves. The South Carolinians fought one major battle with the Indians and had many skirmishes.

In the North, the French and their Indian allies carried raids deeper into New England than ever before. In 1704, they raided and nearly destroyed Deerfield, Massachusetts, a prosperous farm town on the Connecticut River. A New England fleet

Discussion Question: In what ways did the colonies behave like independent states? Include the facts that they had their own separate government and charter, money, laws, militia.

again captured Port Royal, and this time it remained English.

The Long Peace: 1713–1739.

During the long peace following Queen Anne's War, France built its chain of trading posts up the St. Lawrence River, around the Great Lakes, and down the Mississippi. The English colonies expanded during these years, too. But, being farmers rather than trappers, the line of settlement moved more slowly. Instead of striking boldly into the wilderness, colonial Americans cleared forest little by little. Once a region was developed, however, it was firmly joined to the older parts of the colonies.

It was also during the long peace that Robert Walpole dominated English politics. Walpole's theory of government was to leave well enough alone. Because the colonies were returning huge profits to British merchants, Walpole ignored increasing violations of British trade laws. When his constituents complained, Walpole acted. But once the fuss died down, he again ignored the violations.

For example, during the early 1730s, British sugar growers in the West Indies protested that New England merchants were buying French and Spanish sugar and molasses because it was cheaper than their own products. Parliament enacted the *Molasses Act* of 1733, placing a high *duty*, or import tax, on all sugar and molasses bought outside the empire. If New England merchants had obeyed the law, they would have been ruined.

But they did not obey it. They bribed customs officials to record the illegal molasses as originating in the British West Indies, and therefore not taxable. Because Walpole's approach to government spread to the colonies, the bribes were almost always accepted. Another example was the Iron Act of 1750. The colonists were forbidden to compete with the English iron manufacturers, but the law was allowed to die quietly.

King George's War.

In 1740, a woman, Maria Theresa, became Empress of Austria. According to traditional Austrian law, a woman could not wear the imperial crown. But before Maria Theresa's father died, he persuaded every important European ruler to accept his daughter's right to be empress. In truth, she proved to be one of Austria's greatest rulers.

However, the King of Prussia (in northern Germany), thought he could expand Prussian territory at Austria's expense, and invaded Austria. France was Prussia's ally and England backed Austria. Once again all Europe was at war.

In the colonies the conflict was called King George's War. Fighting flickered along the New England and New York frontier. There was only one major action involving colonials. On June 17, 1745, Massachusetts troops won the single greatest military victory of colonial history to that time by capturing the French fortress of Louisbourg.

After the French lost Port Royal in 1713, they built another, stronger fortress at Louisbourg to provide an Atlantic port for New France. The fort was thought to be invincible. But in 1745, an army of 4,000 New Englanders surrounded Louisbourg, intending to starve the French out of the fort. Finally, hungry and with no hope of a French fleet arriving in time, the commander surrendered. It was an amazing victory. A force of colonial troops had defeated a professional French force.

The joy in Massachusetts was short-lived. In the Treaty of Aix-La-Chapelle (ĕks′lä′shä-pĕl′) in 1748, England traded Louisbourg for Madras, India, which had been lost to a French army. Parliament reimbursed Massachusetts for its efforts, but there was no way to bring back men who lost their lives in the war. The colonists began to realize that the English were not really concerned about their problems. Then, soon after the treaty was signed, England and France began preparing for another war. This war would decide who would rule North America, and would create a split between England and the American colonies.

SECTION REVIEW

1. Write a sentence to identify: Marquette and Joliet, La Salle, petit guerre, Port Royal, Louisbourg.

2. Give three reasons why New France's population grew much more slowly than that of the 13 British colonies.

3. French and English colonists opposed each other in extensions of three European wars between 1689 and 1748. By what names were each of these wars called?

CHAPTER REVIEW

TIME LINE

- 1600
- 1610 — Founding of Quebec (1608)
- 1620
- 1630 — Virginia becomes a royal colony (1624)
- First Navigation Act (1660)
- 1640 — Marquette and Joliet explore Mississippi (1673)
- 1650 — Bacon's Rebellion (1676)
- La Salle navigates the Mississippi to its mouth (1682)
- 1660 — King James II crowned (1685)
- 1670 — Dominion of New England (1685)
- Glorious Revolution (1688)
- 1680 — Massachusetts becomes royal colony (1691)
- 1690 — King William's War (1689–1697)
- 1700 — Peace conference returns Port Royal to French (1697)
- 1710 — Queen Anne crowned (1702)
- Queen Anne's War (1702–1713)
- 1720 — Treaty of Utrecht (1713)
- 1730 — Molasses Act (1733)
- 1740 — Surrender of Louisbourg (1745)
- King George's War (1740–1748)
- 1750 — Treaty of Aix-La-Chapelle (1748)

1. In what year did American colonists win a great victory over the French?
2. What European wars were fought in part in North America, and when was each war fought?
3. When was the first attempt made by the British Parliament to control the commerce of the American colonies?

SKILLS STRATEGY

SLAVE POPULATION IN THE NORTHERN AND SOUTHERN COLONIES-SELECTED YEARS

SLAVES (in thousands) — vertical axis: 25, 50, 75, 100, 125, 150, 175, 200, 225, 250, 275, 300

YEARS — horizontal axis: 1670, 1700, 1730, 1750

SOUTHERN / NORTHERN

Historical Statistics of the United States

LINE GRAPHS

Graphs show relationships between sets of data. On *line graphs*, one set of numbers appears on the left side of the graph (the *vertical axis*). Another set of numbers appears along the bottom of the graph (the *horizontal axis*). Points connected by a line refer to both a numeral on the horizontal axis and a numeral on the vertical axis. To decide what each point represents, read down from the point to the numeral listed on the horizontal axis, and then read across from the point to the numeral on the vertical axis. For points that fall between the lines on the graph, you must estimate. Compare the growth of the slave population in the South between 1670 and 1750 with the growth in the North during those years. Then compare the total slave populations in those two years.

APPLYING SKILLS

Use the graph above to answer these questions.

1. Approximately how many slaves lived in the North in 1750? How many were in the South?
2. Between which years did the number of slaves in the South increase from 20,000 to over 200,000?

Making Connections: Review the questions and topics presented in the Making Connections section at the opening of this chapter. Present students with the idea that although the colonies

UNIT 1 TEST

CHAPTER SURVEY

In a few sentences, summarize the content of the chapter from which these terms come, and write a sentence to identify *one* of the terms.

1. *Chapter 1*: The Inca, League of the Iroquois, the Indies, Prince Henry the Navigator, conquistador.
2. *Chapter 2*: Junipero Serra, viceroy, *Golden Hind*, Roanoke, John Smith.
3. *Chapter 3*: Great Migration, blue law, Fundamental Constitutions of Carolina, Society of Friends, The Holy Experiment.
4. *Chapter 4*: enumerated article, Middle Passage, Dominion of New England, Marquette and Joliet, Louisbourg.

TEXT REVIEW

5. Who were the first settlers of the continents we call North and South America? What theory explains how they arrived?
6. Name one ancient Indian civilization that developed in Central or South America, and briefly describe its culture.
7. Identify the European country that took the lead in exploring the world. Explain why this country did not concentrate exploration and colonization in the Americas.
8. Give reasons for the use of the word *Indians* to name the groups of people who first inhabited the Americas.
9. What countries were able to claim lands in the Americas because of the explorations of the following men: Verrazano, Columbus, Cabot, Ponce de Leon, Cartier, Cortez, Pizarro, Coronado.
10. Identify the Spanish Armada. Describe what happened to it, and how Europe was affected by this event.
11. List at least one colony founded in America by each of these countries: England, France, the Netherlands, Sweden.
12. List the English colonies that later became the first states of the United States.
13. Discuss the status of slavery in the English colonies before the American Revolution.

14. Define *mercantilism*. Which two groups of English colonies opposed mercantilist practices? Why did they oppose the practices?

CRITICAL THINKING

15. In a three-column chart, show the areas of the Americas settled by the English, the Spanish, and the French.
16. Put yourself in the place of an American Indian whose land is being settled by Europeans. Explain how your viewpont about this would differ from that of the Europeans.
17. Trace religious tolerance in the United States to principles or practices in the American colonies.

SKILLS REVIEW

18. List these events in order: Dutch settle Manhattan Island; Tenochtitlán built; James Oglethorpe founds Georgia; Columbus lands at San Salvador; King William's, Queen Anne's, and King George's wars; Jamestown founded; Puritans found Massachusetts Bay Colony.
19. The following outline is incorrect and incomplete. Keep the first head, "Some Cities in New England." Decide what organizing feature should precede this head. Then correct the outline and add at least a *B* section to it.

    Some Cities in New England
    A. Providence was founded in Rhode Island Colony
      (a) founded in 1636
      (b) Roger Williams was its founder.
      (c) he founded it after disagreeing with Massachusetts Puritan leaders
20. Use the information in the table to construct a line graph showing the rise in population in the 13 English colonies from 1660 to 1750.

Year	Population
1660	75,058
1670	111,935
1700	250,888
1750	1,170,760

were much more different in many ways than alike, the seeds of discontent that were beginning to sprout in this period served as a unifying factor for the colonies.

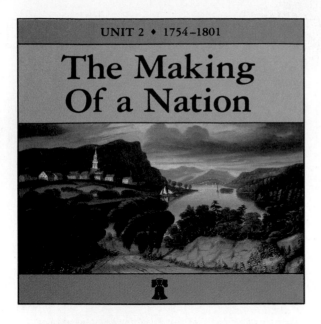

UNIT 2 ♦ 1754–1801

The Making Of a Nation

Unit 2 Overview

Unit 2 begins with an account of the war in which the colonists helped England expel the French from North America, then quarreled constantly with England about the right of Parliament to tax the colonies. The unit continues with the colonists' declaration of their independence from Great Britain; the successful revolution that made independence a reality; the postwar struggle for power between the state governments and the weak national government under the Articles of Confederation; the writing of the Constitution, a plan for a new, strong national government; and the attempts of the first two presidents—George Washington and John Adams—to make the plan work.

Basic Unit Concepts

1. The American colonists' resistance to British tax laws and the resulting revolution were based on the principle that Parliament did not have the right to tax them and that only the colonial legislatures had that right.
2. The Declaration of Independence was a brilliant statement of the natural rights of all people.
3. Motivated by the ineffectiveness of the Confederation representatives of the states wrote the Constitution.
4. The Constitution provided a workable structure for strong national government with certain powers for the states.
5. After the ratification of the Constitution, George Washington and Congress worked successfully to give reality to the government blueprint in the Constitution.
6. Constitutional issues raised during the terms of the first three presidents were loose vs. strict construction of the Constitution, states' rights to nullify federal laws, and the principle of judicial review of state and federal laws.

Chapter 5: The Quarrel With Great Britain (1754–1774)

In Chapter 5, students learn how the colonists helped England drive France out of North America in the French and Indian War. They follow the increasingly bitter and violent

disputes between England and the colonies over the question of who had the right to tax the colonies—the British Parliament or the colonial legislatures. They witness the Boston Tea Party that provoked Britain's Intolerable Acts which, with the Quebec Act, led to the convening of the First Continental Congress.

Features
Movers and Shapers: Benjamin Franklin (page 99)
Going to the Source: An excerpt from Benjamin Franklin's *Autobiography* (page 104)

Learning Objectives
History Generalizations. Students will gain knowledge that supports the following generalizations:
1. In the French and Indian War, the American colonists joined with Great Britain in attempting to break French power in the Ohio Territory.
2. In the Treaty of Paris, France gave up Canada to England.
3. In the aftermath of the war, Great Britain had to find a way to govern French Canadians and the Indian allies of France.
4. Once the French threat ended, many of the American colonists felt more confident and independent.
5. Because Great Britain was on the verge of bankruptcy after the war, Parliament imposed a series of tax laws on the American colonies.
6. Colonial resistance —violent and nonviolent—was based on the principle that, since they were not represented in Parliament, Parliament had no right to tax them.
7. American resistance culminated in the convening of the First Continental Congress one step away from an open break with Great Britain.

Study Skills. In addition to the three skills noted in Chapter 1 which are standard to every chapter, students will:
1. recognize the function of the title, legend, compass rose, and scale of a physical map.
2. write a paragraph contrasting two points of view.
3. relate graphic materials to the text of the chapter.
4. practice these **critical thinking skills**: generating questions about materials to be read, recognizing propaganda, and recognizing bias.

Chapter 6: Independence Declared (1774–1783)

In this chapter, students learn why the delegates to the First Continental Congress loyally toasted King George III after demanding the repeal of the Intolerable Acts, when and where the first shots of the Revolution were fired, and how Thomas Paine influenced the Second Continental Congress to declare independence. Students are given the opportunity to analyze the Declaration of Independence in detail and to follow the ups and downs of George Washington and the Continental Army on their way to the final victory at Yorktown and the achievement of the goal of independence.

Features
Going to the Source: Patrick Henry's "Liberty or Death" speech (page 122)
Going to the Source: Excerpt from Thomas Paine's *The Crisis* (page 126)
Text of the Declaration of Independence (pages 130–131)

Learning Objectives ***History Generalizations.*** Students will gain knowledge that supports the following generalizations:

1. Following Parliament's issuance of the Intolerable Acts, the First Continental Congress appealed to the monarch to permit colonials to make laws for Americans.
2. As a result of Great Britain's refusal to compromise, open warfare between Americans and British troops began in New England and New York.
3. While the initial battles of the War for Independence were being fought, Patriot delegates to the Second Continental Congress declared the independence of the American colonies from Great Britain, but not without objection.
4. With the crucial help of France, the outnumbered American Continental Army won the War for Independence.
5. Despite important inconsistencies, the Declaration of Independence was a brilliant statement of the natural rights of all people, including the right to govern themselves.

Study Skills. In addition to the three skills noted in Chapter 1 which are standard to every chapter, students will:
1. write a paragraph, tracing a given development chronologically.
2. gain information by using a map grid.
3. relate graphic materials to the text of the chapter.
4. practice these **critical thinking skills**: generating questions about materials to be read, recognizing propaganda, determining possible effects.

Chapter 7: Molding a Nation (1783–1789)

In Chapter 7, students discover how the newly independent Americans caused the ineffectiveness of the national government under the Articles of Confederation by insisting upon strong state governments. They learn that a Constitutional Convention was called six years after the Confederation government was established to write a plan for a new government—the United States Constitution—and they follow the sometimes thorny path of ratification. Students examine the complete text of the Constitution.

Features
Movers and Shapers: Robert Morris and Haym Salomon (page 155)
Profiles of the Presidency: George Washington (page 161)
Going to the Source: Excerpt from Thomas Jefferson's "Letter on the Constitution" (page 166)

Learning Objectives
History Generalizations. Students will gain knowledge that supports the following generalizations:
1. Although they formed a nation in many senses of the word after declaring independence, Americans were not united politically in any effective way.
2. In forming thirteen new state governments, the people insisted on written constitutions listing their rights and the powers of the state governments.
3. The national government under the Articles of Confederation was deliberately deprived of many powers.
4. Land ceded to the national government by the states was organized into the Northwest Territory, opened to American settlers, and parts of it eventually became new states.
5. Moved by the ineffectiveness of the Confederation, representatives from twelve states wrote the Constitution.
6. Although some people opposed the Constitution, it was ratified by all thirteen states within a few years.
7. The Constitution provided a workable structure for a strong national government and reserved states' powers.

Study Skills: Besides the three skills noted in Chapter 1, which are standard to every chapter, students will:
1. write a paragraph, arranging the supporting sentences in the order of importance.
2. use a primary source (the Bill of Rights) to gain knowledge.
3. relate graphic materials to the text of the chapter.
4. practice these **critical thinking skills**: generating questions about materials to be read, organizing information, classifying information in a two-level outline.

Chapter 8: The Federalist Era (1789–1801)

In this chapter, students observe how President George Washington and John Adams aided by Congress set the course for the new nation, using the Constitution as their guide. They learn what contributions Alexander Hamilton, Thomas Jefferson, and John Marshall made to the new government, and how the different political views of Hamilton and Jefferson resulted in the formation of the Federalist and (Democratic) Republican parties. They witness the growing assurance of leaders in dealing with challenges from within the country and from abroad. Finally, they watch the decline of Federalists and the rise of Republicans.

Features
Going to the Source: George Washington's *Farewell Address* (page 201)
Profiles of the Presidency: John Adams (page 204)
American Ingenuity (pages 208–209)

Learning Objectives
History Generalizations. Students will gain knowledge that supports the following generalizations:
1. After the ratification of the Constitution, George Washington and Congress worked together to give reality to the government blueprint in the Constitution.
2. Through the efforts of Alexander Hamilton, the new United States was put on a sound financial basis.
3. At home, the new national government proved its strength by passing and enforcing the Tariff of 1789 and putting down a rebellion over another national tax law.
4. Despite their best efforts, leaders of the new government were forced by circumstances to develop a foreign policy.
5. The differing political philosophies of Alexander Hamilton and Thomas Jefferson gave rise to the first two political parties in the United States—The Federalists and the (Democratic) Republicans.
6. Federalist influence on governmental policy had declined by the end of President John Adams's administration, except through the work of John Marshall and other Federalist judges appointed by Adams.
7. With the election of Thomas Jefferson, Republican political thinking directed government policies.
8. Important Constitutional issues were raised during the administrations of the first three Presidents: loose vs. strict construction of the Constitution, the states' right to nullify federal laws, the principle of judicial review.

Study Skills. In addition to the three skills noted in Chapter 1 which are standard to every chapter, students will:
1. summarize information in a scratch outline.
2. use a scratch outline to write a summary paragraph.
3. relate graphic materials to the text of the chapter.
4. practice these **critical thinking skills**: generating questions, classifying information in an outline.

CHAPTER 5

THE QUARREL WITH GREAT BRITAIN

1754–1774

*Every revolution was once a thought in one man's mind,
and when the same thought occurs to another man, it is the key to
that era.*   RALPH WALDO EMERSON

Making Connections. In 1754, the American colonies were drawn into one more worldwide war between France and England. The English colonists helped fight the French and won some major victories. But after the war, England had to pay for maintaining its huge empire, and began to assess heavy taxes on the American colonies. The colonists resented these taxes and sometimes resisted them forcefully.

In this chapter you will learn:
- Who first proposed a plan to unite the colonies
- How the map of North America was redrawn in 1763
- Why the colonists said Parliament had no right to tax them
- Why Americans boycotted British goods
- Who led a group of Americans to destroy a cargo of British tea
- How British laws for Quebec pushed Americans toward a break with England

You have read that European wars sometimes spilled over into North America, and that the English colonists in America willingly fought and died for England. As you read, note how the American colonists became less and less willing to help England after the French and Indian War.

Sections
1. French and Indian War
2. The Aftermath of War
3. Quarrel Over Taxation
4. The Road to Revolution

1. FRENCH AND INDIAN WAR

In 1754, France and Great Britain went to war again in North America. However, the *French and Indian War* (known in Europe as the Seven Years' War) demonstrated an important shift in how Europeans viewed North America. For the first time, the European governments decided that the war in North America required as much attention as the war in Europe. Under a new and energetic prime minister, William Pitt, Great Britain intended to concentrate its energies in North America and break French influence there.

The Ohio Territory. Today, the place where the Allegheny and Monongahela rivers join to form the Ohio River is downtown Pittsburgh, Pennsylvania. In 1754, the site was woodland wilderness. But every Indian and frontiersman who wandered that country knew it was a strategic location. With rivers serving as the highways of travel and trade in the interior of America, whoever controlled that juncture of the three rivers controlled the whole Ohio River Valley.

The river junction was within the boundaries of Virginia's 1609 charter, which gave the colony all the land west and northwest of the seaboard settlements. Therefore, Virginia's Lieutenant

Paul Revere, an American silversmith, made an engraving (right) depicting the Boston Massacre of March 5, 1770. In that action, Samuel Gray, Samuel Maverick, James Caldwell, Crispus Attucks, and Patrick Carr were killed by British Redcoats.

Engrav'd Printed & Sold by PAUL REVERE

Skills Review: Have students reinforce the knowledge learned in the previous Skills Strategy. Have students use their knowledge of graphs to make a graph illustrating some aspect of the information presented in this chapter. They should explain the graph's usefulness. If your school has computer facilities, have students use them in constructing the graphs.

97

Governor Robert Dinwiddie summoned an ambitious 22-year-old surveyor named George Washington, assigned him 150 men, and told him to secure the area from French threat. When Washington arrived at the junction, however, he discovered that the French were a step ahead of him, having already built Fort Duquesne there. After a minor skirmish, Washington set up Fort Necessity nearby and waited for reinforcements from Virginia. Before they arrived, his stockade was forced to surrender. After a gentlemanly discussion, Washington led his troops home.

Ben Franklin Proposes a Union. Other colonies were concerned about growing French power in the Ohio Valley. They agreed completely on the importance of keeping the French out. While George Washington was fencing with the French far to the west, Benjamin Franklin of Philadelphia was trying to get all the colonies to unify to fight the war that everyone knew was coming.

Franklin was the best-known American of his time. He owned a printshop in Philadelphia, and between 1732 and 1757 wrote and published *Poor Richard's Almanack*, probably the second most-read book in the colonies after the Bible. He was also active in politics, and worked hard for the intensive settlement of Indian lands in western Pennsylvania.

Ben Franklin was regarded as a wise man. Thus, when a meeting of the colonies was called in Albany, New York, to firm up the alliance with the Iroquois and plan for a united war effort against the French, the delegates listened intently to what Franklin proposed.

Franklin explained his idea, which came to be called the *Albany Plan of Union*. It called for each colony to elect delegates to an assembly that would manage relations with the Indians and control all land taken in the impending war with France. The assembly would have the power to levy taxes on the colonists to finance itself. King George II would appoint a presiding officer with veto power over the assembly's actions.

In calling for union, Franklin was, as usual, ahead of his time. The colonies, however, rejected the plan because they wanted no outside assembly to control any of their actions, and they did not want to give up their claims to western land.

Colonel George Washington fought under General Braddock during the French and Indian War.

Class Activity: Using the special sections on pages 99 and 104 of this chapter, examine the information by and about Ben Franklin and discuss how primary and secondary source materials differ.

MOVERS AND SHAPERS

Benjamin Franklin

The extraordinary life of Benjamin Franklin (1706–1790) is perhaps unmatched in the annals of American history. In a lifetime studded with accomplishments, he was the prototype of the man of humble origins who rose to international fame. The Boston-born son of a soapmaker, at the age of 12 he learned the printing trade from his brother James, launching a career that might have satisfied any normal citizen. For Franklin, it was only the first of many.

Starting at the ripe young age of 20, the industrious and resourceful Franklin scored a series of successes that brought him wealth and fame. His print business got the contract for Pennsylvania's paper currency. He started the *Pennsylvania Gazette* and began writing his celebrated *Poor Richard's Almanack,* a book of wise sayings extolling the virtues of hard work, thrift, and honesty.

Franklin's dizzying variety of interests included the establishment of a circulating library, a philosophical society, and a fire company; he was post master of Philadelphia, and he started a college that later became the University of Pennsylvania. In his spare time he organized a militia to defend the city, and he drew up plans to improve the paving and lighting of city streets. A prolific inventor and internationally known scientist, he was elected to England's prestigious Royal Society.

Franklin became increasingly involved in the growing tensions between the colonies and England. He vigorously opposed the Stamp Act of 1765, and made a dramatic appearance before the House of Commons in 1766, arguing for American self-government. From 1765 to 1775, he lived in London, acting as agent for Pennsylvania, Georgia, New Jersey, and Massachusetts, and writing articles about the American cause.

Returning home at the age of 70, Franklin plunged into numerous activities in support of American independence, the most notable being his work in drafting the Declaration of Independence. In October 1776, Franklin sailed across to France to enlist French aid in the American cause. For seven years he used his immense talents and prestige to arrange for French financial support for America. Single-handedly, he obtained desperately needed money and supplies for the fledgling nation. With John Adams and John Jay, he signed the Treaty of Paris in 1783 that guaranteed the independence of the new nation. In his eightieth year, the indefatigable Franklin wrote the last part of his *Autobiography,* summing up a life as rich as it was full.

Franklin's famous lightning experiment is shown here.

Research Assignment: You may choose to follow up on the preceding Class Activity by having students compare similar incidents in Franklin's autobiography to secondary accounts of the same incidents.

The War Goes Badly. In the spring of 1755, General Edward Braddock and 1,400 British soldiers arrived in Virginia. He was joined by George Washington, eager to avenge his defeat at Fort Necessity, and 450 Virginians. The British were well-trained and Braddock was an able commander. But Braddock was unprepared for the wilderness tactics of the French and Indians. Ambushes, little skirmishes followed by retreat, and sniping from hidden positions were new to him.

The British and Virginians set out to restore British power in the Ohio River Valley, but the expedition turned into a disaster. Just a few miles from Fort Duquesne, a smaller French and Indian force surprised and defeated them. Braddock himself was killed, and George Washington again led a humiliated army back to Virginia.

Until 1757, the war went against Great Britain.

In Europe, where war was declared in 1756, French armies marched deep into the lands of Britain's new ally, Prussia. British warships were defeated in the Mediterranean Sea. In the forests of North America the French and their Indian allies raided frontier settlements at will, tightening their grip on the inland waterways.

In October 1755, the British secured their hold on Nova Scotia by forcing 6,000 French farmers and fishermen from their homes. Some of these people settled in Louisiana and were called *Cajuns*. (Cajun is a slurred form of the word *Acadian*, the French name for a Nova Scotian.)

William Pitt Takes Charge. Then, at the war's darkest hour, the English government changed hands. The extraordinary William Pitt became prime minister and committed England to

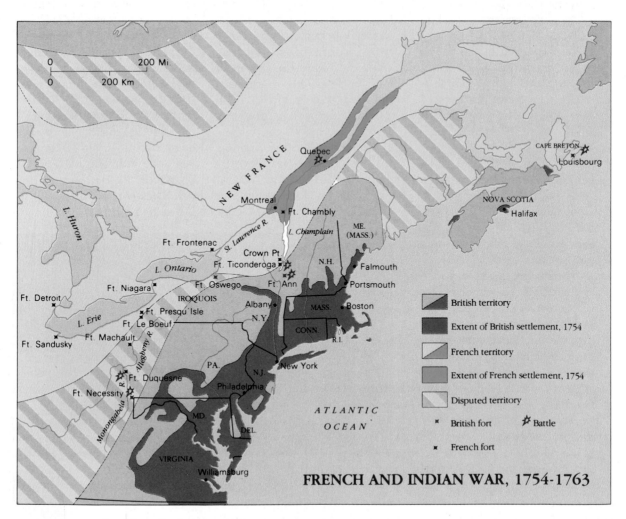

FRENCH AND INDIAN WAR, 1754-1763

	British territory	
	Extent of British settlement, 1754	
	French territory	
	Extent of French settlement, 1754	
	Disputed territory	

× British fort ☆ Battle

× French fort

Research Assignment: Have students write a report contrasting the different techniques of fighting employed in the Seven Years War in Europe and the French and Indian War here. (The first of these featured more traditional open field combat, the latter more guerilla tactics). Why

William Pitt, the British prime minister, assigned General James Wolfe the task of capturing the French city of Quebec. Wolfe launched a bold surprise attack, and his troops captured the city. However, Wolfe died in the attack.

winning the war. He appointed brilliant, young James Wolfe to command the largest British force in North America and instructed him to attack Louisbourg, on Cape Breton Island off the coast of Nova Scotia. In July 1758, with 9,000 Redcoats (as British soldiers were called) and 500 colonials, mostly from Massachusetts, General Wolfe captured the French fortress and hatched the plan that brought him both fame and death.

Wolfe Wins Canada. Wolfe thought of New France as if it were a tree. His idea was that the tree's roots—the source of French power in America—was the city of Quebec. The weakness of earlier British strategy, Wolfe insisted, was that instead of striking at these roots, the army had merely picked away at outlying posts such as Fort Duquesne and Louisbourg. Wolfe reasoned that he could fell the tree (French lands in North America) by striking at its roots.

But Quebec would not fall easily. The town was situated at the foot of high cliffs, and was defended by a fortress above. An army staging a frontal attack would be exposed to the fort's cannon, and would be thrown back with ease.

There was another possibility. Wolfe's scouts discovered a path up the cliffs by which, under cover of night, the whole army could climb the heights to the Plains of Abraham behind the city. However, this plan risked disaster, for if the British were defeated there, no retreat was possible. They would be wiped out or captured.

Wolfe did not hesitate to take such a chance. At dawn on September 12, 1759, his 3,000 troops were arrayed in ranks on the Plains, ready to challenge the French.

The French commander, Louis de Montcalm, should have had an edge. With 4,500 soldiers and a strong base, he could afford to take his time. But Montcalm panicked and sent his army out to fight without proper preparation. Within moments, the French suffered 1,400 casualties, including Mont-

these differences existed should be discussed in the report. Included should be tactics used by the Indians.

101

A general at the age of 30, James Wolfe proved to be a brilliant military strategist.

calm. Wolfe was killed, too, but Quebec fell to the British; and the next year, all of Canada surrendered. As Wolfe had calculated, French morale and strength collapsed after the fall of Quebec.

The Treaty of Paris. The treaty ending the French and Indian War was signed in Paris in 1763. Under its terms, the map of North America was completely redrawn. Spain, France's ally, gave up Florida to Great Britain. As compensation for this loss of territory, Spain received Louisiana from France.

France also surrendered all of Canada to Great Britain. Nowhere on the North American continent did the French flag continue to fly. France retained only the sugar islands of Martinique and Guadeloupe, which had been captured during the war, and two small islands off the coast of Nova Scotia.

Some Britons wanted to keep the sugar islands and return Canada to France. They argued that Martinique and Guadeloupe produced a profitable commodity, while Canada was mostly wilderness populated by Indians who had been enemies of

NORTH AMERICA IN 1754

NORTH AMERICA IN 1763

Discussion Question: Did Britain do the right thing by taking Canada? Affirmative answers should include the following: no need to fight France again; long-term economic benefits. Negative answers should include the following: French would check on U.S.; short-term economic benefits in Caribbean; France would have given Canada up eventually.

Benjamin Franklin—American patriot, politician, diplomat, scholar, writer, publisher, scientist, and inventor—was respected by people on both sides of the Atlantic. In the painting above, he is seen addressing the Lords of the Privy Council in London.

CHAPTER 5

Great Britain for more than a century. A few people even raised another point: the American colonies would remain loyal to Great Britain only as long as Americans felt threatened by the French.

But the new British prime minister, the Earl of Bute, wanted to take Canada. He was supported by Benjamin Franklin, then in England as an agent for Pennsylvania. Franklin convinced many members of the British Parliament that, in the long run, the vast Canadian forests would be far more valuable than the tiny West Indian islands. Many of the people to whom he spoke were interested in speculating in American land and preferred keeping Canada. In the end, Great Britain decided to keep Canada with its huge potential riches, rather than have the immediate benefit of the sugar islands.

SECTION REVIEW

1. Write a sentence to identify: William Pitt, Fort Duquesne, General Braddock.

2. Name Benjamin Franklin's 1754 proposal, and explain what threat to the colonies it was meant to eliminate.

3. Why was the junction of the Ohio, Monongahela, and Allegheny rivers so important?

4. Explain the connection between the city of Quebec and General Wolfe's theory of New France as a tree.

5. Explain this statement: "Under the terms of the Treaty of Paris, the map of North America was completely redrawn."

103

GOING TO THE SOURCE

I have been the more particular in this description of my journey, and shall be so of my first entry into that city, that you may in your mind compare such unlikely beginnings with the figure I have since made there. I was in my working dress, my best clothes coming round by sea. I was dirty from my being so long in the boat; my pockets were stuffed out with shirts and stockings; and I knew no one, nor where to look for lodging. . . .

I walked toward the top of the street, gazing about, still in Market Street, where I met a boy with bread. I had often made a meal of dry bread, and, inquiring where he had bought it, I went immediately to the baker's he directed me to. I asked for biscuits, meaning such as we had at Boston; that sort, it seems, was not made in Philadelphia. I then asked for a threepenny loaf, and was told they had none. Not knowing the different prices nor the names of the different sorts of bread, I told him give me threepenny worth of any sort. He gave me, accordingly, three great puffy rolls. I was surprised at the quantity, but took it, and, having no room in my pockets, walked off with a roll under each arm and eating the other. Thus I went up Market Street as far as Fourth Street, passing by the door of Mr. Read, my future wife's father; when she, standing at the door, saw me, and thought I made, as I certainly did, a most awkward, ridiculous appearance. Then I turned and went down Chestnut Street and part of Walnut Street, eating my roll all the way, and coming round, found myself again at Market Street wharf, near the boat I came in, to which I went for a draft of the river water. . . .

Thus refreshed, I walked again up the street, which by this time had many clean-dressed people in it, who were all walking the same

> *Thus I went up Market Street as far as Fourth Street, passing by the door of Mr. Read, my future wife's father; when she, standing at the door, saw me, and thought I made, as I certainly did, a most awkward, ridiculous appearance.*
>
> BENJAMIN FRANKLIN,
> *AUTOBIOGRAPHY*

way. I joined them, and thereby was led into the great meetinghouse of the Quakers near the market. I sat down among them, and, after looking round awhile and hearing nothing said, being very drowsy through labor and want of rest the preceding night, I fell fast asleep, and continued so till the meeting broke up, when someone was good enough to rouse me. This, therefore, was the first house I was in, or slept in, in Philadelphia.

I then walked down toward the river, and, looking in the faces of everyone, I met a young Quaker man, whose countenance pleased me, and, accosting him, requested he would tell me where a stranger would get a lodging. . . . And he conducted me to the Crooked Billet in Water Street. There I got a dinner; and, while I was eating, several questions were asked me, as from my youth and appearance I was suspected of being a runaway.

After dinner, my sleepiness return'd, and being shown to a bed, I lay down without undressing . . . and slept soundly till next morning. Then I made myself as tidy as I could, and went to Andrew Bradford the printer's. I found in the shop the old man his father, whom I had seen at New York. . . . He introduc'd me to his son, who receiv'd me civilly . . . but told me he did not at present want a hand, being lately suppli'd with one; but there was another printer in town . . . who, perhaps, might employ me; if not, I should be welcome to lodge at his house. . . .

An entertaining account of life in colonial Pennsylvania was written by Benjamin Franklin. This passage from his Autobiography *describes his first impressions of Philadelphia in 1723 as a 17-year-old youth.*

Colonials on the southern frontier had learned long ago that the most effective way of combating the Indians was to destroy their villages and crops.

2. THE AFTERMATH OF WAR

The war had nearly bankrupted England. Pitt's government had borrowed heavily to win the great empire. More urgent was the challenge of peacefully governing the French in Canada and their Indian allies who lived in the area around the Great Lakes. Great Britain could not exile all of the French Canadians, as they had the Acadians. Somehow, their loyalty must be won.

The Indians presented an even more serious problem. They had not, like the French, been decisively defeated. Their homes were in small forest settlements that few Britons or colonials had ever seen. The tribes had not surrendered or signed the Peace of Paris. West of the Appalachians, the Indians waited to see what their old enemies would do.

The Canadian Problem. The French Canadians were Roman Catholics, members of a faith that was generally disliked in England and the colonies. In Great Britain, Catholics were denied some civil rights, including the right to vote. The Americans generally allowed all people to worship as they pleased. But there was a big difference between tolerating small numbers of Roman Catholics in Maryland, Philadelphia, and New York City, and coming to terms with the totally Catholic province of Quebec.

Language and culture were problems, too. The French Canadians loved their French language and culture as deeply as the British loved theirs. They could not be forced to abandon French and speak English. Moreover, as part of their culture, the French Canadians had no experience with British political institutions, such as representative government, in which citizens could vote and affect government policy and taxation. French colonials were used to a king who ruled with absolute power. The Estates General, France's equivalent of Parliament, had not met for 150 years, and a military commander had ruled New France in the king's name.

This tradition, at least, helped the British. Because the Canadians had no experience in self-government, they did not rebel against British military commanders. There was not much difference between taking orders from an officer in a red coat than from one dressed in French blue.

During the 60-year reign of King George III (above), England lost its American colonies.

Like the Indians of the Great Lakes Basin, the French Canadians were willing to wait and see.

Pontiac and the Proclamation of 1763. An Indian uprising was the first sign that the war had caused new problems. In the summer of 1763, General Jeffrey Amherst, commander of all British troops in North America, informed the Ottawas and other tribes that he would not continue the French practice of giving them regular gifts —blankets, iron tools and pots, firearms, and liquor. However, the tribes regarded these presents as their right, as compensation for the land the Europeans had taken from them. Led by an Ottawa chief named Pontiac, several tribes revolted. They attacked the frontier forts and raided farms deep within Virginia and Pennsylvania. In a few months more than 2,000 people were dead.

The British troops were finally able to defeat Pontiac at Bushy Run near Pittsburgh. Nevertheless, the lesson of the uprising was very clear. The Indians who lived west of the Appalachians were capable of inflicting huge losses on the British

Army and the colonists. Unless the British and American people were willing to continue fighting a more difficult war than the one they had just concluded, they had to make some concessions to the Indians.

No one was willing to fight a new war. The British were tired of fighting, and their treasury was empty. General Amherst adopted the French custom of giving gifts to the tribes. Then, in October, 1763, the Royal Privy Council, which advised the Crown on important matters, forbade further British settlement on Indian lands.

In the *Proclamation of 1763*, King George III drew a line on the map of North America that followed the crest of the Appalachian Mountains. Regarding the land west of the mountains he proclaimed, "we do strictly forbid, on pain of our displeasure, all of our loving subjects from making any purchases or settlements whatsoever."

Few Americans protested the proclamation. A few people had already settled in the forbidden territory, building cabins in what is now Kentucky. They were forced to return and they were probably not happy about it.

However, most Americans realized they were not strong enough to challenge the Indians at that time, and no one considered the boundary permanent. In fact, British agents immediately began to negotiate with the Indians to purchase territory west of the mountains. However, after the colonies and Great Britain began to quarrel over taxation during the 1760s, some Americans would look back on the Proclamation of 1763 as the first attempt by King George III to control their lives in America.

The Redcoats. As a result of Pontiac's uprising, General Amherst asked Parliament to send him 5,000–6,000 more soldiers to maintain the strength of the frontier forts. Defense against the Indians was uppermost in his mind. In response to his request, Parliament passed the *Quartering Act* of 1765. Much to Amherst's surprise, the act gave him a garrison of 10,000 men!

But the British government did not have the money needed to maintain such an army in America. Therefore, Parliament included in the act the provision that the government of each colony in which the soldiers were stationed pay the costs of the soldiers' housing, food, drink, and wages.

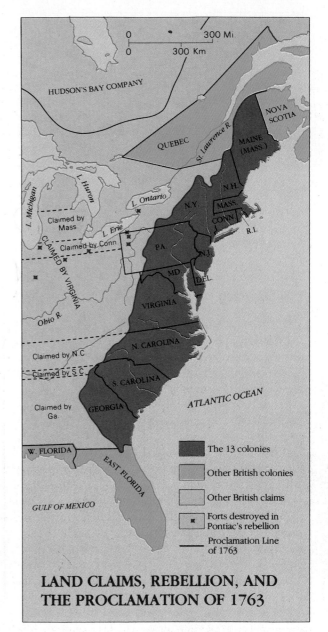

LAND CLAIMS, REBELLION, AND THE PROCLAMATION OF 1763

The cost to the colonies was high, but few colonials protested at first. They also recognized the need for protection against powerful Indian tribes. Nevertheless, the seed was planted for a quarrel between the Americans and Parliament. The Quartering Act raised a critical question: Did Parliament have the authority to pass laws that applied to the colonies? It was the dispute over this question that would lead to the War for Independence.

Discussion Question: The Quartering Act and other laws that followed were the more immediate events that signalled the beginning of the move for independence. Are there signs of the impending break with England that can be traced back further than these laws?

SECTION REVIEW

1. Write a sentence to identify: General Amherst, Bushy Run, King George III, Proclamation of 1763.

2. Name at least three ways in which French-Canadian culture differed from that of the English colonists.

3. Describe Pontiac's actions in Virginia and Pennsylvania, and explain why he acted as he did.

4. Why didn't the colonies object to the Quartering Act of 1765 when it was first passed by Parliament?

3. QUARREL OVER TAXATION

Two motives lay behind the British Parliament's attempt to tax the American colonies after 1763. The first was that Parliament needed money. Great Britain was on the verge of bankruptcy because of the French and Indian War. A huge debt of £130 million needed to be repaid, and the cost of governing the colonies had jumped from £70,000 a year to about £350,000 a year. The British were already taxed heavily. Property owners paid an annual tax equal to 20 percent of the value of their land. Therefore, Parliament concluded during the 1760s that the American colonists, who had gained security from French and Indian attack, should help repay the war debt, or at least assume the expenses involved in governing the colonies.

The second motive was that Great Britain needed to reorganize the government of the vast empire. Great Britain now had colonies all over the world. There were outposts in India and Africa. In the Americas alone, more than 20 colonies flew the British flag. Parliament could no longer neglect the colonies. A rational, uniform system of government for the far-flung possessions was needed.

George Grenville.

The man who believed he had the solution to the colonial problem was George Grenville, who became prime minister in 1763. Grenville had broad vision. He imagined an ever-growing British Empire and sought to develop a way to govern it.

Grenville also had a fault. Like many British politicians of the time, he knew little about England's most valuable colonial subjects, the Americans, and he did not care to learn about them. He regarded colonials as half-civilized people who were to do what their betters in London told them to do. Grenville was annoyed that the colonials did not pay a fair share of taxes. He reasoned that the colonists came from England, were governed by England, were treated like English subjects, and so should be taxed like English subjects.

The Sugar Act of 1764.

Grenville's first action was to reform the Molasses Act of 1733, which had established an import tax on molasses from the French and Spanish West Indies. The tax was so high that New England merchants had no choice but to break the law to get enough molasses. Instead of paying the tax, the Americans bribed British customs collectors to allow their cargoes into port. Because the customs officers were overworked and found it impossible to convict American smugglers in American courts, the officials usually went along and the molasses came in tax-free.

In the *Sugar Act* of 1764, Grenville struck at all the problems: no revenue from the importing of molasses; the impossibility of convicting smugglers in colonial courts; and overwork and corruption in the Customs Service. The duty on molasses was cut to three pennies a gallon and was applied to molasses brought in from the British West Indies as well as the French and Spanish West Indies. This and other new taxes would raise money.

In order to enforce the law, Grenville organized new *Vice-Admiralty Courts* to try violators. No longer would smugglers be able to count on friendly judges and juries to acquit them. Grenville also enlarged the Customs Service in the colonies, and allowed the Vice-Admiralty Courts to prosecute corrupt officers. These provisions were aimed at removing the temptation to take bribes.

Although the law seemed fair to the English, wealthy merchants in Boston, New York, and other seaports protested. Some people boycotted molasses products. But Grenville was unmoved.

THURSDAY, *November 7, 1765.*   THE   NUMB. 1192.

NEW-YORK GAZETTE;
OR   THE
WEEKLY   POST-BOY.

With the freſheſt Advices   Foreign and Domeſtick.

The united Voice of all His Majeſty's *free* and *loyal* Subjects in AMERICA,-- *LIBERTY* and *PROPERTY*, and NO *STAMPS*.

The Stamp Act of 1765 required a tax to be paid on colonial newspapers, pamphlets, handbills, and posters. Most American colonists were opposed to this tax.

He believed that the Americans were being stubborn and simply did not want to pay any taxes, no matter how just the taxes were.

Taxation and Representation. Grenville was only partly right. Throughout the taxation crisis of the 1760s, many colonials, like some taxpayers of all times and places, just wished to avoid paying taxes. However, there were also some important principles involved in the dispute. By ignoring them, Grenville showed his shortsighted disdain for Americans and widened the rift that was coming between Great Britain and her 13 American colonies.

The Sugar Act, as Daniel Dulany of Maryland pointed out in a pamphlet, differed from the Molasses Act in one important way. The Molasses Act had taxed molasses and sugar imported from outside the empire. The purpose of that law, Dulany said, was to regulate trade—to give British sugar growers an advantage over foreign sugar growers in selling to the mainland colonies. Parliament had the right and duty to do this. Parliament had the right to regulate trade for the good of the empire as a whole.

But Dulany asserted that the Sugar Act did not regulate trade by favoring British sugar growers, since it taxed British and foreign molasses equally. The law—whose official title was the "American Revenue Act"—was simply intended to raise money. Dulany claimed that Parliament had no right to tax the colonials, who were not represented in Parliament, for the purpose of raising money. According to the cherished right of British subjects to consent to all taxes levied on them, only the colonial assemblies, where Americans were represented, could enact such duties.

We cannot know what would have happened if the Sugar Act had been the last of Grenville's tax laws. Possibly, the protest would have faded and died. In 1766, when the duty was reduced to one penny a gallon, (the level of the traditional bribes), protest against the Sugar Act practically ceased. But the Sugar Act was not the end of the Grenville reforms.

The Stamp Act. The English people had paid a stamp tax since 1694. All legal documents such as wills, bills of sale, licenses, deeds, and insurance policies had to be printed on paper bearing a

Stamps like the ones pictured below were used to indicate taxes assessed under the Stamp Act.

government stamp. This stamp, pressed into the paper rather than stuck on it, meant that a tax had been paid. Without the stamp, the document was not legal.

The *Stamp Act* Grenville pushed through Parliament in 1765 went somewhat farther than earlier stamp taxes. In addition to existing requirements, it stated that all newspapers, pamphlets, handbills, posters, and even playing cards had to be printed on the special taxed paper. When news of the Stamp Act arrived in the colonies, the Americans protested strongly. (Consider the protest if a person who hands out advertisements at a supermarket had to pay a nickel tax for each sheet of paper.)

Colonial protest did not, however, fasten on the cost of the stamps. John Dickinson, a Pennsylvanian who wrote a stinging attack on the act, stated that the stamp tax was illegal. Parliament, Dickinson argued, had the right to enact *external taxes*, which placed duties on goods that came into the colonies. But Parliament had no right to levy *internal taxes*, or taxes on transactions that occurred entirely within the boundaries of a colony. Like Dulany, Dickinson said that only the colonial assemblies, which represented the people of the colonies, could enact internal taxes. This was an ancient right of British subjects.

Bostonians were so angered by the Stamp Act that they used the stamps to make bonfires in 1765.

Riot.

Thoughtful John Dickinson was the quietest of the American protesters. Other Americans took to the streets. Local societies called the *Sons of Liberty* pledged to disobey the law. When the special stamped paper arrived in some colonies, the societies broke into warehouses and burned the paper.

A British official in Maryland fled to New York for fear of his life. He picked the wrong refuge, since the New York Sons of Liberty were the most riotous of all. Led by Isaac Sears, they forced the Marylander to write a letter of resignation. In Boston, Sons of Liberty looted the homes of several British officials to protest their authority.

The Stamp Act Congress.

Parliament had not expected such widespread and violent opposition to the Stamp Act, nor had the leaders of colonial society who had begun the protest. Worried that riot by the common people on behalf of the cause could lead to riot against their own leadership, they attempted to channel the popular anger into a law-abiding protest. In October 1765, 27 delegates from nine colonies assembled in New York City. This *Stamp Act Congress* adopted 14 resolutions criticizing the Stamp Act, the Sugar Act, and other Parliamentary acts.

It was the first time since the unsuccessful Albany Convention that people from different colonies attempted to act together. Whereas the Albany Convention had been called to do something about the French, the Stamp Act Congress issued a protest against British policies. Since such a protest could be seen as treason, the delegates were careful to state that they were loyal subjects of George III. They were not revolutionaries, not even delegate James Otis of Massachusetts, the fiery lawyer who had first used what had become the rallying cry of the protesters: "Taxation without representation is tyranny!"

In fact, Otis proposed a logical solution to the problem. Since the principle at stake was taxation

Discussion Question: Which do you feel were the most important causes of the war for independence, economic (too much taxation) or political (no representation)? See that students present logical, well-defined arguments.

Political cartoonist M. Darley drew this cartoon showing "Poor Old England" (right) trying to reclaim rebellious American colonists.

without representation, Otis noted, why couldn't the colonists have the right to elect their own members of Parliament? The colonists would be represented, and Parliament would have its taxes!

The American Stand. No one paid attention to Otis's plan. The Americans did not want to be represented in the British Parliament. Even if the colonial population was fairly represented in the House of Commons, the elected branch of Parliament, a colonial delegation would be small and weak. What the Americans wanted was Parliament's recognition that they could be taxed only by their own colonial assemblies.

The British Position. The British were not interested in Otis's plan either. Almost everyone in Parliament, including strong friends of the Americans, claimed that the colonials already were represented under the principle of *virtual representation.* According to Edmund Burke, the most famous British supporter of the Americans, the House of Commons represented every person in England and the Empire. Members of the House, who were elected by the voters in their districts, were supposed to act with the interests of all British subjects at heart. The purpose of election

districts was to simplify the election. Nationwide or empire-wide elections were impossible, for there was no way a voter could be familiar with every candidate standing for election to the 554-member House of Commons.

Although Parliament had the better argument, the Americans still did not pay the taxes. Whether their reason was a dislike for all taxes or a principled insistence on the power of their own assemblies, the Americans successfully resisted the Stamp Act. Only in Georgia was the tax ever collected. Parliament repealed the act in 1766.

The Declaratory Act. Parliament still did not recognize that the Americans were determined to have some say in how they were governed. On the day the Stamp Act was repealed, Parliament passed the *Declaratory Act.* This statement of principle said that Parliament had and ought to have "full power and authority to make laws and statutes of sufficient force and validity to bind the colonies and people of America, subjects of the crown of Great Britain, in all cases whatsoever."

Few colonists even took note of the Declaratory Act. But it was important, for it hardened Parliament's stand that it had the right to pass laws concerning the colonists without their consent.

Class Activity: Get a book of political cartoons (available in most libraries) and make overhead transparencies of some of the cartoons for use during the year. Interpretation of these cartoons is a useful skill.

The Townshend Acts. Charles Townshend, the British Chancellor of the Exchequer (a cabinet post equivalent to Secretary of the Treasury in the United States), announced in 1767 that he had a formula answering American objections, but promising large revenues for the British government. His plan, which became known as the Townshend Acts, called for a tax on goods imported into the colonies from Great Britain, including paper, paint, lead, glass, and tea. Because, under the Navigation Acts, the colonials had to buy these goods from England, Townshend thought he had solved the problem of taxes on interior, as opposed to exterior, goods.

The weakness of the Townshend Acts was that, except for tea, the plan taxed goods the colonists could provide for themselves. The Americans decided to *boycott,* or refuse to buy, taxed goods from Great Britain. In boycotting the taxed goods, people sacrificed. However, in losing an important market, the merchants of England who handled paint, glass, tea and the other boycotted goods suffered severe financial losses.

The boycotters hoped to keep the protest nonviolent, and to pressure powerful British merchants to demand that Parliament repeal the Townshend Acts. The strategy worked. There was no repetition of the Stamp Act riots, and trade between Britain and the colonies was cut in half. Townshend had predicted that the duties would bring in £40,000 a year. The actual payments by the spring of 1769 were no more than £3,500. By this time, the loss to British merchants from American nonimportation was £7,250,000. Facing bankruptcy, British merchants called for repeal of the Townshend Acts, and in 1770 they got it. Except for a tax of three pennies a pound on tea, which Parliament left in the spirit of the Declaratory Act, all duties were lifted. Britain would not yield in principle what it was willing to give up in fact. The tea tax was to show their right to tax.

Some colonial protesters tried to keep the tea boycott alive. But most Americans took satisfaction in the repeal of the other taxes and resumed trading with Great Britain. Imports into New England rose from a low of £330,000 to £1.2 million. Total colonial exports were valued at £1.7 million in 1770, and £4.5 million in 1772. Between 1770 and 1774, it appeared as if England and America were through with their quarrel.

SECTION REVIEW

1. Write a sentence to identify: Sugar Act, Sons of Liberty, Stamp Act Congress.

2. Why did Prime Minister Grenville insist on taxing the Americas to help England out of its financial difficulties?

3. What was the American view about James Otis's proposal to have colonists elect members to the House of Commons?

4. Contrast the American colonists' reactions to the Stamp Act and the Townshend Acts.

4. THE ROAD TO REVOLUTION

The calm of 1770–1774 was deceiving. There were no massive protests in the colonies, but not all was well between Great Britain and the Americans. Anti-British feeling was still present, kept alive by a few radical agitators who were waiting for the spark that would light the fuse of rebellion.

Samuel Adams and the Boston Massacre. On March 5, 1770, Boston was locked in a severely cold New England winter. The streets were icy. Heaps of gritty snow blocked the gutters. Unemployed men wandered about in search of jobs or, perhaps, just a warm place. On a crowded street, a group of workers were jostled by a patrol of British soldiers. Words were exchanged. Many Bostonians had resented the presence of soldiers in their city ever since the Quartering Act of 1765. And more troops had come to Boston to help enforce the hated Townshend Acts. This time, all the anger and resentment exploded. A growing mob of men and boys surrounded the soldiers and backed them against a wall. Ignoring an order to disperse, the rioters pelted the Redcoats with snowballs and chunks of ice. The soldiers opened fire. Five in the crowd, including a black sailor named Crispus Attucks and a young boy, fell dead.

Samuel Adams, a shrewd agitator and a leader of Boston's protest against the Sugar Act, Stamp Act, and Townshend Acts, was enraged. He was one of the earliest proponents of an independence movement, and may have thought that what he called the *Boston Massacre* would be the revolutionary spark. He published a pamphlet depicting the incident as a case of brutal military action against innocent citizens. In several colonies, newspapers printed the story with a black border, the symbol of mourning. But no massive protest resulted. In fact, Samuel Adams's cousin, John Adams, was the soldiers' lawyer when they were tried for the shootings. He argued that the mob threatened the Redcoats' lives, and that the soldiers had had no choice but to fire.

John Adams did not believe that British troops belonged in American cities. At the same time he insisted that the individual soldiers involved in the Boston Massacre were innocent of wrongdoing, he criticized Great Britain for stationing "lobsters," as the colonials sometimes called the Redcoats, in American cities. "Soldiers quartered in a populous town," he said, "will always occasion two mobs where they prevent one. They are wretched conservators of the peace."

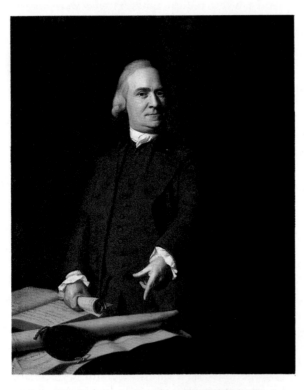

Samuel Adams, an American radical, believed that the American colonies should be independent. Through speeches and pamphlets, he argued for revolution, and signed the Declaration of Independence.

The Hated Redcoats.

The garrison of 10,000 soldiers that had been sent to America was stationed for the most part in frontier forts. However, after the Stamp Act riots, more and more had been posted in cities and towns and few Americans liked them.

Soldiers of the eighteenth century were not the most civil people, either. Military life was so unpleasant that only the poorest, toughest men joined the army. Some soldiers were *impressed*, or forced into service, by "press gangs" because they had no jobs, and some were even taken out of prisons. They were generally loyal to their commanders and comrades, but they were inclined to be suspicious of civilians. In turn, civilians did not want them around. Tension was inevitable, especially in highly populated cities.

In the Declaration of Independence, one of the American complaints that Thomas Jefferson listed was that troops were stationed amidst the citizens. When Americans adopted their own Bill of Rights in 1791, the Third Amendment read: "No soldier shall, in time of peace, be quartered in any house, without the consent of the owner, nor in time of war, but in a manner to be prescribed by law." Although the presence of the hated Redcoats in cities was not a direct cause of the Revolution, it increased American resentment.

Trouble in the Carolinas.

While New Englanders worried about violence between Americans and British soldiers, some Americans actually took up arms against their fellow colonists. In the Carolinas, backcountry settlers protested the refusal of the wealthier eastern colonists to allow them to organize county governments of their own. Living far from the colonial capitals, the westerners needed local government to maintain law and order and also to provide for local needs.

Those who lived in the eastern, older part of South Carolina feared that western counties might grow so large that they would gain control of the colonial assembly. Devoted to keeping taxes on their plantations as low as possible, they did not want westerners making decisions about the colonial treasury. After repeated frustrations, the western farmers formed counties anyway. They stopped paying taxes to the colonial government, giving the money to their local governments instead. Because they were determined to regulate

Most Americans were heavy tea drinkers, but the tea tax only affected well-to-do colonists since these were the only ones who legally bought tea. Most Americans drank a cheaper tea, smuggled into the colonies from Holland.

Paul Revere's engraving (above) shows British troops landing in Boston. The colonists thought that quartering of soldiers in their homes and inns was a denial of their rights.

their own affairs, they became known as *Regulators*.

The dispute was settled peacefully in South Carolina, but in North Carolina, Regulators took up arms in May 1771. Whether or not they were thinking in terms of shooting or protesting, they got a battle. The North Carolina militia marched into Regulator territory and met them at Alamance Creek on May 16, 1771. In the short battle that followed, over 200 Regulators were killed or wounded; only 9 militiamen were killed. Western bitterness toward the eastern elite grew when 6 Regulator leaders were hanged for treason.

This bitterness was so deep that when the Revolution broke out, many of the Regulators fought on the British side.

The Gaspee. In June 1772, the *Gaspee*, a British patrol boat chasing smugglers, ran aground in Rhode Island's Narragansett Bay. When night fell on the crippled vessel, a group of men boarded it, chased the crew, and set the *Gaspee* afire.

Obviously the deed had been done by local farmers. However, when the British investigated the incident, not a single person would testify.

The Tea Act of 1773. The incident that set colonial feelings aflame was the *Tea Act* of 1773. The chief purpose of the law had nothing to do with the colonies. The prime minister, Lord North, was concerned that an old established trading firm, the East India Company, was near bankruptcy. Because the Crown depended on the company to handle many government responsibilities in its colonies in India, North was determined to save it.

In its warehouses, the East India Company had 17 million pounds (7.6 million kilograms) of tea. The market in England was glutted, so the price was low. The directors of the company suggested to Lord North that they be permitted to sell tea directly to the colonies, instead of selling to English merchants, who then sold to the colonies. Because the price of tea was low in the colonies, too, the East India Company would need a monopoly to drive out the competition and sell its tea profitably.

Most Americans did not support the war until 1776. Even then, some historians have said that more Americans fought with the British than against them.

On December 16, 1773, Samuel Adams led a group of Americans aboard a British ship in Boston Harbor and dumped the cargo of tea overboard. The Bostonians were protesting the Tea Act of 1773.

Lord North agreed. All tea not sold by the East India Company was declared to be illegal. In order to further encourage the East India Company's prosperity, North got rid of one of the taxes on tea sold in the colonies. Because it did not have to pay heavy taxes, the East India Company was able to sell tea at a lower price than Americans were accustomed to paying. However, when the directors of the company suggested that the remaining duty on tea should be repealed as well, Lord North refused. North believed that the Americans would accept East India Company tea because of its cheap price. In doing so, they would demonstrate their obedience to the king by being willing to pay the taxes levied by Parliament.

The Tea Parties.
Lord North was wrong. When a dozen ships carrying 1,700 chests of tea sailed into American ports, they set off the angriest round of defiance since 1765. The Americans would not be bought by a cheap cup of their favorite beverage. As agitators like Samuel Adams told them, if they accepted the taxed tea, other Parliamentary taxes would follow. The Tea Act was only the first step in denying them their liberties.

In Charleston, South Carolina, the tea was taken off the ships, but it never left the warehouse in which it was stored. In New York and Philadelphia, officials ordered the tea ships to return to England, fearing a riot if the tea was unloaded. In Annapolis, Maryland, the tea ship was burned. But the reaction in Boston triggered the final crisis.

Massachusetts Governor Thomas Hutchinson wanted to avoid a riot, but not at the price of surrendering to the mob and sending the ships back to England. He thought he could get the tea ashore by seizing the cargo for refusal to pay an obscure port tax. He felt that the Sons of Liberty might destroy the property of the East India Company, but would surely not defy the royal governor of Massachusetts.

Hutchinson was wrong. Samuel Adams assembled his supporters, dressed them like Indians, and led them to the wharf. In full sight of a cheering crowd, they boarded the tea ship and dumped the chests into the harbor. This action came to be called the *Boston Tea Party*.

Adams knew what he was doing. He made defiance of the British government look like a festive party. He also calculated correctly that, unlike the incident at Annapolis, where a private company's ship was destroyed, Great Britain itself had to respond to the Boston Tea Party. However, even Adams could not have foreseen Parliament's actual response.

Class Activity: Many modern disputes are settled by arbitration by a neutral party. Divide the class into three groups. Have each group take the side of either the colonists, Grenville and his

The Intolerable Acts. Instead of discovering, arresting, and punishing the individuals who destroyed the tea, Prime Minister Lord North tried to punish all of Boston and the whole colony of Massachusetts. He angrily replied to the colonists' disobedient acts by hurriedly pushing the *Coercive Acts* through Parliament. These four laws were designed to *coerce*, or force, Massachusetts to obey the Crown. The colonists called the laws the *Intolerable Acts*. To Americans they represented completely unacceptable interference with their rights as British subjects.

The first law closed the port of Boston to all trade until the people of the city paid for the spoiled tea. The second law empowered the British government to replace the royal governor of Massachusetts with a military governor. Governor Hutchinson stepped down and was replaced by General Thomas Gage. Gage was given the power to transfer out of the colony the trials of any soldiers accused of killing protesters. To Samuel Adams, now in hiding, and many other Bostonians, this seemed to be an open invitation to the Redcoats to do as much wanton killing of colonists as they wished.

The third law overhauled the entire structure of the Massachusetts government. Officials appointed by the king replaced elected officers. The power of the colonial assembly was diminished and the Boston City Council was abolished. The city was, in effect, placed under martial law.

The fourth law, a new Quartering Act, pushed relations between civilians and soldiers to the breaking point. It provided that Redcoats, who now streamed into Boston, could be housed in occupied private homes. English law held that a person's home was a very private place, and law officers were required to apply for warrants from judges before searching houses. The Quartering Act of 1774 seemed to mock this right of privacy, one of the most prized rights of British subjects.

The Quebec Act. Although it did not apply to the Americans, the *Quebec Act* of 1774 also angered many colonists. In the act, Parliament recognized French laws as valid in the province of Quebec, and Roman Catholics were allowed to practice their religion. The boundaries of Quebec were extended into the Ohio River Valley, just west of Pennsylvania and Virginia. And the government of Quebec would be headed by an appointed royal governor, with no elected assembly.

Most historians see the Quebec Act as an example of enlightened, liberal government of a conquered people. Rarely had a conqueror been so generous to a conquered people. To the American colonials in 1774, however, the Quebec Act was nothing of the sort. They saw it as another step toward tyranny—no elected assembly—and an attempt to deny them the right to expand to the west by including country they claimed in a French province. Why, Virginians and Pennsylvanians asked, had they fought the French and Indian War except to win the Ohio Valley from the French Canadians?

The Turning Point. The Quebec Act caused Americans from other colonies to help Massachusetts. Several sent food to the isolated colony. Others drafted letters and resolutions of protest. Most importantly, when Massachusetts called for a "continental congress" to meet in Philadelphia to discuss the protest, every colony except Georgia sent delegates.

This was the turning point. Before the summer of 1774, conflict between Great Britain and the colonies had been a series of scattered incidents. Only a handful of radical agitators had contemplated an open break with Great Britain. Although most of the delegates who came to Philadelphia insisted they were loyal to the Crown, the mere fact that they came to a meeting called a "continental congress" pointed unmistakably toward a serious break with England.

SECTION REVIEW

1. Write a sentence to identify: Crispus Attucks, Lord North, Quebec Act.

2. Why were a large number of British soldiers in Boston on March 5, 1770?

3. Was the presence of Redcoats in the colonies a direct cause of the American Revolution? Explain your answer.

4. How did the Tea Act of 1773, the Tea Parties, and the Quebec Act contribute to a turning point in the quarrel between the American colonies and Great Britain?

men, or neutral arbitrators. Setting up the situation as it was for each of the two arguing parties, stage a mock arbitration to see if conflict can be avoided.

CHAPTER REVIEW

TIME LINE

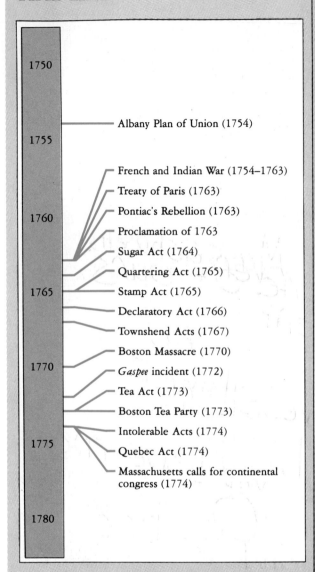

- 1750
- Albany Plan of Union (1754)
- 1755
- French and Indian War (1754–1763)
- Treaty of Paris (1763)
- Pontiac's Rebellion (1763)
- 1760
- Proclamation of 1763
- Sugar Act (1764)
- Quartering Act (1765)
- 1765
- Stamp Act (1765)
- Declaratory Act (1766)
- Townshend Acts (1767)
- Boston Massacre (1770)
- 1770
- *Gaspee* incident (1772)
- Tea Act (1773)
- Boston Tea Party (1773)
- Intolerable Acts (1774)
- 1775
- Quebec Act (1774)
- Massachusetts calls for continental congress (1774)
- 1780

TIME LINE QUESTIONS

1. How many years are shown on this time line?
2. In which year did the French influence in North America come to an end?
3. In which years did events that directly fueled the quarrel between Great Britain and the American colonies take place?
4. How many years after the first of these events was a continental congress called?

SKILLS STRATEGY

THE COLONY OF MASSACHUSETTS, 1774

— Colonial boundary
• Town

N.H.

• Deerfield

Concord • • Lexington

MASS.

Boston •

N
W — E
S

CONN.

R.I.

Plymouth •

0   50 Mi.
0   50 Km

PHYSICAL AND POLITICAL MAPS

Maps are a visual presentation of facts and concepts, as are other illustrations in a textbook. Maps can show some kinds of information more clearly and more exactly than can words alone.

A *physical*, or *topographic*, map shows such natural features as mountains, plateaus, escarpments, valleys, plains, swamps, and bodies of water. To read a physical map effectively, you should pay attention to its title, *scale, legend,* and *compass rose.*

The title gives the main idea of the map. On most maps the scale indicates the distances represented by a given measurement on the map, allowing you to figure out actual distances between places. The legend shows what each map symbol represents. The legend on the map (right) shows a color symbol for each range of elevation (height in feet above sea level). The compass rose shows the map orientation: its points north, south, east, and west.

A political map, such as the one shown above, shows man-made features and may contain such things as boundaries, countries, states, cities,

Making Connections: Review the questions and topics presented in the Making Connections section opening this chapter. Leave students with the impression that the war was caused by a

roads, airports, and railroads. Like physical maps, political maps should have a title, a legend, a scale, and a compass rose. Standard symbols are used on most political maps. For instance, a circle always indicates a city or town. However, you must look at the legend to find out whether capital cities are designated in a special way. Boundaries are usually shown by a black line, but certain boundaries may be shown by a broken line.

A map may contain both physical and political features. For example, physical maps often show boundaries, cities, and towns. All political maps show bodies of water in the mapped area, and some show mountains, too.

APPLYING SKILLS

1. Write the title of the physical map above.
2. Compare the two maps. Name the colonies in which the average elevation is high.
3. From information on these maps, draw a conclusion about where people settled.
4. Use the scale to determine the number of miles between the northernmost boundary and the southernmost boundary of the colonies.

CHAPTER 5 TEST

TEXT REVIEW

1. Why did France and Great Britain go to war in North America in 1754?
2. Why did General Wolfe think it important for the British to strike the French city of Quebec?
3. Explain how the provisions of the Treaty of Paris ended the French threat to England's American colonists.
4. Name two groups of people who came under British rule at the end of the French and Indian War.
5. Why did some Britons recommend that England return Canada to France and allow the French to stay in North America?
6. Tell how the Proclamation of 1763 and the Quartering Act of 1765 affected the American colonists.
7. Give the two motives that lay behind the British Parliament's attempt to tax the American colonies after 1763.
8. Explain why the calling of the continental congress in 1774 is referred to as the "turning point" in British-American relations.

CRITICAL THINKING

9. Give two examples of the use of the Boston Massacre as propaganda—that is, one-sided information distributed by supporters of a cause to win others to their viewpoint.
10. Explain how Lord North showed bias in his decisions related to the Tea Act of 1773.

WRITING A PARAGRAPH

Write a paragraph comparing the reactions of John Adams and Samuel Adams to the Boston Massacre. After you make a statement with details supporting one man's reaction, use words or phrases such as *however, on the other hand,* or *although* to show that the next sentence will contain details supporting a contrasting point of view.

Topic Sentence: Both Samuel and John Adams deplored the Boston Massacre, but each viewed the incident in a different way.

series of events that built on each other and which might have been avoided. Ascertain how the personalities of the individuals involved may have compounded the problems that existed.

CHAPTER 6

INDEPENDENCE DECLARED

My country need not change her gown,
Her triple suit as sweet
As when 'twas cut at Lexington,
And first pronounced "a fit."
EMILY DICKINSON

1775–1783

Making Connections. In 1775, despite their grievances, most Americans were still loyal to the British king. Within a year, however, representatives of the 13 colonies agreed on a Declaration of Independence, which meant war with England. What had happened to change people's minds in such a short time?

In this chapter, you will learn:

- Why the First Continental Congress toasted King George III
- Who the Minutemen were, and how they chased British soldiers from Concord to Boston
- How Thomas Paine helped destroy American loyalty to King George III
- What the Declaration of Independence really meant
- Why it was important for George Washington to hold his army together
- Why France is called America's "oldest friend"

You know that Parliament's attempt to control the colonies after years of neglect caused great resentment. Yet British actions grew harsher in the face of American resistance. As you read, note the ideas that led the colonists toward revolution.

Sections

1. THE CALL FOR FREEDOM

The delegates to the *First Continental Congress,* which opened on September 5, 1774, were as angry as Samuel Adams and the other radicals. They had no intention of buckling under to Lord North and Parliament by accepting the Intolerable Acts. But they were not opposed to compromise. They were proud to be British subjects, and did not meet to declare their independence. Only after a year and a half of Great Britain's refusal to compromise, and the outbreak of fighting in New England, would a second continental congress declare for independence and a Revolutionary War.

The First Continental Congress. The First Continental Congress met for a little more than seven weeks. The 56 delegates adopted a list of demands called the *Suffolk Resolves,* which declared that the Intolerable Acts violated the rights of British subjects. The Resolves also called for Massachusetts to form its own government, keep the taxes that usually went to the royal governor, and hold the money until the Intolerable Acts were repealed. The Resolves called on all colonies to form and train armed militias. Finally, they called for a boycott of trade with Great Britain.

George Washington (right) was born in Virginia in 1732. He served as a colonel with the British forces in the French and Indian War and as a general in the American Revolution.

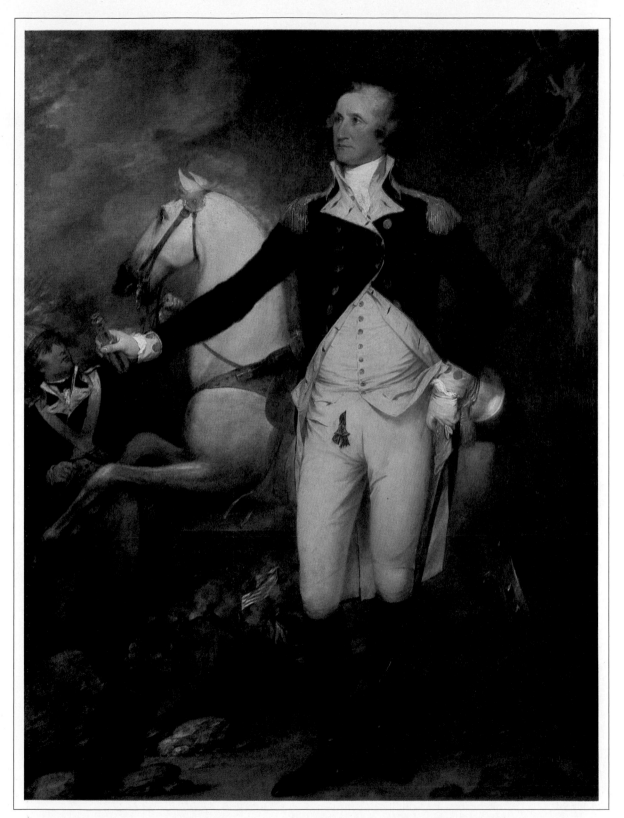

Skills Review: Have students reinforce the knowledge learned in the previous Skills Strategy. Have students use their knowledge of maps to make a map illustrating some aspect of the information in this chapter. They should explain the map's usefulness.

The Battle of Lexington took place on April 19, 1775. Amos Doolittle captured a scene of that battle in an engraving (above) that he made in the same year.

To call for the formation of a government and the training of soldiers was rebellion, and very close to treason. However, the delegates clearly stated their loyalty to the Crown. They drank public toasts to King George III, and phrased their protests in such a way as to appeal to him to bring Parliament to its senses.

King George III. Parliament, and not King George, was responsible for the actions that drove the colonists to rebellion. Although the king was the head of England and the empire, Parliament made the laws in the king's name. The Americans addressed their appeals to King George because they were objecting to Parliament's attempt to make laws for them. They insisted that only their local assemblies could do that.

Americans generally liked King George III. He had been crowned in 1760, at almost the same time the tide turned in the French and Indian War. Americans connected the king with the great victory of 1763. And he had personally put pres-

sure on Parliament to repeal the Stamp Act and Townshend Duties. Not only did the Americans recognize his authority, they believed the king was their friend.

To the PUBLICK.

NEW-YORK, October 5, 1774.

BY Mr. Rivere, who left Boston on Friday last, and arrived here last night, in his way to the General Congress, we have certain intelligence that the Carpenters and Masons who had inadvertently undertaken to erect barracks for the soldiers in that town, upon being informed that it was contrary to the sentiments of their countrymen, unanimously broke up, and returned to their respective homes, on the 26th of last month; which, it is hoped, will convince the Mechanicks of this city, how disagreeable it will be to the inhabitants of that place, for them to afford any manner of assistance to those, who are made subservient to the destruction of our American brethren.

Printed by JOHN HOLT, near the COFFEE HOUSE.

As the broadside above shows, solidarity among the colonists was a political issue in 1774.

Only 16 percent of able-bodied American males fought in the Revolutionary War.

Colonials in Arms. In the winter of 1774–1775, American men met by the thousands on village greens to train as soldiers. Training involved formal teamwork; a line of soldiers aimed and fired all at once rather than firing individually. The goal as two lines of soldiers faced one another was to frighten the other side into forgetting their training and breaking into a run. When the enemy army broke up in panic, the battle was won.

The First Shot. Nowhere was training for this kind of war harder than in the colony suffering under the Intolerable Acts. British control was tight, yet all over Massachusetts groups of farmers and craftsmen, called *Minutemen* because they promised to be ready on a minute's notice, drilled and drilled.

Early on the morning of April 19, 1775, British General Thomas Gage sent 700 Redcoats out of Boston under the command of Lieutenant Colonel Francis Smith. His instructions were to seize the military supplies the Minutemen had stored at Concord. Learning of their plans, Paul Revere, William Dawes, and Samuel Prescott galloped

Paul Revere, 1735–1818

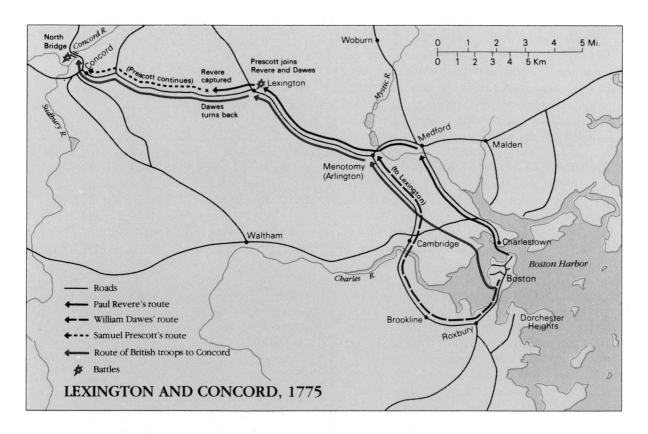

Roads ———
Paul Revere's route ◄——
William Dawes' route ◄— —
Samuel Prescott's route ◄- - -
Route of British troops to Concord ◄▬▬
✸ **Battles**

LEXINGTON AND CONCORD, 1775

GOING TO THE SOURCE

Let us not, I beseech you, sir, deceive ourselves longer. Sir, we have done everything that could be done to avert the storm which is now coming on. We have petitioned; we have remonstrated; we have supplicated; we have prostrated ourselves before the throne and have implored its interposition to arrest the tyrannical hands of the Ministry and Parliament. Our petitions have been slighted; our remonstrances have produced additional violence and insult; our supplications have been disregarded; and we have been spurned, with contempt, from the foot of the throne. In vain, after these things, may we indulge the fond hope of peace and reconciliation.

There is no longer any room for hope. If we wish to be free; if we mean to preserve inviolate those inestimable privileges for which we have been so long contending; . . . we must fight! I repeat it, sir, we must fight!! An appeal to arms and to the God of hosts is all that is left us!

They tell us, sir . . . that we are weak, unable to cope with so formidable an adversary. But when shall we be stronger. Will it be the next week or the next year? Will it be when we are totally disarmed, and when a British guard shall be stationed in every house? Shall we gather strength by irresolution and inaction?

> *The next gale that sweeps from the north will bring to our ears the clash of resounding arms! Our brethren are already in the field! Why stand we here idle? Forbid it, Almighty God—I know not what course others may take; but as for me, give me liberty, or give me death!*
>
> PATRICK HENRY, "LIBERTY OR DEATH" SPEECH

Shall we acquire the means of effectual resistance by lying supinely on our backs and hugging the delusive phantom of hope, until our enemies shall have bound us hand and foot? Sir, we are not weak if we make a proper use of those means which the God of nature has placed in our power. Three million people armed in the holy cause of liberty and in such a country as that which we possess are invincible by any force which our enemy can send against us. . . .

It is vain, sir, to extenuate the matter. Gentlemen may cry, peace, peace; but there is no peace. The war is actually begun! The next gale that sweeps from the north will bring to our ears the clash of resounding arms! Our brethren are already in the field! Why stand we here idle? What is it that gentlemen wish?

Forbid it, Almighty God—I know not what course others may take; but as for me, give me liberty, or give me death!

In March 1775, Virginia's leaders met to protest British threats against American "liberties." At this meeting, Patrick Henry asked that the state's militia be organized. Defending his proposal, Henry delivered the stirring "Liberty or Death" speech for which he is best remembered.

through the still, dark countryside, rousing Minutemen from their beds with cries like, "The British are coming!" When the British arrived in Lexington, they found about 77 farmers with muskets standing on the common in the center of town. Major John Pitcairn, who was commanding a group of Redcoats, ordered the colonists to disperse. According to several eyewitnesses, the Minutemen were doing so—they knew they were no match for the larger, more professional British force. Suddenly, a shot rang out. No one knows whether it was fired by a soldier or by a colonial. Pitcairn's troops unleashed a deafening volley, killing eight Americans and wounding ten. The British then regrouped and started off for Concord, eight miles down the road. Smith divided his

Discussion Question: In reading the above document, what sense do you get about the speaker's main concern?

troops, sending some of the Redcoats to the center of Concord and some toward the North Bridge.

The War Begins. The Minutemen from Concord and surrounding towns had gathered on a hill near the North Bridge just outside of town. From this point they saw smoke coming from Concord Center. While the British were looking for the hidden military stores a building was set on fire, either by accident or on purpose. In any case, the Minutemen thought that the British were burning the town, and they started toward Concord Center to stop them. The British detail assigned to hold the North Bridge tried to halt the Minutemen, and a battle began. Only two British soldiers were killed, but the British broke rank and retreated back along the Lexington road.

All the way to Boston, snipers hiding behind trees and stone fences fired at the retreating Redcoats. A relief force of 1,000 British soldiers joined the original force in Lexington, but they only provided more targets for the snipers. By the time the Redcoats reached Boston at dusk, they had suffered 73 killed, 174 wounded, and 26 missing. The American toll was 49 dead and 41 wounded.

Other Massachusetts Minutemen came to the scene, too. In a short time 16,000 Americans were camped outside Boston, and·the city was under siege. By June 16, 1775, colonial officers with military experience had taken charge of the colonists. They ordered the farmer-soldiers to occupy high ground called Bunker Hill and Breed's Hill, on a narrow peninsula to the north of Boston harbor.

Three newly arrived British generals, Henry Clinton, William Howe, and John Burgoyne, told General Gage he had to move before the Americans could move cannon to the heights. On June 17, over 2,000 crack British troops crossed the harbor to challenge the Americans in what· was called the Battle of Bunker Hill. According to tradition, either William Prescott or Israel Putnam gave the command to the Minutemen, "Don't fire until you see the whites of their eyes!" This was a practical order, too, as the Americans were short on ammunition.

Three times the British made frontal assaults on the American positions. Twice they were thrown back, with shocking losses. The third assault would have been turned back as well, but the defenders ran out of powder and the British drove away the Americans with bayonets. However,

On June 16, 1775, Americans took the high ground of Bunker Hill in Boston. The next day, Redcoats suffered terrible losses in two assaults. Their third assault proved successful when the Americans ran out of ammunition.

On June 17, 1775, British General Howe bombarded Charlestown, Massachusetts.

when General Clinton heard that 226 Redcoats had been killed and 828 wounded, he said that too many victories of that kind and the British would lose a war.

Clinton was right. By standing up to some of the best soldiers in the world, the Minutemen had shown that they could fight a war on their own.

Ticonderoga.

Ticonderoga. American morale got another boost when Benedict Arnold and Ethan Allen teamed up to capture Fort Ticonderoga, a former French outpost on New York's Lake Champlain. Benedict Arnold, a well-trained officer, set off with a small force to capture the fort when he learned that Ethan Allen, head of a kind of guerilla group called the Green Mountain Boys, was planning the same thing. (Vermont, which means "green mountain" in French, was not a colony but mostly wilderness claimed by New York, New Hampshire, Massachusetts—and by independent-minded Ethan Allen.)

Arnold and Allen disliked one another, but on May 10, 1775, they cooperated long enough to surprise the British garrison and capture the fort. The Americans also took the British fort at nearby Crown Point, and began to move the heavy cannon from those forts to the troops that were besieging Boston.

Invasion of Canada. After the fall of Ticonderoga, Arnold led more than 1,000 troops through the Maine wilderness to invade Canada. After almost four months of marching through almost trackless land, hauling heavy boats along portages, and fighting terrible winter weather, Arnold arrived at Quebec in December 1775. However, his force was too small and too weary to capture the walled, heavily defended city. Arnold besieged Quebec for the rest of the winter, but he had to give up when spring came and the British navy could again sail up the St. Lawrence River to Quebec.

Arnold retreated to Fort Ticonderoga. However, word soon came that Sir Guy Carleton was leading a large British army south from Canada. Arnold realized that if Carleton were allowed to

Ethan Allen's Green Mountain Boys were not a product of the Revolution, as most people believe. They were organized around 1770 to fight the New Yorkers. The states of New Hampshire and New York had a boundary dispute over the region that today is Vermont. The Green Mountain Boys were New Hampshire's answer to the problem.

march down the Hudson River, he could link up with the British in New York City. This would cut off New England from the other colonies.

Carleton had reached Lake Champlain, and had stopped to build boats to sail part of his army down the lake. Arnold rushed to the lake, and set his troops to building their own ships. The two fleets met on October 11, 1776, and the American ships were destroyed. However, Arnold still emerged the hero, because he had cost Carleton precious time. Winter was setting in, and Carleton did not want to be stuck in the New York wilderness. The British returned to Canada.

The Second Continental Congress.

By May 1775, the *Second Continental Congress* was meeting in Philadelphia. The delegates were generally more belligerent than those at the first congress. Young, fiery radicals like Thomas Jefferson of Virginia came for the first time.

Nevertheless, the delegates still hoped to find a formula to restore peace. They too drank toasts to the king, and in a letter entitled *A Declaration of the Cause and Necessity of Taking Up Arms*, appealed to him to support their cause. But George III was infuriated with the colonials. He told Lord North that "blows must decide whether they are to be subject to the country or independent," and refused even to read the Americans' letter.

Edmund Burke, William Pitt, and John Wilkes begged the king to let tempers cool. Instead, Lord North pushed through Parliament an act designed to crush the New England economy. It forbade Massachusetts citizens to fish the Grand Banks of Newfoundland.

As the situation around Boston grew more tense, the delegates to the Continental Congress feared that events would leave them behind. In order to establish their authority, and to make the fight an American rather than a Massachusetts fight, they sent George Washington of Virginia to take command of the Minutemen.

Snipping the Thread of Loyalty.

The person who stepped forward to snip the thread of colonial loyalty to the king was not a member of the Continental Congress, nor even an American. Thomas Paine was an English artisan who had come to the colonies in 1774. Over the next 25

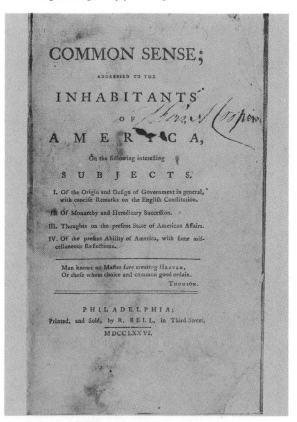

Thomas Paine (above) wrote a political pamphlet titled Common Sense *(below). Published in early 1776, it was widely read throughout the colonies. It argued eloquently for independence.*

Class Activity: Obtain a copy of the movie *1776* and show it in class. Although it is a light view of the events surrounding the Declaration of Independence's signing, the character portrayals of Jefferson, Adams, and Franklin are fairly accurate. The movie runs 80 minutes. Follow this presentation with a discussion about how the movie depicts these people.

125

GOING TO THE SOURCE

These are the times that try men's souls. The summer soldier and the sunshine patriot will, in this crisis, shrink from the service of his country; but he that stands it now deserves the love and thanks of man and woman. . . . Why is it that the enemy have left the New England provinces and made these middle ones the seat of war? The answer is easy: New England is not infested with Tories, and we are. I have been tender in raising the cry against these men, and used numberless arguments to show them their danger, but it will not do to sacrifice a world either to their folly or their baseness. The period is now arrived in which either they or we must change our sentiments, or one or both must fall. . . . Every Tory is a coward, for servile, slavish, self-interested fear is the foundation of Toryism; and a man under such influence, though he may be cruel, never can be brave. . . .

Quitting this class of men, I turn with the warm ardor of a friend to those who have nobly stood and are yet determined to stand the matter out. I call not upon a few but upon all; not on this state or that state, but on every state.

> *I call not upon a few but upon all; not in this state or that state, but on every state. Up and help us; lay your shoulders to the wheel. . . . Let it be told to the future world that in the depth of winter . . . the city and country, alarmed at one common danger, came forth to meet and to repulse it.*
>
> THOMAS PAINE,
> *COMMON SENSE*

Up and help us; lay your shoulders to the wheel; better have too much force than too little, when so great an object is at stake. Let it be told to the future world that in the depth of winter, when nothing but hope and virtue could survive, that the city and country, alarmed at one common danger, came forth to meet and to repulse it. Say not that thousands are gone, turn out your tens of thousands; throw not the burden of the day upon Providence, but "show your faith by your works," that God may bless you. It matters not where you live, or what rank of life you hold, the evil or the blessing will reach you all. The far and the near, the home counties and the back, the rich and the poor will suffer or rejoice alike. The heart that feels not now is dead; the blood of his children will curse his cowardice who shrinks back at a time when a little might have saved the whole, and made them happy.

In 1776, Washington's army suffered a series of disheartening defeats. The talented propagandist, Thomas Paine, wrote Common Sense *in December 1776, in hopes of lifting the morale of the dispirited revolutionaries.*

years, Paine would write eloquent essays condemning tyranny and praising liberty. During the fall of 1775, he was laboring over a pamphlet called *Common Sense*.

Published in January 1776, *Common Sense* was an attack on King George in particular ("the Royal Brute") and the idea of monarchies in general. Paine wrote that all kings were enemies of human liberty. Having taken the first step in rebelling against monarchy, Paine said, the Americans should take the second—declaring their independence of the corrupt British monarchy.

Paine's eloquence gave the revolt in Massachusetts a significance for all people. It was not just a rebellion in defense of the rights of British subjects. It was a revolution on behalf of liberty. Thomas Paine shattered the loyalty and affection many Americans held for King George. Eventually, a country of only 2.5 million people would buy 500,000 copies of *Common Sense*. Every American who could read must have at least skimmed the pamphlet.

Discussion Question: What elements of propaganda can be found in "The Crisis?" Have students support their observations with facts presented in the text.

2. THE DECISION TO BE FREE

We can be sure that most of the delegates to the Second Continental Congress read *Common Sense.* Many of them must have spoken with Paine, who lived in Philadelphia in 1776. It was his voice, as well as that of Richard Henry Lee, which rang out in the Pennsylvania statehouse on June 7, 1776. Be it resolved, Lee said, that "these United Colonies are, and of right ought to be, free and independent States."

Americans Debate. The delegates, the people of Philadelphia, and others who heard of the resolution debated the pros and cons of independence. In the Continental Congress, the delegations from New England and the southern colonies were almost solidly in favor of the resolution. Those from the middle colonies were divided.

The New Englanders were, with good reason, the angriest Americans. Boston was occupied by British troops and the people of New Hampshire, Rhode Island, and Connecticut feared the same fate. The southern delegates were strongly for independence because they believed that mercantilist restrictions drained their wealth. One of their leaders was Patrick Henry, the radical Virginian famous for his 1775 "Liberty or Death" speech. The delegations from New York, Pennsylvania, New Jersey, and Delaware were divided, because those colonies had prospered as part of the British Empire.

The debate over independence among the other colonists was just as strong as in the Continental Congress itself. The people who supported independence came to be called *Patriots.* However, there were people who remained loyal to Great Britain in every colony. These people, called *Loyalists* or *Tories,* were often influential, and did not think that the Americans had the right or the reason to rebel. Other colonists, whether Patriot or Tory, simply believed that rebellion was wrong, and argued that change should come through the political process.

Writing the Declaration of Independence. The delegates soon realized that they would need a document to work from, or their time would be consumed by unimportant matters. Therefore, a committee was formed on June 11 to write a draft of a proclamation stating the Americans' case.

The committee consisted of five men from five different colonies. They were John Adams of Massachusetts, a lawyer; Roger Sherman of Connecticut, who had begun his career as a shoemaker's apprentice; Robert Livingston of New York, a wealthy landowner; world-famous Benjamin Franklin of Pennsylvania; and the young Virginian, Thomas Jefferson.

These men knew that a committee could never produce a document as eloquent and forceful as the occasion demanded. They decided to leave most of the writing to Jefferson, who was already famous as a writer of fine polished prose.

Jefferson retired to the room he had rented near the statehouse. He worked around the clock and came out with a masterpiece. The other committee members made a few changes, and then recommended that the Continental Congress accept their document—the *Declaration of Independence.*

The Vote Is Taken. On July 2, 1776, the Second Continental Congress, by then referred to simply as Congress, voted for independence. The New Englanders and southerners generally favored the resolution, but the delegates of the middle colonies still wavered. The Pennsylvania delegation voted for the resolution only because John Dickinson, who as a Quaker hated war, and the conservative banker, Robert Morris, agreed to

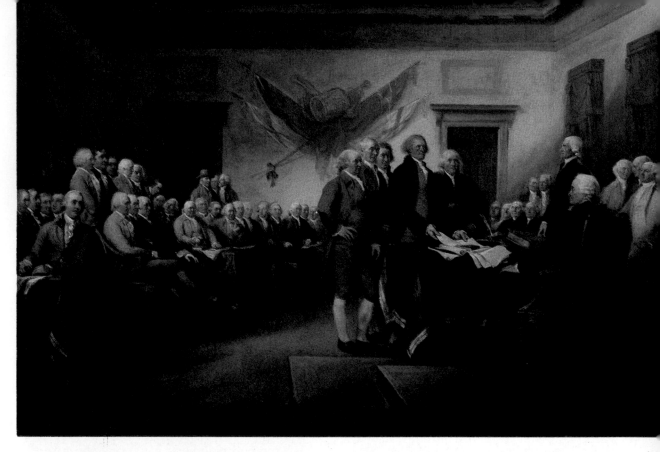

The Declaration of Independence was more than a message for King George—it was a message of intention, explanation, and political philosophy addressed to the whole world.

be absent when the vote was taken. Delaware voted for independence only because Caesar Rodney of Dover galloped 80 miles (128 kilometers) to Philadelphia to break a tie within Delaware's delegation. Then, on July 4, the Congress formally accepted the Declaration of Independence as the formal statement of their act.

SECTION REVIEW

1. Explain who the Patriots and the Loyalists were, and explain why each group felt as it did about independence.

2. What five delegates were chosen by the Continental Congress to write a draft of the Declaration of Independence, and what colonies did they represent?

3. On what date did the delegates to the Continental Congress formally accept the Declaration of Independence?

3. DECLARING INDEPENDENCE

The Declaration of Independence, one of the world's greatest political statements, was the work of Thomas Jefferson, a 33-year-old tobacco planter from the Virginia Piedmont. In order to understand the Declaration, it is necessary to understand Jefferson's philosophy and the purpose he meant the Declaration to serve.

A Proclamation to the World. Carefully read the first paragraph of the Declaration of Independence (*page 130*). In it, Jefferson does not simply declare that the colonies are independent. Nor does he address the document to the American people, to King George, or to Parliament.

The Declaration is addressed to the whole world. "When in the course of human events," Jefferson wrote, one people breaks the bands that have tied it to another, "a decent respect to the opinions of mankind" requires that the action be explained. Jefferson and most of the delegates to the Second Continental Congress believed that what they did in Philadelphia in July 1776 had meaning for all the world's people.

Enlightenment Philosophy.

The second paragraph of the Declaration is the most important part of the document. It expresses the philosophy on which the Americans' right to independence was based. During the *Enlightenment*, or the Age of Reason, as the eighteenth century is known, many educated people in Europe and America had come to believe that all human beings possessed certain natural rights. These were not rights granted by governments, and which governments could take away. These rights, the philosophers said, were granted to all humans by the Creator, and could not be taken away.

These thinkers also believed that God had created the universe, setting it in motion like a clock, and gave human beings the intelligence to understand the universe. Although the universe was not easy to understand, it did work according to definite laws. If humans studied nature, they would discover its laws. Knowing these laws would make what had appeared to be mysterious actually quite logical and "self-evident."

Natural Rights.

Among the truths that were self-evident in the 1700s were the rights of all human beings to life, liberty, and property (economic security). Jefferson borrowed these concepts from the English philosopher of the preceding century, John Locke, who had written *Two Treatises on Human Government* in 1690. These essays were written to justify England's overthrow of King James II in 1688. They attacked the idea of the divine right of monarchs, whereby kings and queens claimed to take their right to rule directly from God. Instead, Locke wrote that any government had the right to rule only as long as it protected the three natural rights of its subjects. When the government ceased to do so, its subjects had the right to rebel and replace the old government with a new one.

The natural rights philosophy made it possible to address the Declaration of Independence to the entire world. The message that all human beings were entitled to the same rights found eager listeners everywhere. In the first half of the Declaration of Independence, Thomas Jefferson wrote one of the noblest statements of human rights in history.

King George as a Tyrant.

What the Declaration does not mention is as important to understanding the American Revolution as what it does mention. Parliament was never mentioned, yet it was Parliament that exercised real power in Great Britain. All the laws that drove Americans to rebel were acts of Parliament, not of King George.

Jefferson did not directly attack Parliament because the Americans had denied that Parliament had any authority to make laws for them. According to the Americans, the colonial assemblies were equal to Parliament and independent of Parliament. Parliament's laws did not tie the Americans to Great Britain; only loyalty to George III did.

There was another reason that what Jefferson called an attempt to establish "an absolute Tyranny over these States" was blamed on George III. Because of Thomas Paine's *Common Sense*, the formerly popular king had become extremely unpopular among Americans. Throughout the colonies, Patriots destroyed paintings and statues of the king. People would be more likely to support a document that expressed what they were feeling.

The Declaration as Propaganda.

Close examination of the Declaration shows that Jefferson might have had another reason for choosing the wording he did. The document is a strong piece of *propaganda* favoring the Americans.

Although we usually think of propaganda in a negative sense, it actually refers to any information distributed to support an idea or cause. It is designed to convince others that an idea or cause is right. However, propaganda is one-sided—it tells only the information that will help a cause.

One of Jefferson's purposes in writing the Declaration was to win the American people to the cause of independence. In the final part of the document, Jefferson listed more than two dozen violations of the colonials' natural rights that he blamed on George III. His descriptions of the violations were not totally accurate. But Jefferson was not concerned with accuracy as much as he wanted to stir the Americans' imaginations.

For example, there was little in the events leading up to the Declaration to justify the statement that "He [King George] has plundered our

Discussion Question: Propaganda usually has negative connotations. Yet some of our country's most stirring speeches had elements of propaganda in them. Is the use of propaganda good or bad?

129

The Declaration of Independence

IN CONGRESS, JULY 4, 1776

The Unanimous Declaration of the Thirteen United States of America

When in the Course of human events, it becomes necessary for one people to dissolve the political bands which have connected them with another, and to assume among the Powers of the earth, the separate and equal station to which the Laws of Nature and of Nature's God entitle them, a decent respect to the opinions of mankind, requires that they should declare the causes which impel them to the separation.

We hold these truths to be self-evident, that all men are created equal, that they are endowed by their Creator with certain unalienable Rights, that among these are Life, Liberty and the pursuit of Happiness. That to secure these rights, Governments are instituted among Men, deriving their just powers from the consent of the governed, That whenever any Form of Government becomes destructive of these ends, it is the Right of the People to alter or to abolish it, and to institute new Government, laying its foundation on such principles and organizing its powers in such form, as to them shall seem most likely to effect their safety and Happiness. Prudence, indeed, will dictate that Governments long established should not be changed for light and transient causes; and accordingly all experience hath shown, that mankind are more disposed to suffer, while evils are sufferable, than to right themselves by abolishing the forms to which they are accustomed. But when a long train of abuses and usurpations, pursuing invariably the same Object evinces a design to reduce them under absolute Despotism, it is their right, it is their duty, to throw off such government, and to provide new Guards for their future security. Such has been the patient sufferance of these Colonies; and such is now the necessity which constrains them to alter their former Systems of Government. The history of the present King of Great Britain is a history of repeated injuries and usurpations, all having in direct object the establishment of an absolute Tyranny over these States. To prove this, let Facts be submitted to a candid world.

He has refused his Assent to Laws, the most wholesome and necessary for the public good.

He has forbidden his Governors to pass Laws of immediate and pressing importance, unless suspended in their operation till his Assent should be obtained; and when so suspended, he has utterly neglected to attend to them.

He has refused to pass other laws for the accommodation of large districts of people, unless those people would relinquish the right of Representation in the Legislature, a right inestimable to them and formidable to tyrants only.

He has called together legislative bodies at places unusual, uncomfortable, and distant from the depository of their Public Records, for the sole purpose of fatiguing them into compliance with his measures.

He has dissolved Representative Houses repeatedly, for opposing with manly firmness his invasions on the rights of the people.

He has refused for a long time, after such dissolutions, to cause others to be elected; whereby the Legislative Powers, incapable of Annihilation, have returned to the People at large for their exercise; the State remaining in the mean time exposed to all the dangers of invasion from without, and convulsions within.

He has endeavoured to prevent the population of these States; for that purpose obstructing the Laws for Naturalization of Foreigners; refusing to pass others to encourage their migration hither, and raising the conditions of new Appropriations of Lands.

He has obstructed the Administration of Justice, by refusing his Assent to Laws for establishing Judiciary Powers.

He has made Judges dependent on his Will alone, for the tenure of their offices, and the amount and payment of their salaries.

He has erected a multitude of New Offices, and sent hither swarms of Officers to harass our people, and eat out their substance.

He has kept among us, in times of peace, Standing Armies without the Consent of our Legislature.

He has affected to render the Military independent of and superior to the Civil Power.

He has combined with others to subject us to a jurisdiction foreign to our constitution, and unacknowledged by our laws; giving his Assent to their acts of pretended Legislation:

For quartering large bodies of armed troops among us:

For protecting them, by a mock Trial, from Punishment for any Murders which they should commit on the Inhabitants of these States:

For cutting off our Trade with all parts of the world:

For imposing taxes on us without our Consent:

For depriving us in many cases, of the benefits of Trial by Jury:

For transporting us beyond Seas to be tried for pretended offences:

For abolishing the free System of English Laws in a neighboring Province, establishing therein an Arbitrary government, and enlarging its Boundaries so as to render it at once an example and fit instrument for introducing the same absolute rule into these Colonies:

For taking away our Charters, abolishing our most valuable Laws, and altering fundamentally the Forms of our Governments:

For suspending our own Legislature, and declaring themselves invested with Power to legislate for us in all cases whatsoever.

He has abdicated Government here, by declaring us out of his Protection and waging War against us.

He has plundered our seas, ravaged our Coasts, burnt our towns, and destroyed the lives of our people.

He is at this time transporting large armies of foreign mercenaries to compleat the works of death, desolation and tyranny already begun with circumstances of Cruelty & perfidy scarcely paralleled in the most barbarous ages, and totally unworthy the Head of a civilized nation.

He has constrained our fellow Citizens taken Captive on the high Seas to bear Arms against their Country, to become the executioners of their friends and Brethren, or to fall themselves by their Hands.

He has excited domestic insurrections amongst us, and has endeavoured to bring on the inhabitants of our frontiers, the merciless Indian Savages, whose known rule of warfare, is an undistinguished destruction of all ages, sexes and conditions.

In every stage of these Oppressions We Have Petitioned for Redress in the most humble terms: Our repeated Petitions have been answered only by repeated injury. A Prince, whose character is thus marked by every act which may define a Tyrant, is unfit to be the ruler of a free people.

Nor have We been wanting in attention to our British brethren. We have warned them from time to time of attempts by their legislature to extend an unwarrantable jurisdiction over us. We have reminded them of the circumstances of our emigration and settlement here. We have appealed to their native justice and magnanimity, and we have conjured them by the ties of our common kindred to disavow these usurpations, which, would inevitably interrupt our connections and correspondence. They too have been deaf to the voice of justice and of consanguinity. We must, therefore, acquiesce in the necessity, which denounces our Separation, and hold them, as we hold the rest of mankind, Enemies in War, in Peace Friends.

We, therefore, the Representatives of the United States of America, in General Congress, Assembled, appealing to the Supreme Judge of the world for the rectitude of our intentions, do, in the Name, and by Authority of the good People of these Colonies, solemnly publish and declare, That these United Colonies are, and of Right ought to be Free and Independent States; that they are Absolved from all Allegiance to the British Crown, and that all political connection between them and the State of Great Britain, is and ought to be totally dissolved; and that as Free and Independent States, they have full Power to levy War, conclude Peace, contract Alliances, establish Commerce, and to do all other Acts and Things which Independent States may of right do. And for the support of this Declaration, with a firm reliance on the protection of Divine Providence, we mutually pledge to each other our Lives, our Fortunes and our Sacred Honor.

human rights violations listed by the founding fathers. Also show how the wording indicates that the signers of the Declaration felt that separation from Britain was considered a last course of action. Also initiate a discussion about whether the injustices cited really did exist.

131

seas, ravaged our Coasts, burnt our towns, and destroyed the lives of our people." The sentence conveys a picture of a people undergoing unspeakable horrors. This was obviously not the case when the Second Continental Congress could meet openly in the largest colonial city. But Jefferson knew Americans had a war to fight. He wanted to rally as many supporters as possible.

The Pursuit of Happiness.

John Locke had said that the three natural rights were life, liberty, and property. The Declaration calls the "self-evident" truths life, liberty, and the pursuit of happiness. Why the change?

Benjamin Franklin had pointed out that not every American owned property, and neither he nor other wealthy colonials were prepared to give their own property away. What people had a natural right to, Franklin argued, was the opportunity to own property. America offered them the right to pursue economic security and riches. This right was called the "pursuit of happiness" because people of the eighteenth century understood "happiness" to mean independence, security, and material comfort.

Exclusion of Blacks.

Not every American had the opportunity to own property. The almost 500,000 blacks who were slaves were denied not only the right to pursue happiness but the right of liberty. Many of the delegates to the Second Continental Congress, including Thomas Jefferson, owned slaves.

The denial of liberty to the blacks bothered many colonials, including Franklin (who later urged Americans to free their slaves). However, because a great deal of colonial wealth and power was supported by slaves, the Congress ignored the inconsistency of saying "all men are created equal" while denying black men and women their natural rights. Slavery was legal in every colony, and was particularly important in the southern colonies. The Continental Congress needed support from slaveholders, too, so the issue was not dealt with in the Declaration.

Exclusion of Women.

When Jefferson used the word *men*, did he mean men and women? It is difficult to say for sure. The word *man* can mean all humankind as well as just males. However,

Abigail Adams wrote intelligent, eloquent letters. Charles Adams, her grandson, later published two volumes of her letters.

almost everyone of the time believed that the head of a household should be a male and that the woman occupied a lower position.

A married woman was required to turn over the management of her property to her husband in every colony. Married women could not engage in business without their husbands' permission. They had to live where their husbands said they should live and obey almost every order he gave. Also, women were not represented in the elective assemblies because they could not vote.

Such limitations on women bothered Abigail Adams, who successfully managed the business affairs of her husband, John Adams, during the Revolutionary War. In a letter she wrote to her husband, she urged him and the Continental Congress to "remember the ladies and be more generous to them than your ancestors. Do not put such unlimited power in the hands of husbands. . . . If particular care and attention is not paid to the ladies, we are determined to foment rebellion, and will not be bound by any laws in which we have no voice or representation." But her views went unheeded.

Despite the inconsistencies of Jefferson's document, the Declaration of Independence was a brilliant call for the right of a people to govern themselves. Although John Adams, who became Jefferson's political opponent, said later that there was not an original word in the Declaration, this does not detract from Jefferson's work. Jefferson borrowed his ideas from others. But if he had expressed a completely new philosophy of government, no one would have listened. The genius of the Declaration is that it took current ideas and put them into such eloquent words.

SECTION REVIEW

1. Write a sentence to identify: Enlightenment, John Locke, propaganda, natural rights.
2. To whom is the Declaration of Independence addressed? Why?
3. In the first draft of the Declaration, what natural rights were said to be self-evident?
4. Why did Thomas Jefferson never mention Parliament in the Declaration of Independence?

---

4. THE CRITICAL WAR YEARS

The signers of the Declaration had good reason to celebrate in July 1776. The war had gone well during the first half of the year. Although General William Howe replaced General Gage as commander of British troops in America, Washington and the Continental Army (as Washington's soldiers were called) had chased the British out of Boston.

When the Americans around Boston received the 43 cannon and 16 large mortars from Fort Ticonderoga and Crown Point, General Washington placed them on Dorchester Heights, south of the city. The guns commanded the city and the harbor, and made General Howe's position unsafe. Howe decided to get out of Boston. With the help of the British fleet, which was commanded by his brother, Richard Howe, the General moved his troops and about 1,000 Boston Loyalists down the coast to New York.

British Advantages. Howe did not think of his evacuation of Boston as a defeat. He was confident he could stamp out the rebellion in a short time. The Redcoats he commanded were as good as any in Europe—tough, well-trained professionals. In addition, Britain's great wealth enabled Lord North to hire *mercenary* soldiers —soldiers who fought for money, not for national causes. In January 1776, North signed a contract with the little German state of Hesse-Kassel to "rent" 17,000 (later 30,000) Hessians to fight in America.

In contrast to the British professionals, the Continental Army and the state militias that Washington commanded were amateurs. They were farmers and artisans whose training amounted to some practice on the village green. General Washington himself wrote that "to place any dependence on" his soldiers "is assuredly resting on a broken staff."

The British were also helped by the many Americans who fought on their side. One historian estimates that 50,000 Loyalists took up arms for King George at one time or another. These Loyalists included many blacks who ran away from their patriot owners because the British promised them freedom after the war. These black soldiers later left the country for Canada and other British possessions along with as many as 100,000 white Loyalists.

Patriot Chances. The fact that the British had to transport most of their soldiers and supplies across the Atlantic did not amount to a colonial advantage. Great Britain was used to fighting overseas. By 1778, there were about 50,000 British, Hessian, and Loyalist troops in North America. Except at the beginning of the war, Washington could rarely put more than 10,000 in the field.

The Patriots probably had an edge in morale. They were fighting for their independence while the Redcoats and Hessians were fighting to deny liberty. Many Hessians came to hate the war, and when they saw the abundance of land in America, deserted to the rebel side. Some British soldiers sympathized with the Americans, too.

There was also some pro-American feeling in the British Parliament. Many Patriots believed that if their army could simply hold out long enough, the British people would grow weary of the war.

Class Activity: Using a chart, list the advantages each side had in the war. Include money, type of arms, troop strength, tactics, training.

133

AMERICAN REVOLUTIONARY WAR, 1775-1781

☆ Battles
✕ Fort
⚓ French fleet

Also, although the British navy seemed to be over-powering, the Americans did have some success at sea. During the war, they built more than 50 warships of varying sizes. The most memorable American victory occurred when John Paul Jones, in command of the *Bon Homme Richard,* engaged the British ship *Serapis* in 1779. Jones won the day by lashing his sinking ship to the *Serapis* and defeating the British in hand-to-hand combat. At the height of the battle, when asked to surrender, Jones uttered his famous remark, "I have not yet begun to fight!"

Most important of all, the Americans had reason to hope for help from the French. King Louis XVI and his ministers had not forgotten their humiliation by Great Britain in 1763. They saw the rebellion in America as an opportunity to take revenge, and perhaps even regain Canada and Louisiana. As early as May 1776, the French began to funnel money and arms secretly to the Americans. During the first two years of the war, the French provided 80 percent of the gunpowder the Americans used.

Ben Franklin in Paris.

The Continental Congress, which held some poorly defined governmental powers, made Benjamin Franklin ambassador to France in September 1776. His job was to keep the assistance flowing and, if possible, to persuade the French to join the war on the American side.

Congress could not have picked a better ambassador. Franklin was well known in France for his scientific experiments. When he learned that the elegant ladies and gentlemen at Louis XVI's court thought of Americans as "noble savages," he played the part. Much as he preferred elegant living, Franklin dressed in suits made of homespun wool and never donned the powdered wigs that were then fashionable in European high society. He even pretended he was a Quaker, even though he had generally opposed the Quakers at home.

The French foreign minister, Count Vergennes (vêr-jĕn′) dealt cautiously with Franklin. France might be interested in an alliance with the United States if the Americans could prove they could defeat the British in battle.

Defeat in New York.

Washington's army set out to gain the victory that Franklin needed. In high spirits, the Continental Army marched to New York City to meet Howe's army. It was the last high-spirited march the army would make until the war was almost over.

Howe's strategy was to meet Washington in battle, defeat him, and then go north along the Hudson River. He planned to link up with the British army under Sir Guy Carleton that was coming south from Canada. Having thus cut off New England from the other colonies, the two armies would march through Massachusetts, retaking Boston. If that did not convince the southern colonies to surrender, Howe would then move south and force them to give up.

On July 2, 1776, Howe landed 10,000 soldiers on Staten Island, just south of New York City. More British soldiers arrived, and when his force numbered 32,000, he moved to Long Island to attack Washington's troops, who were dug in on Brooklyn Heights.

Brooklyn Heights was high ground, but it also backed on the East River. With dozens of warships controlling the river and New York Harbor, it seemed that Howe had the Americans trapped. But after driving the Americans off the heights, Howe stopped the attack and let Washington escape across the East River to Manhattan Island.

Howe then pressed after Washington in a series of running battles. From Washington Heights at the northern tip of Manhattan, Washington was forced to retreat north to White Plains, across the Hudson River, then south to Fort Lee in New Jersey, and across New Jersey to Pennsylvania. Washington had started the New York campaign in July with about 23,000 soldiers. By December, because of death, desertion, and surrender, he had fewer than 8,000. But his army, although overmatched, was still in the field.

The Fox Turns on the Hounds.

It seemed like the favorite sport of the English aristocrat, the fox hunt. Indeed, Howe infuriated Washington by sounding the traditional bugle call of the hunt when the Americans were on the run. But Washington's army was in the situation of a weary fox. Men were beginning to desert, and news arrived from Philadelphia that a worried Congress had moved to Baltimore. In December 1776, just a few months after the celebrations of independence, the American cause appeared doomed.

On September 6, 1776, in New York City, the "Turtle" was launched. It was a one-man submarine invented by David Bushnell, used by the Americans to set explosives on the undersides of British warships.

REVOLUTIONARY WAR CAMPAIGNS
AND BATTLES, 1775-1779

The British could have continued chasing Washington during the winter of 1776–1777. But Howe commanded by the book, and the book said that an army did not fight in the winter. Because Carleton had turned back to Canada after his battle with Arnold in October, the bold plan to cut off New England had to be postponed. Also, the warmth and nightlife of New York City beckoned. Leaving small garrisons of Hessians to watch Washington and to guard Trenton and Princeton in central New Jersey, Howe called off the war for the season.

George Washington also believed in commanding by the book, but he was desperate. To go into winter quarters in Pennsylvania meant to have no army in the spring. He had to win a battle, to pick up the spirits of his soldiers and convince the Continental Congress that he should remain in charge.

Washington chose Christmas night to strike. He guessed correctly that the Hessians would celebrate the holiday with plenty of drinking. Washington recrossed the Delaware. His tiny force marched nine miles to Trenton, and at dawn

Research Assignment: Have students do a report on the weapons used during the war. Include in the report the amount of time it took to move troops and how this affected strategies.

completely surprised the Hessians. Washington captured the whole garrison.

In reply, Howe sent General George Cornwallis to retake Trenton. Washington surprised one of Cornwallis's forces at Princeton and forced the British back to New Brunswick, close to their base in New York City. Washington then took his soldiers into winter quarters at Morristown, having practically cleared New Jersey of British troops.

The Battles of Trenton and Princeton were not very large battles. They were more like raids. But they were extremely important. Washington's success after four months of nothing but defeats kept the dream of independence alive. And Washington had his revenge for Howe's bugle calls.

British Successes. In the spring of 1777, Howe had his choice of plans. He could move up the Hudson River to Albany and revive the plan to isolate New England, or he could move southward and attack General Washington. He decided to go after Washington, capture Philadelphia, and con-

quer Pennsylvania. As slow as ever, Howe did not get started until July. Leaving General Henry Clinton and an army in New York, he sailed to the Chesapeake and marched toward Philadelphia.

Howe and Washington fought twice, at Brandywine Creek and at Germantown, a suburb of Philadelphia. The Americans had to withdraw from the field both times, and Howe occupied Philadelphia on September 26. However, Howe controlled little more than Philadelphia and the coastal areas. Washington's army was still intact, and the Patriot war effort continued.

Howe's occupation of Philadelphia was to have other effects on the British war effort. For in June, a British army of 8,000 soldiers under General John Burgoyne had begun to move from Montreal down Lake Champlain and the Hudson Valley, expecting to meet Howe at Albany. The Americans scoffed because he brought tons of personal baggage they considered unnecessary: dozens of changes of clothing, heavy furniture, white linen tablecloths and real silver, crystal, and china for Burgoyne's meals.

General Washington, following a brilliant plan, crossed the Delaware River on Christmas night, 1776, and attacked the surprised Hessian troops stationed at Trenton, New Jersey. His troops were victorious and their victory boosted the Patriots' morale around America.

Major General Benedict Arnold, although wounded (above center), helped win the Battle of Saratoga and force the British commander, General Burgoyne, to surrender with his whole army.

The chief reason for Burgoyne's delay was that he was moving a huge army over narrow footpaths meant for Indians and fur traders. American guerillas made his progress more difficult by chopping down trees across the narrow road. And Burgoyne's inexperience in frontier living made picking a route difficult.

Saratoga! By July, although Burgoyne had taken Fort Ticonderoga back from the Americans, he sensed that he was in trouble. Another British force was supposed to move eastward from Lake Ontario to Albany, but it had been cut off and driven back by a Patriot force under Benedict Arnold. When Burgoyne sent a detachment to seize supplies in Bennington, Vermont, it was wiped out by local militia. In two pitched battles near Saratoga, the British lost hundreds of men.

By this time, Burgoyne knew that General Howe would send no help from Philadelphia. Burgoyne might have returned to Montreal. Instead, he requested help from General Clinton in New York, and waited at Saratoga. But the American forces, commanded by Benedict Arnold and General Horatio Gates, grew stronger. They sur-

rounded Burgoyne's army, and on October 17, 1777, Burgoyne surrendered 5,000 troops.

The Battle of Saratoga was the most important in the war to that time—and the Americans had won it. Because of Saratoga, New England was saved. Just as important, the news of the battle was exactly what Benjamin Franklin, still in Paris, was waiting to hear. The capture of Burgoyne's army paved the way for a French alliance.

SECTION REVIEW

1. Write a sentence to identify: General William Howe, Continental Army, mercenary, Count Vergennes.

2. Make a chart classifying each of the following as either a British or an American advantage in the war: (a) help from France, (b) help from Loyalists, (c) higher morale, (d) powerful navy, (e) sympathizers in Parliament, (f) Hessian troops.

3. Explain how the outcome of the Battle of Saratoga saved New England.

Although a less important battlefront, the Revolutionary War was also fought in the frontier areas of Ohio, Kentucky, and western Virginia. British gains in these areas until 1778 were partially the result of help from the Indians. The tables turned somewhat in 1778 and 1779. However, the skirmishes were not critical to the war's outcome.

5. THE ROAD TO VICTORY

When Lord North heard the news of the American victory at Saratoga, he sent a message to Franklin. He was willing to end the war by meeting all the demands the Americans had made up to July 2, 1776. The Intolerable Acts would be repealed, the colonials would control their own internal affairs, and no one would be punished for their part in the rebellion. They only had to swear loyalty to the Crown.

The generous offer conceded victory to the Americans. Although Lord North did not use the terms, he was suggesting that the colonies become self-governing commonwealths within the British Empire, much like Canada, Australia, and New Zealand were later to become.

But North's offer came too late. The Patriots no longer trusted George III's government. After so many years of demanding the rights of British subjects, they no longer wanted to be British subjects.

Help From France. On December 17, 1777, Count Vergennes formally recognized the United States of America as an independent nation. In February 1778, he and Franklin signed a treaty of alliance that would take effect if France and England went to war (which they did in June 1778). The treaty called for close commercial contacts after the war. Franklin hoped that France would replace Great Britain as the chief customer for American products.

The treaty also stated that if the Americans conquered Canada, France would make no claims on their old province. Instead, France would receive the British West Indies as compensation for its help.

As the events of the next several years showed, the Revolution could not have been won without foreign help. France supplied the fleet that neutralized Great Britain's control of the American waters. Individual Patriot captains, such as John Paul Jones and John Barry, won extraordinary naval victories in one-to-one encounters with British warships, and privateers caused some disruption in the British merchant marine. But until the French entered the war, the American coastline was at the mercy of the British Navy.

French assistance also paved the way for Spain and the Netherlands to join the war on the American side. Britain was quite alone in fighting the Americans. That is why France is known as

General Burgoyne's surrender to the American Patriots at Saratoga proved to be the turning point of the war. In December, France decided to recognize the United States of America as an independent nation, and a French-American alliance became a possibility.

John Paul Jones, captain of the Bon Homme Richard, *defeated the larger British ship* Serapis.

Marquis de Lafayette was commissioned a major general in the Continental Army on July 31, 1777.

"America's Oldest Friend." In fact, except for Russia, France is the only major European power with which the United States has never fought a declared war.

Foreign Soldiers Fight for Independence.

Professional soldiers from several countries fought on the American side in the War for Independence. Some were mercenaries, looking for nothing but a salary. Others liked the chance to "twist the Lion's tail," as defying Great Britain was called. Others were inspired by the natural rights philosophy of the Declaration of Independence. Such a figure was the Marquis de Lafayette (lä-fä′ĕt), a 19-year-old aristocrat who was an excellent field commander and became a close friend of George Washington's. Another idealist was Casimir Pulaski, a Polish noble who had fought unsuccessfully to win his country's independence from Russia. Recruited by Franklin, Pulaski was a dashing cavalry commander. He lost his life leading a charge at the Battle of Savannah in October 1778. Another cavalry officer, the German Johann Kalb,

was also killed in the Revolution, at the Battle of Camden, in South Carolina.

Probably more valuable than combat officers were specialists like the Polish Thaddeus Kosciusko (kŏs′ē-ŭs′kō). Kosciusko was a military engineer who knew how to build fortifications. Friedrich Wilhelm von Steuben (shtoi′bən), a Prussian, was an expert in training troops. During the winter of 1777–1778, he transformed Washington's army from a ragtag group of artisans and farmers into a professional fighting force.

A Bleak Winter.

Steuben arrived just in time. The winter of 1777–1778 was the most difficult the Continental Army faced. While Howe's Redcoats enjoyed the comforts of Philadelphia, Washington's troops camped at Valley Forge outside the city. Supplies were scarce and the winter was bitterly cold. Many soldiers died, and many deserted and went home to their families. But a strong core of soldiers remained, drilling, practicing, and growing more confident that they could win the war.

Lafayette was a major general at the age of 19. His full name was Marie Joseph Paul Yves Roch Gilbert du Motier, Marquis de Lafayette.

During the winter at Valley Forge, General von Steuben (below), helped Washington (above, with Lafayette) to train his troops in professional military techniques and discipline.

The War Drags On. General Clinton, who replaced William Howe as commander of British forces in May 1778, developed a new strategy. Clinton reasoned that New England was lost, at least for the time being, because of the defeat at Saratoga. His plan was to conquer the southern colonies while the British Navy *blockaded* the American coast and strangled the American economy.

Beginning with the occupation of Savannah, Georgia, in December 1778, Clinton's forces won a series of victories in the South. However, as in the North, southern Patriot commanders like Francis Marion of South Carolina (the "Swamp Fox") were somehow able to keep their beaten armies in the field. The British were seldom able to completely crush American resistance.

Then, in May 1780, a British force under General Clinton captured Charleston, South Carolina, and destroyed the defending American army under General Benjamin Lincoln. At this time, Clinton turned over command of the southern forces to General George Cornwallis and

141

returned to New York, confident that the southern colonies would be quickly subdued.

Cornwallis began successfully. He defeated a large force of Americans at Camden, South Carolina in August, and appeared to have the Carolinas in his grasp.

At this point, the Americans returned to the frontier warfare they had used so well when the British retreated from Concord in 1775. They knew that they would not be able to stand against the British in a pitched battle, so they took to hit-and-run attacks. These actions took their toll in British casualties and lost supplies.

Eventually, the Americans felt powerful enough to face the British openly. A force of Americans under General Daniel Morgan defeated a British force at Cowpens, South Carolina, on January 17, 1781. Then, at Guilford Courthouse, North Carolina, on March 15, 1781, Americans under Nathanael Greene battled Cornwallis's troops. The British won that battle, but lost more than a quarter of their army. Cornwallis abandoned his Carolina campaign, and retreated to the coast and the protection of the Royal Navy.

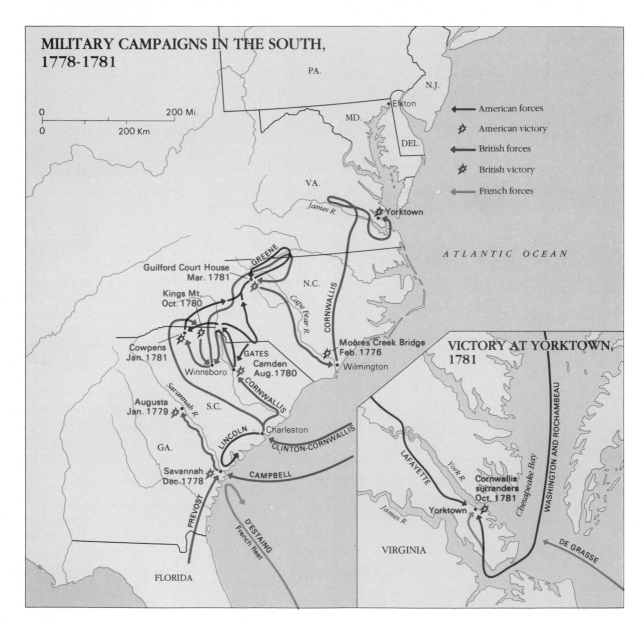

MILITARY CAMPAIGNS IN THE SOUTH, 1778-1781

American forces
American victory
British forces
British victory
French forces

Guilford Court House Mar. 1781
Kings Mt. Oct. 1780
Cowpens Jan. 1781
Winnsboro
GATES
Camden Aug. 1780
Moores Creek Bridge Feb. 1776
Wilmington
Augusta Jan. 1779
Savannah Dec. 1778
Charleston
CLINTON-CORNWALLIS
CAMPBELL
PREVOST
D'ESTAING French fleet
LINCOLN
CORNWALLIS
GREENE
Yorktown

VICTORY AT YORKTOWN, 1781

LAFAYETTE
York R.
Cornwallis surrenders Oct. 1781
Yorktown
James R.
Chesapeake Bay
WASHINGTON AND ROCHAMBEAU
DE GRASSE
VIRGINIA

American Problems Off the Field. The war wore heavily on the Americans. Because of the British blockade, the price of imports and even home-grown necessities soared. The members of the Continental Congress continued to bicker, failing to send Washington the money and supplies he needed. In 1780 and 1781, troops from Connecticut, Pennsylvania, and New Jersey mutinied when they were not paid. Washington just barely kept them in the army.

Support from Home. The mutineers were probably worried about their families at home. A soldier's pay was low, and could not support a family. Soldiers that were away at war for two or three years had to leave the farmwork or family business to their wives and children. And they could never be sure that the British wouldn't raid their towns and destroy their homes.

Since the British blockade was so complete, the Patriot women became important suppliers of the Continental Army. They collected metalware to be melted down and turned into cannonballs. Bandages for the medical corps came from cloth the women spun. They made many of the army's uniforms.

Women also contributed at the front. Many worked as camp cooks. Others cared for the wounded and sick in the military hospitals. A few lived more dangerously. Some women, such as Deborah Sampson, disguised themselves as men and fought in battles. And quite a number of women acted as spies for the Continental Army.

Betrayal. In September 1780, British Major John André was captured. He was delivering a message from General Benedict Arnold, commander of the American fort at West Point on the Hudson River, to the British commander. When the message was made known, the Americans were shocked. Arnold had been plotting to turn West Point over to the British!

Although Arnold had won fame on the battlefield, he had been passed over for promotions. Disillusioned with the American leaders, and convinced that the American cause was lost, he intended to sell his services to the British. If his plans had gone through, the British would have controlled the Hudson River and been in position to retake New England.

Deborah Sampson, disguised as a man, actively participated as a soldier in the American Revolution. She was wounded and received a pension.

Although the British, who were encamped in New York City, did not try to move up the Hudson after Arnold's plot was discovered, the threat to New England kept Washington in the North while the Americans were battling Cornwallis in the Carolinas. In fact, after the Battle of Stony Point, New York, on July 16, 1779 (which the Americans won), the British and American armies in the North did little more than watch each other until 1781.

The Sudden End. Then, in August 1781, Washington realized that General Cornwallis could be trapped. After Cornwallis abandoned the Carolinas, he took his troops to Virginia. Tired of chasing the elusive Americans, he set up camp at Yorktown, Virginia, on the same narrow neck of land where Jamestown had been founded in 1607 American forces commanded by Lafayette were watching the British. Washington knew that if he could get enough troops to Yorktown, he could bottle up Cornwallis. This would leave the British only one escape route—by sea. But Washington

Research Assignment: In keeping with the topic of women in U.S. history, mention the numerous books about women who fought in the Revolutionary War. Assign a report on them.

143

Benedict Arnold became disillusioned when he was passed over for a military promotion. Becoming a traitor, he offered to aid the British, but his plans were discovered.

also knew that a French fleet under Count François de Grasse was already on its way from the West Indies to Chesapeake Bay.

Washington decided to gamble. He left a small force in New York to occupy General Clinton, and rushed to Virginia. His army marched quickly to the head of Chesapeake Bay near Elkton, Maryland. Part of his army then marched down to get in front of Cornwallis, while meeting up with the force commanded by Lafayette. The other half boarded ships and sailed down the bay, and came up behind Cornwallis.

When General Clinton realized what was happening, he sent his fleet to rescue Cornwallis. The British ships reached the mouth of Chesapeake Bay at the beginning of September, but De Grasse and the French fleet had already set up a blockade. In the sharp naval battle that followed, the French drove the British fleet back to New York.

Washington, with almost 10,000 American and 7,000 French soldiers, then began the siege of Yorktown. The American and French gunners constantly bombarded the British. Cornwallis, encircled and with only about 7,000 troops, held out for another month. On October 19, 1781, Cornwallis surrendered.

The World Turned Upside Down. Yorktown was an extraordinary victory. Lowly colonials (with French help) had defeated English soldiers, supposedly the best in the world. General Corn-

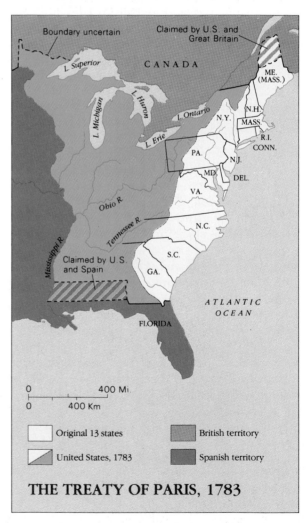

THE TREATY OF PARIS, 1783

Boundary uncertain

Claimed by U.S. and Great Britain

CANADA

L. Superior
L. Michigan
L. Huron
L. Ontario
L. Erie

ME. (MASS.)
N.H.
MASS.
R.I.
CONN.
N.Y.
PA.
N.J.
MD.
DEL.
VA.

Ohio R.
Tennessee R.
Mississippi R.

Claimed by U.S. and Spain

N.C.
S.C.
GA.

FLORIDA

ATLANTIC OCEAN

0 — 400 Mi.
0 — 400 Km.

☐ Original 13 states
▨ United States, 1783
▨ British territory
▨ Spanish territory

144

Research Assignment: Have one or more students design a three-dimensional model or a diagram of the battle of Yorktown. Because of the topography and the various parties involved, such an illustration can prove useful in explaining the battle to the class.

wallis acknowledged the effect of his defeat when, to accompany the surrender, he ordered the British band to play the hymn "The World Turned Upside Down."

Cornwallis was not so graceful in the actual surrender ceremony. Instead of personally giving his sword to Washington, he sent one of his aides. Perhaps remembering the call of the fox hunt in New York four years earlier, Washington directed one of his aides, General Benjamin Lincoln, to take the sword. Washington would not be humiliated this day.

Despite the stunning victory at Yorktown, the war did not officially end for two more years. More than 54,000 British troops continued to occupy some of the most important American cities, and George III wanted to fight on. However, Parliament was not willing to make the effort needed to win the war. Lord North was forced to resign, and was replaced by Lord Rockingham, a noble who had been friendly to the Americans. In the spring of 1782, Rockingham sent negotiators to Paris to meet with Benjamin Franklin, John Adams, and John Jay. While the treaty commissioners met, Patriots and Loyalists continued to skirmish. Fighting finally stopped in April 1783. Then, in September 1783, nearly two years after the Battle of Yorktown, the *Treaty of Paris* officially ended the war between Great Britain and the United States.

SECTION REVIEW

1. Write a sentence to identify: John Paul Jones, "America's Oldest Friend," "Swamp Fox," "The World Turned Upside Down."

2. After the Battle of Saratoga, what offer did England's prime minister, Lord North, make to the Americans?

3. Name and briefly describe the roles of some Europeans who fought on the American side.

4. How might Benedict Arnold's betrayal of West Point have seriously damaged the struggle for independence?

The last major fighting of the American Revolution ended on October 19, 1781, at Yorktown. There, the British general, Cornwallis, surrendered a large British army to General Washington. America's independence had been won.

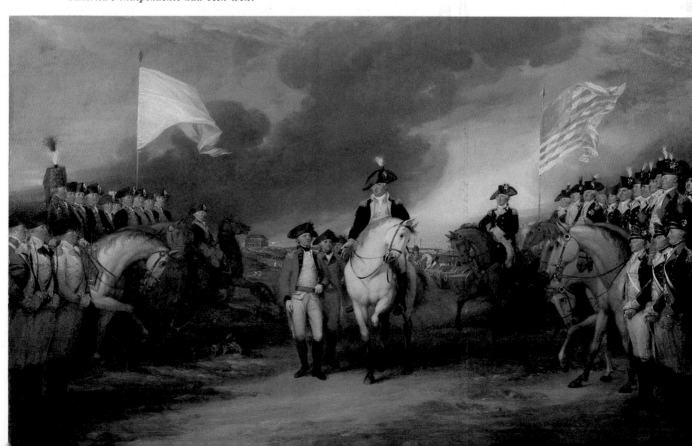

CHAPTER REVIEW

TIME LINE

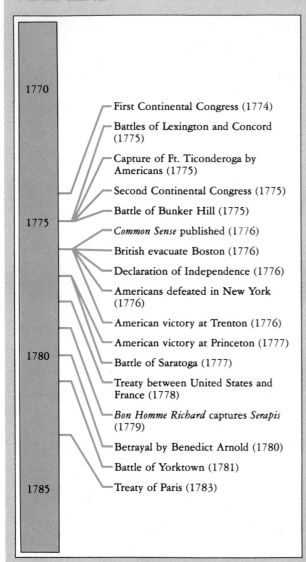

- First Continental Congress (1774)
- Battles of Lexington and Concord (1775)
- Capture of Ft. Ticonderoga by Americans (1775)
- Second Continental Congress (1775)
- Battle of Bunker Hill (1775)
- *Common Sense* published (1776)
- British evacuate Boston (1776)
- Declaration of Independence (1776)
- Americans defeated in New York (1776)
- American victory at Trenton (1776)
- American victory at Princeton (1777)
- Battle of Saratoga (1777)
- Treaty between United States and France (1778)
- *Bon Homme Richard* captures *Serapis* (1779)
- Betrayal by Benedict Arnold (1780)
- Battle of Yorktown (1781)
- Treaty of Paris (1783)

TIME LINE QUESTIONS

1. Which occurred first—the first battle of the American Revolution, or the colonies' declaration of their independence?
2. How many years passed between the first battles in the War for Independence and the final defeat of the British forces?
3. When did the French enter the war?
4. What 1776 event happened in Boston?

SKILLS STRATEGY

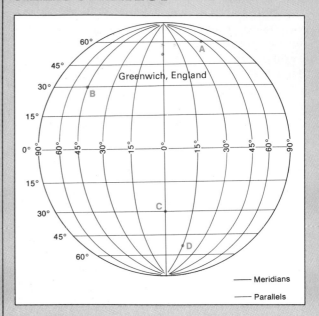

Greenwich, England

— Meridians
— Parallels

MAP GRIDS

An essential part of a map is the *map grid,* made up of one set of lines called *meridians* and another set of lines called *parallels*. Meridian lines are shown above in black, and parallel lines are in red. Meridians show degrees of longitude and allow you to locate any place in relation to the *prime meridian,* or 0° longitude. The prime meridian was set at Greenwich, England, because the observatory there was an important one in the 1400s and 1500s, when both navigation skills and mapmaking skills were becoming important.

Meridians go 180° east and 180° west from 0°. The 180° meridian, east or west, is called the International Dateline. You know that there are 360° in a circle. There are, therefore, 360° marked by meridian lines on a globe.

All meridians converge at the North and the South poles. Lines of latitude, however, are called parallels because they never meet, but run parallel to each other. These lines allow you to find a location in its position relative to the North or South poles. The longest parallel is at the equator (0°). The higher the number of the north or south parallels, the farther away from the equator the

Making Connections: Review the questions and topics referred to in the Making Connections section opening this chapter.

THE NEW ENGLAND AND MIDDLE ATLANTIC STATES, TODAY

State boundary
★ State capital
• Other city

lines are. Any place on the earth's surface can be pinpointed on the grid if the exact degrees of the meridian and parallel that pass through the place are known.

Use parallels and meridians to locate the following on the hemisphere diagram above. Point A is located at 60° N and 45° E. Where are points B and C located? Point D is located about halfway between 45° S and 60° S. Since the parallel on which it is located is neither shown nor labeled, you have to estimate the location of point D.

APPLYING SKILLS

1. Which parallels north of the equator are labeled on the diagram above?
2. Use a parallel to locate each of these cities on the map: Newark, New Jersey; the capital of Maryland; Syracuse.
3. Estimate the north–south distance in miles and kilometers between the capital of Delaware and the capital of Connecticut; between Harrisburg and Richmond.
4. Summarize the functions of parallels and meridians on a map or globe.

CHAPTER 6 TEST

TEXT REVIEW

1. Did the delegates to the First Continental Congress meet to declare the independence of the American colonies from Great Britain? Give facts to support your answer.
2. Name the places where the first four battles of the Revolution occurred.
3. Which American officer commanded the ships that defeated Sir Guy Carleton's ships on Lake Champlain?
4. What was happening in Philadelphia while the initial battles of the Revolution were being fought?
5. Give two ways in which *Common Sense* may have changed the ideas of Americans.
6. Did all Americans support the ideas in the Declaration of Independence? Explain your answer.
7. What three self-evident natural rights of all human beings were included in the version of the Declaration adopted on July 4, 1776?
8. Why was the battle in which Americans finally won their independence such an extraordinary victory?

CRITICAL THINKING

9. How might your life be different if the Americans had accepted the British offer to end the fighting after the American victory at Saratoga in 1777?
10. Give some examples of the persuasive language Jefferson used in the Declaration of Independence.

WRITING A PARAGRAPH

Write a paragraph beginning or ending with the topic sentence that follows. Arrange the supporting sentences of your paragraph in chronological order, starting with the time of the First Continental Congress. Use words and phrases such as *at first* or *by the following year* to show time order.

Topic Sentence: The general American attitude toward King George III gradually changed for the worse as difficulties with Great Britain developed.

Quotation: from the novel *O Pioneers!* Other works by Willa Cather (1873–1947) include *April Twilights, Alexander's Bridge, The Song of the Lark, My Antonia, Youth and the Bright Medusa, My Mortal Enemy, Death Comes for the Archbishop, Shadows on the Rock,* and *Obscure Destinies.*

CHAPTER 7

MOLDING A NATION

1783–1789

The history of every country begins in the heart of a man or a woman.   WILLA CATHER

Making Connections. When the American colonials broke away from England, they had to create their own government to carry on the war and bind the 13 states together. The first central government they created, based on the Articles of Confederation, seemed to be just what was needed—loose central authority, and strong state governments. But could this government work?

In this chapter, you will learn:
- Why many of the new state constitutions called for elections every year
- How England and Spain plotted to exploit the weaknesses of the United States
- Who led a rebellion against Massachusetts
- Why a constitutional convention was called in 1787
- What compromises were needed to satisfy both large states and small states in order to produce a new form of government
- How each of the three branches of the new government was given powers to balance the other two branches

You know that the American colonists rebelled against England because they felt their rights were being violated. Consequently, their first central government was weak. As you read, note the problems that this weak national government caused, and how most of the problems were solved by adopting the Constitution.

Sections
1. The State Governments
2. The Confederation
3. Writing a Constitution
4. Ratification
5. The Constitution

1. THE STATE GOVERNMENTS

When the American colonists rose against their British rulers, they had to create new local governments for themselves. Each state had to carry on the war, keep order in its towns, collect taxes, and supply its militia. Since British control and virtual representation in Parliament was no longer accepted, the Patriots had to set up their own system of control.

The governments that the states created resembled the British government in many respects. After all, the Americans were mostly British or of British descent, and their customs were rooted in British culture. But the Americans had been working for years to ensure their rights as British subjects, and in their new state governments, they made sure that those rights could never be taken away.

Written Constitutions.   One of the most important breaks with British tradition was the value Americans placed on *written constitutions*. England has no one document on which the government is founded. What is called the British constitution consists of the *Magna Carta*, a list of rights the powerful nobles won from King John in 1215, and the *English Bill of Rights*, adopted in 1689. But most of the duties and powers of the Crown, Parliament, and the judiciary are not written down. They developed over time as custom, and were accepted as law. This law was interpreted by Parliament and the judiciary system.

Philadelphia, Pennsylvania, as seen in this 1790 engraving by William Birch, was the scene of the national convention called to amend the Articles of Confederation.

Skills Review: Reinforce knowledge of the map skills learned in the preceding Skills Strategy by using maps to illustrate the information in this chapter. Have students label a blank map; give them coordinates of cities, lakes and other items.

Disagreement about the interpretation of this unwritten constitution lay at the heart of the American Revolution. If the colonists thought that Parliament's interpretation was wrong, they had no documentary proof to turn to. Consequently, the Americans wanted their system of government, and particularly their rights as citizens, written out for all to see. As Thomas Jefferson said, written constitutions "furnish a text to which those who are watchful may again rally and call the people."

State Constitutions.

When possible, the Americans used familiar sources as models for their state constitutions. Connecticut and Rhode Island adjusted the wording in their old colonial charters. They simply struck out references to loyalty to the Crown and continued to govern themselves as before. Connecticut used its colonial charter as the basis for its government until 1818, and Rhode Island did not write a new state constitution until 1842.

In states that had not had charters, written constitutions were drafted early in the war. Many features of these state constitutions reflected American resentment of British rule. For example, British officials (including colonial governors) held their posts as long as the Crown approved of their behavior. The citizens had no say in the matter. To make officials accountable to the people they governed, most of the new constitutions called for yearly elections. This assured that if an official did not act for the common good, the people could choose another official. The number of years a person could serve in an office was also limited. The Americans did not want a permanent privileged class of any kind, especially one based on unlimited political power. As John Adams said, "Where annual elections end, there slavery begins."

The constitution makers feared executive power most. As colonials they had controlled the elected assemblies—the legislative branch of government. But the governors, who enforced the law, had been appointed by the Crown, and were often beyond the colonials' control. The new state governors, although elected, were usually powerless ceremonial figures. Pennsylvania's constitution, which was written in 1776, provided for no governor at all.

Separation of Church and State.

The new American states differed in their approach to the relationship between church and state. In the southern and middle colonies, the Church of England (the Anglican or Episcopal Church) had been *established* during the colonial period. That is, the clergy and the churches had been supported at taxpayer expense. Most Anglican priests had strong ties to England and had opposed the Revolution. Consequently, church and state were separated by law in these states. Financial support of churches became a private affair.

In New England, the Congregational, or Puritan, churches were the strongest, and most of their ministers had supported the Revolution. In those states, the Congregational Church remained established, and continued to be so well into the nineteenth century.

Democracy Spreads Slowly.

In every state, more people were *enfranchised*, or given the right to vote, than in colonial times. In Pennsylvania, every male who paid taxes could vote. Vermont, which was not officially a state but was run like one by Ethan and Levi Allen, also followed this rule. In most other states a man could not vote unless he owned property. For a short while, women who met the property qualification could vote in New Jersey.

There were other limits to democracy. In 1807, the New Jersey legislature decided that women should not be allowed to vote, and disenfranchised all women in the state. Roman Catholics were not allowed to hold office in North Carolina until 1835. In most states, many men who could vote could not hold office, for the higher the office, the higher the property qualifications were. This rule was accepted because most Americans of that time believed that wealthier people were better qualified to govern.

Rights and Liberties.

The Patriots went to war because they believed Great Britain had trampled on their rights and liberties. These same people guarded against the possibility that their fellow Americans might try to take away these hard-earned rights. A *bill of rights* was a consistent feature in the state constitutions. It listed those rights that the people felt no government could take away. Most of the freedoms later written into

Discussion Question: Before reading the chapter, ask students how they would go about starting a government. What kind of model would they have used if they were involved with setting up the first U.S. government? Answers should indicate some reliance on past models—either colonial or British.

150

the Bill of Rights of the United States Constitution can be found in one or another of the original state constitutions.

Even these supposedly *inalienable* rights were qualified. Only in Massachusetts were black people thought to be covered by a bill of rights. The Massachusetts Supreme Court ruled that slavery was abolished because the state constitution said that "all men are born free and equal," and the state bill of rights guaranteed personal liberty. Nowhere else was this action taken soon, and some southern states explicitly stated that their bills of rights did not apply to slaves or even to free blacks.

SECTION REVIEW

1. Write a sentence to identify: Magna Carta, separation of church and state, enfranchise.
2. Why can it be said that the English have an "unwritten constitution"?
3. After the American colonists declared their independence from Great Britain and were forming their new state governments, why did they insist upon having written constitutions?
4. List some limits to democracy in the new American states.

---

2. THE CONFEDERATION

Organizing state governments was relatively easy. However, most American leaders recognized the need for a national government. The states were united by their common dislike of British rule, but this would not keep them together through the trials of the long war and adjusting to independence. Therefore, on June 12, 1776, the Second Continental Congress formed a committee to write a constitution.

The document that the committee wrote was the *Articles of Confederation.* Accepted by almost the entire Continental Congress in 1777, it was not officially adopted until 1781, when Maryland finally ratified the Articles. This framework of government reflected the ideas and feelings that went into the state constitutions. Consequently,

the document created the type of government the Americans thought they wanted—a weak central government that would not deny them their rights.

Principles of the Articles of Confederation
The United States had no president under the Articles of Confederation. The person who presided over the Confederation Congress was called "president," but had no power or responsibility outside of conducting meetings. The Confederation Congress was the sole governing body. It was supposed to make the laws, and execute them as well.

Members of the Confederation Congress were elected annually by the state legislatures, and could serve only three years out of every six. That is, if a delegate was elected three years in a row, he was not eligible for office at the next three elections.

Under the Articles, the United States was not a nation like Britain or France. It was a *confederation*, a group of loosely joined states. Each of the states retained its sovereignty, freedom, and independence. Major decisions had to be approved by only nine of the 13 states, but changes in the Articles themselves had to be approved unanimously.

Powers of the Congress. Congress had the power to raise and maintain an army and navy, to wage war, to send ambassadors abroad, to make treaties with foreign countries, and to negotiate with the Indian nations on behalf of all the states. It also had the power to establish a post office, to coin money and print paper money, and to adopt standards of measurement.

Powers of the States. The states retained complete control over their economic policies. Trade between states was regulated by the states involved. The individual states also set their own policy for trade with foreign countries. Of course, each state also regulated trade that went on within its own borders.

Each state also had the right to fight a war alone (with the consent of Congress), in case of invasion by a foreign country. Each state could also send ambassadors to foreign countries, again with the consent of Congress, and keep its own army and

Discussion Question: Why might the states want more power than the central government? List the states, economic and political differences and how these might cause competitiveness rather than cooperation. Also mention pre-war differences and mistrust of central power from experience with Britain.

 151

navy. In fact, the state *militias* were important to the American War effort in the Revolution. However, they were controlled by the states and were intended to be used to defend their own states only.

The individual states could also coin their own money if they so chose. They could set their own standards of measurement, and could make laws that conflicted with other states' laws. Since each state was sovereign, there was no higher authority to resolve the conflicts.

It is important to know that these seeming weaknesses of the government under the Articles of Confederation were not accidental or the result of inexperience. On the contrary, the people who called King George a tyrant, and went to war to escape British authority, had no intention of creating a powerful American government. The Revolutionary generation insisted that any government outside their independent states be a government controlled by the states.

The Western Lands.   Most governmental powers were reserved by the states. But there were certain issues that the states could not resolve by themselves, and which were taken up by the Congress. One such issue was the conflicting claims to land west of the Appalachians. In fact, this problem blocked the ratification of the Articles.

When the British Crown granted land to form colonies, little was known about North America. Consequently, lines were simply drawn on maps, and some colonies were granted land from the Atlantic to the Pacific. Seven states carried these claims over from the colonial period —Massachusetts, Connecticut, New York, Virginia, North Carolina, South Carolina, and Georgia. Virginia claimed to own every acre of land between the crest of the mountains and the Mississippi River, the western boundary of the United States. The other six claimants said that their colonial charters had canceled most of Virginia's claims.

Another complication was that New Hampshire, Rhode Island, New Jersey, Pennsylvania, Delaware, and Maryland had no western claims. Their western boundaries had been clearly set by their charters. They worried that the landed states would be able to finance their governments by

The engraving above from the April 1787 issue of Columbian Magazine *depicts a typical farm of the late 1700s, located near the Delaware River.*

selling western lands, and would not have to tax their citizens. Naturally, the leaders of these six states thought their citizens would leave to settle in tax-free areas. They also believed that the balance of power within the Confederation would shift overwhelmingly to the states with western land claims.

Maryland, one of the states with no land claims, came up with an answer. The landed states should *cede*, or give up, all their western land to Congress. In this way, all the citizens of the Confederation would share equally in the riches of the West. Maryland was adamant about this. It would not accept the Articles of Confederation until the other states ceded their claims.

This was a bold resolution because it involved millions of acres of land. Fortunately, Virginia, the

Research Assignment: Have students investigate and report on the kinds of people already living in the western lands. How many were there? Were they taken into consideration when the laws were passed?

152

state with the most land to give up, had good reasons to do so. Virginians had played an important part in the Revolution, and wanted to see the Confederation succeed. Moreover, many Virginians believed that large states would be impossible to govern with a republican government.

In January 1781, Virginia offered to cede to Congress its land claims north of the Ohio River. (This land was turned over in 1784.) Maryland then joined the Confederation. New York had already ceded its claims, and within a few years, every other state but Georgia did the same. Virginia surrendered its claims south of the Ohio in 1792, and Georgia finally gave up its western land in 1802.

The Northwest Territory. In 1785 and 1787, the Confederation Congress adopted two laws that dealt with this new public land, or *national domain*. These laws, known as the *Northwest Ordinances*, were so effective that they served as models for the incorporation of new land into the United States for years afterward. In this case, the ordinances applied to the *Northwest Territory*, which was bounded by the Great Lakes, the Ohio River, and the Mississippi River.

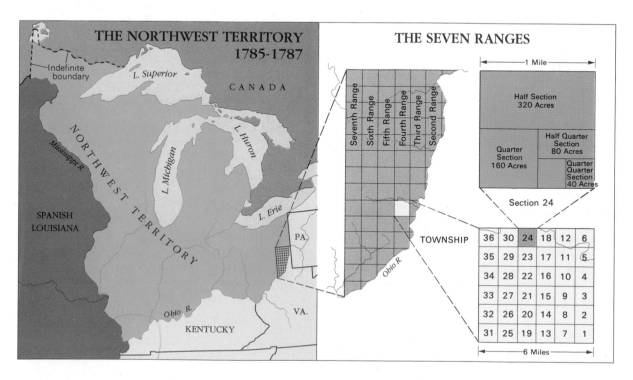

THE NORTHWEST TERRITORY 1785-1787

THE SEVEN RANGES

Land Ordinance of 1785.

The first law, the *Land Ordinance* of 1785, established the *rectangular survey system*. Before western land was offered for sale, it was carefully surveyed into townships six miles square. Each township was divided into 36 *sections*. A section was 1 square mile (2.6 square kilometers), or 640 acres (260 hectares). The government would sell the land for $1 an acre.

At first, a section was the smallest parcel of government land an individual could purchase. But very few farm families could afford such a large plot. Congress reduced the size of the minimum tract for sale, until eventually the size of the standard farm was set at 40 acres (16 hectares).

Besides raising money for the national treasury and promoting an orderly settlement of the frontier, this ordinance had a great civil effect, too. In each township, the revenues from the sale of one of the 36 sections were reserved for the support of a public school in the township. Therefore, everybody in the territory who wanted an education could get one, although a person might have to walk miles to reach the school.

Northwest Ordinance of 1787.

The *Northwest Ordinance* of 1787 dealt with the division of the territory into regions, and the regions' subsequent admission to statehood. Congress was saying that, unlike Great Britain, the United States would not keep the new land as colonies. The law provided a governor for the Northwest Territory, who was appointed by Congress. When the territory had 5,000 adult white males, it could elect its own legislature and send a nonvoting representative to Congress. When any region in the territory reached a population of 60,000, it could write its own constitution and apply to Congress for statehood. Upon approval of its constitution, it would become a state, and have equal footing with the other states. Eventually, the region was divided into five states—Ohio, Indiana, Illinois, Wisconsin, and Michigan.

The act also forbade slavery in the Northwest Territory. It called for the encouragement of education and guaranteed freedom of religion.

Monetary Difficulties.

The Confederation Congress was not so successful in meeting the country's money problem. Gold and silver coins

By 1779, $200 million of paper currency, called continentals, *had been issued by Congress.*

were quite scarce during the colonial period. Imperial trade laws required Americans to exchange their products for British manufactured goods instead of money. One reason Americans adopted the Spanish dollar as their basic unit of money was that, at the time of the Revolution, there was more Spanish coin (from the West Indies) than British pounds in the colonies.

The expenses of the war made the money problem more serious. When the states were slow to vote money for Congress, Congress issued large amounts of paper money, called *continentals*. Only $6 million in continentals were printed in 1775, but $63 million were printed in 1778 and $90 million in 1779.

These continentals had value only because Congress said they could be redeemed in gold and silver. When faith in Congress was low, and it seemed unlikely people would ever be able to redeem their paper money, its value dropped. By 1781, it took almost 150 continentals to buy what one gold dollar would buy.

Bankers like New York's Haym Salomon, a Jewish immigrant from Poland, and Pennsylvania's Robert Morris managed to finance the war. However, the currency crisis went unresolved because Congress had very restricted taxing powers, and an amendment was needed to give Congress more power. In 1781, 12 states voted to approve an amendment that would allow Congress to place a five percent tax on imported goods. Rhode Island refused and the bill died.

In addition to the dollar, one-fourth of a dollar became known as a quarter. Before coins valued less than a dollar were made, change was made by sawing a dollar into 8 wedge-shaped pieces. Two of these equaled a quarter, and since they consisted of two bits of paper, they became known as "two bits."

MOVERS AND SHAPERS

Robert Morris

A wealthy Philadelphia merchant, Robert Morris (1734–1806) was a major force in financing the American Revolution. Born in Liverpool, England, he came to America in 1747 and in a few years established a prosperous mercantile firm, engaged principally in overseas trade. While maintaining his business connections, he soon plunged into the political life of the young country, first as a legislator from Pennsylvania, then as a signer of the Declaration of Independence and a delegate to the Continental Congress from 1775 to 1778.

After outstanding service in Congress, Morris was chosen for the new post of Superintendent of Finance and raised crucially needed funds to support General Washington's campaign against Cornwallis at Yorktown, the last decisive battle of the war. He also strengthened the new government's finances by issuing "Morris notes" based on personal credit, establishing the first national bank in American history, and arranging for French and Dutch loans to restore government solvency.

After the war, however, Morris lost his personal fortune in land speculation in the West and was thrown into debtors' jail. Released in 1801, he returned to Philadelphia and died there in obscurity in 1806.

Haym Salomon

O n December 15, 1941, one week after the Japanese attack on Pearl Harbor, a unique bronze monument was unveiled in Chicago, honoring three heroes of the American Revolution. George Washington, standing tall in the center, was flanked by two men who never carried a rifle—Robert Morris and Haym Salomon, both financiers whose unselfish support helped the struggling colonies to gain their independence.

Haym Salomon (1740–1785), a Polish Jew, arrived in New York City at the age of 32, a penniless immigrant. He soon had success as a commission merchant and financier, and after the outbreak of war associated himself with the Patriots' cause.

In 1781, with the Revolution in grave financial trouble, Superintendent of Finance Morris appealed to Salomon for help. Salomon, who was more than willing to aid the Patriot cause, used the wealth he had accumulated to subscribe heavily to government bonds. He also endorsed notes, equipped soldiers at his own expense, and loaned Morris's office over $350,000 at minimal interest during the period of crisis.

Salomon gave years of illustrious service to his adopted country and to the financial community. However, when he died in 1785, he was penniless. The government of the United States, still struggling to get on its feet, could not pay Salomon the $600,000 it owed him.

Rhode Island also frustrated attempts by Congress to stabilize the value of paper currency in 1786. The assembly of the state was dominated by farmers who were deeply in debt. The state printed $100,000 in its own money and declared it legal tender. Although the Rhode Island money was worthless elsewhere, farmers rushed to pay off their debts within the state. The story was told of bankers galloping for the Connecticut line chased by people who owed them money, waving handfuls of Rhode Island paper.

The Economy.

The money problem was made worse by another difficulty over which the Confederation Congress had no control. A postwar depression occurred in the 1780s. The government was no longer feeding, clothing, and paying wages to a large army. In addition, by leaving the British Empire, the United States lost many economic advantages.

For example, mercantilist law required American tobacco growers to send their entire crop to Great Britain. The same law prevented British merchants from buying tobacco outside the colonies and forbade English farmers to grow tobacco. The Americans were the sole source of tobacco for the world's leading consumer and distributor.

With independence, however, the Americans were themselves outside the empire. The same laws that once benefited American tobacco growers now shut them out of the British market.

In the same way, New England merchants who had once traded within the British empire were prevented from calling at familiar ports. The ships of the Royal Navy, which once protected American merchant vessels, now threatened them.

The solution was to develop new trade routes, which the American seafarers did with great ingenuity. As early as 1784 the American flag was seen in Chinese ports. But the job of completely replacing a colonial economy with an independent economy could not be done overnight.

Disrespect for the United States.

The weakness of the Confederation government made it difficult for the United States to borrow money abroad. Even France, which had helped to finance the war, refused to loan money to the Confederation Congress in peacetime. Seeing the inability of Congress to tax the states, French bankers thought the Americans would not repay their debts.

Great Britain never considered lending money to the former colonies. Indeed, British officials missed no opportunity to heap scorn on the infant country. Although the Treaty of Paris provided for an exchange of ambassadors, Britain never sent one. In London, the American ambassador, John Adams, was ridiculed at diplomatic functions.

The Barbary States of northern Africa, whose economies were based on piracy, also ignored United States sovereignty. Great Britain paid annual bribes to the Barbary States in return for free passage of empire ships in the Mediterranean. But American ships were left unprotected and were captured and their crews sold into slavery. Congress was unable to raise the money for ransom or to finance an expedition against the pirates.

Diplomatic Setbacks.

Much more serious than insults was Great Britain's refusal to honor the Treaty of Paris. According to the treaty, the western boundary of the United States was the Mississippi River, and the northern boundary was the Great Lakes. Great Britain refused to withdraw troops from a number of forts within these bounds. American demands that the soldiers be removed were simply ignored.

The British also schemed to detach Vermont from the United States. Ethan and Levi Allen, who controlled Vermont, had fought for independence. However, they distrusted the Confederation government, in part because Congress was unable to force New York and New Hampshire to give up their claims to Vermont. So the Allen brothers attempted to make a deal with the British. Congress was powerless to stop them. Only because the British were slow to act did Vermont remain in the Confederation.

Spain, too, tried to exploit the weakness of the Confederation. In 1785–1786, Spanish Ambassador Diego de Gardoqui (dā gär-dō′ kē) attempted to split the northern and southern states. He offered to open Spanish colonies to American ships, which meant northern ships because there were few seagoing merchants in the South. In return, he asked that Congress give up its claims to free navigation of the Mississippi River for 25 years.

The northern states were willing. The Mississippi meant nothing to them. But the river was

Discussion Question: How do you think people in the U.S. might have felt about the way they were treated by European powers after the Revolutionary War? Compare these feelings to the way the Indians might have felt in response to European and U.S. treatment.

156

vital to the southerners and to the development of the western areas. Tens of thousands of North Carolinians and Virginians had moved west to what are now Kentucky and Tennessee. If those people were to trade with the outside world, they needed the right to use the Mississippi.

The treaty was made, but southerners and westerners blocked its ratification by Congress. Had the treaty been accepted, the United States would surely have split in two.

States Fight Among Themselves.

Squabbles between the states also threatened to break up the Confederation. When New York passed laws forbidding the importation of some goods from other states, some Connecticut and New Jersey merchants resorted to the old custom of smuggling. When New Jersey requested that New York contribute to the upkeep of a lighthouse at Sandy Hook, the New York assembly refused to pay. Although the light was essential to New York shipping, the New Yorkers knew that the lighthouse would operate whether or not New York contributed. The state refused to do its share.

Shays's Rebellion.

By 1787, the economic depression was lifting, and Congress seemed to be coping with its many problems. But a crisis in Massachusetts illustrated the government's weaknesses and made people think of change.

Daniel Shays was a veteran of the Revolution who lived in western Massachusetts. Like many other farmers, he resented the fact that Boston dominated the state government. The farmers claimed that they paid too many taxes, and that the Bostonians favored trade over agriculture. Boston bankers loaned them money and, when they could not pay back the loans, took their land.

Daniel Shays led a rebellion against the Massachusetts government because of what he and other farmers saw as their lack of representation in matters of taxation in the state.

At first, Shays and his followers merely protested. However, when the state assembly adjourned without enacting any of the laws the farmers requested, representatives of 50 towns met in Hatfield. Shays and other leaders warned against using violence. But tempers were up and mobs attacked state officials, judges, and lawyers.

Late in November 1786, Shays led an army of about 1,200 men toward Springfield. Another group of about 800 men joined them. They planned to seize an arsenal, but Congress decided to act. In cooperation with the government of Massachusetts, an army was raised to meet Shays. Commanded by General Benjamin Lincoln, the force easily defeated the Shaysites, and by March 1787 the rebellion was over.

To some Americans, including Thomas Jefferson, the rebellion was a natural result of oppression. To others, however, the rebellion was a sign of danger. To George Washington and Alexander Hamilton, the Revolution was over. It was time to build a nation that was safe and strong. There must be no more such rebellions; or if there were, there must be a government that was able to put them down immediately.

SECTION REVIEW

1. Write a sentence to identify: Confederation, national domain, continentals, Sandy Hook lighthouse.

2. Explain how and why the Articles of Confederation were written.

3. What was the Northwest Territory, and what were its boundaries?

4. What caused the currency crisis that faced the Confederation Congress?

5. Describe difficulties each of the following countries presented to the United States: Great Britain, France, Spain.

---

3. WRITING A CONSTITUTION

Fifty-five men gathered in Philadelphia in the spring of 1787. They had come from every state except Rhode Island. The purpose was to amend the Articles of Confederation to provide a government that could truly govern.

Some Americans disapproved of the convention. Rhode Islanders sent no delegates because they thought the convention would give more power to the central government. Samuel Adams worried that the convention might try to cut back the rights and liberties that had been won in the Revolution.

An early action of the convention seemed to confirm these fears. After electing George Washington to preside over them, the delegates voted to meet in secret. Although it was hot and humid in Philadelphia, they barred the doors and sealed the windows of the Pennsylvania State House (Independence Hall).

There was nothing sinister in their secrecy. Everyone knew what the convention was doing. The delegates decided to close the doors because they knew they were engaged in a historic act. They were designing a living government on paper. The job required caution, calm, and frank discussion by everyone present. They wanted to speak without risking their political careers back home.

Starting Anew. Although the announced purpose of the convention was to improve the Articles of Confederation, and Congress had approved the meeting for that purpose alone, Edmund Randolph of Virginia stood up on the third day of discussion and proposed that the delegates forget the Articles. They should write an all new "supreme law of the land." Almost everyone agreed with Randolph. The few who did not had no choice but to leave.

The delegates had a practical reason for starting from scratch. In order to *amend*, or change, the Articles, every state would have to agree. But Rhode Island was satisfied with the Articles, and would probably veto any change the convention suggested. Therefore, the Founding Fathers, as the men who wrote the Constitution are known, decided to start anew. They decided that only nine of the 13 states would need to approve their document for it to go into effect.

The Founding Fathers. The men who wrote the Constitution were a talented and able group. They had been active in politics their entire adult lives. Some of them were scholars of political philosophy. Most of them were practical politi-

Research Assignment: Have students report on the European philosophers (Locke, Rousseau, Hobbes) whose thinking influenced the writers of the Constitution. Show specifically where their ideas might appear in the document.

cians and had helped to write state constitutions. Seven of the 55 had been state governors. Thirty-nine had served in the Continental Congress.

The youth of the delegates is important to understanding the government they created. They had been teenagers during the Stamp Act crisis, and had been very young men during the Revolutionary War. Unlike their elders, who thought of themselves as North Carolinians or Marylanders first, and citizens of the United States second, the delegates to the Philadelphia convention thought *nationalistically*. They were Americans, and they wanted to create a government suitable for a great nation.

A Conservative Movement. A majority of the men who wrote the Constitution were conservatives who believed that well-educated people and people who owned property should have more say in government than the uneducated and the poor. They thought that education enabled people to see through unscrupulous leaders and false promises. Those who owned property had a stake in society that poor people did not.

They also believed that if government was not strong enough to restrain the worst human in-

The Constitution of the United States was written in Philadelphia, Pennsylvania (above and below) in 1787.

When referring to Washington, Hamilton, and Adams as conservatives, do not confuse their ideology with modern conservative ideology. The founding fathers believed in a strong central government with great economic control and were suspicious of human nature. Today's conservatives believe in little government control of economics and a weak central government, with greater individual powers.

stincts, social disorder would result. This is why Shays's Rebellion shocked them. They believed that the Confederation government had been too weak to head off "mob rule" in western Massachusetts.

The most conservative of them all was Alexander Hamilton. He believed that an excess of democracy was the major flaw in the Articles of Confederation. Hamilton proposed that some officials in the new government be elected for life so that, once in office, they would not have to respond to the mood of what he called the "common run" of people. A few others agreed with him. But most realized that Americans would not agree to be governed by people who were not accountable to the electorate.

The Connecticut Compromise.

The Founding Fathers differed on many questions. In general, though, they were willing to compromise. But the resolution of one conflict was essential to the making of the Constitution. The conflict pitted the small states against the large states on the issue of representation, and began when Edmund Randolph proposed the *Virginia Plan*.

The Virginia Plan, reflecting the views of quiet, thoughtful James Madison, provided for a national legislature divided into two houses. The lower house, or the Assembly, would be elected by popular vote. All eligible voters would take part in selecting members of the Assembly. The Assembly would then select the members of the upper house, the Senate. The plan called for the number of a state's representatives in both houses to be based on the state's population.

Delegates from the small states protested. They feared that under this plan their states would be constantly out-voted in the legislature by the large states. In response, William Paterson of New Jersey offered the *New Jersey Plan*, which provided for a Congress much like the Confederation Congress. There would be a single house, in which each state would have equal representation.

The New Jersey Plan alarmed Madison. He saw it as a threat to his dream of a truly national government. For two weeks he argued and pleaded for the Virginia Plan. But the small states would not give in.

It was Roger Sherman of Connecticut, a small state, who finally hit on the solution. According to the *Connecticut Compromise*, the identities of the smaller states would be protected by equal representation in the upper house, the Senate. Each state legislature would select two senators. However, the people of the country as a whole would be represented in the lower house, the House of

Although North Carolina and Rhode Island were not eager to ratify the new Constitution, they did eventually do so in November 1789 and May 1790, respectively. The "Rise it will" claim of the wood engraving below, thus came true.

Class Activity: Referring to the previous chapter's Class Activity, involving interpretation of political cartoons, have students figure out what the cartoon (wood engraving) on page 160 means. Its meaning should become obvious once students read page 164, where Carolina and Rhode Island's positions are explained.

PROFILES OF THE PRESIDENCY

GEORGE WASHINGTON

1789–1797

George Washington's charismatic leadership was evident in his words to the Continental Army before the Battle of Long Island:

The time is now near at hand, which must probably determine whether Americans are to be free men or slaves; whether they are to have any property they can call their own; whether their houses and farms are to be pillaged and destroyed, and themselves consigned to a state of wretchedness from which no human efforts will deliver them. The fate of unborn millions will now depend, under God, on the courage and conduct of this army. Our cruel and unrelenting enemy leaves us only the choice of a brave resistance, or the most abject submission. We have, therefore, to resolve to conquer, or to die. . . . The eyes of all our countrymen are now upon us. . . . Let us, therefore, animate and encourage each other, and shew [show] the whole world that a free man . . . is superior to any slavish mercenary on earth.

ARMY ORDERS, AUGUST 27, 1776

Representatives. Each state's delegation in the House would be determined by the size of the state's population. The compromise worked. Although many on both sides were not happy, they knew it was the only solution.

The Three-Fifths Compromise. In accepting the principle of representation according to population, the delegates opened another conflict. This time the conflict pitted the North against the South. Should slaves be counted in calculating the size of a state's delegation in the House?

The northerners, whose states had abolished slavery or were near to doing so, said that slaves should not be counted. According to law, slaves were property and could not vote. Therefore, the argument went, they should not be counted as part of the population to be represented. The northerners' argument had a second point. Because slaves were legally property, they should be counted when taxes were levied on the states.

If this point of view had been accepted, the size of the southern delegations in the House of Representatives would have been drastically reduced. In South Carolina, for example, more than 50 percent of the people were slaves. If they were not counted in assigning seats in the House, South Carolina's representation would be cut by half. Southerners insisted that slaves be counted as people.

The *Three-Fifths Compromise* exposed once again the human tragedy of slavery. To settle their dispute, both North and South were willing to define the blacks as something less than human beings. The Constitutional Convention decided that for purposes of both representation and taxation, five slaves would be counted as three people. In the original Constitution, a slave counted as only three-fifths of a person.

The Presidency. Almost all the delegates agreed that the new government would be headed by a single executive, a president. Discussion of the presidency must have been uneasy at times because everyone knew who would probably be the first to fill that position—George Washington.

Washington's close friend, Alexander Hamilton, suggested that an elected president should serve for life. But few delegates supported Hamilton's idea. The plan sounded too much like monarchy, and Americans had had their fill of kings.

On the other hand, if the president were to have real power, the presidential term needed to be longer. After some debate, the delegates agreed on a term of four years.

A more difficult problem was how the president

Thomas Jefferson originally put a clause in the Constitution abolishing slavery. The clause had to be removed because of pressure from pro-slavery factions.
Discussion Question: In regard to the fears of conservative members of the constitutional committee, what do you think the phrase "tyranny of the majority" might mean?

was to be elected. Nationalists like James Madison and James Wilson of Pennsylvania wanted the president to represent all of the people. Therefore, they proposed that all eligible voters participate in the presidential election. The candidate who received the most votes would win the office.

Once again, the delegates from states with small populations objected. They felt that their states would have too little influence in such an election. Every president would come from a large state.

The small states were joined by strong conservatives, like Hamilton and Gouverneur Morris of New York, who did not want the common people to have a direct say in the election of the president. They felt that such a powerful office must be filled by a member of the educated elite. After the convention rejected a proposal that the Senate elect the president, George Mason of Virginia suggested another compromise.

All voters would participate in the election, thus making the president a representative of the people and not of the states. However, the voters would not vote directly for the president. They would choose *electors*, who would convene as an *electoral college* after the popular vote was taken. They would then vote for president. If a majority of the electoral college was unable to agree on a president, the House of Representatives, with each state having one vote, would make the decision.

This plan satisfied the strong nationalists because all voters would participate in the presidential election. It satisfied the strong conservatives because the common people would not participate directly in the final choice. Electors would almost certainly represent the elite. It satisfied the small states because an election that went to the House of Representatives would be decided by the states voting as equals.

Amending the Constitution.

Perhaps the most essential part of the new plan of government was the ability to amend the document. The writers were setting out into new territory—who knew if something they included was unworkable? Who knew if conditions would change? The delegates made sure to include a specific process for amending the Constitution, requiring a three-fourths majority of the states, not unanimity as in the Articles of Confederation.

SECTION REVIEW

1. Write a sentence to identify: Edmund Randolph, the Founding Fathers, nationalist, conservative.

2. For what purpose did Congress approve the gathering of 55 delegates in Philadelphia in the spring of 1787?

3. What conflict was the Connecticut Compromise designed to resolve, and how did it resolve it?

4. How was the dispute over the method of electing a president settled to the satisfaction of all?

---

4. RATIFICATION

On the final day of the Constitutional Convention in September 1787, Ben Franklin spoke about the document they had prepared. The frame of government they had written, he said, was not perfect. But he had lived long enough to know that nothing was perfect. He urged the delegates to forget their disappointments. Everyone disliked something in the document. The point was that the Constitution promised a better government than the Articles of Confederation provided.

This point was important for the delegates. Their job was now to urge the people of their states to *ratify*, or approve, the Constitution. To some of them, coming up with the new government would be much easier than getting others to accept it.

The Federalists. Americans who supported ratification called themselves *Federalists*. In speeches, in newspapers, and at political meetings, they argued that to cling to the Articles of Confederation was to guarantee a weak and divided United States. Weakness invited powerful European countries to meddle in American affairs. It was time for the United States to take its place among the great nations as a single country.

James Madison, Alexander Hamilton, and John Jay of New York were the most effective supporters of the new type of government. In the *Federalist Papers*, a series of 85 essays published in

Research Assignment: Have students write a report on one of the Federalist papers. You might consider assigning one for each student. Reports should discuss the meaning and the impact of each of the Federalist Papers. Attention should also be given to distinguishing propaganda.

THE

FEDERALIST

A COLLECTION

O F

E S S A Y S,

WRITTEN IN FAVOUR OF THE

NEW CONSTITUTION,

AS AGREED UPON BY THE FEDERAL CONVENTION,
SEPTEMBER 17, 1787.

IN TWO VOLUMES.

VOL. I.

NEW-YORK:

PRINTED AND SOLD BY J. AND A. M°LEAN,
No. 41, HANOVER-SQUARE.
M,DCC,LXXXVIII.

The Federalist Papers *argued for ratification.*

newspapers throughout the colonies, they answered every objection to the Constitution with carefully thought-out ideas. The *Federalist Papers* still rank among the most important political essays ever written.

The Anti-Federalists. Some delegates to the convention refused to sign the Constitution. They joined other *Anti-Federalists* who urged voters to reject the Constitution. They did not claim that the Articles of Confederation were perfect. However, the Anti-Federalists claimed that the Articles could be improved without abandoning them completely.

They pointed out that the Confederation government was just beginning to work well, and that the independence of the states was guaranteed. This Anti-Federalist argument appealed to people who thought of themselves as citizens of particular states rather than as citizens of the United States. It also appealed to the many Americans who believed that their freedom was safe only when smaller state governments were more powerful than the federal government. The common people could control a state government. They could not control one that ruled from far away.

Edmund Randolph, who had taken an active part in writing the Constitution, refused to sign it and joined the Anti-Federalists. So did Luther

John Jay (left), Alexander Hamilton (center), and James Madison (right) wrote the Federalist Papers *to deal with objections people had to the new Constitution.*

Class Activity: Have a panel of students stage a debate pitting "Federalists" against "anti-Federalists."

Martin of Maryland. He had stormed out of the convention because he believed the new document was anti-democratic.

At the beginning, Samuel Adams objected that the Constitution included no protections of a citizen's rights. When the Federalists agreed to support a Bill of Rights in the form of ten amendments to the Constitution, Adams withdrew his objections.

Early Federalist Victories.
It can be difficult to understand that many Americans of the 1780s, and perhaps a majority, did not want the new government. While a few states ratified the Constitution very quickly, both Federalists and Anti-Federalists used every means at their disposal to sway their fellow citizens. Some of these tactics were of doubtful legality, and debate continues as to whether or not the Constitution would have been ratified in an open election.

Delaware was the first state to ratify, on December 7, 1787. Unlike Rhode Islanders, the people of Delaware thought the Constitution protected small states. Pennsylvania was second, on December 12, although the Pennsylvania convention was able to vote only because two Anti-Federalists were forced to be present in order to make a *quorum* (the minimum number required before a meeting is legal). New Jersey also ratified the Constitution before the end of 1787.

Success!
Early in 1788, Georgia and Connecticut became the fourth and fifth states to ratify the Constitution. The Massachusetts ratifying convention met in the depths of winter. Some Anti-Federalists claimed that the Federalists had chosen the date because farmers from the western part of the state, who generally opposed the Constitution, could not get through the snows to attend. Even so, the Massachusetts Anti-Federalists, led by Samuel Adams, had a 192 to 144 edge in the convention. The state was won over only when the Federalists agreed to support the Bill of Rights.

Maryland, South Carolina, and New Hampshire all ratified in the spring. New Hampshire had the honor of being the ninth state to ratify, and therefore the state that put the Constitution into effect.

However, Virginia and New York had still not ratified. The Federalists realized that without the

POGHKEEPSIE
July 2d, 1788.

JUST ARRIVED

BY EXPRESS,

The Ratification of the New Conſtitution by the Convention of the State of Virginia, on Wedneſday the 25th June, by a majority of 10 ; 88 agreeing, and 78 diſſenting to its adoption.

"WE the Delegates of the People of Virginia, duly elected   With theſe Impreſſions, with a ſolemn Appeal to the Searcher of Hearts for the

Virginia was the tenth state to ratify the new Constitution.

participation of these two large states, the new government could not work. Virginia ratified the Constitution on June 25, 1788. This news was enough to sway New York. At first the New York convention had rejected the Constitution. But Alexander Hamilton managed to keep the delegates together and, on July 26, the Federalists won by the narrow vote of 30 to 27.

Rhode Island and North Carolina were overwhelmingly opposed to ratification. With the old Confederation dead, however, their alternatives were to join the new government or become independent but weak countries. North Carolina ratified in November 1789. Rhode Island held out until May 1790. By then it was obvious the new government was going to succeed and would not tolerate an independent Rhode Island. With little enthusiasm, Rhode Island became the thirteenth state to join the new union.

SECTION REVIEW

1. Write a sentence to identify: ratification, the Federalist Papers, quorum, Samuel Adams.

2. Explain the position Federalists and Anti-Federalists took on the Constitution.

3. Which state was first to ratify the Constitution in 1787? Why was New Hampshire's ratifying vote important? Is it surprising that Rhode Island was last to ratify in 1790? Why or why not?

Discussion Question: Was our Constitution designed to be truly democratic? Discuss direct versus indirect democracy (the latter being in the Constitution). Some groups were favored (the "wiser" and business classes); some groups were excluded from the Bill of Rights (women, blacks).

5. THE CONSTITUTION

The best way to understand the Constitution of the United States is to read it and discuss it. As you read, keep in mind certain basic principles that influenced the people who wrote it.

Federalism. James Madison and a majority of the Founding Fathers wanted to replace the weak Confederation with a stronger, national government. Only with a strong central government, they believed, could the United States take its rightful place among the nations of the world.

However, state loyalties were too strong to be ignored, even among the delegates who attended the Philadelphia convention, and Madison had to compromise. He did not get as powerful a central government as he would have liked. The states retained a number of powers with which the central government could not interfere. This division of powers between state and federal governments is known as *federalism.*

The Constitution expresses a more conservative view of government than the Declaration of Independence and the Articles of Confederation. It was not, in its original form, as democratic as the earlier documents. The people were allowed to vote directly for only members of the House of Representatives. Although few delegates to the convention shared Alexander Hamilton's deep distrust of democracy, they did ensure that senators and the president would be elected indirectly. (The senators were to be chosen by state legislatures; the president by the electoral college.) Justices of the federal courts would not be elected at all. They would be appointed by the president. It was only later in American history that the Constitution became as democratic as it is today.

Mixed Government. John Adams, the chief American spokesman for mixed government, or a government made up of monarchic, aristocratic, and democratic elements, did not attend the Philadelphia convention. Nevertheless, his views strongly influenced the delegates because he had helped write the Massachusetts state constitution, which for many was a model for the national Constitution.

Adams believed that *monarchy* (rule by one person), aristocracy (rule by an elite few), and democracy (rule by the many) all had advantages and disadvantages. Monarchy was more efficient because one person can act more decisively than a committee. However, monarchy easily turned into *tyranny.* Rule by an elite few guaranteed that society's best minds would make policy. However, aristocratic governments easily became self-serving. They neglected the common good for the good of the rich or powerful. Democracy allowed many people to have a stake in government. However, rule by the many was often inefficient and could degenerate into mob rule, as in Shays's Rebellion.

Adams's solution was to mix the three principles. In the Constitution, the single strong president embodied Adams' monarchic principle. The Senate and the Supreme Court embodied the aristocratic. The House of Representatives embodied the democratic. When the powers of these three branches balanced each other, government would work well. Only if one of the branches became too powerful would problems arise.

Separation of Powers. One way that the three branches were kept balanced was the *separation of powers.* The Founding Fathers hated tyranny because one person could make and enforce the laws, and also judge offenders. There was no recourse if citizens felt their treatment was unjust. The Constitution separated these three powers. The *legislative* branch, the Congress, would make the laws. The *executive* branch, the president and advisors, would oversee the enforcement of the laws. The *judicial* branch, the Supreme Court and other federal courts, would judge according to the law, ensuring that the executive branch did not act unjustly.

Checks and Balances. The power of the courts to judge executive actions was just one of a number of *checks and balances* written into the Constitution. The president had the power to *veto* an act passed by Congress. But Congress could *override* the president's veto and establish an act as law. The Supreme Court established the principle that it could declare a federal law to be unconstitutional. But the president had some control over the Supreme Court because the president appointed justices to sit on the Court. The Senate had to approve the president's appoint-

GOING TO THE SOURCE

You say that I have been dished up to you as an Anti-Federalist, and ask me if it be just. . . . I am not a Federalist, because I never submitted the whole system of my opinions to the creed of any party of men whatever, in religion, in philosophy, in politics, or in anything else, where I was capable of thinking for myself. . . . Therefore, I am not of the party of Federalists.

But I am much farther from that of the Anti-Federalists. I approved, from the first moment, of the great mass of what is in the new Constitution: the consolidation of the government; the organization into executive, legislative, and judiciary; the subdivision of the legislative; the happy compromise of interests between the great and little states by the different manner of voting in the different houses; the voting by persons instead of states; the qualified negative on laws given to the executive which, however, I should have liked better if associated with the judiciary also, as in New York; and the power of taxation. I thought at first that the latter might have been limited. A little reflection soon convinced me it ought not to be.

What I disapproved from the first moment, also, was the want of a bill of rights to guard liberty against the legislative as well as the executive branches of the government; that is to say, to secure freedom in religion, freedom of the press, freedom from monopolies, freedom from unlawful imprisonment, freedom from a permanent military, and a trial by jury, in all cases determinable by the laws of the land. I disapproved, also, the perpetual reeligibility of the President.

With respect to the reeligibility of the President, I find myself differing from the majority of my countrymen; for I think there are but three states out of the eleven which have desired an alteration of this. And, indeed, since the thing is established, I would wish it not to be altered during the life of our great leader [Washington], whose executive talents are superior to those, I believe, of any man in the world, and who, alone . . . is fully qualified to put the new government so under way as to secure it against the efforts of opposition. But, having derived from our error all the good there was in it, I hope we shall correct it the moment we can no longer have the same name at the helm.

> *I am not a Federalist because I never submitted the whole system of my opinions to the creed of any party. . . . But I am much farther from that of the Anti-Federalists. I approved, from the first moment, of the great mass of what is in the new Constitution. . . .*
>
> THOMAS JEFFERSON, "LETTER ON THE CONSTITUTION"

Thomas Jefferson, who wrote the Declaration of Independence, was not present at the Constitutional Convention. This excerpt from his "Letter on the Constitution," written on March 13, 1789, summarizes what Jefferson liked and disliked about the new plan of government.

ments, and the House of Representatives had the power to *impeach,* or charge with misconduct, Supreme Court justices or any other federal official, including the president.

The fact that both houses of Congress had to approve a law gave each a check on the other. Finally, the division of powers between states and federal government was another example of checks and balances.

Amending the Constitution. The most important feature of the Constitution may have been the amendment process. It would not be easy to amend the Constitution, as the Founding Fathers

Class Activity: With students, design a chart comparing the Articles of Confederation with the Constitution. Compare general powers of the government in both.

intended. The Constitution was to be the nation's basic law, a framework within which other laws were to be made. The delegates to the Constitutional Convention were thinking of the future—if changing the basic law was very difficult, later generations would be forced to think carefully before doing so. Although hundreds of amendments have been proposed, only 26 have been ratified.

The Bill of Rights. The first ten amendments to the Constitution, known as the Bill of Rights, were practically part of the original document. They were proposed as one of the first actions of the Congress under the Constitution in September 1789, and were ratified by the states in 1791. These ten amendments were the condition for ratification by Massachusetts, and the New Hampshire, Virginia, and New York conventions also insisted that the new Congress protect individual liberties. In looking at the Bill of Rights, it becomes obvious why Americans clamored for it. In those amendments were the United States citizens' most valuable heritage. They prevent a government, even a democratic, constitutional government, from interfering with basic American liberties.

SECTION REVIEW

1. Write a sentence to identify: federalism, mixed government, separation of powers, Bill of Rights.

2. In what way was each of these men's wishes satisfied in the Constitution: James Madison, Alexander Hamilton, John Adams?

3. Describe the people and groups that make up the branches of government.

4. Give three examples of how the different branches of government check and balance each other's powers.

CONSTITUTIONAL SEPARATION OF POWERS
(CHECKS AND BALANCES)

LEGISLATIVE

Pass legislation
Confirm executive appointments
Ratify treaties
Appropriate money
Impeach the President
Override presidential veto

Impeach judges
Create courts and judgeships
Approve federal judge
   appointments
Propose constitutional
   amendments to overrule
   judicial decisions

EXECUTIVE

Propose legislation
Veto legislation
Recommend appointments
Negotiate treaties

Appoint judges
Grant pardons

JUDICIAL

Declare legislation
unconstitutional

Declare executive actions
unconstitutional

Constitution of the United States of America

PREAMBLE

We the people of the United States, in order to form a more perfect Union, establish justice, insure domestic tranquility, provide for the common defense, promote the general welfare, and secure the blessings of liberty to ourselves and our posterity, do ordain and establish this Constitution for the United States of America.

The Constitution derives its authority from the people of the entire nation, not merely from the state governments as under the Articles of Confederation. As stated in the preamble, the major purposes of the Constitution are (1) to create a better balance between state power and national power ("a more perfect Union"), (2) to improve the court system, (3) to prevent outbreaks of civil disturbances or riots such as Shays's Rebellion, (4) to protect the nation from foreign dangers, (5) to encourage national growth and social progress, and (6) to safeguard the freedom of citizens.

ARTICLE 1. LEGISLATIVE BRANCH

The first part of the Constitution, Article 1, concerns the organization and powers of the law-making or legislative branch of government: the Congress.

SECTION 1. CONGRESS

All legislative powers herein granted shall be vested in a Congress of the United States, which shall consist of a Senate and House of Representatives.

The writers of the Constitution decided to divide the law-making power between two houses that were to conduct business separately. Such an arrangement is known as a *bicameral*, or two-house, system for making laws. Though this clause gives "all legislative powers" to Congress, the president shares in law-making when signing a law enacted by both houses of Congress.

SECTION 2. HOUSE OF REPRESENTATIVES

1. Election and Term of Members. The House of Representatives shall be composed of members chosen every second year by the people of the several States, and the electors in each State shall have the qualifica-

tions requisite for electors of the most numerous branch of the State Legislature.

Every two years, members of the House of Representatives are chosen by the people of the different states. Anyone qualified by state law to vote for a state legislator is automatically eligible to vote for a Representative to Congress. When this clause was written in 1787, all 13 states placed restrictions on who could vote. These requirements have since been removed.

2. Qualifications. No person shall be a representative who shall not have attained to the age of twenty-five years, and been seven years a citizen of the United States, and who shall not, when elected, be an inhabitant of that State in which he shall be chosen.

A member of the House must be (1) at least 25 years old, (2) a United States citizen for at least seven years, and (3) a resident of the state in which he or she is elected.

3. Apportionment of Representatives and Direct Taxes. Representatives and direct taxes shall be apportioned among the several States which may be included within this Union, according to their respective numbers,* which shall be determined by adding to the whole number of free persons, including those bound to service for a term of years, and excluding Indians not taxed, three-fifths of all other persons. The actual enumeration shall be made within three years after the first meeting of the Congress of the United States, and within every subsequent term of ten years, in such manner as they shall by law direct. The number of representatives shall not exceed one for every thirty thousand, but each State shall have at least one representative; and until such enumeration shall be made, the State of New Hampshire shall be entitled to choose three, Massachusetts eight, Rhode Island and Providence Plantations one, Connecticut five, New York six, New Jersey four, Pennsylvania eight, Delaware one, Maryland six, Virginia ten, North Carolina five, South Carolina five, and Georgia three.

A state's representation in the House is based on the size of its population. The more populous the state, the greater is its number of elected Representatives. Every ten years, a *census*, or official count, is made of the nation's population, and a state's representation in the

*Note: Parts of the constitution no longer in use are crossed out.

Discussion Question: See the English Bill of Rights on page 86 in the text. What elements of the U.S. Bill of Rights derives from the English Bill of Rights?

House is adjusted accordingly. The current size of the House, 435 members, was fixed by law in 1929. Indians were not counted in the census for purposes of representation until 1940. The practice of counting every five slaves ("all other persons") as equal to only three free citizens was nullified by the adoption of the Thirteenth and Fourteenth Amendments after the Civil War.

4. Vacancies. When vacancies happen in the representation from any State, the Executive authority thereof shall issue writs of election to fill such vacancies.

The governor of a state is the "executive authority" referred to in this clause. When a Representative dies or retires before his or her term expires, the state governor may call for a special election to fill the vacancy.

5. Officers and Impeachment. The House of Representatives shall choose their Speaker and other officers; and shall have the sole power of impeachment.

Members of the majority party of the House select their presiding officer, the Speaker, in addition to other officers. The selection is made every two years after the newly elected House convenes to begin its term.

The Speaker is always a member of the political party to which the largest group of House members belong, and has great influence both in selecting members for important committees and in conducting the business of the House.

To *impeach* an officer of government, such as a president or judge, is to accuse the officer of wrongdoing. Only the House has the power to pass a bill of impeachment.

SECTION 3. SENATE

1. Term and Number of Members. The Senate of the United States shall be composed of two senators from each State, chosen by the legislature thereof, for six years; and each senator shall have one vote.

Since the Seventeenth Amendment was adopted in 1913, senators are elected by the voters of the states at a regular election. Before 1913, senators were elected by state legislatures, and the people had no direct part in their selection. This was because in the early days of the Constitution the senators were supposed to represent the state governments to see that the small states got equal treatment with the large states. Every state is represented by two senators, each of whom serves a six-year term.

2. Three Classes of Senators. Immediately after they shall be assembled in consequence of the first election, they shall be divided as equally as may be into three classes. The seats of the senators of the first class

shall be vacated at the expiration of the second year, of the second class at the expiration of the fourth year, and of the third class at the expiration of the sixth year, so that one-third may be chosen every second year; and if vacancies happen by resignation, or otherwise, during the recess of the legislature of any State, the executive thereof may make temporary appointments until the next meeting of the legislature, which shall then fill such vacancies.

Unlike the House, all of whose members are elected at the same time, the Senate has a staggered membership. Only one-third of the senators are elected in any one election year.

If a senator dies or retires in midterm, the current procedure is for the state's governor to call a special election to fill the vacancy. Earlier, before the Seventeenth Amendment was adopted, the state legislature was empowered to make the selection.

3. Qualifications. No person shall be a senator who shall not have attained to the age of thirty years, and been nine years a citizen of the United States, and who shall not, when elected, be an inhabitant of that State for which he shall be chosen.

A Senator must be (1) at least 30 years old, (2) a citizen for at least nine years, and (3) a resident of the state where elected.

4. Vice President's Role. The Vice President of the United States shall be President of the Senate, but shall have no vote, unless they be equally divided.

The only duty that the Constitution assigns to the vice president is to preside over meetings of the Senate. The only time that the vice president may vote on a Senate bill is when there is a tie. Modern presidents have given their vice presidents important political and diplomatic duties to perform, but none of these are required by the Constitution.

5. Other Officers. The Senate shall choose their other officers, and also a President pro tempore, in the absence of the Vice President, or when he shall exercise the office of President of the United States.

The Senate votes for one of its members to preside over debates whenever the Vice President is absent. The position is called *pro tempore* because it is a temporary position. The members of each political party represented in the Senate meet at the beginning of each new Congress and select a "floor leader" and appoint various senators of their own party to help the leader.

6. Trial of Impeachments. The Senate shall have the sole power to try all impeachments. When sitting for that purpose, they shall be on oath or affirmation. When the President of the United States is tried, the Chief Justice shall preside; and no person shall be convicted without the concurrence of two-thirds of the members present.

If a bill of impeachment is passed by the House, then the Senate must act in the manner of a court to try the case of alleged wrongdoing. The Senate sets the date for trial and provides the accused with a written statement of the charges. The accused has the same legal rights of any person on trial.

7. *Penalty for Conviction.*
Judgment in cases of impeachment shall not extend further than to removal from office, and disqualification to hold and enjoy any office or honor, trust or profit under the United States; but the party convicted shall nevertheless be liable and subject to indictment, trial, judgment and punishment, according to law.

If the Senate convicts an accused officer of the impeachment charges, that person may be forced to leave office. This is the only penalty that the Senate may impose. However, the person can still be tried in a regular court for any crimes committed.

SECTION 4. MEETINGS AND ELECTIONS

1. *Holding Elections.*
The times, places and manner of holding elections for senators and representatives, shall be prescribed in each State by the legislature thereof; but the Congress may at any time by law make or alter such regulations, except as to the places of choosing senators.

Congress set no election requirements until 1842, when it required members of the House to be elected from specific districts in a state. In 1872, it set the same day in even-numbered years as the date for Congressional elections.

2. *Meetings.*
The Congress shall assemble at least once in every year, and such meeting shall be on the first Monday in December, unless they shall by law appoint a different day.

Since members of the House of Representatives are chosen every two years, the life of a Congress is considered to be two years. The Twentieth Amendment of the Constitution provides that the Congress shall convene in regular session at noon on January 3 of each year unless it shall pass a law to fix a different date. It meets in the Capitol at Washington, D.C. It remains in session until its members vote to adjourn. The president may call a special session whenever it is necessary.

SECTION 5. RULES OF PROCEDURE

1. *Quorum and Membership.*
Each house shall be the judge of the elections, returns and qualifications of its own members, and a majority of each shall constitute a quorum to do business; but a smaller number may adjourn from day to day, and may be authorized to compel the attendance of absent members, in such manner, and under such penalties as each house may provide.

A quorum is the number of members who must be present for either house to conduct business. Currently, in the Senate, a quorum is 51; in the House, it is 218.

2. *Discipline.*
Each house may determine the rules of its proceedings, punish its members for disorderly behavior, and, with the concurrence of two-thirds, expel a member.

The rules adopted by each house include procedures for censuring and expelling members. A two-thirds vote is required for expulsion.

3. *Journal.*
Each house shall keep a journal of its proceedings, and from time to time publish the same, excepting such parts as may in their judgment require secrecy; and the yeas and the nays of the members of either house on any question shall, at the desire of one-fifth of those present, be entered on the journal.

Two journals, one for the House and the other for the Senate, are published at the end of each session of Congress. A third journal, the *Congressional Record*, is published every day that Congress is in session and provides a complete account of debates, resolutions, and other business conducted in both houses. The purpose of these journals is to make it possible for the general public to watch the conduct of their elected representatives.

4. *Adjournment.*
Neither house, during the session of Congress, shall, without the consent of the other, adjourn for more than three days, nor to any other place than that in which the two houses shall be sitting.

This clause gives Congress the power to determine when and where to meet. Both houses, however, must meet in the same city. Adjournment by one house for more than three days is not allowed unless the other house agrees to it.

SECTION 6. PRIVILEGES AND RESTRICTIONS

1. *Compensation and Privileges.*
The senators and representatives shall receive a compensation for their services, to be ascertained by law, and paid out of the Treasury of the United States. They shall in all cases, except treason, felony and breach of the peace, be

Class Activity: Use the preceding activity to make a similar collection of modern applications of the system of checks and balances.

privileged from arrest during their attendance at the session of their respective houses, and in going to and returning from the same; and for any speech or debate in either house, they shall not be questioned in any other place.

The first Congress voted to award members $6 a day in compensation for their services. More recently (1981), the Congress adopted a yearly salary of $60,663 for all regular members and $79,125 for the Speaker of the House.

Members cannot be arrested for what they say in speeches and debates in Congress. They are immune, however, only in the Capitol building itself, and not in their private lives.

2. Restrictions. No senator or representative shall, during the time for which he was elected, be appointed to any civil office under the authority of the United States, which shall have been created, or the emoluments whereof shall have been increased during such time; and no person holding any office under the United States, shall be a member of either house during his continuance in office.

While they are members of Congress, legislators cannot hold positions in either the executive or judicial departments of the government. This clause was intended by the Founding Fathers to uphold the principle of separation of powers.

SECTION 7. HOW BILLS BECOME LAWS
1. Money Bills. All bills for raising revenue shall originate in the House of Representatives; but the Senate may propose or concur with amendments as on other bills.

This clause provides that all tax and appropriation bills for raising money must originate in the House of Representatives. However, the Senate usually amends the money bills voted by the House and may even substitute an entirely different bill.

2. President's Veto Power. Every bill which shall have passed the House of Representatives and the Senate, shall, before it become a law, be presented to the President of the United States; if he approves he shall sign it, but if not he shall return it, with his objections to that house in which it shall have originated, who shall enter the objections at large on their journal, and proceed to reconsider it. If after such reconsideration two thirds of that House shall agree to pass the bill, it shall be sent, together with the objections, to the other House, by which it shall likewise be reconsidered, and if approved by two thirds of the House, it shall become a law. But in all such cases the votes of both Houses shall be determined by yeas and

nays, and the names of the persons voting for and against the bill shall be entered on the journal of each House respectively. If any bill shall not be returned by the President within ten days (Sundays excepted) after it shall have been presented to him, the same shall be a law, in like manner as if he had signed it, unless the Congress by their adjournment prevent its return, in which case it shall not be a law.

After a bill has been passed by both houses, it is sent to the president. The president may approve the entire bill or disapprove it. If the president has not signed the bill within ten days after it reaches him (not counting Sundays), it becomes a law without his signature. However, if Congress adjourns in the meantime, the bill does not become a law unless the president signs it within the ten-day limit. This way of preventing a bill from becoming a law is known as a *pocket veto.*

If the president vetoes a bill while Congress is in session, it does not become a law unless each house passes it over the president's veto by a two-thirds majority vote.

3. Actions Other Than Bills. Every order, resolution, or vote to which the concurrence of the Senate and House of Representatives may be necessary (except on a question of adjournment) shall be presented to the President of the United States; and before the same shall take effect, shall be approved by him, or being disapproved by him, shall be repassed by two thirds of the Senate and House of Representatives, according to the rules and limitations prescribed in the case of a bill.

Besides acting on regular bills, Congress may also adopt resolutions of two different kinds. A *joint resolution* results from a declaration passed by both houses on the same subject. When signed by the President, it becomes a law. A *concurrent resolution* is merely an expression of opinion on the part of either house of Congress. Since it can never become law, this kind of resolution does not require the President's approval.

SECTION 8. POWERS DELEGATED TO CONGRESS
1. Taxes. The Congress shall have power to lay and collect taxes, duties, imposts and excises, to pay the debts and provide for the common defense and general welfare of the United States; but all duties, imposts and excises shall be uniform throughout the United States.

Congress's power to tax may be used only to pay the federal government's debts and to provide for the common defense and general welfare. The taxes it collects must be the same everywhere. An excise or sales tax on gasoline, for example, cannot be higher in Texas than in Hawaii.

Class Activity: Examine and briefly discuss each clause in the Constitution and its significance. A different or a complementary approach to the same idea would be to come back to the various sections of the Constitution as they are mentioned throughout the year.

171

2. Borrowing. To borrow money on the credit of the United States;

Selling government bonds is the most common of the government's methods for borrowing money. This clause, extended by Clause 18 below, has enabled Congress to create a national banking system.

3. Commerce. To regulate commerce with foreign nations, and among the several States, and with the Indian tribes;

Congress derives considerable authority from this clause, which gives it exclusive power to regulate trade between the states and trade with foreign countries. Interstate commerce, as defined by the Supreme Court, involves more than transportation and the sale of goods. It also can mean communication by telephone or television across state lines.

4. Naturalization and Bankruptcy. To establish a uniform rule of naturalization, and uniform laws on the subject of bankruptcies throughout the United States;

Naturalization is the process by which foreign-born individuals may become citizens. Bankruptcy is the condition of being unable to pay one's debts to creditors. Congress has power to pass laws on both these matters.

5. Coins and Standards. To coin money, regulate the value thereof, and of foreign coin, and fix the standard of weights and measures;

Under this provision, Congress not only mints coins but also prints and circulates paper money in various denominations. In 1838, Congress adopted the English system of pounds, ounces, feet, and yards as a national standard for weighing and measuring objects.

6. Punishment of Counterfeiting. To provide for the punishment of counterfeiting the securities and current coin of the United States;

The current penalty for counterfeiting American money is a fine of up to $5,000 and/or imprisonment for up to 15 years.

7. Post Offices and Roads. To establish post offices and post roads;

Any turnpike, canal, river, street, and airway may be considered a "post road" if mail travels over it.

8. Patents and Copyrights. To promote the progress of science and useful arts, by securing for limited times to authors and inventors the exclusive right to their respective writings and discoveries;

Congress may protect authors by enacting copyright laws and may encourage scientists and inventors by enacting patent laws. Patents may be obtained on processes as well as products. Copyrights protect an author from acts of plagiarism for the period of his or her life plus 50 years.

9. Lower Courts. To constitute tribunals inferior to the Supreme Court;

From this clause, Congress derives the authority to establish all federal courts except the Supreme Court. Courts created by act of Congress are known as "inferior" or "lower" courts because they are under the final jurisdiction of the Supreme Court.

10. Punishment of Piracy. To define and punish piracies and felonies committed on the high seas, and offenses against the law of nations;

Piracy was common at the time this clause was written. Today, the only significant function that Congress derives from this clause is the power to protect Americans at sea.

11. War. To declare war, grant letters of marque and reprisal, and make rules concerning captures on land and water;

The Founding Fathers probably intended that the power to declare war should lie exclusively with Congress. Many presidents, however, have used their power as commander in chief to carry on acts of war without a formal declaration by Congress.

A letter of marque and reprisal is a commission authorizing private citizens to outfit vessels (privateers) for capturing and destroying enemy ships in time of war. Such letters have been forbidden under international law since 1856.

12. Army. To raise and support armies, but no appropriation of money to that use shall be for a longer term than two years;

13. Navy. To provide and maintain a Navy;

14. Regulation of Armed Forces. To make rules for the government and regulation of the land and naval forces;

Americans in the 1780s were fearful of standing armies like the British army, which had been their enemy. This explains the provision that appropriations for an army be limited to two years. Congress has the power to vote supplies for a navy for an unlimited period.

15. Militia. To provide for calling forth the militia to execute the laws of the Union, suppress insurrections and repel invasions;

Class Activity: Have a lawyer from your community who specializes in civil rights cases come in to class to give a special lecture on due process and civil liberties. Have students ask questions on due process and civil liberties' issues that affect us today.

A state's militia is its troop of citizen soldiers who may be called into service in time of emergency. Better known as the National Guard, the militia may be called into the federal service by either a vote of Congress or a declaration of the president.

16. *Organizing the Militia.* To provide for organizing, arming, and disciplining the militia, and for governing such part of them as may be employed in the service of the United States, reserving to the States respectively, the appointment of the officers, and the authority of training the militia according to the discipline prescribed by Congress;

The National Guard, when called into federal service, must follow the same rules that Congress has set for the regular armed services of the United States.

17. *District of Columbia.* To exercise exclusive legislation in all cases whatsoever, over such district (not exceeding ten miles square) as may, by cession of particular States, and the acceptance of Congress, become the seat of the Government of the United States, and to exercise like authority over all places purchased by the consent of the legislature of the State in which the same shall be, for the erection of forts, magazines, arsenals, dock-yards, and other needful buildings;

At the time this clause was written, a permanent capital for the United States had not been selected. During Washington's presidency, a piece of land on the Potomac River was named Federal City, and later the District of Columbia. Committees of Congress governed the city until 1874, when presidentially appointed commissioners took over its government. Under the *Home Rule Act* of 1973, the city has governed itself through a mayor and a city council.

18. *Elastic Clause.* And to make all laws which shall be necessary and proper for carrying into execution the foregoing powers, and all other powers vested by this Constitution in the Government of the United States, or in any department or officer thereof.

This is often called the "elastic clause" because its meaning can be stretched to fit many circumstances. The constitutional basis for the concept of *implied powers* is found in this clause. Unlike the other 17 powers directly delegated to Congress, this clause gives no specific grant of power. But its liberal interpretation by both Congress and the Supreme Court has contributed greatly to the federal government's ability to adjust to changing circumstances.

SECTION 9. POWERS DENIED TO THE FEDERAL GOVERNMENT
1. *Slave Trade.* The migration or importation of such persons as any of the States now existing shall think proper to admit, shall not be prohibited by the Congress prior to the year one thousand eight hundred and eight, but a tax or duty may be imposed on such importation, not exceeding ten dollars for each person.

According to this defunct clause, Congress could make no law before 1808 to forbid the sale of slaves. Congress was allowed, however, to place a tax as high as $10 on each slave brought into the country.

2. *Habeas Corpus.* The privilege of the writ of habeas corpus shall not be suspended, unless when in cases of rebellion or invasion the public safety may require it.

A *writ of habeas corpus* ("produce the body") is a court order directing a sheriff or warden who is holding a person in prison to show before a court that the prisoner is being held legally.

3. *Special Bills.* No bill of attainder or ex post facto law shall be passed.

A *bill of attainder* is a legislative act that inflicts punishment without a legal trial. An *ex post facto* law is a law that punishes a person for doing something that was legal before the law was passed.

4. *Direct Tax.* No capitation, or other direct, tax shall be laid, unless in proportion to the census or enumeration herein before directed to be taken.

A direct tax is a tax imposed on each person, such as the poll tax on persons voting. This provision was inserted to prevent Congress from taxing slaves per person for the purpose of abolishing slavery. This clause was overruled by the Sixteenth Amendment, which allows for an income tax.

5. *Export Duties.* No tax or duty shall be laid on articles exported from any State.

This clause also resulted from a commerce compromise. The southern states wanted to make sure that Congress could not use its taxing power to impose taxes on Southern exports, such as cotton and tobacco.

6. *Interstate Commerce.* No preference shall be given by any regulation of commerce or revenue to the ports of one State over those of another; nor shall vessels bound to, or from, one State, be obliged to enter, clear, or pay duties in another.

7. *Treasury Withdrawals.* No money shall be drawn from the Treasury, but in consequence of appropriations made by law; and a regular statement and account of the receipts and expenditures of all public money shall be published from time to time.

Since Congress controls expenditures, it can place limits on a president's powers by deciding how much the chief executive may spend for different purposes. This could well be the single most important check on the president's power in the Constitution.

8. *Titles of Nobility*. No title of nobility shall be granted by the United States, and no person holding any office of profit or trust under them, shall, without the consent of the Congress, accept of any present, emolument, office, or title, of any kind whatever, from any King, Prince, or foreign State.

This clause prohibits the establishment of a nobility, and also discourages bribery of American officials by foreign governments.

SECTION 10. POWERS DENIED TO THE STATES

1. *Treaties, Coinage*. No State shall enter into any treaty, alliance, or confederation; grant letters of marque and reprisal; coin money; emit bills of credit; make any thing but gold and silver coin a tender in payment of debts; pass any bill of attainder, ex post facto law, or law impairing the obligation of contracts, or grant any title of nobility.

When this clause was written, Shays's Rebellion was still fresh in the minds of the delegates to the Constitutional Convention. The delegates decided to protect creditors once and for all by denying states the right to pass laws that would impair obligations of contract. During the 1930s, the Supreme Court upheld state laws relieving debtors or mortgagees from paying their debts on the due dates.

2. *Duties and Imposts*. No State shall, without the consent of the Congress, lay any imposts or duties on imports or exports, except what may be absolutely necessary for executing its inspection laws; and the net produce of all duties and imposts, laid by any State on imports or exports, shall be for the use of the Treasury of the United States; and all such laws shall be subject to the revision and control of the Congress.

A state may not put taxes on goods sent in or out of a state, unless Congress agrees.

3. *War*. No State shall, without the consent of Congress, lay any duty of tonnage, keep troops, or ships of war in time of peace, enter into any agreement or compact with another State, or with a foreign power, or engage in war, unless actually invaded, or in such imminent danger as will not admit of delay.

States are forbidden to keep troops or warships in peacetime or to make a compact with another state or a foreign nation unless Congress agrees. States can maintain a militia, but a militia's use is limited to internal disorders that arise within a state unless the militia is called into federal service. States can enter into interstate compacts regarding problems that require joint or regional action. These compacts, however, require the approval of Congress.

ARTICLE 2. EXECUTIVE BRANCH

The second part of the Constitution concerns the powers and duties of the president as the head of the executive branch.

SECTION 1. PRESIDENT AND VICE PRESIDENT.

1. *Four-Year Term*. The executive power shall be vested in a President of the United States of America. He shall hold his office during the term of four years, and, together with the Vice President, chosen for the same term, be elected, as follows:

The Constitution says that the executive power in the federal goverment shall be legally delegated to a president of the United States of America (often called the chief exective). All other executive officers are responsible to the president, and receive from the president the right to perform executive duties as the chief executive's delegates. The president and vice president are the only officers elected by the vote of the whole people.

2. *Electors From Each State*. Each State, shall appoint, in such manner as the legislature thereof may direct, a number of electors, equal to the whole number of senators and representatives to which the State may be entitled in the Congress; but no senator or representative, or person holding an office of trust or profit under the United States, shall be appointed an elector.

The number of presidential electors is determined by a state's representation (senators and representatives) in Congress. No member of Congress or federal officer may be an elector.

3. *Former System of Election*. ~~The electors shall meet in their respective States, and vote by ballot for two persons, of whom one at least shall not be an inhabitant of the same State with themselves. And they shall make a list of all the persons voted for, and of the number of votes for each; which list they shall sign and certify, and transmit sealed to the seat of the Govern-~~

ment of the United States, directed to the President of the Senate. The President of the Senate shall, in the presence of the Senate and House of Representatives, open all the certificates, and the votes shall then be counted. The person having the greatest number of votes shall be the President, if such number be a majority of the whole number of electors appointed; and if there be more than one who have such majority, and have an equal number of votes, then the House of Representatives shall immediately choose by ballot one of them for President; and if no person have a majority, then from the five highest on the list the said House shall in like manner choose the President. But in choosing the President, the votes shall be taken by States, the representation from each State having one vote; a quorum for this purpose shall consist of a member or members from two thirds of the States, and a majority of all the States shall be necessary to a choice. In every case, after the choice of the President, the person having the greatest number of votes of the electors shall be the Vice President. But if there should remain two or more who have equal votes, the Senate shall choose from them by ballot the Vice President.

This clause outlines the original method of selecting the president and vice president. It has been replaced by the method outlined in the Twelfth Amendment. The framers of the Constitution did not foresee the rise of political parties, the development of primaries and conventions, or the broadening of democracy whereby the presidential electors would be elected by the people rather than chosen by state legislatures.

4. *Time of Elections.* The Congress may determine the time of choosing the electors, and the day on which they shall give their votes; which day shall be the same throughout the United States.

In 1845, Congress set the first Tuesday after the first Monday in November of every fourth year as the general election date for selecting presidential electors.

5. *Qualifications for President.* No person except a natural born citizen, or a citizen of the United States at the time of the adoption of this Constitution, shall be eligible to the office of President; neither shall any person be eligible to that office who shall not have attained to the age of thirty-five years, and been fourteen years a resident within the United States.

This clause provides that the President (1) must be a natural-born citizen of the United States, (2) must be at least 35 years old on taking office, and (3) must at that time have been a resident within the United States for at least 14 years.

The president's term of office, as provided in the Constitution, is four years. The Twenty-second Amend-

ment to the Constitution limits the number of times a person may be elected president.

6. *Succession of the Vice President.* In case of the removal of the President from office, or of his death, resignation, or inability to discharge the powers and duties of the said office, the same shall devolve on the Vice President, and the Congress may by law provide for the case of removal, death, resignation, or inability, both of the President and Vice President, declaring what officer shall then act as President, and such officer shall act accordingly, until the disability be removed, or a President shall be elected.

Until the adoption of the Twenty-fifth Amendment, which expressly provides for the vice president to succeed to the presidency, succession was based on a precedent set by John Tyler in 1841. Tyler followed William Henry Harrison as president after the latter's death. He interpreted the ambiguous wording in this clause to mean that the vice president actually became the president, not just a temporary acting head of government.

7. *President's Salary.* The President shall, at stated times, receive for his services, a compensation, which shall neither be increased nor diminished during the period for which he shall have been elected, and he shall not receive within that period any other emolument from the United States, or any of them.

Originally, the president's salary was $25,000 per year. The president's current salary of $200,000 plus a $50,000 taxable expense account per year was enacted in 1969. The president also receives numerous fringe benefits.

8. *President's Oath of Office.* Before he enter on the execution of his office, he shall take the following oath or affirmation: "I do solemnly swear (or affirm) that I will faithfully execute the office of President of the United States, and will to the best of my ability, preserve, protect and defend the Constitution of the United States."

On January 20 following election in November, the president begins official duties with a ceremony called the Inauguration. It is customary for the president to go to the Capitol to take the oath of office, which is administered to him by the Chief Justice of the United States.

SECTION 2. POWERS OF THE PRESIDENT

1. *Commander in Chief.* The President shall be Commander in Chief of the Army and Navy of the

United States, and of the militia of the several States, when called into the actual service of the United States; he may require the opinion, in writing, of the principal officer in each of the Executive Departments, upon any subject relating to the duties of their respective offices, and he shall have power to grant reprieves and pardons for offenses against the United States, except in cases of impeachment.

This provision places the armed forces under civilian control. The president is a civilian but is superior in military power to any military officer. The phrase "principal officer in each of the executive departments" is the basis for the creation of the president's cabinet. Each cabinet member is the head of one of the executive departments. The president chooses the cabinet members, with the consent of the Senate, and can remove any cabinet official without asking Senate approval.

The president may grant a full or a conditional pardon to any person who has been convicted of breaking a federal law, except in a case of impeachment. He may shorten the prison term or reduce the fine that has been imposed as punishment for a crime.

2. *Treaties and Appointments.* He shall have power, by and with the advice and consent of the Senate, to make treaties, provided two thirds of the Senators present concur; and he shall nominate, and by and with the advice and consent of the Senate, shall appoint ambassadors, other public ministers and consuls, Judges of the Supreme Court, and all other officers of the United States, whose appointments are not herein otherwise provided for, and which shall be established by law; but the Congress may by law vest the appointment of such inferior officers, as they think proper, in the President alone, in the courts of law, or in the heads of departments.

This clause identifies some of the president's major powers, which include the power to make treaties with foreign countries, provided that the Senate gives its concurrence in a vote of two-thirds of its participating members; and the power to appoint ambassadors, Supreme Court judges, and other government officials. Most of the president's appointments to office must be submitted to the Senate for its approval.

3. *Vacancies.* The President shall have power to fill up all vacancies that may happen during the recess of the Senate, by granting commissions which shall expire at the end of their next session.

When Congress is not in session, the president may appoint people to federal offices for a temporary period. These appointments terminate at the end of the next meeting of the Senate.

SECTION 3. DUTIES OF THE PRESIDENT

He shall from time to time give to the Congress information of the state of the Union, and recommend to their consideration such measures as he shall judge necessary and expedient; he may, on extraordinary occasions, convene both houses, or either of them, and in case of disagreement between them, with respect to the time of adjournment, he may adjourn them to such time as he shall think proper; he shall receive ambassadors and other public ministers; he shall take care that the laws be faithfully executed, and shall commission all the officers of the United States.

In compliance with this clause, it is the president's custom to present to Congress an annual report known as the State of the Union message. In this message, the president sets forth a legislative program for the year, thus giving Congress leadership in solving the nation's problems. In an emergency, the president may call a special meeting of either or both houses of Congress.

This clause also gives the president the duty of meeting with ambassadors and heads of state from other countries. Another presidential duty is to see that federal laws are observed. The president must sign the papers that give federal officials the right to hold their positions.

SECTION 4. IMPEACHMENT AND REMOVAL

The President, Vice President and all civil officers of the United States, shall be removed from office on impeachment for, and conviction of, treason, bribery, or other high crimes and misdemeanors.

Treason means giving help to the nation's enemies. "High crimes and misdemeanors" are serious abuses of political power. For either or both of these offenses, a president and vice president may be impeached (or accused) by the House and removed from office if convicted by the Senate.

ARTICLE 3. JUDICIAL BRANCH

The third branch of the federal government, the judicial branch, is made up of federal courts. It has the duty of explaining and interpreting laws, settling lawsuits between citizens of different states, and punishing those who break the federal laws.

SECTION 1. FEDERAL COURTS

The judicial power of the United States shall be vested in one Supreme Court, and in such inferior courts as the Congress may from time to time ordain and establish. The judges, both of the supreme and inferior courts, shall hold their offices during good behaviour, and shall, at stated times, receive for their services, a compensation, which shall not be diminished during their continuance in office.

The creators of the Constitution did not write the details of the court system into the Constitution. They left to Congress much authority over the federal courts. Congress can decide when to establish more federal courts and judgeships, and what cases each kind of federal court shall hear. It can even change or abolish any federal court except the Supreme Court.

Congress has established two kinds of federal courts (besides special courts). These are (1) the district courts and (2) the courts of appeals for the various circuits. These lower federal courts keep the work of the Supreme Court from becoming too heavy. Congress has passed laws which require that most litigation (trial of cases) in the federal courts shall start in the district courts. If persons in certain kinds of cases are not satisfied with the district court's decision, they can appeal to a higher federal court. Sometimes such cases can be taken directly to the Supreme Court; sometimes they must be appealed to a court of appeals. In some cases, the decision of a court of appeals is final.

SECTION 2. JURISDICTION OF FEDERAL COURTS

1. Cases Under Federal Jurisdiction. The judicial power shall extend to all cases, in law and equity, arising under this Constitution, the laws of the United States, and treaties made, or which shall be made, under their authority; to all cases affecting ambassadors, other public ministers and consuls; to all cases of admiralty and maritime jurisdiction; to controversies to which the United States shall be a party; to controversies between two or more States; between a State and citizens of another State, between citizens of different States, between citizens of the same State claiming lands under grants of different States, and between a State, or the citizens thereof, and foreign States, citizens or subjects.

Cases presented to federal courts for settlement include the following: (1) cases having to do with the Constitution, the laws and treaties of the United States, ships and shipping; (2) cases in which the federal government is one of the two opposing sides; (3) disputes between two or more states; (4) disputes between citizens of different states; (5) disputes about certain claims to grants of land; (6) disputes between a state and a foreign country; and (7) disputes between an American citizen and a foreign country.

2. Cases for the Supreme Court. In all cases affecting ambassadors, other public ministers and consuls, and those in which a State shall be a party, the Supreme Court shall have original jurisdiction. In all the other cases before mentioned, the Supreme Court shall have appellate jurisdiction, both as to law and fact, with such exceptions, and under such regulations as the Congress shall make.

The Supreme Court has *original jurisdiction* in all cases involving a representative from a foreign country or involving a state. It hears the facts of the case and decides which side wins the case. All other cases must be tried in the lower courts first. The decision of the lower courts can then be appealed to the Supreme Court.

3. Conduct of Trials. The trial of all crimes, except in cases of impeachment, shall be by jury; and such trial shall be held in the State where the said crimes shall have been committed; but when not committed within any State, the trial shall be at such place or places as the Congress may by law have directed.

If a person is accused of committing a crime against the United States, he or she has the right to a trial by jury. The accused is tried in a federal court in the state where the crime was committed. If the crime was committed in a territory, not a state, Congress decides where the trial shall be held.

SECTION 3. CASES OF TREASON

1. Treason Defined. Treason against the United States shall consist only in levying war against them, or in adhering to their enemies, giving them aid and comfort. No person shall be convicted of treason unless on the testimony of two witnesses to the same overt act, or on confession in open court.

Treason means carrying on war against the United States or helping enemies of the United States. At least two witnesses must testify in court that the accused person committed the same act of treason. Any confession by the accused must be made in court.

2. Punishment. The Congress shall have power to declare the punishment of treason, but no attainder of treason shall work corruption of blood, or forfeiture except during the life of the person attainted.

Congress has the power to decide the punishment for treason. It can only punish the guilty person. *Corruption of blood* is punishment of the family of a wrongdoer. It is prohibited by this clause.

ARTICLE 4. RELATIONS AMONG THE STATES

SECTION 1. TREATMENT OF OFFICIAL ACTS

Full faith and credit shall be given in each State to the public acts, records, and judicial proceedings of every other State. And the Congress may by general laws prescribe the manner in which such acts, records and proceedings shall be proved, and the effect thereof.

States must honor the laws, records, and court decisions of other states. Regarding judicial proceedings, there are two exceptions. A state does not have to enforce another state's criminal code. A state does not have to recognize another state's grant of a divorce if legitimate residence was not established by the person obtaining the divorce.

SECTION 2. TREATMENT OF CITIZENS

1. Privileges. The citizens of each State shall be entitled to all privileges and immunities of citizens in the several States.

This clause means that a resident of one state may not be discriminated against unreasonably by another state. However, a state may require a person to live there for a certain length of time before he or she may vote or hold office.

2. Extradition. A person charged in any State with treason, felony, or other crime, who shall flee from justice, and be found in another State, shall on demand of the executive authority of the State from which he fled, be delivered up, to be removed to the State having jurisdiction of the crime.

If a criminal travels from one state to another, the second state, on request of the governor of the first state, will usually send the criminal back to the state in which the crime was committed. In this way, states cooperate in enforcing state laws.

3. Fugitive Slaves. No person held to service or labour in one State, under the laws thereof, escaping into another, shall, in consequence of any law or regulation therein, be discharged from such service or labour, but shall be delivered up on claim of the party to whom such service or labour may be due.

This provision applied to fugitive slaves. It was made obsolete by the Thirteenth Amendment.

SECTION 3. ADMISSION OF NEW STATES

1. Process for Admitting States. New States may be admitted by the Congress into this Union; but no new State shall be formed or erected within the jurisdiction of any other State; nor any State be formed by the junction of two or more States, or parts of States, without the consent of the legislatures of the States concerned as well as of the Congress.

When a group of people living in a particular area that is not part of an existing state wishes to set up a new state, it petitions Congress for permission to do so. Congress may then tell the people of that area to prepare a state constitution. The people organize to do this and offer to Congress a state constitution, which sets up a representative form of government for the group, and is in no way contrary to the federal Constitution. If a majority of Congress approves of the proposed constitution, it votes favorably on a statehood bill. The new state is then admitted as a member of the national group of states.

2. Public Lands. The Congress shall have power to dispose of and make all needful rules and regulations respecting the Territory or other property belonging to the United States; and nothing in this Constitution shall be so construed as to prejudice any claims of the United States, or of any particular State.

For many years, the federal government owned large areas of western lands (territories) that were not part of any state. This clause gave the federal government exclusive right to administer those lands.

SECTION 4. GUARANTEES TO THE STATES

The United States shall guarantee to every State in this Union a republican form of Government, and shall protect each of them against invasion; and on application of the legislature, or of the executive (when the legislature cannot be convened) against domestic violence.

A "republican form of government" is one in which the people choose their own representatives to govern and make the laws in accordance with delegated power.

The federal government can use whatever means are necessary to prevent foreign invasion and to put down domestic violence.

ARTICLE 5. METHODS OF AMENDMENT

The Congress, whenever two thirds of both Houses shall deem it necessary, shall propose amendments to this Constitution, or on the application of the legislatures of two thirds of the several States, shall call a convention for proposing amendments, which, in either case, shall be valid to all intents and purposes, as part of this Constitution, when ratified by the legislatures of three fourths of the several States, or by conventions in three fourths thereof, as the one or the other mode of ratification may be proposed by the Congress; provided that no amendment which may be made prior to the year one thousand eight hundred and eight shall in any manner affect the first and fourth clauses in the Ninth Section of the First Article; and that no State, without its consent, shall be deprived of its equal suffrage in the Senate.

The fifth article of the Constitution provides two different ways in which changes can be proposed to the states and two different ways in which states can approve such changes and make them a part of the Constitution. The Senate and House of Representatives may each approve an amendment by a favorable vote of two thirds of those present. The proposed amendment is then sent to the states for adoption. If, on the other hand, the legislatures of two thirds of the states apply to Congress for an amendment, Congress must call together a national convention to discuss and prepare such an amendment. In either case the consent of three fourths of all the states must be gotten for the proposed change to become effective. In sending the proposed amendment to the states for their consent, Congress may direct that the legislatures of the states shall decide the question or it may call upon the states to hold special conventions.

There have been 26 amendments in all. For all except the Twenty-first Amendment, Congress proposed the amendment and the state legislatures adopted it. In proposing the Twenty-first Amendment, Congress directed that each state call together its own convention.

ARTICLE 6. NATIONAL SUPREMACY

1. *Existing Obligations.* All debts contracted and engagements entered into, before the adoption of this Constitution, shall be as valid against the United States under this Constitution, as under the Confederation.

This provision assured the nation's creditors that the new federal government would assume the existing financial obligations of the country.

2. *Supreme Law.* This Constitution, and the laws of the United States which shall be made in pursuance thereof; and all treaties made, or which shall be made, under the authority of the United States, shall be the supreme law of the land; and the judges in every State shall be bound thereby, anything in the Constitution or laws of any State to the contrary notwithstanding.

This "supremacy clause" guarantees that federal law will take priority over state law in cases of conflict. To be valid, however, any law must be constitutional.

3. *Oath of Office.* The senators and representatives before mentioned, and the members of the several State legislatures, and all executive and judicial officers, both of the United States and of the several States, shall be bound by oath or affirmation, to support this Constitution; but no religious test shall ever be required as a qualification to any office or public trust under the United States.

Almost all government officials must affirm or take an oath to uphold the Constitution. No religious qualification can be set as a requirement for holding public office.

ARTICLE 7. RATIFICATION

The ratification of the conventions of nine States shall be sufficient for the establishment of this Constitution between the States so ratifying the same.

Done in convention by the unanimous consent of the States present the seventeenth day of September in the year of our Lord one thousand seven hundred and eighty seven and of the Independence of the United States of America the twelfth. In witness whereof we have hereunto subscribed our names.

For the Constitution to become operable, nine states were required to ratify. Delaware was first and New Hampshire ninth, but not until Virginia (tenth) and New York (eleventh) ratified was the Constitution assured of going into effect.

George Washington—President and deputy from Virginia
Attest: William Jackson, Secretary

New Hampshire
John Langdon
Nicholas Gilman

Massachusetts
Nathaniel Gorham
Rufus King

Connecticut
William Samuel Johnson
Roger Sherman

New York
Alexander Hamilton

New Jersey
William Livingston
David Brearley
William Paterson
Jonathan Dayton

Pennsylvania
Benjamin Franklin
Thomas Mifflin
Robert Morris
George Clymer
Thomas FitzSimons
Jared Ingersoll
James Wilson
Gouverneur Morris

Delaware
George Read
Gunning Bedford, Junior
John Dickinson
Richard Bassett
Jacob Broom

Maryland
James McHenry
Daniel of St. Thomas Jenifer
Daniel Carroll

Virginia
John Blair
James Madison, Jr.

North Carolina
William Blount
Richard Dobbs Spaight
Hugh Williamson

South Carolina
John Rutledge
Charles Cotesworth Pinckney
Charles Pinckney
Pierce Butler

Georgia
William Few
Abraham Baldwin

AMENDMENTS

Since the ratification of the Constitution in 1788, it has been modified by amendment a total of 26 times. The first ten amendments, adopted by the first Congress in 1791, are popularly known as the Bill of Rights.

AMENDMENT 1. RELIGIOUS AND POLITICAL FREEDOM (1791)

Congress shall make no law respecting an establishment of religion, or prohibiting the free exercise thereof; or abridging the freedom of speech, or of the press; or the right of the people peaceably to assemble, and to petition the Government for a redress of grievances.

Government is to be kept separate from religion. Citizens are free to join any religious body (or none at all), and each religious body is free to practice its own beliefs and form of worship. The government may not interfere.

This amendment also prohibits any government action that will interfere with a citizen's right to say, write, print, or publish the truth about anything. There are important limitations to the practice of free speech. If false or harmful statements, spoken or printed, unjustly damage someone's reputation, the speaker or publisher may be sued in a court of law. But within these limits, citizens can discuss any question freely and criticize the government.

Furthermore, the First Amendment provides that Congress cannot make laws that stop people from holding peaceful meetings. This is "the right of the people peaceably to assemble." Finally, the amendment guarantees that people may send petitions to the government without fear of penalty.

Originally, all of these guaranteed freedoms applied to Congress and the federal government, not the state governments. Adoption of the Fourteenth Amendment in 1868, as later interpreted by the Supreme Court, guaranteed basic freedoms in the First Amendment against infringement by the states.

AMENDMENT 2. RIGHT TO BEAR ARMS (1791)

A well regulated militia, being necessary to the security of a free State, the right of the people to keep and bear arms, shall not be infringed.

This guarantee, like others in the Bill of Rights, is a limited right. It means more than the citizens' right to possess firearms. It protects their right and duty to serve in the armed forces.

This amendment also prevents the national government from absolutely prohibiting the ownership of firearms by citizens. The federal government has, however, passed laws to exercise some control over the interstate commerce in guns.

AMENDMENT 3. QUARTERING OF SOLDIERS (1791)

No soldier shall, in time of peace be quartered in any house, without the consent of the owner, nor in time of war, but in a manner to be prescribed by law.

The Third Amendment provides that in peacetime no soldiers can be lodged in any private house without the consent of the owners, and in wartime soldiers can be quartered in private houses only according to laws passed by Congress.

AMENDMENT 4. SEARCH AND SEIZURE (1791)

The right of the people to be secure in their persons, houses, papers, and effects, against unreasonable searches and seizures, shall not be violated, and no warrants shall issue, but upon probable cause, supported by oath or affirmation, and particularly describing the place to be searched, and the persons or things to be seized.

Under totalitarian governments, no guarantees of individual privacy are observed. In the United States, the Fourth Amendment and the strictness of courts in upholding it keep citizens free. The word warrant means "justification," and in the legal sense it refers to a document issued by a magistrate indicating the name, address, and possible offense committed. The person asking for the warrant (a police officer, for example) must convince the magistrate that an offense probably has been committed.

AMENDMENT 5. CRIMINAL PROCEEDINGS; DUE PROCESS (1791)

No person shall be held to answer for a capital, or otherwise infamous crime, unless on a presentment or indictment of a Grand Jury, except in cases arising in the land or naval forces, or in the militia, when in actual service in time of war or public danger; nor shall any person be subject for the same offense to be twice put in jeopardy of life or limb; nor shall be compelled in any criminal case to be a witness against himself, nor be deprived of life, liberty, or property, without due process of law; nor shall private property be taken for public use, without just compensation.

Juries are of two types. There are small or *petit* juries consisting of 12 jurors who hear a case tried and decide it. There are also larger, or *grand* juries, made up of as many as 23 persons, who listen to the testimony of witnesses and decide whether enough evidence exists to bring the matter to trial. Indictment by a grand jury means that the jurors think there is sufficient reason to hold a trial. The Fifth Amendment gives all citizens accused of major crimes the right to have their cases considered by a grand jury before being brought to trial.

Furthermore, this amendment states that a citizen who has been tried and acquitted in a criminal case may not be tried for the same offense again. This is his or her protection against "double jeopardy," that is, endangering his or her life or freedom twice. Double jeopardy does not work against a person, however, once he or she has been convicted. The amendment also guarantees protection against "self-incrimination." This clause means that people are not expected to be witnesses against themselves.

The last two sections of the Fifth Amendment provide protection against the violation of "due process" and the arbitrary confiscation of property. The "due process" clause means that all the protections listed in the Bill of Rights and in the body of the Constitution must be extended to the accused person in a criminal action.

AMENDMENT 6. RIGHT TO JURY TRIAL (1791)

In all criminal prosecutions, the accused shall enjoy the right to a speedy and public trial, by an impartial jury of the State and district wherein the crime shall have been committed, which district shall have been previously ascertained by law, and to be informed of the nature and cause of the accusation; to be confronted with the witnesses against him; to have compulsory process for obtaining witnesses in his favor, and to have the assistance of counsel for his defense.

Trial by jury is one of the cornerstones of the American legal system. Accused persons may usually waive this protection if they so choose. If, on the other hand, they demand a jury trial, 12 jurors must reach a unanimous verdict in order to convict. The right to a speedy trial protects citizens from being indefinitely under a criminal charge, something that could cause much hardship.

AMENDMENT 7. CIVIL TRIALS (1791)

In suits at common law, where the value in controversy shall exceed twenty dollars, the right of trial by jury shall be preserved, and no fact tried by a jury, shall be otherwise reexamined in any court of the United States, than according to the rules of the common law.

Either side in a dispute can insist on having a jury trial in cases involving more than $20. On the other hand, both can agree not to have a jury. Judges may not interfere with a jury's decision.

AMENDMENT 8. PUNISHMENT FOR CRIMES (1791)

Excessive bail shall not be required, nor excessive fines imposed, nor cruel and unusual punishments inflicted.

Bail is the money (or property) given to a court by an accused person in order to guarantee that he or she will appear for the trial. This amendment states that bails, fines, and punishments must not be excessive, cruel, or unusual.

AMENDMENT 9. OTHER RIGHTS (1791)

The enumeration in the Constitution, of certain rights, shall not be construed to deny or disparage others retained by the people.

This amendment says that the rights already described in the Constitution and the first eight amendments are not the only rights of the people, and that other rights are not taken away from the people because the Constitution and amendments do not mention them.

AMENDMENT 10. POWERS RESERVED TO THE STATES (1791)

The powers not delegated to the United States by the Constitution, nor prohibited by it to the States, are reserved to the States respectively, or to the people.

Any powers not delegated by the Constitution to the federal government, or definitely taken away from the states, are *reserved* (belong) to the states, and to "the people."

The states pass many laws for the welfare of their citizens under the authority usually known as their "police powers." This means the power delegated to a state by its people to protect their lives, health, and morals and to provide for their safety, comfort, and convenience.

AMENDMENT 11. SUITS AGAINST STATES (1798)

The judicial power of the United States shall not be construed to extend to any suit in law or equity, commenced or prosecuted against one of the United States by citizens of another State, or by citizens or subjects of any foreign State.

Unless it gives its prior consent, a state cannot be sued in the federal courts either by citizens of other states or by foreign countries.

AMENDMENT 12. ELECTION OF PRESIDENT AND VICE PRESIDENT (1804)

The electors shall meet in their respective States, and vote by ballot for President and Vice President, one of whom, at least, shall not be an inhabitant of the same State with themselves; they shall name in their ballots the person voted for as President, and in distinct ballots the person voted for as Vice President, and they shall make distinct lists of all persons voted for as President, and of all persons voted for as Vice President, and of the

number of votes for each, which lists they shall sign and certify, and transmit sealed to the seat of the government of the United States, directed to the President of the Senate; The President of the Senate shall, in the presence of the Senate and House of Representatives, open all the certificates and the votes shall then be counted; The person having the greatest number of votes for President, shall be the President, if such number be a majority of the whole number of electors appointed; and if no person have such majority, then from the persons having the highest numbers not exceeding three on the list of those voted for as President, the House of Representatives shall choose immediately, by ballot, the President. But in choosing the President, the votes shall be taken by States, the representation from each State having one vote; a quorum for this purpose shall consist of a member or members from two-thirds of the States, and a majority of all the States shall be necessary to a choice. And if the House of Representatives shall not choose a President whenever the right of choice shall devolve upon them, before the fourth day of March next following, then the Vice President shall act as President, as in the case of the death or other constitutional disability of the President. The person having the greatest number of votes as Vice President, shall be the Vice President, if such number be a majority of the whole number of electors appointed, and if no person have a majority, then from the two highest numbers on the list, the Senate shall choose the Vice President; a quorum for the purpose shall consist of two-thirds of the whole number of Senators, and a majority of the whole number shall be necessary to a choice. But no person constitutionally ineligible to the office of President shall be eligible to that of Vice President of the United States.

In the original Constitution (Article 2, Section 1.3), electors cast a single ballot for president and vice president. This caused confusion in the election of 1800 when Jefferson and Burr as candidates of the same party received an identical number of electoral ballots. The Twelfth Amendment was adopted to prevent this from happening again. It specifies separate ballots for president and vice president.

The amendment provides that at least one of the candidates voted for by the electors must live in a different state. The electors are instructed to make two lists, one that gives the total votes cast for president and another that gives the total votes cast for vice president. The lists are then sealed and sent to the president of the Senate in the nation's capitol.

When the votes are counted, the candidate who receives a majority of presidential ballots is declared the president elect. The same rule applies to the list of vice presidential candidates. On the other hand, if the vote was divided among many candidates and none received more than half the votes, then the House of Representatives must select the president from the three candidates who have the largest number of electoral votes. Each state's delegation in the House casts just one vote. The candidate who receives a majority of the votes of the states is declared the president-elect. A similar procedure is followed in the Senate if no candidate for vice president receives a majority of electoral ballots. In that case, the Senate chooses a candidate from the two candidates with the most votes. A majority of Senators (currently 51 or more) must agree upon one candidate for a vice presidential candidate to be elected. No person can be vice president who lacks any of the qualifications for being president.

AMENDMENT 13. ABOLITION OF SLAVERY (1865)

Section 1. Neither slavery nor involuntary servitude, except as a punishment for crime whereof the party shall have been duly convicted, shall exist within the United States, or any place subject to their jurisdiction.

This amendment was adopted in 1865, after the Civil War, and was aimed at eliminating the ownership of one person by another. Because of the amendment, four million black Americans gained their freedom from bondage.

Section 2. Congress shall have power to enforce this article by appropriate legislation.

Congress has the power to carry out this amendment by enacting appropriate laws.

AMENDMENT 14. RIGHTS OF CITIZENS (1868)

Section 1. All persons born or naturalized in the United States, and subject to the jurisdiction thereof, are citizens of the United States and of the State wherein they reside. No State shall make or enforce any law which shall abridge the privileges or immunities of citizens of the United States; nor shall any State deprive any person of life, liberty, or property, without due process of law; nor deny to any person within its jurisdiction the equal protection of the laws.

The first part of the amendment overruled the Dred Scott decision of 1857 by declaring that a person was a citizen if he was born or naturalized in this country. Americans were to have dual citizenship, on the state and federal levels. The other parts of this section were designed to insure that states would not discriminate against freed slaves. The due process clause, which in the Fifth Amendment limited the federal government, now was used to limit states as well.

The citizenship guarantee means that even children of aliens are citizens of the United States.

The due process clause of the Fourteenth Amendment is intended to protect the citizen from state oppression, through the federal Bill of Rights.

The extremely significant "equal protection" clause makes it unlawful for states to discriminate on unreasonable grounds against any category of citizen. It was this clause which caused the Supreme Court in 1954 to decide that racially segregated schools violated constitutional guarantees.

Section 2. Representatives shall be apportioned among the several States according to their respective numbers, counting the whole number of persons in each State, excluding Indians not taxed. But when the right to vote at any election for the choice of electors for President and Vice President of the United States, Representatives in Congress, the executive and judicial officers of a State, or the members of the legislature thereof, is denied to any of the male inhabitants of such State, being twenty-one years of age, and citizens of the United States, or in any way abridged, except for participation in rebellion, or other crime, the basis of representation therein shall be reduced in the proportion which the number of such male citizens shall bear to the whole number of male citizens twenty-one years of age in such State.

This section voided the provision in Article 1, section 2 about slaves being counted as three-fifths of a free person. Indians were still not counted in the process described here for determining the apportionment of seats in Congress.

Section 3. No person shall be a Senator or Representative in Congress, or elector of President and Vice President, or hold any office, civil or military, under the United States, or under any State, who, having previously taken an oath, as a member of Congress, or as an officer of the United States, or as a member of any State legislature, or as an executive or judicial officer of any State, to support the Constitution of the United States, shall have engaged in insurrection or rebellion against the same, or given aid or comfort to the enemies thereof. But Congress may by a vote of two-thirds of each house, remove such disability.

This clause was designed to penalize southern states by keeping former Confederate leaders out of political office. Such leaders were barred from holding office either in their state governments or the national government. Congress, however, had the power to rescind this prohibition by a two-thirds vote of each house.

Section 4. The validity of the public debt of the United States, authorized by law, including debts incurred for payment of pensions and bounties for services in suppressing insurrection or rebellion, shall not be questioned. But neither the United States nor any State shall assume or pay any debt or obligation incurred in aid of insurrection or rebellion against the United States, or any claim for the loss or emancipation of any slave; but all such debts, obligations and claims shall be held illegal and void.

Neither the states nor the federal government could pay any portion of the Confederate debt. Southern states could not demand compensation for slaves who had been emancipated. Payment of the Union debt, on the other hand, could not be questioned.

Section 5. The Congress shall have power to enforce, by appropriate legislation, the provisions of this article.

Congress had the power after the Civil War to make laws that put this amendment into effect, and it did so during Reconstruction.

AMENDMENT 15. RIGHT OF SUFFRAGE (1870)

Section 1. The right of citizens of the United States to vote shall not be denied or abridged by the United States or by any State on account of race, color, or previous condition of servitude.

After the Civil War, Congress required the former states of the Confederacy to adopt constitutions which provided for universal suffrage of male citizens before they could come back into full partnership with the other states of the Union. Many states did this, but still there was fear that once they had returned to the Union they might then repeal the right to vote from their constitutions. Moreover, even after the Civil War, many northern states denied Negroes the right to vote. To solve these twin problems, Congress adopted the Fifteenth Amendment.

Section 2. The Congress shall have power to enforce this article by appropriate legislation.

Congress may make laws that put this amendment into effect.

AMENDMENT 16. INCOME TAX (1913)

The Congress shall have power to lay and collect taxes on incomes, from whatever source derived, without apportionment among the several States, and without regard to any census or enumeration.

This amendment gives Congress the power to put a tax on income *without* dividing the amount due among the states according to population. Income taxes were collected by the federal government after this amendment was adopted.

AMENDMENT 17. DIRECT ELECTION OF SENATORS (1913)

Section 1. The Senate of the United States shall be composed of two senators from each State, elected by the people thereof, for six years; and each senator shall have one vote. The electors in each State shall have the qualifications requisite for electors of the most numerous branch of the State legislatures.

Section 2. When vacancies happen in the representation of any State in the Senate, the executive authority of such State shall issue writs of election to fill such vacancies: *Provided*, that the legislature of any State may empower the executive thereof to make temporary appointments until the people fill the vacancies by election as the legislature may direct.

Section 3. This amendment shall not be so construed as to affect the election or term of any senator chosen before it becomes valid as part of the Constitution.

This amendment changed the method of selecting senators described in Article 1, Section 3, clause 2 to say that senators would be elected by the people of each state, not by the state legislatures.

AMENDMENT 18. NATIONAL PROHIBITION (1919)

Section 1. After one year from the ratification of this article the manufacture, sale, or transportation of intoxicating liquors within, the importation thereof into, or the exportation thereof from the United States and all territory subject to the jurisdiction thereof for beverage purposes is hereby prohibited.

One year after this amendment was ratified it became illegal in the United States and its territories to make, sell, or carry intoxicating liquors for drinking purposes. It became illegal to send such liquors out of the country and its territories or to bring such liquors into them.

Section 2. The Congress and the several States shall have concurrent power to enforce this article by appropriate legislation.

Enforcement duties were shared by the states and the federal government.

Section 3. This article shall be inoperative unless it shall have been ratified as an amendment to the Constitution by the legislatures of the several States, as provided in the Constitution, within seven years from the date of the submission hereof to the States by the Congress.

This amendment had to be ratified by the state legislatures within a period of seven years. The need for ratification within seven years was written into several amendments.

AMENDMENT 19. WOMEN'S SUFFRAGE (1920)

Section 1. The right of citizens of the United States to vote shall not be denied or abridged by the United States or by any State on account of sex.

Section 2. Congress shall have power to enforce this article by appropriate legislation.

Neither the United States nor any state can keep a citizen from voting because she is a woman. Congress has the power to make laws that put this amendment into effect.

AMENDMENT 20. "LAME DUCK" AMENDMENT (1933)

Section 1. The terms of the President and Vice President shall end at noon on the 20th day of January, and the terms of Senators and Representatives at noon on the third day of January, of the years in which such terms would have ended if this article had not been ratified; and the terms of their successors shall then begin.

Section 2. The Congress shall assemble at least once in every year, and such meeting shall begin at noon on the third day of January, unless they shall by law appoint a different day.

Section 3. If, at the time fixed for the beginning of the term of the President, the President elect shall have died, the Vice President elect shall become President. If a President shall not have been chosen before the time fixed for the beginning of his term, or if the President elect shall have failed to qualify, then the Vice President elect shall act as President until a President shall have qualified; and the Congress may by law provide for the case wherein neither a President elect nor a Vice President elect shall have qualified, declaring who shall then act as President, or the manner in which one who is to act shall be selected, and such person shall act accordingly until a President or Vice President shall have qualified.

Section 4. The Congress may by law provide for the case of the death of any of the persons from whom the House of Representatives may choose a President whenever the right of choice shall have devolved upon them, and for the case of the death of any of the persons from whom the Senate may choose a Vice President whenever the right of choice shall have devolved upon them.

Section 5. Sections 1 and 2 shall take effect on the 15th day of October following the ratification of this article.

Section 6. This article shall be inoperative unless it shall have been ratified as an amendment to the Constitution by the legislatures of three-fourths of the several States within seven years from the date of its submission.

The political term "lame duck" refers to any office holder who expects to be replaced by someone else. Such officials generally lose a great deal of influence. Before 1933, this was true of "lame duck" presidents, who attempted to govern for five months between election day in November and the swearing in of a new president on March 4. Now, because of this so-called Lame Duck Amendment, new presidents are inaugurated in January, thus reducing the lame duck period.

AMENDMENT 21. REPEAL OF PROHIBITION (1933)

Section 1. The eighteenth article of amendment to the Constitution of the United States is hereby repealed.

This amendment repeals Amendment 18. Prohibition is no longer a national law.

Section 2. The transportation or importation into any State, Territory, or possession of the United States for delivery or use therein of intoxicating liquors, in violation of the laws thereof, is hereby prohibited.

Carrying liquor across state boundaries for use in a "dry" state is a crime against the United States as well as against the state.

Section 3. This article shall be inoperative unless it shall have been ratified as an amendment to the Constitution by conventions in the several States, as provided in the Constitution, within seven years from the date of the submission hereof to the States by the Congress.

This amendment had to be ratified by state conventions chosen specifically for their views on the issue. The conventions had to approve the amendment within seven years.

AMENDMENT 22. TWO-TERM LIMIT FOR PRESIDENTS (1951)

Section 1. No person shall be elected to the office of the President more than twice, and no person who has held the office of President, or acted as President, for more than two years of a term to which some other person was elected President shall be elected to the office of the President more than once. But this Article shall not apply to any person holding the office of President when this Article was proposed by the Congress, and shall not prevent any person who may be holding the office of President, or acting as President, during the term within which this Article becomes operative from holding the office of President or acting as President during the remainder of such term.

This amendment wrote into the Constitution a custom begun by George Washington whereby presidents limited themselves to two terms in office. The precedent was not broken until Franklin D. Roosevelt was elected to a third term in 1940 and a fourth term in 1944. The amendment prevents any president from serving more than two terms.

Section 2. This Article shall be inoperative unless it shall have been ratified as an amendment to the Constitution by the legislatures of three-fourths of the several States within 7 years from the date of its submission to the States by the Congress.

For this amendment to take effect, the states were required to ratify it within a period of seven years.

AMENDMENT 23. VOTING IN THE DISTRICT OF COLUMBIA (1961)

Section 1. The District constituting the seat of Government of the United States shall appoint in such manner as the Congress may direct: A number of electors of President and Vice President equal to the whole number of Senators and Representatives in Congress to which the District would be entitled if it were a State, but in no event more than the least populous State; they shall be in addition to those appointed by the States, but they shall be considered, for the purposes of the election of President and Vice President, to be electors appointed by a State; and they shall meet in the District and perform such duties as provided by the twelfth article of amendment.

Section 2. The Congress shall have power to enforce this article by appropriate legislation.

This amendment gives to citizens living in the District of Columbia the right to vote in elections for president and vice president. The District of Columbia is now given three presidential electors. Before this amendment was adopted, it had none.

AMENDMENT 24. ABOLITION OF POLL TAXES (1964)

Section 1. The right of citizens of the United States to vote in any primary or other election for President or Vice President, for electors for President or Vice President, or for Senator or Representative in Congress, shall not be denied or abridged by the United States or any State by reason of failure to pay any poll tax or other tax.

Section 2. The Congress shall have power to enforce this article by appropriate legislation.

Neither the states nor the national government may require a person to pay a poll tax in order to vote in a federal election. For many years before this amendment was adopted, poor citizens were effectively denied the right to vote because they could not pay poll taxes collected by state governments.

AMENDMENT 25. PRESIDENTIAL DISABILITY AND SUCCESSION (1967)

Section 1. In case of the removal of the President from office or of his death or resignation, the Vice President shall become President.

When the President dies, resigns, or is removed from office, the vice president becomes president.

Section 2. Whenever there is a vacancy in the office of the Vice President, the President shall nominate a Vice President who shall take office upon confirmation by a majority vote of both Houses of Congress.

When the office of vice president is vacant, the president appoints a vice president. This appointment must be approved by a majority vote of both houses of Congress.

Section 3. Whenever the President transmits to the President pro tempore of the Senate and the Speaker of the House of Representatives his written declaration that he is unable to discharge the powers and duties of his office, and until he transmits to·them a written declaration to the contrary, such powers and duties shall be discharged by the Vice President as Acting President.

When the President writes to the president pro tempore of the Senate and the Speaker of the House declaring that he is unable to perform the duties of office, the vice president serves in the role of acting president.

Section 4. Whenever the Vice President and a majority of either the principal officers of the executive departments or of such other body as Congress may by law provide, transmit to the President pro tempore of the Senate and the Speaker of the House of Representatives their written declaration that the President is unable to discharge the powers and duties of his office, the Vice President shall immediately assume the powers and duties of the office as Acting President.

Thereafter, when the President transmits to the President pro tempore of the Senate and the Speaker of the House of Representatives his written declaration that no inability exists, he shall resume the powers and duties of his office unless the Vice President and a majority of either the principal officers of the executive department or of such other body as Congress may by law provide, transmit within four days to the President pro tempore of the Senate and the Speaker of the House of Representatives their written declaration that the President is unable to discharge the powers and duties of his office. Thereupon Congress shall decide the issue, assembling within forty-eight hours for that purpose if not in session.

If the Congress, within twenty-one days after receipt of the latter written declaration, or, if Congress is not in session, within twenty-one days after Congress is required to assemble, determines by two-thirds vote of both Houses that the President is unable to discharge the powers and duties of his office, the Vice President shall continue to discharge the same as Acting President; otherwise, the President shall resume the powers and duties of his office.

When the vice president and a majority of the cabinet (or some other body designated by Congress) write the president pro tempore of the Senate and the Speaker of the House informing them that the presi-dent is unable to perform the duties of office, the vice president immediately becomes the acting president.

The president may resume his duties by writing to the president pro tempore of the Senate and the Speaker of the House informing them that he is able to take up the duties of office. If within four days, however, both the vice president and a majority of the cabinet (or some other body designated by Congress) write the president pro tempore and the Speaker of the House informing them that, in their judgment, the president is still unable to perform presidential duties, Congress must decide the issue. Congress has 21 days to decide, by a two-thirds majority of both houses, that the president is still unable to serve. The vice president then continues as acting president. If Congress determines that the president is able to discharge his duties, the president resumes office.

AMENDMENT 26. VOTING AGE LOWERED TO 18 (1971)

Section 1. The right of citizens of the United States, who are 18 years of age or older, to vote shall not be denied or abridged by the United States or by any State on account of age.

Section 2. The Congress shall have power to enforce this article by appropriate legislation.

No person 18 years of age or older may be denied the right to vote in either a federal or a state election. Congress has the power to make laws for putting this amendment into effect.

CHAPTER REVIEW

TIME LINE

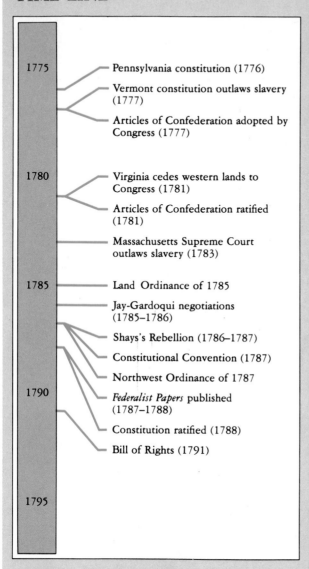

1775

— Pennsylvania constitution (1776)

— Vermont constitution outlaws slavery (1777)

— Articles of Confederation adopted by Congress (1777)

1780

— Virginia cedes western lands to Congress (1781)

— Articles of Confederation ratified (1781)

— Massachusetts Supreme Court outlaws slavery (1783)

1785

— Land Ordinance of 1785

— Jay-Gardoqui negotiations (1785–1786)

— Shays's Rebellion (1786–1787)

— Constitutional Convention (1787)

— Northwest Ordinance of 1787

1790

— *Federalist Papers* published (1787–1788)

— Constitution ratified (1788)

— Bill of Rights (1791)

1795

TIME LINE QUESTIONS

1. In what year did Virginia cede its western land claims to the Confederation Congress? What other events shown on the time line were made possible by Virginia's action?
2. How many years after the ratification of the Articles of Confederation did the Constitution legally become the "supreme law of the land" in the United States?

SKILLS STRATEGY

AMENDMENT 1. Congress shall make no law respecting an establishment of religion, or prohibiting the free exercise thereof; or abridging the freedom of speech, or of the press; or the right of the people peaceably to assemble, and to petition the Government for a redress of grievances.

AMENDMENT 2. A well regulated Militia, being necessary to the security of a free State, the right of the people to keep and bear Arms shall not be infringed.

AMENDMENT 3. No Soldier shall, in time of peace, be quartered in any house, without the consent of the Owner, nor in time of war, but in a manner to be prescribed by law.

PRIMARY SOURCES

Your knowledge of history has come from *primary* and *secondary* sources. This textbook is a secondary source of historical information. It is an account of historical events written by a modern author, who could not be closely involved with any but the most recent of the events.

To write this textbook, the author used primary sources such as newspaper articles, books, letters, diaries, and official documents that were produced by people who lived during the historical periods that the book covers. A primary source is valuable because it gives a firsthand record of an event.

In order to give you a keen sense that history involves real people, this textbook has reproduced portions of primary sources in the special feature Going to the Source. One important primary source document reprinted in its entirety is the Constitution. The first ten amendments of the Constitution are called the Bill of Rights. Commentary is given on the Constitution. This commentary is a secondary source of information.

APPLYING SKILLS

The first five amendments in the Bill of Rights are reproduced above. Refer to them as you answer the following questions.

Making Connections: Review the questions and topics presented in the Making Connections section opening this chapter. Pay particular attention to the idea that there were historical reasons why the states were suspicious of each other and of a strong central government. Stress

AMENDMENT 4. The right of the people to be secure in their persons, houses, papers, and effects, against unreasonable searches and seizures, shall not be violated, and no Warrants shall issue, but upon probable cause, supported by Oath or affirmation, and particularly describing the place to be searched, and the persons or things to be seized.

AMENDMENT 5. No person shall be held to answer for a capital or otherwise infamous crime, unless on a presentment or indictment of a Grand Jury, except in cases arising in the land or naval forces, or in the Militia, when in actual service in time of War or public danger; nor shall any person be subject for the same offence to be twice put in jeopardy of life or limb; nor shall be compelled in any criminal case to be a witness against himself, nor be deprived of life, liberty, or property, without due process of law, nor shall private property be taken for public use, without just compensation.

1. Which of the amendments guarantees that your home will not be searched by the police unless they have a court order?
2. Which amendment assures that you will not be asked to testify against yourself during a trial?
3. If you were brought to trial for writing an article that attacked government policy, which amendment would your lawyer use in your defense?
4. Which amendment gives you the right to take part in a public protest with other citizens?
5. Could someone stop you from being a member of any religion you wanted to belong to? Which amendment is about religious preference? What does this amendment say about a national, or established, religion?
6. Which amendment guarantees people convicted of a crime the right to receive humane punishments, or punishments that are appropriate to their crimes?
7. What are the exceptions to the guarantee of a grand jury investigation if a person is accused of a crime?
8. Which amendment prohibits the government from unlawfully quartering troops in private homes?

CHAPTER 7 TEST

TEXT REVIEW
1. Why did the Americans insist on having written state constitutions?
2. How effective was the central government formed under the Articles of Confederation?
3. How did the lands known as the "national domain" and the Confederation Congress's policies toward them figure in the later growth of the United States?
4. Why could Rhode Island legally prevent the Confederation Congress from raising money by taxing the states in 1781?
5. Did the Founding Fathers accomplish a second, peaceful revolution by writing the Constitution? Explain your answer.
6. Give facts from the chapter that support the following idea: The Constitution was, in a sense, a set of compromises.
7. Explain how the Constitution provided for checks and balances among the three branches of the federal government.
8. Why was Rhode Island the last state to ratify the Constitution? Why did Delaware ratify the Constitution so quickly?

CRITICAL THINKING
9. Make a list of the steps that people in the Northwest Territory had to follow to make a region a state.
10. Make a two-level outline of the separation of powers among the three branches of the national government.

WRITING A PARAGRAPH
You know that the situation described in the topic sentence given below had several important causes. Write a paragraph to explain why the sentence is true. You might use phrases such as *a critical reason, of almost equal importance,* or *somewhat less importantly* to indicate the order of impact that each cause had. Your sentences should support the topic sentence with details.

Topic Sentence: The government of the United States under the Articles of Confederation was largely ineffective.

that although many of the individual ideas expressed in the Bill of Rights were not novel, the Constitution was a unique document and a very daring experiment, given the time in which it was created.

Quotation: from *In the American Grain*. Others works by William Carlos Williams (1883–1963) include *A Voyage to Pagany*, *White Mule*, *In the Money*, and *The Completed Collected Poems of William Carlos Williams: 1906–1938*.

CHAPTER 8

THE FEDERALIST ERA

1789–1801

. . . America must remember what in its hour of excitement it had promised, its declarations, its pronouncements, its Patrick Henry speeches. Were these just expedients of war to spur to battle or was it serious?

WILLIAM CARLOS WILLIAMS

Making Connections. Washington, Jefferson, Adams, Hamilton—all are familiar people. We think of them as being four of the founders of our country. But when these men were together in government, they did not always agree. Like today's politicians, they fought bitterly over what course was right for the country.

In this chapter, you will learn:

- How Congress decided to pay for the expenses of government
- Who the first cabinet members were
- What five-point plan Alexander Hamilton had for the new government
- Who favored loose construction of the Constitution, and who favored strict construction
- Why the United States signed two new treaties with England and Spain
- How the dispute between Adams and Jefferson nearly made Aaron Burr president

You know that some people favored a strong central government and others favored a relatively weak one. Even after the new Constitution was written, this disagreement continued. Therefore, two political parties grew up around the two positions. As you read, note how each side fought for its policies in the early years of the federal government.

Sections

1. The Course Is Set
2. The Federalist Position
3. Foreign Policies
4. The Federalists Decline

1. THE COURSE IS SET

Shortly after the Constitution was ratified, the state legislatures chose senators for the new Congress and the voters elected 59 representatives and 69 presidential electors. Everyone agreed on the name of the first president. The electoral college unanimously chose George Washington.

The New Government Takes Shape. On April 16, 1789, Washington left his plantation at Mount Vernon. In a week he was in New York City, the nation's temporary capital. On April 30 he was sworn in before a cheering crowd as the nation's first president. Taking the oath as vice president was John Adams of Massachusetts.

The Importance of George Washington. George Washington inspired confidence and trust, and he knew how to blend others' talents and abilities to serve the country. He did not make suggestions at the Constitutional Convention, and in cabinet meetings he listened. He understood that debate was better left to brilliant young thinkers like Madison, Hamilton, and Jefferson. Major policies of his administration originated with others.

Washington understood his talents and knew exactly where his abilities lay. He knew he was a leader, born and raised to command as the master of a plantation and a member of the Virginia

George Washington was inaugurated on April 30, 1789, at Federal Hall (right) in New York City. At that time, Federal Hall was where Congress met.

Skills Review: To reinforce the skills learned in the preceding Skills Strategy, refer to the Bill of Rights and the Constitution throughout the course of this chapter and the remainder of the year whenever it is applicable to the material being studied.

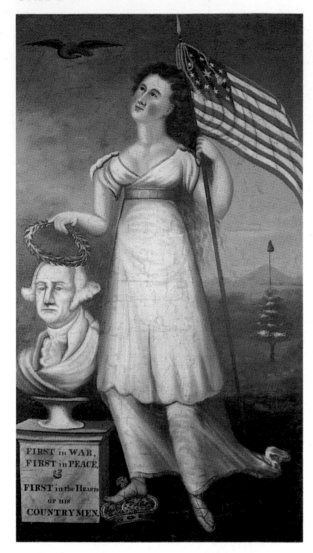

This painting shows Liberty placing a wreath on a sculpture of Washington. It indicates the reverence Americans had for their first president.

Washington lived at a time that produced many remarkable people. And yet, no other person could have done what George Washington did. During the Revolution, he kept an army together against overwhelming odds. He remained above squabbling in a quarrelsome time. And he placed the republic on a solid foundation by approving policies that most other southern planters would not have approved.

An Active Congress. The early days of the first Congress were busy with activity. One of the first things the new Congress did was to pass the *Judiciary Act* of 1789. It provided for 13 district courts, one for each state, and with powers over the state governments. Three circuit courts were to hear appeals of the district court decisions. Higher than all federal and state courts was the Supreme Court, consisting of a chief justice and five associate justices. Shortly after he signed the bill, Washington named John Jay of New York to be the first chief justice.

Congress also approved the Bill of Rights and sent it to the states for ratification. The Northwest Ordinance, adopted earlier by the Confederation Congress, was reenacted under the Constitution.

In order to pay the expenses of government, Congress adopted the *Tariff of 1789,* a tax on goods imported into the United States from abroad. It was not much of a tax. The rate ranged from only five percent to 15 percent of the value of the goods and applied only to some imports, such as glass, pottery, nails, and the like. But the tariff had great importance as a symbol of the new government's strength. The Continental Congress had never been able to enact a tariff because the Articles of Confederation did not give it that power. The Tariff of 1789 was also important because it opened the doors of Congress to a financial policy that reached much farther than a simple tax.

The Cabinet. Congress also created several executive offices and departments, each headed by a Secretary, to assist Washington with his many responsibilities. Edmund Randolph, whose change of heart helped to ratify the Constitution in Virginia, was rewarded with the post of Attorney General. He advised the President on legal matters. The Post Office, inherited from the Confed-

aristocracy. People naturally looked to him for guidance. Using his natural dignity, he remained aloof from petty disputes.

As president, Washington cultivated a presence that was almost royal. He drove about the streets of New York in a gleaming yellow coach pulled by six matching cream-colored horses. He understood that every action he took was a *precedent.* That is, as the first president, he was setting standards that would be looked to long after he was dead.

In the painting above, General Washington receives a hero's salute as he crosses the Hudson River between New Jersey and New York on the way to his inauguration.

FEDERAL SYSTEM		
Powers of Federal Government *(Delegated Powers)*	**Powers Shared by Federal and State Governments** *(Concurrent Powers)*	**Powers of State Governments** *(Reserved Powers)*
• Maintain armed forces • Establish postal and monetary system • Set standards for weights, measures, copyrights, and patents • Regulate interstate and foreign commerce • Establish laws of citizenship and immigration • Declare war	• Provide for general welfare • Establish criminal justice system • Levy taxes • Charter banks • Borrow money and issue bonds	• Establish schools and local governments • Determine structure of state government • Create and administer corporations • Determine regulations for marriage and divorce • Regulate intrastate commerce

Although he was the first president under the new Constitution, Washington was not the first president of the United States. Under the Articles of Confederation, eight men presided over the Congress between 1781 and 1789, when the Constitution was ratified. The title for each in the year in which he served was 'President of the United States in Congress Assembled.'

eration, was supervised by Postmaster General Samuel Osgood.

Although Randolph often met with Washington's *cabinet,* or committee of advisors, he did not head a department. (The Department of Justice was not established until 1870.) Only three men held full cabinet rank. Henry Knox became Secretary of War, although there was no navy and an army of only 600 soldiers. In charge of foreign affairs was Secretary of State Thomas Jefferson. The Secretary of the Treasury, soon to be the second most powerful person in the United States, was Alexander Hamilton.

Washington's cabinet included (from left) Henry Knox, Thomas Jefferson, and Alexander Hamilton.

2. THE FEDERALIST POSITION

Hamilton had a clear vision of what the new United States should be, and the energy to turn that vision into reality. Even Jefferson, the only member of the cabinet whose talents and energy rivaled Hamilton's, soon found himself reacting to the Treasury Secretary's program rather than proposing one of his own.

Hamilton wanted to put the government on a firm financial footing and to encourage American economic development. In a series of reports to Congress, Hamilton outlined a five-point plan. First, he proposed that the government repay the debts of the Confederation both to foreign countries ($12 million) and to American citizens ($44 million). There was no money to pay them immediately, but the Constitutional government could reassure its creditors by funding the debt with new *bonds.*

Second, Hamilton wanted the federal government to assume the debts of the states. Third, he called for Congress to charter a national bank patterned on the Bank of England. Fourth, Hamilton proposed that the government promote manufacturing in the United States by adopting a protective tariff. Fifth, he wanted an *excise tax* on whiskey to raise money to pay government's bills.

Unlike the first actions taken by Congress, Hamilton's economic policy aroused widespread opposition. However, with Washington's support,

Research Assignment: Have students do a report on George Washington and the myths that became popular about him. They can examine these myths and find how they contributed to Washington's power as president and how they have affected our picture of him as a historical figure.

Alexander Hamilton, Secretary of the Treasury, moved decisively to strengthen the economy.

and by making compromises, he won four of his five proposals. (He lost only on the protective tariff.) The Hamilton program earned the United States a solid financial footing. At the same time, it paved the way for the development of political parties and caused a rebellion.

Funding the National Debt.

The Confederation government had never been able to repay the $12 million borrowed from France, the Netherlands, and Spain during the Revolutionary War. If the new government moved to fund this debt by issuing bonds to pay it off gradually, it would establish good credit abroad. The United States needed this credit because it was a cash-poor country, and in future times of crisis, the government would again need to borrow money abroad.

However, when Hamilton insisted that Congress also fund the $44 million the Confederation government had borrowed from American citizens during the war, James Madison, his old ally in the fight to ratify the Constitution, rose to oppose the plan.

Madison believed in repaying debts, particularly to people who had put up money by buying bonds when the country was fighting for its independence. (Selling bonds is how governments borrow money.) But few of the people who had purchased bonds during the Revolution still owned them. During the Confederation years, when it looked as if the bonds would never be repaid, the original lenders had sold them to speculators for a tenth, or less, of the original price. Indeed, during the months before Hamilton's proposal was made public, speculators who knew about it in advance spread the rumor that the new government would not honor the bonds, and so were able to buy them up at bargain rates.

Madison felt that the United States government should not reward such *unscrupulous* and dishonest people. If it was not possible to locate the original owners of the public paper, those who had actually loaned money to the government in its time of need, the domestic debt should be funded at less than face value.

Hamilton faced the issue directly. He admitted that wealthy speculators and not ordinary people would benefit most from funding the domestic debt at face value. However, it was essential that the government win the support of the wealthy. Hamilton believed that the rich were the most important social class, and that they would invest their money in enterprises that would benefit the country. Hamilton's arguments finally swayed Congress, and the funding bill was approved.

Assumption of State Debts.

Several of the states were also in debt. Together, they owed about $22 million, mostly to foreign lenders and speculators who had also bought the state bonds at a discount. Hamilton proposed that the federal government assume these debts. By doing so, the federal government would improve its credit and increase its prestige in relation to the states.

Although he was also a nationalist, Madison, with the support of most southern senators and representatives, opposed this plan. For the most part, the southern states had been repaying their war debts. North Carolina and Georgia were almost completely caught up and Virginia had reduced its debts by half. They had accomplished this by thrifty state spending and by taxing their citizens during the Confederation period.

Discussion Question: What might have been the reasons Washington chose both Jefferson and Hamilton, two men politically opposed to each other, to serve on his cabinet? Discuss the wisdom of this arrangement.

Hamilton was successful in establishing the First Bank of the United States.

The northern states, on the other hand, had practically ignored their debts, allowing interest to pile up. What Hamilton was asking, Madison said, was for southern taxpayers to help pick up the debts of the irresponsible northern states.

In April 1790, the bill came to a vote in the House of Representatives (where all financial bills must originate) and was closely defeated by a vote of 31 to 29. But Hamilton did not give up. Instead, he made a deal with Jefferson. Southern leaders wanted the site of the permanent national capital to be in the South. If Hamilton would persuade some northern representatives to support a southern site for Federal Town (as Washington, D.C., was first known), Jefferson would persuade some of his followers in Congress to vote for assumption. Thus, in July 1790 the House approved assumption by 34 to 28.

The Bank of the United States.

In December 1790, Hamilton asked Congress to establish a national bank. Hamilton argued that the benefits of this *Bank of the United States* would be several. It would earn additional money for the government from interest on loans to states and businesses of various kinds. The economy would be stimulated by the availability of money for investment. Finally, the Bank would provide what the United States always lacked, a reliable currency. The government could print money, and since the notes would be backed by the Bank, they would be worth the same everywhere in the nation. Interstate business, always troubled by the lack of gold and silver and by distrust of paper money, would now flourish.

Hamilton proposed that the Bank be started with $10 million. The federal government would

At the time of the controversy over the Bank of the U.S., there were in existence three banks: the Bank of Massachusetts in Boston, the Bank of North America in Philadelphia, and the Bank of New York. Hamilton's experiences with these banks convinced him that they were not reliable or adequate for the national purpose he had in mind for the Bank of the U.S.

contribute $2 million, and so own one-fifth of the Bank. The other four-fifths of the money would be raised from private investors who would buy 20,000 shares at $400 a share. To ensure that the Bank would be profitable and would attract private investors, Hamilton proposed that all the government's money be deposited in the Bank.

The Bank Bill brought Jefferson and Madison together in opposing Hamilton. It did not seem right to either man that any bank would be issuing so much paper money backed up with so little gold or silver, as Hamilton proposed. Moreover, the few wealthy investors who could afford $400 for a share of Bank stock would make profits on tax money that justly belonged to all the people. Finally, because most American commerce and industry was located in the North, Hamilton's policy seemed once again to favor that section over the South. Despite these concerns, though, Hamilton again had his way. Although Washington was not sure the Bank would be good for the country, he signed the bill in 1791.

Loose Versus Strict Construction.

The Bank debate was also a battle over the Constitution. Jefferson said that the Bank was unconstitutional. He argued that nowhere in the Constitution was the federal government given the power to charter a bank.

Hamilton replied that even though the Constitution did not strictly give the power to charter a bank to the federal government, that did not mean the government did not have that power. On the contrary, the government had the right to exercise any power the Constitution did not explicitly deny to it or reserve for the states. He based his argument on the *elastic clause* in the Constitution, which allows Congress to make any laws that are "necessary and proper" to execute the government's powers.

Hamilton's approach to interpreting the Constitution is known as *loose construction*. Jefferson's, which demanded a specific Constitutional provision for each government power, is known as *strict construction*.

Hamilton Loses on the Tariff.

Hamilton's tariff proposal was defeated. Hamilton's tariff was unlike the Tariff of 1789, which was basically a revenue-raising tariff designed to make money for

the government. The bill Hamilton proposed in 1791 was a *protective tariff*. For example, the Tariff of 1789 levied a tax on imported pottery equal to five percent of the value of the pottery. This increased the selling price of British pottery in the United States by five percent. However, British manufacturers made their product so efficiently that, even with this tax, British pottery was much cheaper in the United States than any American pottery. With so many dishes, bowls, and pots coming into the country, the low tariff simply meant revenue for the United States government.

Hamilton's tariff would make the import duty on pottery so high that the price of the imports would be more than the price of American pottery. Thus, American pottery manufacturers would be *protected* from British competition. It was true, Hamilton agreed, that a protective tariff meant higher prices for consumers. However, the short-term sacrifice was worthwhile. Future generations of Americans would benefit from a strong industrial base.

Hamilton's tariff proposal made little headway in the House of Representatives. Southerners solidly opposed the tariff. Many, like Jefferson, did not want to see the United States become an industrial nation. They believed that manufacturing created ugly, unnatural cities populated only by the very wealthy and the very poor. They did not think a society with sharp class lines was a healthy society. Moreover, the tariff would again benefit the northern states, where most manufacturing was located. The agricultural South, which consumed manufactured goods, would once again pick up the bill by paying higher prices.

The Excise Tax.

Hamilton's fifth proposal, a 25 percent *excise tax* on distilled liquor, passed Congress. (An excise tax is a tax on the manufacture and sale of goods, usually luxury items and other non-essential goods, within a country.)

In eastern cities, the tax raised the price of rum, the favorite homemade drink, and people grumbled. However, it was difficult to pretend persecution over a drink of liquor. West of the Appalachian Mountains, however, the tax struck at the heart of the economy. The farmers in Kentucky, Ohio, and western Pennsylvania not only liked to drink whiskey, they depended on producing it for the small cash income they had.

Discussion Question: Whose interpretation of the Constitution was correct, the strict constructionist's or the loose constructionist's? There is no correct answer to this question; it is meant as an exercise in developing and defending one's point of view. Make sure arguments are coherent and logical. Have students use specific clauses of the constitution to support their argument.

Before 1795, the Mississippi River was closed to American shipping. Farmers west of the mountains could not float crops down the Ohio and Mississippi by raft. Their only trade routes lay to the east, over steep, narrow, and rocky trails through the Appalachians. Horses or mules that carried four bushels of grain cost more to feed along the way than the selling price of their cargo.

However, twenty-four bushels of grain could be turned into a gallon of whiskey that could be sold for 25 cents or more in the East. Even then, the profit was small, and much hard work went into that small profit. Hamilton's tax, at seven cents a gallon, wiped out that profit. The western farmers responded with a rebellion.

The Whiskey Rebellion.

Like the supporters of Daniel Shays in 1787, farmers on the Pennsylvania frontier protested the tax by roughing up tax collectors, closing county courthouses, and patrolling towns with firearms. It was actually more of a riot than a rebellion. Nonetheless, in the late summer of 1794, Washington set out from Philadelphia (the temporary capital since 1790) at the head of 15,000 state militiamen. Hamilton, who rode at his side, made sure that troops from Virginia and Maryland as well as from Pennsylvania were present in the column. He wanted every-

one to know that the federal government, and not just Pennsylvania, was taking action.

On hearing that the militia was on its way, the rebels quickly disbanded. Washington returned home, but Hamilton pushed on. By the time the army reached western Pennsylvania, there was no rebellion to be found. Hamilton arrested four persons anyway and tried them for treason. Two were convicted and sentenced to death. Wisely, Washington pardoned them. Hamilton's point had been made, and no bloodshed was necessary.

SECTION REVIEW

1. Write a sentence to identify: government bond, national debt, protective tariff, excise tax.

2. What was the purpose of the five-point plan that Treasury Secretary Hamilton presented to Congress?

3. Explain the position of the southern states on Hamilton's proposal that the federal government assume state debts from the Revolutionary War.

4. What is loose construction? To which of Hamilton's proposals was it related?

The federal government's exise tax on whiskey proved extremely unpopular to farmers on the Pennsylvania frontier, seen below having tarred and feathered a tax inspector in 1794.

3. FOREIGN POLICIES

It seems almost impossible that Americans could be bothered to consider foreign problems when they were facing such revolutionary changes at home. But despite their best efforts, Americans became involved in European affairs, and the government had to decide how to deal with the world at large.

The French Revolution. In 1789, just as the Constitution was taking effect, a revolution in France toppled King Louis XVI and plunged Europe into turmoil. Many of the revolutionaries claimed that they were following the example of the United States in fighting for liberty. Others went further, adding that the French Revolution was also dedicated to equality and fraternity.

At first, almost all Americans favored the French Revolution, including George Washington, who had been disgusted by Shays's Rebellion. Most Americans also approved when the new French government abolished the special privileges of the aristocracy. Most Americans disliked the notion of a class possessing privileges by right of birth.

However, when the revolutionaries beheaded the king and queen and then executed nobles and political enemies by the thousand, conservatives such as Washington and Hamilton backed off. Other Americans, however, still supported the French.

War or Neutrality. Many nobles fled France for fear of their lives. In neighboring countries, their plans to retake the country by force were backed by rulers who feared the revolution would spread among their own people. In 1793, France and Great Britain went to war and put the United States in a touchy situation. The alliance with France signed during the American Revolution seemed to require the United States to help the French against the British.

Jefferson believed the alliance should be honored. With some reservations, he supported the French revolutionaries. Hamilton opposed the revolutionaries, and viewed any challenge to established order, especially a challenge in the name of rule by the people, as dangerous. He told Washington that the 1778 alliance with France was not binding, arguing that it was an agreement between the Confederation and the French monarchy, neither of which existed anymore.

Washington did not like the French revolutionaries any more than Hamilton did. He also knew that the United States was not prepared to fight a war. So, he proclaimed that America was neutral —"impartial toward the belligerent powers." Unfortunately, neither France nor Great Britain was impartial toward the United States.

Citizen Genêt. France threatened Washington's policy of neutrality with an undiplomatic diplomat. The French ambassador, Edmond Genêt (zhə-nĕ′), acted as if he had official power over the United States. Genêt empowered a group of adventurers to invade Spanish Louisiana. This absurd expedition never got started, but the ships Genêt commissioned as privateers captured and brought into American ports more than 80 British merchant vessels.

Washington was furious. Genêt's behavior insulted the dignity of the presidency, a delicate point with Washington. Much worse, Genêt threatened to drag the United States into a war that Washington had decided to avoid. The President ordered Genêt to cease his political activities and to bring no more captured British ships into United States waters. When Genêt ignored him, Washington ordered the ambassador to leave and go back to France.

Genêt did not go. His party had lost power back home. To return would have meant the guillotine. But he did silence himself and Washington permitted him to stay. The crisis with France was over for the moment.

England Challenges America. In the meantime, the British were also testing Washington's determination. The French, fearing their West Indian islands would be starved out by British naval power, had revoked the mercantilist law that forbade American ships to trade in the West Indies. Vessels from New England and the Mid-Atlantic states rushed to take advantage of the new market.

Great Britain quickly responded, citing the *Rule of 1756*. This rule provided that trading privileges denied during peacetime could not be permitted in time of war. To enforce the rule, British war-

Research Activity: Have students develop a timeline using outside resources to compile a list of events leading to the French Revolution. Relate this to events leading up to the American Revolution and past it, up to the time of the French Revolution. Ask students to discuss any possible relation between the two events.

 199

ships and privateers began to seize American vessels, taking about 600 before the end of 1794. Captains of the British ships also impressed sailors from American ships, forcing them to enter the British Navy.

Impressment was an old practice. When a warship needed more crew members, British law allowed naval captains to board British merchant vessels and force sailors into service. Although American vessels did not, of course, fly the British flag, Britain insisted that many British subjects worked on American ships—which was true—and that they could be legally impressed into the Royal Navy. This justification seemed weak to Americans, especially when American sailors were also impressed.

Hundreds of American sailors were forced into service on British ships. Americans regarded impressment as an illegal action and an insult to their nation. People who lived in the seaports began to call for war.

Washington Saves the Peace.   In the spring of 1794, Washington sent Chief Justice John Jay to Great Britain. His instructions were to sign a treaty that would enable the United States to avoid war. The British were willing to talk. Unfortunately for Jay, the British held the upper hand. The treaty they offered did not provide much for the United States but the promise of peace.

According to *Jay's Treaty*, the British agreed to turn over the western forts they were occupying in the United States. But this was merely agreeing to do what the British had promised in the Treaty of Paris in 1783. The British also agreed to pay Americans £1.3 million for ships lost in the West Indies and for slaves lost during the Revolution. In return, the British would receive £600,000 in debts owed to British subjects by southern planters. Although the subject of impressment was turned over to a commission, nothing in the treaty mentioned the problem.

Washington knew people would protest Jay's Treaty. For four months he kept its terms secret. When the treaty was revealed, there were riots. Supporters of Thomas Jefferson burned effigies of John Jay. They began to speak of the Washington administration as *toadies* of the British. Not even the President was spared from abusive personal attacks.

Pinckney's Treaty.   If the United States gained little from England in Jay's Treaty, a great deal was gained from Spain as a result of the treaty. Spain, fearing that the new Anglo-American pact meant that the United States and Britain would together attack Louisiana, offered to make genuine concessions in 1795 in order to keep the peace.

Calling in South Carolina's Thomas Pinckney, the American envoy to Madrid, the Spanish government offered to recognize American claims to disputed territory on the border of Louisiana, the right of western farmers to use the Mississippi River, and most important of all, the *right of deposit* in the city of New Orleans.

The right of deposit meant that Americans could unload their riverboat cargoes in New Orleans and reload the cargoes on seagoing vessels without paying a tax. By opening the western United States to the seas, *Pinckney's Treaty* (officially known as the *Treaty of San Lorenzo*), encouraged the rapid settlement of the lands west of the Appalachians.

SECTION REVIEW

1. Write a sentence to identify: impressment, Treaty of San Lorenzo, Louisiana, right of deposit.

2. Describe American attitudes toward the French Revolution when it first began, and then later American attitudes toward the revolutionaries.

3. Explain how Citizen Genêt insulted the dignity of the presidency and almost dragged the United States into war.

4. Describe and explain the reactions of some Americans to Jay's Treaty.

4. THE FEDERALISTS DECLINE

After two terms as president, George Washington announced he would not stand for reelection in 1796. As the Founding Fathers intended, his vice president, John Adams, succeeded him. However, as the Founding Fathers had not foreseen, Adams's supporters had to fight to make him president. For during Washington's presidency, two political parties had arisen.

Until 1796, the region that became known as Tennessee was named Franklin, after Benjamin Franklin.

GOING TO THE SOURCE

Europe has a set of primary interests which to us have none or a very remote relation. Hence she must be engaged in frequent controversies, the causes of which are essentially foreign to our concerns. Hence, therefore, it must be unwise in us to implicate ourselves by artificial ties in the ordinary vicissitudes of her politics or the ordinary combinations and collisions of her friendships or enmities.

Our detached and distant situation invites and enables us to pursue a different course. If we remain one people, under an efficient government, the period is not far off when we may defy material injury from external annoyance; when we may take such an attitude as will cause the neutrality we may at any time resolve upon to be scrupulously respected; when belligerent nations, under the impossibility of making acquisitions upon us, will not lightly hazard the giving us provocation; when we may choose peace or war, as our interest, guided by justice, shall counsel.

Why forego the advantages of so peculiar a situation? Why quit our own to stand upon foreign ground? Why, by interweaving our destiny with that of any part of Europe, entangle our peace and prosperity in the

> *Why quit our own to stand upon foreign ground? Why, by interweaving our destiny with that of any part of Europe, entangle our peace and prosperity in the toils of European ambition, rivalship, interest, humor, or caprice? It is our true policy to steer clear of permanent alliances. . . .*
>
> GEORGE WASHINGTON,
> FAREWELL ADDRESS

toils of European ambition, rivalship, interest, humor, or caprice?

It is our true policy to steer clear of permanent alliances with any portion of the foreign world, so far, I mean, as we are now at liberty to do it; for let me not be understood as capable of patronizing infidelity to existing engagements. I hold the maxim no less applicable to public than to private affairs that honesty is always the best policy. I repeat, therefore, let those engagements be observed in their genuine sense. But in my opinion it is unnecessary and would be unwise to extend them.

Taking care always to keep ourselves by suitable establishments on a respectable defensive posture, we may safely trust to temporary alliances for extraordinary emergencies. . . .

In September, 1796, a lengthy essay by President Washington appeared in city newspapers announcing that he chose not to be a candidate for a third term. The essay came to be known as Washington's "Farewell Address." In the essay, Washington offered advice on American policy toward Europe.

Federalists and Republicans. Alexander Hamilton's proposals, and Thomas Jefferson's opposition to them, caused a split that, for the most part, followed economic and sectional lines. Hamilton's policies favored commerce and manufacturing over agriculture. In general, he found support among the wealthy people of the North. However, rice and indigo growers from the deep South also supported Hamilton, as did strong nationalists in Jefferson's own Virginia, such as John Marshall and George Washington. Plenty of New Englanders who were not rich, but who depended on trade and manufacture for their livelihood, also liked Hamilton's policies.

In contrast, Jefferson thought that agriculture should be promoted. He believed that "those who labor in the earth are the chosen people of God, if ever He had a chosen people." Jefferson and Madison claimed to speak for the ordinary people and found most of their support in the South and

Discussion Question: How was George Washington's farewell address as much a policy statement as a farewell speech? Discuss the precedent Washington set by using such innocuous situations to drive home important political policies.

When George Washington stepped down from the presidency in 1797 after two terms in office, he retired to Mount Vernon (above), a Virginia estate he had inherited from his older brother, Lawrence. In the portrait below, Washington is seen with his wife, Martha, and his two stepchildren.

West, where almost everyone lived by farming. Jefferson also had supporters in the North among farmers who disliked city merchants and manufacturers. And he had plenty of wealthy backers. A majority of southern planters shared Jefferson's dislike of Hamilton's plans for the United States.

This political disagreement hardened into political parties. Hamilton's group called themselves *Federalists,* the name given to the people who had worked for ratification of the Constitution. Jefferson's supporters were known as *Democratic Republicans,* or *Republicans.*

George Washington Goes Home.
George Washington was happy to leave office. He was angered and hurt by the insults hurled at him because of Jay's Treaty. He was also worn down by a long and glorious career in the front ranks of his country. However, he wanted to leave his people with a course for the future. Therefore, in his *Farewell Address* to the nation, Washington indirectly defended his foreign policy by urging Americans not to get involved in Europe's "frequent controversies." The President also warned the country against "the baneful effects of the spirit of party."

The Election of 1796.
Washington's successors followed his advice in the matter of staying out of European wars. However, it was too late to reverse the growth of political parties. The election of 1796, in which the second president was chosen, was contested not so much by individual candidates as by Federalists and Jeffersonian Republicans.

Under the original Constitution, presidential electors wrote two names on a ballot. The candidate who received the most votes became president. The candidate who came in second became vice president. In this way, the Founding Fathers thought, the best person for the job would be president, and the second best would be vice president.

In 1789, there had been no difficulty with this procedure. In 1796, however, Federalist candidate Adams faced challenges from both outside and inside his party. The Republican party nominated Jefferson for president and fought for electors. Inside Adams's own Federalist party, however, Alexander Hamilton plotted secretly to keep

Adams out of office. Hamilton instructed his supporters among the electors to write the name of Thomas Pinckney, the Federalist vice presidential nominee, on their ballots, but not Adams's name. Hamilton hoped that this scheme would put Pinckney first and Adams second.

The plot might have worked if New England Federalists had not heard of it. When they did, they left Pinckney's name off their ballots! The result was that Adams won a slim majority of the electoral college. Second on the list was not Pinckney, but Jefferson, the Republican candidate. Therefore, Adams's vice president was his chief political opponent.

John Adams.
Looking back, it is hard not to admire John Adams. He was "always honest and often great," as Ben Franklin observed. Yet, as Franklin also knew, Adams's vanity and pride denied him the admiration he craved.

During the four years of his presidency, John Adams struggled to keep the United States at peace. He succeeded, but that was just about the

John Adams was the nation's first vice president and its second president.

Class Activity: With students, compile a chart comparing the Federalist and Republican parties. The chart should include which segments of the population supported each of these parties, what their views were on Constitutional interpretation, what their views were on government and its powers, what each one's leanings were toward France or Great Britain?

203

PROFILES OF THE PRESIDENCY

U naware that history would choose to immortalize July 4 as America's birthday, John Adams wrote to his wife:

The second day of July, 1776, will be the most memorable epoch in the history of America. I am apt to believe that it will be celebrated by succeeding generations as the great anniversary festival. It ought to be commemorated as the day of deliverance, by solemn acts of devotion to God Almighty. It ought to be solemnized with pomp and parade, with shows, games, sports, guns, bells, bonfires, and illuminations, from one end of this continent to the other, from this time forward forevermore. You will think me transported with enthusiasm, but I am not. I am well aware of the toil and blood and treasure that it will cost us to maintain this Declaration and support and defend these States. Yet, through all the gloom, I can see the rays of ravishing light and glory. I can see that the end is more than worth all the means.

—LETTER TO ABIGAIL ADAMS, JULY 3, 1776

extent of his success. Opposition within his Federalist party led by Alexander Hamilton, the steady drift of voters to the Republicans, and Adams's own personality and blunders were to cost him re-election in 1800.

War Scare With France. While the British did not stop seizing American ships after 1796, the chief threat during Adams's presidency came from France. Angered by Jay's Treaty, the French government ordered its navy to raid American shipping. By March 1797, when Adams took the oath of office, more than 300 American merchant vessels had been seized. The French also threatened to hang Americans they captured on British ships, even though they had been impressed against their will.

Following Washington's example, Adams sent Charles Pinckney, brother of Thomas Pinckney, to seek a treaty in Paris. Along with Elbridge Gerry and John Marshall, Pinckney attempted for weeks to see the French foreign minister, Charles Maurice de Talleyrand. Instead of meeting them himself, Talleyrand sent three agents, identified by the Americans as X, Y, and Z, who said the price of a meeting was an agreement to loan France $10 million and a personal gift to Talleyrand of $240,000.

Pinckney, whose patience had been worn thin by the waiting, snapped back, "not a sixpence." Back home, this remark became "millions for defense but not one cent for tribute," a rallying cry for those Federalists who wanted war with France. The incident, when made public, became known as the *XYZ Affair.*

Hamilton Calls for War. No one shouted "millions for defense" more loudly than the *High Federalists*, as the pro-Hamilton, anti-Adams Federalists were called. Hamilton put great pressure on Adams to raise an army of 10,000 men to fight the French, but Adams resisted. He realized that the United States had to respond to Talleyrand's action. But, as a New Englander, he was more comfortable with a navy than with an army. He asked Congress to authorize the construction of 40 *frigates* and other warships, a huge increase over the three-vessel navy of Washington's time. Without a formal declaration of war, Americans captured 80 French ships by the end of 1798. It was enough to calm those who wanted all-out war, and at least officially to keep the peace.

In 1799, a new government headed by Napoleon Bonaparte took over in France. In 1800, a commission sent by Adams arrived in France to see if Napoleon would agree to end the unde-

Discussion Question: What difficulties might John Adams have faced in having to follow George Washington as president? The discussion should examine the differences between the two men as individuals and also relate some of the difficulties which might be attributed to following Washington's mythological stature in the eyes of many Americans.

clared war. Napoleon was eager to be quit of foreign engagements, and peace was soon arranged. However, this courageous act was Adams's high point. Although some people recognized what Adams had done, his actions generally went unappreciated. He was left with little support in the country.

The Alien and Sedition Acts. In 1798, the High Federalists passed four laws against the wishes of Adams. These laws were known as the *Alien and Sedition Acts.* Although the proponents of the acts said they would benefit the country, the acts were aimed directly at the Republican party.

The first act made it more difficult for an immigrant to become a United States citizen. Instead of five years, a newcomer was now required to reside in the country for 14 years. The Federalists passed this law because most immigrants became Republican voters. It was never very effective because, in practice, the states de-

Congressional debate over the Sedition Act of 1798 prompted cartoons like the one above.

cided who could vote and Republican states ignored the law.

The second and third acts provided that in time of war the government could take action against aliens residing in the United States. The acts authorized the government, even in peacetime, to deport any foreigner deemed "dangerous to the peace and safety of the United States." They were dangerously vague laws. They left the definition of "war" and "peace and safety" up to the government. Fortunately, Adams never enforced the laws.

Adams did, however, enforce the fourth law, known as the *Sedition Act.* This law provided stiff fines and prison terms for any person who uttered or published a statement that held the government in "contempt or disrepute." To the Jeffersonians, it was an intolerable attack on the rights of free speech and free press.

Dozens of people were arrested. Of the 25 Jeffersonians who went to trial, ten were convicted and put in jail.

The Republican Response. Although his own High Federalists helped pass the Alien and Sedition Acts, Alexander Hamilton opposed them. He was no friend of civil liberties, but he did believe the laws would provoke the Republicans and help them at the polls.

ALIEN AND SEDITION ACTS 1798	
Alien Act	President could expel from the United States foreigners who were suspected of threatening the safety and security of the nation.
Sedition Act	Persons could be imprisoned for two years and fined $2,000 for saying, writing, or publishing any false or malicious statement against the American government or its officials.
Naturalization Act	Required 14-year residency of immigrants before citizenship.
Alien Enemies Act	President allowed to imprison or expel dangerous foreigners during time of war or invasion.

Discussion Question: What particular clauses in the Constitution would Jefferson have used to protest the Alien and Sedition Acts? Explain why these clauses are relevant. This exercise combines the importance of building a good speculative argument with skills necessary for reading and interpreting important documents and primary sources.

Hamilton was right on both counts. Jefferson and Madison responded by writing state laws based on a theory of government that would haunt the country for 60 years and eventually contribute to the Civil War. In the *Kentucky Resolutions*, drawn up by Jefferson for the Kentucky state legislature, and the *Virginia Resolutions*, written by James Madison, the two men argued that any state had the right to *nullify* a federal law within its boundaries. That is, if Kentucky declared the Sedition Act null and void, that law could not be enforced within the state.

Jefferson and Madison argued that the union of the states was a compact in which the individual states agreed to give up their independence. But the states still remained sovereign. Therefore, the state legislatures had the right to rule on whether a federal action was constitutional. If it was not, they had the right to nullify it within the state.

This *compact theory* of the United States meant that the constitutional government was not much different from the abandoned Confederation government. It was a curious position for Madison to take. Fortunately, the Kentucky and Virginia Resolutions were never put into effect. However, along with the threatening Alien and Sedition laws, they helped assure a Republican victory in the election of 1800.

The Peculiar Election of 1800.

In 1800, the presidential candidates were once again John Adams for the Federalists and Thomas Jefferson for the Republicans. The vice-presidential candidates were Federalist Charles Pinckney and Republican Aaron Burr of New York. When the vote was in, the Jeffersonian Republicans had won 73 electoral votes and the Federalists had won 65 electoral votes.

But it was not that simple. In the election of 1796, problems arose when electors wrote two names on a ballot without stating who was to be president and who was to be vice president. The rules were the same in 1800, but the Federalist electoral votes clearly showed who they favored for president: Adams got 65 votes, Pinckney 64, and John Jay 1. However, the Republicans made a colossal error. They forgot to agree on which of them would leave Burr's name off the ballot so he would finish second. As a result, Thomas Jefferson and Aaron Burr were tied at 73 votes each.

Hamilton's Final Contribution.

In such a case, the Constitution provided that the House of Representatives, with one vote per state, would choose the president. The winner needed to have the votes of the majority of the states present (at that time, nine states). If the Federalist representatives had sat out what was a Republican party problem, Jefferson would have been named president immediately.

However, most of the Federalists voted for Burr. They believed that if they gained the presidency for him, he would join or at least be friendly to their party. By *deadlocking* the House, they may have hoped to force the election of a compromise candidate: John Adams, Charles Pinckney, or John Jay.

The first ballot was eight states for Jefferson, six for Burr, and two evenly divided. The results were the same after the thirty-fifth ballot. Finally, only weeks before the March 4 inaugural day, a shift took place. Delaware Federalist James A. Bayard, fearing for the survival of the Constitution, changed his vote from Burr to Jefferson.

Hamilton himself had already decided to support Jefferson. He still feared Jefferson's democratic principles, but he believed Burr was far more dangerous because he had no principles at all. At least, Hamilton wrote, Jefferson had a "pretension to character." It was not much of a compliment but it was enough. On the thirty-sixth ballot, several Federalist congressmen simply *abstained*, and Jefferson was elected.

The Federalist Legacy.

The Federalist party never regained the presidency. However, the influence of the party persisted as a result of John Adams's decision, as the date approached for him to leave office, to fill the federal courts with Federalist judges. Because he appointed a few in the final hours of his presidency, they were called *midnight judges*.

By far the most important midnight judge was John Marshall, who became Chief Justice of the Supreme Court in 1801. Although he was a distant cousin of Jefferson, Marshall intensely disliked the new president. More important, Marshall was determined to strengthen the power of the federal government, and of the Supreme Court within the federal government. For 34 years, under five Republican presidents and long

Class Activity: Have students read the actual court case for *Marbury* v. *Madison*. The class should examine the issue of judicial review discussed in the case and relate this to Article III, Section 2 of the Constitution. The actual decision of whether to uphold Marbury's claim or

John Marshall, Chief Justice of the Supreme Court, set the precedent of judicial review.

after the death of the Federalist party, Marshall wrote Federalist principles into American law. He was the author of more than half the Supreme Court's 1,100 majority decisions between 1801 and 1835.

Marbury v. Madison.

One of Marshall's most important decisions concerned events that took place during Jefferson's first days in office. The case of *Marbury v. Madison* decided by the Supreme Court in 1803, involved a Federalist, William Marbury, whom Adams appointed to a judgeship.

Unfortunately, Marbury's appointment was made so late that Marshall, who was then Adams's Secretary of State, was unable to deliver it. The document was waiting when Jefferson's Secretary of State, James Madison, took office. Madison, of course, refused to deliver it and Marbury sued on the grounds that it was Madison's duty to do so.

John Marshall, as Chief Justice, could have issued an order requiring Madison to deliver the document. However, he guessed correctly that Madison would ignore him, thus weakening the

prestige of the Supreme Court. Instead, Marshall ruled that while it appeared Marbury had a right to his judgeship, the section of the Judiciary Act of 1789 under which Marbury was appointed was unconstitutional and therefore null and void. Madison did not have to deliver the appointment to Marbury.

Judicial Review.

Jefferson and Madison immediately realized what Marshall had done. He had avoided a direct conflict with the executive branch, which he would have lost. Instead, Marshall had richly scolded them and claimed for the Supreme Court the power of *judicial review*, or the authority to declare unconstitutional a law passed by Congress and signed by the president. This was the power that, in the Kentucky and Virginia Resolutions, Jefferson and Madison had claimed for the state legislatures.

The Constitution provided for *judicial review* by federal courts over state laws. But it was silent as to the final authority over federal laws. Therefore, Marshall was extending the power of the judiciary.

Jefferson and Madison may have planned to challenge Marshall the next time he used judicial review to cancel a federal law. If so, Marshall outsmarted them. He never declared another federal law unconstitutional, being content to have asserted the Supreme Court's right to do so. Not until 1857, in the case of *Dred Scott* v. *Sandford*, would the Court put Marshall's prize to work.

SECTION REVIEW

1. Write a sentence to identify: Farewell Address, High Federalist, Aaron Burr, midnight judge.
2. What political parties grew out of the ideas of Hamilton and Jefferson?
3. Discuss the theory of government on which the Kentucky and Virginia resolutions were based.
4. How did Alexander Hamilton help Jefferson win the presidency in 1800?
5. What Supreme Court case established the concept of judicial review? What was Marshall's purpose in making this ruling?

Madison's was never decided by the Supreme Court. Marshall ruled that the case's jurisdiction was with a lower court. Use this to stress the often political nature of the court. The case of *Marbury* v. *Madison* was, in effect, a forum for the political opinions of the Supreme Court.

In the 1700s, Oliver Evans invented grain-handling machines that
soon became standard equipment in
mills. An Evans flour mill was so
highly automated that it could be
operated by one person.

Noah Webster's elementary spelling
book helped to standardize American spelling and pronunciation. In
1828 Webster published a dictionary whose popularity made Webster's
name synonymous with the word
dictionary.

C H A N G I N G   T E C H N O L O G Y

17 70		17 80
Tin discovered	Stethoscope developed	"The Writer"—first programma-
Paddle wheel invented	Steam engine condenser patented	ble machine produced
Oilcloth developed	Three-wheeled iron gun carriage	Practical submarines built
Aluminum produced	invented	Argand burner introduced
Pedometer introduced	All-iron ploughboard designed	
	Spinning Jenny introduced	

Research Assignment: Have students prepare a report on the use of interchangeable parts in
machines during this period in history. Reports should discuss uses of interchangeable parts

The development of interchangeable parts for machinery laid the foundation for the industrial revolution. An example was Eli Whitney's cotton gin, a simple machine that eliminated the tedious process of separating by hand the cotton fibers from the seeds.

The first American steamboat was invented by John Fitch in the 1780s. Steamboats were small vessels used for river transportation before the development of railroads.

17	90	18	00	18	10
Kitchen range introduced Rotative steam engine designed Montgolfier hot-air balloon demonstrated Power loom patented Bifocal lenses invented	Bleaching powder produced Vaccination process used Nitrous oxide ("laughing gas") discovered (See also p. 258.)	Steamship used commercially Jacquard loom introduced Percussion lock for guns designed Electric battery invented (See also p. 258.)

today. You may also wish to assign reports examining the concept of separation of labor, since this practice developed during this period.

CHAPTER REVIEW

TIME LINE

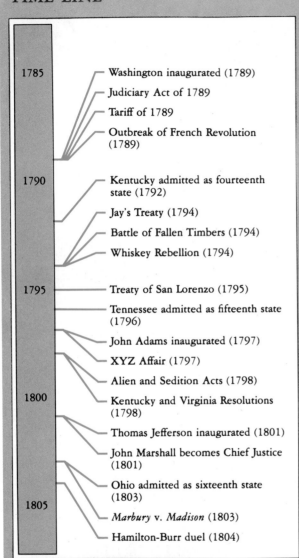

1785 — Washington inaugurated (1789)
— Judiciary Act of 1789
— Tariff of 1789
— Outbreak of French Revolution (1789)

1790 — Kentucky admitted as fourteenth state (1792)
— Jay's Treaty (1794)
— Battle of Fallen Timbers (1794)
— Whiskey Rebellion (1794)

1795 — Treaty of San Lorenzo (1795)
— Tennessee admitted as fifteenth state (1796)
— John Adams inaugurated (1797)
— XYZ Affair (1797)
— Alien and Sedition Acts (1798)

1800 — Kentucky and Virginia Resolutions (1798)
— Thomas Jefferson inaugurated (1801)
— John Marshall becomes Chief Justice (1801)
— Ohio admitted as sixteenth state (1803)

1805 — *Marbury* v. *Madison* (1803)
— Hamilton-Burr duel (1804)

TIME LINE QUESTIONS

1. How long did Washington serve as president?
2. Who was president when each of the following events occurred: *Marbury* v. *Madison*, establishment of first national bank, XYZ Affair, Sedition Act?
3. List the following states in the order of their admission to the union: Tennessee, Ohio, Kentucky.

SKILLS STRATEGY

The Course Is Set

The New Government Takes Shape
• _____
• _____

The Importance of George Washington
• _____
• _____

An Active Congress
• _____
• _____

The Cabinet
• _____
• _____

SUMMARIZING

A summary is a short account of something you have seen, heard, or read. Summarizing is an important study skill because it forces you to select and concentrate on important ideas. Since a summary should not be long, it must include only major points, and exclude minor details.

In preparing a summary, it is helpful to make a *scratch outline* like the unfinished one in the exhibit above. As you might surmise, this kind of quick outline does not have much form and is a kind of note-taking. Completing this scratch outline will help you to write a summary for the main section of this chapter indicated by the outline's title.

APPLYING SKILLS

1. Which main section of Chapter 8 is the scratch outline for?
2. From where do the outline's title and headings come?
3. Complete the scratch outline. Skim the appropriate section of the chapter and jot down the missing points. Save your outline for use as a guide in completing item 20 of the Unit Test.

Making Connections: Review the questions and topics presented in the Making Connections section opening this chapter. Stress the idea that our nation's beginning—one of its strengths—lay in its being based on the premise that people could disagree and work out their differences.

UNIT 2 TEST

CHAPTER SURVEY

In one or two sentences, summarize the content of the chapter from which these terms come, and write a sentence to identify *one* of the terms from each chapter.

1. *Chapter 5:* Proclamation of 1763, Sons of Liberty, Stamp Act Congress, Crispus Attucks, Boston Tea Party.
2. *Chapter 6:* Minutemen, Breed's Hill, Continental Army, Valley Forge, "The World Turned Upside Down."
3. *Chapter 7:* separation of church and state, Confederation, the Founding Fathers, Samuel Adams, Bill of Rights.
4. *Chapter 8:* President John Adams, Alexander Hamilton, impressment, Farewell Address, midnight judges.

TEXT REVIEW

5. In what North American war did English colonists and French settlers, both with Indian allies, fight each other? Give some reasons explaining why this war occurred.
6. How did the terms of the Treaty of Paris after this North American war change the map of the continent? Why did some English people think that the gains made by England would be dangerous for the Empire?
7. List several important events that led to the calling of the Continental Congress, and explain why this action could be considered a turning point in the relations between England and the American colonies.
8. Contrast the intentions of the delegates to the First Continental Congress with the intentions of the delegates to the Second Continental Congress.
9. Explain the importance of the following to the Americans in the War for Independence: Lexington and Concord; General George Washington; Benjamin Franklin, French, Prussian, and Polish friends; Saratoga; Yorktown.
10. What accounts for the ineffectiveness of the national government under the Articles of Confederation, as opposed to its effectiveness under the Constitution?
11. Give the essential facts about the Connecticut Compromise and the Three-Fifths Compromise at the Constitutional Convention. What issues did they resolve?
12. Name some of the leaders of the first administration under the Constitution. Evaluate the importance to the country of the work of one of the leaders.
13. List two foreign problems and two domestic problems faced by the first government under the Constitution. Discuss the government's successful or unsuccessful attempts to resolve each problem.

CRITICAL THINKING

14. Summarize the functions of parallels and meridians on a map or globe.
15. Explain the influence that the ideas of Thomas Paine and Enlightenment philosophers had on the writing of the Declaration of Independence.
16. What arguments did the Federalists give for ratifying the Constitution? Compare these arguments with those of the Anti-Federalists. Evaluate the arguments of both sides in light of the events of that period. Use specific examples in your answer.

SKILLS REVIEW

17. List the following events in chronological order: Boston Tea Party; Declaration of Independence; John Adams inaugurated; Constitutional Convention; Battle of Yorktown; surrender of Canada.
18. Compare a physical map with a political map. How do the two types of maps differ? Name four elements that appear on these and all other good maps.
19. Distinguish between a primary source and a secondary source of historical information. Give one example of each.
20. Turn to Section 1 of Chapter 8—"The Course Is Set." Use one of the section's subheadings and the information following it to make a scratch outline. Then, use the outline to write a paragraph summarizing the information in the subsection you chose.

Explain how this idea is built into the system of checks and balances, the separation of powers, and the two-party (or multi-party) system. Also highlight how this premise is as important an element of our government today as it was during the formative years of the country.

211

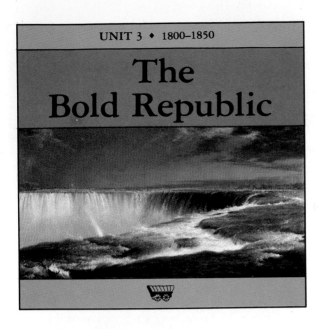

The Bold Republic

Unit 3 Overview

Unit 3 takes students from the presidency of Thomas Jefferson through the War of 1812, the industrialization of the United States, the settlement of western lands, the growth in democracy (for some) during the two terms of President Andrew Jackson, to an era marked by religious innovation, utopian quests, literary achievements, and social reforms.

Basic Unit Concepts

1. During the Jefferson and Madison administrations, the United States increased its land area won a second war with Great Britain, took its place in the community of nations, and began a dispute over slavery.
2. During the early 1800s, the Industrial Revolution came to America, a new machine revived slavery in the South, restless Americans built farms and cities in "the West," a national transportation network was begun, and sectional differences became more pronounced.
3. Between the 1820s and the 1840s, a democratic revolution took place, but Indians and other groups were exluded from its benefits; nullification briefly threatened to divide the nation; a presidential attitude toward banks and money plunged the nation into depression; and a long-standing dispute about the boundary between Canada and the United States was settled.
4. The first half of the nineteenth century was marked by the rise of a variety of religious and utopian groups, a flowering of American literature, attempts to reform many areas of American society, an increase in immigration, and the birth of the women's rights movement.

Chapter 9: "Jeffersonian Republic" (1801–1824)

In Chapter 9, students watch the United States grow with President Jefferson's purchase of Louisiana and President Monroe's purchase of Florida. They learn why the United States and Great Britain fought the War of 1812 and the negligible results of that war. They witness, in James Monroe's presidency, an explosion of nationalism expressed in the Monroe Doctrine, Chief Justice John Marshall's decisions that established the supremacy of the federal government. They understand why Thomas Jefferson saw the Missouri Compromise as "a fire bell in the night," and recognize Andrew Jackson as a man to be reckoned with when he is defeated by John Quincy Adams in 1824.

Features

Profiles of the Presidency: Thomas Jefferson (page 216); James Madison (page 224); James Monroe (page 230); John Quincy Adams (page 235)
Movers and Shapers: Tecumseh and Sequoyah (page 226)

Learning Objectives

History Generalizations Students will gain knowledge that supports the following generalizations:

1. Thomas Jefferson's presidency saw many changes of Federalist policy, the purchase and exploration of French Louisiana, and the mysterious "Burr conspiracy."
2. The attempts of Presidents Jefferson and Madison to avoid war were unsuccessful, and from 1812 to 1814, the United States fought with Great Britain.
3. Victory in the War of 1812 gave rise to a surge of nationalism and ushered in an "Era of Good Feelings."
4. President Monroe's administration was marked by achievements in foreign affairs and the Monroe Doctrine.
5. Chief Justice John Marshall, in a series of critical decisions, established the authority of the Supreme Court and the federal government over the state governments.
6. The admission of new states as "free" or "slave" were only temporarily settled in the Missouri Compromise.
7. In 1824, traditions associated with the selection of presidential candidates were put aside.
8. Because neither presidential candidate received an absolute majority of electoral votes in 1824, the choice of a president went to the House of Representatives.
9. The House's choice of John Quincy Adams provoked charges from Andrew Jackson's camp, and brought Jackson into focus as a national political figure.

Study Skills In addition to the three skills noted in chapter 1 which are standard to every chapter, students will:

1. use an encyclopedia index to locate information.
2. write a one-paragraph thumbnail personality sketch.
3. relate graphic materials to the text of the chapter.
4. practice these **critical thinking skills**: generating questions about materials to be read, forming a hypothesis based on given data, drawing conclusions.

Chapter 10: "Machines, Cotton, and Land" (1800–1825)

In this chapter, students trace the first steps taken towards the industrialization of the United States as the Northeast developed its manufacturing potential. They learn why slavery almost disappeared in the South and what new machine and crop revived slavery while thwarting the development of southern industry. They follow pioneers who settled what was then "the West," and they learn how uncontrolled speculation in western lands brought about the Panic of 1819 and, eventually, changes in the federal government's land policies. They learn how advances in transportation helped to tie the nation together while sectional differences were threatening the country.

Feature

American Ingenuity chart (pages 258–259)

Learning Objectives

History Generalizations Students will gain knowledge that supports the following generalizations:

1. With machines spirited from England, mass production made possible by Eli Whitney's invention of interchangeable parts, the North began to industrialize.
2. In spite of attempts to keep industry from disturbing traditional ways, the momentum of industrialization caused a permanent industrial working class to arise.
3. Before the invention of the cotton gin made cotton a profitable cash crop, slavery was dying out in the South.
4. After the invention of the cotton gin, production of cotton soared, and the South turned away from industry.
5. Adventurous pioneers rapidly settled in the West.
6. Frantic speculation in western lands led to bank failures and, eventually, the Panic of 1819.
7. To discourage speculators and make western land available, the federal government instituted policies favoring the farmers.
8. A network of turnpikes, canals, steamboat routes began to tie the growing nation together , but sectional differences became more pronounced.

Study Skills In addition to the three skills noted in chapter 1 which are standard to every chapter, students will:
1. judge the validity of opinions.
2. write a persuasive paragraph.
3. relate graphic materials to the text of the chapter.
4. practice these **critical thinking skills:** generating questions about materials to be read, summarizing information, making comparisons, problem-solving.

Chapter 11: The Age of the Common Person (1824–1844)

In Chapter 11, students recognize that the democratic revolution, limited though it was to free white males, constituted a turning point in American history. They encounter again the specter of Civil War in South Carolina's nullification arguments. They learn how President Jackson's feelings toward banks and paper money caused a boom, a bust, and a depression. They witness a presidential election decided in the House of Representatives and discover how John Tyler became president, why he was expelled from his party, and what treaty with Britain was negotiated.

Features
Profiles of the Presidency: Andrew Jackson (page 267), Martin Van Buren (page 277), William Henry Harrison (page 278), John Tyler (page 280)
Going to the Source: Daniel Webster's *Liberty and Union* speech (page 271)

Learning Objectives
History Generalizations Students will gain knowledge that supports the following generalizations:
1. With the election of Andrew Jackson in 1828, the Age of the Common Person was underway.
2. The upsurge in democracy during the Jackson years applied to free white adult males.
3. Under President Jackson, loyal party members were rewarded with government jobs under the spoils system.
4. Sectional disagreements over protective tariffs led to the revival of the theory of nullification.
5. Although South Carolina rescinded its nullication of a federal tariff, nullification and secession, remained alive.
6. President Jackson's attitude toward banks and hard

money was manifested in his battle against renewing the chapter of the Bank of the United States and his transfer of federal government funds from the Bank to state "pet" banks—contributing to a boom, bust and depression.
7. The newly founded Whig party ran three candidates in the 1836 presidential election to throw the election to the House of Representatives; the strategy failed, for the House made Democrat Martin Van Buren president.
8. John Tyler's chief accomplishment was the Webster-Ashburton Treaty that settled a long-standing border dispute between the United States and Canada.

Study Skills In addition to the three skills noted in chapter 1 which are standard to every chapter, students will:
1. compare and construct circle graphs.
2. write a paragraph based on notes taken in research.
3. relate graphic materials to the text of the chapter.
4. practice these **critical thinking skills:** generating questions about materials to be read, distinguishing fact from-opinion, supplying details to support a main idea.

Chapter 12: "American Reform Movements" (1815–1850)

In Chapter 12, students learn how the philosophy of Transcendentalism contributed to a flowing of American writers. They witness the reforms in insane asylums, prisons, schools for the blind and deaf, and in the abuse of alcohol. They discover the reason for the founding of the anti-Catholic Native American party and how a convention in Seneca Falls, New York, was connected with the rights of American women.

Features
Movers and Shapers: Elizabeth and Emily Blackwell, Dorothea Dix (page 297)
Going to the Source: Excerpt from the *Seneca Falls Declaration of Sentiments and Resolutions* (page 304).

Learning Objectives
History Generalizations Students will gain knowledge that supports the following generalizations:
1. The first half of the nineteenth century saw the rise of religious groups—Unitarians, Universalists, revivalists, Millerites (Seventh-Day Adventists), Mormons.
2. At the same time, various "perfect societies" were founded, including religious and social utopias.
3. Influenced by Emerson's philosophy of Transcendentalism, a group of American writers created literary works during a period known as The Flowering of New England.
4. American writers produced works that departed from the Transcendentalist view.
5. Nineteenth century reformers sought to improve society through improvements in treatment of the insane, prisoners, deaf and blind people, and alcoholics.
6. A changing pattern of immigration gave rise to the formation of the anti-Catholic Native American party.
7. Missionaries sought to convert those of other beliefs.
8. Outstanding women led the feminist movement which led to the *Declaration of Sentiments and Resolutions*.

Study Skills In addition to the three skills noted in chapter 1 which are standard to every chapter, students will:
1. relate text information, pictures, and captions.
2. write a paragraph to expand a picture caption.
3. relate graphic materials to the text of the chapter.
4. practice these **critical thinking skills:** generating questions about materials to be read, contrasting facts, classifying information, recognizing causes of given effects.

CHAPTER 9

THE JEFFERSONIAN REPUBLIC

1801–1824

Our lives are in the hands of the Great Spirit. He gave to our ancestors the lands which we possess. We are determined to defend them, and if it is His will, our bones shall whiten on them, but we will never give them up.   TECUMSEH

Making Connections. In 1801, Americans were still preoccupied with making their country and government work. Unfortunately, they also became involved in foreign affairs. The British and French were still at war, and Presidents Jefferson and Madison had to find a way to satisfy both European countries while maintaining American pride.

In this chapter, you will learn:
- How Jefferson nearly doubled the size of the United States
- Why Jefferson forbade American trading ships to go to sea
- What caused the War of 1812
- Where the United States won a great victory after the war was officially ended
- Who established the power of the federal government over the states
- When a presidential election was decided in the House of Representatives

You know that the Federalists had managed to keep the United States out of European conflicts. After 1801, Republican efforts to keep the nation out of war were thwarted by foreign pressure. As you read, notice how the United States grew and changed, and how the country emerged from the period as an important nation with international responsibilities.

Sections
1. Success at Home
2. More Troubles Abroad
3. The War of 1812
4. Postwar Problems

1. SUCCESS AT HOME

Thomas Jefferson is best known as a political figure and the author of America's birth certificate, the Declaration of Independence. But Jefferson was many other things. He was a philosopher. He read and spoke several languages. He exchanged letters with hundreds of people on dozens of subjects. Jefferson wrote with clarity and style, using English more eloquently than any other president except Abraham Lincoln. He founded the University of Virginia down the hill from his home. Not only did he design the buildings, the walks, and the beautiful serpentine brick wall that all still exist, he also had the students to dinner and even decided what subjects they would study.

Jefferson was also an inventor. He invented the dumbwaiter and the swivel chair. He dabbled in natural science and experimented with agriculture. His interests were broad, and his intelligence was keen. In 1962, President John F. Kennedy said to his guests, an assembly of Nobel Prize winners, "This is the most extraordinary collection of talent, of human knowledge, that has been gathered at the White House, with the possible exception of when Thomas Jefferson dined here alone."

When Thomas Jefferson took office, Washington, D.C. was still being built along the Potomac River. The watercolor at the right shows the incomplete Capitol building.

214

Skills Review: Reinforce the skills learned in the preceding Skills Strategy section. Have students use the method of outlining learned in the preceding chapter to outline this chapter.

PROFILES OF THE PRESIDENCY

Thomas Jefferson was not totally pleased with the early draft of the Constitution:

I will now tell you what I do not like. First, the omission of a bill of rights, providing . . . for freedom of religion, freedom of the press, protection against standing armies, restriction of monopolies. . . .

The second feature I dislike, and strongly dislike, is the abandonment, in every instance, of the principle of rotation in office, and most particularly in the case of the President. Reason and experience tell us, that the first magistrate will always be re-elected if he may be re-elected. He is then an officer for life. . . .

After all, it is my principle that the will of the majority should prevail. If they (the people) approve the proposed constitution in all its parts, I shall concur in it cheerfully, in hopes they will amend it, whenever they shall find it works wrong.

—LETTER TO JAMES MADISON, DECEMBER 20, 1787

Republican Simplicity. George Washington carefully surrounded himself with ceremonies that reminded Europeans of a royal court, and sensitive John Adams insisted on strict formality. But when Jefferson dined or entertained visitors, there were gourmet dinners but little fuss and formality in the service. Jefferson believed that citizens of a republic should be informal. His dinner guests simply gathered around a table as if in an ordinary home instead of the White House. Jefferson answered the door himself, more than once in an old bathrobe and worn slippers. He did not wear a powdered wig, as his predecessors had done, but allowed his red hair to hang loosely over his shoulders.

Republican simplicity was made easier by the fact that the capital had been moved from elegant Philadelphia to the new city of Washington just a few months before Jefferson became president. This was not the Washington of white marble buildings that we know today. The city then was the brand-new White House and Capitol, where Congress met, joined by a muddy dirt track hacked through the forest. Senators and congressmen lived in ramshackle boarding houses. Their wives and children stayed back home. If a person got lost in Washington, D.C., it was not on confusing busy streets, it was in the wilderness. European-style formality would have been ridiculous in such a place.

Republican Changes. More than style changed under Jefferson. In 1801, he allowed the Alien and Sedition Acts to expire and pardoned the people who had been jailed under them. At his request, Congress repealed the law that required a foreigner to reside 14 years in the United States to become a citizen.

Jefferson also abolished the excise tax that had led to the Whiskey Rebellion of 1794. This action increased his popularity among western farmers. Having cut taxes, Jefferson also cut expenditures. He reduced the size of the army and navy that John Adams had built to meet the French threat. Civilian government was reduced, too. Jefferson believed that the government that governed least governed best. However, he also believed his own supporters would govern better than Federalists. He replaced 180 Federalists holding government jobs with Republicans.

Jefferson also tried to strike at the Federalist-controlled courts. After his bout with Chief Justice John Marshall in the case of *Marbury* v. *Madison*, Jefferson aimed at Marshall and the courts from another direction in 1803. His followers successfully removed from office John Pickering, the district court judge in New Hampshire.

The Pickering case was easy. Next, however, the Republicans impeached Supreme Court Justice Samuel Chase. Chase may have been a poor judge, but he had committed none of the "high crimes and misdemeanors" that the Constitution says are the grounds for removal from office. Sensing that Jefferson was aiming at Marshall himself and at the independence of the judicial branch, the Senate refused to find Chase guilty. It was Jefferson's first defeat, and he never again attacked the courts directly.

Some Things Stay the Same. Some Federalist policies remained in force under Jefferson. Although in 1791 Jefferson had called the Bank of the United States unconstitutional, it was working too well for Jefferson to abolish it. The conflict over the Bank had been a basic difference between Federalists and Republicans, or so it seemed. But Jefferson was to show that Republicans, too, could use a broad interpretation of the Constitution.

Louisiana For Sale. In 1799, Napoleon Bonaparte came to power in France. Napoleon was a dynamic leader and France was one of the most powerful countries in the world. When Napoleon gained control of Spain in 1802, France regained Louisiana, which had been given to Spain after the French and Indian War. Louisiana was a huge territory that included the middle third of the present-day United States. Napoleon needed the fertile province to provide grain and livestock to feed the slave population of the French West Indies.

At about the time France took control of Louisiana, however, rebellious slaves won independence for the most valuable French possession in the West Indies, the island of Santo Domingo (present-day Haiti). Under the leadership of Toussaint L'Ouverture (tōō-săn′ lōō-vĕr-tür′), the "Black Napoleon," an army of former slaves killed or captured 20,000 French troops.

With that defeat, Louisiana became worthless to Napoleon. The Santo Domingo slaves were now citizens of an independent nation, and Napoleon no longer had to feed them. In fact, it was potentially even a greater loss. In the event of war with Great Britain, which Napoleon was planning, the enemy could conquer thinly populated Louisiana with ease. Rather than lose it, Napoleon decided to sell it.

A buyer was already in Paris. When Thomas Jefferson learned that Louisiana had become

Toussaint L'Ouverture

On December 20, 1803, the United States purchased the Louisiana Territory from France.

French, he worried that Napoleon would not honor Pinckney's Treaty, which won western farmers the right to use the port of New Orleans. With the approval of Congress, Jefferson sent James Monroe to France where, with ambassador Robert Livingston, he was to offer Napoleon $10 million for the city of New Orleans and West Florida.

A few days before Monroe arrived, the French foreign minister, Talleyrand, offered to sell the whole Louisiana Territory to the United States for only $15 million! It doubled the size of America, and it was the greatest real estate bargain in history—500 million acres (200 million hectares) at less than three cents an acre.

The bargain was also unconstitutional according to Jefferson's theory of strict construction. The Constitution said nothing that allowed Jefferson to buy territory. Congress had authorized Jefferson only to purchase the city of New Orleans.

Monroe and Livingston decided that Napoleon's offer was worth risking Jefferson's disapproval. They accepted, thereby spending $5 million Congress had not voted them. They need not have worried about the President. Whatever Jefferson thought, he was willing to sacrifice principle for such a prize. "What is practicable must often control what is pure theory," he wrote. The

THE LOUISIANA PURCHASE AND
WESTERN EXPLORATIONS, 1803-1808

Discussion Question: Many of Jefferson's White House policies were not in keeping with his values on "strict construction" of the Constitution. Federalists who, in principle, should have opposed the purchase of Louisiana and the president's method of funding the purchase, supported both. Were these people hypocrites, or political realists?

Federalists took pleasure in calling Jefferson a hypocrite. But they too had no intention of passing up the deal. With the Stars and Stripes floating over Louisiana, both banks of the great river were American. Rafts loaded with crops could flow to the sea unmolested.

The Magnificent Journey. Jefferson probably wished that he had been free to explore Louisiana. The President worked long hours on the smallest details of an expedition he organized to explore the West even before Louisiana became part of the United States. The explorers were led by Meriwether Lewis, Jefferson's neighbor in Virginia, and Lewis's former commanding officer in the army, William Clark.

With about 45 men—Americans, Indians, and French Canadian fur trappers—Lewis and Clark left St. Louis, then little more than a fort, in May 1804. Poling, pulling, and rowing their boats, they made their way up the Missouri River to the spectacular cascade at present-day Great Falls, Montana. With the help of Mandan, Shoshone, and Nez Perce Indians, and especially of their interpreter, the Shoshone woman Sacajawea, who traveled the difficult journey with her baby strapped to her back, the expedition found a river

Zebulon Pike explored the West (above) from 1805 to 1807. Meriwether Lewis (below) and William Clark began an expedition in 1804 that took them all the way to the Pacific Ocean.

flowing to the west—the Columbia. By following the Columbia, they reached the Pacific Ocean in November 1805 and camped for the winter.

In September 1806, when Lewis and Clark arrived back in St. Louis, they were national heroes. Not only were they the first people to cross the continent, they also brought back a large amount of information about geography, plant and animal life, and the Indians of the interior.

Lewis and Clark were among the last white people to meet Indians who were unaffected by the new American way of life. They had a few close scrapes, and one expedition member died after an accident, but they never had a real fight. On the contrary, almost every tribe they met was curious, hospitable, and anxious to help. They were particularly interested in York, a black man who was Clark's slave. Each time the explorers met a new tribe, York had to prove he was not a white man wearing paint by standing still while the Indians scrubbed his skin.

Pike's Explorations.

Another explorer of the new lands was Lieutenant Zebulon M. Pike. In 1805, he traveled 4,000 miles (6,400 kilometers) up the Missouri River, deep into Minnesota, and then down the Mississippi. Pike also received good treatment from the Indians.

In 1806 and 1807, Pike led another expedition up the Arkansas River and into territory claimed by Spain. On this trip he discovered the snow-covered mountain in Colorado that bears his name, Pikes Peak. Returning along the Rio Grande, Pike was captured by the Spaniards and briefly imprisoned in Santa Fe, New Mexico.

Pike's published account of his explorations excited American interest in the West. However, his writings discouraged settlement on the grassy, rolling prairies and plains of the central United States, which he called "the Great American Desert."

The Mysterious Adventures of Aaron Burr.

In 1804, Alexander Hamilton published comments about Aaron Burr that Burr regarded as *slanderous*. Burr responded by challenging Hamilton to a duel, in which Hamilton was killed. In 1804, Burr had hoped to run again as Jefferson's vice president, but Jefferson chose George Clinton. Burr's political prospects were shattered.

Burr looked west. In April 1805, he set out for Pittsburgh. There he lived with Harman Blennerhasset, a wealthy Irish refugee who lived on an island in the Ohio River.

The two men had about ten flatboats built. With about 70 men, their fleet floated down the Ohio and Mississippi rivers as other frontiersmen joined them. In Tennessee, they spoke with Andrew Jackson, one of the wealthiest men in the state. In New Orleans, Burr and Blennerhasset conferred secretly with other powerful people. Then, in February 1807, Thomas Jefferson had Aaron Burr arrested and charged with treason.

The Burr Conspiracy.

John Marshall presided over the trial. According to the prosecution, which Jefferson backed, Burr was plotting a revolution that would detach Louisiana from the United States. However, the only hard evidence offered to support this accusation was the testimony of James Wilkinson, the commander of United States forces in the Mississippi Valley and a questionable character. John Marshall did not like Aaron Burr. But he took pleasure in angering Jefferson again by acquitting Burr.

What was Burr doing in the West? No one really knows. Jefferson may have been right. However, some historians believe that Burr's target was not the United States but Spanish lands to the west. It has been suggested that the *Burr Conspiracy* was nothing less than a plan to conquer Mexico and make Aaron Burr its emperor.

SECTION REVIEW

1. Write a sentence to identify: Justice Samuel Chase, James Monroe, Robert Livingston, Sacajawea.

2. Give two reasons that explain why Napoleon was willing to sell Louisiana.

3. Describe the explorations of Lewis and Clark and those of Zebulon Pike. What were the experiences of these explorers with the Indians they met?

4. What are the two theories about what Aaron Burr was trying to do in the West? What happened to Burr as a result of his "conspiracy"?

Research Assignment: Students may wish to do a report on the scientific findings of Lewis and Clark. Encourage students to illustrate the project. Perhaps the more artistically inclined might like to replicate some of the drawings found in journals of the expedition.

In 1804, the American ship Philadelphia *was captured by Barbary pirates. To keep the ship out of their hands, Stephen Decatur led a force into Tripoli harbor to burn the ship.*

2. MORE TROUBLES ABROAD

Jefferson was generally successful in his domestic policies and triumphant in acquiring Louisiana, but relations with Europe undid him. The same question of how the nation was to prosper while remaining neutral when England and France were at war proved to be difficult for Jefferson, and impossible for his successor, James Madison.

The Barbary Pirates. In 1801, Jefferson reluctantly approved the annual payment of *tribute* to North Africa's Barbary States. The Pasha of Tripoli (present-day Libya) was given $40,000 in gold and silver, $12,000 in Spanish money, and an odd assortment of diamond rings. In return for this gift, (as the pasha considered it), the ships of Tripoli were expected not to attack American trading vessels in the Mediterranean.

The practice of paying tribute grated on Jefferson's sense of national dignity, especially when the Barbary pirates continued to take American sailors prisoner and ask for ransom. Jefferson sent American warships to the Mediterranean to protect merchants and to punish the Barbary states for violating their agreements.

BARBARY STATES, 1804

Discussion Question: The Barbary states considered the giving of gifts, and the acts of piracy that drove the U.S. to war with them, commonplace in the dealings of nations. One of the recipients of their gifts was Thomas Jefferson, who received four Arabian stallions from the pasha. Was war the correct response to a "cultural misunderstanding"?

 221

In February 1804, Lieutenant Stephen Decatur led 80 marines into Tripoli harbor, seized the frigate *Philadelphia*, which had been captured, and set it afire. Decatur led other *forays* against the pirates, but not until a combined British and American fleet broke the Barbary power in 1815 could Americans stop paying tribute.

Caught in the Middle Again.

By 1805, England and France were once again at war. With each side attacking the shipping of the other, the conflict meant rich profits for neutral American merchants, who traded with both sides. Between 1803 and 1806, the value of West Indian goods brought first to the United States and then shipped to Europe increased from $13 million a year to $60 million.

The British were happy to have the Americans help sell their products. The French were delighted to be able to dispose of what their colonies produced. Because the navies of both warring countries were preoccupied with one another, few American vessels were bothered.

Then, in 1805, at the battle of Trafalgar, the British admiral Horatio Nelson devastated the French fleet, and Great Britain became supreme on the seas. Napoleon then defeated the armies of Austria, Prussia, and Russia in rapid succession,

and France became supreme on land. The only way the two powers could do battle was indirectly —on the economic front. France and England each set out to destroy the other's economy.

In 1807, great Britain issued the *Orders in Council*, which forbade neutral nations, such as the United States, to trade in European ports unless their ships first stopped in England to be inspected and "licensed." Also in 1807, Napoleon issued the *Milan Decree*. According to this decree, any neutral ships that observed the Orders in Council would be seized by the French.

There was so much money to be made in the wartime trade that most merchants were willing to defy either Great Britain or France. Within a year, the British seized 1,000 American ships and the French took 500. Nevertheless, wartime trade was so profitable that even if a ship owner lost two out of three vessels, the ship owner still came out ahead from the third that completed its voyage.

Impressment.

The British continued to impress sailors from American ships stopped at sea, as they had in the 1790s. Anyone, even naturalized American citizens, whose accent betrayed English, Scottish, or Irish birth was fair game.

In addition, about 10,000 native-born Americans were forced to serve on British warships. The

Research Assignment: Students should be made aware of the judiciary's function as a political institution. Assign a report examining the definition of the Supreme Court's powers in the Constitution and detailing how these powers developed in the early years of the court. As part of

222

British government did not officially approve of this practice. About 4,000 of the Americans were released as soon as their ships reached England. Still, captains in need of sailors at sea were inclined to overlook the fact that the Americans were no longer colonials.

The impressment crisis came to a head in June 1807 when HMS *Leopard* ordered the American frigate *Chesapeake* to stand by for boarding within swimming distance of Virginia beaches. The captain of the *Chesapeake* refused, but after three broadsides from the larger *Leopard*, had no choice but to comply.

The nation was outraged. The *Chesapeake* was not a merchant vessel but part of the United States Navy. To worsen the insult, the boarding had taken place in or near American waters. Jefferson had no choice but to act.

The Embargo.

Jefferson's cure was worse than the disease. Under the *Embargo Act* of 1807, American ships in port were forbidden to sail. Foreign vessels in American ports were required to leave "in ballast," that is, with no cargo except worthless rocks in their hulls. The United States would not import European manufactured goods, export its own mostly agricultural products, or carry freight for any foreign country.

Under the Embargo Act of 1807, American ships in port were forbidden to sail. The painting above shows American frigates alongside a Salem, Massachusetts wharf.

It was a logical action for the President who, as a young man, had seen nonimportation agreements force England to repeal its tax laws. However, his plan did not work. People who depended on trade disliked ship seizures and impressment, but no trade at all was far worse. Ships rotted at anchor in New England ports. Some capsized from neglect. Recognizing that his policy was a failure, Jefferson canceled the Embargo shortly before he left office in 1809.

James Madison Takes Over.

The unpopularity of the Embargo in New England allowed the Federalist candidate, Charles Pinckney, to increase his party's vote in 1808. Nevertheless, Jefferson's Secretary of State, James Madison, won the election easily.

Madison cut an unimpressive figure. Short, with pinched features, he reminded writer Washington Irving of "a withered applejohn," a doll made from an apple that had dried into the shape of a face. In fact, Madison was one of the most intelligent people ever to occupy the presidency.

this report, or as a separate assignment, students could examine the influence of Justice John Marshall, one of the most prominent figures in court history.

PROFILES OF THE PRESIDENCY

*T*he last of the Founding Fathers, James Madison, wrote these words to be read after his death:

As this advice, if it ever see the light will not do it till I am no more, it may be considered as issuing from the tomb, where truth alone can be respected, and the happiness of man alone consulted. It will be entitled therefore to whatever weight can be derived from good intentions, and from the experience of one who has served his country in various stations . . . who . . . adhered through his life to the cause of its liberty, and who has borne a part in most of the great transactions which will constitute epochs of its destiny. The advice nearest to my heart . . . is that the Union of the States be cherished and perpetuated. Let the open enemy to it be regarded as a Pandora with her box opened; and the disguised one, as the Serpent creeping with his deadly wiles into Paradise.

—"ADVICE TO MY COUNTRY," FALL, 1834

His contributions to the *Federalist Papers* are still considered masterpieces of political theory. Unhappily, political theory did not help in an impossible political situation. With the resumption of American shipping, the ship seizures and impressment by the British and French began again.

Offering a Prize. Madison tried a new approach. Instead of cutting off trade completely, his *Nonintercourse Act* of 1809 allowed trade with all nations except Britain and France. It also provided that the United States would resume trade with whichever of the two warring powers stopped seizing American ships.

It seemed to work. David Erskine, the pro-American ambassador from Great Britain, signed a treaty and Madison reopened trade with Great Britain. However, in London the British foreign minister, the anti-American George Canning, rejected the Erskine treaty, and Madison was humiliated.

In May 1810, the President introduced a new policy. Under a law called *Macon's Bill No. 2*, Americans were permitted to trade with both England and France. As soon as one of the powers ceased to bother American ships, the United States would cut off trade with the other. If France and England wanted to fight an economic war, Madison would offer them a way to hurt each other financially.

Macon's Bill No. 2 worked. Napoleon lifted the Milan decree and Madison cut off trade with Great Britain. On June 16, 1812, British Prime Minister Lord Castlereagh repealed the Orders in Council. Unfortunately, he had given no hint of his intention to do so, and British warships continued to seize American ships. On June 18, 1812, long before the news from England could possibly arrive, Madison asked Congress for a declaration of war against Great Britain.

Why the United States Went to War. Actually, there was more to the decision to go to war in 1812 than just the violation of American shipping on the high seas. Although New England opposed the action, Madison was pressured into going to war by a group of young and extremely patriotic congressmen called the *War Hawks.* Made up mostly of southerners and westerners, the War Hawks had many motives. Their national pride was stung by the "injuries and indignities" the British had heaped on the United States. The westerners feared that the British would capture New Orleans and close the Mississippi River, on which western exports were shipped. Finally, some of the War Hawks wanted a war so that the United States could annex Canada. Because Great Britain had to keep most of the army at home to guard against Napoleon, the War Hawks thought that conquering Canada would be easy.

Discussion Question: Was the War of 1812 a political war or an economic war? Lead students into discussing the War of 1812 as a consequence of interference with U.S. shipping and commerce or as a war contrived by self-interested and power-seeking war hawks. This should be an exercise in students' ability to take and defend a position.

SECTION REVIEW

1. Write a sentence to identify: Tripoli, Stephen Decatur, *Leopard* and *Chesapeake*, War Hawks.

2. Explain why France and England set out to destroy each other's economy. How did the United States get caught in the middle?

3. Why was President Jefferson's response to the British impressment of American sailors unsuccessful?

4. What two responses did Madison make to continued problems with the French and British? Explain why Madison's first response failed and why his second response succeeded.

3. THE WAR OF 1812

According to the numbers, the United States should have won the War of 1812 on the land and lost it on the sea. To fight the war on land, Congress voted money to raise an army of more than 100,000 soldiers, whereas there were fewer than 5,000 British soldiers in Canada. Furthermore, the Americans believed that the Canadians would welcome them as liberators. Even the Indian allies of Great Britain seemed a minor threat. In November 1811, before the war began, the tribes of the Great Lakes region had been dealt a stinging defeat by General William Henry Harrison at the Battle of Tippecanoe, in Indiana. A confederation organized by the great Shawnee leader Tecumseh and his brother Tenskwatawa, a religious leader

WAR OF 1812

American victories / American forces / British victories / British forces / Fort

Class Activity: List two columns on the chalkboard: "If the U.S. had won" and "If the British had won." List possible ways that the terms of war might have been different if either side had won a clear military victory. Ask students why each side was willing to end the war with its issues unsettled. Mention that it was not a popular war in either country.

MOVERS AND SHAPERS

Sequoyah

Two great American Indian leaders, Tecumseh (tə-kŭm′sə) and Sequoyah (sĭ-kwoi′ə), contributed to their people in different ways.

Sequoyah (1773–1843), the son of a Cherokee woman and a British trader, invented a writing system for the Cherokee language. He was born in Tennessee and was raised by his mother. As a young child he spoke only Cherokee. Later he learned French, Spanish, and English. As a young man he became an accomplished painter and silversmith, but his important work did not begin until he was 36. Sequoyah believed that the Cherokee culture was in danger and that the Cherokee people needed to record their history. Since they had no written form of the Cherokee language, Sequoyah developed one. The "alphabet" he invented was really a *syllabary,* a system based on syllables or consonant/vowel units. Sequoyah used 86 symbols to represent Cherokee speech. This task took him 12 years.

In 1821, Cherokee leaders accepted Sequoyah's writing system, and by 1823 thousands of Cherokees could read and write their own language. In 1829, the first Indian newspaper was started, the *Cherokee Phoenix.*

Tecumseh

Tecumseh (1768–1813) was the kind of person legends are made of. This chief of the Shawnees was swift and sure-footed, was an expert with bow and arrow, and was a spellbinding orator. He also fought for a united Indian nation.

In 1783, when Tecumseh was 15, the Revolutionary War ended, and the number of white settlers moving into Indian territory increased. The Shawnees saw their land invaded, their crops destroyed, and their people killed. The tribes under Tecumseh's leadership began to form an Indian confederation.

White settlers, led by William Henry Harrison, did their best to block Indian unification, because they knew they would have more difficulty dealing with one powerful Indian nation than with many small tribes. Despite the opposition, Tecumseh received pledges of allegiance from the Sioux, the Chippewa, the Kickapoo, the Illinois, and others.

However, not all Indians were as independent as Tecumseh, and Harrison signed the Treaty of Fort Wayne with a few village chiefs. This treaty gave the settlers rights to extensive tracts of Indian land. Tecumseh exclaimed: "Sell a country! Why not sell the air, the great sea, as well as the earth? Did not the Great Spirit make them all for the use of his children?"

In 1811, Indian forces were badly beaten by Harrison's army in the bloody Battle of Tippecanoe. In the War of 1812, Tecumseh and his supporters joined the British, and fielded the most formidable force ever commanded by a North American Indian. Tecumseh's army was defeated in 1813 and Tecumseh was killed. His death ended Indian resistance.

Research Assignment: To promote a better understanding of the role of the Indians in the War of 1812, have students prepare a report on the roles played by various Indian nations. Another possibility is a report on Tecumseh.

The "Star-Spangled Banner," the national anthem of the United States, was written by Francis Scott Key after seeing the American flag still flying atop Fort McHenry after a night-long bombardment by the British Navy during the War of 1812.

known to whites as The Prophet, had been driven into Canada; and their capital at Tippecanoe had been burned to the ground.

At sea, however, the Americans seemed to have little chance. The navy consisted of 16 oceangoing frigates and ships, compared to a British fleet numbering hundreds of vessels. As she would for nearly a century to come, Britain ruled the waves.

But things did not go according to the numbers. Relatively few men joined the federal army, and the state militias were poorly trained. The Canadians fought alongside the Redcoats to drive the Americans back, and American land forces were routed in the Canadian campaign. At sea, however, the Americans did quite well. Consistent American victories on the Great Lakes were the only reason the United States was not successfully invaded from Canada.

Stalemate on Land.

Instead of concentrating their troops and invading Canada in force, the Americans tried to attack at three different points. General William Hull crossed into Canada from Detroit, lost his nerve, and returned to his base. There he was surrounded by British regulars and

surrendered without firing a shot. A second American force marched toward Montreal by the Lake Champlain route. At the border, the poorly trained New York militia refused to cross the Niagara River to aid an American detachment that was being badly defeated on the other side.

In 1813, General William Henry Harrison defeated the British and Canadians at the Battle of the Thames and destroyed the Canadian capital of York in Ontario. However, that was the end of American offensive action in the north.

In August 1814, a surprise British landing at Chesapeake Bay caught the Americans entirely by surprise. The Redcoats marched into Washington so quickly that they very nearly captured President Madison. At the White House, British officers ate a meal that had been prepared for the Madisons. However, when they marched on Baltimore, they met stiff resistance from the American forces at Fort McHenry. Although the British ships bombarded the fort throughout the night, the Americans kept firing. Francis Scott Key watched this action from a British vessel. When he saw the American flag still floating above the fort in the morning, he wrote the song that became our national anthem—the "Star-Spangled Banner."

Victory on the Waves.   Much to the surprise of both Americans and British, several American vessels defeated ships of the Royal Navy. The frigate _Constitution_ won the name "Old Ironsides" as cannonballs bounced off its tough oak hull in victories over the British ships _Guerriere_ and _Java_.

Most important of these encounters was the victory of Commodore Oliver Perry's gunboats at Put-in-Bay on Lake Erie in September 1813. "We have met the enemy, and they are ours," Perry reported. American control of Lake Erie for the rest of the war discouraged British attempts to invade the United States on that front.

Then, in 1814, Captain Thomas Macdonough turned a Canadian and British army back when he defeated a British flotilla on Lake Champlain.

First Lady Dolly Madison (above) and President Madison had to flee the White House when the British burned the capital on August 24, 1814 (below).

Two political opponents, Adams and Jefferson, died within hours of each other on July 4, 1826—the fiftieth anniversary of the signing of the Declaration of Independence. Coming out of a coma before he died, Adams last words were, "Thomas Jefferson survives!" Jefferson had been dead for 5 hours.

In the Battle of New Orleans, on January 8, 1815, the American army under General Andrew Jackson soundly defeated the British army under General Packenham.

Peace—And a Great Victory. By 1814, both sides wanted peace. The United States sent Henry Clay, a War Hawk, the diplomat John Quincy Adams, and several other negotiators to talk to British representatives in Ghent, Belgium. While the discussions dragged on, Britain decided to invade Louisiana. General Sir Edward Packenham sailed for New Orleans with 7,500 excellent troops, part of the army that had defeated the great Napoleon.

While they were on their way, the peacemakers of Ghent signed a treaty in which neither side won or lost territory. Nor was the issue of impressment resolved. However, the slowness of communications again became a factor. On January 8, 1815, two weeks after the signing of the *Treaty of Ghent,* Packenham's troops marched against a strong position below New Orleans held by a motley collection of defenders commanded by General Andrew Jackson of Tennessee.

General Packenham was too confident against Jackson's army of Tennessee frontiersmen. He saw them as raw recruits. There were untrained free blacks from New Orleans, Choctaw Indians, and even pirates employed by Jean Lafitte (lä-fēt′),

who furnished Jackson with cannon. To the sound of bagpipes and drums, the Redcoats marched on Jackson's position through the morning fog. When they were 200 yards away, the Americans let loose "a leaden torrent no man on earth could face." The British casualties exceeded 2,000, but fewer than ten Americans died in the fighting.

An Explosion of Nationalism. Jackson's amazing victory at New Orleans made it easier for Americans to forget the losses and humiliations of the war. National pride welled up anew. Orators boasted that Americans did almost everything better than anybody else. The Fourth of July became a time of noisy, rowdy celebration. Songwriters produced patriotic songs.

It was a time of patriotic books. In 1817, William Wirt published a biography of Patrick Henry that presented the orator as a national leader. Wirt emphasized statements by Henry like his speech to the First Continental Congress, "I am not a Virginian, but an American." Mason Locke Weems's *Life and Memorable Actions of George Washington* depicted the first president as perfectly moral and almost superhuman. It was

Research Assignment: Some students may wish to report to the class on some of the words that Webster added to the "American" language. Where possible, have students relate the origins of these new words.

PROFILES OF THE PRESIDENCY

J ames Monroe is best remembered for the Monroe Doctrine.

The American continents . . . are henceforth not to be considered as subjects for future colonization by any European powers. . . . We owe it, therefore, to candor, and to the amicable relations existing between the United States and those powers to declare that we should consider any attempt on their part to extend their system to any portion of this hemisphere as dangerous to our peace and safety. With the existing colonies or dependencies of any European power we . . . shall not interfere. But with the governments . . . whose independence we have . . . acknowledged, we could not view any interposition for the purpose of oppressing them, . . . by any European power, in any other light than as a manifestation of any unfriendly disposition towards the United States.

—MESSAGE TO CONGRESS, DECEMBER 2, 1823

Weems who made up the stories of young George Washington and the cherry tree and of him throwing a silver dollar across a river.

Noah Webster added to the patriotic feeling by emphasizing the differences between American English and British English in his *American Spelling Book*. In his *American Dictionary of the English Language*, published in 1828, Webster included 12,000 more definitions than in any previous dictionary, many of them American Indian words Americans had adopted.

James Monroe's Happy Presidency.
James Monroe, elected in 1816, had the good luck to be president during this period of proud nationalism called the *Era of Good Feelings*. Monroe was a cautious, conservative leader. No excitement surrounded him, nor did any conflicts turn truly ugly during his eight years in office. In 1820, Monroe ran for reelection without opposition. One elector cast a vote for John Quincy Adams (Monroe's Secretary of State) so that only Washington would have the honor of unanimous election.

Monroe was unopposed because the Federalist party had ceased to exist. Discredited because of their opposition to the war, the Federalist delegation in the House of Representatives declined from 68 in 1813 to 25 in 1821. With only one political party, popular interest in elections declined. In 1820, only seven of 24 states chose presidential electors. In Richmond, Virginia, a city of 12,000, only 17 people bothered to cast ballots.

Monroe's Accomplishments.
The chief accomplishments of the Monroe presidency were in foreign affairs. In the *Rush-Bagot Agreement* of 1817, the United States and Great Britain agreed to limit the number of armed vessels on the Great Lakes. The treaty set the pattern for what later became the longest unfortified national boundary.

In 1818, Britain and the United States established the southern boundary of Canada from the Great Lakes to the Rocky Mountains at 49° north latitude. West of the Rockies, in what was called the *Oregon Country* (the future states of Oregon and Washington and the province of British Columbia), England and the United States agreed to share sovereignty. Spain and Russia also claimed the territory, but no single nation had many settlers there.

Monroe's busy Secretary of State, John Quincy Adams, was even more successful with Spain. By 1819, the Spanish Empire was breaking up as such South American liberators as Simón Bolívar, José de San Martin, and Bernardo O'Higgins defeated Spanish armies. Mexico was also on the verge of independence. Taking advantage of Spain's troubles, Adams persuaded the Spanish to sell Florida

The Rush-Bagot agreement was signed in 1817. However, it was not until 1871 with the signing of the Treaty of Washington that all border fortifications on the U.S.-Canadian border were finally dismantled.

CANADA

OREGON
COUNTRY
Disputed between
Britain and U.S.

UNITED STATES

• Boston
• New York
• Washington

ATLANTIC

OCEAN

• Charleston
• St. Augustine

New
Orleans

GULF OF MEXICO

MEXICO

Mexico •

CUBA   HAITI

PUERTO RICO

BR. HONDURAS   JAMAICA

CARIBBEAN SEA

UNITED PROVINCES OF
CENTRAL AMERICA

Cartagena   • Caracas

Panama

VENEZUELA

BRITISH GUIANA

DUTCH GUIANA

FRENCH GUIANA

Bogotá

GREATER COLOMBIA

Quito •

Guayaquil • ECUADOR

Manaos

Belém

Marañon R.

Amazon R.

Tapajós R.

BRAZIL

Pernambuco

PACIFIC

OCEAN

PERU

Lima •

Cuzco •

San Francisco R.

Bahia

La Paz •

BOLIVIA

Sucre •
Independent 1825

Paraguay R.

Paraná R.

Rio de Janeiro

PARAGUAY

Asunción •

São Paulo

UNITED
PROVINCES
OF RIO DE
LA PLATA

CHILE

URUGUAY

Valparaiso •

Independent 1828

Santiago •

Buenos Aires •

Montevideo •

PATAGONIA

0   1000 Mi.

0   1000 Km

British territory

Spanish territory

French territory

Dutch territory

▲   Area protected by Monroe Doctrine

THE AMERICAS AND THE
MONROE DOCTRINE, 1823

Research Assignment: Have students do a report on South American wars of liberation that were
taking place during this period. In writing the report, students should examine how these wars
were similar to the U.S. war for independence. What forms of government were instituted in
these countries as a result of the war?

to the United States for $5 million. In the *Adams-Oñis Treaty*, Spain also agreed to set the boundary of the United States at the Rockies and the eastern boundary of present-day Texas.

The Monroe Doctrine.

Adams was also the author of the American policy statement known as the *Monroe Doctrine*. In December 1823, the President declared to Congress and to Europe that the United States was no longer to be considered part of the European world.

The United States pledged not to interfere in European affairs. In return, the United States expected Europe not to interfere in the Western Hemisphere. Americans would respect those European colonies that still existed. However, Americans would not tolerate any European, and particularly Spanish, attempts to gain new colonies.

Curiously, the idea of the Monroe Doctrine originated in England. British merchants, profiting from trade with the independent Central and South American republics, did not want the Spanish back. John Quincy Adams persuaded President Monroe to declare his support of Latin American independence before Britain did. Therefore, the United States was able to gain the prestige of recognizing the new countries.

John Marshall's Nationalism.

While Monroe and Adams proclaimed America's national dignity to the world, John Marshall continued to proclaim the supremacy of the national government at home. In a series of critical decisions, he firmly established the power of the federal government over the states.

In both *Fletcher* v. *Peck* (1810) and *Dartmouth College* v. *Woodward* (1819), Marshall declared a state law unconstitutional, thus establishing the authority of the Supreme Court and the federal government over the state legislatures. In *Martin* v. *Hunter's Lessee* (1816), Marshall asserted the power of the Supreme Court to reverse a decision of a state court. In *Gibbons* v. *Ogden* (1824), the Court told New York State that it could not regulate commerce on the Hudson River because New Jersey also touched on that river, thus making it an *interstate* waterway, which only Congress could regulate.

In *McCulloch* v. *Maryland* (1819), Marshall prevented the state of Maryland (and all states) from taxing the nationally chartered Bank of the United States. "The power to tax," Marshall wrote, "is the power to destroy." The states were not permitted to destroy a federal institution. In the McCulloch case, Marshall committed the Supreme Court to the Hamiltonian principle of loose construction of the Constitution. If government's goal was a legitimate one serving the public good, Marshall wrote, it did not matter that the Constitution did not specifically authorize a particular action. So long as the Constitution did not specifically forbid that action, Congress and the president had the authority to take it.

SECTION REVIEW

1. Write a sentence to identify: General Harrison, Put-in-Bay, Treaty of Ghent, General Andrew Jackson.

2. Describe the land and sea advantages of the Americans and the British at the beginning of the War of 1812.

3. Describe three of Monroe's achievements, including the Monroe Doctrine, and how they affected the United States.

4. Explain the significance of the decisions made by Chief Justice John Marshall during this period.

---

4. POSTWAR PROBLEMS

The Monroe years were not without problems. In 1819, when Missouri applied for statehood, Congress discussed the immorality of slavery for the first time. The dispute ended in compromise. Most political leaders of the North, where slavery had been abolished, and the South, where it lived on, believed they had resolved the issue. In reality, the Missouri debate of 1819–1820 was only an early rumbling of a storm that would engulf the United States in civil war.

Its effects were first felt in 1824, as James Monroe's presidency drew to a close. The Republican party, which had united the country, was torn apart by dissension. By the time the sixth president was sworn in on March 4, 1825, everyone knew that the Era of Good Feelings was over.

Class Activity: Divide the class into groups. Have each group prepare a brief report detailing the facts and findings in one of the following cases heard by the Supreme Court under John Marshall: *Marbury* v. *Madison*, *McCulloch* v. *Maryland*, *Fletcher* v. *Park*, *Gibbons* v. *Ogden*, *Brown* v.

Slave States Versus Free States. By 1819, all of the original states north of the *Mason-Dixon Line* (the Maryland-Pennsylvania border) had abolished slavery or were in the process of doing so. Slavery had never existed in the western states of Ohio, Indiana, and Illinois.

In the states south of the Mason-Dixon Line, including Delaware, slavery was still legal. Even in the new southwestern states of Kentucky, Tennessee, Alabama, Mississippi, and Louisiana, which were settled largely by southerners, citizens were permitted to own other humans.

So, although no one had planned it, a more or less straight line ran from the mouth of the Delaware River in the East to the mouth of the Ohio River in the West and divided the 11 free states from the 11 slave states. When Missouri applied for admission to the Union as a slave state in 1819, it threatened to undo the balance. In the debate, Congressman James Tallmadge of New York argued that because slavery was immoral, Congress should admit no more slave states. The *Tallmadge Amendment* said Missouri could enter the Union, provided that it prohibit importation of additional slaves and that children of slaves be freed at age twenty-five.

"A Fire Bell in the Night."

Southerners protested. Some admitted that slavery was a tragedy but they refused to admit that slaveowners were immoral. Let the southern states work out their problem, they said. Northerners had no right to lecture them on the morality of their social institutions. Most southern members of Congress insisted that Missouri be admitted as a slave state.

Henry Clay of Kentucky, a border state where slavery was legal but not vital to the economy, worked out a compromise. The balance of free states and slave states would be preserved by also admitting Maine, then a part of Massachusetts, as a free state. Southerners had no objection to this.

Clay appealed to northerners who wanted to stop the expansion of slavery by proposing that the southern boundary of the state of Missouri, at 36° 30′ north latitude, be extended to the Rocky Mountains. All states created out of land lying north of that line must be free states. South of the line, slavery would be permitted but not protected. New states entering the Union from south of the line could be either slave states or free states.

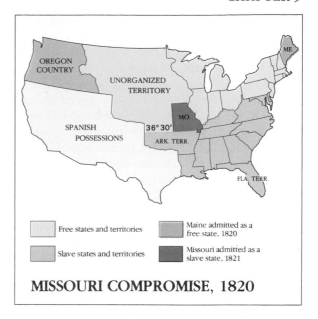

Free states and territories

Slave states and territories

Maine admitted as a free state, 1820

Missouri admitted as a slave state, 1821

MISSOURI COMPROMISE, 1820

In 1820, Congress accepted the *Missouri Compromise.* Most Americans relaxed, believing that the issue was resolved for all time. John Quincy Adams, unconvinced, wrote in his diary that "the present question is a mere preamble—a title-page to a great tragic volume." In retirement at Monticello, Thomas Jefferson used an even more striking image. When he heard that northerners had attacked southern slaveowners as immoral, he said that the news sounded "like a fire bell in the night," terrifying because of what it might mean for the country.

The Life and Death of King Caucus.

The Missouri crisis divided Americans along sectional lines. Before 1824, the Republican presidential candidate had been nominated by members of Congress, meeting in a *caucus* (an informal meeting of people who agree on an issue). The old Federalists had also nominated candidates in this way. Another orderly tradition held that the Secretary of State should succeed to the presidency. Madison, the fourth president, had served Jefferson as Secretary of State. James Monroe, the fifth president, had served Madison as Secretary of State. In 1824, however, the Republican caucus broke with tradition and nominated William Crawford of Virginia, the Secretary of the Treasury.

However, the caucus was poorly attended. Other individuals who wanted to be president returned to their states and were nominated by state legislatures. King Caucus was dead.

Four Candidates.

Massachusetts nominated John Quincy Adams, the son of John Adams. A majority of New Englanders supported Adams —he was a New Englander himself, he had been Secretary of State, and they resented Virginia's monopoly of the presidency. Although Georgia was Crawford's home, he had been born in Virginia, as had Jefferson, Madison, and Monroe. This was called the *Virginia Dynasty*.

Henry Clay, the Speaker of the House of Representatives, was nominated by his home state of Kentucky. He claimed to be the spokesman for the new western states, both slave and free, and hoped that their support would carry him into the White House. However, the western state of Tennessee nominated its own hero, Andrew Jackson. As events soon proved, his popularity in the West was greater than Clay's, and the memories of the glorious Battle of New Orleans brought him support from east of the Appalachians, too.

Adams and Clay.

Both Clay and Adams were strong nationalists. Both wanted the federal government to play an active part in the national economy. They supported the Second Bank of the United States, chartered in 1816. Both wanted a high protective tariff in support of American industry, and both wanted the federal government to help finance internal improvements in the West: canals, good roads, and good river harbors.

Crawford and Jackson.

William Crawford represented the Jeffersonian philosophy. He did not like protective tariffs because they raised the price of manufactured goods for the farmers and southern planters. He opposed federal funding of internal improvements because they were expensive and Crawford believed government should be economical. Crawford believed the states and private enterprise should be responsible for building roads and canals and for dredging harbors and river channels.

Because Crawford had little support outside the South, he had very little chance to be elected. When he suffered a stroke in 1823 and temporarily lost his ability to walk and talk, even that chance disappeared.

No one knew where Jackson stood on the issues. Although he served two terms in the Senate, his mark had been made not in politics but in business and the military. Born in North Carolina, he went west to Tennessee as a young man. Practicing law and speculating in land, he built up a huge plantation called "The Hermitage." By 1824 Jackson was the wealthiest man in the state.

Best known for his great victory at New Orleans, Jackson also had other military feathers in his cap. He crushed most of the powerful Indian tribes of the southeastern states. In 1818, he followed the unbeaten Seminoles into Spanish Florida, an illegal and potentially dangerous action, and there he performed the even more controversial act of hanging two British subjects for treason against the United States! Some members of the government criticized him for this action. But the incident only added to his popular reputation as a man of action, a great national hero who got things done.

The House Decides the Election.

Jackson's reputation as a hero won more votes than any other candidate (a *plurality*) in both the popular vote and the electoral vote, but not an *absolute majority* (more than half the total votes). In addition, Jackson was the only national candidate, carrying states in the West, the South, and the Northeast.

Adams was second. However, he was clearly a sectional candidate. He carried only the New England states and New York. Crawford and Clay were sectional candidates, too. Clay's three states were in the West. Crawford won only the state of his birth, Virginia, and his adopted state, Georgia.

Because no presidential candidate won a majority of electoral votes (131 were needed in 1824), the choice of the sixth president, as in 1800, went to the House of Representatives.

Clay was not eligible in this phase of the election because the Twelfth Amendment to the Constitution required the House, voting by states, to choose from among the top three candidates. Nevertheless, the Kentuckian was in a powerful position. As Speaker of the House, he could influence the votes of many representatives by promising them favors.

Clay's power worried the Jackson supporters. Clay and Jackson both claimed to be the leader of

Class Activity: Review Article II, Section 2 of the Constitution as changed by the 12th Amendment. It provides for House of Representative involvement in elections such as that of 1824.

To his diary, John Quincy Adams confided that he preferred a seat in Congress to being President:

No one knows, and few conceive, the agony of mind that I have suffered from the time that I was made by circumstances, and not by my volition, a candidate for the Presidency till I was dismissed from that station by the failure of my reelection. They were feelings to be suppressed; and they were suppressed. No human being has ever heard me complain.

But this call upon me by the people of the district in which I reside, to represent them in Congress, has been spontaneous and, although counteracted by a double opposition, federalist and Jacksonite, I have received nearly three votes in four throughout the district. My election as President of the United States was not half so gratifying to my inmost soul.

—DIARY, NOVEMBER 7, 1830

the West, and they disliked one another intensely. Jackson, with more votes than anyone else, was the only candidate to win states in all three sections of the country. The Jacksonians argued that the House of Representatives should simply ratify what the American people wanted.

"Corrupt Bargain!" It was a good argument but it did not carry the day. Clay supported Adams because the two men believed in the same nationalistic economic policy, and because Clay felt he had a better chance to succeed Adams as president.

Therefore, the Adams and Jackson forces each went into the House with 12 states. New York held the key vote; and its delegation was evenly divided, with Steven Van Rensselaer holding the deciding vote. Van Rensselaer had promised his vote to both Jackson and Adams supporters. No one, including himself, knew what he would do.

When it was his turn to put his ballot in the box, Van Rensselaer said he prayed for guidance. Looking at the floor he saw a piece of paper bearing the name of John Quincy Adams. He took it as a sign and made John Quincy Adams president.

The Jacksonians protested that the will of the people had been betrayed. A short time later, when President Adams named Henry Clay to be Secretary of State, the Jackson forces screamed, "Corrupt Bargain!" They claimed that Clay had

supported Adams in return for the office that had been the stepping-stone to the presidency since 1808.

There was, almost certainly, no deal between Adams and Clay. Clay was a dealer but Adams, with his strict Puritan conscience, was not.

Nevertheless, the cry of "Corrupt Bargain!" was a powerful political slogan. Andrew Jackson resigned his Senate seat in a fury. His supporters vowed to put him in the White House in 1828. For four years they worked to organize voters behind their hero and to make Adams as unhappy in the presidency as his father had been.

SECTION REVIEW

1. Write a sentence to identify: Tallmadge Amendment, Henry Clay, Virginia Dynasty, Twelfth Amendment.

2. Give the two most important provisions of the Missouri Compromise. Explain the effects each provision had.

3. Why was the presidential election of 1824 settled in the House of Representatives? Which candidate did the House select?

4. How did Andrew Jackson react to the House's vote in 1824? Why did he think the result was unfair?

CHAPTER REVIEW

TIME LINE

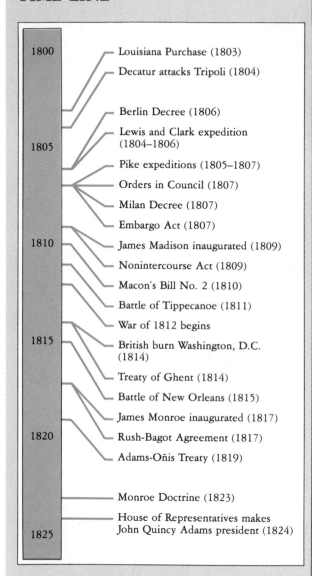

1800	Louisiana Purchase (1803)
	Decatur attacks Tripoli (1804)
	Berlin Decree (1806)
1805	Lewis and Clark expedition (1804–1806)
	Pike expeditions (1805–1807)
	Orders in Council (1807)
	Milan Decree (1807)
	Embargo Act (1807)
1810	James Madison inaugurated (1809)
	Nonintercourse Act (1809)
	Macon's Bill No. 2 (1810)
	Battle of Tippecanoe (1811)
	War of 1812 begins
1815	British burn Washington, D.C. (1814)
	Treaty of Ghent (1814)
	Battle of New Orleans (1815)
	James Monroe inaugurated (1817)
1820	Rush-Bagot Agreement (1817)
	Adams-Oñis Treaty (1819)
	Monroe Doctrine (1823)
1825	House of Representatives makes John Quincy Adams president (1824)

TIME LINE QUESTIONS

1. In which president's administration was the War of 1812 fought?
2. List the following events in chronological order: Adams-Oñis Treaty, Louisiana Purchase, Battle of New Orleans, Monroe Doctrine, start of Lewis and Clark expedition, Treaty of Ghent.
3. Name the events leading to the War of 1812.

SKILLS STRATEGY

Jefferson, Peter [father of] Jefferson, Thomas [Boyhood] **J:58**
Jefferson, State of [U.S. history] **J:57**
Jefferson, Thomas [U.S. President] **J:58**
  with pictures
  Early years
    Alien and Sedition Acts **A:351**
    Declaration of Independence *picture on* **D:68a**
    Democratic-Republican Party **D:111**
    Kentucky and Virginia Resolutions **K:214**
  President
    Lewis and Clark Expedition (Making Plans) **L:198**
    Louisiana Purchase **L:434**
    Marshall, John **M:185**
    Nonintercourse Act **N:351**
    White House (The Original Building) **W:242**

ENCYCLOPEDIA INDEXES

Encyclopedia articles are alphabetically arranged and bound in volumes that look like this:

If you wanted to find information about Thomas Jefferson, you might do your initial research in the J-K Volume. You could find information on the War of 1812 in the W-X-Y-Z volume. However, you may not be able to find all the information you need in these specific articles; that's where the *encyclopedia index* comes in. The index is in a separate volume, usually the last one. Look at the first excerpt from the encyclopedia index above.

Index *headings* are printed alphabetically in heavy type. Index *entries* are listed alphabetically under some headings. Each index entry is a title of

Making Connections: Review the questions and topics presented in the Making Connections section opening this chapter. Pay particular attention to reviewing how our political leaders' attitudes were sometimes tempered when faced with the realities of office; why the national

236

an encyclopedia article that gives information about the subject in the entry. A word or phrase in brackets after a heading identifies the subject. A word or phrase in parentheses after an entry (always the title of an article) refers you to the section of an article where information can be found. Every entry (and heading that is the title of an article) ends with a letter and number in heavy type (**J:57**) referring to a particular volume and page where information is located. References to illustrations are printed in italic type.

APPLYING SKILLS

1. Where can you find information about Jefferson and the Declaration of Independence?
2. In which section of what article can you find out about Jefferson's father?
3. Which article relates to Jefferson's presidency: Alien and Sedition Acts, or Marshall, John?
4. Where can you find information and a picture on the United States Marines in the War of 1812?
5. If the index headings and entries under War of 1812 do not give you the information you want, where does the index recommend you look?

CHAPTER 9 TEST

TEXT REVIEW

1. Under which president was Justice Samuel Chase impeached, and why did the Senate refuse to find Chase guilty?
2. Explain why the Louisiana Purchase was an example of a loose interpretation of the Constitution.
3. Why did President Jefferson agree to the Louisiana Purchase?
4. Discuss the reasons behind the declaration of war against England in 1812.
5. Name three events that show why James Monroe's presidency was the "Era of Good Feelings."
6. Describe the circumstances leading to the Missouri Compromise.
7. Using the reactions of John Quincy Adams and Thomas Jefferson, explain whether the Missouri Compromise successfully settled the issue of slavery.
8. Name the candidates in the 1824 presidential election, and the states they came from. Did any of the candidates gain support nationwide? Explain your answer.

CRITICAL THINKING

9. How might the information brought back by the Lewis and Clark expedition have been different if a president other than Jefferson had been in office?
10. Considering Andrew Jackson's behavior after the House made John Quincy Adams president in 1824, what conclusions can you draw about Jackson's desire to be president?

WRITING A PARAGRAPH

As its name implies, a *thumbnail personality* sketch is a brief, "sketchy" word-drawing of the outstanding personality traits of a subject. It is not a detailed word-portrait. Write a one-paragraph thumbnail sketch of one of the following people: Thomas Jefferson, James Madison, Andrew Jackson. Begin your sketch with an interesting topic sentence that sums up one or more outstanding traits of the person you are sketching.

character of Americans became less chauvinistic about their states and more concerned with themselves in terms of the region of the country they came from and as Americans.

Quotation: from the novel *The Works of Love.* Other works by Wright Morris (born 1910) include *The Inhabitants, The Deep Sleep, In Orbit, Love Among the Cannibals, Earthly Delights, Unearthly Adornments,* and *Real Losses, Imaginary Gains.*

CHAPTER 10

MACHINES, COTTON, AND LAND

1800–1825

. . . towns, like weeds, spring up when it rains, dry up when it stops. WRIGHT MORRIS

Making Connections. The early years of the nineteenth century saw the beginning of great changes in the United States. A mostly rural country took the first steps toward becoming a great industrial nation. Factories grew in the Northeast, a new crop revitalized southern agriculture, and settlers began to move west. All these changes, however, put strains on the nation's unity.

In this chapter, you will learn:
- Why the use of machines in manufacturing caused cities to grow
- How the United States obtained the secrets of industrialization
- What new crop kept slavery from dying out in the South
- Who invented a machine that changed an entire region
- Why the government's land policies touched off the Panic of 1819
- What new transportation systems solved the West's isolation

You know that Thomas Jefferson thought the United States should remain an agrarian nation. But the energies of the new nation's growing population could not be confined to farming, and the Industrial Revolution turned the United States away from Jefferson's ideal. As you read, note the reasons why the regions of the United States developed differently between 1800 and 1825.

Sections
1. The Northeast Industrializes
2. The South Changes
3. Winning the West
4. Tying the Nation Together

1. THE NORTHEAST INDUSTRIALIZES

One of Alexander Hamilton's dreams headed for fulfillment in the early nineteenth century. Hamilton had perceived that the *Industrial Revolution,* then underway in England, was the key to a nation's prosperity. He believed that if a country could make its own goods instead of importing them, it would grow wealthier and more powerful than any agricultural country ever could.

Thomas Jefferson, on the other hand, preferred the farming life. But he also saw the benefits of industrialization. It was clear that Great Britain was growing richer as a result of the new cloth-making machinery that the British monopolized. However, Jefferson observed that industry caused changes in British society. People were moving from farms to cities in ever greater numbers. Jefferson felt that, without a strong core of land-owners, democracy could not work.

Jefferson's vision of the United States was based on conditions at that time. He wanted to perpetuate those conditions, and therefore urged the government to adopt policies that encouraged Americans to remain farmers and to take up the land that the government owned in the West.

Preindustrial Society. At the beginning of the nineteenth century, only a few crafts were

This painting, entitled Pat Lyon at the Forge *(right), shows a typical blacksmith in the early 1800s. Although the Industrial Revolution had already come to the United States, the individual artisan was still important to the economy.*

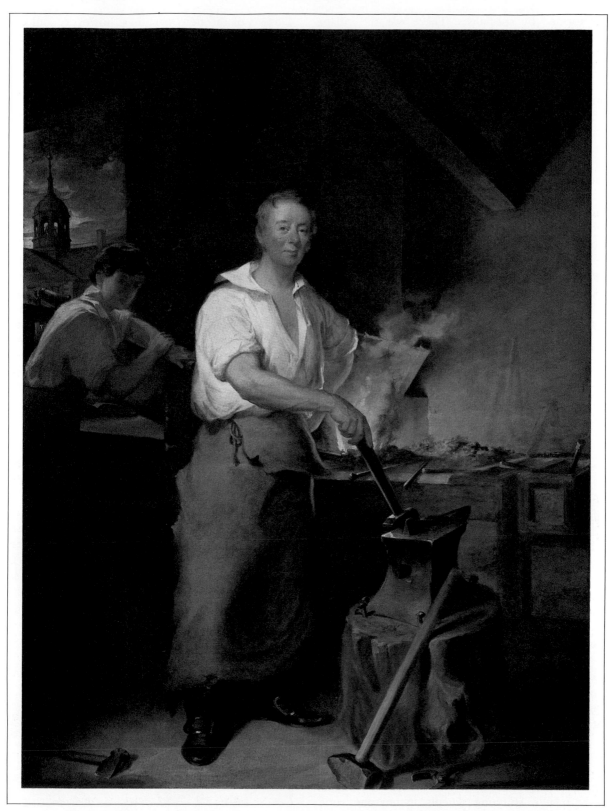

Skills Review: Reinforce the skills learned in the preceding Skills Strategy section. In preparing Research Assignments, have students use the encyclopedia as a research source. In those assignments done for this chapter, have students detail their use of the encyclopedia index they used in their research.

performed by specialists. There was the village blacksmith, who needed special equipment and skills to fashion iron objects. Everyone needed the blacksmith for horseshoes, wheel rims, nails, and so on. And it was a rare region that didn't have a miller who, with the power of animals or of a running stream to move the giant millstones, ground each farmer's grain in return for a share of it, which the miller then sold in towns and cities.

The wealthy bought their clothes, shoes, and other goods from artisans who made them with hand tools. But people in the middle, who were not rich but not poor either, made most of the goods they consumed themselves and treasured those they had to buy.

The broom to sweep the floor was handmade, not purchased. In 1800 American girls learned how to use a needle and thread with passable skill. The job of making clothing and mending worn garments was considered a regular part of women's domestic work.

A majority of American women probably knew how to spin yarn and thread out of natural fibers or to weave it into cloth. People growing up on farms, westerners, in fact anyone who lived far from towns and artisans, learned to be "handy," not expert but good enough, at a large number of crafts. The phrase "jack-of-all-trades" comes from preindustrial times.

The Industrial Revolution.

Life began to change in England in the middle of the eighteenth century, when machines began to appear. Driven by waterwheels, James Hargreaves's *spinning jenny* carded wool or cotton. *Carding* means to comb the tangled fibers so that they could be spun into yarn or thread. (*Jenny* is short for "engine.") Sir Richard Arkwright invented a machine that did the spinning. It twisted wool or cotton into yarn and thread many times faster than the most skillful person with a hand-turned spinning wheel could do it. Edmund Cartwright also helped to found another industry by inventing a rope-making machine. Machines to produce other goods followed at a dizzying rate.

When cloth-making and other crafts were done by hand and depended on human muscle for power, they were done at home. It would have made no sense to have 50 women working at hand-turned spinning wheels under one roof.

Dozens of the new machines, however, could be turned by a fast-running river or by a steam engine, which had also been invented in England. Workers, mostly girls and women at first, had to be brought to the riverside factory or mill, with its whirring belts and pulleys. Because they worked 14 or 16 hours a day and walked to work, they could not live too far from the mill. Among its many effects, the Industrial Revolution caused the rapid growth of cities and towns.

England's Secret Turned Loose.

The Industrial Revolution made Great Britain the world's richest nation and, in time, the most powerful. The textiles that English mills turned out by the ton were better and cheaper than handmade cloth. Every country in the world wanted to buy them.

Understandably, the British placed a high value on their machinery. The cloth was for sale, but not the spinning jennies and power looms that made it. In fact, it was illegal for anyone who worked in a textile mill to leave the country, because with them would go their knowledge of the machines.

Samuel Slater (below), with Moses Brown, built the first successful American spinning mill. He eventually owned mills in three states.

Research Assignment: Beginning with the information presented in the text, have students reseach and contrast Jefferson's and Hamilton's ideas on the ideal social setting for people in society. Have them research what philosophical views of people and society influenced both of these men and their views.

Manufacturers, like the owner of this factory built beside the Hudson River in the nineteenth century, used rivers as power sources and as highways to transport materials and products.

In 1789, Samuel Slater, a 23-year-old English machinist, heard that American state legislatures had offered large sums of money to machine experts who would defy the British law and come to the United States. He managed to slip out of Great Britain and get to New York. There he announced that he had memorized the plans for an entire spinning factory and was prepared to build one. Moses Brown, a wealthy Quaker merchant, was quicker than anyone else. He wrote to Slater, "If thou canst do this thing, I invite thee to come to Rhode Island and have the credit of introducing cotton-manufacturing into America."

Brown and Slater's little factory housed only 72 spindles. Still, that was the equivalent of 72 spinning wheels in 72 cottages. But instead of paying 72 highly skilled women, the men ran their mill with one supervisor and nine children. The total of all their wages came to less than $5 a week.

Paul and Arthur Scholfield were two brothers who also brought English industrial secrets to the United States. They built America's first woolens mill in Byfield, Massachusetts. Francis Cabot Lowell, an American, smuggled plans for a power loom out of England and became a millionaire in the weaving industry.

Yankee Ingenuity. Americans soon began to make their own contributions to industrial technology. Indeed, Europeans came to think of *Yankee ingenuity*, or "a peculiar aptitude for mechanical improvements" in Alexander Hamilton's words, as one of the unique characteristics of the American people. It is not surprising that Americans were clever at solving problems. A people who, for the most part, lived on farms some distance from the cities where artisans lived, had to be handy. Even in the cities, because labor was scarce in the United States, Americans took quickly to machines that did the work of many people.

Oliver Evans of Philadelphia earned an international reputation when he invented a continuous operation flour mill. Old-fashioned mills required several workers, or had to be run in fits and starts as the miller hurried to do different jobs. Evans's mill ran without stopping, with only two men on the job. The first dumped the grain into one end of an ingenious complex of machinery. Without human attention, the grain was weighed, cleaned, ground, and poured into barrels. Only at this point was a second worker needed to hammer the lids on the barrels. In time, of course, the second worker would be replaced by a machine.

Discussion Questions: Was Great Britain wrong in its attempt to keep all industrial patents and inventions for itself? Would you consider Slater a traitor to his country? Relate the first question to the present conflicts between the U.S. and Japan regarding computer technology. Direct the discussion to interpret this issue in light of laissez-faire capitalism.

The painting above is of Eli Whitney's gun factory, where Whitney (below) revolutionized United States industry after 1800 by introducing interchangeable, mass-produced parts.

Mass Production.

A revolutionary invention by Eli Whitney introduced the textile industry's principle of cheap *mass production* to the manufacture of iron and steel products—and therefore to the manufacture of machines themselves!

It started with rifles and muskets. In 1798, guns were handmade by extremely skilled gunsmiths. The lock, or firing mechanism, consisted of a dozen or more tiny parts that were fitted to one another by hand. When wear or abuse caused one of these parts to break, the gunsmith had to take the lock apart and "custom make" the broken piece so that it worked with the others. It was a time-consuming job and therefore expensive.

Whitney persuaded Secretary of the Treasury Oliver Wolcott to give him a contract to produce 10,000 muskets that anyone could repair. His secret was the principle of *interchangeable parts*. By making even the smallest parts of a lock in molds just precise enough that the parts fit together and worked, it would no longer be necessary to take a broken gun to a skilled artisan. Anyone with standard spare parts could fix it.

In 1800, Whitney demonstrated the interchangeable parts to the President's cabinet. He disassembled ten muskets, mixed the parts together, and proceeded to assemble ten muskets that

Discussion Question: Why is the Industrial Revolution referred to as a "revolution"? Discussion should center on the meaning of revolution as a term having to do with great and rapid change, rather than with military history.

fired. They were not as fine as handmade guns—any more than a suit of clothes made by machine is as fine as a suit made by a skilled tailor. But the guns all worked and they were cheap. That was the principle behind mass production and the basis of modern industry.

New England Industrializes.

New England was ready for industry. Most early factories were powered by water, and the northeastern part of the United States had many fast-flowing rivers and streams. When steam challenged waterpower, New England was ready with its rich resources of wood for fuel.

The War of 1812 also encouraged industrialization. Financial losses caused by the British seizure of ships convinced some American merchants to take their capital out of marine trade and put it into manufacturing. Jefferson's embargo and Madison's Nonintercourse Act, by preventing ships from sailing, turned even more businesses toward investing money in spindles and looms. After the war, 130,000 spindles hummed in 213 factories in Massachusetts, Connecticut, and Rhode Island.

The growing American banking system also helped to finance industrialization. In 1811, President Madison allowed the Bank of the United States to go out of existence. Over the next five years, the number of state banks tripled.

In New England, loans from state banks made it possible for investors to build mills they could not otherwise afford. In 1816, even the Jeffersonian Republicans recognized the value of well-managed banks. In that year, with New England's support, Congress chartered a national bank, the *Second Bank of the United States*.

Working People.

New England farm families provided a ready-made labor force for the new industry. Although the growing season was short and the soil difficult to work, New Englanders had large families, too large for small farms to support. Many families and single young men went west. However, this opportunity was not available to a young single woman who wished to remain respectable. New England's strict moral code required that girls and young women be closely supervised until they married.

Francis Cabot Lowell offered hard-pressed farm families a way in which these young women could earn money while remaining respectable. His recruiters visited village meetinghouses and explained to farmers that their daughters would be paid $3 a week for working in Lowell's mill at Waltham, Massachusetts. They would send half of their wages home.

The other half of their income would pay for room and board at a Lowell-approved rooming house where they would be supervised as strictly as if they were at home. All day, as long as there was light, the "Lowell girls" worked in the mill. In the evenings they would read, discuss the Bible and other good books, and practice the needle-craft they would need as homemakers. They would be in bed at an early hour. On Sunday, they were required to attend church.

After several years, Lowell expected his employees to return to their families, marry, and

In the Northeast, easy access to water power, financing, raw materials, workers, and major ports, along with an acceptance of innovative methods, spurred the rapid growth of factories.

Discussion Question: What effects might the Lowell system and the Industrial Revolution have had on family life? (If students have trouble with this, assign it as a report.) Changes should include disintegration of the family; for example, those who lived in the same household saw less of each other, whereas farm work and household manufacturing had previously involved family members with each other.

 243

Harriet Hanson Robinson's Loom and Spindle *tells of her 13 years from age ten as a "Lowell girl."*

raise a family. Lowell did not believe a person's whole life should be spent working in a factory. He believed, with Thomas Jefferson, that farm life was more natural than factory life. He designed the *Lowell system* as a means to make cloth without disturbing traditional ways.

Of course, *industrialization* was more powerful than Lowell's good intentions. By 1825, an increasing number of New Englanders had left their farms for good and had become part of a permanent industrial working class.

Daniel Webster. Industrialization also caused changes in New England politics. These changes can be seen in the career of the man who, with the passing of the Revolutionary generation, became New England's most admired political spokesman.

Daniel Webster was born on a poor New Hampshire farm in 1782. He graduated from Dartmouth College and became a lawyer. Because of his booming voice, his dignified appearance, and his eloquent speeches to juries, he became famous almost immediately. According to one admirer, Webster was "a living lie because no man

on earth could be so great as he looked."

In 1813 Webster was elected to Congress. There he opposed the high protective tariff of 1816. The people he represented were farmers who wanted cheap manufactured goods, regardless of whether they were made in England or America, and Portsmouth ship owners who wanted cargoes to haul, regardless of whether they originated in Great Britain or America.

In 1816 Webster moved to Massachusetts, a larger state that offered great opportunities. There he began to associate with bankers and newly wealthy industrialists. He became the attorney for the Second Bank of the United States and his sympathies began to go to the mill owners who complained that as soon as the War of 1812 ended, English merchants *dumped* cheap cloth into the United States, hoping to destroy the infant American industry. When Webster reentered Congress from Massachusetts in 1823, he had been transformed into a defender of high tariffs.

Daniel Webster's dark, piercing eyes and compelling voice earned him the nickname "Black Dan."

The practice of flooding foreign markets with goods to eliminate surpluses without hurting domestic prices was actually known as "dumping." It was a very common commercial practice.

2. THE SOUTH CHANGES

John C. Calhoun of South Carolina knew Daniel Webster very well. The two men were the same age. They first came to Congress as young men during the early 1800s. For four decades they crossed one another's paths in Washington, mostly in the Senate but also in the executive branch of the government. Webster was Secretary of State under two different presidents and ran for the presidency once. Calhoun was vice president under two presidents, Secretary of War under a third, and Secretary of State under a fourth. They died within two years of one another, Calhoun in 1850, Webster in 1852.

The two men were also political enemies. Webster spoke for the industrial Northeast and Calhoun for the agricultural South when the two sections once again became hostile toward one another. Where Webster spoke for high tariffs and a strong, sovereign national government, Calhoun insisted on low tariffs and believed that the states should have more authority than the central government.

It was not always that way. When Calhoun first came to Congress in 1811, he was a strong nationalist, a superpatriotic advocate of military force, and a spokesman for a high protective tariff. In his political turnabout in the 1820s, there is a reflection of the effects of the Industrial Revolution on the South.

Slavery Almost Dies Out. When Calhoun was born in 1782, the plantation system and slavery itself appeared to be dying out in the South. Tobacco was the chief cash crop raised on plantations. Many slaves were used in growing and marketing it. But the price of tobacco declined steadily in the early years of the republic as a result of the loss of the British market. Indigo, a major slave-raised crop in Calhoun's South Carolina, was also less profitable without British subsidies. Even rice growers had difficulty finding markets for their product. Slavery seemed to be losing its reason for existing—a profitable cash crop that could be grown efficiently on large plantations.

In addition, many white southerners were troubled by the proclamation in the Declaration of Independence that "all men are created equal." Some planters freed their slaves because of their belief in natural rights, and it became almost common for planters to free their slaves in their wills. James Madison, James Monroe, and John

John C. Calhoun was one of the South's greatest statesmen in Congress.

In 1816, the Virginia legislature petitioned the president to establish an area in Africa for freed slaves to return to. By 1829, only 1,400 ex-slaves took advantage of it. Many did not want to return, and the cost of returning the slaves became too high. The cotton revolution also made slaves a commodity again.

Marshall all supported the *American Colonization Society,* which encouraged slaveowners to free their slaves and pay the passage of free blacks who wished to return to Africa. The African republic of Liberia was founded by free blacks from the United States.

The Cotton Gin.

In 1793, seven years before he demonstrated the principle of interchangeable parts, 28-year-old Eli Whitney was visiting a friend in Georgia. There he saw his first cotton plants and learned that they grew very well in the upland South.

Unfortunately, the cotton of the upland South could not be sold to English textile manufacturers at much profit, even though the British could not get enough cotton fiber. The fibers in the cotton boll were *short staple,* and the seeds of the plant very sticky. Slaves could separate the seeds from the fiber by hand. But in a long day's work, a man or woman produced only a few pounds of cleaned fiber.

Planters who grew *long-staple* cotton on the sandy sea islands of South Carolina had a machine for separating fiber from seeds. However, the seeds of the long-staple plant were smooth and slippery. Merely passing the bolls between rollers spat the seeds out. When short-staple upland cotton was put into these machines, the oily seeds were crushed and the fiber ruined. If someone could invent a machine that worked on upland cotton, a lot of money could be made.

In only ten days, Eli Whitney built an "absurdly simple contrivance" he called a "cotton engine," or *cotton gin.* It was too simple. Almost anyone who saw a cotton gin could build one. In 1790, Congress had passed a law providing that for 14 years after an inventor registered an invention with the United States Patent Office, anyone who used that invention had to pay a fee. But Eli Whitney's cotton gin patent was simply ignored. He never made a cent from the machine that enriched the South.

The South Expands.

Cotton production soared. In 1792, the year before the cotton gin was invented, the South exported 150,000 pounds (68,000 kilograms) of the snowy fiber, pressed and tied into bales. In 1825, 176 million pounds (80 million kilograms) were exported, with northern mills consuming another 100 million pounds (45 million kilograms).

Cotton was the reason the South expanded so quickly in the early nineteenth century. The rich

Eli Whitney's cotton gin made cotton-raising profitable for upland Southern plantations. The gin rapidly and cleanly separated the sticky seeds from the cotton fibers. Although Whitney patented the simple machine, he made no money from it.

Sugar plantations, like this one along the Mississippi River, sprang up in the deep South, particularly in Louisiana. Much of the sugar was used to make rum, which was then shipped to West Africa and traded for slaves.

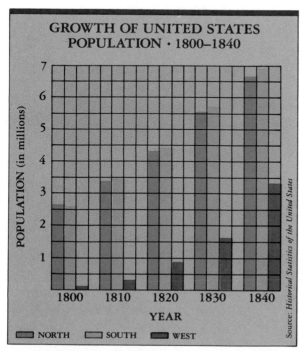

GROWTH OF UNITED STATES
POPULATION · 1800–1840

POPULATION (in millions)

1800   1810   1820   1830   1840

YEAR

☐ NORTH   ☐ SOUTH   ☐ WEST

Source: Historical Statistics of the United States

soil of Alabama and Mississippi was ideal for the crop. In 1800, excluding Indians, there were about 1,000 people in what is now Alabama. In 1810 there were 9,000, and in 1820 there were 128,000. Mississippi's population rose from 8,800 in 1800 to 75,000 in 1820.

Among these pioneers were a great many black slaves. In 1800, there were about 4,000 blacks in Alabama and Mississippi combined. In 1810 there were 17,000, almost all slaves, and in 1820, 75,000. Nearly half the population of Mississippi consisted of black slaves.

The Revival of Slavery.   Like tobacco, cotton could be grown efficiently on large plantations worked by gangs of cheap, dependable workers. A cotton plantation was busy 11 months out of the year. During the growing season the fields had to be tended constantly. Picking time was the busiest of all. The bolls had to be harvested before the fall storms. Then the cotton was ginned and baled.

Research Assignment: The more science-minded or artistically inclined students in class may construct working models of some of the inventions they will read about. Once completed, these projects should be brought in to class and an oral presentation given explaining the machines, the designs and how they worked.

247

During the winter, equipment was repaired, hogs slaughtered and salted for the year's meat supply, and a score of other tasks performed. In spring it was time to plant again, not just cotton but also corn and vegetables to feed the people of the plantation.

People who owned small farms could and did raise cotton. Nevertheless, it was a crop that, with slaves and many acres, could make a planter quite rich. An institution that appeared to be dying out in 1793 was suddenly very valuable. A single slave cranking a small gin could clean ten pounds of cotton a day. A larger machine attended by several slaves and turned by a horse could clean 50 pounds a day. Once steam-powered gins were introduced, the capacity for producing cotton was unlimited. A planter could produce as much cotton as there were acres to grow it on.

Dreams of Industry Are Dashed. The boom in cotton led the young John Calhoun and other southerners like him to support the protective tariff of 1816. They reasoned, logically enough, that the best place to build cotton mills was near the cotton in the southern states. They wanted to protect their future factories and voted for the tariff, which put a tax on English textiles and many other goods. But Calhoun's dream of an industrialized South Carolina, shipping cloth all over the world, was not realized. Only a few mills were built.

There were several reasons for the failure of industry to develop in the South. For the most part, the South lacked the fast rivers, so abundant in New England, that were necessary for the mills. Second, with their rich lands and long agricultural tradition, southerners were less inclined to turn to other ways of making a living than were New Englanders, whose poor farming prospects had turned them to other employment from the beginning. Growing the cotton was so profitable in the South that it seemed pointless to waste money and energy manufacturing cloth.

Consequently, by 1824, Calhoun joined with most other southerners in opposing a protective tariff. In fact, Calhoun would later sacrifice his chances to be elected president by supporting his state's attempt to nullify a tariff. The one-time nationalist changed as Daniel Webster had. Section was becoming more important than nation.

3. WINNING THE WEST

When most people think about the West, they think of the wide-open spaces of Montana, Wyoming, Colorado, and west Texas. They think of Indians hunting bison and living in tepees, and of cowboys moving gigantic herds of cattle. They think of a prospector wading in a frigid stream, trying to find a nugget of gold among the pebbles and sand in his shallow pan.

These are the images of the West because they represent the last part of the United States to be settled or "tamed." These images are the West that writers, film-makers, and television shows have fixed in people's imaginations.

But in the early nineteenth century, the West was the forested country beginning at the Appalachian Ridge and running perhaps 100 miles (160 kilometers) west of the Mississippi River. To many Americans who lived during the early nineteenth century, that was the frontier, the zone where civilization was taking root and wilderness was disappearing.

A few adventurers traveled much farther. Following the trails blazed by Lewis and Clark, Pike, and others, fur trappers—*mountain men*—penetrated the Rockies as early as 1815. During the 1820s, Missouri merchants began to trade with the Mexicans in Santa Fe, and a New England family opened the Mexican state of Texas to cotton cultivation and cattle raising by Americans.

But the American West has been as much an idea as a particular place or region. To Americans,

Class Activity: Have the class brainstorm to come up with attributes that would exemplify the average American today. By consensus, have the class remove attributes they can't agree upon. See how this idealized version of today's Americans compares to the average Americans of the early 1800s.

During the 1840s, thousands of settlers followed the Oregon Trail (above) in search of fertile western lands. The trip west covered 2,000 miles and took four to six months.

the West has meant opportunity, the place where people who could not get ahead in the settled areas could go to make a good living and where people with a little money could get rich. The story of American expansion was the story of constant settlement of new country, as older frontier sections became settled. The West was always somewhere still farther ahead.

People on the Move.

To Europeans, Americans were a people who never put down roots. The young couple who said their marriage vows and promptly climbed atop a wagon was a common sight in New England. "Come all ye Yankee farmers, who wish to change your lot," a popular song went, "And leave behind the village where Pa and Ma do stay. . . ."

Virginians headed across the mountains in greater numbers than any other group. A wagon road across Pennsylvania was so popular that the economy of the towns along the way was geared to supplying the needs of emigrants. The people of the Conestoga Valley in Pennsylvania specialized in building the high-wheeled wagons that could traverse deep-rutted roads or even no roads at all. They gave the name of their valley to the *Conestoga wagon*.

Europeans, geared to a life in which people were born, lived, and died in the same place, were amazed by the ease with which Americans moved from one home to another. Alexis de Tocqueville (tōk'vĭl), a famous French observer of American ways, wrote that "in the United States a man builds a house in which to spend his old age, and he sells it before the roof is on."

Tom Lincoln, the father of Abraham Lincoln, moved several times. In 1782 he left his native Virginia for Kentucky. There Abraham was born. Soon the Lincolns moved to Indiana and, four years later, to Illinois. Other pioneers moved even more often. Americans joked that their chickens crossed their legs in spring so they could be tied up for the next trip west.

Cities on the Frontier.

Most areas of the West were opened by families in buckskin who wrested a subsistence farm from the forest wilderness with muscle, sweat, courage, and tears. In other places, however, cities were founded before farms. Soldiers stationed in isolated forts to guard against Indian attack had to be fed, clothed, and entertained, so shopkeepers clustered around the log stockades. The security of a fort attracted trappers and hunters and other individuals who wandered

In this painting, the Yellowstone *steams down the Mississippi River at St. Louis, Missouri. By the early 1800s, St. Louis was a thriving starting point for westward-bound settlers.*

the forest. Indians came to trade. Soon the town around the fort was larger than the fort itself. Only then did farmers arrive to take advantage of the ready-made market. An example of how a frontier was opened this way is southeastern Michigan. The military installation at Detroit, taken over from the French, had a long history as a trading center before the farmers settled the region.

Along western rivers, townspeople often preceded farmers in opening the West. Cincinnati, Ohio; Louisville and Lexington, Kentucky; and Nashville, Tennessee, were small cities before agriculture developed fully in the surrounding forests. They were built at good locations for keelboats and rafts to tie up and became jumping off points and supply stations for emigrants headed into the wilderness.

When the cotton boom in Alabama and Mississippi created a demand for cheap foodstuffs, river cities like Cincinnati became processing centers where hogs were slaughtered and the pork salted and packed to be floated down the Ohio and the Mississippi rivers. Cincinnati was famous as the "Queen City of the West," a bustling trade center. Just ten miles farther into the interior of Ohio, the hardwood forest was so dense that sunlight could barely reach the earth.

The Industrial Revolution reached parts of the West before it reached much of Europe. Steam engines were manufactured in Pittsburgh and Lexington by 1815. In Kentucky that same year, six steam mills turned out cloth and paper. Before the War of 1812, St. Louis had a steam mill that was six stories high. In Cincinnati there was a mill nine stories high.

Research Assignment: Have students do a research assignment on the history of one of the western cities referred to in this chapter. They should include the facts surrounding its origins, its early industry, and major routes leading to the city (where these went and why they were important). If applicable, use a city in your area.

Speculating in Land. The rapid settlement of the West led to heated and sometimes frantic land speculation. Many people who went to Ohio, Michigan, and Alabama did not plan to farm, open a shop, or invest in a meat-packing plant. They were the *speculators,* people who brought some money with them to the frontier. They hoped to get rich quickly by buying land when prices were low because few wanted it, and selling it at a profit when settlers arrived.

Except for a few old French grants in the Louisiana Purchase, all western land was owned by the government. Under a law of 1785, purchasers had to pay a minimum of $1 an acre for at least 640 acres (259 hectares). Farmers protested that 640 acres was more than a family could possibly farm, and $640 was much more cash than an ordinary farm family could raise.

The Federalists ignored the protests. Their land policy favored land speculators, and they were quite content to let people with money buy at $1 an acre, divide their holdings into smaller farms, and sell those plots at $2 or $3 an acre.

The Jeffersonians, who favored farmers over speculators, disagreed with this policy. In 1804, a Republican Congress reduced the minimum size of the tract to 160 acres (64 hectares). The minimum price was set at $1.64 an acre, or $262

for the whole tract. However, a buyer could make a down payment of as little as $80 and pay the balance of $182 over four years.

This reform did not shut out speculators as it was intended to do. On the contrary, the credit provision of the law actually encouraged speculation. By applying all their money to down payments, speculators could lay a claim to much more land than was possible under the cash-only rule. Of course, they did not intend to farm the land. They gambled that buyers would come along before the payments were due. They would make a profit, and the new buyers would assume responsibility to pay off the government.

Often, buyers did come along. In 1815, the government sold 1 million acres. In 1819, land sales totaled 5 million acres. Many speculators made extraordinary profits. Some land in the cotton belt of Alabama and Mississippi, purchased from the government for as little as $2 an acre, was sold to planters for as much as $100 an acre.

Western banks fueled the speculation by making loans to any speculator or planter who was willing to go into debt in order to pay the inflated prices. These banks were called *wildcat banks* because of their irresponsible lending policies. The wildcat bankers gambled that the price of western lands would continue to rise.

Bales of cotton at Memphis Landing, Tennessee, wait to be loaded onto steamboats. Memphis grew rapidly as a river port, railroad depot, and wagon train departure point.

Class Activity: Have students provide you with the chronological events needed to make a cause-and-effect.flow chart of the events leading to the Panic of 1819. If possible, have students do research to provide details to add to those given in the book.

The Panic of 1819.

Of course, prices could not continue to rise indefinitely. In every speculation, whether in land, stocks, or gold, there comes a moment when there are no more buyers because everyone believes that prices are too high and can only fall. That moment came in 1819.

Speculators stuck with large tracts of land had no cash with which to pay the government or the wildcat banks. Rather than lose all their land by failing to pay, they offered some for sale at a lower price. Once prices started to drop, they crashed as speculators threw their land on the market.

The Bank of the United States, which had provided money to the wildcat banks, panicked. The directors of the Bank told the wildcat banks to pay the money they owed the Federal bank. In order to do this, the wildcat banks ordered speculators and farmers to pay off their debts. The whole tangled network of credit purchases came tumbling down. No one had the money to repay these loans. Much of the land the federal government believed had been sold reverted to government ownership. Wildcat banks closed by the dozen, and depositors lost all their money.

Thomas Hart Benton.

Stunned by the Panic of 1819, Congress tried to discourage speculation by giving the actual farmer an advantage at government land sales. A law adopted in 1820 abolished credit purchases of government land, reduced the minimum tract to 80 acres (32 hectares), and set the minimum price per acre at $1.25.

More important for future land policy, Thomas Hart Benton was elected to the Senate from the new state of Missouri. Benton was short-tempered and quick-witted. He hated paper money and banks, which, he believed, were the chief causes of land speculation that ruined frontier farmers. Shortly after entering the Senate he began his campaign to shut speculators out of the West and encourage settlers. He became the West's leading spokesman for a pro-settler land policy.

One of Benton's pet projects was the principle of *pre-emption* or, as frontier farmers called it, "squatter's rights." Under this principle, a person who settled government land and improved it prior to the official sale of the land would be allowed to purchase it at the minimum price rather than bidding for it against others.

Another Benton program was *graduation*. Land that remained unsold after an auction would be offered for sale at half the government minimum. If it was still unsold, it would be offered at a fourth of the minimum. In other words, the price of land would be graduated downward in order to make it available to poorer farmers. In fact, several years after Benton's death in 1858, the federal government began to offer land free to settlers.

Thomas Hart Benton introduced policies meant to keep speculators from buying western farmland.

SECTION REVIEW

1. Write a sentence to identify: Conestoga wagon, Alexis de Tocqueville, squatter's rights, Thomas Hart Benton.

2. Give the location of "the West" as United States pioneers perceived it in the early nineteenth century.

3. Name five cities founded on the frontier in the early 1800s.

4. Explain how each of the following contributed to the Panic of 1819: land speculators, wildcat banks, the Bank of the United States. Describe two ways in which Thomas Hart Benton tried to keep western lands out of the hands of speculators.

Discussion Question: How did U.S. experiences in foreign affairs affect or prompt the Industrial Revolution in this country? Answers should relate foreign disdain for the U.S., events leading to the Embargo Act, the Non-intercourse Act, and the War of 1812 to already existing desires for

4. TYING THE NATION TOGETHER

In many ways, Thomas Hart Benton's West was tied more closely to the South than to the Northeast. Much of the land beyond the Appalachians had been settled by southerners, especially Virginians. Like the people of the South, most westerners were farmers. In the southwestern states of Tennessee, Alabama, and Mississippi, cotton was the cash crop. In Louisiana, sugar cane competed with cotton for the top spot, but it too was raised by slaves. A common interest in the institution of slavery bound much of the West to the South.

Ohio, Indiana, and Illinois, the states of the Old Northwest where slavery was prohibited, were settled by New Englanders as well as by southerners. Those states produced foodstuffs and lumber with free men and women working on small farms. Nevertheless, they were closely tied to the South by the dictates of geography. The Appalachians isolated the northwestern states from the Northeast. Farmers could no more ship their corn, wheat, hogs, and logs directly to the east than could the Pennsylvanians who started the Whiskey Rebellion in 1794. They depended on the Mississippi River to float their products to southern markets or to New Orleans where they went by sea to the West Indies or to Europe.

Solving the Problem of Isolation.
Isolation —the difficulty of transportation—was the westerners' chief economic problem. Indeed, the difficulty of overland transportation was a national problem. The United States was notorious for bad roads, even in parts of the country that had been settled for 200 years.

With a fairly good water transportation system in use, the southern states built few roads. Between Boston and New York City, the Old Post Road allowed year-round travel. In other heavily populated areas, private investors built *turnpikes*. These roads were so named because entrance to them was blocked by a pike, a long spear-like weapon. When a customer paid the toll required to use the road, the pike was turned aside.

By 1811, about 1,400 miles of toll roads were in operation. By 1820, there were about 4,000 miles of graded and paved roads in the United States, mostly in the Northeast. They were surfaced in crushed rock, parallel wooden planks, or in *macadam*, a blacktop paving invented in England. The cheapest surface was the *corduroy* road, which was made by laying down logs. It also provided the bumpiest ride.

Turnpike companies would not build roads in the West because there were not enough people to make such projects profitable. With small populations, and therefore a small tax base, the western state governments could not afford the many improvements they needed. The western states were caught in a vicious circle. They needed good roads if they were to attract people. Yet they did not have enough people to finance the construction of good roads.

Henry Clay and Internal Improvements.
The solution seemed to lie in the national treasury. Only the federal government could afford the huge outlay of money necessary to build roads and finance other internal improvements such as dredging river channels and maintaining river ports. The man who became the West's voice in Washington in this matter was the Kentuckian Henry Clay. Clay had been a War Hawk in 1812, a member of the commission that signed the Treaty of Ghent, and one of the four presidential candidates in 1824.

Clay was called "Handsome Harry of the West." He had been born in Virginia, moved to Kentucky as a young man, and prospered as a planter and a land speculator. He liked to have a good time. He was charming with women and admired by western men for his willingness to fight a duel. Like Webster and Calhoun, he was an excellent orator.

Clay's first success in persuading Congress to pay for internal improvements was the *National Road*. Costing $13,000 a mile to build, the road connected Cumberland, Maryland, on the Potomac River, with Wheeling, in present-day West Virginia, on the Ohio River. Clay then worked to have the National Road extended. Eventually it reached Vandalia, Illinois, where another highway connected it with St. Louis.

Not all of Clay's proposals were successful. While most western congressmen supported him, some southerners opposed federally financed internal improvements because of the traditional Jeffersonian belief that government should be

neutrality and isolationism. These events also created a need to find new sources of manufactured goods as well as a new market for selling the raw products still being produced.

253

CANALS, ROADS, AND WESTERN TRAILS, 1850

Canals
Roads
Western trails

CANALS

economical. Some New Englanders opposed Clay because they had already built their roads. They would not share directly in the benefits of his internal improvements bills, and some factory owners feared that if the roads to the West were too good, their workers would leave, thus driving up wages at home. Clay's problem was to devise an economic program that would provide something for all three sections.

The American System. To his fellow westerners, Clay offered federally financed internal im-

provements and the sale of government land at reasonable prices. To northeasterners, Clay argued that a populous West would provide a huge market for their manufactured goods. Also, if there were good roads, food prices would drop and mill workers would not need high wages.

Clay's *American System,* so named because he believed it would tie the sections together in a national economy, also included a high tariff to protect northeastern industries against English competition. Clay overcame westerners' hostility to the promise of higher prices for manufactured goods by arguing that flourishing industrial cities in the Northeast would provide a huge market for western agricultural products.

But what did the *American System* offer the South? Clay said that southerners would benefit because northeastern mills would buy their cotton and western farms would supply their food needs. Capping the nationalistic program would be the Second Bank of the United States, which would maintain a sound financial structure.

This argument did not sway Southerners. The American System did not offer southern cotton planters anything they did not already have—except higher prices for manufactured goods and higher taxes to pay for internal improvements. English mills were willing to buy every bale of cotton the South produced. Southerners saw no need to subsidize New England mills through a protective tariff. The Ohio, Indiana, and Illinois farmers already supplied southern plantations with food via the Mississippi River system. Southern leaders saw no benefit to connecting the West with the Northeast.

The Erie Canal. As it turned out, the West was first joined to the Northeast not by a federally financed project but by one built by New York State. In 1817, prodded by Governor DeWitt Clinton, the New York legislature voted funds to connect the Hudson River at Albany with the Great Lakes at Buffalo.

With picks, shovels, mules, and wagons to haul the dirt, gangs of muscular laborers, many of them recent Irish immigrants, dug a ditch four feet (1.2 meters) deep, 40 feet (12 meters) wide, and 364 miles (584 kilometers) long. The Erie Canal was later enlarged to seven feet (2.1 meters) deep and 70 feet (21 meters) wide.

It was expensive, $8.4 million, or more than $23,000 a mile. But when the Erie Canal was finished in 1825, it opened up the entire Northwest to New York's merchants. It cost only $12 a ton—one-seventh of the overland cost—to move factory goods west or farm products east on the canal. Thanks to the Erie Canal, New York City quickly outstripped Philadelphia and Boston as the nation's leading commercial center.

The Erie Canal, 364 miles long and originally four feet deep, took eight years to complete. It was a major connection between the East Coast and the frontier.

Ten of the Erie Canal's 83 locks are shown above. The great gates of a lock made it watertight. By filling or emptying a lock with water, boats could be raised or lowered safely.

Canals Boom and Bust. Before the Erie Canal was dug, there were only about 100 miles of canal in the United States. The longest canal ran 27 miles. After the Erie Canal was completed, others frantically imitated the Erie's example. Two systems, the Ohio and Erie out of Cleveland and the Wabash and Erie out of Toledo, eventually made money.

More common, however, was the experience of the poorly advised Mainline Canal in Pennsylvania. Designed to join Philadelphia with Pittsburgh, the Mainline was actually shorter than the Erie. However, where the Erie ran over a route that reached only 650 feet (195 meters) above sea level, requiring only 83 *locks* to control the muddy water, the Mainline route rose up to 2,200 feet (660 meters), and required 174 locks. Even then, at several points the clumsy canal boats had to be hauled out of the water and over ridges on huge inclined planes. Amazingly, the Mainline Canal was actually completed, but it almost bankrupted Pennsylvania in the process.

Even the best canals could not be used during the winter months, when they froze solid. Not until 1829, when railroads began to stretch out from the cities, would Americans find an all-season way to connect the West to the Northeast. In the meantime, another revolution in transportation made the Mississippi-Missouri-Ohio River system even more important.

Steamboats. An American, John Fitch, built the first practical steamboat in 1787. He ran his 45-foot vessel up and down the Delaware River, but he could not make a profit from his invention. Fitch was a demanding, difficult man and no investors were willing to back him. Moreover, American merchants looked to the sea rather than the inland waterways. It was difficult to imagine how a steamboat, with its heavy burden of fuel, could compete with a sleek sailing ship that traveled on the wind, its entire hull free to hold cargo.

The merchants were right, of course. Not until the second half of the nineteenth century would steamboats challenge sailing ships on the ocean. Even into the twentieth century, some shipping companies continued to prefer wind-powered vessels.

But rivers were another matter. Sailing ships had difficulty navigating up rivers. Rivers were too

Although Robert Fulton is credited with the invention of the first practical steamboat, he had a predecessor. George Washington saw James Ramsey cruise his steam-powered motorboat on the Potomac River in 1784.

Three great rivers—the Mississippi, the Missouri, and the Illinois—meet at St. Louis, Missouri. Even by 1840, the city's harbor was a busy place.

narrow for tacking into the wind, and high river-banks stole the wind from the sails. When conditions were poor, an oceangoing sailing ship had to be rowed against the current or pulled upstream with cables and winches.

Inventor Robert Fulton understood that the steamboat's future was on the rivers, and in 1807, his *Clermont* wheezed and chugged up the Hudson River from New York to Albany at five miles per hour. The *Clermont* was three times as long as Fitch's boat. But the dimension that mattered most was the mere seven feet (2.1 meters) of water the *Clermont* needed in order to float.

Old Man River. This made the flat-bottomed steamboat ideal for the Mississippi and Missouri rivers, where shifting sandbars could turn a clear channel into an obstacle overnight. In 1817, 17 steamboats splashed up and down the "Father of Waters." By 1830, 230 paddle-wheelers were engaged in a busy river commerce.

Designers competed to build the fastest boats —speed sold tickets—and also to reduce the depth of water a boat needed to sail. The shallower the water a steamboat could navigate in, the more

river ports it could visit. In 1841, the *Orphan Boy,* carrying 40 tons of freight plus passengers, skimmed through water only two feet deep. That was the record.

SECTION REVIEW

1. Write a sentence to identify: turnpikes, National Road, DeWitt Clinton, Mainline Canal.

2. For what two reasons were westerners tied more closely to the South than to the Northeast?

3. Why was Henry Clay's American System opposed by southerners?

4. What bodies of water did the Erie Canal connect? Of what value was the canal to New York's merchants?

5. Explain why Robert Fulton's steamboat was ideal for the Mississippi and Missouri rivers. What conclusions can you draw about steamboats by considering the increase in their numbers between 1817 and 1830?

Cyrus McCormick's reaper could harvest grain four times as fast as a person using a cradle and scythe. Mechanical reapers quickly revolutionized agriculture throughout the world.

As early as 1842, Crawford Long, an American physician, performed surgery after using ether to make his patient unconscious. But he did not make his discovery known. Credit for the discovery of using ether as an anesthesia went to William Morton, a dentist, who first demonstrated its use at Massachusetts General Hospital in 1846.

C H A N G I N G   T E C H N O L O G Y

18 10

18 20

Food canning introduced
Parachute demonstrated
Diving suit developed
(See also p. 209.)

Engine lathes introduced
Carbon arc light designed
Mowing machine developed
Locomotive produced
(See also p. 209.)

Hot-air engine patented
Miner's safety lamp produced
Milling machine developed
Tin can patented
Hydraulic press constructed

Class Activity: Using a large topographical map, identify areas where different inventions took place and discuss how the environment helped to spawn their creation. (Have students provide the research to create the map.) Possible examples: cotton gin—needed because of the nature

The telegraph was the fastest way to communicate long distance during the nineteenth century. Words were tapped out letter by letter using Morse Code, whose dots and dashes were changed into electrical impulses that then went out over telegraph wires.

The first sewing machine with a foot-operated treadle was patented by Isaac Singer in 1851. Singer improved the sewing machines of the time into more efficient appliances.

Clipper ships with deep, narrow hulls answered the need for speed when trade expanded in the nineteenth century.

18	30	18	40	18	50

Photograph first taken
Steam-railway tunnel built
Water turbine developed
Diving helmet patented
Floodlighting introduced
(See also p. 330.)

Usable rubber developed
Daguerrotype process released
Electric carriage built
(See also p. 330.)

Safety match introduced
Pneumatic tire produced
Safety pin designed
(See also pp. 330 and 432.)

of short seed cotton; steamboat—needed because water travel upriver was difficult; flatboats—had new design for travel in shallow water.

CHAPTER REVIEW

TIME LINE

1780

Fitch builds first practical steamboat (1787)

1790

Patent Act (1790)

Whitney invents cotton gin (1793)

Slater's factory opens (1793)

1800

Whitney demonstrates interchangeable parts (1800)

Land Act (1804)

Fulton's *Clermont* steams from New York to Albany (1807)

1810

Second Bank of the United States founded (1816)

Tariff of 1816

Panic of 1819

1820

Credit abolished in purchase of public land (1820)

Tariff of 1824

Erie Canal built (1817–1825)

1830

TIME LINE QUESTIONS

1. List the following events in order: invention of the cotton gin, voyage of the *Clermont*, inter-changeable parts demonstrated, Fitch builds the steamboat.
2. How many years did it take to build the Erie Canal?
3. How long after Slater's mill opened was the Erie Canal finished?

SKILLS STRATEGY

1. Speculation in government lands in the West must be stopped! Although land prices continue to rise, experience has proven that eventually they must fall. History has shown what will happen at that moment: The speculators will then be unable to pay the banks which loaned them money to buy the land. Because of a lack of funds, banks will have to close their doors, and their many hard-working depositors will lose their life savings. Government leaders should take steps to avoid this train of events before it is too late.

2. Speculation in government lands in the West must be stopped! Every speculator is little more than a greedy, profit-grabbing thief and should be brought to immediate and severe justice. What's more, all land speculators are in cahoots with bankers, the biggest thieves of all. Government leaders, how long will you let this crime against the people continue?

JUDGING OPINIONS

In the study of American history, one often finds opinions stated in *primary sources* (newspapers or books from a certain historical period) and *secondary sources* (textbooks). The writers are trying to convince readers to agree with their opinions. It is important to be able to distinguish opinions from facts. Your judgment of the validity of an author's opinions will often decide what you think of the author's writing.

A *statement of fact* expresses a truth that can be proved. A *statement of opinion* gives a person's idea or feeling and it cannot be proved, although it may or may not be true. A statement of opinion often contains qualifying words, such as *I believe, probably, perhaps, seems to be, may or might, could,* and *ought.*

Sometimes an opinion is, or contains, a genera-lization that cannot be proved. Many generaliza-tions can be recognized by the qualifying words they contain. These words will often make the statement include every related incident, instead of speaking about specifics. Some examples are the following sentences: *Every* right thinking

Making Connections: Review the questions and topics presented in the Making Connections section opening this chapter. Pay special attention to describing how the Industrial Revolution contributed to changing the way of life for Americans and how this, in turn, affected political,

The steamboat may be the ideal means of transporting people and goods on the Mississippi and Missouri rivers.

* * *

The people who settled cities in some part of the West should receive more credit for their pioneering efforts than farmers.

* * *

Europeans were, perhaps, somewhat justified in their belief that all Americans were people who never put down roots.

* * *

American knows that slavery is no longer honorable. *No* American Indians know how to use land wisely. The Yankees are *all* ingenious people. Robert Fulton's steamboat was the *finest* and *most creative* invention *in the history of the world*.

To judge whether an author's opinion is valid, and whether to accept it or not, analyze the information given to support the opinion. Does the information warrant your agreement? Careful authors will support their opinions with facts, and support strong opinions with facts, reasons, and examples.

APPLYING SKILLS

Refer to the exhibits above before answering the following questions.

1. Which opinion paragraph on the preceding page would you judge valid and acceptable? Explain your answer.
2. Which opinion paragraph would you judge to be unacceptable? Why?
3. Complete the paragraphs in the above exhibit by listing factual information from the chapter to validate the opinions given.

CHAPTER 10 TEST

TEXT REVIEW

1. Contrast the positions of Thomas Jefferson and Alexander Hamilton on the possible effects of the Industrial Revolution.
2. Briefly describe the contributions of three of the following to the Industrial Revolution in the United States: Samuel Slater, Eli Whitney, state banks, Francis Lowell, Daniel Webster.
3. Explain how the American Colonization Society contributed to the decline of slavery. What other factors contributed to this decline?
4. Why might southern cotton planters be more interested in reviving slavery than in building southern industry?
5. Give three facts the author uses to support this statement: "To Europeans, Americans were a people who never put down roots."
6. Discuss why average settlers were unable to buy western land, and why speculators were able to buy so much land.
7. Describe actions taken by the following people that helped tie the nation together: Henry Clay, DeWitt Clinton, Robert Fulton.

CRITICAL THINKING

8. Summarize the reasons for the failure of industry to develop in the South.
9. For which region was a high tariff most favorable? Explain your answer.
10. In what sense could it be said that Eli Whitney's cotton gin created a far more serious problem than it solved?

WRITING A PARAGRAPH

Henry Clay had to convince people in three different regions of the country that his American System would benefit them. Put yourself in his place, and write a persuasive paragraph to the people of one of the three regions. The topic sentence should state the position you are trying to persuade the people to accept. The supporting sentences should give sound reasons. Anticipate some of the objections the people might have, and answer them in the supporting sentences.

social, and economic development in this country. Discuss the emergence of a new national character in this period.

CHAPTER 11

THE AGE OF THE COMMON PERSON

1824–1844

Their plots were America's first subdivisions called home-steads. . . . EDWARD DORN

Making Connections. Andrew Jackson was the first president to have been born in a log cabin. To his supporters, he represented the common people. His enemies, however, portrayed him as an arrogant tyrant—"King Andrew I." Either way, his administration was a turning point in American history.

In this chapter, you will learn:

- Why the number of voters casting ballots rose sharply between 1824 and 1840
- Who argued that states could nullify a federal law
- How the wife of a cabinet member caused a crisis in Jackson's administration
- Why Jackson's attempt to close the Bank of the United States caused the failure of many state banks.
- How John Tyler became president, and why his party deserted him

You know that Jackson was not elected president in 1824 even though he received the most popular votes. For the next four years, he built political alliances, and he easily won the 1828 election. As you read, note how Jackson changed the federal government and helped make the nation more democratic.

Sections
1. Growth of Democracy
2. The Jackson Presidency
3. Jackson, Calhoun, and Van Buren
4. The Rise of the Whigs

1. GROWTH OF DEMOCRACY

A dark cloud hovered over the presidency of John Quincy Adams. He was haunted by the charge that he won the White House only because he made a "corrupt bargain" with Henry Clay. The supporters of the defeated Andrew Jackson never let Adams forget that fewer people voted for him in 1824 than for their own hero. Jackson was silent but busy. As he waited for the presidential election of 1828, he invited a steady stream of powerful politicians to visit him in his Tennessee mansion and make plans.

In 1828, the Jackson forces buried Adams in a landslide vote. The hero of New Orleans was president, and the Age of the Common Person was under way. By the end of Jackson's first term, most states had changed their laws so that all adult white males could vote. Election campaigns, dignified and quiet as recently as 1820, were now marked by parades, parties, stump speeches, and noisy torchlight rallies.

Jackson's new *Democratic party* was supreme as long as "The General" was president. Jackson's reputation as an ordinary person who distinguished himself through hard work never faded. He became even more popular because of policies he said favored the "common person" over the "rich and powerful" and a strong, democratic, central government over state governments controlled by small groups of selfish aristocrats.

Citizen participation in the election process increased dramatically in the 1820s and 1830s. The painting at the right shows a county election.

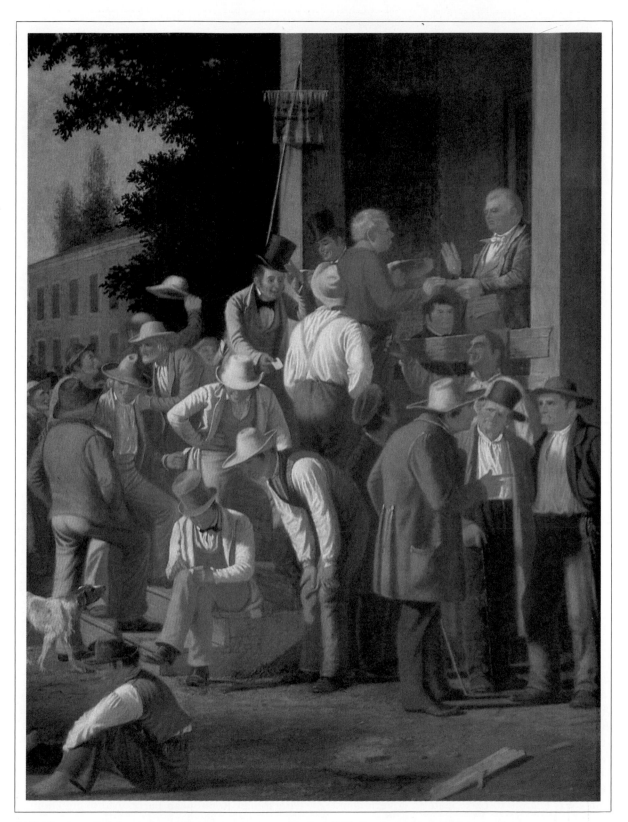

Skills Review: Reinforce the skills learned in the preceding Skills Strategy section. Using various passages from the text and ideas presented in the Annotations, have students further develop their critical ability to judge the validity of opinions of various people mentioned.

263

The political cartoon above shows John Quincy Adams and Andrew Jackson in a race for the White House (below). Jackson won easily in 1828, making up for his bitter defeat by Adams in 1824.

John Quincy Adams. In an age when politicians with magnetic, *charismatic* personalities were most popular—leaders like Jackson, Clay, Calhoun, and Webster—John Quincy Adams's personality was cool and unexciting. He was a private man, aloof from the crowd, at his best working quietly in private.

During a time when ordinary Americans liked their leaders to claim that they too were ordinary, Adams took pride in his distinguished ancestry, his superior intelligence and education, and his record of accomplishment. He thought that as a member of America's talented "natural aristocracy," he deserved to be president. Although he was the same age as Andrew Jackson (they were both born in 1767), Adams was out of date in the Age of Jackson.

The Upsurge of Democracy. In 1824, about half the states still insisted that in order to vote a person had to own some property. By 1830, only three states had that requirement. In 1824, a quarter of the states still chose presidential electors in the state legislatures. By 1832, only South Carolina still used this system. By the end of the 1820s, nearly every adult white male in the United States was eligible to participate in government.

Not only could they vote, but they did, in increasing numbers. In 1824, the first election in which there was widespread participation, only one-fourth of the nation's eligible voters voted. In 1828, half the eligible voters cast ballots. By 1840, three-quarters of the voters actually voted, a much higher proportion than today.

What caused this upsurge in democratic feeling? One reason was the long dominance of the Jeffersonian Republican party. Although Thomas

Jefferson agreed with John Quincy Adams that only talented people should be elected to office, he also believed that the "common person" should participate in elections. After 25 years of hearing this message, Americans demanded that their election laws put it into practice.

The growth of the West also promoted democratic reforms. Partly because the West was settled largely by people who were not members of privileged classes, and partly as a way of attracting more emigrants, the western states generally opened the polls to all white adult males. Eastern states, fearing the loss of population to the West, countered by reforming their own election laws.

The "Workies."

In New York and other eastern cities, new voters among the mechanics, as skilled craftspeople were known, organized *Workingpeople's parties* that pushed for additional democratic reforms. Inspired by Kentucky, which was the first state to abolish debtors' prisons in 1821, the "Workies" called on their own state governments to do likewise.

Mechanics lived in fear of imprisonment for debt. They often had to borrow money in order to buy tools and practice their crafts. If they were unable to repay these loans on time, their creditors (those who loaned them money) could have them jailed until the debt was paid. Of course, once in prison, the debtor could not earn money to get out of debt. Hence, unless someone loaned or gave the debtor money, there was no reason to hope for release.

Another Workie reform was the *mechanic's lien law*. This provided that an artisan's tools could not be seized by creditors. The Workingpeople's parties also called for free public education for all children.

The most effective leader of the Workies was Scotland-born Frances Wright. At a time when women were rarely seen and heard in public. she was an exciting and unapologetic platform speaker, a great favorite of New York mechanics who knew her by her nickname, "Fanny." Frances Wright also attacked the institution of marriage, claiming that it meant slavery for women. Because of this stance, she lost a great deal of support.

The Anti-Masonic Party.

Another political movement that reflected the surge of democratic

Frances "Fanny" Wright was a dynamic speaker who campaigned for the Workingpeople's parties.

feeling in the 1820s was the *Anti-Masonic Party*. This organization was founded in 1826 after the mysterious disappearance of William Morgan, a former member of the *Masonic Order*, a men's fraternal lodge. It was believed that Morgan was writing a book that would reveal the secret rituals of the Masons—secret handshakes by which Masons recognized one another and similar signals. Many people believed that Masons had murdered Morgan for this reason.

The Anti-Masons claimed that the secret organization, most of whose members were affluent business people, was much more than a social club. The Masonic Order was a conspiracy of the rich to keep the common person from improving himself or herself. Masons discriminated against non-Masons in business, in hiring, and in politics. The chief aim of the Anti-Masons was to outlaw all secret organizations. Their party also called for other reforms aimed at providing equal opportunity for the common person.

For a time, the Anti-Masonic Party was very powerful in New York and other northeastern states. Young politicians who would become very powerful in future years were members. Among them were future president Millard Fillmore and future senator and Secretary of State William Seward, both of New York.

Discussion Question: How was Jackson's Democratic Republican party similar to today's Democratic party? Answers should include these items: both liked to think of themselves as more closely tied to the common man, and both were a conglomeration of separate factions.

Because Andrew Jackson was a member of the Masonic Order, the Anti-Masons opposed him. But it was Jackson's Democratic party that benefited most from the democratic spirit of the 1820s.

2. THE JACKSON PRESIDENCY

In the 1820s, presidential candidates did not take an active part in political campaigns. The very idea of asking people to vote for him would have disgusted John Quincy Adams. The President even refused to reward political leaders who supported him by favoring them over opponents for appointments to political office. Officially, he ran as the *National Republican* candidate in 1828.

Andrew Jackson did not ask for votes either. He made no speeches during the campaign of 1828. However, throughout the four years of the Adams presidency, Jackson had quietly formed alliances with political leaders in the Northeast and South. Jackson believed that his popularity in the West was great enough that he would sweep that section. In order to win in the South, he agreed to take Vice President John C. Calhoun as his own vice presidential candidate.

To be sure of victory, Jackson needed to win at least one of the large Middle Atlantic states. The man who stepped forward with a promise to deliver New York was the shrewdest politician of

the era, Martin Van Buren. Van Buren believed that a party built a majority by offering local politicians rewards in return for their support. The party Van Buren built around Andrew Jackson in this way was known as the *Democratic Republicans*, later shortened to the Democratic party.

The Campaign of 1828. Both sides *slung mud* at one another in 1828. Democratic stump speakers claimed that Adams was an elitist, a snob, that he preferred fancy British manners to honest, forthright American ways. They said he was given to gambling and was personally immoral.

Adams's supporters replied that Jackson was a murderer. They published a poster listing the names of the men Jackson had killed in duels or sentenced to death when he was a commanding general.

The attack that bothered Jackson most was the

Andrew Jackson was viewed as a hero and a reformer by the majority of voters in 1829.

Discussion Question: Based on what you've read so far in this chapter and also based on what is written about Jackson on page 234 of this text, what qualifications did Jackson have to hold the office of president? Answers should indicate that he had few qualities that set him apart from other possible choices, except for popularity.

PROFILES OF THE PRESIDENCY

Andrew Jackson was proud of his military record, and bristled when others used it against him:

He who fights, and fights successfully, must . . . be held up as a "military chieftain." Even Washington, could he again appear among us, might be so considered, because he dared to be a virtuous and successful soldier, a correct man, and an honest statesman. . . . I became a soldier for the good of my country. Difficulties met me at every step, but I thank God it was my good fortune to surmount them. The war over, the peace restored, I retired to my farm to private life, where, but for the call I received to the Senate of the Union, I should have contentedly remained. I have never . . . been willing to hold any post longer than I could be useful to my country, not myself; and I trust I never shall. If these things make me one, I am a "military chieftain."

—LETTER TO SAMUAL SWARTOUT, FEBRUARY 22, 1825

accusation that he had married Rachel Jackson before her divorce from a previous husband was final. Jackson loved and respected his wife. When she died shortly before he assumed the presidency, he blamed her death on the National Republicans and their *smear campaign.*

Jacksonian Democracy. As expected, Jackson was elected easily with 178 electoral votes to Adams's 83. And on Inauguration Day, 1829, the worst dreams of those who feared the new democracy seemed to come true.

Ten thousand people, many of them boisterous westerners, crowded the streets of Washington. Invited into the White House by the new president, Jackson's supporters muddied expensive carpets, broke crystal glasses, and stood on elegant chairs and couches in the hope of catching a glimpse of their hero.

The crowd was so unruly that the new president, "Old Hickory," was nearly trampled. He had to escape through a window and spend his first night as president in a hotel. The mob was persuaded to leave only when punchbowls were set up on the White House lawn.

The man the crowd idolized was by no means a common person. On the contrary, Andrew Jackson was the richest man in Tennessee, the owner of thousands of acres and 150 slaves. However, Jackson's origins were quite common. He was the first president to have been born in a log cabin, the symbol of hard frontier life. Even as president he was just as comfortable swapping tales with rough backwoods people as making small talk with European ambassadors. Jackson took pride in the fact that he had earned every cent he owned.

The key to Jacksonian Democracy was Jackson's belief that every American should have the opportunity to do what he had done. He believed that the government's job was not to punish or to penalize successful people, but to make sure everyone had an equal opportunity to succeed.

Women in the Age of Jackson. Equal opportunity to Jackson and to most of the voters in America during that era meant equal opportunity for free white adult males. Women, black people, and all Indians did not have a right to participate in public life, either business or politics.

The people of Jackson's era, including many women, believed that women had an essentially different role in society than men. Men's place was in public life. Women's place was in the home.

This did not mean that a woman's role was inferior. On the contrary, the Jacksonians, none more than Andrew Jackson himself, believed that women were more moral, gentle, and cultured than men. It was believed that by preserving the home as a refuge of morality, women prevented men from lapsing into savagery.

Thousands of Cherokee men, women, and children died during their forced relocation to Oklahoma in the winter of 1838. The journey was called the "Trail of Tears."

Jacksonian Democracy and Race. The Jacksonian principle of equality of opportunity did not apply to black people or to Indian people. Jackson was himself a slaveowner. He believed that black people were inferior to white people. Therefore, he believed white people were justified in holding black people as slaves. Indeed, some white slaveowners believed they did their slaves a favor by protecting them from the need to compete, in return for their labor. Northerners and the large majority of white southerners owned no slaves. Nevertheless, the belief that it was both right and just to own black people as slaves was widespread.

Jacksonians looked at Indian people somewhat differently. Westerners like Jackson saw Native Americans as culturally different, and incompatible, rather than inferior. And Indian people were their competitors for ownership of the land. Because few tribes intensively developed the land in the same way that white settlers did, the Jacksonians believed they had a greater right to the land.

President Jackson's belief in this principle led him to defy a ruling of the Supreme Court. However, he was not the simple "Indian hater" that critics like Henry Clay described. Jackson, the old Indian fighter, respected the courage and closeness to nature of his old enemies.

Government by Party. Attitudes are not policies. But President Jackson lost no time in making his policies known. He was the first president who frankly admitted that he represented a single political party. As soon as he took office he made it clear that he would replace National Republicans who held government jobs with his own Democratic party supporters. "To the victor belong the spoils," said a New York Jacksonian, William Marcy. The practice of rewarding political supporters, and thereby strengthening a political party, became known as the *spoils system.*

When critics complained that educated and trained government officials were losing their jobs to uneducated followers of Jackson, Jackson replied that the common man was quite able to perform any government job in a democracy. It was just the kind of statement that was guaranteed to win popular approval in a time of strong democratic feeling.

Discussion Question: What were the merits and drawbacks of the spoils system? Is it useful? Does it, or something like it, exist in government today?

The debate over the spoils system was noisy but brief. For Jackson's opponents, who became known as *Whigs* after 1834, had themselves used government jobs as rewards to faithful party members, with even more enthusiasm than the Jacksonians. In fact, Jackson did not replace all the government workers. Of 20,000 federal jobs when he became president, only about 4,000 were given to Democratic party workers.

The Trail of Tears. With the Indians who lived in the settled parts of the United States,

Jackson was quite ruthless. There was no danger of attack by the Creeks, Choctaws, Chickasaws, and Cherokees of Georgia, Alabama, and Mississippi. Jackson had defeated them in war.

Indeed, the so-called "Civilized Tribes" had made peace with the white people and even with many of their customs. A Cherokee silversmith named Sequoyah (sĭ-kwoi′ə) had invented a way to write the Cherokee language. All of the tribes of what is now the Southeast lived in villages and farmed the land intensively, and some even owned black slaves.

INDIAN REMOVALS, 1828-1842

Land from which Indians were removed

Reservations to which Indians were moved

Extent of settlements to 1830

Discussion Question: Was the Age of Jackson "democratic"? Students should list the topics that are brought up in answering this question in a yes/no list. Jackson represented the common person on many issues but had very undemocratic attitudes toward slavery, women, and the Indians. He came from common stock, but was one of the richest men in Tennessee.

Nevertheless, their white neighbors wanted their land. The Cherokee Nation, however, insisted that the federal and state governments observe the treaty of 1791 that guaranteed them broad powers of self-government in northwestern Georgia. In 1831, Georgia defied the Cherokees by trying and convicting Samuel A. Worcester, a white minister living in Cherokee land, for refusing to take an *oath of allegiance* to the state. Worcester sued, claiming that Georgia had no authority in Cherokee lands.

In 1832, led by Chief Justice John Marshall, the United States Supreme Court ruled that Worcester was correct. Georgia was ordered to release him and recognize that the state had no authority over the Cherokees.

Georgia ignored the court and Jackson refused to enforce the decision. By 1835 the Cherokees too were worn down and agreed to move to Oklahoma. Their tragic 800-mile (1,300-kilometer) trek in 1838 became known as the "Trail of Tears." Neglected and abused by the soldiers that accompanied them, the Cherokees and other southeastern tribes lost thousands of people to disease and starvation.

The Tariff of Abominations.

Andrew Jackson was not particularly interested in the ongoing tariff controversy that pitted protectionists like Henry Clay and most New Englanders against low tariff southerners like his own vice president, John C. Calhoun. However, an extremely high tariff passed in 1828, the year of his election, led to a conflict between federal power and state power that he approached quite differently than he approached the subject of Indian removal.

That is, when the Supreme Court ordered the state of Georgia to observe the federal government's treaty with the Cherokees, Jackson supposedly said, "John Marshall has made his decision. Let him enforce it." He encouraged a state to defy the federal government. However, when South Carolina defied the tariff law of 1828, Jackson threatened to lead an army into the Palmetto State to collect the tax.

The *Tariff of Abominations*, as southern planters called the 1828 tariff, put a tax as high as 50 percent on manufactured goods imported from Europe. This meant that American manufacturers would have no foreign competition.

Many southerners were infuriated. With few factories of their own, they had to buy manufactured goods either from England or the northern states. Cotton growers were hit especially hard because they had to feed and clothe their large slave labor forces.

In the opinion of many southerners, the Tariff of Abominations meant that southerners were subsidizing overblown profits in New England. They were particularly resentful because their export, cotton, brought more money into the United States than any other export.

Nullification Again.

Secretly, because he was Jackson's vice president and heir-apparent, John C. Calhoun wrote the *South Carolina Exposition and Protest*. In this document, Calhoun revived the compact theory of government. Calhoun argued that the Union was not formed by the people of the United States as a whole, but by people acting through their state governments. The states were sovereign, not the federal government. The states had indivisible power. The federal government was an agreement, a "compact" of the states.

Therefore, when the compact passed a law that a sovereign state protested, as South Carolina protested the Tariff of Abominations, a state had the right to nullify, or remove the authority from, that law within its boundaries.

Nullification in Practice.

Jefferson and Madison had been content to let the compact theory remain a theory. However, when Congress passed a slightly lower protective tariff in 1832, South Carolinians met in a convention and declared the tariff "null and void" within the state.

Jackson, who had shrugged off the South Carolina Exposition, exploded at this defiance. He asked for, and Congress passed, the *Force Bill* granting him the power to use force to ensure that the tariff was observed. South Carolina responded by nullifying the Force Bill, and prominent politicians announced they would fight any army that "invaded" the state.

It is difficult to imagine Andrew Jackson backing down from such a challenge. Fortunately, the crisis cooled when Henry Clay, a high tariff man but also "The Great Compromiser," sat down with Calhoun and worked out a settlement. A new tariff in 1833 removed the tax on some goods

Discussion Question: What did Jackson mean when he said, "John Marshall has made his decision, let him enforce it"? (See this page, under The Tariff of Abominations.) This, of course, alludes to the fact that the Supreme Court has no power if the chief executive does not choose to enforce the law.

270

GOING TO THE SOURCE

I have not allowed myself, sir, to look beyond the Union, to see what might lie hidden in the dark recess behind. I have not coolly weighed the chances of preserving liberty when the bonds that unite us together shall be broken asunder. I have not accustomed myself to hang over the precipice of disunion, to see whether, with my short sight, I can fathom the depth of the abyss below. . . . While the Union lasts, we have high, exciting, gratifying prospects spread out before us, for us and our children. Beyond that I seek not to penetrate the veil.

God grant that in my day, at least, that curtain may not rise! God grant that on my vision never may be opened what lies behind! When my eyes shall be turned to behold for the last time the sun in heaven, may I not see him shining on the broken and dishonored fragments of a once glorious Union. . . . Let their last feeble and lingering glance rather

> *While the Union lasts, we have high, exciting, gratifying prospects spread out before us, for us and our children. . . . When my eyes shall be turned to behold for the last time the sun in heaven, may I not see him shining on the . . . fragments of a once glorious Union.*
>
> DANIEL WEBSTER,
> "LIBERTY AND UNION"
> SPEECH

behold the gorgeous ensign of the Republic, now known and honored throughout the earth, still full high advanced, its arms and trophies streaming in their original luster, not a stripe erased or polluted, nor a single star obscured, bearing for its motto, no such miserable interrogatory as "What is all this worth?" nor those other words of delusion and folly, "Liberty first and Union afterwards"; but everywhere, blazing on all its ample folds, as they float over the sea and over the land, and in every wind under the whole heavens, that other sentiment, dear to every true American heart—Liberty *and* Union, now and forever, one and inseparable!

During the nullification conflicts in 1830, Massachusetts Senator Daniel Webster spoke for the need to follow federal laws. This text is from his powerful "Liberty and Union" speech in the Senate on January 26, 1830.

---

cotton planters bought in quantity, like woolens, and provided for an annual reduction of rates on all imports. South Carolina then rescinded its nullification and Jackson allowed the issue to fade.

It faded, but it did not die. South Carolina did not deny that nullification itself was illegal. Indeed, the state's nullification of the Force Bill remained in effect. In later writings, Calhoun explored an important objection to the doctrine of nullification. That is, what was to happen if a state nullified a law and, through the Constitution's amendment process, two thirds of the states made that law a part of the Constitution and therefore binding on all. In that case, Calhoun replied, the nullifying state could either obey or secede from the union. This doctrine, ten years after Calhoun's death, would lead to civil war.

SECTION REVIEW

1. Write a sentence to identify: "Old Hickory," Whigs, "Trail of Tears," Force Bill.

2. How would you characterize the campaign of 1828? Give some examples to support your answer.

3. Describe the status of women, blacks, and American Indians in the Age of Jackson. Did they benefit at all from Jacksonian democracy?

4. What was the Supreme Court decision regarding the Cherokee Nation? What was President Jackson's role in the removal of the Cherokees from their lands?

Nullification is a key term in understanding much of what will be going on in the next few chapters. Make certain that students understand what it means.

3. JACKSON, CALHOUN, AND VAN BUREN

When Jackson became president in 1829, many who knew him doubted that he would live through one term. The people might call him "Old Hickory," as strong and sturdy as the tree of that name. However, personal friends knew that Jackson had become frail and was frequently ill.

Given Jackson's illness and Calhoun's own position as vice president, it would seem that Calhoun was in a strong position to become the next president. However, by 1832, Calhoun had lost Jackson's support. By then, Jackson favored Martin Van Buren to succeed himself.

The Peggy Eaton Affair. Jackson first began to distance himself from Calhoun because of a scandal in Washington involving the wife of his Secretary of War, John Eaton. Eaton married a woman of questionable virtue. As a member of Jackson's cabinet, Eaton quite naturally attended Washington social functions accompanied by his bride.

Other women at the balls and parties would not speak to Peggy Eaton nor invite her to their homes. Still mourning the death of his own wife, which Jackson blamed on the effects of scandalous gossip, the President instructed his niece, who acted as hostess at the White House, to accept Peggy Eaton. When she refused, he told her to move out of the White House.

At a meeting of the cabinet, Jackson ordered his appointees to socialize with Peggy Eaton. Except for Secretary of State Martin Van Buren, they did not do so. Women were excluded from business and politics, but morality and social standards were entirely within their accepted roles, and the women of Washington had made up their minds about Mrs. Eaton. The men honored their collective decision. Both women and men continued to shun Peggy Eaton. Because Mrs. Calhoun was the informal head of Washington society, Jackson believed she was behind the women's rebellion and held her husband responsible.

The Rise of Martin Van Buren. Martin Van Buren was an exception. His sensitivity to the

The political cartoon below is of an imaginary cabinet meeting called by President Jackson to discuss the scandalous gossip about Peggy Eaton, the wife of Secretary of War Eaton.

Although the eighth U.S. president, Martin Van Buren was the first to be born in the U.S. He was born in 1782, six years after the signing of the Declaration of Independence.

Martin Van Buren served as a senator from New York, Secretary of State, vice president, and president between 1821 and 1841.

Calhoun Seals His Political Doom.

At the same time Van Buren gained Jackson's favor, Vice President Calhoun lost it. While the Eaton Affair was still simmering, Jackson found out that when he was fighting Indians and hanging British subjects in Florida, Secretary of State John Quincy Adams had supported Jackson while Secretary of War Calhoun wanted Jackson punished.

In April 1830, their relations took another bad turn. Nullification was in the air and at a formal dinner, 20 of Calhoun's supporters offered toasts to the doctrine that a state could defy federal authority. Jackson sat silently. However, when it was his turn to offer a toast, he lifted his glass and stared directly at Calhoun. "Our Union," Jackson said, "it must be preserved." Calhoun had the last word. "The Union, next to our liberty, the most dear."

Finally, Calhoun sealed his political doom in a personal slap at Van Buren. The Senate vote to confirm or reject Van Buren's nomination as ambassador to England ended in a tie. As vice president, it was Calhoun's responsibility to cast the deciding vote. He did so: he voted against Van Buren. This action meant that Van Buren was at home when it came time for Jackson to run for reelection, and Jackson named Van Buren as his new running mate.

Second Bank of the United States.

Unlike the presidential election of 1828, when personalities and mud-slinging obscured issues, Jackson's reelection campaign in 1832 turned on a very important issue—the future of the Second Bank of the United States. Chartered in 1816, the Second Bank of the United States was scheduled to go out of existence in 1836, unless Congress were to vote to renew its charter and the President were to sign the bill.

The head of the Bank, an aristocratic Philadelphian named Nicholas Biddle, tried to win Jackson's friendship well in advance of the critical date. He made generous loans to Jackson supporters and proposed that the national debt be paid off—a goal dear to Jackson's heart—on the anniversary of the Battle of New Orleans.

Jackson responded politely but bluntly to Biddle. Jackson said that he did not dislike the Bank of the United States more than other banks, but that he did not like banks at all.

feelings of Peggy Eaton may have been quite sincere. However, his willingness to chat with her in public when no one else would served to win him President Jackson's friendship. When hard feelings over the scandal threatened to paralyze the administration, Van Buren improved his position by showing Jackson a solution.

Van Buren would resign as Secretary of State and Eaton would resign as Secretary of War. Those actions would allow the other members of the cabinet to resign without losing face. Jackson would not lose their support. The President would be rid of the Eaton problem without offending the groups within the Democratic party that the members of his cabinet represented. And he would surely not lose the support of the New York Democrats, of whom Van Buren was the leader.

Jackson appreciated Van Buren's strategy and his sacrifice of high office. The President rewarded Van Buren by naming him ambassador to England, the most prestigious diplomatic position.

In the published record of their interchange, Jackson had the final say over Calhoun. To further emphasize his intent, Jackson changed the printed record of his toast to read "Our Federal Union." In his day, this was the political jargon emphasizing the doctrine that the Constitution was a compact between states.

*Andrew Jackson strongly opposed the Bank of the United States, which he called, "The Monster."
A firm believer in hard money, Jackson believed that banks should not issue bank notes without
having enough gold and silver to back up each note.*

Like many westerners, including his strong supporter, Missouri Senator Thomas Hart Benton, Jackson believed in *hard money*—gold and silver coin. He and Benton disliked the fact that banks loaned more money out in the form of bank notes than they had gold and silver in their vaults with which to redeem those notes. If too many people who held a bank's notes presented them at the same time, demanding the coin that was their right, the bank went broke. Everyone who had deposited money in the bank lost it, a common experience in the West. Both Jackson and Benton had witnessed the Panic of 1819 when thousands of people were ruined. Although the Bank of the United States was only partly responsible for the disaster, and Biddle was not then its head, Jackson never forgave the institution he and his supporters called "The Monster."

Moreover, like Thomas Jefferson, Jackson and Benton believed the Bank of the United States was unconstitutional. Finally, and most importantly, while the Bank had the use of the government's money, it was controlled by a very few wealthy citizens who owned 80 percent of the stock in the Bank. Jackson and Benton could not tolerate such power in the hands of a few wealthy people.

Politics Makes Strange Bedfellows. The Bank of the United States had other enemies. Oddly, while hard-money men like Jackson and Benton disliked the Bank because they feared it would use its power irresponsibly, some of their allies were owners of state banks who believed the Bank of the United States was too conservative.

That is, at any given time, the Bank of the United States held millions of dollars in state bank

Class Activity: The bank issue is often the cause of confusion for students. To help illustrate it more clearly, have one student play Jackson and another portray Clay and present the issues and positions held in this conflict. To further illustrate them, list the issues and positions on a chart.

notes. If the Bank presented these notes for redemption, it could destroy the state banks. Nicholas Biddle usually exercised his great power with caution. Rather than ruining state banks, he preferred to hold the threat of action over them, forcing them to practice more conservative lending policies. So Jackson and Benton found themselves in alliance with the most reckless bankers of all.

Finally, New York bankers, suddenly very rich as a result of the busy trade on the Erie Canal, resented the fact that the single most powerful bank in the country, holding a third of all bank deposits in the United States, was located in Philadelphia. They reasoned that if the Bank of the United States could be dismantled, much of that money would come their way.

Clay Fires the First Shot.

Once he knew that Jackson would not sign a new bank charter in 1836, Biddle could do nothing but wait. But then, Henry Clay and Daniel Webster told Biddle that if Clay could defeat Jackson in the presidential election of 1832 using the Bank of the United States as the major issue, then the Bank could be saved.

With Biddle's reluctant agreement, Clay introduced a bill to renew the Bank's charter in 1832, four years early. It passed Congress but, as Clay anticipated, Jackson vetoed the new charter. Up and down the country, members of Clay's National Republican party argued for the Bank. Jackson's Democratic followers campaigned against it. To Clay the issue was a stable financial system. To Jackson, it was the Monster's power over the lives of the common person.

Jackson won. He received 219 electoral votes to Clay's 49. The Anti-Masonic party candidate, William Wirt, won 7 electoral votes, and Calhoun's South Carolina, at odds with both Jackson and Clay, gave its 11 electoral votes to John Floyd of Virginia.

Jackson Attacks.

There would be no Bank of the United States. But that was not enough for Jackson. In September 1833, Jackson ordered the Secretary of the Treasury to cease depositing the government's money from taxes and land sales in the Bank of the United States. Instead, the government opened accounts in 89 state banks, which became known as Jackson's "pet banks."

In the meantime, as it was required to do by law, the Bank of the United States continued to pay the government's bills out of the money deposited with the Bank. Government deposits dropped by $17 million in about a year. Biddle felt he had no choice but to call in money that state banks owed. The result was a wave of bank failures that wiped out the savings of thousands of people, precisely what Jackson wanted to avoid.

Boom, Bust, Depression.

Under pressure from his friends in business and banking, Biddle agreed to reverse his policy of calling in money from the state banks. He began to loan money to state banks so that the bank failures would cease. This sudden infusion of money into the economy resulted in a rash of easy bank loans that promoted speculation in western lands and eastern industrial cities alike. And to Jackson's dismay, his pet banks were the least responsible of all. Using both government deposits and Bank of the United States loans, the state banks made money available to practically every borrower who asked.

In 1836, the year the Bank's charter expired, Henry Clay made his contribution to the financial crisis. He convinced Congress to pass the *Distribution Bill,* which provided $57 million to state governments for the purpose of building internal improvements. Presented with this windfall, the states spent freely. Seeking to share in the rapidly circulating money, new banks were founded at a fast rate. In 1830 there had been 330 state banks. By 1837 there were almost 800. Only a fraction of the new banks were responsibly run.

The Specie Circular.

Now, however, there was no Bank of the United States that, by putting what Biddle called "a mild and gentle but efficient control" on the economy, could cool things down gradually. Instead, President Jackson had to take direct action. In July 1836 he issued the *Specie Circular*, which required that anyone buying government land had to pay for it in *specie*, meaning gold or silver. Paper money issued by banks would no longer be accepted.

Because there was much less gold and silver available than paper money, Jackson's executive order did slow down the number of easy bank loans. However, it had two less desirable effects. Speculators who owed the government money and did not have enough gold or silver could not pay their debts. People who were not even involved in speculation lost faith in paper money. The chain reaction of the Panic of 1819 was repeated, but on a greater scale. Banks failed. Money deposited in them ran out. People who believed their paper money was redeemable in gold found that it was worthless. Honest farmers lost their land. Businesses deep in debt or losing money went bankrupt when the banks failed. People were thrown out of work. By 1837, the United States was locked in a *depression* worse than any since the days of Jefferson's Embargo. By the time the economy hit bottom, however, Andrew Jackson had retired to his mansion in Tennessee. The president who wound up presiding over the depression and who was ultimately blamed for it was Martin Van Buren.

SECTION REVIEW

1. Write a sentence to identify: Nicholas Biddle, hard money, "the Monster," pet banks.

2. Trace the events that led to the split between President Jackson and Vice President Calhoun. Who succeeded Calhoun as Jackson's vice president in 1832?

3. What were the results of President Jackson's attempts to destroy the Second Bank of the United States?

4. How were the depression of 1837 and the Specie Circular related? Describe some of the conditions of the depression.

---

4. THE RISE OF THE WHIGS

Van Buren became president in one of the oddest presidential elections in American history. The two-party system was functioning again. Van Buren was the Democratic party nominee. However, the Whig party, founded in 1834, could not decide on a single candidate. Instead, the Whigs ran three of their leaders, one from the Northeast, one from the South, one from the West. Their strategy was to throw the election into the House of Representatives. Once in the House, the Whigs believed, they could out-vote the Democrats.

Their strategy failed, as the three candidates —Daniel Webster from New England, Hugh L. White from the South, and General William Henry Harrison from the West—did not carry enough states. Van Buren rode the Democratic machine he had helped build to win with 170 electoral votes.

The Whigs. The Whigs were unable to agree on a single candidate in 1836 because they were united on little except a dislike of Andrew Jackson and resentment of various Democratic policies. According to the Whigs, Jackson acted like an arrogant monarch—"King Andrew I." They felt that Jackson had increased the power of the presidency beyond the intentions of the Founding Fathers. Some Whigs were disgusted by his defi-

Whig Party supporters disliked President Jackson and his policies. Calling him "King Andrew I," they complained that he had exercised more power than the Constitution permitted.

Class Activity: The Whigs felt Congress was meant to be the most powerful branch of government; Jackson saw it as the presidency; Marshall made it clear that he felt decisions made by the Supreme Court were law. Divide the class into three groups. Using the text of the Constitution, have each group defend the view that either the executive branch, Congress, or the courts were meant to have ultimate power to decide matters of state. In a three-way debate,

PROFILES OF THE PRESIDENCY

*M*artin Van Buren's glowing picture of prosperity seems ironic in view of the financial panic that began a few months later:

Though not altogether exempt from embarrassments that disturb our tranquillity at home and threaten it abroad, yet in all the attributes of a great, happy, and flourishing people we stand without a parallel in the world. Abroad we enjoy the respect and, with scarcely an exception, the friendship of every nation; at home, while our Government quietly but effi-

ciently performs the sole legitimate end of political institutions—in doing the greatest good to the greatest number—we present an aggregate of human prosperity surely not elsewhere to be found. How imperious, then, is the obligation imposed upon every citizen . . . to exert himself in perpetuating a condition of things so singularly happy! . . . We have risen to a people powerful in numbers and in strength; but with our increase has gone hand in hand the progress of just principles.

—INAUGURAL ADDRESS, MARCH 4, 1837

ance of the Supreme Court in his high-handed treatment of the Cherokee Indians. Many Whigs were shocked by his personal war against the Bank. Others believed he used the veto too often. To the Whigs, Congress was meant to be the most powerful branch of the federal government.

The Whigs were a mixed lot. Former National Republicans like Clay, Webster, and John Quincy Adams became Whigs. Anti-Masons like William Seward drifted into the party. Those few blacks who still retained the right to vote tended to be Whigs. But so did some of the wealthiest slave-owners in the country, Louisiana sugar planters who wanted a high tariff to protect them from West Indian competition.

Most Whigs were nationalists. They wanted a Bank of the United States. They supported the high protective tariff and federal financing of internal improvements. They believed in a national economy and, therefore, a federal government that was stronger than the states. However, supporters of state sovereignty, like John C. Calhoun, cooperated with Whigs simply out of hatred for Jackson and Van Buren. Finally, most educated people in the Northeast and some western and southern cities became Whigs because they were offended by what they believed to be the vulgarity of the Jacksonian appeal to the common person.

In 1834, this patchwork alliance of Whigs was strong enough to win 98 seats in the House of Representatives and almost half the Senate, 25 seats to the Democrats' 27. However, the Whigs' failure to agree on much beyond their common dislike of the Democrats was to prevent them, throughout their party's 20-year existence, from exercising as much political power as their numbers would seem to justify.

Van Buren and the Depression. When the economic depression dragged on, the Whigs in Congress demanded that President Van Buren take action. Clay and Webster called for the President to infuse money into the economy by financing internal improvements. The plan called for the government to deposit money into the banks. Then the banks were to loan this deposited money out, thereby stimulating business.

But Van Buren did not believe that government should play a role in national economic life. Indeed, he attempted to separate the government completely from the national financial system by taking government money out of banks and keeping it in *subtreasuries*, or government-operated depositories. The depression simply worsened. Everyone blamed President Van Buren, even Democratic voters.

have members of each group defend their powers based on an interpretation of the Constitution most favorable to their own interests. Afterwards, have them come to some consensus of what the powers of each branch really should be and what limits should be set to the powers of each.

PROFILES OF THE PRESIDENCY

William Henry Harrison was chosen by the Whigs as their presidential candidate. The most surprised person was Harrison himself, as he wrote to a friend:

The last correspondence between us was a letter from you dated about 18 months ago. I did not answer it—for at the time and long after I was greatly afflicted in mind and frequently so in person. I could not write to you without telling you all the tale of my woes. . . . In the midst of my difficulties, however, I . . .

resolutely resolved to apply every remedy within my reach to overcome what I could overcome and palliate what I could not. My efforts . . . have so far approached success as to give me every encouragement to persevere. . . . But I have news still more strange to tell you. . . . Some folks are silly enough to have formed a plan to make a President of the United States out of this Clerk and Clodhopper!

—LETTER TO GENERAL SOLOMON VAN RENSSELAER, JANUARY 15, 1835

Voters almost always blame hard times on the government in power. For this reason, the Whigs looked forward to the presidential election of 1840. They were sure that anger toward Van Buren would translate into votes for the Whigs.

The Whigs Adopt the Democrats' Methods.
Young Whigs like New York's Thurlow Weed argued that victory was certain in 1840—but only if the Whigs learned the political lessons of the preceding twelve years.

When Jackson was first elected president, Weed pointed out, no one knew where he stood on any important issue. He won the election of 1828 because he was a military hero who appealed to the common person.

Weed wanted to nominate the Whig's military hero, the candidate who had done far better than any other Whig, William Henry Harrison of Ohio. No one knew where he stood on the issues. The Whigs would emphasize his career as an Indian fighter.

Weed's reasoning carried the day. Harrison was nominated and, in order to attract southern votes, his vice-presidential running mate was John Tyler of Virginia. The Whig slogan was: *Tippecanoe and Tyler, Too.* Early in the campaign, an unsuspecting Democratic politician gave the Whigs their symbol too. He sneered that while Van Buren was a

distinguished *statesman*, Harrison would be just as happy with a jug of hard cider, a $2,000-a-year pension, and a bench on which to sit and doze in front of his log cabin.

The Whig party, taking a lesson from the successful Democratic Republican strategy of 1828, nominated a popular war hero, William Henry Harrison, to run for president in the election of 1840.

Discussion Question: Why was Martin Van Buren blamed for the depression? Should he have been blamed? What does this tell you about the executive office? Assuming students will take a sympathetic view of Van Buren's problem, try relating his situation to that of a more recent president or political leader.

The election of 1840 saw the careful use of campaign slogans ("Tippecanoe and Tyler Too") and emotional images (Harrison and Tyler as candidates with simple, American tastes).

be campaigned without great fussing over slogans and symbols. The Whigs had a right to celebrate, and they did. However, in making the Democratic party's appeal to the common person their own, they demonstrated that the democratic upheaval of the Age of Jackson was complete.

Fate Takes a Hand. We will never know how William Henry Harrison stood on issues dear to the hearts of leading Whigs like Clay and Webster. Although his inaugural address still holds the record as the longest ever given, his term of office also holds the record as the shortest. For, after delivering his long speech in wet and windy weather, the 67-year-old President caught a cold. He took to bed but the illness went to pneumonia. While Whigs hoping to get appointed to public office waited in the White House, President Harrison died exactly one month after he was sworn in.

Tyler Becomes President. At first, Henry Clay did not miss a stride. He had believed he would be able to dictate policy to Harrison, but he was sure he could dictate policy to the new president, John Tyler. He explained to Tyler that, because he was not actually elected as president, Tyler should act as a figurehead with a committee of congressional Whigs, headed by Clay, making important decisions.

Tyler would have none of it. He knew the Constitution. It said that if a president died in office, the vice president succeeded him as president, not as acting president.

He tried to get along with Clay. He went along with the abolition of Van Buren's subtreasury system. Although as a planter he favored low tariffs, Tyler even agreed to an increase in import duties. Tyler also signed Clay's *Pre-emption Act* of 1841. In this attempt to steal the thunder of western Democrats like Benton, Clay's bill provided that a family that had "squatted" on public land before it was offered for sale could purchase up to 160 acres at the minimum price of $1.25 an acre.

A President Without a Party. But Tyler drew the line at Clay's proposal to establish a new national bank. The fact was, the president was closer in his views to John C. Calhoun and even Andrew Jackson than to Clay. He had become a

Tippecanoe and Tyler, Too. Such snobbery toward simple tastes, the humble life, and the kind of home in which many westerners lived was poor politics. The Whigs, who usually suffered Democratic accusations that they were the party of snobbery, grabbed at the opportunity. They hauled out miniature log cabins at political rallies. They tapped thousands of barrels of hard cider. Although Harrison in fact lived in a large mansion, the Whigs presented him as just an ordinary man. Van Buren, the Whigs said, sipped champagne, ate fancy food, and perfumed his whiskers.

It worked. The popular vote was close. Van Buren won 47 percent of the total, but he was trounced in the electoral college by a vote of 234 to 60. Never again would a presidential election

PROFILES OF THE PRESIDENCY

The first vice president to become president, John Tyler faced bitter abuse from political enemies, who called him "acting president." On the day he stepped down from office, he said:

In 1840 I was called from my farm to undertake the administration of public affairs, and I foresaw that I was called to a bed of thorns. I now leave that bed which has afforded me little rest, and eagerly seek repose in the quiet enjoyment of rural life. . . . I rely on future history, and on the candid and impartial judgment of my fellow citizens, to award me the meed due to honest and conscientious purposes to serve my country.

. . . The day has come when a man can feel proud of being an American citizen. He can stand on the Northeastern boundary, or on the shores of the Rio Grande del Norte and contemplate the extent of our vast and growing Republic, the boundaries of which have been settled and extended by peaceful negotiation. . . . The acquisition of Texas is a measure of the greatest importance. Our children's children's children will live to realize the vast benefits conferred on our country by the union of Texas with this Republic. . . .

—FAREWELL SPEECH, MARCH 3, 1845

Whig because he regarded Jackson's use of power as arrogant. However, he shared Jackson's view that a national bank was unconstitutional and benefited northeastern financial interests at the expense of southern and western farmers. He vetoed Clay's attempts to design a new Bank of the United States.

Furious, the Clay Whigs expelled Tyler and his whole cabinet from the party, with the exception of Secretary of State Daniel Webster, who resigned. Senator Clay resigned from the Senate. He intended to win the Whig nomination for president in 1844 and to resume work that Tyler had ruined.

Most of the men Tyler appointed to his new cabinet were southern Whigs like himself. However, as the end of his term approached, he moved closer to the *states' rights* philosophy of John C. Calhoun. In 1844, he named Calhoun Secretary of State.

Resolving Disputes with England.
The major accomplishment of the Tyler presidency was a treaty that resolved several dangerous differences between the United States and Great Britain. Daniel Webster had remained in the cabinet temporarily when the other Whigs resigned for the purpose of completing the negotiations he had begun.

One problem was a boundary dispute between Maine and the Canadian province of New Brunswick. In 1838 Canadian lumberjacks began cutting trees on land Maine claimed. Maine and New Brunswick militias exchanged gunfire with no deaths, and Van Buren managed to calm things down. But he could not resolve the boundary dispute.

The Canadian-American line just west of Lake Superior was also in question. Finally, there was tension between the two countries because of assistance given to unsuccessful Canadian rebels by American citizens and the fact that some Americans still purchased slaves in West Africa in violation of both British and American law.

The Webster-Ashburton Treaty.
Any one of these problems could have resulted in war if left uncorrected. Webster managed to get the British to agree to a treaty resolving all of them by making a big concession in Maine. He recognized the Canadian version of the boundary line, which gave the Canadians almost half of the disputed land.

Quite a few people did not believe that Tyler could assume the office of president according to the Constitution. Congressman John McKeon of Pennsylvania even submitted a resolution in the House of Representatives in order to change Tyler's title to "acting president." The resolution was, however, defeated.

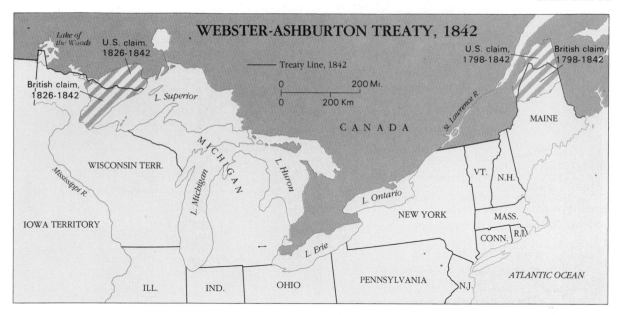

WEBSTER-ASHBURTON TREATY, 1842

Lake of the Woods
British claim, 1826-1842
U.S. claim, 1826-1842
—— Treaty Line, 1842
U.S. claim, 1798-1842
British claim, 1798-1842
L. Superior
CANADA
St. Lawrence R.
MAINE
0   200 Mi.
0   200 Km
MICHIGAN
WISCONSIN TERR.
L. Michigan
L. Huron
VT. N.H.
Mississippi R.
L. Ontario
IOWA TERRITORY
NEW YORK
MASS.
CONN. R.I.
L. Erie
ILL.   IND.   OHIO
PENNSYLVANIA
N.J.
ATLANTIC OCEAN

Lord Ashburton, who wrote the treaty with Webster, granted territory to the United States in what is now northern New York and Vermont. He also agreed to Webster's claim to about 6,500 square miles (16,800 square kilometers) west of Lake Superior. Although nothing but forest in 1842, this land later proved to be the site of some of the richest iron ore deposits in the world.

When the Senate ratified the treaty in 1842, Webster had good reason to be pleased with himself. He had settled every boundary dispute between the United States and Canada. When the vote was taken, he resigned from Tyler's cabinet.

SECTION REVIEW

1. Write a sentence to identify: "King Andrew I," subtreasuries, "Tippecanoe and Tyler, Too," Lord Ashburton.

2. Name the presidential candidates and their parties in the election of 1836. Discuss the strategy of the Whigs in the election. Why did their strategy fail?

3. Describe Thurlow Weed's strategy for defeating the Democrats in 1840.

4. How did John Tyler become president? Why were he and almost his entire cabinet expelled from the Whig party?

The old chamber of the House of Representatives (above) was the forum for many colorful debates on extremely important issues that shaped the nation.

CHAPTER REVIEW

TIME LINE

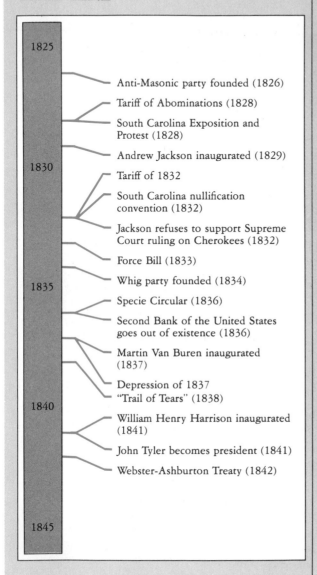

1825

Anti-Masonic party founded (1826)

Tariff of Abominations (1828)

South Carolina Exposition and Protest (1828)

Andrew Jackson inaugurated (1829)

1830

Tariff of 1832

South Carolina nullification convention (1832)

Jackson refuses to support Supreme Court ruling on Cherokees (1832)

Force Bill (1833)

Whig party founded (1834)

1835

Specie Circular (1836)

Second Bank of the United States goes out of existence (1836)

Martin Van Buren inaugurated (1837)

Depression of 1837

"Trail of Tears" (1838)

1840

William Henry Harrison inaugurated (1841)

John Tyler becomes president (1841)

Webster-Ashburton Treaty (1842)

1845

TIME LINE QUESTIONS

1. Trace the events on the time line that had a direct bearing on the nullification issue.
2. What events that occurred during Martin Van Buren's presidency were brought on by actions taken by President Jackson? Name the related events.
3. What two new parties were founded in this period?

SKILLS STRATEGY

ELECTION 1824 DATA

CANDIDATE	ELECTORAL VOTES	POPULAR VOTES
Adams	84	108,740
Jackson	99	153,544
Crawford	41	46,618
Clay	37	47,136

ELECTION OF 1824

CANDIDATES

Adams

Jackson

Crawford

Clay

16% 14% 38% 32% 13% 13% 43% 31%

TOTAL ELECTORAL VOTES 261

TOTAL POPULAR VOTES 356,038

Source: *Hammond's Advanced Reference Atlas*

PIE GRAPHS

Circle or *pie* graphs, like all graphs, show relationships between or among sets of data and allow a great deal of information to be presented in limited space. To get the information you need from a pie graph, begin by reading the title, any labels, symbols, and the key. The pie graphs above convey more clearly than words can certain data about the 1824 presidential election. The data on the chart was used to construct the two pie graphs. Notice that each wedge in the graph at the left expresses as a percentage the number of electoral votes won by each candidate listed in the chart and shown on the key for the graph. The sum of the percentages shown in all the wedges is 100 percent, which represents 261 votes, or the total number of electoral votes cast. The chart shows that John Quincy Adams received 84 electoral votes, and a quick calculation will show you that Adams received 32 percent of the electoral votes (84 ÷ 261 = 0.32, or 32 percent).

The label below the pie graph on the right

Making Connections: Review the questions and topics presented in the Making Connections section opening this chapter. Emphasize the dramatic increase in the involvement of the election

ELECTION 1828 DATA

CANDIDATE (PARTY)	ELECTORAL VOTES	POPULAR VOTES
J. Q. ADAMS (National Republicans)	83	508,084
A. JACKSON (Democratic Republicans)	178	647,286

PARTY

NATIONAL REPUBLICAN

DEMOCRATIC REPUBLICAN

178
83

TOTAL ELECTORAL VOTES 261

TOTAL POPULAR VOTES 1,155,370

Source: *Hammond's Advanced Reference Atlas*

indicates that this graph shows the percentages of popular votes received by each candidate in 1824. In this case, 100 percent is equal to 358,038 popular votes, the total number cast. If you study the two graphs on the preceding page, you will understand why the election of 1824 was decided in the House of Representatives, and why Andrew Jackson felt cheated.

APPLYING SKILLS

Refer to the chart of the 1828 election data and the pie graphs above, and answer the following questions.
1. What should the title of the two graphs be?
2. How will you find the percentage of electoral votes each candidate received?
3. What number of electoral votes is equal to 100 percent?
4. What number of popular votes is equal to 100 percent?
5. Summarize the information about the election of 1828 that is presented in the pie graphs.

CHAPTER 11 TEST

TEXT REVIEW

1. How do the Workingpeople's parties and the Anti-Masonic party typify the upsurge of democratic sentiment in the United States in the early nineteenth century?
2. What two principles constitute the key to Jacksonian Democracy?
3. How did President Jackson use political patronage? Cite evidence from the chapter that Jackson did not abuse this practice.
4. From Jackson's point of view, which of John Calhoun's actions could justly be called disloyal?
5. Describe President Jackson's attitude toward banks and hard money.
6. What unintended results occurred because of actions Jackson took to lessen the influence of banks and to promote hard money?
7. Name the new political party that became important in the election of 1836. Explain why this party lost the presidential election of 1836, but won in 1840.
8. Give the important details about either John Tyler's political difficulties or the Webster-Ashburton Treaty.

CRITICAL THINKING

9. In the author's opinion, the Peggy Eaton affair was "overblown" (pages 272–273). If you agree, list some facts that would give weight to the opinion. If you disagree, explain why.
10. Back up the following statement with facts from the chapter: "The campaign of 1828 could be called a propagandist's dream."

WRITING A PARAGRAPH

Space limitations usually prevent history textbooks from including all the important and interesting details about the lives and careers of the people who made history. Choose such a person from this chapter. Consult an encyclopedia to find at least three details about the person not included in this or previous chapters. Take notes as you research. Then, use your notes to write a paragraph about the person you have chosen.

process. Also pay attention to the practice of using "image" to sell a candidate and to the beginnings of organized political machines and their use.

Quotation: from the novel *The House of the Seven Gables.* Other works by Nathaniel Hawthorne (1804–1864) include *Twice-Told Tales, Mosses From an Old Manse, The Scarlet Letter, The Blithedale Romance, The Marble Faun,* and *Our Old Home.*

CHAPTER 12

AMERICAN REFORM MOVEMENTS

1815–1850

The world owes all its onward impulses to men ill at ease. The happy man inevitably confines himself within ancient limits.

NATHANIEL HAWTHORNE

Making Connections. Free to worship as they pleased, many Americans developed their own forms of religious expression. Some formed their own communities where they could lead "perfect" lives. Others set out to cure the evils they saw in society. Religion and reform reflected the American belief that people could change things for the better.

In this chapter, you will learn:
- Who founded some new religions
- Which groups believed that an ideal society could be created in the United States
- How the philosophy of Transcendentalism influenced American writers
- What nineteenth century reformers did to improve insane asylums, prisons, and the treatment of blind and deaf people
- How changing immigration patterns gave rise to an anti-Catholic political party
- Who were the leaders of the women's rights movement

You have read that some of the original American colonies were founded by those who wanted the freedom to practice their own religion, and that the writers of the Constitution made sure there would be no state-supported religion. As you read, note how a diversity of religious ideas found an outlet in the early 1800s.

Sections
1. Religion in America
2. American Utopias
3. The Flowering of New England
4. American Reformers

1. RELIGION IN AMERICA

At the beginning of the nineteenth century, organized religion was perhaps weaker than at any other period of American history. Most national leaders in the Confederation and Federalist period were *deists.* They believed in God but did not think that church services and rituals were important forms of worship.

The Anglican Church (Church of England) lost members because many Anglican priests had been Loyalists during the Revolution. The Congregationalists lost ground in New England because people who now felt that their economic and political lives were in their own hands found it difficult to continue believing in the old Puritan doctrine of predestination.

The Congregationalists also suffered losses when most of their ministers opposed the triumphant Jeffersonian Republicans. In 1828, the same year Andrew Jackson became president, the last two states to pay salaries to ministers out of tax money, Massachusetts and Connecticut, ceased to do so.

Unitarians and Universalists. Many educated New Englanders, such as Oliver Wendell Holmes, became Unitarians. This religious denomination's American roots began in 1785 when

The first Shaker community in the United States was established in 1787 at New Lebanon, New York. Shakers received their name because visitors to their meetings observed them shake with emotion when participating in group dance rituals (right).

Skills Review: Reinforce the skills learned in the preceding Skills Strategy section. Have students create a circle graph representing the national origins of new immigrants to the U.S. in the 1830s and 1840s as a percentage of the total number of immigrants entering the U.S. in those years. Students can use a library's U.S. statistical abstracts to compile the numbers of immigrants.

Unitarians like Oliver Wendell Holmes (left) and William Ellery Channing (center) and Universalists like Charles Grandison Finney (right) rejected the doctrine of predestination.

a Boston church rejected the Christian doctrine of the Trinity (three persons in one God—the Father, the Son, and the Holy Ghost) because it seemed like idolatry to them. Their God was one; thus the name *Unitarians.*

The Unitarian God was believed to be a kind, well-wishing father. In the words of William Ellery Channing, the most famous of the early nineteenth century Unitarians, God "had a father's concern for his creatures, a father's desire for their improvement, . . . a father's joy in their progress, a father's readiness to receive the penitent, and a father's justice for the incorrigible."

Unitarianism appealed mainly to middle and upper class New Englanders. *Universalism,* founded by the Universalists in 1779, appealed mainly to working people interested in reforms aiding laboring people. Universalists rejected the doctrine of predestination; they believed that salvation was extended by God to all—universally.

Revivalists.

Other religious developments did not liberalize teachings as the Unitarians and Universalists did. Instead, devoted and talented preachers like Charles Grandison Finney crisscrossed New England and New York with a "democratic" version of the old Puritan faith. The Puritans were right, Finney told enthusiastic crowds, in their belief that human nature was essentially sinful. However, instead of choosing just a few people as His "Elect," God made it possible for anyone who was truly sorry for sinning to be saved.

Revivalist sermons almost always began with an emotional description of human sinfulness. From there, the skillful preacher moved on to discuss the sufferings awaiting sinners. Finally, revivalists concluded on a note of hope: any person could be saved if he or she repented of sins and declared complete faith and trust in God.

Finney was a Presbyterian who later became a Congregationalist. However, he and his followers preached their message of "free and full salvation" to people of all faiths. After their revivals, they urged those who were "born again" in the Lord to choose the denomination that suited them best and to strive to lead good lives.

Camp Meetings.

In cities, because churches were usually too small for the crowds revivalist preachers attracted, preachers spoke in large halls. On the frontier, where there were few large halls, revivalists held *camp meetings,* a week or more of outdoor sermons and hymn singing held in clearings in the forest. These meetings were usually announced months in advance.

At the turn of the century, beginning at Cane Ridge and Gasper River, Kentucky, ministers like James McGready drew crowds as large as 20,000. Such a concentration of normally scattered and

Discussion Question: Why do you think Europeans visiting the U.S. found the camp meetings interesting? How did this reflect European attitudes toward Americans of that period? The discussion of these questions should find that the Europeans were probably not at the meetings as participants but were there as critical observers.

sometimes lonely frontier people camping in one place was itself exciting. The preachers, as many as 40 at one time, enlivened things further with emotional "fire and brimstone" sermons.

Camp meeting religion was emotional. People were frequently so deeply affected by the powerful sermons that they would break into tears and fall to the ground in convulsions. Due to the emotional drama that was to be found at these camp meetings, it is not surprising that one of the two American sights European tourists frequently wanted to see was a camp meeting. (The other was a slave auction.) Because the Baptists and Methodists were particularly active in organizing these frontier revivals, they became the most popular denominations in the trans-Appalachian West.

Circuit Riders. Because some people came to camp meetings for entertainment rather than religion, Methodist ministers designed a new way to serve the religious needs of westerners. A minister would be assigned to visit a dozen or more settlements that were too poor to support a permanent parson. These traveling ministers came to be called *circuit riders.* They preached, performed marriages and baptisms, counseled the people who housed and fed them, and rode on—carrying both a Bible and a rifle—to their next stop.

Camp meetings like the one shown below were held in forest clearings because local churches were not big enough to hold the large crowds that the traveling revivalist preachers attracted.

Small western settlements that could not afford their own parson were visited by traveling preachers (above) called "circuit riders."

Circuit riders were usually young and unmarried. It was a difficult life. The rider was constantly on the move in territory that was sometimes still wilderness. As the circuit riders grew older and the population in their respective territories grew larger, they would settle down at one church or another that was now able to pay them a salary, however low it might be. Eventually, even the smallest western communities were likely to have several churches. Baptists and Methodists were most numerous in the West, but the Presbyterian churches of the Scotch-Irish were also common, as were the Disciples of Christ, founded by revivalists.

The Millerites.

Another new sect was the Millerites, founded in 1831 by a New Yorker, William Miller. His studies of the Bible showed him that Christ's second coming—the end of the world—would occur between March 21, 1843 and March 21, 1844. Most of the people to whom he preached hooted at him, but Miller convinced tens of thousands that he was right.

Along with a disciple, Joshua V. Himes of Boston, Miller published a newspaper and regularly delivered two or three long sermons a day. When the fateful year began, thousands of new converts flocked to Miller's *advent* (*advent* means "coming" or "arrival"). Many of them sold their possessions and contributed the money they received to the Millerite sect, which led critics to accuse Miller and Himes of fraud.

On March 21, 1844, several thousand people in New York dressed in "ascension robes" sold by Himes, and climbed hills in order to be the first to greet the Lord.

When Christ did not come, Miller discovered an error in his calculations and set a new date for the end of the world, October 22, 1844. Again people climbed the hills. Again they were disappointed. Miller himself was bewildered and broken-hearted. But one of his disciples, Hiram Edson, concluded that while the second coming was not far in the future, it could not be dated. He organized the Millerites into a church that observed the Jewish sabbath, Saturday instead of Sunday, and were therefore called the *Seventh-Day Adventists.*

The Latter-Day Saints.

Another religious group was the *Church of Jesus Christ of the Latter-Day Saints,* founded by Joseph Smith, a poor Vermont-born farmboy living in upstate New York. Smith liked to wander the hills near his home where, he told a few friends, he was visited by an angel, Moroni. Smith claimed that the angel showed him where some mysterious gold plates were buried. Smith claimed to have been able to read the inscriptions on these plates.

The story he translated became *The Book of Mormon,* a Bible of the New World that told of the Nephites, one of the lost tribes of Israel that supposedly had come to America. According to the story, in the year 384 the Lamanites, or American Indians, wiped out the Nephites in a war with the exception of the prophet Mormon, who wrote the book Smith claimed to have found.

Smith made many converts. However, many neighbors of the Mormons ridiculed them, and eventually Smith led them to Missouri and then in 1840 to Nauvoo, Illinois.

There the Mormons were not ridiculed but hated. In part this was because of their practice of

The engraving above shows the Mormon settlement at Provo, Utah in 1858. The Mormons moved west in 1847, into what was then Mexican territory, to escape religious persecution.

polygamy, one man having several wives. Also, holding all property in common, the Mormons prospered, while in the wake of the Panic of 1837, their neighbors struggled to make ends meet. And the Mormons shut themselves off, referring to all non-Mormons as "Gentiles." As the Anti-Masonic party had shown earlier, Americans tended to dislike and mistrust secret societies.

The crisis came in 1844 when Joseph Smith announced he was a candidate for president of the United States. He was arrested on a trumped-up charge. On June 27, a mob took him from the jailhouse and murdered him. The Latter-Day Saints might well have buckled under the persecution except for the emergence of a strong new leader—Brigham Young. Young concluded that the Mormons would never flourish in the United States. Consequently, in 1847, he took his followers west, outside the existing boundaries of the United States.

SECTION REVIEW

1. Write a sentence to identify: deists, William Ellery Channing, Seventh-Day Adventists, Joseph Smith.

2. Name two New England religious denominations that lost much of their influence at the beginning of the nineteenth century. What caused them to lose their influence?

3. What religious movement preached a "democratic version of the old Puritan faith"? Explain what camp meetings and circuit riders were and how they were connected with this movement.

4. Trace the steps that led Brigham Young to take the Mormons west of the existing boundaries of the United States.

the communal experiments of the 1960s).

The U.S. Congress passed a law against polygamy in 1862. The Supreme Court upheld the constitutionality of this law in 1890, and the Mormon Church has disapproved of polygamy since 1890.

2. AMERICAN UTOPIAS

In 1516, the Chancellor of England, Sir Thomas More, wrote a book called *Utopia*. In it he spun a tale of a nonexistent country where the evils that plagued the real world had been overcome. Subsequently, people have referred to plans to create a perfect society as *utopian*.

Not all Utopias have been in books. In the early nineteenth century, many Americans and Europeans who came to the United States believed that conditions were such that they could actually create an ideal society. The American utopians did not try to convert all Americans to their beliefs through politics. Instead, they withdrew from participation in mainstream American life— "resigned" from society—and founded communities based on their ideals. In a way, the Mormon community Brigham Young would found in isolated Utah was a utopia.

The utopian hope was that others would admire their example and imitate them. But even if that did not happen, they at least were living as they believed people should live.

Religious Utopias.

The earliest American utopias were founded by religious groups. The *Rappites* were approximately 600 followers of a German minister, George Rapp, who came to the United States in 1803. Like the early Mormons, they held property in common. Unlike the Mormons, the Rappites practiced celibacy. They did not marry or have children.

For a time the Rappites prospered. Their utopian communities at Harmony and Economy, Pennsylvania and New Harmony, Indiana, were very successful. However, because they did not have children and discouraged non-Germans from joining them, their utopian experiment ended after a generation or two.

The *Shakers,* mostly English followers of Mother Ann Lee, held beliefs much like those of the Rappites. They too forbade marriage and held property in common. However, Shakers survived longer because they welcomed any true believer into their communities and adopted children from orphanages to carry on the faith. The Shakers practiced celibacy because they believed Christ would return to earth soon. Therefore, they believed there was no need to perpetuate the human race. They got their unusual name because of a dance in which, visitors observed, they shook with emotion.

Social Utopias.

Utopian communities that were held together by a social rather than a religious ideal were generally less successful. The most famous of the utopian communities fell apart quickly.

In 1825, a wealthy Scottish industrialist, Robert Owen, purchased New Harmony, Indiana, from the Rappites. He put out a call to people who believed that private property was a source of hatred among men and women to join him in building a model for a better society. At New Harmony, all property would be held in common. Everyone would work for the good of the whole rather than for individual enrichment.

Unfortunately, genuine idealists were joined at the Indiana community by people who enjoyed the weekly philosophical discussions but disappeared when there was hard work to do. The generous Owen could not bring himself to throw the lazy members out. He believed in his message so deeply that he was sure they would learn to work. After only two years he returned to Scotland, deeply disappointed.

The *Icarians*, who followed the teachings of a Frenchman, Etienne Cabet, established communities in Texas and on the site of the abandoned Mormon town of Nauvoo, Illinois. One branch of this movement survived until 1895.

Another Frenchman, Charles Fourier, founded more than 20 *Phalanxes*, as he called his communities. Most of them fell apart after a few months.

Brook Farm, near Concord, Massachusetts, functioned somewhat better. Most of the writers, poets, and philosophers who lived there tried to do their share of the heavy labor.

However, the idea of establishing an essentially communistic society with people who quarreled about the fine points of everything seemed bound to fail. Many distinguished New Englanders spent at least a short time at Brook Farm. One of them, Nathaniel Hawthorne, wrote a critical novel about the community called *The Blithedale Romance.*

Oneida.

Virtually all the utopias were based on the belief that private property and frantic competition for riches were at the bottom of unhappi-

Class Activity: To help organize the information in this chapter, make a chart comparing the various movements, their leaders, and their goals.

ness in society. Property was held in common in all of the utopian communities.

To private property as a source of evil, John Humphrey Noyes added the institution of marriage. Indeed, Noyes said, marriage was a form of property. Husband owned wife and wife owned husband. Instead of preaching the alternative of celibacy, as the Rappites and Shakers did, Noyes devised the concept of "complex marriage." Each man at his *Oneida* community was married to all women, each woman to all men.

SECTION REVIEW

1. Write a sentence to identify: Sir Thomas More, George Rapp, Mother Ann Lee.
2. Define *utopia*. Name two religious utopias founded in the nineteenth century, and tell why one survived longer than the other.
3. Name and locate the social utopias that were founded by these people: Etienne Cabet; a group of New England writers and philosophers; Robert Owen.
4. Contrast the utopia founded by John Humphrey Noyes with the other utopias of the time.

3. THE FLOWERING OF NEW ENGLAND

Numerous utopian philosophers were what is known in philosophy as *perfectionists*. Perfectionist philosophers refused to accept the traditional Christian doctrine that human nature is essentially evil, or at best, a mixture of good and evil. They believed that individuals had it within themselves to be sinless, perfect. People had only to face up to their own perfection and it would be so. Then they would never sin again.

Perfectionism was not so very far out of step with the spirit of the Jacksonian era. It was a time when, dizzy with the opportunities and possibilities of America, many Americans felt that nothing was beyond their capacity. One New Englander, Ralph Waldo Emerson, called Perfectionism by another name, *Transcendentalism*, and became one of America's favorite philosophers.

Many of the men and women who, in the 1830s

and even somewhat earlier, created an impressive body of literature in the United States were *Transcendentalists*. Most of them were New Englanders, and this emergence of American culture is often called *The Flowering of New England*.

The royalties from the books that Louisa May Alcott (above) wrote helped support her family and her father, Bronson Alcott (below), who was a Transcendentalist writer and utopian philosopher.

Discussion Question: Why did many of the utopian communities of the time fail?

Ralph Waldo Emerson. Emerson was a Unitarian minister in Boston who agreed with William Ellery Channing that human nature was essentially good and God a kind father. In 1832, however, he shocked his congregation by resigning his pulpit. Although Unitarian teachings were broad and vague, Emerson found he could not accept some of them. He returned to his home in Concord, Massachusetts, and devised a personal religion which found God not in the Bible and in church but in nature. Emerson came to believe that individuals could find happiness by appreciating nature. He believed that personal morality, defined by the individual, was superior to laws.

Transcendentalism was mystical. That is, it was a philosophy and a form of religion rooted in human feelings rather than reason. The word *transcend* means "to go beyond," or "to rise above."

Emerson was not without critics. One critic was the writer Herman Melville, who called Emerson's Transcendentalism "gibberish." All in all, however, Emerson was immensely popular. At a time when Herman Melville's novels, which dealt with the problem of evil in the world, were read by very few people, Emerson could not honor half the requests to speak that were sent to him.

Thoreau and Fuller. Next to Emerson, the most important Transcendentalist was Henry David Thoreau, the son of a Concord pencil manufacturer. Whereas Emerson delivered lectures about worshiping nature and lived a comfortable middle class life, and spoke about rejecting materialistic American society while pocketing large fees; Thoreau tried to break free of society. In 1845, he got permission from Emerson to build a cabin on some of Emerson's land on Walden Pond, a few miles outside of Concord.

The result of Thoreau's experiment in Spartan-like separation from society was the book *Walden.* Published in 1854, *Walden* was the masterpiece of Transcendentalism and a beautifully written celebration of nature. Not detracting at all from the beauty and power of Thoreau's book, the fact remains that Walden Pond was hardly in the wilderness. It was a short walk to Concord, a walk Thoreau took often when he was lonely or wanted a good meal at Emerson's or his sister's table. As critics have been quick to point out, there is a

Ralph Waldo Emerson (left) and Henry David Thoreau (center) were the leading Transcendentalist writers in America. Margaret Fuller (right), an independent thinker and accomplished writer and editor, became a respected American critic and social reformer.

One story about Thoreau that has been embellished has to do with his going to jail for refusing to pay taxes because the government supported slavery. It is not always mentioned that he spent only one night there. When an unknown party paid his taxes, he was released—forcibly—as an outraged Thoreau argued with the jailer for being let off so easily.

sense of having things both ways about the Transcendentalists, the self-righteous feeling of being superior to American materialism while enjoying its benefits.

Margaret Fuller was one of the people who sensed the Transcendentalists' problem. A brilliant woman who knew five languages before she was a teenager, Fuller was as much a romantic as Emerson and Thoreau. But she grew restless with her conventional life as a successful essayist and editor for *The Dial,* a Transcendentalist magazine, and the *New York Tribune.* Striking out, she wrote a criticism of the inferior status Americans allowed women and went to Italy where she participated in a revolution in 1848.

Dissenters.
Not every American writer belonged to Emerson's group. Nathaniel Hawthorne, author of *The Scarlet Letter* (1850), *The House of Seven Gables* (1851), and other great novels and short stories, disagreed with the Transcendentalists' bubbling optimism about human nature. In his stories, Hawthorne explored evil.

Hawthorne's friend, New York-born Herman Melville, lived a far more romantic life than any of the Transcendentalists. As a young seaman, he jumped ship and lived among the natives of the Marquesas Islands and Tahiti in the Pacific. But his conclusions were rather different from Emerson's and Thoreau's. In his greatest books, *Billy Budd* and *Moby Dick,* Melville, like Hawthorne, explored the problem of evil in the world. Some of his sea stories were successful, but Melville's masterpiece, *Moby Dick,* thought by many to be the greatest American novel, was a commercial failure. And *Billy Budd* was not even published until 1924, more than 25 years after Melville's death.

Other American Authors.
Two other New Yorkers established worldwide reputations as writers. Washington Irving wrote the hilarious *Diedrich Knickerbocker's History of New York* in 1815. And while living in England in 1820, as an agent of his father's shipping company, he published *The Sketch Book,* a collection of tales based on legends of the Dutch who lived in New York's Hudson Valley. In 1832, Irving published *The Alhambra,* about the glorious palace in Granada that was the last stronghold of the Moors in Spain. That book was largely responsible for attempts to

Two of America's finest writers, Nathaniel Hawthorne (left) and Herman Melville (center), were not transcendentalists: they rejected Emerson's and Thoreau's romanticism and wrote powerful novels exploring evil. Washington Irving (right) wrote entertaining sketches.

Research Assignment: Students may have read some of the books mentioned in this section for their literature classes. Have students write a report on one of these books, detailing its story and relating this to the attitudes the author might have had about issues current at that time.

The modern ghost story and the modern detective story were invented by the American poet and novelist, Edgar Allan Poe.

Henry Wadsworth Longfellow was the first American poet to have his statue placed in the famed Poet's Corner of Westminster Abbey in London.

preserve and restore the Alhambra as an international treasure.

England accepted Irving because he adopted European themes. James Fenimore Cooper was lionized in England because his *Leatherstocking Tales*—five novels about Indians and a frontiersman who lived in the wilderness, Natty Bumppo—appealed to European visions of Americans as "noble savages." The most famous of the *Leatherstocking Tales* were *The Last of the Mohicans* and *The Deerslayer.*

Although he was born in Boston, Edgar Allan Poe was a southerner—a Marylander—by inheritance and choice. Embittered by criticisms of his work, he became an alcoholic and died at 40 years of age. Not until the twentieth century was Poe properly recognized as one of America's finest poets and the inventor of both the modern ghost story and the modern detective novel.

Two popular American poets were Henry Wadsworth Longfellow, a professor of languages, and John Greenleaf Whittier. Longfellow was best known for long epics on American themes: *The Song of Hiawatha, The Midnight Ride of Paul Revere,* and *Evangeline.* Whittier's most popular poem was "Barefoot Boy with Cheek of Tan."

SECTION REVIEW

1. Write a sentence to identify: Transcendentalism, Nathaniel Hawthorne, *Moby Dick,* Natty Bumppo.

2. Explain the origin of the term *The Flowering of New England.* Name some of the people involved in the movement who were not from New England.

3. Where did Ralph Waldo Emerson look to find God? Which did Emerson feel was more powerful, personal morality or a society's laws?

4. Describe the connection of Thoreau and Fuller with Transcendentalism.

5. Name five American writers and poets who were not part of the Transcendentalist tradition. Describe a subject or theme used by each author.

As anyone who has ever read James Fenimore Cooper's *Leatherstocking Tales* knows, Cooper seems to have had a propensity for using as many words as possible in his writing. When the stories were first published in Europe, they were serialized in magazines. Cooper's salary was based on the number of words he wrote, so he sought to maximize his profits.

4. AMERICAN REFORMERS

The utopians withdrew from American society because they believed its materialism was dehumanizing. The Transcendentalists criticized American society on a philosophical level. A third important group of Americans in the early nineteenth century, the *evangelical reformers*, did not reject the whole of America. Instead, they directed their attention to specific social problems such as society's treatment of the handicapped, the insane, and other disadvantaged people, and also to behavior they believed was morally and socially destructive, such as drunkenness.

These evangelical reformers looked in many directions. However, almost all of them supported the most important of the campaigns to make a better America, the women's rights movement, which sought equality of the sexes, and the abolitionist movement, which demanded an end to the institution of slavery.

Characteristics of the Reformers.

The reformers of the first half of the nineteenth century were called evangelical because they believed it was the moral duty of Christian men and women to speak out about the evils they found in society. Most of the reformers were New Englanders, descendents of the Puritans. Though they had abandoned the harsh religious doctrines of their ancestors, they still possessed the firm conviction that they were responsible for the welfare of their neighbors.

The New England character of the reformers was also illustrated by the fact that most of them supported the Whig party. The reformers were middle class and tended to be proud of their respectability. To most of them, the Democrats were the party of southern slaveowners, the lower classes, and increasingly, immigrants. To the reformers, the immigrants seemed to be bringing different, undesirable ways of life to the United States.

The reformers also favored the Whigs because that party's leaders believed that government should take an active interest in social and economic questions. In contrast, most Democrats said that government's responsibility ended with defense and maintaining order at home. The Democratic party of the early nineteenth century believed in *laissez faire* (lĕs'ăfâr'). This is the point of view that government should leave the economy to work out its own problems and should leave the solution of social evils to private citizens.

Women were prominent in reform, both as leaders and supporters. Denied the right to participate in business, the professions, and politics, women found they could play a part in movements dedicated to moral and religious issues. Reform was public. But it also dealt in matters of morality, and matters of morality belonged within the "woman's role."

Helping Handicapped People.

Traditionally, handicaps like blindness and deafness were thought to be personal concerns. They were not considered disabilities to be overcome so that blind or deaf people could participate fully in society. They were considered conditions of life for which no one was "responsible."

Thomas Gallaudet (găl'ŭ-dĕt') disagreed. Shocked by the fact that deaf people were simply shunted aside, he devoted his life to educating

Thomas Gallaudet started the first free school for deaf people in the United States in 1817.

Discussion Question: According to the views of the Democratic and Whig parties detailed on this page of the text, how would those parties compare to the present-day Republican and Democratic parties? Which present-day party's views are most similar to those held by the Whigs?

 295

The above engraving shows the Eastern Lunatic Asylum at Williamsburg, Virginia. Until concerned social reformers such as Dorothea Dix brought about changes in the 1840s, insane people were usually kept in prisons rather than asylums like this one.

those who could not hear so that they could participate fully in society. In 1815 he went to Europe to study new techniques for helping the deaf.

In France, Gallaudet met a teacher who, like himself, believed in helping the deaf as a moral duty. They returned to the United States and, in 1817, founded the American Asylum, a free school for the deaf in Hartford, Connecticut. (The word *asylum* means "refuge.") Gallaudet gladly taught his methods to anyone who wished to learn them.

Samuel Gridley Howe was a physician who taught the blind to overcome their disability at the Perkins Institute for the Blind in Boston. Howe toured the country with Laura Bridgman, a girl who was both deaf and blind but had learned to communicate with others. The example of a person who had overcome such serious difficulties proved that with help no physically handicapped person had to live a useless life.

Dorothea Dix. The plight of the insane was understood even more poorly than that of the physically disabled. Insane people were treated as if they were criminals, housed in prisons where they were neglected and even abused.

In the winter of 1841, a 33-year-old Massachusetts schoolteacher, Dorothea Dix, discovered that insane people were kept in an unheated room in the Cambridge House of Corrections. She was shocked. Having lived the very sheltered life of a respectable young lady of the period, Dix had not known such evils existed.

Her discovery changed her life. She investigated insane asylums and found that many were worse than the Cambridge prison. In 1843, she presented a report to the Massachusetts state legislature and demanded a change. The report said that almost everywhere, helpless people were locked in "cages, closets, cellars, stalls, pens." They were fed slops unfit for hogs and "chained, naked, beaten with rods, and lashed into obedience." Massachusetts swiftly enacted a bill to improve conditions. Dix then went on to other states and to urge Congress to establish the St. Elizabeth's Hospital for the Insane. In time, she traveled to Europe and spoke with both Queen Victoria and the pope about the treatment of the insane.

Discussion Question: How does the illustration above compare with Dorothea Dix's description of an insane asylum? Ask students if they would have thought the picture was a prison.

MOVERS AND SHAPERS

Dorothea Dix

Dorothea Dix (1802–1887) had a hard childhood. She lived with her parents in a log cabin in Maine for 12 years, then sought refuge and education with her sympathetic grandmother in Boston. Two years later, at 14, she found employment as a teacher.

In 1841, a friend asked her to give lessons to women prisoners in a local jail. Dix was outraged that insane women were kept in the jail and treated as criminals. From that moment on, she devoted herself to getting the insane out of jails and into decent hospitals.

Dix had to battle the common idea that women should not do public work. But three characteristics kept her going: an independent spirit; intense compassion for fellow hu-

mans; and the belief that any person, ill or well, had spiritual potential, and thus was worth saving. As a result of her crusade, 32 state mental hospitals were built.

Elizabeth and Emily Blackwell

Elizabeth Blackwell (1821–1910) and her younger sister, Emily Blackwell (1826–1910), grew up in Bristol, England. Their father gave his daughters the same education as his sons. The Blackwells emigrated to the United States in 1832. When the father died in 1838, Elizabeth worked as a teacher to support the family.

One day, as Elizabeth was standing at the bedside of a dying friend, the friend proposed a startling idea. She told Elizabeth to study medicine, because suffering women like

herself needed the understanding of a female doctor.

The challenge of becoming a doctor appealed to Elizabeth. She soon came to regard it as "an all-absorbing duty . . . the noblest and most useful path I can tread." However, she encountered resistance at every turn. Because she was a woman, her applications to medical schools were constantly rejected. She was finally admitted to Geneva College in New York. When she graduated from Geneva in 1849, Blackwell was the first professionally licensed woman doctor in the United States.

Through the 1850s, Blackwell struggled to establish herself in New York City. Landlords were horrified at the thought of a woman doctor and refused to rent rooms to her. Hospitals turned her away. But she persevered until, in 1857, she had raised enough money to start her own hospital: the New York Infirmary for Women and Children.

Joining her at the hospital was her younger sister, Dr. Emily Blackwell. Encouraged by Elizabeth, Emily too had pursued a career in medicine, and proved herself to be an able doctor and hospital administrator. Other women followed the Blackwells' example, and by the time the two sisters died, there were scores of women treating hospital patients as fully trained physicians.

Research Assignment: In the Jacksonian era, colleges were all-male institutions. This began to change when Ohio's Oberlin College began accepting women students in 1833. In 1837 Mary Lyon founded the first women's college in the U.S., Mount Holyoke College. Have students write a report detailing the important events leading to the opening of Mount Holyoke and the beginning of higher education in schools for women.

Crime and Punishment. The penitentiary was another institution that attracted the attention of reformers. Large prisons for long-term convicts were new in the early nineteenth century. In earlier times, serious law-breakers were whipped, branded on the cheek (so everyone would know they were dangerous), had their ears cropped, or were hanged.

During the 1790s, the theory of imprisonment became popular. The belief was that jailed criminals would regret their crimes (become penitent) and, when they were released, become useful citizens. Unfortunately, prison life was often extremely cruel and would embitter prisoners further toward society. Connecticut, for example, confined some of its law-breakers in an abandoned mine shaft.

Prison Reform. Another self-defeating feature of the penitentiary system was that juveniles and adults who committed minor crimes were imprisoned together with criminals who had committed much worse and many more crimes. Instead of learning to regret their crimes, many minor offenders were "educated" into more serious crime. In order to prevent juveniles from learning more antisocial behavior from older prisoners, Boston, New York City, and Philadelphia established "houses of refuge" for juvenile offenders.

A lively controversy developed between reformers who favored the *Pennsylvania System* for penitentiaries and those who preferred the *Auburn System,* named for a New York state prison. Pennsylvania kept its prisoners in solitary confinement day and night. This prevented hardened criminals from influencing minor offenders and also, it was argued, gave convicts plenty of time to meditate on the consequences of their crimes. However, the constant solitude drove many convicts insane. Also, with its individual cells, the Pennsylvania System was extremely expensive.

At Auburn, prisoners slept alone in cells at night, but during the day, they were marched to large workrooms where they labored together. Though they were not allowed to speak, fewer people jailed at Auburn cracked under the pres-

New York prisons, like the one shown below, used the Auburn System. Under this system, prisoners were not kept in solitary confinement, but were required to work together in prison workrooms. Reformers encouraged the spread of the system.

Research Assignment: Have students write a report on prison reform in the 1800s. The reform issues should parallel present prison reform issues. Encourage students to use newspapers and magazines as reference sources for present reform issues.

sure and the prison helped pay its expenses with the products the convicts made. The reformers of the Prison Discipline Society eventually converted other states, including Pennsylvania, to the Auburn approach.

An Alcohol Problem. Americans drank heavily and always had. Because grain was cheap in the United States, liquor made from grain was readily available. By 1820 the annual consumption of hard spirits was more than seven gallons for each man, woman, and child.

Ale, beer, cider, and rum were the everyday beverages in New England. Westerners drank so much whiskey made from rye or corn that the "little brown jug" became one of the symbols of frontier life. Middle and upper class Americans tended to drink the more expensive wine and brandy from abroad. Most urban workers insisted they needed liquor for strength.

As early as the 1780s, a famous Philadelphia physician and American revolutionary, Dr. Benjamin Rush, described the numerous physical problems caused by excessive drinking and called for Americans to break the habit. After 1800, diet reformers such as Sylvester Graham, after whom the graham cracker is named, blamed much on "Demon Rum."

In the 1830s, reformers added social and moral arguments to the cause of good health. First, they published statistics showing that large numbers of crimes were committed by drunks. Second, they drew a connection between poverty and drunkenness. A few said that the miseries of poverty caused people to turn to alcohol. But many believed that drunkenness was the cause of poverty.

Once evangelical reformers took up the cause of *temperance* (drinking in moderation), it spread quickly. By 1835 there were 5,000 Temperance Societies in the United States with a membership of more than a million people. In 1840, six reformed drinkers founded a national organization, the *Washington Temperance Society.* Two years later, a more militant association, the *Sons of Temperance,* began to promote sobriety as a basic religious duty. The Sons' most effective lecturer was John B. Gough. He rallied audiences with colorful fire-and-brimstone sermons. Wherever Gough spoke, men and women swore never to touch the bottle and jug.

Benjamin Rush's "tranquilizing chair" was used to restrain unmanageable patients.

In the 1830s, temperance societies encouraged temperance—or moderation—by heavy drinkers.

Temperance Becomes Prohibition. Temperance reformers differed on whether drunkenness or alcohol itself was the problem to be solved. A minority said that alcohol was not evil if it was used in moderation. Others, the complete abstainers or "Teetotalers," said that once an occasional drink was allowed, complete drunkenness followed. They insisted on no alcohol at all.

In 1838, Massachusetts experimented with a law that was designed to cut down on consumption of alcohol by the poor. The *Fifteen Gallon Law* prohibited the sale of whiskey and rum in quantities smaller than 15 gallons. This did not satisfy prohibitionists. Working people protested that it allowed the wealthy, who could afford big purchases, to drink, but not the poor person. In the age of Jackson, the law did not have a chance. It was repealed within two years.

In 1845, New York allowed local governments to forbid the manufacture, sale, and use of alcohol within their jurisdictions. Within a few years, five sixths of the state was dry. In 1846, a Portland businessman, Neal Dow, persuaded Maine to adopt the first statewide prohibition law. By 1860, 13 states had followed Maine's example. However, the laws were widely disobeyed and by 1868, every temperance state but Maine had repealed its laws.

The Response to Immigration. An Irish priest, Father Theobald Mathew, spread the gospel of temperance among Irish-American Catholics who had been attracted to the United States by the chance to work in road, canal, and railroad construction. He administered an oath never to drink to more than half a million Roman Catholic members of the *Teetotal Abstinence Society.*

However, like the other reforms, temperance was largely a Protestant movement. Indeed, the presence in the United States of a large and

Job opportunities brought hundreds of thousands of immigrants to the United States.

Class Activity: Have students do research on rehabilitation techniques employed by Alcoholics Anonymous, various drug rehabilitation programs. *Teetotaler* is a coined word made up of the letter *t* + *total* (abstinence) + the suffix *er*.
Whiskey is derived from a Gaelic word meaning "water of life."

Shiploads of hopeful immigrants regularly arrived in New York. Eager to work hard and better their situations, these immigrants worked in new American factories, built railroads and canals, and contributed in many ways to the tremendous expansion of a young country.

growing Roman Catholic minority worried many evangelical reformers. They did not believe that the Catholic religion, with a pope in Rome, was compatible with American ideals. When the reformers founded organizations designed to convert the new Catholic immigrants to Protestantism or to spread their faith to other parts of the world, they believed that they were improving society.

Changing Pattern of Immigration. In 1820, only 8,400 Europeans came to the United States. More than 23,000 arrived in 1830, and 84,000 in 1840. During the decade that followed, immigration boomed. In 1850, 370,000 people stepped from crowded immigrant ships onto American wharves in eastern seaports.

Not only were the numbers larger than ever, the immigrants of the 1830s and 1840s differed from earlier arrivals in their religion and often their language. Thus, 3,600 Irish men and women entered the United States in 1820, most of them Protestants from the north of Ireland. In 1850, 164,000 Irish immigrants, most of them Roman

Catholic, came to America. Authorities counted only 23 Scandinavian immigrants in 1820. Over 4,000 Scandinavians were arriving annually by the mid-1850s. In 1820, 968 Germans came to the United States. In 1850 the figure was 79,000.

Because the Scandinavian and German immigrants clustered in communities where they were able to preserve their Old World languages and customs, many Americans worried that they would never fit into American society. And some German customs, such as socializing at noisy musical beer gardens, offended the sensibilities of temperance reformers. Despite the efforts of Father Mathew, the more numerous Irish seemed to the temperance reformers even worse than the Germans.

Most of the Irish immigrants were Roman Catholic, as were about half the Germans. Between 1830 and 1860, the Catholic population of the United States increased ten times, from 300,000 to more than 3 million, from three percent of the total United States population to 13 percent.

The term *assimilation* should be introduced here and used as the basis for an on-going discussion in future chapters. Discuss the fairness of this process and the problems presented by it. Emphasize both the negative aspects (racism and prejudice) and the positive by-products (melting pot).

Anti-Catholic Feelings.

Many Americans inherited anti-Catholic prejudices from their Puritan past. In the nineteenth century, suspicion of Catholics took on a new life because the head of the church, the pope of Rome, was not only a spiritual leader but the ruler of central Italy. There the popes allowed few freedoms such as Americans prized. To American Protestants, the Roman Catholic religion seemed opposed to individual liberty. Because the new Irish immigrants were deeply loyal to their faith, some Protestants believed they could never become good citizens.

The Irish also aroused hostility because they were extremely poor. Forced to leave their homeland by the threat of starvation when Ireland's potato crop failed, they were willing to take jobs at almost any wages. Protestant workers blamed them for forcing their own wages down.

In addition to traditional dislike of Catholicism —the suspicion that Catholics were antidemocratic—and economic anxieties, many Protestants believed that priests and nuns, who did not marry, lived immoral lives. The book *The Awful Disclosures of Maria Monk* pretended to be a true story of immorality and the murder of infants in a large convent in Montreal, Canada. Similar rumors led a Protestant mob to burn a convent in Charlestown, Massachusetts, in 1834. Although prominent Protestant clergy members denounced mob action, investigated convents, and assured people the tales of immorality were false, many people continued to believe the stories.

Riots and the Know-Nothings.

The earliest anti-Catholic movement was secret. The Order of the Star-Spangled Banner instructed its anti-immigration members to answer all questions about their organization with the response, "I know nothing," thus earning them the insulting name, the *Know-Nothings*.

After 1850, however, at the urging of such prominent anti-Catholics as the painter and inventor of the telegraph, Samuel F. B. Morse, the Know-Nothings came above ground, formed the *Native American party,* and entered politics. They capitalized on the decline of the Whigs and became a major force in American elections. The Know-Nothings swept to power in several states and controlled Massachusetts. At its peak, the Native American party elected 75 members of Congress. A former Whig president, Millard Fillmore, ran as the party's presidential nominee in 1856. To many Americans, there was nothing unrespectable about being a Know-Nothing.

Missionaries.

A majority of Protestants denounced both violent and political action against Catholics. All Americans, they said, were entitled to the same rights. Even many of these people, however, approved of attempts by Protestant churches to convert Catholic and Jewish people to the traditional American Protestant faiths.

The *American Tract Society* (founded in 1814) and the *American Bible Society* (1816) distributed Protestant pamphlets and Bibles among the Catholic population. By 1836, the Tract Society estimated that it had sold or given away more than 3 million publications that explained Protestant beliefs.

Another group of missionaries worked among the small Jewish population in the United States. However, most missionary activity was directed abroad. With colleges in New England and the United States turning out more ministers than there were churches for them to head, groups like the *American Board of Foreign Missions* collected money to send religious young men and women to Africa, India, China, and the best known of all, to the Sandwich Islands, which we now know as Hawaii.

Americans in Hawaii.

Located in the middle of the Pacific Ocean, the Hawaiian Islands were not discovered by Europeans until 1778 when the English navigator, Captain James Cook, named them after the Earl of Sandwich. At that time, the tribes of the islands were at war. Cook himself was killed in a battle. By 1810, however, with the aid of American and British sailors who provided him with a cannon, King Kamehameha (kä-mä′hä-mä′hä), united the islands under his rule.

By that time, whalers and merchant vessels from New England had been calling at the islands for a generation. They took on fresh water, replenished their provisions, and cured themselves of scurvy by feasting on fresh fruits and fish. They also brought disease and corruption to the native people.

In 1819, a Hawaiian Christian, who had come to New England with some whalers, told graduates

Research Assignment: Have students do a report studying the events in Europe that prompted the surge in immigration to the U.S. from certain countries during this period. Encourage students to use photographs and artifacts from the period to illustrate their reports.

Birth of the Women's Movement. Extraordinary women like Dorothea Dix became famous for their role in reform. The wives and sisters of ministers in Hawaii were at least as important as the men in the missions there. Women were particularly prominent in the greatest evangelical reform movement of all, the movement to abolish slavery. In fact, it was discrimination against women by fellow *abolitionists* that led to the founding of the feminist or women's movement in the United States.

Stanton and Mott. In 1840, Elizabeth Cady of Johnstown, New York, married an attorney, Henry Stanton, whom she had met at meetings of an antislavery society. She took her husband's name but insisted on omitting that part of the wedding ceremony in which the bride promised to obey her husband. Both Stantons believed that husband and wife should be equal.

King Kamehameha I united the warring tribes of the Hawaiian Islands in the beginning of the nineteenth century.

of Andover Theological Seminary that his people needed them, both to learn true religion and as protection against immoral and exploitative sailors. His message was electrifying. The next year, young ministers and their wives shipped out to the Sandwich Islands on the other side of the world to spread their faith.

Once there, they did much good by introducing improved medicine and ideas about sanitation, and by preaching against the lax morality of the visiting American sailors and whalers. However, the missionaries were also criticized for confusing religion and morality with New England customs. In a climate that was ill-suited to such clothing, the missionaries insisted that Hawaiian women dress in long, flannel dresses and men in trousers, stiff white shirts, and stovepipe hats.

Elizabeth Cady Stanton was one of the founders and the guiding spirit of the women's movement.

The kingdom founded by Kamehameha lasted only 83 years. In 1893 a group of American settlers overthrew the reigning monarch in Hawaii, Queen Liliuokalani.

GOING TO THE SOURCE

We hold these truths to be self-evident: that all men and women are created equal; that they are endowed by their Creator with certain inalienable rights; that among these are life, liberty, and the pursuit of happiness; that to secure these rights governments are instituted, deriving their just powers from the consent of the governed. . . .

The history of mankind is a history of repeated injuries and usurpations on the part of man toward woman, having in direct object the establishment of an absolute tyranny over her. To prove this, let facts be submitted to a candid world.

He has never permitted her to exercise her inalienable right to the elective franchise.

He has compelled her to submit to laws, in the formation of which she had no voice.

He has withheld from her rights which are given to the most ignorant and degraded men —both natives and foreigners.

Having deprived her of this first right of a citizen, the elective franchise, thereby leaving her without representation in the halls of legislation, he has oppressed her on all sides.

He has made her, if married, in the eye of the law, civilly dead.

He has taken from her all right in property, even to the wages she earns.

He has made her, morally, an irresponsible being, as she can commit many crimes with impunity [without fear of punishment], provided they be done in the presence of her husband. In the covenant of marriage, she is compelled to promise obedience to her husband, he becoming, to all intents and purposes, her master—the law giving him power to deprive her of her liberty, and to administer chastisement.

> *The history of mankind is a history of repeated injuries and usurpations on the part of man toward woman, having in direct object the establishment of an absolute tyranny over her. To prove this, let facts be submitted to a candid world.*
>
> SENECA FALLS DECLARATION OF SENTIMENTS AND RESOLUTIONS

He has so framed the laws of divorce, as to what shall be the proper causes, and in case of separation, to whom guardianship of the children shall be given, as to be wholly regardless of the happiness of women —the law, in all cases, going upon a false supposition of the supremacy of man, and giving all power into his hands.

After depriving her of all rights as a married woman, if single, and the owner of property, he has taxed her to support a government which recognizes her only when her property can be made profitable to it.

He has monopolized nearly all the profitable employments, and from those she is permitted to follow, she receives but a scanty remuneration. He closes against her all the avenues to wealth and distinction which he considers most honorable to himself. As a teacher of theology, medicine, or law, she is not known.

He has denied her the facilities for obtaining a thorough education, all colleges being closed against her. . . .

Now, in view of this entire disfranchisement of one-half the people in this country, their social and religious degradation—in view of the unjust laws above mentioned, and because women do feel themselves aggrieved, oppressed, and fraudulently deprived of their most sacred rights, we insist that they have immediate admission to all the rights and privileges which belong to them as citizens of the United States.

One hundred women and men convened in Seneca Falls, New York, in July 1848 to write the Seneca Falls Declaration of Sentiments and Resolutions *on women's rights, from which this source was excerpted.*

Discussion Question: What forces in society between 1820 and 1850 influenced the women's rights movement?

Lucretia Mott (left) and Susan B. Anthony (center), were leaders in the women's movement. Amelia Bloomer (right) wanted dress reform, and the trousers she wore were called "bloomers."

The Stantons and a close friend, Lucretia Coffin Mott, traveled to an international slavery convention in England. When they arrived, Mrs. Mott and Mrs. Stanton were told that, as women, they could not participate in the convention. The women were furious. Even people committed to ending the inequalities suffered by black people could not see the inconsistency that went with not believing in the equality of men and women.

The Seneca Falls Convention.

For years the women wondered how to fight their battle. Finally, in the summer of 1848, they called a convention at Seneca Falls, New York, and adopted Elizabeth Cady Stanton's *Declaration of Sentiments and Resolutions.* It was patterned after the Declaration of Independence.

The Declaration stated that the injustices suffered by women included the denial of the right to vote; the fact that a married woman gave control of her property to her husband; the exclusion of women from the professions; and the nearly absolute legal control of women by men.

Only 68 women and 32 men signed the Seneca Falls Declaration. However, the movement attracted attention right away. One of the spectators at the convention was Amelia Bloomer, who crusaded for the right of women to vote. She also wanted to reform women's dress to show equality with men. Susan B. Anthony, who did not attend the convention, would soon join Elizabeth Cady Stanton as a worker on behalf of *women's suffrage* (the right to vote) for more than half a century.

It would take even longer for American women to win legal equality. One reason for the delay was that, by the middle of the nineteenth century, feminists agreed that another cause was more immediately important. That was the movement to abolish slavery in the United States.

SECTION REVIEW

1. Write a sentence to identify: laissez faire, Fifteen Gallon Law, Samuel F. B. Morse, Seneca Falls Convention.

2. Give the names of individual reformers or reform groups that offered help to the following: deaf people, blind people, mentally ill people, prisoners, alcoholics.

3. Describe the circumstances that led to the formation of such groups as the Know-Nothings, the Native American party, and the American Bible Society.

4. List the women who were prominent in the feminist movement. Identify their major achievements or activities.

Class Activity: Have students stage the events that might have taken place at the Seneca Falls Convention. Assign the roles to students of Elizabeth Cady Stanton, Lucretia Mott, Frederick Douglas, Charlotte Woodward, and a newspaper reporter covering the convention. Students should use actual convention text and newspaper accounts of the convention.

 305

CHAPTER REVIEW

TIME LINE

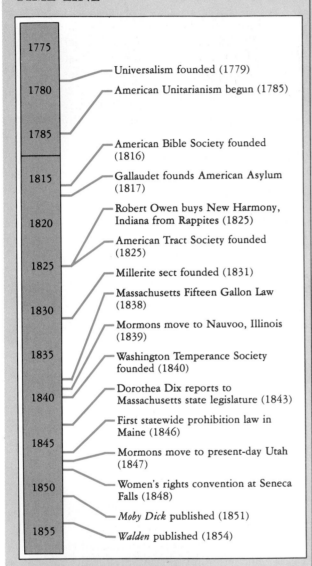

1775

Universalism founded (1779)

1780

American Unitarianism begun (1785)

1785

American Bible Society founded (1816)

1815

Gallaudet founds American Asylum (1817)

1820

Robert Owen buys New Harmony, Indiana from Rappites (1825)

American Tract Society founded (1825)

1825

Millerite sect founded (1831)

Massachusetts Fifteen Gallon Law (1838)

1830

Mormons move to Nauvoo, Illinois (1839)

1835

Washington Temperance Society founded (1840)

1840

Dorothea Dix reports to Massachusetts state legislature (1843)

First statewide prohibition law in Maine (1846)

1845

Mormons move to present-day Utah (1847)

1850

Women's rights convention at Seneca Falls (1848)

Moby Dick published (1851)

1855

Walden published (1854)

TIME LINE QUESTIONS

1. Name the seven events on this time line that deal with religious movements.
2. How long after the Washington Temperance Society was founded did Maine pass its prohibition law?
3. How many years before Dorothea Dix gave her report did Gallaudet open the American Asylum?

SKILLS STRATEGY

To take advantage of the dress reform advocated by Amelia Bloomer, a music publisher brought out "The New Costume Polka." This picture was the cover for the music, and shows a "Bloomer girl" wearing the style Bloomer recommended.

TEXT, PICTURES, AND CAPTIONS

Some textbook pictures, like the one above, can be considered primary sources because they are from the historical period being studied. The caption below it is not a primary source but was written later to clarify the picture for current readers.

APPLYING SKILLS

Reread the material under the heading "The Seneca Falls Convention." Then respond to the following questions:

1. What information in the text is the picture meant to supplement?
2. Why is the woman called a "Bloomer girl" and where did this name come from?
3. What attitude toward Bloomer girls does the picture convey?
4. What information about the picture does the caption give?

Making Connections: Review the questions and topics presented in the Making Connections section that opens this chapter. Emphasize the importance of these reform movements as factors contributing to the Civil War and encourage students' awareness of their long-lasting effects on American values and culture.

UNIT 3 TEST

CHAPTER SURVEY

In a sentence or two, summarize the content of the chapter from which these terms come, and write a sentence to identify *one* of the terms from each chapter.

1. *Chapter 9:* Robert Livingston, Sacajawea, General Andrew Jackson, Twelfth Amendment.
2. *Chapter 10:* Lowell girls, Eli Whitney, Conestoga wagon, National Road, Mainline Canal.
3. *Chapter 11:* "Trail of Tears," Sequoyah, Nicholas Biddle, "Tippecanoe and Tyler, Too."
4. *Chapter 12:* Joseph Smith, Mother Ann Lee, utopia, Transcendentalism, Know-Nothings.

TEXT REVIEW

5. Which achievement of Thomas Jefferson's presidency do you consider most significant for the later history of the United States? Give reasons for your choice.
6. Support the following statement: "There was more to the American decision to go to war in 1812 than just impressment of the nation's sailors."
7. Is the "Era of Good Feelings" a completely accurate description of the Monroe presidency? Explain your answer.
8. Describe three types of machines that made the Industrial Revolution in England possible. Explain how machines came to the United States.
9. How was the revival of slavery in the South aided by inventions and the Industrial Revolution in England and the Northeast?
10. Establish the relationship of the following to the panic of 1819: land speculation in the West, wildcat banks, the Bank of the United States, people who had savings in the wildcat banks.
11. Explain how the growth of the West and Jefferson's and Jackson's ideas contributed to the upsurge of democracy between 1801 and 1844.
12. Explain John Calhoun's "compact theory of government." What action by South Carolina was based on this theory? What did President Jackson do about South Carolina's action?
13. List five religious or utopian movements that arose at the beginning of the nineteenth century. Give important facts about one of them.
14. What types of social problems did the reformers of the first half of the nineteenth century attack? Describe the work of one reformer.

CRITICAL THINKING

15. If Chief Justice Marshall had ruled differently in such cases as *McCulloch* v. *Maryland,* how might the relationship between the states and the federal government have been different?
16. Compare your idea of the location of "the West" with that of an American in the early 1800s.
17. Name some American writers who agreed with Ralph Waldo Emerson's philosophy of Transcendentalism, and other American writers who disagreed with it.

SKILLS REVIEW

18. List the following events in chronological order: Erie Canal built; Louisiana Purchase; Andrew Jackson first inaugurated; Mormons move to Nauvoo, Illinois; Seneca Falls convention on women's rights; British burn Washington, D.C.; South Carolina nullification convention.
19. Which of the statements below expresses an opinion? Explain how the opinion statement could be validated.
    a. Slavery should never have been permitted in the English colonies or the United States.
    b. Southern planters could never have become as rich as they did if slavery did not exist in the United States.
20. The course of history is often determined by a specific idea or event "whose time has come." Choose four ideas or events discussed in Unit 3 which you feel had the greatest long-term importance, and write a sentence for each, briefly summarizing its historical impact.

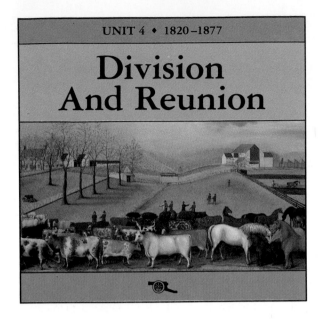

UNIT 4 ♦ 1820–1877

Division And Reunion

Unit 4 Overview

Unit 4 begins when southerners began to argue that slavery was a positive good in opposition to abolitionist contentions that slavery was morally evil. The unit continues with accounts of American expansion to the far west, the war with Mexico, the disputes about whether western territories should be admitted to the Union as free or slave states, and the secession of several southern states after Lincoln was elected in 1860. The last two chapters of the unit are in-depth narrations of the Civil War and Reconstruction.

Basic Unit Concepts
1. Between 1820 and 1860, a bitter national debate over the morality of slavery agitated the American people—slaveholders on one side, abolitionists on the other.
2. Westward expansion of American pioneers brought in its train a war with Mexico and added fuel to the fiery debate over slavery—Which territories should be admitted to the Union as slave states, and which as free states?
3. The election of President Lincoln and the firing on Fort Sumter plunged the nation into a tragic civil war, won by the Union at great cost.
4. An important goal of the Radical Republicans' Reconstruction plan—to guarantee the civil rights of freed slaves—was ultimately thwarted southern state governments.

Chapter 13: "The South and Slavery" (1820–1860)
In Chapter 13, students discover why most white southerners argued that slavery was a positive good. They will learn of the harsh measures taken by whites to suppress the freedom of slaves, and of the courage of slaves in coping with their lot. Finally, they survey the ideas and activities of a variety of abolitionists.

Features
Going to the Source: Excerpt from former-slave Frederick Douglass's Letter to a Slaveholder (page 327)

Movers and Shapers: Isabella Baumfree (page 328)
American Ingenuity chart (pages 330–331)

Learning Objectives
History Generalizations Students will gain knowledge that supports the following generalizations:
1. Fears over slave revolts and a debate in the Virginia legislature over abolishing slavery united most southerners in the belief that slavery should be maintained.
2. Religious, historical, racial, and sociological arguments of the positive good theory were used in defense of slavery.
3. The "peculiar" institution of slavery made possible a gracious, abundant life for a minority of white planters.
4. With few exceptions, the life of a slave was a round of unceasing labor whose greatest benefits went to others and a life devoid of freedom and other human rights.
5. Those black people who did not escape developed a strong cultural life which included music and oral literature that were thinly-masked protests against slavery.
6. After 1820, whites and blacks, northerners and southerners, men and women, contributed to an active movement to abolish slavery in the United States.

Study Skills In addition to the three skills noted in chapter 1 which are standard to every chapter, students will:
1. review and use the parts of a dictionary entry.
2. write a paragraph defining a problem and enumerating proposed solutions.
3. relate graphic materials to the text of the chapter.
4. practice these **critical thinking skills**: generating questions about materials to be read, recognizing viewpoint, distinguishing fact and opinion.

Chapter 14: "Expansion and Division" (1820–1860)
In this chapter, students follow Americans outside the United States to settle lands claimed by other nations. They see the connection among the belief in manifest destiny, a war with Mexico, and the acquisition of new territories for the United States. They evaluate the serious disputes over whether western territories should be admitted to the Union as slave states or free states. Finally, they follow the escalation of events leading to the 1860 election and the resulting secession of several southern states.

Features
Going to the Source: Message from William B. Travis, commander of the Alamo (page 340)
Profiles of the Presidency: James Polk (page 343), Zachary Taylor (page 347), Millard Fillmore (page 349), Franklin Pierce (page 350), James Buchanan (page 353).

Learning Objectives
History Generalizations Students will gain knowledge that supports the following generalizations:
1. In the first half of the nineteenth century Americans settled lands outside the United States that became California, Oregon, Texas, and other states of the Union.
2. The slaughter at the Alamo led to the forming of the Lone Star Republic and the admission of Texas as a slave state.
3. Belief in the manifest destiny of the United States to rule North America led to war with Mexico.
4. The discovery of gold in California led to the admission of the Bear Flag Republic as a state, shattering the previous balance between 15 slave and 15 free states.
5. After the war with Mexico, disputes between North and

South over the admission of western territories as slave or free states grew bitter and sometimes violent.

6. Events such as the Dred Scott decision, a split in the Democratic party, and John Brown's raid on Harpers Ferry widened the gap between the North and the South.
7. The election of Abraham Lincoln in 1860 touched of the secession of South Carolina and six other southern states, making Civil War all but inevitable.

Study Skills In addition to the three skills noted in chapter 1 which are standard to every chapter, students will:
1. compare news stories and editorials as primary sources.
2. write a one-paragraph newspaper editorial and a letter responding to it.
3. relate graphic materials to the text of the chapter.
4. practice these **critical thinking skills**: generating questions about materials to be read, contrasting given political figures, classifying information, recognizing bias.

Chapter 15: "The Civil War" (1861–1865)

In Chapter 15, students witness the founding of the Confederate States of America. They follow the destructive course of the Civil War to the final surrender of the Confederacy at Appomatox. They recognize the importance of the Emancipation Proclamation. Finally, they realize the staggering human and material costs of the war.

Features

Profiles of the Presidency: Abraham Lincoln (page 364)
Movers and Shapers: Matthew Brady and Clara Barton (page 371)
Going to the Source: The Gettysburg Address (page 382)

Learning Objectives

History Generalizations Students will gain knowledge that supports the following generalizations:
1. After the election of President Lincoln, seven southern states formed the Confederate States of America with Jefferson Davis as president; Delaware, Maryland, Kentucky, Missouri and West Virginia remained within the Union.
2. The failure of last-minute attempts at compromise and the attack on Fort Sumter by the Confederacy resulted in the opening of hostilities between North and South.
3. Although both sides expected fighting to end quickly, the Civil War was a long, costly, devastating, and tragic conflict, the first "modern war" in that military leaders sought to destroy the economy and society of their opponents.
4. The caution of some Union generals and the brilliance of some Confederate generals kept the North from winning decisive victories.
5. President Lincoln's Emancipation Proclamation gave Union troops and civilians a morale-boosting goal of "making men free," encouraged black enlistments in the North's fighting forces,and prepared the way for the complete abolition of slavery.
6. Grant employed tactics that eventually resulted in the defeat of the South's armies.
7. A few days before the final surrender of the South, President Lincoln was shot and killed.

Study Skills In addition to the three skills noted in Chapter 1 which are standard to every chapter, students will:
1. use quotations and footnotes.
2. write a paragraph including quotations and footnotes.
3. relate graphic materials to the text of the chapter.
4. practice these **critical thinking skills:** generating ques-

tions about materials to be read, summarizing text information, supporting opinions.

Chapter 16: "Reconstructing the Union" (1865–1877)

In Chapter 16, students learn what domestic changes Congress brought about during the Civil War while southern legislators were absent. They follow the debate over what form Reconstruction should take, ending with the vindictive Radical Republican Reconstruction plan. They witness the southern states' denial of the civil and human rights of the freed slaves, and Congress's attempts to ensure these rights in the Fourteenth and Fifteenth Amendments. Finally, they learn why northern troops were withdrawn from the South ending Reconstruction and leaving the fate of the freed blacks in the hands of white southern leaders.

Features

Going to the Source: Excerpt from *Up From Slavery*, the autobiography of Booker T. Washington (page 396)
Profiles of the Presidency: Andrew Johnson (page 398), Ulysses S. Grant (page 402), Rutherford B. Hayes (page 407)
Movers and Shapers: Walt Whitman and Joseph Pulitzer (page 406)

Learning Objectives

History Generalizations Students will gain knowledge that supports the following generalization:
1. In the absence of southern representatives during the Civil War, Congress enacted legislation on the railroads, tariffs, the national bank, paper money and land policy—all of which brought dramatic changes to the nation.
2. Radical Republicans in Congress strongly opposed the reconstruction plans of Presidents Lincoln and Johnson, and impeached but could not convict President Johnson.
3. The Radicals won the debate over the reconstruction of the South and their reconstruction plan, though vindictive, went into effect, committing the United States to the principle of racial equality under the law.
4. In a variety of ways, the southern state governments subverted the intentions of the Radicals by discriminating against blacks in all areas of life.
5. To counter the leaders of state governments in the South, Congress successfully proposed two Constitutional Amendments: The Fourteenth Amendment was intended to prevent state governments from discriminating against freed slaves; the Fifteenth Amendment was intended to forbid all state governments from denying voting rights to any person on the basis of "race, color, or previous condition of servitude."
6. Disillusionment of northerners occasioned by scandals in President Grant's first term of office, the belief that only white Redeemers could bring stability to the South, and Democratic and Republican partisan political considerations, all contributed to the end of Reconstruction.
7. Despite some weak last attempts to assure their rights, the blacks were abandoned to the policies of southern leaders such as the Redeemers who were intent on keeping blacks in an inferior position.

Study Skills In addition to the three skills noted in chapter 1 which are standard to every chapter, students will:
1. use an atlas to locate places.
2. relate graphic materials to the text of the chapter.
3. practice these critical thinking skills: generating questions summarizing information, recognizing viewpoints.

Quotation: from the novel *Uncle Tom's Cabin.* Other works by Harriet Beecher Stowe (1811–1896) include *Dred—A Tale of the Great Dismal Swamp, The Minister's Wooing, The Pearl of Orr's Island,* and *Oldtown Folks.*

CHAPTER 13

THE SOUTH AND SLAVERY

1820–1860

It was on his grave, my friends, that I resolved . . . that I would never own another slave, while it was possible to free him. . . .

HARRIET BEECHER STOWE

Making Connections. It seems hard to believe now that slavery was ever a major institution in the United States. But until the mid-1800s, most Americans saw no problem with the institution. There were many who argued at the time that slavery was a positive good, for blacks and whites alike. From about 1820 on, however, an active movement to abolish slavery began to gain power in the United States.

In this chapter, you will learn:

• Why slave rebellions nearly caused Virginia to abolish slavery
• What arguments people used to defend slavery
• How slaves were actually treated
• Why slave auctions were particularly shocking to those who opposed slavery
• Who were the first Americans to speak out against slavery
• What effect escaped blacks had on the country when they told of their experiences as slaves.

You know that Thomas Jefferson called the clash in Congress in 1820 over slavery "a fire bell in the night." As Jefferson feared, the Missouri Compromise did not stop the debate over slavery. As you read, note the arguments put forth by proslavery and antislavery forces, and what the institution of slavery was really like.

Sections

1. Slavery Revived
2. The Peculiar Institution
3. The Abolitionists

1. SLAVERY REVIVED

Until the invention of the cotton gin, many white southerners believed that slavery would gradually die out in the United States. Southerners at the Constitutional Convention of 1787 had agreed to allow Congress the right to end the importation of slaves from Africa after 20 years. In 1807, with southern support, Congress did abolish the African slave trade.

But southern opinion was changing in 1820, when southern congressmen insisted that a new state, Missouri, had the right to enter the Union as a slave state. Nevertheless, it was not until after a slave rebellion in 1831 and a famous debate in 1832—when Virginia's legislature considered abolishing slavery in that state—that the majority of white southerners closed ranks and claimed that slavery was a blessing.

Fear of Rebellion. Fear of slave rebellion haunted whites who lived where slaves were numerous. To some extent, the fears were justified. In 1739, a slave known as Cato had led a revolt at the Stono plantation in South Carolina, during which 74 people were killed. Throughout the colonial period and into the nineteenth century, runaway slaves in Georgia joined the Seminole

In this painting by Charles Webber, runaway slaves are helped along the Underground Railroad by northern abolitionists. This "railroad" was actually a series of safe routes, vehicles, and houses runaways could use to get to Canada.

Skills Review: Reinforce the skills learned in the preceding Skills Strategy section. Make use of the photographs in this chapter to reinforce their use as a source of information that complements the text.

Indians and raided outlying plantations. Sometimes, the fear itself was enough. In New York City, two years after Cato's revolt, the mere rumor of rebellion among the city's blacks led to the trial and conviction of more than 100 blacks, on very flimsy evidence, and the execution of 31.

Then, in 1801, a slave named Gabriel Prosser urged blacks to rebel and march on Richmond. He was caught and hanged. In 1822, a free black named Denmark Vesey persuaded slaves and free blacks in Charleston to rise up and kill their masters, or so the authorities thought. Vesey and 36 others, mostly trusted household servants, were executed.

Rumors of slave rebellions circulated throughout the country. No doubt, many of the fears were entirely within the minds of whites, who imagined bloody uprisings simply because two or three blacks were seen speaking quietly together, then breaking up when a white person approached. The point is, the fear was real. And there was nothing imaginary about what happened in Virginia's Southampton County in 1831.

Nat Turner's Rebellion. Nat Turner was a slave. A kind mistress taught him to read and write and he became deeply religious, studying the Bible. He believed that the Bible held a message to slaves like himself to revolt, and he shared his feelings with a few close friends in secret meetings after dark.

On August 21, 1831, there was a solar eclipse that Turner believed was a sign from God. That night, he armed his followers with farm tools, and they spread out across Southampton County. Before the authorities could react, Turner's rebels killed more than 60 whites and convinced many other slaves to join them. When they were rounded up, there were 60 blacks in the band. Nat Turner himself was one of the last to be arrested. When he realized the rebellion was over, he gave himself up.

He and 16 others were hanged. Blacks who were not directly responsible for spilling blood were sold out of state. New restrictions were placed on the slaves who had remained peacefully on the plantations.

Nat Turner (pointing, at left) led a slave revolt in 1831 that frightened slaveowners and inspired slaves. Slaves continued to run away, as the handbill (right) indicates.

$2,500 REWARD!

RANAWAY, from the Subscriber, residing in Mississippi county, Mo., on Monday the 5th inst., my

Negro Man named GEORGE.

Said negro is five feet ten inches high, of dark complexion, he plays well on the Violin and several other instruments. He is a shrewd, smart fellow and of a very affable countenance, and is twenty-five years of age. If said negro is taken and confined in St. Louis Jail, or brought to this county so that I get him, the above reward of $1,000 will be promptly paid.

JOHN MEANS.

Also, from Radford E. Stanley,

A NEGRO MAN SLAVE, NAMED NOAH,

Full 6 feet high; black complexion; full eyes; free spoken and intelligent; will weigh about 180 pounds; 32 years old; had with him 2 or 3 suits of clothes, white hat, short blue blanket coat, a pair of saddle bags, a pocket compass, and supposed to have $350 or $400 with him.

ALSO---A NEGRO MAN NAMED HAMP,

Of dark copper color, big thick lips, about 6 feet high, weighs about 175 pounds, 36 years old, with a scar in the forehead from the kick of a horse; had a lump on one of his wrists and is left-handed. Had with him two suits of clothes, one a casinet or cloth coat and grey pants.

Research Assignment: Have students write a report detailing Cato's revolt.
Discussion Question: Was the use of a "gag rule" in the Congress a suppression of the first Amendment right of freedom of speech? Lead the discussion to an understanding that the gag rule, in this case, was a tool of parliamentary procedure necessary to keep order in the day-to-day

The Last Debate. Virginians were shocked by Turner's revolt, and no one more so than the new governor of the state, John Floyd. As long as there was slavery, Floyd believed, rebellion and bloodshed would threaten Virginia society. In December 1831, Floyd had William B. Preston present a plan to the Virginia legislature providing for the gradual abolition of slavery. Slaveowners would be encouraged to free their slaves by receiving cash compensation for the loss of their property, to be paid out of the state treasury.

For three weeks in January 1832, the legislature discussed the plan. Speeches typically opened with the wish that blacks and slavery had never been introduced into Virginia, that the state would be a better place if it had been developed by free white labor. The majority of representatives recognized, however, that almost half of Virginia's population was black. However, most of the legislators believed that blacks and whites could not live together as equals. By a vote of 94 to 40, the Floyd plan was rejected.

Virginia was considered the cultural heart of the southern states. If Virginia had abolished slavery in 1832, at least the more northerly of the southern states—Delaware, Maryland, Kentucky, and possibly North Carolina—might have done the same. Slavery would have been restricted to the cotton states; and alone, they would not seriously have thought of leaving the Union. As it was, when the debate in Virginia ended, slavery ceased to be a debatable issue in the South.

Suppressing Dissent. Southern congressmen even shut off discussion of abolishing slavery in Congress. This was done by means of the "gag rule." Beginning in 1836, southern congressmen called on the House to table, or set aside without discussion, all petitions calling for Congress to discuss the question of slavery. To abolish or not to abolish slavery, they argued, was entirely up to the individual states and was not Congress's business.

John Quincy Adams, now representing Massachusetts in the House of Representatives, admitted that Congress had no right to abolish slavery. Indeed, Adams was not an abolitionist and regarded agitators as disruptive and destructive citizens. However, he insisted that the spirit of free speech required the House to receive and consider citizens' petitions dealing with slavery. Every year, he fought a battle against the gag rule.

Anyone who seemed to be criticizing slavery in any way was defined as an enemy of the South. By 1857, a southerner named Hinton Helper wrote *The Impending Crisis.* In the book, Helper said nothing about the morality of slavery but pointed out that slavery ruined the South economically. Helper was condemned in most southern states, and was forced to flee his native North Carolina in fear for his life.

"Positive Good" Theory. Southern political leaders were not content to defend slavery as morally "acceptable." Beginning with an 1832 essay by an economics professor, Thomas Roderick Dew, they began to insist that slavery was, in John Calhoun's words, "instead of an evil, a positive good" compared to other labor systems, including the free labor system of the North.

The *positive good theory* included religious, historical, cultural, racial and sociological arguments. The religious argument claimed that because some Biblical figures favored by God had owned slaves, God must approve of slavery. Furthermore, not only had the ancient Hebrews allowed slavery, but Jesus Christ had told a runaway slave to return to his master.

Dew and Calhoun made the historical and cultural arguments, pointing out that the great ancient civilizations, Greece and Rome, were slaveholding societies. Indeed, they argued, the artistic and philosophical accomplishments of the Greek and Roman upper classes were made possible because slaves labored for them. Proslavery southerners who liked to use the cultural argument pointed out that almost three times as many southern planters attended colleges and universities than did New Englanders, even though the populations of the slaveholding states and New England were about the same. When New Englanders pointed out that their primary and secondary school systems were far superior to those in the South, positive good theorists answered that they were interested in providing high culture for the few, not in teaching everyone just to read and write. Few abolitionists believed that these arguments were valid, nor could they possibly justify denying basic freedoms to men and women in the nineteenth century.

proceedings of Congress. Discuss whether this is actually a question of freedom of speech or whether it is a procedural issue involving a political process—the Congressional session. Was Adams in any way hindered from expressing his views outside the formal sessions? Refer to the actual text of the Constitution and, if possible, text from *Robert's Rules of Order.*

Slaves, who had the legal status of property before 1865, were usually bought and sold at auctions, much as livestock is sold today. The engraving above shows a slave auction in the Rotunda in New Orleans. The photograph below is of a street in Atlanta, Georgia, with a company that advertised auctions and slave trades.

Racial and Sociological Arguments.

There was an argument that seemed to justify slavery. George Fitzhugh, a Virginia lawyer, wrote two influential books on the subject in the 1850s. He said that southerners were justified in owning blacks because blacks were racially inferior to whites. They were incapable of competing with whites equally. Slaveowners did black people a favor by protecting them from freedom.

Fitzhugh amassed statistics and other evidence to prove, so he said, that southern slaves actually lived a more comfortable and secure life than most northern industrial workers. Someone had to do the drudgery, heavy labor, and dirty work in every society, he said. In the South, slaves did those jobs. In return, they were cared for from cradle to grave by their masters. Children, the elderly, the handicapped, and blacks who were injured and could not work—all were provided with the necessities of life.

In the northern states, Fitzhugh continued, menial and heavy labor was performed by free workers in return for cash wages. But what happened to children, the elderly, and the disabled in this system? They were simply left to fend for themselves. Northern employers never accepted responsibility for workers who were injured while working for them.

Discussion Question: What did the founding fathers mean when they said that all men are created equal? Students will probably say that the founding fathers meant this to exclude blacks and women. The chapter material will indicate that some of the founding fathers held no such views and disliked slavery. Discuss this phrase as meaning that all people should have the right of

As a result, northern society was plagued by social problems that were unknown in the South: strikes, riots, disruptive reformers, revolutionaries who preached communistic doctrines and threatened revolution. By comparison, southern society was peaceful. The slaves were content, Fitzhugh wrote.

Controlling the Slaves. When Fitzhugh argued that many southern slaves ate better food and enjoyed more secure material lives than many northern workers, he had a point. But when he argued that slaves were happy to be slaves and were devoted to their masters, he had to overlook strong contrary evidence. Every southern state had laws that forced blacks to remain in bondage. If blacks had liked their situation, there would have been no need for such laws. And the slave-owners' fears of rebellion indicated that they knew their slaves were not content.

After Nat Turner's rebellion, the southern states took action to ensure that slave unrest would never again turn into an uprising. Because the presence of free blacks inspired slaves to crave freedom, the cotton states passed laws that made it extremely difficult for a master to free even a single slave. In Virginia, a slave who was freed had to leave the state. Other states required free blacks to live in cities, far from the mass of slaves who worked on farms.

Because Nat Turner got his ideas from the Bible, most southern states made teaching a slave to read a crime. County governments in the South were required to finance *slave patrols*. These mounted and armed posses of rough men had the legal right to break into slave cabins or demand at gunpoint that blacks on the public roads account for themselves. The mere presence of the patrollers, stopping and questioning people at will, lent an air of repression to many areas of the South.

Slaves with permission to leave their master's property were required to carry passes. The 250,000 free blacks in the South by 1860 needed no law to tell them to protect the documentary

This painting by Winslow Homer shows two field hands working in a cotton field. The field hands, forced to do heavy manual labor, received very little in return. The low cost of labor and relatively high prices that cotton commanded made slavery an economical institution.

equal opportunities.
Research Assignment: Have students who wish to write a report on what life was like to a typical free black person in the South during this period. Where did he or she live and make a living, and how was he or she restricted?

proof that they were not slaves. In fact, most free blacks moved to cities whether the law required them to or not. A free black family living in a rural area ran the risk of being kidnaped and sold into slavery by unscrupulous slave traders. In most southern cities, communities of free black people were large enough to provide some security against attack.

SECTION REVIEW

1. Write a sentence to identify: Thomas Roderick Dew, George Fitzhugh, *The Impending Crisis.*

2. List three slave rebellions that took place in the South. Give the important details about Nat Turner's rebellion.

3. List the major points of the Floyd plan, and suggest how and why the South might have changed if the plan had passed the Virginia legislature.

4. List and briefly explain the five arguments used to support the "positive good" defense of slavery. Refute two of the arguments, using material from the text.

2. THE PECULIAR INSTITUTION

During the 1840s, southern leaders began to refer to slavery as their "peculiar institution." By *peculiar* they meant that slavery, as it was practiced in the American South, was unique. Nothing quite like it existed anywhere in the world.

They were right. By 1850, every other western nation except Brazil had abolished slavery, and Brazilian slaves enjoyed many legal rights denied to American blacks. (Brazil did away with slavery in 1888.) Elsewhere in the world, very few other peoples still practiced slavery.

The Planter Elite. Some southerners believed that unique also meant "benign" or "beneficial," and that southern slavery made possible one of the most gracious and cultured societies in the world. Thanks to slavery, well-to-do planters were free to devote themselves to cultural pursuits and to governing the South not for selfish reasons but for the good of all, including the slaves. The planters

The gracious Southern life, with its beautiful mansions and elegant parties, was open to only a small wealthy group of Southern planters.

regarded their role in the South as patriarchal, or fatherly. This was an aristocratic rather than democratic view of society. The planter elite did not deny it. They thought that democracy had made the North disorderly. Some Virginians took pride in claiming they were descendants of noble cavaliers who had fled from England after Oliver Cromwell executed King Charles I. In South

Discussion Question: What do the terms aristocratic and democratic mean as they are used in the text on this page? Initiate a discussion that examines the use of these words to describe a way of life in terms of its social setting. Also have students analyze the use of these terms in a

316

Carolina, planters with French names boasted of their descent from noble French Protestants who had been persecuted for their religion in the old country. Some Louisiana planters also claimed an aristocratic French heritage.

In reality, except in the oldest parts of the South, most great planters had had poor, hard-working pioneers for mothers and fathers. For example, the wealthy Davis brothers of Mississippi, Joseph and Jefferson, had been born in Kentucky log cabins much like Abraham Lincoln's birthplace. The difference was that, where a northerner like Lincoln boasted of humble origins, southern planters tried to hide their own.

However modest their backgrounds, the planter elite did live an elegant life. Mary Boykin Chesnut of South Carolina and other wealthy women left diaries that describe a constant round of balls and parties in magnificent, white-columned "Big Houses" furnished with the best that European artisans could produce. Although she was quite uncommon in her love of learning (and offended many southern men because of it), Chesnut also described a lively intellectual life in her journal. The elegant magnolia-scented world she described was first made famous in the songs of Stephen Foster and became well-known through romantic books and films.

A Hard-Working People.

But the people of leisure whom Mary Chesnut knew were a tiny minority of southern whites. The Heyward family of South Carolina stood at the top of the planter aristocracy, with 200 slaves living on 17 different plantations. However, in the whole South, only 250 families owned that many slaves. Altogether, only 2,200 families—the great planter class—owned 100 or more slaves, and families owning 50 or more slaves numbered only 10,000. The planter elite dominated the South's culture and politics, but it was a very small elite.

About three-quarters of southern whites owned no slaves at all, and most slaveowning families owned only one, two, or three slaves. They lived no gracious life of leisure but worked long, hard hours alongside their slaves. Some of these masters were callous and cruel. Slaves living alone on small farms were sometimes treated worse than livestock. Others were practically family members and even gave their owners advice.

Why Whites Believed in Slavery.

If so few white southerners owned even one slave, and if most white southerners worked hard in a society dominated by a tiny planter class, why did most white southerners approve of slavery?

Whites who owned a few slaves or perhaps none at all supported slavery because they hoped to prosper in the future and become planters. Their ambition in life was to live off the labor of blacks. Others, the ten percent of southern whites who scraped out a bare survival on the fringes of southern society, defended slavery because their only advantage over the blacks was their freedom.

Some whites did not support slavery. Many of the struggling farmers of the Appalachians (western Virginia and North Carolina, eastern Kentucky and Tennessee, northern Alabama and Mississippi) hated slavery because ownership of slaves allowed the minority of great planters to lord it over them. During the Civil War, many young men from the mountains fought for the Union against the Confederacy.

First Light to Last Light.

A small minority of slaves actually lived better than the poorest whites. These were the lucky few who were personal servants or house slaves of the very richest planters—cooks, maids, valets, butlers, and the like. They ate the leftovers from the masters' meals, dressed in good (although cast-off) clothing, and sometimes slept comfortably in the main house instead of in the cabins of the slave quarters that, at best, were little more than shelter.

But the vast majority of slaves worked at hard labor in the fields "from first light to last light" the year around. Cotton was the most important cash crop they grew. During the 1850s, an annual crop of about 4 million bales earned about $190 million. Other crops that were raised by slaves were sugar (mostly in Louisiana), rice (in the Carolinas and Georgia), tobacco (Maryland, Virginia, and North Carolina), and hemp (mostly in Kentucky). No matter what the cash crop was, however, slaves also raised much of the food they ate, particularly corn and hogs.

Slaves were expensive. In the 1850s it cost $1,500 or more to purchase a prime field hand, a healthy male between the ages of 16 and 35. As a result, even the wealthiest planters preferred to hire free labor, free blacks or Irish immigrants, for

strictly political sense. Which use is the text referring to? Are there elements of both of these usages in the South of the early 1800s as compared to the North of this period? Use this discussion as a precursor to the Skills Strategy at the end of this chapter.

the unhealthiest and most dangerous jobs. One such job was constructing levees in malarial swamps for flood control. A dangerous job that was done mostly by free blacks in river ports was the loading of the 600-pound (275-kilogram) cotton bales onto steamboats. Few planters chose to risk their valuable human property at the bottom of the loading chutes where the heavy bales hurtled at high speed.

A Life of Hard Labor.

Field hands worked hard. The more fortunate were organized according to the *task system*. In the morning, each slave was assigned to a job by the owner or overseer. It might be to hoe the weeds out of a certain number of rows of cotton or corn, or to clear drainage ditches of mud. At cotton-picking time, of course, the job was picking, from morning to night. When the task was complete—as early as two o'clock during easy seasons—the slaves could rest, socialize, or work their own garden patches. The task system was most commonly found in the rice-growing areas of South Carolina and Georgia.

Most slaves worked according to the *gang system*. Under the direct supervision of either their owner, a hired overseer, or, on the largest plantations, a privileged slave known as a "driver," men and women alike worked in groups from sunrise to sunset. Even those few planters who owned 100 or more slaves broke them up into gangs of no more than 20 for the day's labor because it was difficult to supervise the work of more than 20 slaves.

A prime field hand on a cotton plantation produced an annual crop valued at about $80 to $120. It cost the owner between $20 and $50 to feed, clothe, and shelter the slave. Receiving so small a share of the fruits of their labor, slaves worked only as hard as they had to in order to avoid punishment.

Whipping was a common punishment. Although hardly unknown, brutal beatings were uncommon, for the simple economic reason that a disabled slave produced no crop at all. But many slaves, probably the majority, felt the sting and humiliation of the lash at one time or another during their lives. Sadly, on large plantations whippings were sometimes administered by fellow slaves. As Frederick Douglass sarcastically remembered of his time spent in slavery, "Everybody in the South wants the privilege of whipping someone else."

The Slave Trade.

Slaves were defined in law as chattel property, personal possessions no different from furniture, tools, hogs, or cattle. They could be bought and sold, given away in wills or as a present. This trade in human beings was the ugliest face of the institution. While many planters could justly claim to be kind and generous to their slaves, no one could cover over the slave auction at which men and women were examined as if they were horses. On the auctioneer's block, blacks were forced to run and jump to prove they were healthy. They were subjected to coarse jokes and other humiliations. Worst of all, slave traders recognized no special relationship between husband and wife or mother and children among slaves. If a buyer wanted a prime field hand but not his wife, the couple was separated. If a buyer was in the market for a young woman but wanted no infants, mother and child were separated.

Nothing was more shocking to northern abolitionists and Europeans than the slave auctions. Harriet Beecher Stowe used the theme of the separation of mother and child as an important part of her best-selling antislavery novel, *Uncle Tom's Cabin*.

The general flow of the slave trade was dictated by the general economy of the South. While cotton was profitable, tobacco continued to decline. Thus, slaves were sold from the older parts of the South, especially the tobacco-growing states of Virginia and Maryland, to the new cotton-growing states of Alabama, Mississippi, Louisiana, Arkansas, and Texas. The only way many Virginia and Maryland planters could continue to live comfortably was by selling their human possessions "down the [Mississippi] river."

In New Orleans, as many as 200 individuals and companies were engaged in the buying and selling of slaves. Few of these traders were accepted in planter society. Because the southern elite took pride in their kindness toward their own slaves, they disapproved of slave traders as vulgar, crude, unworthy men. However, the slave society required slave traders—they did the work that others did not want to do. If human beings were to be property, someone had to buy and sell them, like other property.

Research Assignment: Have students read *Uncle Tom's Cabin* and research its impact on the society of its time.

A northerner, Harriet Beecher Stowe (left), wrote Uncle Tom's Cabin, *a novel depicting the horrors of slavery (title page at right). The 1852 best-seller was banned in the South.*

The Foreign Slave Trade. Importing slaves from Africa was illegal after 1808. Nevertheless, when the price of slaves rose above $1,000, the temptation to break the law was great. It has been estimated that more than 50,000 Africans and Cuban blacks were smuggled into the United States between 1808 and 1861. During the 1850s, travelers in the South reported seeing black men and women with the filed teeth, tribal tattoos, and ritual markings that indicated they were African-born.

The illegal slave trade was a risky business. Although generally under-equipped, the United States Navy patrolled the southern coastline in search of slave traders. The Royal Navy, somewhat more efficient, patrolled West African waters. The British punished slave traders severely, with long prison terms and even hanging. However, even this precaution resulted in atrocities.

When a ship carrying slaves from Africa was spotted and pursued by a British warship, the traders sometimes threw their captives overboard, weighted with chains, rather than be caught with "the evidence" in their possession.

Humans Without Rights. The *slave codes,* southern laws governing the peculiar institution, denied civil rights, and even most human rights, to slaves. Because they were considered property themselves, slaves could not legally own property. Everything they seemed to own or believed they owned, from chickens in a coop to the clothes on their backs, was legally the property of their masters. Unable to own property, slaves could not legally buy and sell anything. Nor could they make contracts.

Marriage between slaves, or between a slave and a free person, was not recognized by the law.

When Abraham Lincoln first met Harriet Beecher Stowe during the Civil War, it is told that he addressed her as "the little woman who started this great war."

If marriage between a slave man and woman were recognized in the law, their owner would not be able to sell one of them without selling the other. But the slaveowner's property rights were more important than the slaves' human rights. When slaves did marry before a minister or their owner, the traditional vow of "till death do ye part" was carefully rephrased as "till death or distance do ye part."

Neither slaves nor free blacks could testify in court against a white person. This meant that one of the few basic human rights allowed to blacks under the slave codes, the right to life, was itself often ineffective. If only black witnesses saw a white man kill a slave, there was no legal case against the murderer. Southern law did not consider it murder or even manslaughter if a slave died "under moderate correction." That is, the master whose slave died while being flogged was guilty of no crime at all.

A Diverse Institution.

The actual experience of slave life had little to do with the letter of the slave codes. Some slaves lived lives of unrelenting misery under callous and cruel masters. However, a slaveowner's economic interests in human property provided most slaves with a guarantee against severe mistreatment. The master who beat a slave to death destroyed a valuable piece of property. The master who fed, housed, and clothed slaves so poorly that they could not work was a poor businessperson.

Self-interest encouraged some masters to allow their slaves to garden, to keep chickens, and even to chop wood for sale to steamboats as fuel and keep the money for themselves. Slaves able to improve their lives, who had something to lose if they ran away, were more likely to be good workers. For the same reason, many masters encouraged their slaves to marry and assured couples they would not be separated. The slave with a wife or husband was less likely to try to escape.

A few slaves lived differently. One was Simon Gray, a skilled flatboatman whose owner paid him a fair wage for those times, $8 a month to haul lumber to New Orleans. Gray commanded crews of up to 20 men, including some whites. He eventually bought his own freedom. In Louisiana, some slaves bought their freedom and became slaveowners themselves.

Some planters ignored the slave codes in other ways. Although the codes made it illegal, there are records of slaves who were allowed to hunt with guns. Mississippi law made it a crime to teach slaves to read and write, but Jefferson Davis's brother, Joseph Davis, provided a school for slave children on his Mississippi estate.

Coping with Adversity.

Resourceful black men and women found ways to keep their spirits and their will to live strong, and to teach their children to have courage. They created a lively cultural and social life that helped them to cope with their enslavement. When the day's work was done, on Sundays when there was usually no work, and at "laying by time," a month around Christmas, blacks lived in a world unknown to whites.

Many slaves were deeply religious. In French Louisiana, they tended to become Roman Catholics. In other parts of the South, they embraced the evangelical Christianity of the Methodists and Baptists. Although very few slaves could read, they treasured the Bible. They identified with the ancient Hebrews because, like them, the Hebrews were held in slavery by the Egyptians and Babylonians and yet remained God's chosen people. The story of the Hebrew exodus from Egyptian captivity gave them hope.

In their retelling of Biblical stories, and in *spirituals,* hymns such as "Let My People Go," and "Go Down Moses," black people were able to protest their slavery in a way that their masters could not prevent.

Tales of Protest.

Another thinly masked form of protest against slavery took the form of stories adapted from African folklore. In these tales, the rabbit, the weakest of the animals and unable to assert his rights by force, survived and flourished by using his wits. In one story, the fox has the rabbit in his hands and is debating with himself whether to barbecue the rabbit, hang him, drown him, or skin him. The rabbit assures the fox that he will be happy with any of these fates but begs piteously not to be thrown in the thorny brier patch. The rabbit says that he fears the brier patch more than anything in the world.

Naturally, the fox throws him into the briers. The rabbit, now safe because the fox is too big to

Research Assignment: Students interested in music can do a research assignment on spirituals such as the ones referred to on this page. These could be compared to the songs of Stephen Foster that are referred to on page 317. These reports might be illustrated by recordings of some of these songs.

The growing opposition to slavery and the Fugitive Slave Act inspired books, poems, and paintings (such as the one above) dramatizing the desperate flight of runaway slaves.

enter the brier patch, begins to laugh. "Bred and born in a brier patch" he shouts as he hops away, "bred and born in a brier patch." Slaves, unable to taunt their masters openly, took pleasure in doing it through stories.

The most direct form of slave protest was running away. Black people who lived in Delaware, Maryland, or Kentucky, states that bordered free states, had a reasonable chance to escape for good. Even then, especially after the *Fugitive Slave Act* of 1850 required federal marshalls in the North to return runaway slaves, the odds were against them. To be truly free, the runaway had to

get to Canada. Nevertheless, southerners estimated that thousands of slaves in the border states made their way to freedom.

Far more common was running away in full knowledge that capture and punishment were inevitable. Even though it meant a whipping, the slim hope of freedom was worth the risk to tens of thousands of slaves each year.

After the Civil War, one South Carolina planter honestly admitted he had been wrong about his slaves. Although he had been generous, his slaves and all those of his neighbors left their homes as soon as they were told they were free. "I believed

Discussion Question: (Refer to the quote of the South Carolina plantation owner given at the bottom of this page and going on to the top of page 322.) Why do you think that the plantation owner who is quoted really felt, at one time, that blacks wanted to be slaves? Discuss what made this notion so believable to the plantation owner.

these people were content, happy, and attached to their masters," he wrote, finally realizing that it was a delusion.

SECTION REVIEW

1. Write a sentence to identify: Mary Boykin Chesnut, task system, Simon Gray, Fugitive Slave Act.
2. Why did slaveowners call slavery the "peculiar institution"?
3. Briefly describe the gap between the life style of the planter elite and that of the majority of white southerners. Give two reasons why the majority of southern whites defended slavery.
4. Explain the following statement by using facts from the text: "A slaveowner's economic interests usually shielded slaves from severe mistreatment."

---

3. THE ABOLITIONISTS

Before about 1830, northerners and southerners were able to discuss the future of slavery calmly and reasonably. In fact, because slavery had already been abolished in the North, the most active *abolitionists* in the early nineteenth century were southerners.

The First Abolitionists. The first Americans to speak out against slavery were Quakers and free blacks. Quakers believed that all men and women had within them a spark of divinity. If this were so, they reasoned, then people did not have the right to own others as if they were things. Quakers were among the first people to *manumit* (individually free) their slaves. In the eighteenth century, Quaker Anthony Benezet (bĕn′ə-zā′) of Philadelphia spoke out against the injustice of the institution, and another Quaker, John Woolman of New Jersey, traveled the countryside urging slaveowners to free their slaves.

During the 1820s, Benjamin Lundy kept this tradition alive. He called on the southern states to abolish slavery and on the entire nation to raise money to help freed blacks move to Haiti, Canada, or Texas, then a state of Mexico. Lundy and

Benjamin Banneker's Almanac was as popular as Benjamin Franklin's had been.

other early abolitionists tried to communicate their ideas to slaveowners rather than attack them for owning slaves. As William Ellery Channing told slaveowners, "We consider slavery your calamity and not your curse."

Benjamin Banneker, a free black born in Maryland, was a mathematician and astronomer who surveyed the District of Columbia. He also published an almanac as popular with Americans as Benjamin Franklin's had been. Banneker wrote to George Washington, urging him to oppose slavery publicly. John Adams considered Banneker's accomplishments "fresh proof that powers of the mind are disconnected with the color of the skin." And Thomas Jefferson, a slaveowner, correspond-

Discussion Question: Was the issue of slavery an economic or a political issue? Why? Answers should indicate that it was both.

ed with Banneker. However, because of the profits to be made growing cotton, neither Banneker nor the Quakers influenced many slaveowners.

Southerners Support Black Colonization.

In the debate over the admission of Missouri to the Union in 1820, Congressman James Tallmadge of New York introduced a new tone to the debate over slavery when he attacked the institution as sinful. His speech disturbed many white southerners. Nevertheless, throughout the rest of the 1820s, the most active antislavery movement in the country was supported largely by southerners.

This movement, called the *colonization movement,* was represented by organizations such as the American Colonization Society. Supporters of colonization agreed that it would be best for the United States to be rid of slavery. But they also believed that blacks and whites could not live together in harmony. Therefore, while they urged slaveowners to free their slaves, members of the society, including John Madison and James Mon-

Some free blacks moved to Liberia, an African country founded on land bought by the Philadelphia Anti-Slavery Society (below). C. D. B. King (above) was an early president of Liberia.

Research Assignment: Have students do a research paper on the history of Liberia.

roe, Chief Justice Marshall, and Henry Clay, also raised money to pay the transportation of free blacks to West Africa.

Cotton continued to boom, however, and slaveowners lost interest in the society's program for abolition, supporting instead only the organization's plan to send free blacks abroad. By 1860, almost 11,000 blacks had gone to Liberia, in West Africa, and helped found and build that country. But many more blacks insisted that the United States, not Liberia, was their country. As a group of Philadelphia blacks said in 1817, "We have no wish to separate from our present homes for any purpose whatsoever."

David Walker and William Garrison. In 1829, discussion of slavery took another new turn. In that year, a free black artisan named David Walker published a pamphlet called *The Appeal.* Walker reviewed the arguments against slavery—it was un-Christian and it made a mockery of American principles of liberty and equality—and called for its *abolition.* If whites did not abolish slavery by law, Walker concluded, then blacks had the right to rise up in violent revolution.

William Lloyd Garrison, a thin, intense young man who worked for Benjamin Lundy in Baltimore, did not believe in violent rebellion. Among the many causes he supported was pacifism. Garrison believed no war was justified.

And yet, in *The Liberator,* an abolitionist newspaper he founded in Boston in 1831, he took so fierce an antislavery position that he seemed to be calling for war. "I am aware," Garrison wrote in the first edition of *The Liberator,* "that many object to the severity of my language; but is there not cause for severity? I *will be* as harsh as truth, and as uncompromising as justice. On this subject I do not wish to think, or speak, or write, with moderation. . . . I am in earnest—I will not equivocate—I will not excuse—I will not retreat a single inch—*and I will be heard.*"

Meetings called to protest slavery were common in the North in the mid-1800s. Among the speakers featured on the handbill at left is William Lloyd Garrison (right).

The Liberator *was a strongly antislavery newspaper founded and edited by William Lloyd Garrison. The illustration shows a slave auction.*

Extremism Versus Moderation.

Garrison was heard. It was difficult to ignore his uncompromising attacks not only on the evil of slavery but on the evil of slaveowners. Garrison described the slaveowner's life as one "of swaggering braggadocio, of haughty domination, of cowardly ruffianism, of boundless dissipation, of matchless insolence, of infinite self-conceit, of unequaled oppression, of more than savage cruelty." Obviously, he was not interested in discussing the question with slaveowners. Indeed, Garrison was also not interested in discussing slavery with northerners who asked about the practical problems involved in any plan to end the bondage of, by 1831, 2 million people. Because the Constitution protected slavery, Garrison burned a copy of that document during a public speech.

Garrison was never a popular man. Even in Boston, a center of antislavery feeling, Garrison was booed and pelted with stones when he gave speeches. On one occasion a mob threw a noose around his neck and led him through the streets. He was saved by a group of women who admired him for his support of women's rights.

In the South, he was despised because many whites believed Garrison was encouraging slaves to rebel. In the deep South, copies of *The Liberator* found in the mails were seized and burned. Georgia's legislature offered a reward of $5,000 to any person who would capture and bring Garrison to the state so he could stand trial on the charge of inciting rebellion.

Another extremist critic of slavery was killed for his beliefs. Elijah P. Lovejoy published abolitionist newspapers in Missouri and in Alton, Illinois. Lovejoy denounced alcohol and Roman Catholicism as well as slavery. But it was his Garrison-like abolitionism that, in 1837, angered people in Alton. A mob destroyed Lovejoy's press, burned his office, and murdered him.

All abolitionists were shocked by Lovejoy's murder. Nevertheless, many of them criticized Garrison and Lovejoy as extremists. They believed that their shrill language and refusal to discuss the practical problems of abolition drove people away from the antislavery movement.

Theodore Dwight Weld.

Connecticut-born Theodore Dwight Weld probably converted many more people to abolitionism than Garrison and Lovejoy together. A modest man who shunned publicity, Weld believed that in order to build a large antislavery movement in the United States, it was necessary to convert farmers to the cause. Most of his career was spent in the rural Midwest where he lectured to church groups, and with financial help from Arthur and Lewis Tappan, two wealthy New York merchants he had converted to the cause, helped to found Oberlin College in Ohio, a state where antislavery feeling ran strong.

In 1839, Weld published *American Slavery As It Is,* a collection of newspaper articles that detailed the mistreatment and outright cruelty that slaves had to endure. Weld deliberately emphasized

more moderate approach of Weld. Contrast the views held by these papers. Articles in the student version should be original but should attempt to use primary sources for information, perhaps issues of *The Liberator* or Weld's *American Slavery as It Is.*

southern newspaper accounts of slaves starving, others freezing to death in winter, and the whipping and branding by which slaves were punished. He did this to counteract the claim by some southerners that northerners only imagined such things.

Within one year, *American Slavery As It Is* sold 100,000 copies. Weld described its message as "heartsickening." Nonetheless, he insisted that abolitionists must not simply denounce slaveowners, but should communicate with them and offer a plan by which slavery could be ended without widespread economic and social disruption.

Abolitionists from the South.

Perhaps because of his moderation, Weld converted several slaveowners to abolition. One of them, Angelina Grimké, married Weld. She and her sister, Sarah, were born into a family of wealthy slaveowners in South Carolina. Convinced by Quakers and by Weld that slavery was wrong, they freed what slaves they could and moved to the North, where they shocked conventional Americans by speaking publicly against slavery. Unfortunately, many people missed their antislavery point because they were so disturbed that women were actually leading a reform movement.

James G. Birney was an Alabama planter persuaded by Weld to free his slaves. Birney believed that slavery should be fought by political debate rather than by attacks and denunciations. In 1840 and 1844, he ran for president as the candidate of the Liberty party.

Two Kentuckians, John Gregg Fee and Cassius M. Clay (a cousin of Henry Clay), criticized slavery in their state. Although slavery was legal in Kentucky, Kentuckians were never as extreme in their hatred of abolitionists as were people in the states farther south.

Black Abolitionists.

The best orator in the antislavery movement was a black man who had escaped from slavery in Maryland. Frederick Douglass taught himself to read and write and, in 1845, published his *Autobiography,* in which he presented a firsthand account of what it meant to be human property. Curiously, while he actually

This print shows the anger aroused by the abolitionist movement. Boston police and a mob are breaking up an abolitionist meeting. The featured speaker at the meeting was Frederick Douglass. Douglass is shown at the center, trying to speak over the chaos.

GOING TO THE SOURCE

I have selected this day on which to address you, because it is the anniversary of my emancipation; and knowing of no better way, I am led to this as the best mode of celebrating that truly important event. Just ten years ago this beautiful September morning, yon bright sun beheld me a slave—a poor, degraded chattel—trembling at the sound of your voice, lamenting that I was a man, and wishing myself a brute. The hopes which I had treasured up for weeks of a safe and successful escape from your grasp, were powerfully confronted at this last hour by dark clouds of doubt and fear, making my person shake and my bosom to heave with the heavy contest between hope and fear. I have no words to describe to you the deep agony of soul which I experienced on that never to be forgotten morning—(for I left by daylight). I was making a leap in the dark. The probabilities, so far as I could by reason determine them, were stoutly against the undertaking. The preliminaries and precautions I had adopted previously, all worked badly. I was like one going to war without weapons—ten chances of defeat to one of victory. One in whom I had confided, and one who had promised me assistance, appalled by fear at the trial hour, deserted me, thus leaving the responsibility of success or failure solely with myself. You sir, can never know my feelings. As I look back to them, I can scarcely realize that I have passed through a scene so trying. Trying however as they were and gloomy as was the prospect, thanks be to the Most High, who is ever the God of the oppressed, at the moment which was to determine my whole earthly career. His grace was sufficient, my mind was made up. I embraced the golden opportunity, took the morning tide at the flood, and a free man, young, active and strong is the result.

> *When yet but a child about six years old, I imbibed the determination to run away. The very first mental effort that I now remember on my part, was an attempt to solve the mystery, Why am I a slave? and with this question my youthful mind was troubled for many days. . . .*
>
> FREDERICK DOUGLASS,
> "LETTER TO A SLAVEHOLDER"

. . . When yet but a child about six years old, I imbibed the determination to run away. The very first mental effort that I now remember on my part, was an attempt to solve the mystery, Why am I a slave? and with this question my youthful mind was troubled for many days, pressing upon me more heavily at times than others. When I saw the slave-driver whip a slave woman, cut the blood out of her neck, and heard her piteous cries, I went away into the corner of the fence, wept and pondered over the mystery. I had, through some medium, I know not what, got some idea of God, the Creator of all mankind, the black and the white, and that he had made the blacks to serve the whites as slaves. How could he do this and be *good,* I could not tell. I was not satisfied with his theory, which made God responsible for slavery, for it pained me greatly, and I have wept over it long and often. I was puzzled with this question, till one night, while sitting in the kitchen, I heard some of the old slaves talking of their parents having been stolen from Africa by white men, and were sold here as slaves. The whole mystery was solved at once. Very soon after this my aunt Jinny and uncle Noah ran away, and the great noise made about it by your father-in-law, made me for the first time acquainted with the fact, that there were free States as well as slave States. From that time, I resolved that I would some day run away.

When Frederick Douglass composed this "Letter to a Slaveholder" on September 3, 1848, he had aready achieved fame in the North as an abolitionist author and lecturer. The Baltimore slaveowner to whom Douglass wrote had been his master.

Class Activity: Students have read about the uses of "fire and brimstone," persuasive speeches by various religious and social reformers. Discuss why such speeches might be effective. Ask students if they think that such techniques are still used today—if so, have them cite examples. Encourage students to develop a persuasive speech on some current issue.

MOVERS AND SHAPERS

Sojourner Truth

Isabella Baumfree (1797–1883) began her life as a slave but ended it as one of the most independent, free-spirited women in American history. As a free woman, she invented another name for herself, Sojourner Truth—a name that she made famous.

New York State still allowed slavery in the 1790s when Isabella was born on the large estate of a Dutch-speaking New York slave-owner. Dutch was the first language that she heard and spoke. As a girl, she was sold several times to different New Yorkers, who whipped and abused her. She married a fellow slave, bore five children, and suffered acute anguish when two of her daughters were sold away.

In 1827, one year before all New York's slaves were emancipated by state law, Isabella fled from her master's household and found refuge in the home of Isaac and Maria Van Wagener. No longer a slave, she adopted her benefactors' last name and found employment in New York City as a domestic servant. Here religion became a dominant force in her life. Joining first the Methodist and then the African Zion Church, she often had mystical experiences and believed that God spoke directly to her through divine voices. Her extraordinary talent for preaching attracted the notice of Elijah Pierson, the wealthy founder of a small religious group. Isabella committed herself to this group and preached for it until 1835.

In 1843 came another major turning point. Her inner voices commanded her to break sharply with her past identity. As she testified later, she was inspired to adopt a new name and a new mission in life. She was to leave her New York home and spread God's truth by traveling and preaching far and wide.

She traveled by foot, setting out from New York with only 25 cents. East across Long Island she hiked, and then north into New England. Whenever the spirit moved her and wherever people congregated, she stopped on the road to sing and preach. Her listeners, often hostile at first, were held in thrall by the magnetic force of her personality and the deep, compelling rhythms of her voice.

As she hiked through Massachusetts in the 1840s, she learned about the abolitionist movement and the feminist movement. She began to speak regularly at abolitionist rallies and preached the rights of women as one aspect of "God's truth."

In 1851, she walked into a church in Akron, Ohio, where feminists were holding their second National Woman's Suffrage Convention. After a male minister suggested that women were the intellectual inferiors of men, the tall visitor rose and delivered an inspired oration in defense of women's strength and intelligence. This spontaneous address in Akron was a peak moment in Sojourner Truth's long career.

There were other triumphs as well. Through the 1850s, she was in great demand as a speaker at abolitionist meetings. The famed author, Harriet Beecher Stowe, wrote about her work. In 1864, President Abraham Lincoln greeted her in the White House. After the Civil War, she tried to persuade the government to grant a huge tract of western land to freed slaves. The government ignored her plea, but the thousands of blacks who migrated to the Great Plains in the 1870s may have been influenced by her.

The wanderings of the aging preacher finally led her to Battle Creek, Michigan, where she died in 1883, an honored citizen.

Despite the North's position on the issue of slavery, black people were still mistreated when they arrived here. Economic opportunities, especially in regard to housing and jobs, were restricted. Many northern states did not allow blacks the right to vote even after the Civil War. Racism has always transcended regional lines.

Harriet Tubman (far left) was called "the Black Moses" because she led her people to freedom as the Biblical character Moses had done. Slaveowners offered $40,000 for her capture.

suffered the sting of the lash, Douglass was better-humored and more humane than most white abolitionists, who often seemed self-righteous. Douglass also continued to fight against injustice after slavery was abolished. Until his death in 1895, he spoke out on behalf of working people and for the right of women to vote.

Sojourner Truth also combined antislavery feeling with support for women's rights. Born a slave and named Isabella Baumfree, she changed her name when she became a free woman to illustrate her purpose in life. She was a *sojourner,* a traveler, on behalf of truth and justice. Unlike Douglass, Sojourner Truth remained illiterate to the end of her days. But she was six feet tall, and there were few more powerful speakers than this woman who, like protesters of a later day, sometimes accompanied her appeals with songs she had composed.

Harriet Tubman, who ran away from her Maryland master in 1849, took direct action against slavery. She was a "conductor" on the *Under-ground Railway,* an informal network of abolitionists who hid runaway slaves fleeing to Canada. Although it meant risking her freedom and possibly her life, Tubman returned to slave states 19 times to guide other blacks to freedom.

SECTION REVIEW

1. Write a sentence to identify: manumit, Benjamin Banneker, Angelina and Sarah Grimké, Underground Railway.

2. Contrast the early abolitionist approach, by such people as Benjamin Lundy, with the approach of later abolitionists, such as David Walker and William Garrison.

3. What was *American Slavery As It Is?* Why did its author publish the book?

4. Name two black abolitionists, and describe the work they did to advance the cause of abolition.

Research Assignment: Have students do projects on the Underground Railroad. Suggest that they draw maps showing the route of the passage, construct artistic depictions of what a stop on the railroad might have looked like, create a fictional account of a traveler on the railroad, or write histories or biographies of people involved with it.

On Christmas Day in 1830, the Best Friend of Charleston, *the first steam locomotive to be used for regular passenger and freight runs in America, began service. The number of steam locomotives operating in the U.S. increased rapidly. By 1870 the locomotives being built were eight-wheeled and heavier and more powerful than earlier models. Improved steam locomotives made the transcontinental railroad a practical reality.*

Combines enabled farmers to cut and thresh crops in a single operation.

C H A N G I N G   T E C H N O L O G Y

18 40	18 50	
Cultivator introduced	Dynamo produced	Bicycle designed
Electric motor produced	Gas refrigeration introduced	Francis turbine developed
Dry-cleaning process developed	Steel plow built	Turret lathe built
Pin-making machine invented	Ice machine invented	Grain binder invented
(See also p. 259.)	(See also p. 259.)	(See also pp. 239 and 432.)

Discussion Question: How did some of the inventions and technological advances of the early 1800s contribute to the development of slavery in both the North and the South? Discuss how the cotton gin spurred a need for slaves to meet renewed production demands. Describe how the various technologies in manufacturing and transportation in the North did not require the same large-scale labor that farming in the South did.

The improved steam engine built by inventor George Corliss in the 1870s used a valve gear to regulate the amount of steam entering a cylinder in response to how much power was needed for a given load.

The modern petroleum industry was born when the nation's first commercial oil well was drilled at Titusville, Pennsylvania on August 26, 1859, by Edwin Drake. Drake's idea of pumping oil from the ground used techniques similar to those of salt mining.

The Bessemer process, developed in the mid-1800s, converted pig iron to steel by using blasts of heated air to burn impurities from the molten pig iron.

18	60	18	70	18	80

18 60

Successful gas engine designed
Safety elevator invented
Hypodermic syringe introduced
(See also pp. 432 and 522.)

18 70

First practical typewriter
  patented
Dynamite produced
Air brake invented
Cellulose acetate introduced
(See also pp. 432, 522, and 584.)

18 80

Telephone patented
Phonograph invented
Barbed wire introduced
(See also pp. 433, 522, and 584.)

CHAPTER REVIEW

TIME LINE

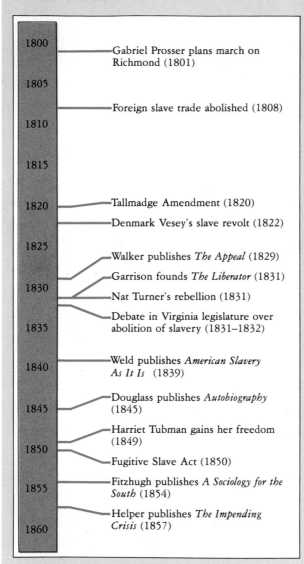

Year	Event
1800	Gabriel Prosser plans march on Richmond (1801)
1805	
	Foreign slave trade abolished (1808)
1810	
1815	
1820	Tallmadge Amendment (1820)
	Denmark Vesey's slave revolt (1822)
1825	
	Walker publishes *The Appeal* (1829)
	Garrison founds *The Liberator* (1831)
1830	Nat Turner's rebellion (1831)
	Debate in Virginia legislature over abolition of slavery (1831–1832)
1835	
1840	Weld publishes *American Slavery As It Is* (1839)
	Douglass publishes *Autobiography* (1845)
1845	Harriet Tubman gains her freedom (1849)
1850	Fugitive Slave Act (1850)
1855	Fitzhugh publishes *A Sociology for the South* (1854)
	Helper publishes *The Impending Crisis* (1857)
1860	

TIME LINE QUESTIONS

1. List the years of the events that show slaves were not content with their condition.
2. In what year was foreign trade in slaves made illegal in the United States?
3. List these publications in the order that they appeared: *The Impending Crisis, The Appeal,* Douglass's *Autobiography, American Slavery As It Is, The Liberator.*

SKILLS STRATEGY

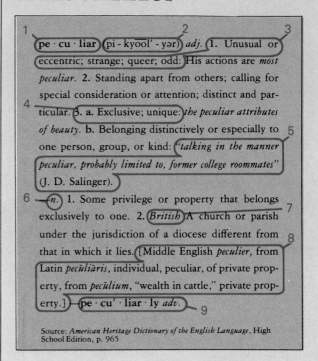

1 2 3
pe · cu · liar (pi - kyōōl′ - yər) *adj.* **1.** Unusual or eccentric; strange; queer; odd: *His actions are most peculiar.* **2.** Standing apart from others; calling for special consideration or attention; distinct and par-
4 ticular. **3. a.** Exclusive; unique: *the peculiar attributes of beauty.* **b.** Belonging distinctively or especially to 5 one person, group, or kind: *"talking in the manner peculiar, probably limited to, former college roommates"* (J. D. Salinger).
6 —*n.* **1.** Some privilege or property that belongs exclusively to one. **2.** *British* A church or parish 7 under the jurisdiction of a diocese different from 8 that in which it lies. [Middle English *peculier,* from Latin *pecūliāris,* individual, peculiar, of private prop- erty, from *pecūlium,* "wealth in cattle," private prop- erty.] **pe · cu′ · liar · ly** *adv.*
9

Source: *American Heritage Dictionary of the English Language*, High School Edition, p. 965

DICTIONARIES

No doubt you have been using the dictionary as a reference both in and out of school for several years. Reviewing the form and content of a typical dictionary *entry* will help you keep your dictionary skills sharp.

The parts of the dictionary entry shown above are labeled with numbers. Refer to the entry as you continue reading.

The first part of a dictionary entry is the *main entry word* in heavy type, which is divided into syllables. You can use it to check spelling or to help you divide a word at the end of a line of writing. The *phonetic respelling* of the word in parentheses comes next. It will help you to pro- nounce the word if you understand the symbols used. If you do not know the symbols, consult the pronunciation key given in the dictionary. The *part(s) of speech* of the word are abbreviated and in italics. Next comes a series of numbered or num- bered and lettered *definitions,* often followed by a *sample phrase or sentence* in italics using the word. Frequently, a definition is preceded by a *usage label*

Making Connections: Review the questions and topics presented in the Making Connections section that opens this chapter. Underscore the changes in slavery that led up to the Civil War.

pi·o·neer (pī'ə-nîr') *n.* 1. One who ventures into unknown or unclaimed territory to settle. 2. An innovator in any field: *a pioneer in aviation.* 3. A military engineer employed in the construction and fortification of positions and the maintenance of communication lines. —*adj.* 1. Of the nature of a pioneer: trailblazing; innovating: *a pioneer chemist.* 2. Of or relating to early settlers or their time: *the pioneer spirit.* —*v.* **pioneered, -neering, -neers.** —*tr.* 1. a. To explore or open up (a region): *Our icebreakers pioneered the Arctic Ocean.* b. To settle: *The taiga is still being pioneered.* 2. To innovate or participate in the development of: *men who pioneered the submarine.* —*intr.* To act as a pioneer. [Old French *pionier,* originally "a foot soldier sent out to clear the way," from *pion, peon,* foot soldier, from Medieval Latin *pedō,* extended use of Late Latin *pedō,* one with large feet, (later) pedestrian, from Latin *pēs* (stem *ped-*) foot.]

Source: *American Heritage Dictionary of the English Language*

in italics, indicating a meaning peculiar to a country or region. Near the end of some entries, you will find the word's *history,* or *origin,* enclosed in brackets. Finally, many dictionary entries give *other forms* of the word in heavy type.

APPLYING SKILLS

Refer to the dictionary entries above to answer the following questions.

1. Write the name of each numbered part of the first dictionary entry.
2. Use the dictionary entry on this page to find the meaning of each underlined word in the sentences below. Write the part of speech and the correct number or number and letter of the meaning of the word beside the letter of each sentence.
    a. Jefferson Davis's parents *pioneered* lands that later became southern plantations.
    b. President Lincoln was proud of his *pioneer* origins.
    c. William Lloyd Garrison was a grim *pioneer* of extreme abolitionist sentiment.

CHAPTER 13 TEST

TEXT REVIEW

1. Name the incident that brought about the last debate on slavery in the Virginia legislature. Describe the subject of the debate and the final outcome.
2. How did southern representatives in Congress block debate on slavery?
3. Name four ways that southern states controlled their slaves.
4. Why did many slaveowners ignore the slave codes? Give examples of such actions.
5. List three ways that black people protested their enslavement.
6. In what ways did many slaves show their resourcefulness and courage?
7. Was the alternative to slavery given by the American Colonization Society a real solution to the slavery question? Give reasons to support your answer.
8. Why were the Grimké sisters not as effective as abolitionists as other speakers were?

CRITICAL THINKING

9. Write a sentence expressing the point of view on slavery that might have been held by the following: a black woman whose husband had been "sold down the river"; an extreme abolitionist; a member of the planter class.
10. Agree or disagree with the following statement: "Many slaves were actually better off than the industrial workers of the time." Give factual reasons to support your opinion of the statement.

WRITING A PARAGRAPH

The people of the United States faced a great problem in the middle decades of the nineteenth century: What was to be done about slavery? Write a paragraph about this problem and the different solutions proposed to resolve it. Your topic sentence should define the problem, and supporting sentences should contain details about the proposed solutions. Include solutions suggested by northerners, southerners, slaves, free blacks, plantation owners, and political leaders.

Discuss how these changes, and the reactions of abolitionists and southern slave owners to them, fueled the debate over slavery that ended in war.

Quotation: from the autobiography *One Writer's Beginnings*. Other works by Eudora Welty (born 1909) include *A Curtain of Green and Other Stories*, *The Delta Wedding*, *The Golden Apples*, *The Ponder Heart*, and *Losing Battles*.

CHAPTER 14

EXPANSION AND DIVISION

1835–1860

Crossing a river, crossing a county line, crossing a state line—especially crossing the line you couldn't see but knew was there, between the South and the North—you could draw a breath and feel the difference. EUDORA WELTY

Making Connections. Americans began to make their way across the continent—to California, to Oregon, and to Texas. These areas would soon become part of the United States. But the new territories caused the debate over slavery to flare up. This time, compromise was not possible.

In this chapter, you will learn:
- Who began the trade between the United States and the northern Mexican territories
- When American slaveowners settled in Texas Why the election of James Polk as president led to war with Mexico
- How the discovery of gold in California threatened the balance between free states and slave states
- Why the repeal of the Missouri Compromise led to the formation of the Republican party
- Whose election as president caused South Carolina and other southern states to secede from the Union

You remember that the Missouri Compromise forbade slavery in the territories north of Missouri. Consequently, the prospect of many free western states entering the Union alarmed southerners. As you read, bear in mind the strong emotions slavery aroused, and note the effect the settling of the territories had on the nation.

Sections
1. Expansion to the Pacific
2. Conflict With Mexico
3. Crisis in the Territories
4. Final Steps to Secession

1. EXPANSION TO THE PACIFIC

American farmers were not attracted to the prairies and plains beyond the Mississippi River. They believed that only land on which trees grew could support crops. In the far west of the Louisiana Purchase, rainfall was so scant that any attempt to farm seemed to be doomed.

Beyond the western boundary, however, in what was then Mexican territory and in the little-known Oregon Country, lay lands that were of considerable interest to a handful of adventurous Americans. "Mountain men"—fur trappers and explorers—were drawn to the Rockies as if by some mysterious force. Missouri merchants, with an eye for a rich opportunity, also began to trade with the mountain city of Santa Fe, New Mexico, and Americans settled in the northeasternmost Mexican state of Texas.

Few of these pioneers thought seriously of adding the lands they entered to the United States. Even further from their minds was the notion that the broad lands they explored and settled could cause a quarrel between North and South that would tear their country apart. But that is exactly what happened.

The print at the right shows Mexican General Santa Anna's army attacking the Alamo in Texas. Though the Alamo fell, the cost to Mexico was high, both in lives lost and in the time the Texans gained for their efforts to raise an army.

Skills Review: Reinforce the skills learned in the preceding Skills Strategy section. As an assignment, have students list all the words they do not know the meaning of in this chapter. Have students use the dictionary to write an analysis of the words following instructions for the exercise in the preceding Skills Strategy section.

The Spanish Heritage of the Southwest.

Before the late 1600s, the Spaniards and Mexicans in Mexico took little interest in the mountainous deserts to their north. However, when the French and British began to expand toward the Mexican borderlands, the viceroys of Mexico moved to confirm Spain's claims in what is now the American Southwest.

Roman Catholic friars from Mexico established two strings of *missions*, along the Rio Grande and the San Antonio River. To protect these tiny outposts in the lands of the fierce Comanche Indians, the Spaniards founded presidios, or forts, at strategic locations, such as the site of present-day San Antonio, Texas.

The northernmost Spanish-Mexican settlement in the North American interior was Santa Fe, in the Sangre de Cristo Mountains of modern New Mexico. Its very existence was threatened by rebellions among the Pueblo Indians in nearby Taos, but Santa Fe held on to become the center of a thriving economy based on mining, fur trapping, cattle raising, and trading with the Indians.

Spanish California.

California was settled later than Texas and New Mexico, in response both to British visits to its magnificent coast and to the lonely little fur-trapping outposts that had been founded by Russians from Alaska. The Franciscan priest Father Junipero Serra hiked tirelessly up and down the coast, urging Indians to build missions at sites where they could improve their standard of living and be converted to Christianity as well. Although he did not live to see the completion of his plan, Serra's idea was to space the missions about a day's walk from one another along the *Camino Real,* the royal road. Soldiers and ranchers followed the missionaries. California became a land of small military posts and large ranches, or *haciendas* (hä′sē-ĕn′dəz). Mexico's long war for independence from Spain, finally won in 1821, hardly touched these northern reaches.

The Santa Fe Trail.

The new Mexican government was friendly with the United States. In 1821 it announced that American traders, formerly banned in Santa Fe, would now be welcome

A string of missions, like Mission Santa Clara (below), were built along the California coast on a road called the Camino Real.

Research Assignment: Have students reconstruct a map of California that outlines the *Camino Real* with an indication of the missions Father Serra designed for it. Information detailing this can be found in a U.S. historical atlas. Display the finished products in class.

there. William Becknell, an alert, enterprising businessperson from Independence, Missouri, immediately set off in a wagon packed with American- and British-made cloth, shoes, tools, and luxury items. By compass and dead reckoning, he made his way 800 miles (1,280 kilometers) across "The Great American Desert"—the prairie —to Santa Fe. The 3,000 inhabitants of that town were astonished and delighted. Becknell made a huge profit on the furs and gold he brought back to Missouri.

Each year for 20 years, a convoy of wagons made a round-trip journey to Santa Fe. Although few Americans actually settled there, a strong link had been forged and an overland route, the Santa Fe Trail, had been permanently marked out by the ruts left by hundreds of heavy wagons.

The Texans. The Mexican government also welcomed Americans to Texas, the thinly populated area that bordered Louisiana. As early as 1820, a Connecticut Yankee named Moses Austin had explored the country and believed it was suitable to both cotton cultivation and cattle grazing. He died before he was able to implement his idea, but in 1821 his son, Stephen Austin, made an agreement with the Mexican government.

Austin agreed to settle 300 American families in Texas, each household receiving 177 acres (72 hectares) of farmland and 13,000 acres (5,300 hectares) of pastureland. In return, Austin promised that the new Mexican citizens would learn the Spanish language and observe the Roman Catholic religion.

No doubt the earliest settlers intended to keep their part of the bargain. But there were few Spanish-speaking Catholics in Texas, and with Mexican authority far away, the settlers from the United States found it easy to ignore Austin's pact. The American population in Texas grew to 20,000 by 1835, and all but a few spoke only English, were Protestant in their religion, and were American in their customs.

Among those customs was slavery. In 1835, about 2,000 blacks toiled in east Texas cotton fields and on cattle ranches. But slavery was illegal in Mexico. According to Mexican law, all slaves in Mexico had been given their freedom in 1830. Trouble was beginning between the Texans and the Republic of Mexico.

In 1821, Stephen Austin and 300 American families settled in Texas under an agreement with the Mexican government.

Santa Anna's Plan. In 1832, General Antonio Lopez de Santa Anna seized control of the Mexican government. Santa Anna feared the growing power of the United States. He therefore canceled American trading privileges in Santa Fe and revoked the broad privileges of self-government enjoyed by the American Texans.

Most historians believed that Santa Anna wanted the Texans to rebel. His hold on the Mexican government was not secure. A war with "foreigners" seemed a good way to unite behind him the many factions in Mexican politics.

The Texans did rebel. They seized the only Mexican military garrison among their farms and

Texas is the only state in the U.S. to have also been an independent republic. One of the provisions for its becoming a state was that it would have the option of dividing to form five individual states. Although this never happened, the prospect had been looked at as a way of increasing Senate representation from 2 to 10.

ranches, the Alamo at San Antonio. Santa Anna would not negotiate with the Texans. Instead, early in 1836, he led an army of about 4,000 into Texas and surrounded the Alamo on February 23.

Less than 200 Texans occupied the fort, mostly Spanish-speaking *tejanos* (tā-yä′nōz), with a handful of Americans, including Jim Bowie, inventor of the Bowie knife, and frontiersman and Whig politician Davy Crockett. A much more serious threat to Santa Anna lay to the east, where Sam Houston was trying to raise an army to fight the Mexicans. But rather than march off to stop Houston before he got started, Santa Anna made the error of attacking the Alamo.

The Lone Star Republic. Commanded from a sickbed by William Travis, the courageous band in the Alamo delayed Santa Anna for thirteen days. In that time, Houston was able to get his army into fighting shape.

When he realized he had blundered, Santa Anna declared that if the Alamo did not surren-

Colonel James Bowie (above) and Davy Crockett (below) fought and died to defend the Alamo in 1836. They and their fellow defenders were memorialized in the cry, "Remember the Alamo!"

Sam Houston (below) raised an army in Texas and defeated Santa Anna's army after the fall of the Alamo. Independent Texas became the Lone Star Republic. Houston became its first president.

Discussion Question: Which side began the war between Texas and Mexico? Answers should indicate that both sides contributed to it.

der, he would take no prisoners after capturing it. The defenders refused to give in. On March 6, the Mexican troops scaled the Alamo's walls. The Texans, out of ammunition, fought with clubs and knives until the last defender was killed.

When news of the massacre reached the eastern part of the state, Spanish- and English-speaking Texans alike swarmed to join Houston. On April 21, the Texan and Mexican forces met at the San Jacinto River. The Texans not only routed the Mexican army, but they captured Santa Anna. In order to secure his release, Santa Anna agreed to an independent Texas, called the Lone Star Republic. Sam Houston was elected president of Texas, and the new republic adopted a constitution much like that of the United States. Immediately, Houston sent agents to Washington requesting that President Jackson annex the republic.

Jackson was Houston's personal friend. But Jackson was also in the final days of his term, and his successor, Martin Van Buren, feared that bringing a new slave state into the Union would anger northern Democrats. Annexation was rejected, but on his last day in office, Jackson formally recognized Texas independence. This at least discouraged the Mexicans from launching a new attack, as Santa Anna wanted to do.

The Mountain Men. Even before Americans began to settle in Texas, mountain men were exploring the mountains and deserts north of Santa Fe. They were not interested in settling down. They were trying to escape settlement, cities, towns, farms, and ranches.

They had learned from the writings of Lewis, Clark, and Pike that the Rocky Mountains teemed

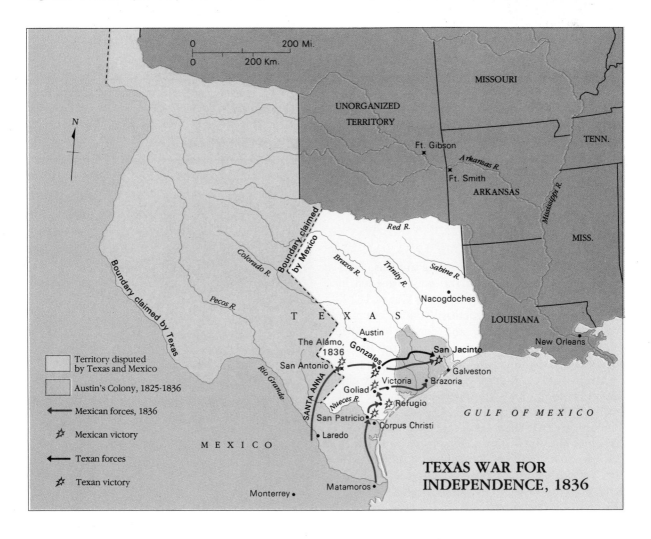

TEXAS WAR FOR INDEPENDENCE, 1836

GOING TO THE SOURCE

Fellow Citizens and Compatriots: I am besieged by a thousand or more of the Mexicans under Santa Anna. I have sustained a continued bombardment for twenty-four hours and have not lost a man. The enemy have demanded a surrender at discretion; otherwise the garrison is to be put to the sword if the place is taken. I have answered the summons with a cannon shot, and our flag still waves proudly from the walls.

I shall never surrender or retreat.

Then, I call on you in the name of liberty, of patriotism, and of everything dear to the American character to come to our aid with all dispatch. The enemy are receiving reinforcements daily and will no doubt increase to three or four thousand in four or five days. Though

Then, I call on you in the name of liberty, of patriotism, and of everything dear to the American character to come to our aid. . . . Though this call may be neglected, I am determined to sustain myself as long as possible. . . .

WILLIAM TRAVIS, "LETTER FROM THE ALAMO"

this call may be neglected, I am determined to sustain myself as long as possible and die like a soldier who never forgets what is due to his own honor and that of his country. *Victory or death!*

W. Barret Travis
Lieutenant Colonel Commanding

P.S. The Lord is on our side. When the enemy appeared in sight, we had not three bushels of corn. We have since found, in deserted houses, eighty or ninety bushels and got into the walls twenty or thirty head of beeves.

In 1836, at the Alamo, a small group of Texans held out against the Mexican Army. This "Letter from the Alamo" was from William Travis, the Texans' commander.

Jim Beckwourth (right), like other mountain men, explored the Rocky Mountains and lived by trapping animals for food and for their fur.

with beaver and other fur-bearing animals. Pelts could always be traded for the goods needed in the wilderness. During and after the War of 1812, men like Jim Bridger, Jedediah Smith, Jeremiah Johnson, Joseph Walker, and Jim Beckwourth explored the meadows and streams of the Rocky Mountains and the deserts beyond.

They lived and trapped in isolation in the winter, spring, and summer, and in the fall brought their pelts to the Sweetwater, Platte, or Bighorn rivers. There they met with agents of Britain's Hudson's Bay Company or John Jacob Astor's American Fur Company and traded their furs for horses, grain, whiskey, guns, traps, blankets, tobacco, and other goods they needed in their wilderness home.

Research Assignment: The story of the mountain men is an often overlooked and exciting part of American history. Encourage students to do reports on some of the mountain men listed on this page of the text. Reports should include details of what their lives were like and how they related to the Indians.

For weeks, the mountain men held riotous parties at the rendezvous points. Then, tiring of so many people in one place, they returned to the mountains. In the meantime, they passed along their enormous geographical knowledge of the mountains to more conventional people back East.

The Oregon Country. Although most of the land they traveled over was officially Mexican, the mountain men aroused the interest of Americans in what was known as the *Oregon Country.* This vague term encompassed more than the present state of Oregon. Altogether, it included present-day Oregon and Washington states, part of Idaho, and British Columbia.

Both Mexico and Russia had vague claims on the territory. So did Great Britain, by virtue of the presence of the Hudson's Bay Company. But Astor's American Fur Company was there too, and beginning in the 1830s, American missionaries —Protestants and Roman Catholics—made their appearance.

The Oregon Trail. These missionaries wrote home of the fertility of the soil and of the mild, rainy climate of the Willamette Valley of central Oregon. Still believing their own prairies could not be cultivated, midwesterners hungry for land decided to go to Oregon. Beginning in 1840, thousands of Americans each year followed the mountain men out from Independence, Missouri, along the *Oregon Trail,* with herds of cattle and lumbering, ox-drawn Conestoga wagons. "Oregon or Bust" was the motto they painted on their wagons.

The emigrants crossed Kansas to the Platte River of Nebraska, followed that broad shallow river to the final American army post at Fort Laramie, and then climbed over Jedediah Smith's South Pass. They struggled through the Rockies to the Snake River, which took them to the Columbia River, and thence into the heart of the Oregon Country.

A wagon train might make up to 20 miles a day, or none at all. At night, exhausted by the tremendous labor of moving a hundred wagons and several hundred head of livestock, the travelers drew their wagons into a hollow square or circle.

While the Indians of the Great Plains and Rockies were hardly delighted to see the intruders

The painting below by Frederic Remington is of a fur trader conducting business in a tepee.

—3,000 Americans in 1845 alone—they rarely threatened to attack. After all, the whites kept moving on and were willing to trade desirable goods for fresh bison meat. Indeed, overland travelers frequently overpacked and had to discard furniture and other curiosities, which the tribes collected. A complete tenderfoot could follow the Oregon Trail by the household goods that lined the ruts left by the Conestoga wagons.

Joint Occupation. The Webster-Ashburton Treaty of 1842 provided that the United States and Britain were to govern the Oregon Country by joint occupation. According to this treaty, Canadians, other British subjects, and Americans would have equal rights everywhere in the territory from California to Alaska. In practice, however, most Americans settled south of the Columbia River; and most British settlers went north of Puget Sound. Only in the huge forested region that is now the state of Washington did joint occupation have real meaning.

What seemed a proper agreement to Daniel Webster and Lord Ashburton did not please the Americans in Oregon. In July 1843, a group met at Champoeg and proclaimed that Oregon was a territory of the United States. They dispatched the news of their action to President John Tyler and, like the Texans, they waited.

SECTION REVIEW

1. Identify: Camino Real, Santa Fe Trail, Stephen Austin, Sam Houston.

2. What was the western boundary of the United States in 1840? Name the two regions west of this boundary that especially interested Americans at that time. Why were Americans so interested in the regions?

3. What two present-day parts of the United States were owned by Spain in the 1840s? What claims did Russia and Great Britain have in the West?

4. Give the main points in the history of Oregon, from the time Americans first settled there to the time they requested annexation by the United States.

---

2. CONFLICT WITH MEXICO

Luckily for the Oregonians, President Tyler believed in expansion. At the same time, a new generation of War Hawks in Congress was willing to challenge Great Britain and was urging the President to annex Texas.

The Texans needed a powerful friend. Their old enemy Santa Anna, still smarting from his humiliation in 1836, was maneuvering to return to power in Mexico. Great Britain was interested in closer relations with Texas, partly because Texas grew cotton, but also because British leaders feared the power of the United States. They felt that with a British presence in Canada and Texas, the young nation could be more easily contained.

Only the hostility of the English people toward slavery kept Great Britain from acting. Having abolished human bondage in the empire, the British did not want to protect Texan slaveowners.

Manifest Destiny. The fact that slavery was legal in Texas was precisely what interested President Tyler and his Secretary of State, John Calhoun. Calhoun had become obsessed with expanding the slave areas. Florida was due to enter the Union as a slave state in 1845. Arkansas had become a slave state in 1836. But the Missouri Compromise line of 1836 effectively shut slavery out of the remaining territories. Three of four territories west of the Mississippi and north of the compromise line would soon be eligible for statehood as free states. Calhoun worried for the future of the southern way of life.

Fortunately, he and Tyler could count on considerable support in the North. Many expansionists were not concerned whether or not slavery was legal in new lands. They mainly wanted the United States to grow.

Americans were feeling their nation's power. A New York editor, John O'Sullivan, coined a slogan for them when he said it was the *manifest destiny* of the United States to rule the North American continent from Atlantic to Pacific. The news from Oregon added fuel to expansionist fires. Americans should have Oregon too, all of it up to the boundary of Russian America. Because the southern tip of Russian Alaska was at 54° 40′ north latitude, expansionists rallied to the cry of "Fifty-four Forty or Fight!"

Class Activity: Lead a discussion on the concept of Manifest Destiny. Consider having students read documents from this period that describe the theory. Explain its importance as a driving force in the movement westward, extending to the Pacific islands.

PROFILES OF THE PRESIDENCY

*J*ames Polk's dream was a United States that stretched from the Atlantic to the Pacific. He especially wanted to acquire California where gold had just been discovered in 1848:

I conversed with several members of Congress . . . and urged upon them the great importance of passing a law to admit California into the Union. . . . I had a casual conversation with Senator Clarke of R.I. on the subject, in which I remarked that there was danger that California would be lost to the Union unless a Government was provided for the inhabitants of that Territory at the present Session of Congress. To which he replied, let her go. I said to him that if California set up an independent Government and separated from the Union, the Eastern States would be much injured by it. He thought not, and said their ships & commerce would derive as much advantage if she was independent. . . .

—DIARY, JANUARY 18, 1849

A "Dark Horse" Candidate for President.
John Tyler believed he could be elected in 1844 by pledging to annex Texas. His problem was that he was a man without a party. The Whigs had expelled him and were about to nominate their old hero, Henry Clay. Nor were the Democrats interested in Tyler. Martin Van Buren had made a comeback after his defeat in 1840. He expected to win the Democratic party nomination and return to the White House.

Clay and Van Buren both wanted to campaign on the issue of economic policy, not on the Texas or Oregon situation. Informally, they agreed that they would take no stand on the question of annexation.

Clay won the Whig nomination. Van Buren, however, ran into trouble. Southern Democrats, who were almost solidly in favor of taking Texas, revived a party rule that two-thirds of the delegates at the nominating convention must agree on a candidate. Van Buren had a majority, but with most southerners opposing him, he could not win two-thirds of the votes.

After eight ballots, the convention compromised by choosing James K. Polk. Polk was the first *dark horse* candidate for the presidency. That is, he had not even been a nominee before the convention began. Indeed, while the Democrats named him "Young Hickory," pretending that Polk was a new Andrew Jackson, no one knew much about him. The Whigs jeered and joked, "Who is Polk?" All anyone could say was that he supported the annexation of Texas. That cheered the Whigs even more. With Polk and independent candidate John Tyler both in favor of annexation, they assumed that Clay would win the votes of everyone who opposed adding another slave state to the Union.

The Fateful Election of 1844. The campaign had a few surprises, however. First, Tyler withdrew his name from the race and supported Polk. Then, as the excitement of expanding the country seemed to be sweeping Polk into the lead, Clay began to worry about his own silence on the issue of annexation. To win, he needed the votes of the North's *Conscience Whigs*, who were against both slavery and annexation (as opposed to proslavery, pro-annexation, *Cotton Whigs*). The result was that Clay never declared himself firmly on either side.

It cost him the presidency. In New York, thousands of Conscience Whigs grew disgusted with him and voted for the tiny antislavery Liberty party. Their votes, subtracted from Clay's total, proved to be just enough to give New York's

---

Discussion Question: Does Manifest Destiny still exist today as a social and political force in the U.S.? Opinions vary, but some variations on the concept of Manifest Destiny, reflecting more of an economic movement than a purely political one, have gained credence in social-science circles.

electoral votes to Polk. With New York went the presidential election of 1844. Polk had a 170–105 majority in electoral votes, but outpolled Clay by fewer than 39,000 popular votes.

A President Who Knew What He Wanted.

James K. Polk may have been an unknown, but he knew exactly what he wanted to accomplish, and the stern, hard-working Tennessean succeeded on all counts.

First, Polk wanted to make Texas part of the United States. This was actually accomplished before he was sworn in as president. Tyler and Calhoun knew they could not get an annexation treaty through the Senate. For a *treaty* to be ratified, two-thirds of the senators had to support it, but more than a third of the senators opposed annexation. However, a resolution of Congress required only that a majority of congressional votes support it. Since Tyler and Calhoun were supported by a majority in Congress, Texas was annexed by means of a joint resolution of the Texan and American congresses.

Polk's second object was to annex as much of Oregon as he could without going to war with Great Britain. This he accomplished by agreeing with England to split the Oregon country at 49° north latitude, the present day Canadian-American boundary east of the Rockies. It was not 54° 40′. But there was no fight, either.

Third, Polk wanted to buy New Mexico and California from Mexico. The United States had no legal claim to either of these Mexican states, and few Americans lived in them. Still, he offered $30 million, which Santa Anna, president of Mexico once again, turned down. Santa Anna refused to

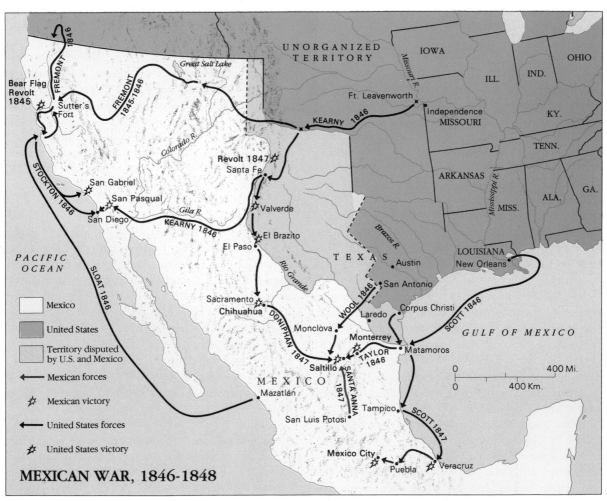

MEXICAN WAR, 1846-1848

Research Assignment: Have students do a research assignment on the leadership of Santa Anna. How long did he remain in power? What were later relations with the United States like? Some students may prefer to do a report on Mexico's history. Such a paper should examine how Mexico's history affected U.S./Mexican relations.

consider the matter, but he did recognize that the Americans were in a warlike mood. He ordered Mexican troops along the Texas border to do nothing to provoke a fight.

War with Mexico. But there was still some question as to whether the Nueces (noo̅-ā′səs) River or the Rio Grande was the southern boundary of Texas. As Polk prepared a message to Congress asking for war with Mexico because of some debts owed to the United States, he ordered General Zachary Taylor to take his army of 1,500 men south of the Nueces to the Rio Grande. In April 1846, 11 American soldiers were killed and five wounded in a *skirmish* with the Mexicans.

Using the fight as a catalyst, Polk took his already prepared speech to Congress. He declared that a state of war already existed between the United States and Mexico and asked Congress to vote money to fight it. This action by Polk was clearly unconstitutional. A president cannot declare war. The power is reserved to Congress.

To the Halls of Montezuma. Constitutional or not, Polk's action was popular. The President became even more popular after a series of rather surprising victories on Mexican battlefields.

The Mexican Army, larger and better trained than the United States Army, was not, however, better commanded. Santa Anna was as poor a general as he was a diplomat, and he led his country into disaster after disaster.

In the summer of 1846, Brigadier General Stephen W. Kearny occupied Santa Fe without resistance. Then Kearny marched to California, where he discovered that along with some *californio* (Mexicans living in California) allies, the 700 Americans who lived there had already defeated the small Mexican garrison and had proclaimed the *Bear Flag Republic.* With their approval, he hauled down the Bear Flag and raised the Stars and Stripes.

In northern Mexico, resistance crumbled after Mexican armies were defeated by the smaller forces of Zachary Taylor. The American victory at Buena Vista gained exceptional attention because Polk, who disliked Taylor, had removed many troops from his command and sent them south to fight for another American General, Winfield Scott. The result was that General Taylor, a crusty old sugar planter from Louisiana, became idolized as "Old Rough and Ready," the hero of Buena Vista.

In March 1847, Winfield Scott landed at Vera Cruz east of Mexico City. He defeated Santa Anna at the battles of Cerro Gordo (cĕr′rō gôr′dō) and Chapultepec (chə-pül′tə-pĕk′) and following Hernando Cortez's route, led his troops into Mexico City—the Halls of Montezuma.

General Zachary Taylor became a hero at the Battle of Buena Vista in Mexico. The painting below is of his field camp after the American victory in that battle.

In the *Treaty of Guadalupe Hidalgo*, signed in February 1848, Mexico was greatly diminished. Fully one-third of the country's territory was attached to the United States. Mexico agreed to recognize the Rio Grande as the boundary of Texas, and in return for a payment of $15 million, ceded California and New Mexico to the United States.

SECTION REVIEW

1. Write a sentence to identify: manifest destiny, "Fifty-four Forty or Fight," Zachary Taylor, Bear Flag Republic.

2. Explain why the annexation of Texas was so important to Tyler and Calhoun. Did their expansionist allies in the North want Texas for the same reason? Explain your answer.

3. Name the Whig and Democratic presidential candidates in 1844. What were their positions on the annexation of Texas?

4. Describe the terms of the Treaty of Guadalupe Hidalgo.

---

3. CRISIS IN THE TERRITORIES

During the Mexican War, Pennsylvania Congressman David Wilmot believed that southerners supported the war primarily to win territory where slavery would be legalized. To call their bluff, he proposed the *Wilmot Proviso*, which stated that slavery would be illegal in any territory taken from Mexico after the war.

Twice the proviso passed the House of Representatives where the North had a majority. Both times the Senate, where slave states commanded half the votes, rejected it. The Wilmot Proviso was the first in a series of events that led directly to the Civil War.

The Election of 1848. In 1848, the Democrats nominated Lewis Cass of Michigan for the presidency. Cass had supported the annexation of Texas and the Mexican War, and was popular in the South. The Whigs also had the war in mind when they nominated the hero of Buena Vista, Zachary Taylor, to head their ticket. Taylor was a southerner and a slaveowner. However, because he had taken no interest in politics before 1848, Old Rough and Ready did not have a reputation in the North as a strong supporter of slavery.

Just as in 1844, the two major parties were evenly matched, with New York State holding the key to the election. This time, however, a third party entered the race. With Martin Van Buren as its candidate, the *Free Soil* party made the Wilmot Proviso its guiding principle.

The Free Soilers did not want to abolish slavery where it already existed. However, they insisted that the western lands be reserved for small family farmers. They argued that wherever there was slavery, wealthy planters dominated politics. Unlike abolitionism, this was an idea with which a majority of northerners could agree. Enough New York Democrats agreed with it in 1848 that Cass lost the state to Taylor. With New York's electoral votes, Taylor became president.

Gold Creates a Crisis. Having won states in both North and South, Zachary Taylor might have presided over a new era of good feelings. That was not to be, however, because of the discovery of gold in California in 1848. Americans rushed to California by the tens of thousands. By late 1849, the population of California topped 100,000, enough for California to be admitted as a state.

It happened so fast that California had no time to become organized as a territory. No matter, President Taylor said, there were enough people there, and California was extremely valuable. He urged Californians to skip the customary territorial phase and apply directly for statehood.

They did. The *Forty-niners* held a constitutional convention during September and October of 1849 and sent the document to Congress for approval. California applied for admission to the Union as a free state.

Proslavery southerners were stunned. They had expected the lands taken from Mexico to be settled slowly and at least some to be settled by people who favored slavery. California's free-state status was politically devastating to the South. In 1850 there were 15 free states and 15 slave states. The southerners had felt they could defeat any antislavery law in the Senate, where each state had two votes. But California statehood would change that, shattering the balance between free and slave states.

President Zachary Taylor spent the bulk of his life as a professional soldier. As such, he moved about the country extensiviely—so much so that he was unable to establish a legal residence until his retirement. Because of this he did not vote until he was 62. He didn't even vote in his own election.

PROFILES OF THE PRESIDENCY

*Z*achary Taylor was a most reluctant presidential candidate. He did not campaign for himself. To his brother-in-law he wrote:

I have said I was not a party candidate, nor am I in that straightened and sectarian sense which would prevent my being the President of the whole people, in case of my election . . . I am not engaged to lay violent hands indiscriminately upon public officers, good or bad, who may differ in opinion with me. I am not expected to force Congress, by the coercion of the veto, to pass laws to suit me, or pass none. This is what I mean by not being a party candidate.

I refer all persons, who are anxious on the subject to this statement for the proper understanding of my position towards the Presidency and the people. If it is not intelligible, I cannot make it so, and shall cease to attempt it.

—LETTER TO JOHN S. ALLISON, SEPTEMBER 4, 1848

The Compromise of 1850.

Southern extremists known as *Fire-eaters* refused to accept California. They soon learned that Zachary Taylor was not their friend. Taylor believed slavery was just, but he was also a strong nationalist. In his view, California must be a state, and if Californians chose not to have slavery, they had that right.

The gruff old general would not even accept a compromise plan designed by Henry Clay. In Clay's *Omnibus Bill* (the name means it contained a great many provisions) northerners would get the admission of California as a free state and the abolition of the slave trade in the District of Columbia, although slavery would remain legal in the capital. To compensate proslavery southerners, Clay's plan organized two federal territories, one to include present-day Utah and Nevada, the other New Mexico and Arizona. He left open the

In 1858, gold was discovered 80 miles north of Pikes Peak in Colorado and a new gold rush began. Thousands of hopeful prospectors, like those below, headed west.

In this engraving, Senator Henry Clay (standing, center) is seen in the Senate on February 5, 1850, offering his Omnibus Bill.

possibility that one or both of these territories might eventually become slave states. The Omnibus Bill also included a new *Fugitive Slave Act*, replacing a weaker one of 1793. Federal marshalls in northern states would receive broader powers in arresting and returning runaway slaves to the South. Texas would agree to give up its claim to the New Mexican land, which had been gained as a result of the Mexican War, in exchange for a federal payment of $10 million. The Texas boundary would then be established.

Proslavery extremists and abolitionists both rejected Clay's plan, each side refusing to make concessions. Then, while southern and northern moderates called for compromise, President Taylor, who seemed to be a moderate, refused to back the Omnibus Bill because it provided for federal payment of money to Texas.

When all seemed lost, and the Fire-eaters spoke of seceding from the Union, a tragedy turned the tide. President Taylor stood in the hot July sun too long at a patriotic ceremony and, returning to the White House, drank huge quantities of ice water.

It was too much for the old soldier. Doctors worsened rather than improved the situation, and he died.

This put Millard Fillmore in the presidential chair. Fillmore was a Whig who favored compromise. During that tense summer, young Senator Stephen A. Douglas of Illinois took over Clay's Omnibus Bill. Douglas was known as the "Little Giant" because, although short of stature, his speech-making powers were great. Douglas split Clay's Bill into five different bills and worked this *Compromise of 1850* through Congress by patching together different majorities for each bill. Many were extremists on one side or the other of the slavery question. Charles Sumner of Massachusetts, William H. Seward of New York, Thaddeus Stevens of Pennsylvania, Salmon B. Chase of Ohio, and many other northerners were determined to fight slavery at every opportunity.

Their young southern counterparts, the Fire-eaters, were as obsessed with protecting slavery as Calhoun had been, but had none of his brilliance. Robert Toombs of Georgia was an example. He

In response to the suggestion by some southern congressmen that the South might have cause to leave the Union, Taylor became incensed. As he explained it in 1850, he would stop such an action without spilling a drop of blood by sending out the navy to blockade all southern harbors.

MILLARD FILLMORE

Millard Fillmore disapproved of slavery but helped avoid civil war by supporting the Compromise of 1850, which provided for return of runaway slaves:

[It is understood that] no human legislation can be perfect. Wide differences and jarring opinions can only be reconciled by yielding something on all sides, and this result had been reached after an angry conflict of many months, in which one part of the country was arrayed against another, and violent convulsion seemed to be imminent.

Looking at the interests of the whole country, I felt it to be my duty to seize upon this compromise as the best that could be obtained amid conflicting interests and to insist upon it as a final settlement, to be adhered to by all who value the peace and welfare of the country. A year has now elapsed . . . I congratulate you and the country upon the general acquiescence in these measures of peace which has been exhibited in all parts of the Republic.

—MESSAGE TO CONGRESS, DECEMBER 2, 1851

---

supported the Compromise of 1850, but within a few years he was denouncing every suggestion of compromise or even discussion with northerners. But at least for the moment, the sectional hatreds faded.

A New Generation.
The Thirty-First Congress, the Congress of 1850, marked a change in American politics from a generation usually able to compromise its differences to one that was not. Henry Clay, Daniel Webster, John C. Calhoun, and Thomas Hart Benton were old and feeble. Within a few years, each would be dead or out of office.

The new, younger leaders were a different breed. With the exception of Douglas, there were few compromisers among them. There were also the *Doughfaces*, northern Democrats who seemed to be moderate because they supported the southern proslavery position. In the political language of the 1850s, a Doughface was a northerner with southern principles.

Election of 1852.
The Whigs began to split along sectional lines in the election of 1852, when they nominated the Mexican War hero Winfield Scott for the presidency. However, he lost so many votes to the Democrats in the South and to the Free Soilers in the North that he was easily

defeated by the Doughface Democrat, Franklin Pierce.

Slavery in the Territories.
Very few northerners were active abolitionists. Some northerners objected to slavery as a moral evil. Some believed that if southerners wanted slavery, that was their business.

What increasing numbers of northern voters did object to was the expansion of slavery into the territories. Small farmers looked to the West as a place where they or their children could build lives for themselves. But that would be possible only if wealthy slaveowners were prevented from establishing slave-run plantations there. Northern farmers believed themselves to be the republic's most valuable citizens. In their view, where there were slave laborers and large plantations, the family farmer could not compete.

Plans to Build a Railroad.
The principal issue of the Pierce presidency was where to construct a railroad connecting California with the rest of the Union. The best route was clearly through El Paso, Texas, and along the southern boundary of the United States. The southern route would have to cross high mountains only in what is now central Arizona. However, to build this route, the railroad would have to pass through

PROFILES OF THE PRESIDENCY

*L*ooking back 75 years to America's beginnings, Pierce reminded people that their ancestors had been practical individuals:

The thoughts of the men of that day were as practical as their sentiments were patriotic . . . They had exhibited not only the power to achieve, but, what all history affirms to be so much more unusual, the capacity to maintain. The oppressed throughout the world from that day to the present have turned their eyes hitherward, not to find those lights extinguished or to fear lest they should wane, but to be constantly cheered by their steady and increasing radiance.

In this our country has, in my judgment, thus far fulfilled its highest duty to suffering humanity. It has spoken and will continue to speak, not only by its words, but by its acts, the language of sympathy, encouragement, and hope to those who earnestly listen to tones which pronounce for the largest rational liberty. But after all, the most animating encouragement and potent appeal for freedom will be its own history—its trials and its triumphs.

—INAUGURAL ADDRESS, MARCH 4, 1853

---

part of Mexican territory. Secretary of War Jefferson Davis solved this problem in 1853 by purchasing a triangular-shaped tract of desert (present-day southern Arizona) from Mexico for $10 million. This last addition to the continental United States was called the *Gadsden Purchase*, after James Gadsden, the agent sent to Mexico to close the deal.

This print shows the Kansas constitutional convention, at which the territory's future status as a free or slave state dominated the debate.

It appeared that the *transcontinental railroad* would be a plum for the South. But that was before Stephen Douglas revealed his central-route plan, which would make Chicago, in his own state of Illinois, the eastern end of the line.

The Kansas-Nebraska Bill.
In order to make a central route to California feasible, Douglas had to organize federal territories in the unorganized prairies of the Midwest. Only in official territories could the federal government provide the law, order, and security such a great construction project would require.

However, southern congressmen were not likely to support any plan to organize territories so far north, particularly since, under the Missouri Compromise, slavery would be forbidden in those territories.

Obtaining the central route was more important to Douglas than was keeping slavery out of the territories. Douglas therefore introduced the *Kansas-Nebraska Act* in 1854. According to this plan, the Missouri Compromise line would be repealed, and slavery would no longer be forbidden north of 36° 30′. Instead, the choice of whether to legalize slavery was left to the voters who would settle the newly organized Kansas and Nebraska territories. *Popular sovereignty*, the will

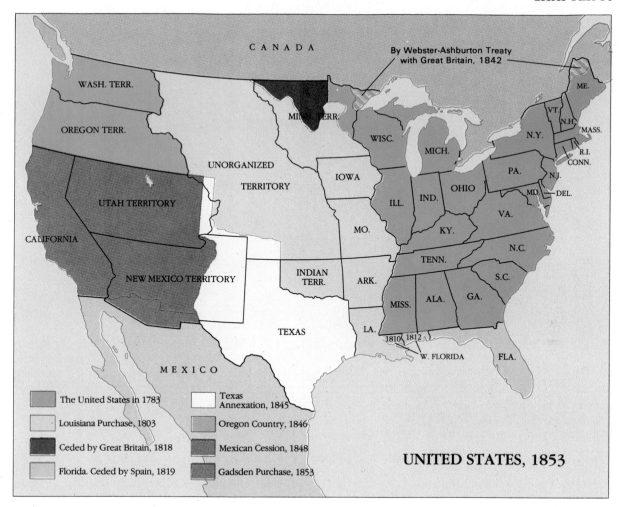

CANADA

By Webster-Ashburton Treaty
with Great Britain, 1842

WASH. TERR.

OREGON TERR.

MINN. TERR.

ME.

VT.

N.H.

MASS.

WISC.

N.Y.

R.I.

CONN.

UNORGANIZED

TERRITORY

IOWA

MICH.

PA.

N.J.

UTAH TERRITORY

ILL.

IND.

OHIO

MD. DEL.

CALIFORNIA

MO.

VA.

NEW MEXICO TERRITORY

INDIAN
TERR.

ARK.

KY.

TENN.

N.C.

S.C.

TEXAS

LA.

MISS.

ALA.

GA.

1810 1812

MEXICO

W. FLORIDA

FLA.

The United States in 1783		Texas Annexation, 1845
Louisiana Purchase, 1803		Oregon Country, 1846
Ceded by Great Britain, 1818		Mexican Cession, 1848
Florida. Ceded by Spain, 1819		Gadsden Purchase, 1853

UNITED STATES, 1853

of the people, would resolve the question of slavery democratically in the territories, Douglas told the Senate.

The Republican Party.

The Kansas-Nebraska Act became law. Many northerners who had never taken notice of the debate over the territories were stunned. For 34 years, slavery had been illegal in the northern part of the Louisiana area. Suddenly, if voters in the Nebraska or Kansas territories chose to have slaves, they could do so. Few northerners worried about Nebraska. It would be settled by people from the free state of Iowa, and would almost certainly become a free state. But Kansas Territory bordered on the slave state of Missouri. If Kansas were settled by Missourians, as seemed likely, it would enter the Union as a slave state.

The first response of antislavery northerners was to form, in 1854, the new Republican party. Later that year, the *Republicans*, committed to keeping slavery out of all territories, won a majority in the House of Representatives.

But in 1856, the Republican presidential candidate, John C. Fremont, was defeated by the Doughface Democrat, James Buchanan. Still, the Republicans had good reason to look forward to 1860. They appealed to farmers on the principle of no slavery in the territories, and by support for a Homestead Act. According to this act, any family that actually settled and developed western land would receive it free. The Republicans wooed the New England states by taking over the old Whig economic policy of a high protective tariff and a liberal immigration policy, thus providing cheap immigrant labor for factories. To the

What persons worked to unify the U.S. in the 1850s? The most obvious answer to this would be Douglas, but there should be some less obvious ones mentioned as well.

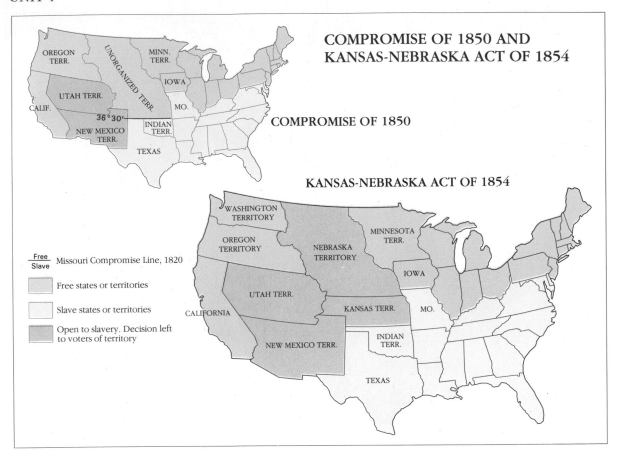

COMPROMISE OF 1850 AND
KANSAS-NEBRASKA ACT OF 1854

COMPROMISE OF 1850

KANSAS-NEBRASKA ACT OF 1854

western Whigs, the Republicans offered the ultimate internal improvement—the transcontinental railroad, subsidized by the federal government.

It was a comprehensive program, offering something to almost every northern voter. But the Republicans were not a national party. Their opposition to slavery kept them off southern ballots.

Bleeding Kansas. After the founding of the Republican party, relations between North and South grew steadily more bitter. In Kansas, southerners discovered that legally opening a territory to slavery did not ensure that slavery would be established there. Northern antislavery groups, such as Eli Thayer's New England Emigrant Aid Company, raised money to get so many free-state voters into the territory that they would out-vote the less numerous Missourians.

Within two years, Thayer's group sent 1,300 people to Kansas and encouraged many others to pay their own way. It seemed quite likely that in an honest election, Kansas would reject slavery. In order to avoid this, proslavery Missourians known as *border ruffians* rode into Kansas for elections, and sometimes terrorized free-state settlers. Abolitionists spoke of the territory as "Bleeding Kansas." Then, on May 21, 1856, a gang of border ruffians burned the antislavery town of Lawrence, killing several people. During the same month, antislavery Senator Charles Sumner of Massachusetts delivered a bitterly anti-South speech about Kansas in which he made reference to a speech impediment of Senator Andrew Butler of South Carolina. The next day Butler's nephew, South Carolina Congressman Preston Brooks, walked up to Sumner and beat him insensible with a club. Sumner was incapacitated for several years.

Nor was all the bleeding done by the antislavery side. Three days after the burning of Lawrence, an abolitionist named John Brown, accompanied by several of his sons, rode up to a small proslavery settlement and brutally killed five men.

Discussion Question: How did the "Bleeding Kansas" violence broaden the base of sectionalism in the U.S. by attracting former moderates?

*T*he storm over slavery, building during James Buchanan's administration, erupted after he left office. He wrote to a friend:

The future of our country presents a dark cloud, through which my vision cannot penetrate. The assault upon Fort Sumter was the commencement of war by the Confederate States, and no alternative was left but to prosecute it with vigor on our part. Up and until all social and political relations ceased between the secession leaders and myself, I had often warned them that the North would rise to a man against them if such an assault were made. No alternative seems now to be left but to prosecute hostilities until the seceding States shall return to their allegiance, or until it shall be demonstrated that this object, which is nearest my heart, cannot be accomplished. From present appearances it seems certain that they would accept no terms of compromise short of an absolute recognition of their independence, which is impossible.
—LETTER TO WILLIAM R. KING, JULY 13, 1861

National Unity Fades. Bitter feelings continued to grow throughout the country. Few southerners condemned the burning of Lawrence by proslavery forces, and Preston Brooks was praised as a hero in many southern states for his beating of Sumner. Few northerners condemned the ugly speech Charles Sumner had given and a few abolitionists actually praised John Brown for murdering proslavery Kansans. The spirit of national unity was dying.

SECTION REVIEW

1. Write a sentence to identify: Wilmot Proviso, Forty-niners, Doughfaces, "Bleeding Kansas."
2. Name the third party that entered the 1848 presidential race, and describe its position on slavery in the territories.
3. How did Clay's Omnibus Bill accommodate proslavery and antislavery forces?
4. Explain the principle of Douglas's popular sovereignty.
5. How did passage of the Kansas-Nebraska Act result in the formation of the Republican party?

4. FINAL STEPS TO SECESSION

Like his predecessor, President James Buchanan was a Doughface. He wanted to resolve the sectional split in a way that would favor his southern supporters. Before he made his view known, however, Chief Justice Roger B. Taney informed him of a Supreme Court decision that, Taney believed, might settle the North-South split for all time.

Taney, a one-time associate of Andrew Jackson, came from an old and respected Maryland family. Although his relatives were slaveowners, Taney was a moderate on the issue. He hoped that his decision in the case of *Dred Scott* v. *Sandford* would resolve the issue of slavery's status in the territories for all time. Instead, it worsened the ill feelings between North and South and pushed the United States farther down the road to civil war.

The Dred Scott Case. Dred Scott was the slave of an army officer who, in the course of his career, had taken Scott into Illinois, where slavery was forbidden by the Northwest Ordinance of 1787, and briefly into Louisiana Purchase lands where slavery was, at the time, forbidden under the Missouri Compromise of 1820. Back in Missouri, where slavery was legal, Dred Scott sued his

The Supreme Court's decision in the case mentioned above was overturned by the Thirteenth Amendment (1865) and the Fourteenth Amendment (1868).

master for his freedom because he had lived where slavery was illegal. Scott was granted his freedom, but the case was appealed, and finally reached the Supreme Court.

In 1857, Taney and the Supreme Court ruled that because Scott was legally a slave in Missouri, he was not a citizen and had no right to sue. Scott remained a slave. The Court could have stopped at this point. But Taney, in writing the majority opinion, said the Constitution provided that citizens could not be deprived of their property in federal territories without due process. Since slaves were considered property, Congress had overstepped its powers in passing the Northwest Ordinance and the Missouri Compromise.

The proslavery forces rejoiced. The Missouri Compromise, under which slavery had been illegal in all territories north of 36° 30', was now invalid. But Taney went even further. Under the Kansas-Nebraska Act of 1854, slavery could be legalized in those territories only if the settlers chose to do so. Taney ruled that territories did not have the same sovereignty as states and therefore could not outlaw slavery, even if the majority of settlers were against it. The Kansas-Nebraska Act was also rendered invalid. Slavery could not be kept out of federal territories.

The legal suit the slave Dred Scott (below), brought against his master ended in the Supreme Court.

The Lincoln-Douglas Debates.

The Dred Scott decision was the major issue of debate in 1858 when Illinois Republicans nominated Abraham Lincoln to run for the Senate against Stephen Douglas. In a series of debates around the state, Lincoln taunted Douglas on the issue of popular sovereignty. How could the Little Giant continue to back his "democratic" solution to the slavery question now that the Supreme Court had ruled against it?

Lincoln's point was that, short of passing a constitutional amendment preventing the expansion of slavery, there was nothing northerners could do. Like other Republicans, Lincoln hinted that under the Democrats, the federal government was in the hands of *slavocrats*, or politicians who supported slavery, who were determined to force their institution on everyone.

In the *Freeport Doctrine*, (so called because Douglas presented it at a debate in Freeport, Illinois) Douglas came up with an ingenious reply. In practice, he said, territorial legislatures could keep slavery out. The Supreme Court might be able to overturn a law of which it disapproved. But the Court could not force a legislature to pass a law. Simply by failing to pass laws protecting the rights of slaveowners, a territorial legislature could, in practice, keep slavery out of the territory.

John Brown's Solution.

In the meantime, John Brown of Kansas surfaced again. In October 1859, with a small band of armed blacks and his own sons, Brown swooped down on the federal arsenal at Harpers Ferry, Virginia (now West Virginia) and captured it. Brown's plan was to use the guns in the arsenal to end slavery with *guerrilla warfare*.

Brown's mistake was to stay in Harpers Ferry too long. Hearing a rumor that slaves in the area were about to rebel and join him, he remained in the town. A detachment of marines commanded by Robert E. Lee surrounded him, killed most of his supporters, and took him prisoner.

Brown was tried for treason and hanged. However, the raid reawakened fears of slave rebellion in the South. When a number of prominent northerners declared that Brown was a saint, even southern moderates began to suspect that their states had no future in the Union.

Class Activity: Have students stage one of the Lincoln-Douglas debates, using actual text if possible. To further add to the activity, students might dress as the two politicians. Follow up with questions to the class covering issues of the debate.

In a series of campaign debates held in Illinois in 1858 between senatorial candidates Stephen Douglas and Abraham Lincoln, the central issue was slavery in the territories.

The Democrats Split.

The northern states were growing rapidly. The South was not. Even if Kansas became a slave state, which was unlikely, it would surely be the last one. Elsewhere in the West, the north's greater population ensured that new states would abolish slavery. In time, free states would number three-fourths of the total, enough to ratify a constitutional amendment abolishing slavery nationwide.

In the meantime, southern Democrats could help isolate the Republicans by cooperating with moderate northern Democrats like Stephen A. Douglas. In 1860, however, the Fire-eaters, who regarded Douglas as an enemy, dominated the

Research Assignment: Have students prepare a report on some aspect of your local history that played a part in this period of history. Topics could include clipper ships, Lincoln's birthplace or a place he lived, "Bleeding Kansas," the Underground Railroad, and gold miners.

John Brown captured a federal arsenal at Harpers Ferry, Virginia, in October 1859. He was captured, tried for treason, and hanged. The painting above shows Brown just before his execution.

FREE STATES AND SLAVE STATES · 1860

	Free States	Slave States
Original 13 States	Massachusetts New Hampshire Rhode Island Connecticut New York Pennsylvania New Jersey	Delaware Maryland Virginia North Carolina South Carolina Georgia
Admitted 1791–1819	Vermont Ohio Indiana Illinois	Kentucky Tennessee Louisiana Mississippi Alabama
Admitted 1820–1839	Maine Michigan	Missouri Arkansas
Admitted 1840–1859	Iowa Wisconsin California Minnesota Oregon	Florida Texas

southern branch of the party. Instead of choosing moderation in 1860, the Democratic party split into a southern and a northern wing. The northerners, with some support from southern *moderates*, nominated Douglas for president. Douglas's program for dealing with the territorial question was still popular sovereignty—plus the Freeport Doctrine.

The southern Democrats nominated Kentucky's John Breckinridge on a platform based on the Dred Scott case—slavery could not constitutionally be kept out of the territories. They demanded that Congress enact a federal slave code to protect slavery in all the territories.

The Republican Challenge. With the Democrats split, the Republicans smelled victory. Instead of gloating, however, and taking an extreme position, they passed over abolitionists and strong Free Soilers, and nominated one of their moderates, Abraham Lincoln.

Lincoln was opposed to the expansion of slavery. However, he had never been an abolitionist. The Republicans chose Lincoln precisely because they expected to win. Already, southern Fire-eaters had said that if any Republican won, their states would leave the Union. By choosing one of their moderates, the Republicans hoped to avoid secession.

The Election of 1860. There were actually four candidates in 1860. The *Constitutional Union* party, made up of former Whigs mostly from the border states of Delaware, Maryland, Virginia, and Kentucky, nominated John Bell of Tennessee. Their program was to wait, to cool down, for both North and South to give the slavery question time to work out on its own.

Stephen Douglas is known as one of the active leaders in the move to avert a war between the states.

Lincoln Wins. As election day drew near, the Fire-eaters warned northern voters that if they elected Lincoln, the southern states would secede from the Union. They claimed that slavery would not be safe with a "Black Republican" in the White House. Lincoln as president would mean more John Browns and decreased southern influence in the government. The southerners would have to form a new nation.

In the election, Lincoln won more popular votes than any other candidate. Douglas was second, followed by Breckinridge and Bell. Lincoln won his majority by sweeping the northern and western states. Breckinridge swept the South, and Bell won only some border states. Douglas was the only truly national candidate, coming in second to Lincoln in the North, and second to Breckinridge in the South. In electoral votes, Lincoln received 180, Breckinridge 72, Bell 39, and Douglas only 12.

The election results could hardly be interpreted as a mandate for Lincoln and the Republican party. Although Lincoln ran 500,000 votes ahead of second-place Douglas, the total for Douglas and Bell, the candidates who stood for compromise, was more than 100,000 greater than Lincoln's popular vote total.

The Deep South Says Farewell. On December 20, 1860, a state convention called by the South Carolina legislature voted unanimously to secede from the Union. In January 1861, six other southern states followed. The southerners also began taking over military installations and federal offices and agencies.

The outgoing president, James Buchanan, was helpless. On the one hand, he said secession was illegal. On the other hand, he would not use force to stop it. Buchanan wanted to leave the problem to the new Republican president.

Just when the Union appeared to be doomed, there was a glimmer of hope. Conventions in the slave states of Kentucky, Virginia, and North Carolina voted against secession. At the same time, these states warned Lincoln not to use force against the states of the deep South. If he did, they would join them in secession.

Although there was still some hope for a peaceful settlement, the hope was slim. It appeared that the war which years of compromise had sought to avoid was about to occur.

The Republican party candidates for president and vice president in 1860 were Abraham Lincoln (left) and Hannibal Hamlin (right).

HON. ABRAHAM LINCOLN, OF ILLINOIS. HON. HANNIBAL HAMLIN, OF MAINE.

FOR PRESIDENT. FOR VICE PRESIDENT.

SECTION REVIEW

1. Write a sentence to identify: slavocrats, Harpers Ferry, James Buchanan, Robert E. Lee.
2. Give the background of the Dred Scott case. How did the Supreme Court's ruling in the case affect slavery in the territories?
3. Explain the point about slavery in the territories that Abraham Lincoln made during his debates with Stephen Douglas in 1858. How did Douglas reply to Lincoln's argument?
4. Name the four candidates and their parties in the presidental election of 1860. How did the outcome of the election affect the country?

Alexander Stephens, the Georgia legislator who, although vice president of the Confederacy, also remained one of the strongest opponents of the secession and wrote about the secessionists, "The people run mad, they are wild with passion and frenzy, doing they know not what."

CHAPTER REVIEW

TIME LINE

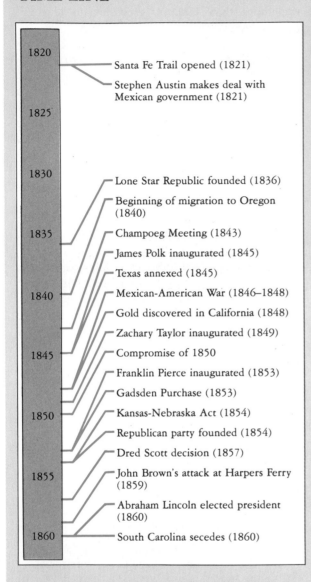

1820

Santa Fe Trail opened (1821)

Stephen Austin makes deal with Mexican government (1821)

1825

1830

Lone Star Republic founded (1836)

Beginning of migration to Oregon (1840)

1835

Champoeg Meeting (1843)

James Polk inaugurated (1845)

Texas annexed (1845)

Mexican-American War (1846–1848)

1840

Gold discovered in California (1848)

Zachary Taylor inaugurated (1849)

1845

Compromise of 1850

Franklin Pierce inaugurated (1853)

Gadsden Purchase (1853)

1850

Kansas-Nebraska Act (1854)

Republican party founded (1854)

Dred Scott decision (1857)

1855

John Brown's attack at Harpers Ferry (1859)

Abraham Lincoln elected president (1860)

1860

South Carolina secedes (1860)

TIME LINE QUESTIONS

1. How long after the Lone Star Republic was founded was it annexed by the United States?
2. How many years separate presidential elections? Assuming that the Republican party nominated a candidate for each campaign after the party's founding, how can you tell from the time line that Lincoln was the Republicans' second presidential nominee?

SKILLS STRATEGY

After the shameful incident in San Antonio last week, all Americans know deep in their bones that it is well nigh time for their leaders to take strong action against General Santa Anna's government. Otherwise, the deaths of Jim Bowie, Davy Crockett, and other Americans at the Alamo will remain a dark stain on our national honor for ages to come. And there is only one action our leaders can take in conscience to honor our dead countrymen: Grant the remaining Americans in Texas what they have so earnestly requested, worked hard for, and, at the Alamo, given up life itself for—territorial status and eventual statehood. Let all those who object think but for a moment of the weeping *American* widows and helpless *American* orphans of those who lost their lives in Texas.

NEWS STORIES AND EDITORIALS

Newspapers of a period are useful and usually interesting primary sources of information. They contain eyewitness accounts and current opinions given by people who were closely involved in or related to historical events. News stories and editorials are often used by historians when they do research.

If facts about an event are needed by a researcher, a *news story* is the place to look. Most news stories give the basic *who, what, where, when, how,* and *why* facts in the first or *lead* paragraph.

On the other hand, if opinions, attitudes, and feelings about an event are wanted by the researcher, an *editorial* is the source to use. Opinions should never be stated in a news story; the opposite is true of an editorial. An editorial gives the opinions of the writer, and should try to persuade readers to accept those opinions.

The editorial page of a newspaper is reserved for articles expressing opinions of the newspaper publisher and its editorial staff and for letters expressing the opinions of the newspaper's readers. These appear on the editorial page to separate them from the straight news reports and feature

Making Connections: Review the questions and topics presented in the Making Connections section that opens this chapter. Explain the Civil War as the culmination of events that caused and resulted from each other. Include an explanation of how the country's expansion contributed to this.

The massacre of 187 American Texans between February 23 and March 6 at a San Antonio fort called the Alamo was revealed today by a government spokesperson. A report of the massacre was sent by Sam Houston—commander of the army of the recently established provisional government set up by Americans in Texas. According to Houston's report, a Mexican force of 3,000 led by dictator General Antonio Lopez de Santa Anna began assault on the Alamo on February 23. The Texans inside the fort, including Jim Bowie, David Crockett, and William B. Travis, held out until March 6, the day Santa Anna's men gained entry to the fort and massacred the entire defenders of the garrison. The Washington spokesperson stressed that the United States government is planning no immediate action.

stories on other pages. The editorial and news pages are identified separately in the index of the paper. However, you can learn to identify each by recognizing the characteristics of news stories and editorials.

One of the above paragraphs could have been the lead of a news story printed in an excerpt from an American newspaper in 1836. The other paragraph could have been an editorial that appeared in the same newspaper. Read each paragraph through once. Then refer to both as you answer the following questions.

APPLYING SKILLS

1. What is the first sentence of the lead paragraph?
2. Which questions are answered in the lead?
3. What opinions, attitudes, and feelings are expressed in the editorial?
4. If you were doing research for a report, why might you use the editorial above?
5. In doing research for the same report, why might you use the lead paragraph?
6. Write the sentence from each paragraph that most clearly shows what kind of an article it is a part of.

CHAPTER 14 TEST

TEXT REVIEW

1. How did the Spaniards and Mexicans protect their settlements in Texas, New Mexico, and California? Why did they begin to protect them?
2. Explain the meaning of this statement: "The Oregon Country encompassed more than the present state of Oregon."
3. Describe the belief expressed by the term *manifest destiny*. How were James Polk's attitudes in accord with manifest destiny's ideals?
4. In what sense was Polk's declaration of war on Mexico unconstitutional?
5. Briefly explain why northerners and southerners argued over admission of western states.
6. Tell how *one* of the following was intended to eliminate sectional hatreds, and comment on its success: Compromise of 1850, Kansas-Nebraska Act.
7. Explain how each of the following led the South farther toward secession: the Wilmot Proviso, California's admission to the Union, John Brown's attack at Harpers Ferry.

CRITICAL THINKING

8. Contrast the "Fire-eaters" with Henry Clay and John C. Calhoun.
9. List each of the following under the heading *proslavery* or *antislavery*: Doughfaces, Free Soilers, Charles Sumner, Republican party, southern Democrats.
10. What bias would you count among Stephen Douglas's motives in having the Kansas-Nebraska Act passed?

WRITING A PARAGRAPH

Put yourself in the place of an editorial writer for a newspaper of the early 1800s whose policy was to oppose the addition of new states to the United States. Write a one-paragraph editorial about why you think the territories should remain territories. Be as persuasive as you can. Then write a letter attacking the editorial, using arguments in favor of statehood for the territories. Again, try to be persuasive.

Quotation: from the poem "For the Union Dead." Other poems by Robert Lowell (1917–1977) are collected in *Near the Ocean, Imitations, Life Studies, The Mills of the Kavanaughs, Lord Weary's Castle,* and *The Old Glory.*

CHAPTER 15

THE CIVIL WAR

1861–1865

On a thousand small town New England greens,
the old white churches hold their air
of sparse, sincere rebellion; frayed flags
quit the graveyards of the Grand Army of the Republic.

ROBERT LOWELL

Making Connections. Most people in the North and the South expected the Civil War to be over in one short campaign. They did not dream that hundreds of thousands of Americans would fight in the war, millions more would be directly affected, and the South would be completely devastated. They did not know that the nation would be torn apart, and put back together in a totally different form.

In this chapter, you will learn:
• What event made the North determined to subdue the South by force
• Why some slave states stayed in the Union
• How each side planned to win the war
• Why the caution of some Union generals and the ability of some Confederate generals kept the North from winning decisive victories that could have ended the war sooner
• How the Emancipation Proclamation helped the Union cause
• What tactics General Grant used to finally defeat the South's forces

You know that the North was more heavily industrialized than the South, which was mostly agricultural. Consequently, the North was more prepared to fight a long war. However, the South, despite considerable weaknesses, had some advantages that allowed it to hold the North at bay until the last year of the war. As you read, note how the North exploited its superior power and numbers, and how the South attempted to counteract them.

Sections
1. Union and Confederacy
2. The Campaign of 1861
3. Stalemate and Breakthrough
4. Grant's War of Attrition

1. UNION AND CONFEDERACY

In February 1861, representatives of South Carolina, Georgia, Florida, Alabama, Mississippi, Louisiana, and Texas met in Montgomery, Alabama, to form a government. They realized that they had to work quickly, or their movement would lose its power. They formed the *Confederate States of America,* and chose Jefferson Davis as president before Lincoln was inaugurated. They wrote a constitution similar to the United States Constitution, and included strong guarantees of slavery and states' rights.

Among the differences was a provision that the Confederate government could never interfere with slavery in the states. Another provision allowed the president only one term of six years.

Jefferson Davis was a moderate from Mississippi. At the Mississippi secession convention, Davis argued that Lincoln should be given a chance before the state seceded. When a majority of delegates disagreed with him, Davis gave in. The Confederate vice president, Alexander Stephens of Georgia, opposed secession to the end. The Fire-eaters chose moderate leaders to win the support of Southerners who did not approve of splitting the Union.

Last Attempts at Compromise. While the Confederacy was being organized, leaders from the border states tried to find a compromise by

The painting at the right by Julian Scott is of the Battle of Chancellorsville. It was at that battle that "Stonewall" Jackson was fatally wounded.

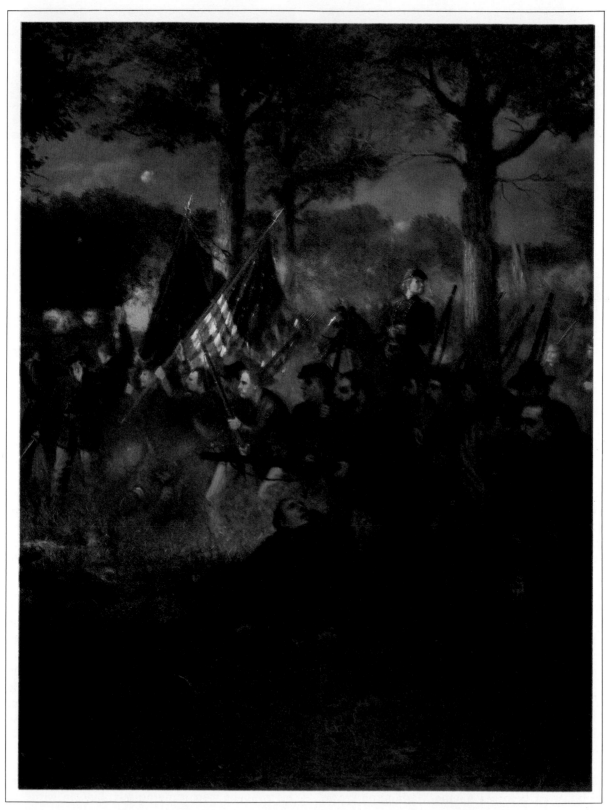

Skills Review: Reinforce the skills learned in the preceding Skills Strategy section. Acquire copies of news and editorial articles written about similar events taking place during the Civil War. Using the methods described in the preceding exercise, have students differentiate between the two.

Abraham Lincoln (left), the sixteenth president of the United States, led the Union through the Civil War. Jefferson Davis (right), former Secretary of War under Pierce, served as the first and only president of the Confederate States of America.

which the Union could be kept together. Senator John J. Crittenden of Kentucky proposed a series of constitutional amendments that would extend the Missouri Compromise line to the California border, thus dividing the remaining federal territories between free states and slave states. Slavery would be forbidden north of the line but guaranteed south of it.

The people of the border states strongly supported this formula. But President-elect Lincoln would not accept it. His Republican party was held together by one all-important principle: slavery must be kept out of all territories. If Lincoln compromised on this point, the Republicans would reject him.

Lincoln did, however, offer to sponsor a constitutional amendment protecting slavery for all time in the states where it already existed. But this did not interest Confederates who were caught up in the excitement of founding a country.

Fort Sumter. On March 4, 1861, Lincoln was inaugurated before a solemn Washington crowd.

By that date, the Stars and Stripes had been hauled down from every flagpole in the Confederate States except a fort in Pensacola, Florida, and at Fort Sumter in the harbor of Charleston, South Carolina. Lincoln decided not to make an issue of the fort at Pensacola. But he was determined not to give up Fort Sumter without a fight.

If Lincoln allowed Sumter to be turned over to the Confederates, the only way he could save the Union would be to invade the southern states. This would cause the border states to join the Confederacy and bring on a strong protest in the North. But if Lincoln held fast to Fort Sumter, the Confederates might be induced to rejoin the Union without fighting. Or, they might fire on the fort. This would allow Lincoln to accuse the seceded states of rejecting his peaceful overtures and of starting the fighting. Therefore, Lincoln would be justified in calling for troops to put down the rebellion.

Something had to be done quickly, for Major Anderson, in charge of Fort Sumter, reported that his supplies were running out. Lincoln wrote to

Class Activity: Construct a time line of the events leading to the Civil War by compiling the events in the time lines at the end of the last four chapters. Examine the relationship between events that occurred in close proximity in the various chapters, and discuss their possible relation. Discuss

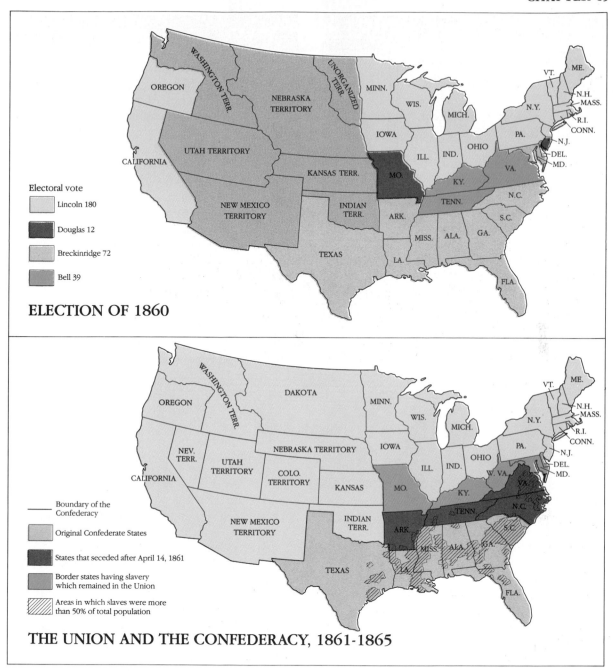

Electoral vote

- Lincoln 180
- Douglas 12
- Breckinridge 72
- Bell 39

ELECTION OF 1860

- Boundary of the Confederacy
- Original Confederate States
- States that seceded after April 14, 1861
- Border states having slavery which remained in the Union
- Areas in which slaves were more than 50% of total population

THE UNION AND THE CONFEDERACY, 1861-1865

the South Carolina governor, F. W. Pickens, that he was sending a supply ship to the fort, but was sending no troops. (Lincoln did not write to Jefferson Davis because he did not recognize the Confederate government.) Pickens sent the note on to Davis, who ordered that any attempt to resupply the fort should be turned back. There-fore, on April 12, 1861, when the supply ship tried to enter the harbor, the South Carolina batteries that ringed the harbor opened fire on the fort.

Sumter was bombarded for 40 hours. Finally, with no more ammunition and the fort almost demolished, Anderson surrendered on April 13.

the question: At what point did the Civil War become inevitable? Was it in 1850, 1858, 1860 and Lincoln's election, or was it never inevitable? If never inevitable, what could have been done to prevent or postpone it?

W hile still a lawyer in Springfield, Illinois, Abraham Lincoln wrote to a friend about his concerns on slavery:

In 1841, you and I had together a tedious low water trip on a steamboat from Louisville to St. Louis. You may remember, as I do . . . there were on board ten or a dozen slaves shackled with irons. The sight was a continual torment to me, and I see something like it every time I touch the Ohio or any other slave border. It is not fair for you to assume that I have no interest in a thing which has, and continually exercises, the power of making me miserable . . . As a nation we began by declaring that "all men are created equal." We now practically read it "all men are created equal, except negroes." When the Know-nothings get control, it will read "all men are created equal, except negroes and foreigners and Catholics." When it comes to this, I shall prefer emigrating to some country where they make no pretense of loving liberty . . .

—LETTER TO JOSHUA SPEED, AUGUST 24, 1855

The first shots of the Civil War were fired when Confederate troops bombarded Fort Sumter in the harbor of Charleston, South Carolina, on April 12-13, 1861. Almost exactly four years later, the war would finally end.

There is no doubt that the attack on Fort Sumter was the beginning of the Civil War. However, these were not the first shots fired between the North and the South. Three months before, on January 9, the Union ship *Star of the West* was fired upon near Morris Island while en route to Fort Sumter. Although hit twice, she sustained no damage.

Two days later, Lincoln asked the governors of the northern states to provide 75,000 soldiers to combat the Confederates. The war had begun.

The Border States Choose Sides.

Lincoln's call for troops forced the border states to choose sides. Reluctantly, Arkansas, Tennessee, and Virginia chose the Confederacy. So did North Carolina, but only because the state was now surrounded by the Confederacy. Many North Carolinians, especially in the mountainous western part of the state, did not want to go to war to protect slavery.

Four slave states—Delaware, Maryland, Kentucky, and Missouri—remained within the Union. Delaware was more Middle Atlantic than southern in culture as well as location. However, had an election been held in Maryland, that state might well have seceded. But Maryland surrounded Washington, D.C., and Lincoln had no intention of being cut off from the Union. Strategically placed troops kept Maryland in the Union.

Kentucky and Missouri were probably divided evenly on the secession question. Swift movement by Union troops in Missouri prevented secession there, and Kentucky was kept in by a combination of force and persuasion. Lincoln assured state leaders in Kentucky that he would not declare war on slavery, but only on disunion. Kentucky was vital to Lincoln's plans because it controlled the south bank of the Ohio River. The President believed that if Kentucky seceded, the war could not be won.

A New State.

The 50 western counties of Virginia also refused to leave the Union. Western Virginians owned few slaves and resented the Tidewater planters' control of Virginia's government. To spite the planters, they rejected secession and in 1861 set up their own state government. In 1863, West Virginia became a state in its own right.

The Odds Against the South.

When the material advantages of North and South in 1861 are compared, it appears that the Confederates had no chance of success. The population of the Confederacy was 9 million, compared with a Union population of 22 million. Even that did not tell the full story, because 3 million Southerners were blacks, most of whom were slaves. In a war to

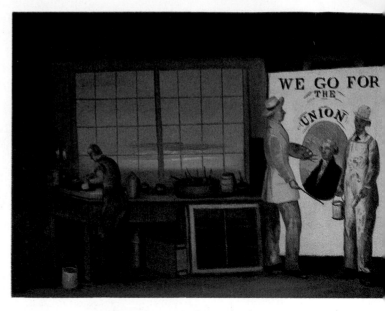

During the Civil War, citizens had to make the choice of allegiance to the Union or to the Confederacy. Such decisions split individual families as well as whole states.

preserve slavery, they could hardly be used in the army. In fact, white overseers had to remain behind to watch the slave population.

There were 30,000 miles of railroad in the North, and only 10,000 in the South. What was worse, the southern railroad system was not a "system" at all. For example, six railways ran into Richmond, the Confederate capital, but none linked up with any other. Different lines had different equipment. And the lines were not ready for the heavy traffic that a war required. In contrast, the North's rail lines were more uniform and newer. Also, Lincoln appointed Thomas Scott, president of the Pennsylvania Railroad, to bring more organization to the northern railroad system.

In industrial capacity, the Union's advantage was overwhelming. There were 120,000 *factories* in the North, compared to only 110,000 industrial *workers* in the South! Ninety percent of American manufactured goods were produced in the northern states. This meant that the Union could make more war products and replace lost materiel faster than the Confederacy could.

Finally, the 40-ship United States Navy remained loyal to the Union. The South depended on cotton trading for its economic health, and its

The Mason and Dixon line did not originate with the Civil War but with a property dispute between the Calvert family (residents of Maryland) and the Penn family (residents of Pennsylvania). The boundary between the states was laid out by Charles Mason and Jeremiah Dixon in 1767.

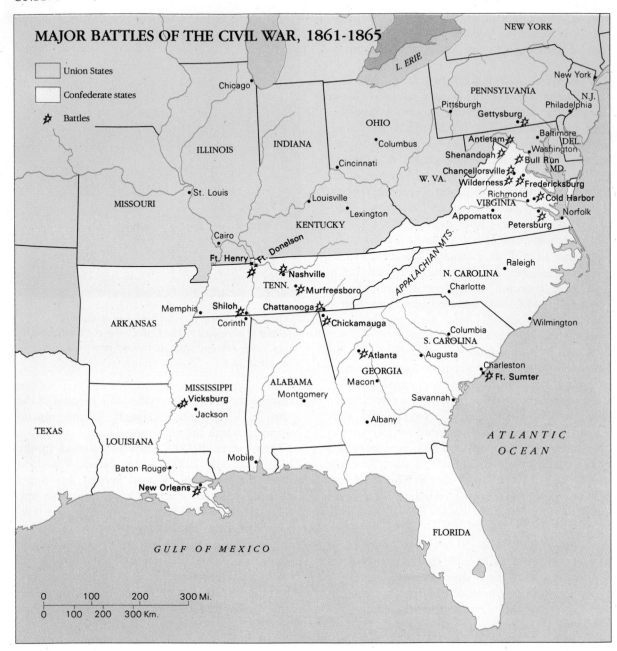

MAJOR BATTLES OF THE CIVIL WAR, 1861-1865

Union States

Confederate states

✬ Battles

nearly complete lack of sea power to protect the trade was a serious handicap.

Why Southerners Thought They Could Win.

With all these disadvantages, why did southerners believe they could win the war? First, the southern goal was not to conquer the North but simply to establish and defend Confederate independence. Fewer numbers and resources were needed to

defend than to attack. The rebels knew the terrain better than the northern enemy did. Although their rail lines were older, all lines of supply and communication were internal. Also, the Union would have to conquer an area almost equal in size to Alaska and Texas combined.

Second, the Confederates thought of the war as being much like the Revolution. They were fighting for independence, and they thought the British

Class Activity: With class participation, develop a chart showing the weaknesses and strengths of the North and the South. Include the following factors: leadership, arms, and preparation. Why was the war a draw for two years?

MAJOR BATTLES OF THE CIVIL WAR • 1861–1865

YEAR		BATTLE	RESULT
1861	April	Ft. Sumter	Union forces surrender fort at Charleston, S.C.
	July	Bull Run	Union army routed by Confederates; Union commander McDowell replaced by McClellan.
1862	April	Shiloh	Union advance into Tennessee halted.
	May	New Orleans	Southern port captured by Union fleet led by Farragut.
	September	Antietam	First major defeat of Lee's Army of Northern Virginia. Union army fails to follow up victory; McClellan replaced by Burnside.
	December	Fredericksburg	Lee defeats Burnside and Union advance toward Richmond is halted. Hooker replaces Burnside.
1863	May	Chancellorsville	Lee defeats Hooker who is replaced by Meade. Following this victory, Lee begins invasion of the North.
	July	Vicksburg	Grant captures Vicksburg and Union controls Mississippi River.
	July	Gettysburg	Lee's northern invasion halted and he retreats into Virginia.
	November	Chattanooga	Grant relieves besieged city and Union army controls Tennessee. Confederacy in half. Grant given command of all Union armies.
1864	May	The Wilderness	First direct military confrontation between Grant and Lee. Both sides suffer heavy casualties.
	June	Cold Harbor	Lee and Grant fight another stalemate but Lee's army is unable to sustain losses. Lee begins a gradual retreat to the defenses of Richmond.
	July	Shenandoah	Union captures important grain-producing region.
	September	Atlanta	Sherman burns city and begins march to the coast.
1865	April	Appomattox	Lee surrenders to Grant.

would sympathize with them and give them support. The southern cotton plantations were the major suppliers of the British textile mills, and the southerners thought the British would not endanger that supply.

Third, many southerners believed that they were better soldiers than the northerners. Although the war bore out no difference in bravery and ability between northern and southern troops, there was no doubt that Confederate commanders, at least in the early part of the war, were superior. A military career was more highly respected in the South than in the North. Both sides agreed that Robert E. Lee of Virginia was America's outstanding soldier. President Lincoln offered him command of the Union Army before Lee sadly announced that his first duty was to Virginia, and therefore the Confederacy.

Although willing to stand by Virginia when she went the way of secession, Robert E. Lee didn't believe that secession was right, either legally or given the circumstances of the time.

Robert E. Lee (above) was the most famous Confederate general. This photograph was taken by Mathew Brady shortly after the Civil War.

SECTION REVIEW

1. Write a sentence to identify Jefferson Davis; April 12, 1861; Robert E. Lee.

2. Name the following: the slave states that formed the Confederacy, the slave states that stayed in the Union, the new state admitted to the Union in 1863.

3. Describe the circumstances leading to the Confederate attack on Fort Sumter, and give the consequences of the attack.

4. List four Union advantages in 1861. Give three reasons for the Confederacy's belief that it could win the war.

2. THE CAMPAIGN OF 1861

The attack on Fort Sumter made it clear that there would be a shooting war. In both North and South, young men rushed to serve in what they considered righteous causes. By the summer of 1861, only weeks after the first shot, the Union had 186,000 soldiers in uniform, the Confederacy 112,000.

The American Civil War was very different from any war the world had known. It was the first modern war. Huge armed forces slugged at one another head-on while generals thought in terms of destroying the economy and society of their opponents.

The Armies: Cavalry and Artillery. The armies of the Civil War were divided into cavalry, artillery, and infantry, with support units such as the Corps of Engineers, to construct fortifications, and the Quartermaster Corps, to supply food and materiel to the combat troops.

The cavalry was a thrilling sight, with its charging horses and flashing sabers. In pitched battle, however, its chief function was *reconnaissance*. Because mounted soldiers could move quickly, the cavalry often rode deep into enemy territory, collecting information about the enemy's size and movements. Because the cavalry was lightly armed, however, horse soldiers could not afford to be trapped in serious battles. Cavalry was useful mostly for reinforcing weak points in the lines, and if enemy troops retreated, for harassing them.

The artillery, on the other hand, was slow to move. But big guns were critical to both attack and defense. An artillery bombardment could "soften up" the enemy's fortifications before the infantry attacked. Conversely, a defender's artillery could destroy an attacker's charge before it got within shooting distance of the defender's lines. Examinations of dead soldiers after Civil War battles showed that many more died from artillery fire than from muskets and rifles.

The Infantry. At that time, and until smokeless gunpowder was invented, a battlefield was soon covered with a thick black smoke. Infantry could not see the enemy to aim at them. Moreover, most fighting took place in hilly or densely forested areas, even in swamps. Opposing foot

The Civil War saw the rapid development of a series of new weapons and innovations in warfare. Have students give a visual presentation depicting the innovations of some of the weapons used in the war.

368

soldiers rarely saw one another until they were close enough for hand-to-hand combat.

Consequently, skill with a bayonet was more important than sharpshooting. But soldiers on both sides disliked bayonet-fighting, so they were more likely to swing their muskets like clubs.

The *foot soldier* was the core of the army. Divided into *brigades* of between 2,000 and 3,000 troops, they were the ones who confronted the enemy, actually won or lost a battle, and suffered the most casualties.

Billy Yank and Johnny Reb. Most Civil War soldiers were between the ages of 17 and 25. Drummer boys, whose rhythmic drumming kept units together, were as young as 12. In both armies soldiers represented every state.

All social classes were represented. However, the Confederate draft law of April 1862 and the Union draft law of March 1863 allowed wealthy men to avoid military service. In the South, owners of more than 20 slaves could stay out of the army. "Johnny Reb," the typical Confederate soldier, resented the fact that the slaveowners

Private Edwin Jennison (above), a young Confederate soldier from Georgia, was killed in battle at Malvern Hill in Virginia during the Seven Days Battle. Belle Boyd (below), at 18 years of age, served as a spy for Stonewall Jackson.

The photograph below is of an unidentified soldier in the Union Army.

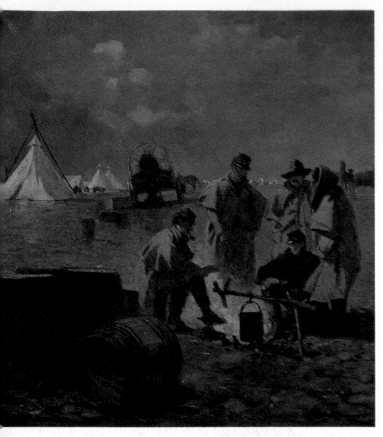

Soldiers on both sides faced difficult field conditions. The detail above is from the painting "A Rainy Day in Camp." It was painted by the American artist Winslow Homer (1836–1910).

were allowed to sit out a war fought largely to protect slavery.

In both North and South, a draftee could pay a substitute to take his place. A rich man in the North could even pay the government $300 directly in order to escape the draft. But the average Union soldier, *"Billy Yank,"* could not afford this. Thus, this ruling also caused resentment. In July 1863, working class rioters in New York virtually captured the city for several days, protesting that the war made the wealthy richer while the draft law made it both a poor man's fight and his graveyard.

Army Life. Drawings in newspapers showed men in blue and gray moving in an orderly way across fields amidst waving flags and puffs of little smoke-like clouds.

The reality was very different. Battle was a horrifying experience and a small part of army life. Mostly the war involved waiting, digging trenches, building fortifications, marching, and being carted about in overcrowded railway cars designed for freight or cattle.

The war meant poor food, poor clothing, and poor shelter. Southern soldiers suffered most. Even when the Confederacy had enough food, equipment, and ammunition—which was seldom —poor administration and an old distribution system meant that soldiers did not get them. Confederate generals told of sending men charging in bare feet over rough ground through thorny underbrush while, ten miles away, there were boxcars filled with shoes.

Union soldiers were usually better supplied. However, many businesspeople who supplied the northern army were corrupt. Some sold tainted, poisonous beef to the government, and others provided blankets that fell apart when it rained. On both sides, well-meaning physicians were unable to cope with the epidemic diseases of dysentery, typhoid fever, and influenza. More soldiers died of contagious diseases than in battle.

The First Battle. In the spring of 1861, Billy Yank and Johnny Reb looked forward to the first battle as if it were a sporting event. Both sides expected a one-battle war. The Confederates spoke of their "Battle Summer," in which they would defeat the Yankees easily, march into Washington, and sign a treaty guaranteeing southern independence. The northern troops expected to march into Richmond, Virginia—the Confederate capital—and be home for the harvest.

Some high officials knew better. Aged General Winfield Scott, Lincoln's Chief of Staff, warned the President that it would be a long and difficult war. Scott wanted to train the troops to perfection first, then fight the battles. He proposed what came to be called the *Anaconda Plan.* The Union navy would blockade the southern coast, and Union armies would encircle, divide, and crush the Confederacy. But most people thought the war would last a season, and Lincoln at first agreed. The first volunteers were called for only three months.

In July 1861, the Union army under General Irwin McDowell left its camp and moved south toward Richmond. Congressmen, their wives, and

Research Assignment: The war was portrayed as glamourous in ads and posters. It was, of course, neither. Have students compile a number of pictures of ads used for enlistment. Students should be able to explain how the ads were persuasive in selling the war to young men.

MOVERS AND SHAPERS

Mathew Brady

Mathew B. Brady (1823?–1896) was a success by the time he was 20. In the 1840s, New Yorkers knew that the best place to go for a daguerreotype portrait was Brady's studio on Broadway.

Daguerreotypes were the forerunners of photographs, but the early process for taking someone's picture was cumbersome and difficult, and required a long posing period, and a longer time to develop the picture. Brady was the first American to truly master it.

Most of the great men and women of the day had their portraits taken by Brady. In 1850, Brady published his best portraits in a book, *Gallery of Illustrious Americans*, which spread his reputation farther.

Brady once said that "the camera is the eye of history," and when the Civil War broke out, he was determined to make a photographic record of it. At his own expense, he organized teams of photographers, each equipped with a special mobile darkroom. With the permission of President Lincoln, Brady accompanied Union armies from battlefield to battlefield. Lugging his heavy camera and tripod, and glass plates, Brady photographed soldiers in camp, soldiers at their guns, and wounded and dead soldiers. Brady and his assistants produced about 3,500 war photographs, which are now prized historical treasures.

Clara Barton

Clara Barton (1821–1912) grew up on a farm in Oxford, Massachusetts. At the age of 15, she accepted a teaching job in a Massachusetts school. In 1852, she started New Jersey's first tax-supported public school in Bordentown.

Barton left teaching and spent the years 1857–1861 in Washington, D.C. When the Civil War erupted, Barton found a new outlet for her energies. She recognized the needs of the wounded for the basic comforts—blankets, food, fresh bandages, and clothing. She gathered these articles and distributed them to grateful soldiers.

Because she wanted to help these men wherever they fought and were wounded, Barton coaxed an army major into writing out a pass that let her go out onto the battlefields. Barton became a familiar figure, dispensing aid on the battlefields. After one bad battle, she arrived with bandages just as the army physicians were running out of supplies. She was often the only comfort the wounded and dying soldiers had, and so they called her the "Angel of the Battlefield."

In 1869, while Barton was traveling in Europe, she heard about a humanitarian organization called the Red Cross. Its purpose was to furnish wounded soldiers with first aid and emergency services. She became interested in establishing such an organization in the United States. It took her 12 years, but finally, in 1882, President Chester Arthur signed the document that gave official sanction to the American Red Cross. For the next 22 years, Clara Barton served as its president.

Research Assignment: Mathew Brady's pictures are a stark and often brutal reminder of the war. Using secondary sources that contain Brady's pictures, have students chronicle the war in a picture essay.

More than a third of the American men who fought in the Civil War were killed, wounded, or imprisoned. The photograph above is of a ward in the Armory Square Hospital, a Union hospital in Washington, D.C.

Confederate General Thomas Jackson, shown above wearing a plumed hat, gained the nickname "Stonewall" after his troops successfully withstood a Union attack at the First Battle of Bull Run.

journalists tagged along carrying picnic lunches. Their dinners, they expected, would be served in Richmond's best restaurants. The pleasant day ended when the Union troops met the Confederates, led by General P. G. T. Beauregard, who had commanded the forces that had taken Fort Sumter. In the South, this meeting was called the *Battle of Manassas Junction.* In the North it was called the *Battle of Bull Run.*

The armies were evenly matched. Soldiers on either side had good morale, but almost none of them had ever been tested in battle. For several hours, the Union soldiers seemed on the verge of breaking through the Confederate lines. But Confederate troops under *"Stonewall" Jackson* held their position during a furious Union charge, and the Confederate lines stabilized. Then, late in the afternoon, fresh Confederate troops arrived by train from the Shenandoah Valley and drove the tiring Yankees back.

The battle ended in a Union rout. Instead of retreating to Washington in an orderly fashion, the Union soldiers threw down their guns and ran in a panic. For several days, Washington was left almost undefended. However, the Confederate armies were nearly as disorganized as the Union's and were not up to an attack on a fortified city.

The Battle of Bull Run is the same as the Battle of Manassas. The Confederacy named all battles by using the name of the town nearest the battlefield. The Union army, however, named battles after the closest waterway to the battle.

The Lesson of Bull Run. Bull Run taught both sides that the war would not be over quickly. The key to victory was to train troops thoroughly. Consequently, the rest of 1861 became a time of recruitment, drilling, and more drilling for both sides. Jefferson Davis placed General Joseph E. Johnston in charge of the Confederate armies during this period. Lincoln replaced McDowell with General George B. McClellan, who was best known for his ability to organize an army.

Union Strategy. The summer and fall of 1861 were also times of planning. Lincoln and Winfield Scott decided that northern strategy would consist of a war on three fronts. First, the *Army of the Potomac,* the principal northern force in the East, would maintain constant pressure on Richmond, Virginia. With Washington and Richmond so close to each other, defense of one meant pressuring the other. Moreover, as Scott pointed out, the most numerous and best-trained Confederate troops were in the *Army of Northern Virginia.* Scott, a Virginian himself, understood that southern commanders Johnston, Lee, and Jackson thought of the war more as a defense of their state than as a war for the Confederacy. If pressed in Virginia, they would not bring their skills to bear elsewhere.

This was important to Union strategy, because its second front was to be in the West. Lincoln readily agreed to a major Union push down the Mississippi River. The object was to reopen the river to trade by the states of the Old Northwest and to split the Confederacy. A loyal Texas force commanded by Sam Houston could fight the Texas Confederates to a draw if Texas were cut off from the rest of the South.

The third part of the Union strategy was a naval blockade. The Confederacy imported most of its manufactured goods, including arms, and paid for them by selling cotton abroad. If the Confederate economy could be choked off, its armies simply would not be able to fight.

Confederate Strategy. British or French aid was central to southern strategy. Davis and his advisors hoped to win a major battle against the Union so that one of these great powers would form an alliance with the Confederacy.

The hope for a French alliance died first. After leading the Confederates on, the French Emperor Napoleon III was distracted by a revolution in Mexico. In return for a promise of French troops, Mexico's threatened elite invited a nephew of Napoleon III, Maximilian, to become Emperor of Mexico. With Americans fighting themselves, Napoleon could ignore the Monroe Doctrine. He decided to establish a French presence in Mexico and forget his plan to dabble in Confederate affairs.

The British government, and particularly textile mill owners and wealthy landowners, felt friendly toward the Confederacy. But antislavery feeling was strong among British working people. The Confederates knew they needed a big victory if they were to gain British support.

SECTION REVIEW

1. Write a sentence to identify draft laws, Anaconda Plan, Army of the Potomac, Army of Northern Virginia.

2. List the three main fighting groups into which Civil War armies were divided. Describe one such unit in detail.

3. When, where, and with what result was the first battle of the Civil War fought? Explain what the Union and the Confederacy learned from this battle.

4. Describe the war strategy of the Union and the war strategy of the Confederacy.

---

3. STALEMATE AND BREAK-THROUGH

After initial victories in the West, the Union advance stalled. In the East, with Stonewall Jackson as his "strong right arm," General Robert E. Lee repeatedly defeated the larger Army of the Potomac. But when Lee attempted to invade the North in search of a decisive victory, he was stopped cold at the Battle of Antietam.

Through the first half of 1863, the Confederacy effectively frustrated every Union attempt at a breakthrough. Then, on July 4, 1863, Lee gave up a second attempt to invade the North, and the last rebel stronghold on the Mississippi surrendered.

The British had another reason for adhering to the blockade. The British doctrine holding that goods from a belligerent country going to a neutral port were contraband upheld their doctrine of the seas—one they had been trying to enforce since the Napoleonic Wars.

The War in the West. Ulysses S. Grant had resigned his army commission in 1854 and then failed at both farming and business. However, the Union forces were happy to have him back, because trained officers were lacking in the Union army. Many of the prewar officers were southerners who heeded the call of the Confederacy.

Grant proved his worth in February 1862, when he played a major role in capturing Fort Donelson and Fort Henry, two important Confederate strongholds in northern Tennessee. The capture of these forts opened up the Ohio and Tennessee rivers, which led right to the heart of the Confederacy.

But on April 6, 1862, Confederates under General Albert Sidney Johnston surprised Grant's army at the *Battle of Shiloh.* Unlike Bull Run, where casualties were light, Shiloh was slaughter.

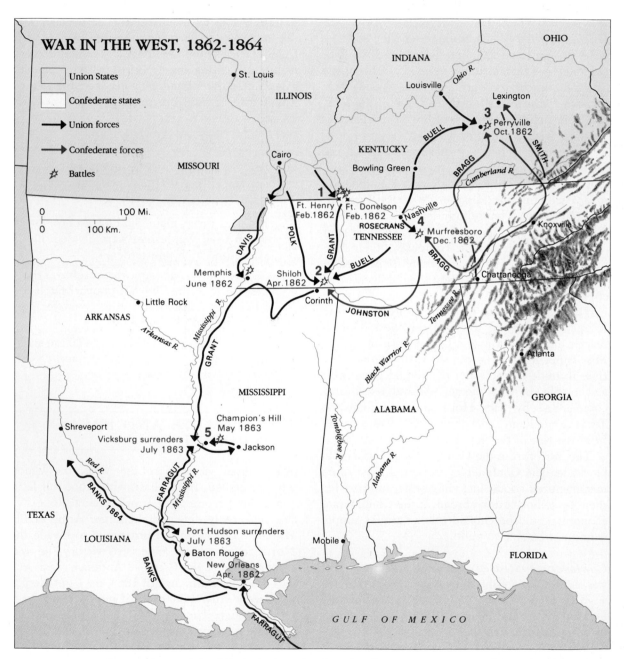

WAR IN THE WEST, 1862-1864

Union States
Confederate states
Union forces
Confederate forces
Battles

The area beyond the Mississippi can be thought of as a separate zone of the war. Although no decisive battles were fought there, there were skirmishes in Missouri, Arkansas, Texas, New Mexico, Louisiana, and the Indian Territory. *Campaign* comes from the Latin word *campania*, meaning "countryside," which is where most battles took place.

General Ulysses S. Grant provided the Union with an experienced and capable officer.

Because of a miscalculation by Grant, many Union troops were shot while still asleep. Among the Confederate dead was General Johnston. It was a major loss to the South, and helped turn the tide of the battle. The Confederates were finally driven off the next day by the arrival of another Union army under General Don Carlos Buell. More than 23,000 Americans died in the battle.

The War at Sea. The major southern effort at sea involved Confederate *commerce raiders,* big, fast, powerfully armed sailing ships that roamed the oceans blasting or capturing northern merchant vessels. During the war, they captured or destroyed more than 250 ships carrying cargos worth more than $15 million. Because the raiders cruised all oceans, northern ships were never secure.

The main northern strategy was the blockade of southern ports. Year by year, the blockade grew more successful as the Union navy grew, so that by 1865 only one Confederate *blockade runner* in five was getting through.

Nevertheless, on March 8, 1862, the rebels almost broke the blockade at Chesapeake Bay. Out of Norfolk steamed a reconditioned wooden warship, the *Merrimack,* now covered with iron

The first battle between ironclad ships occurred on March 9, 1862, at the mouth of Chesapeake Bay. The Union Monitor *(foreground) and the Confederate* Merrimack *fought to a draw. The battle marked the end of the era of wooden naval ships.*

plates, fitted with a ram at the bow, and renamed the *Virginia*. While cannonballs bounced off the *Merrimack*'s armor, the ship disabled several valuable Union ships.

However, the *Merrimack* was not to have all things her way. The next day, the Union rushed in its own ironclad, the *Monitor,* which looked like a cake tin on a raft. The two vessels fought to a draw, but a draw was in effect a Union victory, for the blockade was saved. The *Merrimack* never put to sea again. The Confederates destroyed it a few months later when Norfolk fell to the Union army. The Confederates never built another effective ironclad, but the *Monitor* served as the prototype for a whole fleet of Union ironclad gunboats.

The Peninsular Campaign.

General McClellan performed a great service to the Union by insisting on rigorous military training. That training turned the frightened mob of Bull Run into a true army. But, as President Lincoln learned, McClellan was too cautious. He fended off Lincoln's orders to attack by saying that more training was necessary, or that he needed more soldiers. In the summer of 1862, McClellan's slowness and Lincoln's own error in judgment cost the North a chance to end the war.

The capture of Richmond was essential to a Union victory. Rejecting the Bull Run route, McClellan sailed his army around to Jamestown, on the peninsula between the James and York rivers in Virginia. He planned to attack Richmond from the south, where the Confederates had built fewer fortifications.

McClellan caught the Confederate commander, Joseph E. Johnston, completely by surprise. But McClellan did not believe that his 110,000 soldiers were enough for the job, although the Confederates were greatly outnumbered. After landing he sat, asked Lincoln for more men, and allowed the Confederates to take control.

First, Lincoln would not send McClellan more troops because of diversionary tactics in the Shenandoah Valley by Stonewall Jackson. Lincoln thought Jackson might attack Washington. Then during the indecisive battle of Fair Oaks on May 31, Johnston was seriously wounded, and General Lee took command of the Army of Northern Virginia.

On June 25, McClellan's army was within sight of Richmond. On July 1, they were back where they had started their offensive, at Harrison's Landing on the James River. Lee had turned McClellan's offensive into a desperate defensive

President Abraham Lincoln (center, with top hat) visited Maryland's Antietam Creek after the bloody battle that had taken place there on September 17, 1862. At the Battle of Antietam, over 13,000 northern soldiers and 11,000 southern soldiers died.

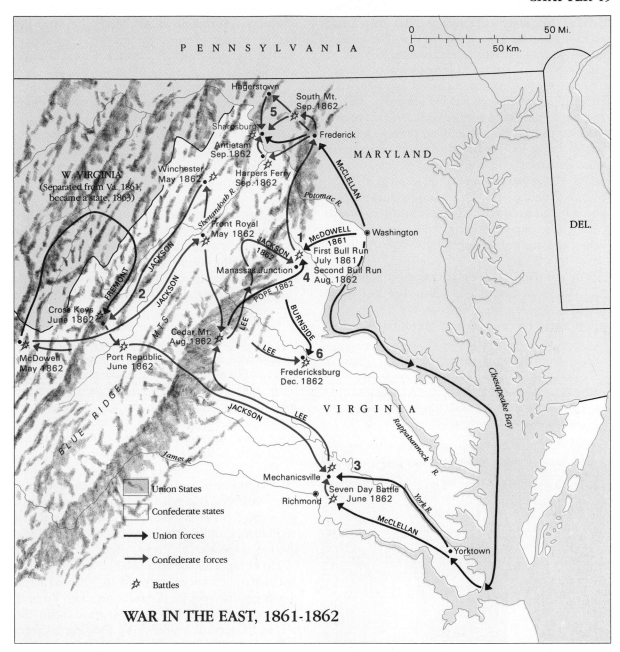

WAR IN THE EAST, 1861-1862

Legend:

- Union States
- Confederate states
- → Union forces
- → Confederate forces
- ✦ Battles

Map labels:

PENNSYLVANIA

Hagerstown
South Mt. Sep. 1862
Sharpsburg
Frederick
MARYLAND
McCLELLAN
Antietam Sep. 1862
Winchester May 1862
Harpers Ferry Sep. 1862
W. VIRGINIA (Separated from Va. 1861, became a state, 1863)
Potomac R.
Shenandoah R.
JACKSON
Front Royal May 1862
JACKSON 1862
McDOWELL 1861
Washington
First Bull Run July 1861
FREMONT
Manassas Junction
Second Bull Run Aug. 1862
Cross Keys June 1862
JACKSON
POPE 1862
DEL.
McDowell May 1862
Port Republic June 1862
Cedar Mt. Aug. 1862
LEE
BURNSIDE
LEE
Fredericksburg Dec. 1862
BLUE RIDGE MTS.
JACKSON
LEE
VIRGINIA
James R.
Rappahannock R.
Mechanicsville
Richmond
Seven Day Battle June 1862
Chesapeake Bay
York R.
McCLELLAN
Yorktown

struggle to stave off destruction. The *Seven Days Battle* showed how hard it would be to beat Lee. Although outnumbered, Lee and Jackson moved their troops so skillfully that they always had an advantage on any given battlefield.

Second Battle of Bull Run and Antietam.

After the Seven Days Battle, Lincoln replaced McClellan as head of the Army of the Potomac with General John Pope. McClellan was ordered to bring his troops north and link up with an army led by Pope that was marching south from Washington. But Lee had no intention of letting the two Union armies meet. Counting on McClellan's slowness to keep him out of the picture, Lee marched his soldiers north to take on Pope.

The meeting place was the old battlefield of Bull Run. In this *Second Battle of Bull Run*, Lee

Because of his position as Commander-in-Chief of the Union forces, Lincoln would come to know military strategy only too well. In 1832, he had gained his other military experience as a captain fighting Indians in the Black Hawk war. Forgetting the command for halt, he once marched his troops past a reviewing platform and into a creek.

 377

divided his army and sent 25,000 men under Jackson to attack Pope from the rear. The Confederates were successful again, although Pope was able to save his army and retreat in good order.

After these two great victories, Lee decided to strike into Union territory. He wanted to take the war out of the South so that farmers could harvest their crops, and he was looking for a victory that would bring in the British on the Confederate side. For several days, the Army of the Potomac, under McClellan's command once more, lost track of him. Then a lost copy of Lee's plans, wrapped around some cigars, fell into northern hands. McClellan found that Lee had divided his army again, and that he had only 40,000 men to McClellan's 70,000.

At Maryland's Antietam Creek on September 17, McClellan caught Lee before Lee had gotten all his troops together. The *Battle of Antietam* was brutal, and Lee was almost surrounded by late

Union General George McClellan was relieved of command by President Lincoln in 1862. In the presidential election of 1864, McClellan ran against Lincoln, but Lincoln was reelected with 212 electoral votes to McClellan's 21.

afternoon. At that point, Confederate troops that had been sent to capture Harpers Ferry arrived on the run and crashed into the Union flank to save Lee.

McClellan might have been able to attack the next day, but once again he was too cautious. While Lincoln fumed in Washington, Lee escaped across the Potomac River. McClellan's caution was probably justified, for Antietam was the bloodiest single day of the war. The North lost over 13,000 men; the South, over 11,000.

Fredericksburg and Chancellorsville.

Lincoln now appointed General Ambrose E. Burnside to head the armies. Burnside was reluctant to take the job, for he knew that the army was McClellan's creation, and the soldiers were loyal to their old commander. But he finally bowed to Lincoln's wishes.

Burnside's command was short and tragic. The two armies faced each other across the Rappahannock River. Lee's men were strongly dug in on Marye's Heights, south of the town of Fredericksburg. On December 13, Burnside ordered his men to cross the river, go through the town, and then climb the cliff-like hills to attack the Confederate lines. All the while, the Confederates were blasting them with musket and cannon fire.

Watching the slaughter of Union soldiers (over 10,000 wounded and killed), Lee remarked to an aide, "It is well that war is so terrible or we would grow too fond of it." Burnside was broken by the terrible loss, and was replaced by Joseph E. "Fighting Joe" Hooker.

However, Hooker also failed to defeat Lee. In May 1863, he took an army of 120,000 men across the Rappahannock to Chancellorsville, Virginia. Lee, outnumbered two to one, once again displayed his tactical brilliance by dividing his force and hitting Hooker from two directions. Once again, the Union forces had to retreat.

However, a major loss to the Confederacy occurred at Chancellorsville. Stonewall Jackson was accidentally shot by his own men and died of the wounds. The Army of Northern Virginia would never be the same. Just as serious, Lee lost more men than Hooker did. The Union could quickly replace its casualties, but the South was running out of manpower. Virtually every able and willing southerner was already in the army.

President Lincoln (seated, holding papers) is shown reading the Emancipation Proclamation to his cabinet. The proclamation paved the way for the abolition of slavery in the United States.

The Emancipation Proclamation.

By early 1863, there were more signs that the tide was turning. In September 1862, Lincoln had issued the *Emancipation Proclamation*. In it he declared that all slaves in territory controlled by the rebels as of January 1, 1863, would then be free. The Emancipation Proclamation did not actually free a single slave, because it applied only to those areas not under Federal control. It did not apply to Delaware, Maryland, Kentucky, Missouri, or those parts of the South, such as New Orleans, occupied by Union troops.

By announcing emancipation in September, Lincoln was telling Confederates that if they laid down their arms before January 1, 1863, they could keep their slaves. (None of the Confederate states did so.) The proclamation helped the Union war effort in other ways.

First, emancipation improved Union morale by giving the troops a positive goal. No longer engaged simply in a war of conquest, they were now fighting "to make men free," as Julia Ward Howe wrote in her great song "The Battle Hymn of the Republic."

Second, Lincoln's action gave blacks a reason to join the army, and free blacks rushed to sign up. Moreover, slaves near northern lines heard of the proclamation and deserted their plantations by the thousands. Eventually, 110,000 blacks—an eighth of the army—served in Union blue.

Third, Lincoln's great proclamation prepared the way for the abolition of slavery. Once the step was taken as a military policy, it was easier for northerners to accept slavery's demise.

Grant Takes Vicksburg.

In July 1863, the war ceased to be a stalemate. By the spring of 1863, Union troops controlled almost all of the Mississippi River except for a short stretch between Vicksburg and Port Hudson, the last two Confederate strongholds on the river. Grant had taken the Mississippi north of Vicksburg. Admiral David Farragut, after his river gunboats had taken New Orleans, had sailed up the Mississippi, but was stopped at Port Hudson.

But Vicksburg itself was a problem. From its high bluffs above the river, Confederates under Joseph Pemberton were able to prevent the North from using the river. Every Union attack from the north led to failure and dreadful casualties. Grant's solution to the problem showed he had a military imagination comparable to Lee's.

Class Activity: Have students read and analyze the Emancipation Proclamation.

Discussion Question: Did the Emancipation Proclamation have any effect on southern slavery? Answers should include the fact that the document had no immediate effect on the release of slaves because Lincoln had no jurisdiction over the slave states.

Grant went on the offensive in the spring of 1863. He moved against Vicksburg and put that city under siege (above). Vicksburg surrendered on July 4, 1863, and Grant became a hero.

Lee had successfully violated traditional rules of war by dividing his troops. Now Grant, defying the rule that said a general should never abandon supply lines, took his army across the Mississippi below Vicksburg. With no supply lines, he charged east to attack Jackson, Mississippi. On May 14, he defeated the Confederate garrison at Jackson, then quickly turned west towards Vicksburg. Pemberton, caught off guard, was defeated in several quick battles and retreated into the city. Grant surrounded Vicksburg and sat down to starve the city out.

The city's defense was heroic. People ate pets and rats rather than surrender to the hated Yankees. But the Confederates had no troops that could rush to Vicksburg and raise the siege. On July 4, Vicksburg surrendered. A few days later Port Hudson also gave up. The South had been split in two.

Lee's Second Invasion of the North.

Instead of sending troops to help Vicksburg, Lee invaded the North again after defeating Hooker at Chancellorsville in May. There was not much hope of a British alliance by then. But a major Confederate win on Union territory would serve several purposes. If Washington could be taken, antiwar feeling in the North would surely mount against Lincoln. Even if Washington did not fall, the President would be forced to bring Grant's troops east, thus relieving Vicksburg.

Lee headed north, aiming for the major Pennsylvania city of Harrisburg. Union General George Meade set off in pursuit. At the small town of Gettysburg in southern Pennsylvania, the two armies bumped into each other when a Union scouting party met Confederate troops who were trying to get shoes. Both armies quickly drew up, and occupied ridges about a mile away from each other. The Confederates held Seminary Ridge; the Union, Cemetery Ridge. On July 1, Lee attacked and pushed the Union lines back. But the Union lines held, and in possibly a better defensive position. On July 2, Lee attacked the left end of the Union position on two steep hills called Little Round Top and Big Round Top. But again the Confederates were beaten back.

On the night of July 2, Lee announced that the next day he would attack the Union center. General James Longstreet protested long and loud that

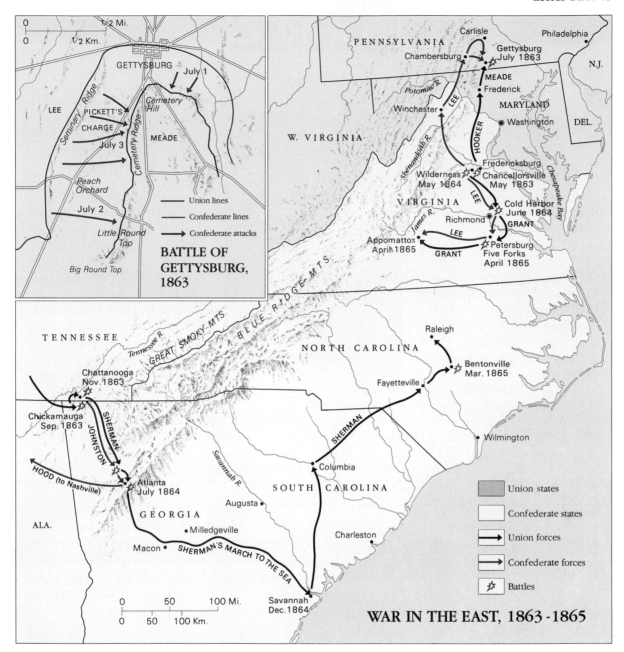

BATTLE OF GETTYSBURG, 1863

July 1

GETTYSBURG

Cemetery Hill

LEE

Seminary Ridge

PICKETT'S

CHARGE

July 3

MEADE

Cemetery Ridge

Peach Orchard

July 2

Little Round Top

Big Round Top

0   1/2 Mi.
0   1/2 Km.

— Union lines
— Confederate lines
→ Confederate attacks

WAR IN THE EAST, 1863-1865

PENNSYLVANIA
Carlisle
Philadelphia
Chambersburg
Gettysburg July 1863
MEADE
Frederick
N.J.
Potomac R.
LEE
Winchester
HOOKER
MARYLAND
Washington
DEL.
W. VIRGINIA
Shenandoah R.
Fredericksburg
Wilderness May 1864
Chancellorsville May 1863
Chesapeake Bay
VIRGINIA
LEE
Cold Harbor June 1864
James R.
Richmond
GRANT
Appomattox April 1865
LEE
Petersburg Five Forks April 1865
GRANT

TENNESSEE
Tennessee R.
GREAT SMOKY MTS.
BLUE RIDGE MTS
Raleigh
NORTH CAROLINA
Chattanooga Nov. 1863
Bentonville Mar. 1865
Chickamauga Sep. 1863
JOHNSTON
SHERMAN
Fayetteville
HOOD (to Nashville)
SHERMAN
Atlanta July 1864
Savannah R.
Columbia
Wilmington
SOUTH CAROLINA
Augusta
GEORGIA
Milledgeville
Charleston
ALA.
Macon
SHERMAN'S MARCH TO THE SEA
Savannah Dec. 1864

0   50   100 Mi.
0   50   100 Km.

Union states
Confederate states
→ Union forces
→ Confederate forces
✵ Battles

Meade would anticipate an attack on his center, and that the Union line would therefore be strongest there. Stonewall Jackson might have persuaded Lee to abandon his plan, but Longstreet could not. He was ordered to lead the attack on the center.

High Tide of the Confederacy.
Longstreet was right. Meade was ready for a frontal assault. Between one and two o'clock on the afternoon of

July 3, 15,000 Confederate troops gave the chilling "rebel yell" and moved at a trot across a mile of open country. This came to be called *Pickett's Charge*, after General George Pickett, one of the generals who commanded a part of the attacking force. Although the most massive Confederate bombardment of the war had been directed at the Federal lines just before the charge, the Union army responded with a withering fire. Only about

Discussion Question: Why do you think that the Civil War is referred to as the first modern war? How was it different from preceding wars fought in the U.S.? Some factors that should be included are weaponry, size of armies, and strategies.

381

GOING TO THE SOURCE

Four score and seven years ago our fathers brought forth on this continent, a new nation, conceived in Liberty, and dedicated to the proposition that all men are created equal.

Now we are engaged in a great civil war, testing whether that nation, or any nation so conceived and so dedicated, can long endure. We are met on a great battlefield of that war. We have come to dedicate a portion of that field, as a final resting place for those who here gave their lives that that nation might live. It is altogether fitting and proper that we should do this.

But, in a larger sense, we cannot dedicate—we cannot consecrate—we cannot hallow—this ground. The brave men, living and dead, who struggled here, have consecrated it, far above our poor power to add or detract. The world will little note, nor long remember what we say here, but it can never forget what they

We here highly resolve that these dead shall not have died in vain — that this nation, under God, shall have a new birth of freedom — and that government of the people, by the people, for the people, shall not perish from the earth.

ABRAHAM LINCOLN, *THE GETTYSBURG ADDRESS*

did here. It is for us the living, rather, to be dedicated here to the unfinished work which they who fought here have thus far so nobly advanced. It is rather for us to be here dedicated to the great task remaining before us—that from these honored dead we take increased devotion to that cause for which they gave the last full measure of devotion—that we here highly resolve that these dead shall not have died in vain—that this nation, under God, shall have a new birth of freedom—and that government of the people, by the people, for the people, shall not perish from the earth.

In November 1863, President Lincoln helped dedicate a cemetery at the Gettysburg Battlefield. Lincoln's talk took only about two minutes. But the Gettysburg Address still moves Americans with its eloquence.

---

100 Confederates reached the Federal lines. Thousands of Confederate soldiers were slaughtered.

Gettysburg was the high-water mark of the Confederacy. In the three-day battle, 25,000 Confederates were killed, wounded, captured, or reported missing. Many officers were killed, too, and the Army of Northern Virginia, the most important Confederate army, would never again be as well led as before Gettysburg.

On July 4, Lee waited for a Union counterattack that could have destroyed his army. As at Antietam, it never came. Meade would not send his tired men across open country. Therefore, the Union forces again missed a grand opportunity, as Lee once more took his shattered army back to Virginia.

SECTION REVIEW

1. Write a sentence to identify: Stonewall Jackson, *Merrimack* and *Monitor*, Admiral Farragut, Pickett's Charge.

2. List five land battles fought in 1862 and 1863, and give the outcome of each of the battles.

3. Contrast the abilities of Lee and McClellan as commanders.

4. What message was President Lincoln sending to the Confederacy in the Emancipation Proclamation? In what three ways did the proclamation help the Union war effort?

Discussion Question: Have students read the text of the Gettysburg Address on this page. What is the purpose of the Gettysburg Address? What is the message President Lincoln was trying to convey?

The Battle of Gettysburg (above), in Pennsylvania, raged for the first three days of July 1863. On the fourth of July, with 25,000 fewer soldiers than he had taken to Gettysburg, Lee began moving his army away from Gettysburg and back to Virginia.

4. GRANT'S WAR OF ATTRITION

Lincoln was unable to make Meade go after Lee. But General Grant's success in the West convinced the President that Grant was the commander who would be able to destroy Lee's army.

The Tennessee Campaign. Grant distinguished himself again after Vicksburg by saving the Union's conquest of Tennessee. In September 1863, Union forces under General William S. Rosecrans pushed the Confederate army under Braxton Bragg out of Tennessee and into northern Georgia. The Union troops then occupied the important railroad city of Chattanooga, Tennessee.

But Rosecrans was also a slow mover who was faced by a commander who could strike quickly. Bragg surprised him by launching a counterattack at Chickamauga Creek. In one of the few battles in which Confederates outnumbered Union soldiers, the Rebels smashed the right side of the Union line. They would have completely routed the enemy had it not been for a Union general from Virginia, General George H. Thomas, who stood firm against the assault. Thomas's stand, which earned him the name "The Rock of Chickamauga," allowed the Union army to retreat into Chattanooga.

Union General William Tecumseh Sherman (below) replaced Grant in the West after Lincoln gave Grant command of the Union forces in 1864.

The field at Gettysburg was littered with 37,000 rifles and muskets. Of these, 24,000 were still loaded and unfired. About one-fourth of these held three to ten charges—soldiers were so excited that they continued to reload their guns without firing them.

The Confederates surrounded the city, but could not capture it. Grant himself marched to Chattanooga with his army, and 25,000 more Union troops arrived from the East by train. Late in November 1863, Grant drove Bragg's forces from their strongholds near Chattanooga back into Georgia.

That was enough for Lincoln. Early in 1864, he called Grant to Washington, promoted him to Lieutenant General, and gave him command of all Union forces. To take his place in the West, Grant nominated William Tecumseh Sherman, a man much like himself. Sherman agreed with his superior officer that war was not a gentle game, but a deadly, serious conflict in which the object was to grind down the enemy.

Grant Before Richmond.

Grant was one of the first modern generals. He believed in a war of *attrition.* With the advantage of much larger numbers than his adversary, Grant rejected the battles of maneuver his predecessors had fought against Lee. In such battles Lee, a master of tactics, had neutralized the Union's superior numbers.

Grant told Lincoln that he would march on Richmond, take his losses, and continue to press the enemy. The *casualty* list would be long, but it would be long on the Confederate side, too. Grant could replace his men, and Lee could not. This was attrition, whittling away at the enemy.

In May 1864, Grant moved 100,000 men into the wilderness, near where Hooker had been defeated. Lee fought him off. Grant then swung east and south. Lee hurried to head him off and the armies clashed at *Spotsylvania Courthouse.* Somehow Lee managed to throw Grant back, again at great loss to both sides. But Grant kept coming, still moving toward Richmond. The armies met again at *Cold Harbor,* and Grant's troops sustained horrible casualties when they made a poorly coordinated attack on solid Confederate positions. And still Grant kept advancing.

Grant's casualties were such that congressmen and newspaper editors called him "the butcher." But Grant knew he was wearing Lee down. He wrote to Lincoln, "I intend to fight it out on this line if it takes all summer." After Cold Harbor, he moved south of Richmond and began the *siege* of Richmond and Petersburg, an important rail center south of the Confederate capital.

Much of the South was destroyed during the war. This photograph shows the ruins of Richmond.

Early's Raid and the Loss of the Shenandoah.

The lull gave Lee a chance to demonstrate his daring once more. In July he sent Jubal Early on a cavalry raid toward Washington. Earlier in the war, the raid would have caused a panic. This time, although Early's troops came within sight of the Capitol building, Grant and Lincoln remained cool. Grant stayed where he was and sent Union cavalry under Philip Sheridan to fight Early.

Sheridan chased the Confederates into the Shenandoah Valley, the beautiful, fertile area that had fed Lee's army for three years. Three times Sheridan defeated Early. He also showed how destructive war could be. Sheridan's men lay waste the valley, burning houses, barns, and crops, slaughtering what livestock they did not eat themselves. Sheridan reported that when he was done, a crow could not fly over the Shenandoah without carrying its own provisions.

Lincoln's Reelection.

As President, Lincoln was not always popular. Northern Democrats vilified him as the war dragged on. The radicals in his own party thought he was too generous with

Discussion Question: Is the use of attrition as a military strategy a sound policy? Take care to lead the discussion in such a way that students who may not be certain of the exact meaning of attrition and the ramifications of its uses in battle come away from the discussion aware of the destruction it involves.

the wounds he had received during the Peninsular Campaign. Then, unaccountably, Jefferson Davis replaced Johnston with John B. Hood. Brave, but not as good a commander as Johnston, Hood was no match for the calculating Sherman. Hood tried to take the offensive against Sherman's larger, better-prepared army, only to be roundly defeated. On September 2, 1864, Union troops occupied Atlanta. The loss of this major rail center in the previously untouched heart of the South was a devastating blow.

But Sherman was himself in a touchy situation. His supply lines ran over an easily raided single-track railway from Chattanooga, 100 miles away. If he waited in Atlanta, he might easily be surrounded and starved out. Once again, the new Union leadership turned challenge into triumph. With Grant's permission, Sherman ordered Atlanta's citizens to leave, and burned the city to the ground.

Sherman then moved his troops southeast in several columns, marching quickly to avoid a major battle. Sherman's troops lived off the land, and what they did not use, they destroyed. A swath 60 miles wide was nearly stripped of buildings, crops, and livestock. Never had such destruction been seen in a war.

Sherman had two purposes for the destruction. First, he wanted to make it difficult for the Confederate army, again commanded by Johnston, to pursue him. They too would be without supplies. Second, he wanted to punish the South for the rebellion.

On December 10, Sherman reached Savannah, where his men could be supplied from the sea. In February 1865, they began to march north to join Grant and attack Lee in one final battle.

Stillness at Appomattox.

That final battle was never fought. In February 1865, Jefferson Davis tried to make peace. He sent Vice President Alexander Stephens to meet Lincoln on a ship near Hampton Roads, Virginia. Stephens was instructed to insist on southern independence. With the South reeling, the demand was absurd and the peace talks came to nothing.

On April 2, Lee tried to draw Grant into a battle in open country. By this time, however, he commanded only 54,000 men to Grant's 115,000, and was easily pushed back. Knowing that his

the South. While most blacks idolized him as the Great Emancipator, black leaders knew that he did not believe in racial equality except until, perhaps, the very end of his life. People of all points of view poked fun at his ungainly appearance.

In the election of 1864, the Democrats chose George McClellan to oppose Lincoln, and for a while, Lincoln thought he was going to lose.

But Lincoln was a shrewd political manipulator. He knew how to give out *patronage* jobs to gain support, and picked his Cabinet members to placate all parts of the electorate.

Lincoln won reelection in 1864 quite easily. He wore down the hostilities and ridicule of his critics by his determination to see the war through, his awesome sense of human decency, his personal humility, and his great eloquence, shown so clearly in the Gettysburg Address of November 1863. Events on the battlefield at that time were going the Union's way, and Lincoln's popularity was rising. The President won the election, receiving 212 electoral votes to McClellan's 21.

Sherman's March to the Sea.

General Sherman had moved his Union troops into Georgia at the same time Grant had moved into The Wilderness. At first Sherman met brilliant resistance from Joseph Johnston, who had recovered from

More Americans died in the Civil War than in all other American wars combined, including the Korean War and the Vietnam War up to 1970.

forces were getting weaker while the Union army was growing stronger, Lee decided to leave Richmond before he was trapped. He made a run to the west, hoping to link up with Johnston's army and make a last stand.

With help from Sheridan, Grant cut off the last escape. With his once proud Army of Northern Virginia reduced to 30,000 ragged men, many without shoes, Lee asked for terms of surrender. He and Grant met in the tiny town of Appomattox Courthouse. The terms were simple and generous. The Confederates surrendered all arms except the officers' revolvers and swords. Officers and enlisted men could keep their horses for the spring plowing. After Lee's soldiers took an oath of loyalty to the Union, they would receive provisions and could go home.

On April 18, Joseph Johnston also surrendered under similar terms to Sherman at Durham, North Carolina. Within weeks, the rest of the Confederate forces dispersed.

The American Tragedy. The United States has never engaged in a more destructive war. More than a third of the men who served were killed, wounded, or captured. In some southern states, more than a quarter of all men of military age lay dead. Black troops, almost always given the dirtiest or most dangerous duty, suffered even more in proportion to their numbers. About 38,000 blacks died in the war.

There was one more casualty to be counted. A few days after he toured ruined Richmond, President Lincoln, his wife, and a few family friends went to a play in Washington. It was Good Friday, April 14, 1865. Shortly after ten o'clock, a fanatical pro-Confederate actor, John Wilkes Booth, slipped into the President's private box and shot him point-blank in the back of the head. Another member of Booth's gang, assigned to kill Vice President Johnson, lost his nerve. A third man seriously wounded Secretary of State Seward before being overcome.

The course of American history might have been changed if Lincoln had not been killed, for he was willing to extend his generosity to the white southerners he had fought so long. In his Second Inaugural Address, delivered just a month before his assassination, he called for northerners to move toward the postwar period "with malice toward none, with charity for all; with firmness in the right, as God gives us to see the right." Perhaps in part because Lincoln did not live to see the postwar period, it was not that way.

On April 9, 1865, General Robert E. Lee (seated, center left) surrendered to General Ulysses S. Grant (seated, center right) at Appomattox Courthouse, Virginia.

On April 15, 1865, just six days after Lee had surrendered at Appomattox, President Lincoln died. The picture above is of Lincoln's funeral procession. The "wanted" poster at the right is for the capture of his assassin.

SECTION REVIEW

1. Write a sentence to identify attrition, "March to the Sea," Hampton Roads, John Wilkes Booth.

2. Who took command of all Union forces in early 1864, and why did President Lincoln appoint him? Who took command of the Union forces in the West at that time?

3. Explain why the loss of Atlanta and the Shenandoah Valley were particularly painful for the Confederacy.

4. Who was the Democratic nominee for president in 1864? Why was Lincoln uncertain of reelection for a time?

5. What hopes for the future of the Union did President Lincoln express in his Second Inaugural Address?

Research Assignment: Have students prepare a report on Lincoln's assassination. The report should examine the various theories about whether the assassination was in fact a conspiracy, who was involved, and why these people might have been involved.

CHAPTER REVIEW

TIME LINE

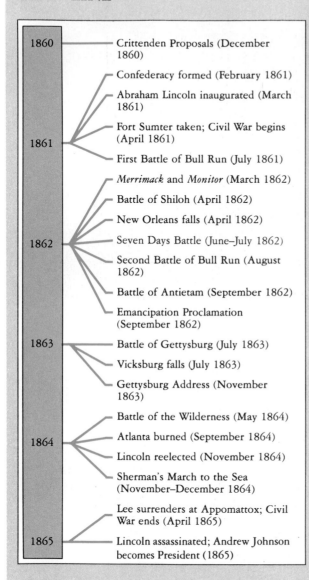

1860 — Crittenden Proposals (December 1860)

— Confederacy formed (February 1861)

— Abraham Lincoln inaugurated (March 1861)

1861 — Fort Sumter taken; Civil War begins (April 1861)

— First Battle of Bull Run (July 1861)

— *Merrimack* and *Monitor* (March 1862)

— Battle of Shiloh (April 1862)

— New Orleans falls (April 1862)

1862 — Seven Days Battle (June–July 1862)

— Second Battle of Bull Run (August 1862)

— Battle of Antietam (September 1862)

— Emancipation Proclamation (September 1862)

1863 — Battle of Gettysburg (July 1863)

— Vicksburg falls (July 1863)

— Gettysburg Address (November 1863)

— Battle of the Wilderness (May 1864)

1864 — Atlanta burned (September 1864)

— Lincoln reelected (November 1864)

— Sherman's March to the Sea (November–December 1864)

— Lee surrenders at Appomattox; Civil War ends (April 1865)

1865 — Lincoln assassinated; Andrew Johnson becomes President (1865)

TIME LINE QUESTIONS

1. How many years did the Civil War last?
2. List the following events in chronological order: Battle of Gettysburg, fall of Fort Sumter, Confederacy formed, Emancipation Proclamation, *Merrimack* versus *Monitor*, Gettysburg Address, Lincoln assassinated.
3. How long after the Battle of Antietam did Lee invade the North again?

SKILLS STRATEGY

Abraham Lincoln's Gettysburg Address was a masterpiece of oratory. One writer described the famous speech as "a sparkling diamond, provocative of profound and valid emotions, brief and simple in expression, gigantic in thought, sensitive and eloquent in every phrase and punctuation mark."[1] The following excerpt from the address proves the writer's point.

" . . . we here highly resolve that these dead shall not have died in vain; that this nation, under God, shall have a new birth of freedom; and that government of the people, by the people, for the people, shall not perish from the earth."[2]

1. Trebor J. Srevart, *Great American Speeches*, p. 12.
2. *World Encyclopedia*, 2nd ed., "Gettysburg Address."

QUOTATIONS AND FOOTNOTES

When writing reports, quoting writers or speakers often helps to support a main idea or to add interest. However, when using quotations, consistent procedures should be followed within the report to credit the writer or speaker quoted. Footnotes are often used because they give complete credit without interrupting the flow of the text. As you read the following rules for proper footnotes, verify each rule by finding an application in the paragraph above.

First, the quoted words must be used exactly as they were written or spoken, and they must be enclosed within quotation marks. Second, the author or speaker of the quoted words must be identified in this way: Each quotation should be followed by a footnote reference number placed after and slightly above the closing quotation mark. This number refers to a footnote with the same number at the bottom of the page on which the quotation appears. The number in the footnote is followed by a period. Then the full name of the author of the source of the quotation is given, followed by the title of the source, and the number of the page on which the quote appears. (Notice the differences between footnotes 1 and 2.)

Making Connections: Review the questions and topics presented in the Making Connections section that opens this chapter. Bear in mind questions relating to whether or not the war solved anything and the possible unseen costs of the war.

> Women played active roles in the Civil War, as one historian pointed out. "(sentence omitted) Northern and Southern women may have considered themselves 'ladies,' but they were not content to sit demurely and hopefully waiting for their men to come home. (sentences omitted) Scornful of social censure, women in both the South and the North worked as nurses tending the wounded of the many bloody battles. Others willingly, and successfully, took over for their soldier spouses on farms and plantations." (page 93 in *The Not So Weaker Sex* by Nancy Jane Weiss) Civil War women made clothes and collected supplies for the armies, worked as government clerks, and even spied. Their work was valuable. Indeed, "Neither the Union nor the Confederacy could long have prosecuted the war without the help of its women." (page 713 in *Civil War Asides* by Edgar Morris)

Find the *ellipsis points* (three periods in a row) in the paragraph on page 516. These punctuation marks indicate that words or sentences have been omitted. Notice that the longer quotation is indented and set off in the text. This is the proper form for quotations of more than five lines.

APPLYING SKILLS
Refer to both paragraphs as you answer the following questions. Then change the paragraph above as directed.

1. How many quotations are used in the above paragraph? Which quotation is longest?
2. How is the longest quotation in the paragraph on page 516 distinguished from the rest of the paragraph?
3. How should the longest quotation in the paragraph above be distinguished from the rest of the text?
4. What punctuation marks are missing from the paragraph above?
5. How many footnote reference numbers and footnotes will be needed for the paragraph above?
6. Write the paragraph above using correct footnote form.

CHAPTER 15 TEST

TEXT REVIEW
1. Name the four border states that joined the Confederacy. Explain why the people in one state were reluctant to secede.
2. Explain how the following border states were kept in the Union: Delaware, Maryland, Kentucky, and Missouri.
3. What political consideration kept President Lincoln from accepting the compromise suggested by Senator Crittenden?
4. Give evidence from the chapter that supports this idea: The Civil War was the first modern war because it was the first war that affected the whole societies of the opponents.
5. Describe Americans' attitudes toward the war before the First Battle of Bull Run.
6. Compare the battle tactics used by Generals Grant and Sherman and those used by General Lee. Why was Grant finally able to defeat Lee whereas others could not?
7. What political abilities, personal qualities, and events on the battlefield helped President Lincoln win reelection in 1864?
8. Describe General Sherman's actions in Atlanta and along the route to Savannah. What were his reasons for these actions?

CRITICAL THINKING
9. Summarize the events that took place from April 2 to April 18, 1865, ending in the surrender of the Confederate armies.
10. Tell what words the author uses in this sentence to show that it is an opinion: "The course of American history might have been different if Lincoln had not been killed." What evidence does the author use in the chapter to lend weight to his opinion?

WRITING A PARAGRAPH
Choose a subject covered in this chapter and write a paragraph about it. Use a quotation from the chapter and credit the author and the book in a correct footnote. Also use a quotation from an encyclopedia or from another book, and credit that quotation in a second footnote.

Quotation: from the poem "Lincoln Monument: Washington." Other works by Langston Hughes (1902–1967) include *Weary Blues, Not Without Laughter, The Dream Keeper, The Ways of White Folks, The Big Sea,* and *Shakespeare in Harlem.*

CHAPTER 16

RECONSTRUCTING THE UNION

1865–1877

And yet a voice forever
Against the
Timeless walls
Of time—
Old Abe.

LANGSTON HUGHES

Making Connections. The great national question after the Civil War was: How should the Confederate states be readmitted to the Union? Lincoln's plan would have made their reentry as easy as possible. But the bitter memories of the war strengthened the Radical Republicans. They wanted to vindictively punish the South.

In this chapter, you will learn:
- What dramatic changes in domestic policy were passed by Congress during the war
- Why the Radical Republicans attacked the policies of Republican presidents Lincoln and Johnson
- How freed slaves were treated by state governments in the South
- What rights were guaranteed by the Fourteenth and Fifteenth Amendments
- Why President Johnson was impeached
- Who the carpetbaggers, scalawags, and Redeemers were, and how their activities denied blacks the right to vote in the South

You have read that the Civil War was a terrible struggle. Some northern leaders wanted to treat the South as a conquered nation. As you read, consider the success (or lack of success) that the harsh Reconstruction policies had in changing the South after the Civil War.

Sections
1. The North During the War
2. The Radicals' Victory
3. Radical Reconstruction
4. Reconstruction Ends

1. THE NORTH DURING THE WAR

The Civil War years were important in American politics because the voice of the South was not heard in Congress. The secession of the southern Democrats meant that the Republicans had comfortable majorities in both the Senate (31–10) and the House (102–75), an edge that increased in the midterm elections of 1862. Republican dominance led to a series of landmark laws that would influence American development for decades to come.

The Republicans were dominant during the war. But they were neither supreme nor united. Northern Democrats were able to mount an opposition to Lincoln's policies that led the President to curtail constitutional liberties in order to maintain political control. Opposition to his policies within the Republican party presented an even touchier problem because Lincoln needed Republican support.

A New Majority. The South had always played a role in national politics out of all proportion to

Cotton, grown on plantations like the one shown at the right, was the most important cash crop grown in the South. Other cash crops that provided significant income for the South were tobacco, sugar, rice, and hemp.

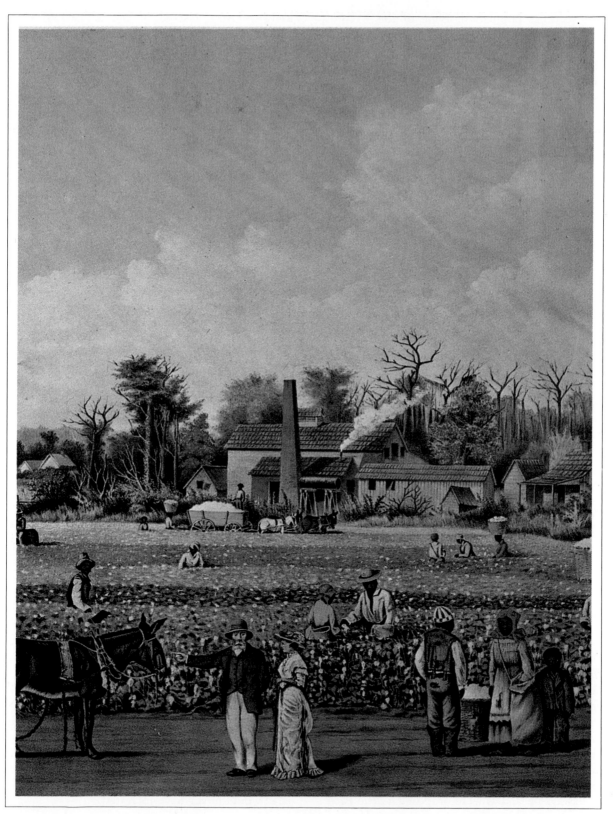

Skills Review: Reinforce the skills learned in the preceding Skills Strategy section. Have students do at least one of the Research Assignments suggested for this chapter, using the methods of footnoting described in the preceding chapter.

the section's population. Nine of the 15 presidents before Lincoln were southerners. At least two of the six northern presidents before Lincoln (Pierce and Buchanan) were strongly prosouthern. In the House of Representatives, southerners and their northern allies were able to restrain if not always prevent Whig, and later Republican, economic policies. In the Senate, the slave states had equal representation until 1850, and even after California's admission, very nearly a working majority because of the Doughface senators. As the Dred Scott decision showed, even the Supreme Court was friendly to southern interests.

All that changed during the Civil War. At that time, all the southern senators except Andrew Johnson of Tennessee and almost all the southern representatives resigned their seats and went with the Confederacy. Beginning in 1861, western farmers, northern industrialists, and businesspeople whose influence had been restrained by southern interests suddenly had a free rein to establish policies favorable to themselves.

A Pacific Railroad—For the North.

In July 1862, about the time of the Battle of Antietam, Congress passed the *Pacific Railways Act.* As modified later in the war, this act gave 6,400 square miles (16,600 square kilometers) of government land in the West to two private companies, the Union Pacific Railroad and the Central Pacific Railroad. These corporations were authorized to sell their land grants and use the proceeds to construct a railroad between California and the eastern states. In 1864, while Grant hammered at Lee before Richmond, another act paid an even richer subsidy to the Northern Pacific Railroad to build a transcontinental line through the northernmost states and territories.

Southerners were also interested in a railroad and supported Jefferson Davis's sponsorship of the Gadsden Purchase in 1853. Before secession, however, South and North had been unable to agree on a route. Both sides wanted the transcontinental line to benefit their sections. With the southern states in rebellion, Republicans were able to ensure that the North reaped the fruits of a link with California. Moreover, southern congressmen were generally opposed to such lavish giveaways of land as were proposed by the Pacific Railways Act. Passage of the act would have been impossible if the southerners had remained in Congress.

A Whiggish Financial Policy.

The tariff was another issue on which the votes of southern agricultural consumers had repeatedly frustrated the northeastern manufacturers. The southern Democratic party had driven tariff rates downward from 1832 to 1860. The last prewar tariff on which southern congressmen had voted, the Tariff of 1857, set rates lower than they had been since the War of 1812.

In March 1861, with most southern congressmen gone, the Republican Congress easily passed the *Morrill Tariff,* which pushed rates up. By 1867, the average tax on imported goods was 47 percent, about the same as it had been with the Tariff of 1828, which southerners had called the Tariff of Abominations.

Southern Democrats had also successfully opposed the old Whig plan for a centralized banking system regulating a national paper *currency.* Opposition to a national bank and paper money were foundation stones of the Democratic party. During the war, however, with the need to finance the war, the Republican Congress reversed the generation-long trend.

The Union financed the war in three ways. First, an excise tax on luxury goods and an income tax were imposed. Second, the government authorized the printing of $450 million in paper money that was not redeemable in gold. That is, *greenbacks,* so-called because they were printed in green on the back instead of the yellow used for notes redeemable in gold, had value only because the government accepted them for payment of taxes. Despite the fact that the Confederacy also resorted to printing paper money during the war, the federal issuing of paper money was something that could not have happened in prewar America because of opposition from southerners.

Finally, the war was financed by borrowing. Jay Cooke's Bank in Philadelphia was empowered to act as agent for the federal government, selling bonds on which the bank took a commission. By the end of the war, the federal government owed $2.6 billion. The debt tied the government to the banking system in a way the prewar Democratic party would never have tolerated.

Class Activity: As students go through the chapter, have them compile a chart comparing problems solved by the Civil War to problems created by it. At the end of the chapter, synthesize these into a final version based on the class's work. Discuss whether or not the war was successful.

Free Land. The wartime Congress also disposed of the national domain in ways the southern Democrats had always opposed. Before the war, southern opposition to new free states dominated by small family farmers had caused most of the South's congressmen to oppose a liberal land policy that made it easy for family farmers to obtain western lands. In May 1862, the Homestead Act completed the work started by Thomas Hart Benton. It provided that every citizen who was head of a family could receive 160 acres (64 hectares) of public land free. The only conditions were a very small filing fee to cover the cost of paperwork, a five-year residence on the land, and the construction of a livable dwelling. Alternately, after only six months of residence on the land, homesteaders could buy it for $1.25 an acre.

A few months after the Homestead Act, Congress passed the *Morrill Land Grant Act.* This law granted each Union state government in the West 30,000 acres for each of the state's congressmen. The states were obligated to use the money they made from selling these grants of land to start agricultural colleges. In the years that followed, 69 land-grant colleges were established, greatly expanding educational opportunities, particularly in the western states. Once again, this was a free-spending policy that a southern-dominated Congress would never have approved.

The War Democrats. Some Democrats remained in Congress during the Civil War. Known as *War Democrats,* many believed that the Union had no choice but to fight for its preservation, and they generally supported Lincoln's policies.

The War Democrats disagreed with the Emancipation Proclamation, believing that freeing the slaves encouraged the Confederacy to fight on. They also hoped for less than a total victory, if total victory meant total destruction of the South. The Democrats wanted the South back in the Union because that would strengthen their party. By the same token, they did not want southern society turned upside down, as abolition would do, because that would weaken their southern allies.

Lincoln and the Copperheads. The Republicans, including Lincoln, tended to see most critics of war policy as *Copperheads,* or pro-Confederate enemies of the Union who, like the poisonous snake of that name, struck with no warning. Lincoln took many controversial actions against those he regarded as threats to the war effort. He suspended the right of *habeas corpus,* a protection

Northern critics of Lincoln's war policies were called "Copperheads," because they were supposedly as treacherous as those snakes. The 1863 political cartoon below shows the Union being threatened by midwestern Democratic congressmen in the shape of snakes.

against arbitrary arrest, so that antiwar Democrats could be jailed. At one time or another, 13,000 critics of the war were imprisoned. Lincoln also used his control of the Postal Service to prevent the distribution of antiwar newspapers.

The noisiest Copperhead was Clement L. C. Vallandigham, a popular Democratic congressman from Ohio. His criticisms of the war unsettled Lincoln so much that the President jailed him. Vallandigham was later released, but only under condition that he live in the Confederate states. In 1863, he ran for governor of Ohio, but had to campaign from exile in Canada.

Identifying Vallandigham with treason was unfair but politically shrewd. Had he been able to plead his case at home, he might very well have won Ohio's governorship. A great many voters of the Ohio River Valley, who were descendants of southerners and had close economic contacts with the South, were either sympathetic to the Confederacy or disapproved of all-out war against the South.

The Radical Republicans.

While Democrats criticized Lincoln for refusing to negotiate with the South, members of his own party attacked him for not pushing the war effort, and particularly the destruction of slavery, with enough enthusiasm. These were the *Radical Republicans,* a powerful minority in Lincoln's party. Most were longstanding abolitionists. In the Senate, Charles Sumner of Massachusetts and Benjamin Wade of Ohio led the Radicals. Thaddeus Stevens of Pennsylvania was the leader of the Radicals in the House. A stern, highly moral man, Stevens hated slavery and therefore the South. He wanted complete military victory so that southern society could be remade in a way more in keeping with his ideals. Confederates disliked him so much that, during the Gettysburg campaign, a cavalry unit was sent on a detour for the express purpose of destroying a factory owned by Stevens.

The Radicals pushed Lincoln constantly for action against slavery. Lincoln delayed, fearing that a blow against slavery would cost the Union the loyalty of such slave states as Kentucky and Missouri. Nevertheless, it was probably Radical pressure that made Lincoln issue his Emancipation Proclamation, and by the end of the war, made the complete abolition of slavery a national goal.

Before the final year of the war, Lincoln had never personally thought of abolition as essential or even desirable.

The Reconstruction Debate Begins.

Lincoln's disagreements with the Radicals continued after emancipation. On December 8, 1863, when northern victory seemed just a matter of time, the President shocked the Radical Republicans with his plan for *reconstructing* the Union at the end of hostilities.

According to this plan, as soon as ten percent of the voters in each rebellious state took an oath of allegiance to the Union, the people of that state could organize a government and elect representatives and senators to Congress. Three states already occupied by Union troops quickly met these "easy" terms.

The Radicals, alarmed, reasoned that if the southern states were reconstructed so easily, they would act much as they had before the fighting. The bloodletting and sacrifice of the war would have gone for nothing. The Radicals had no intention of resuming the prewar bickering with proslavery congressmen.

Although a minority, the Radicals were able to persuade Congress to refuse to recognize the three southern state governments. Moderate Republicans, siding with the Radicals, also did not want to see former Confederates coming to Washington, particularly with the war still raging.

Perhaps more important, many Republicans were alarmed by the broad expansion of presidential powers under Lincoln. The President had done much governing by decree. Even the Emancipation Proclamation had been a presidential act —Congress had had no hand in it. Congress had no intention of allowing Lincoln, or any other president, to continue to rule by decree after the war ended.

The Wade-Davis Bill.

Congress proposed its own reconstruction plan in the *Wade-Davis Bill* of July 1864. First, the Wade-Davis plan insisted that over 50 percent of the registered voters of a rebellious state must take the oath of loyalty in order to set the reconstruction process in operation. This greater demand would buy the time Republicans needed to build their party in the former Confederate states.

Habeus corpus is a legal order directing an officer of the law to bring a person before a court of law to show cause why he or she should be released. Lincoln's suspension of the rule was a violation of Article 1, Section 9 of the Constitution. Examine this section of the document with students.

Second, the Wade-Davis plan ensured that Congress, and not the president, would judge when a state had met the requirements for readmission to the Union. This provision warned Lincoln that Congress had no intention of giving up its constitutional right to rule on whether a person claiming to be a senator or representative would be seated.

The Pocket Veto. Which of these provisions Lincoln disliked we cannot know. Instead of vetoing the bill with a formal message to Congress, Lincoln killed the Wade-Davis reconstruction plan with a *pocket veto.*

The president normally has ten days either to sign an act of Congress or to veto it with an explanation of the action to Congress. If the president does nothing within the ten days, the bill becomes law without the president's signature. However, if Congress adjourns within that ten-day period, as happened in the case of the Wade-Davis Bill, and the president does not sign it, the bill dies without presidential explanation. It is as if the president simply carried the bill around in a coat pocket.

Therefore, on the night Lincoln was shot, there was no set Reconstruction policy. Neither Congress nor the President had established control over the process by which southern states would come back into the Union.

SECTION REVIEW

1. Write a sentence to identify: Pacific Railways Act, Morrill Land Grant Act, Copperheads, Radical Republicans.

2. Give five ways in which the South's role in national politics was larger than its population would seem to call for.

3. Explain why southerners would have opposed legislation in the following areas if they had remained in Congress: railroads, tariff, national bank, paper money.

4. Explain Lincoln's plan to readmit Confederate states to the Union, and describe the reactions of Congress to it.

5. Give the terms of Congress's Reconstruction plan. Why did it never become law?

2. THE RADICALS' VICTORY

In theory, the debate over Reconstruction policy can be stated as an abstract question, similar to Hamilton and Jefferson's disagreement over the interpretation of the Constitution. In practice, the debate was about what obligations America had to the *freedmen,* as the former slaves were called, and what role blacks were to play in American social and political life.

The dispute pitted very real human beings, who had strong feelings on the issue of racial equality, against one another. One reason the Radical-led Congress won the debate and committed the United States to full citizenship for blacks was the stubborn personality and prejudices of the man who succeeded Abraham Lincoln to the presidency, Andrew Johnson of Tennessee.

Andrew Johnson. Johnson, born into extreme poverty, had learned to read and write only as an adult, and had struggled up the political ladder, holding public office at every level before becoming president. Elected to numerous local and state offices, Johnson had also been a congressman, senator, wartime governor of Tennessee, and vice president. Few presidents have had such complete political training.

Johnson hated wealthy slaveowners and considered the Confederacy to be a slaveowners' plot. In 1861, he was the only southern senator to refuse to resign his seat and go with the Confederacy. He had said then that Jefferson Davis and all the leading Confederates should be hanged. This sentiment won him Radical support in 1864.

But Johnson had problems that made him an ineffective president. Lincoln had been an instinctive policitian, sensitive to his critics' feelings and motives, and always ready to outwit or compromise with them. Johnson was blunt, stubborn, and willful. Nonetheless, during his first weeks in office, the Radicals, remembering his earlier statements, thought that they now had one of their own in the White House.

"They Are Already States." Johnson believed that it was constitutionally impossible for states to secede from the Union. According to his view, the United States was a nation formed by its people and not, as Calhoun had said, by the states. In

Research Assignment: Have students research and examine the special powers Lincoln assumed during the Civil War. Was his assumption of these powers constitutional? Was his assumption of these powers the right thing to do?

GOING TO THE SOURCE

The years from 1867 to 1878 I think may be called the period of Reconstruction. This included the time that I spent as a student at Hampton and as a teacher in West Virginia. During the whole of the Reconstruction period two ideas were constantly agitating the minds of the coloured people, or, at least, the minds of a large part of the race. One of these was the craze for Greek and Latin learning, and the other was a desire to hold office.

It could not have been expected that a people who had spent generations in slavery, and before that generations in the darkest heathenism, could at first form any proper conception of what an education meant. In every part of the South, during the Reconstruction period, schools, both day and night, were filled to overflowing with people of all ages and conditions, some being as far along in age as sixty and seventy years. The ambition to secure an education was most praiseworthy and encouraging. The idea, however, was too prevalent that, as soon as one secured a little education, in some unexplainable way he would be free from most of the hardships of the world, and, at any rate, could live without manual labour. There was a further feeling that a knowledge, however little, of the Greek and Latin languages would make one a very superior human being, something bordering almost on the supernatural. I remember that the first coloured man whom I saw who knew something about foreign languages impressed me at the time as being a man of all others to be envied.

Naturally, most of our people who received some little education became teachers or preachers. While among these two classes there

> *In every part of the South, during the Reconstruction period, schools, both day and night, were filled to overflowing with people of all ages and conditions, some being as far along in age as sixty and seventy years. The ambition to secure an education was most praiseworthy and encouraging.*
>
> BOOKER T. WASHINGTON, *UP FROM SLAVERY*

were many capable, earnest, godly men and women, still a large proportion took up teaching or preaching as an easy way to make a living. . . .

During the whole of the Reconstruction period our people throughout the South looked to the Federal Government for everything, very much as a child looks to its mother. This was not unnatural. The central government gave them freedom, and the whole Nation had been enriched for more than two centuries by the labour of the Negro. Even as a youth, and later in manhood, I had the feeling that it was cruelly wrong in the central government, at the beginning of our freedom, to fail to make some provision for the general education of our people in addition to what the states might do, so that the people would be the better prepared for the duties of citizenship.

. . . Perhaps, after all, and under all the circumstances, those in charge of the conduct of affairs did the only thing that could be done at the time. Still, as I look back now over the entire period of our freedom, I cannot help feeling that it would have been wiser if some plan could have been put in operation which would have made the possession of a certain amount of education or property, or both, a test for the exercise of the franchise, and a way provided by which this test should be made to apply honestly and squarely to both the white and black races.

Booker T. Washington (1856–1915) was nine years old when the Union's victory in the Civil War ended slavery. He struggled through the postwar years to pay for his education at Hampton Institute. Later, as a famous educator and reformer, Washington wrote his autobiography, Up From Slavery, *from which this passage comes.*

1861, most northerners, including the Radicals, agreed with him.

Therefore, Johnson believed that the Confederate states were still part of the Union. There had been a war, a rebellion. But that had been fought by individuals. Punish the rebels, Johnson argued, but do not punish the states.

Johnson's plan for Reconstruction was like the Wade-Davis plan in that it called for 50 percent of the voters in each southern state to take an oath of loyalty. Johnson added the provision that the new state governments must ratify the *Thirteenth Amendment* to the Constitution, which ended slavery. However, as in Lincoln's plan, the president and not the Congress would decide when the various states could take full part in political life.

Johnson believed that reinstating the Confederate states was not a Congressional matter. They were already states under the Constitution. Reconstructing them was an administrative matter.

The Radicals Protest. As constitutional theory, Johnson's argument was logical. What it did not take into account was that Americans had just ended a war that had cost 600,000 casualties and had filled survivors in the North with deep resentment of southern whites and considerable sympathy for former slaves.

In the summer of 1865, all the former Confederate states met Johnson's conditions and elected delegates to Congress. Seventy-four southern congressmen had been high Confederate officials, including the Confederate vice president, Alexander Stephens. The Radicals and many northerners who were not Radical Republicans were outraged that the very people responsible for the rebellion were now to make the nation's laws.

The Black Codes. More troubling to the Radicals were the *black codes* adopted by the southern state governments. President Johnson proclaimed that the codes were legal.

These collections of laws varied from state to state, but they had one thing in common. None granted freed people the rights of full citizenship. Instead, they created a second-class status in which blacks enjoyed few civil rights.

Some state codes permitted blacks to work only as domestic servants or in agriculture, precisely the kind of work they had done as slaves. In other codes, blacks were forbidden to live in towns and cities, a scheme designed to force them to do field work. In no southern state were blacks allowed to bear arms or to vote. Louisiana required that freed people sign 12-month labor contracts each year. Those who did not could be arrested.

Southern legislators explained that because the southern economy could not function without them, blacks must continue to work in agriculture. Most northerners agreed. But the Radicals strongly disagreed with a system that forced free people to follow only certain occupations.

If the goal was to get southern agriculture producing again, a few Radicals said, give every former slave family 40 acres (16 hectares) and a mule from the property of the great planters who had caused the Civil War. The solution would serve three purposes. Southern agriculture would recover. Freed people would have an economic basis on which to defend their freedom, and the planter class would lose its anti-democratic power.

One "black code" called for a vagrancy fine to be paid by any man without visible means of support. The engraving above shows a man (holding his hat) who was unable to pay his fine, and consequently, his "services" are being auctioned.

Research Assignment: Have students do a report detailing and examining some of the South's black codes. These laws should be compared with uncodified practices toward blacks in the North. Was there a great deal of difference between the two?

PROFILES OF THE PRESIDENCY

With Lincoln's death and the war's end, Andrew Johnson gave thanks for the nation's survival:

Other nations were wasted by civil wars for ages before they could establish for themselves the necessary degree of unity; the latent conviction that our form of government is the best ever known to the world has enabled us to emerge from civil war within four years with a complete vindication of the constitutional authority of the General Government and with our local liberties and State institutions unimpaired.

The throngs of emigrants that crowd to our shores are witnesses of the confidence of all peoples in our permanence. . . .

Where in past history does a parallel exist to the public happiness which is within reach of the people of the United States? Where in any part of the globe can institutions be found so suited to their habits or so entitled to their love as their own free Constitution? Everyone of them, then, in whatever part of the land he has his home, must wish its perpetuity.

—MESSAGE TO CONGRESS, DECEMBER 4, 1865

Few in Congress supported this solution by itself. But enough disapproved of the black codes to deny seats to the congressmen from the states reconstructed by Johnson.

Five generations of the family below were born on the same plantation in Beaufort, South Carolina.

The Radicals Break with the President.

President Johnson's interpretation of the Constitution was reasonable, but time after time he refused to face political realities. Therefore, in February 1866, the split between Johnson and Congress became final.

In that month, Congress voted to extend the life of the *Freedmen's Bureau.* This government agency had been set up at the end of the war to provide various social services for newly freed blacks and for displaced whites. The Bureau provided food and clothing, served as a kind of employment agency, set up hospitals, and operated schools staffed largely by idealistic northern women who had been abolitionists.

The Bureau was scheduled to expire in March 1866 because Congress assumed that, by then, southern state governments would have taken over these necessary services. But because of the black codes, there were no southern state governments recognized by Congress. However, the life of the bureau was not extended, because Johnson vetoed the bill. He insisted that state governments did exist. In April 1866, Congress voted federal citizenship to blacks. Now, no matter what state governments did, blacks were citizens of the United States. Johnson also vetoed this act, on the

Discussion Question: Was Andrew Johnson a good president? Contrast the content of his policies with his method of getting his policies accepted.

Freed black people, having little money and poor land, had difficulty making a living.

grounds that the Constitution gave the states the power to define who was a citizen.

Finally, in the summer of 1866, white mobs in several southern cities attacked black communities and killed more than 100 people. More and more northerners began to resent what they saw as the arrogance of the white southerners. What, they asked, had the war been about if Confederates claimed seats in Congress, blacks were treated much like slaves, and mobs ran wild without fear of punishment? With the President appearing to support these actions, the Radicals believed that a traitor sat in the White House.

The Fourteenth Amendment.
In 1866, the Supreme Court seemed to support the President and the unacceptable southern state governments. In the case of *Ex parte Milligan,* the Court ruled that the military had no constitutional right to exercise political power in areas free from actual hostilities. This, the Radicals realized, meant that not even the United States Army could protect the freed people from the Johnson-approved governments.

Congress's solution was a constitutional amendment preventing state governments from discriminating against blacks. Proposed in June 1866, the *Fourteenth Amendment* remains the longest and most important in the Constitution.

First, the amendment forbade all states to deny equal citizenship to any person "born or naturalized in the United States." The states were also forbidden to "deprive any person of life, liberty, or property without due process of law," or "to deny any person within its jurisdiction the equal protection of the laws."

After the Civil War, southern black people were able to attend school.

Class Activity: Discuss the Thirteenth, Fourteenth, and Fifteenth Amendments. Examine their texts and discuss what actual changes were effected by their institution—both immediately and later in their histories.

RECONSTRUCTION AMENDMENTS				
		Provisions	Date of Congressional Approval	Date Ratified by States
Amendment	13	Prohibited slavery in United States	January 31, 1865	December 6, 1865
	14	Established that every person born or naturalized in United States was a citizen	June 13, 1866	July 9, 1868
		Provided that a state's representation in Congress would be based on the state's total population (abolished "three-fifths compromise")		
		Prohibited ex-Confederates from holding office		
		Voided Confederate war debt		
	15	Prohibited denial of voting rights based on race or previous condition of servitude	February 26, 1869	February 2, 1870

Second, a state's representation was to be decided on how many people lived in that state. No longer was a black person considered to be only three-fifths of a person.

Third, the amendment provided that high-ranking Confederate leaders, who headed many of the Johnson governments, lost their civil rights until they were pardoned by Congress. They could not vote or hold public office.

Once ratified, the Fourteenth Amendment would invalidate the black codes. However, it would also invalidate laws in many northern states, particularly in the Midwest, that discriminated against blacks. In the local elections of 1866, Johnson saw an opportunity to defeat the Radicals. Thinking that midwestern voters had no strong desire for racial equality, he launched a speaking tour of the Midwest, urging voters to reject Radical candidates for Congress and support instead the Democrats and moderate Republicans who supported him.

The Radical Triumph. Johnson miscalculated. Midwestern voters did not support his Reconstruction plan—not because they believed in racial equality, but for fear the plan would put the Confederate elite back into power. Johnson did not help matters with his gritty oratorical style. Americans liked rough and tumble political debate on a local level. But they expected their president to act with more dignity. Instead, Johnson answered hecklers with harsh language.

When the results of the election were in, the Radicals had won an overwhelming victory. Most of Johnson's candidates were defeated. The Radical Republicans controlled the two-thirds majority necessary to override any presidential veto. Reconstruction policy was in their hands.

SECTION REVIEW

1. Write a sentence to identify: black codes, Freedmen's Bureau, *Ex parte Milligan*, Fourteenth Amendment.

2. Explain the problems that freed people faced.

3. Explain the connection between President Johnson's Reconstruction plan and each of the following: the Constitution, the Thirteenth Amendment, the Wade-Davis Bill, the administrative duties of the president.

4. What miscalculation did Johnson make about the Congressional elections of 1866? What effect did the election have on Reconstruction?

---

3. RADICAL RECONSTRUCTION

The *Radical Reconstruction program* was adopted in a series of laws passed by Congress in 1867. All were passed over the President's veto. But because Johnson believed in the Constitution, which gave Congress power to overrule the president, he enforced the Radical program. Nevertheless, the Radicals tried to remove him from office.

The attempt was unsuccessful, but in the regular election of 1868, the Radicals elected their own presidential candidate, war hero Ulysses S. Grant. During Grant's two terms, the Radicals

Research Assignment: Discuss the provisions in the Constitution dealing with presidential impeachment. Have students compare the impeachment proceedings against Johnson with those against Nixon. How are they the same and how are they different? Did either case have any merit? What impact did each case have on the country and the administration in office?

made a great contribution to American history. For all their faults, they attempted to commit the United States to the principle of racial equality before the law.

The Tenure of Office Act.

Some Radicals came to hate Johnson personally. In 1868, they brought a number of charges against the President as grounds for impeachment.

Impeachment does not mean removal from office, but is only the bringing of charges. In federal impeachment cases, the types of charges are defined in the Constitution, and the Chief Justice of the Supreme Court presides over the hearings, with the United States Senate sitting as a jury. A two-thirds majority is required to remove a federal official, such as the president, from office.

Some of the charges brought against Johnson were simply silly. For instance, the President was charged with undignified behavior and disrespect for Congress. That was true enough, but lack of dignity is hardly one of the "high crimes and misdemeanors" that the Constitution says are grounds for impeachment.

Even the one real charge the Radicals filed against Johnson was weak. They accused the President of violating the *Tenure of Office Act*, a law passed over his veto in 1867 (and repealed in 1887). It said that any presidential appointee whose position was confirmed by the Senate could not be dismissed by the president without Senate approval. When Johnson dismissed Edwin M. Stanton, his Secretary of War and an ally of the Radicals, the House impeached the President.

But there was disagreement over whether the Tenure of Office Act was constitutional. And even if it was, it might not apply to Stanton. Johnson had not appointed him to office, Lincoln had. Moreover, Stanton had been appointed and confirmed before the law was passed.

Of course, these constitutional niceties had little to do with the real issue. The Radicals wanted to humiliate Johnson, to complete their control of the federal government. By a majority vote, the House of Representatives indicted the President.

Impeachment Fails In the Senate.

In 1868, there were 54 senators. The Radicals needed 36 votes to convict the President. They got 35.

In fact, it was not that close. Half a dozen practical Republican senators had agreed privately that if their votes were essential to acquit the President, they would vote for him. They knew that an anti-Johnson vote was popular at home, but if the President were removed from office, it would cripple the independence of the executive branch. Only when they realized that impeachment would fail did they do the politically smart thing and vote against Johnson.

The Radical Program.

Enacted early in 1867, the Radical Reconstruction program provided that, with the exception of already-reconstructed Tennessee, the former Confederacy was to be divided into five military districts governed by martial law.

The army was to enforce order and supervise voter registration. Adult black males were eligible to register, but high Confederate officials disenfranchised by the Fourteenth Amendment were not.

These voters would then elect a statewide convention to ratify the Thirteenth and Fourteenth Amendments and to draw up a constitution, which would then be submitted to Congress for approval. Once it was approved, the thereby reconstructed state could elect a legislature, a governor, two senators, and members of the House of Representatives.

In 1868, largely because of the solidly pro-Radical black vote, six states were readmitted to the Union: Alabama, Arkansas, Florida, Louisiana, North Carolina, and South Carolina. Each sent Republican delegations, including some blacks, to Congress.

In the remaining four states—Georgia, Mississippi, Texas, and Virginia—white opposition to a government in which blacks participated delayed every attempt to set up a reconstructed government until 1870. By that time, states seeking readmission were also required to ratify the Fifteenth Amendment.

Grant's Election and The Fifteenth Amendment.

In 1868, Ulysses S. Grant, the Republican candidate, won the presidency. Grant won the election by a very narrow margin. The electoral vote of 214 to 80 looked comfortable. But in the popular vote, Grant had a nationwide

Discussion Question: How might President Johnson have disagreed with provisions in the Radical Reconstruction Program? Why would he have disapproved of these measures?

ULYSSES S. GRANT

*D*ying of cancer, Ulysses S. Grant struggled to finish his memoirs. He wrote to his doctor:

It seems that man's destiny in this world is quite as much a mystery as it is likely to be in the next. I never thought of acquiring rank in the profession I was educated for; yet it came with two grades higher prefixed to the rank of General officer for me. I certainly never had either ambition or taste for political life; yet I was twice President of the United States. If anyone suggested the idea of my becoming an author, as they frequently did, I was not sure whether they were making sport of me or not. I have now written a book. . . . I ask that you keep these notes very private lest I become an authority on the treatment of diseases. I have already too many trades to be proficient in any.

—LETTER TO DR. JOHN H. DOUGLAS, JULY 8, 1877

---

edge of only 300,000. About 500,000 blacks, nearly all Republican, had voted. This meant that despite his popularity, Grant had won the election only because black voters had given him their support.

Black citizens generally supported the "party of Lincoln" (Republican party) after the Civil War.

The election of 1868 also made it clear that the Republican party's future depended on the votes of blacks, not simply in the southern states, where reconstruction protected them, but also in northern states where anti-black laws were still on the books.

Consequently, early in 1869, the Republicans proposed the Fifteenth Amendment. It forbade all states from denying the vote to any person on the basis of "race, color, or previous condition of servitude." Because Republican governments favorable to blacks were still in power in most of the southern states, the amendment was quickly and easily ratified.

Carpetbaggers, Scalawags, and Black Officials.
These three legends got their start during Reconstruction. *Carpetbaggers* was the name given to northerners who came south during Reconstruction. The name sums up their image as so poor they could keep all their possessions in a carpetbag, a small, cheap suitcase. In fact, many carpetbaggers brought much-needed investment capital to the South. Their intention was to make money, of course. Still, they were no more exploitative than other investors.

Scalawags was the name given to some southern whites. Scalawags have often been represented as "poor whites," the dregs of southern society who used the South's defeat to get revenge on the

President Grant was born Hiram Ulysses Grant and adopted the initials U.S. while a cadet at West Point. The book Grant refers to in his letter above is *Personal Memoirs*. It was published by Mark Twain's publishing company.

planter elite who, with good reason, looked down on them. No doubt many scalawags fit this description. Others, however, were sturdy mountaineers who had opposed secession and found the Republican party a comfortable political home. Nor were all scalawag leaders poor. They were former Whigs whose party had collapsed during the 1850s, but who could not bring themselves to support the Republicans until after the Civil War ended.

Almost all the blacks who served in the House of Representatives and the two who served in the Senate, Hiram Revels and Blanche K. Bruce of Mississippi, were well educated. They had been free blacks before the war, not slaves toiling in cotton fields. No black ever served as a state governor. However, Louisiana's Lieutenant Governor, P.B.S. Pinchback, briefly acted as governor in the absence of the scalawag who held that office.

Images of Reconstruction.

People who lived through the Civil War and Reconstruction usually recalled the postwar period as the unhappier time. Many white southerners came to think of Reconstruction as a time when they were bullied by Union soldiers, exploited by carpetbaggers and scalawags, and lorded over by former slaves.

Southern blacks remembered Reconstruction as a brief interlude of freedom sandwiched between the miseries of slavery and the repression of their rights that followed Reconstruction.

Northern whites saw it as a tragic mistake. They believed that idealistic Radicals were devoured by their vindictiveness toward southern whites. As a consequence, they forced policies on the South that did not work.

There was little glory to be gained in Reconstruction. Few reputations—northern or southern, white or black, Republican or Democratic—

The Fifteenth Amendment forbade all states from denying the right to vote on the basis of race, color, or previous condition of servitude. This poster commemorates the amendment's ratification by the states in 1870.

Research Assignment: Have students do a project in which they depict what life was like for different people in various parts of the country during Reconstruction. Have them get all their information from primary sources. What are the limitations to using these sources?

The Forty-first and Forty-second Congresses included the first black senator and congressmen. Shown here (from left) are Senator Hiram Revels and Representatives Benjamin Turner, Robert De Large, Josiah Walls, Jefferson Long, Joseph Rainy, and R. Brown Elliot.

emerged unstained from that difficult era. Nonetheless, few of the people painted as villains were entirely bad.

The Issue of Race.

A popular legend of whites, both North and South, was that southern blacks used their rights recklessly, forming spendthrift and corrupt governments. The Reconstruction governments did spend a lot of money, some of it corruptly. The scalawag governor of Louisiana, Henry C. Warmoth, deposited $100,000 in the bank during a year when his salary was $8,000. The South Carolina legislature once voted a grant of $1,000 to a Radical black member who had lost that amount in a horse race.

However, a majority of Reconstruction officials were as honest as the majority of officeholders are in any era. Moreover, corruption was not unique to southern Republicans during the 1860s and 1870s. The most crooked government of all was that of "Boss" Tweed in New York City, and Tweed was a Democrat. The champion government thief in the South was the white, anti-black, Democratic treasurer of Mississippi. He absconded with $62,000 in state money.

Most of the high expenditures in the Reconstruction states were necessary. For example, much money was spent on free public education, a social service that had been neglected in many southern states before the Civil War. In some states, the first free schools for whites as well as blacks were established during Reconstruction.

Economic Bondage.

Despite the creditable showing of black officials during Reconstruction, the experiment in racial equality was probably doomed from the start. Failure stemmed from the Radicals' rejection of a plan to confiscate large plantations owned by leading Confederates, and to divide those lands into small farms for the former slaves. If that had been done, southern blacks might have possessed the economic security essential to political freedom.

Instead, the blacks and many poor whites became *sharecroppers.* They farmed small plots owned by others and, as rent, turned over part of each year's crop. The penniless sharecroppers bought provisions on credit from stores, often owned by their landlords. Each purchase sunk them deeper into debt. Then, when the crop was in, sharecroppers often found that they were lucky just to break even. They had little choice but to remain on the same plot of land, caught in a cycle of debt.

The poor, both blacks and whites, of the South were in economic bondage to large landowners. If their landlords told them they could not vote under pain of losing their land, it did not matter very much that they were guaranteed the right to vote. Regular mealtimes for their families were more important to them than voting.

The Redeemers. The economic power of the southern landowners was the most important tool in the hands of the *Redeemers*, white Democrats who regained control of the southern states and "redeemed" them from the Radical Republicans. However, the Redeemers also depended to some extent on terrorism.

In 1866, the *Ku Klux Klan* was founded. Nathan Bedford Forrest, a former slave trader and Confederate general, became its first Grand Wizard in 1868. The Klan was a secret organization designed to frighten blacks away from the polls. Dressing in ghostly white costumes that concealed their identities, the Klansmen rode by night through black communities harassing, beating, and often killing blacks who attempted to exercise their civil rights.

Congress passed several laws designed to suppress the Klan and other such secret societies. But these organizations helped to force blacks out of public life. By 1876, only three southern states —South Carolina, Florida, and Louisiana—were still governed by Radical Republican governments friendly to blacks.

The Ku Klux Klan brought terror to many black communities. Organized to thwart the participation of black people in politics, the "KKK" went so far as to murder black citizens.

Class Activity: Have students discuss their interpretations of the political cartoon above.

4. RECONSTRUCTION ENDS

If northerners had remained committed to the ideal of black civil equality, the Reconstruction aims might have been preserved. However, even before the end of President Grant's first term in office, many northerners, including former Radical Republicans, had become disillusioned with their former ideals. In 1872, Congress passed the *Amnesty Act,* which allowed almost all ex-Confederates to hold office again. In the presidential election of 1872, a group called *Liberal Republicans* broke away from the party and formed a short-lived alliance with the Democrats in an unsuccessful attempt to deny Grant reelection.

Part of the reason for the Liberals' disillusionment was the widespread corruption in Grant's government. In addition, the Liberal Republicans had come to the conclusion that the only way to preserve the rights of southern blacks was to keep large army units stationed in the South. The Liberals treasured social stability and disapproved of terrorism. They concluded that only the Redeemers could bring stability to the South.

Grant's actions during his second term fed this feeling. He became increasingly reluctant to send troops into the South to maintain order and to help keep Republican governments in power.

Last Attempts at Equality. As the Redeemers took over the southern state governments, the

MOVERS AND SHAPERS

Walt Whitman

A love of plain language and an understanding of plain people were the qualities that inspired the poetry of Walt Whitman (1819–1892). Whitman grew up in Brooklyn, New York, and left school at the age of 13 to work for a newspaper. After work, he enjoyed wandering along the shore of Long Island and ambling down the streets of New York City. What most delighted him were his chance conversations with strangers from all walks of life: farmers, shipyard workers, teamsters.

He worked on the *Brooklyn Eagle* for two years, but resigned the job when the editor refused to take a stand against slavery. He took a cross-country trip, and when he returned to Brooklyn in 1848, began his career as a poet.

In 1855, he published 12 poems in a volume called *Leaves of Grass.* The democratic theme as well as the stunningly original style of the poetry impressed Ralph Waldo Emerson, who wrote Whitman a letter glowing with praise. Other readers and critics expressed outrage at Whitman's use of free verse. Despite this criticism, Whitman continued to write poems celebrating the greatness and vitality of America.

During the Civil War, Whitman moved to Washington, D.C., where he visited wounded soldiers. He read to them, wrote their letters, and cheered them with his enthusiasm.

Whitman's poetry was better received after the Civil War, and especially in Europe. Before his death in 1892, he published five more editions of *Leaves of Grass,* including the masterpiece, "When Lilacs Last in the Dooryard Bloom'd."

Joseph Pulitzer

J oseph Pulitzer (1847–1911) was a Hungarian youth of 17 when he emigrated to the United States in 1864 to fulfill his ambition to become a soldier. He served in a Union regiment at the end of the Civil War.

The first part of Pulitzer's remarkable journalism career was spent in St. Louis. After becoming a prominent politician there, he bought two St. Louis newpapers in 1878 and combined them to form the *St. Louis Post-Dispatch*. His editorial judgment turned this newspaper into one of the most influential in the Midwest.

In 1883, Pulitzer purchased the *New York World* from Jay Gould. He made it instantly popular with sensational crime stories, cartoons, bold headlines, and photographs. To compete with William Randolph Hearst's *Evening Journal,* Pulitzer cut the price of the *World* to one cent.

The editorial policies of the *World* were raised to a high standard in the first decade of the twentieth century. It consistently championed liberal and progressive reforms for making American life more democratic. Pulitzer's influence continued after his death. He bequeathed part of his vast fortune to founding a school of journalism and to honoring outstanding Americans with Pulitzer prizes.

Research Assignment: Have students interested in American literature study the works of Walt Whitman and analyze those poems that in some way reflect political or social concerns or events of his period of history.

PROFILES OF THE PRESIDENCY

Rutherford Hayes's philosophy was "He serves his party best who serves his country best":

Fifty-five years old today! Lucy absent, gone to New York. My official life in the Presidency has so far been successful, in the main, and happy. The country does seem to be coming back to the ancient concord; and good people approve what I am trying to do. . . . I must resolve on this birthday to do better in the future than ever before.

With good health and great opportunities, may I not hope to confer great and lasting benefit on my country? I mean to try. Let me be kind and considerate in treatment of the unfortunate who crowd my doorway, and firm and conscientious in dealing with the tempters. The Southern question seems to be on a good footing. The currency also. . . . The improvement of the civil service, I must constantly labor for.

—DIARY, OCTOBER 4, 1877

---

black southerners lost the right to vote and other civil liberties. Even the Republicans abandoned the freed people, for the new western states were predominantly Republican, and southern votes were no longer needed to maintain a Republican majority. A final attempt at equality was Senator Charles Sumner's *Civil Rights Act* of 1875. Passed after Sumner's death, the act was much weaker than Sumner had wished.

Hayes's "Lily-Whites." The final blow to Reconstruction policies came when Rutherford B. Hayes was elected president in 1876. He had run against Samuel J. Tilden, a Democrat. Tilden had won a majority of the popular vote and appeared to have swept the electoral college vote by 204 to 165.

Party leaders quickly realized that Hayes could gain the majority of electoral votes if they could switch the electoral votes of the three southern states they still controlled: South Carolina, Florida, and Louisiana. Party officials in those states immediately declared that Hayes had carried their states and won the presidency by one electoral vote, 185 to 184. Another set of returns showed that Tilden had won.

To resolve the problem, a commission was established to determine which set was valid. The commission voted on party lines to accept the

Hayes returns. Thus, he won the presidency and almost caused another North/South rift.

However, at a series of meetings, a group of northern and southern politicians and businessmen agreed informally to what was called the Compromise of 1877. The South agreed to go along with the electoral vote, making Hayes president. Some conservative southerners also agreed to build a "lily-white" Republican party in the South, based on views they shared with northern conservatives. In return, Hayes removed federal troops from the South. Reconstruction was now over.

SECTION REVIEW

1. Write a sentence to identify Liberal Republicans; "Lily-Whites"; Civil Rights Act of 1875; South Carolina, Florida, and Louisiana in 1876.

2. What group of Republicans voted against President Grant in 1872? Explain why.

3. Describe how the actions of President Grant and his successor, Rutherford B. Hayes, contributed to southern blacks' loss of political rights and civil liberties. What was the Compromise of 1877? What were some of the agreements?

CHAPTER REVIEW

TIME LINE

1860

Morrill Tariff (1861)

Pacific Railways Act (1862)

Homestead Act (1862)

Morrill Land Grant Act (1862)

Wade-Davis Bill (1864)

1865

Johnson's Reconstruction Proclamation (1865)

Thirteenth Amendment ratified (1865)

Ex parte Milligan (1866)

Ku Klux Klan founded (1866)

1870

Tenure of Office Act (1867)

Johnson impeached (1868)

Fourteenth Amendment ratified (1868)

Ulysses Grant inaugurated (1869)

Fifteenth Amendment ratified (1870)

1875

Grant reelected (1872)

Rutherford B. Hayes inaugurated (1877)

Reconstruction ends (1877)

1880

TIME LINE QUESTIONS

1. In which year were two acts passed that would lead to the eventual formation of new western states?
2. Between what two events on the time line would you insert Andrew Johnson's accession to the presidency?
3. What court decision in 1866 led to a change in the Constitution?

SKILLS STRATEGY

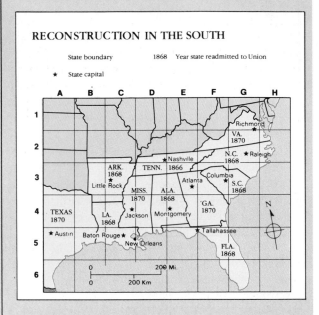

RECONSTRUCTION IN THE SOUTH

State boundary   1868 Year state readmitted to Union

★ State capital

ATLAS REFERENCES

An *atlas* is a collection of maps. The text of a history book tells the reader what happened. An atlas shows the reader exactly where the events occurred, and makes the text more realistic.

The map above shows the South after the Civil War. Like all maps in an atlas, this map has a grid made up of squares that are identified by letters and numbers. The grid, when used with the atlas *gazetteer* (an index of place names at the back of an atlas), helps you to find a place on the map. Notice the sample gazetteer below. Beside each place name goes a letter and number reference to a square on the map grid. For example, Atlanta can be found in square E-3.

APPLYING SKILLS

Use the map above to complete this gazetteer with the correct letter and number references.

Atlanta	E 3	Montgomery	__ __
Austin	__ __	Nashville	__ __
Baton Rouge	__ __	Raleigh	__ __
Columbia	__ __	Richmond	__ __
Jackson	__ __	Tallahassee	__ __
Little Rock	__ __		

Making Connections: Review the questions and topics presented in the Making Connections section that opens this chapter.

UNIT 4 TEST

CHAPTER SURVEY

In one or two sentences, summarize the content of the chapters from which these terms come, and write a sentence to identify *one* of the terms from each chapter.

1. *Chapter 13: The Impending Crisis,* the peculiar institution, chattel property, *The Liberator,* Angelina Grimké.
2. *Chapter 14:* Wilmot Proviso, Alamo, "Oregon or Bust," Bear Flag Republic, Harpers Ferry.
3. *Chapter 15:* Jefferson Davis, Johnny Reb, Billy Yank, the *Monitor,* "the butcher," John Wilkes Booth.
4. *Chapter 16:* Radical Republicans, black codes, Fourteenth Amendment, carpetbaggers, "Lily-Whites."

TEXT REVIEW

5. Verify this statement with facts: "It is incorrect to say that all slaves passively accepted their lot in life."
6. Explain and evaluate *three* of the following arguments of the "positive good" theory: religious, historical and cultural, educational, racial, sociological.
7. Describe the approach to abolition exemplified by each of the following: Theodore Dwight Weld, James G. Birney, William Lloyd Garrison, Sojourner Truth.
8. Name four western areas that became states of the Union before 1860. Explain why the admission of western states was bitterly disputed by northerners and southerners.
9. Explain why President Polk's declaration of war against Mexico was popular with many of the American people. What were the results of this war?
10. Why is the election of 1860 considered a turning point in United States history?
11. Name the eleven Confederate states, their president, and their capital city. What action of the Confederacy began the Civil War?
12. What is the significance of these dates and locations: April 9, 1865, at Appomattox, Virginia, and April 18, 1865, at Durham, North Carolina; April 14, 1865, in Washington, D.C.

13. Name or describe three changes made in domestic policy by Congress during the Civil War. Explain why southerners would have opposed them if they had stayed in Congress.
14. Explain the reconstruction plan proposed by each of the following: President Lincoln, the Wade-Davis Bill, the Radical Republicans.
15. Which reconstruction plan was put into operation? What short-term and long-term effects did this plan have on the civil and political rights of southern blacks?
16. What events in the first administration of President Grant caused the Liberal Republicans to become disillusioned? How did their disillusionment contribute to the end of Reconstruction in the South?

CRITICAL THINKING

17. Summarize the negative conditions under which southern slaves were forced to live, indicating what, in your view, was their greatest deprivation.
18. Make a three-column chart with these headings: *Thirteenth Amendment, Fourteenth Amendment, Fifteenth Amendment.* Then, list each of the following under the appropriate heading: Confederate leaders must be pardoned by Congress; voting rights guaranteed to all citizens; southern states had to ratify before readmission to Union; ended slavery; equal citizenship guaranteed to all persons born or naturalized in the United States.

SKILLS REVIEW

19. Decide whether the following is an excerpt from an editorial or a news story, and explain your decision.

    "Those members of the House of Representatives who voted to impeach President Johnson yesterday should hang their heads in shame. Not only have they shown their own ineptness as leaders, but they have brought disgrace upon the nation."
20. In an atlas, where would you find symbols like the following: D7, I3, B10? How would you use these symbols?

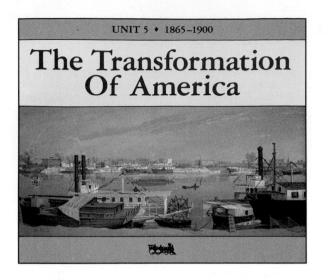

UNIT 5 • 1865–1900

The Transformation Of America

Unit Five Overview

Unit 5 takes students through the period between the end of the Civil War and 1900—an era of expansion and progress, as well as setbacks, in the development of technology and inventions; transportation and cities; industry, big business, and labor; and local and national government. The last chapter points out the growing pains that accompanied these enormous changes.

Basic Unit Concepts

1. Between 1865 and 1900, aided by the ingenuity of American inventors and entrepreneurs, the American nation transformed itself from a largely agrarian society to a first-rate industrial power.
2. During this period, the rapid expansion of rail transportation and the phenomenal growth of industry was sometimes accompanied by greed and corruption of "robber barons" whose power the federal government would not or could not control effectively.
3. Corruption and a "politics as business" attitude were the hallmarks of city, state, and national governments of the times, and although reforms were attempted by some groups, this brand of politics seemed to suit most voters.
4. As the United States was changing, tensions developed between different groups: the very wealthy and citizens of ordinary means, business owners and managers and labor unions, immigrants and long-time Americans; and the problems of growing cities cried for solution.

Chapter 17: "America Becomes an Industrial Nation" (1865–1900)

In Chapter 17, students follow the transition of the United States from an agricultural to an industrial nation between 1865 and 1900. They witness the impressive consolidation of the railroads into a transcontinental transportation system. They learn of the development of the food, steel, and oil industries and survey the inventors and inventions that contributed to this development. They recognize the role of greed and corruption in the growth of some industries, and they examine the supportive and restrictive responses of the federal government to the powerful new industrial leaders.

Features

Going to the Source: Excerpt from an article by Ida Tarbell (page 426)
Movers and Shapers: George Washington Carver and Thomas Edison (page 429)
American Ingenuity chart (pages 432–433)

Learning Objectives

History Generalizations Students will gain knowledge that supports the following generalizations:

1. A stable political environment, foreign and domestic capital, large pools of labor, and a great abundance of natural resources all contributed to changing the United States from an agrarian to an industrial nation between the end of the Civil War and 1900.
2. In the same period, population doubled, the number of states increased to 45, and industrial wealth increased more than six times, placing the United States first among the industrial nations.
3. The vastness of the United States, the one handicap to industrial development, was overcome by the building of, first, regional railroads and, finally, transcontinental lines.
4. The genius of American inventors and entrepreneurs led to the development of the food, steel, and oil industries, among others.
5. The federal government encouraged the building of the railroads and industry with favorable legislation and other actions.
6. Greed and corruption often accompanied the building of the railroads and the development of industry.
7. Responding to public pressure, Congress passed legislation meant to curb corruption and excessive power of industrial leaders.

Study Skills In addition to the three skills noted in chapter 1 which are standard to every chapter, students will:

1. gain information by reading and comparing thematic maps showing historical developments.
2. write a paragraph including sentences giving details that support an opinion stated in the topic sentence.
3. relate graphic materials to the text of the chapter.
4. practice these **critical thinking skills**: generating questions about materials to be read, supporting opinions, recognizing propaganda.

Chapter 18: "Politics and Politicians" (1868–1896)

Chapter 18 discusses a new kind of politics at the local and national levels between 1868 and 1896—corrupt city machines such as that headed by Boss Tweed in New York City, the "politics as business" philosophy of both local and national politicians, the scandals caused by dishonesty in the Grant administration, the doling out of patronage, the acquiescence of the voters, and the response to all this as seen through the eyes of political cartoonists of the times. The last section of the chapter surveys the important national political issues of the era.

Features

Profiles of the Presidency: James A. Garfield (page 449), Chester A. Arthur (page 451), Grover Cleveland (page 452), Benjamin Harrison (page 453)

Learning Objectives

History Generalizations Students will gain knowledge that supports the following generalizations:

1. In the last half of the nineteenth century, the political machines that took over American big city governments introduced political corruption and politics as business to the American scene.
2. In national politics during the same period, corrupt practices were common, most notably during the first Grant administration.
3. Reform was attempted at both city and national levels and succeeded, but only for brief interludes because this brand of city and national politics suited the voters of the time.
4. The national goals of both the Republican and Democratic parties were much the same—to get into power and stay in power in order to distribute the spoils-of-victory patronage.
5. The two national parties remained evenly matched throughout the period, largely because of emerging voting patterns in different regions and among some social classes.
6. The big issues in national politics included the tariff, the backing of American currency with gold, and relations with American neighbors and Great Britain.
7. The lines of division over these national issues were not so much between the Republican and Democratic parties as within them.

Study Skills In addition to the three skills noted in chapter 1 which are standard to every chapter, students will:

1. interpret political cartoons.
2. write a paragraph contrasting two given elements.
3. relate graphic materials to the text of the chapter.
4. practice these **critical thinking skills**: generating questions about materials to be read, recognizing different viewpoints, hypothesizing.

Chapter 19: "Growing Pains" (1865–1900)

In Chapter 19, students contrast the ostentatious lives of the newly wealthy industrial leaders and their families with the lives of working class families whose response to the flaunting of the new wealth was ambivalent. Students examine the arguments of the defenders and detractors of the very rich. They follow the turbulent rise of labor unions in response to wages, hours, and general working conditions of the times. They recognize the prejudice that often greeted immigrants. Finally, they examine the positive and negative aspects of the growth of American cities.

Features

Movers and Shapers: A. Montgomery Ward, Richard Sears, and Alvah Roebuck (page 473); Jane Addams and Florence Kelly (page 480)

Learning Objectives

History Generalizations Students will gain knowledge that supports the following generalizations:

1. The period from 1865–1900 was a time of painful growth in the United States.
2. New wealth that resulted from the growth in industry formed what was perceived as an aristocracy that threatened the American ideals of economic democracy and the "gospel" of hard work.
3. The increase in industry was accompanied by the growth of factories with generally low wages, long hours, poor physical working conditions, and negative psychological effects for the men, women, and children who worked in them.
4. Dissatisfaction with wages, hours, and working conditions led to the gradual, often stormy, development of labor unions—from the early radical unions to the more conservative American Federation of Labor.
5. Starting in 1800, the national origin of immigrants changed from a predominance of Northern and Western Europeans to a growing number of people from Southern and Eastern Europe and Asia, the latter groups not welcomed by all Americans.
6. By 1900, an influx of New Immigrants and dissatisfied farm people contributed to the striking increase in the growth of cities and metropolises in the United States.
7. Along with their advantages, the cities and metropolises had problems which city governments, private groups, and individuals made attempts to solve.

Study Skills In addition to the three skills noted in chapter 1 which are standard to every chapter, students will:

1. summarize information and draw conclusions.
2. relate graphic materials to the text of the chapter.
3. practice these **critical thinking skills**: generating questions about materials to be read, recognizing viewpoint, summarizing information, drawing conclusions.

Quotation: from *Leaves of Grass.* Other works by Walt Whitman (1819–1892) include *Drum Taps, Democratic Vistas, Memoranda During the War, Two Rivulets, Specimen Days and Collect, November Boughs,* and *Goodbye, My Fancy.*

CHAPTER 17

AN INDUSTRIAL NATION

1865–1900

Mark the spirit of invention everywhere, thy rapid patents,
Thy continual workshops, foundries, risen or rising,
See, from their chimneys how the tall flame-fires stream.

WALT WHITMAN

Making Connections. At the end of the Civil War, the United States was still largely a farming nation. Yet between 1865 and 1900, it became the world's leading industrial power. By the 1890s, several industries were so large that the federal government took steps to control them. How did this rapid change in the country happen? What industries led the transformation of America?

In this chapter, you will learn:

- Why the size of the United States was an obstacle to its development
- Why the government gave the railroad owners an area larger than France or Belgium
- Who the robber barons were and how they got their power
- How vertical and horizontal integration made Andrew Carnegie and John D. Rockefeller rich
- What famous inventor took out more than 1,000 patents
- How corporations gained the rights of human beings but avoided the responsibilities

You have read that American inventions such as the telegraph and the cotton gin brought changes in the way Americans lived and worked. After the Civil War, Americans once more turned to building a strong nation. As you read, notice how inventions and discoveries caused explosive growth in many industries between 1865 and 1900.

Sections
1. Growth and Technology
2. The Food Industry
3. Steel and Oil
4. American Inventors
5. Big Business

1. GROWTH AND TECHNOLOGY

Putting the Civil War behind them, Americans faced the future and started an era that would see a basically agrarian, or farming, society become a modern industrial nation. With the Civil War over, the United States again achieved a stable political environment. As a result, both foreign and domestic *capital,* or money, became available for investment. Having vast stretches of usable land, large pools of *labor,* and seemingly unlimited *natural resources,* the United States found itself to be the right country, at the right place, at the right time. Growth seemed inevitable.

An Era of Movement, Growth, and Progress.

The period between 1865 and 1900 was an era of rapid growth and rushing progress. Immigrants poured into the United States from all over Europe. Both immigrants and native-born Americans spread out over the West and settled more land in one generation than had been settled during all the years since 1607. Between 1865 and 1900, the population of the United States more than doubled, from fewer than 36 million people to 76 million people. Including the former Confederacy, there were 36 states in 1865. By 1900, there were 45.

The second half of the nineteenth century was a time of rapid industrial growth in the United States. New factories sprang up in towns such as the one pictured on the next page.

413

The wealth of the American people grew even more rapidly than the population. At the end of the Civil War, the annual production of goods was valued at $2 billion. It increased more than six times in 35 years, to $13 billion in 1900. At the center of this burst of activity was the machine.

America Becomes an Industrial Nation.

Even in 1860, the United States had been a major industrial power, the fifth largest in the world with more than 140,000 factories capitalized at $1 billion. But before the Civil War the United States was still a farmers' country. Not only did more than 70 percent of the people live on farms or in small farm towns, but even more thought in the traditional terms of the farmers, and the majority of politicians catered to their point of view. In 1860, scarcely more than 1.5 million people worked in industrial jobs. Because many of them were women and children who did not vote, factory workers were an insignificant political force, scarcely more important to policy makers than were black people or Indians.

By 1877, this was rapidly changing. In that year, a nationwide *strike* by railway workers shook the nation to its foundations, and more upheavals were to come. By 1900, $8 billion was invested in American factories, and 5.5 million people worked in industrial jobs. During the first years of the 1890s, the industrial production of the United States surpassed that of Great Britain to put the United States in first place in the world, a position it still holds today.

By 1900 the American people understood that, for good or ill, they lived in an industrial, capitalist nation and no longer in an agrarian republic. Their fate was rooted more deeply in black coal and red iron than in the soil.

America's Awesome Geography.

In only one respect was the United States handicapped in its drive toward massive industrial development. The very vastness of the country, the reason for its bountiful supply of resources, was an obstacle. In England, the first industrial nation, a manufacturer could easily assemble raw materials, and the market for everything from heavy machinery to hairpins was concentrated in a relatively small area. But the United States spanned a continent and was divided by rivers, mountains, and deserts into regions as large as some countries. If nature had had the last word, the United States would have remained a patchwork of self-dependent manufacturing areas, in which small local factories produced goods only for the people of the vicinity. Indeed, this is a fair description of manufacturing in the United States through the Civil War period.

The Railroads.

The steam railroad conquered America's awesome geography. The steam-powered locomotive made it possible for steel-makers in Pittsburgh, Pennsylvania, to bring together the coal of Scranton, Pennsylvania, and the iron of the Mesabi Range of Minnesota as though the mines of both regions were just across the county line. Thanks to the railroad, the great steam-powered flour mills of Minneapolis, Minnesota, were able to scoop up the cheap spring wheat of the distant Northwest, grind it into flour, and put their trademarked sacks into every cupboard in the country.

As a result of the Kansas-Nebraska Act, most western railroads found their way into Chicago, Illinois. It was only a matter of time before Chicago became the meatpacking center of America. Livestock fattened on a distant range rolled into Chicago alive in railroad cars. Once in Chicago, the livestock would be butchered and packed in cans, barrels, and refrigerated cars. Then the meat would be shipped by rail to the East Coast, and from there, around the world.

Regional Railroads.

By 1865, the United States was already the world's leading railway country, with about 35 *systems*, integrated lines that tied together distant regions. With the exception of the Baltimore and Ohio and the Erie railroads, American rail lines had been built by entrepreneurs who thought in regional terms. They had constructed their lines to connect two nearby cities, or they had run tracks from a city into the surrounding countryside. While useful, such "feeder" lines reinforced the traditional local patterns of commerce rather than encouraging the development of factories with national and international markets.

Thus the older, more populous regions of the country where immediate profits were to be had were criss-crossed by railroads. Sparsely settled areas, where there were only potential profits, had

Discussion Question: How did the Civil War, and those issues leading up to it, help promote the expansion of railroads? Two things that could be cited are the issue of a transcontinental railroad before the war as a unifying/sectionalist factor and the North's extensive use of railroads during the war.

414

In small towns throughout the United States, railroad depots were centers of town activity.

few, if any, lines. The result was continued isolation in the central part of the country, and fierce, often destructive competition in the densely populated Northeast and South.

The first generation of American railroads was inefficient because few independent companies linked up with one another. The lines went to the same towns, but did not use the same tracks. Goods being shipped over long distances, and therefore on several lines, had to be unloaded at one terminal, carted across town by horse and wagon to another terminal, and reloaded onto another train. In Richmond, Virginia, none of the six railroads shared a common depot. Before the Civil War, Chicago and New York were linked by rail on the map, but a cargo going the entire distance had to be unloaded and reloaded as many as six times.

Still another problem was created by differences in *gauges,* or the distance between the rails. Every independent railroad was free to lay track at whatever gauge they chose, and of course bought locomotives and cars that fit the tracks. This meant that one company's trains could not be run on another company's tracks.

Railroad Consolidation.

It became clear to many Americans that something would have to be done if railroads were to serve the national economy efficiently. The advantages of long consolidated lines seemed obvious to a number of forceful businesspeople. Some of them rose to the challenge of railroad *consolidation* and became the first American big businesspeople. The goal of these railroaders was to bring technological and economic order to American transportation, and to become personally rich in the process. A handful of these *capitalists* achieved both goals in a relatively short period of time.

The Big Railroad Builders.

J. Edgar Thompson pieced together the Pennsylvania Railroad by secretly purchasing stock in small lines in Pennsylvania and Ohio and, once in a commanding position, by declaring all-out *rate wars* against the companies that resisted his takeover attempts. Thompson was all business, a no-nonsense efficiency expert with little celebrity outside his offices.

The founder of the New York Central, the Pennsylvania's chief rival in the Northeast, was

Cornelius Vanderbilt. Vanderbilt built an efficient and safe railroad. In doing so, however, he frequently acted in a ruthless manner. Like many of the great capitalists of the era, he regarded his fortune—$100 million when he died—as adequate justification for what he did.

Another railroad, the Erie, was controlled by Daniel Drew, James Fisk, and Jay Gould. These three men were notorious for their dishonesty and lack of concern for public safety.

The *Big Four* of California were the most powerful of the railroad barons. Collis P. Huntington, Leland Stanford, Mark Hopkins, and Charles Crocker had been well-to-do merchants in California when, in 1862, partly through luck and partly because Huntington was a quick man with a payoff, they won the concession for the Central Pacific, one of the companies that built the first transcontinental railroad. Almost overnight, the four became the bosses of the growing state of California. The successors of the Big Four sometimes used the railroad's leverage to drive small farmers and ranchers out of business.

To some people, the very existence of the big railroads was proof of the greatness of their builders. But to other people, these builders were *robber barons*, or people who became rich by unethical means.

Financing a Transcontinental Railroad.

The small population between eastern Kansas and California made it impossible to attract private investment to construct a transcontinental railroad. With no customers along the way, there would be no profits and, without profits, no investors. However, because the federal government had political and military interests in binding California and Oregon to the rest of the Union, there was a way out of this dilemma. In federally held land, the *public domain*, the government had the means with which to subsidize railroad construction. In 1862, Congress had committed the American people to underwriting the construction of a transcontinental line by giving away large amounts of this land.

The Pacific Railway Act of 1862 granted to two companies, the Union Pacific and the Central Pacific, a right of way 200 feet (60 meters) wide between Omaha, Nebraska, and Sacramento, California. For each mile of track that the companies

With thousands of miles of new track being laid, railroads began advertising new routes.

built, they were to receive, on both sides of the tracks, ten alternate sections (square miles) of the public domain. The result was a checkerboard-pattern belt of land 40 miles (64 kilometers) wide, of which the Union Pacific and Central Pacific owned half. The rest was reserved for disposition by the government under the Homestead Act or by direct government sale.

Building the Transcontinental Railroad.

As in the consolidation of eastern trunk lines, the business end of the transcontinental railroad was marred by gross *corruption*. However, the actual construction of the line was a heroic and glorious feat. The Union Pacific, employing thousands of Civil War veterans and newly immigrated Irish

Thousands of Chinese immigrants helped build the Central Pacific Railroad.

pick-and-shovel workers, laid over 1,000 miles (1,600 kilometers) of track. The workers lived in shifting cities of tents and freight cars built like dormitories.

The builders of the Central Pacific had trouble with the Sierra Nevada Mountains. There were high passes in the mountains through which the line could snake, but they were narrow and steep. The workers—10,000 Chinese immigrants organized in cruelly disciplined work gangs—had to chip ledges into the slopes, build roadbeds of rubble in deep canyons, construct trestles out of huge wood girders, and mine their way through granite when there was no way around.

The Union Pacific and Central Pacific joined at Promontory Point, Utah, on May 10, 1869. An American dream had been fulfilled.

Expanding the National Rail System. Having made multimillionaires of its owners, the land grants to the first transcontinental railroad encouraged other groups to seek similar subsidies. In 1864, Congress authorized the construction of the Northern Pacific Railroad from Lake Superior to Puget Sound. The Northern Pacific's grant was doubly generous. In the territories through which the railroad would be built, the company received 40 alternate sections for every mile built. By the 1870s, under the control of a German immigrant, Henry Villard, the Northern Pacific owned half the acreage in a land belt 80 miles (128 kilometers) wide! It was completed in 1883, connecting Duluth, Minnesota, to Portland, Oregon, and Tacoma, Washington.

The next year, two more lines of track joined

big business toward their employees? How did it reflect their attitudes toward race? Do these last two items give a negative view of business? Why or why not?

On May 10, 1869, at Promontory Point, Utah, an ambitious idea became a reality because of the industriousness of American immigrants: the transcontinental railroad was completed.

the two coasts, and a third was completed just across the Canadian border. The Atchison, Topeka, and Santa Fe Railroad ran from Kansas to Los Angeles, California. Also completed in 1884, the Texas Pacific Railroad and the Southern Pacific Railroad came to an arrangement in El Paso, Texas, that made it possible to ship freight straight through from New Orleans, Louisiana, to San Francisco, California. In the same year, the Canadians (who were even more generous with government land) completed the first of their two transcontinental lines, the Canadian Pacific Railroad. There had never been such an expenditure of effort and wealth for one purpose in so short a time.

The costs were considerable. The federal government gave the *land-grant* railroads a total of 131 million acres (53 million hectares) of land. The state governments added 45 million acres (18 million hectares). This amounted to an area larger than that of France and Belgium combined. In addition, towns along the proposed routes enticed the builders to choose them as depot sites by offering land, money, and tax exemptions.

These gifts were not always offered with a glad hand. If a railroad bypassed a town, that town frequently died. Aware of this, railroaders did not hesitate to set communities against one another. The Atchison, Topeka, and Santa Fe, popularly known as "the Santa Fe," did not even enter the city of Santa Fe. Nearby Albuquerque, New Mexico, offered the better deal and got the depot.

Greed and Corruption. In the Mississippi Valley, farmers discovered that the coming of the railroad did not necessarily mean prosperity. In most parts of the West, there was no competition among railroads; one line handled all the traffic. As a result, the railroad could charge whatever it wished to ship wheat, corn, or livestock to mar-

Class Activity: Set up a panel debate on the topic, Industrial Practices for All Industries, Mercenary or Moral? Confine the material to the time period covered in this chapter. Have one panel of students defend industry practices and another criticize them. Have all members of the class observing the proceedings decide whether industry was mercenary or moral. Some of the issues kets. Farmers often saw their margin of profit consumed to the penny in transportation costs.

Most infuriating to the farmers was the railroads' control of storage facilities, the grain elevators that stood close to the depot in every railway town. The farmer had to pay the company storage fees until the railroad sent a train to haul away the grain. It was often in the railroad's interests to delay scheduling a train as long as possible.

The Interstate Commerce Commission.

Abuses of power and the general corruption of many railroad officials resulted in attempts to have laws passed that would regulate the railroad industry. In 1887, the *Interstate Commerce Act* was enacted by Congress. On the face of it, the law brought the national railroads under control. Excessive rates were outlawed, and Congress created an independent regulatory commission, the *Interstate Commerce Commission* (ICC), to keep an eye on railroad charges.

However, the act did not forbid *mergers* or *interlocking directorates,* both of which were far more effective means of avoiding competition than were the informal pools. Moreover, the Commission was given little real power; it had to take its decisions to the same courts that had favored the railroads over the state legislatures; within a few years railroaders and lawyers friendly to them held a majority of seats on the ICC.

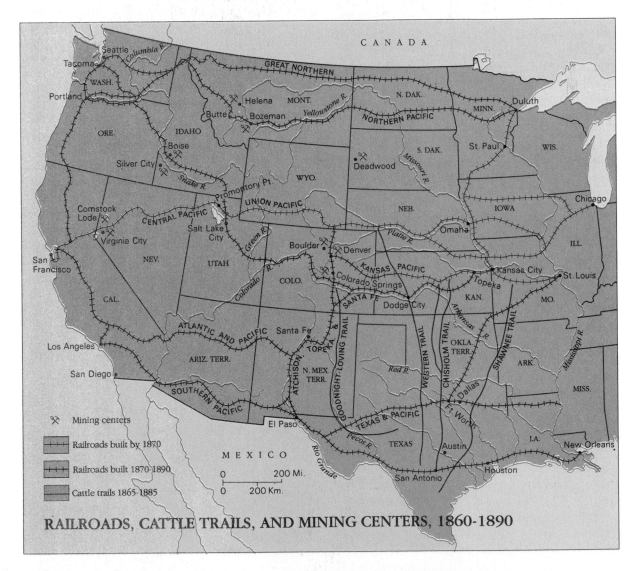

RAILROADS, CATTLE TRAILS, AND MINING CENTERS, 1860-1890

the debate should touch upon are benefits provided to society, business self-interest and its negative effects on society, monopolies, treatment of the worker and salaries, and business as a provider of employment for the masses.

The Money Power. By the early 1890s, the trunk lines of the country had been consolidated into seven great systems. By 1900, even these had fallen under the effective control of two large New York investment banks, J. P. Morgan and Company and Kuhn, Loeb and Company. The latter was in partnership with Union Pacific president Edward H. Harriman.

Because every large railroad needed financial help at one time or another—every transcontinental but the Great Northern went *bankrupt* during the *depression* of 1893–1897—Morgan's and Kuhn and Loeb's men soon sat on every major corporate board, creating an interlocking directorate. Like all bankers, their goal was a steady, dependable flow of profit, and their means to that end was to eliminate wasteful competition.

Banker control had its beneficial side. No more did *unscrupulous* pirates like Drew, Fisk, and Gould of the Erie Railroad ruin great transportation systems for the sake of short-term financial gains. The integration of the nation's railways resulted in a gradual but significant lowering of fares and freight rates.

But the control of so important a part of the economy by only a few people reminded Americans of some of their very basic ideals. Where was individual freedom and opportunity, many people asked, when a sinister "money power" headed by the imperious J. P. Morgan could decide on a whim the fate of millions of farmers and working people?

SECTION REVIEW

1. Write a sentence to identify: agrarian, robber barons, Promontory Point, "money power."

2. Explain how the character of the United States changed between 1860 and 1900.

3. Give two examples of how the steam railroad conquered America's awesome geography.

4. Name at least two of the entrepreneurs who consolidated America's regional railroads, and describe their dual goal.

5. Tell why the ICC was formed, and give several reasons it proved to be ineffective.

---

2. THE FOOD INDUSTRY

Technology and the *entrepreneurial* spirit reached into the American home as they never had before during the latter part of the nineteenth century. Several inventors and business organizers devised new ways to process food that altered American patterns of marketing and cooking and, within a generation, changed the way Americans ate.

Gail Borden. The first of these remakers of food was Gail Borden (1801–1874). Living on the Texas frontier, Borden was aware of the monotony of the diets of overland travelers, and he began to experiment with ways to preserve and make more portable one of the most perishable and bulky foods, milk. Borden's solution was condensation and canning. In 1856, he took out a patent on a process for evaporating milk in a vacuum and preserving the product in cans. Union soldiers in the Civil War did not find Borden's condensed milk particularly tasty, but it was milk and it was

The women below, employees of H. J. Heinz, hand-wrapped cans of preserved food.

Research Assignment: Have students create a flowchart of the processing system of one of the industries discussed in this chapter. For example, they can look at the process of making condensed milk and chart the steps involved. Models should be supplemented by photos if possible.

healthful, too, as many military rations were not. Back home again, they continued to use it because, except on the farm where cows could be milked daily, that perishable food was risky eating. Before the pasteurization process, which came to the United States only at the end of the century, uncanned milk was the source of numerous serious diseases.

H. J. Heinz.

H. J. Heinz of Pittsburgh, Pennsylvania, calculated that by using industrial methods, he could make preserved foods such as were put up in many American homes, and sell them at prices that would tempt buyers, particularly in the cities, to forgo the tedious task of canning. He went bankrupt once but stuck by his idea, canning and bottling pickles, vegetables, fruits, and the mainstay of his prosperous company, ketchup. Before Heinz, the word *ketchup* referred to any number of sauces and relishes. Only after the success of Heinz's tomato ketchup did Americans forget about the others.

Processing America's Staples.

Much more fundamental was the revolution in processing America's staples—wheat flour and meat. The bread and fresh meat that Americans ate had always come from the region in which they lived. Local or regional millers received the grain from farmers and ground it into flour, returning some to the grower and selling the rest. The butcher shops in every town and city were also slaughterhouses. Without refrigeration, the only fresh meat was meat that had been on the hoof a day or two earlier in the butcher's backyard.

The railroad was the key to changing this. Reaching westward into lands where wheat and livestock could be grown on a larger scale and, therefore, much more cheaply than in the East, the trains funneled grain and cattle into Minneapolis-St. Paul, Chicago, St. Louis, and other cities that had railroad connections with the East Coast. In the transfer cities, gigantic processing companies such as General Mills, Ralston, Purina, Swift, Armour, Wilson, and Cudahy, turned the raw materials into consumer goods.

Flour.

Using huge steam-driven steel rollers instead of the slow and cumbersome water-

Grain grown in the Midwest was shipped by rail to other parts of the country. Huge grain elevators like the one above were used for storage.

powered grindstones, the great *milling* corporations were able to undersell and quickly destroy local millers almost everywhere in the country. Their flour did not spoil because the living germ had been *refined* out of it. Although refined flour was fine and white, and therefore considered a much more elegant baking ingredient than previously had been available to ordinary people, it was, as numerous critics pointed out then and in the twentieth century, far less nutritious than unrefined flour.

Packaged Meat.

Chicago was the center of the new meatpacking industry. From vast corrals in the yards of the western railroads, cattle and hogs were processed by applying industrial methods to slaughtering and butchering. The mass-produced meat sold so cheaply in the East that the combination slaughterhouse-butcher shop became a thing of the past.

The pioneers of centralized meatpacking were Gustavus Swift and Philip D. Armour. Armour perfected the "disassembly line," a continuously

Pioneers in the centralized meatpacking business, such as Philip Armour and Gustavus Swift, had to overcome consumer resistance to the idea of buying meat that was more than a day or two old. One approach was to advertise. Colorful posters like the one above were distributed throughout potential markets in an attempt to win customers.

moving chain in which hogs ran in one end under their own power, and pork packed for retailing came out the other. Armour kept his prices down by using what previously had been waste: bones, blood, hides, and even bristle (which was made into hairbrushes). It was said that he made money on every part of the pig but its squeal, and he was working on that.

Gustavus Swift pioneered the use of ice and, later, refrigerated railroad cars to ship fresh sides of beef from Chicago to the East Coast. He had to overcome popular suspicions of any meat from animals that had been slaughtered more than a few days before the meat was set on the table, and the resistance of local butchers. By opening his own

shops in the major eastern cities and underselling even locally raised steers with his Texas, Wyoming, and Montana beef, Swift had his way. Other meatpackers soon followed his example.

By the end of the nineteenth century, a middle class family in Portland, Maine, would likely sit down to a loaf of bread baked with flour from Minneapolis, a beefsteak from Chicago seasoned with ketchup from Pittsburgh, and oranges from Florida or California for dessert. Vegetables alone were local, and were canned at home for storage. It was only in the twentieth century that the food revolutionaries were able to find a way to preserve green vegetables and ship them any considerable distance.

Class Activity: Obtain a copy of Fanny Farmer's *Boston Cooking Cookbook.* Compare the recipes found in it with recipes found in a modern cookbook. If some students would like to try some of these older recipes, encourage them to do so and have them bring in samples for the class.

Fannie Farmer standardized cooking measurements.

Fannie Farmer. Once all of this food was in the American home, it was up to the cook to prepare a tasty meal. Up in Boston, Fannie Merritt Farmer started the Miss Farmer's School of Cookery. More importantly, however, Miss Farmer started the practice of advising the beginning cook to use precise, *standardized* measurements in the preparation of meals. Her recipes were the first to indicate teaspoon, tablespoon, and cup-type measurements. Before then, recipes tended to be written with phrases such as "add a pinch." Miss Farmer's cookbook, the *Boston Cooking School Cookbook*, first published in 1896, remains in print today.

SECTION REVIEW

1. Write a sentence to identify: condensed milk, refined flour, "disassembly line," *Boston Cooking School Cookbook*.

2. Name two of the "food revolutionaries" in the later part of the nineteenth century, and discuss the "revolutions" they led.

3. Describe the role of the railroads in the "revolution" in processing America's food staples.

4. Who was Fannie Merritt Farmer, and what contributions did she make to America's way of eating?

3. STEEL AND OIL

The discovery of an inexpensive method of producing steel revolutionized American industry. Oil, a new source of fuel used to run machinery, also had a great impact. The rise of the oil and steel industries turned the United States into a highly industrialized nation.

The Steel Industry. Steel is much stronger than iron per unit of weight. Produced in quantity, steel could be used in buildings, bridges, and, of particular interest in the late nineteenth century, superior rails for railroad tracks. By the Civil War period, two ironmakers, Henry Bessemer of England and William "Pig Iron" Kelly of Kentucky, working independently developed a method to make steel in quantity at a reasonable price. Cheaper steel would become the essential building material in the explosive growth of the United States.

Andrew Carnegie. Andrew Carnegie saw the business possibilities that would come from this new technology, and he built the country's largest steel factory. Once the factory was operational, Carnegie paid particular attention to one area of his business—costs. Cutting costs was the heart of his business method. Slash expenses, Carnegie said, and profits would take care of themselves.

Andrew Carnegie expanded the steel industry.

"Forging the Shaft," painted by John Weir, reflected the rise of heavy industry.

PRODUCTION OF RAW STEEL

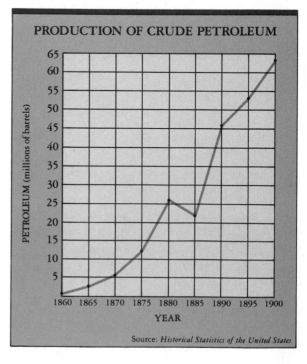

PRODUCTION OF CRUDE PETROLEUM

Class Activity: Have students compile a chart of the 500 largest companies in 1890 and the Fortune 500 today. Have them see how many are the same, noting that some may have merged with other companies or may have changed their names. They should research what happened to those that don't appear on both lists. How many of the companies are U.S. companies on both lists?

Cost-cutting could be as simple as paring down the wages of workers to the least they would accept without rebelling, or increasing the work hours. Or it could be as complicated as replacing a whole factory with an improved, cheaper technology, and using inventions to make his factories run better and less expensively. Whereas other companies tended to contract during depressions, Carnegie expanded, often buying other companies. He knew that during depressions, the cost of everything was down.

Vertical Integration. Carnegie's fundamental means of reducing costs was the *vertical integration* of the steel business. Instead of buying iron and coal from independent mining companies, which were often inefficient and had to take their own profit, Carnegie purchased his own iron and coal mines, often taking advantage of bankruptcies. Although he was never completely independent of the trunk-line railways, Carnegie assumed control of as much of his own shipping as he could. By eliminating from his final product price the profits of independent suppliers, distributors, and carriers, Carnegie was able to undersell competing companies that were not vertically integrated, and therefore, had to include the profits of independent suppliers in their final product price.

The Oil Industry. It was the flammability of oil that attracted the attention of the chemist Benjamin Silliman. With the world population of whales declining in the 1850s because of thoughtless overharvesting, he and others were looking for an illuminant to replace whale oil.

During his experiments with *crude oil*, Silliman isolated kerosene, which became a major lighting and heating source. As Silliman showed how to use oil, a former military engineer, Edwin Drake, showed how to get it in quantities large enough for commerce. At Titusville, Pennsylvania, Drake perfected a drill and pump system in 1859 to tap seemingly infinite quantities of crude oil deep within the earth. Drake's breakthrough caused a rush to Titusville much like the California gold rush of 1849. Oil soon became an essential energy source for the machines that were being built. Without oil, the phenomenal industrial growth of the second half of the nineteenth century would not have been possible.

John D. Rockefeller (above) saw the new business possibilities of the oil industry after Edwin Drake proved at Titusville, Pennsylvania (below), that crude oil could successfully be pumped in quantity from deep within the earth.

Research Assignment: Prepare a report on John D. Rockefeller and the Rockefeller family. Note how the role of the Rockefellers changed, in the mind of society, from villain to hero and back again from one period of history to the next. Have students explain the reasons for this.

GOING TO THE SOURCE

The Standard men as a body have nothing to do with public affairs, except as it is necessary to manipulate them for the "good of the oil business." . . .

Ever since 1872 the organization [Standard Oil] has appeared in politics only to oppose legislation obviously for the public good. . . .

From that time to this Mr. Rockefeller has had to fight the best sentiment of the oil country and of the country at large as to what is for the public good. He and his colleagues kept a strong alliance in Washington fighting the Interstate Commerce Bill from the time the first one was introduced in 1876 until the final passage in 1887. Every measure looking to the freedom and equalization of transportation has met his opposition, as have bills for giving greater publicity to the operations of corporations. In many of the great state legislatures one of the first persons to be pointed out to a visitor is the Standard Oil lobbyist. Now, no one can dispute the right of the Standard Oil Company to express its opinions on proposed legislation. It has the same right to do this as all the rest of the world. It is only the character of its opposition which is open to criticism, the fact that it is always fighting measures which equalize privileges and which

And what are we going to do about it, for it is our business? We, the people of the United States, and nobody else, must cure whatever is wrong in the industrial situation, typified by this narrative of the growth of the Standard Oil Company.

IDA TARBELL, "STANDARD OIL"

make it more necessary for men to start fair and play fair in doing business. . . .

And what are we going to do about it, for it is *our* business? We, the people of the United States, and nobody else, must cure whatever is wrong in the industrial situation, typified by this narrative of the growth of the Standard Oil Company. That our first task is to secure free and equal transportation privileges by rail, pipe, and waterway is evident. It is not an easy matter. It is one which may require operations which will seem severe; but the whole system of discrimination has been nothing but violence and those who have profited by it cannot complain if the curing of the evils they have wrought bring hardship in turn on them. At all events, until the transportation matter is settled, and settled right, the monopolistic trust will be with us—a leech on our pockets, a barrier to our free efforts.

The article from which this source was excerpted was written by Ida Tarbell for McClure's magazine in 1903. The article attempted to expose what Tarbell felt were the ruthless business methods of John D. Rockefeller and the Standard Oil Company. This article was one of a series.

John D. Rockefeller. John D. Rockefeller saw the business possibilities of an oil industry and accordingly went on to build the Standard Oil Company. Like Andrew Carnegie, Rockefeller integrated his oil business from top to bottom. His creations, especially the Standard Oil Company, which was to become the first billion-dollar corporation, controlled oil wells, refineries, pipelines, and even retail sales.

Horizontal Integration. Refinery control of most gas stations is a legacy of Rockefeller's vertical integration. But his distinctive innovation in the movement to consolidate American industry was *horizontal integration*, or control of an industry by dominating the *strategic stage* in the flow of manufacture. In the oil industry, that stage was the refining process. *Refining* was open to few people because of the large investment required.

4. AMERICAN INVENTORS

The national transportation system made it possible for entrepreneurs to draw on the resources of the entire country and to market their products in Maine, California, and points in between. Many of the new products were the result of technological breakthroughs by American inventors like Alexander Graham Bell, Christopher Sholes, Thomas Edison, George Westinghouse, Cyrus McCormick, and Elisha Otis.

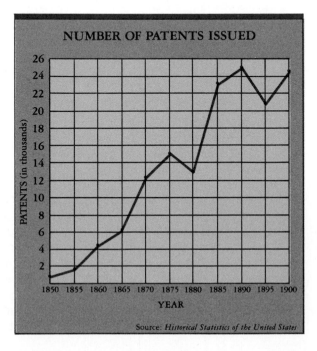

NUMBER OF PATENTS ISSUED

PATENTS (in thousands) / YEAR

Source: *Historical Statistics of the United States*

In 1876, Alexander Graham Bell (seated), demonstrated his new American invention—the telephone.

Alexander Graham Bell. Alexander Graham Bell was the son of a man who was a famous teacher of the deaf. Bell took up his father's work and was instructing teachers of the deaf in Boston in the mid-1870s when he had an idea for a device that would enable some people to hear: a mechanical eardrum made of paper and metal, and powered by low-voltage electricity.

After making his instrument, Bell recognized other possibilities for it. If two of the hearing aids were connected by wire, voices could be transmitted over long distances. Bell successfully tested the telephone early in 1876 and took it to the Centennial Exposition in Philadelphia.

Bell's invention was one of the hits of the show. Millions of people picked up the odd-looking receivers and, alternately giggling and awed, chatted with companions across the room. Scarcely a report on the fair did not dwell on Bell's marvelous toy. But he could not sell it. Western Union, the telegraph company and most likely buyer of a new means of communication, showed no interest whatsoever.

The flurry of inventions and patents coming into the U.S. Patent Office during the late 1800s was astronomical. By 1875 the director of this office recommended that it be closed as he sent in his resignation. He claimed that there was nothing left to invent. 427

Bell was forced to set up his own pilot company in New York, and he saw his "toy" quickly seize the American imagination. President Rutherford B. Hayes put a phone in the White House in 1878. By 1880, only four years after they had first heard of the thing, 50,000 Americans were paying monthly fees to hear it jangle on their walls. By 1890, there were 800,000 telephones in the United States; by 1900, 1.5 million. People in the tiniest hamlets knew all about "exchanges," "party lines," and nasal-voiced "operators."

Many systems were useful only locally. But as early as 1892, eastern and midwestern cities were connected by a long-distance network. Bell's invention became the nervous system of American business, as the railroad was its circulatory system. His American Telephone and Telegraph Company became the most thorough monopoly in American industry.

Christopher Sholes.

Because handwriting was often illegible and potentially costly in business, dozens of inventors had tried creating a "writing machine." But the first practical—easily manufactured and reliable—typewriter was perfected only in 1867 by Christopher Latham Sholes, and first marketed in 1875 by the Remington Arms Company, a firearms manufacturer in search of a product with which to diversify its interests.

The American invention of the typewriter brought more women into the business sector.

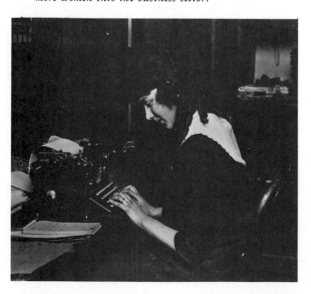

Thomas Edison.

Thomas Alva Edison was the ultimate American tinkerer. He was attuned to the practical and was a genius at making, fixing, and remaking things. Edison did not come upon his creations as the result of other interests, as Bell did. Nor were his inventions lucky accidents such as Harvey Firestone's discovery of the vulcanizing process, by which rubber was transformed into a stable, versatile material. Nor did Edison's breakthroughs come about in a miraculous flash of insight, as had happened when Eli Whitney invented the cotton gin only a day and a half after being presented with the problem of removing cottonseeds from the fibers.

Edison approached invention in a gruff, nononsense, American way. Invention was just another kind of hard work. Edison once said that his genius was "1 percent inspiration and 99 percent perspiration." He took up problems on assignment and, with a large corps of assistants, attacked them in the first research and development laboratory, at Menlo Park, New Jersey. His and his assistants' resourcefulness are still unparalleled. Between 1876 and 1900, Edison took out more than 1,000 *patents*.

Most of these patents were for improvements in existing processes. (He perfected a transmitter for Bell.) However, a few of Edison's inventions were seedbeds for wholly new industries: the storage battery, the motion-picture projector, and the phonograph. The most important of his inventions was the incandescent light bulb, a means of converting electricity into stable, controllable light.

Cyrus McCormick.

Cyrus Hall McCormick was a carryover from the previous age. He invented his first *reaper* for harvesting grain mechanically in 1831. For two decades he battled other inventors of farm machines in the courts, and by the Civil War he had bought out or driven out of business virtually every important competitor in the production of farm machinery. He was quick to purchase the inventions of younger inventors, and by the time of his death in 1884, his International Harvester Company owned hundreds of valuable patents. Headquartered in Chicago, the McCormick works manufactured more agricultural machines than every other company in the world combined.

It wasn't until 1910 that electric lighting was available for use on a competitive, widescale system. The development of the tungsten-filament lamp replaced Edison's original bamboo filament. In the 1890s the development and use of gas lighting had been more prevalent.

MOVERS AND SHAPERS

George Washington Carver

George Washington Carver (1861–1943) and Thomas Alva Edison (1847–1931) changed American life with their scientific discoveries and practical inventions.

Carver was born to slaves in Missouri. Several years after the abolition of slavery, Carver traveled to Kansas to pursue a high school education. After completing high school, he applied to college. He was denied admission to a Kansas college because he was black, but was admitted to Iowa State University. There, he turned a life-long interest in plants to scientific study. After receiving his master's degree, he accepted Booker T. Washington's invitation to teach at Tuskegee Institute in Alabama. For the next 47 years at Tuskegee, Carver taught, experimented, and demonstrated scientific farming techniques.

When the boll weevil devastated the South's cotton crop in 1914, Carver was prepared to show why farmers should diversify their crops. He had developed some 300 products that could be derived from peanuts, more than 100 from sweet potatoes, and 75 more from pecans.

In his whole career, Carver took out only one patent. He felt that denying others the rights to his inventions would limit their helpfulness. His entire estate was used to help black youths go to college and study botany, chemistry, and agronomy.

Thomas Edison

One of the people who sought to hire Carver was the proprietor of a research laboratory in Menlo Park, New Jersey—Thomas Edison. Edison had grown up in a prosperous Ohio family, but he was educated at home because he didn't fit in school. He was an avid reader and an early chemist, but he hated math all his life.

As a teenager, Edison published a newspaper on a train that ran from Port Huron, Michigan, to Detroit. He became acquainted with telegraph operators and their equipment. He learned to be an operator and began inventing improvements for the telegraph at 16, primarily to make more time for his reading. A few years later he invented an electronic voting machine and a stock ticker. Although others had built similar machines, Edison's were more sophisticated.

Eventually, he sold his stock ticker inventions and used the money to set up an "invention factory" with 50 people working for him. A shrewd judge of ability, he hired many people who would one day become famous inventors themselves. This "factory" formed the basis of the General Electric Company.

In 1877, Edison produced his most imaginative machine, the phonograph. Two years later, he refined the light bulb so that it could be mass produced. Then, he designed a central power plant to provide electricity for the lights. He lived long enough to see the fiftieth anniversary of his successful bulb.

Both Carver and Edison were beacons to American science and technology. They pioneered new techniques in research, and led the way in applying their developments to everyday problems.

George Westinghouse.

George Westinghouse became a multimillionaire from his invention of the air brake for railroad trains. By equipping every car in a train with brakes operated from a central point by pneumatic pressure, Westinghouse solved the problem of stopping long strings of cars. His air brake saved lives and meant profits for railroads by making longer trains possible.

Well established, Westinghouse turned his inventive genius to electricity. Because direct current could not be transmitted over long distances, Westinghouse tried to find a way to transmit alternating current. Again, he was successful.

Westinghouse was comfortable enough with the intricacies of business to retain control of the Westinghouse Electric Corporation and to see it expand its operations into the industry's hundreds of possibilities.

Elisha Otis.

As the railroad harnessed steam to move heavy burdens across the land, Elisha Otis devised an elevator to move them up and down. His first safe elevator—stopping a load, not raising it, was the big problem with earlier hoists—went on the market in 1852. Through the rest of the nineteenth century, his company (with competition from Westinghouse) regularly improved the device, converting to electric power and making possible both the digging of deeper mines and the construction of taller buildings. And tall office buildings—skyscrapers—encouraged the centralization of business administration.

SECTION REVIEW

1. Write a sentence to identify: American Telephone and Telegraph Company, Harvey Firestone, Menlo Park, reaper.

2. Give the full name and the most important invention of each person: Edison, Otis, McCormick, Sholes, Westinghouse.

3. Briefly explain how each of the following contributed to the growth and improvement of American business: elevators, telephones, "writing machines," air brakes for trains.

4. What was the purpose of Bell's original invention? What followed?

---

5. BIG BUSINESS

The chief agency of business consolidation in the late nineteenth century was not the partnership or individual ownership, but the *corporation*. Corporate organization was not in itself a new idea. It had originated in early modern times as a means of financing business ventures that were too expensive or too risky to be undertaken by individuals.

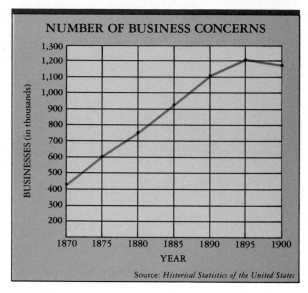

NUMBER OF BUSINESS CONCERNS

BUSINESSES (in thousands) — YEAR 1870–1900

Source: *Historical Statistics of the United States*

Limited Liability.

By the post-Civil War period, courts usually guaranteed the privilege of *limited liability*. Before limited liability was recognized, owners of bankrupt businesses could have everything they owned, even home and personal possessions, seized and sold by *creditors*, to whom the businesses owed money. The new principle limited a corporation's liability to the corporation's assets. Once creditors had seized these, they had to stop. They could not touch the personal property of the shareholders or their shares in other corporations. This privilege made it easier for entrepreneurs to raise capital for high-risk ventures.

The Fourteenth Amendment.

The Fourteenth Amendment also served the interests of corporate managers and shareholders. Under the meaning of the Fourteenth Amendment, a corporation came to be legally viewed as a person. Consequently, the states were forbidden to pass laws that applied specifically to corporations and

The final step in the development of the modern corporation did not occur until 1934, when corporations were legally allowed to declare bankruptcy, a right allowed individuals since the 1830s.

not to flesh-and-blood persons, because those laws would deny the corporate person the civil rights that were granted to others.

However, while a corporation could legally be granted the civil rights of a human being, it was difficult to exact the same responsibilities of it. A walking and talking man or woman could be sent to jail for violating the law. A corporation could not. In the freewheeling business atmosphere of the late nineteenth century, it was not surprising that entrepreneurs found this kind of organization to their liking.

Trusts.   Another kind of business structure was the *trust*. In a trust, the owners of a number of companies engaging in the same business activity surrendered controlling interest in their companies to a board of trustees. In return, they re-

ceived trust certificates (*shares*) that gave them claims on the profits of the consolidated company.

The trust structure was most useful in industries in which there was a single critical stage of manufacture that involved relatively few companies. This was the situation in the oil refining business. In fact, the first trust was the Standard Oil Trust created by John D. Rockefeller. Some of Rockefeller's most successful imitators were in sugar refining (the sugar trust controlled about 95 percent of the nation's facilities) and whiskey distilling. In 1890, James Buchanan Duke of Durham, North Carolina founded the American Tobacco Company, which coordinated the activities of practically every cigarette manufacturer in the United States. Duke even came to an agreement with a similar cartel in England.

The Sherman Antitrust Act.   By 1890, many Americans had become convinced that when a few men could control a whole industry, the principle of economic opportunity was mocked and the very foundations of American democracy were jeopardized. Responding to public pressure in that year, Congress passed the *Sherman Antitrust Act*, which declared that "every contract, combination, in the form of trust or otherwise, or conspiracy, in restraint of trade or commerce among the several states, or with foreign nations, is hereby declared to be illegal." The Sherman Act authorized the *Attorney General* to move against such combinations and force them to dissolve.

Some citizens and members of Congress, believing that no corporation should gain a monopoly position within an industry, tried to break up monopolies and end monopolistic practices.

SECTION REVIEW

1. Write a sentence to identify: corporation, shareholders, trust, James Duke.

2. How did the courts' guarantees of limited liability protect shareholders in corporations and help American business to grow?

3. Explain how the Fourteenth Amendment served the interests of entrepreneurs in the late nineteenth century.

4. What motivated Congress to pass the Sherman Antitrust Act? What did it say about trusts, and what power did it give the Attorney General?

Discussion Question: Should trusts be illegal? Why? Aside from the expected flood of negative comments, students should examine any positive aspects of trusts and monopolies.

Trolley cars powered by electricity and connected to overhead wires on city streets provided mass transportation in the 1800s.

When the Brooklyn Bridge was completed in 1883, its span of 1,595 feet made it the longest suspension bridge in the world.

Christopher Sholes's typewriter revolutionized business communication. This model from the 1860s printed only capital letters.

C H A N G I N G   T E C H N O L O G Y

18|60   18|70

Safety razor introduced
Washing machine produced
Rotary printing press developed
Practical arc lamp built

Shoe sewing machine produced
Internal combustion engine designed

Universal milling machine built
Vacuum tube invented
Pin-tumbler cylinder lock developed

Research Assignment: Have students write reports on the inventors and inventions of this period. Examine how they changed society, both positively and negatively. How were these

Modern skyscrapers became practical when Elisha Otis invented the safety elevator in 1853.

The light bulb invented by Thomas Edison in 1878 used carbonized cellulose fiber for its filament.

The use of turbines to drive the large generators in power stations made supplying electricity to almost every home, factory, and farm in the country possible.

Alexander Graham Bell's telephone, invented in 1875, used electricity to carry sound.

18	80	18	90	19	00
Pneumatic drill designed	Linotype machine introduced	Paper clip invented
Four-cycle gas engine built	Skyscraper built	Diesel engine produced
Cash register introduced	Successful alternating-current induction motor developed	Zipper invented
	Aluminum used industrially	Aspirin developed

inventions improvements over their predecessors? Encourage students to use photographs or art work to illustrate their reports. Also encourage them to create models of inventions as well.

CHAPTER REVIEW

TIME LINE

1830	McCormick invents reaper (1831)
1835	
1840	
1845	Otis perfects elevator (1852)
1850	Borden patents evaporated milk (1856)
1855	Oil strike in Pennsylvania (1859)
	Pacific Railway Act (1862)
1860	Sholes invents typewriter (1867)
	First transcontinental railroad completed (1869)
1865	Bell invents telephone (1876)
1870	Edison develops incandescent light (1879)
1875	Northern Pacific Railroad completed (1883)
1880	Southern Pacific Railroad completed (1883)
	Canadian Pacific Railroad completed (1885)
1885	Interstate Commerce Act (1887)
1890	Duke founds American Tobacco Company (1890)
1895	Sherman Antitrust Act (1890)
	Boston Cooking School Cookbook (1896)
1900	

TIME LINE QUESTIONS

1. In what year was the first transcontinental railroad completed?
2. When was the telephone invented?
3. Name a law permitting the Attorney General to break up big businesses into smaller ones, and tell what year it was passed.
4. When and where were crude oil wells first drilled?

SKILLS STRATEGY

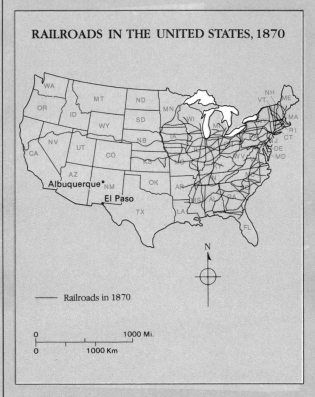

RAILROADS IN THE UNITED STATES, 1870

Railroads in 1870

0   1000 Mi.

0   1000 Km

THEMATIC MAPS

A *thematic map* gives you information in a concise, easy-to-grasp way. When two thematic maps with similar titles appear side by side in a text, you should compare or combine the data they present. The titles of the maps usually imply the relationship between the two maps. After studying each map, you should decide what the relationship is between the maps and what you can learn from them. Be sure you understand what each symbol in the legend means and how it relates to the title. Also, be aware of the scale of miles and the compass as you examine data on the maps.

After you compare two paired thematic maps, you should be able to draw a series of conclusions. Look at the titles of the maps shown above. What difference do you note? From a quick glance at the maps, was there an increase or decrease in railroads between 1870 and 1900? Summarize railroad growth between 1870 and 1900. In which section of the country was there the greatest

Making Connections: Review the questions and topics presented in the Making Connections section that opens this chapter. Emphasize the way in which worker and owner attitudes about

434

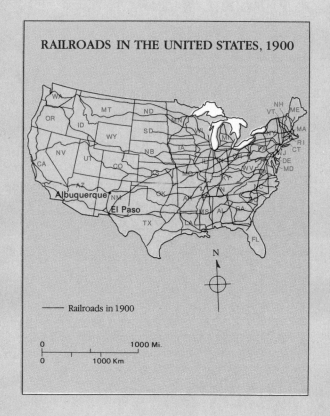

RAILROADS IN THE UNITED STATES, 1900

— Railroads in 1900

0   1000 Mi.
0   1000 Km

CHAPTER 17 TEST

TEXT REVIEW

1. Name four factors accounting for the transformation of the United States from an agrarian to an industrial nation.
2. Describe the changes that occurred in population, number of states, and wealth of the American people between 1865 and 1900.
3. Women, children, black people, and American Indians were not considered important by most politicians at this time. Why?
4. Evaluate the effectiveness of the American regional railroads in 1865.
5. Explain how an entrepreneur or a group of entrepreneurs consolidated some of the regional railroads into one of the following lines: Pennsylvania Railroad, New York Central, Erie, Central Pacific.
6. Explain how the following industries were revolutionized: food industry, oil industry.
7. Describe the provisions of the following laws: Pacific Railway Act of 1862, Fourteenth Amendment, Sherman Antitrust Act.
8. What effect did the growth of railroads have on the western farmers?

CRITICAL THINKING

9. Do you agree or disagree with the following statement: "Many of the entrepreneurs who built the big railroads were corrupt and greedy robber barons." Support your answer with details from the text.
10. Write two propaganda statements, one favoring the railroads, and one opposing them.

WRITING A PARAGRAPH

Write a paragraph beginning or ending with the topic sentence given below. Note that the topic sentence states an opinion. Therefore, the supporting sentences that you write should state facts to support that opinion. (Skim the appropriate sections of the chapter for details you can include in the supporting sentences.)

Topic Sentence: If not for the inventive genius of Americans, farmers and industrial leaders could not have made the progress they did.

growth? In which section was there the least growth?

Based upon your knowledge of this time period, give several reasons why railroad growth occurred where it did. What kinds of changes in people's lives do you think the increase in rail lines brought about?

APPLYING SKILLS

Refer to the maps above to answer the following questions.

1. How many miles of railroad were there between Albuquerque and El Paso in 1870?
2. Could you make a complete trip across the country by rail in 1870?
3. Name at least five states that had no railroads in 1870, but did have railroads by 1900.
4. Which half of the country has the most railroad mileage in both maps? Why do you think this is true?

each other changed during this period. Discuss the ramifications of this. Also note how this period of industrial and technical change might have affected attitudinal changes in society.

POLITICS AND POLITICIANS

1868–1896

*Can history show us nothing
but pieces of ourselves, detached,
set to a kind of poetry,
a kind of music, even?*

ADRIENNE RICH

Making Connections. The late nineteenth century was one of the most colorful times in American politics. Party bosses and their political machines controlled many of the large cities. On the national scene, the two parties traded charges of corruption and invoked memories of the Civil War. Politics was part business and part theater, but few people seemed to care.

In this chapter, you will learn:
- How political machines turned politics into business
- Who the Goo-Goos were and why they seldom defeated political machines
- What the "bloody shirt" was and who waved it
- Which states were "swing states" and why they were important
- Who the Mugwumps, the Half-Breeds, and the Stalwarts were, and how they influenced the Republican party
- Why farmers wanted low tariffs, and industrial workers wanted high tariffs

You know that the late 1800s were a period of prosperity and growth in the United States. Neither political party wanted to rock the boat; in fact, politicians frequently cut themselves in on such projects as the transcontinental railroad. So, there was little to divide the parties except for symbols, slogans, and sentiments. As you read, note the real stakes each party was fighting for in the political battles of this period.

Sections
1. Big City Politics
2. National Politics
3. National Political Issues

1. BIG CITY POLITICS

City government in America traditionally had been town government on a larger scale. A small elected board of *aldermen* or supervisors and an elected mayor made day-to-day administrative decisions. They would turn to the entire *electorate* when major issues were to be decided. However, in the ballooning cities of the late 1800s the electorate was simply too large and fragmented to function as a community.

Moreover, the tremendous responsibilities of running a large, crowded city—the supervision of huge fire and police departments, sanitation, tax-collection, and education, housing, and health *bureaucracies*—called for efficient and powerful political organizations. Such organizations came into being in the form of *political machines*.

Politics as Business. The need for management of the diverse groups in the cities, and the growth of urban tax *revenues* accounted for the evolution of the political machine. Ambitious individuals realized that if they could command the loyalty of a majority of voters in a *ward*, or neighborhood, and could form alliances within a party with other ward *bosses* like themselves, they could take over *municipal* government and use it for their own gain. All they needed was votes, and

This 1880 presidential campaign poster promoting James A. Garfield was created by Currier and Ives. Garfield won the election.

Quotation: from the poem "Readings of History." Other works by Adrienne Rich (born 1929) include *A Change of World, Diving into the Wreck, The Diamond Cutter & Other Poems,* and *Snapshots of a Daughter-in-Law: Poems, 1954–62.*

PUBLISHED BY CURRIER & IVES   COPYRIGHT 1880, BY CURRIER & IVES, N.Y.   115 NASSAU ST.

Skills Review: Reinforce the skills learned in the preceding Skills Strategy section. Have students examine population density maps of the U.S. for 1850, 1865, and 1890 and interpret the significance of the shifts in population and how they relate to events in the text.

Thomas Nast, an immigrant and accomplished cartoonist, published this political cartoon on the eve of the 1871 New York municipal and state elections. The caption read: "The Tammany Tiger Loose—What are you going to do about it?"

they were in business. And business was how they looked at politics.

The machines acted as very personalized social services among a hard-pressed people. During the bitter winter of 1870, Boss William Tweed, the head of the New York City Democratic machine known as *Tammany Hall*, spent $50,000 on coal that was dumped by the ton on street corners in the poorest parts of the city. It was the duty of every boss to find out when marriages and births occurred in the ward. The sensible ward boss had a gift delivered.

Making Money. A political machine made money in a number of ways. There was outright bribery. In return for regular cash payments, law enforcement officials would wink at the operations of illegal businesses.

There was *influence peddling.* For example, William Tweed was on Cornelius Vanderbilt's payroll as a "legal adviser" although Tweed was not a lawyer. What Vanderbilt was buying were the rulings of judges in Tweed's organization.

Kickbacks and *sandbagging* were also prevalent. Companies desiring government contracts were asked to submit artificially high bids, and then give, or kick back, a large sum to the machine. As a result, public works cost much more than they should have.

The machines used sandbagging when dealing with the streetcar lines that needed permission to lay tracks on public streets. John Coughlin and Michael "Hinkey-Dink" Kenna in Chicago would, for a bribe, grant a line the rights to lay tracks on only a few blocks at a time. Building a line this way, the streetcar owners would have to pay again and again to open a complete line.

Another tactic was to threaten an existing trolley line with competition on a nearby street. Rather than have their traffic decline by half, traction companies paid the political machine to prevent new construction.

Research Assignment: Have students prepare a report on a famous political boss of the late 1800s or perhaps a boss involved with a political machine in your area on a city, state, or county level.

A well-established member of a political machine could expect to be on the city payroll for jobs that did not really exist. In one district of New York City where there were four water pumps for fighting fires, the city had 20 pump inspectors. Probably none of them ever looked at the pumps. They were working to keep the political machine in power at public expense.

It was possible to hold several meaningless city jobs simultaneously. Cornelius Corson, who kept his ward safe for the New York Democratic party from an office in his saloon, was on the books as a court clerk at $10,000 a year, as chief of the Board of Elections at $5,000 a year, and as an employee of four other municipal agencies at $2,500 a year per job. Another ward boss, Michael Norton, held city jobs that paid him $50,000 a year.

Altogether, the Tweed Ring, which controlled New York City for only a few years after the Civil War, looted the city treasury of as much as $200

The Nast cartoon at right shows the result of the 1871 election—Tweed lost much of his power.

[127]   November 25, 1871

"What Are You Laughing at? To The Victor Belong The Spoils."

Tweed's greatest monument—the New York County Courthouse—cost New York taxpayers millions more than it should have.

Class Activity: Using the skills taught in this chapter's Skills Strategy section, have students interpret the political cartoons shown in this chapter.

million. Tweed eventually went to jail, but his chief henchman, Controller "Slippery" Dick Connolly, fled abroad with several million dollars.

Staying in Office.

Despite their generally obvious *profiteering*, machine politicians stayed in office. Few were above *stuffing ballot boxes* or marching gangs of "repeaters," who cast more than one vote, from one polling station to the next, but they won most elections fairly. The majority of city voters freely chose them over candidates who pledged honesty.

Ward bosses brought fun into dismal lives by throwing parties. They fixed up minor, and major, scrapes with the law and gave out jobs. In control of the municipal government, the machines had jobs at their disposal, not only phony ones, but jobs that provided work and that poor people were grateful for. Gratitude for such favors was the key to success for the big city politician.

The Goo-Goos.

Not everyone was grateful. The property-owning middle classes, who paid the bills with their taxes, periodically raised campaigns for good government—the bosses called them *Goo-Goos*—and sometimes won elections. The fall of the *Tweed Ring* in New York in 1873 led to the election of a reform organization. Chicago's "Gray Wolves" were thrown out of city hall, and a major wave of indignation swept Abe Ruef and Mayor Eugene Schmitz out of power in San Francisco in 1906. But until the turn of the century, reform governments were generally short-lived. The machines came back.

To millions of people in other countries, the United States offered the promise of refuge and opportunity. Though life was not always easy after they arrived, a large percentage of immigrants, with hard work, did indeed find a better life in America.

Discussion Question: Were political machines good or bad? Have the discussion cover the issues of the morality of the machines. How did one's position in society (lower or middle income) affect perceptions of the machines as good or bad? Were the machines efficient? Were they just filling a niche that so-called honest government couldn't fill?

One weakness of the Goo-Goos was that they did not offer an alternative to the informal social services that the machine provided. They believed instead that honest government was the same as inexpensive government. New immigrants, who were faced with great material problems and were inclined from their European backgrounds to think of government as an institution that one used or was used by, preferred the machines to the government reformers.

Indeed, Goo-Goos often combined their attacks on political corruption with attacks on the new ethnic groups. In contrast, the machine bosses, many of whom were recent immigrants, served as role models for the new immigrants. They were people making good in a difficult situation in a new country.

Ethnicity and Political Power. Although not all the city bosses were of Irish lineage, the Irish were prominent in nineteenth-century machines: Richard Connolly, "Honest" John Kelley, Richard Croker, George Plunkitt, Charles Murphy, and Tim Sullivan of New York; James Mc-Manes of Philadelphia; Christopher Magee and William Finn of Pittsburgh; and Martin Lomasney of Boston. The Irish were so successful in politics in part because they were the first of the large ethnic groups in the cities, and in part because they had been highly political in their homeland as a consequence of Irish protest of British rule in Ireland.

The frequently dominant role of the Irish did not mean that the newer immigrants were shut out of politics. On the contrary, the political machine exhibited little ethnic prejudice. If a ward became Italian and an Italian ward boss delivered the votes, he was welcomed into the organization and granted a share of the spoils equal to his contribution on election day. In many cities, while the police forces retained an Irish complexion, sanitation departments and fire departments often were mostly Italian.

In this way, the urban political machine was beneficial, acting to *assimilate* ethnic groups and therefore speeding their entrance into full citizenship. When the big-city machines became vital to the success of the national parties, anti-ethnic feelings among national political leaders were rarely voiced.

2. NATIONAL POLITICS

To some degree, national politics in the late nineteenth century worked just like municipal politics. Like the no-nonsense bosses of the cities, some politicians on the national level thought of their calling as a business. Others thought of politics as a profession that involved organizing majorities, winning public office, and using the power of government to bestow benefits on members of the party. There were politicians who were fascinated by government and who experienced a call to public service. Most politicians were colorful individuals, and many were *charismatic orators* and talented organizers.

They had to be, for the two major political parties were evenly balanced in voter strength in the last quarter of the nineteenth century, and each vote counted. Slogans, symbols, and sentiments characterized each campaign. Late nineteenth century politics was magnificent theater.

Neither of the national parties at that time truly had an overreaching *ideology,* or set of principles according to which members believed the nation should be governed. On the contrary, Republicans and Democrats pretty much agreed on policy. Indeed, there was more political conflict within the two major parties than between them. The national parties were loose coalitions of regional, state, and city political organizations, and each group had its own particular programs that it wanted to have enacted.

One of the services provided by the political machines in New York City was the instant naturalization of immigrants. The one-day record was set by the Tweed ring on October 14, 1868, when 2,109 (or three a minute) new citizens were sworn in.

Despite the very cautious approach to change in national politics during the final quarter of the nineteenth century, national politics suited the Americans of the time. In no other period of American history did a higher percentage of eligible voters actually vote—more than 80 percent, as compared with less than half those eligible to vote in a typical election of the late twentieth century.

"Waving the Bloody Shirt."

The Civil War still haunted the period. The Republican party specialty was "waving the bloody shirt," or reminding northern voters that Democrats had caused the Civil War. Lucius Fairchild, a Wisconsin politician who had lost an arm in battle, literally flapped his empty sleeve during campaign speeches. With *veterans* like Fairchild hobbling about every sizable town to remind voters of the bloodletting, it was an effective technique.

Of the seven presidents between 1869 and 1901, every one but the Democrat Grover Cleveland had been an officer in the Union Army, and every one of them but William McKinley had been a general. The man who defeated Cleveland in 1888, Benjamin Harrison, was still waving the bloody shirt after 20 years, and did not apologize for it. "I would a thousand times rather march under the bloody shirt, stained with the lifeblood of a Union soldier," Harrison told voters, "than march under the black flag of treason or the white flag of cowardly compromise." Dwelling on the past was not constructive, but it did help win elections.

Civil War Pensions.

In their pension policy, the Republicans converted the bloody shirt into dollars and cents. Soon after the war ended, Congress had provided for pensions to Union veterans who were disabled from wartime wounds and diseases. The law was strictly worded, and many genuinely handicapped veterans did not qualify under its terms. Instead of changing the law, however, northern representatives took to introducing special *pension bills* that provided monthly payments for specific constituents (voters from their home congressional districts) who had persuaded them that their cases were just.

By the 1880s, the procedure for awarding the special pension had become grossly abused. Congress took little interest in the truthfulness of a

Rather than alienate any voter, Congress approved almost every request for Civil War pensions.

petitioner. (One applicant for a pension had not served in the army because, he said, he had fallen off a horse on the way to enlist.) Every bill that any voter requested was introduced. Instead of declining as old veterans died, the cost of the pensions climbed to $65 million in 1885 and $79 million in 1888.

In 1888, Congress passed a new general pension bill that granted an income to every veteran who had served at least 90 days in the wartime army and was disabled for any reason whatsoever. An old soldier who fell off a stepladder in 1888 would be eligible under its terms.

President Cleveland vetoed the bill. In the election that year, the Republicans ran against Cleveland with the slogan "Vote Yourself a Pension." They won the election, and in 1890 Benjamin Harrison signed the even more generous *Dependent Pensions Act*. Harrison also appointed James Tanner, the head of the veterans' *lobby*, to distribute the money. "God help the *surplus*," Tanner said, referring to the money in the Treasury. By the end of Harrison's term in office, the annual expenditure on pensions had increased to $140 million.

Northern Democrats posed as the party of principle in the controversies over the bloody shirt and pensions. In the South, however, Democrats provided pensions for Confederate veterans, and candidates for public office reminded white voters that the Democratic party had rid *Dixie* of *carpetbaggers*.

In the South, the Democrats were more effective than the Republicans. Except in areas where black voters continued to vote, and in mountain regions where white voters had been Unionists during the war, the Republican party simply disappeared in the South. With good reason, Democrats spoke of the "Solid South." Between 1876 and 1896, no former Confederate state voted Republican in a national election.

Politics as Business. Politics also meant concrete benefits for party activists as a result of a spoils system that vastly exceeded the patronage that Boss Tweed or Richard Croker had at their disposal. Most government jobs—50,000 in Grant's time, 250,000 at the end of the century—involved real work. There was a postmaster in every town and other postal employees in the cities. Indian agents administered the government's treaty obligations to the different tribes. In some federal bureaucracies like the Customs Service, there was enough paperwork to keep thousands of clerks busy.

For the most part, the people who got these jobs were supporters of the party in power. Political activists who worked to get the vote out were rewarded with government employment. In return, their party required them to contribute a modest percentage of their income in election years to finance the campaign. The result was politics for its own sake.

The higher the ranking of a party official, the more rewarding the job. Not only was corrupt income possible in some positions, but it was possible to grow quite rich legally in government service. The post of Collector of Customs in large ports was particularly lucrative. In addition to a handsome salary, the collector was paid a share of

all import *duties* on goods reclaimed from smugglers who had been caught at their work. This curious incentive system made for a remarkably uncorrupt *Customs Service*; there was more to be made in catching violators than in taking bribes from them.

Other party supporters were rewarded with contracts for government work in *pork-barrel bills*. At the end of each congressional session, congressional alliances pieced together bills to finance government construction projects in each member's district. Thus, the *River and Harbor Bill* of 1886 would have provided $15 million to begin 100 new projects, although 58 government projects that had been started two years before remained unfinished. (President Cleveland *vetoed* the bill.) The idea was not so much to get needed work done, but to reward businesspeople who supported the party in power.

Party leaders were professional organizers. They built up state organizations in much the same way as the city bosses built up their wards, and they bargained with other like-minded politicians as to how the patronage would be divided.

Republican state bosses such as Roscoe Conkling and Thomas C. Platt in New York, Matt Quay in Pennsylvania, and the *Bourbon Democrats* of the South (so-called because of their extreme conservatism, like that of the Bourbon dynasty in prerevolutionary France) were in business. They had little time for lofty principles. They were interested in holding office and in the power and wealth that came with the office.

Voting Patterns. The two parties remained evenly matched between the end of the Civil War and the turn of the century. For only two years between 1869 and 1897 did either Republicans or Democrats control the presidency, Senate, and House of Representatives at the same time. In large part, this balance owed to unvarying voting patterns in New England and the South and among some social classes.

New England voted heavily Republican, largely in response to the bloody shirt. In the region where abolitionism had been strongest, distaste for the South was a potent political motivation.

The upper and middle classes throughout the North and Midwest were generally Republican. They thought of the "Grand Old Party" (*GOP*) as

The origin of the expression *pork barrel* is uncertain. However, the word *pork*, meaning graft or patronage, was in common use during this period. Omnibus bills like the River and Harbor Bills suggested barrels in which to hold all this pork.

a bastion of morality and respectability that was fighting against the former slave owners and the corrupt big-city bosses backed by immigrants in the Democratic party. (Except for Philadelphia, big cities voted Democratic.) Black voters voted Republican for a somewhat different reason. To black voters, the GOP was the party of Lincoln and emancipation. And the Democrats whom they knew—whether other ethnics in the cities (with whom they competed for jobs) or southerners— were usually seen as *white supremacists.*

As a result of these steady voting patterns, the outcome of national elections turned on the vote in a handful of swing states, particularly Indiana, Ohio, and New York. In each of these states, with their large blocs of electoral votes, hard-core Republicans and Democrats were about equal in number. The decision was thus in the hands of independents who might swing either way depending on local issues, the personalities of the candidates, or mere whim.

Party leaders believed that the personal popularity of a candidate in the *swing states* could make the difference. Thus, a disproportionate number of late nineteenth-century presidential and vice-presidential nominees came from Indiana, Ohio, and New York. Neither party was dedicated to finding the best person for the job. They wanted to win, and to do so they had to carry the swing states.

Ulysses S. Grant. In 1868, the still potent *Reconstruction* issue carried Ulysses S. Grant into the White House. Grant came to appreciate the *perquisites* of his office, and thus was vulnerable to manipulation by those who catered to his wishes. Both he and his wife were overwhelmed by the adulation heaped on them. When towns and counties took his name, and when cities made gifts of valuable property and even cash —$100,000 from New York alone—Grant accepted them willingly. He never fully understood that political gift-givers were actually paying in advance for future favors. Or, if he did understand, he apparently saw nothing wrong in returning kindness with the resources at his disposal.

Black Friday. Grant was hardly settled in the White House when he stumbled. Unlucky in business himself, he reveled in the flattery that was lavished on him by wealthy men, and had struck up a friendship with Jay Gould and Jim

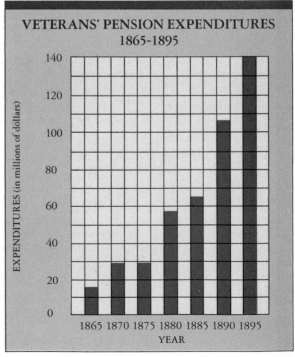

Class Activity: Use the bar graphs on this page to review student skills in gaining information from graphs. Ascertain what the value of comparing the two graphs might be.

In the engraving above, President Ulysses S. Grant is nominated by the Republican party to run for a second term as president in the election of 1872.

Fisk, the dishonest owners of the Erie Railroad. Delighted by their attachment to Grant, the two hatched an ingenious scheme to use their well-publicized friendship with the President to corner the nation's gold supply. And they nearly did!

After having won the assurance of Grant's brother-in-law that Grant would not put government gold on the open market, Gould and Fisk bought as much gold and as many gold *futures* (commitments to buy gold on a given date at a low price) as their resources allowed. Then, they let it be known that the President would not increase the amount of gold in circulation.

With dozens of *speculators* obliged to get gold to sell to the pair, the price of the precious metal soared. It was not, however, only speculators who got stung. Businesspeople who were not involved in speculation needed gold to pay their debts and their employees' wages. Banks needed gold to meet their commitments. Both had to buy from Gould and Fisk at the exorbitant price of $162 an ounce. The two scoundrels were on the verge of making a record killing when Grant finally realized that he was being used. On Friday, September 24—"Black Friday"—the President dumped $4 million in gold on the *New York Stock Exchange*. The price collapsed, not soon enough to harm Gould and Fisk but just in time to bankrupt hundreds of legitimate businesses, throw thou-

sands of working people out of jobs, and darken Grant's reputation.

The Election of 1872.

It was Black Friday, along with their unhappiness with Grant's *Radical Reconstruction* program, that led prominent,

On "Black Friday," panic struck Broad Street in New York City (below) as the collapse in the price of gold caused widespread bankruptcy.

mostly eastern Republicans such as Charles Sumner and E. L. Godkin, editor of the influential *Nation* magazine, to break with Grant in 1872 and form the *Liberal Republican* party.

In a sense, the Liberals were a throwback to the period when, as they believed, the people voted into office the "best candidate," not a candidate promoted by party bosses. Their idealistic view of the past was not entirely accurate. There had been political bosses before Tweed, and collusion between government officials and speculators before Black Friday. But the baldness of politics for self-benefit that the liberals saw around them after the Civil War was something new.

Unfortunately, as is often the case with nostalgic political movements, the Liberal Republicans not only loathed the circumstances of the present, but were unwilling to compromise with the spirit of their time. Their impracticality was most obvious in their choice of a presidential candidate.

Horace Greeley, the editor of the New York *Tribune*, was a lifelong eccentric. Throughout his 61 years, he had advocated almost every reform from abolitionism and women's rights to vegetarianism, spiritualism (communicating with the dead), and phrenology (reading a person's character in the bumps on his or her head).

To make matters worse, Greeley needed the support of the Democrats to make a race against Grant, and he proposed to "clasp hands across the bloody chasm." This was asking too much of Republican party regulars. Voters who disapproved of Grant disapproved much more of southern Democrats. Moreover, throughout his editorial career, Greeley had always vilified the Democrats—particularly southerners.

The Democrats did give him their nomination. But southern white voters found it difficult to support such a leader, and a large vote by black voters for Grant in seven southern states helped give the President a 286 to 66 victory in the electoral college. Thus, in 1872, despite rumors of scandal in his administration that, along with their disillusionment with Reconstruction, drove the Liberal Republicans into an alliance with the Democrats, Grant was reelected by a comfortable margin.

The Mugwumps. After the election of 1872, the Liberals sheepishly returned to the Republican party. For all their contempt for Grant, they found their flirtation with the Democrats humiliating. The Republican regulars took them back—votes were votes—but they joked at the Liberals' self-proclaimed righteousness by dubbing them *Mugwumps*, from an Algonkian Indian word meaning "great men" or "big chiefs." The Mugwumps were never more than a fringe of the GOP. Nevertheless, they helped keep corruption in check by their vigilance and morality.

The political cartoon below shows James G. Blaine, dressed as "Little Bo-Peep," trying to lure Mugwumps back to the Republican party.

Half-Breeds and Stalwarts.

The major part of the Republican party was divided into two factions—the *Half-Breeds* and the *Stalwarts*. In practical politics there was not much difference between them. Rather, they were competitors for patronage and groups devoted to their leaders.

James G. Blaine of Maine was the leader of the Half-Breeds. Blaine believed in Radical Reconstruction; he waved the bloody shirt with as much gusto as anyone, and he coveted patronage as avidly as any Tammany Democrat. But Blaine's ambition, which was enormous, several times brought him into conflict with Grant, and he urged the party, if not quite to stamp out corruption, then to reject the man who silently allowed it. The term *Half-Breed* was tacked onto Blaine in order to convey what his Republican enemies considered to be his hypocrisy.

Blaine's chief rival and Grant's chief henchman was Roscoe Conkling of New York. To this day, Conkling remains distinguished by his total loyalty in political matters. "I do not know how to belong to a party a little," he said. Conkling meant that a politician should support the president, as the leader of his party, regardless of what mistakes the president makes. People who agreed with this position became known as *Stalwarts.*

Conkling had no apologies for doling out the patronage to party faithful. He was the designer of the system of *senatorial courtesy,* by which Republican senators and representatives submitted lists of worthy party members and the jobs they wanted to the president, who then appointed them to office. Naturally, those people worked for the senator who had been their sponsor, and the senator, in turn, was loyal to the president. To Conkling, a party was a machine.

Grant's Second Term.

Conkling wanted Grant to run for a third term in 1876. With three southern states still governed by Republicans, he believed that the party could stay in power if its great leader would head the ticket. He may have been right. But by 1876, Grant and many of his advisors were demoralized. Scandals that had been only rumors in 1872 had burst into the open during Grant's second term, and the President refused to run.

Actually, the biggest scandal of the era was the Credit Mobilier affair, which had occurred during

This cartoon suggests that supporting a third term for Grant would mean supporting a continuation of corruption in his administration.

the Johnson years. It involved a bogus construction company, set up by the Union Pacific owners, that overcharged the government several million dollars. The agents for the company used bribes and favors to government officers and congressmen to hide their misconduct. The scandal involved some of Grant's supporters. Among the beneficiaries was Schuyler Colfax, Grant's vice president. Speaker of the House James A. Garfield also accepted a small payment.

Grant's Secretary of War, William W. Belknap, took bribes from companies that operated trading posts on Indian reservations under his authority. He and his subordinates shut their eyes while the companies defrauded the tribes of goods due them under the terms of federal treaties. Grant removed Belknap from his post, but refused to punish him otherwise. Nor did Grant punish his personal secretary, Orville E. Babcock, when he learned that Babcock sold excise stamps to whiskey distillers in St. Louis, letting the distillers dodge the tax on their products.

Conkling is associated with a cynical attitude toward patronage and party loyalty. However, until his death he instructed members of his law firm to charge little or nothing for legal services afforded to black people.

The Hayes-Tilden presidential election results were referred to the Electoral Commission of 1877. Cornelia Adele Fassett's painting of the Commission (above) has hung in the Capitol since 1886.

Rutherford B. Hayes. Conkling was still a power in Republican circles, but he failed with the Republican nominating convention of 1876. For reform's sake, both major parties nominated men with reputations for honesty.

The Democratic candidate, Samuel J. Tilden of New York, took credit for having crushed the Tweed Ring, although he had cooperated closely with Tweed until the cartoonist Thomas Nast and others had exposed Tweed's larceny. The Republican candidate, Rutherford B. Hayes, also had a reputation for bold honesty. But Hayes was a Half-Breed, in fact if not in name. As long as his subordinates were not overt profiteers, as so many of Grant's people had been, Hayes was content.

The election results seemed to show a clear victory for Tilden. He won the popular vote and appeared to have won in the electoral college by a margin of 204 to 165. However, the votes included those of the last three Rebublican-controlled states in the South, and Republican leaders instructed the governors of those states to submit their own returns, which showed Hayes as the winner. Those electoral votes would give Hayes a 185 to 184 victory in the *electoral college.*

The Democrats were infuriated with the Republicans' tactics. Finally, the decision of which set of returns to accept was turned over to a commis-

American presidents have often been associated more closely with the common man because so many of them had humble beginnings or lacked the pretentiousness of some of their European counterparts. To illustrate, Rutherford B. Hayes was attending a Grand Army of the Republic encampment when he was admonished by a policeman for walking on the grass.

448

A few days before James Garfield's election, he wrote of ordinary matters to his young sons, who were away at school:

When this reaches you the election will be in progress; and a few hours later, the result will be known. . . . It would make me very proud to know that during the first week of November 1880, my boys marked a little higher in studies, decorum, punctuality and industry than in any previous week of the term—and that they were in no wise thrown off

their balance by the Presidential Election. The family are all well, although a little tired out by the crowds of visitors. . . . The buckwheat will be threshed before the week ends, and we will greet you with Indian pudding and buckwheat cakes when you come home for the holidays. Five loads of apples have gone to the cider mill, and twelve barrels [barrels] of cider are fermenting on the north side of the office. . . . This, in brief is the situation on the eve of battle.

—LETTER, OCTOBER 31, 1880

sion made up of five Senators, five Representatives, and five Supreme Court justices. Seven of the commissioners were Republicans, seven were Democrats, and one, Justice David Davis, was an *independent*. It appeared that the deciding vote would be cast by Davis, but he declined that dubious honor by resigning from the Court and the commission. His replacement was a Republican, and on a straight party vote, the commission accepted the Republican votes. Rutherford B. Hayes became president.

Once the disputed election of 1876 was resolved, Hayes moved into the White House and proceeded to please no one. Stalwarts were disappointed by his abandonment of southern black voters; Half-Breeds believed that Hayes did not provide them with as much patronage as they deserved. There never was a question of renominating him. Long before Hayes retired, Blaine announced that he would seek the Republican nomination. Fearing that Blaine was too popular for any ordinary Stalwart candidate, Roscoe Conkling persuaded former president Grant to run against him.

James A. Garfield.

Neither Blaine nor Grant was able to win the support of the majority of the delegates to the Republican convention. They

were frustrated by the ambitions of several *favorite son* candidates who hoped to *deadlock* the convention and force the tired delegates to turn to them as compromise candidates.

After 34 ballots, the Blaine supporters saw that their hero's cause was lost. But instead of turning to a favorite son, they switched their votes to James A. Garfield of Ohio, who had not even been nominated. Delegates began to switch sides, and on the thirty-sixth ballot, Garfield became the Republican candidate.

Garfield was a Half-Breed, a Blaine supporter, but he played on Conkling's vanity by traveling to New York to seek his blessing and promise him a share of the patronage. Garfield went to the polls with a unified party behind him.

The Democrats, having lost with an antiwar Democrat in 1868 (Seymour), a Republican maverick in 1872 (Greeley), and a reformer in 1876 (Tilden), tried a Civil War general, Winfield Scott Hancock. An attractive if uninspiring man, he made the election extremely close. Garfield drew only 39,000 more votes than Hancock, out of over 9.1 million cast.

This close election was typical of the period. Between 1876 and 1896, no winning presidential candidate won as much as 50 percent of the vote. In 1876, Hayes had fewer popular votes than

RESULTS OF PRESIDENTIAL ELECTIONS
1868-1900

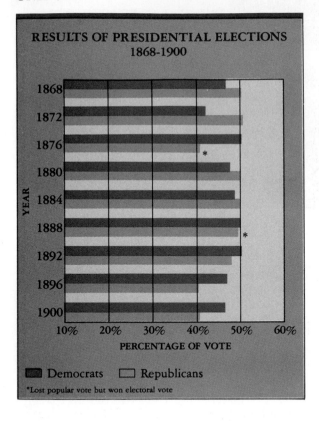

Democrats ☐ Republicans
*Lost popular vote but won electoral vote

landslide by the standards of the time. Even so, Cleveland won only 46 percent of the popular vote.

Garfield's downfall did not come from the slim mandate, but from the burden of distributing federal patronage. During the first months of his term, he sorted out the claims of Republican campaign workers to patronage jobs. Garfield tried to placate both wings of the party, but they were so strongly opposed that it was impossible. The Conkling group finally deserted Garfield when the post of Collector of Customs for the port of New York was given to a Blaine supporter. By the summer of 1881, it seemed that Conkling would lose the battle. The issue was finally resolved by two gunshots in a Washington train station.

The Assassination of President Garfield.
On July 2, 1881, Charles Guiteau, a preacher and bill collector who had worked for the Stalwarts but had not been rewarded with a government job, walked up to Garfield as he was about to depart a Washington, D.C., train station on a holiday and shot him twice in the small of the back. After living in extreme pain for eleven weeks, Garfield died on September 19.

"I am a Stalwart and now Arthur is president!" Guiteau allegedly shouted when he fired the fatal shots. He meant that the new president was none other than Conkling's longtime ally, Chester A.

Tilden. In 1884, Grover Cleveland won with 48.5 percent of the total. In 1888, Grover Cleveland outdrew Republican candidate Benjamin Harrison, but lost in the electoral college. In 1892, Cleveland won by 360,000 votes, which was a

With the growth of the civil service system between 1883 and 1900, more and more women filled jobs within the various branches of government.

PROFILES OF THE PRESIDENCY

CHESTER A. ARTHUR

1881–1885

*C*hester Arthur's unexpected rise to the presidency distressed many voters, but public opinion soon mellowed:

For the fourth time in the history of the Republic its Chief Magistrate has been removed by death. . . . Men may die, but the fabrics of our free institutions remain unshaken. No higher or more assuring proof could exist of the strength and permanence of popular government than the fact that though the chosen of the people be

struck down his constitutional successor is peacefully installed without shock or strain except the sorrow which mourns the bereavement. . . . Prosperity blesses our country, our fiscal policy is fixed by law, is well grounded and generally approved. No threatening issue mars our foreign intercourse, and the wisdom, integrity, and thrift of our people may be trusted to continue undisturbed the present assured career of peace, tranquility, and welfare.

—OATH OF OFFICE SPEECH, SEPTEMBER 22, 1881

Arthur. Indeed, the deranged Guiteau expected Arthur to free him from prison and reward him for his patriotic act.

Once in office, however, President Arthur proved to be an able and uncorrupt president who signed the first law to limit a party's use of government jobs for political purposes.

Chester A. Arthur. Chester A. Arthur did a good job in the White House, acting with good judgment and dignity as head of state and attempting to placate both wings of his party. During his term in office, the fates of current and future government workers were affected by reforms following passage of the *Pendleton Act* of 1883. The Pendleton Act established the *Civil Service* Commission, a three-member bureau that was empowered to draw up and administer examinations that applicants for some low-level government jobs were required to pass before they were hired. Once in these civil service jobs, employees could not be fired because the political party to which they belonged lost the presidency.

At first, only 10 percent of 131,000 government workers were protected by civil service. But the Pendleton Act also empowered the president to add job classifications to the civil service list. Ironically, because the presidency changed party every four years between 1880 and 1896, the

incumbents all desired to protect the jobs of their own appointees. This violated the spirit of civil service reform but led, by the end of the century, to a fairly comprehensive civil service system.

By 1900, 40 percent of the 256,000 federal employees held civil service positions. About 30 percent of government clerks were women.

Another provision of the Pendleton Act was the abolition of the *assessment system.* That is, the parties were forbidden to insist that those of their members who held government positions "donate" a percentage of their salary to political campaign chests each election year. Until the presidency of Benjamin Harrison, the professional politicians were at a loss as to how to replace these revenues. Harrison's Postmaster General, John Wanamaker, came up with the solution, at least for the Republicans. He established a system of levying "contributions" on big businesspeople who had an interest in Republican victory at the polls. This remained the chief means of financing political campaigns until the 1970s.

Grover Cleveland. Twice, President Arthur tried to regain Roscoe Conkling's support by offering the Stalwart leader a seat on the Supreme Court. Arthur also tried to woo the Half-Breeds so that he might run for reelection in 1884 with their support. However, it was not to be. Frustrat-

Discussion Question: Have students research why the Republican practice of soliciting campaign contributions from businesses stopped in the 1970s. Should this practice be allowed? Why or why not?

451

PROFILES OF THE PRESIDENCY

*I*n his first inaugural address, Grover Cleveland warned Americans not to take their rights for granted:

. . . He who takes the oath to-day to preserve, protect, and defend the Constitution of the United States only assumes the solemn obligation which every patriotic citizen—on the farm, in the work-shop, in the busy marts of trade, and everywhere—should share with him. The Constitution which prescribes his oath, my countrymen, is yours; the Government you have chosen him to administer for a time is yours; the suffrage which executes the will of freemen is yours; the laws and the entire scheme of our civil rule, from the town meeting to the State capitals and the national capital, is yours. . . . Every citizen owes to the country a vigilant watch and close scrutiny of its public servants and a fair and reasonable estimate of their fidelity and usefulness. . . This is the price of our liberty and the inspiration of our faith in the Republic.

—FIRST INAUGURAL ADDRESS, MARCH 4, 1885

ed in 1880, James Blaine did not care how reasonable Arthur was. He resigned from the cabinet and, with Conkling's career in eclipse, won the Republican nomination in the summer of 1884.

Blaine expected to win the election as well. As usual, New York State seemed to be the key to victory, and Blaine believed that he would run more strongly there than most Republicans. The Mugwumps had deserted the party, announcing that the Democratic candidate, Grover Cleveland, was the more honest man. But Blaine expected to make up this defection and more by winning the Irish-American vote, which usually did not go Republican. He was popular in the Irish-American community because, in an era when Republican leaders frequently disdained the Catholic Church, Blaine had Catholic relatives. Added to this advantage was news about Cleveland: he had fathered an illegitimate child while a lawyer in Buffalo.

Cleveland was able to neutralize the morality issue. Indeed, the Democrats turned the scandal to their advantage when they argued that if Cleveland was indiscreet in private life, he had an exemplary record in public office, whereas Blaine, who was admirable as a husband and family man, had engaged in several dubious deals while in Congress. Put Cleveland into public office where he shined, they said, and return Blaine to the private life that he richly adorned.

The most damaging blow of the campaign struck the Blaine coalition on just a few days before the election. The confident Blaine made the mistake of publicly dining lavishly with a group of millionaires—not a good idea when he wanted the votes of many poor voters. Before another group, he let pass a statement of a Presbyterian minister, Samuel Burchard, who denounced the Democrats as the party of "rum, Romanism, and rebellion" —that is, of the saloon, the Roman Catholic Church, and southern secession.

Since Blaine was wooing Irish-American votes, and the Irish were sensitive about their religion, he should have repudiated the statement immediately. But he did not, and when Democratic newspapers plastered the insult across their front pages, Blaine rushed to express his sincere distaste for this kind of bigotry. But the damage was done. The Irish voters voted Democratic, giving New York and the presidency to Grover Cleveland.

Benjamin Harrison. In 1888, Cleveland was undone in his bid for reelection by a trivial incident. A Republican newspaper reporter, pretending to be an Englishman who was a *naturalized* American citizen, wrote to the British *ambassador* in Washington asking which of the two

When it was discovered that Grover Cleveland had hired someone to take his place in the service during the war, Cleveland's opponent Blaine attempted to make it an issue in the presidential election. At least, he did until it was discovered that he had done the same thing.

BENJAMIN HARRISON

Benjamin Harrison crusaded to have the flag flown over the White House and every school building:

The old-time Fourth of July celebration, with its simple parades and musters, the reading of the Declaration, and the oration that more than supplied the lack of glitter and color in the parade—once the event of the year—went out of fashion. We allowed ourselves to be laughed out of it. . . .

The day as a patriotic anniversary was almost lost, and a family picnic day or a base-ball day substituted. It is coming back, and we ought to aid in reinstating it. . . . Do not be ashamed to love the flag or to confess your love of it. Make much of it; tell its history; sing of it. It now floats over our schools, and it ought to hang from the windows of all our homes on all public days.

—*THIS COUNTRY OF OURS, 1897*

---

candidates, Cleveland or Benjamin Harrison, would be the better president from the British point of view. Foolishly, the ambassador replied that Cleveland seemed to be better disposed toward British interests. The Republican press immediately labeled Cleveland the British candidate. Thousands of Irish Democrats in New York, who were automatically hostile to anything or anyone the British favored, voted Republican and gave that swing state to Harrison. But Cleveland's political career was not to end here. In 1892, he would become the only American president re-elected to the presidency after having lost it.

SECTION REVIEW

1. Write a sentence to identify: "waving the bloody shirt," Black Friday, Mugwumps, "rum, Romanism, and rebellion."

2. In what four ways did national politics work like city politics?

3. Describe some Republican abuses in awarding pensions to Union war veterans.

4. Explain why President Grant was able to defeat Horace Greeley in 1872.

5. Into what two major factions was the Republican party divided after the election of 1872? Who was the leader of each faction?

3. NATIONAL POLITICAL ISSUES

Until the 1890s, the lines of division in late nineteenth-century politics were not so much between parties as within them. The big issues included the *tariff*, the backing of American currency with gold, and foreign relations with the country's American neighbors and with Great Britain.

Foreign Affairs. Despite the tendency of politicians of both parties to oppose Great Britain, relations with the British generally improved during the final decades of the century. In 1871, President Grant's Secretary of State, Hamilton Fish, concluded the *Treaty of Washington* with Great Britain. The *treaty* resolved a number of aggravating differences between the two nations. Great Britain compensated American shipowners for damages that had been done to their ships during the Civil War by the British-built Confederate *raider*, the *Alabama*. Squabbles between New Englanders and Canadians over fishing rights in the North Atlantic were smoothed, and a minor but locally bothersome boundary dispute between Washington Territory and the province of British Columbia was ironed out—the last point of contention on the long Canadian-American border.

President Grant was less successful in his pet foreign scheme. Encouraged by American inves-

---

Class Activity: Have the class collect newspaper and magazine clippings of stories involving present political corruption. Display these on a bulletin board. Compare the types of corruption found today with that in the late 1800s.

tors and a pro-American political faction in Santo Domingo (the Dominican Republic today), the Spanish-speaking half of the island of Hispaniola, Grant tried to annex it to the United States. He came very close to success and was foiled only because of the opposition of the Liberal Republican party.

In a related matter, James Blaine, who was Secretary of State under both Garfield and Harrison, attempted to assert American economic primacy in Latin America. The Latin American countries were primarily producers of *raw materials*, and Blain wanted them to tie their fates to the United States rather than to Great Britain, which was then the major supplier of manufactured goods in the Western Hemisphere.

After years of campaigning for closer relations between the United States and the Latin American republics, Blaine succeeded in hosting a *Pan-American Congress* in Washington in 1889. Of all the Latin American nations, only Santo Domingo refused to attend.

The delegates agreed to the establishment of a permanent *Pan-American Union* in Washington, to be a clearinghouse for diplomatic relations within the Americas. But they would not agree to Blaine's proposal for a customs union—that is, free trade within the Americas and tariff protection against the rest of the world. Blaine had to be satisfied with *unilateral* action. In the *McKinley Tariff* of 1890, Congress included a *reciprocal trade clause.* The president was empowered to reduce *duties* on the goods of nations that lowered their own tariffs on American goods.

The Tariff.

The tariff was an emotional issue in the late nineteenth century. Most southern and western Democrats, who represented agricultural sections, and some Republicans from rural districts, urged low import duties. With the exception of a few who grew specialized crops such as sugar cane, American farmers had no fear of foreign competition because of the abundance of farm products. Moreover, low duties on imported manufactured goods meant lower prices on the commodities that consumers of manufactured goods, such as farmers, had to buy. Railroaders and bankers often supported the low-tariff forces, too. As far as they were concerned, the more goods being transported, the better.

American manufacturers and most industrial workers insisted on *protective*, or high, *tariffs*. The size of their profits and wages, they believed, depended on keeping out foreign competition.

Increasingly in the late nineteenth century, high tariff interests had their way. After bobbing up and down from a low of 40 percent to a high of 47 percent, rates were increased to 50 percent in the McKinley Tariff. When a *depression* followed quickly on the act, however, Grover Cleveland and the Democrats campaigned against the McKinley rates in 1892 and won the election. But the tariff that Congress prepared in 1894, the *Wilson-Gorman Act,* lowered duties by only 10.1 percent —to 39.9 percent. Cleveland knew that this rate was not low enough to satisfy many of his supporters, so he unsuccessfully attempted a pocket veto.

Backing the American Dollar.

Another issue that generated a great deal of heat during the final third of the nineteenth century was the money question. What should be the basis of the nation's medium of exchange? Should it continue to be gold, with every piece of paper money backed by gold in a vault and *redeemable* in the precious metal? Or should the money supply be increased by the government to benefit workers and, particularly, farmers?

The monetary question predated the Civil War, but the form it took in the early 1880s was a result of wartime policy. In order to help finance the war effort, the federal government had issued about $431 million in paper money that was not redeemable in gold. The *greenbacks*, so called because they were printed in green ink instead of gold on the front, were accepted at *face value* by the federal government. That is, they were accepted at face value in payment of taxes.

As long as people had doubts about the Union's ability to survive (and thus redeem the greenbacks), individuals involved in private transactions insisted on discounting the greenbacks, or redeeming them at something less than face value. Bankers were particularly suspicious of any paper money that was not redeemable in gold, and after the war, secretaries of the treasury who shared the conservative views of the bankers adopted the policy of retiring the greenbacks. When the notes flowed into the Treasury, they were destroyed and were not replaced by new bills.

Research Assignment: Students may wish to develop an ongoing research assignment chronicling U.S./Latin American relations. Emphasis should be placed on the attitudes based on political and economic relations that each side has developed toward the other.

454

The result was *deflation*: a reduction in the amount of money in circulation and, therefore, an increase in the value of gold and of paper money that was redeemable in gold. Prices dipped; so did wages. It took less to buy a sack of flour or a side of bacon than it had when the greenbacks had flowed in profusion. Of course, the farmers who grew the wheat and raised the hogs received less for their trouble.

Farmers, who were generally debtors, were hit hardest by deflation. They had borrowed heavily to increase their acreage and to purchase machinery when the greenbacks had been abundant and prices therefore high. After the Treasury began to retire the greenbacks, they found themselves obligated to repay these loans in money that was more valuable and more difficult to get. For example, one economist calculated that a $1,000 *mortgage* taken out on a farm during the 1860s represented 1,200 bushels of grain. By the 1880s, when a farmer was still paying off his debt, $1,000 represented 2,300 bushels.

The Greenback Labor Party.

Protesting the retirement of the greenbacks as a policy that enriched bankers/creditors at the expense of producers/debtors, farmers formed the Greenback Labor party in 1876. In an effort to convince industrial workers that their interests lay in an abundant money supply, the party chose as its presidential candidate Peter Cooper, a New York philanthropist and model employer.

Cooper made a poor showing. But in the congressional race of 1878, the Greenbackers elected a dozen representatives, and both Republicans and Democrats backed their inflationary policy. However, President Hayes's monetary policy was as *conservative* as Grant's had been, and in 1879, retirement of the greenbacks proceeded swiftly. In 1880, the Greenback Labor ticket, led by James B. Weaver, a Civil War general from Iowa, won 309,000 votes. They denied Garfield a popular majority, but once again failed to affect policy.

In 1884, Benjamin F. Butler led the Greenbackers one more time, but received only one-half of the votes that Weaver had won in 1880. Although the demand to increase the money supply was not dead, the greenbacks were gone and soon forgotten. The new symbol of abundant money

In 1876, the Greenback Labor party chose Peter Cooper to run for president. The cartoon above pokes fun at Cooper (whose head is on the donkey's tail) and his party's platform.

that farmers rallied around was silver, a precious metal that almost had been forgotten in the United States until huge stores of it were discovered during the extraordinary development of the American West.

SECTION REVIEW

1. Write a sentence to identify: Pan-American Union, Wilson-Gorman Act, deflation, Greenback Labor party.

2. Describe American dealings with the following in the late nineteenth century: Great Britain, Canada, Latin America, Santo Domingo.

3. What American groups favored a lower tariff? Why? What groups favored a protective tariff? Why?

4. What questions about money generated controversy during the final third of the nineteenth century?

5. How was the money controversy resolved, and what effect did the resolution have on western farmers?

Research Assignment: In keeping with the work done in this chapter on interpreting political cartoons, have students who wish to make transparencies for the overhead projector of the cartoons of Thomas Nast. Students should accompany the cartoons with an oral presentation about Nast's life and interpretations of the cartoons they show.

CHAPTER REVIEW

TIME LINE

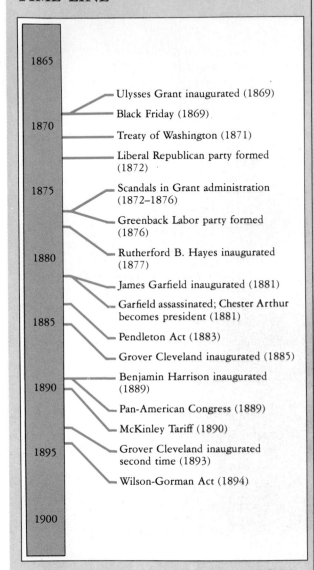

1865

Ulysses Grant inaugurated (1869)

Black Friday (1869)

1870

Treaty of Washington (1871)

Liberal Republican party formed (1872)

1875

Scandals in Grant administration (1872–1876)

Greenback Labor party formed (1876)

1880

Rutherford B. Hayes inaugurated (1877)

James Garfield inaugurated (1881)

Garfield assassinated; Chester Arthur becomes president (1881)

1885

Pendleton Act (1883)

Grover Cleveland inaugurated (1885)

Benjamin Harrison inaugurated (1889)

1890

Pan-American Congress (1889)

McKinley Tariff (1890)

Grover Cleveland inaugurated second time (1893)

1895

Wilson-Gorman Act (1894)

1900

TIME LINE QUESTIONS

1. During which president's administration did each of the following events occur: the Pendleton Act, the Pan-American Congress, the formation of the Greenback Labor party, the McKinley Tariff.
2. Which president served two separate terms?
3. Which president served for less than one year? Why?

SKILLS STRATEGY

POLITICAL CARTOONS

Political cartoons appear in history books to show you how some people who were living during a particular time reacted to a political situation or person. These cartoons, by their nature, are always biased and contain propaganda. The aim of a cartoonist is to persuade readers to agree with the point of view in the cartoon. Humor and exaggeration are used to give the argument punch and to get the reader's attention. Political cartoons first appeared in American newspapers in the *Pennsylvania Gazette*. They quickly became a popular vehicle for political attack because people enjoyed them. They were and are effective weapons.

Since a political cartoon is drawn by a cartoonist who lived during the time of the event shown in the cartoon, it supplements text treatment of the event with a humorous reflection of the attitudes of people who were directly affected.

Reread the last paragraph in the subsection "Chester A. Arthur" on page 451 in the text. Although the cartoon above was drawn recently, long after John Wanamaker made his suggestion for raising campaign contributions, it reflects an attitude about this continuing problem.

In 1974, the Federal Campaign Reform Act

---

456   *Making Connections:* Review the questions and topics presented in the Making Connections section that opens this chapter. Discuss the positive and negative aspects of the political malaise

suggested a different solution for financing politicians' campaigns. Taxpayers were allowed to indicate on their tax returns whether they wanted to contribute $1 of their taxes toward the payment of campaign expenses of the candidates. The second cartoon reflects an attitude toward this solution.

In the first cartoon, the fat cat represents big business people who, until recently, were expected to "contribute" to the campaigns of certain candidates. The cartoonist suggests that the businesspeople attached strings to their "contributions" by showing the fat cat in the process of eating a figure labeled "Public Morality." What the cartoon is saying in a humorous way is that by "contributing" money, the fat cats are gaining undue political influence.

APPLYING SKILLS

1. In the second cartoon, what group does the larger figure represent?
2. How does the cartoonist arouse a negative feeling toward the larger figure?
3. How does the taxpayer seem to feel?
4. How does the cartoon make you feel about public financing of political campaigns?
5. Why are political cartoons propaganda?

CHAPTER 18 TEST

TEXT REVIEW

1. Give the essential ideas you learned from the section titled "Big City Politics."
2. Use facts to support this statement: "To some degree, national politics in the late nineteenth century worked just like municipal politics."
3. Explain President Grant's attitude toward corruption.
4. Explain why voters consistently elected corrupt politicians instead of voting for candidates offered by reform groups.
5. Give some examples of the abuse of patronage by city and national politicians.
6. Make a two-column chart showing voting patterns in the basic geographical regions of the country and among social classes during this period.
7. Describe the political roles of James G. Blaine and Roscoe Conkling.
8. List the big issues in national politics between 1865 and 1900. Give the essential details about one of these issues.

CRITICAL THINKING

9. Explain the point of view of each of the following toward city political machines: working-class poor voters in a city, recent immigrant voters, property-owning middle-class reformers.
10. If President Chester Arthur had been reelected in 1884, in what ways do you think the national political scene might have been different?

WRITING A PARAGRAPH

Write a paragraph contrasting the good and bad points of big city political machines. Begin with sentences that discuss the good points. The first sentence in the group that discusses bad points should begin with words or phrases such as *however* or *on the other hand* to show that it contains contrasting details.

Topic Sentence: The political machines that controlled the governments of some American cities had both good and bad points.

CHAPTER 19

GROWING PAINS

1865–1900

*" . . . but now, they did not know what to do, and perhaps they
would do nothing; or perhaps they would go to a city, where, somehow,
they would continue to live in the woods. . . .*   DAVID PLANTE

Making Connections. The rapid growth of United States industry made fortunes for some Americans. But for most Americans, industrialization meant a new kind of life, one that was not always as good as they wanted it to be. In response to the growing power that industrialists and the machines seemed to have over their lives, workers began banding together in unions to bargain for better pay and safer work places. Cities also saw the beginnings of organizations dedicated to improving people's lives.

In this chapter, you will learn:

- Who criticized the growth of a wealthy class, and what his solution was
- Who approved of the growth of the wealthy class, and how he justified it
- What the typical wages, hours, and working conditions were for working people during this time
- How newly formed labor organizations dealt with employers, and which organization was most successful
- Who the New Immigrants were, and how they adapted to their new country
- What problems were caused by the rapid growth of cities

You know that the population of the United States doubled between 1865 and 1900. Consequently, large numbers of people came to the cities in search of work. As you read, note what kinds of lives the working people led, and how they sought to improve their lives.

Sections

1. NEW WEALTH

Between the end of the Civil War and the turn of the century, the annual production of goods in the United States increased from $2 billion to $13 billion. America made the shift in these years from a basically agricultural to a basically industrial nation. The opportunities for success made the United States an example of economic democracy. Most Americans could now reasonably believe that they did not have to remain at the economic level at which they had been born. Native-born citizens and immigrants alike felt that all one needed to do to improve one's situation was to work hard and practice thrift.

Most of the new wealth in America was not the traditional type—land and its produce. Rather, this new wealth tended to be industrial wealth. And industrial wealth was different from land in an important way. The amount of land in the United States was limited. Industry, however, produced wealth that was potentially limitless because a *capitalist's* property could be expanded indefinitely. There was a danger that this new wealth could be concentrated in the hands of a small industrial *aristocracy*. If that happened, the much treasured equality of economic opportunity would be threatened. Some people thought that the rich might try to control the country to advance only their own interests.

In the second half of the nineteenth century, horse-and-buggy transportation began to give way to clanging trolleys, hissing trains, and a new, horseless carriage called the automobile. As the painting at the right shows, the period was a time of clamorous change.

Quotation: from the novel *The Country*. Other works by David Plante (born 1940) include *The Ghost of Henry James, Slides, Relatives, The Darkness of the Body, Figures in Bright Air, The Family, The Woods,* and *Difficult Women*.

The Very Rich.
In 1837, the richest man in the United States was a Philadelphia merchant, Stephen Girard. When Girard died in 1837, his estate of $7 million awed Americans. They heaped praise on him, not so much for having amassed such a treasure, but for what he did with it. Girard left his money to various *philanthropic* societies and to the city of Philadelphia. He reaffirmed America's belief in equality of opportunity by showing what an *enterprising* American could do and by plowing his fortune back into the society.

Just a decade later, John Jacob Astor died and left $40 million to his son. Those who had praised Girard now condemned Astor. America wanted no aristocrats, Astor's critics said; no heirs and heiresses whose fortunes were unearned. Inherited wealth was Europe's way, not America's. Astor had mocked the ideal of equality and the ethic of hard work.

After the Civil War, it became extremely common for fortunes to be passed from one generation to the next. Moreover, the fortunes that were made in the new industries grew larger, as did the size of the millionaire class. In 1892, there were more than 4,000 millionaires in the United States, most of them richer than Girard had been. Cornelius Vanderbilt left $100 million when he died in 1877. His son, William, doubled that amount in only eight years. By 1900, Andrew Carnegie made $500 million in a single transaction.

The new industrial millionaires flaunted their wealth in ways that offended traditional American values. Thorstein Veblen, a sociologist, observed in several books that the very wealthy literally lived to spend money for the sake of proving that they had money. Veblen called this showy extravagance *conspicuous consumption* and labeled the tendency to practically throw money away "conspicuous waste."

Having much more money than they could possibly put to good use, the very rich competed in spending it. They hosted lavish parties for one another, built extravagant palaces, and purchased

With an expanding economy and few taxes, wealthy American capitalists were able to amass huge fortunes. For them, spending money on lavish parties (top left), expensive clothes (center), and fine automobiles (bottom) was a way of flaunting their success to other millionaires.

"The Breakers" (above) was the summer "cottage" built in Newport, Rhode Island by William Vanderbilt, the son and heir of Cornelius Vanderbilt (inset).

huge yachts that were good for little but show.

Nowhere was consumption more conspicuous and lavish than at upper-class resorts such as Newport, Rhode Island. A summer "cottage" of 30 rooms, used for only three months a year, cost $1 million. William K. Vanderbilt outdid everyone with a cottage that cost $2 million to build and $9 million to furnish.

Public Reaction. In newspapers, popular songs, and theatrical melodramas, the idleness and extravagance of the "filthy rich" were favorite themes. The wealthy were depicted with a mixture of envy and resentment. In the popular melodramas of the day, right-living poor people were pitted against rich and unscrupulous villains. "You are only a shopgirl," said the high-society lady in a typical play. "An honest shopgirl," replied the heroine in stilted language, "as far above a fashionable idler as heaven is above earth!" However, at the end of the play, as a reward for her virtue, the shopgirl married a millionaire and joined high society.

Working Americans were both fascinated and appalled by the habits of the idle rich. Many were attracted by the ideas of social critics who wrote books and articles about the new industrial wealth and its consequences for American society. Perhaps the most influential of these critics was Henry George.

Henry George. A lively writing style and a knack for simplifying difficult economic ideas made journalist Henry George and his single tax the center of a briefly momentous social movement. In *Progress and Poverty*, published in 1879, George observed that instead of freeing people from onerous labor, as it had promised to do, industrialization had put millions to work under killing conditions for long hours. Instead of making life easier and fuller, the mass production of goods had enriched the few in the "House of

Research Assignment: Compare attitudes toward the wealth displayed by John Jacob Astor and Stephen Girard in a report that looks at both of their lives in detail.

461

Political cartoons poked fun at the tax complaints of millionaires.

Have," and had impoverished the millions in the "House of Want."

George did not blame either industrialization or capitalism as such for the misery he saw around him. Like most Americans, he believed that the competition for comfort and security was a wellspring of the nation's energy. Trouble began when those who were successful grew so wealthy that they could live off the "rents" from their property.

The Single Tax.
George called income derived from mere ownership of property "unearned increment" because it required no work, effort, or ingenuity. The property grew more valuable and its owners richer only because other people needed access to it in order to survive. Such value was false, George said. Government had every right to levy a 100 percent tax on it. Because the revenues from this tax would be quite enough to pay all the expenses of government, George called it the *single tax*. All other taxes would be abolished. The idle rich would be destroyed as a social class. The competition that made the country great would

take place without the handicaps of taxation. Everyone would compete on an equal basis.

George's theory was both easy to grasp and firmly within American traditional attitudes. It made him immensely popular among people who resented the power and life style of the very rich. In 1886, George narrowly missed election as mayor of New York, a city where real estate values and "unearned increment" from land were among the highest in the world. Within a few years, however, the single-tax movement lost ground to other reform ideas.

A Defense of Wealth.
At the same time that great wealth was being criticized, it was also being defended and praised. The defenders' strongest argument touched the heart of the American Dream. The United States had been built on the desire for a better life. Therefore, if competition for riches was a virtue, what was wrong with winning? Far from a source of anxiety, as the critics said, or evidence of social immorality, the fabulous fortunes of America's wealthy families revealed their virtue. Defenders of great wealth contended that the Rockefellers, Carnegies, and Morgans deserved their money because they had worked hard for it.

Horatio Alger and "Ragged Dick."
Through the 130 boys' novels written by the minister Horatio Alger, this wealth-as-good manifesto was conveyed to the younger generation. Alger's books sold 20 million copies between 1867 and 1899.

The plots of all the short novels were variations on two or three simple themes. The most popular plot told of a poor lad who was honest, hard working, loyal to his employer, and clean living. "Ragged Dick," Alger's first hero and the prototype of dozens of others, was unfailingly courteous and always went to church.

Curiously, the hero did not get rich slowly through hard work. At the beginning of the final chapter, he was usually as bad off as on page one. Then, however, Ragged Dick was presented with what amounted to a gift that rewarded his virtues. In one story, the daughter of a rich industrialist fell off the Staten Island Ferry; in another, she slipped into the Niagara River just above the falls. Invariably, the heroic lad rescued the young

Class Activity: Examine the pictures of the rich on pages 460 and 461 of this chapter and the pictures of the poor on pages 465 and 466. Are the impressions they give accurate in relation to the images given in the text?

woman at the last minute. His reward was a job in her father's business, marriage to the daughter, and eventually the grateful father's fortune.

The Best Rise to the Top.

Andrew Carnegie was one of the few industrialist millionaires who understood the writings of Herbert Spencer, a British philosopher who preached that great wealth was justified.

Spencer seemed to apply a biological theory to human society. In the world of animals and plants, Spencer said, species competed for life and those best adapted survived, while the weaker species died out. In the same way, he argued, the "fittest" people rose to the top in the social competition for riches. Eventually, in the dog-eat-dog world, they alone survived. "If they are sufficiently complete to live," Spencer wrote, "they do live, and it is well that they should live. If they are not sufficiently complete to live, they die and it is best they should die."

Spencer's use of biological terms crept into the vocabulary of politicians who represented business interests. They used his ideas to argue against government relief of the poor because, they said, such welfare policies would interfere with natural processes.

William Graham Sumner.

The most important American disciple of Herbert Spencer was a Yale professor, William Graham Sumner. His Spencerian ideas made him a staunch opponent of giving aid to the poor, regulating business, or interfering in any way with the economic system.

On some issues, Sumner's belief in free competition made him oppose special favors for business, such as a high protective tariff. To *subsidize* American industry by taxing imports was just as unnatural to him as was regulating the growth of trusts. If American manufacturers were not fit to compete with European manufacturers in a *free market*, Sumner said, they were not fit to survive.

Philanthropy.

Some industrialists like Rockefeller had made a life-long habit of giving money to worthy causes. He and other wealthy industrialists also gave a portion of their great wealth back to society by founding philanthropic organizations and schools. Horatio Alger supported institutions that housed homeless boys in New York City.

Russell B. Conwell founded Temple University, where poor young students could study very cheaply and improve themselves. Leland Stanford built a wholly new "Harvard of the West" in California and named it Stanford University.

Andrew Carnegie justified enormous fortunes on the basis of *stewardship*. In a widely publicized essay entitled "Wealth," he argued that the unrestricted pursuit of riches made American society vital and strong. Any person who succeeded in business became a steward, or trustee, of society. This wealthy steward had an obligation to distribute money where it would provide opportunities for poor people to join the competition of the next generation. Indeed, Carnegie said that the rich person who died rich, died a failure. He retired in 1901 and devoted the rest of his life to granting money to libraries, schools, and useful social institutions. He was so rich, however, that despite extraordinary generosity, he died a multimillionaire.

SECTION REVIEW

1. Write a sentence to identify: Newport, Rhode Island; *Progress and Poverty;* Horatio Alger; philanthropy.

2. What two ideas lay behind the American belief that the United States was an economic democracy?

3. What was Herbert Spencer's theory about how natural competition in human society justified great wealth?

4. Give some examples of what the sociologist Thorstein Veblen called "conspicuous consumption" and "conspicuous waste."

---

2. NEW WORK PLACES

The population of the United States rose rapidly during the last part of the nineteenth century, more than doubling between 1860 and 1900, from 32 million to 76 million. During the same time period, the size of the working class soared. In 1860, 1.5 million Americans made their living in workshops and mills, and another 700,000 Americans worked in mining and construction.

Discussion Question: Are the views of Spencer and Carnegie contradictory? If so, in what way? Are there ways in which their views would not necessarily be contradictory?

At the time of the Civil War, most Americans were still working on farms or working alone or in small family businesses. However, by the end of the century, America had become industrialized. The typical worker in 1900 was a *wageworker*, a person who worked for a company or corporation as an employee. Wageworkers, previously a minor part of the American population, now comprised a distinct and significant social class. American industrialists and American workers led the way as industry changed the American life-style.

Factories. The size of the work place also grew, a fact of profound importance for the quality of working people's lives. In 1870, the average workshop in the United States employed eight people and was owned by an individual or by partners who lived nearby and who personally supervised the business, sometimes working at the bench with their employees. Like it or not, employers were personally involved in the lives of their workers. They heard of events ranging from the birth of a child to the death of a parent. They discussed wages, hours, and shop conditions with the people who were affected by them.

In 1870, not one American factory employed as many as a thousand men and women. By 1900, such gigantic plants were common, and a few companies listed 10,000 people on the payroll. The typical employer of 1900 was a large company that was directed by owners or managers who rarely stepped onto the floor of a shop. They lost the close contact that had been commonplace with small, family-owned businesses.

The increased application of steam power and constantly improved machinery affected workers in other ways. The highly skilled craftsperson, trained for years in the use of hand tools, ceased to be the principal factor in the manufacturing process. Not many crafts actually disappeared and some, like the *machinist's* trade, increased in importance. But in almost every area, machines took over from artisans and "mechanics," performing their jobs quicker and often better.

Into their places came the unskilled or semi-skilled machine tenders—men, women, and children who guided the machine at its task. Unlike craftspeople, these workers required little training. For this reason, they were poorly paid. They had little or no job security, because other un-

When factories grew in size and became whole complexes, like the one shown below, they frequently became the major source of employment for people living in the area. In such instances, the fate of the town became tied to the success or failure of the factory.

The photograph on the left shows "spindle boys" in a Georgia cotton mill, whose job was to make sure the spindles threaded properly. The photograph on the right shows a young girl tending a spinner in a Carolina cotton mill.

skilled workers were readily available to take their places if they got sick or could not work.

Wages. The cash wages of working people remained the same or declined during the final decades of the nineteenth century. However, *real wages*, or purchasing power, actually rose. The cost of food, clothing, and housing dropped more radically than did hourly pay during the deflationary final decades of the nineteenth century. American workers at the end of the century were better off than ever before. Taken as a whole, the industrial working class enjoyed almost 50 percent more *purchasing power* in 1900 than in 1860. The American Dream became a reality for many.

The skilled "aristocracy of labor"—locomotive engineers, machinists, master carpenters, printers, and other highly trained craftspeople—improved their earnings much more than did the unskilled workers. The average annual wage for manufacturing workers in 1900 was $435, or $8.37 a week. Unskilled workers were paid about ten cents an hour on the average, about $5.50 a week. A girl of 12 or 13, tending a loom in a textile factory, might take home as little as $2 a week

after various fines (for being late to work, for example) were deducted from her pay.

Hours. Hours on the job varied as widely as wages. Most government employees had enjoyed an eight-hour day since 1840. Skilled workers, especially in the building trade (bricklayers, carpenters, plumbers), generally worked ten hours. Elsewhere, such short hours were virtually unknown. A factory worker was accounted lucky if he or she worked a 12-hour day. During the summer months, many mills ran from sunup to sundown, as long as 16 hours in some parts of the country—with only one shift.

Because of erratic swings in the business cycle of the period, factory workers were regularly laid off. Some work was seasonal. Coal miners, for example, could expect to be without wages for weeks or even months during the summer, when city people did not heat their homes. Coal companies delivered ice in the summer to offset slack time. In times of depression, of course, unemployment was worse. During the depressions of the 1870s and 1890s, about 12 percent of the working population was jobless.

Research Project: Have students refer to a population density map of this period and discuss the following questions. Where does there seem to be the greatest concentration of people? What about these areas would have attracted people during this time in history? What parts of the country seem to be the most industrialized? What makes you conclude that?

Working Conditions. While some employers attended carefully to safety conditions, a safe work place was by no means the rule. Railroads had a particularly bad record. Every year, one railroad worker in 26 was injured seriously, and one in 400 was killed. Textile workers without some fingers and ex-textile workers without hands were common in every mill town.

Between 1880 and 1900, 35,000 American workers were killed on the job, an average of almost five a day. In many cases, their spouses or dependents received nothing. Usually, employer compensation amounted to little more than burial expenses. In the coal fields, it was considered generous if a dead miner's teenage son, who was younger than the regulation age, was allowed to take a job in the mines in order to support his family.

What compensation the employees received applied only to accidents. Diseases such as the coal miner's "black lung" were not recognized as the employer's responsibility in America or in Europe, because they were not considered "occupational." Poisoning resulting from work with chemicals was rarely identified as related to the job.

The Company Town. In the *company towns*, in which employers owned not only the factory but also houses, stores, schools, and even church buildings, workers usually had a difficult time.

Some company towns were built because there were no residential settlements near where businesses were established. This was true, for example, of isolated Pennsylvania coal fields, and logging and lumber mill towns. Others were built because an idealistic industrialist wanted employees to live better than workers elsewhere. These employers set up their towns as utopias, but later owners did not continue the founders' good intentions.

Once established, the company town soon came to appeal to some factory owners as a way of controlling their employees. Thus, when textile companies began to move from New England and New Jersey to the southern states late in the nineteenth century, their owners deliberately built in the pine woods rather than near established towns. They wanted to keep their employees from organizing and pushing up wages, as workers had done in the North.

When the company owned the store at which food was purchased, workers could be paid in *scrip,* or substitute money, rather than in cash. Scrip was redeemable only at the company store; thus, the factory owner could take profits by charging higher prices than did independent mer-

The photograph below shows workers in a steam locomotive factory. People of all ages worked in factories during the late nineteenth century.

chants who had to compete. Moreover, when employees went into debt at the company store, they gave the bosses additional leverage against them in case of a dispute over wages or conditions. Finally, if workers went on strike in a company town, they risked not only losing a job, but being evicted from a company-owned house.

Women in the Factories.

Cultural lag played a part in the large numbers of women in industry. The first industrial workers had been women, partly because the founders of the first American textile mills had not been able to imagine factory work as a suitable lifetime career for the head of a family. Instead of recruiting men to work in their mills, the early cloth manufacturers had persuaded New England farmers to send their unmarried daughters to towns like Lowell, Massachusetts. The plan had been that they would work for a few years, save their money, and return to the farm to take up their true calling as wives of farmers. Their factory earnings provided them with a dowry that their fathers could not afford.

In devising this *Lowell system* , the pioneers of the factory system had believed that they had reconciled industrialization with farm life. But the increasing demands of growing industry and the heavy nature of much factory work soon resulted in a work force that was predominantly male. Nevertheless, the difficulty of supporting a family on one person's income forced working-class women to continue to labor for wages even after they married. In 1900, almost 20 percent of the total work force was female. About half the workers in textiles were women, and the percentage in the needle trades and other home manufactures was much higher.

With very few exceptions, women were paid much less than men, sometimes half as much for performing the same tasks for the same number of hours.

Children in the Factories.

In 1900, child labor was a common thing in industrialized countries. In America an estimated 1,750,000 children under 16 years of age were employed full time. They did all but the heaviest kinds of work. Girls as young as 12 tended dangerous looms and spinning machines in textile mills. "Bobbin boys" of ten hauled heavy wooden boxes filled with spindles from spinning rooms to weaving rooms and back again. Children swept filings in machine shops. Boys as young as eight were found working at coal mines, hand picking slate from coal in filthy, frigid wooden sheds. In city tenement sweat shops, whole families and their boarders sewed clothing or rolled cigars by hand, and children worked as soon as they were able to master the simplest tasks.

On the grounds that children had no nonworking dependents to support, employers paid them less than adults. The justification was not always convincing, however. In southern textile towns, the "mill daddy" became a familiar figure. Unable to find work because his own children could be hired for less, the mill daddy was reduced to carrying his children's lunches to the factory and tossing them over the fence each noon.

Child labor, as such, was not new. Children had always worked on farms and in small workshops. In the small shop, however, a child's fatigue when set to tedious, repetitive tasks, was easy to recognize and take into account. Placed in a massive factory, the child laborer became little more than a number on an accountant's sheet. It took time for society to realize that industrial life was something radically different from what had existed earlier, and that children had no place in it.

SECTION REVIEW

1. Write a sentence to identify: cash wages versus real wages, "black lung," scrip, Lowell system.

2. What changes occurred between 1860 and 1900 in the size of the American work place and the rate of work? Cite specific examples.

3. What effect did child labor and women workers have on pay scale and the workforce in general?

4. Why were many craftspeople and artisans replaced by unskilled or semiskilled workers during the late nineteenth century?

5. Give the most important facts about the following aspects of the late nineteenth century: (a) wages, (b) hours, (c) working conditions, (d) company towns.

Research Assignment: Have students do some "herstory" research. Have them do a report examining the ways women worked in your locale at the turn of the century. Have them use libraries, historical societies, women's groups, and individuals they know as sources. Have them examine how industrialization affected the kinds of work women did.

3. A NEW LABOR MOVEMENT

In the new industrial age, the rhythms of life were unnatural for people who had been raised on farms or in small towns. Factory workers had to live by the clock, work many hours at a stretch, and perform the same monotonous tasks over and over. American workers resisted the new discipline in a number of ways.

Individual Resistance. Despite the penalties, absenteeism plagued the factories of the late nineteenth century. The long hours and the six-day week caused a significant number of workers to take an unscheduled day off, from time to time. Monday's production was routinely half as much as on other days. Most employers could expect a slow start to each week's output.

Sabotage was also an effective way to slow the pace of work. Workers found it easy to damage a machine so that it appeared to be an accident. When the pace became too taxing, it was easy enough to "throw a monkey wrench into the works" or slash a leather power belt for the sake of a few moments' rest.

Group Resistance. Workers joined together in groups to resist the conditions of their work place. Violence was often the result. Denied any means of changing conditions under which they worked and lived, desperate workers turned to the riot, the gun, and the well-placed stick of dynamite. A nationwide railroad strike erupted in 1877 as an unorganized, spontaneous outbreak. Mobs of striking workers stormed into railroad yards and set trains and buildings on fire. In a few places they fought pitched gun battles with company guards and with troops.

At Andrew Carnegie's Homestead works in 1892, striking steel workers actually besieged the giant factory and forced the withdrawal of a barge bringing 300 armed guards into the town. Similar conflicts characterized labor disputes in many industries. Strikes were most bloody and bitter in the coal mines of Pennsylvania and in the hard-rock gold and silver mines of the West.

The Molly Maguires. During the early 1870s, many Irish coal miners in northeastern Pennsylvania gave up on the possibility of improving the conditions of their unhealthful and dangerous work through peaceful means. Within the semisecret atmosphere of a fraternal lodge, the Ancient Order of Hibernians, they formed a totally secret society called the Molly Maguires. The Mollies then launched an effective campaign of terrorism against the mine owners and particularly the supervisors. They systematically destroyed

The engraving below is of a mass meeting of working people in New York City on July 25, 1877, demonstrating their support of the national railroad strike.

mine property, beat up loyal company workers, and even murdered some workers.

The mine owners finally brought in an Irish-American detective, James McParland, from the Pinkerton Agency. McParland infiltrated the Mollies and gathered evidence that led to the hanging of several men and the destruction of the organization.

Labor War in the West.

In the gold and silver mines of the West, labor violence was chronic. In an attempt to spot leaders, the mine owners employed Pinkerton agents, and these men and the miners engaged in violent confrontations that were more like small battles than industrial disputes. Miners and company guards shot at each other from behind barricades in "territories" that were clearly worker- or company-controlled.

Where the mine owners controlled local law enforcement, beatings and arbitrary arrests of strikers were common. In 1890, authorities in northern Idaho built a bull pen, a ramshackle wooden structure in which virtually every striking miner was confined under wretched conditions.

The miners, as well as the owners, were capable of initiating violence. An independent breed, imbued with the culture of the frontier, they "deported" workers who were unfriendly to them. After beating them, they walked them to the county line and warned them not to return. Resentful of absentee mine owners who lived in San Francisco, New York, and England, they often dynamited company property during labor disputes.

Strength in Numbers.

Long before the industrial age, workers had discovered the advantages of acting together in groups. Before 1800, shoemakers in Philadelphia had banded together for mutual protection in the Knights of St. Crispin. Workingmen's associations had been the backbone of the Jacksonian political movement in the eastern states. By the early 1870s, skilled workers such as machinists, iron molders, carpenters, and locomotive engineers and firemen had formed thousands of local trade groups whose total membership was about 300,000.

For the most part, these organizations had little to do with one another. Developing at a time when industry was decentralized, the unions lagged behind the employers in recognizing the need for national organization. The first labor leader to see the need was a solemn, visionary iron puddler from Philadelphia, William Sylvis.

The National Labor Union.

In 1866, William Sylvis founded an organization called the National Labor Union (NLU). He devoted his life to its cause, traveling around the eastern states and speaking to workers of every occupation in churches, fraternal lodges, and outdoors under the stars.

Sylvis believed that the workers' future depended on political involvement. He formed alliances with a number of reform groups, including the women's suffrage movement and farmers' organizations that were lobbying for a cheap currency. After Sylvis died in 1869, the National Labor party put up candidates in the presidential election of 1872. So poor was their showing, however, that the party and the NLU itself broke up, its members demoralized. From a membership of 400,000 in 1872, the NLU completely disappeared within two years.

The Knights of Labor.

By this time, a different kind of national labor organization had already emerged to take the place of the NLU. The Noble and Holy Order of the Knights of Labor was organized in 1869 by a group of tailors led by Uriah P. Stephens. Unlike Sylvis, Stephens recruited members of the Knights of Labor in secret because, as Stephens well knew, employers usually fired anyone suspected of being in a union.

The Knights of Labor also differed from the NLU by avoiding political action. Members were urged to vote, but Stephens believed that the interests of working people would ultimately be served by solidarity in the work place in opposition to their enemies.

Stephens disliked the idea of class conflict and looked forward to a day when men and women of good will in all social classes would abolish the wage system and establish a cooperative commonwealth. The Knights welcomed into their ranks women, blacks, and unskilled workers—groups that were usually overlooked as union material in the nineteenth century. However, the Knights failed to appeal to one group that was essential to the success of any labor organization: Roman

Research Assignment: Have students conduct an on-going project examining the history and impact of labor unions. Have students compare present-day union practices with those management practices criticized by the unions.

Under Terence Powderly (center) membership in the Knights of Labor grew over 600 percent in one year.

Catholics, particularly Irish-Americans, who were the largest ethnic group in the working class.

Stephens surrounded the Knights of Labor with the mystery, symbolism, ritual, and secret handshakes common to fraternal organizations. A lifelong *Freemason,* Stephens based the Knights' ritual on that of his own lodge.

In Europe, the Masons were known to be an anti-Catholic organization. Catholics were therefore suspicious of the Knights. Without Catholic support, no labor organization could prosper.

Terence Powderly.

In 1879, Stephens was succeeded as Grand Master Workman of the Knights of Labor by Terence V. Powderly. Himself a Roman Catholic, Powderly brought the Knights into the open and toned down the Masonic flavor of the ritual. He persuaded an influential Catholic bishop, James Gibbons, to prevail on the pope to approve Catholic membership in the union.

Then the Knights grew at a dazzling rate. By 1885, there were 110,000 members, and in only one year, the union grew to 700,000. Powderly disliked strikes, so it was ironic that the major reason for this increase was a successful strike by the Knights against Jay Gould's Missouri Pacific Railroad. Gould had vowed to destroy the union. "I can hire half the working class to kill the other half," he growled. But when he tried to cut wages, the Knights closed down his railroad line and forced him to meet with their leaders and agree to their terms.

Following this great victory, the explosive growth of the union proved to be a problem. Powderly and the union's general assembly were unable to control the new members. Instead of working together according to a national policy, local leaders, who were often new to the concept of unionism, were encouraged by the victory in the Missouri Pacific strike to go it alone in a dozen unrelated directions. Powderly fumed and refused to back the rash of *strikes* in 1885 and 1886. But he could not stop them.

Haymarket Square.

In 1886, after an incident for which they were not responsible, the Knights fell to pieces. Defying Powderly and demanding an eight-hour day, Knights in Chicago called a strike against the McCormick International Harvester Company, the world's largest manufacturer of farm machinery. Almost immediately, everything went wrong. The Chicago police were blatantly on the side of the employers, and over several days, they killed four workers. On May 4, a group of *anarchists* (who advocated the ultimate destruction of the political state) called a rally in support of the strikers at Haymarket Square, just south of the city center.

The oratory was red-hot; but the speakers broke no laws and the crowd was cool and orderly. Indeed, the rally was about to break up when a platoon of police entered the square and demanded that the people disperse. At that instant, someone threw a bomb into the crowd, killing seven people and wounding 67 officers. The police fired a volley, and four more workers fell dead.

News of the incident fed an anti-anarchist hysteria in Chicago. Authorities rounded up several dozen individuals who were known to have attended anarchist meetings, and authorities brought eight to trial for the murder of the officers. Among them were a Confederate Army

In Ireland the *Molly Maguires* was a group formed in 1843 to prevent eviction of tenants from houses owned by absentee landlords. The name emphasizes the fact that members of the group sometimes disguised themselves as women.

Tragedy struck on May 4, 1886, at a rally in Haymarket Square in Chicago. A bomb was thrown by an unknown person and the police responded with gunfire.

veteran from an old Virginia family, Albert Parsons, and a prominent German agitator, August Spies.

The trial was a farce. No one on the *prosecution* knew or even claimed to know who had thrown the bomb. Nor did the prosecution present evidence to tie any of the eight accused people to the bombing.

Nevertheless, fearful of more violence, the city's citizens were determined to punish someone as a warning to others. Four were hanged. One committed suicide in his cell. Three were sentenced to long prison terms.

In the meantime, because they were unfairly linked to the Haymarket bombing, the Knights of Labor fell to pieces. The majority of American workers were not interested in violence and shied away from even the suggestion of it. Within four

years, membership in the union plummeted from 700,000 to 100,000. In this reduced form, the organization dragged on until almost 1900.

The Modern Labor Movement. Only with the founding of the *American Federation of Labor (AFL)* in 1886 did a nationwide labor organization establish itself permanently in the United States. The AFL was put together by several dozen existing local associations of skilled workers. Its separate unions of workers, each of which practiced a different trade, retained considerable freedom of action independent of the federation's central office.

Samuel Gompers. The founder of the AFL was Samuel Gompers, a cigarmaker. Born in London of Dutch Jewish parents, Gompers had emigrated

Class Activity: Have a member of a local union organization come to class and give a presentation on the present-day activities of unions and their importance.

471

Samuel Gompers (election ballot in hand) founded the American Federation of Labor.

to New York as a boy. While still in his teens, he had astonished his fellow workers with his intelligence, toughness in bargaining, and oratorical eloquence. He had very definite ideas about how organizations of labor could not only survive in the United States, but also become a part of the interlocking forces that governed the country.

A Union for Skilled Workers.

First of all, Gompers believed that only skilled craftspeople could effectively force employers to negotiate with them. When all the skilled bricklayers in a locality went on strike, the employer who wanted bricks laid had no choice but to talk. On the other hand, if unskilled haulers of bricks went on strike, employers had no difficulty in finding other unskilled people with strong backs and empty stomachs to take their places. Therefore, Gompers concluded, the AFL would admit only skilled workers.

Second, the goals of the AFL unions were higher wages, shorter hours, and better working conditions. Gompers had no patience with socialistic or other utopian dreamers. Unions with utopian programs, he thought, distracted workers from the concrete issues that counted. Furthermore, such unions were easy targets for bosses who wanted to

convince Americans that labor organizations threatened the very stability of their society.

Third, Gompers believed that the strike, as peaceful coercion, was the union's best weapon. He also made it clear, however, that AFL unions would cooperate with employers who recognized and bargained with them. Gompers proposed that moderate unions like his be accepted as partners in industry, rather than rejecting all unions as a threat to the capitalist system. In effect, the AFL would strike against companies that refused to deal with the AFL, and cooperate with those who accepted unions.

Conservative Unionism.

Gompers lived until 1924 and served as president of the AFL every year but one (when AFL socialists defeated him). He did not see his hopes come to fruition, but he made a start. The AFL grew under his leadership from 150,000 members in 1888 to more than one million shortly after the turn of the century.

Most employers continued to distrust Gompers and the AFL as they did socialists and revolutionary labor unions. Their argument was that workers who did not like their pay had the right to quit. In 1893, some employers formed the National Association of Manufacturers (NAM) to counteract unionism wherever it appeared. The NAM remained the most important pro-employer organization into the twentieth century.

In 1900, another group of manufacturers led by Frank Easley and Marcus A. Hanna, a former Rockefeller associate, came to the conclusion that labor unions were a permanent part of the American industrial scene. The choice was not between unions and no unions. The choice was between conservative, procapitalist unions that were willing to cooperate with employers and revolutionary unions that were determined to destroy capitalism. These manufacturers chose Gompers's AFL and joined with him in 1900 to form the National Civic Federation, which was to work for industrial peace through employer-union cooperation.

By 1900, there was no doubt that the AFL would survive. Nevertheless, the conservative trade union movement failed to recognize some of the most serious questions that would face working people in the twentieth century. The AFL remained inflexible in its opposition to organizing unskilled workers. On more than one occasion,

Class Activity: Have a student pretend to be a newspaper reporter doing a follow-up to either the Haymarket Square incident or the trials that followed. Other students should portray people the reporter might interview and, in these roles, should present the point of view each character might have had toward the events. Roles might include: a policeman from the square; an

MOVERS AND SHAPERS

A. Montgomery Ward

Richard Sears

Alvah Roebuck

In 1872, a young midwestern salesman had a business idea that he believed would make farmers happier and himself richer. Aaron Montgomery Ward (1843–1913) had worked selling goods to stores, which would then sell them to farmers at high prices. Ward decided to sell directly to the consumers.

Ward's first office in Chicago was only 14 feet wide, just big enough to store the textiles he had bought at a low price. On a sheet of paper he listed his merchandise, along with their low prices. This was his first catalog that he mailed to potential customers.

Thousands of farmers and rural consumers mailed in orders for his goods. The prices they paid Ward made them satisfied customers, as Ward had predicted, and Ward expanded the catalog every year. By 1888, Ward was taking in $1 million a year.

In 1893, another mail order business was formed in Chicago by Richard Sears and Alvah Roebuck.

Richard Sears (1863–1914) had discovered early in life that he had a talent for buying and selling at a profit. He was only 23 when he made his first small fortune selling watches wholesale to the freight agents of a midwestern railroad company. The agents made good profits by reselling Sears's inexpensive watches directly to customers. Sears made only about $2 on each watch, but he sold so many that his profits in six months amounted to $5,000. This sum, quite substantial for the times, put Sears on the road to becoming one of America's millionaires.

Sears discovered that the best way to attract customers for his watches was through newspaper advertising. One of his ads caught the attention of Alvah Roebuck (1864–1948), who was a watchmaker in

Hammond, Indiana. He went to Chicago to seek a job with Sears. In a short time, the new employee of the Sears Watch Company became a partner in the business. In 1893, the two partners formed the company that soon became known nationwide—Sears, Roebuck and Company.

In 1893, the principal means for reaching American consumers and tempting them to buy was to issue a thick catalog. The Sears, Roebuck catalog for that year had 322 pages filled with advertisements for clothing, watches, bicycles, sewing machines, and any other household products. It also included pianos and organs.

In 1895, Roebuck sold his interest in the company to Sears for $25,000. Nineteen years later, Sears died a very rich man. But financial trouble eventually forced Roebuck to go back to the very company he had founded to ask once more for a job.

anarchist, such as Parson or Spies; a McCormick Harvester executive; or Terence Powderly, the judge. Have the reporter end with a commentary speculating on who would benefit from creating such an incident. Students should use sources from the actual incident, if possible.

Gompers used AFL unions to get rid of other unions that had been formed by the unskilled.

The AFL was particularly hostile to the immigration of unskilled laborers from eastern and southern Europe. The AFL wanted immigration restricted on economic grounds. By stopping immigration of workers from abroad, American workers would be better able to improve their own situation.

The AFL unions also generally opposed the organization of women (20 percent of the work force) and blacks and Chinese. The result was that skilled workers who were white and male steadily improved their lot through union membership. However, by the turn of the century, only three percent of gainfully employed Americans were members of labor organizations.

SECTION REVIEW

1. Write a sentence to identify: Molly Maguires, William Sylvis, Haymarket Square incident, AFL.

2. Name two labor unions formed before the AFL was founded, and explain why they did not survive.

3. List three definite ideas that Samuel Gompers held about labor organizations.

4. Who said the following, and for what reason: "I can hire half the working class to kill the other half."

5. In 1900, which groups of workers were still not unionized?

---

4. NEW CITIZENSHIP

Between 1860 and 1900 the population of the United States more than doubled. Much of this increase was due to immigration.

Immigration—An American Tradition. Immigration was essential to the American experience. Not even the Native Americans had originated in the Western Hemisphere. Throughout most of the colonial period, immigrants were as important to American growth as the natural increase in population. During the late nineteenth century, Europeans came over in numbers that increased almost annually.

But there was more to immigration after 1880 than a mere increase in numbers. Before 1880, a large majority of immigrants listed Great Britain, Wales, Scotland, Ireland, Germany, or Scandinavia as their place of birth. While these northern and western Europeans continued to arrive in large numbers after 1880, an annually larger proportion of newcomers after that year came from Italy, Turkey, Greece, and the Slavic, Hungarian, and Rumanian parts of the Austro-Hungarian Empire. And from Russia, which then included much of Poland, came Russians, Poles, Lithuanians, Latvians, Estonians, Finns, and Jews.

Before 1880, only about 200,000 people of southern and eastern European origin lived in the United States. Between 1880 and 1910, about 8.4 million arrived. In 1896, this New Immigration exceeded the flow from northern and western Europe for the first time. By 1907, the New Immigrants were almost the whole of the influx.

Promoting Immigration. For the most part, American industrialists welcomed immigration and actively courted it. Until the *Foran Act* of 1885 made it illegal to do so, some companies paid immigrants' fares if they signed contracts agreeing to work for their patrons when they arrived in the United States. James J. Hill plastered every sizable town in Sweden and Norway with posters that described the rich soil along his Great Northern Railroad to attract immigrants to South Dakota.

Employers liked immigrant labor because it was invariably cheaper than American labor and because immigrants were less inclined to join unions. So far from familiar surroundings and customs, the newcomers hesitated to complain. Since many intended to work in America only temporarily and then return to their homelands, they generally accepted very low wages.

Irish Immigrants. In the 1840s Ireland was hit by one of the greatest natural disasters in modern history. The potato crop began to die from a blight that had spread slowly across Europe. When it hit Ireland, as many as 1 million people out of a population of 8 million died of starvation or nutrition-related diseases. In addition to the deaths, about 3 million people left

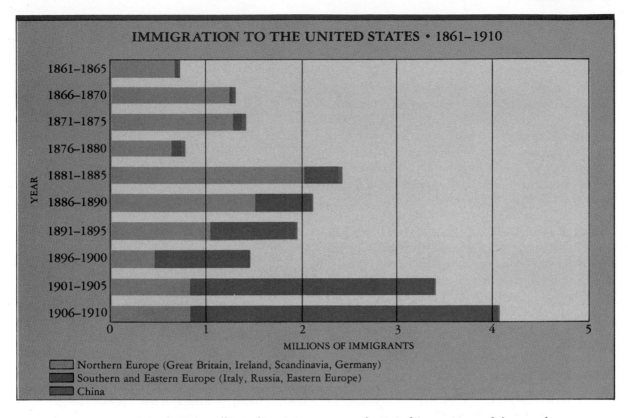

IMMIGRATION TO THE UNITED STATES • 1861–1910

YEAR

| 1861–1865 |
| 1866–1870 |
| 1871–1875 |
| 1876–1880 |
| 1881–1885 |
| 1886–1890 |
| 1891–1895 |
| 1896–1900 |
| 1901–1905 |
| 1906–1910 |

0   1   2   3   4   5

MILLIONS OF IMMIGRANTS

Northern Europe (Great Britain, Ireland, Scandinavia, Germany)
Southern and Eastern Europe (Italy, Russia, Eastern Europe)
China

Between 1865 and 1900, millions of immigrants came to the United States. Many of these people passed through the immigration center on Ellis Island in New York harbor. The photograph below shows some of the new arrivals in the center's dining hall.

Ireland for good during the 1840s and 1850s. They emigrated all over the world, but particularly to the United States.

Chinese Immigrants in California.

In 1849, sailors brought the news to the Chinese port of Canton that a "Mountain of Gold" had been discovered in California. In a country plagued by overpopulation, flood, famine, epidemic disease, and civil warfare, the people of southern China listened avidly to the rosy pictures of life across the ocean. But by the time the Chinese immigrants arrived in any numbers, the rich mines had been exhausted.

By 1860, there were 35,000 Chinese immigrants in California. Most of them were young men who hoped to return home to marry after they had made their fortune. Some Chinese men did stay in America. They sent passage money home so their wives, parents, or other family members could join them. In San Francisco and Sacramento, California, and in most mining camps of any size, Chinese sections flourished, though they were at the bottom of the economic ladder.

The Exclusion Act.

After the construction of the transcontinental railroad began in 1864, Chinese immigration stepped up. As long as there was plenty of work, American hostility to the Chinese was restrained. But in 1873, the country lapsed into a depression.

In 1877, when the Chinese represented 17 percent of California's population, a San Francisco teamster named Denis Kearney began to speak to white working people at open-air rallies in the city's sandlots. He blamed their joblessness on the willingness of the Chinese to work for less than an American's living wage. Kearney's anti-Chinese movement inspired politicians to choke off the Asian immigration. In 1882, Congress enacted the *Exclusion Act*, which forbade the Chinese to enter the United States. A few hundred were able to enter legally every year, and illegal immigration via Canada added somewhat to the Chinese-American population.

To some extent, immigrants from the Philippine Islands and Japan replaced the Chinese in the Asian immigration. Filipinos had free access to the United States after their country was made an American colony in 1898. Japanese began to trickle into the United States, usually via Hawaii, where they were an important part of the agricultural labor force.

German and Scandinavian Immigrants.

After 1848, the failure of a series of liberal revolutions in several German states forced the exile of many leading German liberals. The most famous German exile in the United States was Carl Schurz, who became a senator from Missouri and who was briefly a member of President Grant's cabinet.

Because many of them had been landowners in Europe, German immigrants generally had enough money when they reached the United States to move west and take up free or cheap land. Wisconsin became heavily populated by German-born and German-descended people in the last half of the nineteenth century.

Like the Germans, Scandinavians were inclined to become farmers in the United States. Norwegians predominated in whole counties in Wisconsin and Minnesota. Swedes settled in Minnesota and the Pacific Northwest, while Finns settled in yet other regions, particularly in logging country and in the iron mines of the Mesabi Range.

New Immigrants From Russia and Italy.

In 1881, Russian Jews were the objects of a series of deadly *pogroms*, a term that comes from the Russian word meaning "riot" or "devastation." Peasants and soldiers vented their wrath on the helpless people. They beat and killed Jews with no fear of the law. Between about 1881 and 1914, fully one-third of the Jewish population of Russia left the country, most of them for the United States. Because of the constitutionally provided freedom of religion, America was the hope of the oppressed in most of the world.

The Jews were not the largest group of people to come to the United States during the late nineteenth and early twentieth centuries. Between 1890 and 1914 (when the outbreak of the First World War choked off immigration), some 3.6 million Italians arrived. They came seeking economic prosperity and freedom of opportunity.

Adapting to a New Country.

Early ethnic groups that settled together in America had found adaptation to the New World comparatively easy since they could approximate familiar Old World

The population of Ireland in 1840 was about 8 million. The 1980 population was a little less than 4 million. Ireland is one of the few places in the world whose population was less in 1980 than it was 140 years earlier.

ways of life. They founded schools and churches or synagogues that used their native languages. They started and supported newspapers, periodicals, and European-style fraternal organizations and athletic clubs. They continued to eat familiar food and raise their children by traditional rules. They were numerous enough to deal with America from a position of strength.

However, adapting to their new homes was not so easy for most of the New Immigrants. Very few of the newcomers after 1880 had much money when they arrived. Most were illiterate, and their Old World experience in peasant villages did not prepare them for life in the world's greatest industrial nation.

American Ghettos.

Most of the New Immigrants clustered in the northeastern quarter of the United States, where they were soon an important part of the overall population. Eighty percent of them lived in the Middle-Atlantic and Great Lakes states.

The newcomers were especially visible in the cities, where most of them congregated. By 1890, one-third of the population of Boston and Chicago had been born abroad. When their children were added to the total, it was not unreasonable to think of the cities as centers of the New Immigration.

Within the cities, members of each ethnic group clustered together into *ghettos* that were exclusively their own. Although housing and sanitary conditions were generally poor, within each ghetto immigrants found solace in a familiar language, familiar customs, and familiar foods.

Prejudice Against New Immigrants.

Many people whose families had been in America for several generations looked on the miniature Polands, Chinas, and Greeces in their midst as detrimental to the culture they loved. Unlike older immigrants, including the once-despised Irish, the New Immigrants seemed determined not to become Americans. Around the turn of the century, this cultural anxiety took the form of pressure groups such as the Immigration Restriction League, which began to call for an immigration law that would keep southern and eastern Europeans from entering the United States in any significant numbers.

5. THE GROWTH OF THE CITIES

The proportion of city dwellers in the total population, the number of cities, and the size of cities all increased at a faster rate in the United States than in any other country in the world. In 1790, when the first national census was taken, only 3.4 percent of Americans lived in towns of 8,000 people or more. By 1860, 16 percent of the population was urban, and by 1900, 33 percent.

The increase in the number of cities was rather more striking. In 1790, only six American cities boasted populations of 8,000 or more. The largest of them, Philadelphia, was home to 42,000 people. In 1890, 448 municipalities had at least 8,000 people within their limits. Fully 26 cities were larger than 100,000 in 1900, and six of them topped 500,000. Philadelphia counted 1.5 million people at the turn of the century, but slipped to third place behind New York and Chicago.

Immigration.

Massive immigration had a lot to do with the growth of the urban population. If the native-born children of the New Immigrants were counted, most big cities were largely foreign by the end of the century.

Many newcomers stayed in the first American city they set foot in because most of them were penniless when they stepped ashore, and those who had some money were liable to be fleeced

Class Activity: Make a pie chart such as the one made for the early 1800s to illustrate the percentage of immigrants coming to the U.S. from the various countries in the 1890's. Compare the two. Which groups are the same and which groups are new? Did this new flood of immigrants have the same reasons for coming as did the earlier groups?

477

within a day or so by people who met the "green-horns" at the docks and offered to help them adjust to American life. New Immigrants did get inland, however. Large concentrations of Greeks, Italians, and Poles could be found in Colorado coal-mining towns, for example. But the city of disembarkation, most often New York, was the farthest into America that many immigrants penetrated. By 1900, New York City was the largest Irish and Jewish city in the world, and the second largest Polish city.

Leaving the Farm.

Important as it was, however, the influx of foreigners alone was not responsible for the explosive growth of urban America. Throughout the nineteenth century, men and women from American farmsteads flowed into the cities. Dismayed by the isolation of farm life, ground down by the heavy tedious labor, and often as not reaping few rewards for their toil, they heard of well-paying jobs for literate, mechanically inclined people. Or they visited cities and were dazzled by the bright lights, the abundance of company, the stimulation of a world in constant motion, and the stories of the fortunes that might be made in business.

During the 1880s, more than half the rural townships of Iowa and Illinois declined in population. In New England, while the overall population of the region increased by 20 percent, three rural townships in five lost people to the dozens of bustling mill towns and to the metropolises of Boston and New York.

Metropolises.

While rapid growth was the rule in cities large and small, the most dramatic phenomenon of American urbanization in the late nineteenth century was the emergence of the gigantic metropolises, the six cities of more than 500,000 people that dominated regions in which they sat like imperial capitals. Philadelphia doubled in size between 1860 and 1900, when it claimed 1.5 million people. New York, with over 1 million people in 1860, quadrupled its numbers until, by 1900, 4.8 million lived within its five boroughs. New York was then the second largest city in the world, smaller only than London.

Chicago's rate of growth as the hub of the nation's railroad system amazed Americans and foreigners alike. With only a little more than 100,000 people in 1860, Chicago increased its size 20 times in a generation, numbering 2.2 million inhabitants in 1890.

Innovations in Mass Transportation.

The first means by which wealthy and middle-class people could put some distance between their residences and the working people who swarmed in city centers was the horsecar line. With charters from city hall, entrepreneurs strung light rails down major thoroughfares and ran horse-drawn carriages with seats open to the public.

Upon arrival in cities like New York, immigrants tended to join earlier immigrants of similar backgrounds. Thus, neighborhoods developed distinctly different atmospheres. The photograph below is of Orchard Street, looking south from Hester Street, in New York City.

However, it was the electric trolley car, pioneered by inventor-businessman Frank J. Sprague, that really ensured the sprawl of the great metropolises. Economical and fast, the trolleys were the key to the growth of big cities. Richmond was the first to build a system in 1887. By 1895, fully 850 lines crisscrossed American cities on 10,000 miles of track.

Another innovation, the subway, was a twentieth century development in the United States. London had a subway line by 1886, but the first subway in the United States, in Boston, did not open until 1897.

Skyscrapers and Suspension Bridges.

The streetcars made it possible for many more people to congregate in city centers for work and entertainment. This caused real estate values to soar and created a need for multistoried structures.

Using strong I-shaped girders, architects designed skeletons of steel on which, in effect, they hung decorative siding of iron or of stone. The potential height of steel buildings seemed almost limitless. They could rise so high as to scrape the sky.

Another technological innovation that contributed to the expansion of cities was the *suspension bridge*, which erased wide rivers as barriers to urban growth. Its pioneer was a German immigrant, John A. Roebling, who contended that a bridge could be hung from strong cables instead of being built up on massive pillars.

Roebling planned his masterpiece for the East River, which separated downtown New York from the independent and roomy seaport of Brooklyn on Long Island. The Brooklyn Bridge, completed in 1883, was admired for its beauty as well as its engineering.

Overcrowding and Sanitation Problems.

Many city dwellers died because of impossibly crowded living conditions. Given the very high real estate values in the largest cities, poor people were forced to share small apartments with relatives and frequently had to take in boarders.

In 1866, the New York Board of Health found 400,000 people living in overcrowded *tenements* with no windows. Twenty thousand lived in cellars below the water table. At high tide, their homes filled with water.

John A. Roebling, an immigrant engineer, manufactured the first wire rope in America. He also designed the Brooklyn Bridge (above).

The overcrowding of the cities led to epidemic outbreaks of serious diseases like smallpox, cholera, measles, typhus, scarlet fever, and diphtheria. Even less dangerous illnesses like chicken pox, mumps, and influenza were killers in the crowded cities.

All city governments provided for waste collection, but *sanitation* departments simply could not keep up. Horses compounded the problem. They deposited tons of manure on city streets daily, and special squads could not begin to keep pace.

In the poorest tenements, piped water was available only in shared sinks in the hallways. Wells in the streets were inevitably fouled by runoff. Tenement apartments did not have bathrooms. Children washed by romping in the water of open fire hydrants or by taking a swim in polluted waterways.

Crime.

Slums were breeding grounds of vice and crime. There were 14,000 homeless people in New York in 1890, many of them children, and work was difficult to get. Many found the temptations of sneak thievery, pocket picking, and robbery too much to resist. As early as the 1850s,

Elevated train systems built during this period in Boston, New York, and Chicago are still in use today, although these systems are now electrically powered. The first two sections of New York City's vast subway system began operating in about 1904.

MOVERS AND SHAPERS

Jane Addams

J ane Addams (1860–1935) was in the forefront of the movement to bring social justice to the United States. When Addams began her work, the *Industrial Revolution* was transforming the country. But millions of people had to live in wretched inner city tenements. Their children had no time or place to play. Many children worked for long hours beside their parents in factories. Industrialists took little interest in their workers' welfare, and many officials were convinced that government had no right to intervene in the situation.

Hull House, which Addams founded in the heart of Chicago's slums, had a day care center, a kindergarten, a public park, a boys' club, and sewing and cooking classes. It even offered showers.

Addams wanted to change the system that allowed children to work in factories and millions of women to work unlimited hours. With the help of Florence Kelly, Addams began a movement that would lead to strict federal rules about *child labor*.

From 1915 on, Addams as president of the International Congress of Women, worked to reconcile the conflicts that eventually pushed the United States into World War I. She worked after the war to help women and children in wartorn countries. However, it was not until the Great Depression of the 1930s that her views on aid to the needy became more popular. In 1931, she shared the Nobel peace prize.

Florence Kelly

F lorence Kelly (1859–1932) was one of a group of women, led by Jane Addams, who helped found Hull House. Kelly's first job at Hull House was to investigate slum conditions. Her work led to a new *housing code* in Chicago. Next, she studied the clothing industry, and helped bring about an eight-hour day for Illinois workingwomen. After that, she earned a law degree from Northwestern University, while taking care of her children and working at Hull House.

After graduation, she was appointed by the Illinois governor as an inspector to make sure the state's new labor laws were being followed. She published four shocking reports about poor factory conditions before the governor was pressured into having her resign. But Kelly kept working.

The eight-hour day law in Illinois was struck down, and new challenges to factory reform appeared. Although Congress passed laws to end child labor, the Supreme Court declared them unconstitutional. But with Kelly's aid, fellow lawyer Louis Brandeis (later a Supreme Court justice) wrote a legal brief in which he declared that the Constitution could be used to protect citizens against social ills. With Kelly and Brandeis supporting the movement, several states passed new child labor laws.

The war against abuse of child labor was not won until 1938. Kelly did not live to see the victory, but her influence was unmistakable. Felix Frankfurter, who also later became a Supreme Court justice, wrote that Kelly had the "largest share of shaping the social history of the United States during the first 30 years of this [twentieth] century."

Research Assignment: Have students report on architects and their work during this period. Where possible, photographs and/or actual models should be used to illustrate the reports.

police in New York were vying with strong-arm gangs that were named after the neighborhoods where they lived and operated. The homicide rate tripled in American cities during the 1880s, and the prison population rose by 50 percent.

Coping with the Situation.

City governments attempted to alleviate these problems in many ways. Ordinances that regulated housing conditions were on the books. Idealists such as Frederick Law Olmstead designed and *lobbied* for parks so that, at least for a few hours on Sunday, poor people might get away from the crowds.

Police reformers established detective departments to fight organized gangs. Saloons were licensed, and water supplies were tested. Fire inspectors examined buildings for safety hazards. Sanitation departments increased in size. Yet conditions continued to deteriorate until the very end of the century.

One reason was the inadequacy of private charities to deal with problems of such immensity. Another was that city government remained, for the most part, under the control of politicians who viewed government not as a way to serve society, but as a way to make themselves wealthy.

Social Organizations.

The Young Men's Christian Association (*YMCA*), founded in 1851, came into its own after the Civil War, providing sanitary and moral residential and recreational facilities in city centers at a nominal cost. In 1881, the *Salvation Army*, an evangelical group founded in England, began to give hot meals to the city's hungry and seemingly hopeless men, requiring only their attendance at religious services. They also gave them clothes and began a work program to enable the men to get back their self-esteem. The Salvation Army's "soup kitchens" undoubtedly saved many lives. And Sephardic and German Jewish families who were comfortably established in the United States founded the *Hebrew Immigrant Aid Society* to minister to the needs of the penniless Eastern European Jews who flocked into the cities.

Settlement Houses.

The most important charitable response to urban problems came not from established institutions, but from individuals who were shocked by what they saw around them and were determined to do something useful with their own lives. Their creation was the *settlement house*, whose model was Toynbee Hall in Whitechapel, a notorious slum in London.

During the 1880s, a number of middle-class Americans traveled to England to learn how Toynbee Hall worked. They found that the house provided food and drink as traditional charities had. In addition, working mothers came to Toynbee Hall for child care, recreation, and courses of study in everything from household arts to the English language. Equally important, the young men and women who worked at Toynbee Hall told the Americans that they had been morally elevated by their sacrifices and exposure to a misery that they had not known in their own lives.

The first American settlement house was the Neighborhood Guild, set up in New York City in 1886. More famous, however, because of the intelligence and powerful personalities of their founders, were Jane Addams's Hull House in Chicago (1889), Robert A. Woods's South End House in Boston (1892), and Lillian Wald's Henry Street Settlement in New York (1893). From comfortable middle-class backgrounds, Addams, Woods, and Wald were from the old American middle class. They were determined to fight the *materialism* of their time and keep traditional values alive. Their personal contributions were significant, but they found it very difficult to affect the way in which cities were governed.

SECTION REVIEW

1. Write a sentence to identify: metropolis, John A. Roebling, tenements, Jane Addams.
2. What two groups of people added to the growth of population in American cities and metropolises in the later part of the nineteenth century?
3. List some innovations in mass transportation and architecture that occurred in the nation's cities at about this time.
4. What were some of the challenges that faced city governments? Name some ways in which the governments, private groups, and individuals tried to meet these challenges.

Class Activity: Have students examine the kinds of problems that existed at the turn of the century in the city nearest where you live. Which problems are still present and which no longer exist? Examine how some problems were rectified.

CHAPTER REVIEW

TIME LINE

1850

— YMCA founded (1851)

1855

— YM-YWHA founded (1854)

1860

— National Labor Union founded (1866)

— Knights of Labor founded (1869)

1865

— New York City opens first elevated railroad line (1870)

— Nationwide railroad strike (1877)

1870

— *Progress and Poverty* published (1879)

— Chinese Exclusion Act (1882)

— Brooklyn Bridge completed (1883)

1875

— Foran Act (1885)

— AFL founded (1886)

1880

— Haymarket Square incident (1886)

— Hull House opens in Chicago (1889)

1885

— South End House opens in Boston (1891)

— Homestead strike (1892)

1890

— National Association of Manufacturers founded (1893)

— Immigration Restriction League (1895)

1895

— Henry Street Settlement opens in New York City (1895)

— Boston subway line opens (1898)

1900

TIME LINE QUESTIONS

1. In what year did the event that destroyed the Knights of Labor take place?
2. In which years were achievements made by organized labor?
3. List these in chronological order: New York elevated line, Boston subway, Brooklyn Bridge.
4. When did Jane Addams open her settlement house?

SKILLS STRATEGY

The Life of a Child Factory Worker

Wages

Hours

Working Conditions

SUMMARIZING AND DRAWING CONCLUSIONS

A brief, or scratch, outline can be helpful in preparing a summary. A summary omits less important or redundant details about the information being summarized, and so a summary is always brief.

To complete the scratch outline above, skim the three subsections in section 2 of this chapter, "New Work Places." You can include a fourth item in the outline—"Children's Feelings About Work." You must use the information in the text about working conditions and pay, and then draw on your own reactions to complete this item.

APPLYING SKILLS

1. Complete the outline above, or prepare another one for one of these subjects: "The Life of a Male Factory Worker," "The Life of a Female Factory Worker," or "An Immigrant Worker." Skim related parts of the text for details.
2. Use your scratch outline to write a summary. Read your completed summary to be sure it includes only important details that are directly related to your topic sentences. Eliminate any details that are redundant.

UNIT 5 TEST

CHAPTER SURVEY

In one or two sentences, summarize the content of the chapter from which these terms come, and write a sentence to identify *one* of the terms from each chapter.

1. *Chapter 17:* Big Four, robber barons, Promontory Point, condensed milk, *Boston Cooking School Cookbook,* William "Pig Iron" Kelly, Titusville, Harvey Firestone, James Duke.
2. *Chapter 18:* Boss William Tweed, Goo-Goos, Mugwumps, "waving the bloody shirt," patronage, Charles Guiteau, Pan-American Union, Wilson-Gorman Act, Greenback Labor party.
3. *Chapter 19:* Newport; Horatio Alger, scrip, Lowell system, Molly Maguires, New Immigration, tenements, Robert A. Wood.

TEXT REVIEW

4. What great change took place within the United States between the years 1865 and 1900? Name at least two important factors that help to account for this change.
5. Relate each of the following people to a particular industry: Jay Gould, Gustavus Swift, Gail Borden, John D. Rockefeller, Andrew Carnegie.
6. How did technological breakthroughs by the following inventors affect life in the United States: McCormick, Sholes, Otis, Bell, Westinghouse, Edison?
7. Explain how each of the following affected the activities of big business in the United States: Fourteenth Amendment, Interstate Commerce Act, Pacific Railway Act of 1862, Sherman Antitrust Act.
8. Summarize the effects of dishonesty and corruption on city and national politics between the years 1865 and 1900.
9. To what extent do you consider President Grant personally responsible for the widespread dishonesty and corruption during his first administration? Give facts from the text.
10. Voters at this time consistently voted for corrupt politicians rather than for reform candidates. Give facts that account for this behavior, and describe your reaction to it.
11. Give the important details about two of the following national political issues of the time: foreign affairs, the tariff, the money question.
12. Compare the theories of Henry George and Herbert Spencer that attempted to explain and justify great success and riches.
13. Describe the status of working people during the years between 1865 and 1900. In your description, mention specific details such as wages, hours, working conditions, company towns, and women and child laborers.
14. List the following items in chronological order, and give the important details about one of the items: Knights of Labor, National Labor Union, American Federation of Labor, Haymarket Square incident, National Civic Federation.
15. Compare the immigrants who came to the United States after 1880 with the immigrants who had come before that year. Were the later immigrants welcomed by all Americans? Cite facts from the text to explain.
16. Write what your impressions would be of a large city such as New York in the late nineteenth century if you were an immigrant.

CRITICAL THINKING

17. Discuss the pros and cons of the formation of business corporations as seen by each of the following: a business manager, an ordinary working person, a shareholder in a company. Give facts from the text to explain.
18. Describe and evaluate the contributions of the immigrants to the United States in such areas as the growth of industry, the labor movement, and the improvement of transportation. Refer to individuals where possible.

SKILLS REVIEW

19. Compare the information given in thematic maps with that given in political maps. Explain what you would use each type of map for.
20. What should readers remember about the aim of political cartoons and the methods cartoonists use to achieve this aim?

Class Activity: Ask students to formulate an idea of what life was like in a settlement house. Have them give as much detail as possible. Then have them do research to find out how close their imagined image matches with the actual way of life in these places.

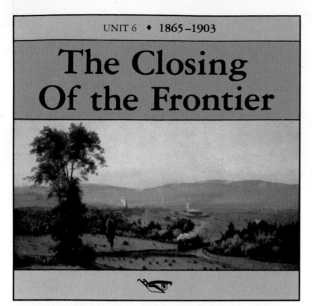

UNIT 6 ◆ 1865–1903

The Closing Of the Frontier

American artist George Inness (1825–1894), "The Lackawanna Valley," (1855).

Unit 6 Overview

Unit 6 begins with a survey of activity on the western frontier between 1865–1900—the brave but unsuccessful encounters of the Plains Indians with the advancing whites; the struggles and triumphs of the farmers, ranchers, and miners. The unit continues with accounts of the revolt of the hard-pressed American farmers in the Populist movement and the development of industry in the South. The last chapter of the unit discusses the Spanish-American War and traces America's imperialist ambitions in Latin America, the Pacific, and Asia.

Basic Unit Concepts

1. American pioneers migrated to the West in increasing numbers and developed the ranching, farming, and mining industries.
2. The cost of American westward expansion and development was paid for by the Plains Indian people, whose way of life was destroyed by the advancing whites.
3. American farmers, angered by their exclusion from the general prosperity of the times, formed various economic and agricultural organizations and, finally, the Populist party.
4. The failure of populism in the south contributed to the rise of racial demagoguery in southern politics which continued for half a century.
5. At about the same time, the lumber, steel, oil, textile, and tobacco industries gave a new face to the South.

Chapter 20: "The West" (1865–1900)

In Chapter 20, students are presented with a picture of the western frontier as it really was between 1865 and 1900. They meet the Plains Indians and witness the tragic destruction of their way of life as white settlement of the West advanced. In studying the ups and downs of the cattle industry, they follow the cowboys on the long and difficult cattle drives to the railroads. They recognize and appreciate

the tenacity and spirit of farmers on the "Sod House Frontier." Finally, they encounter the "risk-all" miners whose strikes of gold and silver changed the value of American money.

Features

Going to the Source: Sioux leader Red Cloud's "Speech for Peace and Justice" (page 490)
Movers and Shapers: Sarah Winnemucca and Helen Hunt Jackson (page 495)

Learning Objectives

History Generalizations   Students will gain knowledge that supports the following generalizations:
1. Between 1865 and 1900, the line of settlement was constantly changing as American and immigrant pioneers and adventurers pushed westward across North America.
2. Native American peoples often paid the bill for the westward expansion with their lives, their homelands, and their traditional ways of life.
3. The white newcomers' virtually complete destruction of the huge bison herds brought on the Indian wars and the near-extinction of the culture of the Plains people.
4. Protests of some Americans over treatment of the Indians brought on attempts at reform by the United States government.
5. After the Indians lost the West, Americans used the land and resources of this region to develop thriving cattle, farming, and mining industries.
6. The conception many Americans had of the West and its people was most often at variance with the harsh reality.
7. Americans who followed them owe a debt of appreciation to the brave, hardy, and determined pioneers who settled the West.
8. Because of an increase in the supply of gold, silver was demonetized, and gold became the sole basis of United States paper currency.

Study Skills   In addition to the three skills noted in Chapter 1 which are standard to every chapter, students will:
1. examine and interpret primary sources of historical information.
2. write a paragraph from the point of view of a cowboy on the trail.
3. relate graphic materials to the text of the chapter.
4. practice these **critical thinking skills**: generating questions about materials to be read, summarizing chapter information, distinguishing fact and opinion, contrasting points of view.

Chapter 21: "The Revolt of the Farmers" (1873–1896)

In Chapter 21, students learn of the new techniques and machinery that helped farmers of the late nineteenth century produce more food than ever before. They recognize the reason for the farmers' frustration at not sharing in the general prosperity of the times. They witness the farmers' crusade for justice that culminates in the formation of the Populist party. They learn of the failure of populism in the South and of the tragic deterioration of race relations in that region. Finally, they follow the development of new southern industries.

Feature

American Ingenuity   chart (pages 524–525)

Learning Objectives

History Generalizations Students will gain knowledge that supports the following generalizations:

1. Growing domestic and overseas markets, improved farming techniques, and new farm machinery resulted in an unprecedented expansion of American agriculture in the final three decades of the nineteenth century.
2. During this same period, western farmers who raised staples and southern cotton growers suffered severe effects from a depression of agricultural prices.
3. Adding to the farmers' woes was a change in the public's image of them and a decline in their political power and status.
4. Spurred on by angry social reformers, farmers tended to see control of money and government policy by the wealthy and powerful—especially the bankers—as the cause of their problems.
5. After attempting to solve their problems by forming various economic and agricultural organizations, farmers finally formed a new political party—the Populist party.
6. Although the Populists captured no significant political power nationally or locally, many of the reforms they proposed in their party platform became law and are part of our lives today.
7. In the South, the failure to form an alliance of poor farmers across racial lines helped to usher in a style of racist demagoguery that contaminated southern politics for half a century.
8. By the 1890s, the South turned from dependence on agriculture to the development of large industries—lumber and turpentine, steel, oil, and tobacco.

Study Skills In addition to the three skills noted in Chapter 1 which are standard to every chapter, students will:

1. appreciate news articles as valuable sources of historical information and recognize bias in reporting the news.
2. write a lead paragraph and headline for a news story
3. relate graphic materials to the text of the chapter.
4. practice these **critical thinking skills**: generating questions about materials to be read, recognizing point of view, classifying information.

Chapter 22: "American Expansion" (1896–1903)

In Chapter 22, students recognize that the election of 1896 marked the end of the Civil War era and the beginning of an era when the United States became more involved with the rest of the world. They discover the role played by the "yellow press" in the Spanish-American war, and learn of the results of that war. They witness the steps the United States took to build an American empire. Finally, they follow the American activities in Latin America that planted the seeds of an enduring resentment of the United States.

Features

Going to the Source: Conclusion of William Jennings Bryan's "Cross of Gold" speech (page 529)

Profiles of the Presidency: William McKinley (page 531), Theodore Roosevelt (page 544)

Learning Objectives

History Generalizations Students will gain knowledge that supports the following generalizations:

1. The 1896 presidential election marked the end of the Civil War era and the beginning of a period in which the United States became a world power.
2. By 1898, racist ideas, belief in the need for a strong navy, and a historian's theory about the influence of the frontier all contributed to growing imperialist ambitions which were countered by a long anti-colonial tradition.
3. Partly as a result of the agitation of the "yellow press," the United States fought a surprisingly short war with Spain and, as a result, gained new territories in the Caribbean and the Pacific.
4. At about the same time, the United States annexed the nation of Hawaii and two other small Pacific islands.
5. With the assassination of William McKinley, the presidency went to Theodore Roosevelt, who led the United States to greater involvement in world affairs: in Asia and Latin America.
6. Roosevelt's interventionist Latin American policy aroused an enduring deep resentment towards the United States among the people of Central and South America.

Study Skills In addition to the three skills noted in Chapter 1 which are standard to every chapter, students will:

1. use cards to take notes.
2. relate graphic materials to the text of the chapter.
3. practice these **critical thinking skills**: generating questions about materials to be read, comparing events, identifying causes, classifying information.

CHAPTER 20

THE WEST

1865–1900

To the land vaguely realizing westward,
But still unstoried, artless, unenhanced,
Such as she was, such as she would become.

ROBERT FROST

Making Connections. The settlement of the West is one of the most exciting parts of our country's history. Even today, the idea of the frontier holds a strong appeal for Americans. Yet the "Wild West" lasted only from about 1865 to about 1890. What was life on the frontier really like? Why did the West change so drastically in such a short time?

In this chapter, you will learn:
- What two animals the lives of the Plains Indians revolved around
- How the fighting style of Native Americans frustrated the United States Army
- Why the Dawes Severalty Act, which was intended to help the Native Americans, actually helped destroy their way of life
- Who was first to use cowhands to drive cattle overland to the railroad
- When the last large unsettled area of the West was opened to homesteaders
- How the rich gold and silver strikes in the West changed the value of American money

You have read that construction of the transcontinental railroad made it possible to cross the United States quickly. Consequently, settlers poured into the sparsely populated areas west of the Mississippi River. As you read, try to get a feeling of how the American Indians, the cattle ranchers, the farmers, and the miners lived in the West.

Sections
1. The Frontier
2. The Indian Wars
3. The Cattle Industry
4. Pioneer Farmers
5. Mining

1. THE FRONTIER

In the United States, the *frontier* was where the nation's settled lands ended and its undeveloped region began. Because the course of American expansion had begun on the eastern rim of the continent, the frontier usually took the form of a line that ran from north to south and that was more or less constantly moving westward. On and beyond that line was the area that Americans called *the West*—the frontier.

At the time of the Civil War, the part of the United States that was unsettled comprised roughly half the total area of the nation. Farther west, there were three major pockets of settlements. The first of these was on the Pacific coast, 440,000 people lived in California, Oregon, and Washington Territory. The Great Salt Lake basin formed the second area of settlement and was home to a population of 40,000. Finally, New Mexico was home to 94,000 mostly Spanish-speaking citizens. Much of the American frontier was then only 150 to 200 miles west of the Mississippi River. Settlement barely spilled over the far boundaries of Minnesota, Iowa, Missouri, and Arkansas. Half of Texas was still not settled at the end of the Civil War.

Southwestern Tribes. The West was not without many of its own people. In addition to the Mormons and the people of the Mexican border-

Wolf Chief, in full ceremonial dress, is shown in the painting (right) by George Catlin. The chief was one of the Mandan Indians, a tribe that lived on the northern Great Plains.

Making Connections: Review the questions and topics presented in the Making Connections section that opens this chapter. Have students consider the implications of the infusion of such a large number of new types of people into society and the effects it would have had. Have students understand that this caused a significant change in the mores of American society. Also examine the effects that this infusion would have had on political and economic development.

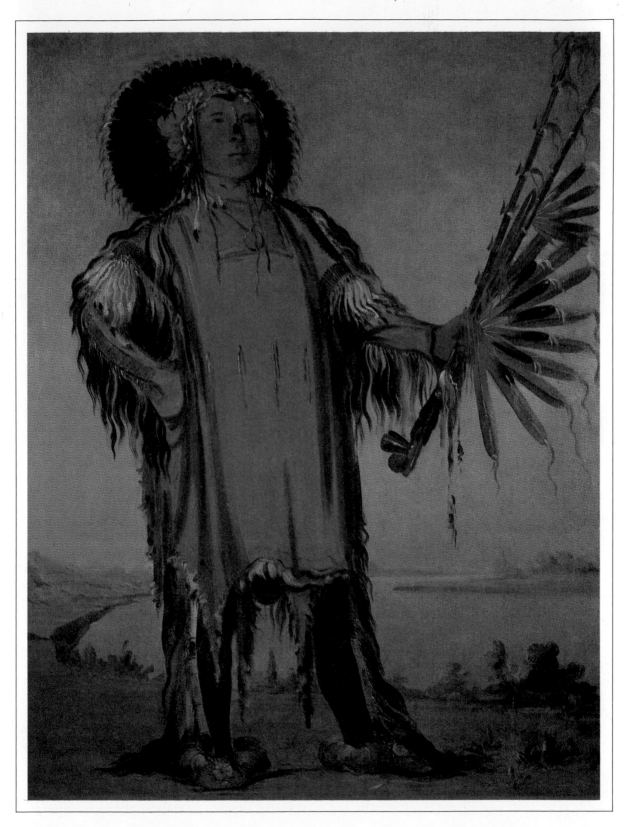

Skills Review: Reinforce the skills learned in the preceding Skills Strategy section. Have students use the skills, or summarizing and drawing conclusions, to answer some of the Discussion Questions presented in this chapter.

Great herds of bison, commonly called buffalo, roamed the western plains. The Indians hunted bison, not for sport, but because they needed the flesh for food, and the hides for clothing.

lands, there were groups of Native Americans living throughout the country. Even the most forbidding parts of the Great Basin supported a few thousand Ute, Paiute, and Shoshone who coped with the extremely hot summers by dividing into small, wandering bands. Farther south, in the seemingly more hostile environment of present-day Arizona and New Mexico, the Pima, Zuñi, and Hopi had developed methods for farming the desert intensively. They lived in *pueblos*, communal groups of houses, sometimes perched high on sheer cliffs, where a finely integrated urban culture evolved.

The tribes that occupied the so-called *Indian Territory* (present-day Oklahoma) had been forced out of their former homeland in Georgia and Alabama decades earlier. Indian Territory came to loom large in the American imagination after the Civil War because, outside the reach of state and territorial law, it was an attractive sanctuary for some of the most famous outlaws of the era.

The Plains Indians. The Indians who most intrigued Americans were those who were most determined to resist the Easterners and their ways—the tribes of the Great Plains. Best known were the Comanche, Cheyenne, and Arapaho peoples of the central and southern plains, and the Mandan, Crow, Sioux, Nez Perce, and Blackfoot peoples of the northern half of the grasslands. Thanks to the writings of historian Francis Parkman and the paintings of George Catlin, these tribes were a source of awe and admiration to easterners and of dread to settlers who came into their country.

Everything in the lives of the Plains Indians—economy, social structure, religion, diet, dress—revolved around two animals: the native bison and the Spanish horse. The bison not only provided food, but its hide was made into clothing, footwear, blankets, portable shelters (the conical *wickiups,* or tepees), bowstrings, and canvasses on which artists recorded the heroic legends, tribal histories, and genealogies. The bison's manure made a tolerable fuel for cooking and warmth in a treeless land where winters were harsh.

The Plains Indians were *nomadic.* Except for the Mandan, they grew no crops. They trailed after the herds of bison on their horses—to southern grazing grounds in the winter, and back north to fresh grass in the summer. It was by no means an ancient way of life. Runaway horses from Mexican herds had been domesticated only about 150 years before the Plains Indians were confronted by European-Americans. Nevertheless, in that short time, the Indians developed their own way of riding, which was quite independent of the Mexican example and awe-inspiring to Americans.

The wandering ways of the Plains tribes brought them into frequent contact with one another and with Indians who had developed different cultures. While they traded and could communicate with remarkable subtlety through a common sign language, the tribes were just as likely to fight. Since the Indians had no concept of private ownership of land, their wars were not aimed at conquest, but at capturing horses, tools, and sometimes women, and at demonstrating bravery, the highest quality of which a Great Plains male could boast. But with only about 225,000 Native Americans roaming the Great Plains in 1860, war was not massive in scale.

By 1860, every Plains tribe knew about the "palefaces." The wagon trains had traversed their homeland for two decades, and various tribes occasionally skirmished with the white-skinned wayfarers. Nevertheless, the outsiders did move on and were welcome to the extent that they traded (or abandoned) horses, textiles, iron tools, and rifles that the tribes needed.

The nomadic Plains Indians were always moving, following the bison herds. The men hunted, and the women were responsible for keeping the family and its possessions together.

Discussion Question: In what ways was the life-style of the American Indian different from that of the other people who came to settle in the western plains? How might these differences affect relations between these groups?

GOING TO THE SOURCE

My brethren and my friends who are here before me this day, God Almighty has made us all, and He is here to bless what I have to say to you today. The Good Spirit made us both. He gave you lands and He gave us lands; He gave us these lands; you came in here, and we respected you as brothers. God Almighty made you but made you all white and clothed you; when He made us He made us with red skins and poor; now you have come.

When you first came we were very many, and you were few; now you are many, and we are getting very few, and we are poor. You do not know who appears before you today to speak. I am a representative of the original American race, the first people of this continent. We are good and not bad. The reports that you hear concerning us are all on one side. . . .

The Great Father made us poor and ignorant—made you rich and wise and more skillful in these things that we know nothing about. The Great Father, the Good Father in Heaven, made you all to eat tame food—made us to eat wild food—gives us the wild food. You ask anybody who has gone through our country to California; ask those who have settled there and in Utah, and you will find that we have treated them always well. You have children; we have children. You want to raise your children and make them happy and prosperous; we want to raise and make them happy and prosperous. We ask you to help us to do it.

At the mouth of the Horse Creek, in 1852, the Great Father made a treaty with us by which we agreed to let all that country open for fifty-five years for the transit of those who were going through. We kept this treaty; we never

When you first came we were many, and you were few; now you are many, and we are getting very few. . . . I am a representative of the original American race, the first people of this continent. We are good and not bad. The reports that you hear concerning us are all on one side. . . .

RED CLOUD, "SPEECH FOR PEACE AND JUSTICE"

treated any man wrong; we never committed any murder or depredation until afterward the troops were sent into that country, and the troops killed our people and ill-treated them, and thus war and trouble arose; but before the troops were sent there we were quiet and peaceable, and there was no disturbance. . . .

Colonel Fitzpatrick of the government said we must all go to farm, and some of the people went to Fort Laramie and were badly treated. I only want to do that which is peaceful, and the Great Fathers know it, and also the Great Father who made us both. I came to Washington to see the Great Father in order to have peace and in order to have peace continue. That is all we want, and that is the reason why we are here now.

In 1868 men came out and brought papers. We are ignorant and do not read papers, and they did not tell us right what was in these papers. We wanted them to take away their forts, leave our country, would not make war, and give our traders something. They said we had bound ourselves to trade on the Missouri, and we said, no, we did not want that. The interpreters deceived us. When I went to Washington I saw the Great Father. The Great Father showed me what the treaties were; he showed me all these points and showed me that the interpreters had deceived me and did not let me know what the right side of the treaty was. All I want is right and justice. . . .

Red Cloud had led the Sioux people through the 1860s. In 1870, he traveled to the East to plead for fair treatment of his people. His "Speech for Peace and Justice" of which this is an excerpt, was warmly applauded.

Class Activity: Collect other famous speeches given by the Indian chiefs of this period to add to those in this chapter. Have some students volunteer to give dramatic recitations of these speeches.

Passengers and train crew shoot buffalo crowding the track of the Kansas-Pacific Railroad in 1871. Twenty years later there were only 551 bison still alive in the United States.

The Bison. Things began to change as soon as Congress authorized the construction of a railroad to the Pacific. The crews that laid the tracks of the Union Pacific and Kansas Pacific across the plains were not interested in staying. But unlike the California and Oregon emigrants, their presence led to the destruction of the bison, the basis of the native peoples' way of life.

The killing began in order to feed the big work crews. The Union Pacific Railroad hired hunters like William F. "Buffalo Bill" Cody to kill bison. The workers could hardly consume enough of the beef-like meat to affect the size of the herds, which numbered perhaps 15 million in 1860.

Destroying the Bison Herds. A few of the hides were shipped back east and caused a sensation when made into "buffalo robes." The demand for these fashionable robes led to wholesale slaughter of the bison. A team of sharpshooters, reloaders, and skinners could down and strip a thousand of the great beasts in a day. With dozens of sharpshooting and skinning teams at work, the bison population declined rapidly.

The railroad companies encouraged the slaughter when it was discovered that their flimsy iron tracks were destroyed whenever a herd of bison crossed over them. To add to the slaughter, wealthy eastern and British hunters chartered special trains to take them to the plains. Sometimes without even stepping to the ground, they could shoot trophies for their mansions and clubs. By the end of the century, when *preservationists* rushed in to save the species, only a few hundred buffalo remained alive. It was not only the near-*extinction* of a species, but also the near-extinction of the culture of the people whose fate was tied to them.

Research Assignment: Have students research the bison in America today or some other endangered species of wildlife endemic to your area. Have students report on what efforts are being made to help preserve these animals.

1. Write a sentence to identify: the frontier, Indian Territory, "Buffalo Bill" Cody, buffalo robes.

2. How was the American frontier related to the settled and unsettled lands in the United States? Describe the approximate location of the frontier after the Civil War.

3. Name and locate four groups of Native Americans other than the Plains Indians who lived throughout the West.

4. Explain what caused the near-extinction of the culture of the Native Americans whose fate was tied to the bison. Why were they unable to find other sources of food, clothing and shelter?

The Battle of Wounded Knee marked the end of the Indian wars. Burial of the dead is shown above.

2. THE INDIAN WARS

The United States cavalry accompanied the railroad construction crews, ostensibly to enforce the Indians' treaty rights as well as to protect the workers. Many of these troops were black —former slaves who had enlisted and found army life preferable to hard-scrabble farming and menial jobs open to them at home. Some soldiers and officers respected the tribes and their rights and tried to deal fairly with them. This was true, for example, of General George Crook, perhaps the greatest of the army's Indian fighters. Crook was, however, the exception. For the most part, the sympathies of the army were with the newcomers —the railroaders, miners, cattle owners, and eventually farmers who intruded on Indian lands. One rationale was that they thought the Indians used land so inefficiently, their claim to it was not equal to that of the newcomers.

Fighting the Wars. In 1862, the first of the Indian wars began with a Sioux uprising in Minnesota. In 1890, the power of the last resisting tribe was shattered at Wounded Knee. Between these years, the United States cavalry joined with the buffalo hunters in the destruction of a way of life.

Indian war was characterized by many small skirmishes and few pitched battles. Between 1869 and 1876, the peak years of the fighting, the army recorded 200 "incidents," a number that did not include many unopposed Indian raids and confrontations between civilians and the tribes. The army preferred to fight decisive battles. But the Indians generally clung to traditional hit-and-run attacks and exploited their mobility to escape fights in which, with their inferior arms and numbers, they were at a disadvantage. The soldiers were frustrated by this style of fighting, and retaliated with acts of cruelty against Indian warriors, women, and children. In 1871, Commissioner of Indian Affairs Francis Walker explained that "when dealing with savage men, as with savage beasts, no question of national honor can arise. Whether to fight, to run away, or to employ a ruse, is solely a matter of expediency."

By 1876, the army's victory seemed complete. Little by little, they had hemmed in the wandering tribes and had whittled away at their ability to support themselves. The typical state of a surrendering tribe was near-starvation, with a goodly proportion of the young men dead.

Research Assignment: Compare the arms and fighting techniques employed by both the Indians and the U.S. Army in their various military confrontations. Explain how these reflect the cultures that produced them.

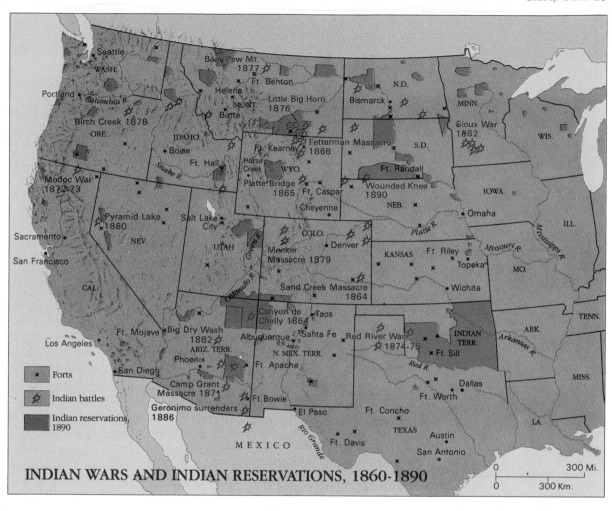

INDIAN WARS AND INDIAN RESERVATIONS, 1860-1890

Map legend:
- ✕ Forts
- ✩ Indian battles
- Indian reservations, 1890

Map labels: Seattle, WASH., Portland, Columbia R., Birch Creek 1878, ORE., Bear Paw Mt. 1877, Ft. Benton, Helena, MONT., Butte, Little Big Horn 1876, Bismarck, N.D., MINN., WIS., Sioux War 1862, S.D., Fetterman Massacre 1866, Ft. Kearney, IDAHO, Boise, Ft. Hall, Snake R., Horse Creek, WYO., Platte Bridge 1865, Ft. Caspar, Ft. Randall, Wounded Knee 1890, IOWA, Modoc War 1872-73, Cheyenne, NEB., Omaha, Platte R., Missouri R., ILL., Pyramid Lake 1860, Salt Lake City, NEV., Green R., UTAH, Sacramento, COLO., Denver, KANSAS, Ft. Riley, Topeka, MO., San Francisco, Meeker Massacre 1879, Colorado R., Sand Creek Massacre 1864, Wichita, CAL., Canyon de Chelly 1864, Taos, Santa Fe, Red River War 1874-75, INDIAN TERR., Arkansas R., TENN., ARK., Ft. Mojave, Big Dry Wash 1882, Albuquerque, Ft. Sill, Los Angeles, ARIZ. TERR., N. MEX. TERR., Red R., MISS., Phoenix, Ft. Apache, Dallas, San Diego, Camp Grant Massacre 1871, Ft. Bowie, Ft. Worth, LA., Geronimo surrenders 1886, El Paso, Ft. Concho, Rio Grande, MEXICO, Ft. Davis, TEXAS, Austin, San Antonio, 0 300 Mi., 0 300 Km.

The last important Indian victory took place at the Little Bighorn River, Montana, in 1876. Despite Custer's famous "last stand," the Sioux wiped out his force to the last man.

Little Big Horn. But Indian resistance was not quite at an end. In June 1876, Colonel George Armstrong Custer led 265 men of the Seventh Cavalry into a battle with the Sioux on Montana's Little Bighorn River. In a total victory for the Indians, every one of Custer's men was killed. Although a completely unexpected defeat, "Custer's Last Stand" thrilled Americans. Only in the next century would it be recognized that the Little Big Horn was most significant as the final victory of a doomed people.

Reform. In 1881, a Colorado writer, Helen Hunt Jackson, published *A Century of Dishonor*, which became a best-selling book. In meticulous detail she described how the United States government had dealt with the Indians since independence. The broken treaties were listed. Time and again, according to Jackson, "Christian" whites had cheated "savage" Indians of their land, had herded them onto reservations on lands judged to be the least useful, and even chipped away at those reservations.

By 1876, the government had ceased to make treaties with the Indians. Those Indians who did not resist American control were defined as *wards* of the federal government. They were not citizens, but were under Washington's protection. After the publication of *A Century of Dishonor*, many people and groups demanded that the government use *wardship* in a just manner.

The Dawes Severalty Act. In 1887, reformers were strong enough in Congress to pass the Dawes Severalty Act. Assuming that the traditional Indian life was no longer feasible, the supporters of the Dawes Act agreed that the Indian peoples must be Americanized. In other words, they must become self-sustaining citizens through adoption of the ways of the larger society. Under the Dawes Act, the tribes were dissolved. Their lands were divided into 160-acre (64-hectare) parcels and distributed to each household. Leftover land was to be sold to white settlers.

The easterners who pushed for the Dawes Act overlooked several facts. First, few of the western Indians were farmers; traditionally they had been hunters, gatherers, and traders. Second, the *reservation* lands were rarely suited to agriculture; they had been allotted to the Indians precisely because they were unattractive to farmers. Third, no west-ern tribe thought in terms of private ownership of land. The tribe, which the Dawes Act aimed to abolish, was a basic social unit that could not be successful when subdivided or scattered.

Defeated, demoralized, and frequently reduced by idleness and alcohol, the Indians were now susceptible to being defrauded of what land was left to them. Because they owned the land on which they lived as individuals, they could sell it. When whites found oil on Indian lands, they generally had little difficulty in talking the individual owners into accepting cash, whereas dealing with a whole tribe would have been more difficult.

Wounded Knee. Among the demoralized people appeared a religious reformer. Wovoka, a Paiute who had lived with a white Christian family and had been fascinated by the religious doctrine of redemption, began to wander through the West and preach a religion that appealed to thousands of Indians. His message was that by performing a ritual dance, the Indians, who were God's chosen people, could prevail on the Great Spirit to make the white people disappear. This *Ghost Dance* would also bring back to life the buffalo herds, the many Indians who had been killed, and the old way of life that many Indians remembered.

To understand the appeal of the Ghost Dance religion, it is necessary to recall just how rapidly the way of life of the Plains Indians was destroyed. This loss made the people vulnerable to a strongly presented idea that promised them a return to the old days. For example, the Dakota Sioux did not go to war with the whites until the end of the 1860s. Within another decade, the survivors had been herded onto the Pine Ridge Reservation in South Dakota.

There, on Wounded Knee Creek, the Dakotas took avidly to the Ghost Dance religion. When the soldiers guarding them heard that there were guns in the camp, they grew nervous. In December 1890, there was a shoving incident, which caused the soldiers to open fire with rifles and *artillery*. About 200 Dakotas were massacred.

The West Changes. As the Indians lost the West, the Americans of European descent won it. Indeed, the final decades of the nineteenth century stand as the era of greatest economic expansion in American history.

Research Assignment: Have students report on some of the Indian tribes mentioned in this chapter and what became of them. Do they still exist? If so, how are their life-styles different?

MOVERS AND SHAPERS

Helen Hunt Jackson

Sarah Winnemucca

Of all the defenders of the American Indians, few have been more passionate and effective than Sarah Winnemucca (1844?–1891) and Helen Hunt Jackson (1830?–1885). Born in widely different circumstances in different parts of the country, they never met. But it is easy to imagine that they would have admired each other.

Boston-born Helen Hunt Jackson went with her husband to live in Colorado, where she became concerned about the plight of western tribes. In 1881, she published a report on the Poncas tribe, *A Century of Dishonor*, and mailed it to every member of Congress. This 457-page book documented the government's mistreatment of the Poncas. In it she wrote, "The story of one tribe is the story of all . . .

Colorado is as greedy and unjust in 1880 as was Georgia in 1830, and Ohio in 1795; and the United States Government breaks promises now as deftly as then. . . ."

The next year, she was appointed by the government to study California's Mission tribe. Determined to publicize the mistreatment of the Indians, she decided to tell the story through fiction. Her novel, *Ramona*, published in 1884, had broad appeal. But its impact was received more as a work of literature than as social protest, and did not precipitate the strong action Jackson desired.

Sarah Winnemucca might have been a heroine in a romantic novel. She was a princess, the daughter and granddaughter of chiefs of the Southern Paiute tribe of Nevada. As a young girl, she

changed her Indian name, Thocmetony (or Shell Flower), to Sarah. She was a brilliant student and was sent to a convent school in California. The prejudiced parents of other students complained bitterly and she was sent home after a few weeks. Nevertheless, Sarah learned both Spanish and English as well as three tribal languages, and used these skills to help her people.

It was a treacherous world in which she lived. The Southern Paiutes were at the mercy of government agents. Sometimes they were treated well, sometimes not. Also, although the Southern Paiutes were relatively peace-loving, there was tension with other tribes. Once when a neighboring tribe, the Bannocks, captured 75 Southern Paiutes, Winnemucca made a grueling three-day trip across the Idaho desert to rescue them. Having accomplished this, she rode ahead of the group for another three days to get help from the United States cavalry.

The rest of Winnemucca's life was spent teaching and working for a better life for her people. Her book, *Life Among the Piutes: Their Wrongs and Claims*, was published in 1883. She earned enough money from the book and her lectures to buy land for a school in Nevada. She taught there until her husband's death. Then she moved to Montana where she died at the age of 47.

The Five Civilized Tribes of the Muskogean-speaking nation of the southeast U.S. were admitted as U.S. citizens in 1901. It wasn't until 1924 that all Indians were given this right, and even then there were some restrictions on their rights. Not until 1947 did Congress *begin* removing all these restrictions from America's first citizens.

When Europeans first arrived in America, over 1 million Indians lived in villages like the one pictured above. The tribes fought desperately to keep their land and way of life. After their defeat, they were forced to live on reservations throughout the West.

In 1870, American forests yielded about 12.8 billion board feet of lumber. By 1900, this output had almost tripled to about 36 billion. Although this increase reflects in part the development of forest industries in the southern states, the region of greatest expansion was a new one, the Pacific Northwest.

In 1870, Americans were raising 23.8 million cattle. In 1900, 67.7 million cattle were fattening on grasslands, mostly in the West, and in feedlots.

Annual gold production continued only slightly below the fabulous levels of the *gold rush* era, and by the end of the century, it was nearly double the totals of 1850. Annual silver production, only 2.4 million troy ounces (3.7 million grams) in 1870, stood at 57.7 million troy ounces (88.6 million grams) in 1900.

SECTION REVIEW

1. Write a sentence to identify: General George Crook, *A Century of Dishonor*, Wovoka, Pine Ridge Reservation.

2. When and where did the Indian Wars begin and end, and what were the peak years of the wars?

3. Give a brief account of the battle that occurred at the Little Big Horn River.

4. Explain the relationship among the Dawes Act, the Ghost Dance religion, and the massacre at Wounded Knee.

5. Briefly describe the American economic expansion at the end of the nineteenth century.

Discussion Question: Do the American Indians have just reason for anger against the U.S. today? What might be done about this? The discussion should cite continuing injustices against the Indians.

3. THE CATTLE INDUSTRY

Acre for acre, cattleranchers won more of the West than any other group of pioneers. They wanted to feed the appetite of the burgeoning cities for cheap meat. They were also encouraged in their venture by the rolling arid grasslands unclaimed by anyone save the Indians. Their story thrills us to this day, partly because it was romantic, partly because the cattle kingdom was established quickly and just as quickly destroyed.

The Cowboy. The cowboy first rode into American legend just before the Civil War. In the late 1850s, several groups of enterprising Texans rounded up herds of the half-wild longhorns that ranged freely between the Nueces (no͞o-ā′səs) River and the Rio Grande. They drove the cattle north over a Shawnee Indian trail to Sedalia, Missouri, a railroad town with connections to Chicago, Illinois. Although the bosses were English-speaking, the actual workers were Mexican. The Mexicans called themselves *vaqueros* (vä-kär′ōz).

Vaquero, which translates roughly as "cowboy," entered the English language as *buckaroo.* Much of what became part of American folklore about the buckaroos was of Mexican derivation. The cowboy's colorful costume was an adaptation of functional Mexican workdress. The bandanna was a washcloth that, when tied over the cowboy's mouth, served as a dust screen, no small matter when riding with 1,000 cattle. The broad-brimmed hat was not selected for its picturesque qualities but because it was a sun and rain shield. Made of first-quality beaver pelt, the sombrero also served as a drinking pot and washbasin.

The pointed, high-heeled boots, awkward and even painful to walk in, were designed for riding in the saddle, where a vaquero spent the workday. The "western" saddle itself was of Spanish design, quite unlike the English type that was used by Americans in the East. Leather leg coverings, known as chaps got their name from chaparral, the low-growing brush of the plains against which they were designed to protect the cowboy.

The Cowboy's Life. Even in the days of the long drive, the world of the cowboy bore scant resemblance to the legends that survive today. A large proportion of cowboys were Mexican or black. In some cases, these workers and the whites acted and mixed socially. Just as often, however, they split when they reached the end of the trail.

The spirit of the Old West was best recorded by artist Frederic Remington. First visiting Montana in the 1880s, he began to gather his material—bronco-busting cowboys (left) and Indian trappers (right). Soon these and the frontier would be no more than a memory.

The term *cowboy* was coined in the American Revolution and referred to British troops who worked in small groups on the land between the British and American forces. They drew unsuspecting soldiers into ambush by using a cowbell to disguise their presence. Have students use the dictionary to find the origin of hoodlum, rustler, and maverick.

The word "boy" in cowboy is nearly accurate. Photographs that the buckaroos had taken in Abilene and Dodge City, as well as arrest records, show a group of very young men, few apparently much older than twenty. The life was too hard for anyone but youths—days in the saddle, nights sleeping on bare ground in all weather. Moreover, the cowboy who married could not afford to be absent from his own ranch or farm for as long as the cattle drives required.

Gunslinging may have been the specialty of cowboys on the movie screen. But the most important skills of the historic buckaroos were riding horses and roping calves. Indeed, toting guns was forbidden in all the trail-head towns. With a binge on almost every cowboy's town itinerary, the sheriff or marshall in charge of keeping the peace did not tolerate shooting irons on every hip. Those who did not leave their revolvers in camp outside town, checked them at the police station.

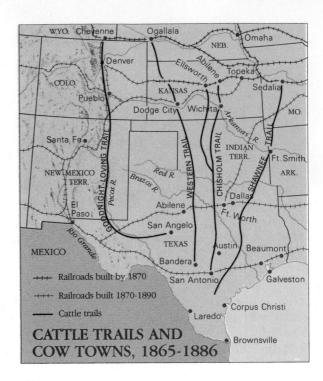

CATTLE TRAILS AND COW TOWNS, 1865-1886

Getting Meat to the Market. Missouri laws against importing Texas cattle stifled the first long-distance commerce in beef before it really got started. However, in 1866, when the transcontinental railroad reached Abilene, Kansas, a dealer from Illinois, Joseph G. McCoy, saw the possibilities of underselling steers raised in the East with the longhorns of Texas. McCoy built a series of holding pens on the outskirts of Abilene, and arranged to ship the cattle with the Kansas Pacific Railroad. He dispatched agents to southern Texas to induce Texans to round up longhorns and drive them north to Abilene on an old trading route called the Chisholm Trail.

In 1867, McCoy shipped 35,000 "tall, bony, coarse-headed, flat-sided, thin-flanked" cattle to Chicago. In 1868, 75,000 beasts, nearly worthless in Texas, passed through Abilene with Chicago packers crying for more. In 1871, 600,000 "critters" left the pens of several Kansas railroad towns to end up on American dinner tables.

High Profits. The profits were immense. A steer that cost $5 when raised on open public lands would be driven to Kansas at the cost of one cent a mile and sold for $25 or, occasionally, as much as $50. Investors from as far as England went west to establish ranches that were as com-

fortable as big-city private clubs. The typical cattle owner at the famous Cheyenne Club never touched a gun and rarely sat on a horse. Instead, he wore expensive clothes and worked on account books and balances.

The Railroad. The railroad continued to move westward, and so did the cowboys, who were soon coming from the North as well as the South. After a few years, the citizens of towns like Abilene concluded that the money to be made as a cattle-trading center was not worth the damage done to their own ranches and farms by hundreds of thousands of cattle. The wild atmosphere given their towns by the rambunctious cowboys was even less conducive to respectable civic life. As a cowtown grew, its "better element" demanded churches and schools in place of saloons and casinos, and the stage was set for the taming of a town.

The Cattle Drive. It took three or four months to drive a herd of cattle from San Antonio, Texas, to a railhead town in Kansas. To be asked to join a trail crew was a coveted honor among the young men of the country. The wages were low, only $1 a day plus board and as good a bed as the

---

Cattle branding did not originate in the West, nor with cows. A Connecticut law in the mid 1800s required the branding of all pigs by farmers.

The cowboys' job of driving cattle to the railroad meant a hard, lonely life. Days in the saddle and nights sleeping on the ground appealed mainly to youths, hence the name "cowboy."

sod of the Great Plains provided. But because a lot of money and many lives rested on every member of a crew, only those men who had impressed a trail boss with their skills and reliability would be invited along.

A trail crew was led by a trail boss, who was responsible for the drive. He brought along a *segundo*, or assistant, a cook, and a wrangler, who was in charge of the *remuda*, or large herd of horses that accompanied the expedition. One cowboy was assigned to each 250–300 cattle. Most herds were made up of between 2,500 and 3,000 cattle, so 10–12 cowboys was the typical number for a trail crew.

The Cowboys' Job.

A herd moved about 10–15 miles a day, the animals grazing as they got the chance. The usual procedure for getting a herd along was for two men to ride "lead," or "point," one on either side of the milling beasts. Two others rode "swing" and "flank," in pairs at regular intervals alongside the herd. Two or three cowboys rode "drag," behind the herd to hurry up stragglers.

Each position had its peculiarities. Riding point was the most dangerous position in the event of a stampede, but it was also the most pleasant in terms of dirt and odor. Conversely, riding drag was the safest but also the least desirable job, not only because of the dust that 3,000 animals raised, but also because there was not a moment in which some independent-minded "dogies" were not determined to leave the herd and set off on their own trail.

The day's drive started at first light and ended as late toward dusk as the trail boss could find satisfactory grass and water. Even then the cowboy's work was not done. After a big dinner at the chuckwagon, the hands had to "ride night." In two-hour shifts, pairs of riders circled the herd in opposite directions, looking out for predators and soothing the nervous steers.

Indeed, night riding was as dangerous as it was detested. Almost all stampedes started at night, tripped by a bolt of lightning or a steer dodging a coyote. Except for drownings during river crossings—there were four major and numerous minor watercourses between Texas and Kansas —the stampede was the most frequent cause of death written on the wooden markers that dotted the Shawnee, Chisholm, and Goodnight-Loving trails.

Disaster Strikes. The profits to be made in cattle were so great that cattle owners ignored the natural limits of the range in supporting huge herds. Vast as the plains were, they were over-stocked by the mid-1880s. Clear-running springs were trampled into unpotable mud holes. Weeds never before noticed replaced the grasses that had invited overgrazing. Hills and buttes were scarred by cattle trails. Some species of migratory birds that once passed through twice a year simply disappeared, for the steers had beaten them to their food.

On January 1, 1886, a great blizzard buried the eastern and southern plains. Within three days, three feet of snow fell, with drifts of 20 and 30 feet. About 300 cowboys could not reach shelter and were killed. Between 50 and 85 percent of the livestock froze to death or died of hunger. When spring arrived, half the American plains reeked of death.

The summer of 1886 brought ruin to many cattle owners who had survived the snows. Grasses that had weathered summer droughts for thousands of years were unable to do so in their overgrazed condition. They withered and died, and the cattle, weakened by winter, starved on the grassless plain. Then, the next winter, the states that had escaped the worst of the blizzard of 1886 got 16 inches of snow in 16 hours and suffered with intermittent periods of heavy snow for weeks.

Cattle Industry Reorganized. The cattle industry eventually recovered, but only when owners who used more methodical practices of cattle raising took over from the speculators. *Cattle barons* like Richard King of southern Texas decided not to risk all on the open range. He built a ranch that was as large as the state of Rhode Island. Others followed King's example in Texas, Wyoming, Montana, and eastern Colorado.

Even more important in ending the days of the long drive and the legendary cowboy was the expansion of the railroad network. When new east-west lines snaked into Texas and the states on the Canadian border, and the Union Pacific and Kansas Pacific sent feeder lines north and south into cow country; the cowboy became a ranch hand, a not so freewheeling employee of large commercial operations.

Western Culture. The legend of the cowboy as romantic, dashing, and quick-drawing was not a creation of a later era. On the contrary, all the familiar themes of the Wild West were well formed when the cold, hard reality was still alive on the plains. Rather more notable, the myths of the Wild West were embraced not only by easterners in their idle reveries, but by the cowboys themselves.

The most important creator of the legendary Wild West was a shadowy character named E. Z. C. Judson. After being dishonorably discharged from the Union Army, Judson took the pen name Ned Buntline, and between 1865 and 1886 churned out more than 400 romantic, blood-and-guts novels about western heroes. Some of them he invented, but others were believable people drawn from real life. The books by Judson and his many competitors were devoured chiefly, but not exclusively, by boys. Indeed, the mythical world appealed to many who knew much better.

Legendary Characters. Many wishfully romantic Americans decided that the bank and train robbers Jesse and Frank James, and several cohorts from the Clanton family, were really modern-day Robin Hoods who gave the money they took to the poor. When Jesse was killed, his enterprising mother made a tourist attraction of his grave, charging admission and claiming that her son had been a Bible-reading Christian.

Belle Starr (Myra Belle Shirley) was immortalized as "the bandit queen," as pure in heart as Jesse James was socially conscious. Billy the Kid (William Bonney), a Brooklyn-born criminal, was romanticized by word-of-mouth stories as a tragic hero who had been forced into a life of crime. James "Wild Bill" Hickok, a gambler who killed perhaps six people before he was shot down in 1876, was attributed with dozens of killings, all supposedly in the cause of making the West safe for women and children. Calamity Jane (Martha Canary), later said to have been a friend of Wild Bill's, wrote her own romantic autobiography.

Indeed, Calamity Jane and other "living legends" of the West personally contributed to the myth making by appearing in Wild West shows that traveled to eastern and European cities. The most famous of the Wild West shows was "Buffalo Bill" Cody's. Among his featured players was

The King Ranch in Texas is bigger than the state of Rhode Island. The first ranch to have its borders completely fenced in, its borders were at one time guarded by armed patrols.

Sitting Bull, the Hunkpapa Sioux chief who had overseen the defeat of George Custer.

Reality and myth were impossibly confused. After a successful career in show business, Sitting Bull returned to the Rosebud Reservation where, during the Ghost Dance excitement, he was accidentally killed by two Indian police officers who were arresting him on suspicion of fomenting rebellion. For the most part, the Wild West was the invention of highly commercial merchandisers of popular entertainment.

SECTION REVIEW

1. Write a sentence to identify: *vaquero,* Chisholm Trail, Sitting Bull, Abilene.
2. Show the relationship of the following to the long cattle drives that made American cowboys famous: Joseph McCoy's idea, the railroads, Chicago meatpackers.
3. How and why did the West's cattle industry change between 1867 and the years after 1886?
4. Name two legendary characters of the West, and contrast the legends about them with the realities about them. Give your opinion of why such legends begin and spread.

---

4. PIONEER FARMERS

At the same time that cowboys were roaming the broad plains, farmers were swiftly changing the character of the frontier. Farmers crossed the wide Missouri in growing numbers after the Civil War. They came in families, and sometimes as single men and women, in a courageous effort to raise crops on a forbidding land that had been known as the Great American Desert. From 1870 to 1900, these pioneers found ways of making this land produce wheat and corn by the millions of bushels.

The "Sod House Frontier." The western territories that attracted emigrant farmers were the Dakota Territory, Kansas and Nebraska, and the Indian Territory (Oklahoma). A federal law prohibited settlers from moving into Indian Territory, but this law was easily and frequently evaded.

The pioneers' first challenge was to erect some kind of shelter. They could hardly build log cabins since the plains were practically treeless. Instead, they broke up the heavy prairie sod with their horse-drawn plows, cut it into blocks, and erected simple one-room houses. *Sod houses* thus became home for the first hardy settlers in western Kansas, Nebraska, and the Dakotas.

Free Land. The settlement of the open prairie was encouraged by government policy. In 1862, Congress enacted the *Homestead* Act, which granted 160 acres (64 hectares) to anyone who managed to live on it for a minimum of five years. The offer of free land was so attractive that thousands of people rushed to take advantage of it, despite the risks and hardships of prairie living. Among those who joined the great migration west were veterans of the Civil War and farm families from New England whose land was worn out. Thousands of others came from Germany, Scandinavia, and Russia.

Between 1870 and 1900, the size of this western migration was truly staggering. Sod house pioneers settled more land in this period than had all previous generations combined. They turned 430 million acres (172 million hectares) of unsettled frontier into cultivated land.

Fencing Problems. Building a house out of sod bricks was only the first of the challenges to confront the pioneering families. Without trees, farmers could not fence in their crops and protect their land from the ranchers' cattle. Farmers experimented with hedges of various kinds as well as wire strung between widely spaced posts. These fencing materials, however, were generally ineffective against the roaming and stampeding cattle. The answer did not appear until 1874 when Joseph Glidden invented barbed wire.

Water Problems. There were many other obstacles, the most terrible of which was the shortage of water. How could a farmer grow corn in such a dry climate? On the Great Plains, rain was maddeningly infrequent and unreliable.

Water did exist deep below the hard sod—but too deep to be reached with simple tools. But during the 1860s, petroleum companies developed new machinery that could drill deep beneath

---

Research Assignment: Have students write a report on any of the legendary western characters mentioned in this chapter. These people should be presented in a realistic light rather than as romantic heroes.

After the Civil War, black families began to join the pioneers moving west in search of new lands. The family posing above were Nebraska farmers. They built their house of sod (the only material available on the treeless plains) and they made the land yield crops.

the surface. The drilling machines, though invented for oil, were soon adapted by sod house farmers to tap the underground water.

Windmills helped bring the water up to ground level. High winds whipping across the plains propelled windmill blades which in turn activated the water pump. Flowing up from a deep shaft, the pumped water irrigated the dry sod and made prairie farming feasible.

Hazards of Prairie Life. The barbed wire and the windmills made survival possible, but prairie life was still hard and fraught with natural perils. Violent storms swept across the flat terrain. Howling blizzards in the winter caused any unsheltered horse or human to freeze to death. Swirling cyclones in the summer wrecked homes and fencing. Worst of all were the swarms of grasshoppers that unpredictably swooped down over the plain and devoured a farmer's entire crop.

The Oklahoma Land Rush. By no means, however, did these hardships deter the continuing push westward. So great was the desire for free land that, on April 22, 1889, about 100,000 eager pioneers responded to President Benjamin Harrison's *proclamation* opening up the territory of Oklahoma to settlement. Lining up along the Oklahoma border, they waited for the officer in charge to fire the signal gun, and then dashed madly across the line to stake out a homestead claim. Within a few hours, the Oklahoma Territory (formerly reserved for Indian tribes) was completely overrun with homesteaders. Thus, the last unsettled area in the United States came under the plow, and the western frontier was closed.

SECTION REVIEW

1. Write a sentence to identify: Great American Desert, Indian Territory, Joseph Glidden, President Benjamin Harrison.

2. What natural obstacles did pioneers in the western territories face? What solutions did they find for these obstacles?

3. How did the Homestead Act encourage settlement of the open prairie? Name four groups that took advantage of the opportunities offered by the law.

4. Describe the event that marked the closing of the western frontier. How long did it take for this last frontier to close? For what group of Americans was this event a disadvantage? Why?

5. MINING

The folklore of the precious-metal mining frontier is second only to the legend of the cowboy in the American imagination. Deadwood Gulch, for example, where Wild Bill Hickok was gunned down and Calamity Jane spent much of her life, was no cowtown but a gold-mining center.

Readers of the dime novels of the time and film viewers since have avidly absorbed the images of boisterous, wide-open mining towns, complete with saloons rocking with the music of pianos and the shouts of bearded men. The live-for-today miner, the gambler, and the lucky gold strike are permanent parts of American folklore. Nor is the picture altogether imaginary. The speculative mining economy fostered a risk-all attitude toward life.

Wild Bill Hickok was a frontier scout and peace officer. Stories circulated about him claimed that he never killed except in self-defense or in the line of duty.

Calamity Jane (below), born Martha Jane Canary, was an expert horsewoman and crack shot who claimed to have scouted for General Custer.

Mining Camps and Towns. Efficient exploitation of underground mining required a great deal of capital and technical expertise, both to finance the operation and to build the railroads that hauled the ore. Consequently, the mining camps became home to 5,000 and even 10,000 people within a year of their founding. They offered a variety of services and a social structure similar to older industrial towns. In 1877, only six years after gold was discovered on its site, Leadville, Colorado boasted several miles of paved streets, gas lighting, a modern water system, 13 schools, five churches, and three hospitals.

Towns like Virginia City in Nevada, Deadwood Gulch in South Dakota, and Tombstone in Arizona are best remembered as places where legendary characters like Doc Holliday and Wyatt Earp fired their revolvers. But they were also the sites of huge ore-crushing mills that towered over the landscape, and of busy exchanges where mining stocks were traded by agents for San Francisco, New York, and London banks.

The mining West was no mere colorful diversion for readers of dime novels. It was instead an integral and important part of the national economy. In Goldfield, the last of the wide-open mining towns, one of the most important people in the

Class Activity: This period of American history is a source of great romantic stories. Compare fictional accounts and artifacts from the period with realities. Have students add to the list of those already mentioned in the annotations, and stress the importance of distinguishing between the two when studying history.

Miners are shown digging for gold at Placerville, California about 1852.

camp was an urbane financier from Wall Street, Bernard Baruch. The Anaconda Copper Company of Butte, Montana, was one of the nation's ranking corporate giants. The Guggenheim mining syndicate was supreme in the Colorado gold fields. Rockefeller's Standard Oil was a major owner of mines in the Coeur D'Alene of Idaho.

Gold and Silver Rushes.

After the richest of the California gold fields played out, prospectors fanned out over the mountains and deserts of the West. For more than a generation, they discovered new deposits almost annually and very rich ones every few years. In 1859, there were two great strikes. A find in the Pikes Peak area of Colorado led to a rush that was reminiscent of that of 1849. At about the same time, gold miners in northern Nevada discovered that a "blue mud" that had been fouling their operations was one of the richest silver ores ever discovered. This was the beginning of Virginia City and the Comstock

Lode, which, before it pinched out in the twentieth century, yielded more than $400 million in silver and gold.

In 1862, Tombstone, Arizona, was founded on the site of a gold mine; in 1864, Helena, Montana, rose atop another. In 1876, rich placer deposits were discovered in the Black Hills of South Dakota (then forbidden to whites by Indian treaty). The next year, silver was found at Leadville, Colorado, almost two miles above sea level in the Rockies.

During the 1880s, the Coeur D'Alene in the Idaho panhandle drew thousands of miners, as did the copper deposits across the mountains in Butte. In 1891, the Cripple Creek district in Colorado began to out-produce every other mining town. As late as 1901, there was an old-fashioned rush when a prospector, Jim Butler, drove his pick into a mountain in southern Nevada and found it "practically made of silver."

United States Currency.

Before 1849, paper money in the United States had value according to the amount of gold and silver that the issuing banks kept in their vaults. The two precious metals were not equal in value, because silver was much more abundant than gold, and therefore cheaper. Traditionally, the value of silver was pegged to that of gold at 16 ounces of silver to one ounce of gold.

This system worked well enough until 1849. Thereafter, despite the Comstock Lode, the American gold supply increased far more rapidly than the supply of silver. Indeed, by 1873, the miners on the Comstock appeared to have reached the bottom of their treasure trove; flooding and other problems prevented them from bringing out silver ore in any quantity. The value of silver on the open market therefore rose. By 1873, 16 ounces of silver could be sold privately for more than one ounce of gold. Silver dollars ceased to circulate because they brought more than 100 cents if melted down and sold to jewelers, speculators, or foreign buyers. Recognizing this, Congress passed the *Demonetization Act* of 1873. This act *demonetized* silver, meaning the silver dollar was dropped from the coinage list. With the Civil War greenbacks in the process of retirement, gold was now the sole basis of American paper currency.

A historian calculated that the gold taken from one South Dakota mine would fill the average bedroom but would weigh about 35 million tons and would be worth about $14 billion at today's gold prices.

The Crime of '73.   No sooner was the Demonetization Act on the books when Nevada miners made rich new silver discoveries. Silver flooded the market, and since the government was buying none of it, the price plunged. *Greenbackers,* fighting for inflation of the currency through the issuance of paper money, realized that they would have had their cheaper, more abundant money if the new silver was being coined into dollars. In Congress, inflation-minded representatives of the Democratic, Republican, and Greenback Labor parties spoke of the "Crime of '73," as though the Demonetization Act had been designed by the nation's bankers to keep money scarce.

There was no "crime." Although silver production began its upswing in 1870, it was a gradual one and the price of the metal had not decreased. In 1873, no one could have predicted that the nation's silver production would increase from 22,000 ounces in 1872 to 64,000 in 1892. The open market price of the metal continued to drop, from $1.32 an ounce to 87 cents an ounce, and then to 67 cents in 1896. Banking interests, of course, were delighted with the results. They were opposed to the inflation that would have resulted had the price of the now-abundant silver been pegged to that of gold.

The Bland-Allison Act of 1878.   In 1878, Richard "Silver Dick" Bland introduced a bill in the House of Representatives to remonetize silver. It proposed to peg the price of silver at the old ratio with gold. However, financial conservatives in the Senate forced a compromise. Under the *Bland-Allison Act,* the Secretary of the Treasury was required to purchase $2–$4 million in silver each month at the market price. Although the government's silver would be minted into dollars, silver was not monetized. In effect, the silver dollars were tokens. They had value only in the same way that dollar bills had value, because they were backed by gold stored in the vaults of the banks and federal Treasury.

Inflationists, mostly from western farming states, were not happy. Nor were the silver mine owners and the miners. Because the Treasury Department was controlled throughout the 1880s by financial conservatives, whether Republican or Democratic, the secretaries invariably bought the minimum amount of silver required by law, while production steadily increased.

The stage was set for a political eruption. It came to a head as the farmers of the West, suffering from an ever-deepening depression, increasingly attributed their problems to bankers' manipulation of the currency. The eruption finally occurred in 1890, after six new agricultural and mining states were admitted to the Union.

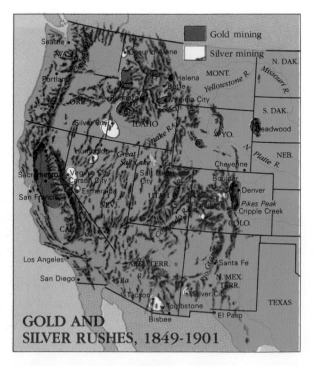

GOLD AND SILVER RUSHES, 1849-1901

SECTION REVIEW

1. Write a sentence to identify: Virginia City, Jim Butler, Demonetization Act of 1873.

2. Name five mining towns of the West. Contrast the fictional pictures of these towns with the reality about them.

3. Before 1849, on what was the value of United States paper money based? Explain how and why this changed in 1873.

4. Explain why the market price of silver decreased as its production increased.

5. Whom did western farmers blame for their financial difficulties? Did mine owners agree or disagree with these farmers? What would have made them happy?

Dungaree comes from the Hindu word *Dungri,* a northern suburb of Bombay, India, where the blue cloth had been manufactured since the 1600s. Levi Straus merely made use of an old standby of the natives and British in India.

CHAPTER REVIEW

TIME LINE

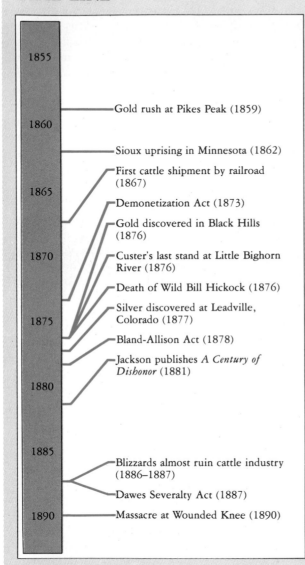

- 1855
- 1860 — Gold rush at Pikes Peak (1859)
- — Sioux uprising in Minnesota (1862)
- — First cattle shipment by railroad (1867)
- 1865 — Demonetization Act (1873)
- — Gold discovered in Black Hills (1876)
- 1870 — Custer's last stand at Little Bighorn River (1876)
- — Death of Wild Bill Hickock (1876)
- — Silver discovered at Leadville, Colorado (1877)
- 1875 — Bland-Allison Act (1878)
- — Jackson publishes *A Century of Dishonor* (1881)
- 1880
- 1885 — Blizzards almost ruin cattle industry (1886–1887)
- — Dawes Severalty Act (1887)
- 1890 — Massacre at Wounded Knee (1890)

TIME LINE QUESTIONS

1. How much time passed between the year silver ceased to back up United States paper money and the year Congress authorized the coinage of silver dollars?
2. What event ended the Indian Wars?
3. How many years after Helen Hunt Jackson wrote her report were Indian tribes dissolved and their lands divided by Congress?

SKILLS STRATEGY

. . . Black Hawk is an Indian. He has done nothing for which an Indian ought to be ashamed. He has fought for his countrymen, the squaws and papooses, against white men, who came, year after year, to cheat them and take away their lands. You know the cause of our making war. It is known to all white men. They ought to be ashamed of it. The white men despise the Indians, and drive them from their homes. But the Indians are not deceitful. The white men speak bad of the Indian, and look at him spitefully. But the Indian does not tell lies; Indians do not steal. . . . Things were growing worse. . . . The opossum and beaver were fled; the springs were drying up, and our squaws and papooses without victuals. . . . The spirit of our fathers arose and spoke to us to avenge our wrongs or die. . . .

PRIMARY SOURCES

A thorough understanding of history can be obtained by reading both *primary* and *secondary sources*. Your history textbook is a secondary source. It is an interpretation of historical events by a person who did not experience most of the events, but who did extensive research on the subject. Some other examples of secondary sources include historical novels, encyclopedia articles, and research reports. On the other hand, a primary source is an oral or written account given by a person who witnessed an event.

The first primary source shown above is from a speech by Black Hawk, a Sauk-Fox chief. He made this speech after his tribe was defeated and he was taken prisoner. Notice that Black Hawk refers to himself in the third person.

The second primary source is from an article by Timothy Flint, a frontier missionary from Massachusetts. Flint's purpose for writing was to explain to easterners the ways of the West.

Examine a primary source carefully before deciding on its reliability. The speaker or writer may not be objective if he or she is closely involved or has a personal bias. But when several primary sources agree, they will probably be accurate.

> In the whole history of the incipient [beginning to exist] settlement of our country, not one solitary instance of an attempt to settle an unoccupied tract, claimed by the natives, is to be found, which was not succeeded by all the revolting details of Indian warfare. . . . Either this great continent, in the order of Providence, should have remained in the occupancy of half a million of savages, . . . or it must have become, as it has, the domain of civilized millions. It is vain to charge upon the latter race results, which grew out of the laws of nature, and the universal march of human events. . . . Give them [the Indians] scope, development, and an object, place them in view of an equal or inferior enemy, and their instinctive nature would again raise the war-hoop . . . and renew the Indian warfare of the by-gone days.

APPLYING SKILLS

Read each of the above sources through once; then refer to both of them as you answer the following questions. Note that ellipsis points . . . mean that some portion of the original text has been left out. Brackets ([]) are used to show a definition or a change in text.

1. What event is the subject of both sources?
2. How closely involved in the event were Black Hawk and Timothy Flint?
3. What is the balance between facts and feelings (or opinions) in each source?
4. What personal feelings may have influenced Black Hawk's view of the event he is speaking about?
5. What does Timothy Flint seem to assume about the right of white settlers to take over Indian lands?
6. What picture do you get of American Indians from Flint's article?
7. Why might ellipsis points be used instead of having the complete original text?
8. Would you see Black Hawk's and Flint's words as sources for accurate facts or as reflections of attitudes and feelings? Explain why.

CHAPTER 20 TEST

TEXT REVIEW

1. Define *frontier* and *the West*, and describe the location of both between 1865 and 1900.
2. List four ways by which the huge herds of bison were brought to near-extinction.
3. Explain the reasons for *one* of the following: the resistance of the Plains Indians to white settlement, the massacre at Wounded Knee.
4. Contrast the attitude of General George Crook toward the Indian tribes with the typical attitude of officers and soldiers in the United States Army.
5. Trace the development of the western cattle industry from its origins in the late 1850s to its reorganization after 1886.
6. Name and give the important details about two ways that the federal government encouraged settlement of the Great Plains.
7. Give the most important steps that led to the demonetization of silver, and explain how demonetization brought about passage of the Bland-Allison Act.

CRITICAL THINKING

8. Summarize the effects of white expansion on the original inhabitants of the West.
9. Support or attack the validity of this statement with text data: "Reality and myth about the West were impossibly confused in the minds of most Americans."
10. Contrast the point of view of westward-moving pioneers with that of American Indians. Express both in terms of daily life.

WRITING A PARAGRAPH

Write a possible primary source. Put yourself in the place of a cowboy on a cattle drive from San Antonio to Abilene. You've been on the trail for over a month, and you want to let the folks back home know you're all right. Write a paragraph that might appear in a letter from such a cowboy. Make the paragraph authentic by writing to a specific friend or relation, and by using terms associated with your duties on the range. Tell how you like the life. Use chapter data for validity.

THE REVOLT OF THE FARMERS

1873–1896

*That's my Middle West—not the wheat or the prairies or the lost
Swede towns, but the thrilling returning trains of my youth. . . .*

F. SCOTT FITZGERALD

Making Connections. New techniques and machinery enabled farmers to produce far more in the late nineteenth century than ever before. Yet many farmers did not share in the national prosperity of the period. Prices for farm products dropped as quickly as supply rose. Farmers were not sure who or what to blame for their condition, but they were determined to strengthen their political power, as other Americans had done.

In this chapter, you will learn:
- What new farming techniques farmers used after 1870
- How the sharecropper system replaced slavery in the South
- Why the increased productivity of farmers failed to bring them prosperity
- What kinds of organizations farmers formed to fight for their common interests
- How the Populists proposed to change the United States
- Who began a new type of industry for the South

You know that the transcontinental railroad opened the large land area west of the Mississippi River to settlement. The amount of cultivated farmland therefore increased greatly. As you read, note what effects this increased farm production had on national politics in the latter part of the nineteenth century.

Sections

1. AGRICULTURAL ADVANCES

Ever since the first farmer poked a hole in the ground and inserted a seed, tillers of the soil have understood that they were engaged in a game of chance with nature. Farming involved gambling a year's living on such uncertainties as winter's final frost, summer's yield of sunshine and rain, and an autumn storm's driving winds and hailstones. Farmers accepted the fact that they were at the mercy of insects and birds. They knew that illness at the wrong time, particularly when the harvest was begun, resulted in a year of little money or food.

But farmers also knew that they produced the necessities of life. Come what may, people must eat, and they must have fibers from which to make clothing. The farmer would always be society's most valuable citizen. Indeed, Thomas Jefferson and four generations of politicians had told American farmers that those who toiled on the earth were the "bone and sinew" of the republic.

However, in the final decades of the nineteenth century, the farmers of the West and South discovered that these century-old truisms were not necessarily so. The power of nature paled in comparison with the power of certain people. Railroad barons, industrial millionaires, landlords, bankers, lawyers, newspaper editors, and

Harvest season meant celebrations for farmers who lived most of the year in isolation. But social activities were often combined with labor. The farmers at right used sword-shaped sticks to beat the flax fiber so that it would be ready for spinning.

Quotation: from the novel *The Great Gatsby.* Other works by F. Scott Fitzgerald (1896–1940) include *Tender Is The Night, This Side of Paradise, The Beautiful and the Damned,* and *The Last Tycoon.*

Skills Review: Reinforce the skills learned in the preceding Skills Strategy section. Have students use both primary and secondary sources in doing one of the research topics assigned in this chapter. Have them explain the use of their sources in a separate section attached to the main report.

politicians—all were viewed by many farmers as social parasites. They were accused of living off of and devouring producers while contributing nothing in return but exploitation and arrogance.

The farmers learned that they were no longer the bone and sinew of the republic, but just one interest group among many. And, in an urban and industrial America, they were not a particularly important one. Indeed, the new America was apt to view farmers disparagingly as hayseeds and yokels to be mocked on the vaudeville stage as well as in joke books.

Farming in the West.

Farmers rarely led the way on America's last frontier. Miners, loggers, cattle owners, and soldiers generally got there first. The farmers settled in the West only when there were enough people in an area to provide a local market for foodstuffs. Large-scale commercial agriculture was not feasible until the railroad arrived to carry crops in quantity to hungry eastern and foreign cities.

Once settled, farmers often clashed with other westerners. The *Grangers* battled the railroads. In California hydraulic miners washed down whole mountainsides to win their gold. This polluted the rivers with mud, and California farmers had to fight in the state legislatures for control of the precious water.

Homesteaders.

On the Great Plains, homesteaders were in competition with open-range cattle owners. They fenced in their holdings with barbed wire, which prevented some cattle from reaching streams and water holes. The cattle owners fought back by damming up streams before they reached the homesteaders' lands and by cutting fence wire. In Johnson County, Wyoming, a shooting war erupted. However, as in the conflict between farmers and miners in California, most of these disputes were resolved in the legislatures and courts. As long as the conflicts were local, the farmers usually had their way. On the national level, against other forces, the story had a different plot and outcome.

A Success Story.

Never in the history of the world has there been anything to rival the expansion of agriculture in the final three decades of the nineteenth century. As of 1870, when the takeoff occurred, American farmers had put 408 million acres of land under cultivation, an average of 1.6 million acres of new farmland a year. Between 1870 and 1900, a single generation of farmers put 431 million acres of virgin soil to the plow, an average of 14.4 million acres each year.

Crop production increased just as sharply. By 1900, American farmers were producing up to 150 percent more of the staples—cotton, corn,

The Homestead Act offered 160 acres of land to anyone who would live on and farm the land for five years. The Kincades (below) were one of thousands of homesteader families in Nebraska.

wheat—than they had in 1870. Hogs, which may be considered a byproduct of corn (corn is good feed for hogs), numbered 25 million in 1870 and 63 million in 1900.

The ravenous appetites of American and foreign city dwellers encouraged this amazing growth. The expansion of the railroads made it possible for crops raised by Great Plains farmers to feed the inhabitants of Chicago and New York, even London and Warsaw.

Improved Farming Techniques. Improvements in farm machinery furthered agricultural expansion. Farmers in the late nineteenth century worked with steel plows that sliced through the sod. They had disc *harrows* that cultivated wide swaths with each pass. There were other machines that planted seeds, shucked corn, threshed wheat, bound shocks, and shredded fodder to make food for livestock. Thus equipped with mechanical aids, farmers were able to cut down on waste, raise more animals, and tend to more acreage than earlier generations had dreamed possible.

The value of farm machinery in use in the United States increased from $271 million in 1870 to $750 million in 1900. This extra machinery greatly reduced the number of hours that a farmer had to devote in a season to produce wheat on an acre of land. Without the machinery, a

Local farm groups called "granges" were organized in the 1860s to promote farmers' interests. Many built their own halls, but this grange in Scott County, Illinois, held its meetings in the woods.

Women threshers on a Minnesota farm stand next to their steam-driven tractor. The photograph was taken in 1896.

farmer had to spend between 50 and 60 hours to harvest about 20 bushels of wheat per acre. With the new harrows, reapers, and threshers, a farmer produced a much larger crop after only eight to ten hours of work per acre. Potentially, a single farmer could cultivate six times as much land in 1890 as before the Civil War.

SECTION REVIEW

1. Write a sentence to identify: "bone and sinew," Johnson County, staples, harrows and threshers.

2. Describe the change of attitude toward United States farmers between the time of Thomas Jefferson and the final decades of the nineteenth century.

3. Give several causes of the conflicts between farmers and cattle owners on the Great Plains. On the local level, how were most of these conflicts settled?

4. Discuss the increase in crop and livestock production between 1870 and 1900. In general, what led to this expansion?

---

2. HARD TIMES

Amidst these marvels and feats, many farmers suffered. Those who lived in the Northeast or in the Ohio and upper Mississippi watersheds stopped growing staples and began producing perishable crops such as dairy goods, poultry and eggs, and garden vegetables to supply nearby urban markets. For the most part they prospered. But the western raisers of wheat, corn, and livestock, and the southern growers of cotton, watched their incomes sag beginning about 1872, and collapse by the 1890s. A crop that in 1872 had brought a farmer $1,000 in *real income* (actual purchasing power) was worth only $500 in 1896. The farmers had to produce twice as much to make the same money.

With their machinery, many farmers were doing just that. But it was not comforting to know that a quarter century of back-breaking toil and new methods yielded nothing but more struggle. By the 1890s, the price of corn was so low (eight cents a bushel) that farmers could not afford coal, and burned their grain for winter warmth.

Between 1889 and 1893, some 11,000 Kansas farm families lost their homes, *foreclosed* by the banks for failure to make their mortgage payments. In some of the western counties of Kansas and Nebraska during the same period, nine out of every ten farmsteads changed hands. Thousands of farms lay abandoned until after 1900, houses and barns decaying amidst thistles and dust. The number of farm *tenant* families—those who did not own the land they worked—doubled from 1 to 2 million between 1880 and 1900, most of the increase coming after 1890.

Southern Cotton. The price of a southern farmer's cotton crop fell to six cents a pound during the 1890s, and below five cents in 1893. In every particular, southern farmers were worse off

The main street of a farm town was usually one block long and supplied most of the farmers' necessities. Signs for a post office, printer, and harness shop can be seen on the right.

Some southern farmers, to escape the sharecropper life, moved west to find land. One such family was the Burdens who moved to Pleasant Hill, Nebraska, and built a farm.

than farmers anywhere save in the western counties of Kansas and Nebraska. Half of them were too poor to own their own land. Landowners outnumbered tenants three to one in the North and West, but in the South, tenants were as numerous as owners. Among southern blacks, *tenant farmers* outnumbered landowners by almost five to one. So poor were many southern farmers that *pellagra,* a fatal niacin-deficiency disease unknown even in slavery times, was common among them by the turn of the century.

These difficulties accompanied a success story. Southern agriculture made a remarkable recovery after the Civil War. The land survived, and the work force remained. Few of the South's 4 million black people went north or west. Cotton production reached the 1860 level in 1870 and exceeded the prewar record (1859) within a few more years. This was accomplished with a system of *cultivation* that was born of expediency and survived only by exploitation of the people on the bottom of southern society.

Tenants and Sharecroppers.

A radical change in the labor force posed a major challenge to the South after the Civil War. Black people were free and would no longer work for nothing. The Radical Republicans missed an opportunity to make them independent farmers when, instead of dividing the old plantations into homesteads for

former slaves, they left the land in the possession of its prewar owners. The landowners had no cash with which to pay wages to farm laborers. Indeed, even if a gang-labor system based on wages had been financially possible, black people would probably have resisted it as being too much like the way they had lived under slavery.

The solution was the share-tenant or the *share-cropper* system. The owners of the old plantations partitioned their land into plots the size of family farms and built a cabin on each plot. In return for the use of the house and the land, the tenants turned over to the landlord one quarter to one third of each year's crop. No money changed hands. Both tenant and landlord marketed their share of the crop.

Sharecroppers, who were likely to be black, were tenants who were too poor to supply their own mules, plows, and seed. The landlord provided everything in return for one half of the crop. In practice, the landlord or sometimes an independent merchant took the other half of the crop as well. In order to live day by day, the sharecropper bought on credit from a general merchandiser, using as collateral a lien on the fall's harvest. All too often, with the price of cotton and corn declining steadily during the late nineteenth century, the sharecropper family found that it had no share left to sell when the books were balanced at the store. All the family had was an open line of

Niacin is found in liver, lean meats, and whole-grain breads and cereals. *Pellagra* is characterized by eruptions of the skin, disturbances of the digestive and nervous systems, and, eventually, mental impairment.

credit and a *lien* on a crop that was not yet in the ground.

There was an element of security in this debt bondage. The cropper who owed money to the landlord was not likely to be evicted. But there had been an element of security in slavery, too.

The Agricultural Depression.

Who or what was to blame for the agricultural depression? Most economists answered that the blame lay in the complex, invisible operation of the international marketplace. The weather in western China affected the price that a South Dakota farmer received for wheat. The decision of a British colonial administrator in Bombay, India influenced the quotations on the Mobile, Alabama cotton exchange.

The beginning of the long slide in agricultural prices dated from the bankruptcy in 1873 of the prestigious Jay Cooke & Company, a respected Philadelphia bank. When Cooke went broke, manufacturers who depended on his bank for credit shut their doors. Tens of thousands of workers lost their jobs. The unemployed cut their food expenditures, thus reducing demand and forcing down prices. During the depression of the 1870s, the average wholesale price of agricultural products dropped almost 30 percent. This ruined farmers who had mortgage payments to meet. A similar disaster, the failure of the Reading Railroad, launched an even worse depression in the 1890s.

The farmers knew that they were part of a complex international economy. They were prepared to accept this fact and its negative possibilities as another condition of farming life. But it seemed to many of them that only they bore the brunt of misfortunes in the end. When a New York banker stumbled in his office, it was the Iowa pig raiser or the Mississippi sharecropper who broke a leg.

Supply and Demand.

As economists explained, the farmers suffered most because there were too many of them producing too much grain, livestock, and fiber. American agricultural capacity had expanded too quickly, far beyond the capacity of society to consume it all. Supply was greater than demand and therefore prices dropped.

Some leaders of the protesting farmers agreed. Jerry Simpson of Kansas urged the federal government to create new markets abroad. Others vehemently disagreed. Among them was Mary Elizabeth Lease from Kansas, one of America's first woman lawyers. How could overproduction be blamed, Lease asked, while American cities teemed with hungry people? "The makers of clothes are underfed," she said. The problem lay not with production but with distribution and exchange of foodstuffs for industrial goods.

Debt.

Angry agitators such as Lease blamed bankers as "the sinister forces at work in the night" who cheated both farmers and industrial workers. It was thought that bankers defrauded people by the artificially small amount of currency in circulation. Workers suffered because scarce currency meant low wages. Farmers suffered even more because so many of them were debtors. They had taken out loans to develop new land or to buy machinery when money was abundant —thanks to greenbacks and freely coined silver. But now they had to pay back their *creditors* in ever scarcer and more valuable gold.

Consider, for example, the case of a typical Great Plains farmer who borrowed money to buy machinery in 1882. If prices were stable, the farmer could devote 20 percent of income to pay off the obligation. However, the *deflation* of the currency and the decline of wholesale prices in only four years forced the farmer to use 30 percent of the income to pay the bank in 1886. If the farmer still owed on the loan in 1896, almost 40 percent of the income had to be devoted to making mortgage payments.

Flight to the City.

A more subtle blow to the farmers was the decline in their political power and status. One reason for this was the annual drop of the proportion of agriculturalists in the population. Equally important, legislators in Washington and the state capitals often seemed to forget about their farm constituents once they made the acquaintance of *lobbyists* for the railroading, manufacturing, and banking industries.

Socially, too, farmers were losing ground. A newly confident urban culture depicted the person of the soil in popular fiction, songs, and melodramas as a ridiculous figure in a tattered straw hat.

Discussion Question: How does supply and demand affect prices consumers pay today? If students have trouble with this question, it may be due to difficulty in understanding the notion of supply and demand. Review it with the class if necessary.

Serious writers such as Hamlin Garland understood the hardships of the agricultural life but also rejected them. In his popular 1891 book, *Main Travelled Roads*, Garland depicted farm life as dreary and stultifying. Tens of thousands of farmers' sons and daughters agreed with Garland and went to the cities. In part, they despaired of ever making a living on the land. In part, they were lured by the social and cultural attractions of the city. "Who wants to smell new-mown hay," playwright Clyde Fitch wrote in 1909, "if he can breathe gasoline on Fifth Avenue instead?" With each son and daughter who opted for urban fumes, farmers who clung to the Jeffersonian image of themselves became further dejected and agitated.

SECTION REVIEW

1. Write a sentence to identify: real income, sharecropper system, Mary Elizabeth Lease, Hamlin Garland.
2. What accounted for the numerous bank foreclosures and abandoned farms in the West between 1889 and 1893? What kept the same events from occurring in regions such as the Northeast?
3. How did the failure of Jay Cooke & Company cause a drop in agricultural prices?
4. Give two reasons to explain the flight of young farm people to the cities.

---

3. THE FARMERS' CRUSADE

Farmers were tardy in organizing to fight their battles collectively. At the center of the agrarian mystique in the United States was the vision of Jefferson's independent farmer. The American farmer stood on two feet, beholden to no one. However, the farmers began to see the trend toward large organizations in corporations, labor unions, and the women's suffrage movement. Eventually, farmers decided to join together to fight for their common interests.

The Cooperative Movement. The first type of organization to which the farmers turned was the *cooperative*. In consumer cooperatives, farmers banded together to obtain essential machines more cheaply by buying them in large numbers.

Money pools, associations much like contemporary *credit unions,* sprouted all over the Midwest. Through these associations, which were capitalized by members and operated on a nonprofit basis, farmers hoped to eliminate their dependence on the hated banks. Money pools, however, suffered from the opposition of the banks and the inexperience of amateur administrators. Distrusting professionalism almost as much as exploitation, farmers too often put friends rather than experts in charge of the money pools, and the rate of mismanagement and *embezzlement* was sadly high. Failed farmers who were suddenly entrusted with large sums of money frequently did not know how to manage it.

Another kind of farm organization was *producer cooperatives,* which attempted to counter the great power of the railroads. In 1886, the Supreme Court decided in the case of *Wabash, St. Louis & Pacific Railway Co.* v. *Illinois* that railroads could set their own rates for storing and carrying grain. Fearful of high rates, corn-belt farmers decided to build and operate their own grain elevators. Members of producer co-ops believed that their own storage facilities would enable them to hold their crops at low cost until the railroads were ready to move them. They could also withhold their products from the market until they liked the selling price.

Regional and State Alliances. Those co-ops that succeeded greatly benefited their members. But their effect on farm conditions was limited. Farmers believed that control of the currency by bankers and control of government policy by bankers, railroaders, and industrialists were the ultimate cause of their problems. By the late 1880s, therefore, they began to stress political action.

The major farmer organizations at this time were the *Agricultural Wheel*, the *Texas State Alliance*, and the *Colored Farmers' National Alliance and Cooperative Union*. At first, they contented themselves, as had the Grangers before them, with endorsing politicians of any party who agreed to support their programs. But they were disappointed when many of these legislators began to be

---

Research Assignment: Have students write a report comparing issues faced by farmers in the late 1800s and those faced by farmers today. Similarities and differences should be noted, as should solutions to old problems that no longer exist.

influenced by lobbyists for opposing interests. The state and regional organizations then moved decisively toward the idea of forming a new party.

By 1889, the various alliances and wheels had merged into three large associations of farmers. One represented mostly western farmers. A second was made up of southern whites, and the third of southern blacks. In December 1890, delegates representing all three organizations gathered in Ocala, Florida, to draw up a list of grievances.

The Populist Party. After the Ocala Conference, it took more than a year for the farmers to break away from the Republican and Democratic parties. Finally, in February 1892, they made the break by meeting in Omaha, Nebraska, and organizing a new political party, the People's party. It was commonly known as the *Populist party.* Once the new movement was proclaimed, emotionally

Populist party reforms were derided in the 1891 cartoon below as a "Platform of Lunacy."

charged enthusiasm swept over the delegates. Far from just a pressure group or a political organization, the Populists believed that they were engaged in a sacred cause. Not only would they capture the American government, but they would also remake the republic of democratic virtue that the Founding Fathers had envisioned.

To symbolize that farmers from both North and South had overcome the sectional chasm that had separated them, the Populists nominated former Union General James B. Weaver for president and former Confederate General James G. Field for vice president.

Reforms in the Populist Platform. At Omaha, the Populists drafted a comprehensive platform that would have significantly altered American history had it been enacted. As a means of crippling the political influence of the special interests, the Populists demanded a series of reforms. They wanted United States senators, who were elected by state legislatures, to be chosen in popular elections. The Populists also endorsed the adoption of the *secret ballot.* In many states at that time, particularly in the South, a voter's choice was a matter of public record. The Populists believed that this practice led to intimidation by employers and landlords.

The new party also introduced the concepts of the *initiative, recall,* and *referendum.* The initiative would allow voters, through petition, to put measures on the ballot independent of action by legislatures and thus free of manipulation by powerful lobbies. The recall would allow voters, also through petition, to force a public official to stand for election before his or her term expired. The Populists hoped that the recall would discourage politicians from backing down on campaign pledges. The referendum would allow voters to vote directly on laws rather than indirectly through their representatives. It was the means by which initiative measures and recall petitions could be decided.

Public Ownership of Monopolies. The most controversial Populist demands were for the abolition of national banks and for government ownership of railroads and the telegraph. Since so many of them were landowners, they could hardly advocate state ownership of all productive property.

Class Activity: Take some time to discuss the importance of the concepts of referendum, recall, initiative and the use of the secret ballot. Through newspaper and magazine clippings, have students point out incidents of recent uses of some of these in national and local politics.
Discussion Question: Should natural monopolies be publicly owned? Why or why not?

Delegates to an 1892 Populist convention in Nebraska brought along their families.

What they wanted was for the public to take over *natural monopolies*, enterprises that could be run efficiently only under a single management. The most effective way to run a railroad, they thought, was as a natural monopoly. Since railroads affected everyone in society, they argued, decisions about them should be made democratically. The "socialistic" parts of the Populist program were actually designed to protect the property of the common person and provide opportunities for self-improvement.

Other Populist Issues.

The Populist platform also called for a postal savings system, so that ordinary people might avoid depositing their money in the hated banks. It also advocated a

The Populists were defeated in the 1892 election by Grover Cleveland (far left).

graduated income tax. In 1892, the federal income tax was two percent for all. The Populists wanted the wealthy, who were supposedly better able to pay, to pay a higher percentage of their income than the modest farmer or wageworker paid.

In the Wilson-Gorman Tariff of 1894, provision was made for an income tax of two percent on all incomes of $4,000 or more, a modest tax by today's standards. It was widely condemned by people of means. In the case of *Pollock* v. *Farmers' Loan and Trust Co.* (1895), the Supreme Court ruled that because the graduated tax was a direct tax that did not fall on all equally, it was unconstitutional. Only after the Sixteenth Amendment was adopted in 1913 was it constitutional to tax the wealthy at a higher rate than the poor.

Finally, the Populists addressed the currency problem. They demanded an increase in the money in circulation. This inflation was to be accomplished through the free and unlimited coinage of silver valued at the old ratio with gold of 16 to one.

The Elections of 1892 and 1896.

The Populists did not expect to win their first election, and they did not. In 1892, Grover Cleveland swept back into office over the Republican *incumbent*, Benjamin Harrison. However, the Populist candidate, James B. Weaver, won 1 million votes (22 electoral votes), and the Populists sent a dozen senators and representatives to Washington, including the majority of the Kansas delegation.

That was enough to set the enthusiastic movement working toward 1896. Flamboyant orators like Simpson, Lease, Weaver, Ignatius P. Donnelly of Minnesota, and William A. Peffer of Kansas crisscrossed the western states stirring up intense feelings. The national leaders of the two major parties worried aloud at what sometimes looked like revolution.

The Populists hoped to win a following in the cities. Urban reformers like Henry Demarest Lloyd joined the new party and tried to persuade union leaders and wageworkers to support it. Eugene V. Debs, the head of the American Railway Union, drifted toward Populism. Prominent Democrats such as Governor John Peter Altgeld of Illinois showed interest in the movement. But in the end, Altgeld rejected its message and remained a Democrat.

Populism in the South.

Populism most fundamentally threatened the established order in the South. Here, particularly in Georgia, Populist leaders tried to form an *alliance* of poor farmers across racial lines. The leading advocate of the principle that social class was more important than race was Thomas E. Watson. A short, red-headed man from Georgia, Watson had trained himself in law and had a knack for inflammatory journalism and oratory. "You are kept apart," Watson told

The Sherman Silver Purchase Act was hailed by the press as "the Silver Sun of Prosperity."

Income tax was used once before as a temporary revenue-raising measure during the Civil War. Like so many of Lincoln's other broad uses of presidential power, it was not successfully challenged.

audiences of black and white farmers, "that you may be separately fleeced of your earnings. You are made to hate each other because upon that hatred is rested the keystone of the arch of financial *despotism* which enslaves you both."

He had his successes. In 1890, Watson was elected to Congress in opposition to the Democratic party machine in Georgia and was defeated two years later only because the bosses of the state redrew the lines of the district and probably miscounted the votes. On another occasion, Watson rallied 2,000 white Georgians to protect the home of a black Populist whose life was being threatened.

Race Relations Deteriorate.

In the end, however, Watson failed, and his failure helped usher in the most tragic period of race relations in the South. He failed in part because most southern blacks who retained the right to vote into the 1890s refused to desert the Republican party. Within the Democratic party, at the same time, emerged a canny kind of politician who appealed to poor white farmers on the same class issues that Watson raised. But instead of calling for an alliance with blacks, these politicians attacked the blacks more viciously than ever had been done during Reconstruction.

Democrats like Benjamin "Pitchfork Ben" Tillman of South Carolina promised to preserve white domination of the South by excluding blacks completely from political life. Tillman said blacks should be forced to observe a strict and humiliating color line in every aspect of daily life.

Thus began a style of *racist demagoguery* that was to characterize southern politics for half a century. One of those to capitalize on it was Tom Watson. Embittered by his failed experiment in interracial cooperation, he became after the turn of the century one of Georgia's fiercest race baiters.

The Free Silver Issue.

On the national level, the Populist party had a different fate. It foundered on neither class nor racial issues, but on the silver coinage question.

When the party was founded in 1892, there was no sign that it would become obsessed with the silver issue. Since the enactment of the Sherman Silver Purchase Act of 1890, the silver question

seemed to be settled. The Sherman Act had been pushed through Congress by an alliance of senators and congressmen from both farming and mining states. It required the Secretary of the Treasury to buy what amounted to the entire output of the nation's mines.

However, the act did not peg the purchase price of silver to the value of gold. Nor did it require the Treasury to treat silver as a basis of currency. President Harrison and President Cleveland during his second administration were determined to keep the United States on the gold standard. They therefore refused to pay the government's obligations in silver. Cleveland was particularly inflexible. He called the free coinage of silver a "dangerous and reckless experiment."

In 1893 government gold reserves slipped below the $100 million mark that economists regarded as safe. By the end of the year, the reserves fell to $80 million. The causes of the crisis were complex, but Cleveland blamed the problem entirely on the Sherman Silver Purchase Act. In November 1893, he persuaded Congress to repeal it. The United States was now back on the *gold standard* in law as well as in fact.

The Populists' Response.

Populists and the growing free silver wing of the Democratic party were enraged, especially when they learned that Cleveland had to call on the banker J. P. Morgan to stop the run on government gold. In 1894, William H. Harvey of Chicago published a popular book, *Coin's Financial School.* He argued in easily understood terms that the free coinage of silver was the key to restoring prosperity. Also in 1894, the silver mine operators of the mountain states launched a well-financed campaign demanding government purchase of silver. They had no interest in the more far-reaching Populist reforms. Indeed, as wealthy capitalists they were hostile to most of them.

They therefore threw their influence and money behind pro-silver Democrats like "Silver Dick" Bland and Congressman William Jennings Bryan of Nebraska. While these men sometimes sounded like Populists with their evangelical style of *oratory,* they were only mildly interested in most of the Populist demands and were actively opposed to others, such as the *nationalization* of the railroads and the telegraph.

Demagogue was a term used to refer to a leader of the common people in ancient Greece. The word now refers to a leader who gains power by appealing to the emotions and prejudices of people.

Henry Demarest Lloyd called free silver "the cowbird of the reform movement." A cowbird lays eggs in another bird's nest. The other bird hatches the eggs, and the young cowbirds eat the food and eventually starve to death the birds that belong in the nest. Free silver was like this, said Lloyd, because it attracted all the attention after 1893 and destroyed popular interest in the rest of the Populists' program. The election of 1896 proved Lloyd right.

SECTION REVIEW

1. Write a sentence to identify: cooperative, Agricultural Wheel, Eugene V. Debs, Sherman Silver Purchase Act.

2. List eight reforms in the Populist party platform. Give details for two of these reforms.

3. Contrast the early ideas of Populist Thomas E. Watson with the ideas of some southern politicians. How did Watson's strategy change?

4. Explain the Populists' stand on the free silver issue.

5. Compare the point of view of the silver mine operators and the prosilver Democrats about free silver with the Populist view.

4. THE NEW SOUTH

Henry W. Grady was for several years the influential, charming editor of a southern newspaper, the *Atlanta Constitution*. In speech after speech throughout the South, he told the story of a funeral that he had attended in rural Georgia. "They buried him in a New York coat and a Boston pair of shoes, and a pair of breeches from Chicago and a shirt from Cincinnati." The coffin at the funeral, said Grady, was made from northern timber and northern forged nails. "The South didn't furnish a thing on earth for that funeral but the corpse and the hole in the ground."

Grady's point, to which he devoted most of his short life, was that the South must abandon its reliance on agriculture and promote industrialization. The North's industry explained why the

The Populists wanted to bring the regions of the country together, as this engraving shows.

Confederacy had been defeated. Only by accepting the realities of the modern world would the South prosper.

Lumber, Steel, Oil, and Textiles. Grady lived to see few of his ideas come to fruition. However, in the 1890s, southern industrialists scored the kind of successes that Grady had called for. Beginning with a federal grant of almost 6 million acres of forest land in 1877, southern *syndicates* laid the basis of a thriving lumber and turpentine industry in the vast pine woods of the section.

Birmingham became the "Pittsburgh of the South," the center of a booming steel industry, following the discovery of coal and iron in northern Alabama in the early 1870s. By 1890, Birmingham was making more *pig iron* than was Pittsburgh. ("Pigs" are iron ingots, intermediate products ready for further processing.)

The southern oil industry was largely a twentieth century development; the great Texas gusher, Spindletop, came through in 1901. It was also after 1900 that most of the New England textile mills moved to the South. Even so, before Grady died in 1889, the trend of "bringing the factory to the fields" was already under way.

Duke and the Tobacco Industry. The southerner who was most successful in bringing the factory to the fields was a maker of cigarettes. James Buchanan "Buck" Duke started out as a tobacco grower, a good southern *agrarian* on the face of it. In 1881, he was shown a new machine that rolled cigarettes by the hundreds per minute,

"THE FAMOUS DUKES"

HIGH GRADE
SMOKING TOBACCO

Southern tobacco manufacturers such as James Duke revolutionized the smoking habits of the country.

and he began to think about its possibilities. All cigarettes were then rolled by the smoker.

Like a chess player, Duke had to see several moves ahead. To make money from manufacturing cigarettes, it was necessary not only to mass produce them cheaply, but also to change Americans' smoking habits.

Changing Americans' Smoking Habits. In the late nineteenth century, polite women did not smoke (at least in public). Men of the upper and middle classes smoked cigars or pipes, and workingmen and the lower classes in the South chewed

tobacco. Cigarettes were only a minor product. Soldiers in the Civil War had taken to them because they could carry papers and a pouch of tobacco but not cigars. After the war, however, the white cylinders were considered unmanly, a boy's smoke behind the barn.

Duke would have to change that image, and he did. Buying the patent to the cigarette-rolling machine, he encouraged adolescents to smoke his cigarettes by selling a pack of 20 for only a nickel. He included inside each pack a "trading card" that featured pictures and brief biographies of military heroes and popular athletes, mostly boxers and baseball players. Duke well understood the wisdom of putting together a long-term market for his products. All the while he created consumers, he improved the machinery and bought out competitors. By 1889, his company accounted for half the cigarettes sold in the United States, and Duke had only begun.

A Tobacco Trust. In 1890, Duke set up a *trust* along the lines laid out by John D. Rockefeller. Through it he gained control of his major competitors, R. J. Reynolds and P. H. J. Lorillard, and built an almost perfect monopoly. Indeed, through loose arrangements with British cigarette manufacturers, Duke had a major say in the tobacco-processing industry on two continents. Only federal *antitrust action* in 1911 forced him to disband his gigantic corporation. By that year, he controlled 150 factories.

SECTION REVIEW

1. Write a sentence to identify: "Pittsburgh of the South," "pigs," Spindletop, tobacco trust.
2. What was Henry Grady's reason for telling his "funeral story" in speeches he made throughout the South?
3. What natural resources led to the growth of these southern industries: lumber and turpentine, steel, oil, textiles?
4. Explain why and how James Duke changed America's smoking habits. Why was his operation subject to antitrust action?

Steam-driven tractors were used for cultivating land and pulling combines at harvest time.

Kodak roll-film cameras revolutionized photography. Ads said, "You press the button, we do the rest."

Perishable food can be carried long distances in refrigerated railroad cars, whose cooling systems keep food cold and thus prevent spoilage.

C H A N G I N G   T E C H N O L O G Y

	18	70		18	80	

Steel converter developed
First oil well drilled
Artificial dye produced

Vote recorder designed
Bessemer process developed
Vacuum cleaner introduced

Incandescent light bulb designed
Efficient internal combustion
  engine produced
Conveyor belt reaping machine
  built

Class Activity: Have students surmise the impact of the inventions appearing on this page and on page 523 on the people who first used them. What might their reactions have been initially? What may have accounted for these reactions?

Before Ottmar Merganthaler developed the Linotype, which used metal molds for each character, type was set by hand as it had been in Gutenberg's day. Using the linotype machine, one operator could set as much type in a given amount of time as several people setting type by hand.

Metal windmills generate power by using the force of the wind. During the latter part of the 19th century thousands of metal windmills were being used in rural areas of the U.S. to pump water, thereby irrigating the farmland.

18 90	19 00	19 10

Electric streetcar introduced
Magnetic wire recording
  invented
Electric iron invented
Motion picture camera produced
Electric fan designed
	Automatic loom developed
	Radio telegraph invented
	Electric stove introduced
		Seaplane flight introduced
		Caterpillar tractor produced
		Hydrofoil designed
		Electric-powered submarine
		  designed

CHAPTER REVIEW

TIME LINE

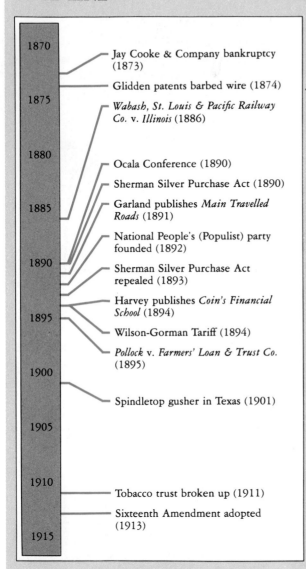

1870	
	Jay Cooke & Company bankruptcy (1873)
	Glidden patents barbed wire (1874)
1875	
	Wabash, St. Louis & Pacific Railway Co. v. Illinois (1886)
1880	
	Ocala Conference (1890)
	Sherman Silver Purchase Act (1890)
1885	Garland publishes *Main Travelled Roads* (1891)
	National People's (Populist) party founded (1892)
1890	Sherman Silver Purchase Act repealed (1893)
	Harvey publishes *Coin's Financial School* (1894)
1895	Wilson-Gorman Tariff (1894)
	Pollock v. *Farmers' Loan & Trust Co.* (1895)
1900	
	Spindletop gusher in Texas (1901)
1905	
1910	
	Tobacco trust broken up (1911)
	Sixteenth Amendment adopted (1913)
1915	

TIME LINE QUESTIONS

1. In what year was legislation passed providing for an income tax? Name the legislation.
2. When was the income of the wealthy first taxed at a higher rate than the income of the poor? What legislation made this action legal?
3. When were two popular books published?
4. What year marked an event that led to a major southern industry? What was the event?

SKILLS STRATEGY

NEW PARTY FORMED IN ST. LOUIS

St. Louis, Feb. 22—A spokesperson for representatives of many of the nation's farmers and industrial workers meeting in this city announced the formation of a new national political party. He said that the political organization would be known as the People's party.

The spokesperson explained that the party was formed to give farmers, industrial workers, and other ordinary Americans a greater say in government at all levels.

Currently, the spokesperson went on, delegates are continuing to work on bold new proposals. These proposals will be revealed in the new party's campaign platform when the national convention meets at Omaha, Nebraska, in July. More information will be available then.

NEWS STORIES AS PRIMARY SOURCES

News stories can be considered primary sources of information about historical periods. However, like all primary sources, news stories should be scrutinized for accuracy and reliability.

The form and content of a news story can be evaluated using certain standards. A good news story is made up of these parts: first, a *factual headline* that states the main idea; second, a *lead*, or first, paragraph that includes essential facts answering *who, what, where, when, how,* and *why* questions, excluding any statement of opinion by the writer; and third a *body* that consists of paragraphs giving less important factual details about the main idea of the news story.

In short, a reliable and accurate news story is the strict reporting of the facts of the event that is its subject. Statements of opinion are never made in a news story. Opinions are reserved for other parts of a newspaper, such as editorial pages, syndicated columns, and feature stories.

The headlines and lead paragraphs of the news stories above might have appeared in American newspapers in 1892, the year the Populist party was founded.

Making Connections: Review the questions and topics presented in the Making Connections section that opens this chapter.

524

LOYAL AMERICANS BEWARE!

Rebel Plot Hatching in St. Louis

St. Louis, Feb. 22—A wild-eyed, agitated spokesperson for a group of disloyal farmers and workers defiantly proclaimed the hatching of the misleadingly named People's party.

The rebel evaded reporters' questions. However, it is reported by reliable, loyal observers inside the well-guarded meeting that the fiery rebels are devising revolutionary plans that would bring about the utter ruin of the American way of life intended for us by our inspired Founding Fathers.

The plans will be made public under the guise of a party platform at the July "convention" of the dangerous revolutionaries in Omaha.

APPLYING SKILLS

Use the form and content standards listed in the second paragraph of this skills lesson as you evaluate the reliability and accuracy of the two news stories above as primary sources of historical information.

1. Which of the above stories contains a nonfactual headline?
2. Which story gives only facts in the lead paragraph? What questions about the subject do the facts answer?
3. What kinds of words in the lead of the other story show the writer's bias or slant?
4. To what feeling on the part of American readers does the writer of the second news story appeal?
5. What less important factual details could have been included in the body of the first story?
6. Which story would be better used as a primary source for historical facts about the founding of the Populist party? How could you use the other story?
7. Briefly explain which of the two news stories appears more reliable and accurate as a primary source, giving reasons to support your answer.

CHAPTER 21 TEST

TEXT REVIEW

1. Name two chief reasons for the phenomenal expansion of American agriculture during the last three decades of the nineteenth century.
2. In what region did agriculture make a remarkable recovery? Explain why.
3. Explain how the sharecropper system developed in the South. Describe its effects.
4. What factors probably led to the agricultural depression?
5. Give important facts about money pools, regional and state farmers' alliances.
6. What political party did the farmers found? Why did they feel it was necessary?
7. List three reforms proposed by the Populists that passed into laws that are still in effect.
8. According to Henry Demarest Lloyd, how did the free silver issue lessen the chances of a Populist victory in the election of 1896?

CRITICAL THINKING

9. From the point of view of a black Republican farmer in the South, give your reaction to Thomas Watson and his ideas.
10. Write *Populist* or *Democrat/Republican* after the letter of each statement to identify the probable speaker: (a) "The rich should pay the highest taxes." (b) "The country must be placed on the gold standard." (c) "We demand the secret ballot." (d) "Popular election of senators is against the Constitution."

WRITING A PARAGRAPH

Select one of the following events covered in the chapter: (1) the settlement of the dispute between hydraulic miners and farmers in California, (2) a Kansas family's loss of their farm because of a bank foreclosure, (3) Jay Cooke & Company declaring bankruptcy and shutting its doors, (4) President Cleveland announcing that the United States government would no longer pay its debts in silver.

Write an attention-getting factual headline, an unbiased lead, and a first paragraph to begin a news story about the event.

AMERICAN EXPANSION

1896–1903

The world is a fine place and worth the fighting for. . . .

ERNEST HEMINGWAY

Making Connections. In 1890, the American frontier was officially closed. Americans began to look for new challenges. They found them close to home, and half a world away.

In this chapter, you will learn:

- Who was the first presidential candidate in a quarter of a century to win a majority of the popular vote
- Why some people believed the United States had to take a greater role in world affairs
- What the "yellow press" was, and how it drew the United States into war with Spain
- How the poorly trained and equipped American forces won a surprisingly short war
- What Pacific islands were annexed by the United States during the McKinley administration
- How Theodore Roosevelt extended the country's influence over Latin America

You know that for the most part, the United States had avoided playing a leading role in world affairs. Consequently, Americans had not joined the European quest for colonies in Africa and Asia. In this chapter, note how the United States took the first steps toward building its own empire.

Sections

1. THE ELECTION OF 1896

The election of 1896 was strikingly different from earlier elections. For the first time in a generation, neither of the major party candidates looked to the Civil War as the central event of their lives. The Republican, William McKinley of Ohio, had served in the Union army as a teenager and young adult. His Democratic opponent, William Jennings Bryan of Nebraska, had been born in 1860. When the Civil war ended, he was only five years old.

The election was significant as well as novel. Almost everyone who was involved in it recognized that 1896 would be a turning point in history. When the election was over, the old era would be dead and a new one underway. No one knew what the country would be like in the new era. That depended on which candidate won the election.

McKinley and Hanna. The master political strategist for the Republicans was a forceful coal and iron industrialist from Ohio, Marcus Hanna. Hanna was not himself a candidate. He preferred to run the party from the background. His choice for the Republican nomination was his close friend, former congressman and governor William McKinley.

By 1904 the American eagle had spread its wings over half the globe. Historically the people of the United States were opposed to owning overseas colonies. Economics tended to be the reason for expansion from the Philippines to Panama.

Quotation: from the novel *For Whom the Bell Tolls.* Other works by Ernest Hemingway (1899–1961) include *In Our Time, The Torrents of Spring, The Sun Also Rises, Men Without Women, A Farewell to Arms, Death in the Afternoon, To Have and Have Not, The Fifth Column,* and *The Old Man and the Sea.*

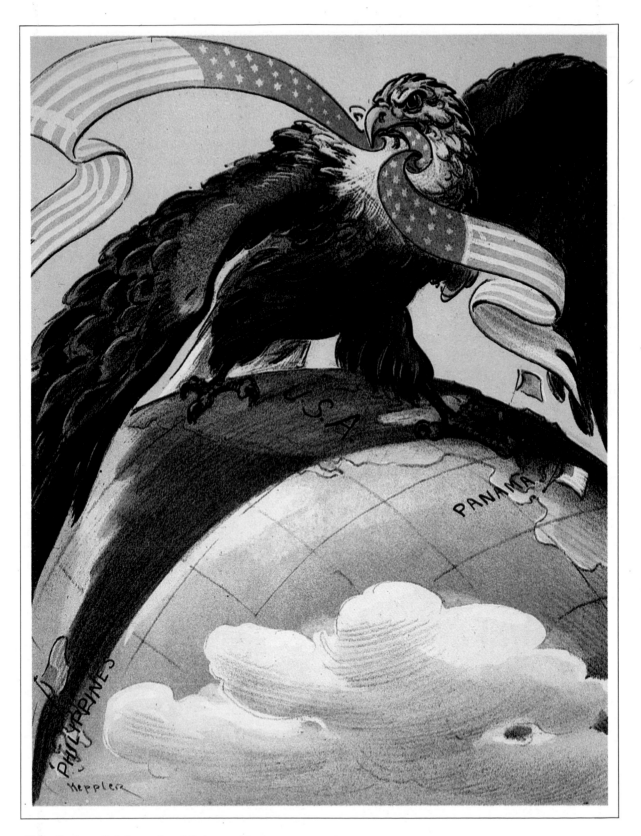

Skills Review: Reinforce the skills learned in the preceding Skills Strategy section. Have students review articles from the "yellow press" that are referred to in this chapter and then have them write a few paragraphs criticizing them.

The energetic William Jennings Bryan (in overcoat) traveled 13,000 miles by train and made 600 speeches as the Democratic candidate in 1896.

McKinley was well known among Republicans as a scholarly expert on the tariff, but some people felt that he was too scholarly. He was not the sort of man whose presence impressed itself on a gathering of political professionals. Nevertheless, he was nominated because of Hanna's persuasive efforts.

William Jennings Bryan. The election of 1896 was so important because, in the opinion of conservatives, the Democratic party had been captured by dangerous, wild-eyed Populists. They were mistaken. The Democratic candidate, William Jennings Bryan, appealed to Populists but was not one of them.

When he went to Chicago in July 1896 to attend the Democrats' national convention, Bryan was by no means the front-running candidate for the nomination. He had achieved fame in his home state of Nebraska as a fiery advocate of the

free coinage of silver. As an orator, he was precise in his phrasing and timing. His "Cross of Gold" speech, which enlisted God in the cause of free silver and identified the gold standard with the crucifiers of Christ, was a masterpiece in oration. Bryan scheduled it to wind up the party's debate on the currency question.

It was a foregone conclusion that the Democrats would endorse free silver. Bryan's speech did not influence their decision on this issue. But his thrilling words so aroused the delegates that they surprised the nation by giving him the party's nomination for president.

It was Bryan's "Cross of Gold" speech that frightened the Republicans. While it was entirely on the subject of silver, they noted a troubling hint of fanaticism in the tone. Indeed, Bryan tended to see disagreements in terms of good versus evil and political causes as crusades. Republicans who simply shrugged when a Democrat like Grover Cleveland was in the White House shuddered at the thought of Bryan residing there.

Bryan was a master orator. His "Cross of Gold" speech at the Democratic convention won him the nomination, but he lost the election to McKinley.

Discussion Question: Why do you think the Republicans would be afraid to have someone like Bryan in the White House? What might he do?

GOING TO THE SOURCE

Ah, my friends, we say not one word against those who live upon the Atlantic Coast, but the hardy pioneers who have braved all the dangers of the wilderness, who have made the desert to blossom as the rose—the pioneers who rear their children near to Nature's heart . . . these people, we say, are as deserving of the consideration of our party as any people in this country. It is for these that we speak. We do not come as aggressors. Our war is not a war of conquest; we are fighting in the defense of our homes, our families, and posterity. We have petitioned, and our petitions have been scorned; we have entreated, and our entreaties have been disregarded; we have begged, and they have mocked when our calamity came. We beg no longer; we entreat no more; we petition no more. We defy them!

. . . There are two ideas of government. There are those who believe that if you will only legislate to make the well-to-do prosperous, their prosperity will leak through on those below. The Democratic idea, however, has been that if you legislate to make the masses prosperous, their prosperity will find its way up

> *Having behind us the producing masses of this nation and the world. . . . we will answer their demand for a gold standard by saying to them: You shall not press down upon the brow of labor this crown of thorns, you shall not crucify mankind upon a cross of gold.*
>
> WILLIAM JENNINGS BRYAN, "CROSS OF GOLD" SPEECH

through every class which rests upon them.

You come to us and tell us that the great cities are in favor of the gold standard; we reply that the great cities rest upon our broad and fertile prairies. Burn down your cities and leave our farms, and your cities will spring up again as if by magic; but destroy our farms and the grass will grow in the streets of every city in the country.

. . . Having behind us the producing masses of this nation and the world, supported by the commercial interests, the laboring interests and the toilers everywhere, we will answer their demand for a gold standard by saying to them: You shall not press down upon the brow of labor this crown of thorns, you shall not crucify mankind upon a cross of gold.

On July 8, 1896, at the Democratic National Convention in Chicago, William Jennings Bryan made himself the hero of the Populists and the presidential nominee of the Democratic party by delivering his great "Cross of Gold" Speech. This excerpt is from the rousing conclusion to that speech.

The Populists Also Nominate Bryan. The Populists were close in spirit to Bryan themselves, and they too favored the free coinage of silver. The majority of the midwestern Populists, for whom the Republican party was the political opposition, immediately called for the nomination of Bryan on the Populist ticket as well as the Democratic. Although Bryan had accepted only the free silver plank of their platform, the Populists reasoned that he would almost certainly win if he had their support. But if Democrats and Populists split the free silver vote, supporters of the gold standard were in for four more years. To keep some of their identity, the Populists nominated their own Tom Watson for vice president.

The Campaign. Bryan was an excellent crusader. Handsome, boundlessly energetic, and at home among farm people, Bryan revolutionized the ways of presidential campaigning. Previously, most presidential nominees had been quiet. Not Bryan. His speaking tour took him more than

Discussion Question: Bryan felt that farmers were the most valuable citizens of any nation. Why would he think so? Would you agree with him? Why or why not?

13,000 miles (20,000 kilometers) by train. He delivered 600 speeches in 29 states in a total of only 14 weeks. The roaring enthusiasm of the crowds that greeted him, at least in the West and South, threw eastern bankers and industrialists into a panic.

This was exactly what Mark Hanna wanted to see. He pressured wealthy Republicans to make large contributions to McKinley's campaign. By the time of the election, Hanna had accumulated a campaign fund of $3.5 million. He spent it on posters, buttons, rallies, picnics, advertisements, and speakers. Hanna was so successful that, before election day, he began to return surplus contributions.

Knowing that McKinley could not hope to rival the colorful Bryan on the stump, Hanna kept his candidate at his modest home in Canton, Ohio. A steady stream of Republican delegations traveled to Canton, where they marched through the town behind a brass band and gathered on McKinley's front lawn. McKinley would deliver a short speech from the porch and answer a few prearranged questions.

The Election.

In the end, McKinley won the election handily—271 electoral votes to Bryan's 176. Bryan received more votes than any previous winning candidate, 6.5 million, but McKinley took more than 7 million. His vote was over 50 percent of the total; this was the first election in 20 years in which any candidate won an absolute majority. Bryan's defeat was caused by several conditions. He appealed to only the hard-pressed staple farmers of the South and West. In the Midwest, many farmers whose situation was not desperate accepted the Republican contention that Bryan was a radical, never a useful tag in American elections.

More importantly, Bryan could not win the support of the industrial workers and city people. He did not make much of an effort to gain their commitment. He made only one speaking tour in vital New York and was quoted as having called New York City "the enemy's country," as though it were inhabited solely by bankers and grain speculators.

Bryan's weakness in the industrial districts was in large part due to the single issue aspect of his campaign. His free silver campaign offered little to factory workers. They found more convincing the

Republican claim that a high-tariff policy would protect jobs.

Finally, Mark Hanna shrewdly judged the instincts of the growing middle class of small business people, professional people, salaried town dwellers, and highly skilled working people. Considering themselves to be the new bone and sinew of the American republic, most members of the middle class were worried about the direction of Bryan's campaign and therefore decided to vote for McKinley.

The End of Populism.

Collaboration with the Democrats sealed the fate of the Populists. They had sacrificed their reform program for the chance of winning free silver with Bryan. They had nothing left when the votes were counted against him. In the South, white Populists turned against the blacks and became the leading exponents of white supremacy. In the West, the party simply withered away, in part because the wholesale prices of farm products began to rise.

The agricultural depression lifted for a number of reasons. Rich new gold deposits that had been found in Canada and Alaska inflated the currency somewhat and helped to raise prices. Several years of poor weather in Europe created demand for American farm products. Finally, farmers, like other Americans, were distracted in 1898 by the McKinley administration's decision to win the United States a place among the empires of the world.

SECTION REVIEW

1. Write a sentence to identify: Marcus Hanna, "Cross of Gold" speech, Canton, "the enemy's country."

2. Explain how each candidate received his party's nomination.

3. Compare the campaign styles of William McKinley and William Jennings Bryan.

4. Explain why these groups did not vote for Bryan: farmers of the Midwest, industrial workers and city people, the growing middle class.

5. Of what significance was the election for the Populists?

    The Populist Party was not formally scrapped for a few years. The party ran candidates for president in 1900 and 1904.

PROFILES OF THE PRESIDENCY

WILLIAM MCKINLEY   1897–1901

*U*nder William McKinley, the country enjoyed prosperity at home and prestige abroad. McKinley marveled at his country's growth:

At the beginning of the nineteenth century there was not a mile of steam railroad on the globe. Now there are enough miles to make its circuit many times. Then there was not a line of electric telegraph; now we have a vast mileage traversing all lands and all seas. God and man have linked the nations together.

My fellow-citizens, trade statistics indicate that this country is in a state of unexampled prosperity. The figures are almost appalling. They show that we are utilizing our fields and forests and mines, and that we are furnishing profitable employment to the millions of workingmen throughout the United States, bringing comfort and happiness to their homes and making it possible to lay by savings for old age and disability.

That all the people are participating in this great prosperity is seen in every American community. . . .

—SPEECH, SEPTEMBER 5, 1901

2. AMERICA REACHES OUT

McKinley hoped for an administration of peace and quiet. His implicit confidence in American business convinced him that prosperity was just around the corner. All he had to do was wait patiently. He got his prosperity. Even before McKinley was inaugurated in March 1897, the economic indicators were on the upswing. But there would be little peace and quiet during his presidency.

Trade. Despite the great oceans to east and west, the United States had never been isolated from world affairs. Trade made the United States an active participant in the affairs of other nations.

Commodore Matthew Perry met the Japanese Imperial Commissioners at Yokohama in 1854 and persuaded Japan to abandon its policy of isolationism and begin trading with the United States.

American ships and sailors were a common sight in the world's ports. As early as 1844, the United States had signed a trade treaty with the Chinese Empire, as far off and foreign a place as Americans could imagine. In 1854, a naval squadron under Commodore Matthew Perry had anchored off Tokyo, Japan. Perry successfully *negotiated* a treaty with the Japanese, in which the Japanese would abandon their isolation and begin to purchase American goods.

By 1890, $960 million in American-made goods were sold abroad. American manufacturers competed with Europeans in selling steel, textiles, and other products in Asia, Latin America, and Europe itself.

A Reluctance to Own Colonies.

Though not isolated, the United States before McKinley had had no ambition to acquire overseas colonies. With the exceptions of Alaska and the tiny Pacific island of Midway (annexed in 1867), the United States possessed no territory that was not *contiguous* to the states.

Two deep convictions worked against the occasional proposals that the United States take such colonies. First, the country had been founded in a war against imperial control. Could the heirs of the first great anti-colonial rebellion take over other peoples? Most Americans answered with a decisive no. Second, the vastness of the American continent provided a more than adequate outlet for American energies. There was plenty of work to be done at home. William McKinley took office holding these beliefs. In all sincerity, he said in his inaugural address that "we must avoid the temptation of territorial aggression."

An International Push for Colonies.

But the times were moving more quickly than was the easygoing McKinley. The United States was no longer a minor country that could sit on the international sidelines. By 1897, it was the single most important industrial power in the world. Aware of this new greatness, many Americans believed that the United States should assume its rightful place among the great nations. In the 1890s, the other great nations were all empires.

The European powers had partitioned Africa so that only two countries there, Ethiopia and Liberia, maintained their independence from *imperial-*

ist rule. In Asia, Indochina was a French colony. The Dutch flag flew over Indonesia. The Japanese had seized Korea and the Chinese island of Taiwan, which they had renamed Formosa. Russia had designs on northern China. Germany and Italy, latecomers to the scramble, searched Africa and Asia for areas to *annex*. India, the biggest prize of all, was British.

The primary motive of imperialist expansion was economic. Colonies were a source of raw materials and a market for the products of the parent country. *Colonialism* also generated an emotional justification of its own. Colonies were a source of pride. The Germans seized parts of Africa that had little economic value just for the sake of having colonies. In England and later in the United States, this energetic chauvinism was known as *jingoism.*

Theories of Racial Supremacy.

Some young American politicians such as Henry Cabot Lodge of Massachusetts and Theodore Roosevelt of New York wanted to join the competition. They said openly that the United States must seize colonies before there were none left to be taken. They worried publicly that, in their wealth and prosperity, Americans were becoming soft and flabby.

Lodge, Roosevelt, and other *expansionists* were profoundly influenced by Josiah Strong's book *Our Country,* published in 1885. Strong argued that the Anglo-Saxons (British and Americans) were obviously more fit to govern than were other peoples. The Anglo-Saxons were "divinely commissioned," according to Strong, to spread their institutions.

Mahan and the American Navy.

In 1890, the expansionists found another spokesman in naval captain Alfred Thayer Mahan. In his book *The Influence of Sea Power Upon History,* Mahan argued that the great nations were always seafaring nations that had powerful navies. He chided Americans for having allowed their fleet to fall into decay. Mahan urged a massive program of ship construction. Congress subsequently agreed to this proposal and responded by authorizing large *appropriations.*

A modern navy of steamships needed coaling stations at scattered points throughout the world. That in itself required taking colonies, even if they

Although military spending as a whole decreased sharply after the Civil War, substantial funds were appropriated for building the navy. Under Cleveland's administration the navy was reorganized and converted to steel and steam. By the late 1800s it consisted of 22 heavily armed warships. The significance of these factors would become apparent.

were only small islands like Midway in the Pacific. It also meant building bases in Hawaii, where in 1887, the United States established a port at Pearl Harbor.

The Frontier Theory.

Another theory of history that fueled the expansionist movement was based on the announcement of the Director of the Census in 1890 that the frontier no longer existed. At the 1893 meeting of the American Historical Association, a young historian named Frederick Jackson Turner propounded a theory that the frontier had been the key to the vitality of American democracy, social stability, and prosperity. With the frontier gone, was the United States doomed to stagnation and social upheaval? To some who found Turner convincing, the only solution was to establish new frontiers abroad. Throughout the 1890s, many American financiers pumped millions of dollars into China and Latin America. They felt that investment opportunities within the United States were shrinking, and wanted to invest in "new" areas.

By 1898, America's attitude toward the world was delicately balanced. Pulling in one direction was the tradition of anti-colonialism. Tugging the other way were jingoism, Anglo-Saxonism, and apprehensions for the future. The decisive event that tipped the balance between these forces was a Cuban war for independence that began in 1895.

SECTION REVIEW

1. Write a sentence to identify: Alaska and Midway Island, jingoism, expansionists, Pearl Harbor.

2. What two American convictions against territorial expansion were reflected in President McKinley's inaugural address?

3. Why was colonialism felt to be contrary to the country's founding principles?

4. Explain how the following fueled the expansionist movement in the United States: Henry Cabot Lodge and Theodore Roosevelt, Alfred Thayer Mahan.

5. Explain how Frederick Turner's philosophy resulted in significant American investments in foreign countries.

---

3. THE SPANISH-AMERICAN WAR

Of the old Spanish possessions in the Americas, only the islands of Cuba and Puerto Rico remained under Spanish rule. Cuban rebels periodically had taken up arms, but weak as Spain was, the Spanish monarchy was able to hold on to the colony.

An uprising in 1895 was more serious. Smuggling in arms and munitions provided by Cuban exiles in the United States, the rebels for the first time won the support of a large number of Cubans, perhaps the majority.

It was a classic *guerrilla war.* By day, Spanish soldiers moved with little trouble among a seemingly peaceful peasant population. By night, however, innocent peasants turned into fierce rebels and sorely punished the Spanish troops. As in most guerrilla wars, fighting was bitter and cruel. Both sides were guilty of atrocities and torture.

The Yellow Press.

Americans tended to be sympathetic to the Cubans. However, widespread interest in the conflict was aroused only when two competing newspaper chains decided that the rebellion could be used as ammunition in their circulation war.

William Randolph Hearst's New York *Journal* and Joseph Pulitzer's New York *World* were known as the *yellow press* because they relied on gimmicks rather than on straightforward news reporting to appeal to readers. The nickname yellow press came from one of those gimmicks: it was named after "The Yellow Kid," which was the first comic strip printed in color to appear in a newspaper.

The Hearst and Pulitzer chains also could squeeze the most sensational details out of the personal lives of famous people. It was easy to move from this kind of promotionalism to publicizing the Spanish atrocities, many of which were genuine. The Spanish military commander in Cuba, Valeriano Weyler, was nicknamed "The Butcher" for his repressive policies. Warring against a whole population, Weyler tried to stifle the uprising by herding whole villages into concentration camps. This method was inevitably brutal, and Cubans died by the thousands from malnutrition, disease, and abuse.

Class Activity: Compare the principles of the frontier theory with those of Manifest Destiny. Is the frontier theory just an extension of the concept of Manifest Destiny?

The sinking of the battleship Maine *in Havana harbor helped lead to war with Spain.*
Although the cause of the explosion was uncertain, popular opinion held Spain responsible.

But real atrocities were not enough for Hearst and Pulitzer. They transformed simple incidents into horror stories and actually invented incidents. The yellow press wanted war. When Hearst artist Frederic Remington wired from Havana that everything was peaceful and he wanted to come home, Hearst ordered him to stay. "You furnish the pictures," he said, "and I'll furnish the war."

War Fever. While public outrage grew, McKinley tried to pursue a peaceful policy. He and his advisers wanted Spain to abandon its harsh policies and placate both Cubans and Americans by liberalizing government on the island.

Ironically, when the Spanish attempted to respond to this pressure, the war came anyway. In 1897, a new government in Madrid withdrew the hated Weyler and proposed autonomy for Cuba within the Spanish Empire. McKinley's administration was apparently satisfied, but two events caused a complete change in policy.

On February 9, Hearst's New York *Journal* published a letter that had been written by the Spanish ambassador in Washington, Enrique Dupuy de Lôme. In it, de Lôme told a friend that McKinley was "weak, a bidder for the admiration of the crowd." It was insulting and McKinley himself was angered. War fever flared higher.

U.S.S. Maine Sunk. Six days later, on February 15, the battleship *Maine* exploded in Havana harbor with a loss of 260 sailors. To this day, the cause of the disaster is unknown. The explosion may have been caused by a fire that spread to the powder magazine. A bomb may have been planted by Cuban rebels in an attempt to provoke the United States into declaring war on their behalf. Or it may have been the work of Spanish diehards who opposed the new liberal policy in Cuba. Influenced by the yellow press, American public opinion accepted the least credible explanation. Though the Spanish government was trying to

Class Activity: Obtain copies of actual articles appearing in the "yellow press" prior to and during the Spanish-American War. Discuss how these might have incited the strong emotional response to Spain's activities.

avoid war at all costs, it was blamed for destroying the *Maine.*

McKinley flooded Spain with demands for a change in policy. On April 9, in a last desperate attempt to avoid war, the Spanish government gave in on every count. In the meantime, fearing that to continue resisting the war fever would cost the Republicans control of Congress in the fall elections, McKinley caved in. On April 11, practically ignoring the Spanish capitulation, the President asked Congress for a declaration of war, and he got it.

The Philippines.

The United States Navy was the first force to take action. Much to everyone's surprise, it struck not at Cuba but halfway around the world in Spain's last Pacific colony, the Philippines. On May 1, acting on the instructions of Undersecretary of the Navy Theodore Roosevelt, Commodore George Dewey steamed a *flotilla* into Manila Bay and completely surprised the Spanish *fleet* and *garrison.* The American ships were better armed than the Spanish, and they consequently destroyed all of the Spanish ships, with little harm done to themselves.

But Dewey had no soldiers with which to launch a land attack on the shore garrison. He

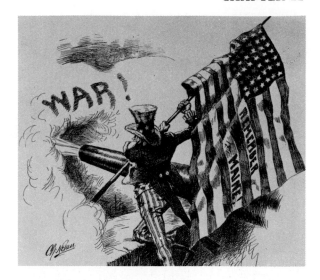

"Remember the Maine" was a popular slogan in American newspapers. The "yellow press" carried sensational stories about conditions in Cuba.

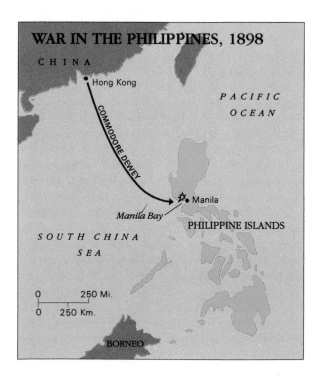

supplied Filipino rebels with arms, but they were not strong enough to take the forts. The Americans had to wait more than three months before a force of American troops arrived. They helped surround the fort, and in August arranged a Spanish surrender to the American forces.

Training Volunteers to Fight.

The cause of Dewey's wait was the slow and inefficient development of the American army. The young men who rallied to arms in every state preferred to join the state militias or new units of volunteers instead of the regular army. Army officers were reluctant to use these units because of their low level of professionalism. They did not have to use the militias extensively, however, because about 270,000 volunteers eventually did join the regular army.

Even in the regular army, training was generally inadequate, and supplies were even worse. Companies were issued heavy woolen winter uniforms to wear in the tropical climate they would be fighting in. They received Springfield rifles that dated back to the Civil War. Much of the meat given the recruits was tainted, and sanitary conditions in the camps were terrible. In fact, when the casualties were counted, 379 Americans were listed as killed in combat, and 5,083 died of disease.

At the Battle of Manila Bay, Commodore Dewey destroyed the entire Spanish Pacific fleet without loss of American lives. Waiting for reinforcements, he blockaded Manila.

The Rough Riders.   One of the volunteer units in the regular army was a group organized by Theodore Roosevelt called the *Rough Riders.* Roosevelt had resigned his office in the Navy Department to accept a colonel's position, and helped mold what was a very unmilitary group. The Rough Riders included cowhands from Roosevelt's North Dakota ranch, show business people, upper-class polo players, and even some ex-convicts. Although the Rough Riders were supposed to be a *cavalry* unit, they had to fight on foot because the army had been unable to transport their horses to Cuba. And even though the popular image of the Rough Riders galloping up San Juan Hill is inaccurate, the unit actually did fight bravely in the war.

Black Soldiers.   About 10,000 black soldiers served in the war and played a large part in both the Cuban and Philippine campaigns. When the war broke out, there were four black regiments in the regular army—two infantry and two cavalry. All four saw action.

Blacks shared in the most celebrated victory of the war—the Battle of San Juan Hill in Cuba. The Rough Riders led the attack and got most of the glory. However, the Tenth Negro Cavalry, immediately to the Rough Riders' left during the charge, saved Roosevelt's company from destruction. As their commander, John J. Pershing, said of them after the battle: "The Tenth Cavalry charged up the hill, scarcely firing a shot, and being nearest the Rough Riders, opened a disas-

Research Assignment: Write a report on the formation of the Tenth Cavalry under General "Blackjack" Pershing. Also do a study of the general himself. Why were his attitudes about the black soldiers who served under him different from attitudes held by other members of the military establishment? When, if ever, did these attitudes change for the military as a whole?

trous *enfilading fire* upon the Spanish right, thus relieving the Rough Riders from the volleys that were being poured into them from that part of the Spanish line."

A Short War. The fighting in the war was completed in only three months. Although the Spanish army in Cuba outnumbered the Americans, Spanish soldiers were paralyzed by defeatist feelings. The Spanish might have been overcome more easily if the Americans had been more organized in their effort.

Despite shortages of food, clothing, transport vehicles, medical supplies, ammunition, and horses, an army of 17,000 Americans was landed in Cuba in June 1898. Meeting some unexpectedly tough resistance from the Spanish, the Americans under General Shafter advanced toward the capital, Santiago. By July 2, Americans had won the Battle of San Juan Hill and taken the fortified village of El Caney. The Spanish troops were forced back to the defenses of Santiago.

On July 3, the Spanish fleet under Admiral Cervera tried to slip out of Santiago harbor. However, an American fleet commanded by Admiral William Sampson and Commodore W. S. Schley caught the Spanish ships and destroyed or captured every one. This was the final straw for the Spanish in Cuba, and on July 15, the Spanish commander surrendered.

The Rough Riders (above) fought in Cuba. Americans also fought in the Philippines (below).

SANTIAGO CAMPAIGN

SPANISH-AMERICAN WAR, 1898

American forces →
American naval blockade ▼▼▼
Spanish fleet →

SECTION REVIEW

1. Write a sentence to identify: "yellow press," Rough Riders, Commodore George Dewey, *U.S.S. Maine.*

2. Who was Valeriano Weyler? Why was he nicknamed "The Butcher"?

3. Describe the role played by Hearst's *Journal* and Pulitzer's *World* before the start of the Spanish-American War.

4. Why did President McKinley finally ask Congress to declare war?

5. Evaluate the importance of the Tenth Negro Cavalry to the Rough Riders at the Battle of San Juan Hill.

6. What event brought an end to Spanish rule in Cuba? When did it occur?

---

4. POSSESSION PROBLEMS

In August 1898, the Spanish gave up and the war ended. American troops occupied not only Manila in the Philippines, but also the island of Puerto Rico, which had been seized without resistance.

Peace Treaty. A treaty officially ending the war was signed in Paris on December 10, 1898 by Spanish and American commissioners. Spain agreed in this treaty to surrender all claim to Cuba. It also agreed to cede to the United States the Pacific island of Guam, the Caribbean island of Puerto Rico, and all of the Philippines. In exchange for these territories, the United States agreed to compensate Spain with $20 million.

But what should be done with these possessions? Suddenly, the imperialism controversy was no longer an academic debate. It involved three far-flung island countries. Each was inhabited by

---

Research Assignment: Have students write reports on the present status of Puerto Rico, the Philippines, Guam, or Cuba and their relations with the U.S.

Spanish-speaking people who clung to traditions very different from those of Americans, and who did not want to become part of the United States.

Cuban Independence. The independence of Cuba had been guaranteed before the war had begun. In order to get money from Congress to fight Spain, the McKinley administration had accepted a rider drafted by an anti-imperialist senator from Colorado, Henry Teller. The *Teller Amendment* forbade the United States to take over Cuba.

After the war, however, American forces continued to occupy and govern Cuba for three years. Doctors in the army of occupation attacked an enemy far deadlier than the Spanish when they attempted to find a cure for the fatal tropical disease, yellow fever. Major William Gorgas and Dr. Walter Reed performed a remarkable medical feat by successfully tracing the disease to a mosquito's bite. Cuba was a much healthier place when the American army left in 1902.

Political independence was also granted to the Cubans, but there were certain conditions attached to independence that kept Cuba subject to American influence and control for many years. The congressional act that imposed these conditions was known as the *Platt Amendment.* Attached to an army *appropriations bill* in 1901, this unusual law placed four major restrictions on the Cuban government. First, Cuba could make no treaty with a European power that might interfere with its independence. Second, whatever debts were incurred by the Cuban government had to be small and capable of being repaid. Third, Cuba had to permit American forces to intervene in the island's affairs whenever there was serious political trouble. Fourth, Cuba had to lease certain lands to the United States for use as coaling or naval stations.

As a condition for withdrawing American troops from Cuba in 1902, the Cubans were required to write the Platt Amendment into their constitution. Thus, Cuba became a self-governing country that was continually watched and guarded by the United States. In effect, it was a *protectorate* rather than a completely *sovereign nation.*

The Anti-Imperialists. What to do about Cuba, however, was a minor issue compared to

questions about other island territories taken from Spain. Most perplexing was the status of the faraway Philippines. Should they be annexed to the United States or given their independence? Those who strenuously opposed the idea of annexation were known as *anti-imperialists.*

The anti-imperialists were a mixed group, and their arguments were sometimes contradictory. In Congress, they included idealistic old Radical Republicans like George Frisbie Hoar of Massachu-

AMERICA BUILDS AN EMPIRE 1854-1903		
DATE	**REGION**	**ACTION**
1854	Asia	Perry opens Japan to trade
1867	North America	Alaska purchased
	Pacific Ocean	Midway annexed
1875	Pacific Ocean	Reciprocity Treaty brings Hawaii into sphere of influence
1878	Pacific Ocean	Naval base established in Samoa
1887	Pacific Ocean	Permanent naval base at Pearl Harbor in Hawaii
1898	Pacific Ocean	Hawaii annexed
		Treaty of Paris ends Spanish-American War; Spain cedes Guam; Wake and Baker Islands annexed
	Asia	Philippines occupied
	Caribbean Sea	Spain cedes Puerto Rico
1899	Asia	Open Door policy
1901	Asia	Philippines becomes a territory
1902	Caribbean Sea	Cuba becomes a protectorate
1903	Central America	Recognition of Republic of Panama; control over Panama Canal Zone

setts and former Liberal Republicans like Carl Schurz. A substantial part of the Democratic party, led by William Jennings Bryan, opposed annexation of any former Spanish lands.

The anti-imperialists reminded Americans of their anti-colonial heritage. "We insist," declared the American Anti-Imperialist League in October 1899, "that the *subjugation* of any people is 'criminal aggression' and open disloyalty to the distinctive principles of our government. We hold, with Abraham Lincoln, that no man is good enough to govern another man without that man's consent."

The Issue of Race. Some of the anti-imperialists appealed to racist feelings. With many people unhappy about the size of the nation's black population, they asked, was it wise to bring millions more nonwhite people under the flag? But racist feelings worked mostly in favor of the *pro-expansion* group. Brilliant *propagandists* like Theodore Roosevelt, Henry Cabot Lodge, and Senator Albert J. Beveridge from Indiana, preached that the white race had a duty and right to govern "inferior" peoples. One of the reasons that was given for annexing the Philippines was that the United States had a duty to Christianize the natives of the islands. What the propagandists failed to say was that the majority of Filipinos had become Catholic Christians long before the first church bell had rung in the United States.

Annexation. Well-grounded fears that if the United States abandoned the Philippines, Japan or Germany would seize them motivated other politicians to support annexation. Such anxiety was especially significant in deciding McKinley's mind on the question. But most of all, the American people seemed to be in an emotional, expansive mood. Coming at the end of the troubled, depressed, and divided 1890s, annexation of colonies seemed a way to unite the country. This idea swayed McKinley, who, like it or not, was forced to take a stand. In December 1898, he announced that the United States intended to govern the Philippines.

Hawaii. Before the annexation of the Philippines and Puerto Rico, the United States already had taken its first real overseas colony. In July 1898, Congress had annexed the seven main islands and 1,400 minor ones that made up the mid-Pacific nation of Hawaii. Shortly thereafter, Guam and Wake were added as coaling stations for the navy.

The annexation of Hawaii was long in the making. The descendants of American missionary families in the islands had grown rich by exporting sugar to the United States, and they had won the confidence and support of the Hawaiian king, Kalakaua. Then in 1890, the McKinley Tariff introduced a two-cent-per-pound bounty on American-grown sugar. This encouraged enough mainland farmers to produce cane or sugar beets so that Hawaiian imports declined sharply. Unable to affect American tariff policy from outside, American planters in Hawaii concluded that they must join the islands to the United States and benefit from the bounty.

The plan was squelched before it got started. In 1891 Kalakaua died and was succeeded by his anti-American sister, Queen Liliuokalani (lē-lē'ōō-ō-kä-lä'nē). She announced that the

Lydia Liliuokalani was queen of Hawaii before the islands were annexed by the United States.

The racist condescension of people like Lodge and Roosevelt is clearly expressed in Rudyard Kipling's poem "The White Man's Burden." Kipling subtitled it "The United States and the Philippines" and addressed the last stanza to the U.S.

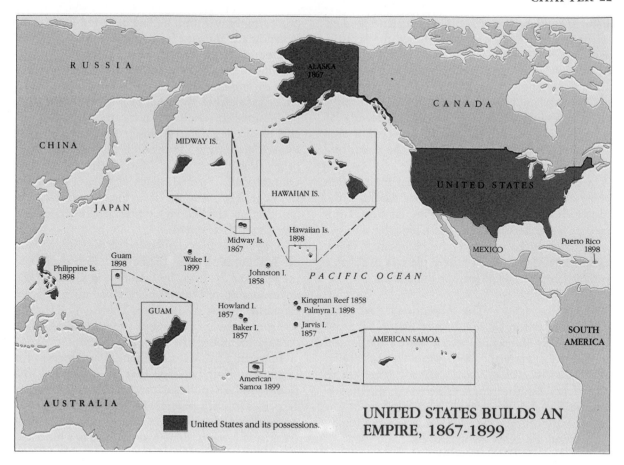

Midway Is. 1867

Guam 1898

Wake I. 1899

Philippine Is. 1898

Howland I. 1857

Baker I. 1857

Kingman Reef 1858
Palmyra I. 1898

Jarvis I. 1857

Johnston I. 1858

Hawaiian Is. 1898

Puerto Rico 1898

American Samoa 1899

United States and its possessions.

UNITED STATES BUILDS AN EMPIRE, 1867-1899

theme of her reign would be "Hawaii for the Hawaiians." Then the Queen introduced a number of reforms that were aimed at dismantling foreign control of both the Hawaiian economy and the *legislature.*

Alarmed, the Americans in Hawaii acted quickly with help from the American ambassador in Honolulu. This diplomat declared that American lives and property were in danger and thus landed marines from the U.S.S. *Boston,* who quickly took control of the peaceful islands. Back home, some members of the Senate introduced a treaty of annexation. Before they could push it through, Grover Cleveland was sworn in as president and he withdrew the proposal.

Cleveland was not opposed to annexation on principle. But he wanted to know how the Hawaiian people felt, and he sent an investigator, James H. Blount, to the islands. Blount reported that very few nonwhite Hawaiians wanted to be part of the United States. Instead, they wanted independence and the restoration of Queen Liliuokalani. Cleveland ordered the marines to return to their ships and to the naval base at Pearl Harbor.

However, the Hawaiians who wanted annexation had gone too far to take a chance in restoring Queen Liliuokalani. They maintained control and declared Hawaii a republic. As long as Grover Cleveland sat in the White House, the Hawaiians bided their time and quietly cultivated Republican senators. Annexation was finally achieved under President William McKinley. Republicans pushed through the treaty on July 7, 1898.

Alaska Gold Rush. At about this time, Americans awoke to the importance of an immense territory to the north that, during 30 years of American possession, had seemed like nothing but a frozen wilderness. This territory, Alaska, had been purchased from Russia in 1867 by President Andrew Johnson's Secretary of State, William Seward. Although the purchase price had been little more than $7 million, the land seemed worthless to critics, who condemned the acquisition as "Seward's Folly."

In 1896, however, gold was discovered in the Klondike region of northern Canada. The best route to the gold lay across the Alaska *panhandle*. In the last years of the 1890s, thousands of fortune hunters trekked across Alaska in a mad rush for Klondike gold similar to the California gold rush of 1849.

Suddenly Americans realized that their nation ruled a vast empire consisting of icy Alaska to the far north and balmy Hawaii to the far west. Even farther west, near the coast of China, lay another recently acquired territory, the Philippines. Here, as anti-imperialists had warned, the task of ruling a remote empire posed serious difficulties.

The Philippines.

The Filipinos adamantly resisted annexation by the United States. Like the Cubans, the Philippine people were experienced in guerrilla warfare. They were led by Emilio Aguinaldo, a well-educated patriot who was as comfortable in the jungle as he was in the library. Aguinaldo and the rebels withdrew from the American-occupied cities to the jungle and fought only when the odds favored them.

In response, the American army was expanded to 70,000 men by early 1900. It made little progress, however, outside the cities. The American commanders were unable to draw the *insurrectos* into a conventional battle in which superior firepower would win.

The war took a vicious turn. The Filipinos frequently cut off the heads of their victims. The Americans felt frustrated because of their failures, the intense tropical heat, insects, and diseases. They retaliated by slaughtering whole villages that were thought to be supporting the rebels.

The American army never did defeat the Filipinos. The rebellion ended only when, in March 1901, General Arthur MacArthur succeeded in capturing Aguinaldo. Weary of the bloodshed, Aguinaldo took an *oath of allegiance* to the United States and ordered his followers to do the same. More than 4,300 Americans had died in the war.

Presidential Politics.

In the same month that Aguinaldo was captured, William McKinley took the presidential oath for the second time. The preceding November, he had defeated Democratic candidate William Jennings Bryan by an even greater electoral margin than in 1896. Bryan's attempt to make the election of 1900 a referendum on imperialism proved to be a fiasco. Most Americans either were happy with their overseas possessions or simply did not care. McKinley was able to sidestep the issue and point to the prosperity of the country. Indeed, the Republican campaign slogan was "Four More Years of the Full Dinner Pail." Several states that had voted for Bryan in 1896 slipped into the Republican column. Bryan, the "Great Commoner," even lost his own state of Nebraska.

A new vice president stood at McKinley's side on Inauguration Day. Theodore Roosevelt had moved quickly from his exploits in Cuba to the governorship of New York. He had alienated the Republican boss of the state, Thomas C. Platt, by refusing to take orders and even attacking some corrupt members of Platt's machine.

In getting the vice presidential nomination for Roosevelt, Platt believed that he was ending the Rough Rider's political career. Roosevelt sourly agreed. The vice presidency was thought of as a political burial ground, a nearly powerless post that usually was assigned to politicians who could help carry swing states.

The Open Door Policy.

Toward Asia, McKinley followed a policy that had been designed by his Secretary of State, John Hay. It was called the *Open Door policy*. China, one of the largest countries in the world, had been left behind by modernization. Although there was a nominal emperor, powerful local chieftains ruled whole provinces as personal estates. Japan and most of the imperialistic countries of Europe had gained spheres of influence in which their own troops maintained order and their own law governed their resident citizens' behavior.

Great Britain opposed further colonization in China. The British were well aware of the high expense of direct imperial rule. They also believed that their efficient industries gave them a competitive advantage in selling to the Chinese.

British interests accorded with American policy, particularly because the United States had no clear sphere of influence in China. In 1899 and 1900, John Hay circulated a series of memoranda

Class Activity: The views that U.S. vice presidents and other observers of U.S. government have held about the importance, or lack thereof, of the vice president's job are very much in keeping with what is stated in the text above. In light of the frequency of presidential deaths and the powers described in the Constitution, discuss this attitude.

Roosevelt's New Diplomacy declared that the United States was to police the Western Hemisphere and Europeans were to stay away. A 1905 cartoon pictured him as "The World's Constable."

that pledged the imperial powers not to seize any Chinese territory. Germany and Japan were reluctant to go along. However, faced with British and American support for maintaining the independence of China and for keeping a door open to the trade of all, they agreed.

The Boxers.

In May 1900, international domination of China was put to the test by a rebellion encouraged by the empress dowager of the country. The rebels were called *Boxers* because the Chinese name for their secret religious, antiforeign society meant "righteous harmonious fist." The Boxers terrorized and murdered westerners and besieged 900 foreigners in the British legation in Peking.

An international army made up of American, British, French, German, Austrian, Russian, Japanese, and Italian troops marched on Peking in August. It defeated the poorly armed rebels and wreaked havoc on the surrounding countryside. The victory ensured the continuation of the Open

Door policy. China remained subject to the imperial powers.

President McKinley Assassinated.

But the international order was shaken in 1901. On September 6, McKinley paid a ceremonial visit to the Pan American Exposition in Buffalo. Greeting a long line of guests, he found himself faced by a man who extended a bandaged hand. The gauze concealed a pistol. Leon Czolgosz (chôl'gôsh), an anarchist who "didn't believe one man should have so much service and another man should have none," shot the President several times. Eight days later, McKinley died.

Roosevelt Becomes President.

The new president, Theodore Roosevelt, known affectionately as "Teddy," left an indelible mark on the presidency. He was completely unlike his predecessors as far back as Lincoln. The exuberant young New Yorker (42 years old when he took office) knew only one way to do anything: take the lead.

One person was present at the assassinations of Lincoln, Garfield, and McKinley. He was Lincoln's son, Robert Todd Lincoln. After the last incident, he refused to attend any meetings with a president and stayed away from state functions.

THEODORE ROOSEVELT

PROFILES OF THE PRESIDENCY

1901–1909

*A*bout to be nominated for president in 1904, a contented Theodore Roosevelt wrote to his young son:

Tomorrow the National Convention meets, and barring a cataclysm I shall be nominated. . . . Of course I hope to be elected, but I realize to the full how very lucky I have been, not only to be President but to have been able to accomplish so much while President, and whatever may be the outcome, I am not only content but very sincerely thankful for all the good fortune I have had. From Panama down I have been able to accomplish certain things which will be of lasting importance in our history. Incidentally, I don't think that any family has ever enjoyed the White House more than we have. I was thinking about it . . . when Mother and I took breakfast on the portico and afterwards walked about the lovely grounds and looked at the stately historic old house. It is a wonderful privilege to have been here and to have been given the chance to do this work. . . .

—LETTER TO KERMIT ROOSEVELT, JUNE 21, 1904

Nowhere was his assertive personality more pronounced than in his foreign policy, an extension of the zest that had taken him up San Juan Hill.

Roosevelt's actions varied according to the part of the world with which he was dealing. With the European nations he insisted that the United States be accepted as an equal, active imperial power. In Asia, he maintained the Open Door policy. Toward Latin America, however, he was arrogant. He told both Latin Americans and Europeans that the whole Western Hemisphere was an American *sphere of influence* in which the other nations had to bow to American wishes.

The Russo-Japanese War. In 1905, Roosevelt applied his policy of equilibrium in China by working through diplomatic channels to end a war between Russia and Japan in the Chinese province of Manchuria. Much to the surprise of most Europeans, Japan was handily defeating Russia and threatened to seize complete control of Manchuria and other parts of northern China. Through threats and cajolery, Roosevelt got both sides to meet at Portsmouth, New Hampshire, to work out a treaty that maintained a balance of power in Asia and upheld Chinese independence.

Latin America. In Latin America, Roosevelt was not so compromising. He made it clear to the European nations that the United States held a preeminent position in the Western Hemisphere. In 1904, several European nations threatened to invade the Dominican Republic to collect debts owed to their citizens. Roosevelt responded by proclaiming what came to be called the *Roosevelt Corollary* to the Monroe Doctrine. In order to protect the independence of American states, he said the United States would, if necessary, exercise an "international police power" in the Western Hemisphere. In other words, while European nations still had to keep out of Latin American affairs, the United States could intervene there when it felt the need to.

Roosevelt immediately put his corollary to work. In 1904, United States Marines landed in the Dominican Republic and took over the collection of customs, seeing to it that European creditors were paid off. From then until the 1930s, the United States intervened in a number of Latin American countries: Cuba, Nicaragua, the Dominican Republic, and Haiti. These actions may have pleased European investors, but they created a reservoir of ill will among Latin Americans who felt bullied by the great "Anglo" power to the north. Probably no action offended Latin Americans more than Roosevelt's seizure of the Panama Canal Zone, which was the President's proudest foreign accomplishment.

Class Activity: Do a document analysis of the Roosevelt Corollary and discuss how it is an extension of the Monroe Doctrine. Are there things in either the letter or the spirit of the two documents that are contradictory? How would you think a Latin American might view the two documents?

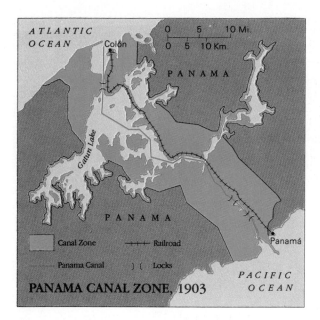

PANAMA CANAL ZONE, 1903

Map legend: Canal Zone · Railroad · Panama Canal · Locks

The next day, the province erupted in riots and declared its independence from Colombia. On November 6, the United States recognized the new republic of Panama. On November 18, the first foreign minister of Panama, Philippe Jean Bunau-Varilla, signed a treaty with the United States, granting the United States perpetual use of a ten-mile-wide *canal zone* across the isthmus on the terms that Colombia had refused.

In 1911, the canal nearly completed, Roosevelt reflected that only his decisiveness had moved the project along. "If I had followed traditional, conservative methods," he said, "the debates on it would have been going on yet; but I took the Canal Zone and let Congress debate; and while the debate goes on, the Canal does also."

Dollar Diplomacy. None of Roosevelt's presidential successors were quite so self-assured in dealing with Latin America. Roosevelt's hand-picked successor, William Howard Taft, tried to replace *gunboat diplomacy* with *dollar diplomacy*. This meant trying to influence Latin America and China through investment, not armed force.

In 1921, the United States attempted to make amends to Colombia for Roosevelt's high-handed actions. Colombia received from the U.S. government the $25 million that it originally had demanded for the right to dig the Panama Canal. But such gestures could not change America's "big brother" behavior or the resentment of Latin Americans. *Intervention* was established as an essential part of the United States' diplomacy.

The Panama Canal. Naval officers had long recognized the value of a quick route between the Atlantic and the Pacific. During the Spanish-American War, this was brought home with new urgency when U.S. warships took more than two months to steam from San Francisco to Cuba.

In 1881, a French company had started to dig across the *Isthmus* of Panama, then a part of Colombia. But the project was abandoned because of financial difficulties and the ravages of tropical diseases among the laborers. The French company's rights to continue construction were to expire in 1904. In 1902, an agent of the company, Philippe Jean Bunau-Varilla (bü-nō' vä-rē'-ya), began prodding U.S. leaders to buy its titles.

Most political leaders, including anti-imperialists, realized that the United States needed the canal to protect and supply its scattered empire. But some wanted to allow the existing rights to expire in order to reopen negotiations with Colombia. Others argued for a route across Nicaragua rather than Panama.

The Colombian government turned down an American offer to buy construction rights for $10 million and to pay an annual rental of $250,000. (The Colombians wanted $25 million.) This delay so infuriated Roosevelt that he supported Bunau-Varilla and his plan for revolution in Panama. On November 2, 1903, several United States warships were stationed near the Panamanian coast.

SECTION REVIEW

1. Write a sentence to identify: Queen Liliuokalani, Open Door policy, Roosevelt Corollary, dollar diplomacy.
2. List each of these places under one of these headings: *Gained in Peace Treaty with Spain* or *Gained at Another Time*— Hawaii, the Philippines, Puerto Rico, Alaska, Guam.
3. What was the motivation of the Republicans in nominating Roosevelt as their vice-presidential candidate in 1900?
4. Briefly note the actions taken by Roosevelt in Asia and Latin America.

Panama is the only place where you can see the sun rise on the Pacific Ocean and set on the Atlantic.

CHAPTER REVIEW

TIME LINE

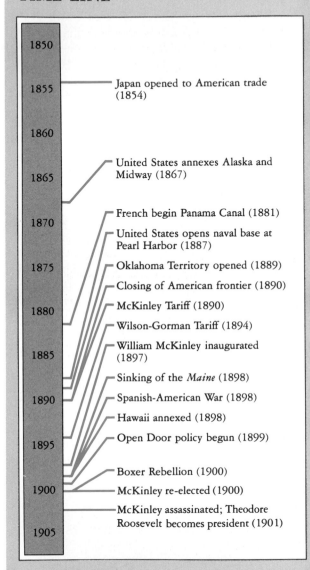

1850

1855 — Japan opened to American trade (1854)

1860

1865 — United States annexes Alaska and Midway (1867)

1870 — French begin Panama Canal (1881)

— United States opens naval base at Pearl Harbor (1887)

1875 — Oklahoma Territory opened (1889)

— Closing of American frontier (1890)

1880 — McKinley Tariff (1890)

— Wilson-Gorman Tariff (1894)

1885 — William McKinley inaugurated (1897)

— Sinking of the *Maine* (1898)

1890 — Spanish-American War (1898)

— Hawaii annexed (1898)

— Open Door policy begun (1899)

1895

— Boxer Rebellion (1900)

1900 — McKinley re-elected (1900)

— McKinley assassinated; Theodore Roosevelt becomes president (1901)

1905

TIME LINE QUESTIONS

1. In what year did the United States acquire two overseas territories?
2. Which event occurred first: the loss of an American battleship, the opening of a United States naval base in Hawaii, or the Boxer ·Rebellion in China?
3. In what year was an American president assassinated?

SKILLS STRATEGY

NOTE-TAKING

Sometimes the information needed to write a paragraph or report is not all in the same place. A reference book and other source books may be needed. In such cases, taking notes on separate cards like the ones shown above will help you.

Notice that one card has a writing topic. Some of the other cards have notes that support this topic.

These cards are shown in no particular order. Before the note cards can be used to write a paragraph or report, they must be sorted to eliminate irrelevant information and then placed in order.

APPLYING SKILLS

Use the cards shown above to answer the following items.

1. What would be the main idea of a paragraph based on the note cards?
2. Which card would have to be eliminated?
3. What would the information on the rest of the cards be used for?
4. ·What other note card(s) would be needed?
5. Use cards to take notes on information that supports the writing topic.

Making Connections: Review the questions and topics referred to in the Making Connections section that opens this chapter. Discuss the significance of this move toward being a world

power in terms of how other nations viewed it and also in terms of the effects it might have had

UNIT 6 TEST

CHAPTER SURVEY

In one or two sentences, summarize the content of the chapters from which these terms come, and write a sentence to identify *one* of the terms from each chapter.

1. *Chapter 20:* Indian Territory, "Buffalo Bill" Cody, Little Big Horn, General George Crook, Chisholm Trail, Homestead Act, Demonetization Act of 1873.
2. *Chapter 21:* "bone and sinew of the Republic," "hayseed," Mary Elizabeth Lease, Populist party, "Pittsburgh of the South," Spindletop, James Buchanan Duke.
3. *Chapter 22:* "Cross of Gold," Frederick Jackson Turner, *New York Journal,* Tenth Negro Cavalry, Queen Liliuokalani.

TEXT REVIEW

4. Give facts that verify this statement: "To show the American frontier between 1865 and 1900, you would have to draw many maps."
5. For what reason did the Plains Indians, more than any other group of Native Americans, resist white settlement of their lands? Describe and comment on the battle that shattered the last resistance.
6. What kind of people invested in the cattle industry in the 1870s? How did they differ from the people who actually took care of the cattle?
7. In what ways was the western cattle industry reorganized after 1886? What made the reorganization necessary?
8. Name two pieces of national legislation that encouraged American pioneers to leave their homes in the East and settle lands in the West. What problems awaited the pioneers when they reached these western lands?
9. Write a brief explanation of the demonetization of silver in 1873, and explain the provisions of an 1878 law that was enacted because of this demonetization.
10. How would you characterize the advance of agriculture in the last three decades of the 1800s? Cite information from the text.
11. Give some of the effects of the agricultural depression that occurred during the late 1800s. Did the economic law of supply and demand have anything to do with the depression? Explain your answer.
12. By what group was the Populist party founded, and what were the reasons for the party's founding? Describe five reforms proposed in the Populist platform.
13. What influence did southern newspaper editor Henry W. Grady have on the rise of the New South? Give some examples of activities that typified the New South that Grady dreamed of.
14. How was American expansion during the latter years of the nineteenth century different from earlier expansion? Explain how each of the following fueled this movement during McKinley's presidency: the international push for colonies, theories of racial supremacy, naval captain Alfred Thayer Mahan, Frederick Jackson Turner's frontier theory.
15. Define the "yellow press," and explain how it drew the United States into war with Spain.
16. Give the essential details about *two* of the following: the annexation of Hawaii by the United States; guerrilla warfare in the Philippines; the Open Door policy and the Boxer Rebellion; the death of President William McKinley.

CRITICAL THINKING

17. In a sentence or two, write the point of view of *two* of the following on American imperialist expansion: President McKinley, Senator Henry Cabot Lodge, Alfred Thayer Mahan, Queen Liliuokalani, Emilio Aguinaldo.
18. Summarize the actions that brought the huge bison herds to the edge of extinction.

SKILLS REVIEW

19. Explain the difference between a primary source and a secondary source, and give an example of each.
20. What standards can be used to evaluate the factuality of a news story? Why must readers be able to make such an evaluation?

on U.S. attitudes about itself. Might Roosevelt's personality have reflected the attitudes of society?

The Progressive Era

American artist Thomas Hart Benton (1889–1955),
"Threshing Wheat," (1939).

Unit 7 Overview:

Unit 7 begins on a mostly bright note with a discussion of turn-of-the-century society and the badly needed governmental reforms brought about by the Progressives. The unit continues with a careful examination of the accomplishments and setbacks of Presidents Roosevelt, Taft, and Wilson as they apply, sometimes unwillingly, Progressive ideas. The last chapter of the unit follows Woodrow Wilson's presidency—from his failure to keep the United States out of World War I to his lack of success in bringing about a just peace and making the United States a member of the League of Nations.

Basic Unit Concepts

1. The turn of the century in the United States, symbolized in many ways by President Theodore Roosevelt, was an era of opportunity for a growing middle class.
2. For the most part, blacks, Indians, and many workers did not benefit from the educational, social, and economic opportunities enjoyed by other Americans of this period.
3. The Progressives, a diverse middle-class reform group aided by muckraking writers, introduced governmental reforms that have endured until the present.
4. The political power of the Progressives greatly influenced the policies of three presidents—Theodore Roosevelt, William Howard Taft, and Woodrow Wilson.
5. Between 1912 and 1920, the United States became involved in a war with Mexico and a war in Europe, but American politics and revived isolationist sentiments kept the United States out of the League of Nations after World War I.

Chapter 23: "The Good Old Days" (1890–1910)

In Chapter 23, students realize why the "good old days"—the last decade of the nineteenth century—must have seemed "the bad old days" to some Americans. They

encounter the ebullient TR, President Theodore Roosevelt, who typified the age. They learn of the increase in educational opportunities and leisure-time activities. They recognize the part muckraking magazine writers played in the Progressive movement. Finally, they follow the rise of the middle-class Progressives and witness the lasting reforms they brought to American governments at all levels—local, state, and national.

Learning Objectives

History Generalizations   Students will gain knowledge that supports the following generalizations:

1. The last decade of the nineteenth century and the first decade of the twentieth were the best of times for some Americans and the worst of times for many others, including Indians, blacks, and workers.
2. During this period, educational opportunities and leisure-time activities greatly increased for the newly emerging middle class.
3. In the late nineteenth century, middle class readers created a demand for writers who departed from the themes and styles of the past and for mass-circulation magazines, many of which featured muckraking exposés.
4. Spurred on in part by the muckrakers, middle class Americans determined to introduce reforms in government and other areas of American society.
5. Middle-class demands gave rise to the Progressive Era, during which Progressives introduced far-reaching governmental reforms whose effects are present in local, state, and national governments today.
6. The American Socialist party grew steadily during the first decade of the twentieth century but lost influence because their goals were so similar to those of the Progressives.

Study Skills   In addition to the three skills noted in Chapter 1 which are standard to every chapter, students will:

1. use the Dewey Decimal System.
2. write a paragraph for a social science book.
3. relate graphic materials to the text of the chapter.
4. practice these **critical thinking skills:** generating questions about materials to be read, comparing political goals, recognizing different viewpoints.

Chapter 24: "The Progressives in Power" (1901–1916)

In Chapter 24, students encounter Theodore Roosevelt again, this time as a popular reformer president. They follow his inimitable dealings with big business, the growing labor movement, the safety of drugs and food, and conservation of the nation's natural resources. Students also meet President William Howard Taft, TR's hand-picked successor whose actions as president did not meet TR's or the Progressives' expectations. They learn how Roosevelt's formation of a third party helped Democrat Woodrow Wilson win the presidential election in 1912. Finally, they trace the gradual change in President Wilson's idealistic New Freedom program to a program consonant with Progressive and Republican demands.

Features

Movers and Shapers: John Muir and John Wesley Powell (page 574)
Profiles of the Presidency: William Howard Taft (page 577), Woodrow Wilson (page 582)
American Ingenuity   chart (pages 584–585)

Learning Objectives

History Generalizations Students will gain knowledge that supports the following generalizations:

1. After assuming the presidency on the death of William McKinley, Theodore Roosevelt proved himself an astute politician and an implacable enemy of radical workers and politicians, but his reputation as a trust buster and a friend of the workers was not consistently deserved.
2. Acting on his belief that socialism would lose its popularity if the worst business practices of the late nineteenth century could be eliminated, President Roosevelt successfully advocated a variety of progressive reform legislation to Congress during his second term.
3. Though, technically, President Roosevelt could have run for reelection in 1908, he deferred to the unwritten rule concerning presidential third terms; however, he hand-picked William Howard Taft as his successor.
4. President Taft's personal style and his nineteenth century view of the presidency along with a lack of political savvy earned him an undeserved reputation as a reactionary and led to the formation of the Progressive party with Theodore Roosevelt as its unsuccessful presidential nominee.
5. Because of the split in Republican voting and a good showing by the Socialist candidate, the Democrat Woodrow Wilson became President in a sweep of the electoral vote.
6. By the end of President Wilson's first term, his concern for reelection in the upcoming presidential contest coupled with an increasing need to attend to foreign affairs had turned him from the policies of his New Freedom program to support of policies close to those of the Republicans and Progressives.

Study Skills In addition to the three skills noted in Chapter 1 which are standard to every chapter, students will:

1. use the card catalog to locate books in a library.
2. write a one-paragraph reaction to an historical event.
3. relate graphic materials to the text of the chapter.
4. practice these **critical thinking skills:** generating questions about materials to be read, hypothesizing, recognizing bias.

Chapter 25: "America Goes to War" (1914–1920)

In this chapter, students learn how President Wilson was forced to abandon his foreign policy ideals, first, in his dealings with Mexico, and then again, by reluctantly involving the United States in World War I. They recognize the contributions that Americans made on the European battlefields and at home. They follow the American government's attempts to control the economy, political dissent, and the press during the war. They witness the happy ending to American women's long struggle to have their right to vote recognized in a Constitutional amendment. Finally, they follow the ailing President Wilson's unsuccessful attempts to apply his Fourteen Points at the peace conference following the war and to bring the United States into the League of Nations.

Features

Going to the Source: Excerpt from Woodrow Wilson's 1917 war message to Congress (page 599)

Learning Objectives

History Generalizations Students will gain knowledge that supports the following generalizations:

1. Woodrow Wilson set moral diplomacy as a goal in dealing with other nations, but as incidents in Mexico and the Caribbean developed during his first term, he sometimes turned to the "gunboat" and "dollar" diplomacy of his predecessors.
2. Although President Wilson tried to steer a neutral course, German hostile activities and the pro-British sympathies of the American people brought the United States into the savage and futile battles of World War I.
3. Once war was declared, the national government took a large hand in organizing the American economy to equip and supply the fighting forces through the work of thousands of government agencies.
4. In exchange for pledging not to strike during the war, the conservative AFL received many government concessions, and its leaders were regarded as partners in running the country.
5. Women's valuable contributions to the war effort eventually resulted in the recognition of their right to vote in the Nineteenth Amendment.
6. Segregated black units led by black officers served with distinction during the war, and black workers from the South worked at relatively high-paying factory jobs in northern cities.
7. Government-directed propaganda and other activities led to the suppression of the civil rights of some people, including Americans of German ancestry, radical union members, and Socialists.
8. Because of a combination of circumstances, including President Wilson's failing health, he was unable to apply his Fourteen Points at the peace conference ending World War I or bring the United States into the League of Nations.

Study Skills In addition to the three skills noted in Chapter 1 which are standard to every chapter, students will:

1. interpret a thematic map.
2. relate graphic materials to the text of the chapter.
3. practice these **critical thinking skills:** generating questions about materials to be read, determining possible effects, tracing a sequence of events, hypothesizing.

THE GOOD OLD DAYS

1890–1910

*Any fool can destroy trees. They cannot run away; and if
they could, they would still be destroyed—chased and
hunted down as long as fun or a dollar could be got
out of their bark hides. . . .* JOHN MUIR

Making Connections. The "Gay Nineties" was a name often given to the lively last decade of the nineteenth century. A growing middle class found leisure time for sports, exercise, reading, and other popular entertainments. The middle class also led the drive toward progressive reforms in government.

In this chapter, you will learn:

- Why President Theodore Roosevelt was an appropriate symbol of this active, enthusiastic age
- How educational opportunities expanded for many people, including minorities and women
- Why spectator sports such as baseball and boxing enjoyed wide popularity
- Who the muckrakers were and what part they played in the Progressive movement
- How Progressive political leaders changed local, state, and national governments
- Why the middle class provided most of the leaders of the Progressive movement

You have learned that government at all levels in the late nineteenth century was often controlled by corrupt political machines. Consequently, reformers often challenged corrupt government practices. As you read, note how the Progressives were successful, whereas many other reformers were not.

Sections

1. Turn-of-the-Century Society
2. A Time to Play
3. The Progressives
4. Progressives in Action

1. TURN–OF–THE–CENTURY SOCIETY

The decade before and the decade after the turn of the century were very important years, when an old way of life passed away and a new one began. The new way was not a good way for everyone. How people remembered it—whether as good times or bad—depended in large part on their race, where they lived, and what they did for a living. The 1890s and the 1900s were, indeed, the best of times and the worst of times.

Indians, Blacks, and Workers. The 1890s and 1910s were not good years for Indians. After the Wounded Knee Massacre of 1890, they were alternately neglected and exploited. Stripped of independent tribal power, confined to bleak reservation lands without the benefits of citizenship, most Indians faced the new century in increasing poverty and decaying cultural vitality.

The turn of the century was not a good time for most blacks. In the South, the rise of political movements based on white supremacy eliminated the last black officeholders. Lynching of black prisoners was so accepted in some communities that in 1899 a mob in Palmetto, Georgia, actually announced in advance that an accused man would be lynched.

Nor were the 1890s very good years for workers. Clashes between strikers and bosses occurred

This lighthearted, bustling 1901 watercolor by Maurice Prendergast shows the spirit of the good life that many Americans enjoyed at the turn of the century. Its title is "Madison Square."

Quotation: from the book Our National Parks. Other works by John Muir (1838–1914) include The Mountains of California, Stickeen, My First Summer in the Sierra, The Yosemite, and Travels in Alaska.

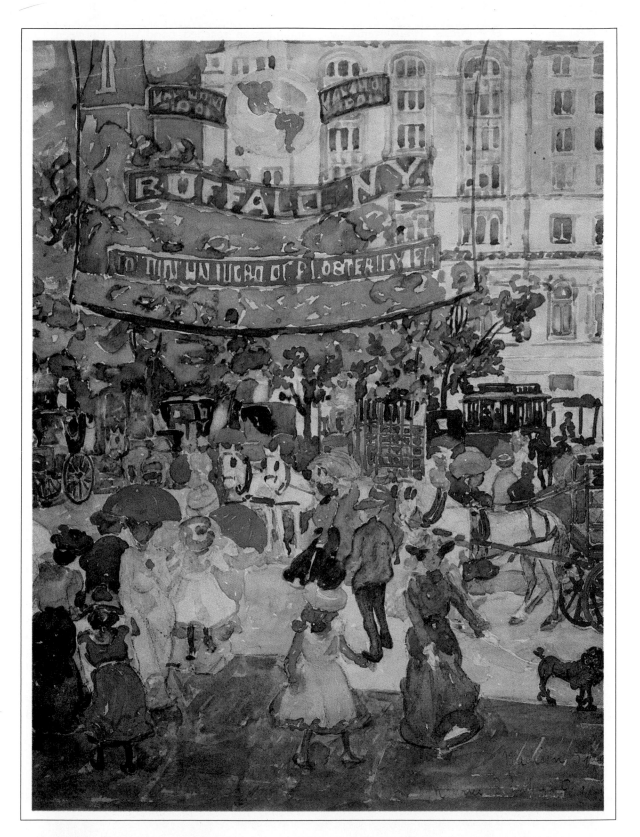

Skills Review: Reinforce the skills learned in the preceding Skills Strategy section. Have students do one of the Research Assignments from this chapter, using cards to take their notes, in the manner described in the preceding chapter.

at steel plants in Homestead, Pennsylvania; at railroad car factories in Pullman, Illinois; and in the mining area of Coeur D'Alene, Idaho. Unemployment reached such high levels in the depression years after 1893 that, in 1894, thousands of workers, known as Coxey's Army, followed an Ohio businessperson, Jacob Coxey, on a march to Washington to demand that the government provide jobs for them.

Immigration at Flood Tide.

Working conditions and wages improved after 1900. But still, in March 1911, Americans opened their newspapers to read that 146 people, mostly women and girls, had died in a fire at the Triangle Shirtwaist Company factory in New York City. The fire had begun slowly. There had been no cause for alarm and plenty of time to escape. But the doors of the workroom had been locked to keep the workers on the job the entire day, until the final bell.

Most of the Triangle fire dead were immigrants or the children of immigrants. Despite the hardships that most newcomers endured, it was a time of promise for them. During the 1890s, 3.7 million people, mostly southern and eastern Europeans, entered the United States. After 1900 immigration reached flood tide. Between 1901 and 1910, 8.8 million peasants and craftworkers, mostly destitute, entered American ports.

The Gay Nineties.

In spite of the troubles many Americans faced, the last decade of the nineteenth century is often described as the "Gay Nineties." In books and in films, it is portrayed as a time of cheerful nickelodeon music and outings at Coney Island, of vaudeville and ice cream parlors, of leisure and the enjoyment of life.

This is the prevailing image of the turn of the century because of the rise of the middle class in American culture during that period. In the years just before and after 1900, the American middle class came of age. The rapid economic expansion of the United States also increased the number of people who, while not rich, were comfortable and secure. Increasingly well-educated, freed of old restraints, "Middle America" set out to enjoy its spare time.

The early twentieth century was also a time when the middle class was determined to improve, or reform, the United States. So far-reaching were these reforms that historians call the first decade or so of the twentieth century the *Progressive Era.*

This middle-class family at holiday time displays evidence of its new affluence—carved chairs, lace curtains, Celluloid collars, leg-o'mutton sleeves, and patterned carpets.

President Theodore Roosevelt's obvious enjoyment of rugged, outdoor activities endeared him to many Americans. He became popularly known as "TR" or "Teddy."

Teddy. The hearty spirit of the times was embodied in Theodore Roosevelt, who succeeded William McKinley as president. Roosevelt, just 42 years old, was climbing a mountain in the Adirondacks when he received the news that McKinley had died.

He rushed to Buffalo, New York, took the oath of office, and told a friend, "It is a dreadful thing to come into the presidency in this way. But it would be a far worse thing to be morbid about it." And, indeed, no other president seems to have had such a wonderful time in the White House.

Roosevelt's foreign policy motto was "Speak softly, and carry a big stick." Friends observed that Roosevelt often carried a big stick, but they rarely knew him to speak softly. On the contrary, everything Roosevelt did was accompanied by fanfare. He loved center stage. One of his sons later remarked, "Father wanted to be the bride at every wedding and the corpse at every funeral."

The Active Life. Roosevelt shattered the long-standing image of solemn presidential dignity. He stormed about the country more than any predecessor. When he visited the site of the Panama Canal, he became the first American president to leave the boundaries of the nation during his term of office.

He loved to mix with crowds and would pose for photographers at the slightest suggestion. When a movie photographer asked him to move for the camera he picked up an axe and began wildly to cut down a tree. As Police Commissioner of New York City between 1895 and 1897, he accompanied officers on dangerous beats. As a rancher in North Dakota, he rode with a posse to capture robbers. When the Spanish-American War broke out in 1898, he resigned his government job and helped organize the famous Rough Riders.

The Symbol of His Age. Roosevelt had many critics. But a large majority of the vibrant new middle class found him a grand fellow. They called him "TR" and "Teddy" and named a new toy, the teddy bear, after him.

Although Roosevelt believed in the superiority of what he called the "Anglo-Saxon race," he was popular with blacks because he ignored segregationists and invited Booker T. Washington to the White House. Women suffragists, then gearing up for their successful push to win votes for women, approved of him. Most college professors and intellectuals liked the president because he was himself a scholar, the author of more than a dozen books. As happens only rarely, the person who occupied the White House between 1901 and

Lynching at this time was as common in the West as in the South. Of the 1,203 recorded lynchings by mobs in the 1890s, 669 of those hanged were white. In the South the mobs were almost always white, the victims black.

 553

Teddy Roosevelt and Booker T. Washington (president of Alabama's Tuskegee Institute) converse before speaking to an assembly of students.

for the purpose of financing schools that would teach courses related to agriculture and mechanical arts. Many of today's great state universities in the West owe their start to the Morrill Act.

Millionaires competed for popular esteem by constructing university buildings, endowing fellowships and salaries for professors, and even founding new universities. Stanford University of California had its start in 1885 as a memorial to the dead son of Leland Stanford, the head of the Southern Pacific Railroad. Cornell (1865), Drew (1866), Johns Hopkins (1876), Tulane (1834), and Vanderbilt (1873) also bear the names of wealthy benefactors from the business world. In 1884, Russell Conwell established Temple University in Philadelphia explicitly to educate poor but ambitious young men. John D. Rockefeller pumped millions of dollars into the University of Chicago.

The midwestern and western state universities generally admitted women to at least some of their programs. In the East, however, separate women's colleges remained the rule. These colleges too were often founded by large contributions. Barnard (1885), Bryn Mawr (1880), Radcliffe (1879), Smith (1871), Vassar (1861), and Wellesley (1875) offered courses as challenging as those given at the best men's colleges.

1909 was so much in tune with the forces of his times that he was truly the symbol of an age.

An Educated People. In this period, educational opportunities for ordinary people multiplied several times over. In 1860 there were no more than 300 junior and senior high schools in the United States, and only 100 had free tuition. By 1900, there were 6,000 free public secondary schools, and by 1915, 12,000.

Higher education was transformed even more radically. Just after the Civil War, only 52,000 people, mostly well-to-do males, attended colleges and universities. Almost all studied the traditional *liberal arts curriculum* courses built around Latin, philosophy, mathematics, history, and public speaking. Higher education was intended not for practical purposes but to prepare gentlemen to be leaders of society. The only women enjoying higher education attended "female seminaries" that were more like finishing schools than colleges. But by 1910, 266,600 young people were registered in universities and colleges.

New Kinds of Schools. Colleges were no longer clinging to the liberal arts. The *Morrill Land Grant Act* of 1862 provided federal land to states

Studying for Careers. Some colleges broadened their offerings by adopting the *elective system.* That is, although students still had to take mostly liberal arts courses, they were permitted to select career-oriented major areas of study and could concentrate on courses related to the major.

Another innovation of the period was the professional graduate school. After completing four years of college, students could remain in school and earn advanced degrees in the professions. Previously, these professions were learned by working as an *apprentice* for a lawyer or engineer. The idea of the graduate school originated in Germany, and was pioneered in America by Baltimore's Johns Hopkins University. As late as 1875 there were only 399 graduate students in the United States. By 1900 there were 5,000.

Minorities in Higher Education. Higher education remained largely a privilege of white males. However, the older colleges and universities, including the West Point Military Academy,

Teddy Roosevelt was extremely fond of meeting with the common man and made every effort to do so. Perhaps one of the best-known incidents of this occurred on New Year's Day, 1907, when he shook hands with 8,513 people.

admitted a few blacks. Blacks who were willing to stand up to prejudice could even complete graduate training. W. E. B. Du Bois earned a Ph.D. at Harvard University.

Most college-educated blacks attended segregated institutions. Beginning with Lincoln University in Pennsylvania, the number of colleges for blacks increased because of the contributions of idealistic benefactors. Fisk University at Nashville (1867) and Howard University in Washington (1867) were two of the best. The most famous black college was Alabama's Tuskegee Institute, founded in 1881 and presided over by a self-educated former slave, Booker T. Washington. Tuskegee's most famous professor was the botanist George Washington Carver, whose discoveries helped to finance the school.

The Catholic Church also founded its own universities. The best known of many Catholic colleges were Notre Dame in Indiana (1842), and Boston College (1863) and Holy Cross (1865) in Massachusetts.

Exceptional women, willing to live with discrimination and even ridicule, attended most of the state universities. By the mid-1880s, coeducational classes were common. Women doctors and lawyers were more conspicuous by the end of the century, and women's advances in medicine were particularly dramatic. Elizabeth Blackwell, the first woman doctor in America, graduated in 1849. In 1868 she founded a medical school for women in New York City. By that time, the Women's Medical College of Pennsylvania was training female physicians. Blackwell's sister-in-law, Antoinette, also paved the way for professional women when she was ordained as a Protestant minister.

Libraries and Lyceums. The hunger for education also found expression in the construction of free public libraries. Enoch Pratt donated $1 million to enable Baltimore to establish a library open to all. Samuel J. Tilden gave New York City $3 million for the same purpose. William Newberry founded one of the world's greatest collections of books and manuscripts in Chicago with a gift of $2.1 million. Beginning in 1881, Andrew Carnegie made libraries his principal *philanthropy.* Before his death in 1919, Carnegie helped to found 2,800 public libraries.

The *lyceum* was a program by which experts

Dr. Sara Josephine Baker began to operate the Bureau of Child Hygiene in New York in 1907. In the next 35 years, infant deaths fell sharply.

went to lecture in towns that were otherwise isolated from cultural centers. Popular before the Civil War, the lyceum idea was revived in 1868 by James Redpath. Offering large fees, Redpath persuaded the era's most distinguished statesmen, ministers, and college professors to deliver addresses in hundreds of small cities and towns.

The *Chautauqua* took its name from a resort town on Lake Chautauqua in upstate New York. Unlike the lyceum, which sent lecturers to the people, the Chautauqua brought middle-class people to a resort, where they rested, played, and also learned and were entertained.

Beginning as week-long training programs for religion teachers, Chautauquas soon attracted people who wanted a break from work and the opportunity to enjoy varied programs. The programs included lectures by famous people, such as William Jennings Bryan; slide shows on China, Persia, or some other distant land; acrobats and German "oom-pah" bands, and Indian fire eaters. More than 200 Chautauqua-type resorts flourished at the turn of the century.

2. A TIME TO PLAY

The Chautauqua resorts were popular because, at the start of the twentieth century, large numbers of Americans had enough time and money to travel and live away from home for a few weeks each year. This was a new and stimulating experience. Only a generation earlier, a vacation was something only the wealthy could realistically think about. Now, tens of thousands of ordinary Americans looked forward to summer as a time to hop trains bound for mountain resorts or seaside towns. There they could escape the heat and humdrum of daily life by participating in the activities provided by the resorts—educational, religious, or healthful. The old Puritan suspicion of idleness was dying, but it was by no means dead. Even vacations had to be useful.

Health Resorts. Resorts that did not specialize in lectures or religious observances often specialized in health. Owners of mineral springs lured vacationers by claiming miraculous curative powers for the baths in their naturally heated mineral waters or hot muds. In the middle of the nineteenth century, Saratoga in New York and White Sulphur Springs in Virginia did a busy summer business in wealthy vacationers who came to "take the cure." By the end of the century, middle-class people were also flocking to these resorts.

Working Class Leisure. By the turn of the century, all but the very poorest working people enjoyed some leisure time. To accommodate them, city governments constructed large, green public parks within walking distance of most

Atlantic City, with its famous Steel Pier and beautiful sandy beach, attracted strollers (with and without straw hats and parasols), "bathers," and a few who came to swim.

Trolley cars like this one took city dwellers to the edge of town for a Sunday outing.

In 1895, both spectators and cyclists attended the opening of the Cycle Path at Coney Island.

neighborhoods. New York's Central Park, in the center of the city, was the most famous. Philadelphia's Fairmount Park, scene of the Centennial Exposition of 1876, was even larger.

Rivaling public parks in popularity were amusement parks, usually constructed by trolley line companies. On weekdays and in built-up parts of the cities, public transportation companies had plenty of riders. On weekends, however, and on the outskirts of cities, the cars usually ran empty.

Goat carriages gave city children novel rides around Central Park in the early 1900s. The carriages were elegant miniatures of adult vehicles, with shiny leather seats.

To remedy this, trolley companies built dazzling, noisy centers with inexpensive places to eat, games of skill and luck that could be played for a nickel, and thrilling mechanical rides like the roller coaster. The amusement parks were jammed with people on weekends and almost every day in summer. A writer in *Harper's Weekly* approved of the "trolley parks" as "great breathing-places for millions of people who get little fresh air at home."

The Bicycle Craze.

Good health was also the reason offered for the sporting crazes that swept the United States during the Gay Nineties. As early as 1858, Thomas Wentworth Higginson urged middle-class people to keep their bodies in shape. By the end of the century, businesspeople and their families were avidly playing croquet, archery, and tennis. Roller-skating was popular in great rinks like San Francisco's Olympian Club, which could accommodate 5,000 skaters at a time.

But no participant sport spread as quickly as bicycling. In 1880, when the League of American Wheelmen was founded, more than 20,000 Americans were devoting their leisure hours to pedaling about parks and paved city streets.

While some praised bicycling as a "health-giving outdoor exercise," a few were critical of the sport. Bicycling made it possible, they complained, for young men and women to escape from their chaperones, the older people who formerly supervised courtship and dating.

Bicycling—and tennis, croquet, and roller-skating—did indeed create opportunities for middle class young women to break away from the parlor and dining room to which they were restricted through most of the nineteenth century. The new, energetic, active women of the 1890s even found an approving role model in the drawings of magazine artist Charles Dana Gibson. His idealized young woman of the period, the *Gibson Girl*, was no *feminist* or supporter of votes for women. She did, however, lead an active life and think of herself as an independent person.

The Wright Brothers.

Two bicycle manufacturers, Orville and Wilbur Wright, went on to greater fame. They became interested in powered flight in the 1890s. Previously, all flight had been in balloons, or as in Otto Lilienthal's experiments in the 1890s, with gliders. The Wrights were intrigued by the possibilities of engine-powered airplanes that could carry people. By 1903, they had used experimental kites and gliders to perfect their ideas, and had built a prototype for their airplane. On December 17, 1903, at Kitty Hawk, North Carolina, they managed to keep their airplane in the air for about 120 feet (37 meters). Humans could fly!

Within a few years, significant advances in airplane design were made. By 1919, an airplane had been flown across the Atlantic, and the first nonstop trip across the Atlantic occurred in 1920.

Baseball.

Increased leisure time also meant the growth of spectator sports played by professionals. By the turn of the century, baseball was already "the American pastime." Baseball grew after the Civil War era, when neighboring towns formed teams to play one another. In the large cities, wealthy young men played for private clubs in matches against clubs from other cities.

The players on these clubs were supposed to be amateurs. However, in the effort to win, the club

Wilbur Wright poses at the controls of the Flyer I, *also called the* Kitty Hawk.

members began, secretly at first, to hire skillful players to represent them. In 1869, the Cincinnati Red Stockings became the first wholly professional team. The Red Stockings went on tour and in their first year won 59 games with no defeats.

Thousands of spectators, mostly middle-class men, willingly paid admission to see well-played baseball. Responding to this demand, major cities in the East and Midwest founded their own professional teams. In 1876, the National League was organized, and in 1900, the American League was founded. The first World Series between the league champions was played in 1903.

Boxing and American Society.

The second most popular spectator sport was boxing. Watching a fight between two men was, of course, an ancient recreation. When the men battled for pay, the contest was called "prize fighting," and just about anything a fighter could do was allowed.

In 1865, however, English noblemen and gentlemen took up amateur "boxing" as a recreation suitable for developing their physiques and their virtue. But gentlemen had to fight like gentlemen, so an English lord, the Marquis of Queensbury, drew up a code of rules to govern fighting. They were not strict rules by any means, but they made it possible to legalize and organize boxing, and attract thousands of ticket-buying spectators. In the United States, the first great heavyweight champion was John L. Sullivan, "the Boston Strongman," who traveled about the country offering $500 (later $1,000) to anyone who could last four rounds with him in the ring. Between 1882 and 1892, Sullivan defeated everyone who took up the challenge.

Boxing and Prejudice.

In 1908, Jack Johnson became the first black heavyweight champion, and he held the championship until 1915. However, because he was black and did not defer to white people, Johnson was never very popular with whites. Still, people of both races attended his matches during the years he defended his title.

In 1912, authorities charged Johnson with violation of a federal morality law. He fled to Europe and then to the West Indies, but he was unhappy away from home and from American boxing. In 1915 he agreed to fight another white challenger, Jess Willard, in Havana, Cuba.

Johnson lost the fight. However, most blacks and many white boxing experts believed that he faked his knockout because losing the championship was the price of being allowed back into the United States. Not until the 1930s would another black prize fighter, Joe Louis, win the heavyweight championship.

A Thriving Culture.

The late nineteenth century also saw an increased interest in intellectual activity. Middle-class readers created a demand for new writers who departed from the themes and styles of the past.

The most popular writer of the time was a Missourian, Samuel L. Clemens, who wrote under the pen name Mark Twain. More than any writer before him, Clemens drew on distinctively American themes and often wrote with a distinctive American quality to his language. He earned an international reputation with *The Adventures of Tom Sawyer* (1876) and *The Adventures of Huckleberry Finn* (1884). While these novels could be read as entertaining books for children and adults, they also were critical of some American customs and points of view.

Twain was known as a *realist* because of his aversion to writing romantic fantasy. Another popular realistic writer of the time was Henry James, whose favorite theme was the relationship of Americans to European culture. James won fame for his deep enquiries into what his characters were thinking, in books such as *Daisy Miller* and *The Turn of the Screw*.

Another popular writer was Edith Wharton. She was very sensitive to the lifestyle of the time, and was particularly interested in the women of the period. One of her favorite topics was how nonwealthy women who were on their own got by in society. Her most popular novel was *Ethan Frome* (1911), and she won a Pulitzer prize in 1920 for her novel *The Age of Innocence*.

Magazines for the Masses.

William Dean Howells, although a novelist, was best known as the editor of a Boston magazine, the *Atlantic Monthly*. Like other well-established magazines— *Harper's*, *Forum*, and *The Arena*—the *Atlantic* published a mix of polite poetry, stories, and elegant essays that sometimes dealt with contemporary affairs, but always in a careful way that appealed to

Research Assignment: Have students prepare a report on an American sport that either originated here or is played here now. The report should include some aspect of the importance of sports as a reflection of society.

Mark Twain, at a dinner in his honor at the Delmonico restaurant, looks ready to deliver a quip to the photographer. Twain, who said, "I came in with Halley's Comet and intend to go out with it," did just that. His life began and ended with appearances of the comet.

a small literary elite. Only a small readership could afford the 35 cents charged for these periodicals.

Beginning in the 1880s, a new kind of magazine appeared. More efficient paper manufacturing and printing presses made it possible for publishers like Cyrus H. K. Curtis to reach a wider readership by charging lower prices. In 1883, Curtis appealed to an increasingly well-educated female readership by publishing the *Ladies Home Journal* for only ten cents. Fifteen years later, he drove the price of his *Saturday Evening Post* down to five cents.

Under the editorship of Edward Bok, the *Journal* was no more daring than the *Atlantic* and *Harper's*. However, other new magazines, such as *McClure's*, *Munsey's*, and *Cosmopolitan*, which also sold for about a dime, began to explore social problems. They were always lively, sometimes scandalous, and enjoyed soaring circulation. By 1900, the combined monthly circulation of the four largest American magazines, none more than 15 years old and all appealing to the middle class, was 2.5 million. This was larger than the circulation of all American magazines in 1880.

The Muckrakers. Early in the twentieth century, the editors of the new journals discovered that no kind of article was more popular than the exposé, an article that revealed corruption and dishonesty in business and government. *Muckraking*, or seeking corruption in supposedly respectable places, began when Samuel S. McClure hired writers Ida M. Tarbell and Lincoln Steffens.

Tarbell and Steffens were idealists, convinced that to expose wrongdoing would inspire middle-class Americans to take action. Both writers were immediately popular. In a series of articles that later became a book, Tarbell examined the sometimes dubious practices that John D. Rockefeller had used to build Standard Oil. Steffens's first venture at muckraking was a series of articles called "The Shame of the Cities." In it he showed that practically every large city government in the United States was laced with corruption, bribery, and outright theft from municipal treasuries.

So popular were these essays that the mass circulation magazines began to concentrate on muckraking. John Spargo, an English-born socialist, discussed child labor in "The Bitter Cry of the

Children." David Graham Phillips, later a successful novelist, made his reputation by depicting the United States Senate as a "Millionaire's Club."

The Jungle. The most famous muckraker was Upton Sinclair. His book, *The Jungle* (1906), sold 150,000 copies in its first year of publication. With its graphic descriptions of Chicago's meatpacking industry, *The Jungle* caused an uproar. As a result, in 1906 Congress moved to pass several *Pure Food and Drug Acts* regulating the processing and contents of foodstuffs.

By 1906, it was not difficult to interest Congress in such reforms. The American middle class was then in the midst of an age of reform so intense that the first decade of the century has been called the Progressive Era.

SECTION REVIEW

1. Write a sentence to identify: Kitty Hawk, Jack Johnson, Edith Wharton, Cyrus Curtis.

2. Describe the changing role of vacations in American society. At what kinds of resorts did many turn-of-the-century Americans spend their vacations?

3. According to some people of the period, what were the benefits and drawbacks of bicycling? What other participant and spectator sports were popular at the turn of the century?

4. Describe the activities of the Muckrakers, and explain what motivated them.

---

3. THE PROGRESSIVES

The spirit of reform that agitated American society after 1900 was fed by the muckrakers. But reform would have been in the air even without them. The rapid expansion of the American economy and population in the late nineteenth century had caused many social problems, and an energetic, educated, and confident middle class could not ignore them.

Who Were the Progressives? Few Progressives came from the industrial and financial *elite*.

Fewer still rose from the masses of laboring people or from the poor farming population. The Americans who wrote and spoke on behalf of reform were lawyers, physicians, teachers, journalists, social workers, small businesspeople, and the wives and daughters of middle-class businesspeople and professionals.

These people believed themselves to be truer to American ideals of democracy and liberty than either great capitalists or working people barely able to survive. They had no overwhelming selfish interests, as did the Morgans and Rockefellers with their huge fortunes. On the other hand, because the middle class did own property, they had a stake in society that those on the bottom did not. They had something to protect.

The Progressives were painfully aware that they were "in-between." They felt themselves—and the best American ideals of democracy and liberty —threatened by big business from above and by the dangerous mob of poor workers and immigrants from below.

An Urban Movement. William Allen White, a newspaperman and an active Progressive, wrote that the Progressives had adopted many reforms, particularly political reforms, that the Populists had already called for.

But unlike the Populists, the Progressives were urban people. White, himself an anti-Populist, had been an editor in Emporia, Kansas, during the 1890s. Progressive politicians who represented rural states had grown up not behind the plow but in towns. It was coincidence that the greatest Progressive president, Theodore Roosevelt, was the only American president to have been born in a big city (New York).

Minorities were represented among the leading Progressives. Louis Brandeis, a Louisville lawyer who crusaded against corrupt railroad practices, was Jewish. Alfred E. Smith and Robert Wagner of New York were Roman Catholics. The black leader William E. B. Du Bois was part of the Progressive movement. However, most Progressives were whites descended from British forebears, and members of Protestant churches.

Limits of Progressivism. Progressives were not a particularly broad-minded lot. Most Progressive leaders were moralistic to the point of self-

Louis Brandeis, who fought for minimum wage laws, became the first Jewish Supreme Court Justice.

Croly called for achieving "Jeffersonian ends"—the good of the common people—through "Hamiltonian means"—a strong, active government. He believed that only the powers of the state could tame the corporations and improve life for the most disadvantaged people so they would not threaten democratic institutions.

A Variety of Reformers.

Progressivism was more a frame of mind than a movement. The unifying belief in the power of government was about all the Progressives had in common.

For example, they differed about labor unions. Many Progressives believed that labor unions had a right to exist and fight for the rights of their members. Others opposed unions, believing they were interested only in the welfare of their members even if that meant sacrificing the welfare of the whole society. On one occasion, leaders of the National American Woman Suffrage Association, a Progressive group, said that women should help to break strikes if by so doing they could win jobs away from men.

Progressives also disagreed on the issue of child labor laws. Most favored keeping children out of factories. By 1907, about two-thirds of the states had adopted laws forbidding the employment of children under 14 years old. However, when Progressives in Congress passed a Federal Child Labor Law in 1916, President Woodrow Wilson expressed grave doubts about it. He feared that the law would deny children their "rights" as citizens to hold jobs.

Progressives and Blacks.

Some Progressives sympathized with the plight of American blacks. A talented muckraker, Ray Stannard Baker, wrote a book called *Following the Color Line*, denouncing the indignities visited daily upon blacks who lived in segregated states.

In 1909, white Progressives, such as social worker Jane Addams, joined with prominent blacks to organize the National Association for the Advancement of Colored People (*NAACP*). Along with W. E. B. Du Bois, they believed that a talented, university-educated black elite would lead blacks to equality.

But other Progressives could not accept the idea of black equality. Some were frank racists who believed that blacks were inherently inferior

righteousness, always looking for the absolute right and the absolute wrong in every political controversy. To many of them, life was a long, holy crusade for what they believed was right.

Even Theodore Roosevelt described an election campaign in biblical terms. "We stand at Armageddon," he said, referring to prophecies about the end of the world, "and do battle for the Lord." The second Progressive president, Woodrow Wilson, would not compromise with political opponents even when his stubbornness meant complete defeat rather than partial victory.

Looking to Government for Answers.

One other characteristic united the Progressives. Unlike many reformers before them, who regarded government as part of the problem, almost all Progressives looked to the government for answers. They believed that once they had captured the powers of the state, they could use those powers to correct what was wrong in America.

In *The Promise of American Life*, an influential Progressive book published in 1909, Herbert

Treatment of blacks in the Progressive Era was not impressive. As mentioned before, lynchings were common. Black voting rights were ignored, an estimated one third of the black population was illiterate (in 1910 there were only 8,000 black high school students) and many blacks continued to face discrimination in housing and jobs.

A crusader for black pride, W. E. B. Du Bois was the first black to earn a doctorate from Harvard.

to whites. Some southern Progressives even worked for reform in some areas while supporting racial segregation.

Other Progressives agreed that the white and black races were probably equal. However, as long as 35 percent of American blacks were illiterate, as was true in 1900, they saw no great injustice in denying them equal political rights.

SECTION REVIEW

1. Write a sentence to identify: *The Promise of American Life*, Ray Stannard Baker, Jane Addams, Louis Brandeis.

2. Describe the kinds of people who made up the Progressive movement. In what sense were they "in between"?

3. Compare the Progressives with the Populists.

4. What one belief united the Progressives? About what issues did they differ?

5. What was the role of some American minorities in the Progressive movement?

6. How did Woodrow Wilson react to political opponents?

---

4. PROGRESSIVES IN ACTION

The Progressive, "good government" movement started in the 1890s when disgust at widespread corruption in city governments aroused middle-class voters to elect mayors committed to honest administrative practices.

There was, of course, nothing new in a candidate for office claiming to represent honesty as opposed to *corruption*. But two features made the Progressives unique. First, because they were effective administrators, they stayed in power and made their reforms permanent. This had not been the case with earlier reformers.

Second, the Progressives went beyond mere honesty in government, making basic structural changes in the way cities, and eventually the nation, were operated. Many of the features of government we take for granted today were introduced by the Progressive movement.

The "Good Government" Movement. One of the first Progressive mayors was Hazen S. Pingree of Detroit. First elected in 1890, he battled the alliance between the City Council and the corrupt public utilities companies for seven years.

More successful was Samuel M. Jones of Toledo, Ohio. An honest businessman who ran his company on the basis of the "golden rule," he became mayor of Toledo in 1897. He rooted *graft* out of Toledo's government, and proved to be a skillful and successful administrator.

Thomas L. Johnson, the Progressive mayor of Cleveland, was first elected in 1901. He cleaned up a dirty government, supported women's *suffrage*, and reformed juvenile courts. He also took over public utilities. With large profits to be made supplying consumers with gas, electricity, water, and transportation, the managements of these utilities regularly bribed city council members to vote them favorable charters. By having the city take over the utilities, Johnson felt they would be run for the good of the community.

Johnson's enemies called him a *socialist*. However, in *The Shame of the Cities*, Lincoln Steffens reported that Cleveland was the best-governed city in the United States. His book, published in 1904, led to the election of many city governments that imitated Johnson's example.

In the year 1900 approximately 5,300,000 women were employed full time. Of these, 960,000 were factory workers and 949,000 had white-collar jobs. About 700,000 children under the age of fifteen worked in factories and related jobs, while about 900,000 worked on farms.

City Managers. Progressives in Staunton, Virginia, went a step further. In 1908, the Staunton city council abolished the office of mayor. Vesting so much authority in one person, they said, made it that much easier for special interests to corrupt government.

In the place of a mayor, the Staunton city charter allowed the democratically elected city council to hire a *city manager*. This official administered the day-to-day workings of the city according to policies adopted by the council. The city manager was a professionally trained expert in administration who would run government more efficiently. The city manager also did not have to face citywide elections and would therefore be free of the influence of special interests.

This plan was most successful in small- and medium-sized cities where the city manager was known personally to most politically active people. By 1915, seven years after Staunton devised the idea, more than 400 American cities had adopted the plan.

The Oregon System. The *Oregon System* of reform was developed by Governor William S. U'ren. U'ren believed that every evil in government could be cured by making government more democratic. Corruption, he said, stemmed from the advantage that special interest groups gained by pressuring lawmakers to depart from the people's best interests. Therefore, the solution was to put more power into the hands of the electorate.

In 1902, U'ren persuaded the Oregon legislature to adopt the *initiative*, the *recall*, and the *referendum*. The initiative allowed citizens to bypass elected lawmakers who might have fallen under the influence of special interests. When a set number of voters' signatures were collected on petitions, the law initiated by the petitioners was put on the ballot for approval or disapproval by the voters. The election in which such questions were decided was called a referendum.

The recall worked in a similar manner. Voters displeased by an elected official could collect signatures calling for that person's recall from office. When a recall petition succeeded, the official under question was forced to resign or submit to an election even if his or her term of office had not expired. The special election was also called a referendum.

The recall was directly aimed at politicians who did not keep their campaign promises once they were in office. The reasoning was that officials who could be recalled at any time would pay more attention to the needs of the people.

Primary Elections. Oregon was one of the first states to choose candidates for public office in *primary elections*. Before U'ren's reforms, party bosses chose the candidates for office. By choosing candidates in a popular election, Oregonians were once again saying that the more democratic the government procedures were, the better they would be.

Another Oregon reform that influenced the nation was U'ren's call for the direct election of United States senators. This was a Populist idea adopted by the Progressives. It became law when the Seventeenth Amendment to the Constitution was *ratified* in 1913.

Battling Bob La Follette. Robert M. La Follette of Wisconsin was a state Progressive leader who rose to national prominence. Born in 1855, he served three terms in Congress as a Republican before 1891. During the last decade of the nineteenth century he was a conventional, rather conservative politician. Then he was approached by an agent of Philetus Sawyer, Wisconsin's political boss, who asked La Follette to help him in bribing a judge.

La Follette, shocked, exploded in a moral fury. He led an "honest government" rebellion against Sawyer's political machine and, in 1900, won election as governor. He then made the railroad and lumber interests squirm as he signed a series of laws closely regulating their activities.

La Follette adopted the initiative, referendum, and recall of the Oregon System, and also primary elections. However, La Follette then went forward with his own reforms.

The Wisconsin Idea. La Follette's *Wisconsin Idea* was based on the belief that in the complex twentieth century, ordinary people needed the help of experts to protect their interests. Since the special interests had armies of lawyers and economists, the only way Progressives could combat them effectively was to organize teams of their own experts.

Class Activity: Have students research and make a chart listing some of the major reforms of the Progressive Era. Included could be manager-council city governments, referendum, recall, initiative, primary elections, and popular election of senators.

La Follette formed a close alliance with the University of Wisconsin, a land-grant institution and one of the country's great universities. He drew on the expertise of economists Richard Ely and John Rogers Commons to draw up progressive laws in which the special interests could not find *loopholes*. In return, the state government financed the university lavishly, making it one of the nation's richest public institutions.

Nor did the Wisconsin Idea neglect farmers, a majority in Wisconsin. Under La Follette, experts at the university researched new farming techniques and sent agents out to inform farmers of their discoveries.

Progressive Machines. La Follette was idealistic, but he was not naive. His greatest contribution to the Progressive movement may have been his realization that the methods of *political machines* could not be left to the corrupt enemies of reform. The political organization he built worked much like that of Boss Tweed's in New York City. That is, political workers who got the vote out to keep people like La Follette in office were rewarded with political *patronage*. But corruption was not condoned as it was in the older machines. Progressives who got the jobs had to work at them, or they were replaced.

Progressives in Other States. In New York, Charles Evans Hughes came to prominence as the result of his investigations into public utilities and insurance companies. Unlike La Follette, who was an impassioned public speaker with a thick mane of hair, Hughes was restrained in his manner, tall, erect, and dignified. In Idaho, William E. Borah was first elected to the Senate in 1906 as a conventional Republican. Once in Washington, however, he usually voted with the growing Progressive bloc.

Prim, humorless, but passionate, Hiram Johnson became famous when he helped prosecute a corrupt city government in San Francisco. During his investigations, Johnson was shocked to learn that the Southern Pacific Railroad was an active partner in the ring that had stolen millions from the city treasury.

The Socialists. Members of the *Socialist* party, which grew steadily during the first decade of the

twentieth century, denied that they were Progressives. Unlike Progressives in both the Republican and Democratic parties, who staunchly defended the *free enterprise system*, the Socialists hoped to overthrow capitalism peacefully by winning the support of the voters.

However, only a few Socialists believed that the day was near when they would accomplish these ultimate ends. In the meantime, they appealed to voters with immediate demands that did not differ in any important respect from the Progressive program. Socialists hoped to win middle-class support by demonstrating that they were responsible, efficient, and democratic—like Progressives— and not wild-eyed *radicals*.

Eugene V. Debs. The most famous Socialist was Eugene V. Debs, a former railroad worker from Terre Haute, Indiana. An impassioned public speaker, Debs thought of socialism as a moral form of government as well as a philosophy.

Debs was the party's presidential candidate five times, in 1900, 1904, 1908, 1912, and 1920. In 1900, he won only 95,000 votes. In 1912, however, he won over 900,000 votes.

That was the high-water mark of American socialism. The major parties began to adopt Progressive ideas, and attracted voters who had previously supported the Socialists. The Progressive movement was not over, however, as Republican Theodore Roosevelt and Democrat Woodrow Wilson carried its ideas into the White House itself.

SECTION REVIEW

1. Write a sentence to identify: city manager, William S. U'ren, Robert La Follette, Wisconsin Idea.

2. Name two ways in which the "good government" reformers were unique.

3. Briefly describe the Progressive political reforms that began in Staunton, Virginia, and Oregon.

4. What were the achievements of Mayor Samuel M. Jones of Toledo, Ohio?

5. How were the goals of the Socialist party like and unlike the goals of the progressives?

CHAPTER REVIEW

TIME LINE

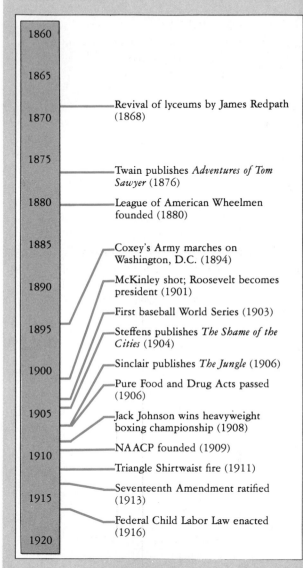

1860

1865

Revival of lyceums by James Redpath
(1868)

1870

1875

Twain publishes *Adventures of Tom Sawyer* (1876)

1880

League of American Wheelmen
founded (1880)

1885

Coxey's Army marches on
Washington, D.C. (1894)

1890

McKinley shot; Roosevelt becomes
president (1901)

First baseball World Series (1903)

1895

Steffens publishes *The Shame of the
Cities* (1904)

Sinclair publishes *The Jungle* (1906)

1900

Pure Food and Drug Acts passed
(1906)

1905

Jack Johnson wins heavyweight
boxing championship (1908)

NAACP founded (1909)

1910

Triangle Shirtwaist fire (1911)

Seventeenth Amendment ratified
(1913)

1915

Federal Child Labor Law enacted
(1916)

1920

TIME LINE QUESTIONS

1. What event was the result of American
workers' need for jobs? In what year did this
event take place?
2. How many years elapsed between the Triangle Shirtwaist fire and the law that controlled
child labor?
3. What are two events that represented
achievements for black Americans?

SKILLS STRATEGY

Table showing the numbers of the general
categories of the Dewey Decimal System:

000–099	General Works (encyclopedias, atlases, others)
100–199	Philosophy (including psychology)
200–299	Religion (including mythology)
300–399	Social Sciences (economics, government, and so forth)
400–499	Languages (all languages, dictionaries)
500–599	Pure Science (mathematics, biology, and so forth)
600–699	Applied Science (agriculture, engineering, and so forth)
700–799	Fine Arts (music, painting, and so forth)
800–899	Literature
900–909 930–999	History
910–919	Travel
920–929	Biography (shelved alphabetically by last name of subject)

LIBRARY SOURCES

The books in a library are kept in three main
sections—the fiction section, the nonfiction section, and the reference section. Works of fiction
are arranged alphabetically on the shelves, according to the last names of the authors. The shelves of
the reference section hold general reference
works such as encyclopedias, atlases, almanacs,
and the *Readers' Guide to Periodical Literature*.

In most libraries, nonfiction books are grouped
according to a system devised in 1876 by Melvil
Dewey, an American librarian. Using this system,
called the *Dewey decimal system*, makes locating
books much easier. The system organizes all
books into the 12 subject-area categories shown
in the table above. All the books in each of these
categories are grouped together. On the spine of
each book is a Dewey decimal number, also
known as a "call number," beginning with the first
three numbers of the category to which the book
belongs. The first three numbers on the spine of a
history book could be any of the numbers 900–
909, and 930–999. For example, the Dewey decimal numbers on all American history books would
begin with the numbers 973.

A decimal point follows the first three num-

Making Connections: Review the questions and topics presented in the Making Connections
section that opens this chapter. Discuss why the Progressives succeeded in creating reforms

bers. The numbers after the decimal point indicate subdivisions of the category *American History*. The Dewey decimal number 973.46 on the spine of a nonfiction book indicates that the book is about American history (973) during the Constitutional period (4) in the administration of Thomas Jefferson (6). The last element in a Dewey decimal number is the first letter of the author's last name.

In most libraries, nonfiction books are shelved by subject-area category and in the order of their Dewey decimal numbers. However, a growing number of libraries are using a similar classification system, called the *Library of Congress system*, instead of the Dewey system. These libraries generally have very large collections. The Library of Congress system allows those libraries to classify their books into more specific categories.

APPLYING SKILLS

Refer to the two exhibits above to do the following exercise.

List the Dewey decimal numbers that appear on the spines of the books pictured above. Beside each number, write the general category to which the book belongs, referring to the table in the exhibit on page 566.

CHAPTER 23 TEST

TEXT REVIEW

1. Describe the situation for Indians, blacks, and workers in the Progressive Era.
2. What American political leader typified the hearty spirit of the Progressive Era? Why?
3. Support this statement with at least four facts from the chapter: "In this period, educational opportunities for ordinary people increased."
4. Explain how either the lyceum or the Chautauqua responded to the American hunger for education at the turn of the century.
5. List five ways that Americans of the 1890s and early 1900s could spend their leisure time.
6. Name several books and magazines that were popular around the turn of the century. Describe the kind of information that would be found in a muckraking magazine.
7. Write a profile of the Progressives, including these points: their "in-between" status, their relationship to cities, their self-righteous tendencies, their view of the role of government, and the issues on which they differed.
8. Describe one reform made by the Progressives in each of the following: city government, state government, national government.

CRITICAL THINKING

9. Compare the ultimate goal of the Socialist party with that of the progressive members of the Republican and Democratic parties, and give one reason to explain why the Socialists made relatively little headway on the national political scene.
10. Explain the viewpoint of each of these men on the use of political machines: Boss Tweed, Robert La Follette.

WRITING A PARAGRAPH

Write a paragraph for a social science book, explaining how one Progressive reform has influenced local government. Supporting sentences should give ways in which this reform has influenced the relationship between citizens and their city or state government.

where others could not. Also discuss the role these reforms played in the development of social mores for the rest of the century.

CHAPTER 24

THE PROGRESSIVES IN POWER

1901–1916

Only a small part of those in the commencing of the twentieth century started it as a twentieth century and not a left over nineteenth century. . . . and then world war came, and that made everybody know it was not the nineteenth century but the twentieth century. GERTRUDE STEIN

Making Connections. With Theodore Roosevelt in the White House, the progressive cause had a national leader. Roosevelt's popular administration took action against the abuses of big business, controlled unsafe drugs, and made strides in conserving natural resources. These policies were carried on by Roosevelt's successors, Taft and Wilson.

In this chapter, you will learn:
- Why Roosevelt was determined to control big business
- How Roosevelt had business and labor leaders sit down together to settle a coal strike
- Who the major leaders of the conservation movement were, and what victories they won during Roosevelt's term
- Why Taft angered Progressives during his term
- How Roosevelt's creation of a third party helped Woodrow Wilson win the presidency in 1912
- What Wilson's "New Freedom" was and how he put his own stamp on government policy

You know that the Progressive movement gained wide popular support. Therefore, a president could find the backing needed to put progressive programs through Congress. As you read, note how the programs of three presidents reflected Progressive demands.

Sections

1. THE REFORMER PRESIDENT

Despite Teddy Roosevelt's distaste for reformers, he was thrown into an alliance with them. The Progressives were members of the middle class, and they felt threatened by the massive economic power of big business. Roosevelt was a descendant of a wealthy *aristocratic* family that was prominent long before industrialization. People of his social class often felt that wealthy industrialists and financiers had rudely shoved them aside. Roosevelt found it easy to describe successful business-people as "malefactors" (evil-doers) of great wealth. When he did, middle-class Progressives cheered him.

Another reason why Roosevelt seized the reins of the reform movement was his desire to be in the thick of things. In the early twentieth century, progressivism was in the thick of things as more and more states elected governors, congressmen, and senators committed to reform.

Roosevelt as Politician. The Republican party bosses were uneasy about Roosevelt. They did not think of him as a reformer. But he did have a reputation as an impulsive, headstrong "cow-

Symbol of turn-of-the-century America was Teddy Roosevelt, who projected an image of being larger than life in war, peace, and politics. At right he is shown campaigning for the presidency in 1912 as the Bull Moose candidate.

Quotation: from the book *Paris, France.* Other works by Gertrude Stein (1874–1946) include *Three Lives, Tender Buttons, Making of Americans, The Autobiography of Alice B. Toklas, Four Saints in Three Acts, Picasso, Ida,* and *The World is Round.*

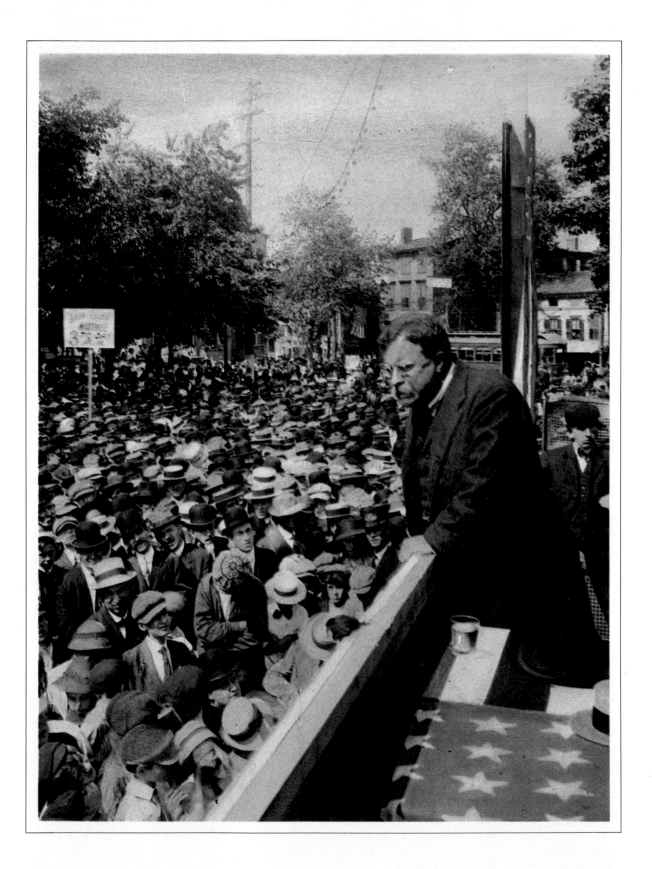

boy." The *political boss* of New York State, Tom Platt, could not control Roosevelt as governor, so he foisted him on the Republican party as its vice-presidential candidate in 1900.

Even before the period of mourning for the murdered McKinley was over, Mark Hanna began to lay plans to challenge Roosevelt for the Republican presidential nomination in 1904. In order to head Hanna off, Roosevelt tried to win the support of the conservative Republicans. He kept most of McKinley's *cabinet*—Secretary of State John Hay, Secretary of War Elihu Root, and the heads of the Justice, Interior, and Agriculture Departments. By allowing these officials more control over their departments than McKinley had given them, Roosevelt won them and their followers to his side.

The Northern Securities Case. Roosevelt also won the hearts of Progressives by taking bold action against the Northern Securities Company in 1902. This was a *holding company*, and it held controlling interest in the three major railroads of the northwestern United States. This transportation monopoly was masterminded by J. P. Morgan with the cooperation of railroaders James J. Hill and Edward H. Harriman.

Morgan had no reason to fear trouble from the government. The Sherman Antitrust law had been forgotten for several years. During the McKinley administration, wealthy businesspeople who expected legal problems worked them out quietly with McKinley's friends and advisors.

Consequently, Morgan was stunned when, without warning, Roosevelt instructed Philander C. Knox, his *Attorney General* and a former corporation lawyer, to institute proceedings against the Northern Securities Company. "We do not wish to destroy corporations," Roosevelt said, "but we do wish to make them serve the public good." In the President's opinion, Morgan's railroad monopoly did not serve the public good, and he insisted that it be broken up.

"If we have done anything wrong," Morgan wrote the President in a pained and revealing moment, "send your man to my man and we can

Striking coal miners in Shenandoah, Pennsylvania, protested harsh working conditions. Not all demands were met, but the strike improved labor unions' status in the United States.

fix it up." It was just the sort of statement to annoy the President. Roosevelt did not believe that a corporation was bad simply because it was big, but he insisted that the United States government must hold ultimate power over business. When Morgan addressed Roosevelt as an equal, Roosevelt determined to see the case through. In 1904, the Supreme Court ruled that the Northern Securities Company was a trust that dealt in illegal restraint of trade and must be dissolved.

Roosevelt as "Trust Buster."

Progressives rejoiced. No more would Morgan and big business run the country. Newspaper editors and cartoonists began to describe Roosevelt as the *"trust buster,"* showing him as a lion tamer in control of corporations.

They spoke too soon. "Trust buster" was an exaggeration. Although Roosevelt instituted 44 antitrust suits and won 25, his more conservative successor, William Howard Taft, filed 90 suits in fewer years in office. Moreover, once Roosevelt felt confident that big business acknowledged the authority of government, he resumed the quiet ironing out of problems that had characterized McKinley's administration. In 1907, when Morgan sent United States Steel president Elbert H. Gary to ask permission for the giant company to gobble up a major regional competitor, Roosevelt quietly gave his blessing.

The Great Coal Strike.

In 1902, 140,000 coal miners in Pennsylvania asked their employers for a 20 percent raise, an eight-hour workday, and recognition of the United Mine Workers (UMW) as their representative in all negotiations with management. The miners believed their demands were reasonable. They worked at a dangerous job for *subsistence* wages. But the mine owners turned them down, afraid to sign long-term wage contracts when the bottom regularly dropped out of the price of coal. The miners went on strike.

As the days grew chilly in October, Americans began to worry. Most city homes were heated by coal-fueled furnaces and the urban coal yards were running out of coal. Under normal circumstances, public opinion would have turned against the workers. Instead, the mine owners came under fire. One reason was the statement by a leader of the employers, George F. Baer, that he would not

deal with the miners' union because God had entrusted him with the management of his mine. Compared with Bauer and that kind of reaction, UMW president John Mitchell seemed moderate.

Roosevelt as the Worker's Friend.

Roosevelt summoned both the union and the mine owners to the White House to work out an agreement. But even when the President requested it, the owners refused to sit in the same room with the union leaders. Roosevelt grew furious at the employers' behavior.

He hinted that if the strike was not settled, he might nationalize the mines (have the government take them over) and use troops to remove the coal. The employers wanted this no more than the workers did. They agreed to submit the dispute to *arbitration*. Impartial *arbiters* would hear both sides, and their decision would be accepted by both employers and employees.

The solution, reached in March 1903, was a compromise. The workday was reduced to nine hours and pay was raised by ten percent. However, the mine owners were not required to recognize the UMW as their employees' representative. Recognition was important to labor unions, but Mitchell was satisfied, because for the first time, a president had treated strikers and employers as equals. In 1904, Roosevelt won the votes of many industrial workers because of his *impartiality* in 1902.

Roosevelt as the Radical's Enemy.

John Mitchell was called a "bread and butter" union leader because he opposed socialism. Socialists were numerous in the UMW, but Mitchell argued that workers should accept capitalism and fight only for higher wages and shorter hours within the system. His conservatism made it easy for Roosevelt to cooperate with him.

Toward union leaders who advocated socialism, on the other hand, Roosevelt was hostile and aggressive. In 1906, for example, the president and secretary-treasurer of the radical Western Federation of Miners were on trial in Idaho, accused of conspiracy to murder the former governor of the state. Roosevelt publicly called the *defendants* "undesirable citizens." Conservatives and radicals both protested his statement, since the President appeared to be trying to prejudice

Although John F. Kennedy is often referred to as the youngest U.S. president, he was not. Kennedy was the youngest elected president at age 43, but Teddy Roosevelt was a year younger when he took office upon the assassination of McKinley.

the jury against the accused men. (They were not convicted.)

Quite unlike the persuasion he used in the coal strike, Roosevelt did use troops in Goldfield, Nevada, when radical unionists nearly took control of the town. There was little violence in Goldfield. Nevertheless, Roosevelt put troops at the disposal of Goldfield employers—and left them there even after he suspected that his action was not necessary.

The Election of 1904. The Republicans unanimously nominated their active president for re-election in 1904. The Democrats, hoping that Roosevelt had angered conservatives in his own party, chose one of their most conservative members, New York lawyer Judge Alton B. Parker.

Parker did not have a chance. A dignified and distinguished man, Parker could not compete with the bombastic, energetic president. Roosevelt won the Progressive vote and that of the conservative Republicans. J. P. Morgan personally donated $150,000 to the President's campaign fund.

Roosevelt won a lopsided 57.4 percent of the popular vote and an electoral college victory of 336–140. It was the biggest margin since Grant's second election in 1872. Roosevelt had completed what Hanna and McKinley had begun in 1896 —he had made the Republican party the nation's "natural majority."

SECTION REVIEW

1. Write a sentence to identify: Northern Securities Company, arbiters, United Mine Workers, John Mitchell.

2. How did Theodore Roosevelt become the Republican vice-presidential nominee in 1900? How did he head off Mark Hanna's plan to deny him the Republican nomination for president in 1904?

3. Explain why the name "trust buster" is not a strictly accurate description for Roosevelt. Explain why the name "the radical's enemy" is accurate.

4. Name the candidates and the winner in the 1904 presidential election. Why did the election turn out as it did?

---

2. ROOSEVELT'S SECOND TERM

The only sour note in the 1904 election was the large increase in the Socialist vote. Socialist party candidate Eugene V. Debs won 400,000 votes, only three percent of the total electorate, but four times what he had attracted in 1900. The totals startled Progressives and conservatives. The Socialist parties of Europe had begun with just such small votes, and by 1904 they were major contenders for political power.

A few conservatives grumbled that the "radical" Roosevelt was to blame for the popularity of socialism. They said that he encouraged attacks on private property by his own criticisms of business.

Roosevelt and other Progressives disagreed. They believed that if they could reform the dubious and often arrogant business practices of the late nineteenth century's worst capitalists, the Socialist solution would lose its popular appeal. Confident in this belief, Roosevelt began his second term by sponsoring a number of reform bills.

Harnessing the Railroads. The railroads remained a major target of Progressive resentment. Reformers Robert M. La Follette, Charles Evans Hughes, and others had done what they could at the state level to regulate the transportation industry for the public interest. But very few railroads lay completely within a single state. Lines that crossed even one state line were subject only to the interstate commerce clause of the Constitution. Thus, it was only at the federal level that effective action could be taken.

In 1903, Roosevelt had signed the *Elkins Act* forbidding shippers to accept *rebates* from railroads. This added power to the Interstate Commerce Act of 1887, which simply forbade railroads to pay rebates. With the Elkins Act, the ICC could prosecute both sides in these schemes to eliminate competition.

In 1906, the *Hepburn Act* brought the nation's railroads under even tighter control. The railroads had made free passes available to politicians and their families in order to win their friendship. The Hepburn Act greatly curtailed this practice. More important, the law authorized the ICC to set maximum rates that the railroads could charge customers. Finally, the act required all railroads to use the same methods of accounting. This made it

Research Assignment: Have students write a report on Eugene V. Debs.

harder for railroad bookkeepers to hide profits and exaggerate losses by falsifying financial records.

In 1906, Congress also passed a law that held railroads liable for injuries suffered by their employees while on the job. By European standards, American railroads were required to pay accident victims only modest amounts. However, American law had previously been unable to prevent railroad companies from wriggling out of the major portion of their responsibility for employee injuries.

Pure Food.   Roosevelt and the Progressives enacted several laws in 1906 designed to stamp out unsanitary, and sometimes dangerous, practices in commercial food processing. Upton Sinclair's novel *The Jungle,* an exposé of the meatpacking industry, helped set the stage for the first of the *Pure Food and Drug Acts.* This gave federal inspectors the right to enter and observe procedures in all slaughterhouses that shipped their products across state lines.

The inspectors ended the worst abuses. However, some critics noted that the law led to monopolization of the meatpacking industry. The larger, wealthier companies such as Armour, Swift, and Wilson were able to observe strict sanitary standards and still make a profit. Smaller, independent slaughterhouses, on the other hand, were often forced out of business by the demands of the new laws.

A common practice by commercial food processors had been to add substances that kept their products from spoiling. For example, some meatpackers used formaldehyde to preserve their products. But a scientist in the Agriculture Department, Harvey W. Wiley, had demonstrated that many preservatives were poisonous, or at least dangerous to humans. The act outlawed the use of many *adulterants*—dangerous additives—by commercial processors.

Safer Drugs.   Even more harmful were addictive drugs derived from opium with which many manufacturers laced *patent medicines,* nonprescription and easily available substances that were advertised as cure-alls. Widely publicized in magazines and newspapers and sold by mail, most also had a high alcohol content.

Not surprisingly, patent medicines made users feel better fast. However, they also made addicts of their customers. The *Pure Food and Drug Acts* strictly regulated the use of narcotics in medicine and required manufacturers to list the contents of their products on the label. Many manufacturers were forced out of business. Those who continued to manufacture the cure-alls were forbidden to make claims that could not be scientifically verified.

The Origins of the Conservation Movement. Roosevelt loved the outdoors. He loved to hike, climb mountains, hunt, and camp. When progressive reformers warned that unregulated exploitation was endangering the nation's wilderness heritage and natural resources, he was very responsive.

Yosemite National Park was a gift from California to the federal government. The park contained many natural wonders, including Yosemite Falls, the highest falls in North America.

MOVERS AND SHAPERS

John Muir

Some of the most beautiful territory in the United States has been preserved because of the life work of a *naturalist* named John Muir (1838–1914) and a geologist named John Wesley Powell (1834–1902).

Born in Scotland, John Muir was a child of 11 years when, in 1849, he moved with his father to settle a homestead on the Wisconsin frontier. He learned about the forested wilderness while performing arduous chores on his family's farm. The inventive young Muir created wonderful contraptions, such as an "early rising machine" which literally propelled him out of bed every morning!

Muir attended the University of Wisconsin but never took a degree. The young naturalist educated himself further by making a number of long journeys through Wisconsin, Iowa, Illinois, Indiana, and part of Canada. He kept detailed diaries of all the plants he saw and wrote his reflections on the relationship between people and nature.

In the 1880s, he married and moved to California. Here Muir lived on a fruit ranch and studied horticulture. His lifelong concern for forests took him into the public arena. He was able to convert the editor of *Century* magazine to the cause of *preservation*. The two men began a campaign that led to the designation of Yosemite National Park.

Muir was also concerned that grazing sheep (or "hoofed locusts," as he called them) were eroding valuable forest lands and causing flooding. He was instrumental in getting presidents Benjamin Harrison and Grover Cleveland to set aside large forest reserves. Partly because of Muir and conservation-minded allies, President Theodore Roosevelt set aside more than 100 million acres of timberland as forest reserve. And Roosevelt established four national parks and 16 national monuments.

Knowing that vested interests would always fight against conservation, Muir helped found the *Sierra Club* in 1892 and served as its president. Americans can thank him today for the continued existence of California's giant redwood trees.

John Wesley Powell

Four years older than Muir, John Wesley Powell had an adventuresome career as a geologist and explorer. After attending both Wheaton and Oberlin Colleges, Powell became a geology professor. His career was interrupted by the Civil War, in which he lost an arm. But this did not deter him in his love of fieldwork.

One day, after climbing a previously unscaled peak of the Rocky Mountains, he saw a portion of the Colorado River that had never been traveled by boat. Deciding to explore it himself, he led an expedition in 1869 that passed through the Grand Canyon. It was a dangerous trip. After three grueling months, Powell's group reached the end of their 900-mile journey.

From 1881 to 1894, Powell acted as director of the *United States Geological Survey*. His energetic leadership led to the publication of a large number of maps, atlases, and bulletins that greatly increased public knowledge of the West.

Class Activity: On a map of the U.S., have students use one symbol to mark the eight national parks in existence when Teddy Roosevelt left office. Have them use a second symbol to show those parks that have come into existence since then.

The *conservation movement* included two distinct groups. One group was the *preservationists*, led by the great naturalist John Muir and the *Sierra Club* he helped to found in 1892. The preservationists urged protection of wilderness and natural wonders, believing that a society without natural retreats from the bustle of modern life would soon lose its vitality and its important spiritual values. Preservationists won their first victory as early as 1872, when Wyoming's Yellowstone National Park was declared off limits to economic development and reserved as a "pleasuring ground." When Roosevelt became president in 1901, there were four national parks in the United States. By the time he left office, four more national parks had been added.

The other major group in the conservation movement was the *reservationists*, led by Gifford Pinchot, the first professionally trained American forester and a close personal friend of Roosevelt's. The reservationists were more interested in conserving economically valuable natural resources for future use. Pinchot argued that unless greedy logging companies were stopped, the next generation of Americans would have few forest resources left.

Roosevelt Saves Resources.

In 1891, Congress created *forest reserves*, or government-owned forests from which loggers were banned. Over the next ten years, Presidents Benjamin Harrison, Grover Cleveland, and William McKinley protected 46 million acres (18.4 million hectares) of valuable forest land from *exploitation*. Roosevelt, in less time, added another 125 million acres (50 million hectares). He also made Gifford Pinchot Chief Forester, and transferred authority over what were then called national forests from the *Interior Department* to the Agriculture Department, where Pinchot believed they would be safer.

Roosevelt also applied conservation to grasslands, which irresponsible cattlemen had allowed their stock to over-graze. Over-grazed land was often permanently destroyed for use as cattle land, since over-grazed land grew back in weeds useless to cattle.

Forests and grasslands could be recovered. However, there were resources that could not be replaced. Roosevelt refused to allow exploitation of 68 million acres (27 million hectares) of coal deposits, 5 million acres (2 million hectares) of phosphate beds (vital to munitions production and, therefore, to national defense), a number of oil fields, and 2,565 sites suitable for the construction of dams for irrigation and hydroelectric production.

The *Newlands Reclamation Act* of 1902 allowed money raised by the sale of federal lands in arid areas to pay for the development of irrigation projects as well as for the *reclamation* of land that had been damaged by unrestricted exploitation in the past.

Roosevelt Loses a Battle.

The President's conservation policy was designed to save the exploiters from themselves. Allowed to do as they chose, the lumber, cattle, coal mining, and other interests would have destroyed the natural resources on which they and the nation depended. Over the last third of the nineteenth century, they had gone a long way toward doing just that for the sake of profits.

Some lumber companies understood the need for conservation. They hired professional foresters who introduced the principle of *sustained yield*, or tree-farming, to privately owned forests. That is, instead of cutting down a forest completely and leaving it that way, which let erosion destroy the land, lumber companies began to harvest their crop. They logged only parts of forests and immediately replanted the cut-over areas with new trees that would supply the nation's demand for wood products in half a century.

In some western states, however, lumber companies handed Roosevelt his first important congressional setback. In 1907 a bill authorizing the government to pay for certain basic services was moving through Congress. It was not a conservation bill, but congressional friends of the lumber companies added a section to it that forbade the president to reserve any additional forestland in the states of Washington, Oregon, Idaho, Montana, Wyoming, and Colorado.

Roosevelt had no choice but to sign the bill. Refusing to do so would have also killed the main part of the bill. But he enjoyed one last blow at his critics. Before he wrote his name on the bill, he reserved 17 million additional acres (7 million hectares) of forest in the six states.

After 40 years of pressure on Congress, the Forest Reserve Act, passed in 1891, was the first attempt at legislating conservation in the U.S.

Roosevelt Steps Down.

Roosevelt was elected to the presidency only once, in 1904, but by 1908 he would have served nearly two full terms. Technically, though, he could have run again. But he agreed with the unwritten rule set down by Washington, Jefferson, and Jackson. During the 1904 election campaign he announced, "the wise custom which limits the President to two terms regards the substance and not the form, and under no circumstances will I be a candidate for or accept another nomination."

By 1908, he almost certainly regretted his promise. He loved being president, and a large majority of the American people loved having him in the White House. Furthermore, he had problems with Congress. In two major speeches, Roosevelt proposed a comprehensive reform program for settling labor disputes fairly, regulating the stock market, and giving the federal government powers to regulate all businesses engaged in interstate commerce. Looking forward to a new president in 1908, however, conservatives in Congress cheerfully ignored every proposal.

Roosevelt Chooses Taft.

The President had to content himself with hand-picking his successor, something no president had been powerful enough to do since Andrew Jackson in 1836. He selected his Secretary of War, William Howard Taft.

Taft would never have been nominated nor would he have run for the office without Roosevelt's blessing. Taft sensed he was not meant for the job. He peppered his letters with the phrase, "I hate politics!" His only other run for election had been for a judgeship in his native state of Ohio. He disliked controversy as much as he disliked running for office. But he was an excellent judge and administrator and would eventually become *Chief Justice* of the *Supreme Court*.

Still, Taft had been doggedly faithful to Roosevelt and served him well. Roosevelt calculated that Taft would carry on the Progressive policies.

The Election of 1908.

In 1908, Taft's Democratic party opponent was William Jennings Bryan. Running for the third time, Bryan was no longer the electrifying "Boy Orator of the Platte." He was middle-aged and getting paunchy. On the speaker's platform, he now was uninspiring.

The Democrats reversed their 1904 strategy and depicted the Republican party as the party of big business and privilege, with themselves as the friends of the common person. It was a lame and unpersuasive argument with crusading Theodore Roosevelt, whom many businesspeople still disliked, campaigning for Taft.

The only excitement in the campaign was provided by the Socialist party. Convinced they were on the verge of becoming a major force in American politics, the Socialists chartered a train, dubbed it the "Red Special," and sent candidate Eugene V. Debs on a nationwide tour. Debs was the thrilling orator that Bryan had once been and Taft would never be. Debs drew larger audiences than the major candidates.

But people came to hear Debs because of a personal fondness for him and a love of a good show. In the polling booth, they chose Taft or Bryan. Despite the expense of the "Red Special," the Socialist party won only 17,000 votes more than it had won in 1904. It appeared that Roosevelt's anti-Socialist strategy was correct. By reforming the worst practices of big business, he had undercut the appeal of anti-capitalist philosophies.

Although Taft's margin of victory was not as great as Roosevelt's in 1904, he still *garnered* 51.6 percent of the vote, and 321 electoral votes to Bryan's 162. Debs received no electoral votes.

SECTION REVIEW

1. Write a sentence to identify: adulterants, John Muir, Gifford Pinchot, forest reserves.

2. With what belief about the impact of the Socialist party did Roosevelt begin his second term? Explain why this was or was not a valid belief.

3. Identify the practices that the following laws were meant to control: Newlands Reclamation Act, Hepburn Act, Pure Food and Drug Acts, Elkins Act.

4. Why did Roosevelt not run for a third term in 1908? Name the candidates of the three parties in this election, and tell which candidate succeeded Roosevelt.

Taft was distinguished among U.S. presidents in two ways: he was the only president who was also Chief Justice of the Supreme Court, and he was the heaviest president, weighing in at 352 pounds.

PROFILES OF THE
PRESIDENCY

Defeated for re-election. William Taft had some tongue-in-cheek remarks to make on the subject of what to do with ex-presidents:

What are we to do with our ex-presidents?... a dose of chloroform or of the fruit of the lotus tree, and the reduction of the flesh of the thus quietly departed to ashes in a funeral pyre to satisfy the wishes of his friends and their families, might make a fitting end to the life of one who has held the highest office, and at the same time would secure the country from the troublesome fear that the occupant could ever come back. His record would have been made by one term and his demise in the honorable ceremony... would relieve the country of thinking how he is to support himself and his family, would fix his place in history, and enable the public to pass on to new men and new measures.

—SPEECH, NOVEMBER 16, 1913

3. THE TAFT PRESIDENCY

The presidency of William Howard Taft is oddly reminiscent of the presidencies of John Adams and his son, John Quincy Adams. Like them, Taft had the bad luck to take over after an immensely popular two-term president. Like the Adamses, Taft lacked the personality the era demanded. He belonged to an earlier age, just as the Adamses had clung to ideals that had gone out of fashion.

Like the Adamses, Taft was a failure as chief executive. He lost the support of a large part of his own party, and he angered representatives of rising political forces and suffered from their opposition at every turn. And, finally, like both Adamses, he ran for reelection in the face of certain defeat and was smothered in the political landslide of 1912.

Taft's Accomplishments. Only months after Taft took office, Progressives were condemning him as a *reactionary*, someone who wants to reverse progress, and as a tool of big business. This was unfair. Taft believed that reform was necessary, and sponsored twice as many antitrust suits as Roosevelt had. The *Mann-Elkins Act* of 1910 gave the ICC authority to regulate telephone, telegraph, cable, and wireless (radio) companies. Taft's administration also cut the workday of companies with government contracts to no more than eight hours.

Taft won his conservative reputation more for his style than for his sentiments. Where Roosevelt would have surrounded the signing of the Mann-

After 1910, telephone companies, with their huge switchboards, were regulated by the government.

Discussion Question: Why was Taft, who began 90 anti-trust suits and supported many reforms, cast as a Progressive?

Elkins Act with fanfare and pronouncements of a glorious new era, Taft merely signed his name. To Taft, the president's job was not to take the initiative, or the publicity, of government but to act as chief administrator and let Congress take the lead. This was very much a nineteenth-century view of the presidency and it, as much as his political blunders, cost Taft the support of the Progressives of his own party.

The Tariff Issue.

Traditionally, the Democrats supported low tariffs, and the Republicans urged high tariffs that would protect American industry from foreign competition. In 1909, however, progressive Republicans also wanted the tariff lowered. Tariff rates, set by the *Dingley Tariff* of 1897, were 57 percent of the value of imports. To Progressives from the midwestern farm states, such a tax was unnecessary. They argued that American industry, far from needing protection from foreign competitors, was now the most powerful in the world, able to undersell the manufacturers of any other country.

These Progressives saw the Dingley rates as nothing more than a generous *subsidy* of big business, since American industrialists who sold cheaply abroad overcharged *consumers* at home. American farmers were twice stung. The Dingley *tariff* had forced most European countries to raise import taxes on American farm products, thus cutting demand.

It was a good Progressive argument, proconsumer and antiprivilege. Taft seemed to agree. He called Congress into special session early in 1909 for the specific purpose of lowering the tariff.

The Republican Split Begins.

In the House of Representatives, progressive Republicans teamed up with Democrats to pass the low-tariff Payne bill. In the Senate, however, Nelson Aldrich of Rhode Island, a spokesman for big business, attached 800 *amendments* to the bill. Although the bill decreased rates overall when it was finally passed, the *Payne-Aldrich Tariff* actually increased rates on many items.

Instead of vetoing a bill quite unlike what he had called for, Taft signed it. He even praised the Payne-Aldrich law as the best tariff law in the nation's history. Robert La Follette, Jonathan Dolliver of Iowa, Albert Beveridge of Indiana, and other progressive Republicans denounced him in harsher terms than even the Democrats used.

Taft was somewhat bewildered by the criticism. He believed he had served Progressive purposes with the Payne-Aldrich Tariff. It did not lower import taxes much, but it did include a one percent tax on corporate profits. Taft also announced his support for a constitutional amendment that would allow a graduated income tax. That is, the government would be able to tax the income of the wealthy at a higher rate than it taxed the income of poorer people. The Sixteenth Amendment, which embodied this idea, was eventually ratified in 1913.

The Insurgents Break With Taft.

Relations between Taft and the Republican Progressives worsened when Taft supported Illinois Congressman Joseph G. Cannon in a battle for control of the House of Representatives. Cannon, known without much affection as "Uncle Joe," had served in the House for 50 years. As the Republican with the most seniority, he was Speaker of the House and used his powers like a dictator.

Cannon appointed Progressives to unimportant committees only. During debate, he often refused

President Roosevelt poses with president-elect Taft before Taft's inauguration in 1909.

Discussion Question: Was Taft a failure as president? If so, why? Have students defend their answers with tangible evidence to support their views.

to recognize them. He also offended Progressives because of his blatant pro-business prejudices.

Calling themselves *Insurgents* (rebels), Republican Progressives joined with House Democrats in 1910 to curtail Cannon's powers. In retaliation, Taft refused to allow them to use funds that the party had raised in the midterm election of 1910. This action, on top of everything else, cost Taft a lot politically. The Democrats gained control of the House for the first time in 16 years. The Socialists also increased their local strength, winning control of several dozen cities.

Conservationists Attack the President.

Taft, who agreed in general with conservationist aims, reserved 59 million acres (24 million hectares) of coal lands, protecting them against exploitation. He also kept Gifford Pinchot on as Chief Forester, and appointed Richard A. Ballinger, an outdoorsman known to be a supporter of conservation, Secretary of the Interior.

However, Taft was much more cautious about using presidential powers than Roosevelt had been. A strict constitutionalist, Taft believed that the president's authority in the matter of conservation was strictly limited. Interior Secretary Ballinger agreed with him and reopened several hundred hydroelectric sites to private development, claiming that they had been wrongly reserved.

Although the Forest Service had no *jurisdiction* over the sites, Pinchot protested loudly to Taft. Taken aback, Taft agreed with Pinchot and overruled Ballinger's action. However, when Ballinger later opened government reserves of forest and coal lands in Alaska to private exploitation, Taft ignored Pinchot's protests and sided with the Secretary of the Interior.

Pinchot and Roosevelt Join the Opposition.

Pinchot seethed with anger. When another government official, Louis Glavis, wrote an article for the muckraking magazine *Collier's* attacking Ballinger, Pinchot supported Glavis. Taft had no choice but to fire Pinchot. Pinchot immediately booked passage to Italy, where Teddy Roosevelt was vacationing.

Roosevelt had left the country soon after leaving the White House. In part he did so because he recognized that Taft's personality was pale com-

pared to his own and he wanted to give his successor a fair chance.

But even from abroad, Roosevelt made better news than Taft. He hunted game in Africa, shooting some 3,000 animals. He represented the United States at the funeral of King Edward VII, and managed to upstage the largest assembly of queens, kings, and emperors in European history. Everywhere he went he was idolized. But by 1910, he was also disillusioned with Taft. He was prepared to hear the worst when his old friend Pinchot arrived in Italy.

The New Nationalism.

Roosevelt returned to his home at Oyster Bay, New York, in June 1910. Instead of paying a call on Taft, he contacted many old followers, who added their criticisms to Pinchot's. At first, Roosevelt seemed to play down the split in the party. Then, in September 1910, in a speech at Osawatomie, Kansas, he proclaimed a progressive program for America that he called the *New Nationalism.*

The New Nationalism went much further than Roosevelt had dared to go when he was president. He called for women's suffrage, an issue he had wavered on in the past. He demanded the restriction of child labor, strict limitations on the power of courts to issue *injunctions* against labor unions, and a national retirement insurance scheme that closely resembles today's Social Security system.

Roosevelt also demanded the establishment of a national commission that would set tariff rates "scientifically." He supported the initiative, recall, and referendum, and called for a provision allowing a referendum on court decisions. This in itself was enough to raise the hackles of the legalistic Taft. When Roosevelt added that he wanted a national primary to replace political conventions in nominating presidential candidates, it became clear what he had in mind. Although he had refused to admit it for nearly two years, he wanted to be president again.

Roosevelt Runs for President.

Taft was not the only political leader who worried about Roosevelt's ambitions. Robert La Follette had decided to challenge Taft for the Republican nomination in 1910. As he rounded up Progressive delegates, he discovered that many preferred Roosevelt as a candidate. Through mutual friends, La Follette asked Roosevelt what his intentions were. Roosevelt waffled but indicated that he was not interested in returning to Washington.

Then, in February 1912, La Follette collapsed from exhaustion during a speech. Although he recovered within days, Roosevelt used the opportunity to declare his candidacy. Progressives deserted La Follette in droves and Roosevelt easily won the primaries in states that held them. Of the 362 delegates chosen in primary elections, Roosevelt won 278 to Taft's 48 and La Follette's 36.

As president, Taft may have lacked Roosevelt's popularity, but he did control the party machinery. Federal officeholders owed their jobs to him and, in the nonprimary states, they picked the delegates to the convention. Taft also controlled the party's major committees. When the committee on credentials awarded 235 of 254 disputed votes to Taft, it was clear that Roosevelt could not win the nomination. Chanting "naked thief," the Progressives walked out of the Republican convention and held one of their own.

At the highly charged Progressive convention, delegates sang as though they were setting forth on a crusade. Roosevelt encouraged the crusading spirit, and, in a reference to La Follette's alleged ill health, he told Progressives that he was "as fit as a Bull Moose." Thus did the Progressive party get its symbol, to compete with the Republican elephant and the Democratic donkey.

SECTION REVIEW

1. Write a sentence to identify: Mann-Elkins Act, Sixteenth Amendment, Insurgents, New Nationalism.

2. Prove or disprove this statement with facts from the text: "It was unfair for Progressives to label President Taft with the term *reactionary*."

3. Explain how President Taft's actions with respect to the following angered progressive Republicans and led to a split in the Republican party: the Payne-Aldrich Tariff, "Uncle Joe" Cannon's methods as Speaker of the House, Interior Secretary Ballinger's decisions on conservation.

4. Trace the circumstances that led to the formation of the Progressive party with Theodore Roosevelt as its presidential candidate.

---

4. DEMOCRATIC PARTY PROGRESSIVISM

United, the Republican party was clearly the majority party, but once it lost its progressive wing to the *Bull Moose party*, the Republicans did not have a chance to win the election of 1912. Roosevelt and the Progressives believed their party did have a chance. If the Democrats nominated William Jennings Bryan again or named a conservative like Taft, the Progressives expected to ride the wave of reform into Washington.

Woodrow Wilson. After 46 ballots, however, the Democratic convention nominated Woodrow Wilson, a man who had been practically unknown until two years earlier, when he was elected governor of New Jersey and won a reputation for honesty, integrity, and a refusal to deal with corrupt party bosses. Wilson was actually a southerner. He had been born in Virginia and had practiced law in Georgia before becoming a pro-

Progressives chose Teddy Roosevelt, who said he was "fit as a Bull Moose," as their candidate for president at their 1912 national convention.

fessor of history and political science. As president of New Jersey's Princeton University, the stern Wilson had fought against elitist fraternities known as "eating clubs" and had transformed Princeton from a finishing school for rich men into an intellectually demanding institution.

In 1910, Wilson won the Democratic party nomination for governor because the party bosses thought it would be easy to control "the professor." Wilson accepted machine support. But he was more independent than the bosses knew.

The New Freedom.

As the Democratic presidential nominee, Wilson proclaimed his program as the *New Freedom*. By emphasizing states' rights and breaking up the trusts rather than regulating them, Wilson's platform echoed the Democratic party's traditional goals, which appealed to southern and rural states. Wilson wanted to restore competition in economic life, and he condemned Roosevelt's demand that the economy be regulated and managed as "a partnership between the government and the trusts."

Wilson won about 6.2 million popular votes, or only 42 percent of the total. But the Republican majority vote was split down the middle. Roosevelt won slightly more than 4 million votes and Taft won less than 3.5 million. The Socialists reached their highest total, with more than 900,000 voters choosing Debs. This allowed Wilson to sweep the electoral college with 435 votes to Roosevelt's 88 and Taft's 8.

Wilson's Cabinet.

Aware of his party's weakness, Wilson tried to unify the Democrats by including in his cabinet a representative of every Democratic faction. Although he had never liked William Jennings Bryan, Wilson named him to be Secretary of State. Bryan was still popular in the rural South and Midwest.

As Secretary of Labor he named William B. Wilson, a congressman from Pennsylvania with strong connections to the AFL. His Secretary of the Treasury was William McAdoo of Georgia (later California), a brilliant lawyer who provided Wilson with good advice on financial questions.

Wilson's three chief advisors did not sit in the cabinet. Joseph Tumulty, Wilson's private secretary, advised him on political reactions in the Northeast. Colonel Edward M. House, a Texan, acted as Wilson's informal contact with influential people both at home and abroad. Self-effacing and completely dedicated to the President, House preferred not to hold an official job.

Louis D. Brandeis, a Progressive corporation lawyer who became an opponent of trusts, provided Wilson with both his New Freedom program and a conscience. When, in 1914, Brandeis realized the limitations of the New Freedom program, he helped to persuade Wilson to move closer to the principles supported by Theodore Roosevelt.

Tariff and Tax Reform.

The Republican split not only elected Wilson, it gave him Democratic majorities in both houses of Congress. With support from the Insurgents on most issues, the President moved quickly to lower the tariff and to adopt progressive tax legislation.

The *Underwood Tariff* of 1913 lowered import duties from about 40 percent to less than 30 percent. The new law also added many items to the *duty-free* list. Among them were several commodities, including iron, steel, woolen goods, and farm machinery, that were controlled by trusts.

After ratification of the Sixteenth Amendment made a graduated income tax constitutional, Congress levied taxes that hit the wealthy harder than they hit lower- and middle-income groups. People with incomes of less than $4,000 a year—good pay in 1913—paid no tax at all. On an annual income of between $4,000 and $20,000, the tax was one percent. People in the highest bracket, with more than $500,000 a year, paid a tax of six percent.

The Federal Reserve System.

The *Federal Reserve Act* of 1913 was a compromise between conservatives and Progressives. Conservatives in both the Democratic and Republican parties preferred to leave banking entirely to the private sector. Progressives of both parties, on the other hand, wanted the government to set up a central bank to regulate the amount of money in circulation and to have the power to control private banks.

The Federal Reserve System established 12 district banks and a semi-public central bank. While the highest officials were appointed by the president, the System was privately owned and was not under direct government control. As chartered by the Act, Federal Reserve banks dealt

The Democratic donkey and the Republican elephant were created by the political cartoonist, Thomas Nast, and are still in use today.

During Wilson's presidency, practically the entire national government was run by southerners.

*D*espite Woodrow Wilson's passionate urging, the United States did not join the League of Nations after World War I:

The isolation of the United States is at an end, not because we chose to go into the politics of the world, but because by the sheer genius of this people and the growth of our power we have become a determining factor in the history of mankind, and after you have become a determining factor you cannot remain isolated, whether you want to or not . . . I do not say it because I am an American and my heart is full of the same pride that fills yours with regard to the power and spirit of this great Nation, but merely because . . . the League of Nations without the United States would merely be an alliance and not a league of nations. There can be no league of nations in the true sense without the partnership of this great people.

—SPEECH, SEPTEMBER 6, 1919

only with other banks. By increasing or decreasing the amount of money in circulation, the Federal Reserve exerted some control over the economy.

The Clayton Act.   In 1914, Congress enacted the antitrust policy of Wilson's New Freedom program as the *Clayton Antitrust Act.* Unlike the vagueness of the old Sherman Act, this law carefully defined the unfair business practices for which a corporation could be punished.

One of those illegal practices was the establishment of interlocking directorates, in which the

Lines such as this one could be seen at income tax windows in 1918. The graduated tax favored low- and middle-income groups. Many people found that they owed no tax at all.

Samuel Gompers referred to the Clayton Act as the Magna Carta of Labor. This was overstated since the act did very little to change the status of unions.

same people sat on the boards of directors of several companies engaged in the same business. By declaring interlocking directorates illegal, the government eliminated the chief loophole by which J. P. Morgan and other bankers had avoided prosecution in the past. Another loophole was closed as the Clayton Act held officers of corporations personally responsible for violations of the law carried out by their companies. That is, businessmen who carried out illegal policies could be fined and imprisoned for their actions, whereas they had previously been able to claim they were just doing what stockholders demanded.

Wilson Changes Direction.

Curiously, Wilson did not use the trust-busting powers of the Clayton Act to their fullest. Just when antitrust forces finally had a law under which they could effectively strike at big business, their leader began to have second thoughts about the advisability of doing so. Furthermore, in 1914, the President approved the establishment of the *Federal Trade Commission (FTC),* which seemed more in line with Roosevelt's New Nationalism than with Wilson's New Freedom.

The FTC was designed not to break up corporations but to control them. The five members of the commission, appointed by the President, were empowered to demand annual reports from major corporations, to investigate unfair business practices, and to order corporations to cease unfair practices.

In the *Smith-Lever Act* of 1914, Wilson also adopted a Roosevelt proposal he had condemned only two years earlier. This law provided direct federal funding to schools in rural areas too poor to maintain high educational standards. Smith-Lever allowed direct federal intervention into affairs traditionally considered to be state or local matters, a position that Wilson, a states-rights southerner, had fought against for years.

More New Nationalism.

By 1916, Wilson had adopted most of the 1912 Progressive party platform. The *Federal Farm Loan Act* provided easy, government-backed loans for farmers. The *Adamson Act* required railroads involved in interstate commerce to institute the eight-hour day without reducing workers' wages.

The *Keating-Owen Act* of 1916 strictly regulated the employment of children in most jobs. In signing it, Wilson approved a law that he firmly believed was unconstitutional. Indeed, in 1916, after a lifetime of firm support for racial segregation, Wilson eased his antiblack policies. He even hinted that he might support a constitutional amendment guaranteeing the right of women to vote, another position he had opposed throughout his political career.

By 1916 Wilson converted to a program that is best described as the Republican Progressive program. One reason for his conversion was the approaching presidential election of 1916. All signs indicated that the Progressive party was about to break up, with Roosevelt's supporters from 1912 returning to the Republican party. Wilson's only chance to win reelection was to convince the Progressive voters that he was more likely to continue reform than anyone the reunited Republicans named to oppose him.

Wilson's second reason for putting his name to policies he had formerly opposed was his waning interest in domestic issues. Wilson found more and more of his attention drawn to foreign affairs. In 1914, the European powers had fallen into a terrible war that raged across the continent. By 1916, the conflict was starting to spread across the Atlantic Ocean. The United States was a major trading partner of all the European nations, and both sides in the conflict wanted American support. Once again, Americans were on the brink of a war that was seemingly not their concern.

SECTION REVIEW

1. Write a sentence to identify: Keating-Owen Act, Colonel Edward M. House, Underwood Tariff, Smith-Lever Act.

2. What two factors allowed Democratic presidential candidate Woodrow Wilson to sweep the electoral college in 1912?

3. Describe the three basic points in President Wilson's New Freedom program. Why did he convert to a program more like Roosevelt's New Nationalism?

4. Give the essential facts about graduated income tax, Federal Reserve System, Clayton Antitrust Act, FTC.

Class Activity: Have students make a time line from 1870 to 1916 that lists 10 to 15 reform acts, labeled as either Progressive or Populist.

This airplane built by Wilbur and Orville Wright made four controlled, engine-powered flights, the first in history, in 1903. The longest of the flights lasted 57 seconds.

Thomas Edison accidentally invented the phonograph in 1877 while working on a carbon transmitter for telephones. It took ten years before the device was perfected.

Experimental radio stations began operating in 1915. Soon stations sprang up all over the country. From 1925 to 1950 radio was a main source of family entertainment.

C H A N G I N G   T E C H N O L O G Y

	18	80		18	90	

Antiseptic first used	Steam shovel invented	Traction engine designed
Watches mass produced	Practical refrigerator developed	Air-cooled transformer patented
Helium gas discovered	Firemen's respirator invented	Ballpoint pen developed
Onimeter for surveying designed	Tarmac roads introduced	Taxi cabs introduced
Ever-pointed pencil patented	Tidal analyzer designed	

Discussion Question: How did the policies of Roosevelt, Taft, and Wilson reflect Progressive demands? Include each one's view of the presidency, means of regulating business, support for reforms and types of reforms, personal style and personality, and racial attitudes.

Aviation came into its own during World War I with the dogfighter. At first the planes were little more than motorized kites used for reconnaissance, but gradually they became the foundation of an American air force.

Henry Ford's Model T, first marketed in 1908, transformed the automobile from a toy for the rich into an everyday item.

19	10	19	20
X-ray examinations used	Offshore oil wells drilled	Aircraft carrier flight
Motion picture projected on	Zeppelin built	introduced
screen	Electric typewriter manufactured	Cellophane manufactured
Escalators introduced	Non-shatter safety glass	Stainless steel discovered
	introduced	Tractor-trailer produced

Discussion Question: With the onset of a major war looming in Europe, how might Henry Ford's concept of the assembly line have revolutionized war? Answers should include the fact that weaponry could be produced faster and in greater quantity.

585

CHAPTER REVIEW

TIME LINE

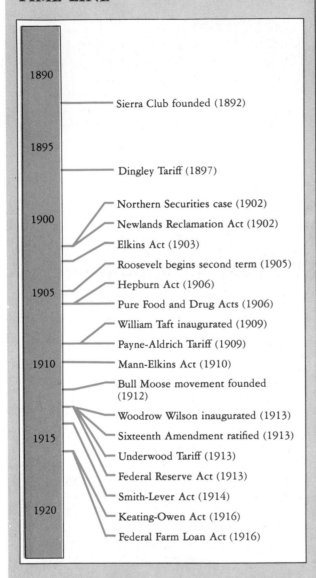

1890

Sierra Club founded (1892)

1895

Dingley Tariff (1897)

Northern Securities case (1902)

1900

Newlands Reclamation Act (1902)

Elkins Act (1903)

Roosevelt begins second term (1905)

Hepburn Act (1906)

1905

Pure Food and Drug Acts (1906)

William Taft inaugurated (1909)

Payne-Aldrich Tariff (1909)

1910

Mann-Elkins Act (1910)

Bull Moose movement founded (1912)

Woodrow Wilson inaugurated (1913)

Sixteenth Amendment ratified (1913)

1915

Underwood Tariff (1913)

Federal Reserve Act (1913)

Smith-Lever Act (1914)

1920

Keating-Owen Act (1916)

Federal Farm Loan Act (1916)

TIME LINE QUESTIONS

1. How many terms did Theodore Roosevelt serve as president of the United States?
2. List two years that were significant to conservation in the United States.
3. Name the events that happened *before* Wilson's inauguration: (a) Northern Securities case, (b) Federal Reserve Act, (c) Payne-Aldrich Tariff, (d) Elkins Act.

SKILLS STRATEGY

CARD CATALOGS

Every library has a catalog of all the books on its shelves. Although the catalog may be in book form or in computer form, most often it is a chest of small drawers filled with cards that give the location and other information about every book in the library. The drawers are arranged alphabetically, as are the cards inside. The catalog cards are meant to help you find the books that you are looking for.

There are three catalog cards for each book in the library. If you know the title of a book you need, the *title card* will help you find it. Title cards are arranged alphabetically by the first word in the title other than *A, An,* or *The.* If you know the name of the author of a book, the *author card* will help you find it. Author cards are arranged alphabetically by the author's last name. If you want to find books on particular subjects, the *subject cards* will help. They are arranged alphabetically, and the subjects are printed in capital letters.

Find each kind of catalog card in the exhibit above. Notice that each card is for the same book, and that the same call number is given in the upper left corner of each.

  Making Connections: Review the questions and topics presented in the Making Connections section that opens this chapter.

```
973.91    The era of Theodore Roosevelt,
  M         1900–1912
          Mowry, G.E.
            The era of Theodore Roosevelt,
          1900–1912. New York, Harper &
          Row, 1958
          416 p. illus


973.91    PRESIDENTS—U.S.
  M       Mowry, G.E.
            The era of Theodore Roosevelt,
          1900–1912. New York, Harper &
          Row, 1958
          416 p. illus


973.91    Mowry, G.E.
  M         The era of Theodore Roosevelt,
          1900–1912. New York, Harper &
          Row, 1958
          416 p. illus
```

The call number directs you to the shelf on which you will find the book. The first three numbers tell you that the books are nonfiction works of American history, and the first letter of the author's last name appears after each call number.

To find the book, go to the nonfiction section where the history (900) books are shelved numerically in the order of their call numbers. Then look at the call numbers on the spines of the books until you find the call number of the book you want.

Remember that works of fiction are shelved alphabetically by authors' last names in the library's fiction section. Biographies are shelved alphabetically by the last names of the people about whom the biographies are written in the nonfiction section.

APPLYING SKILLS

Make three different catalog cards for the book in the exhibit above. Make up the following information: the location of the publisher, the date of publication, the number of pages, and whether there are illustrations or not.

CHAPTER 24 TEST

TEXT REVIEW

1. Discuss the reasons why Theodore Roosevelt allied himself with the Progressives.
2. Give President Roosevelt's motive for introducing to Congress several reform bills at the beginning of his second term.
3. Give the important details about governmental actions during Roosevelt's second term related to harnessing the railroads and curbing destructive exploitation of natural resources.
4. What did Roosevelt expect William Howard Taft to do as president? Did Taft fulfill Roosevelt's expectations? Give at least one example to support your answer.
5. Trace the causes for the formation of the Progressive (Bull Moose) party.
6. How did President Wilson's political program change between 1912 and 1916? Give two important reasons for this change.
7. Why did Eugene V. Debs draw large audiences but few votes?
8. Briefly explain how each of the following affected American business practices: Clayton Act, FTC, Adamson Act, Keating-Owens Act.

CRITICAL THINKING

9. Why did Teddy Roosevelt say he would not run for a third term? Considering his personality, speculate on a motive for his public announcement of his decision.
10. What bias might Roosevelt have had in proposing a national primary to nominate presidential candidates?

WRITING A PARAGRAPH

Theodore Roosevelt was a very popular president, and Americans frequently exchanged their fond reactions to his latest "doings." Select an event from the chapter in which Roosevelt was involved. Write a first person, one-paragraph reaction to the event. Then make up a title, a publisher, and other information that you would need to enter a book about Roosevelt in a card catalog.

AMERICA GOES TO WAR

1914–1920

A peace
Which will again betray
Those silent men,
The dead.

EUGENE O'NEILL

Making Connections. President Woodrow Wilson was devoted to the cause of peace. Ironically, he would become the first American president to send soldiers to fight in a major European war. World events proved stronger than Wilson's good intentions.

In this chapter, you will learn:
- Why Wilson sent troops into Mexico
- What events led the European nations into a major war in 1914
- Where Americans fought major battles that helped turn the tide of the war
- How the United States government tried to control the American economy, political dissent, and the press
- What Wilson's Fourteen Points were, and why he hoped they would prevent future wars
- Why Wilson failed to get the United States into the League of Nations

You know that the United States fought a war with Spain in 1898, and thus began to take a greater role in world affairs. Therefore, when World War I broke out in Europe, many Americans feared the United States would become involved. As you read, note how Wilson tried to keep the country neutral, and what events spelled failure for his efforts.

Sections
1. Wilson, America, and the World
2. The Great War
3. Americans Go to War
4. Planning the War Effort
5. The League of Nations

1. WILSON, AMERICA, AND THE WORLD

Like most Americans, President Wilson was proud that the United States was a major industrial power, and he believed that the United States was unique among nations. While other countries schemed and made war to serve selfish interests, Wilson believed that his country upheld the highest principles of justice and morality.

Moral Diplomacy. Because his principles were so strict, Wilson disliked Theodore Roosevelt's *"gunboat diplomacy."* He believed it was wrong for the United States to bully small nations. Wilson proclaimed that his administration would deal with the weak Latin American republics "upon terms of equality and honor."

As a Progressive who was suspicious of big business, Wilson also disapproved of President Taft's *"dollar diplomacy."* Taft had assured Wall Street investors that the government would protect a big investment they intended to make in China. To Wilson this meant using American armed forces and spilling soldiers' blood to protect the interests of wealthy bankers. He canceled Taft's pledge and the investment plan fell apart.

This painting by the American artist Andrew Wyeth captures the front-line drama of a moment of surrender as battle-weary German troops surrender to allied forces in 1918.

Quotation: from the poem "Fragments." Other works by the Nobel Prize-winning playwright Eugene O'Neill (1888–1953) include *Beyond the Horizon, Emperor Jones, Anna Christie, The Hairy Ape, Strange Interlude, Mourning Becomes Electra, Ah, Wilderness!; The Iceman Cometh,* and *Long Day's Journey Into Night.*

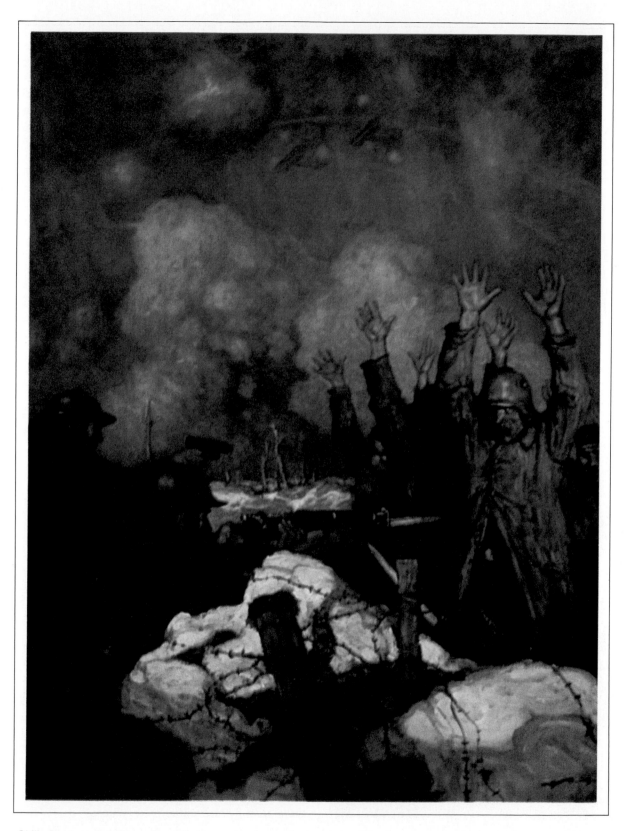

Skills Review: Reinforce the skills learned in the preceding Skills Strategy section. Use the library card catalog to compile a reading list on Mexican and American leaders of the Mexican-American War.

Wilson's Secretary of State, William Jennings Bryan, was strongly opposed to war. As a result, Bryan negotiated "cooling off" treaties with 30 nations. These agreements pledged signers to hold back, or "cool off" for a period of one year when war was threatened. Bryan believed that almost every international dispute could be resolved peacefully if only leaders of nations would pause and think about the horrors that war would mean for their people.

Limits of Moral Diplomacy.

Despite their preference for peace, Wilson, Bryan, and most Americans were also influenced by feelings that could at times defeat their high ideals. When other countries did not act in a way that he thought moral or proper, Wilson was inclined to intervene with military force. He ordered the marines into Haiti in 1915 when rebellion threatened American interests. In 1916, Wilson also used marines to take control of financial and administrative affairs in the Dominican Republic. The marines would not be fully withdrawn from either Caribbean nation until 1924.

These American marines were assigned to keep order in Port-au-Prince and to protect Americans in Haiti during the rebellion of 1915.

The Mexican Revolution.

Mexico presented Wilson with his first major challenge in foreign policy. In 1911, a popular revolutionary leader, Francisco Madero, overthrew the 34-year dictatorship of Porfirio Diaz. This change in leadership worried foreigners who had invested in Mexican property. Diaz had encouraged their investment in return for financial support of his regime. Americans alone owned $1 billion in Mexican mines, oil wells, ranches, and railroads. More than 50,000 American citizens lived south of the Rio Grande.

A short time after winning power, Madero was murdered and replaced by a general, Victoriano Huerta. Huerta intended to protect foreign investors. Nations with large Mexican holdings, including Great Britain, quickly recognized Huerta's government.

But Wilson refused to do so. He called Huerta's government immoral and undemocratic, which it surely was. Nevertheless, in making the virtue of a foreign government the basis of *recognition* or nonrecognition, Wilson was departing from a realistic custom. The United States had recognized the Diaz government for a generation although it was undemocratic. Thus, the break with Huerta was shocking to the Mexicans.

Undeclared War in Mexico.

Wilson's decision led him to interfere in Mexican affairs. When General Venustiano Carranza rebelled against Huerta, Wilson allowed arms to reach Carranza. At the same time the American navy blockaded Mexican ports so that Huerta could not receive weapons purchased in Europe.

In April 1914, some American sailors from the blockade were on shore in Tampico. They were arrested by one of Huerta's colonels. When he realized this could provoke the United States to attack, he immediately released the men with apologies to the fleet.

That was not enough for Admiral Henry T. Mayo. He demanded a 21-gun salute from the Mexicans to show deference to the Americans. To have done so would have been humiliating, and the Mexicans refused. Wilson used the Tampico incident as an excuse to send marines to occupy the Mexican port of Vera Cruz. His real purpose was to prevent the landing at Vera Cruz of a German ship carrying arms to Huerta.

Although dropped with regard to Latin America, Wilson's recognition policy was used with respect to countries elsewhere. For example, it was used with regard to the U.S.S.R., which the U.S. didn't recognize until 1933, and with regard to Red China in the post-World War II period.

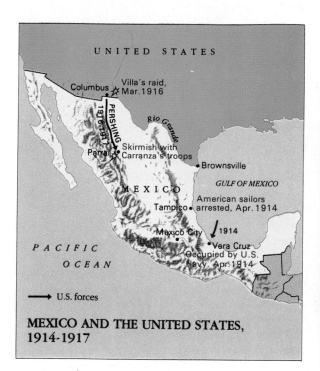

MEXICO AND THE UNITED STATES, 1914-1917

Two heroes of the Mexican Revolution, Pancho Villa (above) and Emiliano Zapata (below) also fought against Huerta and his successor, Carranza. Zapata's land redistribution plan was part of the 1917 Mexican constitution.

To the President's surprise, Mexican citizens in Vera Cruz joined the fight against the invading Americans. There were more than 400 casualties in the street fighting. Even Carranza, at that time moving toward Mexico City, condemned the American action. Alarmed, Wilson agreed to an offer from Argentina, Brazil, and Chile (the ABC powers) to mediate the dispute.

Pancho Villa Invades New Mexico. Within a few months, Carranza simplified the political confusion by defeating Huerta. Now, however, it was time for a rebellious Carranza general, Doroteo Arango, popularly known as Pancho Villa, to take center stage.

A colorful peasant leader and sometimes a plain bandit, Villa hoped to seize power from Carranza by provoking the United States into intervening in Mexico again. Villa stopped a Mexican train, ordered 17 American passengers off, and shot all but one. Early in 1916, he led a raid across the border into the dusty little desert town of Columbus, New Mexico, where his men killed 17 people.

Wilson could have demanded that Carranza punish Villa. Instead, he ordered General John J. Pershing to pursue Villa with 6,000 troops. It was an impossible mission. At home in the mountains

Discussion Question: How would you describe Woodrow Wilson's views on the use of morality and fairness in international politics?

591

"Black Jack" Pershing, who led the search for Pancho Villa, later gained fame in World War I.

of northern Mexico, Villa led Pershing on a zigzag chase for 300 miles (480 kilometers). Never once did the Americans catch sight of Villa's band. They did, however, exchange fire with soldiers loyal to Carranza, whom Wilson had originally supported. Over 40 lives were lost. While accomplishing nothing, Wilson succeeded in angering every faction in Mexican politics and adding to the bitter view many Mexicans had of the United States.

In January 1917, Wilson ordered Pershing to return home. By that time, the United States was facing an even more serious threat in the waters of the Atlantic.

SECTION REVIEW

1. Write a sentence to identify: "cooling off" treaties, Henry T. Mayo, ABC powers, John J. Pershing.
2. What were President Wilson's objections to "gunboat diplomacy" and "dollar diplomacy"? Did Wilson ever use either? Explain.
3. Establish connections among the following: Porfirio Diaz, Francisco Madero, Victoriano Huerta, Venustiano Carranza, Pancho Villa.
4. Explain the presence of an American fleet and American troops in Mexico.

---

2. THE GREAT WAR

What we now call World War I was originally known in Europe as the *Great War*. Though it lasted only four years (1914–1918) it was far more destructive of life and property than any previous war.

From the day the war began in the summer of 1914, Americans had given thanks that it was Europe's affair and had nothing to do with them. On August 4, 1914 President Woodrow Wilson proclaimed American *neutrality*. Days later, he asked Americans to be "neutral in fact as well as in name" and "impartial in thought as well as in action." But as the months passed, Americans learned that neutrality was more easily proclaimed than practiced.

The Origins of World War I. After the final defeat of Napoleon in 1815, Prince Metternich of Austria devised a system of international relations that he believed would prevent major wars in Europe. He called it the *balance of power.* Through a series of interlocking agreements, each European power—England, France, Prussia, Russia, Austria-Hungary, and Turkey—would find itself fighting a force of equal strength if it tried to start a war. In effect, the powers' expansionist tendencies would be kept in check by the threat of having to face several other powers in war.

This system began to weaken and came apart in the last years of the nineteenth century. Italy emerged as a nation, complicating the balance of power. Prussia unified most of Germany into an extremely powerful new state. The German Empire immediately began to challenge Great Britain and France in the race for colonies in Africa and Asia. And the once mighty Turkish empire became the "sick man of Europe," as Arabs and the Balkan peoples of southeastern Europe launched nationalistic rebellions and established the new nations of Greece, Bulgaria, Rumania, and Serbia (present-day Yugoslavia).

The Balance of Fear. By 1907, a simpler but more dangerous balance of power had emerged. In the *Triple Alliance* (also called the Central Powers), Germany was senior partner to Austria-Hungary and Italy with close relations with Turkey. In the *Triple Entente,* or Allied Powers,

---

Discussion Question: For what reasons did the U.S. enter World War I on the allied side? Give as many reasons as possible, and decide which was the most important.

Russia, France, and Great Britain agreed to support one another. Their major fear was Germany.

Russia also thought of itself as the protector of Bulgaria, Serbia, and other Slavic nations in the Balkans. England and France guaranteed the neutrality of Belgium, the small country perched precariously between France and Germany.

In the 1890s and early 1900s, the powers engaged in an arms race. Germany built a navy, although it had never had need for one before. This was a direct challenge to England, which responded by building *dreadnoughts*, or huge, heavily armed battleships. Although all of the powers thought their arms build-up would convince the other side not to attack, the new weapons simply ensured that the coming war would be terrible beyond imagination.

War Begins in the Balkans. On June 28, 1914, in the Austrian province of Bosnia, 19-year-old Gavrilo Princip assassinated the heir to the throne of Austria-Hungary, Franz Ferdinand. Princip was a Serbian who believed the Balkan states should be free of Austro-Hungarian rule.

With the approval of Kaiser Wilhelm II of Germany, the Austrian government issued an *ultimatum* to Serbia. The ultimatum contained many demands. Some the Serbians could accept, but others would have caused Serbia to give up its independence. The Austrians and Germans had carefully calculated the result of the ultimatum, and knew the Serbians would not be able to accept it. Both nations looked forward to an Austrian-Serbian war in which Austria would surely win. They hoped that Russia would not see the Serbian conflict as important enough to intervene. But Serbia did appeal to Russia for help, and Nicholas II, the Russian Czar (zär′), decided to order the massing of his huge army on Austria-Hungary's border. Fearing an attack, Kaiser Wilhelm declared war on Russia and its ally, France. Of course, when Germany declared war on France, England, as part of the Triple Entente, was also pulled into the war.

Deadlock. Germany's greatest strength was its excellent armies. Germany's weakness was that it had to divide its armies and fight on two fronts. In order to meet this challenge, the German General Staff devised the *Schlieffen Plan*.

Because France could mobilize more quickly than Russia, most of Germany's military power would first be hurled against France in the west. While giving up ground to Russia in the east, the army was supposed to surge through neutral Belgium in six days, occupy the Channel ports so England would not be able to land an army, capture Paris, knock France out of the war, and then deal with Russia on the eastern front.

It was a brilliant plan, but it was not carried to completion. The Belgians put up heroic resistance, and Germany took 18 days instead of six to march through that small country. This breathing spell enabled the British to land a large expeditionary force to help the French. Then, the German commanders lost their nerve. The Russians did not advance into German territory any faster than expected. Still, their advance prompted the German General Staff to send crack troops from the western front to fight the Russians.

This resulted in the spectacular German victory at Tannenberg in August 1914. But it also weakened the thrust to the west so that the French and British were finally able to stop the German advance on the outskirts of Paris. When scarcely begun, the war bogged down into deadlock. Two great armies dug into trenches and faced one another across a deadly "No Man's Land."

A Savage, Futile War. The battles of World War I produced unprecedented bloodshed. For example, on the first day of the Battle of the Somme in July 1916, 60,000 British soldiers were killed or wounded, the majority of them in the battle's first half hour. By the end of the meaningless campaign, British losses totaled 400,000, French 200,000, and German 500,000. In April 1917 near Arras, in Belgium, 150,000 British soldiers were killed in six days in order to advance the front line a few miles.

Such carnage resulted from a mixture of new war technology and old-fashioned military tactics. Generals continued to order massive *infantry* charges such as in the American Civil War. But instead of charging into lines of slow-firing soldiers, the attackers were up against nests of machine guns that could fire hundreds of rounds a minute. The machine gun and artillery fire tore gaping holes in the attackers' line. Even when an attack did succeed, the defenders merely fell back

593

WORLD WAR I, 1914-1918

0   200   400 Mi.

0   200   400 Km

ICELAND

ATLANTIC OCEAN

WESTERN FRONT, 1914-1918

NETH.

Dunkirk
Calais
Antwerp
Brussels
Cologne
BELGIUM
GERMANY
Amiens
St. Quentin
Cantigny
Meuse R.
Soisson
Meuse-
Argonne
Belleau Wood
Rheims
Metz
Paris
Château
Thierry
Verdun
St.
Mihiel
Seine R.
Marne R.
Strasbourg
Rhine R.

✱ Battles

- - - - Armistice Line, Nov. 11, 1918

NORWAY

SWEDEN

BALTIC SEA

Petrograd (St. Petersburg)

Moscow

NORTH SEA

DENMARK
Copenhagen

R U S S I A

IRELAND

GREAT BRITAIN

NETH.
Amsterdam
London
Rhine R.
Brussels
BELG.
Cologne
LUX.
Paris
Strasbourg
See inset
Bern
SWITZ.
FRANCE
Lyon
Rhone R.
Venice
Marseilles
SPAIN
ITALY
Rome

Hamburg
Berlin
GERMANY
Dresden
Prague
Danube R.
Munich
Vienna
AUSTRIA–HUNGARY
Budapest
RUMANIA
Sarajevo
SERBIA
MONTENEGRO
ALBANIA
GREECE

EAST
PRUSSIA
Tannenberg
Aug. 1914
Warsaw
POLAND
Brest-Litovsk
Minsk
Kiev
Kharkov
Rostov
Odessa
BLACK SEA
Bucharest
BULGARIA
Constantinople
Gallipoli 1915
TURKEY

MEDITERRANEAN SEA

	Central Powers		Stabilized fronts, 1915-1917
	Allied Powers	- - -	Farthest advance of Central Powers
	Neutral nations		Eastern front Armistice Line, Dec. 1917
	German submarine zone, 1915		1914 boundaries

  Research Assignment: Have students prepare a report on the developments in weaponry during World War I. Reports should discuss the effects of new weapons on the war and afterwards.

to the next line of trenches. Advances were measured in hundreds of yards, not miles.

Other threats to the soldiers were tanks, developed by the British later in the war. These armed and armored vehicles could roll over barbed wire and trenches. Poison gas was a particularly dreadful weapon used by both sides. And airplanes, used only for reconnaissance early in the war, were later armed with machine guns. The famous *dogfights* did not affect the ground war, but were deadly to the pilots.

The War at Sea.

Another frighteningly new element in the war was the German U-boats, or submarines. The *U-boats* were important to Germany as a way of countering England's ability to blockade Germany with its superior navy.

Early in World War I Britain declared a *war zone* in the North Sea and placed explosive mines in the sea to intercept ships trading with Germany. Evading this blockade strategy, neutral Holland, Denmark, and Sweden imported American goods and resold them to Germany. British warships then began stopping American vessels bound for neutral nations as well as for Germany.

As long as the Germans expected a quick victory on land, they ignored the British blockade. With stalemate, however, German commanders began to think in terms of strangling England's economy, which depended on imports of food and other necessities. In 1914, American sales to the Allied Powers stood at $825 million. The U-boat was Germany's only feasible weapon for cutting off this trade.

Early in 1915, Germany declared a war zone in all waters surrounding Britain, including the English Channel. All enemy ships within those waters were liable to submarine attack, and the safety of neutrals could not be guaranteed. President Wilson informed the Germans that regardless of the new weapon, he intended to enforce the traditional American defense of the freedom of the seas. He would hold Germany to "strict accountability."

The Sinking of the Lusitania.

Americans looked on the submarine as uniquely inhumane. Because the U-boats were so fragile, they were

Eager friends and relations wait for arriving passengers to disembark from the Lusitania. *A later voyage ended in disaster and helped sway American public opinion against Germany.*

helpless on the surface, even when faced by a merchant ship with only a light gun mounted on its bow. Therefore, submarine commanders could not with safety give warning, as surface vessels did before sinking a ship with torpedoes.

The issue came to a head on May 7, 1915, when the English luxury liner *Lusitania*, carrying 4,200 cases of small arms and high explosives as well as passengers, was torpedoed off the coast of Ireland. Almost 1,200 people were drowned, including 128 Americans. The German ambassador in Washington rushed to point out that a notice had been run in New York newspapers warning neutrals not to sail on the *Lusitania*. The drowned Americans had sailed at their own risk. This did not calm the furor. *The New York Times* described the Germans as "savages drunk with blood."

President Wilson's reaction was only a little less angry. The second harsh note he sent to Germany seemed so much like a threat of war that William Jennings Bryan resigned as Secretary of State in protest. He was succeeded by an international lawyer with pro-British tendencies, Robert Lansing.

The Sussex Pledge.   After the *Lusitania*, Germany ceased sinking passenger vessels, even those suspected of carrying munitions. Then, in early 1916, the Allies announced that they were arming all merchant ships. Germany responded that all allied ships were therefore subject to submarine attack. On March 24, 1916, a U-boat sank a channel steamer, the *Sussex*, and an American was among the casualties. Wilson threatened to break diplomatic relations with Germany if unrestricted submarine warfare did not immediately stop.

With plans for a major ground offensive about to go into effect, the German General Staff did not want the United States in the war. On May 4, 1916, Germany promised to warn civilian vessels before attacking them.

Wilson had won what seemed a glorious diplomatic victory. Americans believed that Wilson was keeping the country out of war. But Wilson confided to an aide, "I can't keep the country out of war. Any little German lieutenant can put us into war at any time by a calculated outrage." In other words, if a single German U-boat commander decided to strike an American ship, the United States would almost have to go to war.

3. AMERICANS GO TO WAR

The first American reaction to the outbreak of World War I was gratitude that they were not involved in Europe's alliances. Never had American political and social institutions looked so clearly superior to Europe's. Not a single prominent American spoke out against Wilson's declaration of neutrality.

Divided Sympathies.   Impartiality in action seemed easy. To demand impartiality in thought, however, as Wilson did, asked too much of human nature. Most Americans, whose ancestors had come from England, naturally sympathized with England. Wilson himself admired the British.

Other Americans wanted Germany to win. Almost 11 million Americans traced their roots to Germany or Austria-Hungary. They had come to America for its economic opportunities. But many of them continued to harbor fond feelings for the old country. They did not want the United States to intervene on the Triple Alliance's side. But they sympathized with the lands of their origins.

Many of the 4.5 million Irish-Americans favored Germany's cause. They had no love for the Germans, but plenty of hatred for Great Britain. When the British harshly suppressed the Easter Rebellion in Dublin in the spring of 1916, many Irish-Americans openly expressed their hopes that Germany would win the war.

The modern submarine was developed by two Americans in 1897. Unfortunately, Simon Lake and J.P. Holland's *Argonaut* was turned down by the U.S. Navy and was then sold to the Germans. Submarines had been in use, in one form or another, since the *Turtle*, used by David Bushnell and the U.S. in the Revolutionary War.

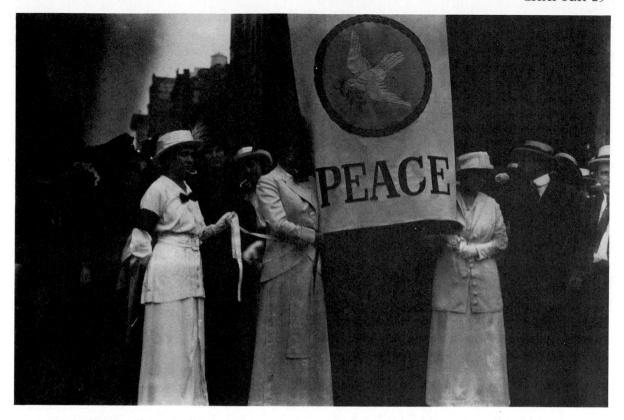

The Women's Peace Movement tried in vain to keep America out of what many considered to be a European war. Increasing pressure from European countries needing help weakened their efforts.

A Shift in Sentiments.

As the war dragged on, more and more Americans came to favor the British side. People with no particular English, Scottish, or Welsh ethnic loyalties could not help but prefer comparatively democratic Britain and France to Germany, which under Kaiser Wilhelm glorified war and the military.

British diplomats in Washington were also extremely successful in their anti-German propaganda campaign. Germany's intention, Britain said, was to force its barbaric culture on everyone. Increasingly, people called Germans "the Huns," referring to the savage invaders of ancient Europe who had settled in lands that became Germany.

Preparedness.

As early as December 1915, Wilson began to prepare for war in the event it was forced on the United States. He asked Congress to beef up the tiny American army to 175,000 soldiers and to authorize the construction of dozens of new naval vessels.

Many Americans opposed preparedness. They pointed out that being prepared with huge armies and munitions had made it easier for the European nations to stumble into the terrible conflict. Congressman Claude Kitchin of North Carolina pointed out that the broad Atlantic was all the protection the United States needed. Midwestern Progressives like Robert La Follette and Nebraska's crusading George Norris opposed building up the military.

The Election of 1916.

Wilson's support for preparedness while also avoiding war was his major appeal in his 1916 campaign for reelection. His supporters used the slogan "He kept us out of war." Wilson's campaign was strengthened when Theodore Roosevelt refused to be the Progressive party's candidate for president, and that party ceased to exist. The Progressives either went back to being Republicans or backed Wilson, who had adopted many of their reforms.

Class Activity: The peace movements of this period were also, in part, an expression of traditional U.S. isolationism. Use a chart to link events in U.S. history that would have fostered isolationism. Be open to any reasonable suggestions that might include physical separation by oceans, European condescension, self-preoccupation, and so on.

The Republican candidate in the 1916 election was Charles Evans Hughes, the reforming ex-governor of New York and Supreme Court justice. He was an impressive, dignified man, but he was unable to establish a clear difference between his positions and Wilson's. Like Wilson, he supported preparedness, but he also expressed the hope that the United States could stay out of the war.

The election was extremely close. It came down to which candidate would carry California, the last state to report returns. When Hughes went to bed on election night he believed he had won. By early the next morning it turned out that Wilson had been reelected. The electoral vote was 277 for Wilson, 254 for Hughes.

Last Ditch Efforts for Peace.

In January 1917, Wilson outlined a peace plan to Congress. The solution, he said, was "a peace without victory." He asked belligerents on both sides to declare an *armistice* and to forge "a peace among equals" in which national self-determination and absolute freedom of the seas were recognized by all. Wilson also proposed the formation of some kind of international organization to prevent future wars. His proposal was beginning to be discussed when two German actions brought the United States to the brink of war.

On February 1, 1917, Germany resumed unrestricted submarine warfare, threatening to sink all ships within the war zone around Great Britain. With the failure of their ground offensives, the German generals had concluded that the only way to win the war was to cut off England's supply lines. The U-boat fleet was bigger than ever, and the Germans expected all-out submarine warfare to force a British surrender within a few months.

The Germans knew that their action would almost certainly bring America into the war. However, they also calculated that Britain could be defeated before the Americans could bring any force to bear in Europe.

Wilson severed relationships with Germany two days later. Then, in early March the British intercepted a message to Mexico from the German foreign minister, Arthur Zimmermann. Zimmermann promised Mexico its "lost provinces" of Arizona, Texas, and New Mexico if it declared war on the United States. The Mexican threat would keep much of the American army at home. The Mexicans ignored the Zimmermann note, but it inflamed anti-German feelings in the United States.

The Declaration of War.

Neutrality was no longer possible. When Germany sank four American ships later in March, American involvement seemed assured. On April 2, saying that "it is a fearful thing to lead this great, peaceful people into war," Wilson solemnly asked Congress for a declaration of war.

For four days Congress debated. Six senators and about 50 representatives tried to argue the majority out of their intentions. Senator La Follette pointed out that in violating the German war zone while observing the British war zone, Wilson had not been impartial. Senator Norris said that the United States was going to war to bail out American bankers who had loaned more than $2 billion to England and feared they would not be repaid. "We are going to war upon the command of gold," Norris said. Ignoring these arguments, the Senate voted overwhelmingly for war, and the House concurred on April 6.

There were strong reasons for going to war. First of all, Wilson feared what a German victory would mean. America's interests in the world had become much the same as England's—to maintain free trading rights all over the globe. Whereas the British permitted other nations to trade in their empire, the German colonies were closed to all but Germans.

This view of freedom of the seas also applied to American shipping rights during wartime. The United States had long been committed to the complete freedom of the seas.

Second, the move to war was not an overnight occurrence. With the mood of the nation slowly moving in an anti-German direction, with an army and navy prepared to fight, the pressure to go to war had been growing for months.

The American Contribution.

Before the United States entered the war, it appeared that the Germans had calculated correctly on their U-boat campaign. It seemed possible they could starve England out of the war. In February and March 1917, German submarines sank 660,000 tons (599,000 metric tons) of shipping bound to or

Class Activity: Discuss why Wilson had to ask Congress for a declaration of war. See the provisions in Article I, Section 8, Clause 11 of the Constitution and talk about how this has changed since Wilson's time.

GOING TO THE
SOURCE

The present German submarine warfare against commerce is a warfare against mankind. It is a war against all nations. American ships have been sunk, American lives taken in ways which it has stirred us very deeply to learn of; but the ships and people of other neutral and friendly nations have been sunk and overwhelmed in the waters in the same way. There has been no discrimination. The challenge is to all mankind.

Each nation must decide for itself how it will meet it. The choice we make for ourselves must be made with a moderation of counsel and a temperateness of judgment befitting our character and our motives as a nation. We must put excited feeling away. Our motive will not be revenge or the victorious assertion of the physical might of the nation, but only the vindication of right, of human right, of which we are only a single champion. . . .

The world must be made safe for democracy. Its peace must be planted upon the tested foundations of political liberty. We have no selfish ends to serve. We desire no conquest, no dominion. We seek no indemnities for ourselves, no material compensation for the sacrifices we shall freely make. We are but one of the champions of the rights of mankind. We shall be satisfied when those rights have been made as secure as the faith and the freedom of nations can make them.

> *The world must be made safe for democracy. Its peace must be planted upon the tested foundations of political liberty. . . . We desire no conquest, no dominion. We seek no indemnities for ourselves, no material compensation for the sacrifices we shall freely make. . . .*
>
> WOODROW WILSON,
> *WAR MESSAGE*

Just because we fight without rancor and without selfish object, seeking nothing for ourselves but what we shall wish to share with all free peoples, we shall, I feel confident, conduct our operations as belligerents without passion and ourselves observe with proud punctilio the principles of right and of fair play we profess to be fighting for.

It is a distressing and oppressive duty, gentlemen of the Congress, which I have performed in thus addressing you. There are, it may be, many months of fiery trial and sacrifice ahead of us. It is a fearful thing to lead this great peaceful people into war, into the most terrible and disastrous of all wars, civilization itself seeming to be in the balance. But the right is more precious than peace, and we shall fight for the things which we have always carried nearest our hearts—for democracy, for the right of those who submit to authority to have a voice in their own governments, for the rights and liberties of small nations, for a universal dominion of right by such a concert of free peoples as shall bring peace and safety to all nations and make the world itself at last free.

Although he was reluctant to go to war, Woodrow Wilson found idealistic reasons for involving the United States in World War I. Wilson's persuasiveness as a speaker is shown in this excerpt from his War Message *of April 2, 1917, in which he asked Congress for a declaration of war.*

from England. In April alone the total jumped to 900,000 tons (816,000 metric tons). A quarter of the British merchant fleet lay at the bottom of the ocean. At one point, England had enough food reserves on hand to feed its population for only three more weeks.

Then, in May, the United States helped turn the tide. Admiral William Sims insisted that American vessels travel in *convoys* guarded by *destroyers* designed for antisubmarine warfare. Sims' "bridge

Discussion Question: If you could rewrite history, what events would you change to keep the U.S. out of World War I?

599

Large convoys such as the "Great White Fleet" (above) used cargo ships and troop carriers flanked by protective destroyers. These huge convoys kept German submarines at bay.

of ships" began to cut the shipping loss. By July, the United States Navy had taken over the defense of the Western Hemisphere and was able to send 34 destroyers to Queenstown, Ireland to assist the British. So effective was the convoy system that of the 2 million soldiers the United States sent to Europe, not one was lost at sea.

Americans manufactured war goods with increased speed and efficiency, out-producing the Germans.

The most important American contribution to the war effort was in material. American farms provided food for their allies. American factories turned out clothing, vehicles, ships, airplanes, and munitions in quantities that the Germans and Austrians could not match.

Russia Leaves the War. The American contribution came not a moment too soon. In the spring of 1917 the Russian government was overthrown by a democratic regime headed by Alexander Kerensky. Kerensky kept Russia in the war and actually helped morale in the West. Now, all of the major allies fighting against Germany were democracies. Wilson's description of a war "to make the world safe for democracy" had more meaning.

But Russia was exhausted. Its army was on the defensive, was poorly commanded, and was often without medicine and food. Exploiting mutiny in the ranks, Bolsheviks, radical Communists led by Vladimir Ilyich Lenin and Leon Trotsky, seized power in the fall of 1917. In March 1918, they signed the treaty of Brest-Litovsk with Germany, ending Russian involvement in the war.

When Rumania also left the war, the Germans no longer had to fight on the eastern front. They could throw their entire army at the western allies. Thus, the German commanders prepared a major offensive in France for the spring of 1918. They hoped to end the war before large numbers of American troops could arrive.

Research Assignment: Have students work on an ongoing research assignment on the development of the Soviet Union under communism.

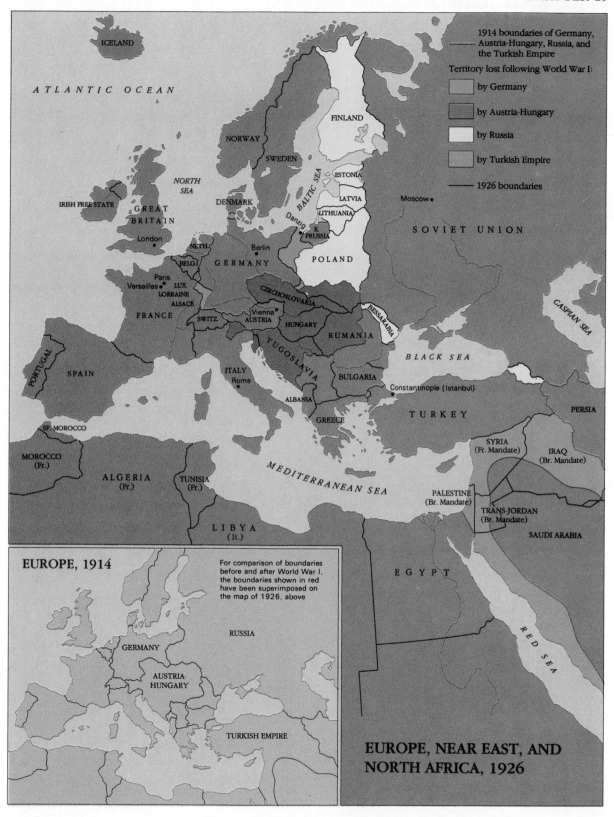

1914 boundaries of Germany,
Austria-Hungary, Russia, and
the Turkish Empire

Territory lost following World War I:

by Germany

by Austria-Hungary

by Russia

by Turkish Empire

1926 boundaries

ICELAND

ATLANTIC OCEAN

NORWAY

SWEDEN

FINLAND

NORTH
SEA

BALTIC SEA

ESTONIA

LATVIA

LITHUANIA

Moscow

SOVIET UNION

IRISH FREE STATE

GREAT
BRITAIN

DENMARK

Danzig

E.
PRUSSIA

POLAND

London

NETH.

Berlin

BELG.

GERMANY

CASPIAN SEA

Paris
Versailles
LUX.
LORRAINE
ALSACE

CZECHOSLOVAKIA

BESSARABIA

FRANCE

SWITZ.

Vienna
AUSTRIA

HUNGARY

RUMANIA

BLACK SEA

PORTUGAL

SPAIN

ITALY
Rome

YUGOSLAVIA

BULGARIA

Constantinople (Istanbul)

PERSIA

ALBANIA

GREECE

TURKEY

SP. MOROCCO

SYRIA
(Fr. Mandate)

IRAQ
(Br. Mandate)

MOROCCO
(Fr.)

ALGERIA
(Fr.)

TUNISIA
(Fr.)

MEDITERRANEAN SEA

PALESTINE
(Br. Mandate)

TRANS-JORDAN
(Br. Mandate)

SAUDI ARABIA

LIBYA
(It.)

EGYPT

RED SEA

EUROPE, 1914

For comparison of boundaries
before and after World War I,
the boundaries shown in red
have been superimposed on
the map of 1926, above

RUSSIA

GERMANY

AUSTRIA-
HUNGARY

TURKISH EMPIRE

EUROPE, NEAR EAST, AND
NORTH AFRICA, 1926

Class Activity: Bring in recordings of World War I songs. Discuss their use as morale builders and
as propaganda.

Chemical warfare, including poison mustard gas, made gas masks necessary (above). The American soldiers shown below wait for the enemy during the Meuse-Argonne offensive.

This photograpah shows American ace Eddie Rickenbacker (center) with some other pilots of the Ninety-fourth Pursuit Squadron in France.

The Last Year of War. The war's last campaign began with a German offensive in March 1918. As they had done in 1914, the Germans pushed to the Marne River, only 50 miles (80 kilometers) from Paris.

American forces were just beginning to arrive in Europe. Because of the urgency of the situation, General Pershing, American commander in Europe, temporarily gave up on his insistence that American troops fight as a unit. The Yanks were rushed to plug holes in British, French, and Belgian sectors of the lines. In May, more than 27,000 fought at Château-Thierry (shä′tō tyĕ-rē′), the bloodiest front in the battle. The Americans helped push the Germans back across the Marne River.

By summer, the Germans were falling back rapidly. Pershing got his wish to make an independent American thrust against the German lines. The final great battle for the Americans was along a 24-mile front in the Argonne Forest. More than 1.2 million Americans took part in the battle, and the rugged country was transformed into a wasteland of smoke and craters by the heavy shelling.

By November, the Germans had been pushed back almost to the Rhine River. The Kaiser realized that defeat was imminent, and abdicated. On November 11, an armistice was declared and the battlefields fell silent. Almost 8.5 million soldiers died in the war either in battle or from disease. An estimated 21 million were wounded. American casualties were small in comparison—about 112,000 killed.

4. PLANNING THE WAR EFFORT

One of the greatest challenges facing the United States on entering the Great War was changing from a peacetime to a wartime economy. President Wilson knew that equipping and supplying the American armed forces and those of its allies would be an unprecedented undertaking. The German threat was too great, and the need was too immediate to let free market practices run the war effort. Consequently, Wilson took steps to plan wartime production in the United States. The government would take a large hand in the American economy.

A Planned Economy. About 5,000 government agencies were founded to organize the American economy during World War I. Some were wasteful, and others did not live up to their expectations. Nevertheless, the major agencies had astonishing success. The *Shipping Board* produced vessels as quickly as German submarines sank them. The *United States Railroad Administration*, headed by Wilson's son-in-law, William G. McAdoo, took control of the nation's railroads and ran them efficiently. Taking over a system that

World War I went by other names as well. Until the U.S. entered it, the British referred to it as the European War. Newspapers in the U.S. also called it the War for Freedom of Europe, the War for the Overthrow of Civilization, and Woodrow Wilson's War to Make the World Safe for Democracy. It became known as the Great War and World War after 1918.

was about 150,000 freight cars short in 1917, the Railroad Administration gave back a surplus of 300,000 cars to railroad owners after the war.

The *War Industries Board*, headed by *Wall Street* financier Bernard Baruch, supervised the operations of the hundreds of boards regulating various industries.

Herbert Hoover's Food Administration.

The most famous and most successful wartime administrator was a mining engineer and self-made millionaire named Herbert Hoover. Only 43, Hoover had already organized food collection and distribution to save the people of Belgium from famine during the first years of the war. He did his job without fanfare or personal acclaim. Hoover was a cool, brilliant administrator who simply got things done right.

Hoover preferred voluntary programs to government coercion. Instead of *rationing* food at home, he urged Americans to conserve food on their own by observing wheatless Mondays, meatless Tuesdays, and porkless Thursdays. Making do without one commodity one day a week was not a great sacrifice for individuals, and it made people believe they were part of the fighting machine. But the savings were astronomical.

Hoover also encouraged Americans to plant "victory gardens" in their backyards so that commercially raised produce could be channeled to the army and the European allies. Americans came to call saving on food "hooverizing."

Selective Service.

In May 1917 Congress passed the *Selective Service Act*. All men between the ages of 21 and 30 were required to register for the draft. (In 1918 the minimum age was reduced to 18 and the maximum was raised to 45.) From the 24 million registered by the end of the war, local draft boards selected 3 million to serve in the armed forces.

Black Americans *inducted* into the army served with distinction. They were segregated into black units but, as a result, more than 1,200 blacks were commissioned as officers. Black progressives like William E. B. Du Bois of the NAACP, who supported the war, looked forward to seeing these men act as a black elite when the war was over.

More important in the long run was black emigration from the South to the North. Wartime

This unit of victorious soldiers had earned the right to the good life in a peaceful America.

factories working around the clock opened opportunities for relatively high-paying jobs in cities like New York, Philadelphia, Detroit, and Chicago.

The AFL Gains Respectability.

In order to keep the factories humming, Wilson made gestures toward organized labor that, before the war, would have been unthinkable. He appointed Samuel Gompers, the patriotic head of the AFL, to sit on the Council of National Security. Another AFL official, William Wilson, became Secretary of Labor. For the first time, labor leaders were regarded as partners in running the country.

In return for this recognition, most AFL unions pledged not to strike during wartime. Because wages rose steadily, most unions kept this promise. AFL membership also rose, going from 2.7 million members in 1914 to 4.2 million in 1919.

The American women's suffrage movement finally resulted in the ratification of the Nineteenth Amendment, guaranteeing women the right to vote, on August 18, 1920. Alice Paul (above), Carrie Chapman Catt, and the Reverend Anna Shaw (far right) were leaders in that movement. The photograph above right shows a group of women suffragists who marched from New York to Washington, D.C., in 1912.

The IWW Is Destroyed. While conservative trade unionists gained respectability, the government moved rigorously against the radical Industrial Workers of the World (*IWW*). The IWW opposed but did not work actively against the war, and gained tens of thousands of members in several critical sectors of the economy.

In 1917, Justice Department agents raided IWW halls from coast to coast. In a trial most historians think was biased, more than 100 IWW leaders were imprisoned for espionage and sedition, and their organization was destroyed.

Women's Victory. For feminists, the happy ending of the long struggle for the vote was at hand. Following French and British examples, the armed forces enlisted women for the first time. Women took industrial jobs that had previously been considered men's work, and took the lead in organizations designed to support the "boys in France." Thousands of women worked for the *Red Cross*. Others rolled bandages, knitted sweaters and socks, and baked cookies and cakes to be sent abroad.

Women's important contributions to the war

effort caused a greater appreciation for women as citizens. As a result of their work during the war, women began to value their own strengths and worth outside as well as inside the home, and they insisted upon being granted full rights as first-class citizens.

In the face of the overwhelming demonstration of women's place in society, most resistance to women's suffrage ended after the war. Even Wilson, who had given no encouragement to the suffragists, announced his support for them. On June 4, 1919, Congress passed the Nineteenth Amendment, granting women the right to vote. The states ratified the amendment on August 18, 1920.

To some feminist leaders like Carrie Chapman Catt, the fight for the right to vote was over. To the more radical Women's Party led by Alice Paul, gaining the right to vote meant that the drive for equality of women and men had just begun. As the 1920s progressed, however, fewer women took an interest in feminist reform. Not until the late 1960s would the movement revive.

The Propaganda War.

George Creel, a journalist from Denver, was named to head the *Committee on Public Information* (CPI). One of his jobs was to screen reports from the front. Unfavorable news about military setbacks was often censored, while accounts of battlefield successes were sometimes blown out of proportion.

The CPI also fought a *propaganda* battle at home. The implied message of Creel's campaign to encourage *patriotism* was that any degree of dissent from the government's policies was disloyal. Through pamphlets, posters, massive rallies, parades, and speeches, the CPI whipped up enthusiasm for the war and hatred of all things German.

Some aspects of the anti-German campaign were silly. Sauerkraut was renamed "Liberty Cabbage" and German measles "patriotic measles." Dachshunds became "Liberty Hounds." There were harmful aspects too, such as the decision of some orchestras to scratch the work of all German composers from their repertoires. Some school districts ceased to offer the German language.

Even worse, people with German surnames were fired from their jobs. German books were burned. People with German accents were beaten by bullies belonging to organizations like the

Some American propaganda posters were meant to enhance the image of working women as contributors with men in the war effort.

"Sedition Slammers" and "Boy Spies of America." Instead of cautioning against such activities, many communities quietly tolerated and even encouraged them.

Suppression of Dissent.

President Wilson, a defender of civil liberties before the war, was so obsessed with defeating Germany that he actively aided subordinates in crushing antiwar groups.

The Socialist party opposed the war. While capitalists grew rich, said party leaders, working people were sacrificed to the war. Opposition to the war helped the Socialists at the polls. A vote for Socialist candidates seemed the only legal way that antiwar sentiment could be expressed.

The Post Office refused to handle Socialist newspapers, and several Socialist assembly members in New York were denied their seats. When Victor Berger of Milwaukee was elected to Congress, the House refused to seat him. Running again against a "loyal" candidate supported by

Class Activity: Have students reproduce propaganda posters used in World War I. Students should be able to interpret the meanings of the posters and explain these to the class. You may wish to hang these posters in your room while discussing World War I.

Republicans and the Democrats, Berger won again. Again, the House refused to seat him.

Two Socialist leaders, Kate Richards O'Hare and Eugene V. Debs, were imprisoned for opposing the draft. Even the Supreme Court's most liberal justice, Oliver Wendell Holmes, Jr., approved a federal law that restricted free speech.

Never had the American tradition of individual liberties been more seriously threatened than during World War I. In 1920, the *American Civil Liberties Union (ACLU)* was founded to act as a watchdog for the Bill of Rights. In so doing, the United States demonstrated that a democracy with a system of checks and balances could both contain and provide for internal differences.

SECTION REVIEW

1. Write a sentence to identify: "victory gardens," Nineteenth Amendment, CPI, ACLU.

2. Name four government agencies that helped to organize the American economy during World War I. Explain how Hoover involved Americans in the war effort.

3. Compare the positions of the AFL and IWW on the war. Describe the government's treatment of each organization.

4. Describe the immediate and eventual effects of women's part in the war effort.

5. THE LEAGUE OF NATIONS

Woodrow Wilson had committed the United States to war because he believed certain important principles were at stake. He wanted to see a world free from war, and countries that were governed by the will of their people. As the war drew to a close, Wilson was determined to end it on the basis of his *Fourteen Points*. These included the promise of no revenge on the defeated powers, national self-determination in place of multinational empires, and freedom of the seas. But the idea that Wilson valued most was a *League of Nations*, an international congress to ensure that World War I was truly "the war to end wars."

In November 1918, Wilson was preparing to go to Europe to represent the United States at the peace conference to be held at Versailles, France. In the congressional election of that year, the Republicans won comfortable control of the House and a narrow margin in the Senate. Instead of recognizing that his Republican opponents would have an important say in ratifying any peace treaty, Wilson departed for Europe without inviting a single Republican leader to join him. It proved to be a critical mistake.

Everywhere Wilson went in Europe, he was greeted by deliriously happy crowds applauding him as the man who won the war. The cheering and confetti blinded the President to the fact that, at home, he did not necessarily have the support of the majority for his peace plan.

Compromising the Fourteen Points. Premier Georges Clemenceau (klĕm′ən-sō′) of France and Prime Minister David Lloyd-George of England wanted Germany to pay their nations huge reparations in money and goods to replace their losses in the war. In addition, they wanted to make Germany acknowledge complete blame for the war. This was a gross violation of Wilson's Fourteen Points.

Wilson hoped that the new nation states of Europe would have boundaries that all would recognize as just. Instead, the allies agreed to the principle of self-determination only when the defeated powers had to give up territory. Thus, Poland was given territory formerly possessed by Germany, Austria-Hungary, and Russia. Czechoslovakia was created out of Austria, and Austrian territory was given to Serbia, which became the new country of Yugoslavia. When national self-determination meant taking territory from the victors, Wilson got nowhere. Ethnic minorities in Italy, France, Poland, and Czechoslovakia remained tied to those countries.

The Fight Over the League. Probably a majority of Americans supported Wilson when he returned home in early 1919. But the enmity of the shrewd Senator Henry Cabot Lodge of Massachusetts was soon to whittle away his backing.

Lodge cared little for Wilson's ideals about a new world order. He detested the President personally, and as a Republican leader, wanted to defeat Wilson politically. Lodge thought that the *covenant* (or constitution) of the League of Nations seemed to limit American freedom of action. The

In 1919, leaders of the Western powers met at Versailles to draw up a peace treaty. From left, these leaders were Vittorio Orlando of Italy, David Lloyd George of Great Britain, Georges Clemenceau of France, and Woodrow Wilson of the United States.

WILSON'S FOURTEEN POINTS

POINT	PURPOSE	RESULT
1	Open covenants of peace	Rejected
2	Absolute freedom of navigation	Rejected
3	Removal of trade barriers	Rejected
4	Reduction of arms to defensive levels	Rejected
5	Impartial adjustment of all colonial claims	Rejected
6	Evacuation of all foreign troops from the Soviet Union	Rejected
7	Evacuation of all foreign troops from Belgium	Accepted
8	German evacuation of France; Alsace-Lorraine restored to France	Accepted
9	Readjustment of Italy's borders	Compromised
10	Self-determination for nationalities in Austria-Hungary	Compromised
11	Evacuation of foreign troops from Rumania, Serbia, and Montenegro	Compromised
12	Self-determination for nationalities in Turkish Empire	Compromised
13	Establishment of independent Poland	Accepted
14	Establishment of League of Nations	Compromised

Class Activity: Do an in-depth document analysis of the Fourteen Points.

provision he and other senators distrusted most was Article 10. It seemed to say that all League members, including the United States, must protect the territory of any other League member, even going to war if necessary. Counting the losses and sacrifices of the war, many Americans had no intention of entangling themselves in another war over some remote country.

Lodge's tactics were to stall for time. He understood very well that every day that passed diminished the idealism of wartime. For this reason, Lodge insisted that the Senate read through the 264–page treaty word by word.

Wilson grew impatient, but it became increasingly clear that he did not have the necessary votes in the Senate to ratify the Treaty of Versailles in the form he wanted.

One group of senators, known as *irreconcilables*, opposed any League of Nations whatsoever. There were only about 16 senators in this group, mostly western isolationists like Hiram Johnson of California and William E. Borah of Idaho. They would vote against anything Wilson offered.

A second group of Republican senators, led by Lodge, were known as *reservationists*. They would vote for the treaty and the League only if "reservations" were inserted in Article 10.

The Democrats, who made up nearly half the Senate, were willing to vote for the treaty with or without reservations.

Wilson Is Felled by a Stroke.

At Versailles, Wilson had made many concessions to his allies. Back in the United States, he refused to give an inch. In September 1919, as the time drew near for the Senate to vote, he set forth on a speaking tour. His purpose was to rally public opinion behind the League, thus forcing the reservationists to support him.

Wilson actually seemed to be succeeding when on September 25, at Pueblo, Colorado, he began to slur his words and openly wept before his audience. The President had either suffered a mild stroke or the beginnings of a nervous breakdown. His physician canceled the tour and rushed Wilson back to Washington. A few days later the President was felled by a massive stroke.

Nobody knew just how incapacitated Wilson was over the next few months. He did not meet with the Cabinet for half a year. The only people who regularly saw the President were his devoted and protective wife and his physicians. Even his long-trusted friends and his secretary, Joseph Tumulty, were stopped from seeing him.

Rejection of the League.

The League could have been ratified with reservations if Wilson had agreed to them. But the Democrats, on Wilson's instructions, voted against the modified treaty in November 1919. Then the Senate voted a second time on the treaty in March 1920. This time, half the Democrats wanted to join with the Republican reservationists in supporting the treaty in modified form. Stubbornly, Wilson refused any compromise. He knew that more changes would ruin the effectiveness of the League. The treaty was defeated again by lacking a two-thirds vote in the Senate.

In the presidential election of 1920, both the Democratic and Republican candidates spoke of a compromise on the League issue. But by November 1920, very few Americans cared about the League. They wanted to put the war and all reminders of the war behind them.

The United States had again entered a period of *isolationism*. Americans became concerned with their life at home, and were content to let the world fend for itself. Although the League of Nations was set up, the United States sent only nonvoting observers. Without American support, the League was unable to prevent events that would lead to a second world war.

SECTION REVIEW

1. Write a sentence to identify: Article 10, irreconcilables, reservationists, isolationism.

2. Explain how the demands of Clemenceau, Lloyd George, and other victorious European leaders compromised Wilson's Fourteen Points.

3. Give Senator Lodge's personal, political, and patriotic motives for opposing the covenant of the League of Nations.

4. How did President Wilson's attitude toward changing the covenant and his physical health contribute to the Senate rejection of the League of Nations?

CHAPTER REVIEW

TIME LINE

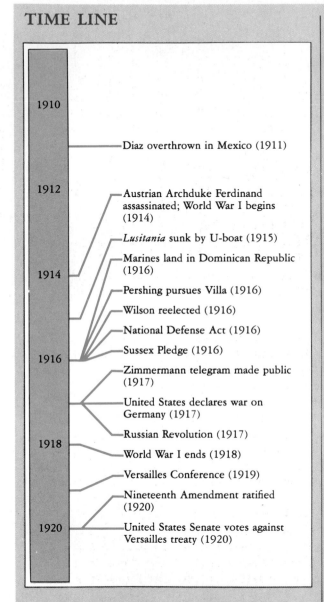

1910

Diaz overthrown in Mexico (1911)

1912

Austrian Archduke Ferdinand assassinated; World War I begins (1914)

Lusitania sunk by U-boat (1915)

Marines land in Dominican Republic (1916)

1914

Pershing pursues Villa (1916)

Wilson reelected (1916)

National Defense Act (1916)

1916

Sussex Pledge (1916)

Zimmermann telegram made public (1917)

United States declares war on Germany (1917)

Russian Revolution (1917)

1918

World War I ends (1918)

Versailles Conference (1919)

Nineteenth Amendment ratified (1920)

1920

United States Senate votes against Versailles treaty (1920)

TIME LINE QUESTIONS

1. How many years had World War I been going on before the United States became involved?
2. For how many years has the right of American women to vote been legally recognized?
3. In what year did the Russian Revolution occur?
4. What events in 1916 could be labeled examples of American "gunboat diplomacy"?

SKILLS STRATEGY

EUROPEAN MILITARY CASUALTIES, WORLD WAR I

0 - 200,000	4,000,000 - 7,000,000
200,000 - 1,000,000	Over 9,000,000
2,000,000 - 3,000,000	

0   800 Mi.
0   800 Km

THEMATIC MAPS

Physical, or topographic, maps show natural features such as mountains and bodies of water. Political maps show boundaries, cities, railroads, and other features made by humans.

Although natural and human features may be included on a *thematic* map, this type of map focuses on facts and ideas. Thematic topics might be average annual rainfall, state-by-state presidential voting patterns, the territorial growth of a country, or distribution of crops. A thematic map makes information of these kinds easily available.

Like all maps, a thematic map should have a title, a legend, a scale, and a compass rose. To interpret a thematic map, you will find the title and legend especially useful.

APPLYING SKILLS

1. What fact or idea does this thematic map illustrate?
2. How are colors used on the map?
3. What colors symbolize the greatest and the least number of casualties?
4. Which countries suffered more than 4,000,000 casualties?

Making Connections: Review the questions and topics presented in the Making Connections section that opens this chapter. Also examine the possible implications of U.S. involvement in the war in terms of how it was viewed by the world and by people in this country.

UNIT 7 TEST

CHAPTER SURVEY

In one or two sentences, summarize the content of the chapters from which these terms come, and write a sentence to identify *one* of the terms from each chapter.

1. *Chapter 23:* Triangle Shirtwaist fire, Kitty Hawk, Red Stockings, Jane Addams, Robert M. La Follette.
2. *Chapter 24:* United Mine Workers, "trust buster," John Muir, Insurgents, "Red Special," New Freedom program.
3. *Chapter 25:* Pancho Villa, Franz Ferdinand, Kaiser Wilhelm II, Sussex Pledge, November 11, 1918, Nineteenth Amendment.

TEXT REVIEW

4. Write a brief personality sketch of President Theodore Roosevelt. In your sketch, make clear why Roosevelt can justly be called the symbol of the Progressive Era.
5. If you were to write a textbook chapter about the turn of the century in the United States, what would be some of the important details you would include under the heading: *Minorities in Higher Education?*
6. What kind of writing is typified by Lincoln Steffens's series called *Shame of the Cities?* In what kinds of publications would this type of writing be found, and what was its purpose?
7. Describe four characteristics that were common to the Progressives. On what issues did many Progressives disagree?
8. Give the essential details about these political reforms of the Progressives: city managers, initiative, recall, referendum, primary elections, popular election of senators.
9. Discuss President Roosevelt's activities as a "trust buster" and "the worker's friend." Explain why these images of Roosevelt were or were not totally valid.
10. Evaluate and give examples of President Roosevelt's performance in *two* of the following areas during his second administration: control of the railroads, making food and drugs safe, natural resources of the nation.

11. Give evidence indicating whether or not President Taft was as in tune with his times as President Roosevelt had been. How did Taft's style differ from the man whom he followed in the presidency?
12. How did President Wilson's actions with regard to the Clayton Act, the founding of the Federal Trade Commission, and the Smith-Lever Act represent a departure from the New Freedom program he advocated in the 1912 presidential election?
13. Describe Roosevelt's "gunboat diplomacy," Taft's "dollar diplomacy," and Wilson's "moral diplomacy." Explain which of the three President Wilson used in dealing with events in Mexico in 1914.
14. Trace the progress of the most important events of World War I that affected the United States up to the date President Wilson asked the United States Congress to declare war on Germany and its allies.
15. Describe some of the American contributions to the war effort at home and in Europe.
16. Explain why the United States never became a member of the League of Nations.

CRITICAL THINKING

17. Write a few sentences expressing the point of view a political boss such as William Tweed might have on the political reforms enacted by the Progressives.
18. Summarize and comment on the actions taken by the federal government to control the press and political dissent during World War I.

SKILLS REVIEW

19. Name and give a general description of the system used to organize books in many libraries. Name a similar classification system that is being put into use in a growing number of libraries with very large collections.
20. Describe the organization of the drawers in a library card catalog and of the cards inside the drawers. Explain how each of the three kinds of cards in the catalog can be used to locate books in the library.

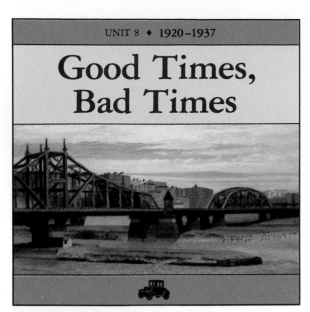

Good Times, Bad Times

American artist Edward Hopper (1882–1967), "Macomb's Dam Bridge," (1935).

Unit 8 Overview:

Unit 8 takes students from the years following World War I, through the administrations of Presidents Harding, Coolidge, and Hoover, on to the Great Depression and the first two terms of Franklin Delano Roosevelt, and leaves them at the point in history when Europe is on the brink of a second world war. Along the way, students follow such important events as the materialism of the Roaring Twenties, and the disastrous crash of the Stock Market in 1929.

Basic Unit Concepts

1. The years between 1920 and 1929 were highlighted by turmoil within the United States: strikes, negative reactions to foreigners, a black nationalist movement, the revival of the Ku Klux Klan, lawlessness growing out of Prohibition, and corruption in the Harding administration.
2. Calvin Coolidge presided over a period of deceptive material prosperity and the giddiness and ballyhoo of the "Roaring Twenties."
3. Short-sighted business and government policies were among the causes of the Great Depression, although people wrongly held President Hoover responsible.
4. Franklin Delano Roosevelt's controversial New Deal policies were pragmatic attempts to lead the American nation out of its economic woes.
5. American's showed spirit and courage in facing the discouragement and hardships of the Great Depression.

Chapter 26: "Changes in Postwar America" (1920–1929)

In Chapter 26, students discover that Americans, desiring a return to peace and normalcy, elected Warren G. Harding president. They witness strikes, discrimination against immigrants, and a growing American xenophobia and notorious trial and execution of two Italian immigrants. They learn of

American women's successful struggle to win recognition of their right to vote. They follow the development of a black nationalist movement and the renewal of activities of the Ku Klux Klan. They recognize the effect of Prohibition on American values. Finally, they learn of serious wrongdoing in the Harding administration and of Calvin Coolidge's accession to the presidency on Harding's death.

Features
Movers and Shapers: Eugene O'Neill (page 621)
Profiles of the Presidency: Warren G. Harding (page 624), Calvin Coolidge (page 627)

Learning Objectives
History Generalizations Students will gain knowledge that supports the following generalizations:
1. The period preceding the "Roaring Twenties" was marked by a postwar depression, a series of unsuccessful strikes by unions, a fear of communism that led to a red scare, a rise in American xenophobia that provoked restrictive immigration laws and culminated in the highly controversial Sacco-Vanzetti trial.
2. Gains made by blacks in this period through an upsurge of black pride were partially negated by race riots, lynchings, and the revival of Ku Klux Klan activities.
3. The Eighteenth Amendment and the Volstead Act brought prohibition and, in its train, disregard for the law—speakeasies, illegal trading in liquor, and gangland wars.
4. Wishing to forget the turmoil of progressivism and World War I, voters overwhelmingly chose Warren G. Harding, the Republican presidential "candidate of normalcy."
5. Under President Harding, Secretary of Commerce Herbert Hoover directed the government to follow a "hands-off" policy toward business and agriculture.
6. Secretary of State Charles Evan Hughes convinced Congress to pass a resolution officially ending the war with Germany and to ratify a treaty limiting the size of the world's navies.
7. Although President Harding was not involved, he was forced to acknowledge the graft schemes hatched and practiced by members of his cabinet.
8. The unexpected death of President Harding gave the nation a new leader—Calvin Coolidge.

Study Skills In addition to the three skills noted in Chapter 1 which are standard to every chapter, students will:
1. use skills needed to locate information in *The Readers' Guide.*
2. write a paragraph based on a magazine article listed in the *Readers' Guide.*
3. relate graphic materials to the text of the chapter.
4. practice these ***critical thinking skills:*** generating questions about materials to be read, drawing conclusions, recognizing bias.

Chapter 27: "Prosperity and Crash" (1923–1929)

In Chapter 27, students follow the United States from the prosperous early years of the 1920s to the collapse of the Stock Market in 1929 and the onset of the Great Depression. They learn of the pro-business Coolidge-Mellon policy that applied to domestic and national activities. They witness the giddiness, ballyhoo, and installment plan material prosperity of the "Roaring Twenties" and the attendant revolution in American morals and spending habits. Finally, they follow the economic policies that resulted in the Stock Market crash and the Great Depression.

Features

Movers and Shapers: George Gershwin and Irving Berlin (page 640)
Profiles of the Presidency: Herbert Hoover (page 647)
American Ingenuity chart (pages 648–649)

Learning Objectives

History Generalizations Students will gain knowledge that supports the following generalizations:

1. President Calvin Coolidge's "New Era" government was marked by favoritism toward business leaders and the wealthy, the introduction of the Bureau of the Budget, shortsighted international economic policies, ineffective attempts to ensure world peace, and Latin American foreign policy designed to protect American business.
2. President Coolidge's admiration of business people was shared by many Americans—Democrats and Republicans—of the 1920s. indeed, some business leaders were adulated as heros.
3. Americans of the time found other heros among athletes in baseball, boxing, and football.
4. A plethora of consumer goods—automobiles, electrical gadgets, radios, phonographs—all ballyhooed by the growing advertising industry—symbolized the deceptive "Coolidge prosperity."
5. Movies, recorded music, sensational tabloid stories, and the automobile contributed to a revolution in morals among the young people of the "Roaring Twenties."
6. Installment buying and a widespread craze for speculation in the stock market by Americans hoping to "get rich quick" touched off but did not cause the Great Depression of the 1930s.
7. Over-reliance on the sale of consumer goods and the government's do-nothing policy toward depression in some sectors of American society were among the most important causes of the Great Depression.

Study Skills In addition to the three skills noted in Chapter 1 which are standard to every chapter, students will:

1. interpret line, bar, and circle graphs.
2. write a paragraph to validate a stated conclusion.
3. relate graphic materials to the text of the chapter.
4. practice these **critical thinking skills:** generating questions about materials to be read, determining effects of a given cause, hypothesizing from given facts, recognizing and validating an opinion.

Chapter 28: "The Depression and the New Deal" (1929–1937)

In Chapter 28, students realize the enormous economic, social, and psychological effects of the Great Depression on the American people, and they recognize their great spirit and courage in surviving it. Students also investigate the reasons for President Hoover's inability to deal effectively with the economic woes of the country. They follow FDR's pragmatic actions in his attempts to put the nation back on a sound economic footing, and they learn of the ideas of his opponents. Finally, they witness the revolution in black voting and the growing power of American unions.

Features

Profiles of the Presidency: Franklin Delano Roosevelt (page 661)
Going to the Source: Excerpt from F.D. Roosevelt's *First Inaugural Address* (page 662)
Movers and Shapers: Eleanor Roosevelt and Mary McLeod Bethune (page 664)

Learning Objectives

History Generalizations Students will gain knowledge that supports the following generalizations:

1. Widespread unemployment, low wages, hunger, breadlines, homelessness, loss of savings, and bank and business failures of the Great Depression left a deep impression upon Americans.
2. Although some protest marked the depression period, Americans generally reacted with a show of faith in the capitalist system.
3. Jokes, movies, and popular adulation of supposed "Robin Hoods" of crime provided Americans with temporary distractions from the cruel realities of hard times.
4. President Hoover's "rugged individualism" and his conviction that prosperity was "just around the corner" prevented him from taking much action against the depression and lost him the confidence of Americans, who inaccurately and unfairly blamed him for the depression.
5. Franklin Delano Roosevelt's promise of a New Deal for the American people gave him and the Democrats in Congress control of the national government in 1932 and 1936.
6. The New Deal in FDR's first administration consisted of pragmatic legislation aimed at saving the nation's banks and farms and providing paying jobs to Americans who most needed the money.
7. Partially in response to critics, the New Deal of the second FDR administration changed character and used government power in attempts to equalize power between employer and employee as well as between people of ordinary means and the wealthy.
8. The 1930s saw a revolution in the voting power of black Americans—from allegiance to the Republican party to the Democratic party—and a dramatic growth in the membership and power of labor unions.

Study Skills In addition to the three skills noted in Chapter 1 which are standard to every chapter, students will:

1. relate text information, pictures, and captions.
2. practice these **critical thinking skills:** generating questions about materials to be read, comparing points of view, recognizing opinion, hypothesizing.

CHANGES IN POSTWAR AMERICA

1920–1929

*Whenever we as Americans have faced serious crises
we have returned to fundamentals. . . .*   RALPH ELLISON

Making Connections. After the war, Americans grew tired of international affairs and progressive crusades. They wanted nothing more than a return to peace and "normalcy." They elected a president who delivered both—Republican Warren G. Harding.

In this chapter, you will learn:

- Why Americans developed a suspicion of anything foreign, and how this suspicion caused a "Red scare"
- How women won the right to vote
- Who led a nationalistic movement among American blacks
- What caused a decline in the American labor movement
- Why a constitutional amendment was passed to outlaw alcoholic beverages, and the effectiveness of the anti-alcohol movement
- How a president was picked in a "smoke-filled room"
- Which of President Harding's friends and appointees discredited his administration with scandals

You have read how the Progressive movement made great gains in the years before World War I. After the war, however, the reform movement lost its energy. As you read, see how the country moved in a new direction in the early 1920s.

Sections
1. Prelude to Good Times
2. Changing American Values
3. Harding's Unhappy Presidency

1. PRELUDE TO GOOD TIMES

The prosperous and happy time known as the *"Roaring Twenties"* did not really begin until 1923. Between the end of World War I and late 1923, Americans were uneasy about an economic depression and social unrest.

Postwar Depression. During the war, most AFL unions kept the no-strike pledge Samuel Gompers had given to President Wilson. Workingpeople's wages increased during the war. For all but a few highly skilled workers, however, pay did not keep up with rapidly rising prices. After the war many workers expected to demand better pay. If necessary, they were prepared to strike in order to get it.

But the postwar period was not a good time for striking. Just as in every postwar era, the government canceled its big orders for products needed to fight the war. Production slacked off, and employers had to lay off thousands of workers who were no longer needed.

While economic depression made life even more difficult for working people, it also made striking very risky. Business was bad, so employers were less inclined to agree to the demands of their workers. Factory owners often found it useful to shut their doors for a short time, or to

During Prohibition, it was illegal to serve alcoholic drinks. The painting at the right was done by the American artist Ben Shahn. It shows government agents pouring a barrel of illegal wine down a sewer.

 Quotation: from the book *Shadow and Act.* Ralph Ellison (born 1914) also wrote the novel *Invisible Man,* published in 1952.

Skills Review: Reinforce the skills learned in the preceding Skills Strategy section. Have students use an outline map to make a thematic map of the states of the U.S. during World War I. Use different colors to represent states in the Union in 1788, 1850, 1900, and 1917.

operate with reduced capacity. Also, there were many unemployed people, so an employer could simply fire strikers and hire new workers to take their places.

Fear of Bolshevism.

The unions also had to overcome popular beliefs that unionism was the same as communism, and that unions had links to the Soviet Union. These beliefs became stronger after World War I, when England, France, and the United States landed troops in Russia near the port of Murmansk to fight the Bolsheviks that had taken over Russia in 1917. They aided the *White Russian* army, which was locked in a brutal civil war with the Communists, or *Red Russians.*

Throughout 1918 and 1919, news of massacres and cruelty filtered out of Russia. Both the Whites and the Reds were guilty of hideous crimes but, because the Reds advocated communism, which was a threat to the American system, American newspapers emphasized Red atrocities and editors portrayed the Soviets as inherently evil.

Some Americans supported the Communists. Two American Communist parties were formed in 1919. Since Communist theory claimed that the working class would rise against the capitalists, many Americans looked upon any unionizing attempt as a step down the road to revolution. Worker discontent, no matter how just the cause, seemed like the same thing as Bolshevism.

Restrictive Immigration Laws.

In the postwar years, there was also a rise in American *xenophobia,* the fear of foreign people and things. We have seen how the federal government whipped up hatred of Germany during the war. After 1917, fear of communism increased people's suspicion of anything foreign. During the postwar depression, they became more aware that the majority of industrial workers were immigrants and the children of immigrants.

Immigration had slowed to a trickle during the war when sea travel was risky and passage hard to find. In 1918, only 110,000 newcomers arrived in the United States. Beginning in 1919, however, enormous numbers of people from southern and eastern Europe began arriving in New York harbor. In 1921, 805,000 immigrants entered the United States, almost matching the record numbers who came during the early 1900s.

The new flood of immigrants, combined with mounting fear of foreign "radicals," led many Americans to demand tighter immigration laws. In 1924, Congress passed the *Johnson-Reed Act,* allowing the admission of only 164,447 immigrants a year, down from 354,000 allowed under a 1921 law. Furthermore, the act said that the United States would accept from other countries only a number of immigrants equal to two percent of the number of people of that nationality who had resided in the United States in 1890.

The base year was selected deliberately to discriminate against southern and eastern Europeans. Most people from Russia, Poland, Greece, and Italy had come to the United States after 1890. The Johnson-Reed Act virtually shut them out while favoring countries of northern and western Europe. For example, Italy's annual quota was a mere 6,000 immigrants per year. The annual quota for Great Britain was 65,000; but because Great Britain was more prosperous than Italy, only about one third of that number arrived from England each year.

Major Strikes of 1919.

Economic hardship resulted in several great strikes in 1919. Fear of radicalism, however, caused them to be quickly suppressed. In Seattle, Washington, a busy seaport during the war, a strike that began with dock workers spread to most of the city's wage workers. Nearly 60,000 people left their jobs in what was one of the rare *general strikes* (strikes affecting all industries in a large region) in American history.

Radicals were a minority among the strikers. However, because they were militant and vocal, Mayor Ole Hanson was able to portray a strike for better wages as an attempt at revolution. With the help of United States marines, he crushed the strike.

In September 1919, steel industry *magnates* used similar methods to fight a walkout of 250,000 workers, mostly in the Great Lakes region. The men had good reason to strike. Most laborers involved in the actual manufacture of steel worked a seven-day week, 12 hours a day. Every two weeks, employees on the day shift changed places with those on the night shift. This meant working 24 hours at a stretch. For this life of toil, steelworkers took home little more than subsistence wages.

Bolshevik is a Russian word derived from the word *bolshoi,* meaning large. The Bolsheviks formed the majority in the Russian Social Democratic party.

Discussion Question: Should police and firefighters have the same right to strike as other unions? Discussion might include the case of the air traffic controller's strike and their subsequent firing.

Ignoring the plight of the workers, many middle class Americans believed the heads of the steel industry, Elbert Gary and Charles Schwab, who said that the strikers were dangerous Communists. Officials of the United States Steel Corporation brought in *strikebreakers* and put them to work under military guard. By January 1920, the bitter strike ended in total defeat for the unionized steelworkers.

The Boston Police Strike.

More frightening was a strike by Boston police officers. The officers of the Boston police force were badly underpaid. Their wages had been held at 1916 levels during the war, while prices for many basic goods had multiplied several times. When the city refused to recognize their union in 1919 and would not negotiate an adequate new wage scale, the entire force went out on strike. The absence of police officers from the streets threatened to cause a jump in the crime rate as professional hoodlums and the desperately poor took advantage of the lawless situation.

Massachusetts governor Calvin Coolidge made a national reputation for himself by ordering the State Guard to enforce the law in Boston. Coolidge said, "There is no right to strike against the public safety by anybody, anywhere, anytime." The strike was broken and the officers' union disappeared. Indeed, a substantial part of the national union movement disappeared during the 1920s. The IWW never recovered from the wartime imprisonment of its leaders. Membership in the conservative AFL declined from 5 million in 1920 to 3.6 million in 1923.

The Red Scare.

Also in 1919, terrorist bombings intensified people's fears of disorder. In April, the Post Office discovered 38 bombs in the mails addressed to prominent capitalists and high government officials. In June, several bombs reached their targets. On Wall Street, the capital of American business, a terrorist planted a bomb in front of the stock exchange in September 1920, and 38 people were killed when the device exploded.

In September 1920, a bomb exploded at the New York Stock Exchange on Wall Street (below). The bomb, which killed 38 people, was planted by an anticapitalist terrorist.

Attorney General Palmer believed that American Communists and anarchists (who opposed all forms of government) were responsible for these outrages. He also calculated that if he moved forcefully against radicals, he could become a national hero like Coolidge. Palmer had ideas of winning the Democratic party's presidential nomination in 1920.

Justice Department agents raided the offices of dozens of radical organizations all over the United States. Amidst a roar of publicity, 249 Communists and anarchists were seized, placed on a steamship, and deported to the Soviet Union.

On January 2, 1920, Palmer launched a new wave of raids in 33 cities. This time 2,700 people were arrested. Many were American citizens who had broken no laws, and some were not even radicals. Even a Western Union messenger delivering a telegram at an unlucky moment was briefly imprisoned.

Palmer's popularity fell in the spring of 1920, when he predicted massive demonstrations on May 1, the international Communist celebration known as May Day. When nothing happened, people lost interest in the career of their crusading Attorney General.

Sacco and Vanzetti.

As Palmer left the spotlight, two Italian anarchists entered it. In 1920, Nicola Sacco and Bartolomeo Vanzetti were arrested for armed robbery in South Braintree, Massachusetts, and accused of the murder of a paymaster and guard. Sacco and Vanzetti insisted that they were innocent, but in a quick trial, they were found guilty and sentenced to die in the electric chair. Further studies in the 1960s led to the belief that Vanzetti was innocent.

Before they could be executed, the ACLU and a number of Italian-American groups investigated the case and found that the evidence against Sacco and Vanzetti was weak. Some of it even seemed to have been fabricated by the prosecution. It appeared as if the two anarchists were sentenced to die not because they had committed a crime, but because they held unpopular political views.

Some people thought that the convicted murderers were the innocent victims of anti-foreign prejudice. For several years, through appeals and demands for a new trial, they delayed their execution. In 1927, however, Sacco and Vanzetti were executed in the electric chair.

SECTION REVIEW

1. Write a sentence to identify: Calvin Coolidge, xenophobia, general strike, Attorney General Palmer.

2. List three strikes that occurred in 1919. Give two reasons why officials were able to suppress these strikes quickly.

3. Describe the provisions of the Johnson-Reed Act. How did the act discriminate against certain European immigrants?

4. Of what crime were Sacco and Vanzetti accused? What role did the American Civil Liberties Union play in their case?

2. CHANGING AMERICAN VALUES

The 1920s were also a time of conflict over race relations, changing moral codes, and the values of an increasingly urban society. The changes begun by the war came to fruition in this decade.

Votes for Women.

In 1920, the Nineteenth Amendment, which guaranteed women the right to vote, was adopted. Tennessee was the thirty-eighth state to ratify the amendment. Although the amendment was adopted only a year after it passed Congress, the actual struggle for the amendment had been much longer.

In 1890, several regional women's suffrage groups had banded together to form the *National American Woman Suffrage Association* (NAWSA). In 1900, Carrie Chapman Catt, an educator and journalist, became president of NAWSA. Within four years, by focusing on women's right to vote, NAWSA became a powerful social force.

Women across the country followed in the path laid out by such people as Elizabeth Cady Stanton and Susan B. Anthony, who had struggled for women's rights since the 1840s. They were strengthened in their resolve to gain voting rights by their growing social role during World War I. Working in the state legislatures, women had gained full or partial suffrage in 37 states by 1919.

A more radical approach to suffrage was undertaken by Alice Paul. She and her followers picket-

---

Research Assignment: Have students do a research project on the Sacco and Vanzetti case. Reports should discuss details of the case and trial and the implications the decision has had for cases that take on the characteristics of a witch hunt. They should also include the implications for the death penalty.

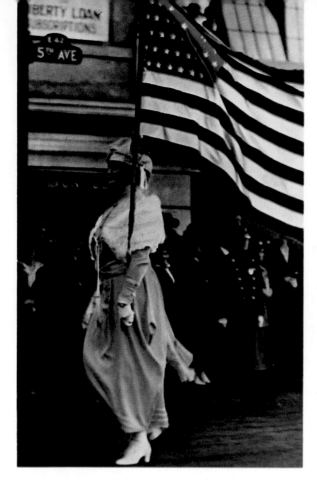

Mrs. Carpenter (above), was one of many women across the United States who participated in marches supporting the women's suffrage movement.

Marcus Garvey (above, wearing gloves) stressed "black pride." He believed that black Americans should move to Africa and start a new nation.

ed the White House. They were jailed, but went on a hunger strike. The ensuing publicity drew international attention to the cause.

Even so, the fight for ratification was not easy. NAWSA had to lobby long and hard in the state legislatures. Some law-makers even hid so that legislatures would not have enough members present to take action. But women were ultimately to win suffrage.

After the amendment was adopted, interest in the women's movement seemed to wane. But NAWSA and Paul continued to work for women's rights. Their efforts began to concentrate on "equal pay for equal work" laws, and on getting an equal rights amendment to the Constitution.

Changes for Blacks.
Black Americans looked forward to greater equality after World War I. Their leading organizations, such as the NAACP, had patriotically supported the war. About

400,000 young blacks had donned khaki, and half of them had served in Europe.

But equality did not arrive. In 1919, 83 blacks were lynched, and ten of them were veterans. Race riots broke out in 26 cities with a death toll of more than 100. The worst conflict was in Chicago, where an argument between blacks and whites on a Lake Michigan beach mushroomed into racial war. Armed gangs roamed the streets, ready to shoot at anyone of a different color.

Black Nationalism.
In this tense atmosphere emerged a remarkable black leader, Marcus Garvey. Born in Jamaica in the West Indies, Garvey came to the United States in 1916. From what he saw of American race relations, he concluded that blacks and whites could never live together in peace and equality.

Filled with a glowing pride in his own race, Garvey told fellow blacks to cease asking for

---

Class Activity: Using a two-column chart, compare the purpose, methods, and results of the actions of Marcus Garvey and the Ku Klux Klan.

equality through integration. He urged them to withdraw from white society and to form *black nationalist* organizations based on pride in being black. Garvey himself formed the *Universal Negro Improvement Association,* which emphasized black accomplishments and minimized white culture. With time and work, Garvey believed, American blacks would be able to return to Africa and establish their own nation.

An Urban Movement.

Garvey's message made little headway in the South, where blacks were faced daily with white prejudice. In the large black communities of northern cities, however, it was possible to feel a sense of shared strength. Especially in neighborhoods like New York's Harlem, blacks took pride in the black culture that was emerging.

The 1920s were the age of the *Harlem Renaissance,* an outpouring of prose and poetry by such black writers as Countee Cullen, James Weldon Johnson, and Langston Hughes. Also during the 1920s, urban blacks supported halls and nightclubs where they turned their rich musical heritage into sophistocated blues and jazz. New Orleans jazz, or *Dixieland*, brought together African rhythms and European instrumentation. Though well formed by 1900, it struck out in different directions in the Twenties as Memphis jazz, Chicago jazz, and Kansas City jazz.

Garvey's ideas on black culture appealed to many urban blacks who saw evidence of a rich culture all around them. W. E. B. Du Bois wrote, "The spell of Africa is upon me. The ancient witchery of her medicine is burning in my drowsy, dreamy blood."

The popularity of black nationalism worried those authorities accustomed to blacks remaining quietly in the background. When Garvey ran afoul of the law with one of his dozens of black business enterprises, he was prosecuted, imprisoned, and in 1927 deported to Jamaica.

The New Klan.

In his disdain for white culture, Garvey used racist ideas. There were white racists as well in the 1920s, who revived the old *Ku Klux Klan.*

The original Klan had died out in the South during the 1870s. In 1915, the great film-maker, D. W. Griffith, featured a romanticized version of the Klan in his movie *Birth of a Nation,* which was about Reconstruction. It inspired a preacher, William Simmons, to revive the organization.

Under Hiram Wesley Evans, who succeeded Simmons as leader, the new Klan grew to as many as 4.5 million members, with groups in the North as well as the South.

As in Reconstruction, the southern Klan preached black inferiority and the necessity of maintaining *white supremacy* in government. While not as violent as the original Klan, its members burned large wooden crosses in front of blacks' homes, churches, and businesses as a warning. Individual blacks (and whites) who criticized the Klan were harassed and beaten.

In the Northeast and Midwest, the Klan preached hatred of foreigners and appealed to anti-Catholic and *anti-Semitic* feelings. The Klan burned crosses in front of Jewish synagogues and Catholic churches.

The Klan's power peaked in 1924, when the organization boasted state legislators, congressmen, and even senators and governors in Oregon, Ohio, Tennessee, and Texas among its members. But after a series of scandals involving its top leadership, it declined rapidly. By 1930, the Klan had only 10,000 members.

Prohibition.

During the war, many Americans learned to live without liquor and beer. The grain that was required to make these beverages was needed to feed the American troops. At the same time, the *temperance* movement became stronger. For years, temperance workers had been trying to get laws enacted prohibiting the sale or manufacture of liquor. They finally settled on a constitutional amendment as the best way of making the United States a liquor-free nation.

The people who supported the amendment were called *Drys.* Those who opposed it were called the *Wets.* Much of the nation agreed with the *prohibitionists.* Liquor was harmful, and its abuse did cause distress for many American families. Congress approved the Eighteenth Amendment in 1917, and it was ratified by the states in January 1919.

The Eighteenth Amendment prohibited the manufacture, sale, and transportation of alcoholic beverages. In October, Congress passed the *Volstead Act,* which defined an alcoholic beverage as

Discussion Question: Should the government legislate moral standards? Discussion should include mention of prohibition and its more recent counterpart, illegal narcotics. The discussion might include ideas about law and the nature of law and the rights of one versus the rights of the many.

MOVERS AND SHAPERS

Eugene O'Neill

Winner of the Nobel Prize for literature and four Pulitzer Prizes for drama, Eugene O'Neill (1888–1953) almost single-handedly invented the serious theater in the United States. Despite his achievements, however, America's greatest playwright lived a hard life and died a bitter, unhappy man.

Before 1900, there were no American writers of serious plays because theaters totally depended on audience support to stay in business and the audiences seemed to want comedies and melodrama. The idea of theater as literature or art had not yet taken root in the United States as it had in Europe.

The American writer who changed this was Eugene O'Neill, the son of a well-known actor, James O'Neill. This early acquaintance with the theater may have given O'Neill's genius its direction. However, he was a troubled young man who spent several years as a drifter, shipping out to sea, drinking in bars and living an almost hand-to-mouth existence as a derelict. He developed an empathy for the down-and-outers that he met during this time, and later used some of them as models for characters in his plays. Suffering from tuberculosis, O'Neill was sent to a sanatorium in 1912, where he gained some perspective on his life. After his recovery, he began to write plays for a small, experimental theater company in Provincetown, Massachusetts. His first plays were produced at Provincetown during World War I, giving O'Neill a chance to develop his craft. Soon his plays became commercial successes in Broadway theaters in New York. The purpose of the Provincetown Players had been to produce experimental plays, not necessarily to make money or become famous. O'Neill and his old friends parted company.

The 1920s were a creative period for O'Neill. *Beyond the Horizon, The Hairy Ape, Anna Christie, The Emperor Jones,* and *Strange Interlude* were all critical and commercial successes. All expressed the playwright's dark vision of the world. Always in search of fulfillment, O'Neill's unhappy characters turn to love, to religion, and to drinking, but they end their searches in despair.

There was an uncanny resemblance between O'Neill's life and his art. The early plays were full of his anger at society. The heroes were rebels who refused to fit in or bow to authority. In his later plays his own withdrawal from the world was evident. His great tragedies, *Mourning Becomes Electra, A Moon for the Misbegotten, The Iceman Cometh,* and *Long Day's Journey Into Night* were psychological dramas that drew on the torment of his own family life for their inspiration.

There is a tragic consistency in O'Neill's plays that was like his own personal tragedy. As a struggling playwright he refused to write the kind of play that would make him popular and rich. He wanted the audiences to come to him. When theatergoers did discover O'Neill, he was pleased with the money his success brought him, but fled in horror from the fame and attention. He could not live at peace with himself or the world.

His last years were marked by ill health and bitterness. He quarreled with his children and separated from his old friends. He became, in many ways, like one of the tragic characters he included in his own plays. He died in Boston at the age of 65.

Speakeasy was the name given to illegal bars of the 1920s because of the method of gaining entrance. A prospective patron would speak in a quiet voice through a peephole.

621

During Prohibition, government agents were required to close any business that sold liquor. In the picture above, agents are destroying an illegal saloon.

anything containing more than one half of one percent alcohol. In effect, this meant the prohibition of beer and wine as well as liquor.

Problems of Enforcement.

The Eighteenth Amendment and the Volstead Act by which it was enforced, were in many ways the last of the progressive reforms. When Prohibition took effect, the Drys believed that poverty and crime would be reduced because working people would no longer squander their money on whiskey and beer. But what occurred was almost the opposite. Although most Americans had supported the amendment, large numbers of them had no real intention of giving up drinking. They immediately created a large market for *bootleggers* who smuggled liquor from Canada, Mexico, or the West Indies. Bootleggers were breaking the law, but many people thought that the Volstead Act was an unfair law. This resulted in a frank and often open contempt for the law as people rushed to buy liquor. The federal government was never able to enforce Prohibition nationally, and local authorities sometimes refused to enforce it.

In Chicago, Republican William "Big Bill" Thompson ran for Mayor on the promise that he would run a "wide-open" city and allow illegal saloons called *speakeasies* to operate. New York's Mayor Jimmy Walker frequented and even advertised glamorous speakeasies. The staid governor of New York and leader of Democratic Wets, Alfred E. Smith, served alcoholic drinks in the state mansion in Albany.

Gangsters.

In cities, shops openly sold the ingredients for making wine and beer. More serious, the huge demand for strong drink created large organizations to supply it. These illegal businesses did not hesitate to branch out into other crime, including murder.

Al Capone, who controlled the supply and distribution of alcohol in Chicago, insisted that he was nothing more than a businessman. "What's Al Capone done?" he told a reporter. "He's supplied a legitimate demand. I call it a business. They say I violate the prohibition law. Who doesn't?" His organization had hundreds of employees and thousands of retail outlets, and Capone needed the administrative skills of a high-ranking executive to run it. In 1927, Capone's organization had a gross income of $60 million from alcohol and $25 million from gambling.

By the late 1800s medical science had already established the existence of *alcoholism* as an incurable disease with the potential of being fatal. Yet the medical effects of alcohol were not taken into account in establishing prohibition.

With such money at stake, the illegal liquor business attracted many people anxious for a part of the profits. Rival gangs fought bloody street wars for the right to sell beer, wine, and whiskey in a neighborhood. In Chicago alone, more than 400 "gangland" slayings were reported. Only a fraction of the killers were ever caught.

SECTION REVIEW

1. Write a sentence to identify: NAWSA, Harlem Renaissance, "Wets" and "Drys," Al Capone.

2. Contrast the methods used by NAWSA and Alice Paul to gain women's suffrage.

3. In what sense could Marcus Garvey's ideas be called racist? What positive effects did his ideas have?

4. Describe the activities of the Ku Klux Klan in the 1920s.

5. Explain the connection among the following: temperance movement, Eighteenth Amendment, Volstead Act, bootleggers, speakeasies, gangland slayings.

Al Capone (above) was one of the most powerful gangsters of the Prohibition era. His gang was responsible for machine-gun deaths of rival gangsters. Jimmy Walker (below) was mayor of New York City from 1926 to 1932.

3. HARDING'S UNHAPPY PRESIDENCY

After the sacrifices of wartime, Americans were generally weary of fighting for idealistic causes. Political issues seemed less important to them now than succeeding in business and having a good time. This change in mood brought an end to the great reform movement known as progressivism. The first two presidents elected after the war —Warren Harding and Calvin Coolidge—were not energetic reformers, as Wilson and Roosevelt had been. They simply made bland speeches and left American business alone.

The Election of 1920. The election of 1920 was supposed to be a referendum on the League of Nations. Democratic candidate James Cox of Ohio and his running mate, Franklin D. Roosevelt, promised that they would complete Woodrow Wilson's work by making the United States a member of the international organization.

Discussion Question: Prohibition of alcohol was a contributing factor to the crime wave of the 1920s. How is the prohibition of drugs today similarly connected to crime? What are the differences between the two periods and the two substances?

*W*ith his adminis-
tration under attack
for corruption, War-
ren Harding told a newspaper
editor about his troubles:

. . . there is a bunch down at
the Willard Hotel coming up
to see me this afternoon, good
friends of mine from Ohio,
decent fellows that I have
worked with thirty years. . . .
Well, there is an energetic young district
attorney . . . and he has gone and indicted
those fellows, is going to put them in jail for
violating the antitrust law . . . they are going to

ask me to dismiss the indictment. I can't do that. The law
is the law, and it is probably all
right, a good law and ought to
be enforced. And yet I sit here
in the White House and have
got to see those fellows this
afternoon and explain why I
can't lift a hand to keep them
from going to jail. [This is a
terrible job!] I have no trouble
with my enemies. . . . But my
friends, my friends, White, they're the ones
that keep me walking the floor nights!

—CONVERSATION WITH WILLIAM ALLEN WHITE,
SPRING, 1923

But the Republicans did not allow the campaign
to turn into a debate on the League. The party's
bosses expected to win because of a series of
congressional and local election victories beginning in 1918. They did not intend to throw a
victory away by guessing wrong about where the
voters stood on such a serious issue. They chose as
their nominee a man who had taken no strong
stand on the League of Nations. In fact, Senator
Warren G. Harding, a small-town newspaperman
from Marion, Ohio, had taken few strong stands
on any issues during his political career. Perhaps
his chief recommendation was that although no
one particularly respected him, no one had any
great grudge against him either.

The Smoke-Filled Room.
Harry M. Daugher-
ty, a blunt-spoken politician from Ohio, told
newspaper reporters what he thought would happen at the Republican nominating convention of
1920. He predicted that the convention would be
deadlocked. The front-runners would be unable
to gain a majority of the delegates, and then the
party bosses would get together in a hotel room
and choose a candidate.

Daugherty's astute prediction was correct. Neither of the front-runners, General Leonard Wood
and Illinois governor Frank Lowden won a majority of delegates. Daugherty then met with Senator
Henry Cabot Lodge and other tired Republican
leaders in a smoke-filled room of the Hotel Black-
stone to pick another candidate.

Daugherty suggested the name of Warren G.
Harding. Lodge thought about the idea and
agreed. Harding was a "reservationist" on the
League of Nations, but he was not particularly
interested in Wilson's dream. Lodge was confident
that with proper pressure, Harding would repudi-
ate the League. Harding was the nominee.

The Candidate of Normalcy.
During the
campaign, Harding waffled on the subject of the
League, sometimes appearing to favor it, other
times hinting that Americans should forget the
League and put the frustrations of the war and its
issues behind them. In most speeches, Harding
hid behind broad generalizations. "America's
need," he told an audience in Boston, "is not
heroics but healing, not nostrums but normalcy,
. . . not agitation but adjustment, not surgery but
serenity, not the dramatic but the
dispassionate. . . ." Harding sensed that what
Americans wanted most in 1920 was a return to
normalcy. They wanted to forget progressivism
and the war. The Republicans were right. Harding
won almost 61 percent of the popular vote.

Discussion Question: In what new directions was the country moving in the 1920s? What can
explain this?

  Eugene V. Debs ran for U.S. president in 1920 once again and received 920,000 votes. This was
an especially difficult achievement given the fact that he had to run his campaign from a jail cell.

A Decent Man. Harding worked his way up in politics with his good looks, a friendly smile, a warm handshake, and a willingness to do whatever the Ohio Republican party asked him to do.

He loved the Senate, where the voters sent him in 1914. Being a Senator was, for him, a little like belonging to a very exclusive club. Harding used his influence to do *favors* for his Ohio friends, and he met with them for all-night poker parties.

Even the work the job entailed suited his temperament. Being a senator called for little more than making an occasional speech—and Harding was good at that. His voice was resonant and he cut a handsome figure that could dominate a platform or even the floor of Congress.

Harding was not a leader, but it did not seem that the country needed to be led. After the war and the excitement about the League of Nations and Wilson's illness, Harding believed that the American people wanted quiet. They wanted a decent, reassuring person in the White House.

Harding was a likable, humane man. He displayed his best side when, at Christmas 1921, he pardoned Socialist party leader Eugene V. Debs and released him from an Atlanta penitentiary. In the wake of the steel strike of 1919, Harding persuaded the leaders of the steel industry to reduce the workday in their mills to eight hours. Harding was an economic conservative. He disliked strikes. He did not believe that government power should be forced on businessmen. But it genuinely disturbed him that steelworkers were forced to work such long hours.

Herbert Hoover's Economic Policy. Harding had several able men in his cabinet. His best appointment was Herbert Hoover, whom he named Secretary of Commerce because Hoover had compiled such a remarkable record as head of the Food Administration during the war. Hoover's goal was to encourage industrialists and farmers to cooperate voluntarily with the federal government to eliminate waste and inefficiency.

Hoover believed that all-out economic competition was destructive and wasteful. He tried to persuade businesspeople and farmers that cooperation among themselves and self-regulation was in their own interests. To do this, each area of the economy would set up *private associations,* to which members would give powers of regulation. Hoover's role as Secretary of Commerce would be to give advice and information to these associations.

Neither Harding nor his successor, Calvin Coolidge, directly interfered with Hoover's work. But Hoover's success was limited. The Secretary of the Treasury, Andrew Mellon, pursued policies that in many ways undercut Hoover's vision of a self-disciplined, self-regulating system of private enterprise.

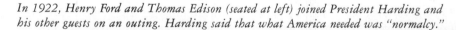

In 1922, Henry Ford and Thomas Edison (seated at left) joined President Harding and his other guests on an outing. Harding said that what America needed was "normalcy."

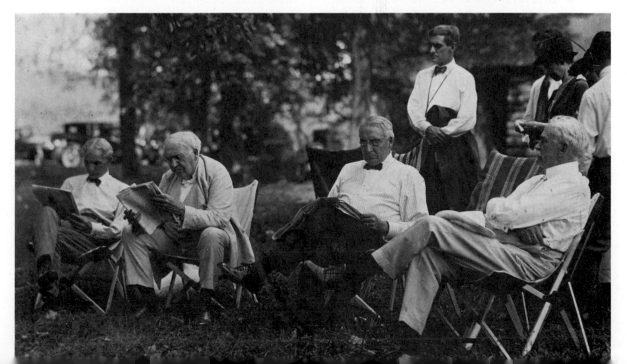

Foreign Policy Under Harding.

Harding was also served well by his Secretary of State, Charles Evans Hughes. Hughes' first task was to bring an official end to the war between the United States and Germany. Because the Senate would not ratify the Treaty of Versailles, Hughes urged Congress simply to resolve that the war was over and a state of peace existed between America and Germany. Then he would legally be able to appoint an ambassador to the former enemy. Congress passed the resolution.

Next, Hughes presented his alternative plan for keeping the peace. Like many world leaders, he believed that the prewar arms race had been a major cause of the war. When the European nations stockpiled weapons and other war materiel, they were too easily tempted to use them.

Hughes called for an international conference in Washington to discuss limiting the size of navies. The delegates arrived expecting no more than the usual round of parties and vague speeches. But Hughes shocked them in his welcoming speech when he proposed a very specific plan, under which the major naval powers would scrap many of their capital ships (battleships and cruisers) and cancel plans for future naval construction.

In the *Treaty of Washington* of 1921, France, Great Britain, Italy, Japan, and the United States agreed to limit the size of their navies in proportion to their defensive needs. America's two coasts and Britain's far-flung empire required them to maintain fleets on two oceans. Therefore, they were allowed the largest navies. Japan was a power only in the Pacific. Therefore, the treaty allowed Japan to maintain a navy three-fifths the size of the American and British forces. Italy and France were allowed fleets just slightly larger than half the Japanese allotment.

Hughes was able to persuade the others partly because the United States offered to give up the most. Thirty American battleships and cruisers that were afloat, under construction, or in the planning stages were scrapped. The Republican administration was happy to lose these ships because it helped to reduce government spending.

Other countries too feared the costs of a naval arms race. Only the Japanese expressed unhappiness with the treaty because of their sensitivity to anti-Asiatic prejudice. Some Japanese leaders believed their nation was left at a disadvantage.

Scandals.

Except for Herbert Hoover and Charles Evans Hughes, Harding's cabinet appointments were unfortunate. Secretary of the Treasury Andrew Mellon supported tax policies that some people felt contributed to the crash of the stock market in 1929. Other appointments went to Harding's poker party cronies and other Republican party favorites.

Harry Daugherty became Attorney General. Far from enforcing the nation's laws, he winked at the corrupt schemes of his friends. Probably with Daugherty's cooperation, Jesse Smith sold favorable policy decisions and appointments to public office for cash. Charles Forbes, another late-night poker partner, headed the Veterans' Bureau. He pocketed tens of thousands of dollars earmarked to build hospitals for the soldiers of World War I.

Most ambitious of all the thefts was the work of Secretary of the Interior Albert Fall. Fall abused his power in disposing of the navy's oil reserves at Elk Hills, California, and Teapot Dome, Wyoming. First, he persuaded Harding to transfer authority over these reserves from the Navy Department to the Department of the Interior. Then he leased the rich oilfields to two oilmen, Harry Sinclair and Edward Doheny. Sinclair and Doheny then generously "loaned" Fall over $400,000.

Harding Faces the Facts.

Harding had no knowledge of Fall's intentions when he gave the Interior Department control of Elk Hills and Teapot Dome, and the President was never involved in large-scale graft himself. His trouble was that he expected his friends to show him the same good will he showed to them. By the summer of 1923, the President was facing up to the cruel facts. He told the prominent Republican progressive, William Allen White, that his political enemies had done him no harm. But his friends had tarred him with scandals that were bound to be on the front pages of the nation's newspapers within a few months.

In the summer of 1923, Harding set out on a vacation trip to Alaska. Photographs clearly showed that he was under great strain. His normally handsome face was haggard, drawn, and gray. On the way back from Alaska, Harding was taken seriously ill, and on July 28, he died in a hotel room. The official cause of death was listed as ptomaine poisoning. But soon there was whis-

*R*eflecting the good times of the prosperous 1920s, Calvin Coolidge spoke about a subject important to most Americans of that time—making money:

After all, the chief business of the American people is business. They are profoundly concerned with producing, buying, selling, investing, and prospering in the world. I am strongly of the opinion that the great majority of people will always find these are moving impulses of our life. . . . Of course the accumulation of wealth cannot be justified as the chief end of existence. But we are compelled to recognize it as a means to well-nigh every desirable achievement. . . . It is only those who do not understand our people who believe that our national life is entirely absorbed by material motives. We make no concealment of the fact that we want wealth but there are many other things that we want very much more. We want peace and honor. . . . America is a nation of idealists. . . .

—SPEECH, JANUARY 7, 1924

pering. Why had no one else in the presidential party of 65 persons been taken ill? They had eaten all their meals together.

In fact, it appears that the diagnosis of ptomaine poisoning was incorrect. Historical researchers have suggested that Harding died of a massive heart attack.

Silent Cal. The new president, Calvin Coolidge, was in some ways the opposite of Harding. He was a person of proper personal habits. His idea of a good time was not poker but a good long nap. Coolidge's political record was without a whiff of scandal. What better person to have in the White House when, late in 1923, the Harding scandals were made public? Whatever corruption there had been, Republican leaders could say there was certainly nothing dishonest going on in Coolidge's administration.

Coolidge Luck. Coolidge was a man of extraordinary good luck throughout his career. Through no particular merit of his own, he always seemed to be in the right place at the right time. In the midst of an undistinguished term as governor of Massachusetts, the Boston police strike provided him with the opportunity to look like a defender of the social order. When he was nominated for the vice presidency in 1920, Coolidge looked forward to nothing but a few quiet years in the nation's second highest post. But when Harding died, Coolidge was catapulted into an office he could not have won on his own at that time. The postwar depression was also lifting, and Coolidge had the good fortune of becoming president on the eve of a period of unprecedented prosperity that would be attributed to him.

SECTION REVIEW

1. Write a sentence to identify: James Cox, Franklin D. Roosevelt, smoke-filled room, Coolidge luck.

2. Why did Harding win the presidency in 1920 as the "candidate of normalcy"?

3. Describe the accomplishments of Secretary of Commerce Hoover and Secretary of State Hughes.

4. Summarize the scandals that involved Attorney General Harry Daugherty, head of the Veterans' Bureau Charles Forbes, and Secretary of the Interior Albert Fall.

5. Under what circumstances did Calvin Coolidge become president in 1923?

When writer Dorothy Parker was told that President Coolidge had died, her unkind, but revealing, response was, "How can they tell?"

CHAPTER REVIEW

TIME LINE

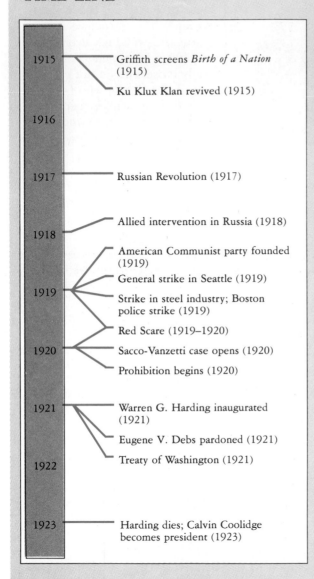

1915 — Griffith screens *Birth of a Nation* (1915)
— Ku Klux Klan revived (1915)

1916

1917 — Russian Revolution (1917)

1918 — Allied intervention in Russia (1918)

1919 — American Communist party founded (1919)
— General strike in Seattle (1919)
— Strike in steel industry; Boston police strike (1919)
— Red Scare (1919–1920)

1920 — Sacco-Vanzetti case opens (1920)
— Prohibition begins (1920)

1921 — Warren G. Harding inaugurated (1921)
— Eugene V. Debs pardoned (1921)
— Treaty of Washington (1921)

1922

1923 — Harding dies; Calvin Coolidge becomes president (1923)

TIME LINE QUESTIONS

1. How long was Harding in office?
2. With which event on the time line was Attorney General Palmer associated?
3. What constitutional amendment and law were connected with an event in 1920?
4. Which event in 1921 was an attempt to prevent another arms race like the one that helped start World War I?

SKILLS STRATEGY

PROHIBITION
    Victory for the "drys": the eighteenth
        amendment I.M. Teetotaler il Natl
        Jrnl 30:50-2 + F '19

TEETOTALER, Isabella M.
    Victory for the "drys": the eighteenth
        amendment il Natl Jrnl 30:50-2 + F '19

THE READERS' GUIDE

If you are looking for a magazine article that contains information you need, you will not find a card for the article in the library catalogue. You will have to go to the reference section and find the volumes of a reference work entitled the *Readers' Guide to Periodical Literature*.

The *Readers' Guide* is a multivolume index to magazine articles published between 1802 and the present. Each volume lists articles published between one date and another; for example, March 1983–February 1984. These dates are shown clearly on the spine of each volume.

Inside the *Guide*, the articles are listed alphabetically under subject headings or headings for authors' names (last names first). The first example above is a *subject listing*. Refer to it as you read.

Notice that the subject heading is in heavy type. The title of the magazine article comes first in the listing. Notice also that only the first word of the article is capitalized.

After the article title comes the author's initials and last name. If the article is illustrated, the abbreviation *il* is placed after the author's name.

Making Connections: Review the questions and topics presented in the Making Connections section that opens this chapter. Discuss how the country's political change of direction was indicative of its social change of direction. Examine the possible reasons for, and consequences of, this change.

Table of Contents

Cover: Maureen Egans as Yum-Yum in a San Francisco revival of *The Mikado* in August
Photograph by Thomas Kramer

Then, an abbreviation of the magazine's name appears. Meanings of abbreviations can be found at the front of the *Guide*.

Next comes the volume number of the magazine, a colon, and the pages on which the article appears. A + means that the article is continued in another part of the magazine. Finally, an abbreviation of the month and the last two numbers of the year the magazine was published are given.

The second example on the preceding page is an *author listing*. The listing under the author's name (which is in heavy type) contains the same information as the subject listing does, except that it omits the author's name.

A subject listing is useful when you want to find several articles about a topic. An author listing is helpful when you want to look up articles written by or about a particular author.

APPLYING SKILLS

Choose two articles listed in the magazine table of contents above. Write a *Readers' Guide* subject listing for one article, and an author listing for the other article.

CHAPTER 26 TEST

TEXT REVIEW

1. Establish the connection between each of these pairs of events: the postwar depression —unsuccessful strikes by unions; the fear of Communists and anarchists—the activities of Attorney General Palmer; anarchist activities —the Sacco-Vanzetti trial.
2. Describe some positive aspects in the lives of black Americans in the 1920s.
3. What laws made alcoholic drinks illegal? How effective were these laws? Give evidence to support your answer.
4. What was the major Democratic issue in the election of 1920?
5. Explain how *one* of the following exemplifies the Harding administration's economic policies: Herbert Hoover's private associations, Andrew Mellon's tax policies.
6. What were the provisions of the Treaty of Washington of 1921?
7. Explain this statement: "With the friends in his cabinet, Harding didn't need enemies."
8. Why was Calvin Coolidge viewed as a good person to have in the White House in 1923?

CRITICAL THINKING

9. What conclusions can you draw about Warren G. Harding as a politician, a national leader, and a person?
10. Newspapers and magazines reported on the Sacco-Vanzetti trial in 1920. Would you use these primary sources to gather factual information, or to gain an impression of the emotions of the time? Explain your answer.

WRITING A PARAGRAPH

Use the *Reader's Guide* to locate a magazine article about current immigration issues or labor-management issues. Use the data in the article to write a paragraph about one topic that the article discusses. Quote a passage from the article, and use a footnote to acknowledge the source. You may wish to review the Skills Strategies in Chapters 15 and 22 before you begin to write.

PROSPERITY AND CRASH

1923–1929

Whiz! She picked up speed with infinite rapidity.
As she ran on there was a clattering behind, the new
noise of the automobile. JOHN DOS PASSOS

Making Connections. The United States enjoyed tremendous prosperity during the Coolidge presidency. For the first time, millions of Americans were able to buy automobiles, refrigerators, radios, and other goods. Overlooked during the prosperity, however, were some significant weaknesses. The 1920s ended with the biggest stock market crash in the history of the United States.

In this chapter, you will learn:

- Why Coolidge's Secretary of the Treasury thought that policies to help the rich would benefit the entire nation
- How American monetary policies hurt the countries of Europe
- What payment plan allowed Americans to buy expensive items for the first time
- How radios, movies, and automobiles changed American life
- Why many Americans put their money into real estate and the stock market
- What economic weaknesses led to the stock market crash and the Great Depression

You have read how the country returned to "normalcy" during President Harding's term. Harding's successor, Calvin Coolidge, continued to give business a free rein. As you read, trace the way in which these policies fueled an economic boom, then created a gigantic bust.

Sections
1. National Policy Under Coolidge
2. Enjoying Good Times
3. Boom and Bust

1. NATIONAL POLICY UNDER COOLIDGE

Unlike President Harding, Calvin Coolidge was not surrounded by a corrupt circle of grasping political cronies. Within months of becoming President, the proper New Englander rid his administration of the hacks who had dragged Harding down. As a result, when he stood for reelection in 1924, American voters held him entirely blameless in the wholesale thievery of the Harding scandals, which were still much in the news.

A Landslide Victory. Actually, the biggest of the Harding scandals, the Teapot Dome Scandal, hurt one of the leading Democrats more than it hurt Coolidge. William G. McAdoo, Woodrow Wilson's son-in-law, was attorney for one of the oilmen involved in the scandal. McAdoo had nothing to do with Teapot Dome, but this association provided ammunition for his rival for the Democratic presidential nomination, Governor Alfred E. Smith of New York.

McAdoo was also handicapped because pro-Ku Klux Klan delegates to the national convention favored him. Smith's supporters from the Northeast, who depended in large part on the good will of Roman Catholic and Jewish voters, opposed McAdoo because of his Klan supporters, and kept

A 1920s "flapper" was a woman whose style included bobbed hair and rolled stockings, and whose behavior some people considered shocking. The illustration of a flapper on the right was for a magazine cover of the time.

Quotation: from *Tin Lizzie,* the biography of Henry Ford. Other works by John Roderigo Dos Passos (1896–1970) include *A Pushcart at the Curb, Manhattan Transfer, The Garbage Man, Airways, Inc., The 42d Parallel, Nineteen Nineteen, The Big Money, Adventures of a Young Man, The Ground We Stand On,* and *Number One.*

Skills Review: Reinforce the skills learned in the preceding Skills Strategy section. Have students use the *Readers' Guide to Periodical Literature* to complete the research for one of the research assignments they do in this chapter. Have them attach an explanation of the sources used and how the *Readers' Guide* was helpful in locating them.

 631

him from winning the nomination.

However, the Smith forces were unable to nominate their own hero, either. McAdoo blocked Smith's nomination, and it took the Democrats 103 ballots to compromise on a Wall Street lawyer, John W. Davis.

Davis was a conservative. His economic views were virtually identical to those of Coolidge and the Secretary of the Treasury, Andrew Mellon. Frustrated at having no clear choice between the major parties, the remnants of the old reform movement formed a new Progressive party and nominated Robert La Follette, the famous reformer from Wisconsin.

La Follette might have had a chance 12 years earlier, when reform was in the air. But times had changed. Coolidge won by a landslide, 382 electoral votes to 136 for Davis and only 13 votes for La Follette.

A Business Government.

Calvin Coolidge believed in business. With eloquent simplicity he once said, "the business of America is business," and "the man who builds a factory builds a temple." Coolidge filled his administration with millionaires and depended on two holdovers from Harding's cabinet to manage the economy of what happy businesspeople called the "New Era."

Herbert Hoover stayed on as Secretary of Commerce and continued his drive to form cooperative associations of farmers and manufacturers. Hoover's intelligence and energy caused Coolidge some anxiety. But the more active Coolidge's aides were, the less the President had to do, so Hoover remained.

More powerful than Hoover was Secretary of the Treasury Andrew Mellon. Mellon was one of the three or four richest persons in the world. With Coolidge's silent approval, Mellon's financial policies were designed to aid wealthy industrialists and merchants.

Trickle-Down Economics.

Mellon agreed with Alexander Hamilton that the wealthy were the nation's most valuable citizens. (The wealthy called Mellon "the greatest Secretary of the Treasury since Alexander Hamilton.") He believed that national prosperity depended on constant economic growth. A man whose bank had grown up with the huge steel industry of Pittsburgh, he believed that larger and newer factories and the steadily increasing production of goods were the key to the future. To encourage this kind of growth, Mellon believed the government should make sure that as much money as possible found its way into the hands of wealthy capitalists, who would then reinvest it. Then, as capital investment expanded the economy, jobs and opportunities for advancement would be created for workingpeople. In this way, prosperity would "trickle down" to working people.

Cutting Taxes.

Mellon proposed slashing taxes that applied mainly to higher incomes. Tax rates would be sharply reduced for people who made more than $60,000 a year, while minor adjustments would be made in the rates paid by people with lower incomes. By 1929, the Treasury was paying refunds to the richest individuals and corporations. United States Steel, for example, received one payment of $15 million.

To make up part of the loss in revenues caused by this policy, Mellon increased many taxes that almost everyone paid, such as *excise taxes* and the price of postage stamps. He also introduced new federal taxes, such as one on automobiles. Mellon's critics complained that an extra cent on a letter or a few dollars on the purchase price of a car meant nothing to well-to-do people, but had a major effect on ordinary consumers. The Secretary's defenders answered that the amount each individual had to pay was not large. It was more important that the rich have money to invest than that the middle and lower income groups have a little more money to spend.

The Fordney-McCumber Tariff.

Mellon also favored industrialists by raising tariff rates. In the *Fordney-McCumber Tariff* of 1922, Congress authorized the President (which, under Harding and Coolidge, meant the Secretary of the Treasury) to raise or lower the tariff on any agricultural or industrial product as much as 50 percent.

Mellon generally raised rates on manufactured products. Tariffs climbed so high that foreign manufacturers were frozen out of the American market. American industrialists had to compete only among themselves.

Like his cuts in income taxes, Mellon's tariff policies reduced the revenues received by the

This view down Pennsylvania Avenue to the Capitol in Washington, D.C., was taken from the United States Treasury building. It shows the hurrying spirit of the 1920s.

federal government. Americans bought fewer foreign products because of the artificially high prices caused by the high import duties. And, of course, the government collected no duties on these lost imports.

Frugal Government. Having reduced the government's revenues, Mellon also had to cut government expenses. The Treaty of Washington of 1921 allowed the United States to get out of the naval arms race. The government saved millions of dollars by canceling the construction of expensive new battleships and cruisers. Mellon also abolished many regulatory agencies created under Wilson and cut the payroll in others.

To introduce business methods into government finance, Mellon sponsored the creation of a new agency, the *Bureau of the Budget,* founded in 1921. The purpose of a government budget, like a household budget, was to avoid going deeply into debt. Before 1921, departments and agencies of the federal government asked Congress for money as they needed it. Congress decided, on the merits of each request, whether to grant the

request, to increase it, or to reduce it. At the end of each session, revenues and expenditures were totaled up. In theory, Congress decided the next year's taxes and expenditures on the basis of whether the Treasury had a *surplus* or a *deficit.* The purpose of the Bureau of the Budget was to predict revenues and expenditures for the *fiscal year* ahead. (A *fiscal year* is 12 months long, but need not start on January 1.) On the basis of these figures, the Bureau suggested a budget for the coming year to Congress and the President. The assumption was that Congress and the President would limit their expenses to the amount of money that was available.

During the 1920s, Mellon's goal was to pay off the $25 billion the government had borrowed from banks during World War I. This sound business practice would put even more capital into the hands of investors. During most of the 1920s, the government spent less money than was collected in taxes. By 1929, Mellon had succeeded in paying off one-third of the national debt that the New Era Republicans had inherited from the Wilson administration.

"Silent Cal" wasn't unwilling to talk—as long as it was on his own terms. If he could control the conversation or interrogation, he was actually gregarious. This was partially the result of the time during which Coolidge served. The press had already made the shift to watchdog and critic, rather than just observer.

 633

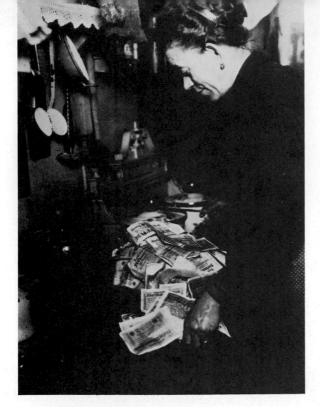

As inflation gripped postwar Germany, people used almost worthless marks as fuel.

Financial Crisis in Europe.
The Mellon-Coolidge financial policy concerned Europeans as much as it did Americans. The former allies, especially Great Britain and France, owed about $10 billion to the American government and American bankers. They intended to repay these debts with the $32 billion in *reparations* owed to them by Germany, according to the Treaty of Versailles.

Unfortunately, the Fordney-McCumber Tariff kept German industry from selling its goods in the United States, the world's richest nation. Germany's cash income decreased but the need to pay debts and buy imports remained. The German economy fell to pieces. With gold and resources flowing out of the country to pay creditors, the German government met its need for money at home by printing increasing amounts of paper money, causing runaway inflation.

Nowhere has inflation been as rapid as it was in Germany during the 1920s. People sometimes had to use large bundles of the almost worthless paper money to buy necessities such as bread and meat. The instability of the German economy worried German citizens and helped extremist political parties, particularly the Communists and Adolf Hitler's Nazis, to gain a large following.

Stabilizing the International Economy.
The stability of Germany was of interest to all European nations and the United States. However, Mellon refused to reduce tariff rates, and President Coolidge rejected every suggestion that the United States cancel French and British debts which in turn, would have allowed France and Britain to cancel German reparations payments. Coolidge's reply was, "They hired the money, didn't they?"

The United States did offer some help to the Europeans. In the *Dawes Plan* of 1924, the United States agreed to *reschedule* the payments of both reparations and debt. That is, France and Britain were given more time to repay their loans, and Germany was given more time to pay reparations. But the total was not reduced.

Instead, the government encouraged American banks to make loans to Europeans. On the surface, this ensured a circular flow of money. Between 1923 and 1929, when the *Young Plan* again rescheduled European debts, Germany paid $2 billion in reparations, Britain and France paid $2.6 billion to American bankers, and the bankers loaned a similar amount to Germany. But in fact, money was still being taken out of Europe to repay the United States. And the American loans to Germany took money that was supposed to trickle down to the working class and reinvested it in a nonproductive balancing of international books.

The Kellogg-Briand Pact.
Although the United States refused to join the League of Nations and demanded that Europeans pay all their debts, it is not quite correct to say that Americans turned their backs on the world. Although the idea of "Collective Security" as embodied in the League was rejected, the New Era administrations did deal actively with foreign countries on a one-to-one basis.

An example was the *Kellogg-Briand Pact* of 1928. Secretary of State Frank B. Kellogg joined French Foreign Minister Aristide Briand to write a treaty that outlawed war between the two nations. Eventually, 62 nations signed the Kellogg-Briand Pact, promising never to war against the other

One of the consequences of the change in the flow of gold during this period was that it drove wheat and, to a lesser extent, other crop prices, up. The flurry of prosperity was short-lived and became known as "the banker's crop."

This photograph shows U.S. Marines boarding a transport enroute to Nicaragua. Military leaders in several Latin American countries asked for American troops to put down rebellions.

signers. But, like the "cooling off" treaties negotiated by Wilson's Secretary of State, William Jennings Bryan, the Kellogg-Briand Pact did not provide any means of enforcing peace.

New Era Diplomacy in Latin America.

American business investments in the Western Hemisphere climbed from about $800 million in 1914 to $5.4 billion in 1929. The United States replaced Great Britain as the major investor in Latin America.

The poorer Latin American countries desperately needed capital to improve the lives of their people. New Era businesspeople took little interest in the masses of Latin Americans. Many countries became ruled by military dictators who exploited and impoverished their own culture.

When rebellion threatened, the dictators turned to American investors for help. In turn, the investors put pressure on Washington, and Washington usually obliged. By 1924, the United States directly or indirectly controlled the finances of ten Latin American countries. For at least part of the decade, marines occupied Nicaragua, Honduras,

Cuba, Haiti, and the Dominican Republic.

In the short run, the interests of United States businesspeople were protected. In the long run, however, United States policy in Latin America caused anger among the people of Latin America.

SECTION REVIEW

1. Write a sentence to identify: William G. McAdoo, fiscal year, trickle-down economics, New Era Republicans.

2. Name the winner of the 1924 presidential election and his opponents.

3. Give the source of this quotation: "The business of America is business." Explain how this spirit was carried out in Secretary Mellon's policies on income tax, tariff, and government revenues and expenditures.

4. Summarize the following: the Dawes and Young plans, the Kellogg-Briand Pact, New Era Latin America diplomacy.

Discussion Question: How does the text's discussion help explain contemporary anti-American attitudes among Latin Americans? Alert students to current examples of why this attitude might still be justified.

 635

2. ENJOYING GOOD TIMES

During the 1920s, a majority of Americans shared President Coolidge's admiration of businesspeople. In 1924, the voters gave Coolidge's pro-business government a comfortable 54 percent of the popular vote. In addition, every Congress between 1920 and 1930 had Republican majorities in both Houses.

Even the Democratic party's national leaders were as pro-business as the Republicans were. Davis, the Democratic presidential nominee in 1924, was a Wall Street lawyer. Alfred Smith, the party's nominee in 1928, was closely tied to New York bankers. Even the grand old man of the Democratic party, William Jennings Bryan, who had once said that no man could make a million dollars honestly, made several million by speculating in Florida real estate.

Businesspeople as Heroes.

On a local level, businessperson's clubs—the Rotary, the Kiwanis, the Lions, the Junior Chamber of Commerce—assumed community leadership and preached *boosterism*, or promoting the good points of business. People looked to successful *entrepreneurs* for answers to questions on every imaginable subject. Even John D. Rockefeller, an arch-villain to the previous generation of progressives, came to be respected by most Americans.

The experience of Bruce Barton, an advertising entrepreneur, showed how idolization of business dominated American culture. In his 1925 book *The Man Nobody Knows*, Barton depicted Jesus Christ as the ultimate salesman. Instead of condemning this as blasphemy, the American people bought so many copies of the book that it remained a best seller for two years.

The vice president of General Motors, John J. Raskob, encouraged the adoration of business-people in articles in popular magazines. Some ministers even urged Americans to thank God for businesspeople.

The American Pastime.

Recreation was an important part of life in the 1920s. Golf courses, swimming pools, skating rinks, and tennis clubs became fixtures of comfortable suburbs.

Spectator sports were even more important, and baseball was the supreme "great American pastime," despite a bribery scandal surrounding the 1919 World Series. Into the early 1920s, the ultimate player was Ty Cobb, the "Georgia Peach." An extraordinary hitter and base runner, Cobb won games for the Detroit Tigers by scrapping out runs with singles, base-stealing, and determined play.

Just when age was slowing Cobb down, George Herman "Babe" Ruth of the New York Yankees changed baseball strategy with his decisive home runs—60 of them in 1927. The baseball itself was made livelier when the team owners saw how popular home runs were: soon, several players were hitting 40 or 50 home runs a year. Ten years earlier, 20 home runs a year was extraordinary.

Blacks were not permitted to play baseball in the major leagues. Instead, they organized their own teams, with players as good as any in the country. However, a black player could never hope to be paid as much or to receive as much recognition as a white player. Black players traveled around in creaky buses and stayed in inferior hotels.

Other Sports.

Boxing ran a close second to baseball in popularity. The premier boxer of the decade was Jack Dempsey, the "Manassa Mauler," who overpowered almost every opponent. In 1921, his fight with Georges Carpentier of France pulled in more than $1 million at the gate. In 1927, a bout between Dempsey and Gene Tunney, the man who replaced Dempsey as heavyweight champion, grossed more than $2.5 million in ticket sales.

Football, a game that had evolved out of the sport of rugby in the late 1800s, became a mania. Middle-class people and working-class people alike identified with local college and university teams. Under coach Knute Rockne, Notre Dame was the most successful college team, almost always turning in a winning season.

Harold "Red" Grange was the most popular individual player of the 1920s. Called the "Galloping Ghost" because he was so difficult to tackle, Grange rarely scored fewer than two touchdowns in a game. Possibly the finest all-around athlete was an American Indian, Jim Thorpe. He won Olympic gold medals in 1912, did well as a professional baseball player, and starred in football in the 1920s.

Discussion Question: Sports heroes and business and political figures still provide fertile ground for hero worship. How is hero worship both a good and a bad thing? Discuss how it can be positive in setting useful values and as a morale builder but how it can be negative if it makes a romantic figure of a person without showing the person's faults.

Athletes were folk heroes and heroines in the 1920s. Tennis champion Helen Wills is shown at Forest Hills in 1929 (above). Jim Thorpe (below) is shown competing in the Stockholm Olympics.

A Car for Everyone. The most important force shaping daily life during the 1920s was the automobile. Manufacturers such as Cord, Duesenberg, La Salle, and Cadillac continued to turn out luxurious, high-powered, expensive cars.

But still more important was Henry Ford's *Model T*, known as the "flivver" or *tin lizzie.* Ford developed the car in 1908 to be the auto that nearly every family could afford. It was an instant success. The public bought 11,000 Model T's in the first year.

The Model T was a starkly simple car, easy to understand, repair, and drive. Riding on high wheels, it could be driven on muddy, rutted, rocky country roads that foiled racy, low-slung, expensive cars.

Most important of all, it was cheap. Ford perfected the assembly line, which enabled him to produce 9,000 cars a day by 1925, one every ten seconds! He could thus cut the price to $290, when most cars cost $800–$1,200. By 1927, 15 million had been sold.

Henry Ford poses next to a Model T. By 1925, assembly-line production made it possible for Ford to manufacture 9,000 cars a day.

Research Assignment: Have students write a report on Henry Ford and his contributions to American industry. Encourage students to illustrate their reports with models or illustrations of an assembly line and the cars invented by Ford.

 637

General Motors soon challenged Ford for control of the mass market with its more stylish and comfortable Chevrolet. The company that became Chrysler Corporation entered the low-priced car market with the Plymouth. Because Henry Ford refused to make changes in a design he thought was perfect, these more advanced competitors gained larger shares of the market each year. The fast-growing used-car market also helped to put America on wheels.

A People on Wheels.

The automobile was one of the keys to "Coolidge prosperity." By 1928, car manufacturing was the country's biggest industry. It consumed 15 percent of the nation's steel, 75 percent of its plate glass, and 80 percent of its rubber. Gasoline for fuel replaced kerosene as the oil industry's best-selling product.

Automobiles also spawned new businesses, such as service stations, parts and accessories shops, and motels—"motor hotels." The industry stimulated road building and indirectly encouraged the growth of chain grocery stores called supermarkets, where a family could stock up on a week's worth of provisions in one trip. Piggly-Wiggly, one of the first such chains, had 515 stores in 1920 and 2,500 in 1929. The Safeway chain had 766 outlets in 1920, 2,660 in 1929.

Turning on the Lights.

Second only to automobiles in transforming American society was electricity. By the end of the 1920s, more electricity was being generated in the United States than in all other countries of the world combined. All the major cities were electrified, as were most areas near the cities. Only farms continued, for the most part, to be illuminated by kerosene lamps.

The electric refrigerator began to replace the messy icebox for cooling foods, and making and delivering ice soon became a forgotten business. Electric washing machines made laundering easier. Imaginative manufacturers hooked up electric motors to almost every household device. Each year during the 1920s, the United States Patent Office recorded the plans for about 90,000 new gadgets, many of them electrified.

This 1923 "dream kitchen" featured the latest model refrigerator, stove, water heater, and fan. Electric appliances revolutionized homemaking by easing or altogether eliminating many of the time-consuming chores that people had performed for centuries.

Radio. The most important electrical gadget did not perform an old job but provided a new kind of entertainment. The radio was the youngest and most successful of the new electronic industries. "Wireless" transmission of sound was perfected by an Italian inventor, Guglielmo Marconi, in 1895. The first commercial radio station, KDKA in Pittsburgh, broadcast the Harding-Cox election results in 1920. Only a few hobbyists with primitive, homemade crystal sets were able to pick out the reports amidst clattering static. But by 1927, 732 stations were broadcasting news, music, and variety entertainment along with raucous commercials for everything from shaving soap to "Holeproof Hosiery." By 1930, more than 12 million families owned a receiver.

Secretary of Commerce Hoover wanted to see the new medium used for educational purposes. Instead, radio's chief functions became entertainment and the sale of consumer goods. Critics of the new culture complained of the constant din of comedians, brassy music, and "buy-buy-buy!" that wafted from the windows of American homes each evening.

Recorded Music. The recorded music industry actually predated electricity. The first phonographs, or *Victrolas*, were powered not by electricity but by a spring-driven motor that had to be wound up between plays.

Electricity ended this inconvenience and also allowed more faithful reproduction of sound. The Radio Corporation of America (RCA) was the most successful early producer of phonographs and recordings. RCA had plenty of competition, because it did not take much money to start a recording company.

Songs were written especially to "fit" the brief time available on a record spinning at 78 revolutions per minute. Families could now listen to their favorite popular music. People could buy recordings of songs performed by stars such as Jimmy Rodgers, "the singing brakeman" of Mississippi, who blended country rhythms with blues. Opera stars such as Enrico Caruso were heard for the first time in American living rooms.

Black singers and instrumentalists were also recorded, and much of what we know of the evolution of jazz and the blues, America's unique musical forms, comes from the recordings of such

In the 1920s, American jazz greats such as Louis Armstrong could be heard at home on records.

black artists as Ma Rainey, Bessie Smith, Blind Lemon Jefferson, Louis Armstrong, Kid Ory, and dozens of others.

The Movies. During the early 1920s, movies were silent. The country's favorite stars were actors specializing in quick-moving, swashbuckling action like Douglas Fairbanks, actresses with faces that could express a wide range of emotions like "America's Sweetheart" Mary Pickford, and slapstick comedians like Charlie Chaplin.

In 1927, the Warner Brothers studio produced the first sound movie, *The Jazz Singer*, starring vaudeville singer Al Jolson. "Talkies" soon became more popular than silents, and although the first movie sound was very scratchy, the industry soon developed more professional equipment.

The stories that the movies told were often sentimental "tear-jerkers," which rivaled comedies and adventure stories for popularity. By emphasizing show business themes, movie producers also helped to make actors and other

Farms and rural areas of the U.S. only began to get electricity in 1910. Electrification of these areas didn't really begin in earnest until about 1923.

Research Assignment: Have students write a report on stars and celebrities of this period. They should pay special attention to the qualities of these people that appealed to the public.

MOVERS AND SHAPERS

George Gershwin

On the night of February 12, 1924, the audience at New York's Aeolian Hall was treated to the first performance of "Rhapsody in Blue," the jazz concerto for piano and orchestra, composed and played by George Gershwin (1898–1935). The concert was an historic success and jazz earned a place as part of the serious tradition of music in the United States.

George Gershwin was remarkably versatile. He was at ease with all types of music: classical, jazz, and popular. Yet he never played any musical instruments until he was 13 years old. It wasn't until he heard a classmate play the violin that he became interested in music and began to study the piano.

Gershwin's teacher soon discovered that he had a great musical talent on his hands. George learned in one sitting what it took other students months to learn. By the time he was 15 he was composing songs. He got a job on *Tin Pan Alley*, the center of the music publishing business in New York, as a "plugger" playing songs for customers. Gershwin was only 21 when "Swanee" made him a famous composer.

After that, Gershwin's success came rapidly. He and his brother Ira worked together. George wrote the music, Ira the words. Besides hit songs, the Gershwin brothers also wrote musical shows for Broadway. The songs in the shows often became hits, too.

Gershwin's songs and concert pieces have become American classics. "Rhapsody in Blue," "Piano Concerto in F," and "An American in Paris," rank with the finest American music. His thrilling work *Porgy and Bess*, the most popular opera ever written by an American, was performed by a cast of black singers, something rarely done in the theater during the 1930s.

Gershwin loved life and his own success. He was equally at ease in high society, Broadway saloons, and Harlem nightclubs. His sudden death from a brain tumor at the age of 37 shocked the nation. Thousands of people stood in the rain to attend his funeral in New York. Although his life was short, he left a melodic legacy to America and to the world.

Irving Berlin

A composer whom George Gershwin greatly admired was Irving Berlin (born 1888). Berlin was born in Russia and came to New York as a young boy. At 13, not wanting to be a burden to his mother, he left home and got a job as a newsboy. He sang for nickels and dimes in saloons before he got a job as a singing waiter.

Eventually, Berlin turned to songwriting. The first song he wrote, with the help of a pianist co-worker, earned Berlin only 33 cents. But he had found a new career, and in 1911 he had his first hit song— "Alexander's Ragtime Band." It was a huge hit and Berlin became the best-known songwriter in the country. He wrote scores for musical comedies and movies. Among his songs are "White Christmas," "Easter Parade," "God Bless America," and "There's No Business Like Show Business."

Research Assignment: Students interested in the music of the period might want to do reports on composers like Berlin and Gershwin. Encourage students to give presentations that use recordings to illustrate their reports.

people in entertainment into a kind of American aristocracy, idolized by millions. When romantic movie star Rudolph Valentino died in 1926 at the age of 31, tens of thousands of his fans attended his funeral.

Revolution in Morals.

Traditionalists were alarmed by such spectacles as the long lines of quietly sobbing people winding past the coffin of Valentino. The Twenties was an era when the young people of the middle classes, particularly women, seemed to be breaking free of the moral codes of their parents. The rebellion was symbolized in dress. "Modern" young men wore outlandish bell-bottom trousers and "loud" argyle sweaters. They slicked their hair down as Valentino had done and carried hip flasks filled with the then illegal whiskey.

Young women bobbed their hair—cut it almost as short as men's—and donned the helmet hats and straight, short dresses of the "flapper." Many wore conspicuous make-up and smoked cigarettes in public, which was regarded as extremely shocking behavior.

The automobile made the greater freedom of young people possible. Cars allowed them to escape not only chaperones but the eyes of people who knew them in their own neighborhoods or small towns. Free of such restraints, they were able to form attitudes and values that did not rely on what their elders had to say.

Advertising.

New styles, such as the flapper costume, were introduced to the entire country in a comparatively short time by the new and energetic advertising industry. Announcing what is for sale is, of course, as ancient as buying and selling. Until the late nineteenth century, however, most advertisements took the form of simple announcements.

The "flagpole sitter" in the photograph below is attempting to draw attention to the two advertisements mounted on the automobile.

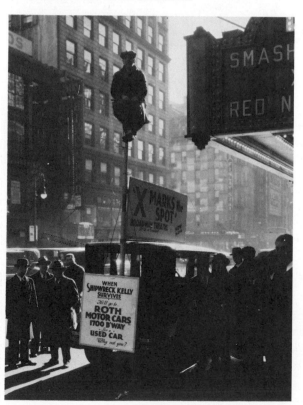

A 1928 advertisement for a Lincoln automobile was typical of the elegant images that were found to result in greater sales.

Charles Lindbergh, the "Lone Eagle," made the first nonstop solo trans-Atlantic flight in his Spirit of St. Louis. *He landed near Paris on May 21, 1927, after 33 hours aloft.*

Then, companies that produced breakfast cereals and patent medicines discovered that if they painted billboards large enough and repeated their message often enough, their sales increased. During the 1920s, advertisers learned how to create demand for products. Automobile advertisements did not list the mechanical specifications of cars, but created an "image" for them. Owning a Pierce-Arrow showed that a person had "good taste." The Stutz Bearcat owner was a fast, sporty type. The Dodge was the proper car for a family. Women who bought Plymouths were liberated and modern. Such were the images created by advertising.

Nor were cars the only objects of image-making. A company offering piano lessons promised greater popularity for people who could play. The producers of Listerine antiseptic, a mouthwash, increased sales by inventing a disease called "halitosis," which the use of Listerine promised to cure. In Listerine advertisements, people lost jobs and even a chance for happiness in marriage because of bad breath.

Ballyhoo. With enough fanfare, it seemed as though Americans of the 1920s could be aroused to fascinated enthusiasm about anything. Newspapers called tabloids specialized in *sensational* stories rather than hard news. Murder trials that might previously have gone unnoticed became objects of rapt national attention when dressed up in colorful language accompanied by "exclusive photographs." When sensational stories did not present themselves, the tabloids invented news. Stories about such daredevil stunts as walking on the wings of airplanes or sitting atop a flagpole for weeks at a time sold millions of newspapers.

Discussion Question: Given the political nature of the times, what might explain the use of sensationalism by the press? Encourage students to discuss modern-day use of sensationalism by the press.

The most famous story of the decade was about the first solo flight across the Atlantic Ocean in 1927 by a quiet, handsome pilot, Charles A. Lindbergh. The flight took 33 hours, and Lindbergh had to navigate by the stars, even as Columbus did in 1492. A serious student of aeronautics, Lindbergh became the object of hysterical adulation on both sides of the Atlantic when he accomplished his feat. For years after his flight he was unable to appear in public without touching off something like a happy riot.

Nor was "hoopla" used only to sell mouthwash and newspapers. To a large extent, Coolidge prosperity was based on encouraging people to believe that everyone could get rich, and get rich quickly.

SECTION REVIEW

1. Write a sentence to identify: boosterism, "tin lizzie," *The Jazz Singer,* Charles Lindbergh.
2. Give three examples of Americans' admiration for businesspeople in the 1920s.
3. Give the names and nicknames of three sports heroes of the 1920s. Identify the sports that they played.
4. List six industries that contributed to the reshaping of American life during the 1920s. Explain the effect each industry had on the American life style.
5. Explain what sort of stories tabloids used to sell newspapers.

---

3. BOOM AND BUST

Many Americans enjoyed the good times of the 1920s by living beyond their means. That is, they bought their automobiles, radios, and household gadgets although they did not have the cash on hand. Instead they bought on the *installment plan.* Installment buying is actually a form of borrowing, and the customer pays back the item's cost plus interest over a period of time.

A customer could have a refrigerator that cost $87.50 installed in the kitchen by paying a $5 down payment, and including interest, make monthly payments of $10. The purchase of a vacuum cleaner that cost $28.95 required a buyer to pay only $2 over the counter and to sign a contract promising payments of $4 a month.

In order to encourage Americans to go into debt, merchants had to overcome deeply ingrained habits of thrift and frugality. Enshrined in the writings of Benjamin Franklin, preached in churches, and taught in schools, traditional American ethics held that people should avoid debt. They should do without goods they could not afford. Money not needed for essentials was to be saved, not spent.

But in the Coolidge era, very few people wanted to save for several years to buy a $600 automobile when it was possible to drive one home for less than $60 and make payments that, because of prosperity, would surely be painless.

As a result, during the late 1920s, 60 percent of all the automobiles on the road had been bought on time payments. About 80 percent of all refrigerators, radios, and vacuum cleaners and some 90 percent of pianos, sewing machines, and washing machines were credit purchases.

Sunny Florida. Consumer goods were not the only things that could be bought on credit. Americans with a little cash to spare were encouraged to turn their hundreds of dollars into thousands and their thousands into tens of thousands by promoters of get-rich-quick schemes.

These schemes were all speculative, but not all of them were sound investments. One of the most famous of the *speculative schemes* centered on real estate along the south Florida coast. Before the 1920s, most of the population of Florida lived in the northern half of the peninsula. In south Florida, citrus fruit was a major crop, and on the magnificent sand beaches of the Atlantic coast, the very wealthy built homes for winter vacations and retirement.

By the 1920s, good rail connections and highways made it possible for middle class people to vacation or retire in the Sunshine State. Miami Beach, Fort Lauderdale, Orlando and other cities catering to this potentially large market sprouted in the subtropical sun. People who owned desirable real estate, including many orange growers, became wealthy overnight by subdividing orchards into lots suitable for building retirement homes and businesses that would serve the new population.

Discussion Question: What are the potential problems of the excessive large scale use of credit? Have students see how using credit in this way affects periods leading to depressions and recessions. Explain that there is an analogy between the way excesses in individual credit create problems for the individual and for society.

The Craze. Promoters not only raved about Florida's sun and warm ocean waters, they also assured people who had no intention of moving to Florida that they could get rich very quickly. The way to do it, they claimed, was to buy real estate cheap, then sell it to others who wanted to live there or to other *speculators* who believed the price of land would continue to rise. There was no need to worry about already high prices. Buyers could make a *down payment*, sign a *note* to pay the balance on easy terms, and probably sell the property before too many monthly payments came due.

As often happens with speculative schemes, the Florida mania fed on itself. Stories of fabulous profiteering appeared in northern newspapers and infected more and more people with the belief that they too could purchase building lots at wasteland prices and sell them to someone else for a profit. In 1925, some lots in Miami Beach changed hands a dozen times within a few months, each new buyer paying more for the property in the belief that someone else would soon offer an even higher price. At the height of the craze, one Miami newspaper ran more than 500 pages filled with advertisements of land for sale. More and more northerners began to buy Florida land they had never seen. Unscrupulous promoters sold alligator-infested swampland and "beautiful beachfront lots" that lay under ten feet of water at high tide.

As long as investors continued to be found, people made money. But the speculators owed banks or other speculators for the greater part of the property's inflated value. When speculators found no other investors, they had to make the monthly mortgage payments themselves, instead of passing them on to the next buyer as they had hoped. Since these speculators did not have the cash to make the payments, they had to sell their properties at reduced prices to raise cash.

As prices began to drop, other speculators panicked. In the general rush to unload properties, the whole speculative balloon collapsed. Banks foreclosed on mortgages, and then were stuck with land that was worth only a fraction of the mortgages.

Many citrus growers who had sold groves for a few thousand dollars at the beginning of the speculation boom and had watched prices inflate into the hundreds of thousands of dollars, often found themselves back in possession of their groves when the people who had bought the farms defaulted on their payments and had to return the land.

Playing the Stock Market. Florida was merely a sideshow in the speculation of the 1920s. The number of people involved in Florida land speculations was only a tiny fraction of the American public. When the boom went bust, it did not affect the American economy except for the failure of a few banks that had loaned money to speculators. However, optimism for the future ran so high during the Coolidge years that a new and far more dangerous speculative craze was in full swing while Florida was still picking up the pieces.

This was the great *bull market*, or tremendous rise in the price of corporation stocks, that began in 1927. The *New York Stock Exchange* attracted people of comparatively modest means all over the country, thanks to Coolidge prosperity and the ticker-tape machine, which allowed stock prices in New York to be flashed almost instantly to cities and towns across the nation.

By 1929, 1.5 million Americans were "*playing the market.*" That is, they were buying stocks in companies, not because they wanted to collect regular dividends, but because of their intention of selling when the price rose, thus pocketing a quick profit. As with Florida land, stock prices went crazy. During the summer of 1929, the price of a share of American Telephone and Telegraph climbed from $209 to $303. General Motors stock rose from $268 to $391 and then soared to $452 on September 3.

Empty Values. In theory, the value of a *share* in a corporation reflected the company's earning power. That is, the purpose of selling stock was to raise money so that the corporation could improve its facilities in order to make more money. The more profitable the company, the more valuable its stock. Thus, when shares of RCA multiplied in value several times during the 1920s, it reflected the amazing success of that company in selling radios, Victrolas, and records.

However, the 300-percent rise in the overall value of stocks between 1925 and 1929 reflected little more than the fact that investors bid up

  Research Assignment: Based on research done from recent newspapers and magazines, have students write brief reports on modern speculative schemes.

prices, believing that someone else would soon be willing to pay even more for them. It did not matter that many companies paid no dividends or that very few corporations used the money raised by selling shares to improve their industrial capacity. In reality, the values were empty.

The problem was complicated by the practice of *buying on margin*, which meant buying on credit. The speculator who had $1,000 to spend in the market did not buy ten shares at $100 per share, but 100 shares on a ten percent margin. The speculator paid $10 down, then borrowed the remaining 90 percent by using the stock as collateral. (*Collateral* is property that a lender can take over if the borrower cannot repay a loan.) As long as the value of the stock continued to climb, everything was fine. If the value sank below the amount of the loan, however, the speculator's margin was called in. It was necessary to put up more cash or lose the shares as well as the money already invested in them.

The Inevitable Bust. Joseph P. Kennedy, a Boston millionaire (and the father of John F. Kennedy), got out of the stock market in 1929. He said he had sold all his shares after the person who shined his shoes said that he too was playing the market. Kennedy knew that if someone in such a low-paying job was buying shares, then there were no people left to bid the stock prices higher. The inevitable *crash* was coming.

On September 3, 1929, it started. The average price of shares on the New York Stock Exchange dipped sharply. For a month prices spurted up and down. Some people began to lose money. Others believed the upward spiral would begin again.

A crowd gathers outside the New York Stock Exchange on October 24, 1929, to hear that their stocks had crashed. The Wall Street crash wiped out small investors, sent shock waves through the financial community, and soon paralyzed the nation's economy.

Then, on October 24, *Black Thursday*, a record 13 million shares changed hands, at ever-lower prices. On Tuesday, October 29, a panic broke out. Believing that prices would continue to fall, speculators trying to get out of the market dumped 16 million shares on the Exchange. Wall Street clerks worked through the night under an avalanche of paperwork. When the dust settled the next morning, more than $30 billion in paper value had been wiped out.

Crash Becomes Depression.

Stock market busts had happened before. In each case, some speculators were ruined, usually those with few financial resources, while others held on, tightened their belts, and waited for prices to rise again. After the *Great Crash* of 1929, however, stock values did not recover. Prices continued to decline for nearly four years.

This was something new. Even investors who believed they were picking up bargains in shares through 1930, 1931, and 1932 saw their money melt away. The *Great Depression* had arrived.

Although only the 1.5 million people who played the market were directly affected by the crash, millions more felt it. Banks that had made easy loans to speculators went bankrupt. Frugal people who had kept their money in savings accounts found that their life savings were gone when the banks closed their doors.

Corporations cut back on operations or even shut down, throwing people out of work. If those people had been buying on credit, they could no longer make the payments. That forced more businesses and more banks into bankruptcy, and the spiral continued.

The Illusion of Coolidge Prosperity.

The stockmarket crash touched off the Great Depression of the 1930s, but it did not cause it. Despite the appearances of sound economic health, Coolidge prosperity had several weak foundations that economists might have seen if they had not been dizzied by sensational rises in stock values.

First of all, the prosperity of the 1920s relied too heavily on the sales of consumer durables, goods that, once purchased, lasted a long time. Most families bought only one car, one washing machine, one sewing machine, and one vacuum cleaner, and then did not replace them for years.

Even very wealthy people, who could afford to buy many automobiles, did not, of course, do so.

This meant that eventually, the demand for automobiles and other consumer durables leveled off. A few economists had noted this even before the market crash.

Depression Within Prosperity.

Not every American family in 1929 owned an automobile or any of the major electrical appliances. Blacks, for example, never really shared as a group in Coolidge prosperity. Those who had moved North during World War I often found that they were bumped out of comparatively well-paying industrial jobs when white soldiers returned after the armistice. For the most part, only menial jobs that paid low wages were open to blacks. As a group, blacks were not able to contribute to the boom because they could not afford the consumer durables on which the boom was based.

Blacks who remained in farming in the South were doubly deprived. Dairy farmers and truck farmers (who grew fruits and vegetables for mostly local markets) did share in the prosperity. But to the nation's *staple* farmers, those who raised wheat, corn, and cotton, there were no good times. For them, the Roaring Twenties was a time of depression. Wheat that had sold for $2.50 a bushel during World War I sank to $1 a bushel during the 1920s.

Poorly Distributed Income.

The farmers' problem was essentially the same as it had been during the 1890s. They were producing more food than the rest of the population could consume, and prices fell. In two acts known as the *McNary-Haugen Bills*, Congress tried to raise the income of farmers to *parity*, that is, to a level that compared favorably with their income in good years. To do this, the federal government would buy whatever part of the annual crop of staples was not needed at home and sell it on the world market for whatever price it would bring. Farmers and companies that transported and processed food would absorb the government's loss in the transaction by paying a special equalization tax. In the meantime, by reducing the domestic supply of their crops, farmers would receive higher prices for the products they brought to market.

President Coolidge vetoed the McNary-

Class Activity: Depict the profound effects of the stock market crash by using pictures and narratives of people who reacted to the disaster. Include narratives of people who picked themselves up "by their bootstraps" and made it through those difficult times. Discuss the reasons for the differences in reactions.

PROFILES OF THE PRESIDENCY

HERBERT HOOVER

1929–1933

Seven months after Herbert Hoover became president, the stock market crashed and the Great Depression began. Looking back, he wrote:

With the October–November stock-market crash the primary question at once arose as to whether the President and the Federal government should undertake to mitigate and remedy the evils stemming from it. No President before had ever believed there was a governmental responsibility in such cases. No matter what the urging on previous occasions, Presidents steadfastly had maintained that the Federal government was apart from such eruptions; they had always been left to blow themselves out. . . . It is not given even to Presidents to see the future. Economic storms do not develop all at once, and they change without notice. In my three years of the slump and depression they changed repeatedly for the worse—and with the speed of lightning. We could have done better—in retrospect.

—MEMOIRS. 1952

Haugen Bills on the grounds that such government intervention in the economy was unnecessary and undesirable. In doing so, he ensured that farmers would not participate in the consumer economy. But farmers made up almost a third of the American population, and without their participation, the boom was bound to end.

Hoover Takes the Blame. Although President Coolidge's do-nothing policy toward the farm depression and his encouragement of stock market speculation contributed to the economic collapse of 1929, Silent Cal did not have to take the blame for it. Early in the election year of 1928, he said, "I do not choose to run for president." Instead, Herbert Hoover stood for election, and easily won the Republican nomination.

Prosperity was at flood tide, and Hoover was, if anything, respected more in the business culture than Coolidge had been. Hoover was a self-made millionaire with an international reputation for intelligence and for getting things done.

Hoover's Democratic opponent was Alfred E. Smith, the governor of New York. Smith was laden with handicaps. Smith dressed like a "city slicker" in well-tailored suits and a derby hat perched at a rakish angle. His nasal New York accent, enhanced on the crackling radio, reminded rural people of their suspicions of big cities.

Smith tried to overcome rural opposition by endorsing the McNary-Haugen idea. But Hoover won by a landslide, 444 electoral votes to 37.

Coolidge handed the presidency over to Hoover in March of 1929. After one last heady summer, the bottom fell out of the boom. Hoover had little to do with the crash and the depression. But he was president on Black Thursday, and he was to end his political career as the villain of the Great Depression.

SECTION REVIEW

1. Write a sentence to identify: buying on margin, Black Thursday, McNary-Haugen Bills, Alfred E. Smith.

2. What was the installment plan? How did it change the American public's buying attitudes and habits in the 1920s?

3. Name which of the following that are considered causes of the Great Depression: stock market crash, speculation in real estate, businesses' over-reliance on sale of expensive consumer goods, playing the stock market, low income of a large portion of the population.

The development of metals that could withstand high heat improved the efficiency of gas turbine engines. They were widely used to power planes, ships, and electric generators.

The first regular TV broadcast started in 1936 with Felix the Cat as star player.

Diesel powered locomotives, traveling power plants whose engines used comparatively low cost oil for fuel, could do heavy duty work such as pulling overloaded freight trains and high-speed passenger trains.

C H A N G I N G   T E C H N O L O G Y

19 00	19 10	
Stereophonic sound equipment introduced	Car engine ignition designed	Gramophone record developed
Staining microscope developed	Steam-driven mowing machine introduced	Drum brake produced
Electric alternator invented	Neon discovered	Acetate rayon patented
	Oscillograph invented	Radiation therapy initiated
		Air conditioning introduced

Discussion Question: Many of the inventions on this page had profound impact on both transportation and communication. Have students discuss what impacts the inventions had and how these inventions contributed to changes in society that are still evident today.

Brine Tank

Freezing Rooms

Cooling Rooms

Poultry

Butter

Meat

Apples

Eggs

The quick-freezing process invented by Clarence Birdseye in the 1920s drastically reduced food spoilage and allowed Americans to enjoy "fresh" food out of season.

The results of the 1920 presidential election heralded the beginning of regular radio broadcasting. Within 5 years radio programs became a major source of family entertainment.

Caterpillar tractors were used for heavy jobs, such as excavating. These huge machines enabled one operator to do the work of scores of hand laborers.

19	20	19	30	19	40
Neon signs demonstrated	Magnetic tapes produced	Practical cyclotron built
Electric oven manufactured	Ship-to-ship communication instituted	Radar developed
Motorized movie cameras introduced	Television demonstrated	Nylon patented
Agitator washing machine marketed	Penicillin discovered	Color film marketed
		Jet aircraft flight initiated

CHAPTER REVIEW

TIME LINE

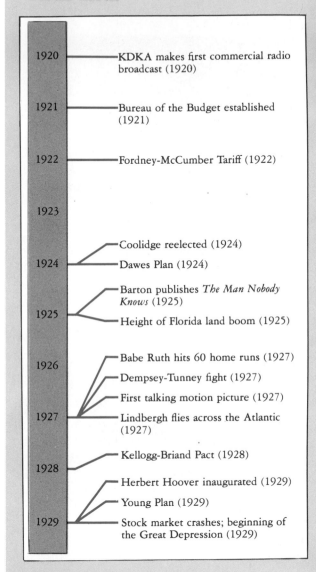

Year	Event
1920	KDKA makes first commercial radio broadcast (1920)
1921	Bureau of the Budget established (1921)
1922	Fordney-McCumber Tariff (1922)
1923	
1924	Coolidge reelected (1924)
1924	Dawes Plan (1924)
1925	Barton publishes *The Man Nobody Knows* (1925)
1925	Height of Florida land boom (1925)
1926	
1927	Babe Ruth hits 60 home runs (1927)
1927	Dempsey-Tunney fight (1927)
1927	First talking motion picture (1927)
1927	Lindbergh flies across the Atlantic (1927)
1928	Kellogg-Briand Pact (1928)
1929	Herbert Hoover inaugurated (1929)
1929	Young Plan (1929)
1929	Stock market crashes; beginning of the Great Depression (1929)

TIME LINE QUESTIONS

1. In what years were the payment of European war debts rearranged?
2. How many years after Coolidge's reelection did the Great Depression begin?
3. List these events in chronological order: Bureau of the Budget established, Lindbergh's flight, KDKA radio broadcasts, Babe Ruth hits 60 home runs, Kellogg-Briand Pact.

SKILLS STRATEGY

THE UNEMPLOYED • 1929–1935

Source: *Historical Statistics of the United States*

LINE, BAR, AND PIE GRAPHS

Graphs relate sets of data and present a great deal of information in limited space. To get information from a graph, read the title, legend, and all labels and symbols.

Note the numbers shown on the graph above. Remember that on line graphs, one set of numbers appears on the vertical axis. Other numbers appear along the horizontal axis. Points connected by a line refer to numerals on both the horizontal and vertical axes. Labels tell you what the numbers mean. Read down from the point to the number on the horizontal axis, and then read across from the point to the numeral on the vertical axis. For points between the lines, you must estimate.

When the bar graph shown on page 651 is completed, it will present the same data as the line graph, but with bars instead of with points and lines. Notice that the bars shown on the graph indicate the same percentages and years as the

THE UNEMPLOYED • 1929–1935

Percent of Work Force Unemployed

YEAR

1933   1934   1935
YEAR

Source: *Historical Statistics of the United States*

corresponding points on the line graph.

Now look at the pie graphs. Why do there have to be seven graphs instead of just one? Which of the kinds of graphs presents data most helpfully?

APPLYING SKILLS

Refer to the line graph above as you respond to questions 1–4. Then refer to the bar graph to complete the exercise in question 5.

1. About what percentage of the work force was unemployed in 1929?
2. When was 16 percent of the work force jobless?
3. Between what two years was there an upward trend in unemployment?
4. What year began a downward trend?
5. Copy the incomplete bar graph on a separate sheet of paper. Then complete the graph. Include all the components of the graph.

CHAPTER 27 TEST

TEXT REVIEW

1. Explain what is meant by this statement: "With President Coolidge's silent approval, Secretary of the Treasury Mellon's financial policies were designed to favor his own kind."
2. Give the chief reason Secretary Mellon created the Bureau of the Budget.
3. Discuss the Coolidge administration's policy in these areas: international economy, world peace, Latin America.
4. What elements contributed to the "good times" of the 1920s? Suggest how some of these led to changes in behavior.
5. Explain how using the installment plan represented a drastic change in America's buying habits and traditional ethics. What role did advertising play in this change?
6. Name the two speculative crazes that swept the nation in the 1920s.
7. Discuss how the over-reliance on the sale of consumer goods and the government's policy toward the depressed sectors of the economy caused the Great Depression.

CRITICAL THINKING

8. Describe the Fordney-McCumber tariff's immediate and long-range effects on Germany.
9. Suggest how United States relations with Latin America might be different today if a bias of the Coolidge administration had not influenced policy toward the nations in Latin America.
10. Defend this opinion: "In 1929, Herbert Hoover was the right man in the right place at the wrong time."

WRITING A PARAGRAPH

Write a paragraph about the effectiveness of the Hoover and Roosevelt administrations in dealing with unemployment during the Great Depression. Your topic sentence should state your conclusion; that is, it should state which government dealt more effectively with unemployment. Then validate your conclusion by citing data from the graphs in the Skills Strategy.

Making Connections: Review the questions and topics presented in the Making Connections section that opens this chapter. Discuss the significance of society's reaction to both the good and bad events of this period.

THE DEPRESSION AND THE NEW DEAL

1929–1937

*. . . the thirties, when the huge middle class of America . . .
were having their fingers pressed forcibly down on the fiery
Braille alphabet of a dissolving economy.* TENNESSEE WILLIAMS

Making Connections. President Hoover tried every way he could to end the depression. But on election day of 1932, it was worse than ever, and he lost in a landslide to Franklin Roosevelt. Roosevelt's policy was "to take a method and try it." He tried many methods in a flurry of legislation, and changed the country in ways that left a permanent mark on the government and society.

In this chapter, you will learn:
- How Americans reacted to the hardships of the depression
- Why President Hoover's policies failed to turn the country around
- When the "Hundred Days" took place, and what programs Congress passed during that time
- How the AAA, FERA, CCC, CWA, WPA, TVA, and NRA were meant to help the country
- How the Supreme Court threatened Roosevelt's program, and how he tried to "pack" the court
- Why labor organizations made great gains during the New Deal period

You know that Hoover was Secretary of Commerce during the Harding and Coolidge years. Therefore, he was tied to past policies. As you read, note how Roosevelt adopted new policies to deal with the crisis of the Great Depression.

Sections
1. Americans Face the Depression
2. The New Deal Triumphs
3. The First New Deal
4. The Second New Deal

1. AMERICANS FACE THE DEPRESSION

More than half a century has passed since the beginning of the Great Depression. And yet, the shadow of the 1930s still hovers over American society. Only America's greatest wars—the Revolution, the Civil War, World War II—play such an important role as milestones in our national imagination.

Not every memory of the depression years is negative. Many Americans took pride in the fact that when the economy hit bottom, they had not just survived, they had carried on vital cultural, social, and personal activities.

President Hoover was not one of those people. Brimming with confidence and energy when he became president in March 1929, he grew nervous and defensive when every action he took failed to halt the economy's downward slide. By the 1932 election, he was a grim, crushed man so unpopular that he hesitated to appear before any audiences but those made up of devoted Republicans. On one occasion when he rode in a motorcade through downtown Detroit, a city hit hard by bad times, thousands of people lined the streets to stare silently at the President. It was a far more effective statement than boos or even rioting would have been.

This somber oil painting, titled "Home Relief Station," shows the patience and quiet dignity of unemployed working-class people as they wait their turn for vital relief money, or "scrip."

Quotation: from the play *The Glass Menagerie.* Other works by Tennessee Williams (1911–1983) include *A Streetcar Named Desire; Cat on a Hot Tin Roof; Sweet Bird of Youth; The Night of the Iguana; Orpheus Descending; Period of Adjustment; Suddenly, Last Summer; Camino Real;* and *Small Craft Warnings.*

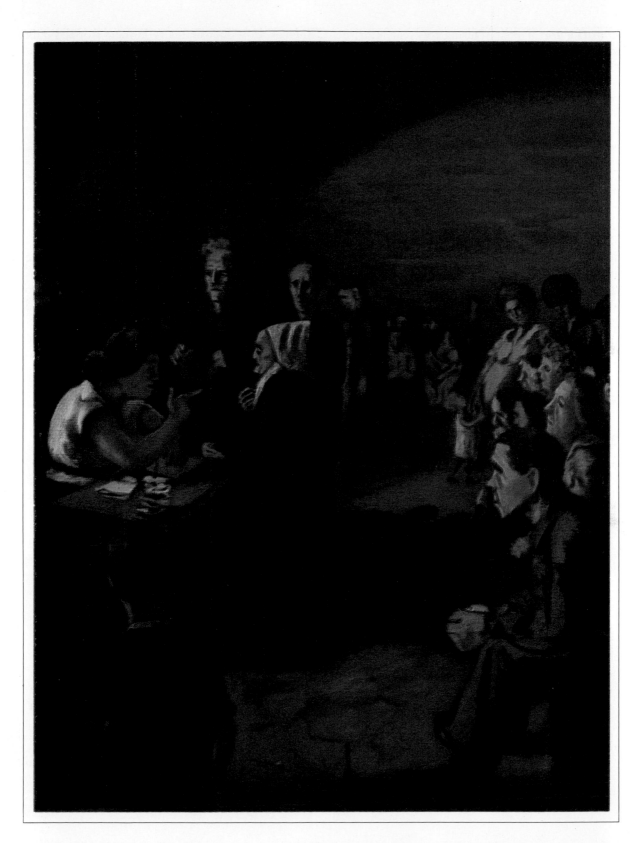

Skills Review: Reinforce the skills learned in the preceding Skills Strategy section. Using the data found on pages 654 and 655 in this chapter, students can construct either a line or a bar graph. If computer facilities are available, have students use them to complete this exercise.

Looking for Work. During the year after the stock market crashed, 4 million workers lost their jobs. By 1931, 100,000 Americans were being laid off each week. By 1932, nearly 13 million people were unemployed, a full quarter of the work force, thus depriving another 30 million people who depended on their support for the necessities of life. Black workers, the last hired and the first fired, had an unemployment rate of 35 percent.

Employees who held on to their jobs took cuts in pay. Between 1929 and 1933, the average earnings of workers in manufacturing fell from $25 per week to less than $17. The income of farmers declined until, by the winter of 1933, many corn and wheat growers were burning their crops to heat their houses because they could only sell their crops at a crushing loss. Wheat farmers estimated that they had to harvest more than ten bushels of grain to earn the price of a pair of shoes. The wholesale price of cotton dropped to 6.5 cents a pound.

Hungry people rioted in St. Paul and in other cities, storming food markets and clearing the shelves. In Wisconsin, dairy farmers stopped milk trucks and dumped the milk into ditches to dramatize the low pay they received for their product. In Iowa, Milo Reno led the *National Farmers' Holiday Association* in holding back hogs from the market. This group also highjacked trucks loaded with farm products.

Bank Failures and Homelessness. Banks failed at a rate of 200 a month during 1932. In one year $3.2 billion in savings was wiped out. When New York's Bank of the United States went under in December 1930, 400,000 people lost their deposits. Much of that money was in small accounts, put aside by workingpeople as a hedge against bad times. Hearing the news, others withdrew their deposits, causing still other banks to fail. By 1932 more than 5,000 banks had closed their doors.

During 1932, the worst year of the depression, 32,000 businesses failed. Untold numbers of peo-

The sign offers hope, but there was little work in Tulelake, California, when Dorothea Lange took this picture in 1939.

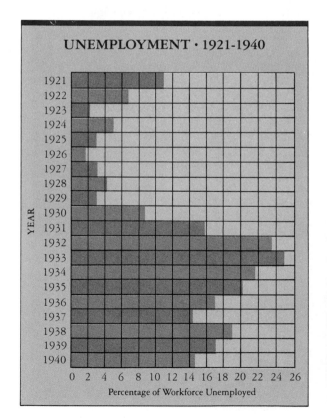

UNEMPLOYMENT · 1921-1940

YEAR — Percentage of Workforce Unemployed

The railroad industry was one of the largest of the many that prospered in the 1920s. The same locomotive company that had produced 600 steam locomotives a year during the 1920s, produced only one in 1932.

A vulture, wind-eroded land, a broken window, a starving cow, and a useless pump symbolize abandonment and despair in Alexander Hogue's 1934 painting "Drouth Stricken Area."

ple lost their homes because they could not keep up mortgage payments. In the South and Midwest, one of every four farm families was forced off the land.

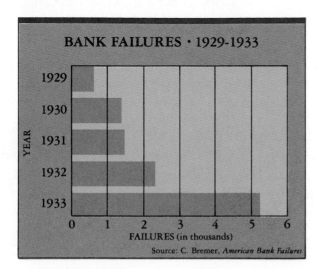

BANK FAILURES · 1929-1933

YEAR	FAILURES (in thousands)
1929	
1930	
1931	
1932	
1933	

0   1   2   3   4   5   6
FAILURES (in thousands)

Source: C. Bremer, *American Bank Failures*

Hitting the Road. In the prosperous year of 1928, about 14,000 hoboes hopped freights on the Missouri Pacific Railroad. By 1931, 186,000 homeless people were estimated to have ridden the same rails. The nation's railroads estimated that about 1.5 million homeless people were wandering about the country in search of work. Many of these wanderers were teenage boys and girls. Some of them told social workers that they had left home so that what money there was could be stretched to feed the younger members of their families.

In 1936 and 1937, natural catastrophe complicated the depression's effects in Oklahoma, Arkansas, and surrounding states. Long periods of drought dried the soil, killing crops and allowing the wind to strip the topsoil from the earth. The dust storms that resulted blotted out the sun. Whole counties in the farm areas of the *Dust Bowl* were depopulated as "Okies" and "Arkies" piled into old Model T Fords and headed toward California in hopes of finding work.

Research Assignment: Have students write a report on the cause of the Dust Bowl. Have them examine the farming techniques of the period that damaged the Dust Bowl area and those that helped it.

"Hoovervilles" sprang up to house unemployed workers who had "hit the road" in search of employment. This one, in the shadow of posh apartment buildings, has a barber shop.

The Face of Catastrophe.

Evidence of the Depression was everywhere. Each day, more than 5,000 people lined up outside a New York employment agency to apply for 300 jobs. When Birmingham, Alabama, put out a call for 800 workers to put in 11-hour days for $2 a day, 12,000 applicants showed up. In 1931, a Soviet agency, Amtorg, announced openings in Russia for 6,000 skilled technicians. Nearly 100,000 people said they would go. On the streets of most big cities, once-proud skilled workers sold apples or shoelaces on street corners in an effort to stay off the bread lines.

Charitable organizations could not keep up with the great number of needy people. At one point, there were 82 bread lines in New York City serving 85,000 free meals a day. Philadelphia's charity workers were able to offer only $4.23 a week to help poor families buy food, and they only reached about one-fifth of the people who needed assistance.

Joking About the Hard Times.

Even in the worst of the bad times, Americans were able to joke about their plight. Will Rogers, himself an "Okie," remained America's favorite humorist with such remarks as, "Let Wall Street have a nightmare and the whole country has to help them get back in bed again," and, "We'll hold the distinction of being the only nation in the history of the world that ever went to the poorhouse in an automobile."

President Hoover was the butt of many jokes. Shantytowns that were built by homeless people sprang up on the outskirts of cities and were dubbed *Hoovervilles.* Boxcars were "Hoover Pullmans." An empty pocket turned inside out was a "Hoover Flag." In the West, people who had never hunted or eaten tough, stringy jackrabbits during good times suddenly found they ate quite well on these "Hoover Hogs."

Midwestern "Robin Hoods."

Disenchantment caused a complete reversal in the popular image of capitalists. Heroes of the 1920s, they became the villains of the 1930s. In popular fiction, on radio, and in movies, businesspeople were at best objects of ridicule, at worst enemies of decent ordinary people.

In the Midwest, new criminals grabbed the attention of law-abiding citizens. They were small-town bank robbers, who with automobiles and wide-open highways, were able to rob banks and then make quick getaways to rural hideouts. John Dillinger, "Pretty Boy" Floyd, "Baby Face" Nelson, "Machine Gun" Kelly, Bonnie Parker and

Class Activity: A presentation of the movie *The Grapes of Wrath* (Twentieth Century Fox, 1939) gives a graphic and accurate picture of the mass exodus that took place in the Great Plains in the thirties.

656

Clyde Barrow, and "Ma" Barker and her gang were in fact dangerous, ruthless thugs, quite willing to gun down anyone who stood in their way. Nevertheless, the fact that their chief victims were bankers, combined with stories that they gave money to the poor, earned them a large, faithful following.

Movies in the 1930s. Movies were one business that did not suffer during the depression. Because of the low cost of admission—about 25 cents, 10 cents for children—85 million tickets were sold each week.

Hollywood featured films about people who "beat the system," even when it meant breaking the laws. Movie makers were careful to ensure that, at the end of the picture, tough-guy heroes played by James Cagney, Humphrey Bogart, George Raft, and Edward G. Robinson paid for their crimes. Nevertheless, criminal-heroes were usually depicted as people who, forced into crime by poverty, deserved sympathy.

Even more popular than gangster films were escapist themes. Shirley Temple, an angelic child star, was paid $300,000 a year to make heartwarming musicals. Warner Brothers had Busby Berkeley, whose movies featured beautiful starlets transformed by mirrors and trick photography into seemingly hundreds of performers. The more fabulous the fantasy, the more attractive it was to people struggling to make ends meet in the real world of the depression.

Faith in Capitalism. Few Americans believed that the depression was proof that the capitalist system itself was at fault. The Socialist and Communist parties, which blamed capitalism itself for the depression, won remarkably few supporters. After polling 267,000 votes in prosperous 1928, the Socialist party, with Norman Thomas as its candidate, won 882,000 votes in the 1932 election. But this was only a small percentage of the more than 40 million votes cast in 1932.

The Communist party polled a mere 49,000 votes in 1928 and 103,000 in 1932. The Communists, whose membership was never much higher than 40,000, were surprisingly powerful because party members and their allies worked hard on behalf of the labor movement. Furthermore, large numbers of articulate intellectuals and literary figures joined, at least temporarily. But the party fell apart rapidly during the 1940s. Communism's foothold in the United States, even during capitalism's greatest crisis, was never strong.

Who Was to Blame? Americans were more likely to blame themselves for their hardship than to blame the capitalist system. A walk through almost any big city park revealed unsuccessful job seekers slumped on benches, wondering where they, not the system, had gone wrong.

But a large majority of Americans did have someone beside themselves to blame for the depression. They blamed the Republican party, the businesspeople with whom the party was associated, and, most of all, the Republican president, Herbert Hoover.

SECTION REVIEW

1. Write a sentence to identify: "Okies" and "Arkies," Will Rogers, "Hoovervilles," Norman Thomas.

2. Cite statistics that show the impact of the Great Depression on three of the following: employment, earnings, savings, hunger, homelessness, business, banking.

3. In what ways did Americans distract themselves from the harsh realities of the depression?

4. How did American voters show their faith in the capitalist system? Whom did they often blame for their condition?

---

2. THE NEW DEAL TRIUMPHS

In 1928, Herbert Hoover won the presidency with almost 21.4 million Americans—58.2 percent of the popular vote—casting their ballots for him and Republican prosperity. In 1932, Hoover received fewer than 16 million votes as his Democratic opponent, Franklin D. Roosevelt, racked up 22.8 million votes. Never before had there been such a sudden shift of voter allegiance from one party to another.

Just as dramatic was the change in Congress brought about by the Depression. In the Seventy-First Congress of 1929–1931, Republicans held a

Much of President Hoover's negative image was undeserved. He had become independently wealthy before entering politics and became a politician because he wanted to serve the U.S. He donated every federal salary check that he received during his 47 years of public service to charity.

Will Rogers, whose humor was often political, tells a joke to Franklin Roosevelt (above). In contrast, the dust bowl farmer and his family (below) had little to laugh about.

237–195 edge over the Democrats in the House of Representatives and a 56–39 edge in the Senate. When Franklin Roosevelt swept into the White House in 1932, he brought with him a 310–117 Democratic majority in the House and a 60–35 edge in the Senate.

Nor was that the end of it. In the midterm congressional elections of 1934, the Democrats increased their control of both houses. The Republican party, the clear majority party in the United States since 1896, became a small minority party. The story of Herbert Hoover's single term in office is the story of a political revolution.

The Tragedy of Herbert Hoover. In 1928, Herbert Hoover won the presidency because of his boundless energy, his skill as an administrator, and his reputation as a humanitarian. In little more than three years, he was being accused of an inability to act, of incompetence, and of callousness toward the suffering of many Americans.

This change was the result of Hoover's failure to stop the deepening of the depression. Hoover was stunned by the economic collapse. He became sullen and withdrawn, a virtual hermit in the White House. Hoover failed in his fight against the depression, not because of inaction, inefficiency, or lack of sympathy for people's suffering. If anything, it was due to the emphasis he put on individual effort.

Rugged Individualism. Hoover was truly a self-made man. He worked hard to put himself through Stanford University. Unwilling to practice the back-slapping, phony sincerity that business-people came to praise during the 1920s, he had few close friends. Nevertheless, he made millions of dollars as an international mining engineer.

Hoover took justifiable pride in his accomplishments. He concluded that his success, and the success of the United States, was due to *rugged individualism*, the willingness of individuals like himself to stand alone and struggle on the basis of their own personal resources. Although he believed in helping other people, he thought that should be done by the private sector of the economy. In Hoover's view, government interference meant that individual initiative, and therefore the genius of America, would be sapped and destroyed.

Class Activity: Bring in recordings of songs popular during the Great Depression. Have students discuss how these songs reflected the mood of society.

As president, he applied this principle rigorously. The national government's potential for harm, with all the resources and power at its disposal, seemed nearly infinite to Hoover.

Just Around the Corner.

Hoover's belief in rugged individualism kept him from taking action during the first year of the depression. He was convinced that prosperity was "just around the corner." By repeating such phrases as conditions worsened daily, he lost the people's confidence.

For a few months in 1931, however, it seemed that he might be right. The rate of unemployment stopped rising, business and bank failures declined, and other indicators seemed to say that recovery was near. Then, in May, a major European bank, the *Kreditanstalt* of Vienna, went bankrupt. A chain reaction spread the economic crisis throughout Europe. England, a strong proponent of allowing paper money to be redeemable in gold, went off the gold standard.

Worried that the United States would do the same, international investors withdrew $1.5 billion in gold from American vaults. This led to a new wave of bank failures and deepened the depression at home.

Hoover could not believe that his policies were wrong. The events of early 1931 convinced him that Europe was responsible for America's depression. In reality, it was more the other way around.

Boulder Dam, completed in 1936, remains one of the largest dams ever built.

Helping the Economy Help Itself.

By late 1931, Hoover recognized that the depression was not going to lift. He searched for a way to pump government money into the private economy without violating his principles.

He found it in a public works program to construct highways, federal office buildings, and other massive projects that served the public good. Hoover released $500 million for such work, creating jobs for some of the unemployed. The largest appropriation went for the construction of Boulder Dam on the Colorado River, a project that would produce electricity and conserve water for irrigation projects. (In 1947, Boulder Dam was renamed Hoover Dam.)

In 1932, Hoover took an even larger step. He established the *Reconstruction Finance Corporation* (*RFC*), which loaned money to major banks, railroad companies, and factories so they could stave off failure and possibly recover from the shock of the depression. The RFC injected more than $2 billion into the economy and probably helped American business escape even deeper disaster.

For his efforts, Hoover received scant praise. Conservatives were convinced that any such government intervention in the economy was wrong. Desperate men and women concerned about their next meal or mortgage payment were not won over when they saw that Hoover catered to the needs of millionaires while steadfastly refusing to provide direct help for less wealthy individuals.

The Bonus Marchers.

Much more damaging to the President's reputation was his reaction to the march on Washington in the summer of 1932 by the "Bonus Expeditionary Force," unemployed World War I veterans whom Congress had awarded life insurance policies in 1924. These policies

Research Assignment: Have students do a research assignment examining the survival of a small company during the Great Depression. Students might pick one in your area so that they can interview the people who lived through this period. Included in the report should be measures taken by the company and federal aid programs.

659

Hoping to persuade Congress to help them, thousands of veterans defied police orders and camped out on the lawn of the Capitol.

could be redeemed in 1943, but because of the depression, the marchers demanded earlier payment. Hoover refused, and about 20,000 veterans and their families poured into Washington. They intended to stay until the President gave in.

The marchers took over several vacant federal buildings and set up a shantytown on Anacostia Flats at the edge of the city. They were peaceful, but made Hoover very uncomfortable. The group was a reminder of the nation's troubles, and a reminder that would not go away. Finally, in July, the police were ordered to clear the marchers from the federal buildings. This action caused riots, and on July 28 Hoover ordered General Douglas MacArthur to clear the bonus marchers out of Anacostia Flats.

Using armored vehicles and tear gas, MacArthur ordered his young soldiers to attack the

veterans. Remarkably, only three people died in the fighting. But along with those casualties died Herbert Hoover's last chance for reelection.

The Democrats Prepare. With victory almost guaranteed, the Democratic party was rich in would-be candidates for the presidency. Al Smith believed he had a claim on the nomination, having run in 1928 when the Democrats had no chance to win. The former McAdoo Democrats of the South backed John Nance Garner of Texas. A few states offered *favorite-son candidates* in case there was a deadlock. Leading the pack was the popular governor of New York, Franklin Roosevelt.

Roosevelt had been stricken with polio in 1921. The disease left him permanently unable to walk without severe pain and with heavy metal braces on his legs. But he never let this affect his campaigning. What people saw was a person with all the attributes of a true leader. He projected cheerful confidence and seemed to be a person who could take charge.

At the Democratic convention, a deadlock at first seemed inevitable. Then, some Garner delegates switched to Roosevelt and gave him the nomination. Roosevelt broke precedent by flying to Chicago and accepting the nomination in person. Few Democrats had reason to regret their choice. In a forceful, confident voice, Roosevelt told the party he would provide a *New Deal* for the American people.

The Election of 1932. Beyond promising an end to Prohibition, Roosevelt did not, in the months that followed, describe what the New Deal would be. In some speeches he would take a more conservative line than Hoover's, warning against excessive government spending. In others he would hint that his new era of reform would be even busier than the one of his distant cousin, Theodore Roosevelt.

In fact, FDR, as newspapers called him in their headlines, did not have a clear idea of what he intended to do. But even if he had known, he would not have spelled out his program. Roosevelt did not want to get into a debate with Hoover over specifics. He felt that such a debate might only lose him votes.

Roosevelt won by a landslide, 472 electoral votes to Hoover's 59. During the four months

Although F.D.R. was the most popular U.S. president ever to hold office, he did not carry his home county of Dutchess, New York, in any of the four presidential elections.

PROFILES OF THE PRESIDENCY

FRANKLIN D. ROOSEVELT 1933–1945

Accepting the Democratic nomination for a second term, Franklin Roosevelt spoke of the depression in terms of America's destiny:

Better the occasional faults of a government that lives in a spirit of charity than the consistent omissions of a government frozen in the ice of its own indifference.

There is a mysterious cycle in human events. To some generations much is given. Of other generations much is expected. This generation of Americans has a rendezvous with destiny...Here in America we are waging a great and successful war. It is not alone a war against want and destitution and economic demoralization. It is more than that, it is a war for the survival of democracy. We are fighting to save a great and precious form of government for ourselves and for the world.

And so I accept the commission you have tendered me. I join with you. I am enlisted for the duration of the war.

—ACCEPTANCE SPEECH, JUNE 27, 1936

---

between the election and inauguration day, FDR went into seclusion. He was not drawn in by Hoover's attempts to commit him to continue Republican policies and instead met confidentially with experts on agriculture, industry, taxation, finance, and public assistance programs. This *Brain Trust*, consisting of university professors and other professionals, was coordinated by Raymond Moley. By the time Roosevelt took the oath of office, he had a formulated a program.

SECTION REVIEW

1. Write a sentence to identify: *Kreditanstalt*, "rugged individualism," "Brain Trust."

2. How do the phrases "rugged individualism" and "just around the corner" sum up Hoover's fight against the depression?

3. Name two steps President Hoover took in order to help the economy help itself.

4. Describe the event that, more than any other event, made President Hoover unpopular with Americans.

5. Who won the 1932 election? What did he promise to provide for the American people?

3. THE FIRST NEW DEAL

Roosevelt's presidency opened with a symbol that any politician would covet. Inauguration day in Washington was cold and gray. But when FDR stepped forth to take the oath of office, the sun burst through a gap in the heavy clouds and shone on the ceremony.

That was the image Roosevelt hoped his New Deal might evoke. Before the debris of the inaugural ball had been swept up, Roosevelt called Congress into special session. For more than three months, he and his Brain Trust sent bill after bill to the Capitol. Congress, desperate for an active course to follow, passed every bill.

There was no ideology or systematic plan to the legislation of the frantic *Hundred Days*. Nor did Roosevelt pretend that there was. "The country demands bold, persistent experimentation," he said. "It is common sense to take a method and try it. If it fails, admit it frankly and try another."

The Man of Action. In this attitude lay Roosevelt's first great strength. He did not insist that every bill his Brain Trust suggested should fit into a comprehensive philosophy. Instead, he approached the problems from many different directions. He discarded failures and kept what worked.

GOING TO THE SOURCE

This is pre-eminently the time to speak the truth, the whole truth, frankly and boldy. Nor need we shrink from honestly facing conditions in our country today. This great Nation will endure as it has endured, will revive and will prosper.

So, first of all, let me assert my firm belief that the only thing we have to fear is fear itself—nameless, unreasoning, unjustified terror which paralyzes needed efforts to convert retreat into advance.

In every dark hour of our national life a leadership of frankness and vigor has met with the understanding and support of the people themselves which is essential to victory. I am convinced that you will again give that support to leadership in these critical days.

In such a spirit on my part and on yours we face our common difficulties. They concern, thank God, only material things. Values have shrunken to fantastic levels; taxes have risen; our ability to pay has fallen; government of all kinds is faced by serious curtailment of income; the means of exchange are frozen in the currents of trade; the withered leaves of industrial enterprise lie on every side; farmers find no markets for their produce; the savings of many years in thousands of families are gone.

More important, a host of unemployed citizens face the grim problem of existence, and an equally great number toil with little return. Only a foolish optimist can deny the dark, realities of the moment. . . .

I am prepared under my constitutional duty to recommend the measures that a stricken nation in the midst of a stricken world may require. These measures . . . I shall seek, within my constitutional authority, to bring to speedy adoption.

> *This great Nation will endure as it has endured, will revive and will prosper. So... let me assert my firm belief that the only thing we have to fear is fear itself—nameless, ...unjustified terror which paralyzes needed efforts to convert retreat into advance.*
>
> FRANKLIN D. ROOSEVELT.
> *FIRST INAUGURAL ADDRESS*

Our greatest primary task is to put people to work. This is no unsolvable problem if we face it wisely and courageously.

It can be accomplished in part by direct recruiting by the government itself, treating the task as we would treat the emergency of a war, but at the same time, through this employment, accomplishing greatly needed projects to stimulate and reorganize the use of our natural resources.

Hand in hand with this we must frankly recognize the overbalance of population in our industrial centers and, by engaging on a national scale in a redistribution, endeavor to provide a better use of the land for those best fitted for the land. The task can be helped by definite efforts to raise the values of agricultural products and with this the power to purchase the output of our cities. . . .

It can be helped by national planning for the supervision of all forms of transportation and of communications and other utilities which have a definitely public character. There are many ways in which it can be helped, but it can never be helped merely by talking about it . . . .

Finally, in our progress toward a resumption of work we require two safeguards against a return of the evils of the old order; there must be a strict supervision of all banking and credits and investments; there must be an end to speculation with other people's money; and there must be provision for an adequate but sound currency.

Few speeches in history have had as great an impact on a nation's morale as did Franklin Roosevelt's First Inaugural Address on March 4, 1933. Millions of Americans heard their new president on the radio.

Class Activity: Have students make a list giving the acronyms of the various programs of the Roosevelt administration.

Eleanor Roosevelt. One of Roosevelt's greatest assets was his remarkable wife, Eleanor. She had no intention of restricting her activities to being a social hostess. She looked outward and became a champion of the poor and weak in American society.

She supported the organized labor movement before her husband found it in his political interests to do so. She became a spokesperson for American blacks when Roosevelt, busy courting segregationist support essential to the success of the New Deal, was still dodging suggestions that he support a civil rights program. She secured high government posts for such black leaders as Mary McLeod Bethune of the NAACP and Robert Weaver, who in 1966, became the first black appointed to a cabinet post.

Conservatives said that Eleanor Roosevelt acted as if she were a vice president in charge of compassion. In a way, though, that was her job. She served as Roosevelt's legs, climbing the stairs of tenement houses and descending into poorly lit mines, while he was confined to his chair. She was also the Roosevelt administration's heart, openly touched by the suffering of the poor.

Saving Banks. The most pressing problems facing the new administration were the collapse of the nation's banks and the farm bankruptcies. The day after he was sworn in, Roosevelt proclaimed a bank holiday. All banks were ordered to close while, under the terms of the hastily approved *Emergency Banking Act*, government examiners determined which banks were beyond saving and which ones, with loans from the Federal Reserve System, could survive.

The bank holiday saved many well-managed banks that might otherwise have failed. Moreover, those banks that did reopen were assumed to be safe. Depositors stopped withdrawing their money out of fear. And the decisiveness of Roosevelt's action encouraged new confidence in the government.

Roosevelt stopped the drain of gold from the treasury by forbidding the export of gold. In April, he followed England's example by taking the United States off the gold standard. At his request, Congress made it illegal for private citizens to hoard gold. People were required to sell to the government at a price fixed by law.

LEGISLATION OF ROOSEVELT'S FIRST HUNDRED DAYS	
March 9	Emergency Banking Relief Act
March 22	Beer-Wine Revenue Act
March 31	Unemployment Relief Act
May 12	Agricultural Adjustment Act
May 12	Federal Emergency Relief Act
May 18	Tennessee Valley Authority Act
May 27	Securities Act of 1933
June 5	Gold Repeal Joint Resolution
June 13	Home Owners' Refinancing Act
June 16	Farm Credit Act
June 16	Banking Act of 1933
June 16	Emergency Railroad Transportation Act
June 16	National Industrial Recovery Act

Saving Farms. The *Farm Credit Administration* was set up to deal with the farm emergency. It refinanced mortgages for farmers who were in danger of losing their land.

The *Agricultural Adjustment Administration (AAA)* was designed to restore the purchasing power of farmers. To raise the price of their crops, farmers were asked to plow under between one quarter and one half of their 1933 crops. In return, they were paid a *subsidy* raised by a special tax placed on companies that processed the foods. This idea and the practice of slaughtering livestock to keep it off the market offended many people. But within two years, farm income increased by 50 percent.

The AAA was one of the first New Deal programs to come under attack. Higher selling prices for farmers meant higher buying prices for consumers. Because AAA subsidies were available to farmowners and not to *tenant farmers,* many nonworking landowners profited while the *sharecroppers* who had actually done the work were thrown off the land.

Movers And Shapers

Eleanor Roosevelt

Eleanor Roosevelt (1884–1962) was First Lady of the United States longer than anyone else —12 years. After her husband's death, she had a distinguished career as a *delegate* to the *United Nations*.

What makes these achievements remarkable was that she was a shy, fearful child, convinced she was an "ugly duckling." Her parents had both died by the time she was ten, and Eleanor lived with her grandmother, who called her "Granny" because of her shy, sober ways. But what young Eleanor lacked in confidence she made up for in energy and conviction. She did not let her fears ruin her life.

As the wife of Franklin Roosevelt, she worked to help people who were disadvantaged: the poor, minorities, children, and older people. She traveled all over the world, and reported her observations to her husband. Some of the reforms of the New Deal resulted from her convictions.

Although she never felt at home with her public role, she did not shirk her duties as she saw them. She wrote a widely read newspaper column and held regular press conferences.

After President Roosevelt's death, she was instrumental in the founding of the United Nations, serving as chairman of the UN Commission on Human Rights. When she died, people referred to her as the "First Lady of the World."

Mary McLeod Bethune

Mary McLeod Bethune (1875–1955) was born in a log cabin in South Carolina. She grew up to found a college and to become a prominent educator.

As a child, Bethune had a passion for education. Teaching slaves to read had been a crime in southern states; and so, few black people could read after the Civil War. But young Mary was determined, and chanted as she picked cotton, "I'm going to read! I'm going to read!" She knew that education was her way out of the fields.

At a missionary school for black children, Mary proved to be a good student and won a scholarship to high school and later to a Bible college in Chicago. After working as a teacher, Bethune opened her own school in 1904 with five students. Their pencils were splinters from burnt logs, and their ink was made from crushed elderberries.

Bethune said that her first school was "prayed up, sung up, and talked up." Her dream was to have a college for black women, and she was not shy about asking wealthy people for funds. One asked her where this "college" was. She replied, "In my dreams." He wrote her a check.

Bethune's dream came true, and she served as president of Bethune Cookman College until 1942. Four presidents appointed her to government posts. In Franklin Roosevelt's administration she was director of the Division of Negro Affairs. Eleanor Roosevelt, a close friend, gave her Franklin's walking stick after his death.

Repeal of Prohibition and FERA.

On March 13, nine days after his inauguration, Roosevelt called for the immediate legalization of near beer (which was not as alcoholic as regular beer) and the ratification of the Twenty-First Amendment. These two actions would end Prohibition by amending the Volstead Act and repealing the Eighteenth Amendment. Congress agreed to changes in the Volstead Act, and in only nine months, the amendment was ratified by the states.

Roosevelt also proposed the *Federal Emergency Relief Act* (FERA). This law distributed $500 million in federal funds to help the states revive their programs to help the destitute.

To administer FERA, FDR appointed a social worker from New York, Harry Hopkins, who had worked for him when Roosevelt was governor. Hopkins disliked handouts. He believed that the government should create jobs so people who received help would have a sense of having earned it. In the spring of 1933, however, even Hopkins admitted that the size of the emergency required that money be distributed quickly.

The CCC.

The *Civilian Conservation Corps* (CCC), was more to Hopkins's liking. With an initial budget of $300 million, the CCC employed 250,000 young men between the ages of 18 and 25, and about 50,000 World War I veterans. Supervised by the army, CCC groups did important conservation work, planting trees on deforested land and building firebreaks, windbreaks, trails, campsites, and other public facilities in the national parks and national forests.

CCC workers were required to send most of their paychecks home to relatives. This helped to relieve distress and also pumped much-needed money into the economy. Eventually, some 2 million people worked for the CCC, of whom about 200,000 were blacks.

The CWA and WPA.

The *Civil Works Administration* (CWA), headed by Harry Hopkins after November 1933, put 4 million people to work within a few months. They constructed post offices, city halls, and recreational buildings, built roads, and taught in bankrupt school systems. After only five months, the CWA had spent almost $1 billion, and FDR called a halt to the program. But private employers could not or would not

WPA works of art, such as the one shown here being painted for the 1939 World's Fair, can still be found all over the country.

Government work programs, such as the one that improved this road behind the White House, kept some unemployed workers off the bread lines.

Research Assignment: Students interested in art may enjoy doing a research project on WPA mural painting projects.

Eleanor Roosevelt supported the efforts of underprivileged people to secure a higher standard of living. Here she entertains students who came from all over the United States to attend a school for the study of labor practices and leadership techniques.

employ the former CWA workers. In May 1935, the President turned to Hopkins again, and Congress soon established the *Works Progress Administration (WPA).*

The WPA broadened the CWA approach. Artists were hired to paint murals in public buildings. Writers prepared state guidebooks. Researchers interviewed elderly people, including former slaves, about their experiences during America's past. The WPA even formed troupes of playwrights and actors to bring theater to people who had never seen live acting. The *National Youth Administration,* part of the WPA, provided jobs for 2 million students. By 1943, when it was dismantled, the agency had spent more than $11 billion and had employed 8.5 million people who could get work nowhere else.

The TVA.

The greatest of the New Deal's public works programs provided for the construction of a series of dams and electric generating facilities along the Tennessee River. The river rose in the mountains of eastern Tennessee, flowed south into Alabama, and then turned north and emptied into the Ohio River. It was a wild watercourse, causing destructive floods every spring and further depressing an already poor region.

Senator George Norris of Nebraska had long proposed that the federal government harness the river's power through the construction of dams.

Not only would the dams control the destructive annual floods, but the government-produced electricity would contribute to the economic development of the valley. The government's power-producing company would be called the *Tennessee Valley Authority* (TVA).

But what would the TVA offer the people in the rest of the United States? Norris said that by generating electricity itself, the government would be able to determine whether privately owned power companies elsewhere were charging a fair price for their services. At that time, no one except the power companies really knew how much electricity cost.

Under Coolidge and Hoover, Norris's dream had been futile. But, in the heady days of the New Deal when the government was seeking ways to put people to work, Norris saw it become reality. In May 1933, Congress authorized the TVA.

The NRA's Blue Eagle.

New Deal policies were designed to provide relief. Often, as with the CCC, WPA, and TVA, they accomplished other goals as well. But during the Hundred Days, the administration's chief purpose was to get money to the people who desperately needed it.

The *National Recovery Administration* (NRA), on the other hand was designed to stimulate recovery. Symbolized by a blue eagle that clutched lightning bolts and a gear wheel in its

  Research Assignment: Make a map and illustrate it with pictures of your area during the 1930s. Have students locate any CCC, CWA, or WPA projects that may have operated in your area and explain what each project accomplished. Information about these projects may be available at local colleges, libraries, and historical societies. Encourage students to interview people who may have worked on these projects.

talons, the NRA tried to promote cooperation rather than competition within each industry. The head of the NRA was a progressive named Hugh Johnson, who raced about the country trying to convince industrial leaders to develop and sign codes regulating almost every aspect of industrial operation.

For example, the NRA code for the steel industry set standards of quality every steel manufacturer was expected to observe. Each company was assigned a share of the national market and told how much steel to produce in a year. The codes also set standards for wages, hours, and working conditions, and provided that if a majority of a company's employees chose to be represented by a union, the company had to recognize the union.

The NRA was a direct outgrowth of Teddy Roosevelt's New Nationalism. The underlying assumption was that by planning and cooperation, wasteful competition could be avoided and economic collapse would not recur. Indeed, the goal of the NRA was not very different from the goal Hoover pursued with his trade associations. The difference was that NRA codes were compulsory, whereas Hoover's associations were voluntary.

The New Deal Threatened.

By 1934, the New Deal was under attack. Former President Hoover and big business conservatives, including former Democratic presidential candidates Al Smith and John Davis, organized the *American Liberty League*, which claimed that programs like the TVA and the NRA violated the American tradition of free enterprise. Roosevelt was angered by this attack from businesspeople, with whom he always tried to cooperate. But the Liberty League was never a serious threat to Roosevelt's programs.

The opposition of the Supreme Court, however, caused Roosevelt more concern. The Court is not subject to popular pressure, and in *Schechter Poultry Corporation* v. *United States* (1935), the Court declared the NRA unconstitutional. In *United States* v. *Butler* (1936), the Court invalidated the AAA because it taxed one group of citizens (the food processing companies) to help another group (the farmers).

Roosevelt was not sorry to see the NRA destroyed, since it had never really been successful.

Moreover, Congress quickly passed the *National Labor Relations Act* of 1935, preserving the right of democratically chosen labor unions to represent employees.

Nor was the loss of the AAA crushing in itself. In 1938, Congress passed a second Agricultural Adjustment Act that avoided the constitutional problems of the first, but helped keep farm income up through subsidies to farmers who curtailed production. What worried Roosevelt and his advisors about the Court's landmark decisions was the possibility that the Schechter and Butler cases were the first shots in a judicial war against all New Deal legislation.

The Court-Packing Plan.

To protect his programs, Roosevelt wanted to "pack" the Supreme Court with justices that supported New Deal laws. In order to do this, he asked Congress to allow him to increase the Court to 15 justices by letting him appoint a new justice each time a sitting justice reached the age of 70 and did not retire.

For the first time, Congress refused to do his bidding. Even strong New Dealers objected to what they saw as an attempt to destroy the independence of the judicial branch.

Roosevelt lost the battle but won the war. Perhaps startled by the *court-packing* plan, the justices upheld the *constitutionality* of several New Deal laws in 1937. Over the next two years, deaths and resignations created enough vacancies on the nine-member Court for Roosevelt to appoint a majority that favored the New Deal.

SECTION REVIEW

1. Write a sentence to identify: Hundred Days, Twenty-First Amendment, Harry Hopkins, American Liberty League.

2. Describe the actions President Roosevelt took to save the banks and farms.

3. Give the name of the law or organization each set of initials stands for: FERA, CCC, CWA, WPA, TVA, NRA.

4. What motivated President Roosevelt's attempt to "pack" the Supreme Court? How did events in the two following years make the attempt unnecessary?

Research Assignment: Students whose areas have been affected by TVA projects might like to create a map showing the extent of present-day TVA facilities.

Class Activity: Discuss F.D.R.'s "court-packing" attempt and its constitutionality. Examine Article 3, Section 2, Clause 16 of the Constitution in your discussion.

4. THE SECOND NEW DEAL

In 1935, Roosevelt decided he would run for reelection in 1936. His major opposition would come from the Republicans, but there were other critics who concerned Roosevelt and his chief political strategist, James A. Farley.

Their fears were caused by the success of the ideas of three anti-New Dealers—Father Coughlin, Dr. Francis Townsend, and Senator Huey Long. Unlike the American Liberty League, they wanted more extreme reforms and an even greater government role in private life.

Father Coughlin.
One of Roosevelt's critics was a Canadian-born priest, Father Charles Coughlin, whose weekly radio broadcast from Detroit was heard nationwide. At first, Coughlin supported Roosevelt. But by late 1934, Coughlin had become disillusioned with the New Deal. Quite correctly, he saw that Roosevelt was trying to bring about cooperation among business, finance, and the population as a whole. But Coughlin believed that the manipulations of bankers had caused the depression, and he wanted an all-out war on the banking establishment. He pushed for a complete overhaul of the monetary system and abolition of the Federal Reserve System. Coughlin was popular among the urban ethnic groups that the Democrats counted on for a solid pro-New Deal vote.

The Townsend Plan.
Dr. Francis Townsend was an elderly California doctor who was enraged that people who had worked hard their whole lives should be forgotten by society. Therefore, he promoted a plan to help these people. His *Townsend Plan* required that the government pay each person over 60 years of age a pension of $200 per month. These pensions would be funded by a national sales tax. The only condition for receiving the allowance was that every cent must be spent within the month.

Townsend believed that his plan would help the aged and also end the Depression by pumping vast amounts of money into the economy.

The sheer simplicity of the Townsend Plan appealed to many elderly people. By 1936, 7,000 Townsend Clubs claimed a membership of 2.5 million people who supported the plan.

The Kingfish.
The most serious threat to the New Deal was posed by Huey P. Long of Louisiana. A master of biting sarcasm and broad comedy, he plunged into politics as a champion of the underprivileged. Running for governor of Louisiana in 1928, Long denounced the railroads and the oil industry that controlled Louisiana. He promised to tax them heavily in order to pay for a massive hospital and road-building program and for improved public education in a state notorious for neglecting its schools.

After his election, Long kept his promises. He introduced state-subsidized lunch programs in public schools, bought textbooks, and made Louisiana State University one of the best universities in the South. Long amused his enthusiastic followers by naming himself "The Kingfish," after a character in a popular radio program.

Long used his personal popularity to make himself virtual dictator of Louisiana. His reputation won him a following throughout the South, and in 1932 he won a Senate seat.

"Share Our Wealth" and Income Tax.
In his autobiography, *Every Man a King*, Long presented his program for ending the depression and reforming the American economy. His *Share Our Wealth* program would levy a 100 percent tax on all personal income over $1 million. That is, any earnings in excess of $1 million in a year would be confiscated. These revenues and heavy corporate taxes would subsidize a minimum adequate income for the poor.

Long's program appealed to many poor southerners, another group whose votes Roosevelt needed in 1936.

Roosevelt's Action.
If the Coughlin, Townsend, and Long forces formed an alliance, Roosevelt thought, the combined opposition might put a Republican back into the White House. Roosevelt combatted them by taking over small parts of their programs and making them into law. By doing this, he could take the credit for the ideas, and would not appear to be as radical as Coughlin, Townsend, and Long were.

For example, the *Social Security Act* of 1935 established government-sponsored insurance that provided smaller *pensions* for the aged than Townsend had promised. But the pensions were

President Roosevelt signs the Social Security Act into law as a group of Senators and Representatives, along with Secretary of Labor Frances Perkins (behind Roosevelt), looks on.

large enough to take the bite out of Townsend's criticisms.

Roosevelt's policies were not determined solely by political considerations. He was a compassionate man who was truly concerned about others. And his reforms did have far-reaching effects.

Adopting programs that put the government squarely on the side of exploited groups, Roosevelt transformed the Democratic party into the party of the underprivileged. In this, the *Second New Deal* differed from what Roosevelt had done before. Up to 1935 Roosevelt tried to get business, agriculture, banks, workers, and consumers to reconcile their conflicts. But beginning in 1935, he began to use the government's power to adjust the balance of power between employees and employers, and between ordinary people and the wealthy.

Roosevelt also sponsored a revision of the income tax law that radically raised taxes in the upper income brackets. Although Roosevelt's tax reform did not satisfy Long, it did win many of Long's supporters back.

The Election of 1936.
Although Roosevelt was able to take some of the sting out of his critics'

attacks, they still persisted. However, Huey Long was silenced in another way. In September 1935, a young physician with a personal grudge against Long walked up to him in the state capitol at Baton Rouge and shot him. The assassin was cut down in a hail of bullets from Long's bodyguards, but the Long supporters were lost without their leader.

Congressman William Lemke of North Dakota stepped in and tried to rally the supporters of Long, Townsend, and Coughlin behind his *Union party* in 1936, but Lemke lacked Long's dynamic personality, and the party was never able to mount a real challenge to Roosevelt.

Roosevelt's major opposition in 1936 came from the Republican candidate, Governor Alf Landon of Kansas. Landon was a *moderate* Republican, and agreed with many of Roosevelt's policies. But as the campaign wore on, Landon realized that Roosevelt was too popular to be defeated by just saying, "I can do it better." Landon became increasingly conservative, and attacked Roosevelt's social security program in particular.

Landon's attacks were to no avail. Roosevelt, confident in his leadership, won an unprecedented landslide. He received 27.7 million popular and 472 electoral votes to Landon's 16.6 million popu-

Secretary of Labor Perkins met with William Green (left), president of the AFL, and John L. Lewis, president of the United Mine Workers, to discuss American industry and organized labor.

lar and 59 electoral votes. Landon won only two states, Maine and Vermont, and Lemke, who polled only 900,000 popular votes, received no electoral votes.

Blacks Become Democrats.

One reason for Roosevelt's landslide victory was a revolution in the voting patterns of American blacks. Since the Civil War, almost all blacks had voted Republican, the party of Lincoln. Southern segregationists —the most conspicuous enemies of the blacks —were all *staunch* Democrats.

Segregationists were still Democrats in 1936. For this reason, Roosevelt refused to support civil rights legislation. Roosevelt even refused to support a federal law to abolish lynching, which continued to be common in parts of the North as well as the South.

Blacks resented this. However, no Americans were hit harder by the depression than they were. On farms and in cities alike, blacks entered the 1930s poor and got poorer with each month that

passed. New Deal programs often made the difference between a black family's survival and its starvation. Black workers on *public works projects* were often segregated, but they usually got the same pay as white workers doing the same job. As a result, 75 percent voted Democratic in 1936.

Labor Faces the Depression.

Drained of members during the 1920s, many labor unions faced the depression decade with the realization that unless they went on the offensive, bad times would completely destroy them.

However, the leaders of the AFL refused to organize unskilled and semi-skilled workers in the mass-production industries. The AFL leaders insisted that only skilled workers could successfully stand up against employers. It would be too easy, they said, for employers to hire new unskilled workers if their old workers went out on strike.

Some in the AFL did not believe this, particularly John L. Lewis of the United Mine Workers. Along with David Dubinsky of the garment workers and Sidney Hillman of the needle trades union, Lewis formed the Committee on Industrial Organizations. This was a group within the AFL that was interested in organizing workers by their industry, not by their skill.

The Committee members tried to remain within the AFL, but eventually their ideas and tactics brought them into conflict with the AFL leaders, and they were expelled in 1936. But they did not disband; instead, they reformed as the *Congress of Industrial Organizations* (CIO). From its start, the CIO's success was immediate and astonishing.

In 1936, the CIO raised $500,000 for Roosevelt's election campaign. Lewis insisted that the President accept the check personally with photographers present. The picture of the President with one of the country's most prominent labor leaders seemed to signify an alliance between the Democratic party and the unions, which was exactly the impression Lewis wanted to convey.

The Growth of the CIO.

In 1936, the CIO set up the Steel Workers' Organizing Committee and began signing up members. Within a year, it had become the United Steel Workers with 400,000 members. The United States Steel Corporation, frequently the leader in anti-union activities, soon recognized the United Steel Workers as the official

Class Activity: Have students gather information and construct a line graph showing the growth of unions from 1935 to 1940 and the industries that these unions were part of. Discuss the relationship between the data on the graph and what the text reveals about industry during that period.

representative of its employees. Some other steel companies quickly followed. After decades of angry and violent confrontations, an astonishing victory for labor was won within one peaceful year.

The United Automobile Workers (*UAW*) had a similar history. Within a year of its founding, the UAW enlisted 400,000 members. The story was the same in other mass production industries. Unions became almost sacred in the eyes of millions of workers, who fought for the right to wear a union button on the job and sang songs with pro-labor messages.

The new unions also used new tactics against the employers. The *sit-down strike* was a seemingly revolutionary tactic pioneered by the United Automobile Workers. Instead of walking out of General Motors' Fisher Body plant in Flint, Michigan, in early 1937, the workers shut the factory down and stayed inside. Friends and relatives brought them food. They simply refused to leave until their union was recognized.

Management Fights Back. In 1937, Tom Girdler, president of Republic Steel, threatened to fight union organizers with force. In Chicago, police attacked a crowd of union demonstrators on Memorial Day. Ten workers were killed in the *Memorial Day Massacre* and about 100 were seriously injured.

In Detroit, the Ford Motor Company hired toughs to attack and beat several UAW organizers. But the attacks did not have the desired effect. Workers rushed to join the union, and in 1941, Ford signed a union contract.

In fact, instead of discouraging the workers, such acts of violence consistently convinced tens of thousands of workers that unions were their only chance of getting a fair deal. Within a few short years, labor unionism went from being nearly powerless to being a major force in American economic life.

The Legacy of the New Deal. The greatest positive accomplishment of the New Deal was the relief it brought to millions of distressed Americans in 1933. By creating jobs that put money into the hands of families perched on the edge of survival, the Roosevelt administration may have headed off widespread riot and rebellion.

The most significant negative consequence of the New Deal was the extraordinary growth in the size of government. The ambitious New Deal programs required huge bureaucracies. The total number of federal employees grew from about 600,000 in 1930 to more than 1 million in 1940, with even greater increases to come during the 1940s.

Roosevelt's popularity caused a revolution in the character of electoral politics in the United States. The Republican party had been the clear majority party of the nation for a generation before 1930. By 1936 the Democratic party had secured that position by forming an alliance among Southern voters, reform-minded liberals, blacks, urban ethnic groups, and organized labor. The Republicans were placed in the position of having to win those groups away from the Democrats in order to take the presidency.

The New Deal did not end the Depression. When the massive public employment programs had reduced the number of jobless workers to just over 6 million early in 1937, FDR began to dismantle the New Deal. Almost immediately the economy sagged and he had to resume massive government spending. The recession of 1937 was never as serious as the depression. Nevertheless, its existence indicated that New Deal programs had not restored the economy to a level where it could function without massive government participation. Prosperity returned only when the threat of another world war stimulated industry and agriculture to full production.

SECTION REVIEW

1. Write a sentence to identify: Social Security Act, John L. Lewis, sit-down strike, Memorial Day Massacre.

2. Name three forces who opposed Roosevelt's New Deal in 1936.

3. Who were Roosevelt's opponents in the 1936 election? Compare the popular and electoral votes of the candidates.

4. Describe the circumstances leading to the formation of the CIO.

5. Explain what is meant by "the revolution in voting patterns of American blacks."

Strikes involving union workers increased during this period. In 1932, 342,000 workers participated in 841 strikes; in 1933, 1,170,000 workers participated in 1,695 strikes; in 1934, there were 1,470,000 workers in 1,856 strikes.

CHAPTER REVIEW

TIME LINE

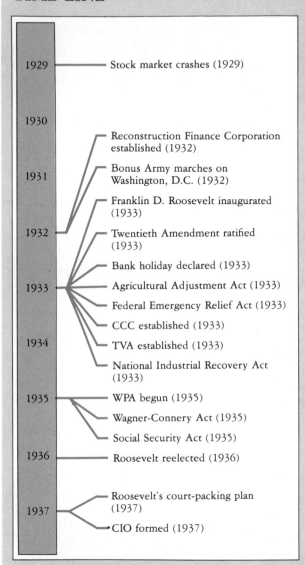

1929 ———— Stock market crashes (1929)

1930

Reconstruction Finance Corporation
established (1932)

1931 —— Bonus Army marches on
Washington, D.C. (1932)

Franklin D. Roosevelt inaugurated
(1933)

1932 —— Twentieth Amendment ratified
(1933)

Bank holiday declared (1933)

1933 —— Agricultural Adjustment Act (1933)

Federal Emergency Relief Act (1933)

CCC established (1933)

1934 —— TVA established (1933)

National Industrial Recovery Act
(1933)

1935 —— WPA begun (1935)

Wagner-Connery Act (1935)

Social Security Act (1935)

1936 —— Roosevelt reelected (1936)

Roosevelt's court-packing plan
(1937)

1937

CIO formed (1937)

TIME LINE QUESTIONS

1. How many years after the Wall Street crash did Roosevelt take office?
2. In what year did Roosevelt start thinking about appointing pro-New Deal judges?
3. Which 1935 event answered the Townsend Plan?
4. List these in order: TVA established, Roosevelt reelected, WPA begun, Wall Street crash.

SKILLS STRATEGY

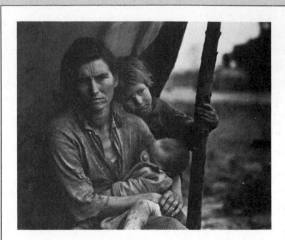

Dorothea Lange and other photographers were assigned by the Farm Security Administration to document the effects of the depression on American farm life. This photograph of a California farm woman was taken by Lange in 1936.

PICTURES AND CAPTIONS

Photographs, such as the one above, are primary sources of information about the Great Depression because they were taken during that time. Details of a good photograph tell you more about a subject than words alone can. Notice the concern on the woman's face, and her obvious poverty. Who might the other people in the photograph be? What do their faces tell you?

The caption, a secondary source, was written later to give additonal information about the phophotograph. The two together make a more powerful statement than either could alone.

APPLYING SKILLS

Read the caption and study the photograph. Then respond to the following questions.

1. What text information is the photograph meant to supplement?
2. What information does the caption give?
3. Is the photograph more important as a primary source of facts about the depression, or as a suggestion of the feelings of the time?

Making Connections: Review the questions and topics presented in the Making Connections section that opens this chapter. How was F.D.R. different in his approach to government from any of his predecessors and how did this affect American politics and society in the 1930s?

UNIT 8 TEST

CHAPTER SURVEY

In one or two sentences, summarize the content of the chapters from which these terms come, and write a sentence to identify *one* of the terms from each.

1. *Chapter 26:* xenophobia, "Red Scare," Marcus Garvey, speakeasies, smoke-filled room.
2. *Chapter 27:* trickle-down economics, Andrew Mellon, *The Jazz Singer, Black Thursday,* Kellogg-Briand pact.
3. *Chapter 28:* "Okies" and "Arkies," "Hoovervilles," "Brain Trust," Hundred Days, John L. Lewis.

TEXT REVIEW

4. Suggest a cause or causes of each of the following events that took place in the years after World War I: strikes of 1919; failure of these strikes; Johnson-Reed Act of 1924; Red Scare of 1919; Sacco-Vanzetti trial.
5. Summarize the positive and negative factors for American blacks after World War I.
6. Give the essential provisions of the Eighteenth Amendment, and discuss the effects it had on American society.
7. How did American voters' feelings about progressivism and World War I lead to the election of Warren G. Harding? Was Harding a successful president? Explain.
8. Explain why the Coolidge administration is aptly called "a business government."
9. Discuss two of these aspects of the 1920s: entertainment and sports; technological advances; advertising, ballyhoo, and hoopla; the revolution in morals.
10. Explain how the following contributed to the stock market crash of 1929 and the Great Depression: over-reliance on the sale of consumer goods; "playing the stock market"; government policy toward the depressed sectors of the American economy.
11. Describe some of the negative effects the Great Depression had on the American people. Give evidence of Americans' courage and spirit in facing up to these negative effects.

12. The text refers to "the tragedy of Herbert Hoover." What does this mean?
13. Give facts from the text explaining this comment: "Especially during his first administration, FDR took what can be called the 'alphabet-soup theory' to solving the nation's economic woes."
14. Give the essential facts about *two* of the following: opposition to Franklin Roosevelt's policies; gains for labor, and management's reaction; "the revolution in the voting patterns of American blacks"; the legacy of the New Deal—positive and negative.

CRITICAL THINKING

15. Explain why wealthy Americans of the 1920s would be likely to have this point of view: "With the possible exception of Alexander Hamilton, Andrew Mellon is the greatest Treasury Secretary in American history."
16. How might American history have been different if, during the Great Depression, Americans had lost their humor or their faith in the economic and political systems?
17. What conclusions can you draw about the abilities of Roosevelt or Hoover as leaders? Cite the facts from the text upon which you base your conclusions.

SKILLS REVIEW

18. What reference work would you consult if you wanted to find a specific magazine article? What two types of listings are included in this reference work? In general, what information is given in the listings?
19. Which type of graph could you use to show each of the following: percentage of electoral and popular votes received by candidates in an election; number (in millions) of homeless people, 1930–1935; federal government expenditures over a ten-year period.
20. Recall a photograph in the chapter that seemed outstanding to you. What text information was the photo meant to supplement? How did the caption help you understand the photo? What did the photo add to your study of the chapter, intellectually and emotionally?

Discuss the ramifications of these differences in the post-war years. Did they leave any sort of lasting mark on U.S. politics and society?

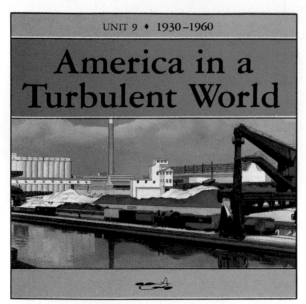

UNIT 9 ◆ 1930–1960

America in a Turbulent World

American artist Charles Sheeler (1883–1965), "American Landscape," (1930).

Unit 9 Overview:

Unit 9 takes students from the years preceding World War II to the eve of President John F. Kennedy's Camelot. In the pages of the unit, students will find the historical roots of many of the names and terms that are part of the living American vocabulary—F.D.R., Pearl Harbor, Midway and Cooregidor, D-Day, atom bomb, Iron Curtain, Cold War, Berlin Wall, Korea, Harry S. Truman, the Marshall Plan, Douglas MacArthur, McCarthyism, television, consumer economy, Ike, Brown v. Board of Education of Topeka, Martin Luther King, Jr., Vietnam, suburbs, Richard Nixon, missiles...

Basic Unit Concepts

1. After the Japanese attack on Pearl Harbor, the American people joined the Allies in fighting World War II and, in the end, defeated the totalitarian Axis powers.
2. President Truman's decision to drop two atomic bombs ended the war with Japan and ushered in the fearful Nuclear Age.
3. Japanese-Americans suffered great injustices at the hands of the American government and people during World War II.
4. After World War II, old emnities between the United States and the Soviet Union erupted in the Cold War that influenced American foreign policy for decades.
5. The Korean War became a ground for confrontation between the United States and Communist China.
6. Fear of communism, fanned by the demagoguery of Senator Joseph McCarthy, deprived many Americans of their civil rights.
7. The Supreme Court decision in Brown v. Board of Education and Martin Luther King's leadership motivated black Americans to actively push for the civil rights that had been denied them since post-Civil War times.
8. The Eisenhower-Dulles foreign policy worsened United States-Soviet relations and caused problems with nations friendly to America.

Chapter 29: "The World in Conflict" (1930–1945)

In Chapter 29, the students investigate FDR's foreign policy. They trace the events that led to the outbreak of war in Europe in 1939. They learn of Roosevelt's difficulties in waging an "undeclared war" against Germany in the face of the traditional isolationism of the American people. They witness the Japanese attack on Pearl Harbor that catapults the United States into World War II. They recognize the positive contributions of the American people to the war effort, and they realize the injustice done to loyal Japanese-American citizens. They follow the fierce fighting in Europe, North Africa, and the Pacific. Finally, they consider President Truman's momentous decision to drop the atom bomb and end the war.

Features
Going to the Source: Excerpt from President Truman's *Statement on the Atomic Bomb* (page 700)
Profiles on the Presidency: Harry S. Truman (page 701)

Learning Objectives
History Generalizations Students will gain knowledge that supports the following generalizations:

1. During his first term, President Franklin D. Roosevelt for the most part continued the foreign policy of President Herbert Hoover in order to concentrate on bringing the United States out of the depression.
2. Aggressive actions by Fascist Italy and Nazi Germany, culminating in the Nazi-Soviet invasion of Poland, led to the outbreak of World War II in Europe.
3. Responding to isolationist pressure, President Roosevelt steered the nation on a narrow course between neutrality and undeclared war against Hitler's *blitzkrieg*.
4. The Japanese attack on Pearl Harbor in 1941 ended the American debate about whether or not to enter the war, and the United States declared war on the Axis Powers.
5. On the home front, government leaders, business leaders, and American civilians combined their efforts to produce a staggering amount of war materials, and in the process American society underwent profound change.
6. Although blacks and women made some gains economically and socially, Japanese-American citizens were deprived of their civil rights and interned in concentration camps.
8. As a result of intense allied bombing of German cities and hard fighting in Africa, Italy, Eastern Europe, and Western Europe, the Allied Powers defeated Italy and Germany.
9. The agreement reached by the "Big Three" at Yalta contained the seeds of many East-West problems that arose after the war.
10. After a period of initial victories, the Japanese were put on the defensive and finally defeated, in large part because of the detonation of atom bombs over two Japanese cities.

Study Skills In addition to the three skills noted in Chapter 1 which are standard to every chapter, students will:
1. recognize and analyze propaganda.
2. write a persuasive paragraph using propaganda techniques.
3. relate graphic materials to the text of the chapter.
4. practice these ***critical thinking skills:*** generating questions about materials to be read, recognizing a point of view, comparing ideas, summarizing information.

Chapter 30: "Cold War Tensions" (1945–1952)

In Chapter 30, students follow events after World War II, at home and around the world. They discover what the Cold War was, how it began, and how the United States used the United Nations, NATO, and foreign aid to wage this war. They learn of the Republican comeback after nearly twenty years of Democratic control of the national government. They investigate the reasons for a red scare fueled by the demagoguery of Senator McCarthy. They witness the unwinnable war the United States fought in Korea. Finally, they consider the great economic and social changes in American life during the post-war years.

Feature

Going to the Source: Excerpt from Eleanor Roosevelt's article, "What I Think of the United Nations" (page 708)

Learning Objectives

History Generalizations Students will gain knowledge that supports the following generalizations:
1. Soon after World War II, old emnities and suspicions between the United States and the Soviet Union led to the Cold War which in large part determined American foreign policy from the late 1940s and into the 1950s.
2. After twelve years of Democratic administrations and Congresses, the Republican Party gained control of Congress in the elections of 1946.
3. In spite of a split in the Democratic party over black civil rights and relations with the Soviet Union, the Democrats held on to the presidency in 1948.
4. In an effort to win the Cold War, the United States government followed a foreign policy that led the country into NATO, the use of foreign aid as a weapon, the loss of Nationalist control in China, and war with Communist China in Korea.
5. A "red scare" at home was marked by passage of the Twenty-Second Amendment, loyalty oaths, the Hiss and Rosenberg trials, and McCarthyism.
6. Excess savings that could not be spent on consumer items during the war tripped off an American affluent society and consumer economy.

Study Skills In addition to the three skills noted in Chapter 1 which are standard to every chapter, students will:
1. interpret and construct flow charts.
2. write a cause-effect paragraph based on a flow chart.
3. relate graphic materials to the text of the chapter.
4. practice these ***critical thinking skills:*** generating questions about materials to be read, recognizing valid predictions, drawing conclusions.

Chapter 31: "Domestic and Foreign Challenges" (1952–1960)

In Chapter 31, students follow President Dwight D. Eisenhower in his two terms of office. They learn how he ended the war in Korea and how the "brinksmanship" of his secretary of state increased tensions with the Soviet Union and caused confusion in friendly countries. They discover which landmark Supreme Court decision initiated a new era for black Americans and what Martin Luther King, Jr. did to give form to the black struggle for civil rights. They investigate the reason for the sudden end to the increasing warmth in U.S.-Soviet relations and witness the growth of a good life for many Americans. Finally, they meet John F. Kennedy, the Democrat who won the 1960 presidential election.

Features

Profiles of the Presidency: Dwight D. Eisenhower (page 730)
Going to the Source: Excerpt from the Supreme Court's opinion in *Brown* v. *Education of Topeka* (page 733)
American Ingenuity chart (pages 742–743)

Learning Objectives

History Generalizations Students will gain knowledge that supports the following generalizations:
1. The first term of Republican president Dwight Eisenhower saw the end of the Korean War and the landmark *Brown* v. *Board of Education* decision that led to violent resistance to integration and the rise of Martin Luther King's nonviolent civil disobedience.
2. The Eisenhower-Dulles foreign policy of brinksmanship and massive retaliation provoked problems in various friendly countries around the world which were met with ineffective responses by the American government.
3. In spite of a mild stroke, President Eisenhower was reelected in 1956: however, because of troubles abroad and at home, American voters gave the presidency back to the Democrats in 1960.
4. Toward the end of President Eisenhower's second term, the growing warmth in U.S.-Soviet relations was cut off dramatically by the shooting down of an American plane over the Soviet Union.
5. During most of Eisenhower's presidency, many Americans enjoyed a "good life" symbolized by material advantages, but domestic and foreign problems forced the American people to face the realities of a changing, challenging world.

Study Skills In addition to the three skills noted in Chapter 1 which are standard to every chapter, students will:
1. use an almanac to locate information.
2. relate graphic materials to the text of the chapter.
3. practice these ***critical thinking skills:*** generating questions about materials to be read, validating opinions with factual evidence, determining causes of given effects.

THE WORLD IN CONFLICT

1930–1945

When the cannons are heard, the muses are silent;
When the cannons are silent, the muses are heard.

TRUMAN CAPOTE

Making Connections. World War II was the most destructive conflict the world has ever known. The United States was the last major nation to enter the fighting, but it played a decisive role. Not only American soldiers, but also American industry, led the Allies to victory.

In this chapter, you will learn:

- What isolationism was, and why many Americans believed in it in the 1930s
- How the United States' neutrality policy sometimes helped aggressor nations
- Who the Axis Powers were, and what they did to start World War II
- What Lend-Lease was, and how it helped draw the United States into the war
- Why the war helped open new opportunities for women and blacks
- How the United States developed a new weapon that ended the war with Japan

You have read that the casualties suffered by American troops in World War I and the debate over the League of Nations left Americans determined not to get involved in Europe's wars again. Therefore, the United States was slow to resist the aggression of Germany in Europe and of Japan in the Far East. As you read, note how the events of the 1930s and early 1940s gradually changed American attitudes.

Sections
1. Roosevelt's Foreign Policy
2. From Neutrality to War
3. The Home Front
4. America's Great War

1. ROOSEVELT'S FOREIGN POLICY

In his early days as president, Franklin D. Roosevelt devoted little time to foreign policy. His Secretary of State, Cordell Hull, was a political figure from Tennessee, not a career diplomat. Together, Hull and Roosevelt adopted the foreign policies of Herbert Hoover and his more professional *Secretary of State*, Henry L. Stimson. Only in matters where foreign policy related directly to Roosevelt's fight against the depression at home did they introduce significant changes.

The Good Neighbor Policy. Roosevelt and Hull adopted Hoover's phrase, "Good Neighbor," to describe the role the United States meant to play in Central and South America. Earlier presidents had responded to instability in Latin America by sending in the marines. Hoover changed this policy by announcing in 1929 that Americans would no longer interfere in the internal affairs of their neighbors to the south.

Following through on Hoover's promise, Roosevelt withdrew marines from Nicaragua, the Dominican Republic, and Haiti. Like Hoover, he refused to intervene in Cuba despite continuing civil war in that country. In 1934, with peace

World War II sent American GIs to fight in the deserts of North Africa, on the beaches of France, and on tiny South Pacific islands with strange names like Iwo Jima and Eniwetok. The marines at right march wearily through a village.

Quotation: from the book *The Muses Are Heard.* Other works by Truman Capote (born 1924) include *Other Voices, Other Rooms; The Grass Harp; A Tree of Night; House of Flowers; In Cold Blood; Local Color; Music for Chameleons; The Thanksgiving Visitor; A Christmas Memory; Breakfast at Tiffany's;* and *Observations.*

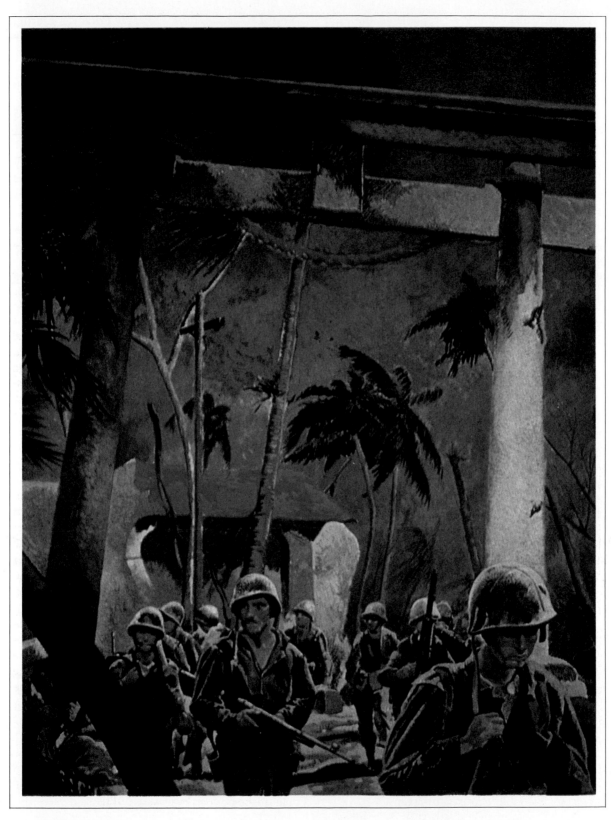

Skills Review: Reinforce the skills learned in the preceding Skills Strategy section. Collect photos of World War II events and have students write captions for them. Have them explain why they chose their captions and relate these responses to what they learned in the last chapter.

restored in Cuba, Roosevelt repudiated the Platt Amendment, which had given the United States the right to interfere in Cuban affairs.

The Good Neighbor policy was put to its most severe test in 1938. The Mexican government seized property owned by powerful American oil companies, paying very little compensation. Roosevelt kept cool, resisted the oil giants' demand for action, remained friendly with Mexico, and a few years later worked out a satisfactory settlement.

By that time the Good Neighbor policy was reaping dividends for the United States. The Second World War had begun and German Nazis were trying to gain a foothold in Latin America. Instead of siding with the Nazis, most of the Latin American republics remained friendly to the United States.

The Stimson Doctrine in Asia.

Toward Asia, Roosevelt also followed the policy laid down by Hoover and Stimson. The challenge in the East, as they saw it, was to maintain American trading rights in China (the Open Door policy) in the face of the growing power of imperial Japan.

Late in 1931, Japan took advantage of the weak Chinese government by moving into the Chinese province of Manchuria, which bordered on Japanese-ruled Korea, and setting up a *puppet government* there. President Hoover rejected the idea of intervening with force, but seriously considered an economic boycott of Japan because Japan depended on the United States for a number of vital raw materials like iron and petroleum. In the end, however, Hoover decided against economic action. Instead, he announced that the United States would not recognize Japan's control of Manchuria or any other changes of boundaries accomplished by force. This policy of *nonrecognition* was known as the *Stimson Doctrine* because the Secretary of State was chiefly responsible for it. But moral pressure, unsupported by force, could not stop Japanese aggression. In 1932, the Japanese launched a devastating air attack on the Chinese city of Shanghai. It was the worst incident of making war on a civilian population to that time.

Nevertheless, Roosevelt continued the Hoover-Stimson policy. Like Hoover, Roosevelt was preoccupied by the depression and reluctant to cut off profitable exports to Japan.

New Directions in Foreign Policy.

During his first term, Roosevelt used foreign policy only as a means of rescuing the American economy from depression. For example, in July 1933, Roosevelt scuttled a 63-nation conference in London called with Hoover's consent to discuss international currency. The conference was designed to save the *international gold standard*. Roosevelt had taken the United States off gold in March.

In November 1933, the United States formally recognized the Soviet Union. The President did not like Soviet communism or Joseph Stalin's dictatorship any more than his predecessors did. But it was clear that the Soviet regime was going to survive. To continue nonrecognition was unrealistic.

Roosevelt hoped that American companies would develop a profitable trade with the Soviets. Unfortunately, there was too little money in the Soviet Union to pay for American goods. The hoped-for trade never developed.

Increasing trade was also the idea behind the New Deal tariff policy. To boost American exports, Hull negotiated *reciprocity* agreements with 29 nations. *Reciprocity* means a mutual exchange. In this case, it meant reducing duties on imports if another nation also reduced its import duties by the same amount. The new policy marked a significant departure from the very high Republican tariffs. Hull cut American import taxes on those nations' goods by as much as half.

Isolationism.

With the exception of these adjustments, the United States remained aloof from European affairs. American public opinion would not have tolerated a more active interest in European politics. The bitter experience of World War I and the League of Nations debate was revived in American minds during Roosevelt's first term by the investigations carried out by North Dakota Senator Gerald Nye.

Between 1934 and 1936, Nye investigated the role of the munitions industry and international investment banks in America's decision to fight in the world war. He showed that the *merchants of death*, as munitions makers were called, and bankers generally favored American participation in the war. No doubt they benefited from the war. In his conclusions, however, Nye went further than his evidence warranted. He said that the

Union of Soviet Socialist Republics is the official name of the country we also refer to as the Soviet Union, the USSR, and Russia. These names will be used interchangeably for the remainder of the book.

678

arms-makers and the bankers were responsible for Wilson's declaration of war. That could not be proved, but some Americans believed it. This made them watch for signs that certain interests were trying to drag the United States into war.

SECTION REVIEW

1. Write a sentence to identify: Cordell Hull, Platt Amendment, Manchuria and Shanghai, reciprocity.

2. Define "Good Neighbor Policy," and give three examples of how President Roosevelt applied it.

3. Toward which country was the Stimson Doctrine directed, and why? Explain President Roosevelt's continuation of this doctrine even after the air attack on Shanghai in 1932.

4. How did Senator Gerald Nye's investigations promote isolationism?

2. FROM NEUTRALITY TO WAR

Numerous acts of military aggression made headlines in the 1930s. The German dictator, Adolf Hitler, hinted in 1935 that he would risk war to fulfill his ambitions for Germany. In 1935, the Italian dictator, Benito Mussolini, invaded the African state of Ethiopia. Between 1936 and 1939 Germany and Italy aided the forces of the conservative Spanish general, Francisco Franco, against the elected government of Spain. In 1937 Japan renewed its effort to make China an economic colony.

The United States responded to these gloomy omens by asserting American *neutrality* in what seemed to be an inevitable world conflict.

Italy Invades Ethiopia. Benito Mussolini came to power in Italy in 1922. Although Italy was a monarchy, the king was a figurehead. As prime minister and head of the *Fascist* party, Mussolini was a *dictator* with virtually *absolute powers*. That is why his government and others like it were

The Munich Agreement sliced up Czechoslovakia in 1938 for the sake of buying peace in Europe. The signers were (left to right) Chamberlain, Daladier, Hitler, and Mussolini.

While the Nazis and the Italian Fascists supported the Fascist forces in Spain's Civil War, the Soviet Union helped the Loyalists.

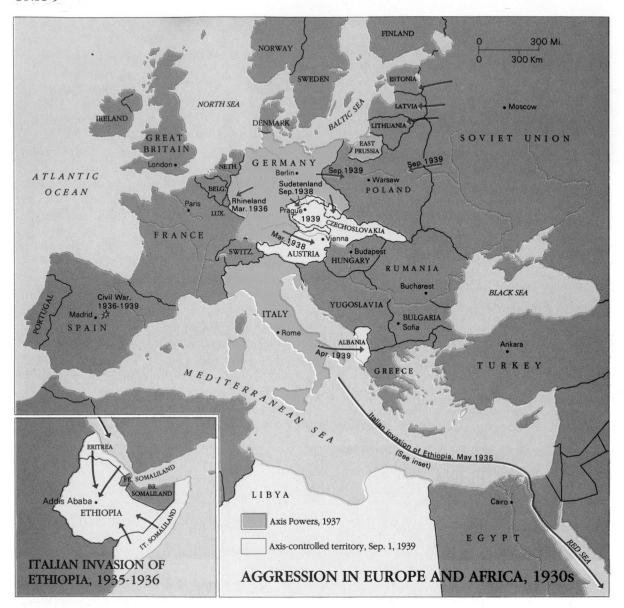

ITALIAN INVASION OF ETHIOPIA, 1935-1936

AGGRESSION IN EUROPE AND AFRICA, 1930s

Axis Powers, 1937

Axis-controlled territory, Sep. 1, 1939

called *totalitarian.* In fascist Italy, through legal action and the uncontrolled brutality of armed bullies, all people who disagreed with Mussolini were forced either to leave the country, silence their dissent, or risk being murdered.

In 1935, Mussolini invaded the ancient kingdom of Ethiopia. Most Americans, particularly blacks who identified with Ethiopia, sympathized with the Ethiopian emperor, Haile Selassie. Although many of them were armed only with primitive weapons against Mussolini's tanks and planes, the Ethiopians put up a heroic resistance.

But sympathy was all the United States offered. An act of Congress, the first of several *Neutrality Acts,* forbade the sale of arms to warring nations. Because Mussolini had other sources of arms while the Ethiopians had none, this policy unintentionally benefited the aggressor nation.

The Neutrality Acts. Congress passed four *Neutrality Acts* between 1935 and 1937. They were designed to avoid the circumstances that most Americans of the mid-1930s believed had entangled their country in World War I.

JAPANESE AGGRESSION IN THE FAR EAST, 1931-1941

First, the Neutrality Acts warned American citizens against traveling on the ships of nations which were at war. No Lusitanias this time!

Second was the principle of *cash and carry*. All nations at war were required to pay cash for American products they purchased and to haul those goods in their own ships. No American ships would be sunk this time because they were trading with a belligerent nation.

Finally, *belligerent nations* were not permitted to purchase any armaments in the United States nor to borrow money to buy arms. This law was designed to stop "merchants of death" from making money on the misery of other countries.

Japan Invades China. Neutrality policy again worked to the benefit of the aggressor nation when, in the case of Japan's invasion of China in July 1937, President Roosevelt did not invoke his powers to cut off arms sales to warring countries. Because American public opinion was strongly in favor of China, Roosevelt announced that he would allow the Chinese to buy weapons and munitions for defense.

Class Activity: Make a two-column chart and list reasons for U.S. involvement in both world wars. Discuss the differences and similarities. Also examine U.S. attempts to remain neutral in both wars.

An air-raid alarm sends workers in the business section of Hankow, China, rushing for shelter.
By 1939, despite stiff resistance, Japan had conquered most of eastern China.

However, this meant that the Japanese also had that right. Because Japan's navy and merchant marine were far superior to China's, and Japan controlled much of the Chinese coast, the aggressor nation was able to purchase tons of scrap metal used to make weapons, while very few American exports made their way to the Chinese.

Germany Advances. Adolf Hitler became Germany's chancellor in 1933 and quickly moved to establish himself as its dictator. His party of *fanatically* nationalistic followers were known as the *Nazis*. Testing very carefully how far he could go, Hitler began to undo the Treaty of Versailles. In 1935, he began to rearm Germany, and then he introduced universal military training in direct violation of the peace accords. France and Britain did nothing.

In 1936, along with Mussolini, he aided Spain's Francisco Franco in a civil war against Spaniards who believed in democracy. Thousands of young men from many nations, including Americans, formed volunteer battalions to fight for the republican side.

Emperor Hirohito of Japan, photographed in uniform during the war.

However, the western democracies gave little direct aid to the republicans for fear of war with Italy and Germany, which provided Franco with massive support. In the United States, President Roosevelt invoked the Neutrality Act. Again, although hardly the American intention, refusal to trade with the Spanish republicans worked to the benefit of the well-supplied Spanish fascists.

Enemies of Democracy. Militaristic Japan, fascist Italy, and Nazi Germany differed in many ways, but they also had much in common. The rulers of all three denounced democracy and human liberties as symptoms of social decay. In the place of the humanistic values of the western nations, they exalted the totalitarian state as personified in a single leader who was to be worshiped almost as a god. The leaders of all three militaristic nations preached a creed of *racism*. In Germany, this belief in a *"master race"* led to massive and brutal *persecution* of German Jews. Hitler's government stripped Jews of their civil rights and seized or destroyed their property. The worst, however, was yet to come.

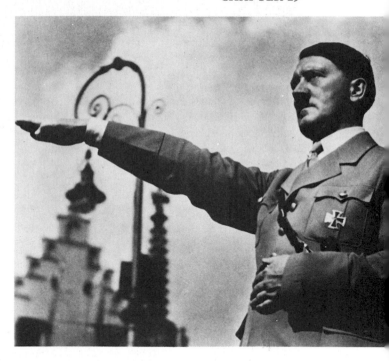

Adolf Hitler, in a typical pose, addresses a rally in 1934 after becoming dictator of Germany.

By 1935, signs like the one below could be seen all over Germany. It says, "Jews not wanted."

The Nazis used rallies to win the German people's acceptance for their "Thousand-Year Reich."

The Holocaust.

During World War II, the Nazis systematically imprisoned, tortured, and murdered Jews of their own country and of conquered lands. Other groups including gypsies, handicapped people, political *dissidents*, and resistance fighters were also treated in this brutal manner. Adolf Hitler led his Nazi followers to commit these atrocities against people who were not members of their "master race." They especially attempted to bring about a "final solution" (total extermination) to what they thought was the "Jewish problem." Using propaganda and force, the Nazis successfully overcame any resistance to their actions to rid their country of "undesirables."

Twelve million people were killed in Nazi *concentration camps* such as Auschwitz, Buchenwald, and Dachau. Six million men, women, and children died because they were Jews. The lesson of the *Holocaust* is that the Holocaust happened and should be remembered. Without moral codes and governmental safeguards, this kind of catastrophe might occur in any place, at any time. Each citizen in every country must protect the rights of all citizens against tyranny.

The Failure of Appeasement.

In 1936, Hitler marched troops into the German *Rhineland*, an area on the frontier of France that was supposed to remain *demilitarized* under the Treaty of Versailles. When France did nothing but protest, Hitler made larger plans. In March 1938, with the help of Austrian Nazis, he joined Austria to Germany in the *Anschluss* (union).

Again France and Britain did not resist. In September 1938, Hitler demanded that Czechoslovakia cede the *Sudetenland* to Germany. The Sudetenland, a section of Czechoslovakia that bordered Germany, was largely German in language and culture. That was Hitler's excuse for his demand: all Germans should live under one flag.

But the mountainous Sudetenland was also Czechoslovakia's natural defense line. The Czech government, the only democracy in central and eastern Europe, appealed to France and Britain to honor their pledge to defend the little country.

However, at a meeting in Munich later that month, Hitler promised French Premier Daladier and British Prime Minister Chamberlain that the Sudetenland was his final territorial demand. So determined were the leaders of the democracies to avoid war that they *appeased* Hitler. They sacrificed the Sudetenland so that, in Chamberlain's words, they could have "peace in our time."

War Comes.

Appeasement had precisely the opposite result. In March 1939, Hitler seized the rest of Czechoslovakia. Then, in August, much to the surprise of the world, because Communists and Nazis claimed to hate one another more than anyone else, Germany and the Soviet Union announced that they had signed a *nonaggression pact*.

This was obviously a prelude to a German and Soviet attack on Poland. France and England warned Hitler against taking this action but, with good reason, the Nazi dictator did not take them seriously. On September 1, Germany invaded Poland. The Soviet Union, acting on secret agreements with Germany, invaded Poland from the east. Within two days, France and England declared war on Germany.

Poland could not be helped. The country fell within a few weeks. Throughout the winter of 1939–1940, British troops poured into France but there was little action anywhere. Journalists wrote of "the phony war." Then they and the world learned about *blitzkrieg,* or lightning war. Hurling their massive strength to the north, German troops overran Denmark, Norway, Luxembourg, Belgium, and the Netherlands in a matter of weeks. In June 1940, France collapsed and the British managed to evacuate 300,000 of their troops from the little port of Dunkirk on the English Channel only by *mobilizing* almost every vessel on the Channel coast.

Then, in September, Germany, Italy, and Japan made an alliance. Thereafter, these three aggressors were called the *Axis Powers*. The forces that opposed them—Great Britain, France, and later the Soviet Union, the United States, and others— came to be called the *Allied Powers*.

The Battle of Britain.

For reasons that are still not clear, Hitler did not invade Great Britain. Instead, he ordered a relentless aerial bombardment of England in November while German land forces struck to the south, joining Mussolini in conquering the *Balkan* countries and most of North Africa.

It was "the *Blitz*," as the British called the almost nightly German bombings, that first began

Research Assignment: First, have students research what took place inside the Nazi concentration camps. Then, have students pretend they were newspaper journalists who were present when one of the camps was liberated and have them write first-person accounts of what they saw and heard.

The dome of St. Paul's Cathedral in London is illuminated by bursting bombs during the Battle of Britain. Almost nightly, German bombers pounded the city. But Hitler's plan for invasion was halted by the Royal Air Force and England's fierce defiance of "the Blitz."

to change Americans' minds about the European war. One of the most influential forces in promoting sympathy for the British was a radio newscaster, Edward R. Murrow. Through his broadcasts from England, Murrow brought the sounds of the Blitz—sirens, the roar of planes—into American living rooms. He also reported the defiance of Prime Minister Winston Churchill and the surprising news that the Royal Air Force (RAF) was actually winning the Battle of Britain.

Europe in 1941. Without control of the air, Hitler could not launch an invasion of England. Therefore, he turned his attention to the East, and on June 22, 1941, invaded the Soviet Union. Meeting little resistance at first, the motorized German army rolled deep into Russia. But after months of advance, the German attack bogged down when Russian resistance stiffened and deep winter snows disrupted their supply lines.

Hitler still held the upper hand. He controlled all of Europe. But, if it was short on supplies, the *Red Army* was a huge armed force. Just as important, in the winter of 1941, England no longer stood alone. In a limited way, without a formal declaration, the United States was helping England fight Germany.

Roosevelt and American Opinion. When the European war began in September 1939,

virtually all Americans opposed involvement. Memories of World War I were sour and strong. Europe's new madness was none of their concern. During the "phony war" of early 1940, only 43 percent of the American people thought that a German victory in Europe would threaten them in any way. By July 1940, after France fell, 80 percent were worried.

The most important force in changing American opinion about the war was President Roosevelt. He was convinced that if Britain fell to the Nazis, it would only be a matter of time before Hitler pushed into Latin America and other areas important to the United States.

The President had to work cautiously within the confines of the Neutrality Acts. His rationale was that the United States had to help England, because the British Isles had become America's first line of defense. Thus, in September of 1940, Roosevelt traded 50 old American destroyers that the British needed to counter German submarines for naval bases in Bermuda and Newfoundland. These bases, Roosevelt said, were essential for defending the United States. Defense was also Roosevelt's justification for asking Congress for a law requiring young Americans to register for military service. The *Burke-Wadsworth Act* of September 1940 was the first peacetime *draft law* in American history. Congress also appropriated $37 billion to build up the navy and the army air corps.

Roosevelt's Third Term. By September 1940, Roosevelt was well on his way to breaking an old tradition. Convinced that there should be no change of administration in that critical time, Roosevelt ran for a third term.

He succeeded. In November, he defeated Republican Wendell Willkie. Actually, there was not much difference between the candidates, as Willkie agreed that the United States must help Britain. He attacked the undeniable waste in many New Deal programs and said that Roosevelt had assumed too much power. Nevertheless, the Republican candidate agreed with the essentials of Roosevelt's policies. Most Americans thought it best to stick to the leader who had already been tested. Roosevelt won 55 percent of the popular vote and 449 electoral votes to Willkie's 82.

Undeclared War. Soon after the election, Roosevelt responded to Winston Churchill's appeal for more help by proposing the *Lend-Lease Bill.* Passed by Congress, it made the United States, in Roosevelt's words, the "arsenal of democracy." American factories turned out arms and other vital materiel that were "loaned" rather than sold to Great Britain. Later, lend-lease was extended to the Soviet Union. Eventually, aid to England and Russia totaled more than $50 billion.

Because no amount of aid could protect British shipping in the Atlantic from "wolf packs" of German submarines, Roosevelt proclaimed a *neutral zone* extending from the United States to Iceland. American destroyers patrolled these waters, warning and protecting British freighters. This informal, limited war with Germany allowed the British to concentrate their naval power around their home islands. Roosevelt stepped up the undeclared war on Germany by sending American troops to occupy Greenland, a possession of occupied Denmark.

The United States was now at war in everything but name. In fact, in August 1941, Roosevelt met with Churchill on a ship off the coast of Newfoundland. In the *Atlantic Charter,* the two agreed on their aims for the postwar world. Among the principles they asserted were these: (1) self-determination of nations; (2) free trade and freedom of the seas; (3) the disarmament of the aggressor nations; and (4) a new organization in which the nations of the world would meet to resolve differences peacefully.

To War or Not To War. In October 1941, a German submarine torpedoed and sank an American destroyer, the *Reuben James.* Americans who favored declaring war claimed that this was reason

At the Atlantic Charter Conference aboard the U.S.S. Augusta in August 1941, Winston Churchill and Franklin Roosevelt (front row center) discussed the postwar world.

enough to do so. However, public opinion was still divided. Many prominent people opposed what they considered "pulling Britain's chestnuts out of the fire." Among them were Charles Lindbergh, Herbert Hoover, and former New Dealer Hugh Johnson. Their *America First Committee* held huge rallies that put Roosevelt on notice that many Americans opposed going to war.

As it turned out, both Roosevelt and the America Firsters were looking in the wrong direction. They feared war with Germany. But it was with Japan that war came first.

Attack on Pearl Harbor.

Throughout 1941, Japanese and American diplomats tried to iron out their differences over China. Roosevelt and Secretary of State Hull put intense pressure on Japan by cutting off trade in vital materials. In 1940, they placed an embargo on the shipment of gasoline, machine tools, scrap iron, and steel. In the summer of 1941, they froze Japan's financial assets in the United States to further block its purchases of American goods. From Japan's point of view, these economic pressures were unbearable, causing severe shortages in the materials needed to continue its war in Asia.

The Japanese peace party, headed by Prince Konoye, hoped to come up with a formula that the United States would accept. But the Japanese insisted on both recognition of Japan's "special interests" in China and the end of the United States embargo on scrap iron and oil. Hull rejected both Japanese demands. The first violated the Open Door policy. The second eliminated America's only bargaining point.

Japan's war party, headed by General Hideki Tojo, gave Prince Konoye until late November to arrange an agreement. After that, Japan would begin irreversible preparations for war—an attack on the base of the American Pacific Fleet in Pearl Harbor, Hawaii.

Ironically, on the same day the war party gave the go-ahead, Cordell Hull concluded that war with Japan was inevitable. He told all American bases in the Pacific to beware of attack.

On the morning of December 7, 1941, it came. Japanese Admiral Isoroku Yamamoto, who had lived long in the United States and opposed war with America, sent waves of Japanese bombers over Pearl Harbor. In just a few hours, the Japanese sank or badly damaged eight battleships, seven other warships, and 188 airplanes. Almost 3,500 American servicemen were killed or wounded.

It would have been worse if Yamamoto had not canceled one final attack. He was concerned be

On December 7, 1941, Japanese bombs began to fall on Pearl Harbor Naval Base in Hawaii, causing much damage to American ships and planes and thousands of casualties.

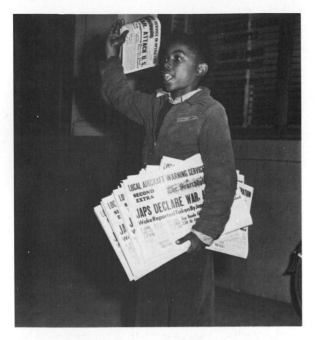

Newspapers such as the one being sold above in California published extra editions carrying news of the Japanese attack on Pearl Harbor.

cause the three American aircraft carriers he thought would be in port were at sea. Yamamoto knew that air power was the key to the war that would follow. His failure to sink the aircraft carriers was a bad sign. He turned grimly to his fellow officers, who were celebrating the victory, and said, "I fear we have only awakened a sleeping giant and his reaction will be terrible."

War Is Declared.   On the day after the attack, President Roosevelt described December 7 as "a date which will live in infamy." Every senator and every representative but one voted to declare war on Japan. The lone holdout was the pacifist congresswoman from Montana, Jeannette Rankin, who had also voted against war in 1917. In the succeeding days, the United States also declared war on Italy and Germany.

SECTION REVIEW

1. Write a sentence to identify: Allied Powers, Edward Murrow, RAF, "Blitz," Tojo.

2. Give three examples of how the policy of neutrality unintentionally aided aggressor nations.

3. In what ways were militaristic Japan, fascist Italy, and Nazi Germany alike?

4. List five steps taken by Hitler's forces that resulted in France and England's declaration of war on Germany.

5. How did the Japanese bombing of Pearl Harbor affect the United States' involvement in the war?

In his radio address President Roosevelt called the Japanese attack on Pearl Harbor "a date which will live in infamy."

3. THE HOME FRONT

World War II was a time of profound change in the United States. In many ways, American society changed more between 1940 and 1945 than in the decade of depression that preceded the war.

Manufacturing Planes and Guns. Prodded by the government, American manufacturers converted their assembly lines from the production of consumer goods (automobiles, cosmetics, civilian clothes) to the production of tanks, airplanes, grenades, and military supplies of every kind. The transformation of the productive forces of an entire nation was accomplished with amazing speed.

The process began during the first war years, when the United States was still nominally uninvolved and acting only as Great Britain's arsenal. After the passage of the Lend-Lease Act early in 1941, American factories hummed with activity, supplying the government's demand for the planes and ships that the British so desperately needed.

After Pearl Harbor, the federal government organized many special agencies to ensure that businesses, labor unions, and consumers adjusted properly to the colossal task of fighting a global war. The *War Production Board* (WPB) supervised the output of factories, and the *War Labor Board* (WLB) helped prevent crippling strikes. The *Office of Price Administration* (OPA) fought wartime inflation by freezing prices and wages at a fixed level.

The wartime performance of American manufacturers, large and small, was little short of miraculous. Production of warplanes went from 5,865 in 1939 to 96,369 in 1944. Construction of merchant shipping, so vital for transporting war supplies, totaled only 1 million tons (900,000 metric tons) in 1941 but skyrocketed to 19 million tons (17 million metric tons) two years later. In addition, American assembly lines rushed into soldiers' hands more than 17 million rifles, 2.7 million machine guns, and 41.4 billion rounds of ammunition.

Going to Work Again. One of the most important consequences of the war was the return of prosperity. Two years before Pearl Harbor, arming for defense and aid to Great Britain reopened factories that had been idle for years. By Decem-

ber 1941, 1.6 million men and women were in uniform, all requiring food, housing, clothing, and supplies. By the end of the war, the armed forces totaled 15 million.

When the war began, the federal government was already spending almost $2 billion a month on the military. During the first half of 1942, expenditures rose to $15 billion a month. By the time the Japanese surrendered in August 1945, the war had cost more than $350 billion! In less than four years, the American government spent more money than it had during its 150 years of existence. The national debt, already considered high in 1941 at $47 billion, topped $259 billion in 1945.

One consequence of government spending was that unemployment vanished as a social problem. The West Coast was especially prosperous. In order to be close to embarkation points for the war against Japan, new factories were founded by the hundreds in cities such as Seattle, Oakland, and Los Angeles. From less than 7 million people in 1940, California grew to more than 10 million in 1950.

Rosie the Riveter. With so many men in the armed forces, women went to work in unprecedented numbers, doing jobs that had previously

"Rosie the Riveter" symbolized the women in slacks and bandannas who worked in defense plants.

Research Assignment: Have students conduct interviews with people who remember what it was like during the Second World War. See if these stories relate to material in the text. Suggest that among the questions that the students pose should be questions about reactions to Japan, about jobs held by people in the U.S., and about the effects of the war on veterans.

been regarded as work for men only. The symbol of the working woman was "Rosie the Riveter," her hair kept out of machines by a polka-dot bandanna, wearing slacks, and wrestling around the noisy rivet guns needed to construct airplanes. In fact, women did every kind of work from operating a farm to serving in huge new government bureaucracies.

The number of government employees grew at a dizzying rate. In 1940, 1 million *civilians* worked for the federal government. In 1945, that number had tripled to 2.8 million. The growth in government opened opportunities for white-collar jobs that earlier generations of men and women could not have dreamed possible.

Gains for Blacks and Unions.

Wartime labor shortages also made it possible for blacks to get high-paying industrial jobs that had always been closed to them. Color was less important to a nation at war. Blacks moved from the South to the West Coast where, until the war, black communities had never been large.

Better jobs did not mean an end to discrimination. In 1943, a rash of race riots broke out in several cities. In Los Angeles, soldiers attacked Mexicans. Nevertheless, prodded by Eleanor Roosevelt and such black leaders as the Reverend Adam Clayton Powell of New York and labor leader A. Philip Randolph, Roosevelt issued an executive order forbidding racial discrimination by companies that benefited from government contracts. Not since Reconstruction had such strides been taken in the direction of racial justice.

Unions, already strong before the war, increased in size and power. With 10.5 million members before the war, membership increased to 14.7 million. There were strikes, but with a few exceptions they were short and did not disrupt production.

Daily Life.

While the government went into debt, civilians saved. One reason for the growth of savings accounts in wartime was that consumer goods were harder to find. Civilian automobile production was completely cut off in 1942 as auto factories turned out tanks, army trucks, jeeps, and airplanes. Even the person who owned a car found gasoline rationed. The President proclaimed a 35 mile-per-hour speed limit, and each automobile was assigned a windshield sticker that stated how much gas its owner was permitted to buy.

Tires were also hard to get. Because the Japanese controlled Malaya, then the source of 97 percent of the world's rubber supply, early in 1942 the government forbade the sale of new tires. The national stockpile of rubber was only 660,000 tons (598,000 metric tons), just about what civilians had consumed in a year, so huge scrap drives were held to collect rubber for the government.

Rationing also extended to some kinds of food. Families were given books of ration stamps. In order to buy scarce commodities such as butter, coffee, and meat, a person had to have not only cash but also ration stamps.

Japanese-Americans.

The citizens who suffered the most from wartime passions and prejudice were Americans of Japanese descent, most of whom lived on the west coast. Early in 1942, despite the objections of some officials, more than 100,000 Japanese-Americans, many of them native-born and therefore American citizens, were forced to leave their California homes to be interned in *relocation camps* as far east as Arkansas. There was no constitutional justification for this action. Japanese-Americans were labeled as threats to security merely on the basis of their race, a clear violation of the Fourteenth Amendment.

In 1944, however, in the case of *Korematsu* v. *the United States,* the Supreme Court upheld the *internment.* The governor of California, Earl Warren, who was considered a liberal politician, even proposed excluding Japanese-Americans from his state permanently.

What caused this tragic violation of civil rights? The shock of Pearl Harbor explains the first impulse. Racist dislike of the Japanese helped sustain it. One factor was the profits to be made from forced abandonment of Japanese-American property. This biased many community leaders against the Japanese-Americans. By the end of the war, $350 million worth of property had been taken from the Japanese-Americans.

Despite persecution, many Japanese-Americans remained highly patriotic. After repeated requests, 17,000 *Nisei* (American-born Japanese) joined the army and fought against the Germans in Italy.

Research Assignment: What was the public's reaction to the Japanese and other similar groups during this crisis? Could something similar happen in the U.S. today?

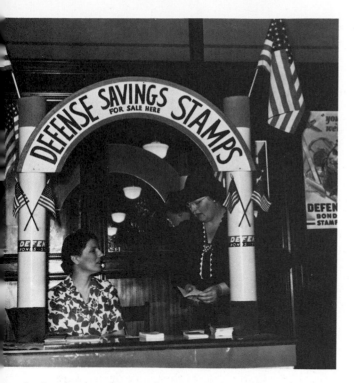

Savings bonds and stamps became patriotic purchases. Booths in public buildings sold defense stamps. Advertising posters (below) appeared in the windows of Japanese stores in Los Angeles.

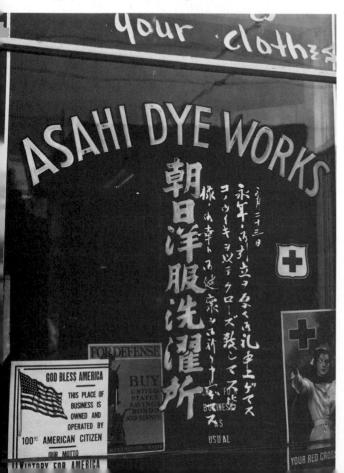

The Election of 1944. Of course no American could have predicted when or how the war would end. President Roosevelt passed his entire third term in office directing the American war effort. In 1944, although his health was noticeably weakening after nearly 12 strenuous years of leadership, Roosevelt decided to run for a fourth term. The Democrats gladly renominated him, but had great trouble choosing a running mate. Finally they settled upon a Missouri senator, Harry S. Truman.

The Republican candidate for president, Thomas Dewey of New York, expressed general agreement with Roosevelt's international policies, but criticized his conduct relating to the war. Again, the country expressed confidence in Roosevelt by reelecting him overwhelmingly. Dewey won only 99 electoral votes to Roosevelt's 432.

SECTION REVIEW

1. Write a sentence to identify: "Rosie the Riveter," Lend-Lease Act, rationing, Nisei.

2. Cite statistics to justify the phrase "little short of miraculous" to describe American wartime production.

3. Explain how each of these groups benefited from military spending: women, blacks, unions, white-collar workers.

4. Give three examples of how the war affected daily life on the home front.

5. Write a description of the plight of Japanese-Americans during the war.

---

4. AMERICA'S GREAT WAR

In the history books of western Europe, World War I is "the Great War." It was the First World War that shattered the confidence of France and England by killing half a generation of young men. By comparison, the American *Doughboys* of World War I arrived late and suffered little.

World War II was America's Great War. Along with the Soviet Union, which suffered the greatest casualties, the United States was a partner in the alliance that defeated Germany, and it was the major nation in the war against Japan.

Early Defeats in the Pacific. Immediately after Pearl Harbor, Japanese troops advanced rapidly in Malaya, Hong Kong, the Philippines, Java, and Guam, and later to the two easternmost Aleutian islands in Alaska. Only on the Bataan peninsula and in the island fortress of Corregidor in the Philippines did the Japanese meet strong resistance. Under General Douglas MacArthur, 20,000 American soldiers and their Filipino allies fought on, expecting help to arrive.

It did not arrive. President Roosevelt ordered MacArthur to flee to Australia, and the Americans and Filipinos were worn down by a far superior Japanese force. On May 6, the last defenders surrendered. Together, Bataan and Corregidor were the worst military defeats in American history. The aftermath was even more tragic. The Japanese forced 75,000 prisoners of war to march to prison camps in the Philippine interior. The unfortunate men on the "Bataan Death March" were so cruelly treated that fewer than 54,000 survived the war.

Stopping Japan's Advance. The Japanese strategy was to establish a defense perimeter far enough from Japan that American bombers based

The painting below is of two American soldiers on an island in the South Pacific.

outside the perimeter could not harm the Japanese homeland. Once this line was secure, the Japanese would push as far to the south and east as they could before the Americans were able to recover from Pearl Harbor and attack. Then, the Japanese government hoped, the United States would have to negotiate a treaty that recognized Japan's imperial supremacy in Asia: what they called the *Greater East Asia Co-Prosperity Sphere.*

By May 1942, Japanese troops were advancing in the Solomon Islands and most of New Guinea. Japan was also planning an invasion of Australia.

On May 7 and 8, however, Japan's advance to the south was halted. At the *Battle of the Coral Sea,* off Australia's northeastern shore, the American and Japanese fleets fought a unique battle. The opposing ships never came within sight of one another, and the fighting was carried out by planes from the aircraft carriers.

Admiral Yamamoto claimed victory in that the Japanese lost fewer ships and planes than the Americans. But he had to call off his move to the south.

The Battle of Midway. Yamamoto next switched his power to the central Pacific. A month later, June 3 to 6, the Japanese and American fleets met at the *Battle of Midway.* Here, the Japanese suffered a decisive defeat. The American fleet under Admirals Raymond A. Spruance and Frank J. Fletcher lost the carrier *Yorktown,* but the Americans sank four Japanese aircraft carriers. The Americans held on to the strategic island of Midway and almost destroyed Japan's seapower.

Like the Confederacy during the Civil War, resource-poor Japan could not replace major warships that were lost. Like the Union in the Civil War, the Americans could. Even while the *Yorktown* was sinking, other carriers were under construction in the United States.

After Midway, Admiral Yamamoto was forced on the defensive and began to build fortifications on the islands Japan controlled. The Americans were almost ready to take the offensive.

Defeating Germany First. Forcing Japan on the defensive so early made it easier for Roosevelt to pursue his first objective, the defeat of Germany. The President and most of his military advisors concluded that Germany was the more dangerous

There was a preoccupation with the belief that Germany was landing saboteurs in the U.S. to bomb defense plants. Of the close to 20,000 such cases reported, the F.B.I. could not trace one to any saboteurs. Of the 4,000 German aliens arrested as spies between 1938 and 1945, only 94 were convicted.

enemy. In control of most of Europe, the Nazis commanded vast resources in both raw materials and industry. Given enough time to dig in, Germany would be almost unbeatable on the continent.

The first priority was to stop Hitler from increasing the territory his army controlled. To strike at German industry and the morale of the people, the RAF and the United States Army Air Corps (later the independent Air Force) unleashed around-the-clock bombing of German cities. Eventually, 2.7 million tons (2.4 million metric tons) of bombs would fall on Germany. Although the bombing did not affect Germany's war effort as much as expected, it hammered away at the German people's morale.

The Second Front. To Soviet Premier Joseph Stalin, aerial attack was not enough. With the Red Army and Russian civilians suffering massive casualties (over 20 million dead by the end of the war),

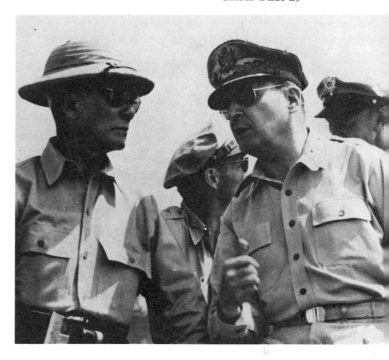

Margaret Bourke-White, a photographer and writer, was a distinguished war correspondent who flew on combat missions. Her photographs, like the one below, appeared regularly in Life *magazine.*

Two colorful generals were Douglas MacArthur (above right), who commanded in the Pacific, and George Patton (below), who won one of the first major Allied victories of the war in North Africa.

WAR IN EUROPE AND AFRICA,
1939-1945

Maximum territory under
Axis control, 1942

Neutral nations

Allied advances

Stalin wanted England and the United States to take direct action. Only an attack in western Europe could relieve the pressure on Russia.

Churchill and Roosevelt agreed that Russia must be relieved. However, neither believed that a full-scale second front could be opened without long preparation. But, in order to calm Stalin's suspicions that his allies wanted to bleed the Soviet Union to death, Roosevelt and Churchill agreed to open a second front. They attacked where they believed Europe to be most vulnerable —"the soft underbelly" of Italy and southern Europe.

First, it was necessary to secure North Africa. In June 1942, with the help of the new Sherman tanks from America, British forces under General Bernard Montgomery halted the German and Italian advance into Egypt at the *Battle of El Alamein*. In November, General Dwight D. Eisenhower landed with an American army in Morocco and Algeria. At Kasserine Pass in Tunisia in February 1943, American tanks fought German Field Marshall Erwin Rommel's seasoned *Afrika Korps* to a standstill. However, when Rommel was recalled to Germany, his army collapsed. American troops had their first victory.

troops had their first victory.

At about the same time, the Soviets won an even more important battle. At Stalingrad, the Red Army destroyed an army of 300,000 German soldiers. The Nazi advance to the east was halted. Slowly, the Soviets began to push the Germans back. But casualties were horrendous, and Stalin renewed his demands for a second front.

Hard Fighting in Southern Europe. In July 1943, American and British armies invaded Sicily. After initial reverses, they conquered the island in eight weeks. Americans got a dashing new hero in the tank commander, George Patton, and Italy was knocked out of the war. Never happy with Italy's dependent relationship with more powerful Germany, Marshall Pietro Badoglio replaced Mussolini and made peace with the Allies.

Peace with Italy did not mean the end of fighting there. German troops occupied almost impregnable positions in the Apennines, the mountains that run the length of the Italian peninsula. The "soft underbelly" of Europe proved to be as hard as granite. With comparatively few troops, Hitler was able to contain the allies in Italy until almost the end of the war. Stalin again had to plead with England and the United States for a genuine second front.

Ike and D-Day. The man whom Roosevelt and Churchill chose to organize the second front was General Eisenhower. "Ike" was not a dashing warrior like Patton. Rather, he was a career administrator who, thanks to a calm temperament, was an excellent diplomat. He had the talent to soothe the feelings of headstrong commanders who disagreed with one another.

These were exactly the qualities Army Chief of Staff George Marshall wanted for the job of preparing to invade Hitler's Fortress Europe. Three million soldiers, millions of tons of weapons, tens of thousands of motor vehicles, 11,000 aircraft, and 4,000 vessels had to be amassed in England and prepared for the greatest amphibious invasion of all time. The invasion project under Eisenhower's command was given the code name *Operation Overlord.*

On June 6, 1944, *D-Day*, the risky invasion was launched. Stalin thought it was two years late, but Eisenhower's cautious planning paid off. With the

Fighting in Italy (above) knocked Mussolini out of the war and made a second front possible. General Eisenhower and England's General Montgomery (below) began to plan the invasion of France.

"D-Day"—the Allied invasion of Europe—began before dawn on June 6, 1944. Among the two million soldiers who rushed the beaches of Normandy was photographer Robert Capa, who almost lost his life taking the above picture at Omaha Beach. Although under heavy fire, Capa did not take his eyes from the camera as he frantically shot frame after frame.

expected high casualties, Americans, Free French, British, and even some Polish forces hit the beaches of Normandy in northwestern France. For a while, the invaders were pinned down on the beaches. But after a breakthrough, they rolled back the German forces with surprising speed. On August 25, the Allies entered Paris. By September 12, they were across the German border.

Winning the War. The British, Canadians, and Americans disagreed about how to finish off Germany. Montgomery wanted to concentrate power in one thrust into the heart of enemy territory. When a tentative attempt to do so failed at Arnheim, Eisenhower returned to the strategy he preferred for both military and diplomatic reasons. The Allies advanced slowly against Germany on a broad front. This conservative approach lacked the high risks of a single thrust, and it allayed Soviet fears that England and the United States meant to keep the Red Army out of Germany.

Battle of the Bulge. Eisenhower's strategy seemed to be working well. But even with all his caution, the Germans turned the tables one last time. In December 1944 they attacked a weak point in the Allied lines. The Allies were pushed back, and were almost broken. Ultimately, the German attack lost momentum, but the *Battle of the Bulge*, as the desperate fighting was called, delayed the Allies for six weeks.

After the battle, German resistance collapsed. On April 30, 1945, with Russian troops on the outskirts of Berlin, Adolf Hitler committed suicide. His "Thousand-Year Reich" (empire) had lasted just 12 years.

The "Big Three" at Yalta. News of the final surrender of Germany was joyfully splashed across the front pages of American newspapers in May 1945. Another major event that newspapers could not fully report had occurred three months earlier: the meeting in February 1945 of Allied leaders in Yalta, a resort city in the Soviet Union. The *Big Three* leaders were Franklin Roosevelt, Winston Churchill, and Joseph Stalin.

Their purpose in meeting was to decide Europe's postwar fate. What they decided at Yalta was kept secret for many months. Their final agreement concerned four main issues.

At the Yalta Conference in February 1945, Stalin, Roosevelt, and Churchill met to discuss postwar Europe and to plan the United Nations. Roosevelt died two months later.

WAR IN THE PACIFIC, 1942-1945

Map legend:
- Territory under Japanese control, Jan. 1943
- U.S. advances
- Battles
- Atomic bombs dropped, Aug. 1945

Map labels: SOVIET UNION, Kamchatka, ALASKA, Sakhalin I., Attu, Kiska, May 1943, ALEUTIAN IS., MONGOLIA, MANCHURIA, Peking, KOREA, JAPAN, Tokyo, Hiroshima, CHINA, Nagasaki, Shanghai, Chungking, PACIFIC OCEAN, Okinawa May 1945, Iwo Jima Feb. 1945, INDIA, Hong Kong, BURMA, PHILIPPINE IS. Manila, Saipan Guam, Leyte Gulf Oct. 1944, July 1944, MARSHALL IS., Eniwetok Feb. 1944, Kwajalein Jan. 1944, Honolulu, HAWAIIAN ISLANDS, SIAM, FRENCH INDOCHINA, CAROLINE ISLANDS, Sept. 1944, DUTCH EAST INDIES, Apr. 1944, Mar. 1943, SOLOMON IS., Tarawa Nov. 1943, GILBERT IS., ELLICE IS., NEW GUINEA, Guadalcanal Aug. 1942, INDIAN OCEAN, NEW HEBRIDES, SAMOA, AUSTRALIA, 1000 Mi., 1000 Km., Sydney, NEW ZEALAND

First, they agreed that, after German surrender, German territory would be divided into four *occupation zones.* The four occupying powers —Britain, France, the United States, and the Soviet Union—would be responsible for governing different zones. The city of Berlin, though located in the heart of the Soviet zone, would be jointly governed by all four powers.

Second, Soviet troops had already occupied eastern Poland when the Yalta conference took place. Roosevelt reluctantly consented to allow the Soviets to remain in Poland and even to annex eastern Poland to the Soviet Union. In return, Stalin pledged that the Soviet Union would allow the government of Poland to be chosen in a free national election.

Third, the Soviets were then at war only with Germany. Roosevelt and Churchill persuaded Stalin to launch a Soviet attack against Japan's armies soon after Germany surrendered. In exchange, England and the United States agreed to allow the Soviets to take the Kurile Islands from Japan. They also promised to recognize Soviet control of Outer Mongolia.

Fourth, and possibly most important, the three leaders worked out some of the details of a new international organization to be called the *United Nations* (UN). To ensure Soviet participation in this body, Roosevelt agreed to an arrangement that, in effect, gave the Soviet Union power to cast three votes on any issue debated in the UN's General Assembly.

When the agreement at Yalta was finally made known, many of Roosevelt's Republican opponents bitterly criticized him for conceding too much to Stalin. Because of Yalta, they said, the Soviet Union gained dominance over the countries of Eastern Europe. The President's defenders argued that nothing could have stopped the Soviets from taking over Poland. After all, they said, Soviet troops were already there. Furthermore, the war against Japan was far from won. At the time, gaining Soviet help in a planned invasion of Japan seemed vitally important to American interests, in the eyes of Roosevelt's defenders.

Warfare in the Pacific.
American troops in Europe, slogging through mud and shivering through frigid winter weather, said that the sailors and Marines in the Pacific were on a picnic. Between battles, that was very nearly true. The balmy weather of the South Pacific islands would be remembered fondly by most sailors who survived the war.

But actual battle in the Pacific theater was a horrifying experience that the soldiers in Europe never knew. An attack always involved landing on islands on which Japanese soldiers were solidly entrenched in concrete bunkers. Japanese fighting men were *indoctrinated* with a fanatical loyalty to the emperor. They were instructed never to surrender, even when the battle was obviously lost. By killing as many of the enemy as they could, they were rendering a valuable service to the homeland.

Perhaps the best illustration of the spirit of the Japanese armed forces was the *kamikaze* pilot. *Kamikaze* means "divine wind." It refers to a storm that destroyed a Mongol invasion force in the Japanese Middle Ages. In World War II, kamikaze pilots were volunteers who flew bomb-laden planes directly into American ships, thus committing suicide in a desperate effort to destroy the enemy's fleet.

Island Hopping.
American strategy involved a three-pronged attack on Japan. On the Chinese mainland, Chinese Nationalists under Chiang Kai-shek (jyäng′ kī′shĕk′) and Communists under Mao Tse-tung (mou′tsĭ-tōong′) would pin down the 2-million-man Japanese army in China. This part of the war was not very successful. Chiang hated his Communist allies more than he hated the Japanese. Despite prodding and taunting from his American advisor, General Joseph Stilwell, he refused to press an all-out attack on the Japanese. As a result, in the last months of the war, the huge Japanese army in China was in splendid condition.

The second and third prongs of the attack were much bloodier, and also more successful. After driving the Japanese out of the Solomon Islands, which was essential to the security of Australia, General MacArthur pushed toward Japan via New Guinea. A second force under Admiral Chester A. Nimitz struck through the central Pacific, capturing islands from which aircraft could bomb Japan.

The casualties were staggering. Some American units that invaded Tarawa in the Gilbert Islands lost 90 percent of their men. Capturing Iwo Jima, little more than a desolate volcano, cost 4,000 American lives. At Okinawa, 45,000 Americans were killed or wounded and more than 100,000 Japanese died. Nevertheless, by the summer of 1945, American troops were poised for an invasion of Japan. Military planners did not look forward to the appointed day. The Japanese army was still 2.5 million strong. Planners said that the invasion would cost the United States a million casualties, as many as had been suffered over three years of fighting in both Europe and the Pacific.

The Atomic Bomb.
Thanks to the contributions of refugees from Hitler's Germany and Mussolini's Italy, American science offered a frightening means of ending the war. The *Manhattan Project* had been launched in 1939 when the physicist Albert Einstein wrote to Roosevelt of the possibility of unleashing unheard-of energy by splitting uranium atoms. It was known that the Germans were working on an atomic bomb.

With $2 billion in secret appropriations, J. Robert Oppenheimer coordinated the work of a team of scientists in Chicago and Los Alamos, New Mexico. In April 1945, the project was three months away from testing a bomb.

Discussion Question: Were we right in giving Poland to the Soviet Union as a part of the settlement of the Second World War? Discussion should center on whether it was ours to give away. (Poland was not an aggressor in the war.) Parallel this to British and French action before the war.

GOING TO THE
SOURCE

Sixteen hours ago an American airplane dropped one bomb on Hiroshima, an important Japanese Army base. That bomb had more power than 20,000 tons of T.N.T. It had more than two times the blast power of the British "Grand Slam" which is the largest bomb ever yet used in the history of warfare.

It is an atomic bomb. It is a harnessing of the basic power of the universe. The force from which the sun draws its power has been loosed against those who brought war to the Far East. . . .

It was to spare the Japanese people from utter destruction that the ultimatum of July 26 was issued at Potsdam. Their leaders promptly rejected that ultimatum. If they do not now accept our terms they may expect a rain of ruin from the air, the like of which has never been seen on this earth. Behind this air attack will follow sea and land forces in such numbers and power as they have not yet seen and with the fighting skill of which they are already well aware. . . .

> *It was to spare the Japanese people from utter destruction that the ultimatum of July 26 was issued at Potsdam. Their leaders promptly rejected that ultimatum. If they do not now accept our terms they may expect a rain of ruin from the air, the like of which has never been seen.*
>
> HARRY TRUMAN,
> "STATEMENT ON THE ATOMIC BOMB"

The fact that we can release atomic energy ushers in a new era in man's understanding of nature's forces. Atomic energy may in the future supplement the power that now comes from coal, oil, and falling water, but at present it cannot be produced on a basis to compete with them commercially. Before that comes there must be a long period of intensive research. . . .

I shall recommend that the Congress of the United States consider promptly the establishment of an appropriate commission to control the production and use of atomic power within the United States. I shall give further consideration and make further recommendations to the Congress as to how atomic power can become a powerful and forceful influence towards the maintenance of world peace.

President Truman was sailing home from the Potsdam Conference when an atomic bomb leveled Hiroshima. Truman released a "Statement on the Atomic Bomb," from which this excerpt is taken.

The decision whether or not to use it was not to be Roosevelt's. On April 12, 1945, shortly after being inaugurated for his fourth term, Roosevelt died of a massive stroke.

The outpouring of grief that swept the nation was real and profound. No other president had led the country for so long. At Roosevelt's funeral, no one was more uneasy than the new president, Harry Truman. He had practically no time to prepare for his new responsibilities.

Truman's Decision. Truman was a senator from Kansas City, Missouri. He had a reputation for honesty and efficiency, but impressed few people as the man to head a nation. Soon, however, Truman proved he had one attribute a president must have, the confidence to make decisions. He ordered that the atomic bomb be used to avoid an invasion of Japan and help end the war.

On August 6, 1945, a bomb nicknamed "*Little Boy*" was dropped on the Japanese city of Hiroshima. It killed 100,000 people in an instant and doomed another 100,000 to death from injury and radiation poisoning. Three days later, when the Japanese showed no signs of surrendering, "*Fat Boy*" was dropped on Nagasaki.

Incredibly, some Japanese generals wanted to fight on. Emperor Hirohito did not. He explained

Numerous historians have begun suggesting that a prime motivation for Truman's use of the A-bomb was to instill a little fear into the Soviet Union. If this is true, Truman should share the blame for starting the Cold War. Would you agree or disagree? Explain your answer.

HARRY S. TRUMAN

PROFILES OF THE PRESIDENCY

1945–1953

A plain-speaking man, Harry Truman described his reaction upon learning he was president:

Mrs. Roosevelt put her arm around my shoulder and said, "The President is dead." That was the first inkling I had of the seriousness of the situation. . . . I am not easily shocked but was certainly shocked when I was told of the President's death and the weight of the Government had fallen on my shoulders. I did not know what reaction the country would have to the death of a man whom they all practically worshipped. I was worried about reaction of the Armed Forces. I did not know what effect the situation would have on the war effort, price control, war production and everything. I knew the President had a great many meetings with Churchill and Stalin. I was not familiar with any of these things . . . but I decided the best thing to do was to go home and get as much rest as possible and face the music.

—DIARY, APRIL 12, 1945

This photograph shows the Japanese surrender aboard the U.S.S. Missouri. Japan's foreign minister signs the document ending the war as General MacArthur, at microphone, broadcasts the ceremony.

on the radio that he personally had ordered surrender. Only that act could ensure the cooperation of the Japanese people. On September 2, 1945, on the deck of the American battleship *Missouri,* representatives of the Japanese government signed the document that ended World War II, a war that had claimed more than 55 million lives. U.S. casualties had exceeded 1,215,000.

SECTION REVIEW

1. Write a sentence to identify: Chiang Kai-shek, Mao Tse-tung, J. Robert Oppenheimer, Hiroshima.
2. Describe the significance of the battles of Bataan and Corregidor.
3. Which two battles gave Roosevelt reason to take the offensive against Japan?
4. Describe the progress and setbacks of the Allies from D-Day through September 12, 1944.
5. List the four main issues agreed to at Yalta by the "Big Three."
6. Why did American military planners hope they would not have to invade Japan?

Discussion Question: Was Truman's use of the atomic bomb right or justifiable? In addition to the material in the text, have students draw upon outside material in discussing this question. It would be useful for them to consult books based on the accounts of survivors of the bombings.

MAJOR EVENTS OF WORLD WAR II

YEAR		ACTION
1939	September 1	Germany invades Poland.
	September 3	England and France declare war on Germany.
	September 17	Soviet Union invades Poland.
1940	May 10	Germany invades Belgium.
	May 11	Winston Churchill elected Prime Minister of England.
	June 10	Italy enters war on side of Germany.
	June 15	Paris occupied by Germans; French government sues for peace.
1941	June 22	Germany invades Soviet Union.
	December 7	Japan attacks Pearl Harbor; U.S. declares war on Germany, Italy, and Japan.
1942	May 4–8	Battle of Coral Sea; U.S. Navy stops Japanese advance in Pacific.
	June 4–6	Battle of Midway; Japanese naval power broken; U.S. begins counterattack in Pacific.
	August 7	Battle of Guadalcanal begins; U.S. begins to move military units into Japanese-held territory.
	November 7	Allies land in North Africa.
	November 19	Battle of Stalingrad begins; German advance into Soviet Union stopped.
1943	January 31	German army surrenders at Stalingrad; Soviets begin counterattack.
	May 13	Germans retreat from North Africa.
	July 10	Allies land in Italy; Mussolini government falls; Italy withdraws from war.
1944	January 19	Leningrad liberated; Germans retreat from Soviet Union.
	June 4	Rome liberated.
	June 6	D-Day; Allies land in France.
	July 8	Soviet army moves into Poland.
	August 25	Paris liberated.
	October 23–26	Battle for Leyte Gulf; Americans return to Philippines.
	December 16–27	Battle of the Bulge.
1945	January 15	American forces cross German border.
	April 1	Americans capture Okinawa, prepare invasion of Japan.
	May 7	Germany surrenders.
	August 6	Atomic bomb dropped on Hiroshima.
	August 9	Atomic bomb dropped on Nagasaki.
	August 14	Japan surrenders unconditionally.
	September 2	Japan signs formal surrender documents.

EUROPE BEFORE WORLD WAR II, 1938

EUROPE AFTER WORLD WAR II, 1945

GERMANY, 1945

EUROPE BEFORE AND AFTER WORLD WAR II, 1938-1945

BERLIN, 1945

Post-war occupation powers

American zone

British zone

French zone

Russian zone

CHAPTER REVIEW

TIME LINE

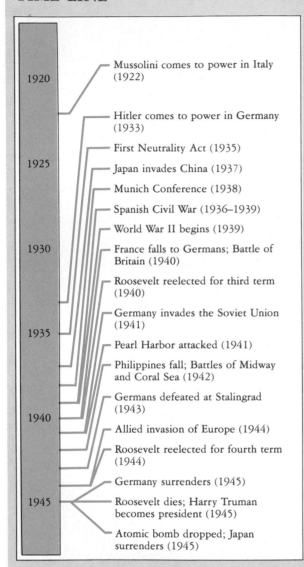

1920	Mussolini comes to power in Italy (1922)
	Hitler comes to power in Germany (1933)
	First Neutrality Act (1935)
1925	Japan invades China (1937)
	Munich Conference (1938)
	Spanish Civil War (1936–1939)
	World War II begins (1939)
1930	France falls to Germans; Battle of Britain (1940)
	Roosevelt reelected for third term (1940)
	Germany invades the Soviet Union (1941)
1935	Pearl Harbor attacked (1941)
	Philippines fall; Battles of Midway and Coral Sea (1942)
	Germans defeated at Stalingrad (1943)
1940	Allied invasion of Europe (1944)
	Roosevelt reelected for fourth term (1944)
	Germany surrenders (1945)
1945	Roosevelt dies; Harry Truman becomes president (1945)
	Atomic bomb dropped; Japan surrenders (1945)

TIME LINE QUESTIONS

1. In what years did dictators assume power in Italy and Germany?
2. How long did World War II last?
3. List these events in chronological order: Japan invades China, atomic bomb dropped, Battles of Coral Sea and Midway, Pearl Harbor attacked, Allied invasion of Europe, President Roosevelt dies.

SKILLS STRATEGY

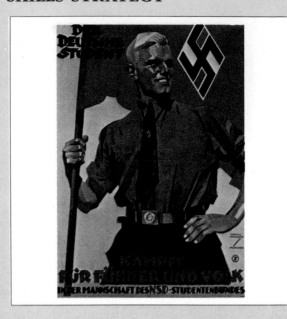

PROPAGANDA

Propaganda is one-sided or biased information written and distributed by supporters of a cause in order to win others to their viewpoint. It is useful to be able to recognize and analyze propaganda in order to grasp facts and form an independent opinion about its content.

Words that evoke deep positive emotions (for instance, *home, flag, love, freedom*) are used to make the propagandist's cause appealing. On the other hand, strongly negative words such as *hate, dangerous,* or *enemy* may be used to frighten or intimidate.

Propagandists might use one or more of the following devices to try to convince you to think as they do. *Name calling* is the use of negative words (such as *bully, crook, traitor*) to identify and discredit a person. Propagandists may tie their viewpoints to *glittering generalities* (such as "the American way" or "equal rights for all"). They may *transfer* the good reputation of a well-known person or group to their viewpoints by claiming that the person or group supports the propagandists' positions. Your desire to be associated with that person can lead you to accept the group's viewpoint or cause.

Making Connections: Review the questions and topics presented in the Making Connections section that opens this chapter. Discuss how the war has left an unmistakable impression on the role of the U.S. in the world. How has the war affected our view of ourselves? Examine the

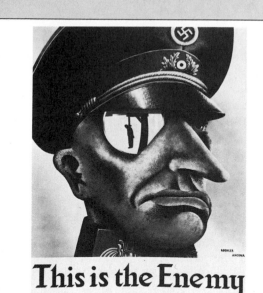

This is the Enemy

Transferring is also done using negative traits in exaggerated or caricatured form. Sometimes the ideas in a propaganda message are presented as ideas that *"just plain folks"* always endorse. *Card stacking* is the use of only those facts that will support a viewpoint (or, similarly, detract from it). Finally, the *bandwagon* technique persuades people to accept a viewpoint because "everyone" does. Propaganda techniques may be found in all forms of mass communication, including movies, songs, books, magazines, television, radio, speeches, and posters.

APPLYING SKILLS

Analyze the propaganda techniques used in the posters above as you answer the following.
1. Which poster is Nazi propaganda? Which is American?
2. Who is shown in the first poster? What emotion or emotions is the poster meant to evoke in the viewer?
3. What message does the propagandist want to give about Germans?
4. What emotion does the second poster evoke?
5. What propaganda techniques are used in this poster? Explain.

CHAPTER 29 TEST

TEXT REVIEW
1. Why did President Roosevelt continue the foreign policy set by his predecessor?
2. Give the important details about two of the following: the application of the Good Neighbor policy to Mexico in 1938, the basis for President Roosevelt's response to the air attack on Shanghai in 1932, and the reason for the United States's formal recognition of the Soviet Union in 1933.
3. List the three main provisions of the Neutrality Acts passed between 1935 and 1937, and explain how American public opinion influenced passage of these acts.
4. Give examples of the "undeclared war" that President Roosevelt led against the Axis Powers both before and after he was elected to a third term of office.
5. Who said the following, and why: "I fear we have only awakened a sleeping giant and his reaction will be terrible"?
6. What were the results of the Battle of Britain and the battle at Stalingrad?
7. Describe the two sea battles that turned the tide of the war against the Japanese forces.

CRITICAL THINKING
8. Identify in detail the following quotation: "a date which will live in infamy."
9. Describe the three beliefs that the Axis Powers held in common.
10. Summarize the provisions of either the Atlantic Charter *or* the Yalta agreement.

WRITING A PARAGRAPH
Propaganda can be a valuable tool for good. You know that everything was in short supply during World War II. It was important not to waste anything, especially items such as rubber tires, tin cans, fats, gasoline, and all food.

Write a propaganda paragraph to be read in a radio message urging all Americans to conserve an item that has just become scarce. Use some of the propaganda techniques discussed in the Skills Strategy for this chapter.

technological changes the war brought about and the positive and negative effects of some of them. Also review those actions against the Soviet Union mentioned in the annotations as a portent of the coming Cold War.

COLD WAR TENSIONS

1945–1952

*I am not willing . . . to bring bad trouble to people who, in
my past association with them, were completely innocent of any
talk or action that was disloyal. . . . I cannot and will not cut my
conscience to fit this year's fashions. . . .* LILLIAN HELLMAN

Making Connections. After the Second World War, the United States found itself the most powerful country in the world. It could not return to the isolation of the prewar years, but instead had to find a new role. It began to send economic and military aid to nations threatened by communism. Before long, American soldiers were once again fighting and dying in a foreign country.

In this chapter, you will learn:
- What the Cold War was, and how it began
- Where the Iron Curtain fell
- Why blacks and union members helped President Truman win a surprise victory
- What events made some Americans feel their country had been betrayed from within
- Why American soldiers were sent to fight in Korea
- How the life-styles of most Americans changed in the years following World War II

You know that Franklin Roosevelt was a popular president. Consequently, people doubted that Roosevelt's successor, Harry Truman, could fill his shoes. As you read, note how Truman led Americans down the paths in difficult postwar years.

Sections
1. The Cold War
2. The Republican Comeback
3. The Red Scare
4. The Beginning of Affluence

1. THE COLD WAR

From the start of the nuclear age on August 6, 1945, the world was shadowed by gloomy anxieties—and one glimmer of hope. The chief source of anxiety was an intense and bitter conflict between the United States and the Soviet Union —a situation known as the *Cold War*. For about two years after World War II, the two superpowers tried to find a way to preserve their wartime friendship. By 1948, it was clear they had failed to do so.

The glimmer of hope was the United Nations. However, by 1948, it was clear that this organization, designed to be more effective than the League of Nations, would have many of the old organization's troubles. Nations were still not ready to give up sovereignty.

The United Nations. Planned in 1944, the United Nations was organized in San Francisco in April 1945 by representatives of 46 countries, all of which had fought against the Axis powers. In the charter they wrote, members vowed "to save succeeding generations from the scourge of war" and "to promote social progress and better standards of life in larger freedom."

*After the United Nations was founded, land was
purchased in New York City for the permanent site
of the organization. The Congress approved an
interest-free loan for construction of the Secretariat
building, which was completed in 1952.*

Quotation: from a 1952 letter to the House Committee on Un-American Activities. Works by Lillian Hellman (born 1905) include *The Children's Hour, Days to Come, The Little Foxes, Watch on the Rhine, An Unfinished Woman, Pentimento,* and *Scoundrel Time.*

Skills Review: Reinforce the skills learned in the preceding Skills Strategy section. Review the uses of propaganda by the U.S. as they related to the events leading to the Cold War.

GOING TO THE SOURCE

We know that the USSR and the Communist parties are making promises for communism that sound very attractive to the downtrodden peoples of the world. We know that we should recognize that the fight today is in Asia, in Africa, and in the islands of the Pacific among the peoples who have felt that they are looked down on by the white race. One cannot observe the United Nations in action—one cannot look around that great table at which now sit the representatives of 59 nations—without realizing that the white race is a minority race in the world and that there are more peoples believing in other religions than there are Christians.

Our first task in finding ways to get along with the Communists is to find ways to make democracy mean what we say it does. And we have to make democracy work in our own country where other peoples can see it function. They can't see inside Russia, but here they can see everything that happens and can see that freedom of information is in itself one of our first advantages.

This country can, and must, show that democracy isn't just a word, but that it means regards for the rights of human beings, that it means that every human being . . . has equal dignity and equal rights, that it means that we

Our first task in finding ways to get along with the Communists is to find ways to make democracy mean what we say it does. And we have to make democracy work in our own country. . . . They can't see inside Russia, but here they can see everything that happens. . .

ELEANOR ROOSEVELT, "WHAT I THINK OF THE UNITED NATIONS"

care about the kind of freedom which allows people to grow and allows them to develop their own potentialities and their own interests; that we recognize that democracy, as a basis for government, has to assume certain obligations to its citizens.

It will not be enough to establish as fact that we have military superiority. It will not be enough to prove our economic superiority. We are going to have to persuade the Russians and their friends that compromise is not only desirable but quite possible. . . .

Finally, if democracy—and the blessings of it both as a way of government and a way life—is going to win this contest for the support of the peoples of the world, we must have moral conviction and spiritual leadership. That is the challenge to America today. That is the challenge that we face in strengthening and making the United Nations work as a whole. Those are the standards that we set ourselves and, in the interest of the future, those are the standards by which we must live.

Eleanor Roosevelt was a champion of human rights and democratic principles. She served as a delegate to the United Nations, and traveled around the world lecturing on international relations. She wrote this article, "What I Think of the United Nations," in 1949.

The three most important bodies of the UN were the *Secretariat*, the *General Assembly*, and the *Security Council*. The Secretariat administered the day-by-day affairs of the UN. The Secretary-General had considerable powers of prestige to bring to bear on members. The first Secretary-General was Trygve Lie of Norway.

In the General Assembly, every member nation was represented by an ambassador. The Assembly had little real power because none of the powerful nations wanted to be bound by the policies of smaller countries. However, it was hoped that as a kind of "town meeting of the world," the Assembly would serve as a place in

Discussion Question: Are we as Americans presently finding ways "to make democracy mean something?" Use this quote from Eleanor Roosevelt to begin a discussion that continues as students read the next few chapters. Have students examine present U.S. policies and their acceptability to each student as an individual and a U.S. citizen.

708

which nations could talk out their differences rather than go to war.

The Security Council was made up of five permanent member nations and representatives of six (now ten) nations, each elected for a two-year term. The temporary members were drawn from among the smaller countries. The permanent seats on the Security Council were held by the major Allied powers: the United States, China, France, the Soviet Union, and Great Britain.

The Security Council had authority to enforce UN policy with military action. However, because each of the five permanent members had the right to veto any Security Council resolution, the Council only had real power in disputes between minor nations and then only when the "Big Five" countries were willing to use force. In disputes between powerful countries such as the United States and the Soviet Union, the UN was ineffective because neither of the two major nations wanted to give up any of its sovereign rights.

The Origins of the Cold War. The origins of the Cold War lie in the period of the Bolshevik (Communist) Revolution in Russia. After the Communists, under Vladimir Ilyich Lenin took power in 1917, they made a separate peace with Germany, refused to pay the debts of Imperial Russia, and seized private property and everything owned by the Russian Orthodox Church.

Americans thought of Soviet Communists as ruthless, brutal atheists who were bent on destroying democracy and capitalism. The United States government worried that the Soviets would spread their doctrine to other nations.

In 1918 and 1919, American, British, French, and Japanese troops landed in northern and eastern Russia to help an anti-Communist army fight an unsuccessful war with the Communists. Many Russians felt that the western nations were bent on destroying their state. The long refusal of the United States to recognize the Soviet Union encouraged this deep mistrust.

During World War II, a common interest in destroying Naziism forced this long-standing suspicion into the background. The Soviets appreciated the massive American aid that enabled them to stop the Germans. In the United States, even staunchly anti-Communist newspapers admired the courage and determination of Soviet people.

On June 26, 1945, in San Francisco, delegates from 50 countries adopted the United Nations Charter. Secretary of State Edward R. Stettinius, Jr., signed for the United States.

Vladimir Lenin, a revolutionary leader and a major force in the Soviet Union, addresses Soviet troops in Red Square, Moscow.

During the Potsdam meeting, Churchill, Truman, and Stalin presented a united front for cameras, even though they disagreed on the issues.

The Problem of Eastern Europe.

After the war, the former feelings of mutual distrust were aroused by political disagreements about Eastern Europe. In the Atlantic Charter of 1941, Roosevelt and Churchill had stated that self-determination of independent and democratic nations was the American and British goal. But at the Yalta Conference of 1945, Stalin had made it clear that the nations of Eastern Europe that separated Germany from the USSR must be "friendly" to the Soviet Union. Roosevelt hoped to solve this dilemma by getting Stalin to agree to hold free elections in Poland. However, when the leaders of the United States, England, and the USSR met at Potsdam, Germany, to make final arrangements, they could not reach agreement. The wartime cooperation was beginning to break down.

The "Iron Curtain."

By March 1946, it was clear that free elections in Poland would result in a government that was more favorable to western Europe than to the Soviet Union. However, the Red Army still occupied Poland so the Soviets were able to prevent the elections from taking place. President Truman was worried and angry by this turn of events.

On March 15, 1946, in the town of Fulton, Missouri, President Truman attended a memorable speech by Winston Churchill, the former British prime minister. "From Stettin in the Baltic to Trieste in the Adriatic," Churchill said, "an iron curtain has descended across the Continent." He said it was time for the western democracies to act to halt the expansion of Communism. The press adopted Churchill's term, *iron curtain*, as the name for the boundary between the Communist regimes of Eastern Europe and the democracies to the west.

Declaring Cold War.

Early in 1947, with Communist guerrillas on the verge of gaining control of Greece, Truman took his first public action against Soviet pressures. On March 12, he asked Congress for $400 million in military assistance to pro-western governments in Greece and Turkey. The principle of supporting anti-Communist regimes with massive military aid became known as the *Truman Doctrine*.

On June 5, 1947, Secretary of State George Marshall proposed a much more ambitious program. He argued that economic hardships in Italy and France were helping the Communist parties of those countries. Marshall therefore urged Congress to invest vast amounts of money in the financial reconstruction of European countries ravaged by the war. In order to soften the anti-Communist aspects of the *Marshall Plan*, the Secretary also proposed to offer assistance to the Soviet Union and Eastern European countries.

As Marshall and Truman expected, the Soviets rejected the offer. By the end of 1947, Stalin was interested only in setting up *satellites*, or pro-Soviet governments, in Eastern Europe.

Containment Policy.
How should the United States respond to Soviet actions? In a long and learned article, a State Department expert on the USSR, George Kennan, said that the United States should seek to contain Soviet power. He pointed out that there was a long Russian tradition of expanding to the west, which was much older than the Soviet Union. Furthermore, the Soviets feared attack from the capitalist nations. For these reasons, wrote Kennan, it was impossible in 1947 to trust any agreement with Stalin.

What the United States must do, Kennan argued, was to draw clear lines beyond which the nation would not tolerate Soviet expansion. Those parts of Europe not already under Soviet control should be protected from Soviet aims.

Kennan warned that the Soviets would test American determination very carefully. But once it was shown that the United States was serious, they would pull back.

The policy of *containment* worked well in Europe. Stalin did not help the Communist rebels in Greece, and may even have worked against them. Nor did the Soviets provide much encouragement to Communist political parties in the Marshall Plan countries of France and Italy.

The Berlin Blockade.
The most serious test of the containment strategy involved the city of Berlin. The former German capital lay far behind the iron curtain. However, West Berlin was occupied by French, British, and American troops in accordance with the Yalta agreement of 1945. West Berlin was supplied by train and truck across Soviet-controlled East Germany. But in June 1948, the Soviet Union cut off access to West

The Marshall Plan, initiated in 1948, provided American money, goods, and services to help European economic recovery after World War II.

The Berlin airlift kept supplies flowing into West Berlin. The airlift foiled the blockade set up by the Communists to keep out Western influences.

Berlin. Stalin went back on his agreement, and declared that all of Berlin was within the Soviet sphere of influence.

For the United States there were three alternatives. The country could go to war against the Soviets, it could abandon West Berlin, or it could take a middle course and show the Soviets without war that it would defend its rights.

Truman chose the third alternative by organizing a massive airlift to West Berlin. For a year, huge supply planes flew in the necessities of life so that West Berlin could hold out. The Soviets responded as Kennan said they would. They neither shot at the American planes streaming into Berlin nor invaded the city. Instead, once they recognized that the United States was prepared to keep up the expensive airlift indefinitely, they canceled the blockade in May 1949. Soviet expansion had been contained.

SECTION REVIEW

1. Write a sentence to identify: Trygve Lie, "iron curtain," Soviet satellites, Berlin airlift.

2. Name the three most important bodies of the United Nations, and describe their compositions and functions.

3. Trace the origins of the Cold War. Explain what part Poland and other Eastern European nations played in the deterioration of relations between East and West.

4. Which American policy document had a broader scope, the Truman Doctrine or the Marshall Plan? Explain your answer.

---

2. THE REPUBLICAN COMEBACK

When Truman became president, the Democrats had controlled the White House for 12 years. That was the longest the Democrats had controlled the presidency since the party was founded in 1828. The Democrats had also controlled both houses of Congress since 1932. Under Roosevelt, the Democrats had nearly destroyed the Republicans as a national political force. With Truman in the White House, however, the Republicans were encour-

aged. Many Americans were beginning to look for new leadership, and they were no longer tied to the Democrats by Roosevelt's personal appeal. Truman could not sway politicians or the electorate by his character alone.

Republicans Gain Control of Congress. The Republicans sensed that voters were in the mood for a change for the sake of change. In the Congressional elections of 1946, they exploited the long Democratic dominance with a two-word slogan—"Had Enough?"

The results of the election seemed to indicate that the voters had, indeed, had enough. When the votes were counted, the Republicans had gained a slim edge in the Senate and a large majority in the House of Representatives.

The next step, the Republicans believed, was to capture the presidency in 1948, and they were very confident about succeeding in this. Their campaign approach was to focus attention on their objections to the Democratic programs, rather than to stress a new program. In Congress, many bills the Republicans introduced were aimed at overturning the New Deal reforms. Because of this, Truman vetoed more than 80 pieces of Republican legislation.

The Taft-Hartley Act. One important Republican measure became law despite Truman's veto. This was the *Taft-Hartley Act* of 1947. In pushing for this law, Republicans argued that labor unions had become too powerful following the passage of the Wagner Act under Franklin Roosevelt. Senator Robert Taft of Ohio, the influential son of a former president, championed the business point of view, which was that New Deal legislation had given unions an unfair advantage.

The Taft-Hartley Act outlawed a number of labor practices that it termed "unfair." Primary among its long list of prohibitions was the so-called *closed shop.* Unions could no longer demand employment contracts that excluded all non-union workers. It permitted employers to sue unions for breach of contract and permitted the president to declare "cooling off" periods before workers in a vital industry could go out on strike.

Siding with organized labor, Truman vetoed the Taft-Hartley Act. But the Republicans in Congress mustered enough support to override the

Research Assignment: Have students write a report examining the Berlin airlift. This report should discuss the kinds of items delivered, how they were distributed, and the feelings of the people in West Berlin at the time.

712

Senator Robert Taft opposed the "closed shop" and other union practices that he considered detrimental to American business.

veto. For years afterward, Democratic platforms called for repeal of the controversial measure.

A Democrat for Civil Rights.

In Truman's support of civil rights legislation, he showed how well he understood post-New Deal politics. The Presidential Committee on Civil Rights recommended legislation banning discrimination against blacks in employment and housing. Truman submitted the report to Congress, where an alliance of southern Democrats and Republicans rejected the civil rights reforms.

Truman responded by using the presidential powers at his disposal. He banned race discrimination in the armed forces, in the federal bureaucracy, and in companies that did business with the government.

It was a moderate program. Truman did not begin to touch the heart of discrimination in the United States, segregation of housing and public facilities. But it was a brilliant political move because it assured Truman of millions of votes at election time.

Blacks Remain Democrats.

During the war, hundreds of thousands of black people had moved out of the South to northern and western states where they could vote. For the most part they were concentrated in industrial states, which cast many of the electoral votes in presidential elections. Most blacks had become Democrats, switching from the party of Lincoln to the party of the New Deal.

But as civil rights organizations like the NAACP began to push for greater equality, there was a strong possibility that the black vote would swing back to the Republicans. Southern segregationists, who voted against every civil rights proposal, were all Democrats. By way of contrast, the leading contenders for the Republican nomination in 1948 all had fairly good records on civil rights questions. By taking direct action against racial discrimination, no matter how moderate, Truman ensured that he would have the support of the most influential black organizations.

The Democrats Split.

By the spring of 1948, Truman's popularity was on the upswing. Americans were becoming familiar with the President's downhome, direct style. Then, just as the Democrats had reason to hope they could win the election, the party split into three quarreling groups.

One group was the *Progressive party*, founded by Henry Wallace. Wallace blamed Truman for the Cold War and attracted some of the Democratic party's most liberal members. Although the Progressives offered a somewhat more ambitious program of social reform than did Truman, Wallace's chief issue was the Cold War. He insisted that the United States and the Soviet Union should cooperate, not attack one another.

Truman was the nominee of the regular Democratic organization. However, when a strong equal rights plank was inserted in the Democratic platform by Hubert Humphrey, then the mayor of Minneapolis, several southern state delegations bolted from the party. They called themselves *Dixiecrats* and nominated Strom Thurmond, gov-

Once, when President Truman's mother was visiting the White House, he arranged for her to sleep in Lincoln's bedroom. She refused, however, protesting that she was a southerner and didn't think it fitting.

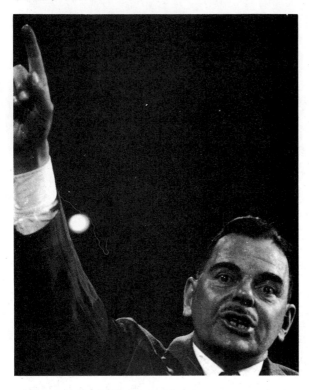

During 1948, Thomas E. Dewey (above) built up a seemingly solid lead over Truman in the public opinion polls. But Truman pulled an upset that surprised almost everyone, including the editors of the newspaper Truman held below.

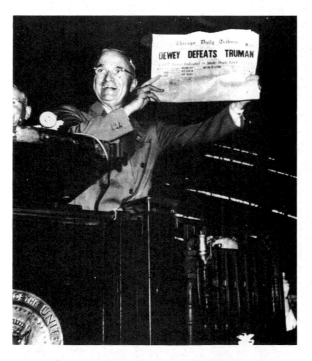

ernor of South Carolina, to run for president. They hoped to help defeat Truman and then win Republican support for continued segregation in the South.

Presented with what looked like a gift victory, the Republicans passed over the party's leading figure, the conservative Senator Robert Taft of Ohio. They renominated their moderate candidate of 1944, Thomas E. Dewey of New York.

The Great Upset. Faced with almost certain defeat, Truman had nothing to lose by speaking out. "Give 'em hell, Harry!" a supporter shouted at a rally, and that was exactly what Truman did. He smothered Congress with proposals, including a comprehensive medical insurance plan. When Congress voted every bill down, Truman denounced it as a "do-nothing Congress," and blamed the Republicans for obstructing social progress.

Truman's cause was helped by Dewey's personality. He aroused little excitement during his campaign. But Dewey was so sure of victory he avoided taking any strong stands whatsoever.

On election night, early returns showed Dewey with a comfortable, but not large, lead over Truman. Anticipating the next day's lead story, some newspapers rushed out early editions saying that Dewey had won.

But Truman was not finished. As late returns came in, Dewey's lead began to shrink. When all the votes were finally counted, Truman was the winner! Although his popular vote was less than 50 percent, Truman won easily in the electoral college with 303 votes to Dewey's 189 and Thurmond's 39.

The Fair Deal. Elected president in his own right, Truman hoped to build upon the reforms of the New Deal by enacting a reform program of his own. In his annual address to Congress, in January 1949, he proposed an ambitious program of legislation that he called his *Fair Deal* for Americans.

Only a small part of the Fair Deal program was adopted by Congress. As Truman requested, the federal minimum wage was raised from 40 to 75 cents an hour. The Social Security Act was amended to increase the benefits for retired workers. And an important housing act authorized construction of housing for low-income families.

Class Activity: Compare the platforms of Dewey and Truman in the 1948 presidential election. Based on the issues presented by each, who would the class have voted for and why?

Other parts of the Fair Deal were rejected by a Congress that tended to be conservative on most domestic issues. Republicans could not accept Truman's proposal for a federally supported health insurance plan. Nor would they permit repeal of the Taft-Hartley Act. At the same time, southern Democrats successfully fended off Truman's efforts for laws protecting civil rights.

SECTION REVIEW

1. Write a sentence to identify: elections of 1946, NAACP, Hubert Humphrey, "do-nothing Congress."

2. Name and give the essential provisions of the act proposed by Republican Senator Robert Taft. Explain why the act became law despite President Truman's veto.

3. Over what issue did each of these groups split from the Democratic party: the Progressives, the Dixiecrats?

4. In one column, list the parts of the Fair Deal program adopted by Congress; in a second, list parts Congress rejected.

---

3. THE RED SCARE

Harry Truman had scarcely begun his second term when Americans were stunned by disheartening news from abroad. In 1949, the Soviet Union exploded a nuclear device, ending the American monopoly on nuclear arms years earlier than American strategists expected. Then, in China, the Communists under Mao Tse-Tung defeated the Nationalist, pro-American government of Chiang Kai-shek. Chiang and his supporters fled to the island of Taiwan, off the Chinese coast. And in 1950, with apparent encouragement from both the Soviet Union and Red China (as Americans called the People's Republic of China), the Communist government of North Korea invaded pro-American South Korea.

A mere five years after the successes of World War II, it seemed as if everything was going wrong. When Americans looked for an explanation, many concluded that their country had been betrayed, subverted from within.

The NATO Alliance and Foreign Aid. How to win the Cold War against Communist pressures was the principal theme of Truman's *inaugural ad-*

Madame Chiang Kai-shek, shown below with her husband and General Joseph Stilwell, was educated in the United States and was a charming and persuasive speaker. She was an important advisor and spokesperson in her husband's government.

dress in March 1949. He announced an ambitious, four-point program which was to be the basis for United States foreign policy in the new era of global challenges.

Giving military support to the democracies of western Europe was one critical part of his plan. This should be done, said Truman, by signing a treaty of alliance with nine nations of Western Europe (including Great Britain, France, and West Germany) as well as other countries of the North Atlantic (Canada and Iceland). Joining in such an alliance represented a drastic departure from the isolationism of the prewar period. But the United States did in fact join the *North Atlantic Treaty Organization (NATO)* when, in July 1949, the Senate ratified the multi-national compact.

Each member nation in NATO agreed that "an armed attack against one or more of them in Europe or North America shall be considered an attack against them all." One year later, it was agreed that the American war hero, General Dwight Eisenhower, should act as supreme commander of the Atlantic Pact forces, which would include troops from all participating nations.

In 1949, Mao Tse-Tung and the Communists gained control of China. Mao's anti-American stand complicated United States foreign policy.

The fourth point in Truman's inaugural address —later referred to as *Point Four*—recommended that the United States stand ready to combat Communist influence in the "underdeveloped areas" of the world by giving various forms of military, economic, and technical aid. Congress supported the Point Four idea by appropriating the relatively modest sum of $10 million for economic assistance. This was the first of dozens of foreign aid bills that Congress would enact in later years to support growth and stability in the struggling *Third World* countries of Asia, Africa, and Latin America.

Asia After the War. In postwar Japan, the United States could claim a success story as great as the Marshall Plan in Europe. Massive economic aid to Japan and the enlightened occupation of the country as directed by General MacArthur produced a prosperous capitalist democracy.

MacArthur had spent much of his life in Asia. He understood Japanese traditions and was able to use his power to promote democratic institutions in a country that had previously been controlled by small ruling groups.

The Republic of the Philippines was also something of a success story. The United States had promised complete independence to the Philippines in 1946. Although the war with Japan interrupted preparations for this event, the United States kept its promise. On July 4, 1946, the government of the islands was formally turned over to the Filipinos.

The China Debate. China was the most important country in Asia and the most populous nation in the world. Throughout the war, the United States had aided the *Nationalists* led by Generalissimo Chiang Kai-shek in their fitful fight against the Japanese.

Some people in the army and the State Department criticized Chiang. They accused Chiang's government of being corrupt. The Generalissimo himself, they argued, was ineffective and unpopular. Others supported Chiang. These people were known as the *China Lobby*, and were a group of influential Americans who believed that the Chinese Communists were working for the Russians. Mao, they said, was Stalin's puppet. If he came to power, China would be a Russian satellite like the nations of Eastern Europe.

Clare Booth Luce, an American political activist and member of the China Lobby, championed Chiang Kai-Shek and opposed Communist China.

Red China.
Because of the discouraging events in Europe, Truman was inclined to listen to the China Lobby. Therefore, when the Chinese Communists defeated the Nationalists and Chiang fled to Taiwan, Truman and the American people were stunned. Until the end, the news from China had been that Chiang was near victory. Instead of pointing out that the China Lobby had misinformed them, newspapers accepted the explanation that the setback was temporary. If only the State Department would "unleash" Chiang, China could be won.

Truman and his new Secretary of State, Dean Acheson, had no intention of unleashing Chiang. They now realized that his Nationalists were far weaker than the Communists. However, it was no longer possible to come to terms with Mao. Because of the long American support of Chiang, Mao had become deeply embittered toward the United States.

Containment Policy in Asia.
Truman and Acheson tried to apply the policy of containment to Asia, too, in order to keep Communist gains to a minimum. But they had difficulty drawing the line. Did containment, for example, apply to Korea? Korea had been divided at the thirty-eighth parallel with the Soviet armies occupying northern Korea and the American armies occupying southern Korea. By 1949, two Korean republics had been formed. North Korea was Communist and friendly to Russia. The Republic of Korea in the south, under President Syngman Rhee, was friendly to the United States. By 1949, Soviet and American troops had been withdrawn from both Koreas. Would the United States defend South Korea in a war with its northern neighbor? Secretary of State Acheson was unclear about this. He did not directly state whether the United States would or would not defend South Korea.

War in Korea.
Both Korean governments claimed the right to rule the entire peninsula. Throughout the first half of 1950, they exchanged threats of war. In June, when Rhee moved troops near to the thirty-eighth parallel, the North Koreans struck. They poured across the border and quickly pushed Rhee's troops south to a tiny enclave around Pusan, at the tip of the peninsula.

Reaction to the invasion was immediate, not only in Washington, but also in the United Na-

These American troops, shown near the Yalu River that separated China from Korea, were part of the huge United Nations army that fought in Korea.

tions Security Council. The Soviet delegate was absent from the UN, because he was protesting the UN's decision to bar Communist China from the organization. This unusual circumstance permitted the Security Council to condemn North Korea as an "aggressor." Furthermore, the UN called on all members to assist the South Koreans. Many nations responded, but only the United States provided massive assistance.

President Truman ordered General Mac-Arthur, who was then in Japan, to take an American force to the peninsula. Instead of joining the desperate South Korean army at Pusan, however, MacArthur landed his soldiers at Inchon on Korea's west coast, deep behind enemy lines. It was a daring, brilliant maneuver. MacArthur cut off and captured 125,000 North Koreans.

With the North Korean army devastated, the Americans and South Koreans moved north. By October 26, 1950, an advance guard had reached the Yalu River, which separates Korea from the Chinese province of Manchuria.

The Unwinnable War. Truman and the United Nations had approved the conquest of North Korea when MacArthur assured them that the Chinese would not intervene. But MacArthur was wrong. In pushing toward China he disobeyed his own advice given years earlier that the United

KOREAN WAR, 1949-1953

→ UN forces
→ Communist forces

CHINA

YALU R.

U.S.S.R.

3 Farthest advance of UN forces Oct.-Nov. 1950

Hungnam

NORTH KOREA

SEA OF JAPAN

Pyongyang

Wonsan

5 Cease-fire line July 1953

Panmunjon

Seoul

38th Parallel

2 UN landing Sep. 1950

Inchon

4 UN Defensive line after Chinese entry Jan. 1951

SOUTH KOREA

YELLOW SEA

Taegu

1 UN Defensive line Sep. 1950

Pusan

0   100 Mi.

0   100 Km

American soldiers in Korea were overjoyed when, after long negotiations, an armistice was signed and they could leave the front line.

Although Truman stripped Douglas MacArthur of command in Korea, the general received a hero's welcome from a grateful nation when he returned home. In New York, he was greeted with a triumphal ticker-tape parade. Other cities gave him similar celebrations.

States should never get involved in a land war in Asia. The sheer numbers of Chinese would ensure that such a venture would be a disaster. Fearing that MacArthur would cross the Yalu River, the Chinese government sent 200,000 "volunteers" across the border. They attacked MacArthur's weary troops, and by the end of the year had pushed the UN troops back to a zigzag line that crossed the thirty-eighth parallel.

There the war stalled. For two years the Americans, South Koreans, and other UN forces battled the North Koreans and Red Chinese along the parallel. Both sides suffered heavy casualties for the sake of capturing forlorn, snow-covered hills. Some ridges for which thousands died did not even have names, but only numbers.

Even after armistice talks began at Panmunjom on the front line, the war dragged on for no apparent reason. The Chinese had achieved their goal of keeping a friendly North Korea on their borders. The Americans had achieved their goal of ensuring the independence of South Korea. But some days the negotiators at Panmunjom simply sat at the table facing one another and saying nothing.

The Fall of MacArthur. The American people were frustrated by this stalemate. The war put 5.7 million young men and women in uniform. About 54,000 Americans died in Korea. The wounded topped 100,000. Military expenditures soared from $40 billion in 1950 to $71 billion in 1952. Truman and Acheson had said the goal was containment, and North Korea was now contained. What was wrong?

In the spring of 1951, MacArthur offered an answer. He complained to reporters that Truman would not let him win the war. The President would not allow him to bomb supply lines in China. In April, MacArthur sent a letter directly attacking the President to a Republican leader.

Truman's military advisors were shocked that an army officer would publicly criticize the commander-in-chief. It is one of the strongest traditions of American government that the military is subordinate to the civilian commander. Unanimously, the *Joint Chiefs of Staff* agreed that Truman had no choice but to replace MacArthur, and on April 11, 1951, Truman relieved MacArthur of his command.

Remembering MacArthur's World War II career, the American people received him as a hero. MacArthur was greeted by ticker-tape parades in every city he visited. When he addressed Congress, more people listened to the speech on radio than had listened to Truman's inauguration in 1948. MacArthur hoped to turn his popularity into the Republican nomination for the presidency in 1952. But the general was no politician, and his ambition was never fulfilled.

The Twenty-Second Amendment and Loyalty Oaths.
Two immediate results of the postwar frustrations were an amendment to the Constitution and loyalty oaths. The Twenty-Second Amendment, proposed in 1947 and ratified in 1951, prohibited any person from being elected to the presidency more than twice. To many, it appeared to be in reaction to Roosevelt's long stay in office.

During Truman's presidency, Republicans began to accuse Democrats of tolerating civil servants who were disloyal to the United States. To defend himself from these charges, Truman ordered all federal employees and applicants for federal assistance to sign a loyalty oath. The signers swore that they were not members of the Communist party nor any group affiliated with the Communist party. They further declared that they did not advocate overthrowing the government of the United States by force. These oaths may not have been constitutional, and they were sometimes used to curtail First Amendment guarantees of free speech. But politics and anti-Communism overrode the concern for civil rights.

Alger Hiss and Richard Nixon.
The fear of Soviet *espionage* took on a new reality in 1948 during hearings held by the *House Committee on Un-American Activities.* A journalist named Whittaker Chambers informed the committee that he had been a Communist agent during the 1930s and had received secret information from Alger Hiss, a high-level government employee.

Hiss was no longer working for the government in 1948. Still, saying his reputation had been defamed, he demanded the right to appear before the committee to deny under oath all of Chambers's charges. Hiss said he did not even know Chambers. Because he was a distinguished person with an outstanding record of public service, most people were inclined to believe him.

But a young California congressman named Richard Nixon did not. While his colleagues said to let the matter drop, Nixon pressed his own investigation. He collected information showing that Hiss was definitely lying about some things. In cross-examination, Nixon several times trapped Hiss and forced him to change his testimony. Hiss was tried and convicted in a second trial for *perjury* (lying under oath) and, for his persistence, Nixon won a national reputation.

The Rosenberg Trial.
Another controversial and much publicized spy case concerned the activities of a married couple, Ethel and Julius Rosenberg. It began in February 1950 when the British arrested Klaus Fuchs, a German-born scientist who had worked on the Manhattan Project that built the American atomic bomb. He and several others admitted their complicity in a plot to pass atomic secrets to the Soviets. Julius and Ethel Rosenberg were implicated in the plot, although critics of the case have asserted that the evidence against them was questionable. The Rosenbergs freely admitted they were members of the Communist party and claimed that they were being tried for their political beliefs. Many liberals believed the government case in their *treason* trial was faulty. However, a jury found the Rosenbergs guilty, and the couple were executed in 1953.

McCarthyism.
The most amazing result of the 1950s *Red Scare* was the rise of Senator Joseph McCarthy of Wisconsin. First elected to the Senate in 1946, McCarthy was considered an ineffective legislator in Congress. He was responsible for no significant piece of legislation, and it was widely believed he would be defeated in the 1952 election.

It was the fear of defeat that sent McCarthy looking for an issue. He finally decided on the issue that had made Richard Nixon a national figure—Communist infiltration of government.

Joseph Welch, (left), the counsel for the Army in the 1954 Army-McCarthy hearings, is shown listening patiently to McCarthy. Using his good manners, down-home style, powerful intellect, and the television cameras, Welch destroyed McCarthy's power and discredited him completely.

Although he did not have the facts, McCarthy held up a piece of paper in front of a Republican audience in Wheeling, West Virginia, and said that it was a list of 205 Communists who were working in the State Department with the full knowledge of the Secretary of State. In other words, McCarthy was indirectly accusing Dean Acheson and his predecessor, George Marshall, of actively supporting subversion of the American government.

McCarthy's claims were fraudulent. But American frustrations ran so deep that many people believed he was telling the truth.

McCarthy viewed it as a game. He confidentially admitted, even to enemies, that he never had a list of Communists. He was amused by his sudden prominence. Yet, after being easily reelected to the Senate, McCarthy had enormous power. Although he never actually named a single Communist working in the government, many politicians were afraid to criticize him. When McCarthy announced an investigation of a government agency, the heads of it meekly rushed to cooperate. People who dared to challenge McCarthy were often fired from their jobs because they were suspected of Communist sympathies. *McCarthyism* meant accusing as a traitor anyone who dis-

sented from approved ideas, or who was even thought to have done so.

Senator McCarthy remained a powerful force until 1954. Then, during nationally televised hearings into the question of Communist infiltration of the Army, McCarthy was suddenly exposed for what he was, a man with no information who was destroying the reputations of innocent people. In December 1954, the Senate censured him. He died in 1957.

SECTION REVIEW

1. Write a sentence to identify: Red China, Third World countries, Dean Acheson, thirty-eighth parallel.

2. What three overseas events in 1949 and 1950 precipitated the "Red Scare" in the United States?

3. Give the important details about the Twenty-Second Amendment, Alger Hiss, the Rosenbergs, McCarthyism.

4. Explain how United Nations forces and the Communist Chinese became involved in the Korean War.

4. THE BEGINNING OF AFFLUENCE

The biggest factor in McCarthy's downfall was not journalists or congressional critics, but the supposedly "neutral" television. By fixing its glaring lights on him for hours on end in the Army-McCarthy hearings, television exposed the falseness and injustice of McCarthy's methods.

Television was just one of the new features of the American scene in the 1940s and 1950s that transformed the way millions of Americans spent their days and nights. The postwar period was a time when the American middle class grew to unprecedented size. It was also a time when a majority of the American people had a great deal of money to spend on goods that were not absolute necessities.

The Affluent Society. Economist John Kenneth Galbraith called American society an *affluent society*. He meant that the large amount of *discretionary income* in American hands, income above what was needed to buy necessary goods, instilled in a large number of people new values based on *consumption,* rather than on thrift and saving.

The affluent society was tripped off by the growth in savings accounts during World War II. Wartime rationing and the conversion of many factories to armaments production prevented American working people from spending money on such things as better housing, automobiles, radios, and other consumer items.

The population entered the postwar period with a great deal of money and the desire to spend it. Rising wages throughout the 1940s and 1950s added to the trend. In 1940, economists estimate, Americans spent $40 billion on nonessential items. In 1950 the figure was $100 billion.

Wedding Bells and Baby Boom. Because of the war, many young couples put off marriage and having children because so many young men were in uniform. Then in 1945 there was a rash of weddings as 4 million men were discharged by the army. Even more impressive was the *"baby boom."* While about 2.5 million children were born annually during the 1930s, 3.4 million were born in 1946 and 3.8 million in 1947. The upward trend continued until 1961, when 4.2 million babies were born, and continued at a high rate until the 1970s.

This tremendous jump in the number of Amer-

The great migration of middle-income families to the suburbs provided a boost to the economy by creating a demand for automobiles, housing, schools, utilities, and highways.

ican children caused a great demand for housing. As the years passed, this demand extended to goods that infants needed (for example, diaper services and baby food), then goods that toddlers consumed (toys), then schoolchildren (schools most of all), and, by the mid-1950s, leisure items for teenagers (records, clothing). The baby boom generation gave a tremendous boost to the consumer economy.

Growth of Suburbs.

Because land in cities was so expensive, contractors supplied housing needs by building large tracts of homes on farmland on the outskirts of cities. The most successful builders were those who got the homes up quickly and cheaply. That meant mass-producing houses, applying the principle of the assembly lines to construction.

The pioneer in suburban home-building was William J. Levitt, who organized armies of construction workers. The first wave graded the terrain. After the bulldozers came gangs laying down water, gas, sewer, and electrical lines. Next came waves of carpenters erecting hundreds of simple and identical houses. They were followed by roofers, plumbers, electricians, carpet layers, painters, and decorators. In only four years, Levittown, New York was transformed from potato farms into a city of 17,000 homes.

The rise of the suburbs was of major importance in American life. It allowed people to satisfy their desire to own a home. But 95 percent of those who moved to the suburbs were white, affluent, and between the ages of 20 and 35. The cities remained home for the poor, the old, and the minorities. These groups normally earned less than the suburban population. The cities were thus faced with the problem of trying to maintain services while collecting less in taxes. The result was the start of decay in the cities.

The GI Bill of Rights.

Many returning veterans were able to buy these new houses because the federal government decided to help them adjust to civilian life. The *Serviceman's Readjustment Act*, which was popularly called the *GI Bill of Rights*, was passed in 1944 to assist veterans in finding housing, medical care, and education. Through loans at low interest rates, the veterans were able to afford low-priced homes developers built.

The GI Bill's greatest contribution came in education. The average soldier was inducted into the armed forces at just the time when he or she would have been finishing high school or going through college. Therefore, the Bill encouraged the veterans to go back to college or vocational school. From 1945 to 1952, the government gave grants totaling $13.5 billion for veterans' education, and about eight million veterans eventually took advantage of the benefits.

The Consumer Economy.

Because the suburbs where the veterans bought houses were far from places of employment and even shops, the automobile became vital in American life. The number of cars Americans drove rose from 26 million in 1945 to 62 million in 1960. Car ownership increased even more quickly than the exploding population of the baby boom years.

More automobiles meant more highway construction and more services to care for the car population. The number of service stations, parts stores, car washes, motels, drive-in restaurants, and drive-in movie theaters increased annually. The suburban shopping mall, with its huge parking lots, began to displace old center-city shopping districts. Stores began to offer easy credit terms to attract shoppers, allowing them to buy *consumer goods* and pay for them over a period of months.

Traffic jams of commuters driving between suburban home and city workplace caused a demand for better highways. This demand eventually resulted in the 1956 *Interstate Highway Act*, which authorized the federal government to spend $1 billion a year on road construction.

Television.

The popularity of television was greater even than that of automobiles. Developed in workable form as early as 1927, television remained a toy of electronics hobbyists until after World War II. In 1946 there were only 7,000 television receivers in the United States, one for each 20,000 people.

Gambling that Americans would spend their money on a new kind of entertainment, the radio networks plunged into telecasting, making a variety of programs available. By 1950, more than 4 million sets had been sold, about one for every 38 people in the country. Throughout the 1950s, 7 million sets a year were sold.

Two possible origins have been suggested for the term *GI*, an enlisted man in the armed services. One version proposes that the initials stand for galvanized iron (used in such items as trash cans). The second version suggests that the letters stand for governnment issue (equipment given to enlisted personnel).

Hans Hofmann, "Golden Blaze"

Mark Rothko, "Number 10"

Louise Nevelson, "Royal Tide II"

Television promoted other leisure activities. Americans listened to slow, romantic, big-band music on the new 45-rpm records. Almost overnight, they bought 30 million hula hoops, an Australian exercise device, for $2 apiece. In six months, they spent $100 million for caps, toy rifles, rubber Bowie knives, lunchboxes, and other spin-offs popularized by Walt Disney's television series based on the life of the early American frontiersman, Davy Crockett.

Teenagers began to come out with their own styles that were different from their parents'. Musicians such as Elvis Presley, Bill Haley, and Chuck Berry popularized a new type of music— rock and roll—that was a total departure from other popular music. Young people wore leather jackets and tight pants, and many emulated Marlon Brando and James Dean, actors who played young, rebellious people in movies such as *The Wild One* and *East of Eden*. As in the Roaring Twenties, teenagers clashed with their parents over just what was proper conduct.

Women in the Postwar Era. With the return of 13 million soldiers to civilian society, most women who had held jobs during the war quickly stepped aside for their brothers and husbands. Female employment in the automobile industry, for instance, declined from 25 percent to ten percent. The proportion of women in colleges also declined. Moreover, colleges came to be looked on as places women attended simply to find suitable husbands. In women's magazines such as the *Ladies' Home Journal* and *Cosmopolitan*, editors preached a "new domesticity." Women were supposed to take pride in their roles as homemakers, wives, and mothers.

Although some women retained the new jobs and roles they had assumed during the war, many seemed to be satisfied with picking up their traditional roles. But their exposure to new roles profoundly affected their outlook on society. In the affluent culture of the 1950s, women became the backbone of suburban churches and synagogues, political clubs, and civic projects. These activities laid the foundation of social activism that contributed to the womens' rights movement of the 1960s and 1970s.

Modern Art. During the time that American ingenuity was being expressed in industrialization and the explosion of technology, there was a concurrent artistic revolution.

The development of good, small cameras and the ability of photographers to capture images with great exactness changed one function of art dramatically. Portraiture, street scenes, and landscapes were no longer the exclusive domain of painting or sculpture. Satisfactory pictures of a subject could be made quickly, and at low cost.

Although many artists continued to follow the charted course of naturalistic painting and sculpture, a significant number of them began experimenting with new forms in art. Many of these artists sought to depict the unseen essence of a subject. They began to extend their media, using color, line, form, and mass in surprising ways. Sometimes they made a normal subject into an *abstract* form. Other times their arrangements were freed from the restrictions of any formal subject. Their efforts brought new life to the arts, and commanded attention from the public.

Painters such as Mark Rothko, Helen Frankenthaler, Willem de Kooning, Jackson Pollock, Adolph Gottlieb, Max Weber, and Franz Kline shook the art world with their bold new approaches. Along with sculptors such as David Smith and Isamu Noguchi, they took the spotlight away from European artists, and for a time made the United States the center of important artistic expression.

Elvis Presley made "rock and roll" a commerical success with his popular style and dynamic presence.

SECTION REVIEW

1. Write a sentence to identify: John Kenneth Galbraith, GI Bill of Rights.

2. What is an affluent society? What accounted for the development of such a society in the United States after World War II?

3. What was the "baby boom"? Explain how it changed the public's demand for goods, services, and housing.

4. Account for the great increase in sales of automobiles in the 1940s and 1950s. Name several businesses that expanded because of these sales.

5. How did the war change women's roles in society? What were the effects of these changes on the postwar United States?

CHAPTER REVIEW

TIME LINE

1940

Wylie publishes *Generation of Vipers* (1942)

United Nations organized (1944)

Yalta Conference (1945)

Churchill's Iron Curtain speech (1946)

1945

Philippines become independent (1946)

Truman Doctrine; Marshall Plan (1947)

Truman elected president (1948)

Berlin blockade (1948)

Soviet Union explodes atomic device (1949)

1950

People's Republic of China proclaimed (1949)

Twenty-second Amendment ratified (1951)

Korean War (1950–1953)

Dwight Eisenhower inaugurated (1953)

1955

Senate censures McCarthy (1954)

TIME LINE QUESTIONS

1. When did McCarthyism stop being a force in American society and politics?
2. What event in 1949 ended the American nuclear monopoly?
3. What 1947 American policy helped European countries rebuild after World War II?
4. During whose administration was the Korean War ended?

SKILLS STRATEGY

MULTIPLE EFFECTS OF

| GI Bill of Rights entitled veterans to | home loans which led to the | move to the suburbs that created an |

FLOW CHARTS

Diagrams are useful adjuncts to written material and can help clarify ideas and details. A *flow chart* such as the one above is a type of diagram.

This flow chart helps to establish the causal connection among a variety of events. Flow charts also help to clarify the chronology of a group of events. As you study the following, refer to the flow chart above.

The first event shown in the flow chart—the GI Bill of Rights—can be considered the first cause in a chain of events. Ultimately, every other event in the flow chart can be traced to the GI Bill. This causal connection is indicated graphically by the arrows joining the events.

The first effect of the GI Bill was the opportunity for veterans of World War II to get loans to buy homes. This effect was also the cause of the next event—an effect—in the flow chart, the move to the suburbs, where contractors were building houses because of the high price of land in the city. In its turn, this effect became the cause of the

---

Making Connections: Review the questions and topics presented in the Making Connections section that opens this chapter. Emphasize the role played by Truman in setting the course of American foreign policy—a role that in many ways we are still acting out as a country.

THE GI BILL OF RIGHTS

increased demand for automobiles that resulted in the	→	expansion of the automobile industry that contributed to the growth of	→	highway construction firms; service stations and parts stores; car washes; drive-in restaurants, theaters, and banks; and shopping malls

next event—the need for automobiles, which caused the growth of the automobile industry. The flow chart continues by showing how the growth of the automobile industry led to the growth of several other businesses that depended upon the automobile for their existence.

Reread the information in the second paragraph under the subheading "Growth of Suburbs" (page 723). The steps William Levitt used to mass-produce homes could be shown chronologically in a flow chart. The information under "Wedding Bells and Baby Boom" (page 722) could be used to show the stages in the lives of the "boom babies" and the effect each stage had on providers of goods and services.

APPLYING SKILLS

Construct *one* of the two flow charts discussed in the last paragraph above. Remember to include arrows, a title for the flow chart, and, if you wish, appropriate illustrations.

CHAPTER 30 TEST

TEXT REVIEW

1. Explain why the General Assembly of the United Nations has little real power, and how it goes about keeping peace.
2. In what sense were the Truman Doctrine and the Marshall Plan Cold War weapons?
3. Discuss the American actions in the Berlin Blockade as a successful application of the policy of containment.
4. Name the ambitious program of reform legislation President Truman proposed in 1949, and tell what happened to it in Congress.
5. From what American tradition was membership in NATO a departure? What motive did the United States have for joining it?
6. Describe the purpose of the loyalty oath as used by President Truman.
7. Make the connection between *one* of the following pairs: the China lobby and the Communist takeover of China; the UN and the war in Korea; the Rosenbergs and atomic secrets; McCarthyism and the 1952 election.
8. What circumstances during World War II led to the development of affluence in the postwar United States? Give some examples of American affluence during this period.

CRITICAL THINKING

9. What did George Kennan correctly predict about the Soviet response to the American policy of containment? Why was this a valid prediction, not merely a good guess?
10. What conclusions could be drawn from McCarthyism about the need to keep informed about national issues?

WRITING A PARAGRAPH

Change the flow chart that you constructed in the Skills Strategy to paragraph form. Include each diagram entry in sentence form. Develop your paragraph sequentially, and indicate causes and their effects. Use words and phrases such as *this led to, as a result, consequently, causing, the outcome was*, and *the end effect* to indicate the cause-and-effect relationships.

CHAPTER 31

DOMESTIC AND FOREIGN CHALLENGES

1952–1960

*The new highway construction had altered everything; the
map bore only a dreamlike relation to the bulldozed countryside.
Road numbers had changed, and the old Indian trail . . .
had melted into the thruway.*   MARY McCARTHY

Making Connections. Most Americans who lived through the 1950s remember them as a time of peace and prosperity. President Eisenhower ended the Korean War, and kept the nation out of major conflicts for the rest of his term. But new issues that would trouble the country in the 1960s were beginning to appear.

In this chapter, you will learn:
- What promise Eisenhower made during the 1952 election campaign that guaranteed his victory
- How the "brinksmanship" policies of Eisenhower's Secretary of State increased tensions with the Soviet Union
- Why the Supreme Court decision in the case *Brown* v. *Board of Education of Topeka* began a new era for American blacks
- Who led a boycott of the Birmingham transportation system, and how his philosophy shaped the civil rights movement
- What Soviet scientific achievement jolted Americans out of their complacency
- How the great increase in suburban households changed American life

You know that under President Truman a cold war began between the United States and the Soviet Union. Therefore, Eisenhower's foreign policy concentrated on dealing with the Communist threat. As you read, note how Eisenhower kept the Cold War between the two superpowers from flaring into a hot war.

Sections
1. Eisenhower's America
2. The Cold War Continues
3. Eisenhower's Second Term

1. EISENHOWER'S AMERICA

The Twenty-Second Amendment did not apply to President Truman. He was eligible to run for president in 1952. But the Korean War and Joe McCarthy's claims that there were traitors in his administration had damaged Truman's reputation. If the Democrats were to have a chance to hold on to the White House, they needed a new candidate.

The new candidate was Adlai E. Stevenson of Illinois. He was a fresh face. Although a solid New Deal liberal, Stevenson had no close connections with the Truman administration.

Many agreed that Stevenson would make a good president. But the American people wanted more of a change than any Democrat could offer, and looked to the Republicans, who nominated the popular hero of World War II, Dwight D. Eisenhower.

Election of 1952.   Americans *liked* Eisenhower, or Ike. ("I Like Ike" was the Republican campaign slogan.) In fact, Harry Truman had asked the General to run for president as a Democrat in 1948. Eisenhower's broad grin and calm, cool temperament seemed to be just what the United States needed after 20 years of domestic reform and foreign wars.

*In 1956, Congress passed the Interstate Highway
Act. In the years that followed, a national network
of highways connected cities to expanding suburbs,
and then stretched on until the entire continent was
ribboned with roads.*

Quotation: from the book *Birds of America.* Other works by Mary McCarthy (born 1912) include *The Company She Keeps, The Oasis, The Groves of Academe, A Charmed Life, Memories of a Catholic Girlhood,* and *Venice Observed.*

PROFILES OF THE PRESIDENCY

DWIGHT D. EISENHOWER   1953–1961

For his first inaugural address, Dwight Eisenhower had difficulty in finding just the right words to the country:

For some weeks I have been devoting harried moments to preparation of my inaugural address—to be delivered next Tuesday. I want to make it a high-level talk. By this I mean I want to appeal to the speculative question of free men more than I want to discuss the material aspects of the current world situation. But how to do it without becoming too sermonlike—how to give it specific application and concrete substance has somewhat defied me. My assistant has been no help—he is more enamored with words than with ideas. I don't care much about the words if I can convey the ideas accurately. . . . I want to tell the American people that, internationally, we are entering a new phase, but I don't want to be using the inaugural address to castigate and indict the administrations of the past twenty years. It's a job.

—DIARY, JANUARY 16, 1953

Eisenhower's supporters made wise use of television commercials to reach as many voters as possible. These commercials showed a deliberate and impressive Eisenhower answering questions posed by ordinary citizens. This use of "packaged" advertisements became common in future political campaigning.

Republican strategists began to worry when polls showed that Stevenson was gaining. But Eisenhower was able to recover his big lead by taking the offensive. He said that if he were elected he would go to Korea to end the war.

Eisenhower won easily, with 55 percent of the popular vote and a 442–89 landslide in the electoral college.

The War Ends. Ike did not have a solid plan for ending the Korean War. Some of his advisors, particularly Secretary of State John Foster Dulles, wanted to wage all-out war on China, as MacArthur had suggested, but Eisenhower vetoed that. He had seen enough prolonged warfare, and, unlike MacArthur, remembered the old rule about avoiding land wars on the Asian continent.

Instead, he made good on his promise to visit Korea. He let it be known that if the North Korean negotiators at Panmunjom did not compromise, he might use nuclear weapons. When

In the presidential election of 1952, Eleanor Roosevelt (at microphone) campaigned for Adlai Stevenson (right).

Discussion Question: Was Eisenhower a good president? In what ways?

Stalin died early in 1953 and was succeeded by a more moderate leadership in the Soviet Union, the Soviet delegate to the UN suggested a settlement. A *truce* was signed on July 27, 1953, and the fighting finally stopped.

A New Style of Government.

With a clean slate, Eisenhower was able to put his conservative economic and social policies into practice. His cabinet was made up almost entirely of millionaires. Under Eisenhower, businesspeople were more directly in power in the United States than since the days of Calvin Coolidge. Secretary of Defense, Charles Wilson, for example, was the former head of General Motors. In his opinion, "what is good for General Motors is good for the United States."

As an excellent administrator himself, Eisenhower put his faith in people who knew how to run large organizations. When Congress created a new cabinet-level department, the *Department of Health, Education and Welfare*, Ike appointed as its head a military administrator like himself, Oveta Culp Hobby, the former commander of the Women's Army Corps.

As a military commander, Eisenhower was accustomed to receiving reports from his aides. Then he would make a decision and expect his orders to be carried out without further bother on his part. This is how he meant to run the executive branch of the government. His cabinet members were given great independent authority as long as they stayed within Ike's policies. Sherman Adams, the former governor of New Hampshire, was a special assistant who screened all people and all information that came to the President. Adams decided what and whom Eisenhower saw.

A Conservative by Nature.

Like Zachary Taylor and Ulysses S. Grant, two other generals who had become president, Eisenhower had taken little interest in politics. But he was an old-fashioned conservative. He believed in the values of his small-town upbringing in Kansas and Texas. As a career soldier, he had been insulated from the profound changes in American life worked by the New Deal and from the abuses that had made them necessary. After the war, most of his friends were wealthy businesspeople who reinforced his suspicion of a government that interfered too much with the workings of private enterprise.

Eisenhower attempted to roll back the federal government's influence in American life. He even wanted to sell the vast government hydroelectric project, the TVA, to private power companies. His advisors also followed this policy. The Secretary of Agriculture, Ezra Taft Benson, wanted to do away with all the federal agencies regulating business and agriculture. When a research physician, Jonas Salk, discovered a vaccine that prevented the dreaded disease polio, Secretary Hobby warned that if the government funded a massive immunization program the United States would drift toward socialism.

A Compromiser in Practice.

In practice, Eisenhower compromised. The government helped pay for the immunization campaign against polio that nearly eradicated the disease among Americans. Benson had to swallow his distaste for feder-

Dr. Jonas Salk (standing) developed a vaccine in 1954 that proved effective in preventing the crippling disease of polio.

Class Activity: Make a chart comparing the Eisenhower administration with that of F.D.R. How did their views on foreign policy, the role of government in a free economy, and their personal styles differ? In which ways were they similar?

Chief Justice Earl Warren (above, left) and Justice William O. Douglas (above, right) served on the Supreme Court during the case of Brown v. Board of Education of Topeka. Thurgood Marshall (below) successfully led the legal attack on the "separate but equal" principle upon which the opponents of integration rested their case.

al agricultural subsidies when farmers produced such huge surpluses that they could not get enough money for their grain to pay the cost of raising it. In fact, when surpluses piled up, sometimes literally in the streets of farm towns, the Eisenhower administration approved the *Soil Bank Act* of 1956. The government paid farmers for every acre they did not cultivate (put in the "bank"). Within a few years, $1 of every $6 in farm income resulted from the government subsidy program.

Eisenhower even adopted New Deal-like programs under which the federal government purchased farm surpluses and provided them free or very cheaply to school lunch programs. He not only learned that a government active in the economy was essential in the modern world, he found out that his business friends were not always trustworthy. When the government awarded a contract to develop electric power in the Appalachian Mountains to a company known as Dixon-Yates, it was revealed that company and government officials were guilty of corrupt practices in arranging the deal. Angry at being embarrassed by his friends, Eisenhower canceled the Dixon-Yates contract and gave it to the city of Memphis.

The President called his compromise between old-fashioned ideals and New Deal practices *Dynamic Conservatism*.

The Supreme Court Attacks Segregation.

Shortly after he took office, Eisenhower appointed Earl Warren to be Chief Justice of the Supreme Court. The President expected that Warren would be cautious and would moderate the New Deal liberalism that had dominated Court decisions for a generation. Instead, Warren took the lead in ushering in a new era of Court-ordered social reform.

In *Brown* v. *Board of Education of Topeka*, a decision handed down in 1954, Warren spoke for a unanimous court. He declared that racially segregated schools violated the Fourteenth Amendment's guarantee of equal treatment for all citizens. This decision revised the Court's 1896 ruling in *Plessy* v. *Ferguson*, which held that "*separate but equal*" public facilities for blacks and whites did not discriminate against the civil rights of black citizens.

The legal attack on this principle was led by Thurgood Marshall, an attorney for the NAACP, and later a Supreme Court justice. Marshall argued that even if separate black schools and white schools were truly equal in facilities and quality of teaching (which they rarely were), the civil equality of blacks was infringed because segregated schools imbued in black children the belief that they were inferior and could not compete in the

After the direction Chief Justice Warren was taking became apparent, conservatives in different parts of the country tried to have him impeached.

GOING TO THE SOURCE

In approaching this problem, we cannot turn the clock back...to 1896 when *Plessy* v. *Ferguson* was written. We must consider public education in the light of its full development and its present place in American life throughout the Nation. Only in this way can it be determined if segregation in public schools deprives these plaintiffs of the equal protection of the laws.

Today, education is perhaps the most important function of state and local governments. Compulsory school attendance laws and the great expenditures for education both demonstrate our recognition of the importance of education to our democratic society. It is required in the performance of our most basic public responsibilities, even service in the armed forces. It is the very foundation of good citizenship. Today it is a principal instrument in awakening the child to cultural values, in preparing him for later professional training, and in helping him to adjust normally to his environment. In these days, it is doubtful that any child may reasonably be expected to succeed in life if he is denied the opportunity of an education.

> *In the field of public education the doctrine of "separate but equal" has no place. Separate educational facilities are inherently unequal. Therefore, we hold that the plaintiffs ... are ... deprived of the equal protection of the laws. . .*
>
> SUPREME COURT, *BROWN V. BOARD OF EDUCATION OF TOPEKA*

We come then to the question presented: Does segregation of children in public schools solely on the basis of race, even though the physical facilities and other "tangible" factors may be equal, deprive the children of the minority group of equal educational opportunities? We believe that it does.

. . . We conclude that in the field of public education the doctrine of "separate but equal" has no place. Separate educational facilities are inherently unequal. Therefore, we hold that the plaintiffs and others similarly situated for whom the actions have been brought are, by reason of the segregation complained of, deprived of the equal protection of the laws guaranteed by the Fourteenth Amendment. . . .

In 1896, the Supreme Court ruled that segregation in public places did not infringe citizen's rights. In the 1954 case Brown *v.* Board of Education of Topeka, *the Court reversed its previous decision. Chief Justice Earl Warren delivered the unanimous opinion of the Court in this landmark case.*

mainstream of American society. To the NAACP, integrated education was the key to black equality in the United States.

The Supreme Court agreed. The Justices ordered segregated school districts in 17 states and the District of Columbia to *integrate* "with all deliberate speed." Blacks and whites were to be enrolled in the same schools as quickly as was reasonably possible.

Resistance to Integration. In border states, racial integration of schools was carried out with reasonable speed and with few incidents of vio-

lence. In the deep southern states of the old Confederacy, however, many whites resisted the order. *White Citizens' Councils* were organized to evade the order. Where they could not have their way, segregationists founded "private" schools for whites only that received tax money from sympathetic state governments. A year after the Supreme Court decision, not a single school in the deep South had been integrated.

The President did not put pressure on southern schools to integrate. Eisenhower had grown up in segregated states and served in a segregated army. He accepted the old ways and he believed his

BLACK MIGRATION FROM SOUTH TO NORTH · 1920–1960		
FROM	GEORGIA	706,000
	SOUTH CAROLINA	637,000
	ALABAMA	499,000
	MISSISSIPPI	442,000
	NORTH CAROLINA	373,000
TO	NEW YORK	793,000
	ILLINOIS	506,000
	MICHIGAN	386,000
	OHIO	323,000
	PENNSYLVANIA	270,000

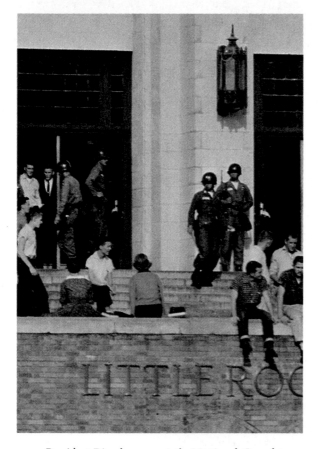

President Eisenhower sent the National Guard to Little Rock Central High School (above) to protect the first black students who enrolled there.

plans for a calm, stable America were threatened by the Supreme Court decision. By the time he left office, only 49 formerly segregated school districts had even begun to integrate.

Violence at Little Rock.

However, when his hand was forced, Eisenhower performed his duty to enforce the law. This happened at Central High School in Little Rock, Arkansas, in September 1957 when the first black students to register were greeted by hundreds of white students and their parents screaming and throwing rocks.

Claiming that integration rather than the segregationist mob threatened public order, Governor Orval Faubus called out the Arkansas *National Guard* to prevent the enrollment of the black children. Eisenhower tried to talk Faubus out of this action. When he failed to do so, the President *countermanded* the governor's orders. Faubus then used local police forces to prevent black registration.

The usually calm Eisenhower had a temper, and he was angered now. He put the National Guard under his command and sent them to Central High. This time the soldiers defended the right of the black students to enroll and protected them from the mob. It was necessary to keep the troops on guard for some time. Eventually, the segregationists lost interest and the soldiers were withdrawn. Without much enthusiasm for his role, Eisenhower had contributed to the movement for black equality.

Nonviolent Civil Disobedience.

In 1955, almost by accident, the *civil rights movement* ceased to be simply a fight in the courts. Ordinary black people began to mobilize and take direct action on their own behalf. It started in Montgomery, Alabama, when Rosa Parks, a secretary who was black, refused to give up her seat on a crowded bus to a white person, as city law required. Parks was arrested and Montgomery's black community rose in protest. The leader was a young Baptist preacher newly arrived from Atlanta, Dr. Martin Luther King, Jr.

King believed in *nonviolent civil disobedience.* That is, he believed citizens had a moral duty to disobey unjust laws in ways that were not violent. The laws that discriminated against black people, he felt, were unjust. This was civil disobedience

Boycott comes from the name of the agent for an absentee landlord in Ireland, Charles Cunningham Boycott, who was ostracized (or boycotted) by tenants for his refusal to lower rents and for heartlessly evicting tenants who couldn't pay their rents.

such as Henry David Thoreau had written of in the nineteenth century.

Moreover, King went on, Christian pacifism specifically required that such civil disobedience must be without violence of any kind. King believed that a Christian's responsibility required that when authorities arrested protesters, or even beat them, the protesters should submit without resistance. Because their action was moral, and the consequences often brutal, public opinion would support the protesters and cause the abandonment of the unjust laws.

King's Movement. In Montgomery, King called for blacks to *boycott* the public transportation system that *discriminated* against them. Because blacks were important customers of the buses, the city-owned bus company was soon in serious economic difficulty. It took considerable time and nonviolent response to violent acts, including the bombing of King's home, but the *Montgomery bus boycott* ended in success. Black riders were no longer subject to special rules.

The victory thrust Dr. King into national leadership. He returned to Atlanta and organized the *Southern Christian Leadership Conference (SCLC)* to sponsor direct action against *discrimination* of all kinds. At the same time, the NAACP continued to fight for equality in the courts. Another organization, the Congress of Racial Equality *(CORE)*, worked for equal rights in the North.

SECTION REVIEW

1. Write a sentence to identify: Adlai E. Stevenson, Jonas Salk, Justice Earl Warren, Thurgood Marshall.

2. Explain nonviolent civil disobedience. How was it practiced in the United States?

3. Give examples of President Eisenhower's economic and social politics, and examples of his ability to compromise.

4. Tell how the following promoted or resisted civil rights: White Citizens' Councils, Governor Faubus, NAACP, CORE

5. What was the Supreme Court decision in the case of *Brown* v. *Board of Education of Topeka?*

---

2. THE COLD WAR CONTINUES

Every president after World War II has faced the same dilemma. Foreign policy has had to be designed around the fact that the United States is locked into a competition with the Soviet Union that seems beyond solution, and which, in a nuclear age, could not be resolved by war.

Eisenhower recognized that a third world war was not a sane alternative. He had some success in relaxing tensions with the Soviets. But partly because of the orientation of his Secretary of State, and partly because of events beyond his control, relations with the Soviet Union were almost as bad when he left office in 1961 as when he had entered the presidency in 1952.

John Foster Dulles. John Foster Dulles was a person with excellent credentials. He had begun his diplomatic career under Theodore Roosevelt, half a century earlier. The somber, serious secretary had a powerful personality. He maintained unswerving convictions about communism and how to oppose it and was very direct and determined about expressing his beliefs.

An unbending belief that "good" nations should not cooperate with "bad" nations influenced and dictated Dulles's approach to Communist bloc countries. He held firmly to the view that Soviet leaders lacked credibility or honest intentions.

Moreover, the Secretary regarded neutral nations that tried to remain on good terms with the Soviet Union as equally suspect. He did not discriminate between a genuine desire for neutrality in the dangerous Cold War world and a surrender to the wishes of the Soviets.

This attitude put the United States at a disadvantage in trying to win friends among the "emerging nations" of the *Third World* (Asia, Africa, and Latin America). The new Soviet leader, Nikita Khrushchev, shrewdly understood how to get along with neutral countries. Therefore, he was able to increase Soviet influence in Third World countries.

Brinksmanship. Dulles believed in brinksmanship. By brinksmanship, Dulles meant that he would win the Cold War by threatening to take the world into nuclear war but stopping at the brink.

In a 1956 magazine article he said, "If you are scared to go to the brink, you are lost." In part, this policy was devised because of President Eisenhower's determination to cut the costs of defense. The easiest way to save money was to reduce the size of the army and navy and to rely instead on nuclear weapons. Brinksmanship meant the threat of *massive retaliation*, or nuclear attack on the Soviets, if they attempted to expand their power.

This diplomatic saber-rattling, which the United States government wisely did not act upon, did, however, injure American prestige abroad. Allies and Third World nations viewed United States diplomacy as uncertain. They were not sure just how far America would go to protect its friends.

Chinese Conflicts. Chinese Nationalists in Taiwan began artillery duels with the mainland Chinese Communist regime. Believing that the Eisenhower administration would "unleash" him, Chiang Kai-shek instructed troops on the tiny islands of Quemoy and Matsu to shell the mainland. The Red Chinese responded by bombarding Quemoy and Matsu. However, to Chiang's surprise, the United States refused to give him the military support that he needed to invade mainland China. So Chiang's limited, senseless war dragged on. The exchange of artillery fire became as ritualistic as a classic Chinese drama. At one point, for instance, the Communists insisted on the right to shell Quemoy and Matsu on alternate days of the month.

The Hungarian Rebellion. In 1956, anti-Communists in Hungary rose in rebellion against the puppet government the Soviets had established there. Budapest, the Hungarian capital, fell under the control of the anti-Communists. The Soviets hesitated to reassert their control, as if waiting to see what the United States would do. When no support for the rebels occurred, Soviet tanks and infantry rolled into Hungary and easily crushed the rebellion.

The Suez Crisis. While the Soviets were preoccupied with Hungary in 1956, Israel, Great Britain, and France invaded Egypt. Their purpose was to regain control of the Suez Canal, which had been nationalized two years earlier by Egypt's leader, Gamal Abdel Nasser.

Egypt was not a Communist country. But when Great Britain and the United States canceled a plan to finance the construction of the huge Aswan Dam, Nasser sought closer relations with the Soviets. Dulles therefore considered Nasser an enemy, and Israel, France, and Britain assumed they had American support in their attempt to seize the Suez Canal.

Eisenhower was prepared to use American troops if the Soviet Union sent military support to Egypt. The Soviets did not send the expected military support, and, to their chagrin, Eisenhower openly criticized Israel, France and England for invading Egypt. Because the United States joined world *censure* against them, the three invaders had no choice but to withdraw. Israel, the only dependable American ally in the Middle East, was resentful. The British, America's best friends anywhere, were angry. France, America's "oldest friend" in Europe, began to pull away from the NATO alliance and to establish an independent defense policy.

Indochina. The French had already become wary of the United States because of what they regarded as betrayal in Indochina (Vietnam). By the time Eisenhower took office, France was losing its fight against an *anti-colonial movement* in Indochina called the *Viet Minh.* Although originally people of many political views belonged to the Viet Minh, it was headed by a Communist, Ho Chi Minh (hō′ chē′ mĭn′). The French believed that the United States would help them because in 1953 the United States gave France $60 million to continue its rule of Indochina.

But, as the United States was eventually to learn, fighting *guerrillas* was a difficult business. The French controlled Indochina's major cities —Hanoi, Hue (hwā′), and Saigon. But much of the countryside was under Viet Minh control, at least at night when ordinary farmers put away their tools and took out their guns.

In order to challenge the ever-growing Viet Minh, the French established a powerful fort at Dien Bien Phu (dyĕn′ byĕn′ foo′) in northern Indochina. The Viet Minh accepted the challenge and attacked. Within weeks the French were surrounded and struggling to survive. They asked the United States to bomb the attackers, and Dulles urged Eisenhower to do so. Concerned that

Ho Chi Minh (above, center) led the Viet Minh in an anti-colonial movement in Vietnam against France. After the French left Vietnam, the United States became more involved there.

bombing would lead to involvement of American ground troops, Eisenhower refused.

Dien Bien Phu fell, and in the *Geneva Accords* of 1954, Indochina was partitioned as Korea was. The Viet Minh governed North Vietnam, north of the seventeenth parallel. A non-Communist Vietnamese, Ngo Dinh Diem (nyō′ dĭn′ dyĕm′), headed the government of South Vietnam. The United States did not sign the Geneva Accords, but promised to support them. However, by 1956 the United States was giving the South Vietnamese government substantial aid, not because it was a democratic government, but because it was anti-Communist.

Brinksmanship Declines. Although Eisenhower thought highly of Dulles and agreed with other statesmen that Dulles's firmness had blocked the Soviet's Cold War strategies, he often had to overrule his Secretary of State. Eisenhower

had seen war and its devastation and hated it, especially nuclear war.

In addition, Ike came to believe that *peaceful coexistence* with the Soviet Union, or peaceful relations between the two completely different societies, might be possible after Stalin's death. In his last years, the long-time Soviet dictator had been obsessed with the belief that the United States planned to attack the Soviet Union.

Although Khrushchev announced that the Soviet Union had developed a hydrogen bomb soon after he came to power, several surprising developments indicated an important change of spirit in the Kremlin. In 1955, Premier Nikolai Bulganin met with Eisenhower in Geneva, and the two leaders promised "a new spirit of cooperation" between the superpowers. Then, early in 1956, Khrushchev condemned the late Stalin for his bloodthirsty policies and for creating a "cult of personality."

Research Assignment: Have students prepare a report on the history of U.S.-Vietnamese relations. Have them go back as far as our relationship with Ho Chi Minh in the Second World War and continue their research to include the present.

President Eisenhower (above, second from left) went to a summit meeting in Geneva, Switzerland, to try to improve relations between the United States and the Soviet Union.

The Election of 1956.

Americans were interested in the implications of Khruschev's speech. It seemed to mark a startling change in Soviet policy. But they also had their own concerns in 1956. It was a presidential election year and there was some reason to believe that Eisenhower would not be able to continue as president.

The reason was health. At the outset of the campaign, Ike was felled by a serious heart attack. It seemed enough to end the career of a 66-year-old man. However, Eisenhower made a remarkable recovery and announced that his doctors regarded him as quite fit to serve four more years.

This was good news to the American people. When all was considered, the President had served well. He had not dismantled the New Deal reforms. More Americans were prospering than ever before. He had ended the Korean War and kept the peace. Relations with the Soviet Union were generally better than they had been since World War II.

With little hope of defeating him, the Democrats renominated Adlai Stevenson. The election was not exciting. As expected, Eisenhower won by a larger margin than in 1952, taking 57 percent of the popular vote and rolling up a 457 to 73 margin in the electoral college.

One exciting event in the election of 1956 was the nomination of the Democratic candidate for vice president. Usually, conventions name the person the presidential nominee chooses. In 1956, however, Stevenson broke with this tradition by making no recommendation. He told the delegates to make the choice.

Estes Kefauver got the nod. Famous and respected for his investigations into corrupt practices among labor leaders, Kefauver had challenged Stevenson for the presidential nomination and had fallen short.

In the race for the second spot on the ticket, Kefauver had to fight back a strong challenge by a 39-year-old senator from Massachusetts, John Fitzgerald Kennedy.

Defeat in 1956 was a blessing in disguise for Kennedy. He did not share in the humiliation of the Democratic defeat. But his name was now nationally known. Quietly but efficiently, his assistants began to work toward the 1960 nomination as soon as the 1956 election was concluded.

SECTION REVIEW

1. Write a sentence to identify: emerging nations, Nikita Khrushchev, Ho Chi Minh, Ngo Dinh Diem.

2. Give reasons that could explain the following opinion: "John Foster Dulles's personality and political beliefs caused difficulties in American relations with other countries."

3. Explain the role played by the inconsistent Eisenhower-Dulles foreign policy in the following situations: Quemoy and Matsu, Hungary, Egypt, Indochina.

4. What developments in 1955 and 1956 indicated a change in the Soviet Union?

3. EISENHOWER'S SECOND TERM

Less than a year after he was reelected in November 1956, Dwight Eisenhower suffered a mild stroke. He remained alert and seemed to regain his health quickly, as he had after an earlier illness, but critics questioned his leadership abilities. Some Democrats and Republicans believed he was not governing actively. In his second term, Eisenhower did leave more decisions to Dulles and Adams.

Changes in the Administration. In 1958, Ike suffered a double blow. Dulles died after a long battle with cancer. The new Secretary of State was an experienced diplomat named Christian Herter who seemed to have no strong ideas on what directions the United States should take.

During the same troubled months, it was revealed that Sherman Adams had accepted a number of expensive gifts from a wealthy businessman, Bernard Goldfine. In return, Adams had used his influence to help Goldfine's business. Adams was forced to resign.

Sputnik. Doubts about Eisenhower's leadership were complicated by the news that the Soviet Union had launched the *Sputnik* satellite into orbit in 1957. The launching called into question American assumptions about their country's technological superiority and the "drift" that, Democrats said, had become the nation's direction under Eisenhower.

Americans had assumed that the Soviet Union had been able to produce the atomic and hydrogen bombs only because they had stolen vital secrets from the United States. It was impossible to say the same thing about *Sputnik*. Soviet space scientists were undoubtedly several years ahead of the Americans.

Americans were not accustomed to being second. They took a brand new interest in their schools and what their children were learning. Science and math were emphasized in order to "catch up" with the Russians. At the same time, more and more critics blamed American failings on the lack of leadership in Washington.

Intervention in Lebanon. Partly in response to these criticisms, Eisenhower asked and received from Congress authority to help any Middle Eastern nation that was threatened by an "aggressor controlled by international communism." In 1958, the assassination of the king of Iraq by army officers friendly to Egypt's Nasser gave Eisenhower a chance to use this power.

When a republic was proclaimed in Iraq, violence broke out in nearby Lebanon. In retrospect, the problem was clearly the age-old one of hostility between Moslems and Christians in Lebanon, but Eisenhower portrayed the rioting as Communist-inspired. In July 1958 he sent 15,000 Marines to Lebanon, where they quickly restored order.

Continued Thaw in the Cold War. During this time, relations with the Soviet Union began to improve markedly. In July 1959, Vice President Nixon toured the Soviet Union. At a trade show exhibit in Moscow with Khrushchev, Nixon caught the attention of the media in what later came to be called the "kitchen debate" or "kitchen conference."

The American exhibit at the show was a model of a typical middle-class kitchen. There was no comparing the abundance and convenience of American middle-class life with the drab, crowded conditions of Soviet life. With reporters and photographers recording the occasion, Nixon surprised Khrushchev with remarks about how the comforts of American life proved that capitalist democracy was superior to communism. Khrushchev was caught so much by surprise that he made only weak replies. Upstaging the Soviet premier was no small accomplishment.

In September 1959, Khrushchev traveled to the United States for a three-week tour. He was the first Soviet leader to visit this country. In good spirits, enthusiastic and at ease, Khrushchev seemed to be able to relate well to the Americans he met on the tour.

The Cold War was never warmer. Eisenhower, popular with many Russians because of his record during World War II, was scheduled to visit Russia in 1960. There was every reason to believe that likable Ike would be as successful as Khrushchev in reducing tensions.

The Friendship Shattered. The trip was never made. On May 5, Khrushchev announced

---

Sputnik is part of the Russian phrase *sputnik zemlyi,* or "fellow traveler of earth."

that an American airplane had been shot down deep within Soviet territory. Eisenhower knew what had happened. For several years, U-2 planes had been flying over the Soviet Union at more than 65,000 feet on missions to photograph Russian defense installations. One of these special planes disappeared on May 1.

The President was confident that the plane had been destroyed and that the pilot had been killed. He announced that a plane used in weather forecasting had apparently lost its bearings and crossed into the Soviet Union.

Khrushchev pounced. The pilot, Francis Gary Powers, had parachuted to the ground and survived. He had also confessed the nature of his mission. Khrushchev was delighted. This was a diplomatic coup, and a major victory in the Russian-American competition. However, Khrushchev hinted that he still wanted Eisenhower to visit Russia, implying that Eisenhower may not have known about the flights.

Eisenhower refused to accept Khrushchev's help. He had known about the U-2 flights. To say otherwise would provide ammunition to Democratic critics who claimed that his subordinates, and not the President, were making key decisions. He acknowledged that he approved every U-2 flight. Khrushchev had no choice but to cancel the invitation. The Cold War was suddenly chillier than ever.

This perfectly suited the Democratic contenders for the party's nomination. Two chief issues that they all exploited were the lack of leadership under the Republicans and what they said was Eisenhower's neglect of defense. John F. Kennedy, for example, spoke of a "missile gap" between Russia and America. As *Sputnik* and the U-2 incident supposedly showed, the Soviet Union was ahead in rocket technology.

The Democratic Hopefuls of 1960.

In addition to Kennedy, the major Democratic candidates for the nomination were Hubert Humphrey of Minnesota and Lyndon Johnson of Texas. Humphrey was a liberal Democrat. Long before it was fashionable to do so, he had fought for legislation to help the poor and assure civil rights for blacks. His liberalism made Humphrey unacceptable to party conservatives.

Johnson was the candidate of the southern Democrats. But far from being conservative, Johnson was a staunch New Dealer who idolized Franklin Roosevelt. He believed in the government's responsibility to help people, but balanced this with political *savvy*, and voted like most southern senators on many civil rights bills.

Johnson knew almost everyone in Congress. As Senate majority leader, he and his fellow Texan, Speaker of the House Sam Rayburn, had seized the initiative from President Eisenhower in legislative matters. Johnson's major handicap as a presidential candidate was the suspicion northern liberal Democrats had of any Southerner.

Kennedy Turns Handicaps to Strengths.

Kennedy had two perceived handicaps. At 43, he was younger than the other candidates, and he was a Roman Catholic. Theodore Roosevelt had been younger than Kennedy when he became president after McKinley was shot. But no one so young had ever been elected to the nation's highest office. And some people continued to believe that because Catholics owed allegiance to the Pope in spiritual matters, they could not govern the country with impartiality.

Kennedy turned his youth to advantage, promising to be a president with "vigor," a backhanded reference to Eisenhower's age and inactivity. Catholicism proved not to be the political liability for Kennedy that it had been for Al Smith in 1928. The American voters, by and large, showed sincere religious tolerance, and indifference toward religion as a critical political factor in a national election. Kennedy found it relatively easy to appeal to a broad range of American voters.

Kennedy Sweeps the Field.

Kennedy easily defeated Humphrey in the New Hampshire primary. Kennedy also edged out Humphrey in the Wisconsin primary, which was unexpected, for Wisconsin bordered Humphrey's home state of Minnesota. Then, in the West Virginia primary, Kennedy knocked Humphrey out of the race. Humphrey had been a good friend of the poor, and West Virginia was a poor state. It was also heavily Protestant. By winning there, Kennedy showed that anti-Catholic prejudice was weaker than the experts thought.

Kennedy's showing got him the backing of influential Democratic bosses like Chicago's Rich-

In the presidential election of 1960, Senator John Kennedy (above, with his wife Jacqueline) successfully overcame political handicaps and won the election.

ard E. Daley and Ohio's Mike DiSalle. By the time of the convention, Kennedy had sewn up the nomination. He won on the first ballot. Shrewdly, he asked his chief remaining rival, Johnson, to be his running mate. It was a brilliant move. Johnson could win the southern states where Kennedy was weakest.

A Media Election.
Eisenhower had shown how important television could be in winning an election. But television had never been used as it was in the 1960 election. Both Kennedy and the Republican nominee, Vice President Richard Nixon, used television to showcase their campaigns in a series of four national debates.

No one actually "won" the debates. Kennedy scored points by firing away at the lack of leadership in Washington and the missile gap. Nixon surprised his many critics by sticking to the issues and backing his positions with a broad knowledge. He managed the difficult trick of defending the Eisenhower record while promising new policies.

But what especially stuck in voters' minds was that Kennedy produced a more positive image than Nixon did. Because of an inept make-up job, Nixon's heavy beard and the dark circles under his eyes were noticeable. Despite his attempt to present the image of a "New Nixon," the Democrats were able to call up old images of Nixon as "untrusting" and a "Communist-hunter." In contrast, Kennedy looked tan, trim, and healthy, and not at all too young for the job.

The Torch Is Passed.
On such images was the election of 1960 decided. The outcome was in doubt until election evening. Kennedy won by less than 120,000 votes out of 68.3 million cast.

Kennedy's popularity in public opinion polls later rose each month of his presidency. But Kennedy's concrete accomplishments were relatively few. He is remembered more for what he inspired than for what he did. His admirers spoke of his brief presidency as *Camelot*, referring to a popular musical of that name based on the ancient legends of King Arthur. For a few short years, in the mythical Camelot and in Kennedy's, the world would seem to be going well.

SECTION REVIEW

1. Write a sentence to identify: Bernard Goldfine, Francis Gary Powers, missile gap, media election.
2. What effect did the launching of Sputnik have on education and American political thinking?
3. Give evidence of improved relations between the United States and the Soviet Union in the late 1950s.
4. What were the details of the U-2 incident?
5. Who were the presidential candidates in the election of 1960? Which candidate won?

Class Activity: In preparation for a class activity in the next chapter involving presidential use of the media, arrange a field trip to a local television station so students can observe how news shows are made. Back in the classroom discuss how the power of the media can make a politician look good or bad.

Xerography, an electrostatic process for copying documents, was developed in 1938 by Chester Carlson.

The first solar-heated house, in Lexington, Massachusetts, used flat plates to collect the sun's energy.

The development of electronic computers to store, retrieve, and process data began in the 1940s. ENIAC, the first computer, weighed 30 tons and had 18,000 vacuum tubes.

C H A N G I N G   T E C H N O L O G Y

19|20   19|30

Paint spray gun introduced	Electric traffic lights set up	Insulin use initiated
Geiger counter invented	Artificial kidney prototype built	Radio compass developed
Domestic oven invented	Mechanical windshield wipers	Lie detector invented
Paper cups manufactured	demonstrated	Band-aids introduced
Aerial photography introduced	Electric food mixer developed	First portable radio marketed

Discussion Question: Why are the 1950s sometimes described as the best of times and the worst of times?

Tape recorders fed electrical impulses to a recorder and then converted them to magnetic patterns on a tape. Some early reel-to-reel models were portable but very heavy.

Tiny transistors made of silicon, a semiconductor material, caused a revolution in electronics.

The first practical single-rotor helicopter was built by Igor Sikorsky in 1939.

A jet engine for aircraft was invented in 1930 by Frank Whittle, although the principle of jet propulsion was known to the Egyptians 2,000 years ago. The first commercial passenger service between New York and London began in 1958.

19	40	19	50	19	60
Parking meters installed Liquid fuel rocket fired DC-3 aircraft produced Cellulose tape marketed	Polyester fibers discovered Nuclear reactor constructed Aerosol device created Plutonium isolated	Electric power produced from atomic energy Optical fibers created Desk-sized computer demonstrated

Research Assignment: Have students prepare a report on the development of computers and the impact they have had on society. Ask students to discuss ways in which computers have had both positive and negative impact.

CHAPTER REVIEW

TIME LINE

- 1953 — Dwight Eisenhower inaugurated (1953)
- — Death of Stalin (1953)
- 1954 — *Brown* v. *Board of Education of Topeka* (1954)
- — *Geneva Accords* end French rule of Indochina (1954)
- 1955 — Montgomery bus boycott (1955)
- 1956 — Soil Bank Act (1956)
- — Hungarian revolt (1956)
- — Egypt invaded by England, France, and Israel (1956)
- — Eisenhower reelected (1956)
- 1957 — Khrushchev makes anti-Stalin speech (1956)
- — Soviets launch Sputnik (1957)
- 1958 — Integration at Little Rock (1957)
- — SCLC formed (1957)
- — Marines sent to Lebanon (1958)
- 1959 — Nixon-Khrushchev kitchen debate (1959)
- — Khrushchev tours United States (1959)
- 1960 — U-2 incident (1960)
- — John Kennedy elected president (1960)
- 1961

TIME LINE QUESTIONS

1. In which year did an event that sparked nonviolent civil disobedience occur?
2. What 1956 event indicated a possible change in spirit among the Soviet Union's leaders?
3. What event was an attempt to regain control of an important canal?
4. What event caused concern in the United States about being beaten in the space race?

SKILLS STRATEGY

QUICK REFERENCE INDEX

SOCIAL SECURITY	73-77
SPACE FLIGHTS	148-149
SPORTS	774-869
STATE GOVERNMENTS	321-324
STATES OF THE UNION	607-634
STRATEGIC ARMS NEGOTIATIONS	333, 335
SUPREME COURT DECISIONS, 1982-1983	902-903

GENERAL INDEX

Space developments	148-149, 151
Astronauts	148-149
Cosmonauts	148-149
First Amer. in space (1961)	148, 660
First person in space	148
First space walk	148
Moonwalk, U.S. (1969)	148, 561
Skylab, II, III, & IV	149
Soviet Union—	
—Cosmonauts die (1971)	148
—Soyuz T-5 & 6 launched	148-149
—Sputnik Satellite	690
Space Shuttle Challenger	884, 889, 894
Space Shuttle Columbia	149,664,872

Source: *World Almanac, 1984*

ALMANACS

The launching of the satellite *Sputnik* began a *space race* between the Soviet Union and the United States. Suppose you want to find out how the space race progressed in recent years. An *almanac* is a good source of up-to-date information, since almanacs are updated every year.

Some almanacs have two indexes (such as those shown above) to help you locate information easily. Try the Quick Reference Index first. Then, if you do not find what you are looking for, consult the General Index. Once you turn to the page(s) indicated in the index, you are likely to find the information in a list, a table, a chart, or a graph.

APPLYING SKILLS

Refer to the indexes above as you answer the following questions.

1. Which index would you consult first to find information on the space race? Which pages does that index tell you to look at?
2. On which pages are there facts about space walks and space shuttles?
3. What other index entries could you consult for information about the space race?

Making Connections: Review the questions and topics presented in the Making Connections section that opens this chapter.

UNIT 9 TEST

CHAPTER SURVEY

In one or two sentences, summarize the content of the chapters from which these terms come, and write a sentence to identify *one* of the terms from each chapter.

1. *Chapter 29:* Manchuria, Edward R. Murrow, RAF, Nisei, J. Robert Oppenheimer.
2. *Chapter 30:* "iron curtain," Third World, thirty-eighth parallel, GI Bill of Rights.
3. *Chapter 31:* Thurgood Marshall, peaceful co-existence, Camelot.

TEXT REVIEW

4. Why is it correct to speak of a "Hoover-Roosevelt foreign policy" in the 1930s? Give an example of how this policy was used in Latin America, Asia, and the Soviet union.
5. Explain how each of the following was part of the "undeclared war" waged by the United States under Roosevelt's leadership between 1939 and 1941: 50 old American destroyers, Burke-Wadsworth Act, Lend-Lease Bill, neutral zone from United States to Greenland, Atlantic Charter.
6. Describe the incident that led Roosevelt to ask Congress to declare war on Japan. Explain why Congress was not unanimous in its response to the certainty of war.
7. Give the essential details about each of the following: Battle of Midway; Stalingrad; D-Day; Battle of the Bulge; Yalta; April 12, 1945; Hiroshima.
8. Define *Cold War,* and discuss the following as "weapons" used in that war: Marshall Plan, policy of containment, Berlin blockade, Berlin airlift, NATO.
9. Which parts of Truman's Fair Deal program were passed by Congress, and which parts were defeated? What did Democratic members of Congress do that resulted in defeat for parts of Truman's program?
10. Discuss *two* of the following: events in China after World War II; Korean War and American containment policy, McCarthyism and its ultimate end; GIs, teenagers, and women in the postwar era.
11. Which party and candidate won the 1952 presidential election? How did the new president bring the Korean War to an end?
12. Make the connection between the struggle by American blacks for civil rights during the 1950s and each of the following: Supreme Court; Central High School; Rosa Parks; nonviolent civil disobedience; Thoreau's philosophy.
13. Discuss the reaction of the Eisenhower administration to developments in *three* of the following places: Taiwan/mainland China; Hungary; the Suez Canal; Vietnam.
14. Give the circumstances surrounding the shooting down of a U-2 plane. Explain how this affected Soviet-American relations.
15. Name the Democratic and Republican candidates in the 1960 presidential election. Explain in what sense this was a "media election."

CRITICAL THINKING

16. Defend this statement with facts from the text: "Indirectly, the American people can have a great influence on the foreign policy of their national government, even though policy-making is in the hands of diplomats and politicians."
17. List groups of people usually considered to be minorities in American society. Why are women often considered to be a minority group when rights are discussed? Summarize and evaluate the gains and setbacks during World War II for two of the minority groups you listed.
18. Evaluate either Truman or Eisenhower as president. Back up your evaluation with facts from the text.

SKILLS REVIEW

19. List at least five communications media in which you might find propaganda. Name and describe four propaganda techniques.
20. Explain what a flow chart is, and describe two types of relationships among events that can be shown on such a chart.

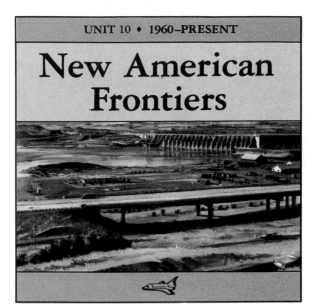

UNIT 10 ♦ 1960–PRESENT

New American Frontiers

American artist Robert Birmelin (born 1933), "Dalles Dam on the Columbia River," (1975).

Unit 10 Overview:

The historical events and issues presented in Unit 10 will be more immediate to students. They will be at most one generation away from these events and issues. The unit takes students from the turbulent Kennedy and Johnson administrations of the Sixties, through the triumphs and governmental crises of the Nixon presidency, to the late 1970s and early 1980s.

Basic Unit Concepts
1. The thousand days President Kennedy spent in office before his assassination were marked by demonstrations for and against black civil rights, a heart-stopping nuclear confrontation with the Soviet Union, and a failure to pass New Frontier social legislation.
2. President Lyndon Johnson had great success in having domestic "Great Society" legislation passed by Congress, but faced strong opposition and finally decided not to run.
3. President Richard Nixon's attempts to expand the Vietnam War provoked widespread domestic disturbances, but he had outstanding success in dealing with Communist China and the turbulent Middle East.
4. A burglary, a cover-up, and the threat of impeachment forced President Nixon to resign his office and made Gerald Ford the nation's leader.
5. President Jimmy Carter's administration was marked by its inability to get Congress to pass domestic legislation, frustration of attempts to deal effectively with the Iranian hostage situation, and a triumph in bringing Egypt and Israel together.
6. President Ronald Reagan chose to allocate money to building up American defense rather than to social programs, and he took a firm attitude towards Communist nations.
7. Americans of the 1980s faced challenges brought about by changes in the ethnic character of life in the United States, advances in technology, competition for markets from abroad, and the possiblility of nuclear warfare.

Chapter 32: "The Vigorous Sixties" (1960–1968)

Students will agree that *vigorous* is an appropriate adjective to describe the Sixties, the topic of Chapter 32. They witness the action-filled thousand days of the Kennedy administration—the riots and violence that accompanied the black struggle for equal rights, the terrifying nuclear confrontation between the United States and the Soviet Union, the exhilarating initiation of the space program, and the tragic assassination of President Kennedy. They follow the outstanding successes of Lyndon Johnson's domestic program and the dismal failure of his Vietnam policy which caused widespread opposition throughout the nation and convinced him not to run for a second term. Finally, they learn of the assassination of Robert Kennedy, the tumultuous 1968 Democratic Convention, and the election of President Richard M. Nixon.

Features
Movers and Shapers: Rosa Parks and Martin Luther King, Jr. (page 752)
Going to the Source: Excerpt from Martin Luther King, Jr.'s *"I Have a Dream"* speech (page 754)
Profiles of the Presidency: John F. Kennedy (page 756), Lyndon B. Johnson (page 759)

Learning Objectives
History Generalizations Students will gain knowledge that supports the following generalizations:
1. Reluctant Republicans allied with conservative Democrats gave little support to John F. Kennedy's New Frontier social programs, although they supported legislation aimed at promoting space technology and landing an American on the moon.
2. During his thousand days, Kennedy had some successes —the Cuban missile crisis, the Peace Corps—and some drastic setbacks—the Bay of Pigs and the Berlin Wall.
3. Many Americans rejected the Warren Commission's findings that the Kennedy assassination was not the result of a conspiracy. Speculation continues today.
4. Lyndon Johnson's Great Society programs, in part an expansion of the Kennedy New Frontier but mostly his own ideas, won easy approval in the Congress.
6. President Johnson's decision to involve the United States more deeply in the Vietnam War led to domestic turmoil that cost him and the Democrats the presidency in 1968.
7. Assassinations and peaceful and violent protests over racism and the Vietnam war caused one American writer to comment that "Shakespeare would grow modest before America" in the Sixties.
8. A growing conservative movement contributed to the victory of Richard Nixon over his opponents in the presidential election of 1968.

Study Skills In addition to the three skills noted in Chapter 1 which are standard to every chapter, students will:
1. formulate hypotheses from photographs.
2. write a paragraph summarizing a point of view.
3. relate graphic materials to the text of the chapter.
4. practice these **critical thinking skills:** generating questions about materials to be read, recognizing a viewpoint, identifying causes, drawing conclusions.

Chapter 33: "Diplomacy, Detente, and Crisis" (1968–1979)

In this chapter, students discover how President Nixon's expansion of the Vietnam War provoked rioting and bloodshed at home and how the war finally ended. They follow the foreign policy successes of the president and his secretary of state in China and the Middle East. They recognize what Nixon domestic policies angered his conservative supporters. They witness the landing of Americans on the moon. They learn why both President Nixon and Vice President Agnew resigned and how Gerald Ford became president. They realize the threat presented by the OPEC oil embargo to the United States and other industrial nations. They share in the celebrations of the nation's two hundredth birthday, and they investigate the "Me-ism" of the 1970s, contrasting it with the social activism of the 1960s. Finally, they consider the revolution in morals, the conservation movement, the revival of ethnic consciousness, and the struggle to have the Equal Rights Amendment ratified.

Features
Profiles of the Presidency: Richard M. Nixon (page 774), Gerald R. Ford (page 784)
Movers and Shapers: Rosalyn Yalow and Barbara McClintock, Nobel Prize winners (page 781)

Learning Objectives
History Generalizations Students will gain knowledge that supports the following generalizations:
1. In his first term, Richard Nixon, with the aid of two secretaries of state, ended United States involvement in Vietnam, established diplomatic relations with the People's Republic of China, negotiated the SALT agreements, and temporarily brought peace to the Middle East.
2. At home, working with a Democratic Congress, President Nixon introduced anti-inflation legislation that angered Republican conservatives; he also restaffed the Supreme Court with conservative judges.
3. President Nixon's attempt to cover up the Watergate break-in resulted in his near-impeachment, his resignation, and the accession of Gerald Ford to the presidency.
4. Although he worked to deal with inflation and recession, President Ford functioned, for the most part, as a caretaker president.
5. The celebration of the bicentennial of the United States restored to some extent the American people's confidence and pride in their country.
6. The political and social activism of the 1960's gave way to a spirit of "Me-ism" in the 1970s, partly as a response to the Vietnam War, the OPEC oil embargo, and Communist initiatives in the world.

Study Skills In addition to the three skills noted in Chapter 1 which are standard to every chapter, students will:
1. compare and construct circle graphs.
2. write a paragraph on a given topic.
3. relate graphic materials to the text of the chapter.
4. practice these **critical thinking skills:** generating questions about materials to be read, identifying multiple effects of a given cause, drawing conclusions from given facts, comparing points of view.

Chapter 34: "America's Third Century Begins" (1976–Present)
As citizens of third-century America, students will have at least a passing familiarity with most of the events and issues discussed in this chapter—President Carter's triumph in bringing Egypt and Israel together and his failure in dealing with the American hostage crisis in Iran; the election of Ronald Reagan, his economic and social policies, his tough attitude towards Communist nations, his trip to China, the invasion of the Latin American nation of Grenada, the terrorist murder of 241 marines in Lebanon, and the school prayer and

ERA issues. In the last section of the chapter, students update their knowledge of the condition of American minorities and preview the changes that technology and challenges from abroad may bring to the nation.

Features
Profiles of the Presidency: Jimmy Carter (page 794), Ronald Reagan (page 800)
American Ingenuity chart (pages 808–809)

Learning Objectives
History Generalizations Students will gain knowledge that supports the following generalizations:
1. Overcoming several political disadvantages, Jimmy Carter became the presidential candidate of the Democratic Party and won the presidency in 1976.
2. Although President Carter was successful in establishing peace between Israel and Egypt, his attempts to deal with the Soviet Union and the hostage crisis in Iran met with frustration and failure.
3. By initiating a moralistic foreign policy that emphasized human rights throughout the world, President Carter hoped to contrast his approach to world affairs with the *realpolitik* of the Nixon administration.
4. President Carter was largely unsuccessful in his attempts to deal with inflation and other domestic problems.
5. In the 1980 election, President Carter was soundly defeated by Ronald Reagan who had the strong support of the Moral Majority and other conservative Republican forces.
6. Interpreting his 1980 victory as a mandate for a conservative revolution in national economic policy, President Reagan pushed through Congress a legislative program that resembled the economic policies of President Coolidge and his Treasury Secretary, Andrew Mellon.
7. "Reaganomics" increased unemployment and resulted in a staggering national debt of over $1 trillion.
8. In foreign policy, President Reagan took a firm position toward the Soviet Union and other communist regimes around the world. In April of 1984 he visited China.
9. Dissatisfaction of the many unemployed people, organized labor, blacks, and women who decried a "gender" gap all contributed to the events of 1984.
10. The 1980s saw some gains for minority groups; shifts in population; increased use of computers, robots, and lasers; threats to American industry from abroad; and the horrifying possibility of nuclear destruction.

Study Skills In addition to the three skills noted in Chapter 1 which are standard to every chapter, students will:
1. review reference materials studied in the text.
2. relate graphic materials to the text of the chapter.
3. practice these **critical thinking skills:** generating questions about materials to be read, recognizing cause, classifying information.

THE VIGOROUS SIXTIES

1960–1968

*. . 1960, that first of the Kennedy years, in which we became a
nation royal with triumphs, tragedies, and ongoing obsessive fears. How
much America becomes the character, no, the protagonist of that novel
no genius is large enough to write. Shakespeare would grow modest
before America.* NORMAN MAILER

Making Connections. President Kennedy's term in office was cut short when he was struck down by an assassin in 1963. His successor, Lyndon Johnson, pushed through laws to help blacks and poor people participate in his "Great Society." But Johnson was forced out of office by the American involvement in the Vietnam War.

In this chapter, you will learn:
- How the civil rights movement grew more powerful in the 1960s
- What events nearly brought the United States and the Soviet Union to nuclear war in 1962
- Where the black struggle for equality led to riots and violence
- Why the United States sent military forces to fight in Vietnam
- How critics of the Vietnam War convinced large numbers of Americans that the war was wrong
- Who were the major American leaders who were assassinated in the 1960s

You know that the Supreme Court decision in *Brown* v. *Board of Education of Topeka* guaranteed equal treatment for blacks in the public schools. After this ruling, blacks sought equal rights in voting, jobs, and housing. As you read, note how the federal government passed laws helping blacks toward full equality.

Sections
1. Kennedy's Thousand Days
2. The Great Society
3. Vietnam Involvement

1. KENNEDY'S THOUSAND DAYS

John F. Kennedy took the oath of office on a frigid but sunny winter afternoon. He delivered a memorable inaugural address that moved many Americans. Kennedy invited the adversaries of the United States to work with him in establishing a lasting peace. He also asked for all people to unite in the struggle against poverty, disease, and war. Kennedy concluded his inaugural address by urging Americans to "ask not what your country can do for you; ask what you can do for your country."

The New Frontier. With a rush of proposals that reminded some of Franklin Roosevelt's first three months in office, Kennedy outlined a program he called *The New Frontier*. There was, however, an important difference between 1933 and 1961. In 1933, Roosevelt had won an overwhelming victory at a time of clear crisis. In 1961, Kennedy was president by a whisker, and the nation faced no urgent crisis to compare to the depression.

As a result, Kennedy often got very little help from Congress. Southern conservatives joined with the Republican minority in both Senate and House to block most New Frontier legislation.

John F. Kennedy told Americans in his inaugural address, "Ask not what your country can do for you; ask what you can do for your country."

Quotation: from the book *Some Honorable Men.* Other works by Norman Mailer (born 1923) include *The Naked and the Dead, The Barbary Shore, The Deer Park, An American Dream, Cannibals and Christians, The Armies of the Night, Existential Errands, Of a Fire on the Moon, The Executioner's Song,* and *Ancient Evenings.*

PROFILES OF THE PRESIDENCY

JOHN F. KENNEDY   1961–1963

*I*n accepting the Democratic nomination in 1960, John F. Kennedy challenged Americans to become pioneers once more:

The pioneers of old gave up their safety, their comfort and sometimes their lives to build a new world here in the West. . . . Today some would say that those struggles are all over—that all the horizons have been explored—that all the battles have been won—that there is no longer an American frontier. But I trust that no one in this vast assemblage will agree with those sentiments. For the problems are not all solved and the battles are not all won—and we stand today on the edge of a new frontier—the frontier of the 1960s—a frontier of unknown opportunities and perils—a frontier of unfulfilled hopes and threats. . . . The New Frontier of which I speak is not a set of promises—it is a set of challenges. It sums up not what I intend to offer the American people, but what I intend to ask of them. . . .

—ACCEPTANCE SPEECH, JULY 15, 1960

Domestic Programs. The domestic reforms Kennedy proposed included *Medicare*, medical insurance for the elderly. Although it was a more modest program than Truman's of a decade earlier, Medicare was easily defeated after heavy lobbying by the American Medical Association, a physicians' organization that opposed government participation in health care.

Other bills either defeated or passed in watered-down form included an act to provide low-interest federal loans to assist college students, federal funds to help depressed Appalachia, and aid to redevelop old cities. Southern Democrats and resurgent Republican conservatives, led by Senator Barry Goldwater of Arizona, were opposed to many of the expensive government programs.

Among the projects that won conservative support was the infant space technology industry, to be centered in the southern states of the nation,

Houston's NASA Space Center worked to put an American on the moon by the end of the 1960s.

"Freedom Riders" challenged the southern custom forbidding blacks to sit with whites on buses. The bus above was set ablaze by a fire bomb tossed through its window.

and a massive space program to put an American on the moon by 1970. Within a few years, 9,000 companies and more than 3 million people were directly or indirectly involved in the *space race*. By 1964, about 30,000 scientists and engineers worked for the National Aeronautics and Space Administration *(NASA)*.

Sit-Ins and Freedom Rides.

Kennedy could not hope to win the Republican conservatives over to the New Frontier. However, with the help of Vice President Johnson of Texas, he thought the southern congressmen in his own party might be brought into line. Kennedy thus decided to move very cautiously on the issues raised by the growing civil rights movement. Kennedy offered no new legislation, but existing laws were enforced. Attorney General Robert Kennedy oversaw the integration of 183 school districts in less than three years.

After the success of the Montgomery bus boycott, black civil rights groups attacked other forms of racial segregation. In 1960, the Student Nonviolent Coordinating Committee *(SNCC),* launched a series of *sit-ins* at lunch counters, beginning in Greensboro, North Carolina. Idealistic black college students took seats in restaurants and cafes. When they were told that local or state law forbade them service, they refused to leave.

"Freedom rides" were sponsored by CORE. Blacks and whites sat together on long-distance buses traveling through states that forbade "race mixing" in public transportation. Because the long-distance buses crossed state lines and were, therefore, subject to federal interstate commerce regulations, the administration had to respond after one such bus was halted and destroyed by a segregationist mob.

"We Shall Overcome."

There were several reasons why Kennedy supported civil rights. First, southern congressmen had not given much support to the New Frontier, so Kennedy did not owe them too much. Second, in the large industrial and urban states, key to Kennedy's election in 1960, more than 80 percent of the black vote was Democratic. Third, a series of events in 1962 and

MOVERS AND SHAPERS

Rosa Parks

On December 1, 1955, a 40-year-old black seamstress made a simple decision that was to have far-reaching consequences. Boarding a bus in Montgomery, Alabama, after a hard day's work, Rosa Parks (born 1915) sat in one of the few available seats—in the rear of the front section. Traditionally, the seats in the front section were reserved for white people. The bus became crowded. Mrs. Parks was asked to give up her seat to a white person, but she refused. She was simply tired and did not want to stand, but she was arrested for her action. Her arrest marked the beginning of a civil rights movement that would see many other acts of courage.

The black population of Montgomery, under the leadership of a young minister, Martin Luther King, Jr. (1929–1968), began a boycott of the city's segregated buses. The boycott ended successfully when the Supreme Court declared the city's bus segregation laws unconstitutional.

A backlash among southern whites began. The firebombing of King's home brought the black community to the brink of violence. But King insisted on a nonviolent response. An admirer of Gandhi and Thoreau, King was convinced that blacks could achieve equality only through peaceful civil disobedience.

As the founder and president of the Southern Christian Leadership Conference (SCLC), King led voter registration drives among blacks and helped organize sit-ins at segregated lunch counters. He also organized black and white volunteers to ride through the South to test federal laws banning segregation in bus station facilities. Southern whites retaliated by overturning and burning buses and attacking the Freedom Riders.

In August 1963, King was an organizer of the March on Washington in behalf of civil rights legislation then pending in Congress. Involving 250,000 blacks and whites, it was the largest civil rights demonstration in American history. King gave his most memorable address, "I Have a Dream," in which he offered a vision of an America where liberty and equality were reali-

Martin Luther King, Jr.

ties for *all* citizens. In 1964, Congress passed the Civil Rights act, and King won the *Nobel Peace Prize*.

In 1965, King led a Freedom March from Montgomery to Selma, Alabama, to demonstrate blacks' determination to vote. King also became increasingly outspoken against the Vietnam War.

Early in 1968, King and other leaders planned a "People's March" on Washington for the end of April. Early that month King went to Memphis, Tennessee, to take part in a demonstration. Faced with threats on his life, he begged his followers to stick to nonviolence. That evening he was felled by an assassin's bullet.

King was widely mourned. Blacks had lost a leader of truly heroic stature, and the world lost an eloquent champion of peace and nonviolence.

Discussion Question: Was Rosa Parks right to disobey the Montgomery city law? Discussion should relate to the different levels of law and where the constitutional liberties of the individual fit into them. Try to include the concepts of civil disobedience in the discussion.

1963 converted at least Robert Kennedy to deep sympathy with the plight of American blacks.

In 1962, James Meredith, a black air force veteran, won a court order entitling him to enroll at the all-white University of Mississippi. Currying favor with segregationist voters, Governor Ross Barnett virtually encouraged a violent reaction to the order. In riots at the Oxford, Mississippi, campus in September 1962, two people were killed and dozens injured. Instead of giving in, Kennedy sent 200 United States marshals to see that Meredith's right to enroll was protected.

The following June, Alabama Governor George Wallace, who had won election on a "Segregation Forever" platform, personally blocked the door when two black students tried to enroll at the University of Alabama. Again Kennedy sent marshals to accompany the new students. Wallace, having made his point that he was a segregationist leader, stepped aside.

More violence followed. Black churches were bombed, black activists were killed, and in June 1963, Medgar Evers, a leader of the NAACP in Mississippi, was shot to death in the doorway of his home. Cautious at first about openly supporting integration, Kennedy soon committed his administration to the cause of civil rights. Nevertheless, Martin Luther King, Jr., and Bayard Rustin, a black labor-union activist, refused Kennedy's suggestion that they cancel or postpone the famous March on Washington of August 1963. More than 200,000 people gathered at the Lincoln Memorial to hear King and others speak, and to demonstrate for equal rights.

Kennedy and the Third World. Another reason Kennedy backed the civil rights movement was his determination to win friends in the Third World nations of Latin America, Africa, and Asia. To achieve this, it was important to counteract the effect of films showing brutal police attacks on nonviolent civil rights protesters in America.

Kennedy also responded to foreign criticism by organizing the *Peace Corps*. For subsistence wages, idealistic women and men with valuable skills to offer traveled to 55 underdeveloped countries to help the local people in their efforts to improve their lives. The Peace Corps accomplished a great deal, and the selfless workers won many friends for the United States.

A sit-in protesting segregation brought out hose-swinging firemen in Birmingham, Alabama.

In August 1963, Martin Luther King, Jr. (below), spoke eloquently of his dream for America.

Marion Anderson said about prejudice, "Sometimes, it's like a hair across your cheek. You can't see it, you can't find it with your fingers, but you keep on brushing at it because the feel of it is irritating."

GOING TO THE SOURCE

I am happy to join with you today in what will go down in history as the greatest demonstration for freedom in the history of our nation.

Five score years ago, a great American, in whose symbolic shadow we stand today, signed the Emancipation Proclamation. This momentous decree came as a great beacon of hope to millions of slaves, who had been seared in the flames of withering injustice. It came as a joyous daybreak to end the long night of their captivity.

But one hundred years later the colored American is still not free. One hundred years later the life of the colored American is still sadly crippled by the manacle of segregation and the chains of discrimination. . . .

We cannot be satisfied as long as a colored person in Mississippi cannot vote and a colored person in New York believes he has nothing for which to vote.

No, no we are not satisfied and we will not be satisfied until justice rolls down like waters and righteousness like a mighty stream. . . .

Let us not wallow in the valley of despair. I say to you, my friends, we face the difficulties of today and tomorrow.

I still have a dream. It is a dream deeply rooted in the American dream.

I have a dream that one day this nation will rise up and live out the true meaning of its creed. We hold these truths to be self-evident that all men are created equal. . . .

I have a dream today.

I have a dream that one day every valley shall be ungulfed, every hill shall be exalted, and every mountain shall be made low, the rough places will be made plains, and the crooked places will be made straight, and the glory of the Lord shall be revealed and all flesh

When we let freedom ring, when we let it ring from every tenement and every hamlet, from every state and every city, we will speed up that day when all of God's children . . . will be able to join hands and sing . . . "Free at last! Free at last! Thank God Almighty, we are free at last!"

MARTIN LUTHER KING, JR.,
"I HAVE A DREAM"

shall see it together.

This is our hope. This is the faith that I will go back to the South with. With this faith we will be able to hew out of the mountain of despair a stone of hope.

With this faith we will be able to transform the jangling discords of our nation into a beautiful symphony of brotherhood.

With this faith we will be able to work together, to pray together, to struggle together, to go to jail together, to climb up for freedom together, knowing that we will be free one day. . . .

And if America is to be a great nation, this must come true. So let freedom ring from the prodigious hilltops of New Hampshire. Let freedom ring from the mountains of New York. . . .

Let freedom ring from the snow-capped Rockies of Colorado.

Let freedom ring from the curvaceous slopes of California.

But not only that, let freedom ring from the Stone Mountain of Georgia.

Let freedom ring from every hill and molehill of Mississippi and every mountainside.

When we let freedom ring, when we let it ring from every tenement and every hamlet, from every state and every city, we will be able to speed up that day when all of God's children, black men and white men, Jews and Gentiles, Protestants and Catholics, will be able to join hands and sing in the words of the old spiritual, "Free at last! Free at last! Thank God Almighty, we are free at last!"

Martin Luther King, Jr., delivered his "I Have a Dream" speech on August 28, 1963 during a huge demonstration for civil rights in Washington, D.C. This excerpt shows the powerful speaker he was.

Research Assignment: Have students examine current U.S. relations with Cuba and the role Cuba plays in international politics. If your school has access to a computer simulation of the Soviet and U.S. gains, losses, and the negotiations surrounding the Cuban Missile Crisis, use the

During the Kennedy Administration, a resurgence of idealism found new expression in programs like the Peace Corps. Americans volunteered to live in poorer nations for two-year periods to assist with local needs. A Peace Corps project in Peru is pictured above.

In Latin America, Kennedy founded the *Alliance for Progress* in a move to change the American reputation for supporting only military dictators. This was an economic and social program to reduce poverty and illiteracy, improve health, and promote democracy. Over a ten-year period, the United States spent $10 billion on Alliance goals. The wealthier Latin American nations contributed a similar sum. Unfortunately, Alliance funds were often diverted to non-social programs, and the people who were supposed to get the aid often did not. By the 1970s, the United States had lost popularity among the people of the fastest growing region of the world.

Castro's Cuba.

Maintaining friendly relations with Latin America was vital to Kennedy because of Castro's Cuba. The island nation, only 90 miles from Florida, was closer to the United States than any other Latin American country except Mexico.

On January 1, 1959, a revolutionary movement under Fidel Castro drove out Cuba's pro-American dictator, Fulgencio Batista. At the start, Castro had few connections with the Soviet Union. However, when the United States banned sugar imports from Cuba and balked at accepting Castro's reforms, which included the seizure of much American property, Castro looked to Russia for aid. By 1961, Castro was praising communism as the solution to Latin America's problems. Believing that the United States was determined to overthrow him by force, Castro allowed the Russians into Cuba in return for weapons and training for his large army.

The Bay of Pigs.

The United States did plan to overthrow Castro. President Eisenhower, who could not run for reelection, approved a Central Intelligence Agency (CIA) plan to train an army of 1,500 anti-Castro Cubans. When Kennedy was informed of the plan, he asked the CIA if it had a chance of succeeding. As soon as the force hit the beach, CIA Director Allen Dulles told him, the Cuban people would rise up to support it.

computer to illustrate the events surrounding this chapter in U.S.-Soviet relations and their effects.

755

CUBA, 1959-1962

In January 1959, Fidel Castro (above) overthrew Batista to become the new dictator of Cuba.

CIA intelligence was tragically faulty. The invasion began on April 17, 1961, at the Bay of Pigs. When Castro told the Cuban people that the invasion was backed by the United States, they rallied behind him instead of the invaders. After three days of fighting, 400 of the invaders were killed and 1,100 were captured.

In the United Nations, Ambassador Adlai Stevenson, who had never been informed of the invasion preparations, denied that the United States was involved. In Washington, President Kennedy took the blame for the assault and its failure. He did not agree with critics' charges that his refusal to provide air support for the invasion was responsible for the defeat. Rather, he blamed

the CIA and his own misjudgment. After a year, Kennedy made partial amends by allowing $53 million to be raised in the United States as ransom for the 1,100 captured soldiers.

West Berlin Crisis. Nikita Khrushchev watched the President's Cuban embarrassment with great interest. The Soviet leader apparently concluded that Kennedy's inexperience provided a rare opportunity to strike again at West Berlin, which Khrushchev called "a bone in my throat." Each month, thousands of East Germans were fleeing into West Berlin, some for political freedom but others, well-educated professionals and technologists, for the greater opportunities the West offered them.

To stop this expensive *brain drain,* Khrushchev threatened to seal off West Berlin entirely. He knew that Kennedy had revised the nation's policy of "massive retaliation" to Soviet provocations to a policy that allowed for "flexible response."

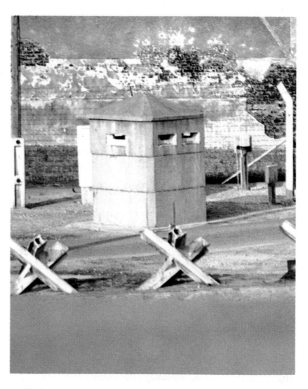

Before Soviet and East German Communists built a wall across Berlin, thousands of citizens fled to the West in search of freedom and opportunity.

Discussion Question: Was J.F.K. a great president? Direct the discussion so that it addresses the issues of his administration, rather than his image.

This meant that the United States would react to Soviet provocations in proportion to the seriousness of the Soviet act. But what was a reasonable response to the sealing off of a city in the midst of a Soviet satellite state? Sensing that Kennedy did not know, Khrushchev invited the president to meet with him in Vienna.

At the meeting, Kennedy informed Khrushchev that he would not tolerate having West Berlin cut off, and that the Russian action could cause war. Khrushchev refused to budge, and the two leaders left the conference with no set agreement. But when he got home, Kennedy increased America's military preparedness, and this convinced Khrushchev that taking over West Berlin was not worth risking war.

A short time later, the East Germans constructed the *Berlin Wall.* This line of brick wall, barbed wire fence, mines, and guard stations stopped most East Germans who tried to flee. Its existence was a defeat for Kennedy, but war had been averted.

The Cuban Missile Crisis.

In October 1962, the jousting between Kennedy and Khrushchev resumed in Cuba, this time with quite different results. The crisis began when American reconnaissance planes flying over the island returned with photographs showing Soviet missile bases under construction at several sites. The missiles appeared to be capable of hitting many large American cities.

Kennedy pored over the photos with Secretary of State Dean Rusk, Secretary of Defense Robert McNamara, Adlai Stevenson, Dean Acheson, and his brother Robert. Kennedy considered staging an invasion of Cuba or a pre-emptive air strike against the missile sites. However, because the bases were not yet operational, he decided to blockade Cuba to prevent the arming of the sites. He announced that any Russian ships bound for Cuba would be stopped. Those carrying weapons would be forced to turn around or, if necessary, would be sunk.

Eyeball to Eyeball.

Several Soviet ships carrying missiles were already on their way. At first, Khrushchev insisted that the weapons were defensive and of no threat unless Cuba were attacked. If Kennedy interfered, Khrushchev hinted, there would be war. The President repeated his intention to maintain the blockade. Nuclear war seemed inevitable.

Then, the Russians backed down. At first, the Russian ships stopped in mid-ocean. Then, on October 26, Khrushchev sent a long, conciliatory letter to Kennedy, offering to dismantle the bases if Kennedy would promise in writing not to attack Cuba. The next day Khrushchev said in a second letter that he would withdraw the missiles from Cuba if Kennedy withdrew American missiles from Turkey, a neighbor of the Soviet Union.

Kennedy had already considered removing the missiles from Turkey. They were obsolete and he was worried about the stability of the Turkish government. But he was determined to have the best of Khrushchev. He ignored the second note and accepted the terms of the first. On the next day, October 28, Khrushchev agreed.

Relations Improve.

Both Kennedy and Khrushchev were shaken by the Cuban missile crisis and their flirtation with nuclear war. As a result, the two leaders agreed to install a *hot line* between the White House and the Kremlin. President and premier would be able to contact one another in an instant in the event of another crisis. Khrushchev also responded positively to Kennedy's proposal that all nations possessing nuclear weapons should ban above-ground testing. Every nuclear nation except France and China signed the agreement.

Kennedy Assassinated.

Most Americans supported Kennedy's actions in the missile crisis, and his popularity had grown. But he was still having difficulty getting his New Frontier programs enacted. Therefore, the President began to push vigorously for his programs.

By November 1963, Kennedy was making some headway. He was confident that he could win reelection in 1964, and so he threw his support behind a sweeping Civil Rights Act to be presented to Congress during the election year. He expected to sweep the northern states, and with the help of Johnson and southern whites who accepted integration, to win at least some southern states. He and Vice President Johnson went to Dallas and Houston to firm up his support in Texas.

Assassin is derived from the Arabic word *hashashin,* a secret, fanatic organization whose members, under the influence of the drug, hashish, attacked and murdered Crusaders occupying the Holy Land.

On November 22, 1963, President Kennedy was assassinated while riding in an open car along a motorcade route through downtown Dallas (above). Vice President Lyndon Johnson immediately flew back to Washington, D.C. En route, he was sworn in as president (below).

PROFILES OF THE PRESIDENCY

LYNDON JOHNSON   1963–1969

In Lyndon Johnson's first address to Congress after President Kennedy's assassination, he used strong words to urge the passage of the civil rights bill:

. . . No memorial oration or eulogy could more eloquently honor President Kennedy's memory than the earliest possible passage of the civil rights bill for which he fought so long. We have talked long enough in this country about equal rights. We have talked for one hundred years or more. It is time now to write the next chapter, and to write it in the books of law. I urge you again as I did in 1957 and again in 1960, to enact a civil rights law so that we can move forward to eliminate from this Nation every trace of discrimination and oppression that is based upon race or color. . . . The time has come for Americans of all races and creeds and political beliefs to understand and to respect one another. So let us put an end to the teaching and the preaching of hate and evil and violence.

—ADDRESS TO CONGRESS, NOVEMBER 27, 1963

As the motorcade crept through the sprawling city to the cheers of a large crowd, shots rang out. The president, seated in an open car with Texas Governor John Connally, slumped forward. Within minutes he was at a hospital, but he was pronounced dead. Governor Connally was slightly wounded. Vice President Johnson was unhurt.

The Assassination Mystery. A few hours after the murder, the police arrested Lee Harvey Oswald as a suspect in the shooting. He had briefly lived in the Soviet Union and had flirted with *left-wing* groups and possibly with extreme *right-wing* organizations as well. When Kennedy was killed, Oswald was in the room at the Texas Book Depository from which shots were fired. Police found a rifle belonging to Oswald and other evidence indicating that he was the killer.

But was he the only one involved? Oswald was never able to confess to his own involvement. Two days after his arrest, he was shot at point-blank range by Jack Ruby, a Dallas nightclub owner who had idolized Kennedy. Suspicious circumstances surrounding the murders led to a number of theories suggesting complex conspiracies.

Lyndon Johnson had been sworn in as president on the airplane trip back to Washington. One of his first acts was to ask Chief Justice Earl Warren to head an investigation into the assassination. Warren doubted that the whole truth could be uncovered. But after much research, the *Warren Commission* found no real evidence of a conspiracy.

But Warren was right in thinking that the commission's report would not end speculation about the assassination. Many people were not satisfied with the report, and to this day, books claiming to shed new light on the killing of President Kennedy continue to be published.

SECTION REVIEW

1. Write a sentence to identify: New Frontier, Robert Kennedy, Fidel Castro, Berlin Wall.

2. Comment briefly on President Kennedy's performance in the following areas: domestic reforms, civil rights, relations with the Third World, Berlin crisis.

3. Describe the circumstances leading to the Cuban missile crisis. How did the crisis change Soviet-American relations?

4. What was the purpose of the Warren Commission? What were its findings? How did many people react to them?

Research Assignment: Have students write a report on the various theories surrounding the Kennedy assassination. Encourage the use of audio-visual and other illustrative materials.

2. THE GREAT SOCIETY

Lyndon Baines Johnson was 55 years old in 1963. He lacked Kennedy's polish, his "class," and his comfort and confidence before large crowds. But Johnson was a master in the closed corridors of power. Where Kennedy failed to put his New Frontier into practice, Johnson took the program, vastly expanded it into the most significant governmental shaping of American society since the New Deal, and steered it through Congress with startling ease.

The first wave of the legislative program that Johnson called the *Great Society* passed Congress in the wake of Kennedy's funeral, when many in Congress wanted to honor the spirit of the dead president. The second, greater wave of laws was passed in 1965, after Johnson won the presidency in his own right.

The Great Society earned Johnson a high place among reformer presidents. It would not have been surprising if those helped most by his program—the elderly and the young, students, liberal professional people, blacks and Hispanics, the poor—had hung portraits of him in their homes, next to the portraits of Lincoln and Franklin Roosevelt.

But it was not that way. Johnson was not beloved like Lincoln or Roosevelt. In part this was because of his personality and manner. Much more important, the domestic reformer led the nation into a bloody, tragic war.

Completing the New Deal. Johnson first came to Washington during Franklin Roosevelt's presidency, and he idolized the New Deal president. Johnson saw his presidential mission as the completion of Roosevelt's programs of social justice for the weak and the poor. His goal was to create an America in which all people had food and clothes, all workers had jobs, and race, creed, or religion did not bar a person from advancement.

Medicare, which Kennedy had failed to move through Congress, passed easily in 1965 with Johnson behind it. It provided government-

President Johnson's "Great Society" program included assistance to poor families, such as the one below in Appalachia.

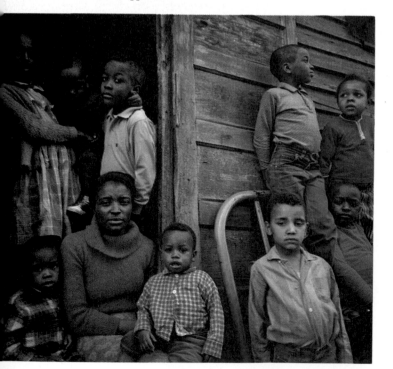

In 1965, Congress passed two major medical programs—Medicare and Medicaid—that brought relief to the elderly and the disabled.

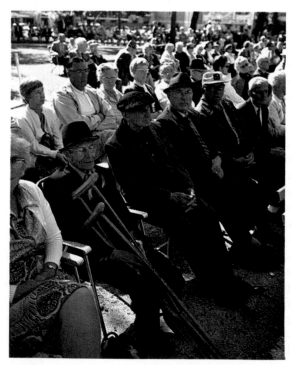

Research Assignment: Have students report on the present status of the Peace Corps and VISTA. Encourage students to seek out people who may have been involved with these organizations in the sixties. Make sure that students are aware of the criticisms of these groups when they write their reports.

funded health insurance for the elderly, and was funded through the Social Security system founded by Roosevelt. *Medicaid*, which gave medical benefits to blind, disabled, or very poor people, passed the same year.

Other Great Society laws conserved wilderness areas for the recreation and edification of future generations. Although the President's wife, Lady Bird Johnson, was not as active as Eleanor Roosevelt had been, she made national beautification and the fight against air and water pollution her special concerns.

Johnson also put into action Kennedy's program for aid to education. He provided over $1 billion to stimulate the economy in Appalachia, and allocated large sums to build public transportation systems and to rehabilitate blighted neighborhoods. The president created a new cabinet-level department, *Housing and Urban Development*, and appointed a black, Robert Weaver, as its first secretary.

Johnson's *War on Poverty*, directed by a new federal agency, the *Office of Economic Opportunity (OEO)*, recruited children from low-income families for catch-up education in the Head Start program and provided grants to allow their older brothers and sisters to attend colleges and universities. The OEO also paid for tutoring of disadvantaged students and administered the *Job Corps*, which retrained people for new jobs when they had been laid off from traditional jobs. Volunteers in Service to America *(VISTA)* was a domestic Peace Corps, sending social workers and teachers into older central city areas and impoverished rural areas.

Civil Rights.

Perhaps the greatest accomplishments of the Johnson years were in civil rights. In the *Civil Rights Act* of 1964 and the *Voting Rights Act* of 1965, Johnson finally fulfilled the promise of equality made to black Americans during Reconstruction a century earlier.

The Civil Rights Act of 1964 forbade segregation and discrimination on the basis of race in all schools and public accommodations, and in all private companies or institutions receiving funds from the federal government. This had been the goal of civil rights demonstrators since 1954. After 1964, anyone who discriminated on the basis of race was subject to punishment under law.

Votes for Blacks.

During the election year of 1964, an attempt by SNCC to register voters in Mississippi exposed another injustice suffered by blacks. Through legal devices such as unfairly administered literacy tests, segregationists had managed to evade the Fifteenth Amendment, which forbade states to deny the vote to anyone on the basis of race. Even more effective were extralegal (outside the law) pressures. By harassing blacks who tried to vote, segregationists were able to keep blacks away from voting places.

After the 1964 election, Johnson proposed the Voting Rights Act. This law put the Fifteenth Amendment into practice. It provided that the Attorney General could send officials into any area where a charge of discrimination at the polls had been filed. With a stroke of his pen, Johnson righted an injustice more than half a century old. Within ten years after the Voting Rights Act, prominent white politicians were actively seeking the support of blacks they once vowed would never approach a voting booth.

After the Voting Rights Act of 1965 became law, the participation of black citizens in elections increased.

Between 1963 and 1968 there were 369 civil rights demonstrations, 239 black riots and disturbances, 214 white attacks on civil rights workers, 104 anti-war demonstrations, 91 student protests on campuses, 54 clashes between segregationists and counter-demonstrators, and 24 anti-integration demonstrations.

Frustration in the black community of Watts, a section of Los Angeles, exploded into extensive rioting in the summer of 1965.

Black Power. Ironically, no sooner had Johnson backed the civil rights movement than most militant young blacks turned away from its goals and from the President. In 1966, James Meredith, the man who had desegregated the University of Mississippi four years earlier, set off on what he called a "Walk Against Fear" across Mississippi. He had barely started when he was shot.

Whites and blacks from all over the country converged on the state to complete Meredith's demonstration. Their purpose was to encourage blacks to vote. However, a young West Indian immigrant named Stokely Carmichael became the leader of the young blacks in the march when he announced that the new slogan of the black movement was *"black power."*

Black power meant different things to different people. To some it meant that blacks should form powerful voting blocs, as white ethnic groups had done. But to most Americans, black power meant that blacks should cut themselves off from whites instead of seeking integration. A few black powerites even said that several states should be set aside for blacks alone. The immediate response to the new slogan was to expel whites from SNCC. The organization was rocked by dissension, and within two years it ceased to exist.

Black Frustration. In part, the black power movement gained in popularity because of the frustration of black people living in northern urban ghettos. Their political rights had been assured, and some had prospered. But the vast majority of northern blacks were underemployed, attended poor schools, and lived in substandard housing. During the mid-1960s a series of violent riots broke out in black neighborhoods as blacks became increasingly angered by their treatment.

New York and Philadelphia had riots in 1964. In 1965, the Watts riot occurred in Los Angeles, and 34 people were killed, 4,000 arrested, and $200 million worth of property destroyed, most of it by fire. In Detroit in 1967, 40 people were killed and the homes of 5,000 people were destroyed by arson.

Most of the damage in these riots was done in the black areas of the city. Therefore, some sociologists have claimed that the riots were not sparked by racial tensions so much as by poverty and poor conditions. But there was a militant minority who were motivated by a dislike of white culture. They did not, they said, wish to be integrated into a white-dominated society.

Black Leaders. The main inspiration for black separatism came from a brilliant and charismatic ex-convict named Malcolm Little who renounced his religion and name to become the Muslim *Malcolm X.* He was a member of the *Black Muslims,* a sect that rejected Christianity and called for blacks to arm themselves in self-defense.

An electrifying orator, Malcolm X crisscrossed the nation calling for blacks to take pride in being black and to break loose from white domination. But his speeches were too radical even for his associates, and Black Muslim leader Elijah Muhammad expelled him from the organization. In 1965, Malcolm X was himself assassinated, apparently by Black Muslim gunmen. Ironically, at the

Discussion Question: How was the black-power movement of the sixties both similar to and unlike the movement led by Marcus Garvey?

time of his death, Malcolm X was calling for a degree of cooperation between blacks and white groups interested in social change.

Martin Luther King, Jr., spokesman for nonviolent disobedience, criticized the black power movement because of the violence preached by its leaders such as Carmichael and H. Rap Brown, and by the *Black Panthers,* a paramilitary group founded in Oakland, California. Although most militants said that blacks should arm only for self-defense, King's philosophy forbade any violent action. King himself was shot and killed in 1968. While in Memphis, Tennessee, to support a strike of black sanitation workers, he was gunned down by James Earl Ray.

Black activist Bayard Rustin opposed black power on the sensible political grounds that by themselves, blacks were a minority among Americans. Only by allying with sympathetic organizations could blacks have real hopes for social justice. Rustin predicted that the enthusiasm of the black powerites would burn out and they would disappear. He was right. By 1970 there was little left of the movement.

Right-Wing Extremism.

The conservative movement of the 1960s also had its extremists. In the South, a new Ku Klux Klan appeared, vowing to fight blacks, Jews, and radicals. Fundamentalist preachers such as the Australian Fred Schwarz of the Christian Anti-Communist Crusade preached that Communist conspirators posing as liberals were destroying American liberty in the name of social progress.

The most important of the *right wing* extremist groups was the *John Birch Society.* Named for a young missionary who was killed in China, whom the Birchers claimed was the first American casualty in the war against communism, the society was headed and funded by a millionaire candy manufacturer, Robert Welch. Welch believed that President Eisenhower had been "a conscious agent" of the Communist conspiracy in the United States. To the Birchers, any attempt to aid the poor, the elderly, or minorities was a Communist plot.

Election of 1964.

The Democrats nominated Johnson as their presidential candidate in 1964. The Republicans nominated the conservative Senator Barry Goldwater of Arizona. Goldwater was

Malcolm X (above) made passionate speeches calling for black citizens to arm themselves in self-defense. Martin Luther King, Jr. (below, center) believed that only nonviolent protest was acceptable.

no John Bircher. But because he claimed that Johnson's social welfare programs ate at the vitality of America, Birchers and other right wing extremists supported him. Moderate Republicans, such as Governor Nelson Rockefeller of New York and Governor William Scranton of Pennsylvania, gave him only lukewarm support.

During the campaign, the Democrats successfully depicted Goldwater as trigger-happy, a man who would start World War III. Their candidate, Johnson, was portrayed as the peace candidate. Johnson won 61 percent of the popular vote. This victory, which helped 100 new Democratic candidates to win seats in Congress, ensured that most of the Great Society programs would be enacted.

SECTION REVIEW

1. Write a sentence to identify: OEO, VISTA, James Meredith, "black power."

2. Explain how President Johnson's Great Society was related to Kennedy's New Frontier and Roosevelt's New Deal.

3. Name and give the provisions of two laws passed during the Johnson years that represented great gains for black Americans.

4. Describe the views of Senator Barry Goldwater, the Republican nominee in the presidential election of 1964. What propaganda did the Democrats use against him?

---

3. VIETNAM INVOLVEMENT

In 1965, Lyndon Johnson was inaugurated after winning a landslide victory at the polls. No president had ever won such a large proportion of the popular vote. Yet 1965 was also the last year Johnson would enjoy such popularity, as the country became increasingly involved in the Vietnam War.

The 1954 Geneva Accords, which had ended the colonial war between the French and the Vietnamese, had divided Vietnam into northern and southern states. They required that a free election be held in 1956 to determine the permanent government of a united Vietnam. The leader of South Vietnam, Ngo Dinh Diem, knew he would lose the election to the popular leader of North Vietnam, Ho Chi Minh. Diem canceled the elections and kept power, but within two years he was fighting a powerful guerrilla force called the *National Liberation Front (NLF),* which wanted to end Diem's dictatorial government. Diem called his enemies the *Viet Cong,* or Vietnamese Communists. He insisted they were not discontented South Vietnamese, but invaders from the north.

In the early years, almost all the rebels were South Vietnamese, and many of them were not Communists. Later, the North Vietnamese took over more and more of the battle. Diem, not a popular ruler, was from a Roman Catholic family and hostile to the Buddhist majority of Vietnamese. Diem also supported the interests of large landowners against the peasants, driving many ordinary farmers to support the NLF. His government was shamefully corrupt. Massive American aid designed to assist ordinary Vietnamese went into the bank accounts of Diem's cronies.

When the NLF murdered government officials, which they did often, they weakened Diem's authority and won the support of Vietnamese peasants who hated their government. By the time President Kennedy took office, the NLF controlled much of the Vietnamese countryside.

Kennedy's Vietnam Policy. President Kennedy's world plan to counter guerrilla rebellion was to use American military personnel to train the armies of friendly governments while urging those governments to eliminate the social injustices that caused uprisings. The 16,000 troops he sent to Vietnam included Army Special Forces known as *Green Berets,* an elite anti-insurrectionary force that trained Diem's army, and Marines who were instructed only to defend American bases.

By mid-1963, Diem's corruption and his repressive policies were such that his American supporters could no longer tolerate him. The CIA backed a military *coup* that replaced Diem with a leader more to American liking. During the action, Diem and several members of his family were murdered.

A rapid succession of ineffectual military dictators replaced Diem. None took interest in reform, and most asked for more American troops. Kennedy refused, resisting any action that would deepen American involvement in the war.

Class Activity: Have students construct a flow chart that shows the events leading to U.S. involvement in the Vietnam War.

During Lyndon Johnson's presidency, the United States became more deeply involved in the war in Southeast Asia. By the time Johnson left the White House, over 500,000 American soldiers were fighting in Vietnam (above). At home, an antiwar movement gained momentum and eventually forced a change in policy.

Escalation. But Johnson did not refuse. Determined not to be "the President who saw Southeast Asia go the way China went," he listened to advisors who said that victory over the Viet Cong was a matter of *escalating*, or increasing by steps, the American presence in Vietnam.

By August 1964, when the Democrats were depicting Goldwater as a threat to world peace, Johnson had decided to step up the war effort. But he needed a reason. An incident in the Tonkin Gulf off North Vietnam supplied it. Johnson told Congress that three North Vietnamese patrol boats had attacked an American destroyer in international waters. He asked for powers to repel any armed attack against the forces of the United States, and to prevent further aggression.

It was later learned that the American destroyer may have been within North Vietnam's territorial waters, and may never have been attacked. Nevertheless, the *Tonkin Gulf Resolution*, which was opposed by only two senators, became the President's justification for sending more troops to Vietnam.

On Election Day 1964 there were 28,000 American troops in Vietnam. By September 1965, there were 130,000, and by December 1965, 184,000. Two months after Johnson left office in 1969, the total was 541,000.

The Unwinnable War. With each American escalation, North Vietnam sent more supplies and troops south. Without getting directly involved, the Soviet Union and Red China supplied North Vietnam. American bombers dropped tons of bombs on Hanoi and the port of Haiphong in an unsuccessful attempt to cut off this foreign aid. Supplies were also transported south along the *Ho Chi Minh Trail*, a narrow road through the jungles of neutral Laos, which bordered North and South Vietnam. United States bombers ravaged the route, but still the enemy fought on. The relatively poorly armed North Vietnamese and Viet Cong were holding their own against the powerful American and South Vietnamese war machine.

Then, in January 1968, shortly after the American commanding general, William Westmoreland,

In response to the Gulf of Tonkin incident, which may not have really occurred, Congress passed an ambiguous resolution that gave L.B.J. the power to escalate the war in the absence of a declaration of war.

AMERICAN INVOLVEMENT IN VIETNAM, 1962-1973

One reason that the Viet Cong and North Vietnamese were so successful was that the South Vietnamese government never won what Johnson called "the hearts and minds of the Vietnamese people." Even the relatively stable regime of General Nguyen Van Thieu (nōō-yĕn′ văn′ tyōō′) refused or was unable to undertake the reforms that would have taken away the appeal of the Viet Cong. American soldiers felt that the South Vietnamese army was more hindrance than help. The North Vietnamese, on the other hand, were dedicated, fierce, and dangerous fighters.

Many South Vietnamese were alienated by atrocities—some unintentional (such as the bombing of civilian targets), and some the result of soldiers cracking under the pressure of a vicious war. The American effort had little support outside Vietnamese cities. Any Vietnamese could be the enemy.

Most important, the sophisticated American weaponry was a disadvantage in this comparatively primitive country. Bombing, for example, was useless against North Vietnamese industry, which was spread out in thousands of tiny shops, not centered in a few giant factories that could be destroyed by air power. Bombing was also useless against the Ho Chi Minh Trail. One bridge along the trail was destroyed more than 20 times. But it was a flimsy log trestle, not a modern steel span, and each time it was rebuilt within days.

had assured Johnson that victory was near, North Vietnam launched a massive offensive. Known as the *Tet offensive*, it proved that the North Vietnamese were far from beaten. They gained control of much of the large city of Hue, and reached the American Embassy in Saigon.

The offensive was contained and pushed back. But increasing numbers of Americans concluded that the war was not going as well as the generals and their president said it was.

Elephant Versus Mosquitoes. Newspaper columnist Walter Lippmann compared the war to a contest between an elephant and a swarm of mosquitoes. The elephant, unquestionably the greater beast, could not use its power against the "mosquitoes," the swarms of Viet Cong and North Vietnamese.

Critics of the War. As the war dragged on, many people were attracted to a new antiwar movement. Political scientist Hans Morgenthau argued that the United States had no genuine interest in Vietnam and was exhausting its power while China and the Soviet Union remained untouched. Senators William Fulbright of Arkansas, Gaylord Nelson of Wisconsin, and Wayne Morse of Oregon said that in warring against the apparent wishes of the Vietnamese people the United States was alienating other Third World nations.

Pacifists, such as the *Quakers* and radical journalist David Dellinger, opposed the war because they opposed all wars. Pediatrician Benjamin Spock and others, who were moralists but not necessarily pacifists, called the war unjust and immoral. Even David Shoup, the former commandant of the Marine Corps, condemned the war as unjustified.

Johnson had no illusions about Diem's government being democratic. L.B.J.'s sole reason for pursuing our involvement in Vietnam was to keep the south free of communism.

Student Radicals.

To many Americans, however, the antiwar movement seemed made up of young people, radical college students, and "long-haired *hippies*." But the movement actually began with an articulate minority of American college students and professors who strongly opposed the war. They were called the *New Left* because their philosophy was liberal and their tactics were novel. Their earlier protests included "teach-ins," a series of lectures and discussions on college campuses at which people explored the reasons for the war and ways to stop it.

Students for a Democratic Society (SDS), was the most important organization of the New Left. Its leading thinker, Tom Hayden, protested the American social "curses" of chronic poverty, racial discrimination, and the failure of wealth to provide a meaningful life. By 1966, the SDS was largely an antiwar organization.

White civil rights workers, many of whom had been expelled from SNCC, joined the antiwar movement. So did many college students who feared that they would be drafted and sent to Vietnam. Blacks made up a disproportionately large part of the army in Vietnam, and many civil rights leaders joined the protest.

The ranks of the antiwar protesters swelled as American involvement deepened, and antiwar leaders began to organize nonviolent demonstrations. In October 1965, 100,000 people demonstrated in 90 cities. In April 1967, about 300,000 people marched in opposition to the war in New York and San Francisco.

The Counterculture.

The demonstrations did not seem to affect the war. Thus by 1966, many disillusioned young people were protesting American society in their own way—"dropping out" to find new values by which to live. In San Francisco's Haight-Ashbury district and New York's East Village, young men and women—"*flower children*"—grew their hair long, donned bizarre clothing, shunned working as a "cop-out" (a compromise with society), and formed *communes* in which, they said, they left American *materialism* and competition behind.

Drugs were an important part of the *counterculture.* Many flower children used marijuana to defy what they saw as senseless rules restricting personal freedom and self-realization.

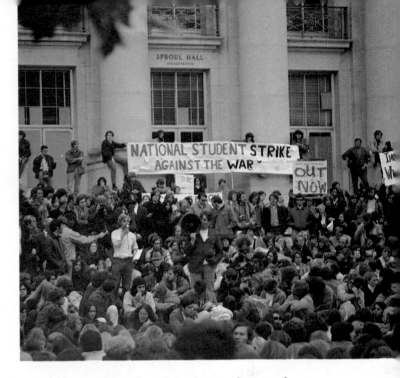

College students such as those above on the steps of Sproul Hall at the University of California at Berkeley were the early leaders in the movement to get the United States out of Vietnam. In time, protest marches like the one below in Washington were capable of drawing several hundred thousand concerned citizens, representing a full spectrum of American society.

When President Johnson took himself out of the 1968 presidential election, the candidacies of (left to right) Senator Eugene McCarthy, Vice President Hubert Humphrey, Senator George McGovern, Senator Robert Kennedy, and Governor George Wallace gained fresh momentum.

Johnson Steps Down.

In January 1968, President Johnson probably intended to run for reelection. If he had won and served a full term, he would have held the office longer than anyone except Franklin Roosevelt. But he did not have that opportunity.

Johnson was challenged in the New Hampshire primary election by Eugene McCarthy, the antiwar senator from Minnesota. Thanks to a great volunteer effort by hundreds of college students, McCarthy won a stunning victory. This showed New York Senator Robert F. Kennedy that an antiwar candidate could win against Johnson. Like McCarthy, he opposed the war. Kennedy felt that with his strong support among minorities and labor, he would be the best Democratic presidential candidate.

President Johnson realized that the war was so unpopular he might not win his own party's nomination. Therefore, on March 31, he announced that he would not be a candidate for reelection.

This brought Vice President Hubert Humphrey into the race. Humphrey automatically had the support of the party professionals, but he also carried a heavy burden. He had to remain loyal to Johnson while hinting that he opposed the war.

On June 5, Robert Kennedy won the important California primary. Then, after addressing his campaign workers in a Los Angeles hotel, Kennedy was shot and killed by Sirhan B. Sirhan. Sirhan, a Palestinian, had shot Kennedy because the Senator was a strong supporter of the Jewish state of Israel. From then on a gloomy pall hung over the 1968 Democratic campaign.

The Democratic Convention.

The Democrats met in Chicago for their *nominating convention.* Vice President Humphrey seemed to be the Democrats' choice, since his major opposition had fallen when Kennedy was killed. But the party was divided into an antiwar faction, which disliked Humphrey for not coming out against the war,

Class Activity: President Nixon, perhaps more than any other president in history, is closely associated with the use of television in politics. As a participant in the first televised presidential campaign debates, as an innovator in TV campaign advertising, as the president who gave the most television appearances during the time he was in office, and as the only president whose and the pro-Humphrey, pro-Johnson faction.

Even more serious trouble awaited the Democrats. A group of young people had started the liberal Youth International Party (YIP), or the *Yippies*. Their motto was "Don't trust anyone over 30." In the spring of 1968, the Yippies had called for people opposed to the Vietnam War to gather for a massive, nonviolent demonstration at the Democratic convention.

The activists were unable to get official permits for the demonstration from Chicago's Mayor Richard Daley. But thousands still came to protest the war.

With hordes of television and print journalists at the Democratic convention, Daley wanted to show off his city's orderliness. He effectively gave Chicago's police permission to take whatever steps necessary, including violence, to control the demonstrators. When the police and demonstrators met, the result was what some investigators called "a police riot." Millions of television viewers saw Chicago's police beating passers-by and journalists as well as demonstrators.

Inside the convention hall, the Democrats nominated Humphrey for president and Edmund Muskie of Maine for vice president. But the demonstrations and violence outside disrupted the celebrations inside, and the Democrats were unable to patch up their differences.

Nixon for the Republicans.

The Republican convention was a strong contrast to the Democratic gathering. Richard Nixon was easily nominated by the Republican convention in Miami. It was the culmination of an astonishing political comeback. After his defeat by Kennedy in 1960, Nixon lost a race for the California governorship in 1962 and had retired from politics.

But Nixon was not out of politics for long. In 1964, almost alone among party leaders, he supported Barry Goldwater, winning the gratitude of Republican conservatives. For four years he made himself available to Republican fund-raising events wherever he was invited. Quietly, tirelessly, he built up a following so strong that in 1968, he walked away with the nomination.

During his election campaign, Nixon said he had a plan to end the war in Vietnam that he could not yet divulge. He presented himself as the person who could end the instability of the John-

son years. While cultivating the image of a statesman, his running mate, Maryland Governor Spiro Agnew, took a hard line. Agnew denounced rioters and antiwar "peaceniks." He said that Nixon would restore "law and order" in the nation.

The American Independent Party.

Agnew's role as a hard-line conservative was invaluable to the Republican campaign. He undercut the appeal of a third party candidate, George C. Wallace, who ran as the candidate of the *American Independent* party. Wallace attacked black rioters and professors who he said encouraged students to be disloyal to their country. He promised not just an end to the war, but victory.

Six weeks before Election Day, Wallace was only slightly behind Hubert Humphrey in the polls while Nixon was running far ahead. Then, a month before the election, Humphrey's popularity soared. In a series of statements, he moved away from his previous support of the Vietnam War. A last-minute campaign on his behalf by organized labor, coupled with fears by liberals and working people that Nixon would dismantle the Great Society, brought him closer to Nixon.

The final results were almost as close as when Nixon lost to Kennedy in 1960. Nixon polled only 500,000 votes more than Humphrey, out of almost 73 million votes cast. Wallace had received 9 million votes. But Nixon received 301 electoral votes to Humphrey's 191 and Wallace's 46. The busy New Frontier-Great Society era was over, only eight years after it had begun.

SECTION REVIEW

1. Write a sentence to identify: New Left, Sirhan B. Sirhan, Yippies.

2. Why were some non-Communist South Vietnamese sympathetic to the Viet Cong?

3. Compare Johnson's and Kennedy's Vietnam policies. Explain the results of Johnson's policy in Vietnam and at home.

4. After President Johnson quit the presidential race, which Democrats tried to win their party's nomination in 1968?

5. Name the candidates of the three parties in the 1968 election. Who won?

CHAPTER REVIEW

TIME LINE

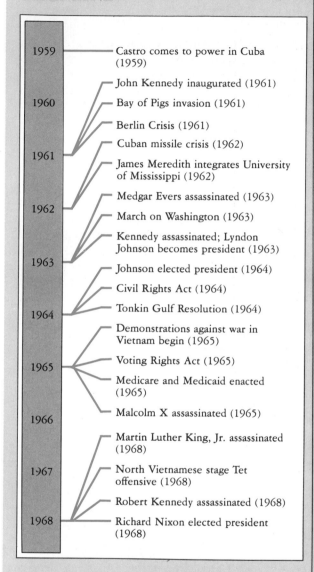

1959	Castro comes to power in Cuba (1959)
1960	John Kennedy inaugurated (1961)
	Bay of Pigs invasion (1961)
1961	Berlin Crisis (1961)
	Cuban missile crisis (1962)
	James Meredith integrates University of Mississippi (1962)
1962	Medgar Evers assassinated (1963)
	March on Washington (1963)
	Kennedy assassinated; Lyndon Johnson becomes president (1963)
1963	Johnson elected president (1964)
	Civil Rights Act (1964)
1964	Tonkin Gulf Resolution (1964)
	Demonstrations against war in Vietnam begin (1965)
1965	Voting Rights Act (1965)
	Medicare and Medicaid enacted (1965)
1966	Malcolm X assassinated (1965)
	Martin Luther King, Jr. assassinated (1968)
1967	North Vietnamese stage Tet offensive (1968)
	Robert Kennedy assassinated (1968)
1968	Richard Nixon elected president (1968)

TIME LINE QUESTIONS

1. How many years was Kennedy in office?
2. List the American leaders who were assassinated during a six-year period.
3. In which years did black Americans make important gains?
4. What event, in what year, brought a confrontation between the United States and the Soviet Union?

SKILLS STRATEGY

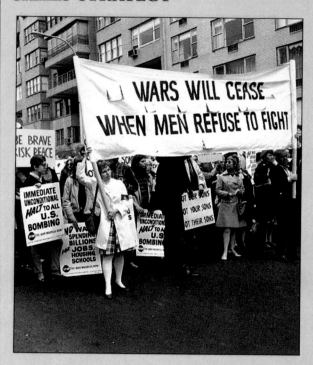

HYPOTHESES FROM PHOTOGRAPHS

A *hypothesis*, or theory, is a tentative conclusion based upon the study of available evidence. You can form a hypothesis about a historical period by thoughtfully examining any of several kinds of primary sources: books, magazines, newspapers, recorded songs, photographs, movies, paintings and drawings, political cartoons, advertisements, laws, statistics, public opinion polls, and the oral testimony of people living at the time. The evidence in such sources can be regarded as the raw material from which you form a hypothesis.

A hypothesis is not a final conclusion. Its degree of validity rests on the accuracy with which the sources used to form it are interpreted. The validity of a hypothesis concerning a given historical period can be tested by reference to conclusions reached by a majority of historians about the same period. Or, where possible, a hypothesis can be tested by interviewing a representative number of reliable people who participated in the events of the time in question.

Making Connections: Review the questions and topics presented in the Making Connections section that opens this chapter. Review the impact of the 1960s on morals. Most political scientists and historians are now convinced that the sixties will be recorded in history as a major

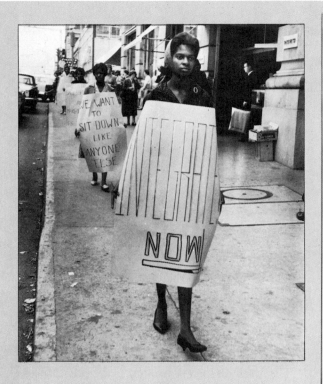

Look at the photos above. Form a hypothesis about the general mood or feelings of many Americans who lived during the 1960s. Base your hypothesis on your response to the photographs, which are primary sources that appeared in the news media of the time. First, try to identify the event shown in each photograph. Study the actions of the people in the photos. Notice other things such as posters and banners. Be sure not to overlook any of the details in the photos.

APPLYING SKILLS

1. What event is depicted in each photo?
2. What feeling or mood do the photos, working together, convey to you?
3. Write captions for the photographs, giving only specific information you observe in each photograph.
4. Write a sentence or two stating a hypothesis about the feeling or mood of the American people in the 1960s as conveyed by the photographs.

CHAPTER 32 TEST

TEXT REVIEW

1. Compare the main thrusts of the domestic legislation programs of the New Frontier and the Great Society. Give reasons for the successes and failures of both.
2. Why did Kennedy go to Texas in 1963?
3. Describe the steps in the country's path to greater involvement in the Vietnam War from August 1964 to September 1965.
4. Describe the significance of two of the following to the civil rights movement: James Meredith, George Wallace, Robert Kennedy, Malcolm X, Martin Luther King, Jr.
5. Explain the importance of the Tonkin Gulf Resolution.
6. Name several individuals and groups who opposed the Vietnam War, and give their reasons.
7. How was the Republican convention in 1968 different from the Democratic convention? How did Richard Nixon win the Republican nomination?

CRITICAL THINKING

8. Put yourself in the place of an American or Soviet citizen during the tense days of the Cuban missile crisis. Tell your thoughts and feelings about what might happen.
9. In what sense did Franklin Roosevelt influence Johnson in formulating the Great Society domestic legislation?
10. Give your reaction to the life style of the "flower children" of the 1960s. Evaluate their reasons for choosing that life style.

WRITING A PARAGRAPH

Suppose that you are in the process of validating the hypothesis you formulated in the Skills Strategy. You have recorded an interview with a woman who worked as a newspaper reporter during the 1960s. You have outlined her responses to your questions about how she perceived the mood or feelings of Americans during the 1960s. Now, write a paragraph summarizing her responses. Write the paragraph from her point of view.

turning point for the United States. Discuss why this might be so. Also discuss how the Vietnam War has affected U.S. foreign policy, at least in terms of military intervention in the world, and how it has changed our world image.

DIPLOMACY, DETENTE, AND CRISIS

1968–1976

The balance of power,
our own,
the world's,
Grows ever fragile

TIM O'BRIEN

Making Connections. President Richard Nixon surprised critics who thought of him as a firm anti-Communist. He had many diplomatic successes, including recognition of Communist China and the withdrawal of American forces from Vietnam. But a burglary in Washington, D.C., caused his downfall. He was the first American president to resign.

In this chapter, you will learn:
- What steps Nixon took to bring an end to United States involvement in Vietnam
- Who served as Secretary of State under Nixon and Ford and what role he played in the nation's foreign policy successes
- How five burglars in Washington, D.C. caused a governmental crisis
- Why Americans became concerned about energy use in the 1970s
- When Americans celebrated an important event in their country's history

In this chapter, you will look at how Richard Nixon began to find new ways to deal with the Communists. As you read, note how Nixon and his Secretary of State opened channels to China and the Soviet Union.

Sections

1. THE DIPLOMAT PRESIDENT

Unlike Johnson, who made high marks in *domestic* affairs and a disastrous decision in foreign policy, Nixon was an imaginative and successful diplomat. He believed the president should specialize in foreign affairs. He said that "the country could run itself domestically, without a president."

His foreign policy was innovative, even daring. Nixon managed to end American involvement in the Vietnam War. He established diplomatic relations with the People's Republic of China, something previous presidents had not dared to do.

Vietnamization. Nixon knew that the growing unpopularity of the Vietnam War had snuffed out Lyndon Johnson's political career. So he determined to end the conflict under any terms but an obvious American defeat. He believed that his first task was to isolate the militant antiwar protesters—the pacifists and radicals—from the increasing number of Americans who disliked the war only because of the heavy casualties American troops were suffering.

America's goal of landing an astronaut on the moon was accomplished on July 20, 1969. The photograph on the right is of Edwin Aldrin, and was taken by Neil Armstrong during their nine-and-a-half hour stay on the moon's surface. Armstrong and the lunar module, the Eagle, *can be seen reflected in Aldrin's face mask.*

Quotation: from the poem "The Nuclear Age." Works by Tim O'Brien (born 1946) include *If I Die in a Combat Zone, Northern Lights,* and *Going After Cacciato.*

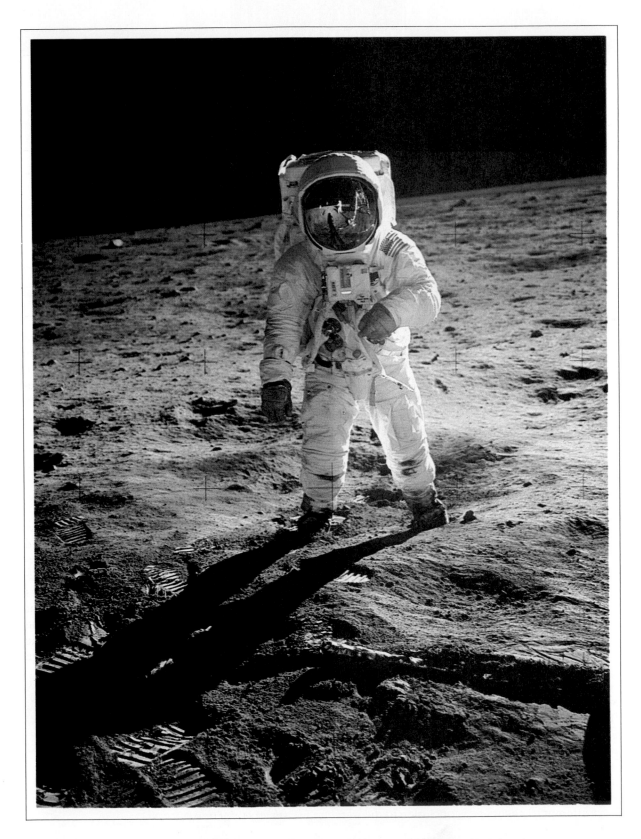

Skills Review: Reinforce the skills learned in the preceding Skills Strategy section. Examine the hypothesis that U.S. industry profited from the Vietnam War. Although a popular theory in the sixties, was this the case? Have students examine this by using skills learned in the previous chapter.

773

PROFILES OF THE PRESIDENCY

RICHARD NIXON   1969–1974

A s a result of the Water-gate scandal, Richard Nixon resigned his office:

Throughout the long and difficult period of Watergate, I have felt it was my duty to persevere, to make every possible effort to complete the term of office to which you elected me. In the past few days, however, it has become evident to me that I no longer have a strong enough political base in the Congress to justify continuing that effort. . . . I have never been a quitter. To leave office before my term is completed is abhorrent to every instinct in my body. But as President, I must put the interest of America first. . . . Therefore, I shall resign the Presidency, effective at noon tomorrow. . . . I regret deeply any injuries that may have been done in the course of the events that led to this decision. I would say only that if some of my judgments were wrong —and some were wrong—they were made in what I believed at the time to be the best interest of the nation. . . .

—RESIGNATION SPEECH, AUGUST 8, 1974

Vice President Spiro Agnew had the job of appealing to the patriotism of middle class and working class Americans. Agnew attacked pacifists as "defeatists," and antiwar university students as privileged snobs. Working people, who proudly called themselves "hardhats," liked his message.

Meanwhile, Nixon and his special adviser on foreign policy, Harvard professor Henry Kissinger, planned the *Vietnamization* of the war. American soldiers were gradually withdrawn from frontline positions and sent home. South Vietnamese troops trained by American advisers took their places. From a high of 541,000 troops in 1969, American forces in Vietnam were reduced to 335,000 in 1970 and 24,000 by 1972.

Nixon and Kissinger were returning the war to where it had been before 1965—Vietnamese fighting Vietnamese. The flaw in their policy was that the South Vietnamese army had been losing in 1965 when there were few if any North Vietnamese troops in the war. In 1969, several hundred thousand North Vietnamese soldiers were in South Vietnam or in sanctuaries in neighboring Laos and Cambodia. Despite some successes in the American training program, the enemy remained a superior fighting force. As long as they were winning, the North Vietnamese rejected every attempt to negotiate a conclusion to the war.

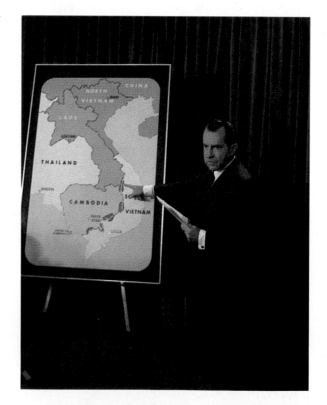

In April 1970, President Nixon authorized an expansion of the Vietnam War to include Cambodia. Public reaction forced him to go on television (above) to explain his actions.

One of the horrors of Vietnam was the stories of massacres caused by the U.S. counteroffensive. When these massacres were revealed by returning troops in 1969, the My Lai Four became a black spot on U.S. ideals of fairness. Although the North Vietnamese perpetrated worse atrocities, the My Lai massacre is remembered because the action was performed by the U.S.

Expanding the War. Frustrated, President Nixon decided to force the North Vietnamese to the bargaining table. While he continued to wind down the American presence on the ground, he increased the air war and actually expanded the scope of the war. In April 1970, the Air Force provided support for a South Vietnamese invasion of the jungles of Cambodia where the North Vietnamese took refuge between battles. The purpose was to destroy their sanctuaries. But the major result of the attack was to contribute to the fall of the pro-American Cambodian government to anti-American rebels.

The invasion of Cambodia also caused students around the country to explode in spontaneous protest. Just when the war seemed nearly over, the president was widening it. Most of the demonstrations were peaceful as worried college administrators closed campuses for as long as a week.

But at Kent State University in Ohio, the demonstrations turned violent. In May, the governor called in the Ohio National Guard. Although the soldiers were not directly threatened, they opened fire, killing four persons. Ten days later, two students at Jackson State College in Mississippi were killed by police. Angry critics of the Nixon administration blamed Agnew's divisive speeches for the killings.

Nixon continued his policy of offering to negotiate while stepping up the war. In January 1971, South Vietnamese troops invaded Laos with American air support. Their goal was to destroy the Ho Chi Minh Trail. The major effect, as in the Cambodian strike, was to strengthen anti-American forces in Laos.

At the beginning of 1972, Nixon revealed that in 1971, Henry Kissinger had held 12 secret meetings with Le Duc Tho (lē′ dŭk′ tō′), Secretary of the Central Committee of the North Vietnamese Communist party. However, late in 1971, Le Duc Tho had withdrawn from the talks and North Vietnam had launched a new offensive in March 1972. Nixon responded by ordering heavy bombing of Hanoi and Haiphong.

Le Duc Tho returned to the bargaining table. In January 1973, a *ceasefire* was signed that enabled Nixon to withdraw the last American troops.

The End At Last. Few people who knew Vietnam expected the ceasefire to last. North Vietnam

Public reaction to the invasion of Cambodia was swift and strong, especially on college campuses. At Kent State University in Ohio, four students protesting American foreign policy were killed by the Ohio National Guard (above).

retained the right to keep 145,000 soldiers in the South. The end came quickly in 1975. North Vietnam launched a major *offensive* that swept rapidly over the country, and concluded with the fall of Saigon. As Saigon fell, the last Americans in the country were evacuated by helicopter from the roof of the American *embassy*.

As Saigon, South Vietnam, fell, residents trying to evacuate the city clogged the highways (below).

Vietnam's Legacy. The Vietnam War was possibly the most tragic war in the history of the nation. More bombs were dropped on Vietnam than on all of America's enemies during World War II. By the time direct American involvement ended, it had cost $140 billion. Of America's wars, only World War II was more expensive. The huge expenditures may have helped cause the nation's economic difficulties into the early 1980's.

The number of Americans killed and wounded exceeded 200,000. Probably 800,000 South Vietnamese and a comparable number of North Vietnamese died. Each day during 1968, the most savage year of the war, 40 Americans were killed and 128 wounded. And yet not one of the goals for which all the blood was spilled and all the money spent was achieved.

Because of Vietnam, the world prestige of the United States sank lower than at any time in the nation's history. The war *demoralized* the American people and ruined the historical reputations of Lyndon Johnson and many of his advisors. Veterans of the war were neglected and shunned, as if they were responsible for it, instead of being its victims. The tragedy of Vietnam haunted the people who lived through the era much as the Civil War had haunted another generation just a century earlier.

A Revolution in Diplomacy. Even while the war continued, a revolution in American diplomacy was underway. Ever since the Chinese Communists had taken control of China in 1949, the United States had recognized the Nationalist government on Taiwan as the legal government of all China. The People's Republic, the actual government of China, was considered undemocratic, immoral, and illegal.

This policy grew increasingly unrealistic as the years passed. For good or ill, the Communists were going to continue to govern the Chinese people. Nevertheless, the United States continued to block Red China's admission to the UN. Even Democratic presidents Truman, Kennedy, and Johnson were particularly careful to condemn Red China in their foreign policy addresses. If they did not, Republican critics like Richard Nixon were apt to accuse them of being "soft on Communism."

The first indication of a change in policy occurred in 1971. An American table-tennis team on a tour of Japan was quietly invited to play some matches in China before they returned home. It was a small thing, and the Chinese regime would suffer no embarassment if the invitation was rejected. But Nixon and Kissinger jumped at the chance. The American athletes were given permission to go.

In the wake of this good-will mission, Henry Kissinger met secretly with Chinese leaders and arranged for a far more dramatic visit. In February 1972, President Nixon himself went to China and laid the groundwork for diplomatic *recognition* of the People's Republic, and for the admission of Red China to the UN in place of the Nationalist government of Taiwan.

Following these events, American companies began selling everything from Coca Cola to heavy machinery to the mainland Chinese. American business had always looked on the most populous country in the world as the largest market in the world as well.

Kissinger's World View. Nixon's diplomatic revolution was politically possible because no one could accuse him of being pro-Communist. His reasons for taking the giant step were drawn from his own beliefs and the theories of international relations held by his chief adviser on foreign affairs and later Secretary of State, Henry Kissinger.

Kissinger was a suave and sophisticated man who frankly and humorously admitted he was something of an egotist. He took as his hero the master of diplomacy, Prince Metternich. Metternich was the Austrian premier who, in 1815, established the balance of power among the nations of Europe that kept the peace for a century.

Kissinger said that ideology should not be the chief force determining how nations acted toward one another. To allow ideas such as morality or anti-Communism to determine national policy was foolish, dangerous, and self-destructive. Instead, Kissinger insisted, the United States should seek a balance of power among nations in which it held the edge and initiative. This viewpoint was known as *realpolitik*, or "realistic policy."

Realpolitik appealed to Nixon. He was himself a practical man who had little time for sentiments and principles. This was why he was able to

Class Activity: Have some members of the anti-war movement of the sixties and some Vietnam veterans come to class separately to answer questions about their experiences.

*In 1972, President Nixon made a dramatic trip to China and changed history. In taking the
initiative and offering American friendship, Nixon paved the way for improved relations.*

reverse his lifelong condemnation of Communist China and fly to Peking, where he drank cordial toasts with Mao Tse-tung and pledged Chinese-American friendship.

Conservative Republicans criticized Kissinger. However, Nixon believed that despite the fact that both Russia and China were Communist, hostility between them was deeper than hostility between China and the United States. It was in the interests of the United States to exploit this rift by expressing friendship for China.

Détente. Because China and Vietnam were traditionally enemies, Nixon's visits to China probably made the North Vietnamese more willing to negotiate. It frightened them to think that China might agree to cut off its military aid to them.

Chinese-American friendship was certainly the inspiration for the Soviet Union's sudden offer to establish a friendly working relationship with the United States. *Détente* was the word that Kissinger

used to describe a gradual relaxation of tension between the superpowers. In May 1972, just three months after Nixon's visit to China and six months before complete American withdrawal from Vietnam, the President flew to the Soviet Union and signed an agreement to limit nuclear weaponry.

This agreement, as well as a formal treaty ratified by the Senate in 1973, were the outcome of a series of diplomatic discussions known as the *Strategic Arms Limitation Talks,* or *SALT.* The Soviets and Americans agreed not to build any offensive missiles for five years. This provision and others made the SALT accords appear to be a major step toward détente and arms control.

Shuttle Diplomacy. In 1973, Kissinger replaced William P. Rogers as Secretary of State. Well into 1974, his diplomatic successes piled up. The most important of these was establishing a cease-fire between Egypt and Syria and the Jewish

Class Activity: Make a comparison chart and study the differences between Kissinger's *Realpolitik* and Ike's Cold War policies. Examine the consequences of both, especially in terms of U.S.-Soviet policies and relations.

Secretary of State Henry Kissinger's frequent trips to the Middle East to conduct secret negotiations became known as "shuttle diplomacy."

President Sadat of Egypt (left, with President Nixon) said, "For great aims, we must dare great things." Seeking peace, he dared to accept Israel.

state of Israel. Because no Arab state would then deal directly with Israel, Kissinger accomplished this nearly miraculous peace by traveling nonstop from Damascus, Syria, to Cairo, Egypt, to Tel Aviv, Israel—and back again. His method was called *shuttle diplomacy.*

The war that originally caused the crisis had broken out on the Jewish high holy day of Yom Kippur in October 1973. Because they attacked by surprise while Israelis were worshiping, the Syrians and Egyptians scored major victories in the first week of war. The superior Israeli armed forces eventually recovered and smashed the Arab offensives. But it appeared as if the Middle East was in for extended instability. There was a real danger that the Soviet Union might intervene on the Arab side.

By ending the tension quickly through shuttle diplomacy, Kissinger managed to head off the Soviets in the Middle East. The Egyptian president, Anwar Sadat, drew closer to the United States. Sadat was finally persuaded that peace depended on Arab acceptance of Israel's right to

exist. Four years later, Sadat flew to Tel Aviv and spoke before the Israeli parliament. Amidst cries of "traitor" from other Arab leaders, Sadat recognized Israel and exchanged ambassadors.

Kissinger's Reputation Declines.
The right wing of the Republican party never approved of Kissinger. Committed to an ideology of anti-Communism, they disliked both recognition of Red China and détente with the Soviet Union. Ronald Reagan of California, the leading spokesman of the Republican conservatives, called for Kissinger's resignation.

After 1974, Kissinger lost the admiration of most liberals as well. This was because *realpolitik* did not always mean seeking a peaceful solution to problems. In Angola, a former Portuguese colony in West Africa, Nixon and Kissinger supported one faction in an ugly civil war while the Soviets supported another. American policy prolonged fighting in that country.

Much more damaging to Kissinger's reputation was the revelation that, with his approval in Sep-

 Discussion Question: Is there a contradiction in U.S. acknowledgement of human rights at home and its supportive relationships with dictatorial, anti-democratic governments abroad?

tember 1973, the CIA cooperated in overthrowing Chile's democratically elected president, Salvador Allende (ä-yān'dä).

Allende was not a Communist. But he was friendly with Cuba's Castro and intended to nationalize many American-owned properties in Chile. In this case, support of democratic regimes was the ideal that Kissinger rejected. Realism, he believed, required that Chile be governed by leaders friendly to the United States no matter how anti-democratic they were.

SECTION REVIEW

1. Write a sentence to identify: Spiro Agnew, Kent State University, SALT, Salvador Allende.

2. Describe the Nixon-Kissinger plan for ending American involvement in Vietnam. How did it lead to an expansion of the war?

3. How did the war in Vietnam finally end? In what sense could the conflict be called the most tragic war in United States history?

4. How did Henry Kissinger's *realpolitik* account for diplomatic recognition of the People's Republic of China?

---

2. THE ECONOMY AND WATERGATE

Richard Nixon was elected in 1968 with the aid of the conservative wing of the Republican party. These politicians believed that government should play little or no part in the workings of the economy. Nixon took some actions that pleased his conservative supporters. But for the most part, Nixon's domestic policies angered conservatives.

Inflation. The most serious domestic problem facing the American people in the 1970s was *inflation*, a constant increase in the prices of both necessities and luxury goods. When income did not keep up with prices, inflation meant a decline in the standard of living.

In some ways, money is like a manufactured product. When the demand for it is high and the supply is low, its value rises. When the supply meets the demand, its value drops. When money

is abundant, people need more dollars and cents to buy goods.

Money was abundant in the 1970s because of huge government expenditures on social programs as well as the immense sums committed to the costly war in Vietnam. President Johnson had avoided raising taxes to pay these costs because he knew that voters hated tax increases. Thus, the government annually ran at a deficit, paying out more money than it collected.

The result was an *inflationary spiral*. With annually greater amounts of money in circulation, prices went up. In order to pay higher prices, working people demanded higher wages. For example, when the wages of workers in the automobile industry increased, the price of cars also went up, creating a need for even higher wages.

Nixon Fights Recession. The traditional approach to stopping an inflationary spiral is to cut government expenditures and to increase taxes. This takes money out of circulation. The money still in circulation becomes more valuable, and prices drop and there is less need to increase wages. The risk of such a policy is a recession or a depression, which hurts people who are laid off from their jobs. If government social services have been cut, the unemployed have nowhere to turn.

This is what happened as Nixon tried to stop inflation using the traditional method. As signs of recession increased in 1971, Nixon abandoned the method, knowing that his administration would probably be blamed for bad times. To correct the recession in time for the 1972 election, the President increased government expenditures and sent to Congress a budget with the largest peacetime deficit in American history. In 1972, the federal government spent $23.2 billion more than was collected in taxes.

Wage and Price Controls. Then, in August 1971, Nixon did something that shocked conservatives in his party. In order to head off the inflationary spiral, he instituted wage and price controls. For a period of 90 days, wages, rents, doctors' and lawyers' fees, and the prices for most goods were to be frozen at August levels.

At the end of the 90-day period, the second phase of the control program started. Beginning in November, Nixon allowed wages and prices to

---

Research Assignment: Have students do a study of inflation since the Second World War. In addition to the study, have students create a bar or line graph showing the rate of inflation. If computer facilities are available, have students use them to analyze this information.

rise if they satisfied guidelines set by the newly established *Cost of Living Council.* Again, conservatives were aghast. The president they had helped elect was now creating a new *bureaucracy* that seemed to be interfering with the workings of *free enterprise.* But Nixon's controls remained in effect, and the rate of inflation slowed down temporarily.

Footprints on the Moon.

The Nixon administration presided over the realization of an American dream that had begun when President Kennedy was in office. On July 16, 1969, the spaceship *Apollo 11* was launched from *Cape Kennedy.* It carried three astronauts—Neil Armstrong, Edwin Aldrin, and Michael Collins. Four days later, the landing module, carrying Armstrong and Aldrin, touched down safely on the moon.

The astronauts stayed on the moon for a short time, but long enough to plant an American flag at

From the first successful flight by the Wright brothers on December 17, 1903, to the landing of the first person on the moon on July 20, 1969, Americans have led the way in aviation pioneering.

the landing site and to perform a series of tests. Americans were able to see what the astronauts did, and the first human step on the moon was recorded by television cameras. Armstrong's comment as he stepped onto the moon's surface was, "That's one small step for a man, one giant leap for mankind."

The Supreme Court.

By 1972, the liberal majority of justices in the Supreme Court had grown old. As they retired, Nixon was able to appoint justices who held conservative philosophies. First to retire was Chief Justice Earl Warren. Nixon replaced him with a conservative jurist from Minnesota, Warren Burger.

The Senate approved Burger's appointment, but the president ran into trouble when he nominated two other conservatives—Clement Haynesworth of South Carolina and Harold Carswell of Florida. The Senate rejected both judges because of their spotty records on civil rights cases. Nevertheless, after appointing a Minnesota associate of Burger, Harry Blackmun, Nixon succeeded in creating a court that broke with Earl Warren's tradition of active liberalism. The Burger Court rulings emphasized the rights of society over those of individuals.

The Congress.

Throughout his presidency, Nixon had to deal with large Democratic majorities in both houses of Congress. The power of the large liberal majority in Congress forced Nixon into actions that disturbed his conservative supporters. For example, he signed laws that protected consumers from shoddy or dangerous goods. He increased Social Security benefits. He backed the ratification of the Twenty-Sixth Amendment to the Constitution, which extended the right to vote in all elections to citizens between the ages of 18 and 21.

In 1970, Nixon signed a bill founding *Amtrak*, a cooperative arrangement between the federal government and the nation's railroads designed to revive passenger travel by rail. Also in 1970, the *Environmental Protection Agency (EPA)* was commissioned to oversee conservation of natural resources. The EPA was empowered to investigate incidents of air and water pollution and other threats to the environment. The EPA could then prosecute companies and individuals in violation of the law.

The Warren Court was very unpopular with archconservatives for its positions on desegregation, legislative apportionment, school prayer, and decisions affecting the civil liberties of communists and people accused of crimes. Students may wish to examine these views in a research assignment.

MOVERS AND SHAPERS

Rosalyn Yalow

In 1977, Rosalyn S. Yalow (born 1921) won a *Nobel Prize* for medicine. She shared the award with two men, but she was only the second woman ever to be so honored. Working with Dr. Solomon A. Berson at the Bronx Veterans Administration Hospital, Yalow developed a revolutionary technique known as *radio immunoassay* (RIA). In RIA, radioactive isotopes are used to trace minute quantities of substances in the blood and other fluids of the human body, animals, and plants.

Yalow and Berson first developed the technique that measures the amount of insulin in adult diabetics' blood. The method was soon being applied to other areas of clinical medicine. Yalow and others used it to measure human growth hormones and to detect the hepatitis virus and other biological substances. Currently, RIA is being used in laboratories all over the world.

The daughter of Jewish immigrants, Yalow pursued graduate work in physics at the University of Illinois at Urbana, becoming the second woman to receive a Ph.D. from that university's physics department. She then taught physics at New York's Hunter College. Shortly after World War II, Yalow was presented with medical applications of radioactive isotopes, and launched her prize-winning research.

Since winning the Nobel Prize, Yalow's pace has not slackened, but now her time is divided between continued lab work on RIA and lectures before scientific groups around the world.

Barbara McClintock

In 1983, Barbara McClintock (born 1902) became the first woman to win the Nobel Prize in medicine without sharing it.

Armed with a Ph.D. in plant genetics from Cornell University, McClintock started out as a researcher at a New York laboratory in the 1940s. She began growing bushels of maize plants for study because maize kernels came in various colors, each determined by a specific gene.

After observing many generations of the maize, McClintock found that the plants did not follow the patterns of color change described in textbooks. Genes were believed to remain locked in position on chromosomes; McClintock made the startling discovery that some genes actually moved from one part of a chromosome to another!

In 1951, McClintock made known her "jumping gene" discovery. The scientific community greeted it with skepticism and outright rejection. Not until 30 years later was the significance of McClintock's work acknowledged. By then, other scientists had had the benefit of more sophisticated techniques, and they began to observe the "jumping gene" phenomenon in bacteria and fruit flies.

In making the award, the committee called McClintock's work "one of the two great discoveries of our times in genetics." Though recognition was long overdue, McClintock accepted the award with characteristic modesty, saying that it "might seem unfair to reward a person for having so much pleasure over the years."

The Environmentalist Movement.

Growing concern for *ecology*, the study of relationships in nature, resulted in the growth of the environmentalist movement in the late 1960s and early 1970s. Organizations like the *Sierra Club* and the *Wilderness Society* doubled and tripled in membership. These groups were committed to preserving America's natural heritage. They expressed the growing concern of Americans that runaway economic development threatened the wild land which had always been an important part of their national heritage.

The Election of 1972.

Despite following policies that did not cater to conservative ideals, Nixon was easily renominated by the Republican party in 1972. His foreign policy initiatives, the winding down of the Vietnam War, and the improvement in the economy gave Republican opponents little to criticize.

However, the nation seemed to be badly split. Antiwar demonstrations continued to grow, and the President continued to ignore them. The gap between the rich and the poor in the country seemed to be growing wider. The Democrats, using these issues as the foundation of their campaign drive, nominated George McGovern, an antiwar senator from South Dakota.

McGovern ran a very strong campaign in the Democratic primaries and appealed to a broad range of Democratic voters, especially young voters, minorities, and women. But he did not win the full support of labor, and his antiwar stance made him unacceptable to many voters. Then, his choice for vice presidential nominee, Senator Thomas Eagleton, revealed that he had been treated several years before for an emotional illness. Concern about Eagleton's health forced McGovern to replace him with Sargent Shriver.

The Democrats were never really a threat to Nixon. The economy continued to improve, and a few days before the election, Henry Kissinger announced that peace in Vietnam was near. Thus McGovern lost his main issue, and even the hoped-for surge of young voters did not appear. Nixon won in a landslide almost as large as Johnson's in 1964, polling 60.8 percent of the popular vote and getting 520 electoral votes to McGovern's 17. McGovern won only Massachusetts and Washington, D.C.

The Watergate Scandal.

Although Nixon's margin of victory was huge, there were some disturbing signs during the campaign. On June 17, Democratic party national headquarters, located in the Watergate complex in Washington, D.C., were burglarized. Washington police arrested five men who were trying to plant electronic listening devices in the offices. One of the men was James McCord, who was security chief for the Committee to Reelect the President. This committee was headed by John Mitchell, one of Nixon's close friends. Mitchell had been Nixon's Attorney General before resigning to head the campaign effort.

Democratic attempts to exploit the break-in fizzled. Gordon Liddy, another man implicated in the burglary, refused to testify in court on his own or others' participation in the affair. His actions were repudiated by Mitchell.

However, two reporters for the *Washington Post*, Robert Woodward and Carl Bernstein, kept the story alive. Following the slenderest of leads, they discovered that several important members of Nixon's administration and campaign committee, including Mitchell, had known about plans for the break-in.

In January 1973, the trial of the five Watergate burglars began. The presiding judge was John J. Sirica, and he soon realized that not all of the information in the case was being presented. He began to press the Nixon administration for more details.

As evidence began to mount, and the public began to take notice, the Senate opened its own investigations. The *bipartisan committee* was chaired by Sam Ervin, a Democrat from North Carolina. The hearings were televised to the nation, and viewers witnessed the unraveling of Nixon's administration.

A parade of Nixon aides came before the cameras, and it became increasingly evident that the people closest to the President had known about the break-in. More important, it seemed that the President himself had been involved in an attempt to cover up the whole affair.

Agnew Resigns.

Another scandal now rocked the Administration. In October 1973, Vice President Agnew resigned after admitting he had falsified his tax returns and accepted bribes when he was governor of Maryland. Nixon chose Con-

Research Assignment: Have students develop profiles on all those individuals connected with the Watergate scandal. Be sure these include updates on what these people are doing now.

Watergate hearings were held by a congressional committee (above) to determine whether there was enough evidence to begin impeachment proceedings against President Nixon. However, when Nixon resigned, the question of impeachment ceased to be an issue.

gressman Gerald Ford of Michigan, the minority leader of the House, to be vice president. But Agnew's resignation did not slow the Watergate investigations.

"Toughing It Out." The President tried to turn aside the rising tide of criticism. He told his aides to "stonewall," or to refuse to cooperate with the investigators. When Special Prosecutor Archibald Cox, whom Nixon had named to lead the Justice Department's investigation, began to challenge Nixon, the President had Cox fired. But the new Special Prosecutor, Leon Jaworski, and Sirica and Ervin kept up the pressure.

As it turned out, the President's own actions caused his downfall. Nixon had recorded many conversations held in his office. Some of the tapes clearly showed that he was involved in the cover up. When ordered by the courts to surrender the tapes to investigators, Nixon at first refused to comply, claiming that presidential immunity allowed him to withhold sensitive information. He then turned over some tapes on which whole sections were missing.

Nevertheless, there was sufficient evidence to suggest the President's wrongdoing. In July 1974, the House Judiciary Committee adopted three resolutions of impeachment for the full House of Representatives to vote on. With Nixon's support amongst even Republicans almost gone, the House seemed certain to pass the resolutions, and the Senate might eventually have found the President guilty.

Nixon avoided the humiliation of a trial by resigning on August 9, 1974. Like Lyndon Johnson, he had slipped from landslide election victory to discredit within a few short years.

SECTION REVIEW

1. Write a sentence to identify: inflationary spiral, Environmental Protection Agency, Burger Court, Twenty-Sixth Amendment.

2. Identify the speaker, time, and place of this quotation: "That's one small step for a man, one giant leap for mankind."

3. Name some Nixon policies that angered his conservative Republican supporters. Why did they react in this way?

4. Trace the circumstances that led to President Nixon's resignation in 1974. In what way did he cause his own downfall?

Discussion Question: What might have happened had President Nixon not resigned? How might it have affected U.S. attitudes toward government? What international ramifications might it have had?

 783

T aking the oath of office, Gerald Ford vowed to heal a shaken nation:

. . . I assume the Presidency under extraordinary circumstances never before experienced by Americans. This is an hour of history that troubles our minds and hurts our hearts. Therefore, I feel it is my first duty to make an unprecedented compact with my countrymen. Not an inaugural address, not a fireside chat, not a campaign speech, just a little straight talk among friends . . . I have not subscribed to any partisan platform. I am indebted to no man and only to one woman, my dear wife, as I begin this very difficult job. I have not sought this enormous responsibility, but I will not shirk it . . . In all my public and private acts as your President, I expect to follow my instincts of openness and candor with full confidence that honesty is always the best policy in the end.

—SPEECH, AUGUST 9, 1974

3. THE FORD PRESIDENCY

Gerald Ford became the first American president who had not been elected to a national office. The vice presidency had come to him by appointment, not by election. After Nixon's resignation the new president was well aware of the uniqueness of his situation. He told Americans in his inaugural remarks that he was just an ordinary man trying to do his best. Ford was from Michigan, the center of the automobile industry, and said that America had "a Ford, not a Lincoln" in the White House.

Ford Pardons Nixon. Ford was immediately popular. Then, in September 1974, Ford seemed to throw this good will away by *pardoning* Richard Nixon for any crimes he might have committed during his term. Many people were shocked by Ford's decision. Why, they asked, were Nixon's top aides going to prison when Nixon himself would not even stand trial? They suspected that a deal lay behind the pardon.

Ford denied this. He said that he had pardoned Nixon so that Americans could put Watergate behind them. Otherwise, the investigation would drag on for years, demoralizing the country.

The Energy Crisis. The most serious domestic problem of the mid-1970s was the discovery that Americans could no longer count on cheap, abundant energy. More than 90 percent of the American economy was powered by fossil fuels—coal and petroleum. Fossil fuels were *nonrenewable.* Once used, they were gone forever. Although experts disagreed on how much coal and oil remained in the earth, there was no doubt that one day these resources would be used up by the growing demand for energy.

One solution was to develop alternative means of power: solar power, wind power, and nuclear energy. Backyard inventors and major corporations made significant strides in all three alternative energy sources during the 1970s.

Another solution was *conservation.* By reducing consumption of nonrenewable energy sources, the day that they ran out could be delayed, thus gaining more time for research into other sources of energy. Nowhere was conservation more an obligation than in the United States. In 1974, Americans made up less than six percent of the world's population and consumed more than 33 percent of the world's oil.

OPEC and Oil Embargo. This hard fact was at the core of the sudden scarcity of petroleum products in the mid-1970s. About 35–40 percent of the oil Americans consumed came from abroad, purchased in Venezuela, Nigeria, and particularly

Discussion Question: How do President Ford's words in the above selection compare with his pardon of Richard Nixon? Does one necessarily reflect poorly on the other?

the Arab countries of the Middle East. In 1960, these oil-rich countries founded the *Organization of Petroleum Exporting Countries (OPEC),* in order to gain more control over their oil resources. In October 1973, the Arab members of OPEC announced an embargo on shipments abroad. They were protesting United States support of Israel, which had just won the Yom Kippur War against Egypt and Syria.

Europeans, Japanese, and Americans were stunned. For several months motorists had to wait in long lines at service stations to fuel up their cars with very expensive gasoline. In some American cities and all over Hawaii, there was little gasoline to be had at any price for weeks on end. The cost of-gasoline never climbed to European levels, as much as $5 a gallon. But for middle-aged Americans who remembered paying 20 cents a gallon, a price of $2 a gallon was startling.

OPEC eventually lifted the embargo, but throughout the 1970s regularly increased the price of crude oil. By the end of the decade the seemingly endless price spiral was suddenly halted because of a split within OPEC. Anti-American oil exporting countries like Libya, and later Iran, wanted to raise prices indefinitely. Their leaders were not concerned that they might bankrupt the industrialized nations. However, pro-American OPEC countries like Saudi Arabia pointed out that if the industrialized nations went bankrupt, the oil-producing countries would suffer, too. Oil sales and revenues would drop. Fortunately for the United States, Saudi Arabia produced so much oil that a threat to undersell the other OPEC nations usually controlled the extremists.

Inflation Again.

Before the 1972 election, when President Nixon had instituted wage and price controls, inflation had slowed to three percent a year. That is, prices were rising only three cents on a dollar over a year's time. During 1973, with controls lifted, inflation rose to 6.2 percent. In 1974, Gerald Ford's first year in office, the rate shot up to 11 percent.

Ford was a conservative in his economics. He did not believe that government should take responsibility for the health of the economy. Instead, he sponsored a voluntary anti-inflation campaign called *Whip Inflation Now* (WIN). He urged consumers to wear WIN buttons and to refuse to buy goods that were overpriced. Employees were urged not to ask for higher wages. Manufacturers were to hold prices down.

Because most people regarded themselves as victims of inflation rather than the cause of it, few paid attention. The WIN campaign was a failure, and the President quietly retired his lapel button.

"Stagflation."

As another remedy for inflation, Ford prompted the Federal Reserve System to reduce the amount of money in circulation by raising the *rediscount rate,* the rate of interest at which Federal Reserve banks loaned money to other banks. When this rate rose, so did the interest that banks charged people borrowing money for a home, a car, or other goods.

Higher interest did discourage spending. But the result was the most serious recession since World War II. With less buying, factories cut their production by laying off workers. Unemployment rose to 8.5 percent. Ford found that he was trapped in the vicious circle that plagued Nixon. Slowing inflation produced unemployment. Putting people to work meant inflation. Trying to steer a middle course produced the unusual situation of *stagflation*—a stagnant economy and inflation at the same time.

Ford's Reputation.

As a congressman, Gerald Ford had been a *hawk* on Vietnam. He had favored pushing the war harder rather than looking for a way to make peace. His first impulse as president, when the North Vietnamese broke the ceasefire and moved against Saigon in early 1975, was to send more military aid to the South Vietnamese. But Congress refused to vote additional funds for South Vietnam. Thus, in a major foreign policy issue, Congress was unwilling to follow Ford's lead.

However, in May 1975, Ford demonstrated his willingness to act decisively when Cambodian troops seized an American ship, the *Mayaguez*. Ford ordered marines to raid Cambodia to rescue the captives. The rescue operation was successful. It relieved many people to see that the United States had not been paralyzed by its humiliation in Vietnam. Thirty-eight marines died in the operation. Despite this action, many politicians still considered Ford as merely a caretaker, and not as a full-fledged president.

Although portrayed by the media as clumsy and therefore politically inept, Ford was neither of these. He was always very athletic and lettered in college sports. He had been an influential congressman for many years before assuming the vice presidency.

SECTION REVIEW

1. Write a sentence to identify: fossil fuels, OPEC, stagflation, *Mayaguez.*

2. What action taken by President Ford diminished his popularity among the American people?

3. Explain why the oil embargo of the mid-1970s was a blow to the United States. What reasoning by Saudi Arabian leaders ended the upward spiral in the price of oil?

4. Explain what is meant by an annual inflation rate of 11 percent. Give the results of the two methods President Ford used to try to reduce the inflation rate.

4. BICENTENNIAL CELEBRATION

On July 4, 1976, the United States of America was celebrating its *bicentennial,* the nation's two hundredth birthday.

Most Americans observed this very special Fourth of July. Unlike in 1876, when the focus of the national celebration was a mammoth exposition in Philadelphia, the bicentennial was celebrated in different ways in almost every village, town, and city. Some Americans restored historic buildings as their contribution to the observance. Others planted trees in public parks. Parades and picnics were held all across the country. Some people retraced historic trails, like the Oregon Trail or Natchez Trace.

The most glorious spectacle of all was the arrival in New York of dozens of antique sailing ships, greeted by hundreds of sailboats. Most seafaring nations sent a vessel to participate in America's celebration.

A Crisis in Confidence. There was another difference from the Centennial celebration in 1876. The confidence of many Americans in their country was low. The Vietnam War had shown that the nation could not do just anything it wanted to. America's power abroad had been cut by OPEC price increases, Communist initiatives, and a drawing-inward of the American people. It seemed that Americans were becoming more concerned with themselves than with large causes.

Sharing in America's Bicentennial celebration, antique ships thrilled spectators in New York.

The Me Generation. Compared to the 1960s, when involvement in political and social issues seemed to characterize the American spirit, the mood of the 1970s seemed to be withdrawal into private, personal concerns. After the deaths of the four students at Kent State in May 1970, young people tended to forget John F. Kennedy's call to help the country and the world. Many Americans in the 1970s seemed to be asking only what they could do for themselves.

Political radicalism disappeared, except for tiny terrorist groups. The black demand for civil rights seemed to evaporate. The peace movement, so strong in the 1960s, was hardly heard. Writer Tom Wolfe aptly called the 1970s "the Me decade."

Class Activity: Using photographs, artifacts, and narratives, have students present a picture of how the bicentennial was celebrated in your community. Going farther back, have students compare this to the community's centennial celebration.

Fads and Fashions.

One reflection of "Me-ism" was the boom in recreational equipment and other commodities designed for self-enjoyment. Americans in the 1970s spent billions of dollars on ski equipment, tennis racquets, ten-speed bicycles, backpacking gear, hang gliders, snowmobiles, skydiving equipment, and other diversions.

Virtually no activity was immune to commercial exploitation. Even running for health and recreation, which would seem to require no equipment whatsoever, spawned multi-million dollar sales of special shoes and fashionable jogging clothes.

Cults.

Preoccupation with self was not confined to personal health and appearance. Many Americans turned to new religions or *cults* with a variety of leaders who claimed to have found the way to be completely happy and entirely fulfilled.

Some of these "religions" were relatively harmless. Others demanded complete loyalty to their teachings and worried many Americans. The members of the Unification Church, for example, were fanatical followers of a millionaire Korean preacher, Sun Myung Moon, who claimed special

Many unhappy adolescents put their faith in a variety of cults, two of which were Hare Krishna (top) and the Unification Church (bottom).

The 1970s found many Americans taking up jogging. The old sweatshirt and sneakers were replaced by new designer clothes and running shoes.

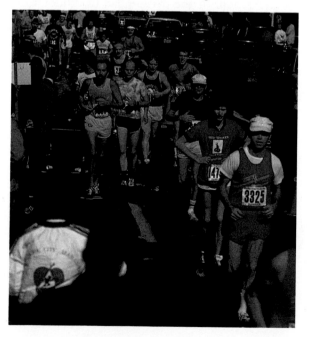

holy status. Thousands of young people joined "Moonie" communities completely closed to outsiders. Moon's critics pointed out that Moonies worked for no wages in a variety of enterprises from packing frozen fish to manufacturing shoes. The Reverend Moon, they said, was really keeping his followers in bondage, helped by their religious fervor. And parents of Moonies claimed that their children were brainwashed into rejecting everyone but fellow Moonies.

A Revolution in Morals.

Only a tiny minority of people looked for fulfillment in cults. But American society was influenced by the increasing belief that traditional moral codes were outmoded

Discussion Question: Should the cults mentioned in this section be protected by the rights associated with freedom of religion? Why or why not?

The Reverend Jerry Falwell became a leader for many fundamentalist Christian Americans who saw themselves as part of a "Moral Majority."

and restrictive. Marriage and raising families, once part of the "American dream," seemed to become less important.

The birth rate had dropped from a high of 25 births per 1,000 people in 1955 to 14.8 in 1975. People were having fewer children for several reasons, including a concern about overpopulation. For many, though, children meant unwanted responsibility.

The family itself seemed threatened. The divorce rate hovered near 50 percent of American marriages. Divorce seemed to be the answer to even minor marital difficulties. Marriage was often viewed as a means of self-fulfillment, rather than as a contract for religious or social purposes.

Preserving Nature.

In only three areas did the idealism and social activism of the 1960s seem to survive. One was in the conservation move-ment. The Sierra Club, Wilderness Society, and organizations like *Greenpeace* worked actively to set aside natural lands for the enjoyment of future generations. Americans had known about the benefits of having wild land ever since the first national parks had been set aside in the early 1900s. But public consciousness about the dangers of pollution, nuclear power, and extinction of species continued to rise. Annual "Earth Days," on which people demonstrated for pollution controls and learned what they could do to help, attracted increasing numbers of supporters.

Ethnic Revival.

Ethnic consciousness also increased during the 1970s. It was inspired by *Roots*, the best-selling book by a black author, Alex Haley. *Roots* was an account of Haley's ancestor, Kunta Kinte, a Mandingo warrior of West Africa who had been enslaved and brought to the United States.

Tens of thousands of people joined the search for their own ethnic heritages. Few could trace ancestors more than a few generations. But the decade saw a great revival in Italian-American, Polish-American, and Irish-American societies and special observances of the many different cultures which went into building America.

Women's Liberation.

The most important social movement of the decade had to do not with ethnic origins but with sexual discrimination. In 1966, Betty Friedan, who had written *The Feminine Mystique* in 1963, founded the *National Organization for Women (NOW)*. Determined to overturn all laws that discriminated against women on the basis of their sex, NOW admitted sympathetic men as well as women.

Other feminist groups, however, refused to admit men. The militant feminists said that only by breaking loose from masculine control could women gain their rightful place in society. For example, in some states, married women were not permitted to have a bank account in their own name. Many such laws that clearly discriminated against women were changed.

Affirmative Action.

Feminists also succeeded in placing at least a token number of women in most occupations formerly held only by men. Almost every large city put women on the regular

Class Activity: Have certain members of the class devise an anonymous questionnaire to administer to the class. Have the questions deal with issues of women's rights and see how the class feels about these issues.

788

police and fire departments. For the first time other than during war, women could be found doing heavy construction work, driving buses, and performing similar jobs formerly thought to be men's work.

To get more than token representation in the professions, women's groups allied with racial and ethnic minorities to demand *affirmative action.* State and federal officials began requiring government agencies, universities, law schools, medical schools, and corporations to hire women, blacks, Hispanics, and the physically handicapped rather than only white males, if the credentials of all applicants were equal.

Equal Rights Amendment. The chief goal of the feminists was to add the *Equal Rights Amendment (ERA)* to the Constitution. The ERA was meant to prohibit states and the federal government from discriminating against women in any way. Approved by Congress in 1972, the amendment was ratified by 35 of the 38 states needed to add it to the Constitution. Then the amendment stalled.

Phyllis Schlafly, a successful writer with conservative sympathies, mounted an active opposition to the ERA. She argued that women would lose certain traditional privileges if the ERA were adopted. Schlafly also claimed that under the ERA, women would be drafted into the army and separate lavatories for men and women would be

Former First Ladies Betty Ford (left) and Lady Bird Johnson (center) actively supported the national campaign for ratification of the ERA.

illegal. When the 1979 deadline for ratification approached, not a single additional state had approved the amendment.

Congress extended the deadline to 1982. But the ERA again did not receive the votes needed for passage. Americans were growing more conservative politically, and coupled with the general decline of interest in political and social issues during the 1970s, feminists' ability to generate interest in their issues declined.

Phyllis Schlafly (left) led the forces opposing the ERA. Gloria Steinem (right) was a leader of the women's movement.

SECTION REVIEW

1. Write a sentence to identify: Natchez Trace, ERA, "Earth Days," Betty Friedan.

2. How did the mood of the American people in the 1970s differ from their spirit in the 1960s? What reflected this difference?

3. Discuss changes in American thinking about marriage and the family during the 1970s.

4. Explain the goal and describe the methods of affirmative action.

5. What forms did the country's bicentennial celebration take?

CHAPTER REVIEW

TIME LINE

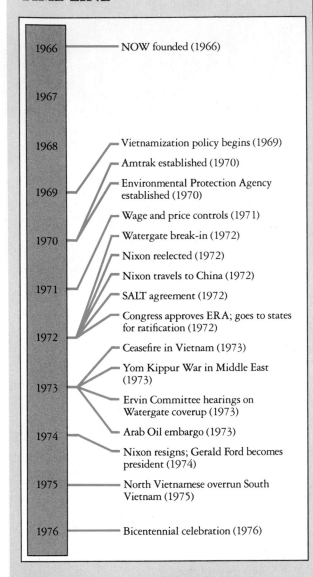

1966	NOW founded (1966)
1967	
1968	Vietnamization policy begins (1969)
1969	Amtrak established (1970)
	Environmental Protection Agency established (1970)
1970	Wage and price controls (1971)
	Watergate break-in (1972)
1971	Nixon reelected (1972)
	Nixon travels to China (1972)
	SALT agreement (1972)
1972	Congress approves ERA; goes to states for ratification (1972)
	Ceasefire in Vietnam (1973)
1973	Yom Kippur War in Middle East (1973)
	Ervin Committee hearings on Watergate coverup (1973)
1974	Arab Oil embargo (1973)
	Nixon resigns; Gerald Ford becomes president (1974)
1975	North Vietnamese overrun South Vietnam (1975)
1976	Bicentennial celebration (1976)

TIME LINE QUESTIONS

1. Name the events that took place *before* Gerald Ford took office: Yom Kippur War, bicentennial celebration, SALT agreement.
2. In which year did the incident that led to Richard Nixon's resignation occur?
3. Name a significant event in the woman's movement.
4. Identify an event important to détente.

SKILLS STRATEGY

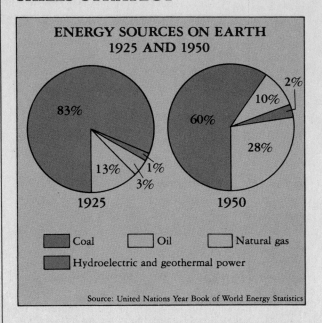

ENERGY SOURCES ON EARTH 1925 AND 1950

1925: 83%, 13%, 1%, 3%
1950: 60%, 28%, 10%, 2%

Coal ◻ Oil ◻ Natural gas
Hydroelectric and geothermal power

Source: United Nations Year Book of World Energy Statistics

PIE GRAPHS

Like all graphs, *pie* (or circle) graphs show relationships between or among sets of data. An advantage of these graphs is that they can present much information in limited space. To get the information from a pie graph, begin by reading the title, any labels, the symbols, and the key.

Each wedge on the three completed pie graphs above is a different color. Refer to the key to learn what source of energy each color symbolizes. The graphs themselves are identified by year, and each wedge is labeled to indicate a percentage. The total of all the percentages shown in a circle graph is 100 percent.

The different-colored wedges in the first three graphs represent all (100 percent) of the resources people all over the world used to produce energy (for example, electricity) in the years 1925, 1950, and 1975. Notice that a new source of energy appears on the 1975 graph, as well as in the key. The 1980 graph is blank. This is the graph you will construct in the Applying Skills exercise.

APPLYING SKILLS

Use the data below to construct a pie graph for

Making Connections: Review the questions and topics presented in the Making Connections section that opens this chapter. In reviewing Nixon's resignation, look at the consequences of

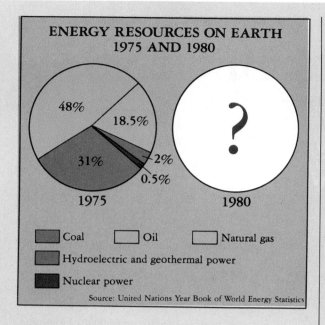

**ENERGY RESOURCES ON EARTH
1975 AND 1980**

48% 18.5% 31% 2% 0.5%

1975   1980

Coal   Oil   Natural gas

Hydroelectric and geothermal power

Nuclear power

Source: United Nations Year Book of World Energy Statistics

1980 on a piece of paper. Note that you must fill in one of the percentages below. (The total for all the percentages will be 100 percent.) Refer to the three completed graphs and the color keys above as you draw your graph and respond to the following questions.

Energy Source	Percentage of Use
(Coal)	27
(Oil)	———
(Gas)	19
(Hydro)	5
(Nuclear)	4

1. In what years was coal the prime energy source?
2. What resource replaced coal in 1975 as the most used source of energy?
3. Did the use of natural gas increase or decrease between 1925 and 1980?
4. Compare the use of nuclear power in 1975 to its use in 1980.
5. What may account for the decrease in the use of oil between 1975 and 1980?

CHAPTER 33 TEST

TEXT REVIEW

1. List President Nixon's successes in foreign policy during his first term.
2. Describe the role that Henry Kissinger played in President Nixon's cabinet.
3. Explain the reason for the decline in Kissinger's reputation after 1974.
4. List President Nixon's nominees to the Supreme Court. Which were appointed? Why were others rejected by the Senate?
5. What government agency was designated by the initials EPA? What is its function?
6. Write a chronological account of Watergate, beginning with the initial incident and ending with Nixon's pardon by President Ford.
7. Give the reason for OPEC's initiation of the oil embargo in 1973. Describe some of its effects in the United States.

CRITICAL THINKING

8. Suggest the effects the Vietnam War had on American prestige and the following aspects of life at home: morale of the American people, attitudes toward returning veterans, economic difficulties of the late 1970s.
9. Consider President Ford's stated reasons for his pardoning of Richard Nixon, and his resolution of the *Mayaquez* incident. What conclusions can you draw about what Ford thought the country needed?
10. Compare the point of view of many Americans of the 1960s toward social problems with that of Americans of the 1970s.

WRITING A PARAGRAPH

In this chapter, you learned that Americans, who make up less than six percent of the world's population, use a disproportionate share of the earth's oil supply. The OPEC oil embargo in 1973 set Americans and other people in industrialized nations searching for alternate energy resources.

Investigate one of the following alternate sources of power, and write a paragraph about its potential for replacing oil in the future: hydroelectric, geothermal, nuclear, solar, wind.

this event. Discuss the positive side—the country was able to survive this enormous blow because the government continued functioning.

AMERICA'S THIRD CENTURY BEGINS

1976–Present

I think the true discovery of America is before us. I think the true fulfillment of our spirit, of our people, of our mighty and immortal land, is yet to come. THOMAS WOLFE

Making Connections. As the United States entered its third century, its people seemed to be looking for new leadership. The two presidents who followed Gerald Ford were newcomers to Washington, D.C. Each had very different ideas about the right direction for the country to take.

In this chapter, you will learn:

- What the Camp David Accords were, and why they were an important diplomatic triumph for President Carter
- How the imprisonment of 53 Americans in Iran affected President Carter's reelection campaign
- What influence political action committees had on the elections of 1980
- Why the Reagan administration faced huge federal budget deficits
- How President Reagan's anti-Communist philosophy shaped his foreign policy
- What changes occurred in the make-up and distribution of the American population in the 1980s

You know that the Vietnam War and the Watergate scandal were wrenching experiences for the United States. Americans were wary of their political leaders. Consequently, they were receptive to new leaders who promised new ideas. As you read, note how presidents Carter and Reagan tried to change the policies of their predecessors.

Sections
1. The Carter Years
2. The Reagan Administration
3. America in the 1980s

1. THE CARTER YEARS

Jimmy Carter was from the small town of Plains, Georgia. He had been a successful farmer, businessman, and governor of Georgia. People respected him. As a young man he had opposed segregation in Georgia when many southern civic leaders had supported it. As governor of Georgia he had won the support of the state's black and white citizens.

But outside of Georgia few voters had heard of him. When Carter announced that he would campaign for president in 1976, one poll showed that only two percent of the Democratic voters knew his name.

The Campaign of 1976. Carter overcame his obscurity through tireless campaigning. In Iowa and New Hampshire, the first states to select delegates to nominating conventions, he presented himself at hundreds of local meetings, shaking hands, smiling, and greeting voters.

Carter said that his lack of experience in federal government was an asset. He had not been involved in any of the decisions responsible for Vietnam, Watergate, or the troubling economy. He emphasized that he could be trusted to do the moral thing, thus reminding voters of Nixon's

Students such as these in the photograph on the right will soon be making American history. Future students of American history will judge their achievements.

Quotation: from the novel *You Can't Go Home Again.* Other works by Thomas Wolfe (1900–1938) include *The Web of Earth, A Portrait of Bascom Hawke, Of Time and the River, The Web and the Rock,* and *Look Homeward Angel.*

Skills Review: Reinforce the skills learned in the preceding Skills Strategy section. Have students make a graph of the information on the Arab OPEC oil embargo, presented on pages 784–785 of this text. Let students figure out how to use the information to make the graphs themselves.

793

PROFILES OF THE PRESIDENCY

*O*n Inaugural Day, Jimmy Carter decided to break tradition and walk to the Capitol:

The inaugural parade route stretched before us with tens of thousands of people lining the streets. I leaned forward and told the Secret Service driver to stop the automobile, then touched Rosalynn's hand and said, "Let's go!" The security men looked all around, saw only friendly faces and opened the doors of the long black limousine. As we stepped into the street . . . a shock wave went through the crowd. There were gasps of astonishment and cries of "They're walking!" The excitement flooded over us; we responded to the people with broad smiles and proud steps. It was bitterly cold, but we felt warm inside. Even our nine-year-old daughter Amy got the spirit, walking in front . . . and carefully placing her small feet on the white centerline. It was one of those few perfect moments in life when everything seems absolutely right.

—MEMOIRS, 1982

deception and Ford's pardon of the Watergate president. Surprising the experts and confounding party professionals, Carter won most of the primaries he entered and was nominated on the Democratic Convention's first ballot.

Although many people assumed that when Gerald Ford gained the presidency he would not run for the position on his own, Ford decided to run. He was opposed in the primaries by former California governor Ronald Reagan, the favorite of the Republican conservatives, who came very close to defeating him at the convention. In fact, the conservatives were so strong despite their defeat that they forced Ford to run on a platform containing many policies the President did not support.

The election was close. Carter won 50 percent of the popular vote to Ford's 48 percent. In the electoral college, Carter won a 297–240 victory.

Poor Relations with Congress.

Carter had just squeaked into the White House, but he had a big Democratic majority in Congress. Or did he? Neither the President nor his staff, made up mostly of friends and business associates from Georgia, had contacts in Congress. Moreover, they showed little interest in cultivating congressional friends.

As a result, none of the major bills the President sent to Congress during his first year in office were adopted in the form Carter wanted. Attempts to solve the energy crisis and to reform social security and the tax structure were debated at great length. The laws finally returned for the President's signature bore little resemblance to the bills he had proposed.

The Economy Worsens.

Many of the problems Carter faced would have frustrated any president. Inflation ran at more than 10 percent each year of his presidency. Prices on some commodities rose almost 20 percent in 1980. By the end of Carter's single term in office, Americans had to spend a dollar to buy what cost fifteen cents in 1940.

But every option open to the president to fight inflation forced people out of work, increasing an already high rate of unemployment. When the Federal Reserve System forced interest rates up in 1979, the jobless rate jumped from 5.8 percent to 7.1 percent. Moreover, high interest rates alienated people with jobs who wanted to buy homes and cars on credit. The nearly universal American dream of home ownership became impossible for all but the prosperous when the annual interest on mortgages rose to more than 20 percent. It meant that the annual interest on a loan of $50,000 was $10,000.

The Energy Crisis. Rising energy costs were a big part of the Carter inflation. The price of a barrel of foreign crude oil rose from $13 in 1978 to more than $31 in 1980. In the same year the total bill for oil purchased from the OPEC nations totaled $73 billion. This affected the price of almost everything that Americans consumed and produced.

Almost all American farmers used gasoline-powered tractors. Much of the nation's electricity was generated by diesel turbines. Practically all of the American transportation system ran on oil. Food, electricity, and even the price of lumber hauled to the Plains states were affected by the cost of crude.

Carter did what he could. He urged Americans to consider it a moral duty to cut down their consumption of petroleum products. But many people believed that the "energy crisis" was a fraud perpetrated by the oil companies. They noted that the big refiners continued to roll up huge profits while actually reducing production of cheaper domestic oil. Carter asked for and Congress eventually approved a *windfall profits tax* that would finance the search for new sources of energy. But he did not get it. Americans imported more OPEC oil in 1979 than they did in 1976.

Carter's Diplomatic Breakthroughs. In foreign policy President Carter was responsible for several important breakthroughs. He appointed fellow Georgian Andrew Young, a black man and former aide to Martin Luther King, Jr., to be ambassador to the United Nations. His mere presence and energetic eloquence made Young immediately popular with Third World nations, especially in Africa.

But Young annoyed the President on several occasions with uncompromising condemnations of apartheid, or strict segregation, in South Africa, a white-dominated African country friendly to the United States. However, Carter seemed to feel that occasional embarrassments were a small price to pay for Young's services. In August 1979, however, it was revealed that Young had met with leaders of the *Palestine Liberation Organization* (PLO), a terrorist anti-Israeli alliance the United States refused to recognize. The public outcry was too great for Carter to ignore, and he asked Young to resign.

Long lines formed at gasoline stations during the worst of the energy crisis. Various rationing measures were used in different states.

OIL IMPORTS · 1972–1980

IMPORTS (in thousands of barrels) / YEAR

Historical Statistics of the United States

Carter also aroused opposition when he negotiated a treaty that gave control of the Panama Canal to the Republic of Panama. The United States leased but did not own the Panama Canal Zone that surrounded the Atlantic-to-Pacific waterway and split Panama in two. Nor was the canal as vital as it once had been, as it had become too small for many of the new, larger ships.

Nevertheless, to many conservatives the canal was a symbol of American power abroad. In speeches, Ronald Reagan expressed the view that the "giveaway" of the Panama Canal was a shameful example of the loss of nerve of the Carter administration.

In 1979, Carter extended formal recognition to the People's Republic of China, finishing a process begun in 1972 by Richard Nixon. Still, recognition meant officially breaking relations with the Nationalists of Taiwan and giving Taiwan's seat in the UN to the People's Republic. Although Carter continued to guarantee Taiwan's security, Republican conservatives denounced his action as the selling-out of an old friend.

Camp David. Carter's accomplishment in the Middle East, on the other hand, was a triumph. Israel and Egypt had laid the foundation for official relations when Egyptian President Anwar Sadat addressed the Israeli legislature. However, relations had broken down over Israeli Prime Minister Menachem Begin's reluctance to return the Sinai Peninsula to Egypt. Begin also would not agree to a state for the Palestinians (Arabs who had once lived in Israeli territory), as Sadat demanded.

In September 1978, Carter brought Begin and Sadat together at Camp David, the forested presidential retreat in Maryland. When Begin refused to make any concessions regarding the PLO, Sadat angrily packed his bags and started to leave. Carter, who had close personal relations with both Sadat and Begin, urged him to stay one more night. When Sadat agreed, Carter persuaded Begin to face up to the fact that the Camp David meeting was an historic opportunity for peace in the Middle East that might never occur again.

Begin's concessions were less than Sadat wanted, but they included the return of the Sinai. These *Camp David Accords* won for Israel formal recognition by an Arab state, Egypt. Sadat and Begin were awarded the Nobel Peace Prize.

A Moralistic Foreign Policy. Just as he appealed to Begin and Sadat, Carter also appealed to Americans' moral sensibilities. He dedicated his

In September 1978, President Carter brought Israeli Prime Minister Menachem Begin (left) and Egyptian President Anwar Sadat (right) together to make peace between their two countries.

MIDDLE EAST IN CONFLICT, 1949- PRESENT

- American fleet
- Oil fields
- Oil tankers

SOVIET UNION

RUMANIA
YUGO.
BULGARIA
ALBANIA
GREECE

BLACK SEA

CASPIAN SEA

Ankara
TURKEY

MEDITERRANEAN SEA

Inset

SYRIA

Nile R.

IRAQ

Baghdad

Tehran

IRAN
Shah of Iran
overthrown, 1979

Iran-Iraq War begins,
Sep. 1980

American hostage
crisis, Nov. 1979

Soviet invasion/
occupation, Dec. 1979

Kabul

AFGHANISTAN

PAKISTAN

KUWAIT

PERSIAN
GULF

BAHRAIN

Riyadh

QATAR

UNITED ARAB
EMIRATES

INDIA

LIBYA

EGYPT
Sadat assassinated

RED SEA

SAUDI ARABIA

OMAN

SUDAN

YEMEN

SOUTH
YEMEN

ARABIAN SEA

0 ____ 1000 Mi.
0 ____ 1000 Km

ARAB-ISRAELI CONFLICT

- Israel in 1949
- Occupied by Israel in Six-Day War, 1967
- Israel withdrawal from Sinai, 1974-1981

Palestinian refugee camps
War in Lebanon, 1975-

LEBANON
Beirut
Damascus
SYRIA

ISRAEL

Tel Aviv
Jerusalem

Jordan R.

Amman

Dead Sea

JORDAN

Alexandria

Port Said

Suez Canal

Cairo
Suez crisis, 1956

EGYPT

Nile R.

Yom Kippur
War, 1973

SINAI PENINSULA

Eilat

Palestinian refugee camps

SAUDI ARABIA

RED SEA

administration to the cause of human rights everywhere in the world. The United States would expose violations of basic rights wherever they occurred and cut off aid to allies who were guilty of them. By emphasizing morality in foreign policy, Carter hoped to contrast his approach to world affairs with Henry Kissinger's *realpolitik*.

In the case of unfriendly nations, Carter found it easy to carry out his human rights policy. He condemned the Soviet Union for punishing protesters like the scientist Andrei Sakharov. Sakharov was exiled from his Moscow home for criticizing the government. Carter also drew attention to Soviet anti-Semitism. Like the old czarist regime, the Soviets discriminated against Jews and

refused to grant passports to many Jews who wanted to leave the country.

When the Soviet Union urged the destruction of Poland's independent labor union, *Solidarity*, Carter spoke eloquently about liberties and rights. When the Soviet Union invaded Afghanistan in December 1979, Carter suspended the six-month-old *SALT II* treaty, designed to head off the nuclear arms race. He also canceled American trade agreements with the Soviet Union. In 1980, because of Afghanistan, Carter did not allow Americans to compete in the Moscow Olympics.

Ignoring Trouble in Iran. In regard to violations of human rights by friendly nations, Carter's

Class Activity: Contrast Kissinger's *Realpolitik* with Carter's moralistic approach. Are they different? If so, how? Direct the discussion to include information about how each person handled situations in the Middle East, in the Soviet SALT talks, and in the Chile and Iran situations.

 797

idealism was difficult to put into practice. He could not alienate the undemocratic and sometimes brutal regimes in Latin America and Africa that the United States supported. Many government officials felt that a friendly dictatorship was preferable to an unfriendly dictatorship.

Much more serious was the case of Iran, a rich, powerful neighbor of the Soviet Union, and an OPEC nation. The United States supported the government of Shah Reza Pahlavi (rē′ zə pä′lə-vē′). The Shah tolerated no dissent and his secret police, the notorious *Savak,* imprisoned and tortured hundreds of political opponents.

The Shah succeeded in alienating almost every segment of Iranian society. The comfortable and modern middle class of Teheran disapproved of Savak and wanted a voice in governing the country. The industrial working class of the country was inclined to favor socialism or even communism as a means of improving their lot. Most important, the Shah had angered the powerful Moslem priests, mullahs and ayatollahs (holy men), by seizing their property and by bringing western ideas, dress, and culture into Iran. The Moslem clergy still dominated the largest group in the population, rural peasants who had hardly been touched by the twentieth century.

Nevertheless, Carter referred to this powder keg of a nation as "an island of stability" in the Middle East. However, in 1978, Iran burst into rebellion. At first, the Shah kept some control, but then his army deserted him. They refused to fire on their fellow Iranians.

The Hostage Crisis.

In January 1979, after months of disorder, the Shah fled Iran. At the same time, the Ayatollah Ruholla Khomeini (kō-män′ē), the hard-line Moslem religious leader who had been exiled by the Shah, returned to Iran. Khomeini began to turn Iran back into a traditional Moslem nation. Consequently, everything that had to do with the Shah, the West, and the United States was condemned as villainous. When Carter admitted the ailing Shah to the United States for treatment in October, Iranian students stormed the American embassy in Iran's capital, Teheran, and took 53 Americans hostage.

This was a blatant violation of international law. But Khomeini's hatred of all Americans put Carter in a helpless position. Every attempt to free the hostages through intermediaries or negotiation failed. Whipped into a nationalistic frenzy, Iranians held the United States responsible for every misfortune Iran had suffered. The Ayatollah used the hostages as leverage for his religious party to seize control of the country.

On April 24, 1980, Carter secretly ordered a specially trained commando unit to free the hostages by force. The force landed in the desert outside Teheran, but a collision of helicopters caused the complete abandonment of the mission. After the failed rescue attempt, the Iranians moved the hostages to unknown locations. Negotiations were eventually reopened, but not until the day Carter stepped down from the presidency —January 20, 1981—were the hostages released.

The Election of 1980.

Ironically, the Iranian hostage crisis won Jimmy Carter the Democratic nomination for president in 1980 and assured his defeat in the general election. In November 1979, before the hostages were taken, Carter's popularity stood at a record low. Not even in the last days of Watergate had so many people disapproved of a president's performance. Polls of Democrats showed that Senator Edward Kennedy of Massachusetts, brother of John and Robert, would easily defeat Carter in the Democratic primaries.

After the hostages were seized, however, the natural desire of the people to unite behind a

Ayatollah Khomeini's followers held 53 Americans (one shown below) hostage for over a year.

president in times of crisis pushed Carter's popularity up. Kennedy continued to campaign, and gained many delegates. But Carter's power as the incumbent president and the voters' anxiety for the hostages gave Carter the Democratic nomination after a hard-fought campaign.

As had happened in 1968 and 1972, the Democrats were badly split. Kennedy backers did not give Carter their full support, and the President's popularity was still not very high. Meanwhile, the conservative Ronald Reagan easily beat back challenges by more moderate Republicans, George Bush and Illinois Congressman John Anderson. Reagan took Bush as his vice presidential candidate. Anderson decided to run as an independent candidate.

Reagan avoided the hostage question. He said he did not want to interfere with Carter's efforts and only hinted that he would have dealt with the crisis more effectively. Instead he focused on the failure of Carter's economic policies and promised to break with the New Deal tradition of government intervention in the economy.

Reagan was helped by the hostage issue. By election day the crisis had dragged on for exactly one year. Negotiations to bring the hostages home dragged on, with no end in sight. This added to the belief that Carter was simply not up to the standards of leadership required of a president.

Reagan also had some formidable political allies. Although federal law put limits on the amount of money a candidate's campaign committee could spend, there was no cap on the amount that other, supposedly independent groups could spend on behalf of the candidates they supported. These *political action committees* (PACs) spent many millions of dollars in 1980 to support Reagan and to oppose certain liberal senators.

One of the leading conservative forces in the campaign was a group known as the *Moral Majority*. Led by such fundamentalist preachers as Jerry Falwell, the Moral Majority appealed to voters on moral issues. Its members wanted to have prayer allowed in public schools, to defeat the ERA, and to reinstate what they perceived as traditional American values. They supported Reagan, and they forced many candidates to adopt more conservative positions so as to appeal to those voters who would be inclined to agree with the Moral Majority.

Almost every political expert predicted a very close election, but the outcome was very different. Reagan won a large majority—43.9 million votes to 35.5 million for Carter, with 5.7 million going to John Anderson. In the electoral college, Reagan won 489 votes to only 49 for Carter.

SECTION REVIEW

1. Identify: windfall profits tax, Andrew Young, PLO, Solidarity.
2. What was remarkable about Democrat Jimmy Carter's nomination and election to the presidency in 1976? Who was his opponent in the election?
3. Give examples of President Carter's domestic policy problems. Cite one diplomatic triumph that he scored.
4. Explain how the hostage crisis helped and hurt President Carter in the 1980 campaign. Who won the presidential election that year? What was his point of view?

---

2. THE REAGAN ADMINISTRATION

Ronald Reagan had been a popular film actor and television show host before serving two terms as governor of California and making several tries to win the presidency. Democrats scoffed at his lack of administrative ability, but Reagan actually made a better impression than did Jimmy Carter. His popularity held firm and even increased. By 1983, signs of an economic recovery even won broader approval for his economic policies, which critics had attacked as being designed to help the rich at the expense of the middle and lower classes. By the time of the 1984 presidential election, continuing signs of renewed prosperity worked to Reagan's political advantage.

A Conservative Movement. Reagan's advisers regarded the stunning 1980 victory as a mandate for a conservative revolution in national economic policy. Not only had Ronald Reagan sailed into office, half a dozen of the Senate's leading Democratic liberals were defeated by conservative op-

*T*he truth about the American economy in the 1980s was not pleasant, Ronald Reagan warned, but had to be faced:

I regret to say that we are in the worst economic mess since the Great Depression. A few days ago I was presented with a report I had asked for—a comprehensive audit if you will of our economic condition. You won't like it, I didn't like it, but we have to face the truth and then go to work to turn things around. And . . . we can turn them around.

Over the years we've let negative economic forces run out of control. We've stalled the judgment day. We no longer have that luxury. We're out of time.

We can leave our children with an unrepayable massive debt and a shattered economy or we can leave them liberty in a land where every individual has the opportunity to be whatever God intended us to be. All it takes is a little common sense and recognition of our own ability.

—SPEECH, FEBRUARY 5, 1981

ponents. For the first time in nearly 30 years, the Republicans had a majority in the Senate. The Democrats maintained a majority in the House of Representatives, but their margin was narrowed. When conservative Democrats, known as *"boll weevils,"* voted for the President's policies, the Democrats' majority disappeared.

The election results may be seen as a reaction to Jimmy Carter and the disillusionment Americans felt during his administration. Ronald Reagan's skill as a speaker and campaigner was also instrumental in the Republican victory. He was able to present more moderate views as well and attract a wider range of support. Perhaps another factor in the election was the poor voter turn out. Only about half the voters had cast ballots and made their wishes known at the polls.

Reagan's Economic Policies.
Reagan wasted little time in implementing his policies. With the help of the *"boll weevils"* in Congress, he introduced the most innovative legislative program since Johnson's Great Society. However, unlike Johnson's attempt to use the government as an equalizer between poor and rich, Reagan felt that the capitalist system could take care of itself if the government kept its hands off.

First, the President argued that huge government expenditures and the resulting deficits were

responsible for inflation. He quickly convinced Congress to cut $35 billion from the budgets of social welfare programs like Medicare, food stamps, and free school lunches for poor children.

Second, Reagan's *supply side* economic theory held that the way to cure unemployment was to cut taxes and reduce government regulations. In theory, the untaxed money of the wealthy would be invested in industry, thus creating jobs for working people. Supply side economics resembled the economic policies of Calvin Coolidge and Andrew Mellon in the 1920s. In fact, Reagan dramatized his admiration for Coolidge by hanging his portrait in a conspicuous place in the White House.

In the short run, his policies would cause higher unemployment, the President warned. But he urged Americans to "stay the course." By 1981 the economy would be swinging upward. In fact, unemployment continued to rise through 1982 when it topped 11 percent, higher than at any time since the 1930s. Then, early in 1983, the unemployment rate began to decline, as did the inflation rate.

The Deficit Grows Larger.
The reduction of spending on social programs and tax cuts for potential investors were compatible policies. However, spending more on the military destroyed any chance of achieving Reagan's goal of balancing the federal budget.

Discussion Question: How are the policies of Presidents Reagan and Coolidge similar?

The Reagan administration proposed increased military spending to match Soviet military spending and restore America's prestige. The resulting arms buildup contributed to huge overall deficits —close to $200 billion yearly by 1983. Increased expenditures on new weapons systems resulted not in balanced budgets but in increases in the *ceiling of the national debt* (the legal limit of borrowing the government allows itself) approved by Congress.

In 1981, as debate continued on how to control spending, the accumulated national debt reached $998 billion. In 1982, for the first time, the national debt owed by the United States rose to over $1 trillion. President Reagan was faced with a larger government deficit than any president before him.

At the same time, the inflation rate and unemployment were on the decline, and the economy seemed on the road to recovery. At the beginning of 1984, a majority of Americans polled thought the Republican party was more frugal with tax revenues than their opponents.

Hanging Tough with China and the Soviets.

President Reagan did not, as he hinted he might, break relations with the People's Republic of China and recognize Nationalist China instead. However, he was less friendly to the People's Republic than Nixon, Ford, and Carter had been. There were no good-will flights to Peking nor invitations to Chinese leaders to call at the White House when Reagan entered office.

Reagan had been a critic of détente when Henry Kissinger first defined it. He believed that the SALT II treaty had been "a one-way street," with Americans making all the concessions to the Soviets. He used his influence in the Senate to block the treaty's ratification. He consistently described the Soviets in the harshest terms, saying that they were untrustworthy and committed to world domination. The relaxation of East-West tensions that had occurred in the Nixon-Ford years seemed to be coming to an end.

When Premier Leonid Brezhnev of the Soviet Union died in November 1982, the world waited to see who would succeed him. Yuri Andropov, who seemed to be a moderate, eventually took Brezhnev's place, but Reagan's opinion about the Soviets did not change. He even referred to the Soviet Union as an "evil empire," and the American-Soviet relationship remained cool. Not until May 1984 did he follow his predecessors' example and pay a visit to the People's Republic of China. Even at that time, Reagan used the occasion to openly express his views about the Soviet Union.

Nervousness in Europe.

Reagan's tough talk about the Soviet Union caused uneasiness among America's European allies. Large numbers of people in Western Europe, especially in West Germany, feared that the Reagan policies might lead to a nuclear war in which they would be the first Soviet targets. Exploiting these anxieties, Andropov proposed several plans for arms reduction in Europe that he knew Reagan would never accept. He hoped to split the NATO alliance, and hoped to have the Soviets appear more friendly to Europe than the United States.

However, European leaders, including Chancellor Helmut Kohl of West Germany, Prime Minister Margaret Thatcher of Great Britain, and even President François Mitterand of France, a *socialist,* remained loyal to the alliance. Even when antinuclear demonstrations were numerous during the installation of new American nuclear missiles in Europe, these leaders remained firm. Andropov's strategy had misfired, and he too began speaking belligerently.

After the nuclear weapons were installed, however, the European leaders asked Reagan to soften his words about the Soviets. Andropov died in early 1984, and the new Soviet leader, Konstantin Chernenko, was not tied to all of the policies of his predecessors. Chernenko used some conciliatory language, and in March 1984, after Chancellor Kohl had visited Washington and urged Reagan to improve Soviet-American relations, the President said that some sort of peaceful arrangement could be made. Then, in April, Reagan traveled to China for meetings with Chinese leaders. Reagan had made the point that the United States would no longer back down from difficult confrontations. Reagan would from then on negotiate from a position of strength.

Troubles in Central America.

When President Reagan took office, Fidel Castro was still in power in Cuba and still promoting revolution in

Central America. In 1979, the armed assistance provided by Cuban "volunteers" was at least partly responsible for the overthrow of a *repressive* military government in Nicaragua. The victorious rebels in Nicaragua, the *Sandinistas,* established a *regime* similar to Cuba's.

The presence of a second pro-Communist regime in Latin America alarmed Reagan and his advisers. They feared that other nations in the region might also fall prey to pro-Communist rebels. Already the smallest country in Central America, El Salvador, was torn between rebels supported by Cuba and Nicaragua and a right-wing military government that, though friendly to the United States, used terroristic tactics against anyone suspected of aiding the rebels. Americans were shocked to learn in 1984 that the murder of several women from the United States, including Roman Catholic nuns, was the work of an army their country supported.

Nevertheless, Reagan insisted that the spread of communism in Central America must be stopped. His Central American policy was given a boost in May 1984 when, in a free election, the people of El Salvador elected a moderate, José Napoleon Duarte, to be president instead of a right-wing extremist believed to be the head of murderous "death-squads."

Marines in Lebanon.

While he insisted that no American soldiers would be sent to Central America, Reagan did, along with Great Britain, France, and Italy, send Marines to Lebanon in the Middle East. That tragic country was locked in a confusing civil war among numerous religious and tribal groups. To complicate matters all the more, Israel occupied the southern third of the country and Syria much of the eastern regions.

Reagan insisted that the troops would remain until a stable government representing all Lebanese groups had been formed. Congressional critics claimed that there were too few Marines to exercise real authority and, fearing another Vietnam, they would never agree to a larger force.

Then, in October 1983, a truck loaded with heavy explosives and driven by an anti-American suicide team, widely believed to be supported by Iran, crashed into marine headquarters just outside the Lebanese capital of Beirut. Digging through the wreckage of the headquarters, the stunned survivors of the blast counted 241 dead Americans.

Grenada Is Invaded.

The tragedy in Beirut caused Americans to wonder why Americans had been sent to Lebanon in the first place, and Democratic members of Congress stepped up their attacks on the president's policies as irresponsible. National attention, however, quickly shifted from Lebanon to Grenada when President Reagan sent American Marines and paratroopers into the tiny island nation of Grenada in the southern Caribbean. He explained that a brief civil war in Grenada had endangered the lives and liberties of 700 American medical students residing there. More important, however, was the nature of the civil war. The victorious rebel forces had been supported in their revolt by Cuban soldiers. Reagan could not tolerate the threat of yet another Communist base being established in the Western Hemisphere.

The invasion force of 6,000 easily took over the island. This apparent victory helped to prevent a blow to the president's prestige in February 1984 when he evacuated the troops from Lebanon, something he had said he would not do.

Prayer in Schools.

As the election year of 1984 began, President Reagan began to speak out on the moral issues that had been important to him in 1980. He backed a proposed constitutional amendment that would allow voluntary prayer in public school activities. The issue had been debated ever since school prayer had been banned by the Supreme Court as a violation of the constitutional separation of church and state. Conservative supporters in the Senate pushed for approval of the amendment. But when the vote was taken in March 1984, they fell 11 votes short of the required two-thirds majority.

The Democrats Prepare.

The defeat of the prayer amendment encouraged the Democrats to believe that despite the president's personal popularity they could win the presidency. When the primary elections began, eight men competed for the Democratic nomination. All the candidates asserted that *Reaganomics* had not reduced the *national deficit.* They claimed the program benefited the rich at the expense of the poor.

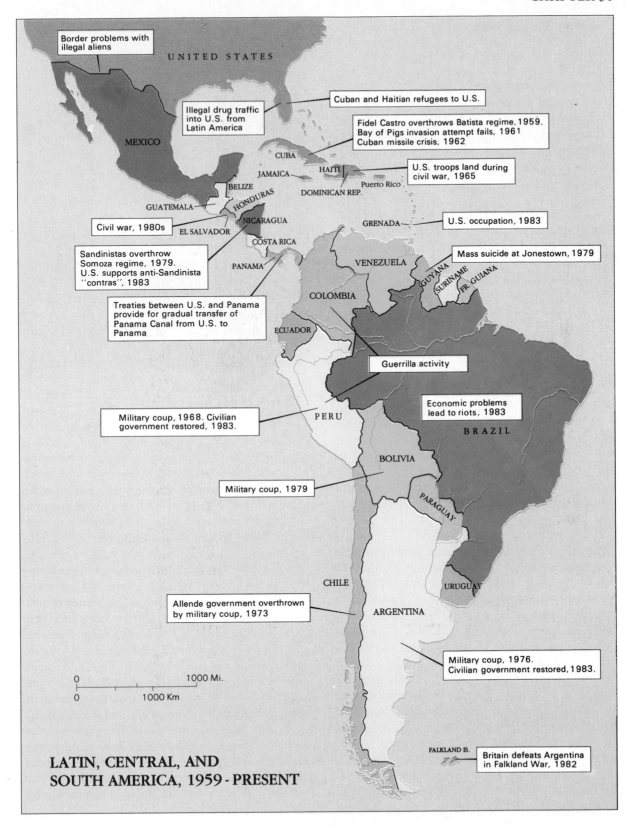

Border problems with illegal aliens

UNITED STATES

Illegal drug traffic into U.S. from Latin America

MEXICO

Cuban and Haitian refugees to U.S.

Fidel Castro overthrows Batista regime, 1959. Bay of Pigs invasion attempt fails, 1961 Cuban missile crisis, 1962

CUBA

JAMAICA

HAITI

BELIZE

HONDURAS

GUATEMALA

DOMINICAN REP.

Puerto Rico

U.S. troops land during civil war, 1965

Civil war, 1980s

NICARAGUA

EL SALVADOR

COSTA RICA

GRENADA

U.S. occupation, 1983

Sandinistas overthrow Somoza regime, 1979. U.S. supports anti-Sandinista "contras", 1983

PANAMA

VENEZUELA

Mass suicide at Jonestown, 1979

Treaties between U.S. and Panama provide for gradual transfer of Panama Canal from U.S. to Panama

COLOMBIA

GUYANA

SURINAME

FR. GUIANA

ECUADOR

Guerrilla activity

Economic problems lead to riots, 1983

Military coup, 1968. Civilian government restored, 1983.

PERU

BRAZIL

BOLIVIA

Military coup, 1979

PARAGUAY

CHILE

URUGUAY

Allende government overthrown by military coup, 1973

ARGENTINA

0   1000 Mi.

0   1000 Km

Military coup, 1976. Civilian government restored, 1983.

LATIN, CENTRAL, AND SOUTH AMERICA, 1959 - PRESENT

FALKLAND IS.

Britain defeats Argentina in Falkland War, 1982

Discussion Question: Nixon and Reagan are both considered conservative presidents. How are their personalities different? Are their policies very different?

The front-runner was Walter "Fritz" Mondale, the former vice president under Jimmy Carter who had the support of organized labor, the *AFL-CIO,* and most big city Democratic party leaders. Astronaut John Glenn of Ohio argued that because Mondale was associated with big-spending liberalism, only he could defeat Reagan. Other candidates included Senator Gary Hart of Colorado; George McGovern of South Dakota; Alan Cranston of California; Ruben Askew of Florida; and Ernest Hollings of South Carolina.

Two Surprises. A surprise candidate was the Rev. Jesse Jackson, a black preacher who had been an aide of Martin Luther King, Jr., and later made a name for himself by telling young blacks they should not blame everything on whites but, rather, that they should study hard in school in order to improve their lives. Jackson's exciting style of public speaking, perfected over many years in the pulpit, stood in sharp contrast to that of the other candidates. He was especially popular among black voters who turned out in the polls in record numbers to vote for him.

Still, it was Gary Hart who emerged from the pack to throw a scare into the Mondale campaign. Hart won several early primaries in New England and was stronger in the western states than the front-runner. Because he appealed to many young, middle-class voters of the baby-boom generation, Hart claimed he was the only Democrat who could defeat President Reagan.

Mondale Chooses a Woman. One by one, the Democratic challengers dropped out. By the time the Democratic convention met in San Francisco in July, only Hart and Jackson remained in the race. However, Mondale had more than enough delegate votes to win the nomination. The only question remaining was: whom would the Democrats pick to run as vice president?

On the eve of the convention, Mondale surprised the nation by selecting as his running mate Geraldine Ferraro, a congresswoman from New York. This choice, making Ferraro the first woman to run on a major party's presidential ticket, seemed to assure the Democrats of an increase in support from those women who had been angered by President Reagan's opposition to ERA. As an Italian-American, Ferraro was also expected to

Former Vice President Walter Mondale and Congresswoman Geraldine Ferraro were the Democratic Party's 1984 presidential ticket.

win the support of blue-collar ethnic voters, some of whom had been drifting away from the Democratic party. Perhaps most of all, her buoyant personality seemed to add life to a ticket that even many Democrats said was dull compared to that of the personable Ronald Reagan.

The Gender Gap. A persistent problem facing Reagan was the so-called *gender gap.* Careful analysis of the 1980 election results showed that women of nearly all political views were less likely to vote for Reagan than were men. The reason for some women's opposition to Reagan was clear insofar as he opposed the ERA, both as a candidate and as president. He also approved some policies that seemed to threaten the social gains women had made in the 1960s and 1970s.

Reagan attempted to answer these criticisms by appointing some women to high government positions. Several women served in his cabinet, and in his first year in office, Reagan named the first woman justice ever to sit on the Supreme Court, Sandra Day O'Connor.

Republican incumbent President Ronald Reagan and Vice President George Bush won the 1984 presidential election.

A Second Term. Despite the efforts of the Democratic Party, President Reagan and Vice President George Bush easily won reelection. Reagan won 525 electoral votes, while Mondale won only 13. Ten of Mondale's electoral votes came from his home state of Minnesota, with the remaining three votes coming from the District of Columbia. In a landslide victory, President Reagan carried the remaining 49 states, winning 59 percent of the popular vote. Whether because of the improving economy or the renewed spirit of confidence and patriotism that characterized the American mood in 1984, the "great communicator," as Ronald Reagan was called, had a second term in which to carry out his policies.

The Olympics. Even more than the 1984 election, the Olympics held in Los Angeles in August 1984 symbolized the new spirit abroad in America. It had seemed impossible to hold a successful Summer games. In recent years people had shown a reluctance to support mammoth shows. (Even in 1984, the New Orleans World's Fair was a finan-

cial disaster.) Then, in May, the Soviet Union announced that its team would boycott the games, and every nation in the Soviet bloc, except Rumania, followed suit.

In part, the Soviets were retaliating for Jimmy Carter's boycott of the Moscow Olympics of 1980. Many also believed, however, that the Soviets feared that too many of their athletes would defect from their teams once they were in the United States. In either case, the competition was injured by the loss of the Russians and East Germans in track and field events, gymnastics, and swimming, and by the Cubans in boxing.

Still, the Olympics were a stunning success. The pageantry was stirring and the contestants kept Americans, and much of the world, glued to

UNITED STATES OLYMPIC TEAM MEDAL BREAKDOWN BY SPORT SUMMER 1984				
SPORT	GOLD	SILVER	BRONZE	TOTAL
Archery	1	1	0	2
Athletics (Track & Field)	16	15	9	40
Basketball	2	0	0	2
Boxing	9	1	1	11
Canoe/Kayak	0	0	1	1
Cycling	4	3	2	9
Diving	2	3	3	8
Equestrian	3	2	0	5
Fencing	0	0	1	1
Field Hockey (women)	0	0	1	1
Gymnastics	5	5	6	16
Judo	0	1	1	2
Modern Pentathlon	0	1	0	1
Rowing	2	5	1	8
Shooting	3	1	2	6
Swimming	21	13	0	34
Synchronized Swimming	2	0	0	2
Volleyball	1	1	0	2
Water Polo	0	1	0	1
Weightlifting	0	1	1	2
Wrestling	9	3	1	13
Yachting	3	4	0	7
TOTALS	**83**	**61**	**30**	**174**

Source: *United States Olympic Committee*

At the 1984 Summer Olympics in Los Angeles, the American Olympic Team won 83 gold, 61 silver, and 30 bronze medals.

their television sets for two weeks. Because of the Olympic Committee's much criticized decision to recruit commercial sponsors for the games, the Los Angeles Olympics actually showed a profit. The money was set aside to finance future American Olympic teams and to promote sports in the underdeveloped nations.

SECTION REVIEW

1. Write a sentence to identify: "boll weevils," Beirut, Jesse Jackson.

2. Explain President Reagan's reasons for the following measures included in his economic program: cutting $35 billion from the budgets of social programs; cutting back income taxes; increasing expenditures for the military.

3. Explain President Reagan's point in "hanging tough" with the Soviet Union.

4. Describe the actions that President Reagan took concerning two Latin American countries.

3. AMERICA IN THE 1980s

As in all previous periods of history, Americans in the 1980s were challenged to make the difficult adjustment to changing circumstances. The pace of change in their time was rapidly accelerating and propelling their society into a future altogether different from what earlier generations had known.

The Sun Belt. The census of 1980 called attention to a remarkable phenomenon. A shift in population was fast changing the political and economic life of every American community. Throughout the 1970s, old cities of the Northeast and Midwest from Boston to St. Louis witnessed the closing of one factory after another. At the same time, in the South and West, such cities as San Diego, Denver, Houston, and Miami experienced unprecedented growth. Responding to the attraction of lower taxes, major corporations shifted their headquarters from colder and older American regions—the so-called *Frost Belt*—to the warmer and newer regions—the so-called *Sun Belt.*

Computers, Robots, and Lasers. One profound change both fascinated and frightened Americans in the 1980s. Although they had known about computers for many years, few were prepared for the coming of the microcomputers, whose moderate prices put them within reach of many American consumers. Advertisements touted the unlimited benefits of owning a home computer. Depending on how it was programmed, it could play video games, keep records, balance bank accounts, edit compositions, teach spelling, conserve heating fuel, and even defend against burglars.

The home computer was not yet as significant as television. But it was a conspicuous symbol of an electronic technology that was rapidly altering every institution in American culture from nursery schools to nursing homes. By 1984, banks, factories, farms, hospitals, stores, airports, schools, publishing firms and others were adopting computerized methods for processing information, delivering services, and distributing goods. Clearly, the country was in the midst of an economic revolution akin to the industrial revolution of an earlier era.

Important as it was, the computer was only one of the new technological marvels. Computerized robots became common on assembly lines in the most advanced American factories. Engineers were also discovering that *laser* beams, high intensity beams of light, had a nearly infinite number of practical applications. They could help surgeons operate on a patient's body and help defend against enemy missiles and satellites from outer space, as well as a variety of other tasks.

It was clear that, because of the computer and other technologies, old methods of producing goods and managing services were becoming outmoded. The need to adapt to the new *high technology* seemed paramount for economic survival of the country's industry.

The Space Shuttle. In the early 1980s, the *National Aeronautics and Space Administration (NASA)* developed the *space shuttle* as a reusable craft that could orbit like a spaceship and land like an airplane. The first shuttle, *Columbia,* successfully completed several flights. Its pilots did tests and even launched *communications satellites.*

The second shuttle, *Challenger,* was first launched in 1983. It was also used for making tests in space, and was equipped to catch satellites and pull them into its cargo bay for in-flight repairs. Two other firsts for the program were the first American woman in space, the physicist Sally K. Ride, and the first black American to orbit the earth, Air Force Lieutenant Colonel Guion Bluford. With the shuttle program, Americans took a long step toward possible human habitations in space.

Challenges From Abroad. Throughout their history, Americans had prided themselves on their inventiveness and industry. In the nineteenth century, they had built an industrial system that, for almost a century, out-produced and out-sold its major European rivals. But in the 1980s, American businesses came under heavy pressure from extremely able foreign competitors, particularly from Japanese automobile and electronics manufacturers. American dominance in world markets and leadership in technological innovation could no longer be taken for granted.

American leaders noted a startling statistic. Between 1972 and 1984, the productivity of the Japanese worker had increased by an amazing 80 percent. By comparison, an average American worker in 1984 was only 15 percent more productive. How could Americans close this gap, which placed United States businesses at a disadvantage in the fierce international competition for markets?

During the recession of the late 1970s and early 1980s, unions were forced to make concessions to keep plants running and hold their members' jobs. Automation increased, and new industries were developed. Productivity began to rise again, partly due to stronger commitment by American workers. Many people, especially young students, learned to cope with the new computer age, and to be more comfortable with the new technology in their daily lives.

There were other challenges from abroad that caused Americans to worry and wonder. Despite President Carter's efforts to win their good will, the nations of the Third World repeatedly denounced the United States on the floor of the United Nations. Furthermore, the threat of nuclear destruction seemed more real in the early 1980s than ever before. Many young Americans wondered if they would live to see the dawn of a new century. But as President Reagan said again and again in his masterful television speeches, the United States had survived past challenges. America's future growth and security were assured, he said, if Americans only remembered their courageous heritage and lived up to the pioneering spirit of earlier generations.

SECTION REVIEW

1. Discuss what the 1980 census revealed about the Frost Belt and the Sun Belt.

2. What happened to American businesses during the early 1980s? What were the causes and what were some of the effects on American workers?

3. Name three technological marvels that were of growing importance in the 1980s. Describe some of the uses of each.

4. According to President Reagan, how could Americans assure the future growth and security of their country?

Discussion Question: How could relations between Japan and the U.S. move us into a new age of protectionism? Do you see this as a possibility? Why or why not?

The microscope used in microsurgery permitted surgeons to operate on delicate tissue in extremely small areas. Surgery heretofore impossible became routine.

BART (Bay Area Rapid Transit), San Francisco's innovative transit system, inspired other urban mass transit networks.

Robotics is the field concerned with the building and use of robots, especially in industry. Robots perform repetitive tasks with great efficiency and accuracy. They work around the clock without stopping and require little supervision.

C H A N G I N G   T E C H N O L O G Y

19|40

19|50

Instant coffee produced
Hip replacement initiated
Pressure cooker perfected
Pre-cooked frozen food sold
Electric slicing knife marketed
(See also pp. 649 and 743.)

Freeze-dried food introduced
Automatic digital computer operational (Mark I, ENIAC, EDSAC)
Polaroid camera developed
Microwave cooker manufactured
(See also p. 743.)

Heart-lung machine invented
Supersonic combat fighter built
Velcro fastener patented
Bifocal contact lenses developed
Transistorized TVs marketed
(See also see p. 743.)

The percentage of American homes with televisions has risen steadily since the 1950s (1950—9.0%; 1955—64.5%; 1960—87.1%; 1970—95.2%; 1978—98%). What impact has this had on U.S. attitudes about its leaders and about itself?

By the 1980s, home computers became a part of everyday life.

The first American to walk in space was Edward H. White during the Gemini 4 flight. Outside the ship, an astronaut wears a many-layered suit and carries a life-support system on his back.

Microchips (integrated circuits) about the size of a fingernail made it possible to build desk-size computers.

The uses of lasers range from cutting metal, to measuring the enormous distances from earth to satellites, to use in the performance of delicate eye surgery.

19	60	19	70	19	80
Light-emitting diode (LED) invented	"Floppy-disc" recorder developed	Computer-aided manufacturing initiated
Artificial heart surgery initiated	Pocket calculator marketed	Mini-computer introduced
Biodegradable liquid detergent introduced	Thermonuclear power station operational	Video games prolifigate
Computer time-sharing developed	Supersonic airliner introduced	Pocket-sized TVs produced
	Mini tape player developed	Magnetic disc camera developed

Discussion Question: Where is technology leading us? Elicit both positive and negative responses to this question.

CHAPTER REVIEW

TIME LINE

1977	Jimmy Carter inaugurated (1977)
1978	Camp David Accords between Israel and Egypt (1978)
1979	United States recognizes People's Republic of China (1979)
	Soviet Union invades Afghanistan (1979)
	Americans in Iran taken hostage (1979)
1980	United States boycotts Moscow Olympics (1980)
	American attempt to rescue Iranian hostages (1980)
1981	Ronald Reagan inaugurated (1981)
	Hostages returned (1981)
	Reagan cuts taxes and government expenditures for domestic programs (1981)
1982	Sandra Day O'Connor becomes first woman Supreme Court Justice (1981)
1983	National debt goes over $1 trillion (1982)
	American troops occupy Grenada (1983)
1984	Reagan visits People's Republic of China (1984)
	Soviet Union boycotts Los Angeles Olympics (1984)

TIME LINE QUESTIONS

1. What event in 1979 provoked the United States boycott of the Moscow Olympics?
2. In what year did a historic meeting between Anwar Sadat and Menachem Begin take place?
3. List these events in chronological order: national debt rises to over $1 trillion, Americans taken hostage in Iran, People's Republic of China recognized, Jimmy Carter inaugurated.

SKILLS STRATEGY

SELECTING REFERENCES

Most libraries contain a card catalog and the basic reference books shown above. In researching a report, all of these sources can be valuable in finding information. If you need to refresh your memory on how to use one or more of these resources, consult the table of contents to find the chapters in which these skills were taught.

APPLYING SKILLS

Refer to the diagram and previous Skills Strategy lessons to answer the following questions.

1. Which source would give you the title of a book on the Iran hostage crisis if you knew the name of the book's author?
2. Which source would you use to get brief biographical information about Anwar Sadat?
3. Which source could tell you the distances between China's major cities?
4. Which source would give the pronunciation of a word you might see while researching robots?
5. Which source would cite recent magazine articles about American Indians?
6. Which source would give you the most up-to-date information on the progress of civil rights in the United States?

Making Connections: Review the questions and topics presented in the Making Connections section that opens this chapter. End the year with the impression that all the events in this chapter and in the book are important to what we will be like as a country in the future. Encourage students to think about what the next few years may be like in this country.

UNIT 10 TEST

CHAPTER SURVEY

In one or two sentences, summarize the content of the chapters from which these terms come, and write a sentence to identify *one* of the terms from each chapter.

1. *Chapter 32:* Peace Corps, Warren Commission, James Meredith, Watts, Ho Chi Minh.
2. *Chapter 33:* Kent State, Strategic Arms Limitation Talks, Burger Court, Organization of Petroleum Exporting Countries, Betty Freidan.
3. *Chapter 34:* Andrew Young, Palestine Liberation Organization, Reaganomics, Jesse Jackson, Sunbelt.

TEXT REVIEW

4. Explain this statement with facts from the text: "President Kennedy gave his support to the civil rights movement in the 1960s, but he moved very cautiously in doing so."
5. List some of the domestic legislation included in the Great Society program that President Lyndon Johnson steered through Congress with such surprising ease.
6. Compare President Johnson's Vietnam policy with the Vietnam policy of President Kennedy. How did President Johnson's policy affect the progress of the war in Vietnam? What was the result of this policy concerning Johnson's popularity with American citizens?
7. Describe the platforms of the candidates of the three parties in the 1968 presidential election. Who was the winner? Give the main reason for the successful campaign of the winning candidate.
8. List the major achievements of President Nixon's foreign policy. Describe one of these achievements in detail.
9. Who was the Secretary of State under presidents Nixon and Ford? Explain the role this Secretary of State played in the nation's foreign policy successes.
10. Describe the circumstances that brought Gerald Ford to the vice presidency and then to the presidency of the United States.

11. Give evidence that tends to support Tom Wolfe's labeling of the 1970s as "the Me decade."
12. Contrast the foreign policy of President Carter with that of Henry Kissinger and *realpolitik*. What was the outcome of the Camp David meeting, and why was it considered such a diplomatic triumph for Carter?
13. Give the important details about the crisis caused by Iran's taking of American hostages. How did this crisis both help and harm Jimmy Carter in his bid for reelection in 1980?
14. Describe the actions taken by President Reagan in *three* of these areas: social program budgets, tax cuts, military expenditures, relations with Latin America, school prayer, the Equal Rights Amendment.
15. Discuss *one* of the following: changes for minorities between 1970 and 1980, high technology in the 1980s.

CRITICAL THINKING

16. Compare the philosophies of Martin Luther King, Jr., the advocates of black power, and Malcolm X.
17. In *The Making of the President, 1968,* author Theodore H. White wrote "Were there no outside world, . . . Lyndon Johnson might conceivably have gone down as the greatest of twentieth-century presidents." Verify this opinion with facts from the text. State why Johnson's strengths as a congressional leader did not save his presidency from severe criticism.
18. Comment on this statement as it applies to people of your age. "America's future growth and security are assured if Americans remember their courageous heritage and live up to the pioneering spirit of earlier generations."

SKILLS REVIEW

19. Define *hypothesis*. Explain how a hypothesis is formed, and how its validity can be tested.
20. Name several basic reference sources you can use in research. Explain how you would use either the *Reader's Guide* or a library card catalog.

ATLAS AND REFERENCE SECTION

MAPS

TABLES AND GRAPHS

WORLD: POLITICAL BOUNDARIES AND CAPITAL CITIES, 1980s

ARCTIC OCEAN

UNION OF SOVIET
SOCIALIST REPUBLICS

GREENLA

ALASKA
UNITED STATES

CANADA

NORTH

AMERICA

Ottawa

UNITED STATES

Washington D C

ATLANTIC OCEAN

PACIFIC OCEAN

HAWAII
UNITED STATES

BAHAMAS

MEXICO
Havana • CUBA
HAITI
Mexico City
Port-au-Prince • DOMINICAN REP.
BELIZE
Puerto Rico
JAMAICA
Santo
GUADELOUPE
Belmopan
Domingo
MARTINIQUE
Guatemala
HONDURAS
BARBADOS
Tegucigalpa
TRINIDAD AND TOBAGO
GUATEMALA
NICARAGUA
San Salvador
GUYANA
EL SALVADOR
San Jose
Georgetown
SURINAME
Managua
Caracas
Paramaribo
COSTA RICA
Panama
FRENCH GUIANA
PANAMA
VENEZUELA
Bogota
COLOMBIA
Quito
ECUADOR

CAPE

BRAZIL

PERU
Lima
SOUTH AMERICA

La Paz
Brasilia
BOLIVIA
Sucre

PARAGUAY
Asuncion

URUGUAY
Santiago
CHILE
Buenos Aires
Montevideo
ARGENTINA

NEW CALEDONIA

NEW ZEALAND
Wellington

EUROPE

NORWAY
Oslo
FINLAND
Stockholm
SWEDEN
Helsinki

DENMARK
Copenhagen

U.S.S.R.

Dublin
IRELAND
UNITED
KINGDOM
NETH.
Berlin
POLAND
The Hague
E.
Warsaw
London
Brussels
Bonn
GERMANY
BELG.
Prague
LUX.
W.
CZECHOSLOVAKIA
Paris
GERMANY
Vienna
Budapest
FRANCE
Bern
AUSTRIA
SWITZ.
HUNGARY
ROMANIA
Belgrade
Bucharest
YUGOSLAVIA
ITALY
BULGARIA
Rome
Sofia
Tirane
PORTUGAL
Madrid
ALBANIA
SPAIN
GREECE
TURKEY
Lisbon
Athens

0   600 Mi.

0   600 Km.

814

UNION OF SOVIET SOCIALIST REPUBLICS

• Moscow

EUROPE
See inset

ASIA

Ulaanbaatar •
MONGOLIA

Ankara •
TURKEY

Beijing •

N. KOREA
• Pyongyang
• Seoul
S. KOREA

• Tokyo

Tunis •

Algiers •
Rabat •

TUNISIA
Tripoli •

LEBANON
ISRAEL
Jerusalem
Cairo •
JORDAN

SYRIA
Beirut
Damascus •
Amman
• Baghdad
IRAQ

• Tehran

IRAN

AFGHANISTAN
Kabul •
Islamabad •

PEOPLE'S REPUBLIC OF CHINA

JAPAN

MOROCCO

ALGERIA

LIBYA

EGYPT

KUWAIT
BAHRAIN
QATAR
UNITED ARAB
EMIRATES

PAKISTAN

BHUTAN
NEPAL
Kathmandu •

New Delhi •

• Dacca

MAURITANIA

AFRICA

NIGER

CHAD

Khartoum •

SAUDI
ARABIA

Riyadh •

OMAN

INDIA

BANGLADESH

BURMA
Rangoon •

LAOS
Vientiane •

Hanoi •

MALI

GAMBIA
UPPER
VOLTA
• Niamey

N'Djamena •

SUDAN

YEMEN
San'a •

S
YEMEN

• Aden
DJIBOUTI

THAILAND
Bangkok •

VIETNAM

PHILIPPINES

GUINEA
IVORY
COAST
GHANA
Monrovia
LIBERIA
Abidjan

NIGERIA

Lagos •

CENTRAL
AFRICAN REP

Addis Ababa •
ETHIOPIA

SOMALIA

MALDIVES

Colombo •

SRI LANKA

KAMPUCHEA
Phnom Penh •

Manila •

BRUNEI

TOGO
BENIN
EQUAT.
GUINEA

CAMEROON
Yaounde •
Bangui •

UGANDA

Kampala •

KENYA

Kuala Lumpur •
MALAYSIA

GABON
Brazzaville •
CONGO
Kinshasa •

RWANDA
BURUNDI

ZAIRE

Nairobi •

TANZANIA

Dar es Salaam •

SINGAPORE

INDONESIA

Djakarta •

PAPUA
NEW GUINEA
Port Moresby •

Luanda •

ANGOLA

MALAWI
ZAMBIA
Lusaka •
Lilongwe •

Antananarivo •

MADAGASCAR

INDIAN OCEAN

NAMIBIA
Windhoek •

BOTSWANA

Gaborone •

ZIMBABWE
Harare •

Pretoria

MOZAMBIQUE
Maputo •

SWAZILAND

AUSTRALIA

SOUTH
AFRICA
Cape Town •

LESOTHO

Canberra •

0   1,500 Mi
0   1,500 Km

815

15°W   0°   15°E   30°E   45°E   60°E   75°E   90°E   105°E   120°E   135°E   150°E   165°E

85°N
75°N
60°N
45°N
30°N
15°N
0°
15°S
30°S
45°S

UNITED STATES: 1980s

MAINE (1820)

• Bangor

VERMONT (1791)

• Augusta

★ Lewiston

Montpelier ★

• Portland

Mt. Washington

Burlington

WHITE MTS.

NEW HAMPSHIRE (1788)

L. Champlain

GREEN MTS.

Concord ★

Portsmouth

ADIRONDACK MTS.

Manchester

Lawrence

Watertown

Worcester

MASSACHUSETTS (1788)

NEW YORK (1788)

Schenectady

Springfield ★ Boston

Cape Cod

L. Ontario

Albany ★

Hartford

New Bedford

Rochester • Syracuse

Providence

Niagara Falls

Ithaca

CATSKILL MTS.

RHODE ISLAND (1790)

Buffalo

Binghamton

Hudson R.

New Haven

CONNECTICUT (1788)

Erie

Scranton

Long Island

Wilkes-Barre

New York

Williamsport

Newark

NEW JERSEY (1787)

Cleveland

Allentown

Trenton

Youngstown

Harrisburg

Reading

Toledo

Sandusky

PENNSYLVANIA (1787)

Philadelphia

Ft. Wayne

Pittsburgh

Camden

OHIO (1803)

Wheeling

Baltimore

Wilmington

Columbus

Dover

Kokomo

Zanesville

Annapolis

DELAWARE (1787)

Muncie

Washington D.C.

MARYLAND (1788)

Dayton

WEST VIRGINIA (1863)

Indianapolis

Cincinnati

ATLANTIC OCEAN

INDIANA (1816)

Portsmouth

VIRGINIA (1788)

Frankfort

Ashland

Richmond

Evansville

Huntington

Charleston

Lexington

James R.

Newport News

Louisville

Lynchburg

Petersburg

Norfolk

KENTUCKY (1792)

Danville

Roanoke R.

Bowling Green

NORTH CAROLINA (1789)

Cape Hatteras

Nashville ★

Winston-Salem

Raleigh

Knoxville

Asheville

New Bern

Clingmans Dome

Charlotte

Fayetteville

TENNESSEE (1796)

Chattanooga

Cape Fear

Memphis

Rome

Athens

Columbia

Cape Fear

Gadsden

Wilmington

SOUTH CAROLINA (1788)

Myrtle Beach

Birmingham

Atlanta ★

Augusta

Charleston

Columbus

Macon

Savannah

MISSISSIPPI (1817)

Montgomery ★

ALABAMA (1819)

Albany

GEORGIA (1788)

Jackson ★

Meridian

Jacksonville

Mobile

Pensacola

Tallahassee ★

St. Augustine

Biloxi

Panama City

Daytona Beach

New Orleans

Orlando

Cape Canaveral

Tampa Bay

Tampa

FLORIDA (1845)

St. Petersburg

West Palm Beach

GULF OF MEXICO

Sarasota

L. Okeechobee

Ft. Myers

Everglades

Ft. Lauderdale

Miami

Miami Beach

Coral Gables

BAHAMAS

Florida Keys

Key West

Lake Superior

SOTA (8)

WISCONSIN (1848)

Green Bay

Oshkosh

Sheboygan

Lake Michigan

MICHIGAN (1837)

Lake Huron

Bay City

Flint

Milwaukee

Grand Rapids

Lansing

Madison ★

Racine

Jackson

Detroit

Kalamazoo

Ann Arbor

Chicago

South Bend

Gary

Lake Erie

Davenport

Peoria

Bloomington

Springfield ★

ILLINOIS (1819)

St. Louis

MISSOURI (1821)

Cairo

Little Rock

ANSAS (36)

Tupelo

Jackson

Monroe

SIANA (812)

Baton Rouge

Elevation above sea level

Feet	Meters
13,124	4000
9843	3000
6562	2000
3281	1000
1640	500
646	200
0	0
Below sea level	Below sea level

★ National capital

★ State capital

• Other city

▲ Mountain Peak

(1812) Year of statehood

| 0 | 100 | 200 | 300 | 400 | 500 Mi. |

| 0 | 100 | 200 | 300 | 400 | 500 Km |

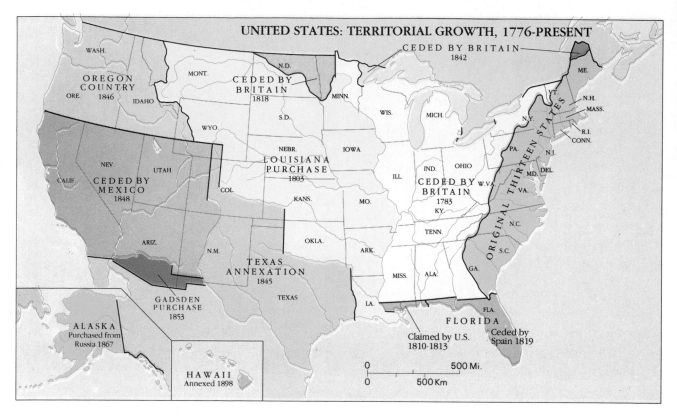

UNITED STATES: TERRITORIAL GROWTH, 1776-PRESENT

CEDED BY BRITAIN 1842

WASH.

OREGON COUNTRY
ORE. 1846

IDAHO

MONT.

N.D.

CEDED BY BRITAIN 1818

MINN.

ME.

VT.

N.H.

MASS.

R.I.

CONN.

N.Y.

WIS.

MICH.

S.D.

WYO.

NEV.

UTAH

CALIF.

CEDED BY MEXICO
1848

COL.

NEBR.

IOWA

LOUISIANA PURCHASE
1803

ILL.

IND.

OHIO

PA.

N.J.

MD. DEL.

W.VA.

VA.

CEDED BY BRITAIN
1783

KANS.

MO.

KY.

ORIGINAL THIRTEEN STATES

N.C.

ARIZ.

N.M.

TENN.

S.C.

TEXAS ANNEXATION
1845

OKLA.

ARK.

GA.

GADSDEN PURCHASE
1853

TEXAS

MISS.

ALA.

LA.

FLA.

FLORIDA
Claimed by U.S.
1810-1813

Ceded by
Spain 1819

ALASKA
Purchased from
Russia 1867

HAWAII
Annexed 1898

0 ——— 500 Mi.
0 ——— 500 Km

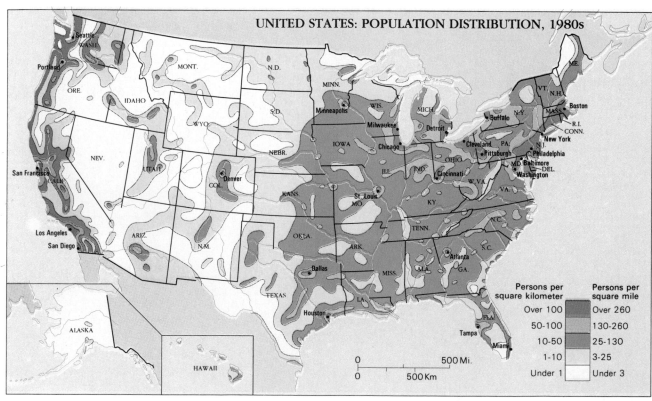

UNITED STATES: POPULATION DISTRIBUTION, 1980s

Seattle
WASH.

Portland
ORE.

MONT.

N.D.

MINN.

ME.

VT. N.H.

Boston

MASS.

R.I.

CONN.

IDAHO

WYO.

S.D.

Minneapolis

WIS.

MICH.

Milwaukee

Detroit

Buffalo

N.Y.

New York

Philadelphia

San Francisco

NEV.

UTAH

COL.

Denver

NEBR.

IOWA

Chicago

ILL.

IND.

OHIO

Cincinnati

Cleveland

PA.

Pittsburgh

N.J.

MD. Baltimore

DEL.

Washington

W.VA.

VA.

CALIF.

Los Angeles

San Diego

ARIZ.

N.M.

KANS.

St. Louis
MO.

KY.

N.C.

OKLA.

ARK.

TENN.

S.C.

Atlanta

GA.

Dallas

TEXAS

MISS.

ALA.

LA.

Houston

FLA.

Tampa

Miami

ALASKA

HAWAII

Persons per square kilometer	Persons per square mile
Over 100	Over 260
50-100	130-260
10-50	25-130
1-10	3-25
Under 1	Under 3

0 ——— 500 Mi.
0 ——— 500 Km

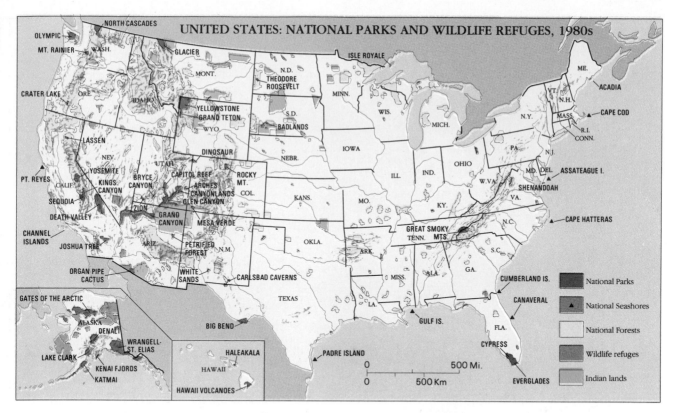

UNITED STATES: NATIONAL PARKS AND WILDLIFE REFUGES, 1980s

NORTH CASCADES
OLYMPIC
MT. RAINIER
WASH.
GLACIER
ISLE ROYALE
ME.
ACADIA
CRATER LAKE
ORE.
IDAHO
MONT.
N.D.
THEODORE
ROOSEVELT
MINN.
WIS.
MICH.
N.Y.
VT.
N.H.
MASS.
CAPE COD
R.I.
CONN.
YELLOWSTONE
GRAND TETON
WYO.
S.D.
BADLANDS
IOWA
NEBR.
PA.
N.J.
LASSEN
NEV.
DINOSAUR
OHIO
MD. DEL.
ASSATEAGUE I.
PT. REYES
CALIF.
YOSEMITE
KINGS
CANYON
UTAH
BRYCE
CANYON
CAPITOL REEF
ARCHES
CANYONLANDS
GLEN CANYON
ROCKY
MT.
COL.
ILL.
IND.
W.VA.
VA.
SHENANDOAH
SEQUOIA
ZION
KANS.
MO.
KY.
N.C.
CAPE HATTERAS
DEATH VALLEY
GRAND
CANYON
MESA VERDE
CHANNEL
ISLANDS
JOSHUA TREE
ARIZ.
PETRIFIED
FOREST
N.M.
OKLA.
ARK.
TENN.
GREAT SMOKY
MTS.
S.C.
GA.
ORGAN PIPE
CACTUS
WHITE
SANDS
CARLSBAD CAVERNS
MISS.
ALA.
CUMBERLAND IS.
GATES OF THE ARCTIC
TEXAS
LA.
GULF IS.
CANAVERAL
FLA.
CYPRESS
ALASKA
DENALI
BIG BEND
WRANGELL-
ST. ELIAS
LAKE CLARK
KENAI FJORDS
KATMAI
HALEAKALA
HAWAII
HAWAII VOLCANOES
PADRE ISLAND
EVERGLADES

0   500 Mi.
0   500 Km

■ National Parks
▲ National Seashores
□ National Forests
■ Wildlife refuges
■ Indian lands

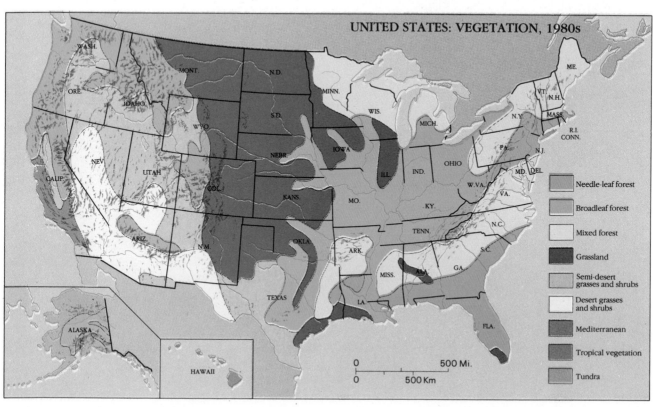

UNITED STATES: VEGETATION, 1980s

WASH.
ORE.
IDAHO
MONT.
N.D.
MINN.
WIS.
MICH.
ME.
VT.
N.H.
MASS.
R.I.
CONN.
WYO.
S.D.
NEBR.
IOWA
N.Y.
PA.
N.J.
NEV.
UTAH
COL.
KANS.
ILL.
IND.
OHIO
MD. DEL.
W.VA.
VA.
CALIF.
ARIZ.
N.M.
OKLA.
MO.
KY.
TENN.
N.C.
S.C.
ARK.
MISS.
ALA.
GA.
TEXAS
LA.
FLA.
ALASKA
HAWAII

0   500 Mi.
0   500 Km

■ Needle-leaf forest
■ Broadleaf forest
□ Mixed forest
■ Grassland
■ Semi-desert
grasses and shrubs
□ Desert grasses
and shrubs
■ Mediterranean
■ Tropical vegetation
■ Tundra

819

WASHINGTON

MONTANA

NORTH DAKOTA

OREGON

IDAHO

SOUTH DAKOTA

WYOMING

NEBRASKA

NEVADA

UTAH

COLORADO

KANSAS

CALIFORNIA

ARIZONA

NEW MEXICO

OKLAHOMA

TEXAS

ALASKA

HAWAII

500 Mi.

0

500 Km

0

150 Mi.

0

50 Km

820

UNITED STATES: AGRICULTURE, LIVESTOCK, AND FISHING, 1980s

OTA

WISCONSIN

MICHIGAN

WA

ILLINOIS   INDIANA   OHIO

MISSOURI

KENTUCKY

ARKANSAS

MISSISSIPPI   ALABAMA   GEORGIA

LOUISIANA

FLORIDA

MAINE

VERMONT

NEW HAMPSHIRE

MASSACHUSETTS

NEW YORK   RHODE ISLAND

CONNECTICUT

PENNSYLVANIA   NEW JERSEY

DELAWARE

WEST VIRGINIA   MARYLAND

VIRGINIA

NORTH CAROLINA

TENNESSEE

SOUTH CAROLINA

Wheat and small grains
Corn, soybeans, and livestock
Dairy cattle
General farming
Cotton
Range livestock
Fruit, truck, special crops
Little or no agriculture

Rice

Pineapple

Sugar cane

Fishing

| 0 | 100 | 200 | 300 | 400 | 500 Mi. |
| 0 | 100 | 200 | 300 | 400 | 500 Km |

ALASKA

500 Mi.

500 Km

HAWAII

150 Mi.

50 Km

UNITED STATES: MINERAL, GAS, PETROLEUM,
AND TIMBER RESOURCES, 1980s

Hardwood forest
Mixed forest
Softwood forest

• Natural gas

Coal

⚒ Petroleum

▬ Iron ore

□ Copper

⚒ Gold and silver

0   100   200   300   400   500 Mi.
0   100   200   300   400   500 Km

823

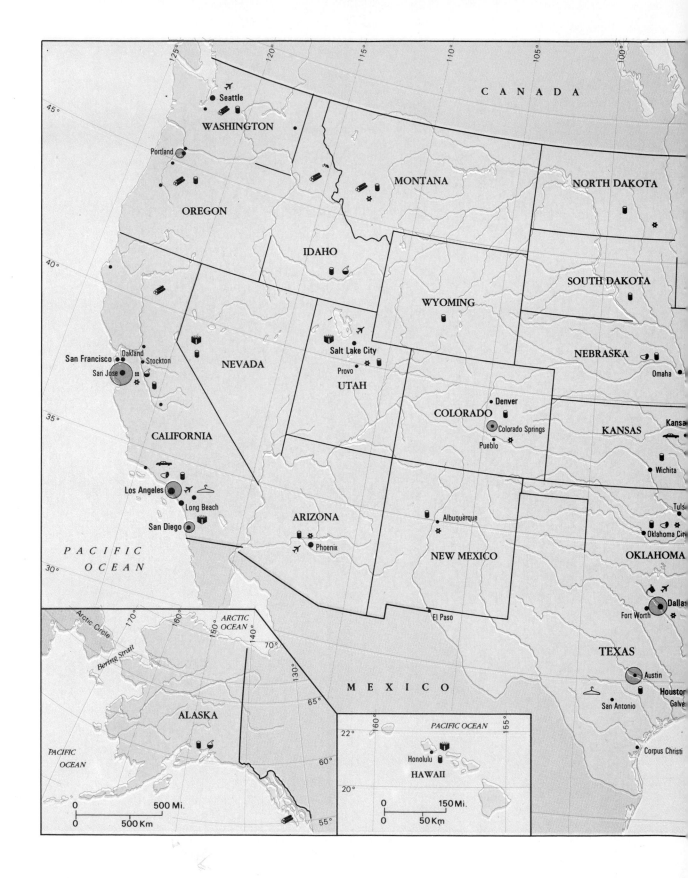

CANADA

WASHINGTON

Seattle

Portland

OREGON

MONTANA

NORTH DAKOTA

IDAHO

SOUTH DAKOTA

WYOMING

NEVADA

Salt Lake City

Provo

UTAH

NEBRASKA

Omaha

San Francisco
Oakland
Stockton
San Jose

Denver

COLORADO

Colorado Springs

Pueblo

KANSAS

Kansa

Wichita

CALIFORNIA

Los Angeles

Long Beach

San Diego

ARIZONA

Phoenix

Albuquerque

NEW MEXICO

Tulsa

Oklahoma City

OKLAHOMA

PACIFIC
OCEAN

El Paso

ARCTIC
OCEAN

Arctic Circle

Bering Strait

Dallas

Fort Worth

TEXAS

Austin

MEXICO

PACIFIC
OCEAN

ALASKA

Houston
Galve

San Antonio

Corpus Christi

PACIFIC OCEAN

Honolulu

HAWAII

0   500 Mi.

0   500 Km

0   150 Mi.

0   50 Km

UNITED STATES: INDUSTRY AND
RESEARCH & DEVELOPMENT 1980s

Legend:

- Major industrial centers
- High-technology research and development centers

Symbol	Industry	Symbol	Industry
Food	Leather
Electronic equipment	Aircraft
Chemicals	Transportation
Meat	Machinery and metals
Clothing	Iron and steel
Textiles	Lumber and paper
Printing and publishing		

Scale:
0 100 200 300 400 500 Mi.
0 100 200 300 400 500 Km

ATLANTIC OCEAN

GULF OF MEXICO

BAHAMAS

825

THE UNITED STATES

STATE	YEAR ADMITTED	POPULATION (1980)	AREA (sq mi)	POPULATION DENSITY (per sq mi)	CAPITAL	LARGEST CITY	*CONG. REP. (1980)
1. Delaware	1787	594,338	1,932	307.6	Dover	Wilmington	3
2. Pennsylvania	1787	11,863,895	44,888	264.3	Harrisburg	Philadelphia	25
3. New Jersey	1787	7,364,823	7,468	986.2	Trenton	Newark	16
4. Georgia	1788	5,463,105	58,056	94.1	Atlanta	Atlanta	12
5. Connecticut	1788	3,107,576	4,872	637.8	Hartford	Bridgeport	8
6. Massachusetts	1788	5,737,037	7,824	733.3	Boston	Boston	13
7. Maryland	1788	4,216,975	9,837	428.7	Annapolis	Baltimore	10
8. South Carolina	1788	3,121,820	30,203	103.4	Columbia	Columbia	8
9. New Hampshire	1788	920,610	8,993	102.4	Concord	Manchester	4
10. Virginia	1788	5,346,818	39,704	134.7	Richmond	Norfolk	12
11. New York	1788	17,558,072	47,377	370.6	Albany	New York	36
12. North Carolina	1789	5,881,766	48,843	120.4	Raleigh	Charlotte	13
13. Rhode Island	1790	947,154	1,055	897.8	Providence	Providence	4
14. Vermont	1791	511,456	9,273	55.2	Montpelier	Burlington	3
15. Kentucky	1792	3,660,777	39,669	92.3	Frankfort	Louisville	9
16. Tennessee	1796	4,591,120	41,155	111.6	Nashville	Memphis	11
17. Ohio	1803	10,797,630	41,004	263.3	Columbus	Cleveland	23
18. Louisiana	1812	4,205,900	44,521	94.5	Baton Rouge	New Orleans	10
19. Indiana	1816	5,490,224	35,932	152.8	Indianapolis	Indianapolis	12
20. Mississippi	1817	2,520,638	47,233	53.4	Jackson	Jackson	7
21. Illinois	1818	11,426,518	55,645	205.3	Springfield	Chicago	24
22. Alabama	1819	3,893,888	50,767	76.6	Montgomery	Birmingham	9
23. Maine	1820	1,124,660	30,995	36.3	Augusta	Portland	4
24. Missouri	1821	4,916,686	68,945	71.3	Jefferson City	St. Louis	11
25. Arkansas	1836	2,286,435	52,078	43.9	Little Rock	Little Rock	6
26. Michigan	1837	9,262,078	56,954	162.6	Lansing	Detroit	20
27. Florida	1845	9,746,324	54,153	180.0	Tallahassee	Jacksonville	21
28. Texas	1845	14,229,191	262,017	54.3	Austin	Houston	29
29. Iowa	1846	2,913,808	55,965	52.1	Des Moines	Des Moines	8
30. Wisconsin	1848	4,705,767	54,426	86.5	Madison	Milwaukee	11
31. California	1850	23,667,902	156,299	151.4	Sacramento	Los Angeles	47
32. Minnesota	1858	4,075,970	79,548	51.2	St. Paul	Minneapolis	10
33. Oregon	1859	2,633,105	96,184	27.4	Salem	Portland	7
34. Kansas	1861	2,363,679	81,778	28.9	Topeka	Wichita	7
35. West Virginia	1863	1,949,644	24,119	80.8	Charleston	Huntington	6
36. Nevada	1864	800,493	109,894	7.3	Carson City	Las Vegas	4
37. Nebraska	1867	1,569,825	76,644	20.5	Lincoln	Omaha	5
38. Colorado	1876	2,889,964	103,595	27.9	Denver	Denver	8
39. North Dakota	1889	652,717	69,300	9.4	Bismarck	Fargo	3
40. South Dakota	1889	690,768	75,952	9.1	Pierre	Sioux Falls	3
41. Montana	1889	786,690	145,388	5.4	Helena	Billings	4
42. Washington	1889	4,132,156	66,511	62.1	Olympia	Seattle	10
43. Idaho	1890	943,935	82,412	11.5	Boise	Boise	4
44. Wyoming	1890	469,557	96,989	4.9	Cheyenne	Cheyenne	3
45. Utah	1896	1,461,037	82,073	17.8	Salt Lake City	Salt Lake City	5
46. Oklahoma	1907	3,025,266	68,655	44.1	Oklahoma City	Oklahoma City	8
47. New Mexico	1912	1,299,968	121,335	10.7	Santa Fe	Albuquerque	5
48. Arizona	1912	2,718,215	113,508	23.9	Phoenix	Phoenix	7
49. Alaska	1959	401,851	570,833	0.7	Juneau	Anchorage	3
50. Hawaii	1959	964,691	6,425	150.1	Honolulu	Honolulu	4
District of Columbia (Washington, D.C.)	—	638,333	63	10,132.3	—	—	—
United States of America	—	226,504,825	3,675,545	64.0	Washington, D.C.	New York	535

Source: *U.S. Bureau of the Census*

*Congressional Representatives (1980)

PRESIDENTS OF THE UNITED STATES • 1789-1984

PRESIDENT	PARTY	TERM OF OFFICE	VICE PRESIDENT
George Washington (1732-1799)	None	1789-1797	John Adams
John Adams (1735-1826)	Federalist	1797-1801	Thomas Jefferson
Thomas Jefferson (1743-1826)	Democratic-Republican	1801-1809	Aaron Burr (1801-1805)
			George Clinton (1805-1809)
James Madison (1751-1836)	Democratic-Republican	1809-1817	George Clinton (1809-1813)
			Elbridge Gerry (1813-1817)
James Monroe (1758-1831)	Democratic-Republican	1817-1825	Daniel D. Tompkins
John Quincy Adams (1767-1848)	Democratic-Republican	1825-1829	John C. Calhoun
Andrew Jackson (1767-1845)	Democratic	1829-1837	John C. Calhoun (1829-1833)
			Martin Van Buren (1833-1837)
Martin Van Buren (1782-1862)	Democratic	1837-1841	Richard M. Johnson
William H. Harrison (1773-1841)	Whig	1841[1]	John Tyler
John Tyler (1790-1862)	Whig	1841-1845[2]	—
James K. Polk (1795-1849)	Democratic	1845-1849	George M. Dallas
Zachary Taylor (1784-1850)	Whig	1849-1850[1]	Millard Fillmore
Millard Fillmore (1800-1874)	Whig	1850-1853[2]	—
Franklin Pierce (1804-1869)	Democratic	1853-1857	William R. King
James Buchanan (1791-1868)	Democratic	1857-1861	John C. Breckinridge
Abraham Lincoln (1809-1865)	Republican	1861-1865[3]	Hannibal Hamlin (1861-1865)
			Andrew Johnson (1865)
Andrew Johnson (1808-1875)	Democratic	1865-1869[2]	—
Ulysses S. Grant (1822-1885)	Republican	1869-1877	Schuyler Colfax (1869-1873)
			Henry Wilson (1873-1877)
Rutherford B. Hayes (1822-1893)	Republican	1877-1881	William A. Wheeler
James A. Garfield (1831-1881)	Republican	1881[3]	Chester A. Arthur
Chester A. Arthur (1829-1886)	Republican	1881-1885[2]	—
Grover Cleveland (1837-1908)	Democratic	1885-1889	Thomas A. Hendricks (1885)[1]
		1893-1897	Adlai E. Stevenson (1893-1897)
Benjamin Harrison (1833-1901)	Republican	1889-1893	Levi P. Morton
William McKinley (1843-1901)	Republican	1897-1901[3]	Garret A. Hobart (1897-1901)
			Theodore Roosevelt (1901)
Theodore Roosevelt (1858-1919)	Republican	1901-1909[4]	
			Charles Fairbanks (1905-1909)
William Howard Taft (1857-1930)	Republican	1909-1913	James S. Sherman
Woodrow Wilson (1856-1924)	Democratic	1913-1921	Thomas R. Marshall
Warren G. Harding (1865-1923)	Republican	1921-1923[1]	Calvin Coolidge
Calvin Coolidge (1872-1933)	Republican	1923-1929[4]	—
			Charles G. Dawes (1925-1929)
Herbert C. Hoover (1874-1964)	Republican	1929-1933	Charles Curtis
Franklin D. Roosevelt (1882-1945)	Democratic	1933-1945[1]	John Nance Garner (1933-1941)
			Henry A. Wallace (1941-1945)
			Harry S. Truman (1945)
Harry S. Truman (1884-1972)	Democratic	1945-1953[4]	
			Alben W. Barkley (1949-1953)
Dwight D. Eisenhower (1890-1969)	Republican	1953-1961	Richard M. Nixon
John F. Kennedy (1917-1963)	Democratic	1961-1963[3]	Lyndon B. Johnson
Lyndon B. Johnson (1908-1973)	Democratic	1963-1969[4]	—
			Hubert H. Humphrey (1965-1969)
Richard M. Nixon (1913-)	Republican	1969-1974[5]	Spiro T. Agnew (1969-1973)[5]
			Gerald R. Ford (1973-1974)[6]
Gerald R. Ford (1913-)	Republican	1974-1977[7]	Nelson A. Rockefeller[8]
James E. Carter (1924-)	Democratic	1977-1981	Walter F. Mondale
Ronald W. Reagan (1911-)	Republican	1981-	George H. Bush

1. Died in office 2. Succeeded to the presidency on death of president; no provision for succession to vice presidency until 1967
3. Assassinated 4. Succeeded to the presidency on death of president; won following election; no provision for succession to vice presidency until 1967 5. Resigned 6. Appointed to the vice presidency on resignation of vice president
7. Succeeded to the presidency on resignation of president 8. Appointed to the vice presidency

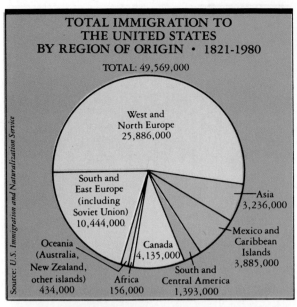

TOTAL IMMIGRATION TO THE UNITED STATES BY REGION OF ORIGIN • 1821-1980

TOTAL: 49,569,000

West and North Europe
25,886,000

South and East Europe (including Soviet Union)
10,444,000

Asia
3,236,000

Mexico and Caribbean Islands
3,885,000

South and Central America
1,393,000

Canada
4,135,000

Africa
156,000

Oceania (Australia, New Zealand, other islands)
434,000

Source: U.S. Immigration and Naturalization Service

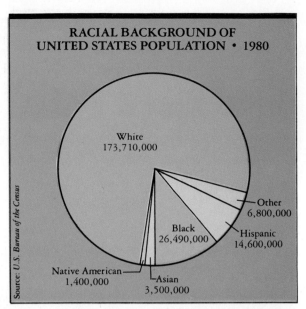

RACIAL BACKGROUND OF UNITED STATES POPULATION • 1980

White
173,710,000

Other
6,800,000

Black
26,490,000

Hispanic
14,600,000

Native American
1,400,000

Asian
3,500,000

Source: U.S. Bureau of the Census

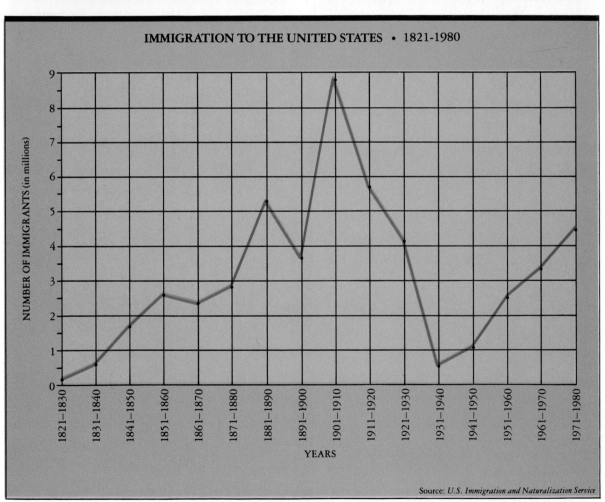

IMMIGRATION TO THE UNITED STATES • 1821-1980

NUMBER OF IMMIGRANTS (in millions)

YEARS

Source: U.S. Immigration and Naturalization Service

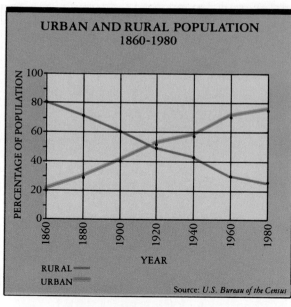

URBAN AND RURAL POPULATION
1860-1980

PERCENTAGE OF POPULATION

YEAR

RURAL
URBAN

Source: *U.S. Bureau of the Census*

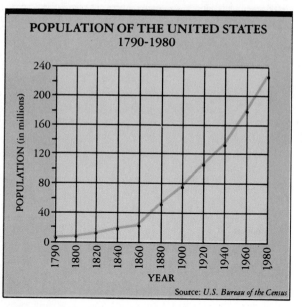

POPULATION OF THE UNITED STATES
1790-1980

POPULATION (in millions)

YEAR

Source: *U.S. Bureau of the Census*

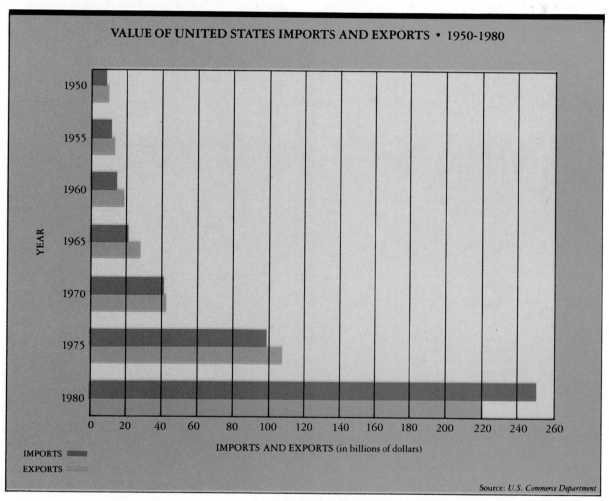

VALUE OF UNITED STATES IMPORTS AND EXPORTS • 1950-1980

YEAR

1950
1955
1960
1965
1970
1975
1980

0 20 40 60 80 100 120 140 160 180 200 220 240 260

IMPORTS AND EXPORTS (in billions of dollars)

IMPORTS
EXPORTS

Source: *U.S. Commerce Department*

829

GLOSSARY

This glossary defines many of the important terms and phrases that are used in this book. All of the entries appear in italics the first time they are discussed in the text. Page numbers refer to the pages on which the terms or phrases are first used. Italic words in the glossary indicate cross-references to other entries.

A

AAA Agricultural Adjustment Administration, organization formed under the New Deal to restore farmers' purchasing power (p. 663).

abolition Act of doing away with totally; putting an end to (p. 324).

abolitionist In the 1800s, one who advocated eliminating the institution of slavery (p. 302).

abridge To cut short or make smaller.

absolute majority More than half of the total votes (p. 234).

absolute power Power to lead a country held by only one person who is completely free from constitutional or other restraints (p. 679).

absolute ruler A monarch who claims to be empowered by and responsible only to God, not his subjects, who must be unquestioning and obedient (p. 33).

abstain To refrain from doing something, such as voting (p. 206).

abstinence Voluntarily and deliberately refraining from an action or practice; often used in reference to alcoholic beverages (p. 300).

abstract art A style of art focusing on mood and feeling rather than realistic representation. Abstract art often uses geometric shapes and designs, interesting textures and bright colors (p. 725).

ACLU American Civil Liberties Union, an organization founded in 1920 to act as a watchdog for the Bill of Rights (p. 607).

acquit To remove an obligation or accusation from (p. 220).

acquitted Found innocent of a crime in a court of law (p. 181).

acronym A word or abbreviation formed from the first letter of each word in the name of an organization or program, such as *VISTA* for "Volunteers *in* Service *to* America."

activist Person who takes direct action, such as intense lobbying or mass demonstrations, in support of or opposition to one side of a political issue (p. 717).

adulterants Preservatives or other chemicals added by commercial food processors to products to enhance their appeal or keep them from spoiling (p. 573).

affirmative action The hiring of women, blacks, Hispanics, and the handicapped in preference to white males if the credentials of all applicants are equal (p. 788).

affluence Wealth (p. 552).

affluent society John Kenneth Galbraith's term for a society in which a large amount of discretionary income is in people's hands—that is, income above what is needed to buy necessary goods; such surplus income instills new values based on consumption instead of thrift and saving (p. 722).

AFL The American Federation of Labor, a nationwide labor organization founded in 1886 to work for higher wages, shorter hours and better working conditions (p. 471).

AFL-CIO The American Federation of Labor and Congress of Industrial Organizations, one of the major modern labor unions, formed by the merger of the *AFL* and *CIO* in 1955 (p. 804).

agrarian Related to farming or a farmer's lifestyle (p. 521).

alcaldes Elected mayors who also served as judges in colonial Spanish-American towns (p. 33).

alderman Member of a city council or other city legislative body (p. 436).

allegiance Loyalty or devotion (p. 226).

alliance A union of individuals formed to further common interests (p. 518).

Alliance for Progress An economic and social program founded by John F. Kennedy to reduce poverty and illiteracy, improve health, and promote democracy in Latin America (p. 755).

Allied Powers 1. In World War I, alliance of Russia, France and Great Britain—also called the *Triple Entente*—against the unified powers of Germany, Austria-Hungary, and Italy—the Central Powers, also known as the *Triple Alliance* (p. 592). 2. In World War II, the United States, Great Britain, France, the Soviet Union, and other countries who united against the *Axis Powers* of Germany, Italy, and Japan. (p. 684).

almanac An annual publication reporting on current events, important people, records, and new discoveries during the year (p. 744).

ambassador The highest ranking representative of the U.S. State Department to another country (p. 452).

ambergris A valuable substance made from whale oil and used for making perfumes (p. 58).

amendment A legal change made in a law (p. 578).

American Colonization Society An organization in the late 1700's that encouraged slaveowners to free their slaves and pay the passage of free blacks who wished to return to Africa (p. 246).

American Independent party A third party of the 1960s that nominated George Wallace for President (p. 769).

American Liberty League An organization of business people formed in 1934 who claimed that programs like the *TVA* and *NRA* violated the American tradition of free enterprise (p. 667).

American System Programs initiated by Henry Clay that included federally financed internal improvements, the sale of government land at low prices, and a high tariff to protect northeastern industries against English competition; it was intended to tie sections of the country together in a national economy (p. 255).

Amtrak Cooperative arrangement founded in 1970 between the federal government and U.S. railroads designed to revive travel by train (p. 780).

anarchist One whose political belief is opposed to all forms of government and authority, often advocating the ultimate destruction of the political state (p. 470).

Anglican Church The established Church of England, a Protestant Episcopal church (p. 284).

annex To incorporate a country or territory into one's own country or state (p. 532).

anthropologist A person who studies the history of mankind, especially in regards to race, physical character, culture, society, and interaction with the environment (p. 4).

anti-colonial movement Effort by a colony to oust a parent government and establish an independent one (p. 736).

Anti-Federalists Americans who wanted to improve the Articles of Confederation

Parts of speech abbreviations: *n.,* noun; *adj.,* adjective; *v.t.,* verb transitive.

©1969, 1970, 1971, 1973, 1975, 1976, 1978, 1979, 1980, 1981, 1983 by Houghton Mifflin Company. The pronunciation system in this glossary is used by permission from the *American Heritage Dictionary of the English Language.*

ă pat/ā pay/âr care/ä father/b bib/ch church/d deed/ĕ pet/ē be/f fife/g gag/h hat/hw which/ĭ pit/ī pie/îr pier/j judge/k kick/l lid, needle/m mum/n no, sudden/ng thing/ŏ pot/ō toe/ô paw, for/oi noise/ou out/ŏŏ took/ōō boot/p pop/r roar/s sauce/sh ship, dish/t tight/th thin, path/*th* this, bathe/ŭ cut/ûr urge/v valve/w with/y yes/z zebra, size/zh vision/ə about, item, edible, gallop, circus/

rather than ratify the U.S. Constitution, stressing the power of the states over the federal government (p. 163).

anti-imperialists A group of old Radical Republicans, Liberal Republicans, and Democrats who opposed the annexation of the Philippine Islands at the end of the 19th century because it violated the United States' anti-colonial heritage (p. 539).

Anti-Masonic party A political party founded in 1826 that aimed to outlaw all secret organizations, especially the Masons, who were seen as discriminating against non-Masons in business, in hiring and in politics (p. 265).

anti-Semitic Showing hostility toward or discriminating against Jews (p. 620).

antitrust action Government effort to protect trade from monopolies by enforcing laws against trusts (p. 431).

Apollo 11 U.S. spaceship that landed on the moon on July 20, 1969, carrying three astronauts—Neil Armstrong, Edwin Aldrin, and Michael Collins (p. 780).

appease To calm or pacify by making concessions at the expense of principles (p. 684).

appellate A court with the power to hear appeals from lower courts and to reverse their decisions.

apportionment The assigning of allotting of representatives or taxes according to U.S. law (p. 183).

apprentice Individual who learns a skill by working under the supervision of a person in a trade or profession (p. 554).

appropriations Federal money set aside for specific purposes (p. 532).

appropriations bill Legislative act setting aside federal money for a specific purpose (p. 539).

aristocracy Small upper class holding control of business or government (p. 165).

aristocratic Upper-class; socially exclusive (p. 568).

armistice Temporary cease-fire established by agreement between opposing parties (p. 598).

arsenal A place where arms and other military equipment are stored (p. 354).

artifact A man-made object from a past civilization (p. 8).

artillery Cannons and other heavy guns, or a branch of an army armed with these weapons (p. 494).

assassin Person who murders a political leader. The term comes from an Arabic word for a secret, fanatical organization whose members, under the influence of the drug hashish, murdered Crusaders occupying the Holy Land (p. 757).

assembly line Manufacturing arrangement in which a product passes from worker to worker, with each completing one step in its manufacture.

assessment system A practice in which a political party insists that its members who hold government positions "donate" a percentage of their salary to political

campaign chests each election year (p. 451).

assimilate To be taken in or absorbed into the culture of a population or group and take on their characteristics (p. 42).

assumption of debt To take over another's debts and be responsible for their payment (p. 195).

astrolabe An instrument once used in navigation to tell location and direction by examining the position of the stars.

atlas A collection of maps in book form (p. 408).

Attorney General Person appointed by the President and approved by the Senate to act as the chief law officer in the U.S., represent the government in litigation, and act as the government's chief legal adviser (p. 431).

attrition Weakening, exhausting, or whittling away of the enemy by making repeated raids and attacks (p. 384).

Auburn System A prison system begun in a New York penitentiary in which inmates slept alone in cells at night but labored together in a large workroom during the day. The system caused fewer cases of insanity and helped pay its own expenses with products made by the inmates. See also *Pennsylvania System* (p. 298).

autobiography The story of a person's life written by that person (p. 326).

Axis Powers Germany, Italy, and Japan, the aggressors in World War II (p. 684). See also *Allied Powers*.

B

baby boom Tremendous increase in the number of babies born in the U.S. from 1946 through the 1960s (p. 722).

bail The money or property given to a court by an accused person in order to guarantee he or she will appear for trial (p. 181).

balance of power Before World War I, a system of international relations to prevent major European wars. The arrangement worked through interlocking agreements designed so that no one European power could start an expansionist war without facing a force of equal strength (p. 592).

Balkan countries Countries on the Balkan peninsula: Yugoslavia, Rumania, Bulgaria, Albania, Greece, and Turkey (p. 593).

banishment Expulsion from a Puritan colony for a serious crime so God would not hold the other members responsible for the sinner's actions (p. 54).

bankrupt State of financial ruin in which a person or corporation is legally declared insolvent, and assets and debts are turned over to an administrator who finalizes them, distributing whatever assets remain to creditors (p. 420).

barcha A Portuguese sea vessel (p. 15).

basin A large depression or hollowed area of land, usually made by a river or lake that has since disappeared (p. 10).

Battle of the Bulge The Germans' last major offensive attack during World War II (p. 697).

Bear Flag Republic The temporary name given to what is now California by a small group of Americans who defeated the Mexicans who lived there (p. 345).

belligerent nations Nations involved in war (p. 681).

Berlin Wall A 29-mile-long brick and barbed wire fence, lined with explosive mines and guard stations, built around East Berlin by communist East Germans in 1961 to prevent massive emigration (p. 757).

Bessemer process A process of making steel from *pig iron* by blasting out impurities in a furnace (p. 522).

bicameral Having two legislative houses, such as Congress, which consists of the Senate and House of Representatives (p. 168).

bicentennial A nation's two hundredth birthday (p. 786).

"The Big Three" Leaders of the three major allied forces during World War II: Russia's Stalin, Roosevelt from the U.S., and England's Churchill (p. 697).

bill of attainder A legislative act that judges a person guilty of a serious crime without a legal trial and that carries the death penalty; this is illegal under the U.S. Constitution (p. 173).

bill of credit A financial instrument that English colonists were supposed to accept as payment for their goods and products instead of gold or silver; under the *mercantile* system, the colonists could redeem the bills only in English manufactured goods (p. 76).

Bill of Rights The first ten amendments to the Constitution which guarantee basic freedoms to individual citizens (p. 86).

"Billy Yank" A nickname for the typical Union soldier in the Civil War (p. 370).

biodegradable Able to be easily broken down into harmless components by natural processes, such decomposition (p. 809).

bipartisan committee Committee made up of people from both the Republican and Democratic parties (p. 782).

black codes Collections of laws adopted by Southern states after the Civil War that denied freed slaves the right of full citizenship (p. 397).

Black Muslims Separatist black sect of the 1960s that rejected Christianity, professed Islamic beliefs, and called for blacks to arm themselves in self-defense (p. 762).

Black Nationalism Black movement advocating withdrawal from white society and the formation of black organizations based on pride in being black (p. 620).

Black Panthers Radical organization of blacks advocating violent revolution and use of armed force to fight oppression and achieve equality (p. 763).

black power Black militant movement in the 1960s advocating that blacks withdraw from political association with whites and work to win their own power (p. 762).

Black Thursday October 24, 1929, the day marking the beginning of the stock market crash and the Great Depression (p. 646).

"Bleeding Kansas" The Kansas territory in the 1850s, so called because proslavery border ruffians from Missouri rode into Kansas for elections, sometimes terrorizing settlers, in order to ensure Kansas would accept slavery (p. 352).

Blitz Intensive air raid during World War II (p. 684).

blitzkrieg Intensive surprise attack by air and ground forces working closely together. The word comes from the German words *blitz* ("lightning") and *krieg* ("war") (p. 684).

blockade To use troops or warships to prevent the passage of people or supplies to or from an area occupied by the enemy during a war (p. 141).

blockade runner A ship that runs through a blockade in order to take in supplies, bring out merchandise for trade, bring in or take out information (p. 375).

bloody shirt Reference used in Republican campaigns blaming the Democrats for causing the Civil War (p. 442).

blue laws Laws in the New England colonies that forbade non-religious activities on Sundays (p. 54).

"boll weevils" Congressmen who vote for policies advocated by the opposing party (p. 800).

Bolshevik Revolution Overthrow of the Russian government in 1917 by Lenin and his followers and the subsequent establishment of the Communist state (p. 616).

bonds A certificate issued by a government promising that the price of purchase will be repaid with interest to the person who buys it; bonds are the way a government borrows money (p. 194).

boom and bust The practice of overspending during a period of prosperity, leading to financial ruin when hard times hit (p. 643).

boosterism Promoting the good points of business (p. 636).

bootlegger Person who bought, sold, made, or transported liquor illegally during *Prohibition* (p. 622).

border ruffians Proslavery Missourians who rode into Kansas for elections and sometimes terrorized free-state settlers (p. 352).

boss Politician who commands the loyalty of a majority of voters in a *ward* (p. 436).

Bourbon Democrats Extremely conservative Democrats of the South, named after the conservative Bourbon dynasty in pre-revolutionary France (p. 443).

boycott Unite in refusing to deal with a business or organization to exert pressure on it and force social change (p. 735).

Boxers Chinese rebels in 1900 who attempted to terrorize foreigners out of China, so called because the name for their secret society meant "righteous harmonious fist" (p. 543).

brain drain Emigration of a nation's top professionals to other countries, where greater opportunities or political freedom exists (p. 756).

Brain Trust Group of experts on agriculture, industry, taxation, finance, and public assistance programs who helped President Roosevelt formulate his New Deal program (p. 661).

brigade A large body of troops (p. 369).

brinksmanship A form of international Cold War diplomacy in which a crisis is resolved through the threat of nuclear war (p. 735).

broadside An advertisement printed on a sheet of paper (p. 30).

buckaroo English form of the Spanish word "vaquero," a cowboy of the American West in the 1800s (p. 497).

bull market Rise in the price of corporate stocks, leading to economic prosperity (p. 644).

Bull Moose Party Nickname for the Progressive party during the candidacy of Theodore Roosevelt, who told reporters he felt healthy and "fit as a bull moose" (p. 580).

bureaucracy 1. A system of government having specialized departments that follow strict rules and have a hierarchy of authority. 2. One of those specialized departments (p. 436).

Bureau of the Budget Government agency founded in 1921 to predict revenues and expenses for the fiscal year ahead, and propose a budget to Congress and the President (p. 633).

buying on margin Buying stocks on credit (p. 645).

C

cabildos Elected governing councils in Spanish American colonial towns (p. 33).

cabinet Committee of top advisors to the President in numerous departments, appointed by the President with approval of the Senate (p. 570).

Cajuns (kā′jəns) *n.* Exiled French colonists from Nova Scotia (Acadia) who later settled in Louisiana (p. 100).

californio Mexicans living in California in the 1800s (p. 345).

Calvinistic Having to do with the teachings of John Calvin and reformed Protestant churches.

Camino Real A road on the California coast along which Father Junipero Serra encouraged Indians to build missions about a day's walk from each other; the term means "royal road" (p. 336).

Camp David Accords Peace-making meeting between Israeli Prime Minister Menachen Begin, Egyptian President Anwar Sadat, and U.S. President Jimmy Carter, held at Camp David, the presidential retreat in Maryland, in 1978 (p. 796).

camp meeting A week or more of outdoor sermons and hymn singing held by revivalists on the frontier (p. 286).

canal zone Ten-mile wide strip across the Isthmus of Panama, encompassing the Panama Canal and its adjacent banks (p. 545).

Cape Kennedy From 1963 to 1973, the name of Cape Canaveral off the Florida coast. It is the principal launch site for U.S. missiles, satellites, and manned space flights (p. 780).

capital Money (p. 412).

capitalist Person who favors the private ownership of goods, self-determined investment, and free market competition. Also, a person who has achieved great wealth through this system (p. 415).

capitalist system The economic system of the U.S. in which property is owned by private investors rather than by the government or society in general (p. 415).

caravel (kar′-ə-vel′) *n.* A small, fast maneuverable sailing ship with three-cornered sails used by the Spanish and Portuguese in the 15th and 16th centuries (p. 14). See also *galleons*.

carpetbagger Northerner who came south during Reconstruction for political or monetary gain (p. 443).

cash and carry The principle of having goods paid for in cash and transported by the purchaser (p. 681).

casualty Death or injury in a war (p. 384).

cattle barons Individuals who refined practices of cattle raising and built huge ranches during the latter 1800s (p. 500).

caucus Meeting of members of a political party to choose candidates or decide on party platforms and policies (p. 233).

cavalry Branch of an army mounted on horseback (p. 536).

CCC Civilian Conservation Corps, a jobs program under Roosevelt's *New Deal* that employed some 2 million people to do conservation work (p. 665).

cease-fire Agreement to temporarily stop fighting; truce (p. 775).

cede To give up or transfer, usually by a treaty (p. 152).

censure Official expression of disapproval or criticism (p. 736).

census An official count of the nation's population, taken every ten years (p. 168).

Central Powers See *Triple Alliance*.

Challenger The second space shuttle, first launched in 1983 and equipped to carry out tests in space and repair orbiting satellites (p. 807).

charismatic Having a strong magnetic charm or appeal (p. 264).

chattel (chăt′l) *n.* 1. Personal property that is movable; any possession other than real estate. 2. A slave (p. 80).

Chautauquas (shə-tô′kwəz) *n.* Resorts popular during the late 19th and early 20th centuries in which middle-class people rested, played, learned, and were entertained; although they began as training programs for religion teachers, Chautauquas attracted people who wanted a break from work and the opportunity to enjoy varied programs (p. 555).

checks and balances A division of power between governmental branches giving each some controls over the others in order to ensure that none acts unjustly (p. 165).

Chief Justice The head presiding judge in a court of law (p. 576).

child labor Employing children to do low-paying, unskilled, menial jobs in large factories (p. 480).

China Lobby Group of influential Americans who supported Chinese Nationalists led by Chiang Kai-Shek in the 1940s and who believed the Chinese Communists were working for the Russians (p. 716).

chronological order Time order in which events occurred (p. 482).

CIA Central Intelligence Agency, a government bureau established in 1947 to gather information about foreign countries and their activities for the use of the President and National Security Council (p. 755).

circuit riders Ministers who traveled around to a limited number of Western settlements, preaching, performing marriages and baptisms, and counseling people (p. 287).

city manager A professionally trained, hired official who administers the daily workings of a city government according to policies adopted by a city council (p. 564).

civil disobedience See *nonviolent civil disobedience.*

civilian Person who is not a member of the armed forces (p. 690).

civil rights movement A movement to secure constitutional rights for all, regardless of race; activists were particularly concerned with overthrowing segregation policies in the South (p. 734).

civil servant Civilian who works for a branch or office of federal, state, or local government or an international agency. Civil service jobs are secured by taking competitive examinations (p. 451).

closed shop A labor union practice by which unions demanded employment contracts that excluded all non-union workers (p. 712).

Cold War A war of chilling words that stops short of actual combat (p. 706).

collateral (kə-lăt′ər-əl) *n.* Property that a lender can take over if the borrower cannot repay a loan (p. 645).

colonial Having to do with the original thirteen American colonies (p. 58).

colonialism Control by a strong government over a smaller, dependent area of *colony* (p. 532).

colonization movement A movement by antislavery southerners to rid the U.S. of slavery by urging slaveowners to free their slaves and pay their transportation to West Africa (p. 323).

Columbia The first space shuttle, which

completed several flights in the early 1980s (p. 807).

commerce Trade; business.

commerce raiders Big, fast, powerfully armed Confederate sailing ships that roamed the oceans blasting or capturing northern merchants vessels (p. 375).

Commission on Human Rights United Nations committee that promotes human rights for all people worldwide (p. 664).

commonwealth A political union of self-governing, autonomous states.

commune Community characterized by collective ownership and use of property, often formed for the purpose of putting a particular philosophy into practice as a way of life (p. 767).

communications satellite Man-made satellite placed in orbit around the earth to provide a link between worldwide radio, telephone, and television signals (p. 807).

compact A written agreement or contract between two or more parties (p. 42).

compact theory of government A theory of government that held that the union of the states was a compact in which the individual states agreed to give up their independence. However, the states remained *sovereign* and therefore had a right to rule on whether a federal action was constitutional; if it was not, they had the right to *nullify* it within the state (p. 206).

company town Town in which an employer owned not only the factory, but also houses, stores, schools, and even church buildings, thus maintaining control over every aspect of workers' lives (p. 466).

compass rose A symbol (+) that shows direction on a map; each point indicates either north, south, east or west (p. 116).

concentration camp A camp where prisoners of war or political prisoners are held (p. 684).

concurrence Agreement.

concurrent powers Power shared by federal and state governments (p. 193). See also *delegated powers, reserved powers.*

concurrent resolution An expression of opinion by either house of Congress that lacks the force of law and does not require the President's approval (p. 171). See also *joint resolution.*

Conestoga wagon A high-wheeled wagon covered by a canvas stretched over wooden frame; the wagons were drawn by horses or oxen and used to transport freight and people across the prairies (p. 249).

Confederacy The eleven states that seceded from the Union and formed the Confederate States of America (p. 363).

Confederate States of America Organization of eleven southern states that seceded from the United States in 1860 and 1861 to form their own government based on guarantees of slavery and states' rights (p. 360).

confederation (kən-fĕd′ə-rā′shən) *n.* A group of loosely joined states, each of which retains its *sovereignty* (p. 151).

Congregationalists Members of a religion

that placed the final authority on church matters with local congregations rather than with a central Church body (p. 284).

Congress of Industrial Organizations Also known as the CIO, a group formed within the *AFL* but expelled in 1936 because they wanted to organize unskilled workers according to their industry. They quickly grew to become the largest union organizer in the U.S. and merged with the AFL again in 1955 (p. 670).

conquistador A leader of the Spanish conquest of Mexico and Peru in the 16th century. The word is Spanish for "conqueror" (p. 21).

Conscience Whigs Northern members of the Whig political party in the 1800s who were against both slavery and annexation (p. 343).

conservation Planned management to preserve and protect natural resources from exploitation, destruction, or neglect (p. 573).

conservation movement Movement beginning in the late 1800s to protect the earth's natural resources, wilderness areas, and natural wonders (p. 573). See also *preservationists; reservationists.*

conservative 1. During the early years of the U.S., a person who advocated a strong central government with great economic control. Most of the men who wrote the Constitution were Conservatives. 2. In modern times, someone who believes just the opposite, that government controls should be lessened and government should change society very slowly or not at all (p. 455).

consolidation Combining companies to form a larger, more powerful corporation (p. 415).

conspicuous consumption Showy, extravagant, and often wasteful spending just to enhance social prestige (p. 460).

Constitution Document containing the basic principles and laws of the U.S. Constitution (p. 87).

constitution The basic law of a nation or state (p. 148).

constitutionality In accordance with provisions of the U.S. Constitution (p. 667).

consumer Person who buys or uses economic goods (p. 578).

consumer goods Goods such as homes, cars, televisions, and appliances that are used directly by consumers (p. 723).

consumption Spending *discretionary income* to purchase expendable goods, rather than saving it (p. 722).

containment policy George Kennan's plan for containing Soviet power in Europe after World War II. Under this proposal, the U.S. drew clear lines beyond which it would not tolerate Soviet expansion; the first test of this policy occurred with the Berlin Blockade of 1948–1949 (p. 711).

contiguous Touching, or sharing a common border (p. 532).

continentals Paper currency issued by the

U.S. Congress prior to the adoption of the Constitution. Its value was extremely unstable (p. 154).

convene To come together or assemble as a group (p. 170).

convention A group of people who meet for a common purpose (p. 167).

convoy Group of vehicles organized to protect each other in travel (p. 599).

Copperheads Pro-Confederate northerners during the Civil War, named after a poisonous snake that strikes without warning (p. 393).

cooperative (kō-ŏp′rə-tĭv, -ə-rā′tĭv) *n.* An organization in which members work together for mutual benefit, sharing all profits and losses among themselves (p. 515).

corduroy road An inexpensive road made by laying down logs. (p. 253).

CORE Congress of Racial Equality, an organization founded in 1942 by black and white citizens to end racial segregation through nonviolent means (p. 735).

corporate colony A self-governing settlement or region of the New World in which authority was based on a corporation charter (p. 44).

corporation Organization formed and authorized by law to act as a single person, even though it may be made up of many people (p. 430).

corruption Bribery, selling political favors, and other illegal conduct reflecting low morality in a government (p. 416).

Cost of Living Council Committee set up by President Nixon to evaluate wages and prices in relation to the economy (p. 780).

cotton gin A machine invented by Eli Whitney in 1793 that separated seeds from cotton fibers (p. 246).

Cotton Whigs Members of the Whig political party in the 1800s who were both proslavery and pro-annexation; Cotton Whigs were generally southerners (p. 343).

counterculture Culture, usually of young people, in which ideals and practices are counter to, or opposite, those of established society (p. 767).

countermand Revoke an instruction by issuing a higher order (p. 734).

counting coup To touch an opponent during battle in front of witnesses; some Indian tribes thought such a touch to be as brave as to wound or kill (p. 11).

coup Military overthrow of a government (p. 764).

court-packing Deliberately appointing to the Supreme Court justices who support certain views or political issues (p. 667).

crash Sudden decline in stock prices (p. 645).

credit 1. Amount of money made available to a person or business by a bank. 2. Time given for payment for goods or services sold (p. 514).

creditor Person or organization to whom a debt is owed (p. 514).

credit union Organization in which members of a group establish their own saving and lending institution (p. 515).

creed Fundamental or religious beliefs (p. 759).

criollos Spaniards born in America (p. 31).

crude oil Oil in its natural, unrefined state (p. 425).

cult Unorthodox or faddish religion, often unconventional, nonconforming, and based on unquestioning acceptance of a revered doctrine or leader (p. 787).

cultivation Tilling soil and growing crops (p. 513).

culture The beliefs, institutions, customs, arts, and other things that make up the way of life of a group of people (p. 4).

currency Paper money in circulation (p. 392).

Customs Service Government agency that supervises the collection of duties on imports and exports (p. 443).

CWA The Civil Works Administration, a jobs program under Roosevelt's New Deal that employed four million people to do construction work (p. 665).

cyclotron Nuclear physics device invented in the 1940s which produces beams of charged particles that can penetrate the atomic nucleus to study its structure. This technology is used in many applications in medicine and industry today (p. 649).

D

daguerrotype An early photograph produced on a silver plate (p. 259).

dark horse candidate A presidential candidate who has not been a nominee before a presidential convention begins (p. 343).

D-Day June 6, 1944, the day the allied forces stormed the beaches of Normandy in France, marking the beginning of Germany's defeat (p. 696).

deadlock Standstill or inaction caused by the opposition of two equal and unyielding powers (p. 206).

defendant Person who is defending himself or herself against charges in a court of law (p. 571).

deficit Excess of money spent over money taken in, resulting in debt (p. 633).

deflation Reduction of the amount of money in circulation, resulting in an increase in the value of money and a decrease in prices and wages (p. 455).

deists (dē′ists) *n.* People who believed in God but did not think that church services and rituals were important forms of worship (p. 284).

delegate 1. *(v.)* To assign responsibility or authority to another. 2. *(n.)* A representative to a convention or conference (p. 664).

delegated powers Power given by the states to the federal government. See also *concurrent powers; reserved powers* (p. 193).

demagoguery Use of appeals to emotion, common prejudices, and false claims and promises to gain power (p. 519).

demilitarized Prohibited from being used for military purposes (p. 684).

democracy Rule by the many, or a government in which all citizens make their own laws, either directly or indirectly through elected representatives (p. 165).

democratic 1. Of a government that is run by the people either directly or indirectly through elected representatives. 2. Of or having regard for the common people. *Jacksonian democracy,* especially, was a belief that all Americans had a right to succeed and that ordinary people should have the same opportunities as wealthy people (p. 267).

Democratic Republican A member of a political party that favored strong state governments and a strict interpretation of the Constitution (p. 203). See also *Federalist.*

demonetization Stopping a metal, such as silver, from being used as a monetary unit (p. 504).

demoralize To weaken the morale and confidence of (p. 776).

depression Period of low economic activity and high unemployment (p. 276).

desegregation The act of eliminating any separations based on race.

despotism Abusive or oppressive exercise of absolute power.

destroyer Small, fast warship that is heavily armed (p. 599).

détente (dā-tänt′) *n.* A term for the gradual relaxation of tension between the U.S. and the Soviet Union during the 1970s (p. 553).

dictator Person who holds absolute power and often rules oppressively (p. 679).

diplomacy Art of skillfully and tactfully conducting affairs between nations (p. 545).

diplomat Person who conducts relations and business between nations (p. 772).

direct election An election in which the people vote directly for leaders. For example, U.S. Representatives are chosen by direct election (p. 162). See also *indirect election.*

directorate Board of directors of a corporation (p. 582).

discretionary income Income above what is needed to buy essential goods (p. 722).

discriminate Treat people differently because of race, age, sex, nationality, or religion (p. 735).

discrimination Denying of rights or privileges to individuals because of race, sex, religion, or national origin (p. 735).

dissidents People who disagree with a prevailing opinion or group (p. 684).

division of labor The breakdown of a job into several parts to be done by different people in order to increase efficiency.

Dixie Southern states of the U.S. (p. 443).

Dixiecrats Conservative, prosegregationist southern Democrats (p. 713).

Dixieland Type of jazz developed by blacks in New Orleans in the 1920s, usually played by a small band and characterized by many improvisations (p. 620).

dogfighter Small, lightweight fighter plane in World War I (p. 585).

dogfights Fights between fighter planes at close range during World War I (p. 595).

dollar diplomacy Attempting to influence other countries and regions by investment rather than by armed force (p. 545).

domestic Related to programs and activities within one's own country (p. 772).

double jeopardy Putting a person on trial for an offense for which he was already tried and acquitted (p. 181).

Doughboys American troops who fought during World War I (p. 691).

Doughfaces Moderate northern Democrats who supported the southern proslavery position in the 1850s (p. 349).

down payment Small portion of the total price of an item, paid at the time of purchase or delivery, with the remaining amount to be paid later (p. 644).

draft law Law requiring young men to register with the U.S. government in case of a wartime necessity of calling them into military service (p. 685).

dreadnoughts Huge, heavily armed battleships built by England in the early 1900s in response to Germany's naval buildup (p. 593).

"Drys" Those who supported the Prohibition Amendment (p. 620).

due process of law Legal action carried out according to rules and protections established by the Bill of Rights (p. 181).

dumping The practice of flooding foreign markets with goods to eliminate surpluses without hurting domestic prices (p. 244).

Dust Bowl Area including Oklahoma, Arkansas, and surrounding states that were struck by severe drought and dust storms in 1936 and 1937, killing all the crops and leading to mass depopulation (p. 655).

duty Import tax placed on certain goods to encourage the purchase of higher priced domestic goods instead (p. 91).

duty-free Not requiring payment of an import tax (p. 581).

E

editorial A newspaper or magazine article that gives the opinions of the writer and tries to persuade readers to accept those opinions (p. 358).

elastic clause A power delegated to Congress to make the "necessary and proper" laws to execute the government's powers; called "elastic" because its meaning can be stretched to fit many circumstances (p. 173).

election returns Results of the popular and electoral votes in an election (p. 714).

elective system College curriculum system in which students can choose career-oriented areas of study and take related courses, in addition to traditional liberal arts courses (p. 554).

elector A member of the electoral college in the U.S., chosen by his or her state. Each state has as many electors as it has Senators and Representatives in Congress (p. 162).

electoral college Group of electors from every state who elect the President and Vice President of the United States (p. 162).

electorate All those who are entitled to vote (p. 436).

elite Group held to be socially superior and powerful (p. 561).

ellipsis points Three periods in a row in a quotation that indicate that words or sentences have been omitted (p. 389).

Ellis Island Small island in the New York harbor with an immigration center through which millions of European immigrants passed in the late 19th and early 20th centuries (p. 475).

emancipation The act of freeing something from slavery or bondage (p. 184).

Emancipation Proclamation Official statement in which Abraham Lincoln declared that all slaves in territory controlled by Confederate rebels would be free as of January 1, 1863 (p. 379).

embargo Government action stopping trade with another nation, or stopping ships from leaving its ports (p. 223).

embassy Official offices of diplomats and ambassadors living in a foreign country (p. 775).

embezzlement The crime of taking money entrusted to one's care. For example, a cashier who steals money from a cash register and an accountant who takes money from accounts are both guilty of embezzlement (p. 515).

emigrate To leave one's native country or home in order to live somewhere else.

emolument Money received for performing the duties of an elected or appointed office (p. 171).

encomenderos Spaniards who owned American land under the encomiendo system (p. 31).

encomienda system (en-ko′me-en′də) *n.* A system in which a Spanish monarch granted tracts of land to Spaniards who settled in the New World; with the land came the right to the labor of the Indians who lived on it (p. 30).

enfilading fire Gunfire directed along the entire length of an enemy's battle line (p. 537).

enfranchise To give the right to vote to someone (p. 150).

engraving An artwork made by cutting lines in a metal or wooden plate, then filling the lines with ink and transferring the design under high pressure onto paper or canvas. Multiple prints can be made from each engraving (p. 120).

ENIAC The first computer, developed in the 1940s (p. 742).

Enlightenment A philosophical movement during the 18th century, also known as the Age of Reason because during this period reason was applied to religion, politics, morality, and social life. It is further characterized by a turning away from traditional doctrines and values, a belief in the natural rights of all men, and the belief that natural laws govern the universe and can be understood through the study of nature (p. 129).

entrepôt (än′trə-pō) *n.* A French word for warehouse; in colonial times, a port for clearing goods from the colonies, in which ships were unloaded, records were made of the cargo, a tax was collected, and ships were reloaded for the return voyage (p. 76–7).

enterprising Ready to take on new projects or experiments (p. 460).

entrepreneur Person who creates, organizes, manages, and is responsible for a business or project (p. 420).

EPA Environmental Protection Agency, commissioned by the federal government in 1970 to oversee the conservation of natural resources by investigating causes of pollution and other enviOnmental threats and prosecuting violators of environmental standards (p. 780).

ERA Equal Rights Amendment, an amendment to the U.S. Constitution proposed by feminists to prohibit states and the federal government from discriminating against women (p. 789).

escalate To increase in number, intensity, or scope (p. 765).

espionage Use of spies to obtain information about the plans and activities of a foreign government (p. 720).

eulogy Formal speech praising an individual, often given at a funeral or in memory of someone (p. 759).

evangelical reformers (ē′văn-jĕl′i-kəl) *n.* A group of reformers in the early 19th century who addressed specific social problems such as society's treatment of the handicapped, the insane, and other disadvantaged people; they also tried to correct behavior they believed was morally and socially destructive, such as drunkenness (p. 295).

excise tax Levy placed on the manufacture and sale of certain products, usually luxury items or other nonessential goods (p. 194).

executive branch The President of the U.S. and his advisors, who are responsible for seeing that laws are enforced (p. 165). See also *judicial branch; legislative branch.*

expansion The process of enlarging or increasing something; particularly of enlarging a nation's land area by claiming new territories and stretching out borders (p. 334).

expansionist One who believed the U.S. should join the race for colonies in the late 1800s (p. 532).

exploitation Using natural resources for one's own profit or advantage (p. 575).

ex post facto Latin for "after the fact" (p. 173).

ex post facto law A retroactive law that punishes a person for having done something that was legal before the law was passed (p. 173).

extinct No longer in existence as a species (p. 491).

extradition Sending an accused criminal from the state or country to which he or she has fled back to the state having jurisdiction over the crime to be tried (p. 178).

external taxes Duties placed by Parliament on goods that were imported by the colonies (p. 109).

extremist Person who supports extreme or radical solutions to political problems (p. 325).

F

face value Dollar amount indicated on the front of a note such as a bond or stock certificate (p. 454).

Fair Deal Legislative program proposed by Truman in 1949 intended to build on New Deal reforms. It included raising the minimum wage, increasing Social Security benefits for retired workers, and funding construction of low-income housing (p. 714).

fanatical Excessively, intensely, and uncritically devoted to something (p. 682).

Fascist Political regime exalting nation and race above the individual and headed by a strong repressive dictator (p. 679).

"Fat Boy" Code name of the second atomic bomb, dropped on Nagasaki, Japan, on August 9, 1945 (p. 700).

favor Special right or privilege granted by an elected official to a political supporter (p. 625).

"favorite son" candidate Presidential candidate specially favored by the delegates of his own home state (p. 449).

federalism (fĕd′ər-ə-lĭz′əm) *n*. The doctrine that formerly independent states should be more closely joined than in a confederation, but still maintain a clear division of powers between state and federal governments (p. 165).

Federalist 1. A person who worked for the ratification of the U.S. Constitution (p. 162). 2. A member of a political party, led by Alexander Hamilton, that favored a strong federal government and a *loose construction* of the Constitution (p. 203). See also *Democratic Republican*.

Federal Reserve System Government banking system set up in 1913 to regulate the amount of money in circulation and control private banks. It includes 12 district banks and a semi-public central bank. The system is privately owned and not under direct government control (p. 581).

felony A serious crime, such as murder, that is tried by a district or circuit court.

feminist Person who promotes women's rights and equality of the sexes (p. 558).

FERA The Federal Emergency Relief Act, a program that distributed $500 million in federal funds under Roosevelt's New Deal to help states revive social service programs (p. 665).

Fire-eaters Southern proslavery extrem-

ists who fought to protect slavery in the Western territories and ultimately brought about the secession of the South from the Union (p. 347).

fiscal year Twelve-month accounting period which may start with any month of the year (p. 633).

flapper Young woman of the 1920s whose bold behavior and dress defied conventional norms (p. 630).

fleet Group of ships under one command (p. 535).

flotilla Fleet of ships, especially a naval unit of small warships (p. 535).

flow chart Diagram showing a step-by-step progression, establishing the casual connections among a variety of events and clarifying chronology (p. 726).

"flower children" Disillusioned young people of the 1960s who espoused love, peace, and beauty and protested modern society's materialism and competitiveness by growing their hair long, wearing unusual clothes, shunning work, forming communes, and using drugs to oppose what they saw as senseless rules (p. 767).

foot soldier Soldier trained and equipped to fight on foot (p. 369).

foray A military invasion or attack (p. 222).

foreclosure Legal proceeding in which property is taken away from an owner who cannot pay off the loan used to buy it and given to the creditor (p. 512).

forest reserves Government owned forests from which loggers are banned (p. 575).

"Forty-niner" A person who went to California in 1849 as part of the gold rush that was triggered by the discovery of gold there in 1848 (p. 346).

Founding Fathers The men who wrote the U.S. Constitution and "founded" the U.S. government (p. 158).

Fourteen Points Reconstruction program proposed by Woodrow Wilson after World War I, based on a moral approach to foreign policy (pp. 607–8).

freedmen People emancipated from slavery; particularly after the Civil War, former slaves (p. 395).

Freedmen's Bureau A government agency established at the end of the Civil War to provide various social services for newly freed black and displaced whites (p. 398).

free enterprise system Economic system in which private business can operate competitively for profit without interference by government, except for minimal regulation to protect public interest and ensure a balanced economy (p. 565).

free market Economic market characterized by free, unrestrained, and unsubsidized competition (p. 463).

Freemasons Fraternal society for men which has secret symbolic rites and ceremonies and is based on liberal democratic principles. The Masonic creed upholds religious tolerance, loyalty to local government, and political compromise (p. 470).

freemen Puritans who owned land and were members of the official church. Only freemen were allowed to participate in Massachusetts government (p. 53).

Freeholder An early New England colonist who owned land, could vote for officials, and approve or disapprove all laws (p. 44).

free silver Political movement during the late 1800s calling for free and unlimited coinage of silver to supplement the gold standard (p. 519).

Free Soil party A national political party in 1848 which argued that slavery should be legal where it already existed, but should be outlawed in any territory taken from Mexico. This would reserve western lands for small family farmers rather than plantation owners (p. 346).

frigate A U.S. warship propelled by large sails (p. 204).

frontier (frŭntîr′) *n*. In American history, the westward-moving line between the nation's settled lands and its undeveloped regions (p. 486).

Frost Belt The northern region of the U.S., where temperatures for part of the year dip to the freezing point or below (p. 806).

FTC Federal Trade Commission, federal agency created in 1914 to regulate corporations. The commission is authorized to demand corporations' annual reports, investigate unfair business practices, and order corporations to cease unfair practices (p. 583).

futures A market term for commitments to buy commodities on a given date in the future at a given date (p. 445).

G

Gadsden Purchase A small desert area (present-day southern Arizona) purchased from Mexico in 1853 for a stretch of transcontinental railroad. The property was named for James Gadsden, the U.S. agent who closed the deal (p. 350).

gag rule A rule that restricts freedom of expression or debate in a legislative body, used by the South to set aside all petitions for Congress to discuss the question of slavery (p. 313).

galleon (găl′ē-ən) *n*. A large, heavy Spanish ship of the 15th and 16th centuries with three or four decks at the stern and one or more at the bow; used as a warship and a trader (p. 35).

gang system A method of working small groups of slaves from sunrise to sunset on as many tasks as could be done in daylight (p. 318). See also *task system*.

garner To acquire, accumulate, or collect (p. 576).

garrison Military post (p. 535).

gauge Distance between rails of a railroad track (p. 415).

gazetteer An index of place names at the back of an atlas (p. 408).

Geiger counter Instrument used to detect and measure radiation (p. 742).

General Assembly Group of ambassadors from every nation who serve as the main working body of the United Nations (p. 708).

general strike A strike that affects all the industries in a large region; for example, the one that occurred in Seattle in 1919 (p. 616).

generator A machine that changes mechanical energy, such as steam, moving water, or pressure from ignited fuel, into electrical energy (p. 433).

Geneva Accords 1954 agreement in which Indochina was divided into North Vietnam, governed by the Communist Viet Minh, and South Vietnam, governed by non-Communist Vietnamese (p. 737).

geology The study of the history of the earth and its life, particularly as revealed or recorded in rocks (p. 574).

ghetto (gĕt′ō) *n.* A section of any city where one ethnic or racial group lives exclusive of others, often preserving its own language, customs, and foods (p. 477).

Ghost Dance religion A 19th century Plains Indian movement; participants believed that by performing a ritual dance they could prevail on the Great Spirit to make the white people disappear and bring back to life the bison herds and Indians who had been killed (p. 494).

G I Bill Also known as the Serviceman's Readjustment Act, a bill passed in 1944 to assist veterans in obtaining housing, medical care, and education by providing them with low interest loans, medical benefits, and federal grants for education (p. 723).

Gibson Girls The new, energetic women of the 1890s; named after the role models in the illustrations of Charles Dana Gibson, these women led active lives and thought of themselves as independent persons—although they were not feminists and did not support votes for women (p. 558).

gold rush Mass migration of Americans to California in 1849 when gold was discovered there (p. 346).

gold standard Use of gold as the basis for the value of currency; i.e., only allowing as much currency in circulation as the government has gold in reserve (p. 519).

"Good Government" movement Effort by reformers in the early 1900s to eliminate corruption in government and political machines (p. 563).

Good Neighbor policy American policy under Franklin Roosevelt of not interfering in the internal affairs of Central and South American countries (p. 676).

Goo-Goos Property-owning middle class who opposed political machines in the late 19th century, so named because they called for *good* government (p. 440).

GOP Abbreviation for "Grand Old Party," the Republican party (p. 443).

graduated income tax Scale according to which the wealthy pay a greater percentage of their annual income in taxes than those who earn less (p. 518).

graduation A government policy in the 1800s in which land not sold at an auction was offered for sale at half the original minimum price in order to make it available to poor farmers (p. 252).

graft Acquiring money dishonestly or illegally (p. 563).

grand jury A group of 12 to 23 people who listen to the testimony of witnesses and decide whether enough evidence exists to bring the matter to trial (p. 181).

granges Local organizations of farmers formed in the 1860s to promote farming interests (p. 511).

Great Crash The stock market crash of 1929 that ushered in the Great Depression (p. 646).

Great Depression Period beginning with the stock market crash in 1929 and lasting through much of the 1930s when unemployment was extremely high, prices fell, and many businesses and individuals went bankrupt (p. 646).

Great Salt Lake Basin Large area in northern and central Utah that was once covered by a huge, salty lake (of which the Great Salt Lake is now a remnant), and now is primarily desert (p. 486).

Great Society Reform program carried out by Lyndon Johnson that guaranteed black voting rights, fought poverty, established Medicare, and generally expanded social services throughout the country (p. 760).

Great War Another name for World War I, which was far more destructive than any previous war had been (p. 592).

Greenbackers Post-Civil War political party that fought for inflation of the currency through the issuance of paper money (p. 505).

greenbacks In the 1880s, paper money not redeemable in gold, so called because they were printed with green ink on the back, instead of the usual yellow (p. 392).

Green Berets Special army group sent to a country at war to train soldiers. The group is named for a part of their uniform —a green woolen, visorless cap (p. 764).

Greenpeace Organization that works to preserve wildlife and set aside natural lands for the enjoyment of future generations (p. 788).

Guadelupe Hidalgo A treaty signed in February 1840, in which Mexico agreed to recognize the Rio Grande as the boundary of Texas, and ceded New Mexico and California to the U.S. for $15 million (p. 346).

guerrilla Member of an independent army practicing guerrilla warfare (p. 736).

guerrilla warfare War waged without regard to established laws, customs, or moral principles, especially by independent groups participating in property destruction and sudden raids (p. 354).

gunboat diplomacy 1. The practice of sending troops to an unstable country to protect it from invasion by an enemy.

2. Using military force as a diplomatic tool (p. 545).

H

habeas corpus (hā′bē-əs kôr′pəs) *n.* Latin for "you should have the body"; a writ issued to bring a party before a court to prevent unlawful arrest.

hacienda A large ranch, especially in a Spanish-speaking country (p. 336).

Half-Breed A Republican faction in the 1870s that advocated stamping out corruption in southern politics while tolerating it somewhat, in the North (p. 447).

half-section A half square mile or 320 acre plot in the western U.S. offered for sale by the government, under the Homestead Act of 1862 (p. 153).

hard money Gold and silver coins, as opposed to paper money (p. 274).

hard money policy A belief that no more money in the form of bank notes ought to be lent out than there is gold or silver in the bank vaults to redeem them (p. 274).

Harlem Renaissance Period during the 1920s characterized by many literary and musical achievements by blacks, particularly the development of Dixieland jazz (p. 620).

harrow Machine that breaks up and smooths soil prior to planting (p. 511).

hawk Person who favors war or war-like policies (p. 785).

headright system A system in which colonists able to pay their passage to the New World were granted 50 acres of land "per head" by a *joint-stock company* (p. 40).

Health, Education and Welfare (HEW) Cabinet-level department created in the 1950s to administer social security, SSI, public health, and mental health programs. Reorganized and renamed the Department of Health and Human Services in 1979 (p. 731).

Hebrew Immigrant Aid Society An organization founded in the late 1800s to aid immigrating Eastern European Jews (p. 481).

High Federalist A member of the Federalist Party who favored Alexander Hamilton's ideas over those of John Adams, believing particularly that more money should be allocated for a war with France (p. 204).

high technology The technical advances in scientific, mechanical, and industrial efficiency that permit computerized rapid access to data and automated control systems (p. 807).

hippies Young people in the 1960s who rejected established values and customs of society, advocated nonviolence, and used drugs or other nonconformist behaviors (p. 767).

hogan Round Navajo houses, usually made of mud and logs and built in small, scattered groups (p. 9).

holding company A monopoly that holds the controlling interest in competing companies and regulates them for its own profit (p. 570).

holocaust Complete destruction or slaughter, as of Jews by the Nazis in World War II, or by nuclear bomb (p. 684).

homestead Piece of land acquired free by filing a small fee with the government and living on and farming it for five years (p. 501).

homesteader A person who acquired a piece of private land free by filing a small fee with the government and living on and farming it for five years (p. 510).

Hoovervilles Clusters of shacks made out of junk wood, cardboard, and metal named after President Hoover, whose policies were thought to have caused the Great Depression of the 1930s (p. 656).

horizontal axis The numbers or scale that appears horizontally along the bottom of a line graph (p. 92). See also *vertical axis*.

horizontal integration A method of controlling an industry by dominating the strategic stage in the flow of manufacture; for example, the refining process in the oil industry (p. 426).

hot line Telephone connection between the White House and the Kremlin by which the U.S. and Russian leaders can contact each other in an instant in the event of a crisis (p. 757).

Housing and Urban Development (HUD) Cabinet-level department established in 1965 to administer housing and community development programs (p. 761).

housing code Body of laws regulating housing-related activities such as construction, rents, and landlord responsibilities (p. 480).

Huguenots French Protestants who, like the English Puritans, based their dissenting beliefs on the writings of John Calvin. However, French kings prevented them from immigrating to the New World, which France was determined should be totally Roman Catholic (p. 88).

Hundred Days The first 100 days of Franklin Roosevelt's presidency, during which an unprecedented amount of legislation was passed in a decisive move to end the Depression (p. 661).

hypothesis Tentative conclusion based on study of available facts and observations; a theory (p. 770).

I

ideograph A form of ancient Mayan writing using pictures to represent ideas (p. 7). See also *pictograph*.

ideology Ideals or belief system underlying a person's or government's actions and opinions (p. 441).

illuminated Decorated with gold or silver or very bright colors and having small, intricate designs (p. 14).

immigration Moving from another country to establish residence in the U.S. (p. 474).

immunity The state of being exempt from or protected against something (p. 178).

impartiality Showing no favoritism or bias; treating all equally (p. 571).

impeach (ĭm-pēch') *n.* To bring charges for wrongdoing against a public official (p. 166).

imperialist Advocating extending a nation's power and dominion by acquiring territories or gaining indirect control over outlying areas (p. 532).

implied powers The powers of Congress to adjust to political and social conditions, granted by the elastic clause in the U.S. Constitution (p. 173).

import duty Tax on goods brought from foreign countries into the U.S. (p. 443).

imposts and excises Types of taxes (p. 184).

impressment Involuntary induction into military service (p. 112).

inalienable Not able to be taken away, transferred to another person, or surrendered (p. 151).

inaugural address Speech given by a newly elected President on the day he is formally sworn into office (p. 715).

inaugurated Ceremoniously initiated into office (p. 190).

income tax A tax levied by Congress on the money earned by an individual or business (p. 184).

incumbent Person who already holds a political office (p. 451).

indenture A contract binding a person to work for someone for a certain length of time, usually in return for travel and living expenses. The contract was so called because the paper on which it was written had indented edges (p. 40).

indentured servant (ĭn-děn'chərd) A worker who gained passage to the New World by signing a legal contract to serve a specific master for a set number of years (p. 40).

independent Candidate for political office who is not aligned with a political party (p. 449).

Indian Territory Present-day Oklahoma, the area to which Indians were forcefully removed (p. 488).

indictment (ĭn-dīt'-mənt) A statement by a grand jury charging a person with an offense after ruling that there is enough evidence to bring the person to trial (p. 181).

The Indies European name for Southeast Asia, including Indonesia, China, and Japan, in the 1400s (p. 12).

indigo Plant used to make a blue dye for cloth (p. 64).

indirect election An election in which the people do not vote directly for a leader, but rather choose a person who votes as a representative for a large group of people. For example, the U.S. president is chosen by electors in an indirect election (p. 165).

indoctrinated Thoroughly taught and imbued with certain opinions, viewpoints, or principles (p. 699).

induct To admit or enroll into military service (p. 604).

industrialization The process of becoming involved in the mechanized and systemic manufacturing of goods (p. 244).

Industrial Revolution Period of rapid economic change caused by introduction of machinery and new manufacturing methods, occurring in England in the late 18th century and in the U.S. shortly afterward (p. 238).

infantry Soldiers trained and equipped to fight on foot (p. 368).

inflation (ĭn-flā'shən) *n.* A sharp and continuing increase in the prices of necessities and luxury goods (p. 779).

inflationary spiral Situation in which prices rise, creating a need for even higher wages. To pay higher wages, manufacturers must raise prices, creating a need for even higher wages (p. 779).

influence peddling Using political influence to benefit someone in exchange for money or a bribe (p. 438).

initiative (ĭ-nĭsh'ə-tĭv) *n.* A specific measure put on the ballot by voter petition, thus allowing citizens to bypass lawmakers who might have fallen under the influence of special interests (p. 516).

injunction Court order requiring someone to do or stop doing something (p. 579).

installment plan A system of buying goods by paying for them, plus interest, over a set period of time (p. 643).

insurgent (ĭn-sûr'jənt) *n.* 1. A person who rises up in revolt; a rebel. 2. Specifically, when capitalized, the name congressional Republican Progressives called themselves in 1910 when they joined with Democrats to oppose a powerful Speaker of the House (p. 579).

insurrection An act of open rebellion against an established government.

integration Ending segregation by bringing groups into common and equal membership in society or an organization (p. 733).

interchangeable parts Components of any mechanism or machine that are designed with enough precision so that they will fit into and work with any model of the mechanism (p. 242).

Interior Department Cabinet-level department established in 1849 to monitor natural resources in the U.S. (p. 575).

interlocking directorate A group of bankers who are members of a number of different corporate boards with the goal of eliminating competition, fixing policy and prices, and ensuring a dependable flow of profits for themselves (p. 419).

internal combustion engine Engine invented in the 1860s in which the fuel burns inside the engine itself rather than in a separate furnace (p. 432).

internal taxes Taxes levied by Parliament on transactions occurring within the boundaries of a colony, such as on the printing of newspapers or handbills (p. 109).

international date line The 180 degree meridian that is on exactly the opposite side of the globe from the *prime meridian*. It is the place where each calendar day begins. For example, if it is Monday morning on the east side of the date line, it is Sunday morning on the west side (p. 146).

international gold standard Basing international currency on a stated quantity of gold (p. 678).

internment Confinement, as in a concentration camp or prison, during a war (p. 690).

interstate commerce Trade or business involving two or more states (p. 419).

Interstate Commerce Commission (ICC) Government organization created in 1887 to regulate the railroad industry and subsequently responsible for regulating trade involving two or more states (p. 419).

intervention Government interference in economic or political affairs of another country (p. 545).

ironclad ships Military ships covered with a layer of iron armor to protect the vessel from gunfire and other attacks; the heavy ships moved slowly and sat very low in the water (p. 375).

iron curtain Imaginary barrier between the Soviet Union and western democracy (p. 710).

irreconcilables Group of 16 senators during World War I who opposed the formation of a League of Nations (p. 609).

isolationism Policy of avoiding foreign entanglements and alliances and not taking sides in international affairs (p. 609).

isolationist During the beginning of World War II, a person who advocated that the U.S. stay out of the war by forming no foreign alliances or otherwise taking sides in international affairs (p. 609).

isthmus Narrow strip of land connecting two large bodies of land, such as the Isthmus of Panama, which connects North and South America (p. 20).

IWW Industrial Workers of the World, a radical organization that opposed U.S. involvement in World War I (p. 605).

J

Jacksonian Democracy Government policy under President Andrew Jackson that encouraged equal opportunity (p. 267).

jingoism Practice of seizing dependent areas for the prestige of having colonies rather than for economic reasons (p. 532).

Job Corps Government program that teaches job skills to disadvantaged young men and women aged 16 to 22. Training programs are designed to meet the job needs of a locality, and often include labor union apprenticeship and on-the-job experience (p. 761).

John Birch Society A radically conservative political group that believes the U.S.

should be fighting a holy war against communism (p. 763).

"Johnny Reb" A nickname for the typical Confederate soldier (p. 369).

Joint Chiefs of Staff Department of Defense military advisory group to the President, consisting of the chiefs of the army, air force, navy, and marine corps. The JCS prepares military plans and reviews overall military requirements (p. 720).

joint resolution A resolution made by Congress resulting from a declaration passed by both Houses on the same subject; it becomes law when signed by the President (p. 171). See also *concurrent resolution.*

joint-stock company A private group of shareholders licensed by royal charter to found colonies in the New World and operate them for profit (p. 38).

judicial branch The Supreme Court of the U.S. and other federal courts responsible for judging according to the law and ensuring the executive branch does not act unjustly (p. 165). See also *executive branch; legislative branch.*

jurisdiction Authority to interpret and apply the law (p. 178).

jury A group of 12 people who collectively determine guilt at criminal and civil trials.

K

***kamikaze* pilot** Japanese pilot who volunteered to fly a bomb-laden plane directly into American ships, committing suicide to destroy the enemy's fleet (p. 699).

Kellogg-Briand Pact 1928 treaty between the U.S. and France that outlawed war between the two nations. Eventually, 62 nations signed the pact, promising never to war against the others who signed (p. 634).

kickback An illegal payment to a political machine by a company desiring a government contract; the company submits an artificially high bid and gives, or kicks back, a large sum to the machine (p. 438).

Knights of Labor Secret labor organization founded in 1869, the first to organize workers of all trades into a single union which was powerful enough to force railroads to meet its demands (p. 469).

Know-Nothings A secret political organization in the 1800s, also known as "The Order of the Star-Spangled Banner," that opposed Roman Catholicism and Catholic immigrants; so called because members claimed to "know nothing" about the organization or its purpose (p. 302).

Ku Klux Klan Group of white racist secret societies that preach black inferiority and hatred of foreigners, Catholics, and Jews, and use terrorism and violence to repress minorities (p. 405).

L

labor union Organization of laborers or workers formed to achieve better work-

ing conditions, wages, hours and benefits (p. 469).

laissez faire (lĕs′ā-fâr′) 1. In economics, the theory that government should allow trade, business and industry to operate with as little regulation or interference as possible. 2. By extension, the belief in letting people do as they please, leaving the solution of social problems to private citizens (p. 295).

lame duck An elected official continuing for what is usually a brief interim between the election and inauguration of a successor (p. 185).

land grant Gift of land from the government for a specific purpose, such as for a railroad or college (p. 418).

landslide Great majority of votes leading to a sweeping victory (p. 450).

laser High intensity light beam with wide applications, from medicine to space technology (p. 807).

Latter-Day Saints Also known as Mormons, members of a church, founded in 1830 by Joseph Smith, who accept The Book of Mormon as scripture along with the Bible and who believe in modern day prophets and revelation. Members were persecuted for practicing polygamy, among other reasons, and eventually migrated to the Utah Territory under the leadership of Brigham Young after Smith was murdered by a mob (p. 288).

lead In a news story, the first paragraph or sentence which includes essential facts (p. 524).

League of Nations International association created to maintain peace after World War I by pledging unified defense against aggression (p. 582).

LED Light-emitting diode, the material used in digital displays in clocks, calculators (p. 809).

left-wing Radical, advocating political reform or overthrow of the established order (p. 759). See also *right-wing.*

legend List that shows what each symbol on a map represents (p. 116).

legislative branch Congress of the U.S., responsible for making the laws (p. 165). See also *executive branch; judicial branch.*

legislature Law-making body of a government (p. 541).

lend-lease Policy of giving or loaning goods and services to an ally during wartime (p. 686).

liberal arts curriculum Courses in school built around traditional subjects such as Latin, philosophy, mathematics, history and public speaking (p. 554).

Liberal Republicans Political party that broke off from the Republican party in 1872 to oppose the corruption of Grant's presidency and promote an idealistic view. Their candidate, Horace Greeley, was badly beaten in the 1872 election (p. 446).

lien A claim on property made by someone who does not own it, resulting from the property being promised as payment for a debt (p. 79).

limited liability (lĭ′ə-bĭl′ə-tē) A principle that limits a bankrupt corporation's creditors to recovering debts on its assets but leaves undisturbed the personal property of shareholders and their shares in other corporations (p. 430).

limited suffrage The restriction of voting rights to a certain group of people such as property owners or male heads of households (p. 87).

line graph A graph with numbers or other information along the bottom and left side so that points inside the graph and connected by a line refer to both a number on the bottom and the side (p. 92). See also *vertical axis, horizontal axis.*

litigation Trial of a case in a court of law (p. 177).

"Little Boy" Code name for the first atomic bomb, dropped on Hiroshima, Japan, on August 6, 1945 (p. 700).

lobby 1. (*v.*) To promote the passage of legislation by influencing public officials (p. 481). 2. (*n.*) A group engaged to promote a special interest by influencing public officials, especially legislators (p. 442).

locks Sections of a canal closed off with gates and used in raising or lowering boats as they pass from level to level (p. 256).

log The record of a ship's voyage, including such things as distance traveled, speed, and location (p. 17).

Lone Star Republic Area which is now the states of Texas and parts of New Mexico and Colorado, won from Mexico in 1836 and established temporarily as an independent nation (p. 338).

long staple A kind of cotton with long fibers and smooth, slippery seeds (p. 246).

loophole An unclear or indefinite part of a law which can be used to avoid the actual intent of the law (p. 565).

loose construction A way of interpreting the Constitution that gives the federal government any powers not explicitly denied it or reserved for the states (p. 197). See also *strict construction.*

Louisiana Territory The center third of the U.S. between the Mississippi River and Rocky Mountains, purchased from France in 1803 (p. 87).

Lowell system System of manufacturing developed by Francis Cabot Lowell in the 1800s in which farm girls were recruited to work for a few years in mills under strict supervision, then returned home to their traditional lifestyle (p. 244).

loyalists People who fought on the side of Great Britain during the Revolutionary War (p. 127).

loyalty oath A statement required of federal employees and applicants for federal assistance that they are not members of the Communist Party, nor any group affiliated with it, and they do not advocate overthrowing the U.S. government by force (p. 720).

lyceums (lī-sē′əmz) *n.* Programs popular before the Civil War in which experts went to lecture in isolated towns (p. 555).

M

macadam Blacktop paving invented in England and composed of small, broken stones and asphalt (p. 253).

machinist Person who operates, makes, assembles or repairs machinery (p. 464).

magnate Person of high rank, influence or power in a specific field (p. 616).

Manhattan Project Secret, government-funded research in Chicago and Los Alamos, New Mexico, leading to the development of the atomic bomb (p. 699).

Manifest Destiny A slogan coined in the 1840s to justify the westward expansion of the U.S. The slogan asserted that the U.S. was obviously fated to rule the continent from the Atlantic to the Pacific (p. 342).

manumit (măn′yŏŏ-mĭt′)   -mitted, -mitting *v.t.* To set free from bondage or slavery (p. 322).

map grid A network of evenly spaced horizontal and vertical meridians on a map used to locate points or indicate longitude and latitude (p. 146). See also *meridians, parallels.*

maritime Related to navigation or sea trade (p. 15).

Marshall Plan Secretary George Marshall's program for combatting communism by investing vast amounts of U.S. money in the reconstruction of European countries ravaged by World War II (p. 711).

Mason-Dixon Line The Maryland-Pennsylvania border that generally divided the eastern U.S. into North and South, free and slave states (p. 233).

Masonic Order A men's secret fraternal society (p. 265).

mass production The manufacture of goods or articles in large numbers, often by using assembly-line machinery and usually at a great saving in cost over hand production (p. 242).

massive retaliation (rĭ-tăl′ē-ā′shən) A response by one nation to an antagonistic action of another, involving the full-scale annihilation of the other in a nuclear attack (p.736).

"master race" According to German Nazis, the white European race was superior and should rule and eliminate all others to preserve its "purity" (p. 683).

materialism Preoccupation with material things, such as possessions, to the exclusion of spiritual or intellectual values (p. 481).

McCarthyism The political tactic of labeling as a traitor dissenters from approved ideas. After Senator Joseph McCarthy, who accused government officials and private citizens of being communists in the 1950s Red Scare (p. 720).

Medicaid Government funded program established in 1965 that gives medical benefits to blind, disabled, and very poor people (p. 761).

Medicare Government-funded health insurance program for senior citizens, established under Lyndon Johnson's "Great Society" (p. 760).

"Me generation" Nickname for the 1970s, a period during which Americans seemed to lose interest in political and social involvement and to withdraw into private, personal concerns (p. 786).

mercantilism (mûr′kən-tēl-ĭz′əm) *n.* An economic doctrine which argues that a country can strengthen itself by exporting more than it imports and by investing the profits in new domestic production and increased military spending (p. 28).

mercenary (mûr′sə-nĕr′ē) *n.* A soldier, usually hired by a foreign state, who serves for pay instead of national patriotism. —*adj.* Serving for money (p. 133).

"merchants of death" The name given to munitions makers after World War I when it was suspected they encouraged and were responsible for the war (p. 678).

merger Absorption of one corporation by another (p. 419).

meridians The set of vertical lines on a map grid that show degrees of longitude in relation to the prime meridian, which is 0 degrees longitude. All meridians are equal in length and meet at the North and South Poles (p. 146).

mestizo A person of mixed Spanish and Indian blood (p. 30).

metropolis Large, important city that is the center of business and activity for a region (p. 478).

microchips Tiny, integrated circuits that make it possible to build desksize computers (p. 809).

midnight judge A judge appointed to fill a vacancy in the federal courts during the final hours of a president's term (p. 206).

militia People available to be called into the armed forces in an emergency, including the Reserves and the National Guard (p. 152).

Millerites A religious sect founded in 1831 by William Miller, who preached the imminent second-coming of Christ (p. 288). See also *Seventh-Day Adventists.*

milling Grinding grain into flour (p. 421).

minutemen Farmers and craftsmen, trained informally on village greens as soldiers, who promised to be ready on a minute's notice for battle just before and after the Revolutionary War (p. 121).

mission 1. Self-sufficient communities of free Indians, founded by Spanish priests (p. 336). 2. A church built to spread Christianity, educate Indians, and provide shelter for travelers (p. 337).

mita Tax paid to the Inca emperor by common people in the form of several days work each year (p. 7).

mobilizing Assembling and readying for war (p. 684).

Model T Simple, inexpensive car developed by Henry Ford in 1908 (p. 637).

moderate A person without extreme political or social views (p. 356).

Molly Maguires Secret society formed in the 1870s by Irish coal miners in Pennsylvania who tried to improve working conditions by terrorizing mine owners and destroying mine property (p. 468).

monarchy Rule by one person, such as a king or queen (p. 165).

money pool A midwestern farm association like a credit union, capitalized by members and operated on a non-profit basis to eliminate dependence on banks (p. 515).

monopoly Company that controls the entire market for one type of service or goods (p. 516).

Moors Moslems from northwestern Africa who had conquered Portugal and Spain in the 700s (p. 14).

Moral Majority A national organization advancing fundamentalist religious and conservative social views in the political arena (p. 799).

mores Customs, standards, or habits of a particular group.

Mormon Church See *Latter-Day Saints.*

mortgage To pledge property as payment for a loan if agreed on payments are not met on schedule (p. 455).

Moslems Arabs who are converts to the religion of Islam (p. 12).

mountain men Fur trappers who explored the Rocky Mountains and deserts beyond in the early 19th century (p. 248).

muckraker (mŭk′rāk-ər) *n.* A journalist in the early 1900s who specialized in magazine articles or books revealing corruption and dishonesty in business and government (p. 560).

mud-slinging Using abusive, insulting, or denouncing speeches against a political opponent (p. 266).

Mugwumps *Liberal Republicans* who rejoined the Republican party after the election of 1872. The name, an Indian word meaning "great men" or "big chiefs," was a poke by Republican regulars at the liberals' self-proclaimed righteousness (p. 446).

mulattoes People of mixed Spanish and African decent (p. 31).

municipal Related to city or local government (p. 436).

N

NAACP National Association for the Advancement of Colored People, a civil rights organization formed in 1909 to end discrimination and promote education and leadership for blacks (p. 562).

NAM National Association of Manufacturers, a pro-employer organization formed in 1893 to counteract unionism (p. 472).

NASA National Aeronautics and Space Administration, a government organization in charge of space exploration and rocket technology (p. 751).

national debt ceiling The legal limit of borrowing that the government allows itself (p. 801).

national deficit Amount the federal government has spent above what it has taken in (p. 802).

national domain Public land owned by the federal or state government (p. 153).

National Guard Reserve military force recruited by each state, equipped by the federal government, and subject to the call of either (p. 734).

nationalism The principle that people who speak the same language and share the same culture should live in their own nation (p. 619).

Nationalist A person who believes the federal government should be more powerful than the state governments (p. 716).

nationalization Turning control or ownership over to the national government (p. 519).

National Labor Relations Act Law Passed by Congress in 1935 to preserve the right of democratically chosen labor unions to represent employees (p. 667).

National Republic Party A political party of the early 1800s that favored a *loose interpretation* of the Constitution and a strong central government (p. 266).

National Road A road built under direction of Henry Clay that connected Cumberland, Maryland, with Wheeling, West Virginia; it was later extended to Vandalia, Illinois (p. 253).

National Youth Administration Division of the *WPA* under Roosevelt's New Deal that provided jobs for two million students (p. 666).

Native American Party A political party formed by the Know-Nothings in the 1850s that advocated barring Roman Catholics and other groups from immigrating to the U.S. (p. 302).

NATO North Atlantic Treaty Organization, an alliance formed in 1949 by nine democratic nations pledging mutual defense (p. 716).

naturalist Person who studies animals in their natural setting rather than in a laboratory (p.574).

naturalized Granted U.S. citizenship (p. 172).

natural monopoly Enterprise that members of the Populist party thought could be run most efficiently under a single management, such as railroads or the telegraph industry (p. 517).

natural resources Materials such as water, oil, and coal, that are supplied by nature (p.412).

natural-rights An 18th century doctrine which held that all human beings were given certain rights by the Creator that could not be taken away by a government; such rights as life, liberty and property (p. 129).

naval stores Tar, pitch, and turpentine used to make wooden ships watertight (p. 77).

Nazis *Fascist* party that controlled Germany from 1933 to 1945 under Adolf Hit-

ler. The term comes from two German words *national* and *sozialist,* or "national socialist" (p. 682).

negotiate Resolve through discussion and compromise (p. 532).

neutrality Not taking sides in an argument (p. 199).

Neutrality Acts Four acts passed between 1935 and 1937, designed to avoid foreign entanglements that could lead to war (p. 680).

neutral zone Area in which no fighting or other war-related activities are to take place (p. 686).

New Deal Program designed by Franklin Roosevelt to promote economic recovery from the Great Depression and social reform. It included several jobs programs, the Social Security system, a steeply graduated income tax, and bank and farm subsidies (p. 660).

"New Era" Period during the Coolidge administration when expanded business and economic growth were encouraged by government policies (p. 632).

New Era diplomacy U.S. practice of controlling finances of Latin American countries in the 1920s through investments and the use of military troops to put down rebellions, thereby protecting American business interests (p. 635).

New France Territory in North America owned by France before 1763 and composed of present-day Canada, Louisiana, and the French West Indies (p. 46).

New Freedom Program sponsored by Woodrow Wilson in 1910 emphasizing states' rights and breaking up trusts to restore competition (p. 581).

The New Frontier Reform program introduced by John F. Kennedy that included government-funded medical care for the elderly and programs such as the Peace Corps (p. 748).

New Immigrants Wave of immigrants entering the U.S. in the late 19th and early 20th centuries, mainly from southern and eastern Europe. Unlike earlier immigrants, they were not as quickly or readily assimilated and tended to retain their former cultures (p. 477).

New Left Liberal college students and professors in the 1960s who strongly opposed the Vietnam War (p. 767).

New Nationalism Progressive program begun by Theodore Roosevelt in his 1910 campaign for the presidency, calling for women's suffrage, restrictions on child labor, stronger labor union rights, national retirement insurance, and other reforms (p. 579).

New Netherland In the 1600s, the area now New York, originally settled by the Dutch (p. 47).

New York Stock Exchange Place, located on Wall Street in New York City, where shares of corporate stocks are bought and sold (p. 445).

Nisei (nē-sā′) *n.* American-born Japanese, many of whom were persecuted during World War II and herded into "relocation camps" in the West and Midwest (p. 690).

NLF National Liberation Front, a powerful guerrilla force opposed to Diem's dictatorial government of South Vietnam (p. 764).

Nobel Prize Annual monetary prize established by Alfred Nobel to honor outstanding contributions in the fields of peace, literature, medicine, chemistry, physics, and economics (p. 752).

nomadic Wandering from place to place according to the season and available food supply (p. 489).

nominating convention A meeting of delegates held by a political party to choose a nominee for elected office (p. 768).

nonaggression pact Agreement between countries not to fight (p. 684).

nonrecognition Policy of refusing official acknowledgement to governments or boundaries established by force (p. 678).

nonrenewable resources Resources such as coal and oil that, once used, are gone forever (p. 784).

nonviolent civil disobedience A theory of political action which holds that citizens have a moral duty to disobey unjust laws without the use of force. Specifically, a tactic used by the civil rights movement to end racial discrimination against black people (p. 734).

normalcy State of being normal and regular (p. 624).

note A written contract to pay a certain amount of money by a specified date (p. 644).

Northwest Territory The area of land bounded by the Great Lakes, the Ohio River, and the Mississippi River. The area today includes Ohio, Indiana, Illinois, Michigan, Wisconsin, and part of Minnesota (p. 153).

NOW The National Organization for Women, a group founded by Betty Friedan to overturn laws that discriminate against women on the basis of sex (p. 788).

NRA The National Recovery Administration, formed under Roosevelt's New Deal to promote cooperation within industries by setting codes for production and quality, wages, working conditions, and unions (p. 666).

nuclear reactor Device in which a controlled chain reaction occurs, producing a tremendous amount of energy. In the U.S. nuclear reactors are used primarily to produce electricity (p. 743).

nullification The act by a state of preventing the operation and enforcement of a federal law within the state's boundaries (p. 270).

nullify (nŭl′-ə-fī) v.t. To render void of legal force or effect (p. 206).

O

oath of allegiance Formal promise of loyalty or support (p. 270).

occupation Seizure and control of a country or area by stationing military forces within it.

occupation zones Four areas into which Germany was divided after World War II, to be governed by Britain, France, the Soviet Union and the U.S. (p. 698).

OEO Office of Economic Opportunity, a federal agency formed to direct Lyndon Johnson's *War on Poverty* program, which funded educational opportunities for disadvantaged children and adults (p. 761).

offensive Aggressive attack on an enemy during a war (p. 775).

"Old Hickory" Nickname given to Andrew Jackson.

omnibus bill Bill containing or providing for many things at once.

onimeter Tool used in land surveying (p. 584).

OPEC Organization of Petroleum Exporting Countries, founded in 1960 by oil-rich countries to gain more control over the world oil market (p. 785).

Open Door policy Policy giving all nations equal opportunity for trade with a country (p. 542).

optical fibers Very thin glass or plastic tubes that carry light and are used in telephone systems and computers. Since light travels faster than electricity, optical fibers can carry more information at a faster rate than wire can (p. 743).

orator Skillful or eloquent public speaker (p. 441).

oratory Art of speaking effectively or eloquently in public (p. 519).

Oregon Country The area of North America that now includes Oregon, Washington, part of Idaho, and the Canadian province of British Columbia (p. 230).

Oregon system Government reforms developed in Oregon in the early 1900s introducing the *initiative, recall, referendum,* as well as *primary elections* and direct election of U.S. senators. The system was based on the theory that the more democratic government was, the better it would be (p. 564).

Oregon Trail After 1840, a route leading westward from Missouri by which emigrants traveled in Conestoga wagons with their cattle and belongings to settle in the Pacific Northwest (p. 341).

original jurisdiction The power of the court to hear and judge a case before any other court can do so (p. 177).

oscillograph Electronic device used by engineers to produce a visual display of an electrical signal on a screen (p. 648).

override To obtain two-thirds of the votes of both Congressional houses in order to annul a Presidential veto of a bill, thus making the bill law without the President's approval (p. 165).

P

Palestine Liberation Organization (PLO) An organization of homeless Arabs who lived in the region that is now Israel and who seek return to a homeland, often by tactics involving violence and terrorism (p. 795).

panhandle Narrow projection of land from a larger body, resembling the handle of a pan (p. 542).

Panic of 1819 A depression caused by uncontrolled land speculation, which finally resulted in many bank failures and crashing land prices (p. 252).

parallels The set of horizontal lines on a map grid that show degrees of latitude in relation to the North and South Poles. The longest parallel is the equator, at 0 degrees latitude (p. 146).

pardon Presidential release or excuse from the legal penalties of an offense or crime (p. 784).

parity (păr′ə-tē) n. A level of farm income that compares favorably with earnings in a good year. Parity is calculated to keep the price of farm produce equal to that of a base period (p. 646).

patent Legal document that guarantees an inventor the exclusive right to make, use, or sell his invention (p. 428).

patent medicines Nonprescription and easily available substances advertised in the early 20th century as cure-alls. Widely publicized in magazines and newspapers, and sold by mail, most had a high alcohol content (p. 573).

Patriot An American colonial who supported independence in the Revolutionary War, in contrast to a *Loyalist* (or *Tory*), who supported Great Britain (p. 127).

patriotism Love for one's country (p. 127).

patronage Distribution of government jobs by an office holder to supporters or friends (p. 385).

patroon A Dutch landowner in the area now New York (p. 47).

Peace Corps Organization of trained volunteers who work in under-developed countries to help improve living conditions (p. 753).

pellagra Fatal niacin-deficiency disease (p. 513).

Pennsylvania System Prison system developed in Pennsylvania in which inmates were kept in solitary confinement night and day, preventing hardened criminals from influencing minor offenders and giving convicts plenty of time to repent their crimes; however, the solitude drove many prisoners insane and the system was very expensive (p. 298). See also *Auburn System.*

pension Fixed sum paid regularly to someone upon retirement (p. 668).

pension bills Legislation introduced by Northern Republicans after the Civil War providing monthly payments to specific Union veterans from their home congressional districts who had persuaded them that their cases were just (p. 442).

perfectionists Utopian philosophers who believed that rather than being essentially evil, individuals had the ability to become perfect (p. 291).

periphery The bare outline or outer boundaries of something (p. 2).

perjury Lying under oath in a court of law (p. 720).

perquisites Expected privileges and gains that result from holding a job or political position (p. 444).

persecution Harassment with intent to inflict injury or suffering because of a person's beliefs (p. 683).

petit guerre (pə-tē′gär) n. French for "little war"; a raid-and-run style of fighting the colonists learned from the Indians.

petit jury (pet′-ē) A panel of 12 jurors who hear a case tried and decide whether or not the accused person is guilty (p. 181). Also see *grand jury*.

petroglyphs Line drawings or carvings on rock done by pre-Columbian Indians (p. 9).

philanthropic Dedicated to improving society, usually by donating money or time to charitable organizations (p. 460).

philanthropy Donation of money or time to charitable organizations (p. 463).

physical map Also called a topographic map, a map showing natural features such as mountains, valleys, and bodies of water (p. 116).

pictograph A form of Mayan writing using pictures to represent objects (p. 7).

pie graph Circular graph divided into sections that show relative percentages of the whole (p. 282).

pig iron Crude iron that is refined to make steel (p. 520).

Pilgrims English Separatists who settled in Plymouth in 1620 to escape religious persecution in Europe (p. 42).

pillory A device used by the Puritans to publicly punish wrong-doers. It consisted of a wooden frame with holes in which the head and hands were locked (p. 54).

Plains Indians Indians living on the Great Plains, including the Comanche, Cheyenne, Arapaho, Mandan, Crow, Sioux, Nez Perce, and Blackfoot tribes (p. 488).

plateau A flat plain that rises above surrounding land (p. 11).

"playing the market" Buying stocks with intent to sell for profit when prices rise rather than to collect regular dividends (p. 644).

plurality More votes than any other candidate, but not more than half the total votes (p. 234).

pneumatic drill Drill invented in the 1880s that is activated by air pressure and is used in mining (p. 433).

pocket veto A way of vetoing a legislative bill without sending a formal explanation to Congress; if Congress adjourns during the ten day period the President has to sign or veto a law, he may "pocket" the bill (do nothing at all with it), and the bill will die without presidential explanation (p. 395).

pogrom (pō-grum′) n. An organized massacre against a minority group, especially Jews (p. 476).

Point Four Point in Truman's inaugural address in which he recommended that the U.S. combat Communist influence in under-developed countries by giving these countries military, economic, and technical aid (p. 716).

Political Action Committees (PACs) Supposedly independent groups that contribute large sums of money to political campaigns, circumventing the federal law limiting the amount a candidate's campaign committee can spend (p. 799).

political boss Politician who controls votes, appointments, and delegation of responsibilities within a political party (p. 570).

political machine A highly effective group organized to achieve a common political goal, usually by all voting the same (p. 436).

political map Map showing political boundaries around cities, states, and/or countries (p. 116).

poll tax A tax that must be paid as a requirement for voting; this tax was abolished in 1964 by the 24th Amendment (p. 186).

polygamy The state of being married to more than one wife (p. 289).

population density Number of people living in a given area, i.e., 100 people per square mile.

popular sovereignty (sŏv′ər-ən-tē) The doctrine, proposed before the Civil War, that settlers of a territory be allowed to decide for themselves whether or not to legalize slavery in the new states from the territory (p. 350).

Populist party Also known as the "People's party," a political party formed in 1892 by farmers advocating reforms such as popular election of senators, a secret ballot, public ownership of monopolies, and an increase of money in circulation (p. 516).

pork-barrel bills Lucrative contracts for government work awarded to businesspeople who have supported the party in power (p. 443).

portage A place where canoes are carried from waterway to waterway (or lake to river) (p. 89).

positive good theory Southerners' justification for slavery, based on religious, historical, cultural, racial, and sociological arguments, which claimed slavery was good for both society and the slaves themselves (p. 313).

potlatch A traditional party of the Northwest Indian culture in which the hosts gave away their accumulated wealth to invited guests (p. 10).

preamble An introduction to a formal document.

precedent A standard occurrence that later events or actions will be compared to or based on (p. 192).

predestination The Puritan belief that some individuals are destined for salvation while others are not, regardless of personal desires or efforts (p. 284).

pre-emption A land sale policy in the 1800s in which a person who settled and improved government land prior to its official sale could buy it at the minimum price rather than having to bid for it against others; also called "squatter's rights" (p. 252).

preservationist (prĕz′ər-vā′shən-ĭst) n. A person who believes that wilderness should be conserved and protected from development so that some natural retreats will always be available to society (p. 575). See *reservationist*.

preside To act as president or chairman or to exercise guidance or control over a group.

presidios Military forts built by the Spaniards in America (p. 32).

primary election A preliminary vote to choose candidates for office from a certain political party (p. 564).

primary source Firsthand record of an event, such as a newspaper article, diary, book, letter, or official document written by someone who was actually present when the event occurred (p. 506).

prime meridian An imaginary line at 0 degrees longitude running between the North and South Poles and through Greenwich, England; all other longitudes are calculated from the prime meridian (p. 146).

private associations Regulatory bodies proposed by Hoover in 1919 that would have overseen large areas of the economy and promoted cooperation between businesspeople and farmers (p. 625).

privateer (prī′və-tîr′) n. A privately owned ship under contract to a government to attack and capture (p. 20).

processing Turning raw materials into consumer goods (p. 421).

proclamation Official public announcement (p. 502).

producer cooperatives Farm organizations formed to counter the great power of railroads by building and operating independent grain elevators rather than using the railroad storage facilities (p. 515).

pro-expansionists Advocates of annexing territories in the late 1890s who used the argument that the white race had a duty and a right to govern "inferior" people and spread Christianity (p. 540).

profiteering Taking unreasonable profits from business activities (p. 440).

Progressive Era Early 20th century movement to clean out corruption in city governments, achieve more democratic state governments, regulate big business, and make other reforms (p. 552).

Progressive party Liberal group led by Henry Wallace that split from the Democrats in 1948 to promote a more ambitious program of social reform and an end to the Cold War (p. 713).

Progressives Members of an early 20th century reform movement that cleaned out corruption in city governments, worked for more democratic state governments, and used the powers of the federal government to regulate big business (p. 561).

Prohibition Fourteen-year period (1919-1933) during which it was illegal to make, transport, or sell alcohol (p. 620).

prohibitionists Advocates of an amendment to the Constitution prohibiting the use or sale of alcohol (p. 620).

propaganda techniques Ways used to win others over to an opinion. These include: name calling, glittering generalities, transfer, "just plain folks," and the bandwagon approach (p. 704).

propagandist Person who uses propaganda to spread opinions and beliefs (p. 540).

proprietary colony (prə-prī′ə-těr′ē) *n.* A settlement or region in the New World, ruled by landowners who were free to develop it for personal profit in any way they wished (p. 59).

proprietor (prə-prī′ə-tər) *n.* 1. Person who has exclusive right to a possession or piece of private property. 2. The owner of a *proprietary colony* (p. 60).

prosecution 1. Act of bringing a criminal case before the court to be tried. 2. The person or party who brings a case to court against an accused individual or party (p. 181).

protectionism Policy of using government controls to protect the economic interests of producers by placing restrictions on foreign competitions.

protective tariff Tax on foreign imports that is levied primarily to protect a nation's own businesses from foreign competition by making imports more expensive than domestic products (p. 197).

protectorate (prə-těk′tər-ĭt) *n.* A self-governing country that is subject to the influence and control of another country in such stipulated areas as treaties, debts, and defense, and thus is not a completely sovereign nation (p. 539).

pro tempore Latin for "temporarily" or "for the time being" (p. 169).

public domain Any land owned by the U.S. government (p. 416).

public lands Lands owned and administrated by the federal government, particularly those to be sold under the homestead laws of the 1800s (p. 178).

public works projects Government projects under Roosevelt in the 1930s providing community improvement jobs for the unemployed (p. 670).

pueblo (pweb′lō) A Hopi or Zuni Indian village comprised of adobe houses, often built in the sides of cliffs (p. 9).

puppet government Government whose "strings" are pulled by a more powerful government, or whose policies and actions are dictated by someone else (p. 678).

purchasing power The amount of actual goods money will buy; i.e., a dollar had more *purchasing power* in 1950 than it does now because prices were lower and more goods could be bought with a dollar (p. 465).

Pure Food and Drug Acts Laws enacted in 1906 and 1938 to set health and safety standards for food and drug production and marketing (p. 573).

Puritans An English group who wanted to reform the Church of England from within by removing all Roman Catholic elements. They migrated to Massachusetts to escape "evil" changes in the Church made by James I and to establish a society where only the Puritan religion would be practiced (p. 50).

Purple Heart Military award given to any member of the U.S. armed forces who is wounded or killed in action.

pyramids Very large stone structures built by the Mayan Indians in ancient Mexico. They have four triangular sides that meet in a point at the top (p. 6).

Q

Quakers A religious sect, also known as the Society of Friends, that holds all life sacred. It believes each person can communicate directly with God and has no formal church hierarchy. Under William Penn, this group settled in Pennsylvania (p. 67).

quarter-section A quarter square mile or 160 acre plot in the western U.S. offered for sale by the government under the Homestead Act of 1862 (p. 153).

quorum (kwôr′əm) *n.* The minimum number of members of Congress who must be present in order to transact business (p. 170).

quit-rent system English custom developed at the end of the Middle Ages in which serfs paid money to landowners to free themselves of the obligation to work for them; in the New World, *proprietors* would give land to immigrants according to the *headright system* and collect quit-rents when the settlers could pay (p. 60).

R

racism Belief that a person's traits and capacities are determined by race and that one race is naturally superior to others (p. 683).

racist Person who believes in the inherent superiority of one race over another (p. 519).

Radical Reconstruction program Government program enacted in 1867 that divided the former Confederacy into five districts governed by martial law and supervised readmission proceedings and the re-establishment of state governments (p. 400).

Radical Republican Northern Republicans who attacked Lincoln for not pushing the Civil War and the elimination of slavery hard enough (p. 394).

raider Fast, armed ship that attacks and loots merchant vessels (p. 453).

rate war Competition between companies for the lowest prices and most customers (p. 415).

ratification The process of formally approving something (p. 162).

ratified Formally approved by Congress (p. 162).

rationing Distributing food or goods equally among groups or individuals, sometimes necessary during wartime when essential items are in short supply (p. 604).

raw materials Materials in a natural, unprocessed state that are used in the manufacture of useful products (p. 454).

reactionary Someone who wants to reverse progress; ultraconservative (p. 577).

Reader's Guide to Periodical Literature Multivolume index to magazine articles published between 1802 and the present (p. 628).

Reaganomics Ronald Reagan's economic policies during his presidency, including program and budget cuts and *supply side economics* (p. 802).

real income Actual purchasing power (p. 512).

realist Writer or artist who tries to depict life and nature accurately and as they really are instead of idealistically (p. 559).

real wages The actual *purchasing power* of a person's wages (p. 465).

reaper Machine designed to cut down a crop of grain (p. 428).

rebate Return of part of a payment (p. 572).

recall A voter petition that would require an elected official to resign or submit to a special election (p. 516).

reciprocal trade clause Clause in a trade agreement reducing duties on imports from nations that also lower their tariffs on American goods (p. 454).

reciprocity (rěs′ə-prŏs′ə-tē) *n.* A mutual exchange, especially the exchange of special privileges to encourage trade between two nations (p. 678).

reclamation Restoring damaged land and water resources to use (p. 575).

recognition Formal diplomatic, acknowledgement of a nation, government, or political action (p. 590).

reconnaissance Exploratory military examination of enemy armies, position, or territory (p. 368).

Reconstruction 1. The policy by which southern states after the Civil War could demonstrate allegiance to the Union, reorganize their governments, hold Congressional elections, and reestablish a relationship with the federal government. 2. Period from 1865 to 1877 when southern states returned to the Union (p. 394).

Red Army Russian army during World War II (p. 685).

Red Cross International organization formed in 1863 to alleviate human suffering and promote public health (p. 605).

redeemable Able to be converted into

something of full value, as paper money was once *redeemable* in gold. (p. 454)

redeemers White Democrats who regained control of southern states and "redeemed" them from Radical Republicans after the Civil War (p. 405).

rediscount rate Rate of interest at which *Federal Reserve* banks loan money to other banks (p. 785).

Red Russians Communist party, also known as Bolsheviks, who violently overthrew the Russian government in 1917 (p. 616). See also *White Russians*.

Red Scare Mass hysteria in the 1950s over alleged Communist infiltration of the U.S. government (p. 720). See also *McCarthyism*.

referendum (ref′ə-ren′dəm) *n.* An election to pass or reject an initiative (or other specific political proposal) put on the ballot by petition (p. 516).

refined Purified or having unwanted elements removed (p. 421).

reform To change for the better by removing faults, abuses (p. 284).

Reformation A 16th century religious movement in which Roman Catholic doctrine and practices were rejected or modified by individuals and groups who established Protestant Churches.

reform movement Movement to change or improve an undesirable condition (p. 284).

regime A form of government (p. 802).

relocation camps Camps in which Japanese Americans were interned in 1942 because of fear of a national security threat (p. 690).

remuda Large horse herd accompanying a cattle drive in the 1800s (p. 499).

renaissance French word for "rebirth," often used in connection with a period of time characterized by much artistic and intellectual activity (p. 12).

reparations Money or materials paid for damages or costs resulting from a war (p. 634).

repeal To officially withdraw or cancel (p. 185).

representation Belief that members of a community have a say in making the laws by which they are governed (p. 40).

repressive Preventing natural or normal activities, development, or expression (p. 802).

republic Government in which laws are made by elected representatives and those they appoint to office (p. 178).

republican (*adj.*) Having the characteristics of a government in which citizens elect officers and representatives who are responsible to the voters and to a body of laws (p. 178).

Republicans Political party formed in 1854 committed to keeping slavery out of all territories (p. 351).

reschedule Give a debtor more time to repay a loan (p. 634).

rescind To take back, cancel or make void (p. 183).

reservation Area of public land set aside for the use of Indians; reservations were usually placed on land unsuitable for farming and therefore unattractive for private ownership (p. 494).

reservationist (rĕz′ər-vā′shən-ĭst) *n.* **1.** A person who believes that economically valuable natural resources should be conserved for future use and development (p. 575). See *preservationist*. **2.** During the Senate debate over the League of Nations, a senator who would vote for the League if certain reservations were inserted in its covenant (p. 609).

reserved powers Power held by the states for themselves alone (p. 193). See also *concurrent powers, delegated powers*.

resolution A formal statement of a decision adopted by Congress.

revenues Taxes collected by the government (p. 436).

revivalist A preacher who conducts an evangelistic meeting, usually describing human sinfulness and suffering and offering salvation through faith and repentance (p. 286).

RFC Reconstruction Finance Corporation, formed in 1932 by Herbert Hoover to loan money to major banks, railroad companies, and factories to keep them from failing (p. 659).

Rhineland Area of Germany west of the Rhine River and near the French border. It was occupied by Nazi troops in 1936 in direct violation of the Treaty of Versailles (p. 684).

right of deposit A concession made by a government to foreign shippers to unload cargoes in a port and reload them on seagoing vessels without paying a tax (p. 200).

right-wing Favoring traditional, conservative attitudes and practices, opposing change, and/or often advocating an authoritarian political order (p. 759). See also *left-wing*.

"Roaring Twenties" Years between 1920 and 1929 when the U.S. economy appeared to boom and lifestyles were often wildspirited and free (p. 614).

robber barons 19th century railroad builders and industrialists who became rich by unethical means (p. 416).

robotics Field concerned with the building and use of robots (p. 808).

romanticism 19th century literary and philosophic movement emphasizing the imagination and emotions, the worth of comman man and an appreciation of nature (p. 293).

Roosevelt Corollary Theodore Roosevelt's expansion of the Monroe Doctrine; he declared that while European nations still had to keep out of Latin American affairs, the U.S. could exercise an "international police power" and intervene when it felt the need (p. 544).

Rough Riders Volunteer unit organized by Theodore Roosevelt that fought in Cuba during the Spanish-American War (p. 536).

royal colony A settlement or region in the New World ruled directly by the Crown (p. 41).

rugged individualism The willingness of individuals to succeed based on their own personal resources (p. 658).

S

saboteur Enemy agent who carries on destructive actions designed to hinder a nation's war efforts.

sachem (sā′chəm) *n.* A leader of a North American Indian tribe or *confederation* of tribes (p. 12).

SALT Strategic Arms Limitation Talks, a series of diplomatic discussions in the 1970s between the Soviet Union and the U.S. in which both agreed not to build any offensive missiles for five years (p. 777).

SALT II A second arms limitation treaty signed between the Soviet Union and the U.S. in 1979 (p. 797).

salutary neglect (săl′yə-tĕr′ē) In the early 1700s, a British governmental policy that favored merchants by doing nothing to disturb the prosperity of the American colonies (p. 84).

Salvation Army Religious and charitable group founded in England (p. 481).

sandbagging A *political machine's* practice of taking bribes from contractors for the right to complete work on a small segment of a city or state project; contractors would then have to pay again and again to complete the project (p. 438).

Sandinistas Nicaraguan rebels who overthrew the government in 1979 and established a pro-Communist regime (p. 802).

Sandwich Islands Early name for the Hawaiian Islands, discovered in 1778 by Capt. James Cook and named for the British Earl of Sandwich (p. 302).

sanitation The practice of maintaining clean conditions to prevent disease (p. 479).

satellite Country that is politically or economically controlled or dominated by a stronger government (p. 711).

savvy Internal understanding and ability; know-how (p. 740).

scalawag A white southerner who joined the Republican party during the Reconstruction (p. 402).

scale A divided line on a map that shows a small length used to represent a larger length, such as an inch to a mile, allowing someone to figure out actual distances between places (p. 116).

SCLC Southern Christian Leadership Conference, a civil rights group organized by Martin Luther King, Jr., to sponsor direct nonviolent action against discrimination (p. 735).

scrip Substitute money given by a company to its workers to pay for goods purchased in company-owned stores (p. 466).

SDS Students for a Democratic Society, an organization of the *New Left*, originally protested chronic poverty, racial discrimination, and the failure of wealth to provide a meaningful life in the U.S. By 1966, the SDS was largely an antiwar organization (p. 767).

sea dog A raider of Spanish colonies in the Americas during the 1500s (p. 34).

secondary source An account of historical events written by a modern author not actually involved in the events (p. 506).

Second Bank of the United States A bank chartered in 1816 to contain most of the major government deposits; it was dissolved by Andrew Jackson in 1836 when its charter expired (p. 273).

Secretariat Administrative department of the United Nations, headed by the Secretary-General (p. 708).

Secretary of State Cabinet member who advises the president on foreign affairs (p. 676).

secret ballot Ballot distributed only at the polls and marked in secret (p. 516).

section A unit of land offered for sale by the U.S. government under the *rectangular survey system*. Originally, a section was one square mile (640 acres); eventually the standard section size was reduced to 40 acres (p. 154).

Security Council United Nations council which has the authority to enforce UN policy with military action (p. 709).

segundo Assistant or "second" to a trail boss on a cattle drive in the 1800s (p. 499).

senatorial courtesy A patronage system in which senators and representatives of the party in power submitted lists of party members and the government jobs they wanted to the President, who then appointed them to office (p. 447).

sensationalism Use of superficial and exaggerated claims or actions in advertising and publishing (p. 642).

sentence outline An outline in which sentences are used to give information in the main topics, subtopics and details (p. 72). See also *topic outline*.

"separate but equal" Policy of maintaining racially segregated facilities, such as schools, supposedly equal in quality (p. 732).

separation of powers A system of dividing governmental functions into different branches (as legislative, executive, and judicial) so that no one branch exercises too much power (p. 165).

Separatists English Protestants who believed in worshiping separately from the official Church of England, which they felt was too much like the Roman Catholic Church. They were given the name "Pilgrims" in the 1600s when they journeyed to the New World to find a place to worship without interference (p. 41).

settlement house Charitable institution created by individuals to provide various community services, such as child care, recreation, and classes, to the poor (p. 481).

Seventh-Day Adventists A religious sect, organized from the Millerite sect by Hiram Edson, that observes the Jewish sabbath, Saturday (the seventh day of the week), instead of Sunday (p. 288).

Shaker A member of a religion that forbade marriage and held property in common; the name comes from a dance with shaking movements the members performed as part of worship (p. 284).

sharecropper system The arrangement by which plantation owners after the Civil War partitioned their lands into one-family farms and rented them to tenants, often black, in exchange for a share of the crop (p. 404).

shares Equal portions into which the capital stock of a corporation is divided, usually owned by private investors (p. 431).

short staple A kind of cotton with short fibers and sticky seeds, making it hard to clean (p. 246).

shuttle diplomacy A means of achieving international agreements by traveling back and forth between the countries involved and urging their heads of state to come to terms (p. 778).

siege A military blockade of a place to force surrender (p. 384).

Sierra Club *Preservationist* club founded by John Muir in 1892 to protect America's wilderness and natural wonders (p. 574).

sit-down strike A tactic in a labor dispute in which workers shutdown the workplace, stay inside, and refuse to leave until their demands are met (p. 671).

sit-in Nonviolent organized protest in which black participants occupied seats in non-black areas of racially segregated restaurants and cafes (p. 751).

skirmish Minor, generally unplanned fight or battle (p. 345).

slander To say false or misleading things that may damage someone's reputation (p. 220).

slash and burn agriculture A type of agriculture used by the Southeastern Indians in which they killed forest trees by cutting a deep circle in the bark around the trunk, thereby preventing soil nutrients from reaching the leaves. After the trees died, they were burned and left to fertilize the soil, which was then planted the following year (p. 11).

slave codes Collection of harsh laws in colonial South Carolina that defined imported Africans as *chattel*—that is, as property or slaves (p. 80).

slave patrols Mounted and armed posses of men who policed the slave populations in the South (p. 315).

slavocrats Politicians who supported slavery during pre-Civil War years (p. 354).

smear campaign A political contest based on attacking the opponent's policies, character, lifestyle (p. 267).

smuggling To trade goods illegally and usually secretly to avoid duties or taxes imposed by law on imports and exports (p. 83).

SNCC Student Nonviolent Coordination Committee, a civil rights group of the 1960s involving black college students who used *sit-ins* and other nonviolent means to force integration (p. 751).

Socialist Member of a political party that advocates collective or government ownership of factories, businesses, and goods rather than private ownership (p. 565).

Social Security A program established by the U.S. government in 1935 that instituted retirement pensions for the elderly (p. 668).

Society of Friends See *Quakers* (p. 67).

sod houses Homes built by settlers in Kansas, Nebraska, and the Dakotas from blocks of turf (p. 501).

Solidarity Poland's independent labor union (p. 797).

Sons of Liberty Secret organizations in the colonies pledged to disobey Stamp Act laws instituted by Parliament; some of these groups actually broke into warehouses and burned paper bearing the government stamp and looted British officials' homes to protest the Act (p. 109).

sovereign nation An independent, self-governing nation (p. 539).

space race Competition between the U.S. and Soviet Union to develop the quickest and most extensive space-related technology (p. 751).

space shuttle A reusable craft that can orbit the Earth like a spaceship and land like an airplane (p. 807).

Spanish Main Waters off the northern coast of South America, explored and raided by Sir Francis Drake (p. 34).

speakeasy Place where alcohol was illegally sold during Prohibition, so called because admission was gained by speaking softly through a peephole in the front door (p. 622).

specie (spē′shē) *n.* **1.** Coined money; coin. **2.** Gold or silver, as opposed to paper money. (p. 275).

speculative scheme Plan to make a big profit on a very risky business venture or investment (p. 643).

speculator Person who assumes business risk in hopes of making a large profit, as in buying and selling stock to profit from changes in its market value (p. 251).

sphere of influence A geographical region in which one country declares it has vital interests to which other countries in that region must bow (p. 544).

spinning jenny A machine invented by James Hargreave in the 18th century that combed wool or cotton fibers so they could be spun into wool or thread (p. 240).

spirituals Deeply emotional religious songs developed by black slaves in the southern U.S. (p. 320).

spoils system The practice of rewarding political supporters with money, office, or favor as a way of strengthening the power of a political party (p. 268).

Sputnik Satellite launched into orbit by the Soviet Union in 1957. The word comes from a Russian phrase meaning "fellow traveler of earth" (p. 739).

squatter's rights See *pre-emption*.

stagflation (stăg′flā′shən) *n*. An economic condition in which prices rise but the economy remains stagnant (p. 785).

Stalwarts A Republican faction in the 1870s that advocated total loyalty in political matters, regardless of what mistakes were made by party leaders (p. 447).

statesman A person who knows a lot about the principles of government and who exercises wise, fair political leadership (p. 278).

states' rights A theory that states should have more power than the federal government (p. 280).

staunch Faithful; loyal (p. 670).

stewardship Responsibility of a successful person to become a steward, or trustee, of society and distribute wealth to provide opportunities for the poor (p. 463).

Stimson Doctrine A policy under Hoover of nonrecognition of Japan's control of Manchuria or any other boundary changes accomplished by force (p. 678).

stocks A device used by the Puritans to publicly punish wrongdoers. It consisted of a wooden frame with holes in which the feet or feet and hands were locked (p. 54).

"Stonewall" Jackson Nickname for Thomas Jackson, a general in the Confederate army during the Civil War (p. 372).

strait A narrow passageway connecting two large bodies of water (p. 20).

strategic stage Step that is necessary or vital to a manufacturing process; for example, *refining* is a strategic stage in the oil industry (p. 426).

strict construction A way of interpreting the Constitution which argues that each governmental exercise of power can be mandated only by a specific and explicit provision in the Constitution (p. 197). See also *loose construction*.

strike Refusal to work by an organized body of workers in an attempt to force an employer to meet certain demands or change conditions or policies (p. 414).

strikebreaker Person hired to replace a worker on strike (p. 617).

stuffing ballot boxes Fraudulently filling out and submitting phony ballots in order to sway the results of an election (p. 440).

subjugation Forceful placing of one country under another's governing and control (p. 540).

subsidize To aid a private business by giving it public money (p. 463).

subsidy Money given to by the government to an individual or company to encourage a certain activity or support business (p. 663).

subsistence Barely enough to provide the minimum food and shelter necessary to live (p. 571).

subtreasuries Government operated depositories for federal funds, as opposed to banks (p. 277).

suburbs Residential areas on the outskirts of a large city (p. 723).

Sudetenland Section of Czechoslovakia bordering Germany that Hitler demanded be ceded to Germany in 1938 (p. 684).

suffrage The right or privilege of voting; franchise (p. 87).

summit meeting Diplomatic conference of heads of government (p. 738).

Sun Belt The southern region of the U.S. where temperatures stay above freezing almost year round (p. 806).

supply and demand Economic principle explaining the fluctuation of prices according to the amount of goods or services available compared to the public's desire and ability to purchase them (p. 514).

supply-side economics A theory that the way to cure unemployment is to cut taxes, particularly for the wealthy; the untaxed money would then be invested in industry, creating jobs for working people (p. 800). See *trickle-down economics*.

Supreme Court The highest court in the U.S., holding jurisdiction over all other courts (p. 192).

surplus Amount left over after debts have been paid; excess (p. 443).

suspension bridge Bridge suspended between cables rather than supported by pillars underneath (p. 432).

sustained yield The practice of logging only parts of forests and immediately replanting cut areas for future use (p. 575).

swing states Large populous states in which voters are evenly divided between Republicans and Democrats; a small number of voters can thus determine the outcome of a national election (p. 444).

syndicate Group of people authorized to transact and carry on business (p. 520).

systems Integrated railway lines that tie together distant regions (p. 414).

T

Tammany Hall Powerful, corrupt, New York City Democratic *Political machine* of the 1870s headed by Boss William Tweed (p. 438).

tariff Tax or duty placed by government on imported or sometimes on exported goods to raise money to pay government expenses (p. 192).

Tariff of Abominations A tax high as 50 percent imposed in 1828 on manufactured goods imported from Europe; the Tariff was particularly damaging to Southerners, who did little manufacturing of their own (p. 270).

tarmac road Road made of layers of crushed stone bound with a layer of tar (p. 584).

task system A method of assigning work to slaves on a daily basis; when a specific job was done, the work day was considered over as well (p. 318). See also *gang system*.

technology Application of scientific knowledge to the development of useful objects and processes (p. 412).

Teetotalers Reformers who insisted on no alcohol and making drinking illegal (p. 300).

tejanos (tā-yä′nōz) The Spanish word for "Texans," used to refer to Texans who spoke Spanish (p. 338).

temperance Moderation or total abstinence from the use of liquor (p. 299).

tenant farmer Farmer who works land owned by another and pays rent either in money or with a percentage of his crop (p. 512).

tenement Inner city apartment building occupied by poorer families and often overcrowded, run-down, and unsanitary (p. 479).

Tet Offensive Massive offensive attack launched by North Vietnamese in January 1968 against South Vietnam and U.S. forces (p. 766).

thematic map Map showing a specific subject or theme, such as railroads in the U.S. (p. 434).

Third World Underdeveloped nations of the world (p. 735).

Thousand-Year Reich The political regime set up by Hitler and the Nazi party which they believed would last 1000 years or longer. "Reich" is the German word for empire or kingdom (p. 683).

Three-Fifths Compromise An agreement reached the Constitutional Convention that for purposes of both representation and taxation, five slaves would be counted as three people (p. 161).

thresher Worker who separates seed from the straw of grain plants (p. 511).

time-sharing Simultaneous use of a computer by many users at scattered locations (p. 809).

tin lizzie Another name for the Model T car of the early 1900s (p. 637).

Tin Pan Alley Center of the music publishing business in New York in the early 1900s (p. 640).

toady Person who flatters in hopes of being granted special favors (p. 200).

topic outline An outline in which phrases are used to give information in the main topics, subtopics, and details (p. 72). See also *sentence outline*.

topic sentence A sentence in a paragraph that expresses the main idea of the paragraph (p. 27).

topographic map See *physical map*.

Tory Also called a *Loyalist*, an American colonist who remained loyal to Great Britain rather than supporting independence (p. 127).

totalitarian (tō-tal′ə-târ′ē-ən) *adj*. Of a government ruling through force and oppression and controlled by one political faction or by a dictator with virtually absolute power (p. 181).

totalitarianism A government controlled by a single person or party, that allows no opposition, and that may use censorship or terrorism to control all aspects of life and economic production (p. 181).

totem pole A tall, carved, painted pole or pillar placed outside Northwest Indian homes to identify the people living in the village or house (p. 10).

Townsend Plan Plan advocated by Dr. Francis Townsend in the 1930s to pay everyone over 60 a pension of $200 a month, funded by a national sales tax (p. 668).

"Trail of Tears" The 800-mile trek made by thousands of Cherokee Indians forced to relocate to Oklahoma in the winter of 1838; many of them died of disease and starvation along the way (p. 268).

traitor A person who secretly aids an enemy to defeat the traitor's own country in a war (p. 144).

Transcendentalism A 19th century American philosophic and literary movement that believed in man's essential divinity and ability to "transcend" the limits of the senses and logic by relying on intuition and the conscience, thereby being able to comprehend higher truths and achieve greater knowledge (p. 291).

Transcendentalists (trăn′sən-dĕn′təl-ĭst) *n.* Utopian philosophers during the Jacksonian era who refused to accept the traditional Christian doctrine that human nature is essentially evil; they believed instead that individuals had it within themselves to be sinless (p. 291).

transcontinental railroad Railroad system that spans an entire continent; in the U.S., a railroad running between the Pacific and Atlantic Oceans (p. 350).

transistors Very small devices that are able to carry and amplify sound (p. 743).

treason Betrayal of one's country, usually by aiding an enemy in wartime or plotting to overthrow the government (p. 720).

treaty An agreement between countries made by negotiating (p. 344).

triangular trade Shipping transactions conducted in colonial times by New England merchants traveling along trans-Atlantic shipping routes that connected three ports: one in the colonies, one in England or Africa, and one in the West Indies. Goods picked up in one port would be sold in the net or used to buy a new cargo (such as slaves or sugar) with considerable profits gained after each leg of the round-trip journey (p. 80).

tribute A payment by one ruler or nation to another in return for protection or a promise not to attack (p. 221).

trickle-down economics An economic theory holding that government should direct as much money as possible toward wealthy capitalists, who then reinvest it; as capital investment expands the economy, jobs and opportunities for advancement are created for working people (p. 632). See *supply-side economics*.

Triple Alliance Also called the Central Powers, a World War I alliance formed in 1907 between Germany, Austria-Hungary, Italy and Turkey (p. 592).

Triple Entente Also called the *Allied Powers*, a World War I alliance formed in the early 1900s between Russia, France, and Great Britain (p. 592).

truce Agreement between groups at war to cease fighting (p. 731).

Truman Doctrine President Truman's plan for sending massive military aid to anti-communist regimes in Europe after World War II (p. 710).

trust A business structure in which the owners of normally competing companies delegate control to a board of trustees in exchange for shares in the profits from the consolidation (p. 431).

trust buster Federal official who prosecutes and breaks up trusts under anti-trust laws (p. 571).

turbine Rotary engine drive by a current of water or steam (p. 433).

turnpike A toll road built by private investors; the entrance was blocked by a spear-like structure which turned aside to allow a customer through once the toll was paid (p. 253).

TVA Tennessee Valley Authority, a New Deal public works program that built a series of dams to prevent floods and generate electricity along the Tennessee River (p. 666).

Tweed Ring New York City *political machine* headed by Boss William Tweed in the 1800s (p. 440).

tyranny Harsh and oppressive authority exerted by government (p. 165).

U

UAW United Automobile Workers, a labor union formed in 1935 (p. 671).

U-boats German submarines first used in World War I. The term is short for *unterseeboot*, or undersea boat (p. 595).

ultimatum A final proposal or demand, which if rejected will end negotiations and result in the use of force (p. 593).

unconstitutional Not consistent with or according to the U.S. Constitution (p. 167).

Underground Railroad An informal network of abolitionists who hid runaway slaves fleeing to Canada (p. 329).

unilateral One-sided; having to do with a contract or agreement in which a restriction or requirement applies to only one of the parties (p. 454).

Unitarian A member of a religion that believes in a single God rather than the Trinity and stresses individual freedom of belief, the use of reason, a unified society and social action (p. 286).

Union party Political party of the 1930s headed by Congressman William Lemke (p. 669).

United Nations (UN) Organization of 159 nations founded after World War II to mediate international relations and promote peace and human dignity worldwide (p. 664).

United States Geological Survey Government bureau organized in 1879 under the Department of the Interior to gather information about U.S. geology, prepare maps, examine potential natural resources, and study irrigation water and power problems (p. 574).

Universal Negro Improvement Association *Black nationalist* organization formed by Marcus Garvey in the 1920s to emphasize black accomplishments and pride (p. 620).

unscrupulous Having no principles or moral integrity; dishonest (p. 195).

urban Having to do with a city (p. 561).

USSR Union of Soviet Socialist Republics, also known as Russia and the Soviet Union.

utopian (yōō-tō′pē-ən) *adj.* 1. Of a plan or idea for a perfect place or state having ideal laws. 2. Visionary; perfectionist; impractical.—*n.* An advocate of visionary reforms (p. 290).

utopian community A community organized in an attempt to form a perfect society (p. 290).

V

vacuum tube Device in which electrons flow in a vacuum and create an electrical current (p. 432).

vaqueros Mexican cowboys in the 1800s (p. 497).

vertical axis The numbers or scale that appears vertically on the left side of a line graph (p. 92). See also *horizontal axis*.

vertical integration A way of reducing costs in industry by buying up independent suppliers, distributors, and carriers and thereby eliminating their profits from the final product (p. 425).

veteran Person who has served in one of the armed forces (p. 442).

veto Power of the president to reject a legislative bill passed by Congress and prevent its becoming a law (p. 165).

viceroy A "deputy ruler" appointed by the Spanish monarch to govern an area of the Americas as his representative (p. 33).

Victrola Early phonograph powered by a spring-driven motor that was wound up by hand between plays (p. 639).

Viet Cong Vietnamese Communists who used guerrilla warfare against Diem's dictatorial government of South Vietnam (p. 764).

Viet Minh Anti-colonial movement in Vietnam in the 1940s headed by Communist leader Ho Chi Minh (p. 736).

Vietnamization Gradual withdrawal of American troops from Vietnam and their replacement with American-trained South Vietnamese troops (p. 774).

Virginia Dynasty The monopoly of the presidency by men from Virginia, including Jefferson, Madison, and Monroe (p. 234).

virtual representation A doctrine which claims that an elected body is said to act on behalf of all citizens even though not all citizens are entitled to vote in the election. On this basis, the British Parliament in the 1760s claimed it fairly represented and taxed the American colonies (p. 110).

VISTA Volunteers in Service to America, a domestic program staffed by volunteers who work to improve life in older central city areas and impoverished rural areas (p. 761).

W

wage and price controls Act of government limiting or freezing the amount wages and prices can rise during a stated period (p. 779).

wageworkers Persons who work for a company or corporation as employees; by 1900 they comprised a distinct and significant social class (p. 464).

Wall Street Street in New York City where the *New York Stock Exchange* is located. The term is also used to refer to influential financial interests or groups in the U.S. (p. 604).

"War On Poverty" Part of Lyndon Johnson's "Great Society" reform movement, an attempt to fight poverty in city slums by educating children and adults in government-funded programs (p. 761).

ward 1. Division of a city by neighborhood for political purposes (p. 436). **2.** Person under the custody and protection of the government (p. 494).

War Democrat Democrats that remained in the mostly Republican Congress during the Civil War (p. 393).

wardship Care and protection of a person or group by the government (p. 494).

War Hawks Group of congressmen who favored going to war with Great Britain in 1812 (p. 224).

War Industries Board Organization that supervised the operation of hundreds of boards regulating production and availability of supplies during World War I (p. 604).

Warren Commission Group headed by Chief Justice Earl Warren to investigate the possibility of a conspiracy behind the assassination of John F. Kennedy. No evidence of any such plot was uncovered (p. 759).

war zone Area, especially on the ocean, designated for war battles and unsafe even for neutral parties (p. 595).

Watergate Scandal Illegal burglarizing and wiretapping of Democratic party national headquarters by Nixon aides during the 1972 presidential election campaign (p. 782).

"The West" Any area west of the settled regions in the U.S. in the late 19th century (p. 486).

"Wets" Those who opposed the Prohibition amendment (p. 620).

Whig 1. In the 1700s, a member of a British political party that favored reform and opposed the Tory party. **2.** American of the Revolutionary era who opposed British colonial rule and supported the Revolution. **3.** After 1834, a member of an American political party that opposed the Democratic party and favored high protective tariffs, federalism, and a loose construction of the Constitution. It was succeeded by the Republican party after 1855 (p. 269).

White Russians Army that fought against the communist takeover of Russia in 1917 (p. 616). See also *Red Russians*.

white supremacist Person who believes the white race is superior to all others (p. 444).

white supremacy The theory that whites are naturally superior to other races, and therefore more fit to govern and hold power (p. 620).

wickiups Portable, cone-shaped homes of the Plains Indians, usually having a wooden frame covered with skins or grasses (p. 11).

wildcat banks Banks that fueled western speculation by irresponsibly lending money to any speculator or planter willing to go into debt in order to pay already inflated land prices (p. 251).

Wilderness Society Environmentalist group committed to preserving wilderness areas as part of America's national heritage (p. 782).

wildlife preservation Efforts to preserve or protect wild animals that are in danger of becoming extinct.

Wilmot proviso A proposal by Pennsylvania Congressman David Wilmot that slavery be illegal in any territory taken from Mexico after the Mexican War (p. 346).

windfall profits tax A government levy on gains made from unexpected new oil strikes (p. 795).

Wisconsin Idea A belief current in the Progressive Era that, like special interest groups, ordinary people in the complex 20th century also need their own teams of experts to protect their interests; state universities were looked to as sources of expertise in many fields, especially farming (p. 564).

women's suffrage Drive by women in the early 1900s to win the right to vote (p. 305).

WPA Works Program Administration, a New Deal jobs program that employed 8.5 million people from many professions who could not get work elsewhere (p. 666).

writ Formal written document issued by a court commanding someone to do or refrain from doing something (p. 173).

X

xenophobia (zĕn′-ə-fōb′bē-ə) *n*. The fear of foreign people and things. Xenophobic feeling was particularly strong after World War I, when many people were suspicious of communism and immigrants, especially those from southern and eastern Europe (p. 616).

xerography Electrostatic process for copying documents, developed in 1938 by Chester Carlson (p. 742).

Y

Yalta Resort city in the Soviet Union where Roosevelt, Churchill, and Stalin met in February 1945 to decide Europe's postwar fate (p. 697).

Yankee 1. A native or resident of New England during colonial times (p. 65). **2.** A northerner during the Civil War.

yellow press Newspapers that rely on gimmicks rather than straightforward news reporting to appeal to readers. (The first colored comic strip of this kind was called "The Yellow Kid") (p. 533).

Yippies Members of the liberal Youth International Party (YIP), which opposed the Vietnam War in the 1960s (p. 769).

YMCA Young Men's Christian Association, a service organization founded in 1851 to provide residential and recreational facilities in city centers at a low cost (p. 481).

Z

zamboes People of mixed Indian and African descent (p. 31).

zeppelin Hard-surface, motor-driven airship with a cylindrical frame (p. 585).

Italicized page numbers preceded by an *m* refer to a *map;* those preceded by a *p* refer to a *photograph* or *picture;* those preceded by a *t* refer to a *table;* and those preceded by a *c* refer to a *chart* or *graph.*

Aztecs, *m5*, 6, 8, 11, 12, 20–1, 24, 30, 31

B

Babcock, Orville, 447
Baby boom, 722–3, 804
Bacon's Rebellion, 84–5, 87
Badoglio, Marshall Pietro, 695
Baer, George F., 571
Baker, Ray Stannard, 562
Baker, Dr. Sara Josephine, *p555*
Balance of power, 592, 776
Balboa, Vasco Nuñez de, 20, *p21*, *m22*, *t23*
Balkans, 592, 593
Ballinger, Richard A., 579
Baltimore, *m134*, 135
Bank Bill of 1791, 196, 197
Bank of the United States: First, 196–7, 217, 232, 243; Second, 234, 243, 244, 252, 273–5, 277
Banks, banking: and the agricultural depression (1880s–90s), 512, 514, 515: and the Civil War, 392; Clay's plan, 279–80; and foreign investment, 588, 590, 598; and the Great Depression, 646, 654, *c655*, 659, 663, 668; Hamilton's programs, 194, 196–7; and industrialization, 243; Jackson's policies, 273–5; and the mining industry, 503–4; Populist programs, 516, 517–18; and railroads, 420; and the Revolutionary War, 154, 155; Van Buren's policies, 277; and Western land speculation, 251–2, 275; and World War I, 598, 678–9. *See also* Federal Reserve System.
Banneker, Benjamin, 322–3
Baptists, 287, 288, 320
Barbados, 65, 77–8
Barbary States, 156, *m221*, 221–2
Barbed wire, 501, 502, 510
Barnett, Ross (Governor), 753
Barry, John, 139.
BART (San Francisco), 808
Barton, Bruce, 636
Barton, Clara, 371
Baruch, Bernard, 504, 604
Baseball, 558–9, 636
Bataan death march, 692
Batista, Fulgencio, 755
"Battle Hymn of the Republic," 379
Bayard, James A., 206
Bay of Pigs invasion (1961), 755–6, *m756*
Beauregard, P. G. T. (General), 372
Becknell, William, 337
Beckwourth, Jim, 340, *p340*
Begin, Menachem, 796, *p796*
Belgium, 229, 593, 603, 604, *t608*
Belknap, William W., 447
Bell, Alexander Graham, *p427*, 427–8
Bell, John, 356–7
Benezet, Anthony, 322
Benson, Ezra Taft, 731–2
Benton, Thomas Hart (Senator), 252, *p252*, 253, 274, 275, 279, 349, 393
Berger, Victor, 606–7
Berkeley, John, Lord, 69
Berkeley, Sir William, 84–5
Berlin, Irving, 640
Berlin, 697, 698, *m703*; blockade, 711–12, Wall, *p756*, 756–7
Bernstein, Carl, 782

Bessemer, Henry, 423
Bethune, Mary McLeod, 663, 664
Beveridge, Albert J. (Senator), 540, 578
Bicentennial celebration, 786
Bicycling, *p557*, 558
Biddle, Nicholas, 273, 274, 275
Big Four (railroad barons), 416
Bill of Rights: English, 86–7, 148; U.S., 112, 150–1, 164, 166–7, 180–2, 192, 216
Bills of credit, 76
"Billy the Kid," (William Bonney), 500
Bingham, Hiram, 6
Birdseye, Clarence, 649
Birney, James, G., 326
Bison, 11, *p488*, 489, 491, *p491*
Black codes, 397–8, 400. *See also* Slave codes.
Black Friday panic (1869), 444–5
Black Hawk (Indian chief), 506
Blackmun, Harry (Justice), 780
Black nationalism, 619–20
Black Power movement, 762–3
Blacks, 553, 561, 583, 646, 767, 804; and abolition, 322–3, 324, 326–9; in the Civil War, 379, 386; in colleges, 554–5, 562; colonial period, 31, 40–1, 62, 87, 151; culture, 620, 639; in the Democratic party, 670, 713, 751; explorers, 220, 340; and the Great Depression, 654, 656–7, 663, 670; in the labor movement, 469, 474, 671; in the 1920s, 620; lynchings, 550, 619, 670; North, emigration to, 604, 646, 713, *c734;* and Populist programs, 518–19; in the Progressive Era, 561, 562–3; and Reconstruction, 395–400, 401, 402, 403–5, 407, 513; in the Republican party, 402, 407, 444, 519, 670; in the Revolutionary War, 111, 133; school integration, 732–4; in the Spanish American War, 536–7; in sports, 559, 636; tenant farmers, 513–14; urban riots (1960s), 763; voting rights, 161, 402, 407, 752, 761; in the War of 1812, 229; in the West, 328, 492, *p502, p504, p513;* in the Whig party, 277; in World War I, 604, 619; in World War II, 690. *See also* Civil rights movement; Free blacks; Slavery.
Black Thursday (1929), 646, 647
Blackwell, Antoinette, 555
Blackwell, Elizabeth, 297, 555
Blackwell, Emily, 297
Blaine, James G., *p446*, 447, 449, 450, 452, 454
Bland, Richard "Silver Dick," 505, 519
Bland-Allison Act, 505
Blennerhasset, Harman, 220
Blitzkrieg, 684, *p685*
Blizzard of 1886, 500
Bloomer, Amelia, 305, *p305*
Blount, James H., 541
Blue laws, 53–4, 61
Bluford, Guion, 807
Bok, Edward, 560
Bolivar, Simon, 230
Bolshevism, 600, 616, 709
Bonds, 155, 195
Bonus Marchers, 659–60
Booth, John Wilkes, 386, *p387*
Bootleggers, 622
Borah, William E., 565, 609
Borden, Gail, 420

Border ruffians, 352
Boston, 52, *m53*, 69, 114, 115, 123, 125, 127, 133, 135, 157, 298, 325; police strike, 617, 627
Boston Cooking School Cookbook, 423
Boston Massacre, *p97*, 111–12
Boston Tea Party, 114, *p114*, 115
Boulder Dam (Colo.), 659, *p659*
Bourbon Democrats, 443
Bourke-White, Margaret, *p693*
Bowie, James (Colonel), 338, *p338*
Boxer Rebellion, 543
Boxing, 559, 636
Boyd, Belle, 369
Braddock, Edward (General), 100
Bradford, William, 42, 43, *p44*
Brady, Mathew, *p368*, 371, *p371*
Bragg, Braxton (General), 383, 384
"Brain Drain," 756
Brain Trust, 661
Brandeis, Louis (Justice), 480, 561, *p562*, 581
Brandywine, Battle of, *m136*, 137
Brazil, 18, 31, *t45*, 316
Breckinridge, John, 356, 357
Breed's Hill, Battle of, 123
Brest-Litovsk, Treaty of, 600
Brewster, William, 42
Brezhnev, Leonid, 801
Bridger, Jim, 340
Bridges, *p432–3*, 479, *p479*
Bridgman, Laura, 296
Brinkmanship, 735–6, 737
Britain, Battle of, 684–5, *p685*
British East India Co., 113–14
British Empire, 107, 110, 139, *m231*, 532, 542, 626
Broadsides, *p61*
Brook Farm, 290
Brooklyn Bridge, *p432–3*, 479, *p479*
Brooks, Preston, 352, 353
Brown, H. Rap, 763
Brown, John, 352, 354, *p356*
Brown, Moses, 241
Bruce, Blanche K., 403
Bryan, William Jennings, 519, *p528*, 528–30, 540, 542, 555, 576, 580, 581, 590, 596, 636
Buchanan, James (President), 351, 353, 357, 392
Buchenwald, 684
Buckaroos, 497
Budget, Bureau of the, 633
Buell, Don Carlos (General), 375
Buena Vista, Battle of, 345, *p345*
Buffalo, *See* Bison.
Bulganin, Nikolai, 737
Bulge, Battle of the, 697
Bull Moose party, *p569*, 580
Bull Run (Manassas Junction), Battles of, *m366*, *t367;* First, *p372*, 372–3, 376; Second, 377–8
Bunau-Varilla, Philippe Jean, 545
Bunker Hill, Battle of, 123, *p123*
Burchard, Samuel, 452
Burger, Warren, (Chief Justice), 780
Burgoyne, John (General), 123, 137–8, *p139*
Burke, Edmund, 110, 125
Burke-Wadsworth Act, 685
Burnside, Ambrose E. (General), 378
Burr, Aaron, 206, 220
Bush, George, 799, 805, *p805*
Business: growth (1870–1900), *c430;* in the 1890s–1910s, *c430*, 568, 570–1, 572–3, 577; in the 1920s, 632, 635, 636, 643–6; in the 1930s, 654, 656,

Evans, Hiram Wesley, 620
Evans, Oliver, 241
Evers, Medgar, 753
Excise taxes, 194, 197–8, 216, 392
Exclusion Act, 476
Executive branch, 165, c167
Explorers (1480–1610), m18, m22, t23

F

Factories, 414, 464–7
Fairchild, Lucius, 442
Fair Deal programs, 714–15
Fair Oaks, Battle of, 376
Falkland Is. War, m803
Fall, Albert, 626
Falwell, Jerry, p788, 799
Farley, James A., 668
Farm Credit Administration, 663
Farmer, Fannie, 423, p423
Farmers, farming, 414; and abolition, 325, 349, 351; colonial period, 57–8; cooperative movement, 515; and currency deflation, 455, 469, 505, 514; and the Great Depression, 646, 647, 654, p658, 662, 663, 667; and industrialization, 243, 244, 467; machinery, 428, 511–12; in the 1920s, 646–7; organizations, 515–16; Populist programs, 516, 518–19, 530; in the Progressive Era, 565; quit-rent system, 60; and railroads, 418–19, 510, 511; standard tracts, 154, 251; urban migration, 478, 514–15; in the West, 249–52, 501–2, 510–11. See also Agriculture; Homesteading; Plantations.
Farragut, David (Admiral), 379
Fascists, 679–80, 683
Fassett, Cornelia Adele, 448
Faubus, Orval (Governor), 734
Federal Campaign Reform Act (1974), 456–7
Federal Emergency Banking Act, 663, t663
Federal Emergency Relief Act (FERA), t663, 665
Federal Farm Loan Act, 583
Federal government: branches, 165, c167; budget, 633; budget deficits, 779, 800, 801; and farm prices, 646; growth, 671, 690; regulatory powers, 576, 577, 581–3, 633
Federalism, federal system, 165, c193, 232
Federalist Papers, 162–3, p163, 224
Federalist party, 203, 205, 216, 217, 219, 223, 233; decline, 230; "High," 204, 205; land policy, 251; legacy, 206–7
Federalists, 162–4
Federal Reserve System, 581–2, 663, 668, 785, 794
Federal Trade Commission (FTC), 583
Fee, John Gregg, 326
Ferraro, Geraldine, 804, p804
Field, James G. (General), 516
Fifteen Gallon Law, 300
"Fifty-four Forty or Fight!", 342
Fillmore, Millard (President), 265, 302, 348–9
Finn, William, 441
Finney, Charles Grandison, 286, p286
Finnish immigrants, 476
Fire-eaters, 347, 348–9, 355–6, 357, 360

Firestone, Harvey, 428
Fiscal year, 633
Fish, Hamilton, 453
Fishing, 58, m81, 125, 453
Fisk, James, 416, 420, 444–5
Fitch, Clyde (playwright), 515
Fitch, John (inventor), 256
Fitzhugh, George, 314–15
Fitzpatrick, Thomas (Colonel), 490
Fletcher, Frank J. (Admiral), 692
Flint, Timothy, 506–7
Florida, 20, t45, m59, 102, m106, 218, 230, 232, 273, 342, 643–4
Flour mills, 240, 241, 414, 421
Flow charts, 726–7
Floyd, John, 275, 313
Food, food industry, 80–1, m81, 82, 253, 255, 420–3, 604. See also Meatpacking industry; Pure Food and Drug Acts.
Football, 344
Foran Act, 474
Forbes, Charles, 626
Force Bill, 270, 271
Ford, Betty, p789
Ford, Gerald (President), 783, 784–5, 794
Ford, Henry, p625, 637, p637, 638
Fordney-McCumber Tariff, 632–3, 634
Foreign aid, 716, 755. See also Marshall Plan.
Forest Service, 574, 579
Forrest, Nathan Bedford, 405
Fort Donelson (Tenn.), 374, m374
Fort Duquesne, 98, m100, 101
Fort Henry (Tenn.), 374, m374
Fort Laramie (Wyo.), 341, 490
Fort McHenry (Md.), m225, 227
Fort Necessity, 98, m100
Fort Orange (N.Y.), 47, 89
Fort Sumter (S.C.), 362–3, p364, m366, t367, 368
Fort Ticonderoga (N.Y.), m100, 124, 133, 138
Fort Wayne, Treaty of, 226
Foster, Stephen, 317
Founding Fathers, 158–9
Fountain of Youth, 20
Fourier, Charles, 290
Fourteen Points (Wilson), 607, t608, 609
Fox, George, 68
France, 34, 156, 199, 204–5, 736–7; and the American Revolution, 135, 138, 139–40, 144, 155, 195, 199; and the Civil War, 373; colonialism, 532; explorations, 20, m22, t23, 34; war with Great Britain (1778), 139; and World War I, 592–3; and World War II, 684, m694, 695, 697, 709. See also French and Indian War; War of the Spanish Succession.
Franco, Francisco (General), 679, 682–3
Frankfurter, Felix (Justice), 480
Franklin, Benjamin, p99, 103, p103, 104, 127, 132, 135, 138, 139, 162; Albany union proposal, 98; and the Declaration of Independence, 127, 132; and the French and Indian War, 103; Ufe, 99; in Paris (1776), 135, 139, 145; Poor Richard's Almanac, 98, 99
Franz Ferdinand, Archduke, 593
Fredericksburg, Battle of, m366, t367, 378

Free blacks, 79, 87, 151, 245–6, 312, 315–16, 317, 318, 320, 322–3, p323, 324, 379, 386, 397
Freedmen, 395, 397–400
Freedmen's Bureau, 398
Freedom rides, 751, 752
Freeholders, 44
Freemen, 53
Freeport Doctrine, 354, 356
Free silver issue, 518, 519–20, 528–30
Free Soil party, 346, 349, 356
Freemont, John C., 351
French and Indian War, 96, m100, 100–3, 105, 107, 115, 120
French Canadians, 105, 115, 219
French colonies, 46, 47, 87–91, m100, m102
French-English wars (1689–1748), 89–91
French Revolution, 199
French Revolutionary and Napoleonic wars, 139, 199–200, 204–5, 222–4
Friedan, Betty, 788
Frontier, m231, 232, 249, 486, 488–91; closing of, 502, 526, 533; colonial land claims, m106, 115, 152–3. See also Louisiana Territory; Ohio Territory; Old Northwest; West.
Frontier theory, 533
Frost Belt, 806
Fuchs, Klaus, 720
Fugitive Slave Act, 321, 348
Fulbright, William (Senator), 766
Fuller, Margaret, p292, 293
Fulton, Robert, 257
Fundamental Constitutions of Carolina, 63
Fur trade, 39, 46, 47, 76, 80, 88, 89, 336, 340–1

G

Gadsden Purchase, 350, m351
Gage, Thomas (General), 115, 121, 133
Gag rule, 313
Galbraith, John Kenneth, 722
Gallaudet, Thomas, 295–6
Gandhi, Mohandas, 752
Gangsters, 622–3
Gang system, of field work, 318
Gardoqui, Diego de, 156
Garfield, James A. (President), 447, 449–50, 455
Garland, Hamlin, 515
Garner, John Nance, 660
Garrison, William Lloyd, p324, 324–5
Garvey, Marcus, 619–20
Gary, Elbert H., 571, 617
Gaspee incident, 113
Gas warfare, 595, p602
Gay Nineties, 550, 552, 556–8
Gender gap, 804
General Motors Corporation, 638, 644, 671, 731
Genêt, Edmond, 199
Genetics research, 781
Geneva Accords (1954), 737, 764
George, Henry, 461–2
George II (King of England), 65, 98
George III (King of England), p105, 106, 109, 120, 125–6, 129, 132, 139, 145
Georgia, 59, 65–6, 78, 110, 115, 153,

Hoover Dam, 659, *p659*
Hoovervilles, 656, *p656*
Horizontal integration, in industry, 426
Hopkins, Harry, 665–6
Hopkins, Mark, 416
Horses, 11, 21, 478, 489
Hot line, 757
House, Edward M. (Colonel), 581
House of Burgesses, 40, 41
House of Commons, 110
House of Representatives, 160–2, 165–6, 206, 234–5, *p281;* Un-American Activities Committee, 720–1
Housing and Urban Development, Department of, 761
Houston, Sam, *p338,* 339, 373
Howe, Julia Ward, 379
Howe, Richard, 133
Howe, Samuel Gridley, 296
Howe, William (General), 123, 133, 135–7, 140, 141
Howells, William Dean, 559–60
Hudson, Henry, *m22, t45*
Hudson River, 47, 66, 232, *p241,* 255, 257
Hudson's Bay Company, *m102,* 340, 341
Huerta, Victoriano, 590, 591
Hughes, Charles Evans, 565, 572, 598, 626
Hughes, Langston, 620
Huguenots, 88, 317
Hull, Cordell (Secretary of State), 676, 678, 687
Hull House (Chicago), 480–1
Hull, William (General), 227
Human rights, 320, 684, 708, 796–7
Humphrey, Hubert H. (Vice President), 713, 740, 768, *p768,* 769
Hungarian rebellion, 736
Huntington, Collis P., 416
Huron Indians, *m5,* 46, 88, 90
Hutchinson, Anne, 55
Hutchinson, Thomas (Governor), 114, 115
Hypotheses, 770–1

I

Icarians, 290
Ice Age, 2, 4, *m5*
Idaho, 469, 504
Ile de Saint Croix (Maine), 46
Illinois, 154, 233, 253, 353
Immigration, 69, 87, 88, 205, 295, 300–2, 351, 412, *p440,* 441, 452, 453, 474–8, 616, 805; growth (1860–1910), 412, 416–7, 474, *c475, p475,* 476, 477, 552; 1920s quotas, 616; and political machines, 441, 444; prejudice against, 477; and urban growth, 477–8; Western settlers, 501
Impeachment, 166, *c167,* 401, 783
Imperialism, 532–3, *c539,* 539–40, *m541,* 543–5, 592
Impressment, 112, 200, 222–3, 224
Incas, 6–7, 12, 24, 28, 30, 31, 33
Income tax, 518, 581, 632–3, 669
Indentured servants, 40, 61–2
Independence (Mo.), *m254,* 337
Independence Hall (Phila.), 158
India, 12, *m13,* 16, 113, 532
Indiana, 154, 226, 233, 253, 444
Indian agents, 443

Indians. *See* American Indians.
Indian Territory, *m352,* 488, *m493,* 501
Indian Wars, 492, *m493,* 494
Indies, 12–13, 16, 18, 20
Indigo, 64, 65, 66, 77, 78, 245
Indochina, 736–7. *See also* Vietnam War.
Industrialization, 197, 412–30, 458; in New England, 241–4; social effects, 461–2, 464–6, 480; in the South, 520–1
Industrial Revolution, 238, 240–8
Industrial wealth, 458, 460–63, 568, 570, 632
Industry, 234, 807; automation, 87; growth (1865–1900), 414, 458; horizontal integration, 426; interlocking directorates, 419, 420, 583; mergers, 419; New Deal programs, 666–7; and railroads, 414, 422; vertical integration, 425; working conditions, 463–7, 480. *See also* Manufacturing; Work force.
Inflation, 634, 779, 785, 794–5
Initiatives, 516, 564, 579
Insane asylums, 296, 297
Installment buying, 643, 723
Insurgents, 579, 581
Interchangeable parts, 242–3
Interest rates, 785, 794
Interlocking directorates, 419, 420, 582–3
Internal improvements, 234, 277. *See also* Public works.
International Congress of Women, 480
International Harvester Co., 428, 470
International Workers of the World (IWW), 605, 617
Interstate commerce, 232, 419–20, 426, 572, 576, 751
Interstate Highway Act, 723, *p729*
Intolerable Acts, 115, 118, 121, 139
Inventions, 214, 240, 241, 246, 427–30, 638, 639. *See also* Technology.
Iran, 785, *m797;* hostage crisis, 797–9
Ireland, 87, 596; potato famine, 302, 474, 476
Irish immigrants, 255, 300, 301–2, 317–18, 416, 441, 452, 453, 470, 474, 476
Iron. *See* Coal and iron industry.
Iron Act, 83, 91
Iron Curtain, 710
Iroquois Indians, *m5,* 11–12, 47, 88, 98
Irving, Washington, 223, 293–4, *p293*
Isabella (Queen of Spain), 15, 17, *p17, t23*
Isolationism, 582, 609, 678–9
Israel, 12, 736, 778, 785, 795, 796, *m797*
Italian immigrants, 441, 476, 616, 618
Italy, 13, 532, 592, *m594,* 679–80, *m680,* 688, *m694,* 695, 710–11
Iwo Jima, Battle of, *m698,* 699

J

Jackson, Andrew (President), 220, 262, 278, 279, 284, 300, 339; bank policy, 273–6; democratic beliefs, 267; Eaton affair, 272–3, *p272;* and the election of 1824, 234–5; and the

election of 1828, 262, *p264,* 266–7; Indian removals, 268, 269–70; and nullification, 270–1; reelection (1832), 273, 275; and the spoils system, 268–9; tariff policy, 270; and the War of 1812, 229
Jackson, Helen Hunt, 494, 495
Jackson, Rev. Jesse, 804
Jackson, Rachel, 266–7, 272
Jackson, Thomas "Stonewall" (General), 372, *p372,* 373, 376, 377, 378
Jackson, (Miss.), Battle of, 380
Jackson State killings, 775
James, Henry, 559
James, Jesse and Frank, 500
James I, (King of England), 38, 39–40, 41, 42, 50, 56, 59, 87
James II, (King of England), 67, 85, 129
Jamestown (Va.), 38, *p38,* 39–41, *m41,* 376
Jamestown Massacre, 41
Japan, 12, *m13,* 16, 18, 542–3, 716, 807; aggression in China (1930s), 678–9, 681–2, 687; colonialism, *p531,* 532, 540; economy and industry (1980s), 807; naval agreement (1921), 626; and World War II, 687–8, 691–2, *m698,* 698–701
Japanese immigrants, 476, 690
Japanese relocation camps, 690
Jaworski, Leon, 783
Jay Cooke & Company, 514
Jay, John, 99, 162, *p163,* 192, 200, 206
Jay's Treaty, 200, 203, 204
Jazz, 620, 639, 640
Jefferson, Thomas (President), 112, 125, 132, 150, 158, 190, 196, 205, 233, 238, 243, 244, 270, 274, 322–3, 515; agricultural and economic policies, 197, 201, 203; and the Declaration of Independence, 127–9; domestic policy, 214, 216–20; and the election of 1800, 206; foreign policy, 221–3; inventions, 214; and the Kentucky Resolutions, 206; and the Louisiana Purchase, 217–9; vs. the *Marbury* decision, 207, 216; as Secretary of State, 194, 199, 200
Jeffersonian Republicans, 203, 204, 205–6, 216, 233–4, 243, 251, 264–5, 284
Jennison, Edwin, *p369*
Jesuits, 88–9
Jews, 31, 65, 154, 155, 302, 476, 478, 481, 561, 683–4. *See also* Anti-Semitism.
Jingoism, 532, 533
Job Corps, 761
John Birch Society, 763, 764
Johns Hopkins University, 554
Johnson, Andrew (President), 386, 392, 395, 397–401, 447; impeachment, 401
Johnson, Hiram, 565, 609
Johnson, Hugh, 667, 687
Johnson, Jack, 559
Johnson, James Weldon, 620
Johnson, Jeremiah, 340
Johnson, Lady Bird, 761, *p789*
Johnson, Lyndon B. (President), 740, 741, 751, *p758,* 759, 772, 776, 779; domestic policy, 760–2; and the 1964 election, 763–4; and Vietnam, 764–6, 768, 776
Johnson, Thomas L., 563
Johnson-Reed Act, 616

P

Pacific coast, settlement of, 486
Pacific Northwest, *m102*, 230, 476, 496; Indians, *m5*, 10
Pacific Ocean, 20, *p21*, 36; U.S. territories, 538, *t539*, 540–1, *m541*. *See also* World War II.
Pacific Railway Act, 392, 416
Packenham, Sir Edward (General), 229
Pahlavi, Mohammed Reza, (Shah of Iran) 798
Paine, Thomas, *p125*, 125–6, 127, 129
Paiute Indians, *m5*, 10, 488, 495
Palestine Liberation Organization (PLO), 795, 796
Palmer, Alexander Mitchell (Attorney General), 618
Panama, 20, *m22*, *t23*, 545, 796
Panama Canal, 544–5, *m545*, 553; treaty (1978), 796, *m803*
Pan-American Union, 454
Panics: of 1819, 252, 274; of 1837, 275–6, 289; of 1869, 445; of 1893, 519; of 1929, 645–6
Paris, Treaties of: of 1763, 102–3; of 1783, 99, *m144*, 145, 156, 200
Paris Peace Conference, 607
Parity, in farm income, 646
Parker, Alton B., 572
Parkman, Francis, 488
Parks, Rosa, 734, 752, *p752*
Parliament, 103, 106–11, 120, 129, 133, 145
Parsons, Albert, 471
Patent medicines, 573
Patents, 246, *c427*, 638. *See also* Inventions.
Paterson, William, 160
Patriots, 127, 129, 133, 135, 139, 145, 150
Patronage jobs, 443, 447, 450, 451
Patroons, 47
Patton, George (General), *p693*, 695
Paul, Alice, *p605*, 606, 618–19
Payne-Aldrich Tariff, 578
Peace Corps, 753, *p755*
Peaceful coexistence policy, 737
Peanuts, 429
Pearl Harbor, 533, 687–8, 690, 692
Peffer, William A., 518
Pellagra, 513
Pemberton, Joseph (General), 379, 380
Pendleton Act, 451
Peninsular Campaign, 376–7
Penn, Sir William (father), 67
Penn, William (son), 67–9
Pennsylvania, 67–9, 87, 136, 137, 140–1, 249, 256, 298, 415
Pennsylvania Dutch, 69, 87
Pennsylvania System (prison reform), 298
Pension bills, 442–3
Perfectionists, 291
Perkins, Frances, *p669*, *p670*
Perkins Institute (Boston), 296
Perry, Matthew (Commodore), *p531*, 532
Perry, Oliver (Commodore), 228
Pershing, John J. (General), 536–7, 591–2, 603
Perth Amboy (N.J.), *m66*, 69
Peru, 33, *t45*, *m803*. *See also* Incas.
Petit guerre, 90
Philadelphia (Pa.), *m66*, 69, 99, 104,

115, 125, 137, 158, *p159*, 275, 298, 460, 477, 478; Centennial Exposition (1876), 427, 557
Philadelphia (ship), *p221*, 222
Philanthropy, 460, 463, 554, 555
Philippine Islands, 20, 476, *m535*, 535, 536, 538, 539–40, *m541*, 542, 716; annexation (1898), 540, *m541*; and World War II, *m681*, 692, *m698*
Phillips, David Graham, 561
Phonograph recordings, *p584*, 639
Photography, 371, *p522*, 725; hypotheses from, 770–1; as an information source, 672
Pickens, F. W. (Governor), 363
Pickering, John, 216
Pickett, George (General), 381
Pierce, Franklin (President), 349–50, 392
Pierson, Elijah, 328
Pig iron, 520
Pike, Zebulon, *m218*, *p219*, 220, 248, 339
Pikes Peak gold rush, 504, *m505*
Pilgrims, 42, 44, *t45*
Pinchback, P. B. S. (Lieutenant Governor), 403
Pinchot, Gifford, 575, 579
Pinckney, Charles, 64, 204, 206
Pickney, Elizabeth Lucas, 64
Pinckney, Thomas, 200, 203
Pinckney's Treaty, 200, 218
Pine Tree Shillings, 83
Pingree, Hazen S., 563
Pioneers, 501–2
Pirates, 34, 156, 221–2
Pitcairn, John (Major), 122
Pitt, William, 96, 100–1, 105, 125
Pittsburgh (Pa.), 96, 414
Pizarro, Francisco, *m22*, *t23*, 24, 31, *t45*
Plains Indians, *m5*, 11, 219, 226, 336, 341–2, 488–94
Plantations, *t45*, 61–2, 64–6, *p64*, 78–81, 245, 247, 312, 313, 316–8, 513
Plateau Indians, *m5*, 11
Platt, Thomas, 443, 542, 570
Platt Amendment, 539, 676, 678
Plunkitt, George, 441
Plymouth colony, *m41*, 41–4, *t45*, 83
Plymouth Company, 38, 39, 42, 44, 66
Pocahontas, 40, *p40*
Pocket veto, 395
Poe, Edgar Allan, 294, *p294*
Pogroms, 476
Point Four program, 716
Poland, 607, 684, 698, 699, *t702*, *m703*, 710, 797
Polio vaccine, 731
Political Action Committees (PACs), 799
Political cartoons, 456–7. *See also* Nast, Thomas.
Political machines, 436, 438–41, 446, 447, 565
Political parties, 201, 203, 441–55. *See also* Congressional elections; Election campaigns; Presidential elections.
Polk, James K. (President), 343–5
Polo, Marco, 13, *p14*
Ponce de Léon, Juan, 20, *m22*, *t23*
Pontiac's Rebellion, 105–6
Poor Richard's Almanac, 98, 99
Pope, John (General), 377–8

Popular sovereignty, 350–1, 354, 356
Population: American Indian, 8, 31; birth rate decline (1955–75), 788; birth rate increase (post-World War II), 722–3; of cities, 477; Civil War period, 365; 1800–1840, *c247*; 1860–1900, 412, 463; seventeenth and eighteenth centuries, 87, *c90*; slave, 79, 365; and statehood, 154; in the Sun Belt, 806; western frontier, 486
Populist party, 516–20, 528–30, 561, 564
Pork-barrel bills, 443
Port Royal colony, 46, 90–1
Portugal, 14–16, *m18*, *t23*, 31, 33, *t45*
Postal savings system, 517
Postal Service, 192, 194, 394, 443
Powderly, Terence V., 470, *p470*
Powell, Adam Clayton, 690
Powell, John Wesley, 574
Powers, Francis Gary, 740
Powhatan Indians, *m5*, 11, 39, 41
Pratt, Enoch, 555
Predestination, 50, 284, 286
Pre-emption, in land settlement, 252, 279
Prendergast, Maurice, *p551*
Presbyterian Church, 87, 288
Prescott, Samuel, 121–2
Prescott, William, 123
Preservationists, 575
Presidency, 151, 161–2; constitutional powers, 165–6, *c167*; indirect election to, 162, 165; under Lincoln, 394–5; succession to, 233; two-term rule, 576, 720
Presidential elections, 162, 264–5, 449–50; of 1789, 190; of 1796, 203; of 1800, 206; of 1808, 223; of 1816, 230; of 1820, 232; of 1824, 233–4, 264; of 1828, 235, 262, *p264*, 266–7, 273; of 1832, 273, 275; of 1836, 276–7; of 1840, 264, 278–9, 326; of 1844, 280, 289, 326, 343–4; of 1848, 346; of 1852, 349; of 1856, 302, 351; of 1860, 356–7, *m363*; of 1864, 385; of 1868, 400, 401–2, 444, 449, *c450*; of 1872, 405, 407, 445–6, 449, *c450*, 469; of 1876, 447–9, *c450*, 455; of 1880, 449–50, *c450*, 455; of 1884, 449, *c450*, 451–2, 455; of 1888, 442, 449–50, *c450*, 452–3; of 1892, *c450*, 450, 516, *p517*, 518; of 1896, *c450*, 518, 520, 526–30; of 1900, *c450*, 542, 565, 570; of 1904, 565, 570, 571, 572; of 1908, 565, 576; of 1912, 565, *p569*, 579–81; of 1916, 583, 597–8; of 1920, 565, 609, 618, 623–4; of 1924, 630, 632, 636; of 1928, 636, 647, 657; of 1932, 652, 657–8, 660–1; of 1936, 668, 669–70; of 1940, 686; of 1944, 691; of 1948, 712, 713–14; of 1952, 728, 730; of 1956, 738; of 1960, 740–1; of 1964, 757, 763–4; of 1968, 768–9; of 1972, 779, 782; of 1976, 792, 794; of 1980, 798–9, 800; of 1984, 802, 804–5
Presley, Elvis, 724, *p725*
Preston, William B., 313
Primary elections, 564, 579, 713–4, 740–1, 768–9, 792, 794, 798–9, 802, 804
Princeton, Battle of, *m136*, 137
Princeton University, 581
Printz, Johann (Governor), 47
Prison reforms, 296, 297, 298–99
Privateers, 20

Proclamation of 1763, 106, *m106*
Progressive Era, 552, 561, 568–73, 580, 581–3, 597, 622, 623, 624; blacks and, 562–3; conservation, 573, 575; election reforms, 564; government reforms, 562, 563–5; end of, 597; tariff issue, 578, 579
Progressive party (1948), 713
Prohibition, 300, *p615,* 620, 622–3, 641, 665
Promontory Point (Utah), 417, *p418, m419*
Propaganda, 129, 132; methods, 704–5; and World War I, 606
Property ownership, 132, 159; colonial period, 40, 44, 53, 56, 59–60, 63; and the slave codes, 319, 320; and voting rights, 87, 150, 264
Prophet, The, 225, 227
Proprietary colonies, 56, 59–60, 63
Prosser, Gabriel, 312
Protective tariff, 197. *See also* Tariffs.
Protectorates, 539
Protestant Reformation, 34
Protestants, 300–3, 341. *See also* Huguenots; Pilgrims; Puritans.
Providence (R.I.), *m53, p55*
Prussia, 91, 100, 222, 592, *m594, m601, m703. See also* Germany.
Public domain, public land, 153–4, 251, 416
Public schools, 371; federal funding, 583; growth (1860–1900), 554; integration, 732–4; and land revenues, 154; in New England, 58–9, 313; prayer issue, 799, 802; during Reconstruction, 404; and *Sputnik,* 739
Public utilities, 563
Public Works, 234, 253–5, 275, 277, 659, 665, 666–7. *See also* Canals; Roads.
Pueblo Indians, 8–9, 25, 336, 488
Puerto Rico, *m22, t45,* 533, 538, *m538, t539,* 540
Pulaski, Casimir, 140
Pulitzer, Joseph, 406, 533–4
Pullman Co. strike, 552
Pure Food and Drug Acts, 561, 573
Puritans, 50–5, 57–9, 61, 62, 83, 150, 284. *See also* Reform movements; Revivalists.
Putnam, Israel, 123

Q

Quakers, *p51,* 67–9, 82, 83, 104, 135, 322, 323, 326, 766
Quartering Act: of 1765, 106; of 1774, 115
Quay, Matt, 443
Quebec, 20, m22, *t23, t45,* 46, 87, 88, *m100,* 101–2; Arnold's siege, 124
Quebec Act, 115
Queen Anne's War, 89, 90–1
Queensbury, Marquis of, 559
Quemoy-Matsu war, 736
Quetzalcoatl, 24
Quivira, 24
Quit-rent system, 60

R

Racial segregation, 397, 407, 519, 553, 619–20, 690, 732–4

Racial supremacy, 444, 519, 532, 540, 550, 620, 683, 684
Radical Republicans, 394, 395, 397–405, 444, 445–6, 513, 539–40
Radio, 584, 639, 649
Radio immunoassay technique, 781
Railroads, 414–20, 508, 510–11, 514, 515, 531; and the cattle industry, 414, 421, 498, 500; and the Civil War, 365–6, 385; and the food industry, 414, 421, 422; government operation, 780; and the Great Depression, 655; and industrial growth, 414, 422; land grants, 392, 393, 416, 417–18; monopolies, 418–19, 517, 518, 570–1; Progressive reforms, 564, 565, 570–3; routes, *m419, m498;* strike (1877), 414, 468; strikes (1880s), 470; system consolidation, 414–5, 418–9; and World War I, 603–4. *See also* Transcontinental railroad.
Raleigh, Sir Walter, 36, *p36,* 63
Randolph, A. Philip, 690
Randolph, Edmund, 158, 160, 163, 192, 194
Rankin, Jeannette, 688
Rappites, 290
Raskob, John J., 636
Ray, James Earl, 763
Rayburn, Sam (Senator), 740
Reactionaries, 577
Reagan, Ronald (President), 794, 796, 799–805; domestic policy, 800–2; foreign policy, 801–2; and the 1976 elections, 794; and the 1984 elections, 802, 804–5
Realpolitik, 776–7, 778
Recall, 516, 564, 579
Recessions (1970s–80s), 779, 801, 807
Reconstruction Finance Corporation (RFC), 659
Reconstruction period, 394–405, *t400,* 407, 444, 445–6, 513, 620
Red Cloud (Indian chief), 490
Redcoats, *p97,* 106, 112, 133
Redeemers, 405, 407
Redpath, James, 555
Red Scare: of 1919–20, 617–18; of 1950s, 720–1
Reed, Dr. William, 539
Referendum, 516, 564, 579
Reform movements, 295–301, 302–5, 469, 494. *See also* Populist party; Progressive Era.
Refrigeration, 421, 422, *p522,* 638
Regulators, 112–13
Regulatory agencies, 731–2
Religion: colonial period, 31–2, 41–2, 60–1, 68–9; cults (1970s), 787, *p787;* freedom of, 61, 63, 154; nineteenth-century movements, 284–90; separation of church and state, 150, 802; of slaves, 320
Religious toleration, 42, 52, 54–5, 61, 63, 67, 69
Remington, Frederic, *p341, p497,* 534
Renaissance, 12
Reno, Milo, 654
Representative government, 40, 53, 109–10, 159, 160–1. *See also* Congress; House of Representatives; Senate.
Republican party, 351, 352; black support, 402, 407, 444, 519, 670; and the Civil War, 390, 392, 393–4, 442–3; and the gold standard, 528–9; and the Great Depression, 657–8;

671; in New England, 351, 443; "New Era" (1920s), 632–5; post-Civil War politics, 442–53; in the Progressive Era, 568, 570, 572, 578, 583; right-wing, 777, 778, 779; and slavery, 351, 362; in the South, 443; split (1910), 578–9; and tariffs, 351. *See also* Bull Moose party; Jeffersonian Republicans; Liberal Republicans; National republicans; Radical Republicans.
Reservationists: conservation movement, 575; League of Nations, 609
Resorts, 556
Revels, Hiram (Senator), 403, *p404*
Revere, Paul, *p97, p113, p121, m121,* 121–2
Revivalists, 286
Revolutionary War, 99, 106, 111–15, 121–5, 133–45, *m134, m136, m142, m144,* 652; British blockade, *m134,* 141, 142; and Canada, 124–5, 135, 136, *m136,* 137, 139; critical years, 133, 135–8; currency crisis, 154–5; debt repayment, 194, 195, 200; early battles, *m121,* 121–4; foreign soldiers, 140; French aid, 135, 138, 139–40, 144, 155, 195, 199; naval battles, 135, 139, 144; in the south, 141–2, *m142;* women in, 143, *p143*
Reynolds, R. J., 521
Rhee, Syngman, 717
Rhode Island, 54–5, 57, 59, 83, 86, 87, 150
Rice, 64, 65, 66, 76, 77, 78, 245, 317, 318
Richmond (Va.), 370, 373, 376, *m377,* 384, *p384–5*
Rickenbacker, Eddie, *p603*
Ride, Sally K., 807
Right of deposit, 200
Right-wing extremism, 763–4
Rio Grande, 32, *m32,* 220, 336, *m339,* 345–6
Rising, Johan (Governor), 47
River and Harbor Bill, 443
Rivers, and industrialization, 243, 248, 250, 256–7
Roads, construction of, 253–4, 723
Roanoke colony, 36, *m41,* 63
Roaring Twenties, 614, *p631,* 636–43
Robber barons, 415–16
Robinson, Harriet Hanson, *p244*
Robots, 807, *p808*
Rock and roll, 724
Rockefeller, John D., *p425,* 426, 431, 462, 504, 554, 560, 636
Rockefeller, Nelson (Vice President), 764
Rockingham, Lord, 145
Rockne, Knute, 636
Rocky Mountains, 10, 232, 248, 339–40
Rodney, Caesar, 128
Roebling, John A., 479
Roebuck, Alvah, 473
Rogers, Will, 656, *p658*
Rogers, William P., 777
Rolfe, John, 40
Roman Catholics, 452, 540, 561; in the colonies, 34, 88, 105, 115; immigration, 301–2, 452; and labor unions, 469–70; in Maryland, 60–1, 86; missions, 31–2, 336, 337, 341; persecutions of, 60, 150, 302, 364, 620; and the presidency, 452, 740; universities, 555
Rommel, Erwin (Field Marshall), 694

ACKNOWLEDGMENTS

QUOTED MATERIAL

For permission to reprint copyrighted material, grateful acknowledgment is made to the following:

American Heritage Publishing Co., Inc.: For excerpts reprinted by permission from *American Testament: Fifty Great Documents of American History.* Copyright © 1971 by American Heritage Publishing Co., Inc. *Archon Books, The Shoe String Press:* For excerpts from *The Life and Times of William Howard Taft, Vol. 2* by Henry Pringle, copyright © 1964, Archon Books. *Chelsea House Publishers:* For excerpts from *State of the Union Messages of the Presidents 1970–1966, Vol. 2.* Copyright © 1966 by Chelsea House Publishers. *Curtis Brown, Ltd.:* For excerpts from *Many Are the Hearts* by Richard Goldhurst. Copyright © 1975 by Richard Goldhurst. *Farrar, Straus & Giroux, Inc.:* For excerpts from *Mr. President* by William Hillman. Pictures by Alfred Wagg. Copyright © 1952 by William Hillman and Alfred Wagg. *Hoover Foundation, New York:* For excerpts from *The Memoirs of Herbert Hoover, Vol. 3* by Herbert Hoover, copyright 1952. *Houghton Mifflin Company:* For excerpts from *The American Heritage Dictionary of the English Language, High School Edition.* Copyright © 1976 by Houghton Mifflin Company; for excerpts from *The American Heritage Dictionary of the English Language.* Copyright © 1981 by Houghton Mifflin Company. *Alfred A. Knopf, Inc.:* For excerpts from *Gentleman Boss: The Life of Chester Arthur,* by Thomas C. Reeves. Copyright © 1975 by Alfred A. Knopf, Inc. *Little, Brown and Company:* For excerpts from *Calvin Coolidge: The Man from Vermont* by Claude M. Fuess. Copyright © 1940 by Little, Brown and Company; for excerpts from *Woodrow Wilson's Own Story,* edited by Donald Day. Copyright © 1952 by Little, Brown and Company. *Macmillan Publishing Company:* For excerpts from *James Madison: A Biography* by Ralph Ketcham. Copyright © 1971 by Ralph Ketcham. *The New York Times Company:* From "Speech by Gerald R. Ford," August 9, 1974; from "Speech by Richard Nixon," August 8, 1974. Copyright © 1974 by The New York Times Company. *W. W. Norton & Company, Inc.:* For excerpts from *The Eisenhower Diaries,* edited by Robert H. Ferrel. Copyright © 1981 by W. W. Norton & Company, Inc. *Rutherford B. Hayes Presidential Center:* For excerpts from *Diary and Letters of Rutherford Birchard Hayes, Vol. 3,* edited by Charles R. Williams. Copyright © 1924, Columbus, Ohio, Ohio State Archaeological and Historical Society. *Charles Scribner's Sons:* For excerpts from John Quincy Adams, excerpted from *The Diary of John Quincy Adams, 1794–1845.* Copyright 1928 Charles Scribner's Sons; for excerpts from Freeman Cleaves, excerpted from *Old Tippecanoe.* Copyright 1939 Charles Scribner's Sons; for excerpts from Theodore Roosevelt, excerpted from *An Autobiography of Theodore Roosevelt;* for excerpts from Theodore Roosevelt, excerpted from *The Works of Theodore Roosevelt, Vol. 19.* Copyright 1913 Charles Scribner's Sons. Copyright renewed 1941 Edith K. Carow Roosevelt. *Mrs. William Allen White:* For excerpts from *The Autobiography of William Allen White* by William Allen White, copyright 1946. *World Book, Inc.:* For excerpts from *The World Book Encyclopedia.* Copyright © 1984 by World Book, Inc.

ILLUSTRATIONS

208–209, 258–259, 330–331, Chris Calle; 522–523, 584–585, 808–809, Jon Friedman; 70–71, 432–433, 567, 586, 628, 648–649, 742–743, 810, Tom Leonard.

PHOTO CREDITS

The following abbreviations indicate the position of the photographs on the page: *t,* top; *b,* bottom; *l,* left; *r,* right; *c,* center.

FRONT MATTER

Detail From iii–iv, "Sunny Morning on the Hudson River," Thomas Cole, Museum of Fine Arts, Boston, M. and M. Karolik Collection; vii, x, The Granger Collection; vi, National Park Service; ix, Independence National Historical Park Collection; viii, xi, Smithsonian Institution, xii, xiii, Metropolitan Museum of Art.

MAPS

All cartographic material
created by Richard Sanderson

UNIT 1

xiv–1, "The Grand Canyon," Thomas Moran, Thomas Gilcrease Institute of American History and Art, Tulsa, Oklahoma; 3, George Gerster, Photo Researchers, Inc.; 4, Van Bucher, Photo Researchers, Inc.; 6 (t), Jack Fields, Photo Researchers, Inc.; (b), Peter B. Kaplan, Photo Researchers, Inc.; 7, Bradley Smith, Photo Researchers, Inc.; 8, American Museum of Natural History, New York; 9 (t), George Gerster, Photo Researchers, Inc.; (b), George Dineen, Photo Researchers, Inc.; 14, Mary Evans Picture Library, Photo Researchers, Inc.; 15 (l, r), The Granger Collection; 16, Scala/EPA; 17, 21, 24, The Granger Collection; 25, Historical Pictures Service, Inc., Chicago; 29, 30, 35 (t, b), 36, 37, 38, 39, The Granger Collection; 40, National Portrait Gallery, Smithsonian Institution, Washington, D.C.; 44, The Granger Collection; 46, New York Public Library, Rare Books; 47, The Granger Collection; 51, Detail from "Penn's Treaty," Edward Hicks, Thomas Gilcrease Institute of American History and Art, Tulsa, Oklahoma; 52 (l, r), Culver Pictures; 54, 55, 56 (l, c, r), 57 (l, c, r), 60, 61 (b), The Granger Collection; 62 (l), Nathaniel Jocelyn, New Haven Historical Society; 62 (r), The Bettmann Archive Inc.; 63, Mary Evans Picture Library, Photo Researchers; 64, The Granger Collection; 67, New York Historical Society; 68, "Quaker Meeting House," Anonymous, Museum of Fine Arts, Boston; 75, "East India Wharf," Peter Monarny, Victoria and Albert Museum, London; 76, American Antiquarian Society, Worcester; 77 (t), The Bettmann Archive Inc.; 77 (b), The Granger Collection; 78–79 "The Plantation," Unknown Artist, Metropolitan Museum of Art, New York; 79 (b), 80, New York Historical Society; 82 (t), American Antiquarian Society, Worcester; 82 (b), "The Sargent Family," American School 19th cent., National Gallery of Art, Washington, D.C., Gift of Edgar W. and Bernice C. Garbisch; 84 (t), The Granger Collection; 84 (b), 85, The Bettmann Archive Inc.; 86 (l, r), The Granger Collection; 88, "Chief of the Taensa Indians Receiving La Salle, March, 1682," George Catlin, National Gallery of Art, Washington, D.C., Paul Mellon Collection; 89, The Granger Collection.

UNIT 2

94–95, "The Hudson Valley, Sunset," Thomas Chambers, National Gallery of Art, Washington, D.C., Gift of Edgar W. and Bernice C. Garbisch; 97, Attributed to Paul Revere, Yale University Art Gallery, New Haven; 98, The Granger Collection; 99 (t), Yale University Art Gallery, New Haven; 99 , 101, 102, 103, 105, The Granger Collection; 108 (t), American Antiquarian Society, Worcester; 108 , New York Historical Society; 109, The Granger Collection; 110, The Bettmann Archive Inc.; 112, John Singleton Copley, Museum of Fine Arts, Boston; 113, 114, The Granger Collection; 119, John Trumbull, Yale University Art Gallery, New Haven; 120 (t), The Granger Collection; 120 , New York Historical Society; 121, John Singleton Copley, Museum of Fine Arts, Boston, Gift of Joseph W., William B., and Edward H. R. Revere; 123, John Trumbull, Yale University Art Gallery, New Haven; 124, American School, National Gallery of Art, Washington, D.C., Gift of Edgar W. and Bernice C. Garbisch; 125, John Wesley Jarvis, National Gallery of Art, Washington, D.C., Gift of Marian B. Maurice; 128, John Trumbull, Yale University Art Gallery, New Haven; 132, The Granger Collection; 137, Anonymous, Philadelphia Museum of Art, Edgar W. and Bernice C. Garbisch Collection; 138 The Granger Collection; 139, John Trumbull, Yale University Art Gallery, New Haven; 140 (l, r), The Granger Collection; 141 (t, b), The Bettmann Archive Inc.; 143, Rhode Island Historical Society, Providence; 144, The Bettmann Archive Inc.; 145, John Trumbull, Yale University Art Gallery, New Haven; 149, William Birch, Historical Society of Pennsylvania, Philadelphia; 152–153, Library of Congress; 154, Chase Manhattan Bank, New York; 155 (t), The Bettmann Archive Inc.; 155 (b), American Jewish Historical Society, Waltham, Massachusetts; 157, The Bettmann Archive Inc.; 159 (t), American Philosophical Society; Linda Bartlett, Photo Researchers; 159 (b), The Bettmann Archive Inc.; 160, New York Historical Society; 161, U.S. Bureau of Engraving and Printing; 163 (t), New York Historical Society; 163 (l), National Portrait Gallery, Washington, D.C., Tom McHugh, Photo Researchers; 163 (c), Library of Congress; 163 (r), National Portrait Gallery, Washington, D.C., Tom McHugh, Photo Researchers; 191, The Granger Collection; 192, New York State Historical Association, Cooperstown; 193, L. M. Cooke, National Gallery of Art, Washington, D.C., Gift of Edgar W. and Bernice C. Garbisch; 194, Scala/EPA; 195, John Trumbull, Yale University Art Gallery, New Haven; 196, The Granger Collection; 198, Culver Pictures Inc.; 202 (t), The Granger Collection; 202 (b), Edward Savage, National Gallery of Art, Washington, D.C., Andrew W. Mellon Collection; 203, Library of Congress; 204, U.S. Bureau of Engraving and Printing; 205, 207, The Granger Collection.

UNIT 3

212–213, "Niagara Falls," Frederick Church, The Corcoran Gallery of Art, Washington, D.C.; 215, The Granger Collection; 216, U.S. Bureau of Engraving and Printing; 217 (t, b), 219 (t), The Granger Collection; 219 (b), New York Historical Society; 221, The Granger Collection; 222–223, Peabody Museum, Salem; 224, U.S. Bureau of Engraving and Printing; 226 (t), Field Museum of Natural History, Chicago; 226 (b), The Bettmann Archive Inc.; 227, New York Historical Society; 228 (t), Unknown Artist, Yale University Art Gallery, New Haven; 228, The Granger Collection; 229, Unknown Artist, Yale University Art Gallery, New Haven; 230, 235, U.S. Bureau of Engraving and Printing; 239, "Pat Lyon at the Forge," John Neagle, Museum of Fine Arts, Boston; 240, Merrimack Valley Textile Museum, N. Andover, Massachusetts; 241, Johann Carmiencke, Yale University Art Gallery, New Haven; 242 (t), W. G. Munson, Yale University Art Gallery, New Haven; 242 (b), Samuel F. B. Morse, Yale University Art Gallery, New Haven; 243, American Antiquarian Society; 244 (t), Boston Public Library; 244 (b), G. P. A. Healy, National Portrait Gallery; Tom McHugh, Photo Researchers; 245, National Portrait Gallery: Tom McHugh, Photo Researchers; 246, 247, The Granger Collection; 249, National Cowboy Hall of Fame: Tom McHugh, Photo Researchers; 250, The Granger Collection; 251, Museum of Fine Arts, Boston; 252, The Granger Collection; 255, New York Historical Society; 256, The Granger Collection; 257, New York Historical Society; 263, Detail from "County Election," George Caleb Bingham, St. Louis Art Museum; 264 (t, b), 265, The Granger Collection; 267, U.S. Bureau of Engraving and Printing; 268, 272, 273, 276, The Granger Collection; 277, 278 (t), U.S. Bureau of Engraving and Printing; 278 (b), Indiana Historical Society; 279, The Granger Collection; 280, U.S. Bureau of Engraving and Printing; 281, Detail from "Old House of Representatives," Samuel F. B. Morse, Corcoran Gallery of American Art, Washington, D.C.; 285, The Granger Collection; 286 (l, c, r), The Bettmann Archive Inc.; 287, 288, 289, The Granger Collection; 291 (t), Sophia Smith Collection, Smith College, Northampton, Massachusetts; 291 (b), The Bettmann Archive Inc.; 292 (l, c, r), The Granger Collection; 293 (l, c), The Bettmann Archive Inc.; 293 (r), The Granger Collection; 294 (l, r), 295, 296, 297 (l), The Bettmann Archive Inc.; 297 (r), National Portrait Gallery; 298, 299 (t), The Bettmann Archive Inc.; 299 (b), The Granger Collection; 300, 301, Museum of the City of New York; 303 (t), Culver Pictures Inc.; 303 (b), The Granger Collection; 305 (l, c), The Bettmann Archive Inc.; 305 (r), Culver Pictures Inc.; 306, The Granger Collection.

UNIT 4 308–309, "The Cornell Farm," Edward Hicks, National Gallery of Art, Washington, D.C., Gift of Edgar W. and Bernice C. Garbisch; 311, Detail from "Underground Railroad," Charles T. Webber, Cincinnati Art Museum; 312 (l), The Granger Collection; 312 (r), American Antiquarian Society; 315, 316, 319, Alanson Fisher, National Portrait Gallery: Tom McHugh, Photo Researchers; 321, "A Ride for Liberty," Eastman Johnson, Brooklyn Museum, Gift of Gwendolyn O. L. Conkling; 322, 323 (t), The Bettmann Archive Inc.; 323 (b), Sophia Smith Collection, Smith College, Northampton, Massachusetts; 324 (l), American Antiquarian Society; 324 (r), Photo Researchers; 326, The Granger Collection; 328, National Portrait Gallery; 329, The Bettmann Archive Inc.; 335, The Granger Collection; 336, The Bettmann Archive Inc.; 337, The Granger Collection; 338 (t, bl), The Bettmann Archive Inc.; 338 (br), Seymour Thomas, San Jacinto Museum of History Association; 340, The Bettmann Archive Inc.; 341, The Granger Collection; 343, U.S. Bureau of Engraving and Printing; 345, Scala/Art Resource; 347 (t), U.S. Bureau of Engraving and Printing; 347 (b), Denver Public Library; 348, The Granger Collection; 349, 350 (t), 353, U.S. Bureau of Engraving and Printing; 354, The Bettmann Archive Inc.; 355, The Granger Collection; 356, "Last Moments of John Brown," Thomas Hovenden, Metropolitan Museum of Art; 357, The Granger Collection; 361, Scala/Art Resource; 362 (l), Sophia Smith Collection, Smith College, Northampton, Massachusetts; 362 (r), The Bettmann Archive Inc.; 364 (t), U.S. Bureau of Engraving and Printing; 364 (b), The Granger Collection; 365, "We Go for The Union," American School, National Gallery of Art, Gift of Edgar W. and Bernice C. Garbisch; 368, The Granger Collection; 369 (t, b), Photo Researchers; 370, Detail from "A Rainy Day at Camp," Winslow Homer, Metropolitan Museum of Art, New York; 371 (l), The Granger Collection; 371 (r), The Bettmann Archive Inc.; 372 (t), New York Historical Society; 372 (b), Scala/Art Resource; 376, 378, Photo Researchers; 379, 380, 383 (t, b), 386, 387, 391, 393, 397, The Granger Collection; 398 (t), U.S. Bureau of Engraving and Printing; 398 (b), Library of Congress; 399 (t), Photo Researchers; 399 (b), Library of Congress; 402 (t), U.S. Bureau of Engraving and Printing; 402 (b), 403, New York Historical Society; 404, The Granger Collection; 405, Library of Congress; 407, U.S. Bureau of Engraving and Printing.

UNIT 5 410–411, "View of Sacramento, California, from across the Sacramento River," George Tirrell, Museum of Fine Arts, Boston, M. and M. Karolik Collection; 413, Yale University Art Gallery, Mabel Brady Garvan Collection; 415, "9:45 Accomodation, Stratford," Edward Henry, Metropolitan Museum of Art; 416, Henry E. Huntington Library and Gallery, San Marino, California; 417, The Granger Collection; 418, The Bettmann Archive Inc.; 420, H. J. Heinz Co., Pittsburgh; 421, The Bettmann Archive Inc.; 422, The Granger Collection; 423 (t), The Bettmann Archive Inc.; 423 (b), Culver Pictures Inc.; 424, "Forging the Shaft," John Weir, Metropolitan Museum of Art; 425 (t), The Bettmann Archive Inc.; 425 (b), Library of Congress; 427, The Bettmann Archive Inc.; 428, Library of Congress;

429 (t, b), The Bettmann Archive Inc.; 431, Culver Pictures Inc.; 437, 438, 439 (b), 440, 442, 445 (b), 446, 447, The Granger Collection; 448, "Electoral College," Cornelia Adele Fassett, Architect of the Capitol; 449, U.S. Bureau of Engraving and Printing; 450, Culver Pictures Inc.; 451, 452, 453, U.S. Bureau of Engraving and Printing; 455, The Granger Collection; 456, Don Hesse; 459, "Bowery at Night," Museum of the City of New York; 460 (t, c), Museum of the City of New York; 460 (b), 461 (t, inset), Culver Pictures Inc.; 462, The Granger Collection; 464, 465 (l, r), 466, The Bettmann Archive Inc.; 468, 470, 471, 472, 473 (l), The Granger Collection; 473 (c, r), The Bettmann Archive Inc.; 475, The Granger Collection; 478, Museum of the City of New York; 479, New York Historical Society; 480 (t), The Granger Collection; 480 (c), New York Public Library, Manuscript Division.

UNIT 6 484–485, "The Lackawanna Valley," George Inness, National Gallery of Art, Gift of Mrs. Huttleston Rogers; 487, George Catlin, Scala/Art Resource; 489, Charles Russell, Amon Carter Museum, Fort Worth, Texas; 491, The Granger Collection; 492, Nebraska State Historical Society; 493, New York Historical Society; 495 (l), Nevada Historical Society; 495 (r), The Bettmann Archive Inc.; 496, "Indian Camp," Jules Tavernier, Thomas Gilcrease Institute of American Art, Tulsa, Oklahoma; 497 (l), "The Cowboy," Frederic Remington, Amon Carter Museum, Fort Worth, Texas; 497 (r), "An Indian Trapper," Frederic Remington, Amon Carter Museum, Fort Worth, Texas; 499, 502, Denver Public Library; 503 (l), The Granger Collection; 503 (r), The Bettmann Archive Inc.; 504, California Historical Society; 509, Detail from "Flax Scutching Bee," Linton Park, National Gallery of Art, Gift of Edgar W. and Bernice C. Garbisch; 510, Nebraska State Historical Society; 511 (t), The Granger Collection; 511 (b), Minnesota Historical Society; 512, 513, Nebraska State Historical Society; 516, The Granger Collection; 517 (t), Nebraska State Historical Society; 517 (b), The Bettmann Archive Inc.; 518, The Granger Collection; 520, Nebraska State Historical Society; 521, 527, The Granger Collection; 528 (l), Nebraska State Historical Society; 528 (r), The Granger Collection; 531 (t), U.S. Bureau of Engraving and Printing; 531 (b), 534, The Granger Collection; 536, The Bettmann Archive Inc.; 537 (t), The Granger Collection; 537 (b), Library of Congress; 540, 543, The Granger Collection; 544, U.S. Bureau of Engraving and Printing.

UNIT 7 548–549, "Threshing Wheat," Thomas Hart Benton, The Sheldon Swope Art Gallery, Terre Haute, Indiana; 551, Detail from "Madison Square, 1901," Maurice Prendergast, Whitney Museum of American Art, Gift of Joan Whitney Payson; 552, Culver Pictures Inc.; 553, 554, Brown Brothers; 555, Sophia Smith Collection, Smith College, Northampton, Massachusetts; 556, 557 (tl), Culver Pictures Inc.; 557 (tr), Brown Brothers; 557 (b), 558, 560, 562, 563, Culver Pictures Inc.; 569, The Granger Collection; 570, Brown Brothers; 573, California Historical Society; 574 (l), The Bettmann Archive Inc.; 574 (r), The Granger Collection; 577 (t), U.S. Bureau of Engraving and Printing; 577 (b), 578, 580, Brown Brothers; 582 (t), U.S. Bureau of Engraving and Printing; 582 (b), Culver Pictures Inc.; 589, N.C. Wyeth, Collection of Mort Kunstler, Courtesy Society of Illustrators' Museum of American Illustration; 590, 591 (t, b), 592, Brown Brothers; 595, The Bettmann Archive Inc.; 597, 600 (t, b), 602 (t), Brown Brothers; 602 (b), The Bettmann Archive Inc.; 603, 604, 605 (tl, tr, br), Brown Brothers; 606, Treidler, Society of Illustrators' Museum of American Illustration; 608, Brown Brothers.

UNIT 8 612–613 "Macomb's Dam Bridge," Edward Hopper, The Brooklyn Museum, Bequest of Mary T. Cockeroft; 615, Ben Shahn, Museum of the City of New York; 617, Wide World Photos; 619 (tl), The Bettmann Archive Inc.; 619 (tr), Brown Brothers; 621, The Bettmann Archive Inc.; 622, 623 (t), Brown Brothers; 623 (b), The Bettmann Archive Inc.; 624, U.S. Bureau of Engraving and Printing; 625, The Bettmann Archive Inc.; 627, U.S. Bureau of Engraving and Printing; 631, Culver Pictures Inc.; 633, 634, 635, 637 (t, bl) The Bettmann Archive Inc.; 637 (br), 638, Culver Pictures Inc.; 639, 640 (l, r), The Bettmann Archive Inc.; 641 (l, r), Culver Pictures Inc.; 642, Wide World Photos; 645, The Bettmann Archive Inc.; 647, U.S. Bureau of Engraving and Printing; 653, Detail from "Home Relief Station," Louis Ribak, Whitney Museum of American Art; 654, Library of Congress; 655 (t), "Drouth-Stricken Area," Alexandre Hogue, Dallas Museum of Art; 656, 658 (t), Culver Pictures Inc.; 658 (b), Library of Congress; 659, Culver Pictures Inc.; 660, The Bettmann Archive Inc.; 661, U.S. Bureau of Engraving and Printing, 664, The Bettmann Archive Inc.; 665 (t), Culver Pictures Inc.; 665 (b), Wide World Photos; 666, Culver Pictures Inc.; 669, Wide World Photos; 670, The Bettmann Archive Inc.; 672, Library of Congress.

UNIT 9 674–675, "American Landscape," Charles Sheeler, Museum of Modern Art; 677, Guiness, Society of Illustrators' Museum of American Illustration, Courtesy U.S. Marine Corps. Art Collection, Washington, D.C.; 679, Imperial War Museum; 682 (t), Magnum Photos; 682 (b), Black Star Photos; 685, Associated Newspapers Group Ltd.; 686, The Bettmann Archive Inc.; 687, Wide World Photos; 688 (t), Library of Congress; 689, Victor Kayfetz, Black Star Photos; 691 (t, b), Library of Congress; 692, Robert Benney, Society of Illustrators' Museum of American Illustration; 693 (t), Owen, Black Star Photos; 693, (bl), Margaret Bourke-White, LIFE Magazine, © Time Inc.; 693 (br), Eliot Elisofon, LIFE Picture Service, © 1941 Time Inc.; 695 (b), Frank Scherschel, LIFE Magazine, © 1950 Time Inc.; 696 (t), Robert Capa, Magnum Photos; 697, UPI, LIFE Picture Service; 701 (t), U.S. Bureau of Engraving and Printing; 701 (b), The Bettmann Archive Inc.; 704, The Granger Collection; 707, Sergio Lorrain, Magnum Photos; 709, Wide World Photos; 710 (l), The Bettmann Archive Inc.; 710 (r), Wide World Photos; 711 (l), David Seymour, Magnum Photos; 711 (r), Walter Sanders, LIFE Magazine, © 1948 Time Inc.; 713, Robert Capa, Magnum Photos; 714 (t), Bob Henriques, Magnum Photos; 714 (b), W. Eugene Smith, LIFE Magazine, © 1948 Time Inc.; 715, Rodgers, Magnum Photos; 716, Magnum Photos; 717 (t), David Seymour, Magnum Photos; 717 (b), Hank Walker, LIFE Magazine, © Time Inc.; 718, 719, 721, Wide World Photos; 722, Wayne Miller, Magnum Photos; 724 (tl), "Number 10, 1950," Mark Rothko, The Museum of Modern Art, Gift of Philip Johnson; 724 (tr), "Golden Blaze," Hans Hofmann, Corcoran Gallery of Art; 724 (b), "Royal Tide II," Louise Nevelson, Whitney Museum of American Art, Gift of the artist; 725, Leviton, Black Star Photos; 729, Tom McHugh, Photo Researchers; 730 (t), U.S. Bureau of Engraving and Printing; 730 (b), Cornell Capa, Magnum Photos; 731, Wide World Photos; 732 (t), Fred Ward, Black Star Photos; 732 (b), Wide World Photos; 734, John Bryson, LIFE Magazine, © Time Inc.; 737, 741, **Cornell Capa, Magnum Photos.** Black Star Photos; 738, Erich Lessing, Magnum Photos; 741, Cornell Capa, Magnum Photos.

UNIT 10 746–747, "Dalles Dam on the Columbia River," Robert Birmelin, Courtesy Sherry French Gallery; 749, Black Star Photos;

750 (t), U.S. Bureau of Engraving and Printing; 750 (b), Erich Hartmann, Magnum Photos; 751, Wide World Photos; 752 (l), Paul Schutzer, LIFE Magazine, © 1972 Time Inc.; 752 (r), Bob Fitch, Black Star Photos; 753 (t), Charles Moore, Black Star Photos; 753 (b), The Bettmann Archive Inc.; 755, Sergio Larrain, Magnum Photos; 756 (l), Andrew St. George, Magnum Photos; 756 (r), Jan Lukas, Photo Researchers; 758 (t), Dallas Herald Time, Black Star Photos; 758 (b), Don McCoy, Black Star Photos; 759, U.S. Bureau of Engraving and Printing; 760 (l, r), Paul Fusco, Magnum Photos; 761, Bob Adelman, Magnum Photos; 762, M. Alexander, Black Star Photos; 763 (t), Leonard Freed, Magnum Photos; 763 (b), Bob Adelman, Magnum Photos; 765 (l), Hiroji Kubota, Magnum Photos; 765 (r), Robt. Ellison-Empire News, Black Star Photos; 767 (t), Eugene Anthony, Black Star Photos; 767 (b), Steve Schapiro, Black Star Photos; 768 (l, r), Burt Glinn, Magnum Photos; 768 (c), Steve Schapiro, Black Star Photos; 770, Ted Cowell, Black Star Photos; 771, Don Uhrbrock, LIFE Magazine, Time Inc.; 773, NASA; 774 (t), U.S. Bureau of Engraving and Printing; 774 (b), Dennis Brack, Black Star Photos; 775 (t), Owen, Black Star Photos; 775 (b), Hiroji Kubota, Magnum Photos; 777, Magnum Photos; 778 (l), Gamma/Liaison; 778 (r), Burt Glinn, Magnum Photos; 780, NASA; 781 (l), Nik Kleinberg, Picture Group; 781 (r), Georgiana Silk, Discover Magazine, Time Inc.; 783, Gamma/Liaison; 784, U.S. Bureau of Engraving and Printing; 786, Burt Glinn, Magnum Photos; 787 (l), Rene Burri, Magnum Photos; 787 (tr), Bill Stanton, Magnum Photos; 787 (br), A. J. Levin, Black Star Photos; 788, Shelly Katz, Black Star Photos; 789 (t), Penelope Breese, Gamma/Liaison; 789 (bl), Shelly Katz, Black Star Photos; 789 (br), Goff, Magnum Photos; 793, Jeff Lowenthal, Woodfin Camp and Associates; 794, U.S. Bureau of Engraving and Printing; 795, Larry Voigt, Photo Researchers; 796, D. Halstead, Gamma/Liaison; 798, Morgan, Gamma/Liaison; 799, D. Halstead, Gamma/Liaison; 800, U.S. Bureau of Engraving and Printing; 801, Greg Mathieson, Gamma/Liaison; 806, Eli Reed, Magnum Photos; 807, Jim Pickerell, Black Star Photos; 812, The Granger Collection.

D 6
E 7
F 8
G 9
H 0
I 1
J 2